Routledge International Encyclopedia of Women

Global Women's Issues and Knowledge

Volume 4   Quakers—Zionism

Index

Editorial Board

Routledge International Encyclopedia of Women

Global Women's Issues and Knowledge

Volume 4 Quakers—Zionism

Index

Cheris Kramarae and Dale Spender

General Editors

Routledge

New York • London

Published in 2000 by
Routledge
29 West 35 Street
New York, NY 10001

Routledge is an imprint of the Taylor & Francis Group

Published in Great Britain by
Routledge
11 New Fetter Lane
London EC4P 4EE

Library of Congress Cataloging-in-Publication Data
Routledge international encyclopedia of women: global women's
    issues and knowledge / general editors, Cheris Kramarae, Dale
    Spender.
        p.   cm.
    Includes bibliographical references and index.
        ISBN 0-415-92088-4 (set) — ISBN 0-415-92089-2 (v.1) —
        ISBN 0-415-92090-6 (v.2) — ISBN 0-415-92091-4 (v.3) —
        ISBN 0-415-92092-2 (v.4)
        1. Women—Encyclopedias. 2. Feminism—Encyclopedias.
    I. Title: International encyclopedia of women. II. Kramarae,
    Cheris. III. Spender, Dale.
    HQ1115 .R69 2000
    305.4'03—dc21   00-045792

10   9   8   7   6   5   4   3   2

ISBN 0-415-92088-4 (4-volume set)
ISBN 0-415-92089-2 (volume 1)
ISBN 0-415-92090-6 (volume 2)
ISBN 0-415-92091-4 (volume 3)
ISBN 0-415-92092-2 (volume 4)

Contents

Alphabetical List of Articles

Routledge International Encyclopedia of Women

Global Women's Issues and Knowledge

Volume 4   Quakers—Zionism

Index

Q

QUAKERS

The Religious Society of Friends, commonly known as the Quakers, grew in England in the mid-seventeenth century and spread to Wales, Ireland, Scotland, the Netherlands, Germany, and the American colonies. After an initial period of expansion, the Quakers became concentrated in the English-speaking countries, with the largest number in the United States. In the twentieth century, Quakers of an evangelical bent established the group in Africa and Latin America, where it has grown considerably. There are also small Quaker meetings in many countries of Europe and Asia.

From the beginning, Quakers have believed that each person has direct access to God and needs no intermediary, no priest or preacher. Friends generally worship in silence, waiting for the stirring of the Holy Spirit within. This belief, that "there is that of God in everyone," has led to Quaker leadership in the abolition of slavery, the advocacy of the rights of indigenous peoples, and especially the rights of women.

Women were among the Quaker ministers who traveled overseas to preach the new religion, and they earned respect for their gender. When George Fox, founder of Quakerism, saw the necessity of setting up small local meetings for business as well as worship, he felt women as well as men should participate. He therefore established separate business meetings for women and nurtured them with the help of Margaret Fell, a strong and independent woman who later became his wife. These separate women's business meetings became training grounds for women to learn to speak, write epistles, raise money, and run schools.

The Quaker grammar schools were coeducational, and later when academies and colleges were established, they too admitted women. Quaker women were therefore well educated and prepared to play a leading role in entering the professions and the reform movements of the nineteenth century. This was particularly true in the United States, where the majority of Friends were concentrated. In Philadelphia, Quakers established the first medical school for women and trained many pioneer Quaker women doctors. They also educated many of the first women scientists and educators. In prison reform and in the abolition of slavery, Quaker women played an important role, while in the development of the women's rights movement, Quaker women gave much of the early direction. Lucretia Mott (1793–1880), of Philadelphia, was a role model to Elizabeth Cady Stanton (1815–1902), and with Stanton and three other women, all Quaker, called the first women's rights convention at Seneca Falls in 1848. Later, Susan B. Anthony (1820–1906), a Quaker, joined the movement, and still later, Alice Paul (1885–1977), a New Jersey Quaker, became a leader first in obtaining suffrage and later in working for an equal rights amendment.

Today, Quaker women are represented in all the professions and are active around the world in working for the rights of women through such organizations as Quaker Peace and Service in Great Britain and the American Friends Service Committee in the United States.

See Also

CHRISTIANITY: STATUS OF WOMEN IN THE CHURCH; FEMINISM: NINETEENTH CENTURY; PACIFISM AND PEACE ACTIVISM

References and Further Reading

Bacon, Margaret Hope. 1986. *Mothers of feminism: The story of Quaker women in America.* San Francisco: Harper and Row.

Brown, Elisabeth Potts, and Susan Mosher Stuard. 1989. *Witnesses for change: Quaker women over three centuries.* New Brunswick, N.J.: Rutgers University Press.

Margaret Hope Bacon

QUEER THEORY

Queer theory emerged as a theoretical concept and a distinct form of political activism during the early 1990s, mainly in North America, with a substantial take-up in the United Kingdom.

The use of the term *queer* marks a reclamation of a term that had previously been used pejoratively in English-speaking countries. In this, queer has much in common with previous episodes of renaming and self-affirmations in gay and other civil rights politics (for example, the reclamation of *gay, dyke, black,* and so on). However, one of the main differences between queer politics and previous modes of lesbian and gay civil rights activism is that queer refuses what it sees as the liberal agenda of civil rights. Such emphatic rejection of earlier models leaves queer in danger of ignoring history and rewriting gay politics as less confrontational and radical than many would argue they indeed were. The queer refusal of an assimilationist position highlights one of the central tenets of queer as theory and politics—that is, that all forms of sexuality are queer: there is no "normality" to appeal to or to be equal with. What is taken to be natural is in fact the result of endlessly repeated performances that have meaning only in relation to the other forms of sexuality they define themselves against (Butler, 1990).

Heterosexuality is only assumed to be "natural" because of the endless repetition of a series of culturally recognized markers that mimic what is, in fact, only a fantasy of an original. In other words, heterosexuality needs homosexuality to give itself meaning. But more than this, according to Sedgwick (1991), the perceived distinction between heterosexuality and homosexuality determines the very nature of thinking in the West. Sedgwick argues that the open secret of the closet (one cannot be "out" as gay unless there is a closet of "in" to be defined against) has in fact been an organizing motif of western epistemology over the past century; knowledge is inextricably linked to sex, and in particular to homosexuality, so that in vastly different debates over meaning the homosexual/heterosexual dichotomy will be found to be one of the organizing principles. This argument can help to explain the bewildering longevity and internal logic of homophobia. Queer theory is in many ways in accord with a constructionist model of sexuality that follows Foucault in arguing that sexuality is not innate but socially constructed (Foucault, 1979).

In academic work and cultural production queer theory has animated research in many cultural, historical, and political fields. It provides a mode of analysis for thinking about the lesbian/gay/queer reader of the past and the present (Burston and Richardson, 1995; Horne and Lewis, 1996; Simpson, 1994). In this way, it has allowed "queer" meanings to be unlocked from a diversity of texts. Queer has also been important in recent theorizations of the body, adding to existing feminist analyses. In all this, queer's potential to disrupt previous codifications of the body and of experience and sexuality has been profoundly important.

Queer activism such as OutRage in the United Kingdom and Queer Nation in the United States valorizes transgression, delighting in contravening heterosexist norms. But it also aims to provide an alternative to what some have come to see as the proscriptiveness of feminist and lesbian and gay politics. In the face of what some experience as the regulatory nature of political correctness, queer offers the possibility of diverse alliances, confrontational "in your face" politics, and an inclusionism that some found impossible under the segregationist regime of identity politics (Smyth, 1992). Whether queer can indeed overcome differences of gender, ethnicity, and sexuality is a much argued point, but it has galvanized debate and provided a forum in which lesbians, gay men, and bisexuals could work together in a politics that also includes transsexuals, transvestites, and other sexual minorities. At its most radical and theoretically rigorous, queer's destabilization of normality allows nominally "heterosexual" people to own—and politically act on—their queerness. It argues that no one is really "straight" (who is queerer: the heterosexual woman who penetrates her husband with a dildo, or the gay male couple who share a mortgage?). In this, queer activism has links with other movements that see themselves as sexually radical, such as sadomasochism. Queer's ability to cross previously institutionalized boundaries of sexual orientation has also been galvanized by the need to respond to the international crisis over AIDS, a disease whose transmission evidences the fluidity of human sexual behavior. Queer politics was also forged in the radical campaigning about AIDS undertaken by such groups as ACT UP (AIDS Coalition to Unleash Power).

Many women are involved in queer politics because they see it as a chance to problematize the nature of racialized and gendered, as well as sexual, experience and identity. Others are critical of queer, worrying that it is still a white masculinist space. To some extent, there is a generational divide with younger people, for whom feminism and gay liberation appear to be an orthodoxy, embracing the radicalism of queer while older people defend gay liberation and feminist politics. Yet, for other seasoned campaigners, queer appears to offer precisely the space to discuss things that they felt were inadmissible in what became the politically correct arena of feminist and gay politics. Queer is also linked to the revitalization of bisexuality as a term of self-identification and sexual activity: in some feminist circles, a queerer climate has made it permissible to act on and make public desires previously seen as reactionary. This aspect of queer, along with its trendy, media-conscious image, can also be understood in relation to the postmodernist validation of pleasure; in art and literature and on the street, queer is pro-sex (of a safer kind) and pro-pleasure.

See Also

CRITICAL AND CULTURAL THEORY; LESBIAN STUDIES; SEXUALITY: OVERVIEW

References and Further Reading

Burston, Paul, and Colin Richardson, eds. 1995. *A queer romance: Lesbians, gay men and popular culture*. New York and London: Routledge.

Butler, Judith. 1990. *Gender trouble: Feminism and the subversion of identity*. London: Routledge.

Foucault, Michel. 1979. *The history of sexuality*. Vol. 1, *An introduction*. London: Allen Lane.

Horne Peter, and Reina Lewis. 1996. *Outlooks: Lesbian and gay sexualities and visual culture*. London: Routledge.

Munt, Sally. 1998. *Butch/femme: Inside lesbians genders*. London: Cassell.

Sedgwick, Eve Kosofsky. 1991. *Epistemology of the closet*. Hemel Hempstead, U.K.: Harvester.

Simpson, Mark. 1994. *Male impersonators*. London: Cassell.

Smyth, Cherry. 1992. *Lesbians talk: Queer notions*. London: Scarlet Press.

Reina Lewis

QUILTING

The term *quilting* refers to the entire process of making a quilt. A quilt is a bedcover, garment, or decorative textile in which a batting is sandwiched between two fabric layers. This layering enhances the quilt's capacity to provide warmth and protection. Running, or quilting, stitches hold the three layers securely together and simultaneously create patterns that complement the patchwork design of the top fabric layer. Quilting has become a metaphor for women's domestic experience within patriarchy.

The origins of Euro-American quilting are unknown, but scholars have documented quilting in the ancient world and in Europe since the Middle Ages. Evidence of quilting and patchwork traditions in Asia and Africa have caused speculation about their influence during the late eighteenth and early nineteenth centuries in contributing to modern quilt design. Industrialization, however, defined the socioeconomic conditions that guaranteed quilting's popularity throughout the nineteenth century and into the twentieth century. The emergence of a middle-class society characterized by a cult of domesticity coincided with an increased availability of inexpensive mass-manufactured cloth. Through quilting, women could demonstrate deference to their moral responsibility as wives and mothers to preserve the sanctity of family life.

With quilting's rise in popularity during the nineteenth century, local women's groups made fund-raising quilts in support of political and religious affairs. The Women's Christian Temperance Union appropriated this practice to build nationwide alliances among women and to advance social reforms improving domestic, employment, and educational conditions. In the late twentieth century, women drew upon similar imagery of quilt making to express activism regarding health issues, including AIDS and breast cancer.

The renewed interest in quilting among feminist scholars and artists overcame the view that women's occupation with needlework indicated their oppression within patriarchal society. Whereas the cult of domesticity bonded many women, it stigmatized others. For women seeking recognition within the public sphere, pressures to pursue domestic activities, such as quilting, restricted these ambitions. Nineteenth- and twentieth-century authors and poets used references to quilting to express their protest.

During the 1970s, women artists and writers, such as Judy Chicago and Alice Walker, found that insights into women's experience and survival in a patriarchal society could be gained through attention to quilts and their relation to the quilters' lives, including questions of feminine sensibility, of originality and tradition, of individuality versus collectivity, of content and values in art (Mainardi, 1973). This interest in the subjectivity of female expression stands in contrast to the acknowledgment of quilt making as an abstract art form, with the 1971 exhibit at the Whitney Museum in New York. Yet together they stimulated its popular revival in the late 1970s. Contemporary quilters, both trained artists and self-taught, now integrate traditional textile practices, modern sewing methods, and artistic trends to realize a creativity often reflective of female experiences.

The spread of quilting during the 1980s and the growth of a quilt subculture based within local communities but with national and international linkages has led scholars to question both the distinctiveness of women's culture and the diversity of women's experience. Art historians and critics assert that the expression of feminity in women's arts, including quilting, is inherent in the materials, techniques, and production process. Studies of African-American quilts pose issues of their inclusion in quilt history as well as recognition of the uniqueness of their contribution.

Scholars in folklore and women's studies have gained understanding of the importance of the creative process to quilters by examining the interactions, activities, and publications of the quilt subculture. Women's participation in a quilt guild empowers artistic expression and contributes to an understanding of self. By drawing on traditional imagery, women can demonstrate a relationship toward home and family. At the same time, the subculture is responsive to the changing society and the changing roles of women. Quilting becomes a context in which definitions of femininity are negotiated. An openness to both old and new conceptions of gender provides women with options in determining what values and meanings are central in defining the self and layering them to fit individual circumstance. Questions persist about the extent that patriarchy mediates the actions and expressions of quilters.

To distinguish reality from myth, historians are compiling a history of quilts and quiltmaking. Questions consider regional and ethnic differences, cross-cultural influences, national trends and international contacts. Through careful authentication of quilts and appraisal of their significance, this scholarship has challenged stereotypes about women's needlework. Recognition is being accorded to women who have resisted the constraints of domesticity by using quilting to achieve autonomy and personal fulfillment, as well as to claim recognition in the public sphere.

See Also

CRAFTS

References and Further Reading

Freeman, Roland L. 1996. *A communion of the spirits: African-American quilters, preservers, and their stories.* Nashville, Tenn.: Rutledge Hill.

Gunn, Virginia. 1993. From myth to maturity: The evolution of quilt scholarship. In Laurel Horton, ed., *Uncoverings 1992,* 192–205. San Francisco: American Quilt Study Group.

Hedges, Elaine, Julie Silber, and Pat Ferrero. 1987. *Hearts and hands: Women, quilts, and American society.* Nashville, Tenn.: Rutledge Hill.

Mainardi, Patricia. 1973. Quilts: The great American art. *The Feminist Art Journal* 2(1): 1, 18–23.

Torsney, Cheryl B., and Judy Elsley, eds. 1994. *Quilt culture: Tracing the pattern.* Columbia: University of Missouri Press.

Catherine A. Cerny

R

RACE

There is no one way to define *race*. Typical definitions of race mention people with some common origin, but referential categories vary widely. Race is often equated with skin color, but this ignores the complexity of racial definition and the purposes for which it is used. For instance, different criteria are used to define such "races" as black (inherited skin color, when including African and Australian peoples), Caucasian (physical characteristics attributed to ancestral region), Japanese (heritage and culture), Jewish (religion and culture), Hispanic (language and geography), Native American (geography), South African colored (color, parentage, and language), and human (species). Though most people in many cultures do not doubt that race originates in biology or a divine source, it is in fact a social construct, built to suit other social beliefs. This is demonstrated by the different taxonomies of humans found within different societies. For instance, in Southern Africa, "black" does not include the Khoi or San (Bushmen) peoples, but in the non-African world, any indigenous Sub-Saharan African is "black." Since race cannot be defined in any objective manner—by physical, cultural, or linguistic measurements—the concept frequently overlaps with that of *ethnicity*, which has stronger associations with culture.

The use of racial concepts originates in the universal need to distinguish between "us" and "them"—our people and everybody else. The coherence of one's own group is based in its differentiation from other groups. Thus, although not every group identifies itself as a race, all groups seem to identify others by race. *Race*, then, can be shorthand for "ways that people differ (from us)." It is not uncommon for groups to have racial labels only for others, and not for themselves. In such cases, members of the in-group may simply use the word for *people* to refer to themselves. These local words for *people* are often adopted by outsiders as the name for the group; to the question "Who are you?" the only possible reply is "We're the people (who live here)"—Inuit (North American Arctic), Bantu (Africa), Khoe or Khoi (Africa). Similarly, though English speakers have used *black* in the racial sense for centuries, self-reference as a racial group (*white,* rather than *Christians* or *citizens*) did not become common until the nineteenth century (Flexner, 1976), the peak of English colonialism.

The conception of race leads rather directly to the practice of racism. The very act of identifying other groups can be demeaning to them. Those who call their own group "the people" may do so in contrast to other groups who are viewed and even mythologized as less than completely human. In the Western world, this judgment has been accomplished through so-called scientific estimations of race. This approach regarded races as separate biological species or subspecies, among which the white race was considered the most highly evolved. In other cultures, the human/nonhuman dichotomy can be seen in racial labeling practices. For example, in the Bantu languages of Sub-Saharan Africa, the word for one's own group is always in the "human" noun class (as indicated by a "human" prefix); however, the names for other racial and ethnic groups are often in "object" noun classes (as are words for other outsiders, such as disabled people and criminals). In Cantonese, words for foreigners (especially European) include an otherworldly, nonhuman element, the meaning "ghost" or "demon" (*gwai* or *kuei*).

Racial or ethnic "others" are identified universally, but the need to identify one's own group in racial terms is often precipitated by racial oppression. Ironically, while modern scientific evidence denies the existence of race, the fight against racism usually reifies the concept of "race"

(Dominguez, 1994). Thus, race has been reinvented as a social rather than a biological concept, and it is unlikely to become less important any time soon.

Biology as Destiny

Even though differences among humans have been noted throughout history, racial taxonomy (formal classification) based on biological features gained currency through European and American attempts to classify races "scientifically" in the eighteenth through twentieth centuries. The drive to identify races coincided with and followed other trends among naturalists, including the advent of the Linnaean classification system for plant and animal life (which demanded taxonomy at many levels) and Charles Darwin's theory of natural selection and evolution. The view that the races constitute separate species (polygeneism) enjoyed some popularity in pre-Darwinian times, when such a view could fit with the biblical creation story. In this view, Adam and Eve had been "Caucasian," and the other races had separate and lesser origins. However, the belief that different races were different species depended on the belief that miscegenation (interbreeding among races) could not produce fertile offspring, so polygeneism was never uncontroversial. Acceptance of Darwinism pushed the balance toward the competing theory, monogeneism. Monogeneism holds that the races are separate subspecies of the same species (*Homo sapiens*) which have adapted in particular ways to different habitats. Within anthropology, no fixed number of subspecies was ever universally accepted. However, the three-way classification of Negroid, Mongoloid, and Caucasoid achieved popularity outside the academy and has become part of the popular myth of race in North America.

Despite the claim that their science was objective, the work of racial taxonomists was biased by the expectation that races differ in abilities and temperament and by the desire to justify racial policy. (See Gould, 1981, for a history and reconsideration of the nineteenth-century data.) Therefore, racial taxonomy was guided by a belief in biological determinism. Because the field was invented and pursued by people of European descent, the white race was associated with virtues and the other races with limitations. Particularly convenient for the justification of slavery, apartheid, and other institutionalized forms of racial oppression were the notions that black African people were less intelligent, more subservient, capricious, and crafty than whites, and more like apes in appearance and ability. Though European interest was most fixed on differences between Africans and Europeans, all groups were considered inferior to the European. For example, East Asian people were classified as severe

and ruled by opinion, and Native American peoples were claimed to be obstinate and ruled by custom (Wolf, 1994).

Early evolutionary science included the belief that the evolutionary process is illustrated in the development of an animal ("ontogeny recapitulates phylogeny"). Thus, the human fetus was said to go through stages in which it is fishlike, reptilelike, and apelike before it reaches a human stage of development. Since some groups, including most nonwhite races and women, were considered inferior to the white male standard, recapitulation allowed for the ranking of human groups. Women, non-Europeans (and, to a lesser extent, the Irish and Southern Europeans), and the lower classes were considered less advanced than adult white males of privilege, and thus they could be likened to white male children in their biologically determined abilities. The argument for limited rights and responsibilities for nonwhites and women could be justified on the basis that these people were adapted to carry no more responsibility than a white boy. Furthermore, the theory of recapitulation allowed for "throwbacks" to be born to those of "higher" races. The best-known application of this theory is John Langdon Down's description of a medical condition he called Mongolism (now known as Down's syndrome). Since people with Down's syndrome were thought to have Mongoloid facial characteristics and some stereotyped behaviors, it was argued that they must be degenerate forms, retarded by some fluke at a lower stage of racial development. (Down's subjects were all of European stock.) Similarly, degeneration was argued to be the cause of criminality, and so white criminals were examined for physical characteristics that might link them to a "lower" race.

During the last decades of the twentieth century, racial classifications were being abandoned by natural scientists. Greater knowledge about genetics and less reliance on singular, superficial appearance traits led naturalists to question the value of differentiating subspecies for any species, including humans (Gould, 1977). For instance, it has been shown that there can be more genetic variation within a so-called racial group than among different groups. Any "black" person is likely to have more genes and genetic characteristics in common with, say, an Inuit person than with another "black" person. The traits that have been associated with any one race are found in varying combinations in others. For instance, the "Asian" epicanthic eye folds are found in the San (Bushmen), nearly every skin color is found among "Caucasians," and racially associated genetic defects cross race lines as well. For example, sickle-cell anemia, usually associated with African peoples, does not occur in the Xhosa, an indigenous South African group, but it does among "white" Mediterranean peoples. The inability to fix firm boundaries among races is not explained away by the possibility of interbreeding among peoples, because the extent of the overlaps and the geographic separation of peoples with similar genetic traits are too great. Though genetic arguments have not convinced every natural scientist to abandon the search for races, the trend is definitely against racial classification. A survey has found that only 50 percent of physical anthropologists and 29 percent of cultural anthropologists believe that biological races exist (Reynolds, 1992).

Social and Cognitive Sources of "Race"

Races, then, are socially constructed divisions of humans, and social conditions bias the composition of races and views toward them. Although little evidence supports the biological reality of races, they certainly have social and psychological reality. Whether one believes in race or not, its effects are undeniable. The specific social functions of race vary according to culture and time, but in general, racial divisions can be seen to perform two major functions. First, racial categorization supports the social coherence of one's own cultural group, even if this is attained by contrast rather than by self-identification. By confirming notions of who "they" are, people develop a notion of who "we" are. This allows positive self-evaluation and the judgment of other groups as different *and therefore worse* (Tajfel and Forgas, 1981). (This is not to say that all groups derive equally positive self-concepts through group differentiation; but while one group might look down on another as intellectually impoverished, the other might view the first as morally corrupt.) Second, differentiation among races can be used to define social roles, just as class or caste divisions do. This is seen especially in the use of racial divisions to justify slavery or unequal distribution of resources.

Since races are created for social and economic purposes, differences in social and economic conditions contribute to different racial taxonomies. The treatment of racially ambiguous peoples demonstrates this. For example, in the United States, where divisions between black and white were firm from the start, people of mixed African and European ancestry were categorized as black. However, as these divisions have become less firm in the wake of civil rights movements, assertion of "mixed" identity (or identities) has arisen (Funderburg, 1994; Motoyoshi, 1990). Mixed identities have also arisen in cultures where social divisions among races were less firm, or where other factors created a need for an additional race. In South Africa, for example, the designation *colored* is a particular mixed-race identity. The social condition of the (mostly male) early white set-tlers created reasons for accepting Khoi wives and "colored" children more closely into the white social fold, especially since black (Bantu language-speaking) groups were considered a common enemy to both. The colored category later served as a mediating one between the extremely defined social roles of the black and white categories. Other treatments of mixed African, European, and Native American heritage are found in Latin American cultures. In some, "mulatto" (African and European) and "mestizo" (Native American and European) identities are strong, though certain people of mixed heritage can be classified as part of the white social group.

The oppression committed in the name of racial role/giving has set in motion a cycle of reifying race. People who have been lumped together into a race and treated uniformly and badly on that basis are likely to develop a racial or ethnic identity that differs from the one they formerly held. The oppressed people are then forced to react to the imposed, unacceptable conditions. Fighting the racism of the oppressing class often involves working within the racial paradigm that the oppressor has defined. Thus, a common strategy in fighting racism is to claim that the oppressed group should have equal rights and is equally valuable to the society. Rather less common is the rejection of the oppressing class's racial taxonomy altogether. It is more usual to claim that "the black race has made many important contributions to society" than to assert that "there's no such thing as a black race." Obviously, the former strategy is preferred because there *is* such a thing as a black race—albeit a socially constructed one. However, if the recognition of races does entail racism, then antiracism work that depends on racial concepts may be able only to change and not to eradicate the practice of racism.

Past thinking about race has focused on thinking about the oppressed races—the Others—because these groups have had the greatest need to react to racism. However, this can have the effect of implicitly accepting the oppressor's race (and roles) as the norm, with other races as deviations. For example, in literary studies, the works of people of color have been examined for the ways in which racial identity informs and shapes the medium and the message. Recent work, especially by feminists, has called attention to the need to view white people as also "racialized"—to look at how having a white identity implicitly affects one's interaction with and views of the world (*see* Frankenberg, 1993; Morrison, 1992).

Race, Sex, and Gender

The social construction of race is underscored in the intersection of race, sex, and gender. Sex is a determinant in racial categorization when, for instance, a woman is placed in a racial category according to her husband's race, or a child's race is categorized solely according to her mother's or her father's race. Both these criteria were used in determining race membership for the purposes of the Group Areas Act in South Africa, whereby a wife or a minor child was categorized according to her husband's or father's race, respectively. Racial classification by paternity also holds in exogamous cultures, where a woman goes to live in the husband's group and raises her children as members of his group.

Racial categorization, in turn, leads to sexual stereotyping. In the colonialist tradition, women of color are seen as more sexual than white women. This was a subject of biological determinist investigation in the nineteenth century. European interest in the allegedly voracious sexual appetites of African women was most strikingly illustrated by the persistent study of genital size in Khoi and San women. This culminated in a museum tour of a live specimen, Saartjie Baartman ("the Hottentot Venus"), whose genitals were removed and stored in a Paris museum after her death.

Racial sexual stereotypes continue, whether they are attributed to biology or to cultural norms. Thus, women of color have come to be fetish items to some white men: Asian women are stereotyped as exotic, sexually knowing, and submissive, and African women as available and insatiable. Black men, in turn, are stereotyped as a sexual threat in the white world. However, such stereotypes are nearly reversed in some postcolonial cultures, where whites are viewed as sexual decadents who have introduced homosexuality, disease, and disregard for sexual tradition into the colonized culture.

Patriarchy and (white) racism are often claimed to be inextricably linked (for example, hooks, 1990). In some senses, nonwhites and white women have been equated—as in the theory of recapitulation, and in denial of rights such as suffrage and property ownership. This equation of nonwhiteness with womanhood has led to what some claim is the "emasculation" of nonwhite men, especially in postcolonial contexts. These similarities in denigration on the basis of race and sex create a "double bind" for women of color and make an antipatriarchal approach to antiracism both necessary and difficult. It is necessary because racism as it exists today feeds off a patriarchal mind-set; it is difficult because the privileges of patriarchal white manhood are very tempting. Thus, it might be easier or more attractive to reverse the positions of the oppressor and the oppressed rather than overthrowing the system of oppression altogether. Women of color feel this pressure when they are asked or assumed to give loyalty *either* to antisexism *or* to antiracism. Feminist movements have often been accused of reflecting only a privileged, white worldview (Spelman, 1988); some antiracist movements have been labeled sexist because they ask that women not assert their own rights but instead help to put men of color into the same class of privilege as white men.

The contrasting argument is that sexism and racism are different and separable types of oppression. For example, Laurence Thomas (1980: 240) argues that racism is more easily abandoned than sexism because sexism is easier to defend as culturally appropriate behavior, and "the positive self-concept of men has been more centrally tied to their being sexists than has been the positive self-concept of whites to their being racists." Thomas's thesis is based on two facts: race is not as biologically determined as sex; and women and men are dependent on each other (for example, for survival of the species) and are thus forced to interact in a way that people of different races are not. Whereas racist positions may claim that the races should not interact at all, sexist positions are based on the assumption that women and men should interact, but in constrained ways. Thomas's argument could lead to the conclusion that it is possible to abolish racism without abolishing patriarchy, although one might then ask whether other forms of differentiation and oppression (for example, by class, religion, or caste) would serve the purposes that racism has served in a patriarchal system.

See Also

ANTIRACIST AND CIVIL RIGHTS MOVEMENTS; APARTHEID, SEGREGATION, AND GHETTOIZATION; BIOLOGICAL DETERMINISM; BLACKNESS AND WHITENESS; ETHNICITY; EUGENICS; EVOLUTION; HYBRIDITY AND MISCEGENATION; IMAGES OF WOMEN: OVERVIEW; RACISM AND XENOPHOBIA; SCIENTIFIC SEXISM AND RACISM

References and Further Reading

Dominguez, Virginia R. 1994. A state for "*the Other*": Intellectual complicity in racializing practices. *Current Anthropology* 35(4): 333–348.

Flexner, Stuart Berg. 1976. The blacks. In *I hear America talking*, 31–59. New York: Van Nostrand Reinhold.

Frankenberg, Ruth. 1993. *White women, race matters: The social construction of whiteness.* London: Routledge.

Funderburg, Lise. 1994. *Black, white, other: Biracial Americans talk about race and identity.* New York: William Morrow.

Gould, Stephen Jay. 1977. Why we should not name human races—A biological view. In Stephen Jay Gould, *Ever since Darwin: Reflections on natural history*, 231–236. New York: W. W. Norton.

———. 1981. *The mismeasure of man.* London: Penguin.

hooks, bell. 1990. *Yearning: Race, gender and cultural politics.* Boston: South End Press.

Morrison, Toni. 1992. *Playing in the dark: Whiteness and the literary imagination.* Cambridge, Mass.: Harvard University Press.

Motoyoshi, Michelle M. 1990. The experience of mixed-race people: Some thoughts and theories. *Journal of Ethnic Studies* 18(2): 77–94.

Reynolds, Larry T. 1992. A retrospective on "race": The career of a concept. *Sociological Focus* 25(1): 1–14.

Spelman, Elizabeth V. 1988. *Inessential woman: Problems of exclusion in feminist thought.* Boston: Beacon.

Tajfel, Henri, and Joseph P. Forgas. 1981. Social categorization: Cognitions, values, and groups. In Joseph P. Forgas, ed., *Social cognition: Perspectives on everyday understanding,* 113–140. New York: Academic.

Thomas, Laurence. 1980. Sexism and racism: Some conceptual differences. *Ethics* 90(2): 329–350.

Wolf, Eric R. 1994. Perilous ideas: Race, culture, and people. *Current Anthropology* 35(1): 1–12.

M. Lynne Murphy

RACISM AND XENOPHOBIA

The term *racism* entered feminist debates when black feminists in the United States and Britain criticized white feminists for being racist (Davis, 1981; hooks, 1981; Hull, Scott, and Smith, 1982). They claimed that using *women* as a universal term to describe a homogeneous group equally oppressed by men, patriarchy, or a sexist system obscured that some (white) women also exercised control over and oppression of other (black) women. By assuming universalist positions feminists were obscuring the different realities faced by black women and women in developing countries. These criticisms of feminist theory and practice focused mainly on forms of racism that are more subtle and unconscious than those usually associated with the concept. To judge this, it is useful to turn to the history of the term *racism.*

The English word *racism* was first used to translate the title of a book written in German by Magnus Hirschfeld: *Rassismus* (published 1938 in English). Hirschfeld was a famous sexologist who founded and directed the first institute of Sexual Science in Berlin. He fought for the right to homosexuality and women's right to abortion. When the fascists came to power in 1933, he fled to France because he was a Jew and had already been beaten up by a fascist group in Munich.

Hirschfeld's book refuted the claim that there are discrete human races, hierarchically ordered, thus challenging the backbone of German fascist ideology. Hirschfeld founded a tradition, adhered to throughout the late twentieth century, that defines racism as the belief that humanity can be classified into a hierarchy of specific races. This theory, known among theories of racism as "scientific racism", originated in the nineteenth century. It defined the "Aryan race" as superior to all other "races". The Jews, defined as an "Asiatic people," were at the bottom of the hierarchy. Therefore, this racism is also called "anti-Semitism," although for instance, blacks were also depicted as inferior and persecuted and killed under German fascism. "Scientific racism" argued for the necessity to secure "race-purity" (*Rassenreinheit*) through eugenics and population politics. This meant "preferential breeding from the choicest stocks" (Lapogue, in Hirschfeld, 1938: 39) and prevention of "degeneration".

Well established by at the beginning of the twentieth century, eugenics became most prominent during German fascism. Its main target was women: those of the "choicest stock" were required to have many children; those of the "lower races" (all except the Aryans) and those with "bad genetic material" (women of the lower classes and those with disabilities) were forced into sterilization. People with disabilities were systematically killed. To produce "racially pure" children, an institution (*Lebensborn*) was founded. German women and men considered to be of pure race volunteered into this institution, and eleven thousand children were born there.

Although the German fascists wanted to enslave the "Eastern races," Jews and Gypsies were to be exterminated. As a result of this, in Germany and in other European countries, racism is now equated with anti-Semitism and its genocidal consequences. Discussions about today's forms of racism are often rejected on the grounds that it would devalue the sufferings of Jews and Gypsies to use the term *racism* for discrimination that does not aim at extermination.

The racism analyzed by Hirschfeld is different from the racism that black feminists identified in white feminists' work and political practices. They derived their analysis from a body of theory that analyzed the enslavement and oppression of people with African origin in the United States as racism.

The Black Power movement, organizing against this oppression, introduced the term into the political and theoretical debate (Carmichael and Hamilton, 1968). Cox

(1976), a black Marxist, was the first to analyze racism in the context of capitalism and colonialism, putting emphasis on the importance of class relations for understanding racism. Subsequently, ideologies legitimating colonialism, the slave trade, and South African apartheid by defining peoples in Africa, Asia, and Latin-America as "inferior races" were analyzed as expressions of racism. The European ideology of the "civilizing mission" constructed the populations colonized by European countries as less intelligent, less able to develop a culture. Domination, exploitation, and oppression were described as bringing civilization and development to the uncivilized. Enslavement of African peoples was legitimated by constructing black people as needing to be controlled and as fit only for unskilled manual work. This history of racism founded a tradition that defines racism as a theory and practice of white people aimed at black people. As in the case of anti-Semitism, racism in general is equated with one instance of racism.

Racism in the form of anti-Semitism was aimed at extermination, whereas racism in the context of colonialism was aimed at the enslavement and exploitation of the racialized group. One should not forget, however, that in Fascism, Jews, Gypsies, and eastern European populations were also enslaved and exploited, and that Africans, Asians, and the indigenous populations in the Americas and in Australia were worked to death or murdered in wars aimed at colonizing them.

Racism is aimed at both women and men, but it constructs women and men differently and discriminates against them in different ways. Societies in which racism occurs are structured through sexism. As a result, racism against women in racialized groups is articulated with sexism. Images of women construct them as sexual beings in a specific way: for example, black women are depicted as matriarchs in some cultures, as seductive in others; Asian women as submissive to men and family; Jewish women as dangerously seductive by some, or as matriarchs by other cultures. The articulation of racism and sexism is also evident in images of the dangerous "mixture" between races or cultures. While men of the dominant group are seen to "purify" the race or culture of the subordinated ethnic group, women of the dominant group are seen to "pollute" their own race or ethnic group by mixing with inferior races or cultures. The articulation of racism and sexism also produces segregated labor markets for men and women of subordinated ethnic groups, where women generally earn less than men.

Racism, like sexism, is a process and an ideology of naturalization, of constructing social relations as natural and unchangeable. Some authors have therefore wanted to incorporate all forms of naturalization—for example, sexism,

homophobia, oppression of the disabled—into the concept of racism (Guillaumin, 1972). Others have talked about the double or triple oppression of women (Smith, 1983). The latter view has been criticized as too simplistic, because the articulation of different forms of oppression changes their character. Instead of adding up, Deborah King (1988) has proposed, oppressions multiply.

Women of the majority are seen as necessary for the biological, social, and ideological reproduction of society and nation-state. As opposed to this, the Others (men and women), defined as a different race, culture or ethnic group, have no legitimate place within the society that defines them in that way.

A majority of scholars agree that there are different racisms and different articulations of racism and sexism, which have to be analyzed in their specific historical and political context (e.g. Anthias and Yuval-Davis, 1992; Cohen, 1988). Miles (1989) has argued in favor of a definition that allows for the different racisms to warrant the term *racism*. He defines racism as an ideology constructing a social group as a race by articulating actual or assumed phenotypic characteristics (size of skull, skin color, form of nose) with assumed or actual social features and behaviors. The "radicalized" group is defined as inferior in relation to those who produce these images. This definition has been criticized for not taking into account instances of racism where cultural rather than somatic features are used to construct social groups as inferior (Anthias and Yuval-Davis, 1992). But one could also argue that "cultural racism" and "biological racism" are difficult to distinguish. All forms of racism naturalize assumed or existing cultural traits. For instance, racisms against black people also have constructed them as culturally different and claimed these differences were determined genetically. In turn, all cultural racisms use (often invented) physical characteristics as signifiers for the target group. The difference lies only in what element is emphasized.

Racisms regard culture as a static, transhistorical feature of a social group. This is also true of newer forms of racism named "new racism," "differentialist racism" (Taguieff, 1987), or "cultural racism" (Balibar, 1988). They argue in favor of cultural variety. In order to preserve it, they claim, people from different cultures need to stay in their respective places. Therefore, migrants ought to be repatriated and borders closed. Differentialist racisms do not explicitly hierarchize cultures. However, only migration of groups who have been defined as inferior within the old racisms is seen as a danger. Neo-racists never demand that white European natives should not cross borders because they pollute other people's cultures.

Cohen (1988) analyzes the way in which different racisms produce different "myths of origin" articulating origin with destiny. The Other is depicted as a group undermining the social order. Cohen points to the fact that racisms are not engendered by those groups who are its objects but rather by the conflicts and contradictions that exist within a society.

Racisms are closely connected to nationalisms. No nation-state is founded on a homogeneous ethnic group, yet ethnic homogeneity is one of the main legitimating ideas of nation-states (Balibar, 1988). One means to construct homogeneity is the construction of a homogeneous Other that serves as an inverted mirror image of an ideal, homogeneous national self. Racisms are a powerful means of constructing homogeneity because they work on all levels of social life: on an individual level as everyday racisms, on the level of social structures as institutional racisms, and as an ideology reproducing the structures of domination (Hall, 1997, Räthzel, 1997). On all levels, racisms serve to exclude those groups defined as not belonging to the legitimated community from equal access to social resources and positions (work, housing, social relations, positions of decision making). Racisms can also have damaging effects on the personality of individuals who are its objects: sometimes they internalize and thus subordinate themselves to racist images (see Fanon, 1952; Memmi, 1982).

Some authors have analyzed racism as the other side of universalism (Balibar and Wallerstein, 1988). If racism is seen as a societal structure, indispensable for the functioning of modern nation-states that dominate global power relations, the term must be confined to Western societies. If racism is defined in terms of exclusion and discrimination against those defined as different and inferior, then racisms can be found all over the world: the Indian caste system; the hostilities among Sikhs, Hindus, and Muslims; ethnic cleansing in former Yugoslavia; the annihilation of the Armenians by the Turks; the conquering of China by Japan; the murdering of Tutsi by Hutu in Rwanda...the list is endless.

Xenophobia is frequently used as a substitute for the term *racism*. It is derived from Greek *xenos*, meaning "guest" or "stranger," and *phobos*, "fear." Traditionally, this concept bears the meaning of an innate anxiety toward strangers which is characteristic of all human beings at all times. It goes hand in hand with the notion of a "threshold of tolerance," according to which human beings can bear only a certain number of aliens without turning aggressive. This usage is problematic because the existence of innate anxieties toward aliens has not been proved, and moreover, many of those subjected to racism are not strangers to those who discriminate against them. On the contrary, they have lived decades or longer among those who discriminate against them.

Another body of theory analyzing the ways in which societies deal with the stranger (who is mostly constructed as male) does not equate this relation with racism. One famous essay is that of Simmel (1908), who defines the stranger as the person who "comes today and stays tomorrow". He is at the same time close to and distanced from the rest of society. Alfred Schütz (1944) defined the incompatibility of the cultures of the stranger and the host country as the source of conflict. This implies a concept of culture as a closed universe without the possibility of communication. For Bauman (1989), the distrust of the state toward the stranger is a general characteristic of modernity. As a guarantee and producer of orderly life, everybody who does not fit into his order is defined by the modern state as a threatening chaos. Bauman uses the term *proteophobia* (from Proteus, the god who could take any form) to express that, in modernity, rejection of the stranger is due to the inability and unwillingness of modern institutions and individuals to endure ambivalence.

In feminist debates of racism, the concepts of xenophobia and of the stranger have not been prominent. They have avoided the trap of essentializing xenophobia as an innate human behavior and of reifying the position of the stranger as one who is always discriminated against—irrespective of the specific power relations. On the other hand, using the term *racism* introduces the danger of reducing this power relation to a question of black versus white, thereby ignoring the fact that any group, irrespective of skin color, can be constructed as threatening strangers, as not belonging to the nation-state.

Feminist debates have been influential in deepening the understanding of racism because they showed not only that the ruling classes exercise racism but also that groups who are themselves oppressed do this. Feminist analysis of racism has also influenced feminist theory by challenging the idea of women as mere victims. Women's active role in supporting racism, colonialism, and fascism has been analyzed (Koonz, 1986; Ware, 1992). Other studies investigate the ways in which belonging to the dominant group shapes the lives and self-conceptions of women and can make them a supporting part of a racist system (Frankenberg, 1993; Rommelspacher, 1994; Räthzel, 1994).

See Also

ANTI-SEMITISM; ETHNIC CLEANSING; EUROCENTRISM; FASCISM AND NAZISM; FEMINISM: AFRICAN-AMERICAN; FEMINISM: ASIAN-AMERICAN; FEMINISM: BLACK BRITISH; FEMINISM: BRITISH ASIAN; GENOCIDE; IMMIGRATION

References and Further Reading

Anthias, Floya, and Nira Yuval-Davis. 1992. *Racialized boundaries*. London: Routledge.

———, and Nira Yuval-Davis. 1983. Contextualising feminism—Ethnic gender and class divisions. *Feminist Review* 15: 62–75.

Balibar, Etienne. 1988. Y a-t-il un neo-racisme? In Etienne Balibar and Immanuel Wallerstein, *Race, classe, nation*, 27–41. Paris: La Decouerte.

Bauman, Zygmunt. 1989. *Modernity and the Holocaust*. Oxford: Oxford University Press.

Carmichael, S., and C. V. Hamilton. 1968. *Black power: The politics of liberation in America*. London: Jonathan Cape.

Cohen, Philip. 1988. The perversions of inheritance. In Philip Cohen and Harwant S. Bains, eds., *Multi-racist Britain*, 9–118. Hampshire: Macmillan.

Cox, Oliver C. 1976. *Race relations*. Detroit: Wayne State University Press.

Davis, Angela. 1983. *Women, race and class*. New York: Vintage Books.

Fanon, Frantz. 1952. *Peau noire, masques blancs*. Paris: Editions du Seuil.

Frankenberg, Ruth. 1993. *White women, race matters*. London: Routledge.

Guillaumin, Colette. 1972. *L'idéologie raciste: Genèse et langage actuel*. Paris-La Haye; Mouton.

Hirschfeld, Magnus. 1938. *Racism*. London: Victor Gollancz.

hooks, bell. 1981. *Ain't I a woman?: Black women and feminism*. Boston: South End Press.

Hull, Gloria T., Patricia Bell Scott, and Barbara Smith. 1982. *But some of us are brave*. New York: Feminist Press.

Jordan, Glenn, and Chris Weedon. 1995. *Cultural politics: Class, gender, race and the postmodern world*. Oxford and Cambridge: Blackwell.

King, Deborah. 1988. Multiple jeopardy, multiple consciousness. *Signs* 14(1): 42–72.

Koonz, Claudia. 1986. *Mothers in the fatherland*. New York: St. Martin's.

Lewis, Reina. 1996. *Gendering Orientalism: Race, femininity and representation*. London and New York: Routledge.

Memmi, Albert. 1982. *Le racisme: Descriptions, définition, traitement*. Paris: Editions Gallimard.

Miles, Robert. 1989. *Racism*. London: Routledge.

Räthzel, Nora. 1994. Harmonious "Heimat" and Disturbing "Ausländer." In Kum-Kum Bhavnani and Ann Phoenix, eds., *Shifting identities, shifting racisms*, 81–98. London: Sage.

Rommelspacher, Birgit. 1994. Frauen in der Dominanzkultur. In Olga Uremovic and Gundula Oerter, eds., *Frauen zwischen Grenzen: Rassismus und Nationalismus in der feministischen Diskussion*, 18–32. Frankfurt: Campus.

Schütz, Alfred. 1944. The stranger: An essay in social psychology. In Arvid Brodersen, ed., *Collected Papers II—Studies in Social Theory*, 91–106. Den Haag: M. Nihoff.

Simmel, Georg. 1950. The stranger. In Kurt H. Wolff, trans. and ed., *The sociology of Georg Simmel*, 402–408. London: The Free Press of Glencoe, Collier-Macmillan.

Smith, Barbara, ed. 1983. *Home girls: A black feminist anthology*. New York: Kitchen Table Press.

Smith, Joan, Jane Collins, Terence K. Hopkins, and Akbar Muhammad. 1988. *Racism, sexism, and the world-system*. Westport, Conn.: Greenwood.

Smith, Valerie. 1998. *Not just race, not just gender*. London and New York: Routledge.

Taguieff, Pierre-Andre. 1987. *La force du préjugé*. Paris. La Decouverte.

Ware, Vron. 1992. *Beyond the pale*. London: Verso.

Young, Lola. 1996. Fear of the dark: "Race," gender and sexuality in the cinema. London and New York: Routledge.

Zack, Naom, ed. 1996. Race/sex: Their sameness, difference, and interplay. London and New York: Routledge.

Nora Räthzel

RACISM, SCIENTIFIC
See SCIENTIFIC SEXISM AND RACISM.

RADIATION

Radiation is a very general term applied to photons or elementary particles emanating from an object. Photons are microscopically small units of electromagnetic energy having both wave and particle properties. Elementary particles, which make up the atoms of our earth, are called electrons, protons, and neutrons.

Electromagnetic Radiation

This photon radiation travels at the speed of light in wave motions. The wave is characterized by its length, that is, the space required to complete one wave (usually designated by the Greek letter λ, or lambda). The entire spectrum of electromagnetic wavelengths has been mapped out and used by humans. For example, the wavelength used for general radio transmission is about 1600 meters. "Shortwave" radio uses waves less than 60 meters in length. Still shorter waves are used for television transmission or for microwave. The intermediate wavelengths include ultraviolet, visible light, and infrared radiation. The shortest waves are used for X-ray or occur naturally as cosmic rays. These may be as short as 4×10^{-14} meters in length (one-hundredth of a micron). Waves can also be measured by the time required for one wave cycle to pass a fixed point, called the *period* and usually designated as *T*. The frequency, *f*, of a wave, is the number of cycles passing a fixed point per unit of time, mathematically expressed as *1/T*. Electromagnetic waves travel at the speed of light, regardless of their wavelength. Therefore, one can calculate the two other parameters when any one is known. Electromagnetic waves are able to travel through a vacuum, unlike sound waves, which must travel through matter.

When electromagnetic radiation strikes matter, it can be so energetic that it knocks an electron out of its normal orbit around the nucleus of the atom. This electron has a negative charge, and when given an escape velocity it becomes a negatively charged ion. The remaining atom, minus one negative charge, loses its electrically neutral status and becomes an electrically positive ion. The process is called *ionization*. Electromagnetic radiation that is capable of giving electrons an escape velocity when it strikes matter, is called *ionizing radiation*. X-rays and cosmic rays are ionizing radiation. Non-ionizing radiation can cause electrons to vibrate, producing heat, but they do not normally escape from their orbit around the nucleus of the atom. Microwave cooking uses this vibration property to heat food.

Ionizing Particles

Some atoms spontaneously erupt in a statistically predictable pattern, emitting photons or ionizing particles. The photons emitted are called X-rays or gamma rays, depending on whether they are emitted from the nucleus of the atom or from its shell. This radiation is the same as the X-rays and cosmic rays that come to us from the sun and outer space.

Ionizing particles are exploded from radioactive atoms with sufficient force to interact with matter and give an electron escape velocity; hence, they are often called ionizing radiation. The electron is very small and is called a *beta particle,* or beta radiation. Tritium, a radioactive form of hydrogen, emits beta particles or beta radiation and is called a *beta emitter.* The beta particle has a negative electrical charge.

Another type of ionizing particle is the neutron. It is the neutron spontaneously emitted from uranium-135 that initiates the chain reaction we call nuclear fission. In nature the uranium-135 atoms are spaced too far apart to be affected by one another's neutron emissions. In the design of nuclear reactors or nuclear bombs, they are concentrated so that the neutron emitted from one atom causes a second atom to

split, releasing more neutrons. This process continues until all the neutrons are absorbed by a "control" rod in a reactor or are blown apart in a bomb. These ionizing particles are called *neutron radiation.* They are electrically neutral.

A final type of ionizing particle is called an *alpha particle.* It is relatively large, about 70 times the size of an electron or beta particle and 4 times the size of a neutron. An alpha particle consists of two protons and two neutrons, and it has a double positive electrical charge.

Uses of Radiation

Non-ionizing radiation is harnessed by humans for transmission of radio or television programs, for heating, for video display terminals, and for microwave ovens. Daylight is a form of non-ionizing radiation, and so is solar energy. Non-ionizing radiation supports the carbon dioxide cycle and photosynthesis, which enables life on earth. Ionizing radiation is used in nuclear power, smoke detectors, medical X-rays, cancer therapy, inspection of welds, and tracers for oil reserves. Radiation is also used by the military: in non-ionizing forms to create invisible fences or for "crowd control," and in ionizing forms for weapons of mass destruction.

Hazards of Radiation

Non-ionizing radiation is hazardous because of its ability to heat living tissue—that is, to cause burns or coagulation of protein, as in the case of cataracts in the eyes. It can cause skin cancers. Research has indicated that at exposure levels below that which causes burns, non-ionizing radiation can disrupt circadian rhythms such as the sleep cycle, and other biological or body rhythms such as the menstrual cycle or the heartbeat. Persons living near broadcasting towers or children hooked on video games can experience sleep-cycle disruption. Women working with video display terminals may experience disruption of menstruation and potentially adverse pregnancy outcomes.

Ionizing radiation causes breakage of chromosomes, leading to genetic damage or cancers. At chronic low exposure levels, it can cause vulnerability of cell membranes to viral invasion, inflammatory cascades in body tissues, and reduction of blood-cell production in bone marrow or lymph nodes. Exposure has been linked to teratogenic effects (birth defects) in children exposed in utero, mental retardation being the best documented. Given the same exposure level to radiation, women and children suffer more severe health effects than adult males. Women develop about three times the number of thyroid cancers as men, and women's breast, uterine, and cervical tissue is very radiosensitive and thus susceptible to cancer. Children, because of their rapid growth rate, take up and store radioactive particles in their bones at a higher rate than adults. Because of their longer potential lifespan, cancers requiring long latency periods are more likely to develop in children; adults often die of other causes before the cancers are fully developed.

Medical X-rays pose a risk and a benefit to the same person. Their use requires a decision on the part of both the doctor and patient that the benefit outweighs the risk. Using X-rays for screening, as in mammography, is controversial because it may initiate or promote breast cancer as well as detect it at an early stage.

Women's Research on Radiation

The French chemist Marie Curie received the Nobel Prize for the discovery of radium, however, she and her daughter also experienced its harmful effects: both died of what was then called aplastic anemia, a bone marrow disease associated with exposure to ionizing radiation. Alice Stewart of the Department of Epidemiology at the University of Birmingham first pointed out that childhood cancers were associated with exposure of the mother to X-rays during pregnancy. Nancy Wertheimer of the University of Colorado discovered the association between exposure to the electromagnetic field around high-tension electrical transmission lines and breast cancer. Rosalie Bertell measured the aging effect of ionizing radiation, and the effect on blood cells of incorporation of radioactive chemicals in bone.

See Also

CANCER; POLLUTION; TOXICOLOGY

References and Further Reading

Axel, Carlson Elof. 1981. *Genes, radiation, and security: The life and work of H. J. Muller.* Ithaca, N.Y.: Cornell University Press.

Bertell, Rosalie. 1985. *No immediate danger: Prognosis for a radioactive earth.* London: Women's Press.

———, ed. 1997. *Chernobyl: Environmental, health and human resources implications.* Geneva, Switzerland: International Peace Bureau.

Busby, Chris. 1995. *Wings of death: Nuclear pollution and human health.* Aberystwyth, Wales: Green Audit Books.

Caldicott, Leonie, and Stephanie Leland, eds. 1983. *Reclaim the earth.* London: Women's Press.

Caufield, Katherine. 1989. *Multiple exposures.* London: Secker and Harbury.

DeMatteo, Bob. 1985. *Terminal shock: The health hazards of video-display terminals.* Toronto: NC Press.

De Vries, Pieter and Han Seur. 1997. *Mururoa and US: Polynesians' experiences during thirty years of nuclear testing in the French Pacific.* Lyons, France: Centre de documentation et de Recherche sur la Paix et les Conflicts.

Greene, Gayle. 1999. *The woman who knew too much: Alice Stewart and the secrets of radiation.* Ann Arbor, Mich.: University of Michigan Press.

Liakouris, Ana G. Johnson. In press. Re: Sickness in the Lilienfield Study: An effect of modulated microwaves? In *Archives of Environmental Health.*

Rosalie Bertell

RADICAL FEMINISM
See FEMINISM: RADICAL.

RADIO

A review of radio must have certain parameters delineated. First, there are different structures of ownership and control in different countries of the world, and within countries there are several varieties of radio. For instance, in the United States the structure of radio is predominantly commercial. However, the public or noncommercial radio sector is significant and must be considered, particularly when we examine women's roles. Other western countries have a mixture of government and private-sector ownership. There are developing countries in Africa, Asia, and Latin America where the government controls the national radio but there is also a growing mix of community, nonprofit radio, and privately owned urban stations. Each country's radio structure is unique, so it is problematic to generalize about this industry. It is even more dangerous to generalize about the intersection of women and radio, for the same reasons.

United States

In the United States, radio began in the 1920s, created, developed, owned, and controlled by the military and commercial sectors, which are dominated by men. Women played no key roles in the early days of radio because broadcasters had positioned radio as a male-dominated—and evening—entertainment. Owners were initially reluctant to include daytime broadcasts or advertising because these were considered unprofitable. Women at home were not thought of as targetable consumers—until the potential for advertising products to them was realized. Announcers were male; their voices were considered authoritative and suitably low-pitched for the airwaves. Women were hired, but only as singers and actors or to conduct preparatory work for radio shows and interviews. They were not doing the important work of on-air announcing, and they were definitely not in the serious business of reporting the news.

Women's voices were finally heard on the air late in the 1920s in programs covering domestic topics and targeting women as consumers of household products. However, women were not regarded as listeners to serious topics like news. Nor, through the 1930s, were women considered credible as news reporters. The only news team to include a woman—newspaper reporter Florence Conley, who contributed "lifestyle" news—was that of CBS in the mid-1930s. A breakthrough came when Margaret Craven was hired by CBS to produce a news show (1936–1938) in which she discussed the news of the day from a woman's perspective.

During World War II, women became news reporters, announcers, and even managers of radio stations. But, as in other industries, at the war's end men returned to reclaim their positions in radio. Although there was little research to support the belief that women's voices were not considered credible by listeners (Whittaker and Whittaker, 1976), this reason was often cited to take women off the air as announcers and news reporters and to replace them with male voices.

In the 1950s and 1960s, women made inroads in the radio industry. The civil rights and women's movements resulted in greater equality in the workplace, and more women graduated from departments of journalism. Television became a major medium in this period, and many male radio employees moved to television, opening opportunities for women in radio. The Federal Communications Commission's (FCC) enforcement during the 1970s and 1980s of the Equal Employment Opportunity Act and the "public interest" standard resulted in the hiring of more women and minority men. Women began working as reporters, announcers, researchers, hosts, producers, and even managers in the radio industry. Their salaries lagged behind those of their male counterparts, but they were making progress. In 1999 there were approximately 18,000 women holding news-editorial positions in radio in the United States (40 percent of all employees), and their average annual salary was $19,000.

Noncommercial broadcasting in the United States began with a commitment to educational programming, news, and public affairs, and "a mission to serve an underserved audience and provide alternatives" (Kosof, 1993: 170). This field did not seem to hold the general, untested assumption that women and minorities were somehow inferior as journalists, or that women's voices were too high, not serious or credible, and not authoritative. Public radio (and public television) was not as characterized by patriarchal attitudes as commercial radio. National Public Radio (NPR) has a record of hiring many women (and minority) journalists, managers, and producers at the local, state, and national levels (Cramer, 1993; Stone, 1994). Salary differentials have all but disappeared. Public radio has also honored its mandate to showcase programming for women and minorities. This has resulted in part from its high proportion of female and minority employees (Stone, 1994).

As research has demonstrated the falsehood of the ideas that listeners prefer men's voices to women's on the air, and that men are more credible as radio journalists, some female public radio reporters have become well known in the United States. They regularly take top awards for news and public-affairs reporting. NPR has as many women correspondents around the world as men and has both sexes reporting from war zones. Research has also shown that women listen to radio programs of all kinds, including news.

By the turn of the twenty-first century, there were more than 11,000 radio stations in the United States (about 250 of them noncommercial), and 6.6 radios per household, or 2 radios for each person. Radio is still the most popular medium for morning news (38 percent of the market), although in the 1990s radio became largely an entertainment medium, with low-cost "canned" programming consisting mostly of music. Nevertheless, 12 million listeners tune to NPR's daily news programs. On average, people in the United States listen to two hours of radio programming each day, but women who work at home tend to listen more. Much radio listening is done in cars, driving to and from work or shuttling children to activities and school. Therefore, women's listening time is estimated to be much higher than men's.

Particular genres of radio programs in the United States typically exclude women. For example, women talk-show hosts are rare on radio (though not on television); this may be because the approach of these radio shows is usually controversial, abrasive, and ego based—qualities not stereotypically associated with women. Listeners to talk radio shows are predominantly white males. There is a great need for more female voices on commercial talk radio as both hosts and callers. Those that have women hosts have included a nationally syndicated radio sports talk show, a financial show, a psychology show, and a few political talk shows (Petrozzello, 1994). This is certainly an area for possible feminist intervention. There are women-owned and women-run community radio stations in the United States. They play a variety of women's music and produce programs of interest to women. Public radio stations around the country offer "womyn's" music programs, as do college stations, but these have not become popular enough to be national in scope. (Some of these stations are WBBU-FM in Baton Rouge, Louisiana; Breakthrough, KTFT in Houston, Texas; Community Radio in Lincoln, Nebraska; Crystal Feminists in Columbia, Missouri; Face the Music in Worcester, Massachusetts; Feminist Frequencies in Boulder, Colorado; and WINGS [Women's International News Gathering Service], which produces radio news in Austin, Texas.)

If women are to become a force in commercial radio, then they will have to enter the highly competitive market and seek the large audiences needed to sustain a commercial venture. Women constitute the majority of journalism graduates, but few of them pursue careers in radio. Noncommercial radio is still the best prospect, with 44 percent of news jobs held by women. However, in the current climate of government defunding of US public broadcasting, the future of public radio is uncertain.

Canada

The Canadian mixed-ownership model of broadcasting, along with government regulation, has resulted in a remarkable variety of radio programming and access to radio by all. However, commercial radio dominates in Canada and has been heavily influenced by and is often affiliated with US networks. Canadians own slightly less than one radio per person, much less than in the United States. The Canadian Broadcasting Corporation (CBC) is much like the British Broadcasting Corporation (BBC) and the US Corporation for Public Broadcasting in that it is the national public service broadcaster and receives its funds from the government but is supervised by an independent public authority. Like its BBC counterpart in the United Kingdom, CBC provides radio services for diverse audiences and has a mandate to serve and employ women. Commercial radio operators have no such mandate and are therefore not compelled either to serve or to employ women. There are at least two companies in Canada producing news and public affairs programs for women. Coop Radio in Vancouver produces women's music shows, a lesbian show, *Women's Visions,* and *Obaa* (women of color). Matrix Women's Radio in Montreal has two weekly programs.

Australia

In Australia, a variety of radio programs for and about women is heard on the public-service Australian Broadcasting Corporation system and on commercial radio stations. The Women's Radio Network in Sydney is a feminist network producing programs and broadcasting daily around the country.

Europe

The situation of women and radio in Europe is somewhat different. Each European country still has a national (noncommercial or public-service) radio network that provides news and educational programming, though each system is unique. Historically underrepresented in both hiring and focus, women now are employed in public service radio. Research in Germany has shown that women listen to the radio much more than men do (Eichhorn and Keller, 1992). Radio ownership figures in western Europe range from 0.6 per person in Ireland to slightly more than one in Great Britain, to 1.8 in west Germany. Those stations best serving the interests of women are the low-power "free" radio stations that are locally owned and operated and are very popular. (An example is RadiOracle in Norway, which "aims at making the strength, resources, activity, and progress of women visible to the public" [Skard, 1989].) Frederick (1993: 146) mentions that "illegal women's radio stations have appeared in France (Les Nanas Radioteuses), Italy (Radio Donna), and the Netherlands (Vrouwenradio)." Feminist radio stations exist in Europe, but they are few. Radio Z Nuernberg is a feminist-run noncommercial station in Germany. In England there are a few feminist stations such as Brazen Radio and VIVA FM in London and Fem FM in Bristol.

The Developing World

Globally, radio is the most ubiquitous, cost-effective medium with the largest penetration. It enables semiliterate and illiterate populations to be consumers of a variety of programs. Radio ownership is relatively high, because most transistor radios are battery-powered. Recently, a hand-cranked radio has been developed that does not require separately purchased batteries to operate. Solar-powered radio sets sell for less than $40, making this technology extremely low cost in low-latitude countries. In Africa, Latin America, and Asia, radio is the only true mass medium for communicating information to millions of people because of its low cost. Governments use radio to communicate with rural people because television is typically restricted to urban areas.

From the national to the community levels, radio is a much loved medium in which women are playing an increasingly important role. In the Caribbean region, women's voices are often heard on FM radio but not on AM, which is more popular (Cuthbert, 1989). In Latin America, feminist radio stations have been founded in Chile, Costa Rica, and the Dominican Republic (Santa Cruz, 1989).

Costa Rica's Feminist International Radio Endeavor (FIRE) in Colon City has done live broadcasts from different countries in the region and also trained women in radio. It was founded as noncommercial, nongovernmental, and listener-supported, with a mandate to "give women world-wide a voice to speak out on all issues—women's human rights, sexuality, education, art, culture, agriculture, politics, and demilitarization. At last we have a forum in which our ideas may be heard without being dismissed by the patriarchy. We intend to cross the barriers of nation, race, class and culture, to strengthen the international consciousness of women" (Luther, 1994). Chile in the early 1990s had women directing 5 of the 45 radio stations in Santiago, but just 10 of the 125 regional stations (Castellon and Guillier, 1993). In Brazil, radio is considered a powerful communication tool for women's political work. A popular program, *Woman Speaks,* was broadcast daily from Rio de Janeiro to millions of women, as was *Nature Women,* in the Amazon region. UNESCO (United Nations Educational, Scientific, and Cultural Organization) has been involved in establishing FM radio networks in many countries, and nongovernmental organizations have trained rural people to operate community radio stations. Radio Baha'i stations in North and South America and in Africa are excellent examples of local radio, with programs for local people by local people. Because one of the tenets of the Baha'i faith is equality between the sexes, these stations have always included women.

In the past there have been "women's" radio shows in most countries of the world, but as women become more integrated into national power structures, they are using radio more and more as a tool for social development and education. Men still own radios in far larger numbers than women and therefore make up the greater share of listeners. Countries that are targeting women in development are designing radio shows run by women for women on topics such as nutrition, family planning, immunization, health, hygiene, AIDS awareness, and farming. In countries such as Zimbabwe there are radio-listening clubs, and the majority of members are rural women. Radio drama has become an important format for development messages, and soap opera–like programs with didactic messages have a big following among rural people. Small, privately owned community radio stations have appeared in countries such as Nepal and India, often assisted by UNESCO or UNICEF (United Nations Children's Fund). These international aid agencies have focused their development projects on women for decades and have realized that providing women with the means to communicate is a way to empower them. Further interventions by bilateral and multilateral donors will surely assist in global development efforts.

Conclusion

As programming on commercial radio becomes more and more irrelevant to women, and radio becomes more commercial, women are getting more involved in community radio wherever it exists around the world. The philosophy of community, or local, radio was always to serve the interests of the community, and women make up an important community. Women's involvement in community radio is the best bet for the future, and surely a legitimate target of feminist interventions for a better world.

See Also

COMMUNICATIONS: AUDIENCE ANALYSIS; JOURNALISTS; MEDIA: OVERVIEW; TELEVISION

References and Further Reading

Castellon, Lucia, and Alejandro Guillier. 1993. Chile—The emerging influence of women in journalism *Media Studies Journal* 7(1–2: Winter/Spring).

Cramer, Judith A. 1993. A woman's place is on the air. In Pamela J. Creedon, ed., *Women in mass communication.* 2nd ed. Newbury Park, Calif.: Sage.

Creedon, Pamela J., ed. 1993. *Women in mass communication.* 2nd ed. Newbury Park, Calif.: Sage.

Cuthbert, Marlene. 1989. "Woman day a come": Women and communication channels in the Caribbean. In Ramona R. Rush and Donna Allen, *Communications at the crossroads: The gender gap connection,* 149–59. Norwood, N.J.: Ablex.

Eichhorn, W., and M. Keller. 1992. The unknown audience: Typologies of radio listeners in Germany. *European Journal of Communication* 7(1: March).

Frederick, Howard H. 1993. *Global communication and international relations.* Belmont, Calif.: Wadsworth.

Kosof, Anna. 1993. Public radio—Americans want more. Radio: The forgotten medium. *Media Studies Journal* 7(3: Summer): 169–75.

Luther, Sara F. 1994. FIRE! *Radio Resistor's Bulletin,* no. 9 (Dec.).

Petrozzello, Donna. 1994. Women talk show hosts. *Broadcasting and Cable.* 22 August.

Rush, Ramona R., and Donna Allen. 1989. *Communications at the crossroads: The gender gap connection.* Norwood, N.J.: Ablex.

Santa Cruz, Adriana. 1989. Alternative communication and Latin American women. In Ramona R. Rush and Donna Allen, *Communications at the crossroads: The gender gap connection,* 251–64. Norwood, N.J.: Ablex.

Skard, Torild. 1989. Norway: Two-edged s(word)s for women journalists. In Ramona R. Rush and Donna Allen, *Communications at the crossroads: The gender gap connection.* 132–41. Norwood, N.J.: Ablex.

Stone, Vernon. 1994. Radio survey. <www.missouri.edu /~jourvs>.

Whittaker, Susan, and Ron Whittaker. 1976. Relative effectiveness of male and female newscasters. *Journal of Broadcasting* 20(2: Spring).

World Radio and TV Handbook. 1998. Vol. 52. New York: Billboard.

Joy Florence Morrison

RAPE

Rape is a pervasive form of human rights abuse to which women and girls universally are vulnerable. A general definition of rape is sexual relations forced on a woman against her desire, including pressuring or threatening her into consenting, or making her intoxicated and incapable of consenting. The crucial difference between "rape" and "sexual relations" is the former's absence of consent from the woman. Very young women or girls are in no position to give consent, so incest is equivalent to father–daughter rape.

Rape and incest are serious hazards to the integrity of women and girls all over the world. According to studies cited in an international overview (Schuler, 1992), 90 percent of young mothers aged between 12 and 16 years old at a maternity hospital in Lima, Peru, had been raped by their fathers or other close male relatives; a government commission in Canada estimated that every fourth female child and every tenth male child would be sexually assaulted before they had reached the age of 17; and 40 percent of Jamaican girls aged between 11 and 15 years old named the reason for their first intercourse as "forced." In the United States, in a sample of nearly 1,000 women, 4.5 percent had been sexually abused by their fathers by the time they reached 18 years of age, 24 percent of adult women had experienced completed rape, and 31 percent had been exposed to attempted rape (Russell, 1984). The Asian and Pacific Women's Resource Collection Network reported that available information indicates that rape appears to be increasing in all countries of the region. Most countries lack adequate and reliable information concerning rape, incest, and other types of sexual violence directed at women, as well as resources for aiding rape victims and preventing rape. This creates problems in comparing statistics and evaluating the need for resources.

Understanding and Defining Rape

Important contexts for the understanding of rape are the family, the community, and the state. The family plays a crucial role in rape and incest as the arena for the violence, as the mediator and reinforcer of social and cultural norms regarding gendered violence, and as the primary place for support and protection. The community is critical in creating and reinforcing both social norms and rights of women regarding their position in the family and in the community. A community's collective understanding of rape and the conditions under which it occurs determines the outcome of a specific rape incident, both for the perpetrator and for the victim. The state is responsible for formulating and upholding laws, but it is also accountable for promoting sexist values and neglecting the protection of women (Schuler, 1992).

The most common perception of rape is that it is committed by a stranger, an unknown, usually armed man suddenly appearing and attacking a woman physically. Careful investigations indicate that stranger rape is not the most common type but is more often seen as a legitimate transgression to report to the police (Russell, 1984). Far more common is acquaintance rape, in which the rapist already knows the woman, has her confidence and trust, and does not show his intention until the victim is in a situation from which she cannot escape—often, her own home or that of the assailant. Violence in acquaintance rape is sometimes even more brutal than that in stranger rapes.

With stranger rape as the prototype, victimization through other kinds of sexual violence is not recognized as rape: there is less recognition of the trauma for the victim; the rape is not reported; and the rapist is not apprehended or dealt with through legal processes. Ideally, the victim's definitions should be the guide for which experiences are perceived as rape. Women's own definitions, however, are never independent of what society—more specifically, legal authorities—have defined as legitimate to label rape (Estrich, 1987). Incidents not corresponding to the stranger-rape stereotype are usually not reported, and this in turn reinforces the narrow definition. Furthermore, the definition of rape usually covers only incidents of penetration or completed intercourse, excluding other kinds of violations. Rape statistics therefore become inaccurate and unreliable.

In countries where young couples see each other alone and go out together without any formally arranged agreement about their relationship, a form of acquaintance rape—date rape—has emerged as a significant problem. Boyfriends use verbal pressure, threats, and even physical violence to force young women to have sex. Koss and Harvey (1991) estimate that about 20 percent of American female college students have been raped on a date or exposed to attempted rape.

Another form of rape is that committed by a husband, known as marital rape. This is probably the most common and also the most underreported form of rape. Other types of abuse and violence against the woman are common in connection with marital rape (Frieze, 1983; Russell, 1990). Marital rape is not recognized by all legal systems. A common understanding of matrimony is that the woman has relinquished her individual right to give consent for each occasion of sexual relations. Instead, her husband has the legal right to use her body for sexual purposes whenever he wishes. Husbands (and sometimes wives, too) embrace this belief, and a wife's attempt to say "no" can become an occasion for rape. Marital rape, like incest, involves the breach of trust: a person who is supposed to give comfort and support becomes the aggressor. When support and understanding are missing in the immediate environment, all rape victims are more traumatized and recover more slowly. In the case of marital rape and incest, all protection is absent. Instead, the wife, like the incest victim, has to live with the very person who has violated her and has the power to continue doing so.

Another form of rape is group rape, also known as gang rape or multiple rape, in which the woman is attacked and violated by two or more men in cooperation. The objective is not primarily sex, but setting oneself above the law and finding excitement and a sense of power strong enough to seek the experience repeatedly (Scully, 1990).

Group rapes occur not only in criminal gangs but also among more privileged young men in all-male environments like fraternities on university campuses. The Association of American Colleges Project on the Status and Education of Women documented 50 fraternity gang rapes over a period of two or three years in 1985. These male environments emphasize narrow, stereotyped masculine values and norms of behavior while polarizing and stereotyping women, degrading female qualities, and emphasizing men's sexual rights over women (Sanday, 1991).

Custodial rape, which frequently is group rape, involves men in positions of authority—for example, police or men in other state institutions—violating women for whom they have responsibility. Especially vulnerable to custodial rape are politically active women and refugee women. Such human rights abuse is not only a sexual violation but also a form of coercive control equivalent to torture, according to Amnesty International.

War rape is prohibited by the international Geneva Convention of 1949 in a specific article protecting civilian women. Statutes of the armed forces of many individual nations have similar prohibitions. However, circumstances of war make it extremely difficult to prevent, document, and prosecute such rapes. There may be no authorities to complain to, or the legal authorities may be replaced with enemy forces.

Raping is part of military conquest, a way of humiliating the enemy. It is committed both by single individuals and in more organized forms. One insidious kind of assault is the rape of wives and daughters of captured men, who sometimes are forced to watch. On record from World War II both in Europe and in Asia, and mentioned in the Geneva Convention, is forcing captured women to perform sexual services in special brothels. A third kind of organized war rape is revenge, either in lieu of expected confrontations with fighters or as reprisals for actions taken by the enemy.

War rape reveals factors behind rape that otherwise are hidden: the motivation for rape in power, domination, and control (of women in general, or of their men), rather than sexual release. Women raped in war are regarded as inferior and different from the women of the rapists' group or nation. Emphasis on the inferiority of the rape victims and their community justifies degrading treatment. However, sexual relations with these women are not avoided. Nazis in Germany, like white male slave-owners in the Americas, defied their own race laws—which prohibited sexual relations between the two groups—by raping Jewish and black women, respectively (Brownmiller, 1976).

Effects of Rape on Physical and Mental Health

Women fear rape. Surviving victims are relieved to have escaped with their lives. Still, the consequences of rape are a serious hazard to women's physical and mental health from which it may take years to recover. Physical injuries are common. Aside from unwanted pregnancy and sexually transmitted disease, ruptures, bleeding, pain and soreness, bruises, scratches, and other injuries, rape also has serious mental, social, and other costs for the victim.

Almost one-third of rape victims experience posttraumatic stress disorder (PTSD) related to the rape event at some time, including flashbacks when the victim relives the attack, which may continue for years. Compared with victims of other kinds of crime, rape victims have very high levels of continuing PTSD, which also carries the increased risk of alcohol or drug abuse. The intensity and frequency of the psychological reactions of rape survivors are related to the conditions of the actual event, to whether the woman was able to defend herself, and to the response of important people in the immediate environment. Women who are able to offer active resistance have a greater chance of escaping being raped and also of being less traumatized by the event. If the family and community do not support the victim and instead blame her, she may have to withdraw from important social contexts. Some cultures indirectly punish the woman by forcing her to marry her assailant. Without support, the psychological trauma is intensified and healing takes longer, if it ever occurs. By contrast, with care and protection from family, friends, and colleagues, the adverse effects can be mitigated and recovery hastened. Others need to show tolerance and generosity toward the rape victim's attempts to rebuild a sense of self and integrity. Support from men appears to be especially important for heterosexual women (Herman, 1992).

There is no particular kind of woman who is raped. Rape victims are of all ages, and come from all social and economic backgrounds, religious, ethnic, and racial groups. Some groups of women, however, are more protected by the circumstances of their lives from being raped by strangers, while the living conditions of others put them at increased risk—for example, women who live in unsafe, crime-infested neighborhoods. Younger women seem to be at greater risk of being raped by men they are acquainted with than are women over 25 to 30 years old. (Russell, 1984).

Rapists tend to be young, like their victims, although both stranger rapists and known rapists are slightly older than their victims, according to most available studies. However husbands who rape are older on the average. Rapists, at least in the United States, tend to be married rather than unmarried (Russell, 1984).

Stranger rape has mostly been interpreted as an expression of pathological sexuality or a disturbed personality in the rapist. However, those studied are mostly convicted and incarcerated stranger rapists, a definite minority among rapists. Moreover, the pathology explanation is cast in doubt by the pervasiveness of rape, the widespread cultural stereotypes and myths ascribing the responsibility for the crime to the female victims' behavior and appearance, and the fact that many men admit that they would commit rape or force women to have sex without their consent if they could get away with it (Malamuth, 1981). Another popular explanation concerns men's need for sexual release because of their strong and uncontrollable "natural" sexual drives. However, no evidence shows that rapists have greater sexual drives than other men, and many rapists are married. Nor does the high premeditation rate of rape indicate uncontrollable urges.

Rape is not equally common across cultures. Anthropological research indicates a common ideology supporting male hegemony and dominance as a characteristic of societies where rapes occur, and where men also rape to punish and threaten women. Yet women in many cultures are blamed for their own victimization. The impact of rape tends to be minimized, the violations even joked about, as a way of diverting attention from the man. Convicted rapists also blame their victims at the same time as they emphasize the right of men to control and dominate women (Scully, 1990). Rape is what many men feel they are entitled to; when women say "no" to sex, the men take it by force. Cultural and social factors—particularly, unequal distribution of power between women and men—provides the foundation for rape, supported by beliefs about men's superiority. The lack of respect for women's right to give consent to sexual relations is the common factor behind rape and other forms of sexual assault in all cultures.

Rape also has importance for nonvictimized women, who have to monitor their everyday life and their interactions with men in order to avoid being victimized. The fear of rape, paradoxically, is reinforced by well-intentioned warnings and safety instructions; it limits women's ability to move about freely and to be involved in activities of their own choice. The most common strategy women use to escape violence from men is to curtail their activities and to barricade themselves in their homes, isolating themselves behind locks, not going out after dark, avoiding all situations of potential risk. All this interferes with women's ability to live normal lives—for example, to take certain jobs or visit friends and relatives. Nonetheless, these concerns are based on realistic assessments; a rape can end with death or injuries that take a very long time to heal. Most precautions concern stranger rape, but protection against rape by a known man is not discussed. How much women's deliberate avoidance of potentially dangerous situations affects the number of actual incidents is unknown.

The behavior of women trapped in rape situations can influence the outcome of such a position. However, this should never be interpreted to mean that every woman threatened by rape can avoid it. This always depends on the attacker, who may kill his victim. Myths and stereotypes surrounding rape often tell women that rape is unavoidable and that the best strategy to save one's life is not to resist. At the same time, it is a common belief, especially in legal contexts, that only a woman's resistance is proof of her lack of consent. Many rapists subscribe to stereotyped ideas about women and rape. They misinterpret an appeal from the victim not to hurt her as an acceptance of the rape, as long as the woman is not seriously injured. Most women attempt to escape a threatening situation by pleading or reasoning with the assailant, strategies that have been found to be useless. Active resistance usually increases the likelihood of avoiding rape. Comparisons between situations in which women avoided being raped and situations in which they did not indicate that injuries are related less to the victim's resistance than to the violence of the initial attack. Because most rapes are planned, the opportunities for a woman to escape are not obvious. More successful avoidance strategies are based on multiple approaches and being flexible. Screaming and physical resistance—scratching, biting, kicking, and hiding behind furniture while looking for an escape route—increase the chances of avoiding rape (Ullman, 1990). Convicted and incarcerated rapists indirectly validate that women who resist and fight back are more likely to escape from stranger-rape situations. Acquaintance rapes occurring indoors are more likely to be completed when weapons are employed, and they also result in more injuries to the victim (Scully, 1990).

Collective strategies against rape require organizing locally, nationally, and internationally. Necessary actions include documenting, protesting, and lobbying for legal change, as well as financing facilities for helping rape victims. Educational programs for men and the public to prevent rape and other sexual violations of women are essential.

See Also

ABUSE; ETHNIC CLEANSING; INCEST; POWER; SEXUAL SLAVERY; TORTURE; VIOLENCE AND PEACE: OVERVIEW; WAR

References and Further Reading

Brownmiller, Susan. 1976. *Against Our Will: Men, women and rape.* Harmondsworth: Penguin.

Estrich, Susan. 1987. *Real rape.* Cambridge, Mass.: Harvard University Press.

Frieze, Irene Hanson. 1983. Causes and consequences of marital rape. *Signs: Journal of Women in Culture and Society* 8: 532–53.

Herman, Judith Herman. 1992. *Trauma and recovery.* New York: Basic Books.

Koss, Mary P. and Mary R. Harvey. 1991. *The rape victim: Clinical and community interventions.* Newbury Park, Calif.: Sage.

Malamuth, Neil, M. 1981. Rape proclivity among males. *Journal of Social Issues* 37: 138–57.

Russell, Diana. 1984. *Sexual exploitation: Rape, child sexual abuse, and workplace harassment.* Newbury Park, Calif.: Sage.

Sanday, Peggy Reeves. 1991. *Fraternity gang rape: Sex, brotherhood, and privilege on campus.* New York: New York University Press.

Schuler, Margaret. 1992. Violence against women: An international perspective. In Margaret Schuler, ed., *Freedom from violence: Women's strategies from around the world.* New York: OEF International.

Scully, Diana. 1990. *Understanding sexual violence: A study of convicted rapists.* London: HarperCollins Academic.

Ullman, Sarah E. 1990. A social psychological analysis of women's resistance to rape. PhD. dissertation, Brandeis University, Waltham, MA.

Mona Lisbet Eliasson

REFERENCE SOURCES

Authors' reference sources are works that assist readers in locating information. Encyclopedias, dictionaries, directories, biographical sources, statistical compilations, handbooks, bibliographies, and indexes are examples of the types of reference sources compiled by librarians and scholars. Since the appearance of a reference source generally awaits the publication of a sizable number of articles and books on a topic, it is a mark of the maturity of the field of women's studies that today there are hundreds of reference works covering all aspects of the field, necessitating metaguides to the reference works (Ballou, 1987; Carter and Ritchie, 1990). The blossoming of women's studies reference materials began in the 1970s, but as late as 1986, librarians writing about reference sources in the field found deficient categories: "statistical sources, encyclopedias, yearbooks, and abstracting and indexing sources including databases" (Josephine and Blouin, 1986: 114). With the exception of adequate representation in mainstream on-line databases, by the late 1990s this situation had changed dramatically. This article surveys reference publishing in women's studies since 1970, examines indexing issues, and mentions the phenomenon of reference sources on the Internet.

Reference Books

Some of the first reference works in women's studies were biographical, reclaiming women ignored or given only scant notice in earlier publications. (Examples are *Notable American Women, 1607–1950* (James et al., 1971), and *American Black Women in the Arts and Social Sciences* (Williams, 1973, and revisions). Throughout the 1970s, other types of reference works appeared: directories (Berkowitz, 1974);

guides to archival collections (Hinding et al., 1979); catalogs of important women's collections, such as the three-volume set (1973), later expanded to ten (1984), of the catalog of The Arthur and Elizabeth Schlesinger Library on the History of Women in America, Radcliffe College, and the *Catalog of the Sophia Smith Collection Women's History Archive,* Smith College (1976); filmographies (Dawson, 1975); financial aid (Schlachter, 1978–); quotations (Partnow, 1977, and revisions thereafter); and general resources (Froschl and Williamson, 1977; Wheeler, 1972 and 1975). Stineman (1979) provided descriptions of 1,763 books and periodicals. The Stineman reference chapters may be consulted for information on other reference works published during the 1970s.

Moving into the 1980s, Searing (1985) led researchers through the intricacies of performing research in women's studies, and Ariel (1987) offered librarians a resource guide to building women's studies collections. The first volume ("Views from the Sciences") of a three-volume Women's Studies encyclopedia, edited by Tierney, appeared in 1989. Loeb, Searing, and Stineman (1987) surveyed more than 1,200 new titles published during 1980–1985, including chapters on reference sources that provide additional reference titles from the first half of the decade. Women's language and usage received attention from Miller and Swift (1980, 1988) and Maggio (1987); Kramarae and Treichler (1985) offered feminist definitions and quotations. Because of the foresight of nineteenth-century curators in the State Historical Society of Wisconsin who amassed the strongest collection of women's periodicals and newspapers in North America, *Women's Periodicals and Newspapers from the 18th Century to 1981: A Union List of the Holdings of Madison, Wisconsin, Libraries* (Danky 1982) became a major source for historians.

Women writers and writing were the subject of numerous reference volumes, with Schlueter and Schlueter (1988) contributing an encyclopedia of British women writers, Mainiero (1979–82 and 1994) a guide to American women writers, and Frost and Valiquette (1988) a bibliography of feminist literary criticism. Humm (1987) provided entreé to the growing area of feminist criticism across many disciplines.

By the 1980s, reference works also reflected the shift from generic research on "women" to examination of issues specific to lesbians and women of various cultural backgrounds. Cruikshank (1982) and Potter (1986) carved a niche for lesbian studies on the reference shelf; Cantor (2nd ed. 1987) did the same for Jewish women, Sakala (1980) for women of South Asia, and Wei (1984) for women in China. Duley and Edwards (1986) produced a comprehensive curriculum guide for cross-cultural courses on women, and

Memphis State University Center for Research on Women maintained an ongoing bibliography on *Women of Color and Southern Women* (Timberlake et al., 1988 and supplements through 1994).

Reference works appeared covering women in all fields of endeavor. Kaye Sullivan (1980, 1985) added two volumes on films for, by, and about women. Legal scholarship was tracked by law students at Benjamin N. Cardozo School of Law, Yeshiva University, (1984). Encyclopedias and dictionaries of women composers (Cohen, 1981) and artists (Petteys, 1985) appeared. In 1986, Nordquist began publishing a bibliographic series that has addressed numerous issues affecting women, including the feminization of poverty, pornography, eating disorders, rape, and aging, along with a second series covering feminist theorists.

The 1990s brought such a proliferation of specialized and general reference works that even large library reference collections have to choose among competing books covering the same territory. Olsen and Trager both published chronologies of women's history in 1994, followed the next year by two more (Franck, Greenspan), and a fifth thereafter (Weatherford, 1997). One-volume encyclopedias of American women's history aimed at the general reader abound (Zophy and Kavenik, 1990; Frost-Knappman, 1994; Weatherford, 1994; Cullen-DuPont, 1996; Mankiller et al., 1998). Additional reference sources on British women writers have been authored by Shattock (1993) and Todd (1989), and the *Feminist Companion to Literature in English* (Blain, Clements, and Grundy, 1990) assists readers of British and American women's literature. The National Council for Research on Women published a *Directory of National Women's Organizations* in the United States (1992), and in 1993 Gale Research issued both a *Women's Information Directory* (Brennan), covering U.S.-based women's organizations and other resources, and an *Encyclopedia of Women's Associations Worldwide* (Barrett). The National Women's Studies Association of the United States issued a directory of women's studies programs in 1990, as did Stafford.

In the 1980s and even more in the 1990s, the internationalizing of women's studies interests provided a ready audience for works on women from all over the world. Isis International, based in Santiago, Chile, and elsewhere maintained an international database of women-focused information, used as a source for several reference publications, including an international directory of women's periodicals (1988–). Conditions for women worldwide were vividly represented in an atlas (Seager and Olson, 1986, rev. by Seager, 1997), while Gibson and Fast used that format to portray the status of women in the United States (1986; rev. by Fast and Fast, 1995). Global statistics on women were compiled by the United Nations (1991 and 1995), and Schmittroth (1991, 1995), with Taeuber (1991, 1996), contributed a detailed statistical handbook on women in the United States. Attention focused on women in the third world in several works, including Kinnear (1997) and Stromquist (1998).

Surveying the breadth of women's studies research and programmatic information remained an important concern in the 1990s. Brownmiller and Dickstein (1994, 1996) covered elusive material published in anthologies. In 1993, Women's International Studies Europe (WISE) issued a detailed *European Women's Studies Guide* (2nd ed. 1997), while Brown et al. provided worldwide information in *The International Handbook of Women's Studies* (1993).

The biographical area was also active in the 1990s, reaching coverage of women absent from the published record except in biographical dictionaries. Telgen and Kamp (1993) surveyed Hispanic-American women, as did Bataille (1993) for Native American women. Three important biographical works on African-American women appeared in rapid succession (Smith, 1992, 1996; Hine, 1993; Salem, 1993), followed by the first biohistorical reference work on American Jewish women (Hyman and Moore, 1997).

The publishers Garland/Routledge, Greenwood, G. K. Hall, ABC-CLIO, Gale, McFarland, Scarecrow, and Oxford produce a steady output of women's studies reference works, occasionally joined by other established publishers, university departments and libraries, and small presses. Weisbard's column, "New Reference Works in Women's Studies," appearing in *Feminist Collections: A Quarterly of Women's Studies Resources,* and the "Reference/Bibliography" chapter of the twice-yearly *New Books on Women and Feminism* (1979–) are ongoing comprehensive sources of information about new reference publications in the English language. Ariel's annual *Reference* core list recognizes the most important women's studies reference works in print.

Indexes and Catalogs

The poor representation of women's studies journals in standard indexes led to the creation of *Women Studies Abstracts* in 1972, followed by *Feminist Periodicals: A Current Listing of Contents* in 1981 and *Women's Studies Index* in 1991 (covering 1989). These indexes are supplemented by *Studies on Women Abstracts* (1983–), which selectively abstracts from a broad range of mainstream academic journals, *Canadian Women's Periodical Index* (1989–94), and *Ny Litteratur om Kvinnor* (New literature on women) (1980–) for additional international coverage. Krikos (1994) compared the strengths and weaknesses of *Women Studies*

Abstracts, Women's Studies Index, and *Studies on Women Abstracts,* concluding that the scope and depth of *Women Studies Abstracts* makes it the most essential of the three for research collections. Retrieval eased considerably with the advent of the CD-ROM version of *Women's Studies Index* (*Women's Studies on Disc*) in 1995, followed the next year by *Women's Resources International,* a database that incorporates *Women Studies Abstracts, New Books on Women and Feminism,* and several other resources. These bibliographic resources were joined in 1997 by two full-text databases. *Contemporary Women's Issues* and *Women "R"* (later called *GenderWatch*). The four products were assessed as reference tools by Dickstein et al. (1998), who concluded that *Women's Resources International* and *Contemporary Women's Issues* are the preferred products in their categories for academic libraries.

Because these products survey women's studies as an interdisciplinary field, they are indispensable to the women's studies researcher. Nevertheless, librarians have observed that many users rely on standard discipline-oriented indexes or broad-brush tables of content services available on-line. Therefore, librarians have repeatedly examined the coverage of women's studies journals in such indexes and services, found them wanting, and advocated additional inclusion (Wheeler, 1983; Sanguinetti, 1984; Mesplay and Koch, 1993; Gerhard, Jacobson, and Williamson, 1993; Koch and Preece, 1995; Faries, 1998).

Being included in indexes is only half the solution, though. *How* women's studies works are indexed has also been an abiding concern. Atkinson and Hudson (1990) provide a detailed look at the anomalies inherent in researching women-related topics in a variety of on-line periodical indexes and catalogs. Marshall (1977) and Capek (1987) list women-specific terms that could be incorporated by catalogers and indexers. Recognizing that most U.S. cataloging is based on Library of Congress subject headings (LCSH), Dickstein, Mills, and Waite (1988) extracted all the women-focused terms in LCSH and presented them in lists structured according to the arrangement in Capek (1987), with the hope of spurring the identification of deficiencies and the need for revisions. Although LCSH has incorporated many of the suggested revisions, Rogers (1993) nevertheless reported on remaining subtle forms of gender bias.

The significance of exact subject heading formulation may be diminishing, however, with the advent of on-line searching mechanisms that allow for keyword retrieval of a term present anywhere in a citation, automatic searching of synonyms, inquiries formulated in natural language, retrieval ranked by number of occurrences of a term, and more full-text databases that can be searched directly, circumventing the problem of second-guessing an indexer. Women's studies will benefit from these advances in database construction, but as the amount of material present in electronic form grows, accurate descriptive terms will continue to be useful for efficiently homing in on relevant information.

Reference Sources on the Internet

Files residing on the Internet constitute the newest reference format available in women's studies. Though many of these files have print equivalents (e.g., National Women's Studies Association, 1990, and miscellaneous women's studies course syllabi), their dissemination is much wider on the Internet. Other material, such as searchable archives of messages sent to electronic discussion lists, is unique to the Internet. The unsystematic explosion of information on the Internet has set the scene for a new category of reference material: subject-arranged guides to Internet resources. Early print guides by Hunt (1993) and Hudson and Turek (1994) provided access to on-line women's studies resources available at that time, while meta–Web sites like *WSSLINKS* (a project of the Women's Studies Section Collection Development Committee of the Association of College and Research Libraries), *Women's Studies/Women's Issues* (maintained by Korenman), and *Selected Women and Gender Resources on the World Wide Web* (maintained by Weisbard) now function as reference sources on the Web itself, providing organized links to content-rich women's studies sites. New resources are routinely announced in *Feminist Collections* and on appropriate discussion lists. In addition, Korenman combines the convenience of a print publication with the need for currency by mounting updates to her *Internet Resources on Women: Using Electronic Media in Curriculum Transformation* (1997) on a Web site: <http://www-unix.umbc.edu /~korenman/wmst/updates.html>.

Conclusion

An expanding array of reference sources, in print and on-line, describe, organize, and distill more than a quarter century of academic women's studies output for use by researchers, students, librarians, and the general public. Most of these works have been book-length subject bibliographies, encyclopedias, directories, and handbooks, akin to reference sources found in other disciplines. Women's studies indexes surveying the full interdisciplinary field began in print but have migrated to electronic format, joined by new products that have no history as print publications. Expansion and enhancements of general academic databases, along with systematic arrangement of material on the Internet, will improve reference capabilities in women's studies in the future.

See Also

INFORMATION TECHNOLOGY; LIBRARIES; WOMEN'S STUDIES: OVERVIEW

References and Further Reading

Ariel, Joan. 1987. *Building women's studies collections.* Middletown, Conn.: Choice.

———. 2000. *Reference: Core List in Women's Studies.* Madison, WI: Women's Studies Section Collection Development Committee of the Association of College and Research Libraries. Also at <http://www.library.wisc.edu/libraries /WomensStudies/core/erref.htm>.

Atkinson, Steven D., and Judith Hudson. 1990. *Women online: Research in women's studies using online databases.* New York: Haworth.

Ballou, Patricia K. 1987. *Women: A bibliography of bibliographies.* Boston: G. K. Hall.

Barrett, Jacqueline K. 1993. *Encyclopedia of women's associations worldwide.* London: Gale Research.

Base de datos mujer: directorio de publicaciones periodicas (Women's data base: Directory of Periodical Publications). 1988. Santiago de Chile: Isis Internacional.

Bataille, Gretchen M. 1993. *Native American women.* New York: Garland.

Berkowitz, Tamar. 1974. *Who's who and where in women's studies.* New York: Feminist Press.

Blain, Virginia, Patricia Clements, and Isabel Grundy, eds. 1990. *Feminist companion to literature in English.* New Haven: Yale University Press.

Brennan, Shawn, ed. 1993. *Women's information directory.* Detroit: Gale Research.

Brown, Loulou, Helen Collins, Pat Green, Maggie Humm, and Mel Landells. 1993. *The international handbook of women's studies (W.I.S.H.).* London: Harvester/Wheatsheaf.

Brownmiller, Sara, and Ruth Dickstein. 1994. *An index to women's studies anthologies: Research across the disciplines 1980–84.* New York: G. K. Hall.

———. 1996. *An index to women's studies anthologies: Research across the disciplines 1985–89.* New York: G. K. Hall.

Canadian women's periodicals index. 1989–94. Ottawa: Canadian Research Institute for the Advancement of Women.

Cantor, Aviva. 1987. *The Jewish woman.* 2nd ed. Fresh Meadows, N.Y.: Biblio.

Capek, Mary Ellen S. 1987. *A women's thesaurus: An index of language used to describe and locate information by and about women.* New York: Harper and Row.

Benjamin N. Cardozo School of Law. 1984. *Women's annotated legal bibliography.* Vol. 1. New York: Clark Boardman.

Carter, Sarah, and Maureen Ritchie. 1990. *Women's studies: A guide to information sources.* Jefferson, N.C.: McFarland.

Catalog of the Sophia Smith Collection Women's History Archive 1976. 2nd ed. Northampton, Mass.: Smith College.

Cohen, Aaron I. 1981. *International encyclopedia of women composers.* New York: Bowker.

Contemporary women's issues [computer file]. 1997. Beachwood, Ohio: Responsive Database Services.

Cruikshank, Margaret. 1982. *Lesbian studies present and future.* New York: Feminist Press.

Cullen-DuPont, Kathryn. 1996. *The encyclopedia of women's history in America.* New York: Facts on File.

Danky, James P., ed., and Maureen E. Hady, Barry Christopher Noonan, and Neil E. Strache, comps., in association with the State Historical Society of Wisconsin. 1982. *Women's periodicals and newspapers from the 18th century to 1981: A union list of the holdings of Madison, Wisconsin, libraries.* Boston: G.K. Hall.

Dawson, Bonnie. 1975. *Women's films in print: An annotated guide to 800 16mm films by women.* San Francisco: Booklegger.

Dickstein, Ruth, Marcia Evans, Lisa German, Jessica Grim, and Sandra A. River. 1998. From zero to four: A review of four new Women's Studies CD-ROM products. *The Serials Librarian* 35(1/2): 59–84.

Dickstein, Ruth, Virginia A. Mills, and Ellen Waite. 1988. *Women in LC's terms: A thesaurus of Library of Congress subject headings relating to women.* Phoenix: Oryx.

Duley, Margot I., and Mary I. Edwards, eds. 1986. *The cross-cultural study of women.* New York: Feminist Press.

Faries (Ingold), Cindy. 1998. Preserving the value of tables of contents online: A critique of Women's Studies/feminist periodicals. *Serials Librarian* 35(1/2): 85–124.

Feminist collections: A quarterly of women's studies resources. 1980–. Madison: University of Wisconsin System Women's Studies Librarian.

Feminist periodicals: A current listing of contents. 1981–. Madison: University of Wisconsin System Women's Studies Librarian.

Franck, Irene M. 1995. *Women's world: A timeline of women in history.* New York: Harper Perennial.

Froschl, Merle, and Jane Williamson. 1977. *Feminist resources for schools and colleges.* New York: Feminist Press.

Frost, Wendy, and Michele Valiquette. 1988. *Feminist literary criticism: A bibliography of journal articles 1975–1981.* New York: Garland.

Frost-Knappman, Elizabeth. 1994. *The ABC-CLIO companion to women's progress in America.* Santa Barbara, Calif.: ABC-CLIO.

GenderWatch [computer file]. 1997. Stamford, Conn.: Softline Information.

Gerhard, Kristin, Trudi E. Jacobson, and Susan G. Williamson. 1993. Indexing adequacy and interdisciplinary journals: The case of Women's Studies. *College & Research Libraries* 54(3): 125–33.

Gibson, Anne, and Timothy Fast. 1986. *The women's atlas of the United States.* New York: Facts on File (rev. ed. 1995, Timothy Fast and Cathy Carroll Fast).

Greenspan, Karen. 1995. *The timetables of women's history: A chronology of the most important people and events in women's history.* New York: Simon & Schuster.

Hinding, Andrea, ed., Ames Sheldon Bower, assoc. ed., Clarke A. Chambers, consult. ed. 1979. *Women's history sources: A guide to archives and manuscript collections in the United States.* New York: Bowker.

Hine, Darlene Clark, ed. 1993. *Black women in America: An historical encyclopedia.* 2 vols. Brooklyn: Carlson.

Hudson, Judith, and Kathleen A. Turek. 1994. *Electronic access to research on women: A short guide.* 2nd ed. Albany, NY: Institute for Research on Women, State University of New York, Albany.

Humm, Maggie. 1987. *An annotated critical bibliography of feminist criticism.* Boston: G. K. Hall.

Hunt, Laura. 1993. *Sources for women's studies/feminist information on the Internet.* 2nd ed. Ann Arbor: University of Michigan.

Hyman, Paula E., and Deborah Dash Moore, eds. 1997. *Jewish women in America: An historical encyclopedia.* 2 vols. New York: Routledge.

James, Edward T., ed., Janet Wilson James, assoc. ed., Paul S. Boyer, assist. ed. 1971. *Notable American women, 1607–1950.* Cambridge, Mass.: Harvard University Press.

Josephine, Helen B., and Deborah K. Blouin. 1986. New reference sources on women: An analysis and proposal. *Reference Librarian* 15(Fall): 109–22.

Kinnear, Karen L. 1997. *Women in the third world: A reference handbook.* Santa Barbara, Calif.: ABC-CLIO.

Koch, Loretta P., and Barbara G. Preece. 1995. Table of contents services: Retrieving Women's Studies periodical literature. *RQ* 35(1): 76–86.

Korenman, Joan. 1997. *Internet resources on women: Using electronic media in curriculum transformation.* Baltimore: National Center for Curriculum Transformation Resources on Women. Updates at <http://www-unix.umbc.edu/~korenman/wmst/updates.html>.

———. 1994. *Women's Studies/Women's issues resource sites.* <http://research.umbc.edu/~korenman/wmst/links.html>.

Kramarae, Cheris, and Paula A. Treichler. 1985. *A feminist dictionary: In our own words.* London: Pandora.

Krikos, Linda. 1994. Women's Studies periodical indexes: An in-depth comparison. *Serials Review* 20(2): 65–78, 82.

Loeb, Catherine, Susan E. Searing, and Esther Stineman. 1987. *Women's studies: A recommended core bibliography, 1980–1985.* Littleton, Conn.: Libraries Unlimited.

Maggio, Rosalie. 1987. *The nonsexist word finder: A dictionary of gender-free usage.* Phoenix: Oryx.

Mainero, Lina. 1979–82 (vols. 1–4) and 1994 (vol. 5). *American women writers: A critical reference guide from colonial times to the present.* New York: Unger.

Mankiller, Wilma, Gwendolyn Mink, Marysa Navarro, Barbara Smith, and Gloria Steinem, eds. 1998. *The reader's companion to U.S. women's history.* Boston: Houghton Mifflin.

Marshall, Joan K. 1977. *On equal terms: A thesaurus for non-sexist indexing and cataloging.* New York: Neal-Schuman.

Mesplay, Deborah, and Loretta Koch. 1993. An evaluation of indexing services for Women's Studies periodical literature. *RQ* 32(3): 404–10.

Miller, Casey, and Kate Swift. 1980. *The handbook of nonsexist writing for writers, editors and speakers.* New York: Lippincott & Crowell (1988, New York: Harper and Row).

National Council for Research on Women. 1992. *Directory of national women's organizations.* New York: National Council for Research on Women.

National Women's Studies Association. 1990. *Directory of women's studies programs, women's centers, and women's research centers.* College Park, MD: National Women's Studies Association. Also at <http://www.inform.umd.edu:8080/EdRes/Topic/WomensStudies/ReferenceRoom/Directories/WomensStudiesPrograms.>

Nordquist, Joan. 1986–. *Contemporary social issues: A bibliographic series.* Santa Cruz, Calif.: Reference and Research Services.

Ny Litteratur om Kvinnor (New literature on women) 1980–. Göteborg, Sweden: Göteborgs Universitetsbibliotek, Kvinnohistoriska samlingarna.

Olsen, Kirsten. 1994. *Chronology of women's history.* Westport, Conn.: Greenwood.

Partnow, Elaine. 1977. *The quotable woman.* Los Angeles: Corwin.

———. 1992. *The new quotable woman.* New York: Facts on File.

Petteys, Chris. 1985. *Dictionary of women artists: An international dictionary of women artists born before 1900.* Boston: G. K. Hall.

Potter, Clare, ed. 1986. *The lesbian periodicals index.* Tallahassee, Fla.: Naiad.

Rogers, Margaret N. 1993. Are we on equal terms yet: Subject headings concerning women in LCSH 1975–1991. *Library Resources and Technical Services* 37(April): 181–96.

Sakala, Carol. 1980. *Women of South Asia: A guide to resources.* Millwood, N.Y.: Kraus.

Salem, Dorothy C. 1993. *African American women.* New York: Garland.

Sanguinetti, Mary Alice. 1984. Indexing of feminist periodicals. *Serials Librarian* 8(Summer): 21–33.

Schlachter, Gail. 1978–. *Directory of financial aids for women.* Santa Barbara, Calif.: Reference Service.

The Arthur and Elizabeth Schlesinger Library on the History of Women in America. 1973, 1984. *The manuscript inventories and the catalogs of manuscripts, books, and periodicals.* Boston: G. K. Hall.

Schlueter, Paul, and Jane Schlueter. 1988. *An encyclopedia of British women writers.* New York: Garland. Subsequently incorporated into (with Katharina M. Wilson) *Women writers of Great Britain and Europe.* New York: Garland, 1997.

Schmittroth, Linda. 1995. *Statistical record of women worldwide.* 2nd ed. London: Gale Research.

Seager, Joni, and Ann Olson. 1986. *Women in the world: An international atlas.* New York: Simon & Schuster (rev. ed.: Seager, Joni. 1997. *The state of women in the world atlas.* New York: Penguin).

Searing, Susan E. 1985. *Introduction to library research in women's studies.* Boulder, Colo.: Westview.

Shattock, Joanne. 1993. *The Oxford guide to British women writers.* New York: Oxford University Press.

Smith, Jessie Carney. 1992. *Notable black American women.* London and Detroit: Gale Research.

———. 1996. *Notable black American women, Book II.* Detroit: Gale Research.

Stafford, Beth. 1990. *Directory of women's studies programs and library resources.* Phoenix: Oryx.

Stineman (Lanigan), Esther. 1979. *Women's studies: A recommended core bibliography.* Littleton, Col.: Libraries Unlimited.

Stromquist, Nelly P., ed. 1998. *Women in the third world: An encyclopedia of contemporary issues.* New York: Garland.

Studies on women abstracts. 1983–. Abingdon, Oxfordshire, Eng.: Carfax.

Sullivan, Kaye. 1980. *Films for, by and about Women.* Metuchen, N.J.: Scarecrow (rev. ed. 1985).

Taeuber, Cynthia. 1996. *Statistical handbook on women in America.* 2nd ed. Phoenix: Oryx.

Telgen, Diane, and Jim Kamp. 1993. *Notable Hispanic American women.* London and Detroit: Gale Research.

Tierney, Helen. 1989. *Women's studies encyclopedia.* 3 vols. New York: Greenwood.

Timberlake, Andrea, Lynn Weber Cannon, Rebecca F. Guy, and Elizabeth Higginbotham, eds. 1988. *Women of color and southern women: A bibliography of social science research, 1975 to 1988.* Memphis, Tenn.: Memphis State University Center for Research on Women (also *Annual Supplements,* 1989–1994).

Todd, Janet. 1989. *British women writers: A critical reference guide.* New York: Continuum.

Trager, James T. 1994. *The women's chronology.* New York: Holt.

United Nations. 1995. *The world's women: Trends and statistics.* 2nd ed. New York: United Nations. Updates at <http://www.un.org/Depts/unsd/gender/intro.htm>.

Weatherford, Doris. 1994. *American women's history.* New York: Prentice Hall.

———. 1997. *Milestones: A chronology of women's history.* New York: Facts on File.

Wei, Karen. 1984. *Women in China: A selected and annotated bibliography.* Westport, Conn.: Greenwood.

Weisbard, Phyllis Holman. 1992. New reference works in women's studies. Column in *Feminist Collections: A Quarterly of Women's Studies Resources.*

———. 1996. *Selected women and gender resources on the World Wide Web.* University of Wisconsin System Women's Studies Librarian's Office. <http://www.library.wisc.edu/libraries/WomensStudies/others.htm>.

Wheeler, Helen Rippier. 1972, and supplement 1975. *Womanhood media: Current resources about women.* Metuchen, N.J.: Scarecrow.

———. 1983. A feminist researcher's guide to periodical indexes, abstracting services, citation indexes, and online databases. *Collection Building* 5(Fall): 3–24.

Williams, Ora. 1973. *American black women in the arts and social sciences: A bibliographic survey.* Metuchen, NJ: Scarecrow (rev. eds. 1978, 1994).

Wilson, Carolyn, ed. 1979 Reference/bibliography. Chapter in semiannual *New books on women and feminism.* Madison: University of Wisconsin System Women's Studies Librarian.

Women Studies abstracts. 1972–. New Brunswick, N.J.: Transaction Periodicals Consortium.

Women's International Studies Europe (WISE). 1997. *European women's studies guide.* 2nd ed. Utrecht: WISE.

Women's Studies index. 1991–. CD-ROM title: *Women's studies on disc.* 1995–. New York: G. K. Hall.

Women's Studies Section Collection Development Committee of the Association of College and Research Libraries.

WSSLINKS: Women and gender studies Websites. Cambridge, Mass.: Humanities Library Massachusetts Institute of Technology. <http://libraries.mit.edu/humanities/WomensStudies/wscd.html>

Zophy, Angela Howard, and Frances M. Kavenik, eds. 1990. *Handbook of American women's history.* New York: Garland.

Phyllis Holman Weisbard

REFUGEES

Everyday, thousands of people flee their homes in terror, carrying what little they can. Of the world's more than 50 million refugees and displaced persons (UNHCR:2000), at least 75 percent are women and small children. The 1951 United Nations Convention Relating to the Status of Refugees (Article I.A. [2]) defines a refugee as a person who is outside his or her country of origin and is unable or unwilling to return owing to a well-founded fear of persecution for reasons of race, religion, nationality, membership of a particular social group, or political opinion.

The phrase *internally displaced persons* refers to individuals who have been forced to flee their homes suddenly or unexpectedly in large numbers, as a result of armed conflict, internal strife, abuses of human rights, or natural disasters, but who remain within the territory of their own country. Because the distinction between refugees and displaced persons is made on political grounds rather than differences in behavior and needs, refugees and displaced persons are both referred to as "refugees" in this article.

Being a female refugee is especially stressful. All refugees have been uprooted from their homes because of persecution, violence, insufficient food, and other life-threatening events and who now have to survive in unfamiliar environments with new social structures, relationships, languages, illnesses, and other difficult conditions. Refugee status automatically carries additional stigmas such as dependence, statelessness, homelessness, and unemployability. Being female makes this adjustment much more difficult because of women's powerlessness and inferior social status vis-à-vis men in most societies.

Women are responsible for generational continuity by giving birth and raising children. They also carry heavy biological, emotional, and economic responsibilities associated with their roles as mother, wife, nurturer, and provider. Refugee women are even more marginalized than women in general; yet as refugees, their responsibilities increase disproportionately to those of men.

It is a truism of human cultures that higher social status and increased responsibilities and functions go hand in hand for men, but not for women. Although in most societies women work harder than men and go through greater biological and physiological hardships owing to pregnancy, childbirth, and lactation, their productive and reproductive contributions are rarely acknowledged as more valuable, and women are rarely, if ever, treated as the social equals of men.

This existential anomaly is even more evident in refugee situations, where women's various roles are all more demanding than in their normal lives. Being a refugee and being female combine with drastic consequences for women's physical and mental well-being.

Gender

Being a refugee is experienced differently by women and men because of their genders. Women generally do not have the same status as men, nor are they treated equally. The power relationship between the sexes is uneven; men often dictate women's ideal roles and behaviors through dominant cultural values. This inequality is exacerbated when women become refugees.

Women flee their homes and start over, often in an alien land, yet they have little decision-making power or control over their own or their children's destinies. Men, either fellow refugees or host government officials, decide almost everything for them. Men are more likely than women to speak a standard language or lingua franca, so all communication with those outside the refugee community is generally done by males. Often, education and vocational training that lead to new economic opportunities are not available to women. Thus, even though women may generate most of the resources that support the household during its refugee period, they have to do so by engaging in informal economic activities that they piece together to obtain little income.

Women are exploited in many ways in these insecure and volatile circumstances. Males make implicit or explicit sexual demands on them, often in exchange for basic needs such as food or health care.

Although gender had not been included in the official definition of refugee status, in July 1991 the Office of the United Nations High Commissioner for Refugees (UNHCR) acknowledged this gap and issued "Guidelines on the Protection of Refugee Women," which list the following problems: physical and sexual attacks and abuse during flight; physical and sexual attacks and abuse in countries of asylum; spouse and child abuse and abandonment; military-related violence and forced recruitment into military operations; sexual exploitation and prostitution; lack of physical protection during repatriation; and difficulties in prosecuting offenders.

Reproduction

Women take responsibility for their children, who are the next generation of a group whose identity may be in jeopardy. This has both emotional and physiological implications. The former have to do with women's attachment to their children. Death of a child is the greatest loss women suffer. In situations leading to displacement, infant and child mortality is often much greater than usual. This grief stays with women for the rest of their life.

According to the Women's Commission on Refugee Women and Children, a group based in the United States, refugee women have higher birthrates than other women. There are a number of speculative reasons for this: (1) women do not have access to family-planning information or services or usable birth-control methods; (2) women get pregnant by their various "protectors" and from prostitution activities; (3) women desire to rebuild the population after losses caused by their flight; (4) cultural and social values accord high status to fertility, especially when other measures of status women may have are lost through displacement; (5) refugees often benefit from better health care than they had in their usual environment, leading to improved pregnancy outcomes; (6) women may become pregnant from increased sexual activity in situations where few pleasurable activities are available; and (7) increasing household size may be desirable in order to increase access to resources, such as food, which are allocated on a per capita basis.

Although pregnancies may be desired, they can also be problematic. In fact, refugee women are often too ill or malnourished to carry through pregnancies and to breast-feed their infants while caring for their existing children (Toole, 1992). Being female heightens susceptibility to malnutrition under these conditions. Refugees also fall prey to nutritional deficiency diseases uncommon among other populations, many of which typically affect women of childbearing age, such as iron deficiency anemia or pellagra.

Women's Social Status and Psychological Well-being

Women are exploited by soldiers, rebels, and other civilians during flight, and upon arrival in a new location by government officials, military personnel, and other refugees. Abandoned and widowed women and girls, especially those unaccompanied by males, are highly vulnerable to sexual and other forms of physical abuse. Young refugee girls have been sold into prostitution or indentured servitude. Sexual harassment and rapes may remain unreported because of shame or fear of ostracism and reprisal, and because of the fact that, in many situations, refugees are illegal and in hiding and do not want to bring themselves to the attention of the authorities.

Refugees generally encounter problems of protection and safety, but women in particular suffer additional forms of physical abuse. It has been found that women are subject to more violence in refugee situations than in normal circumstances (Taft, 1987). In addition to violence from the "outside," domestic violence also tends to increase, because men are under greater stress than usual, and women are the likely victims.

Refugee men often are frustrated by their inability to find employment or other means of supporting their families. Many men resent having to live on charity in substandard conditions, and much of this frustration is manifested at the expense of women, resulting in both mental and physical abuse. Violence against women is considered a significant cause of female morbidity and mortality among refugees (Helse, 1993).

Women suffer mental stress from the trauma of being victims themselves, as well as from witnessing loved ones being tortured. Owing to their greater emotional dependence on other people (that is, children, husbands, parents, siblings), women suffer more from witnessing violence against family members than do individuals without such dependence. Some 85 percent of Central American refugee women living in Washington, DC, for example, had been victims of bombings, gunfire, injury, interrogation, rape, or threats in their home countries (US Committee for Refugees, 1992). Many women fall victim to depression or other forms of mental illness as a result of losing their traditional support system, being uprooted from their homes, or loneliness.

Problems of Resource Allocation

In general, resources available to refugees are very limited. There is usually no cash distributed to them, and items such as blankets, fuel, and soap are distributed only occasionally. Most receive food, however, which becomes the principal component of a household's economic survival strategy. Food has monetary as well as nutritional value. It can be sold, bartered, or traded (Katona-Apte, 1986a). Food therefore becomes a powerful means to generate cash, win influence, and exercise political power (Zwi and Ugalde, 1993).

Food in refugee situations is distributed only to owners of ration cards. In order to receive a ration card, one must be registered. This is a complex procedure subject to much abuse. Although women are often the de facto heads of the household, owing to their higher proportion in adult refugee populations (Taft, 1987), they frequently encounter constraints such as the following:

1.   Many cultures do not permit women to interact with strangers, especially male strangers; therefore, women without adult male household members have no one to facilitate their registration. Even when they are registered, they often have to turn to bribes or prostitution to receive their household's entitlement from male food distributors.

2.   Women are generally not privy to information about benefits or about ways to access resources. Widows and abandoned women are usually not in the "network" or system to receive goods. In situations where supplies are limited, women and children are least likely to receive adequate food.

3.   Generally, men pick up the rationed food for their households. Women without adult males are the last to pick up their allocation, and it is often less than what the male-headed households receive. That is usually the reason for high rates of malnutrition among children, even in situations where the total entitlement of food is considered adequate (prevalence of malnutrition among adults is rarely assessed).

4.   Because decisions regarding food are made by men, inappropriate foods are sometimes distributed: foods that are inconsistent with dietary traditions or those that require much fuel and time for preparation (WFP/UNHCR, 1991).

In addition to overcoming these problems, women have to resort to diverse means of using the resources acquired, as well as finding ways to get more. There are difficulties associated with these additional activities. Specific illnesses, for example, result from carrying water and fuel. The water available in refugee camps is often polluted and of poor quality. Because women handle more water and fuel than men, they are more susceptible to water-borne infections and disease organisms encountered while gathering firewood. Areas surrounding refugee camps are often dangerous because of mines, because they are sites of conflict, or because the villagers resent refugees.

When it comes to priorities in resource allocation, there is no difference between refugees and their counterparts in the general population. While men often use food for political or economic gains—for example diverting it to rebels or selling it for cash—women use food for health care, nutrition, and education (Katona-Apte, 1986b). Therefore, in situations where women receive the food directly, there are fewer cases of misuse and malnutrition (Taft, 1987).

Coping Strategies

Though women bear the burden of coping with their status as refugees and displaced persons, they are rarely, if ever, the cause of the conflicts and wars, nor are they involved in the decision-making processes and events precipitating them. However, the role of women as primary providers of food, comfort, and other essentials for survival of their children, elderly relatives, and spouses increases in refugee life. Women are responsible, regardless of where they are, for most family chores of food acquisition and processing, fuel-gathering, water collection, child care, and cooking, as well as being the primary providers of health care to other family members.

Women attempt to fulfill the responsibilities assigned them even at times of social, political, economic, or environmental upheaval. Although they consider the problems of social status and violence that affect their psychological well-being to be beyond their control, they perceive economic survival through resource generation to be within their reach.

The ingenuity of women for survival in all parts of the world is limitless (Katona-Apte, 1988), and much tested in these extraordinary circumstances. Women try to meet their increased responsibilities by buying and trading small amounts of food, soap, matches, and other essential items; by trading their own and their children's labor; by selling firewood, cooked food, and beer (usually prepared from the food distributed to them); and by prostitution. They work in the informal sector, often illegally and thus for little renumeration. Refugee women are extremely busy caring for their children, generating income, gathering food, fuel, and water, processing the food for cooking, and preparing it. War and other political upheavals or natural disasters affect both men and women, but women bear a much greater burden when they become refugees or displaced persons.

See Also

ABUSE; ETHNIC CLEANSING; FOOD, HUNGER, AND FAMINE; HOUSEHOLDS: RESOURCES; HOUSING; MIGRATION; POLITICAL ASYLUM; WAR

References and Further Reading

Helse, L. L. 1993. Violence against women. *World Health*, no. 1.

Katona-Apte, J. 1986a. A commodity appropriateness evaluation of four WFP projects: A brief exposition; and Food aid as income transfer. Both in M. J. Forman, ed., *Nutritional aspects of Project Food Aid*. Rome: United Nations Administrative Committee on Coordination–Subcommittee on Nutrition.

———. 1986b. Women and food aid: A developmental perspective. *Food Policy* (August).

———. 1988. Coping strategies of destitute women in Bangladesh. *Food and Nutrition Bulletin* 10(3).

Martin, S. F. 1991. *Refugee women*. London: Zed.

Taft, J. 1987. *Issues and options for refugee women in developing countries*. Washington, D.C.: Refugee Policy Group.

Toole, M. 1992. Going home: The prospect of repatriation for refugee women and children. Paper presented at seminar sponsored by the Women's Commission for Refugee Women and Children, 8 June, Washington, D.C.

UNHCR website: <http://www.unhcr.ch/un&ref/un&ref.htm>

US Committee for Refugees. 1992. *World refugee survey*. Washington, D.C.: U.S. Committee for Refugees.

WFP/UNHCR. 1991. Guidelines for calculating food rations for refugees (provisional). 4 Nov. Rome: The World Food Programme.

Zwi, A., and A. Ugalde. 1993. Victims of war. *World Health*, no. 1.

Judit Katona-Apte

RELIGION: Overview

Religion escapes easy definition. It is a phenomenon found all around the world from the earliest times to the present, with myriad and richly nuanced manifestations. It is concerned with intangible beings and forces, concepts that claim transcendence beyond mundane definitions. Despite this, several attempts have been made to formulate a definition that would encompass all the world's religious experience. Some have defined religion as an individual's relation to divinity, as in the Abrahamic traditions of Judaism, Christianity, and Islam. This definition, however, excludes Buddhism, which advocates not worshipping divinities but rather pursuing personal enlightenment. Additional examples of religions not focused on divinity can be found among the rich panoply of ancestor worship from around the world.

Religion has also been defined through its adherence to and reverence for sacred texts, but not all religions privilege the textual. Instead, for many people of faith, practice is the essence: prayer, meditation, ritual, pilgrimage, and so on. In the end, there is no simple definition that allows for the enormous variety among world religions.

The search for a definition, and thus for a univocal conception of religion, was formulated in the West (W. King, 1987). In recent years, this agenda has been justly critiqued for (1) the assumption that Western notions—for instance, the idea of the soul—mean the same thing in radically different cultures; (2) the presumption that one religion is truer, more evolved, or higher than another; (3) the part such definitions have played in the colonial agenda of Western societies; and (4) the exclusion of women's voices and experience from such formulations. However, when the comparative method for the study of religion is utilized with respect for difference, it can provide a basis for dialogue across faiths and a healthy recognition of the cultural limits of one's own faith (Eck and Jain, 1987). The comparative study of religion makes the point, in Max Müller's famous formulation: to know only one religion is to know none (quoted in Sharpe, 1975: 31).

Studying religions from the perspective that there are many different religions, rather than only one true religion, allows feminist scholars and theologians to recognize consistent patterns in religions that are seemingly antithetical with regard to the religious status of women (Cooey et al., 1991; Falk and Gross, 1989; Haddad and Findly, 1985; Young, 1993). For instance, an important common factor of Judaism, Christianity, and Islam is the envisioning of a single, all-powerful male god. Some feminists have criticized this conceptualization of the divine as authorizing a pervasive pattern of suppressing women (Daly, 1978), both through the historical record—which shows the suppression of Goddess religions—and through limiting women's access to positions of prestige in the religious cult: historically, women were not allowed to be rabbis, priests, or imams. Work by other feminist scholars has uncovered or highlighted the feminine aspects of male gods, thereby providing women with a theological basis to participate more fully in their religions (Christ and Plaskow, 1979).

An early and enduring formulation of religion in broad strokes was presented by Émile Durkheim, who postulated that religion creates and maintains two mutually exclusive realms, the sacred and the profane. This approach attempts to define religion through its functions, through what we can observe. Mircea Eliade popularized Durkheim's idea through his voluminous writing and his influential position as an educator of religion scholars (Falk, 1998). In Eliade's view, one function of religion is to articulate what it means to be human by explaining humanity's relationship to the sacred. In this regard, a great deal has been said about women—some of it good and some of it bad, but all of it deeply meaningful for those who live or have lived under the influence of religion.

Mary Daly has criticized Eliade's use of the sacred and profane distinction for being one between male and female activities; in effect, what men do is sacred and what women do is profane. Viewing the activities of women as nonreligious, as profane activities, leads to ignoring the significant participation of women in religion. Until fairly recently, the underlying notion that what women do is profane and therefore unimportant has colored most methodologies in the study of religion. These methodologies, by focusing exclusively on the religious activities of men—as if male experience were representative of human experience—lead scholars to distort human experience; that is, they do not tell us how religion functions for all human beings. Many feminist studies of religion have focused on uncovering this scholarly bias, and one fruitful area of research is within the domestic rites of a tradition. These are religious practices performed by women outside the orthodox spaces of a religion and, sometimes, away from public places. Often they are performed in the home or other informal areas, or at shrines. Frequently they are devoted to generating the welfare of the family by performing rituals of protection. The participants in these activities can be limited to family members or extended to the larger community of female friends and neighbors (Hegland, 1998). Often the rituals revolve around feast-making and attendant food taboos. (A rich collection of other woman-centered rites can be found in Sered (1994).

Other feminist scholars have explored the terms *female* and *male* as symbols that are completely void of meaning until they are invested with meaning by society. Significantly, although *female* and *male* are imbued with different meanings in different societies, those meanings can change within a society and through time (Bynum et al., 1986; Ortner and Whitehead, 1982). Religion is essential to these interpretations of gender because religion has the authority of the divine, or of the ancestors, or simply of tradition. Religion teaches people what it means to be female or male when it expands gender symbols into narratives, laws, customs, and rituals, into the sacred texts and ritual acts of tradition. This is not to say that a society literally acts out these symbolic meanings—although some do—or to deny that meaning varies among individuals, especially those of different status groups; but it is to assert that these symbols can be called up to establish order, to ascertain the divine will, or to maintain commitment to the sacred.

At the same time, because gender is a symbol and therefore needs an interpretation, it has some flexibility. For instance, creation myths may proffer stereotypes of female and male roles, but in reality women and men may diverge from these assigned roles. A certain amount of deviance from the norm is allowed in most societies and indeed may be necessary for the successful running of society.

Not surprisingly, though, the interpretation of what it means to be female or male differs for women and men. Religions in which men dominate in sacral roles reflect the male interpretation of what it means to be female or male. This suggests that Mary Daly is not far off the mark when she says that patriarchy is the religion of the planet because so many religions are controlled by men. Since religion is a social institution, and the social structure has been patriarchal for at least the past 6,000 years, religion—with some notable exceptions associated with innovation and revolution—is concerned with supporting patriarchy. The same should be said of all other social institutions under patriarchal systems: governments, the military, educational institutions, scientific and medical establishments, the workplace, the marketplace, the arts, and so on. An underlying function of social institutions is to maintain the fabric of society, and if that fabric is patriarchal, then patriarchy is what will be maintained.

Another consequence of male dominance in the public sphere of religion has been the allocation and confinement of all positions of prestige within a religion to men. The denial of these positions to women has had far-reaching social and spiritual implications, not the least of which is that, among the so-called great traditions, the ideal religious person is always male—the sage, the priest, the monk. Of even greater significance, the primary deities, especially in the monotheistic traditions, are all male. This has left women with very little social or religious power because no matter how well they fulfill the expectations of their religion, they remain female and therefore excluded on the ideal level as well as on the social level.

Male dominance of religious roles, however, may be a fairly recent development in the long history of the human race, and the concept of male divinity, too, may be recent. According to some scholars, long before men donned sacred attire and began worshipping male gods, women dominated the religious scene as divinities and as religious experts (Young, 1993). Increasingly, women are rehabilitating ancient forms of worship, especially those centering on goddesses. Worshipping divinity in female form has been an empowering experience for many women and for some men (Christ and Plaskow, 1979; Eller, 1993). Though some are doubtful about these new movements, history has shown that women usually have more to gain in terms of prestige and satisfaction in new religious movements than in traditional ones. Recent close studies of such movements around the world attest to this and contextualize problematic areas (Introvigne, 1998).

Feminists of many different faiths are working to undermine patriarchy through religion, not only by highlighting feminine aspects of male gods or turning to female gods, but also by reclaiming women's historical participation in their traditions and reassessing religious concepts about gender. It is their conviction that such feminine revalorizations of faith will inevitably undermine patriarchy. They believe that removing religion as one of the supports of patriarchy—

through enacting a religious life of egalitarian relationships—will go a long way toward defeating patriarchy's hold on us all. In other words, instead of supporting patriarchy, and while remaining true to the tenets of individual faiths, women can enlist religion to destroy patriarchy. One aspect of this is to emphasize the contributions of historical women to their traditions—for example, Khadīja to Islam, Esther to Judaism, and groups of women such as nuns and female Sufis—thereby providing positive role models for women that empower them *within* their faith. Obviously, this will have to occur on a case-by-case basis, given the particularity of religious experience in many parts of the world, and the rise of fundamentalism with its often conservative interpretation of women's place.

One important aspect of reassessing religious concepts about gender requires distinguishing between the function of women in religious imagination and their function in religious reality. In other words, we must distinguish between metaphysical and abstract concepts of "woman" representing Truth, Beauty, Wisdom, Immortality, and so on, and women as addressed by actual religious law, which imposes ritual restrictions on them—especially by limiting their access to positions of prestige and power in the religious hierarchy—or defines women as irrelevant to religious practice (when they are not actually threatening it through potential pollution from menstruation and childbirth). The problem is that male imaginative understandings of women often blind them to the realities of women's lives within religious contexts, which were and in many cases remain the defining reality of women's lives. Further, concepts such as "the feminine" distance us from the actual lives of women; we are prepared for "feminine imagery," but not for flesh-and-blood women.

Conclusion

On one hand, the study of women in the religions of the world radically alters our understanding of religion: not only our understanding of who participates in religion, but also our understanding of what constitutes religious actions and how we read religious texts. Although many religions claim to focus on the afterlife, their actual concern is the social reality of day-to-day life. And though this social dimension is critical to understanding women's relation to religion, one must remember that it is only part of the complexity of religious experience in the lives of women of faith. Throughout history, women have found ways around the social restrictions of religions to pursue lives that were as religiously meaningful as they were socially innovative. Most did this from within their faith positions, out of their own understanding of what their faith required of them (Christ and

Plaskow, 1979; Falk and Gross, 1989; Haddad and Findly, 1985; Young, 1993).

On the other hand, the study of women and religion requires a response because it is value-laden for every one of us on the most basic human level, that of our spiritual life. Further, religion, through its cultural ramifications, affects us, willing or not. Religious realities are social realities, even in such supposedly secular countries as the United States. Feminist challenges to religion are changing contemporary religious life. As in the past, such changes in spiritual life will lead to changes in cultural life; reshaping traditional religious ideas that have been sources of oppression for women can lead to the over-turning of women's oppression in the larger society.

See Also

EDUCATION: RELIGIOUS STUDIES; FAMILY: RELIGIOUS AND LEGAL SYSTEMS; MYTH; PATRIARCHY DEVELOPMENT; PATRIARCHY: FEMINIST THEORY; SACRED TEXTS; SPIRITUALITY: OVERVIEW; THEOLOGIES: FEMINIST; WOMANSPIRIT

References and Further Reading

Bynum, Caroline Walker, Stevan Harrell, and Paula Richman, eds. 1986. *Gender and religion: On the complexity of symbols.* Boston: Beacon.

Christ, Carol P., and Judith Plaskow, eds. 1979. *Womanspirit rising: A feminist reader in religion.* San Francisco: Harper and Row.

Cooey, Paula M., R. Eakin Williams, and Jay B. McDaniel, eds. 1991. *After patriarchy: Feminist transformations of world religions.* Maryknoll, N.Y.: Orbis Books.

Daly, Mary. 1978. *Gyn/ecology: The metaethics of radical feminism.* Boston: Beacon.

Eck, Diane L., and Devaki Jain, eds. 1987. *Speaking of faith: Global perspectives on women, religion, and social change.* Philadelphia: New Society.

Eller, Cynthia. 1993. *Living in the lap of the Goddess: The feminist spirituality movement in America.* New York: Crossroad.

Falk, Nancy Auer. 1998. The sacred. In Serinity Young, ed., *Encyclopedia of women and world religion,* Vol. 2, 860–861. New York: Macmillan.

Falk, Nancy Auer, and Rita M. Gross, 1989. *Unspoken worlds: Women's religious lives.* Belmont, Calif.: Wadsworth.

Gross, Rita. 1996. *Feminism and religion: An introduction.* Boston: Beacon.

Haddad, Yvonne Yazbeck, and Ellison Banks Findly, eds. 1985. *Women, religion, and society change.* Albany: State University of New York.

Hegland, Mary Elaine. 1998. Domestic rites. In Serinity Young, ed., *Encyclopedia of women and world religion,* Vol. 1, 268–270. New York: Macmillan.

Introvigne, Massimo. 1998. New religions: An overview. In Serinity Young, ed., *Encyclopedia of women and world religion,* Vol. 2, 716–718. New York: Macmillan.

King, Ursula, 1998. History of religions; and Religion. Both in Serinity Young, ed., *Encyclopedia of women and world religion,* respectively, Vol. 1, 435–438, and Vol. 2, 837–839, New York: Macmillan.

———, ed. 1995. *Religion and gender.* Oxford: Basil Blackwell.

King, Winston L. 1987. Religion. In Mircea Eliade, ed., *Encyclopedia of religion,* Vol. 12, 282–293. New York: Macmillan.

Ortner, Sherry B., and Harriet Whitehead, eds. 1982. *Sexual meanings: The cultural construction of gender and sexuality.* Cambridge: Cambridge University Press.

Sered, Susan Starr. 1994. *Priestess, mother, sacred sister: Religions dominated by women.* New York: Oxford University Press.

Sharma, Arvind, ed. 1987. *Woman in world religions.* Albany: State University of New York Press.

———, ed. 1994. *Religion and women.* Albany: State University of New York Press.

———, ed. 1994. *Today's woman in world religions.* Albany: State University of New York Press.

Sharpe, Eric J. 1975. *Comparative religion: A history.* New York: Charles Scribner's Sons.

Young, Serinity, ed. 1993. *An anthology of sacred texts by and about women.* New York: Crossroad; London: HarperCollins.

———, ed. 1998. *Encyclopedia of women and world religion.* New York: Macmillan.

Serinity Young

RELIGIOUS AND LEGAL SYSTEMS

See FAMILY: RELIGIOUS AND LEGAL SYSTEMS.

RELIGIOUS BELIEF

See FAITH.

RELIGIOUS COMMUNITIES

See NUNS.

RELIGIOUS STUDIES

See EDUCATION: RELIGIOUS STUDIES.

RELIGIOUS TEXTS

See SACRED TEXTS.

REPRESENTATION

The term "representation" has a range of meanings: one is "making present again" through realistic visual imagery, and another is the indication of an idea through a visual symbol. Feminist critics and historians, however, have preferred to see representation as a symbolic rather than a descriptive system.

Feminism has motivated critical analysis of the way male-dominated visual traditions have represented the feminine and the masculine to serve their interests, in the fine arts and crafts, in film, and in advertising. Within this critical inquiry, women artists play a key role in creating images of women that are wider, more complex, more varied representations of femininities and also question man-made images of masculinity. These are the core activities of what is called the "politics of representation."

This endeavor has been assisted by the interdisciplinary approaches of cultural studies, which treat representation in terms of consumption and production and scrutinize the effect of objects and images in naturalizing notions such as racial and gender characteristics—that is, making viewers think these images coincide with "natural" reality. Many cultures have distinctive regimes of representation which govern what objects women are allowed to make, and how women are allowed to view these images.

Most narrowly, the term *representation* refers to the creation of an illusion of reality. Realistic techniques are used to depict a living person posed for a portrait, or a landscape. Such representation often reflects life and imitates everyday, surface reality. In other forms of representation, however, the emphasis is more obviously on the imaginative act of making visual symbols or indicators to stand for an idea or another object. For instance, realistic techniques may be used to provide a convincing image of a deity, which neither the maker nor viewer has seen, or to evoke a legendary or historical event. Realistic images of human figures may stand for or symbolize abstract ideas like "equality." Representations may also use more suggestive techniques that refer to things or persons more generally, sometimes to evoke a mood in an expressionist manner. More abstractly, a visual shape may conventionally stand for a concept without resembling female appearances much or at all. For instance, the simplified shape of a person wearing a skirt on a lava-tory door indicates the women's restroom, or the astrological sign for the planet Venus denotes the female.

Many feminist critics consider the idea that representations might "show," "describe," "document," or "reflect" what things are to be a conservative tendency. They have consequently favored semiotic theories, which view visual representations as employing systems of signs in which the signifier (that is, the created image) is only conventionally related to the thing signified; the signification—the nature of the relationship—can therefore be changed by women who look at the signifier. From this viewpoint, it is argued that even apparently descriptive forms of representation—for example, photographic snapshots—construct rather than reflect reality. The photographer takes a picture from a specific psychosocial stance, selecting one instance from a multitude, and the print is materially formed by technical processes and by (largely unspoken) conventions which dictate, for example, that snapshots of people who are working, or dead, or not smiling, are not appropriate subjects for the amateur photographer.

Feminism played an important role in disclosing the potential for authoritarian values in modernism, with its insistence on the primacy of a nonrepresentational art which refers to nothing but itself and its own problems. As a result, modernist abstraction is seen by postmodernist artists as a style which women might choose to work in, or which they might choose to avoid, in favor of referential representations which they might consider more communicative for feminist purposes. Equally, feminist artists may decide that it is important to explore nonrepresentational fields to the full and to demonstrate their ownership of the powers of forms of abstraction.

During the last three decades of the twentieth century, the term *re-presentation* has been used (with the hyphen): to convey the power of visual images to present to generation after generation such practices as women's deference to men as normal and correct, or to "re-present" new, revisionary concepts.

"Cultural representation" is differentiated from "political representation." It designates all the ways in which people show their status, fears, or desires, directly and indirectly, through physical and visible signs. These signs include clothing, gesture, touch, bodily appearance, the design of buildings, advertising, and film, as well as images evoked in words, from the poetry people read to the postcards they write.

See Also

AESTHETICS: FEMINIST; FILM; GENDER; IMAGES OF WOMEN: OVERVIEW; OTHER

References and Further Reading

Bonner, Frances, Lizbeth Goodman, Richard Allen, Linda Janes, and Catherine King. 1992. *Imagining women: Cultural representation and gender.* Cambridge: Polity.

Cameron, Deborah. 1992. *Feminism and linguistic theory.* Basingstoke: Macmillan.

Cherry, Deborah, and Griselda Pollock. 1984. Women as sign in Pre-Raphaelite literature: A study of the representation of Elizabeth Siddall. *Art History.* 7: 206–227.

Cottingham, Laura. 1999. *Seeing through the seventies: Essays on feminism and art.* Newark, N.J.: G&B Arts International.

Catherine King

REPRESENTATION, POLITICAL

See POLITICAL REPRESENTATION.

REPRODUCTION: Overview

The biological fact that women reproduce has long been used to define their role in society primarily as that of mothers. The bearing of children, the responsibility for bringing them up, and the general task of maintaining the home have traditionally been identified as constituting a woman's natural vocation. In this sense, a woman's biology is seen as defining her destiny. Although women throughout the ages have implicitly undermined that equation through the practice of birth control and abortion, only since the advent of the women's movement of the late 1960s and 1970s have feminists analyzed and challenged these roles ascribed to women. In that process, they have politicized reproduction by theorizing its contribution to the oppression of women and by mobilizing against instances of that oppression. At issue are the freedom and the right of a woman to choose, safely and without coercion, whether or not she wishes to have a child.

Reproductive Rights

The central concerns regarding reproduction expressed in the early writings of that movement were encapsulated in the claim that without the freedom, and indeed the right, of every woman to control her own body, the full attainment of women's liberation was not possible. In particular, feminists emphasized the right of each woman to choose not to be a mother; they focused on ensuring women's access to contraceptives and on changing the limited access to legal abortion which endangered the health and lives of women by making them resort to illegal abortions (Cisler, 1969). These issues continue to be at the forefront of feminist activism in countries that have not liberalized abortion legislation, but feminists have broadened their investigation of issues within the sphere of reproduction.

The early theoretical analyses of reproduction are now generally accepted as essentially reflecting the concerns of western or Eurocentric feminism (hooks, 1984). Debates around reproduction must be located within the total context of women's lives and must take into account factors such as historical background, class, race, ethnic identity, religion, custom, and access to education and health services. Moreover, developments within reproductive technology—most notably, in vitro fertilization (IVF) and surrogate motherhood, techniques that assist women who are unable either to conceive or to carry a child to full term—have also extended that initial concern toward consideration of the implications of the right to choose motherhood (Stanworth, 1987).

Millions of women are denied these rights. In much of sub-Saharan Africa, for example, women are valued primarily for their fertility; hence, they have limited access to contraception, and they face restrictive abortion laws supported by religious precepts. Fertile women in this region bear an estimated average 6.4 children each. Children may represent a necessary source of labor power for poor families. Widespread poverty means that the diet of pregnant women is deficient in essential nutrients. The extensive practice of female genital mutilation exacerbates the dangers of childbirth. Most women have little access to health care and are especially at risk if there are complications during childbirth in the home. Maternal mortality is often cited as the single most neglected health problem in the third world (*Women: A World Report,* 1985). An increasing number of women on this continent also suffer infertility and social ostracism as sexually transmitted diseases and brutal illegal abortions take their toll.

In the first world, some infertile women have been able to become mothers through access to new reproductive technologies. Feminists have, however, pointed to the potential within those techniques for the control of women's reproduction. For example, in the main in vitro fertilization is available to white, heterosexual, married, wealthy women, with the concomitant denial of its benefits to lesbians. Underlying that discrimination is the implicit assumption that the so-called natural maternal instinct is the prerogative of heterosexual (and preferably, married) women.

Concern has also been expressed about the possible commodification of women's fertility, for example in the way that eggs are bought and sold to supply a commercial market in human embryos. The process of freezing human embryos also has implications for the abortion debate. If such embryos are designated as unborn children with the right to life, this would bolster the position of those who are opposed to the liberalization of abortion laws (Richardson, 1993). Indeed, beginning in the late twentieth century, abortion as a reproductive right was undermined by a vigorous and militant crusade—including the use of violence against abortion clinics and the doctors who perform that service—undertaken by right-wing religious moralists under the umbrella of the pro-life movement.

The scope of reproductive rights also entails challenging the control exercised over women's bodies by the (mainly male) medical profession. Examples include a long record of unnecessary hysterectomies and the medical establishment's appropriation of the birth process.

Motherhood

Early feminists have been accused of devaluing motherhood in the process of encouraging women to question their socially assigned roles. Much more attention is now devoted to the positive side of motherhood, to the unique and joyous intimacy mothers experience and the special bond they forge with their children (Mitchell and Oakley, 1986). While society may value women as mothers in principle, in practice they receive little support. Women cannot necessarily count on the sustained assistance of the men who father their children. Mothers who enter paid employment (either out of necessity or in pursuit of additional fulfillment) find that their biology is used to discriminate against them. The attainment of full reproductive rights, therefore, also requires that there be equality of opportunity and equal pay for equal work, the provision of maternity benefits, and access to childcare.

See Also

ABORTION; CHILDBIRTH; CONTRACEPTION; FERTILITY AND FERTILITY TREATMENT; MATERNAL HEALTH AND MORBIDITY; MOTHERHOOD; OBSTETRICS; PRO-CHOICE MOVEMENT; REPRODUCTIVE HEALTH; REPRODUCTIVE RIGHTS

References and Further Reading

Cisler, Lucinda. 1969. Unfinished business: Birth control and women's liberation. In Robin Morgan, ed., *Sisterhood is powerful*. New York: Vintage.

hooks, bell. 1984. *Feminist theory: From margin to center*. Boston: South End.
Mitchell, Juliet, and Ann Oakley, eds. 1986. *What is feminism?* Oxford: Basil Blackwell.
Richardson, Diane. 1993. *Women, motherhood, and childrearing*. London: Macmillan.
Stanworth, Michelle, ed. 1987. *Reproductive technologies: Gender, motherhood, and medicine*. Oxford: Basil Blackwell.
Women: A World Report. 1985. London: Methuen.

Ros Posel

REPRODUCTIVE HEALTH

Reproductive health was defined in a 1994 global governmental agreement on population as "a state of complete physical, mental, and social well-being and not merely the absence of disease or infirmity, in all matters relating to the reproductive system and to its functions and processes" (United Nations, 1994: para. 7.2). Reproductive health encompasses the full range of "methods, services, and techniques that contribute to reproductive health and well-being by preventing and solving reproductive health problems" (para. 7.1). It also includes sexual health, the purpose of which is the "enhancement of life and personal relations, and not merely counseling and care related to reproduction and sexually transmitted diseases" (para. 7.2). Specific components of reproductive health care include prenatal care, supervised delivery, and post-partum care; choice of contraceptive methods, with careful attention to the appropriateness of methods for each individual woman's needs and health status; safe abortion services; screening and treatment of reproductive tract infections, sexually transmitted diseases, and gynecological problems; treatment for infertility; counseling on sexuality, contraception, abortion, infertility, infection, and disease; and health services for infants and children (International Women's Health Coalition, 1994). No one approach to reproductive health care can cover all needs. Each country needs to establish priorities and strategies within its own context.

The concept of reproductive health was first introduced in 1987 at the International Conference on Better Health for Women and Children through Family Planning (Germain, 1987), held in Nairobi, and by the World Health Organization (Fathalla, 1988), which recognized that the prevailing emphasis in family planning on reducing women's fertility, especially in resource-poor countries, did not suit the realities of women's lives. International women's health advocates have been working since the late 1980s to promote reproductive health services and to ensure that governments, international agencies, and donors make access to reproductive health care a reality for all the world's women and men.

Reproductive health is a political term as well as a technical one. Its grounding principle is that programs should be developed to meet women's real needs, which are multiple and interrelated. By contrast, governments and donors have often promoted narrow, vertical programs for family planning, child survival, or "safe motherhood." Women's health advocates argue that narrow family planning approaches should be avoided for ethical as well as practical reasons. More emphasis should be placed on the quality of care offered, with a standard based on the client's informed choice and access to full information about all services, including contraception. The goal is to build relationships of mutual trust between health care providers and clients so that they will continue using the services with confidence.

Even though the term *reproductive health* is now used by international agencies that support family planning, few programs have truly made the transition to deliver a broad constellation of reproductive health services. Still, reproductive health care programs do exist, and they are working, in some of the poorest, most rural parts of the world. Most of these programs are run by nongovernmental organizations (NGOs), with limited or no support from national governments. The Bangladesh Women's Health Coalition, for example, delivers a wide array of birth control methods, (including early termination of unwanted pregnancy), basic but high-quality women's health care, child services, and sympathetic counseling to more than 100,000 women a year through 10 clinics. In Latin America, NGOs in Colombia, Nicaragua, Peru, and Brazil provide a range of reproductive health services.

A historic international endorsement of reproductive health took place in Cairo, Egypt, in 1994 at the United Nations International Conference on Population and Development, where 184 governments defined reproductive health and rights and the equality of women as central policy concerns. The Cairo Conference called for reproductive health care services to be made universally accessible by the year 2015. The challenge now before governments, donors, and the international women's health movement is to make reproductive health care real for all the world's women and men.

See Also

ABORTION; CHILDBIRTH; CONTRACEPTION; FAMILY PLANNING; GYNECOLOGY; MATERNAL HEALTH AND MORBIDITY; REPRODUCTION: OVERVIEW; REPRODUCTIVE PHYSIOLOGY; REPRODUCTIVE RIGHTS; REPRODUCTIVE TECHNOLOGIES

References and Further Reading

Fathalla, M. F. 1988. Research needs in human reproduction. In *Research in Human Reproduction Biennial Report 1986–1987*. Geneva: World Health Organization, Special Programme of Research, Development, and Research Training in Human Reproduction.

Germain, Adrienne, and Rachel Kyte. 1994. *The Cairo consensus: The right agenda for the right time*. New York: the International Women's Health Coalition.

International Women's Health Coalition. 1994. *More than family planning: A reproductive health approach*. New York: International Women's Health Coalition.

Sen, Gita, Adrienne Germain, and Lincoln Chen, eds. 1994. *Population policies reconsidered: Health, empowerment, and rights*. Cambridge, Mass.: Harvard University Press.

United Nations. 1994. *Programme of action of the International Conference on Population and Development*. New York: United Nations.

Mia MacDonald

REPRODUCTIVE PHYSIOLOGY

This article on reproductive physiology of mammals focuses on twentieth-century western science in the disciplines of biology, medicine, and agriculture as it is related to the functioning of reproductive systems. That science is applied in the medical specialties of gynecology, obstetrics, infertility medicine, urology, andrology (the specialty focused on the male reproductive system), and in animal agricultural and veterinary sciences. With the exception of sperm studies for development of artificial insemination, the focus of human reproductive physiology has been mostly on females, though it is now shifting to include males more fully. Reproductive physiology centers broadly on three lines of work: (1) eradicating or treating pathological conditions and diseases; (2) understanding the mechanisms of reproduction in order to exercise greater control over or transformation of reproductive processes for diverse purposes; and (3) developing technoscientific interventions to implement such control and transformation (for example, contraceptives or infertility treatments). Modern reproductive physiology was historically continuous with reproductive endocrinology, and today both fall under the rubric of *reproductive sciences*. (For a feminist narration of the basic features of human reproductive physiology and endocrinology, see Boston Women, 1998, pp. 269–287. For reviews of major experimental research, see Greep and Koblinsky, 1977; Gruhn and Kazer, 1989; and Setchell, 1984.)

Early History of Reproductive Physiology

Mammalian reproductive physiology as a modern discipline began with the publication in England of the first book-length treatment, Marshall's *Physiology of Reproduction* (1910). The life sciences more broadly were shifting from the anatomical or morphological focus to experimental physiological modes of research. Reproductive physiology as a discipline formed considerably later than the study of other major organ systems, such as circulation or respiration, though it then grew rapidly. It was initially led by physiologically oriented agricultural scientists and endocrinologists in England, by gynecologists in Germany, and by embryologists in the United States (Hall, 1974; Long, 1987).

Over the next decades, researchers in biology focused on analytic problems such as sex determination, sex differentiation, and fertilization, with the species as their basic unit of analysis. Medical physiologists focused on the reproductive system as a system to be treated. Agricultural scientists focused on the reproductive system in particularly profitable and manipulable domestic species (chickens, cattle, mink). Across all three professional domains, the major problems addressed during the 1910–1925 era were describing the "normal" actions and mechanisms of fertilization, sex differentiation, the estrus and menstrual cycles in females, ovarian function, and the corpus luteum. Reproductive endocrinology began as well, including the discovery of estrogens by the mid-1920s. Two key sets of experiments in this era were Frank Lillie's freemartin (a sexually ambiguous, usually sterile, female calf twin born with a male) research, which found that what have been called "sex hormones" contribute to the production of sex in utero, and George Papanicolaou's technology of the vaginal smear, initially used to determine stages of estrus in rodents for experimental purposes and later used to detect cancers and precancerous lesions of the reproductive tract in women—the Pap smear.

Between 1925 and 1940, reproductive physiology coalesced as a line of work focused on biochemical endocrinological problems, a focus sustained even today. International preeminence passed to the United States, signaled by the publication in 1932 by American researchers of *Sex and Internal Secretions,* the second major handbook of the reproductive sciences. During this period, the chief naturally occurring estrogens, androgens, and progesterone were iso-lated and characterized, and the anterior pituitary, placental, and endometrial gonadotropins were also discovered (Oudshoorn, 1994). The key work of this period produced the first clear understanding of the menstrual period in women, knowledge which was used for many medical purposes and for the rhythm method of contraception.

By 1940, American reproductive scientists had garnered close to $2 million in external research support from such major mainstream science sponsors as the Rockefeller Foundation. The prestigious U.S. National Research Council's Committee for Research on Problems of Sex, founded in 1921, had generously funded basic research on reproduction for two decades, receiving fully 10 percent of all research funding of the National Research Council during this period. The new discipline of reproductive physiology provided biologists with a new line of prestigious biochemical research as they sought to expand their discipline. It gave medicine a wide array of scientific nonsurgical diagnostics and therapeutics for functional reproductive problems in gynecology and urology/andrology. And it provided agriculture with revolutionary reproductive technologies that dramatically improved animal production—especially artificial insemination.

Reproductive Science and Birth Control

By the mid-twentieth century, the very nature of what *modern* scientific contraception would be had been negotiated between reproductive scientists and several schools of birth-control advocates—lay feminists, physicians, eugenicists, and neo-Malthusians, largely in the United States and United Kingdom. To recruit reproductive scientists into the birth-control arena, contraception had to be made scientific. This ran counter to the desires of some birth control advocates, such as Margaret Sanger, for improved simple means of contraception (diaphragms and spermicides, preferably with prophylactic capacities against sexually transmitted diseases). Contraception, Sanger and her colleagues argued, should be woman-controlled to enhance women's sexual and reproductive autonomy. However, by this time reproductive scientists had captured definitional authority over what new scientific contraceptives would be. Physicians, eugenicists, and neo-Malthusians moved the birth control movement to a conservative effort of family planning and population control and displaced feminists from key organizational positions.

From the 1920s to the 1960s, reproductive scientists used several strategies to assert their legitimacy, autonomy, and cultural authority. First, they carefully distinguished reproductive physiological and endocrinological research from contraceptive research and refused to participate in studies of *simple* contraceptives such as spermicides, douches, and diaphragms. Any reproductive scientists who did so were made marginal within the profession. Second, they argued with birth-control advocates for basic research as the ultimate source of modern contraception and made token offerings from their work, such as accurate information on the timing of ovulation. Third, they redirected contraceptive research toward new *scientific* methods: hormonal contraception (the Pill) and intrauterine devices (also to spermatoxins and sterilization by radiation—both later abandoned).

Contraception and Conception

By mid-century, there was some focus on the physiology of infertility (Pfeffer, 1993). In fact, the control of fertility for *contra*ceptive purposes involves many of the same physiological problems as understanding the mechanisms of infertility to provide *con*ceptive technoscientific assistance. Both sets of scientific problems can be pursued through the same research. Providing infertility services also legitimated the newly organized family-planning clinics where they were offered and the science that backed them up—reproductive physiology.

The relative lateness of the development of the physiology of reproduction was a key feature of its emergence and disciplinary formation. Historically, the reproductive arena has been a site of considerable and sustained social and cultural controversy which has shaped the scientific discipline itself. For some, reproductive physiology is illegitimate science because of its association with sexuality and reproduction; others associate it with clinical quackery and problematic treatments (fountain of youth drugs, the harmful anti-miscarriage drug DES, contraceptives with negative side effects). For yet others, its links to controversial social movements (eugenics, birth control, abortion, population control) make such science anathema. But it is the creation of brave new worlds in which nature itself is manipulated, transforming and reconfiguring human and animal bodies and reproductive capacities—producing clones or hybrids— that has drawn the most opposition to date and will likely continue to do so. The reproductive technologies of artificial insemination (AI), in-vitro fertilization (IVF), and related conceptive treatments, along with emergent genetic screening and therapies, contraception, and abortion, are major sites of contestation on religious, moral, and other grounds.

Because it was so controversial, reproductive physiology did not share in initial U.S. government research sup-port of the natural sciences, which grew rapidly after World War II. But after concern arose over the social problem of overpopulation by the mid-1950s, private sources of support expanded. The internationally oriented Population Council was founded by John D. Rockefeller III in 1952 and became the locus of development of "low user-responsible contraceptives" such as the IUD and subdermal (under the skin), long-acting hormonal implants such as Norplant. Such means can be called "imposables" because providers rather than women themselves control their installation and (sometimes) removal. The Ford Foundation funded both basic reproductive physiological research and contraceptive development internationally from 1959 to 1983, including major new research centers in the United States and others in England, Sweden, Israel, India, Egypt, and South America. Ford also sponsored the publication of two major new handbooks of reproductive science (Greep et al., 1976, 1977) which reviewed all research to date in physiology and contraception and set agendas for future work. This powerful foundation support consolidated new alliances among the reproductive physiological sciences, birth control, and population control worldwide. After 1960, the U.S. government also became a major funder of the reproductive sciences, and corporate pharmaceutical industry expenditures on research grew dramatically. By 1970, at least six American pharmaceutical companies were each spending several million dollars per year on contraceptive research and development. This was the golden age of reproductive physiology.

Postmodern Reproductive Physiology

Thus, by the 1970s, many of the major technoscientific products of reproductive physiology had been developed and tested: estrogen "replacement" therapies used in menopausal women, DES used to prevent premature labor in pregnant women and as a feed additive for beef cattle (until its carcinogenicity was clear), birth-control pills, plastic IUDs, Depo Provera (a long-acting contraceptive hormonal shot), and several kinds of pregnancy tests. Many of these reproductive technologies were mass-distributed globally. Since the late 1960s, many feminist women's health groups throughout the world have protested against the use of many if not most of these drugs, devices, and technologies on women, their inadequate safety and efficacy testing, the inadequacy of many of the world's local health care systems to provide adequate women's health services around such high-technological interventions, and—most fundamental—the failure of reproductive scientists to address women's own goals and desires vis-à-vis reproductive research and interventions.

The postmodernist reproductive physiology espoused by some in the women's movement differs from its modernist predecessor in goals, means, focus, and definitions of the body. In place of controlling reproductive processes with universal technologies, it aims to transform them for many specific, local, individual purposes. Whereas the modernist strain emphasizes the development, manufacture, and mass distribution of new products and the standardization of reproductive health care, postmodernists prefer to elaborate specific services (such as infertility treatment, sex preselection, or fetal surgery), individualized assistance (genetic and fetal screening and counseling), and technological alternatives individually tailored for specific women and men. The traditional objects of the discipline—childbirth, menstruation, pregnancy, contraception, abortion, and menopause—are still addressed, but they are augmented with attention to conception, infertility, genetice and gene therapies, and male reproduction.

A radically different set of approaches relates to the "bodies": the lived body of the individual, the social body of the intimate group, and the body politic of the state. Modernist science attempts to control the lived body with its innate qualities intact, ideally across its full lifespan, and to plan any new directions that life may take. Postmodernists accept the lived body as something to be transformed and manipulated, even "customized," through technology. Rather than accepting the need to maintain the traditional nuclear family, they propose to transform or "re-construct" heterogeneous families in which new meanings of gender, mother, father, and family can exist; a mother can now be biological, social, surrogate, or donor. Finally, the modernist association of reproductive science and the state takes the form of population control via contraception and the legalization of interventions in the reproductive process. Postmodernists envision the family as a new kind of "industry" and focus on issues of state policy and surveillance.

Many of the new "postmodern" clinical interventions depend on "modern" capacities such as controlling the timing of fertility through hormonal treatment, or abortion in the face of severe fetal abnormalities. At the end of the twentieth century, physiological research at the molecular level centered on receptors and produced RU486 (the "French abortion pill") and was working to develop a fluid "molecular condom" prophylactic against sexually transmitted diseases, including HIV/AIDS. This condom exemplifies the "woman-centered approach" to contraception framed at the Cairo meetings of the UN Decade on Women in 1994. Both modern and postmodern approaches exist simultaneously (Clarke, 1995). Some of the new reproductive technologies

address unmet needs and desires of some women yet have also been staunchly opposed by some feminist groups.

Biological Sex as a Continuous Variable

Another new area of concern centers on challenges to the tradition of conventional reproductive physiology that regards sex as a binary variable: male or female. At the beginning of the twenty-first century, some scientists are asserting instead that what counts as "sex" is instead continuous; here hormonal, genetic, embryogenic, and environmental influences are seen as co-constituitive, producing heterogeneous bodies (Fausto-Sterling, 2000; Terry, 1999). The ambiguous, diverse, and complicated actions of "sex" hormones have long been deliberately obscured by leading reproductive scientists. That is, what have been called "sex hormones" are not *only* sex hormones but have other biological actions as well which have been inadequately studied.

At the end of the twentieth century, the U.S. Institute of Medicine of the National Academy of Sciences sponsored two major assessments of reproductive physiological research, both of which were grim about the future, especially regarding contraceptive research (Harrison and Rosenfeld, 1996; Mastroianni et al., 1990). Most pharmaceutical companies have ceased sponsorship of contraceptive research, largely because profit margins are too narrow; only one large company still has an active research and development program. In response, a new major private funding source has emerged, the Packard Foundation (from the computer industry), which gave $375 million in 1998 for contraceptive research over a period of years. Clearly there remain deep commitments among key American foundations to the development of improved means of control over reproduction—including birth control, population control, eugenics, and family planning. Development and elaboration of new conceptive reproductive technologies (including cloning), genetic screening, and therapies are at the heart of reproductive physiological research today. Many feminists are concerned that cultural, social, ethical, and regulatory frameworks are inadequate to address the complications produced. In contrast, increased attention to male reproductive physiology (for example, Oudshoorn, in prep.; Pfeffer, 1985) is welcome, but also likely to be complicated by social factors.

See Also

CONTRACEPTIVES: DEVELOPMENT; GENETIC SCREENING; GYNECOLOGY; HORMONES; OBSTETRICS; PHYSIOLOGY; PREGNANCY AND BIRTH; REPRODUCTION: OVERVIEW; REPRODUCTIVE HEALTH; REPRODUCTIVE TECHNOLOGIES

References and Further Readings

Borell, Merriley. 1987. Biologists and the promotion of birth control research, 1918–1938. *Journal of the History of Biology*, vol. 19, pp. 51–87.

Boston Women's Health Book Collective. 1998. *Our bodies, our selves for the new century: A book by and for women*. New York: Touchstone/Simon and Schuster.

Clarke, Adele E. 1995. Modernity, postmodernity and human reproductive processes c.1890–1990, or Mommy, where do cyborgs come from anyway? In Chris Hables Gray, Heidi J. Figueroa-Sarriera, and Steven Mentor, eds. *The cyborg handbook*, 139–55. New York: Routledge.

———. 1998. *Disciplining reproduction: Modernity, American life sciences, and "the problems of sex"*. Berkeley: University of California Press.

———. 2000. Maverick reproductive scientists and the production of contraceptives c1915–2000. In Anne Rudinow Saetnan, Nelly Oudshoorn, and Marta Kirejczyk, eds. *Localizing and globalizing reproductive technologies*. Columbus: Ohio State University Press.

Fausto Sterling, Anne. 2000. *Sexing the body: Gender politics and the construction of sexuality*. New York: Basic Books.

Greenhalgh, Susan, ed. 1995. *Situating fertility: Anthropology and demographic inquiry*. Cambridge: Cambridge University Press.

Greep, Roy O., M.A. Koblinsky, and F.S. Jaffe. 1976. *Reproduction and human welfare: A challenge to research*. Boston: MIT (Ford Foundation).

Greep, Roy O., and Marjorie A. Koblinsky, eds. 1977. *Frontiers in reproduction and fertility control: A review of the reproductive sciences and contraceptive development*. Boston: MIT (Ford Foundation).

Gruhn, John G., and Ralph R. Kazer. 1989. *Hormonal regulation of the menstrual cycle: The evolution of concepts*. New York: Plenum Medical Book Company.

Hall, Diana Long. 1974. Biology, sex hormones and sexism in the 1920s. *Philosophical Forum* 5: 81–96.

Harrison, P.F., and A. Rosenfeld, eds. 1996. *Contraceptive research and development*. Washington, D.C.: National Academy Press.

Holmes, Helen Bequaert, ed. 1992. *Issues in reproductive technology*. New York: Garland.

Long, Diana E. 1987. Physiological identity of American sex researchers between the two world wars. In Gerald L. Geison, ed. *Physiology in the American context, 1850–1940*, 263–78. Bethesda, Md.: American Physiological Society.

Marshall, F. H. A. 1910, 1922. *The physiology of reproduction*, 1st and 2nd eds. London: Longmans, Green and Co.

Mastroianni, Luigi, Jr., Peter J. Donaldson, and Thomas T. Kane, eds. 1990. *Developing new contraceptives: Obstacles and opportunities*. [NRC and IOM]. Washington, D.C.: National Academy Press.

Oudshoorn, Nelly. 1994. *Beyond the natural body: An archeology of sex hormones*. London: Routledge.

———. in prep. *Bound by culture: The development of the male pill*.

Pfeffer, Naomi. 1985. The Hidden Pathology of the Male Reproductive System. In Hilary Homans, ed. *The sexual politics of reproduction*, 30–44 Aldershot, U.K.: Gower.

———. 1993. *The stork and the syringe: A political history of reproductive medicine*. Cambridge, U.K.: Polity Press [Blackwell].

Setchell, Brian P., ed. 1984. *Male reproduction: Benchmark papers in human physiology 17*. New York: Van Nostrand Reinhold.

Stanworth, Michelle, ed. 1987. *Reproductive technologies: Gender, motherhood and medicine*. Minneapolis: University of Minnesota Press.

Terry, Jennifer. 1999. *An American obsession: Science medicine and homosexuality in modern society*. Chicago: University of Chicago Press.

Adele E. Clarke

REPRODUCTIVE RIGHTS

Reproductive rights is a concept whose definitions initially grew out of the women's and birth-control movements, feminist political thought, and, later, international legal and human rights instruments. Its basic premise is that individuals—especially women—have the right of ultimate decision over matters that affect them personally in the realms of pregnancy, childbearing, and sexuality; over when, whether, and with whom to have sex, marry, become pregnant, carry a pregnancy to term, or raise a child; and over how to care for the sexual and reproductive capacities of their own bodies. Underlying this notion is a broader ethical and legal principle relevant to many issues of political and social power, such as freedom from torture, rape, or other forms of sexual or bodily abuse; the right to voluntary consent to medical treatment or experimentation; and freedom from slavery or other forms of involuntary servitude. That principle is the one of self-determination, which holds that, in order to act as responsible citizens and moral agents, individuals must have effective control and authority over their own bodies and persons.

Tracing the genealogy of the idea of reproductive rights reveals that the origins of the term's underlying values—if not the term itself—have a long and culturally diverse history. The idea that women—because of their socially and biologically determined situation (with regard to pregnancy and childbearing)—must have freedom to decide about their fertility originated in the feminist birth control movements that developed as early as the 1830s among the Owenite socialists in England and spread to many parts of the world over the next one hundred years. In the 1920s and 1930s, not only western figures—such as Margaret Sanger and Stella Browne—but also women's movement leaders in southern colonial countries (for example, Kamaladevi Chattopadhaya in India) invoked women's need to "own and control" their bodies' sexual and reproductive functions as one basis of their social and political emancipation. We can find earlier philosophical validation of the principle of bodily self-possession for women (as well as men) in Hindu asceticism, Islamic law, and radical Protestant movements in early modern Europe.

The first known use of the term *reproductive rights* came in the context of women's movements in the United States and Europe, as an expression of the right to abortion and contraception. Organizations such as the Committee for Abortion Rights and against Sterilization Abuse (CARASA) and the Reproductive Rights National Network (R2N2) in the United States and the Women's Global Network for Reproductive Rights in the Netherlands emerged in the 1970s and 1980s as a feminist response to both pronatalist ("pro-life") and antinatalist attacks on women's control over reproduction, and especially women's access to safe and legal abortion. The rapid spread of the feminist reproductive rights movement to other parts of the world, particularly in Latin America and South Asia, reflected several international influences: the growth of broad-based women's rights movements in many countries, including a significant component focused on women's health; concern with alarmingly high rates of maternal mortality and morbidity among poor women because of illegal and unsafe abortion and lack of access to adequate prenatal and obstetrical care; increasing opposition among women's groups and ethnic minority groups to coercive methods of population control used by family-planning and other government agencies; and responses to the growing strength of conservative political and religious and groups (led by the Vatican and Islamic fundamentalists) opposed to abortion, homosexuality, and female sexual self-determination.

Against this mounting conservative reaction, feminist advocates of reproductive rights asserted "women's right to decide whether, when and how to have children—regardless of nationality, class, race, age, religion, disability, sexuality or marital status—in the social, economic and political conditions that make such decisions possible" (Women's Global Network for Reproductive Rights, Statement of Purpose). They called for access to safe, effective contraception; safe, legal abortion services for all women, regardless of age or income; access to prenatal care and good-quality maternity and child health services for all women; an end to sterilization abuse and other coercive practices by health and family-planning providers; and adequate education for women of all ages about reproduction, sexuality, and the risks of reproductive technologies.

During the 1980s, the activism of several nationally based women-of-color groups in the United States (for example, the National Black Women's Health Project, the Latina Women's Health Coalition, and the Women of Color Roundtable of the Religious Coalition for Abortion Rights) underscored the racist dimensions of existing family-planning and population policies, including both selective application of "targeted" programs and unequal access to reproductive health services. The concerns of these groups coincided with those of women in South Asia, the Caribbean, and elsewhere that fertility reduction programs were taking the place of primary health care for women and children in their countries' agendas.

As women representing more diverse social positions and cultural perspectives became involved in the movement for reproductive rights, the meanings of "reproductive rights" expanded well beyond the original focus on abortion and contraception. Those meanings came to encompass not only women's self-determination over their fertility and childbearing, but also their freedom from bodily violence, coercion, and abuse (whether by family members, the state, or medical providers); freedom from preventable sexual and reproductive tract diseases; research and resources to cure and prevent breast cancer and other gynecological cancers; access to basic health care for women and children; and freedom for women to express their sexuality in safety, dignity, and pleasure. Moreover, this expanded definition of sexual and reproductive rights entailed a commitment to the necessary enabling conditions—social, economic and cultural—that would make their practical realization possible for even the most disadvantaged women.

Four basic ethical principles lie at the heart of reproductive and sexual rights: bodily integrity, personhood, equality, and diversity. All four have both negative and positive applications—that is, they involve, on one hand, protection against coercion and abuse, whether by state officials, medical personnel, kin, or sexual partners, and on the other, the fulfillment of basic needs and goods. Bodily integrity refers to people's right not only to be free from physical abuse or coercion but also to be enabled to enjoy their bodys' full potential for health, procreation, and safe sexual pleasure. Thus, it involves issues such as sex and gender education—including safer-sex education—for adolescents, as well as the prohibition of child marriage, involuntary sterilization, and female genital mutilation. Personhood refers to a woman's right to be treated as a principal actor and decision-maker in matters of reproduction and sexuality; as a subject, not object, of medical, population, and family-planning policies. Thus, respect for women's personhood would require taking seriously their complaints about contraceptive side effects, removing implants or IUDs on request, and providing safe, unrestricted abortion services.

Reproductive and sexual equality—both between women and men and among women—has to do not only with prohibiting discrimination (for example, population control programs targeted at poor, indigenous, and ethnic or racial minority communities); it also means providing social justice and the conditions of development (for example, comprehensive reproductive health services available to all women, not only those who can pay the market price). Finally, the diversity principle means respecting the differing values, needs, and priorities of different groups of women in their self-defined identities (ethnic, religious, sexual, national)—but as women themselves, not male kin, politicians, or religious leaders, define those values, needs, and priorities. Traditional patriarchal practices that subordinate women, however condoned in local settings or cultures, cannot supersede the responsibility of governments and intergovernmental agencies to enforce women's equality, personhood, and bodily integrity. In other words, although reproductive rights are *context-specific*—with different applications depending on local needs and values—they also have a universal validity that derives from these ethical principles and from their recognition as part of fundamental human rights.

Since 1966, the rights to life, liberty, and security of the person and to equality based on sex, as recognized in the Universal Declaration of Human Rights, have formed the basis for a codification of reproductive rights in international law through a series of United Nations instruments. Until the recent International Conference on Population and Development in Cairo (September 1994), however, the right recognized most consistently in international forums was the rather narrow one of "all couples and individuals...to determine freely and responsibly the number and spacing of their children." In addition, the Alma Ata Declaration of 1978 and the Convention on Economic, Social, and Cultural Rights recognized a right to "primary health care,"

including family planning and maternal and child health; and the Convention on the Elimination of All Forms of Discrimination Against Women (CEDAW) made such rights, and the "information, education and means to exercise [them]," a matter of "equality of men and women."

The 1994 Cairo Programme of Action marked a significant leap in bringing a broader and more "feminist" conception of reproductive rights into the discourse of international law and politics. In that document, an entire chapter (chap. 7) is devoted to defining and elaborating the meanings of and governmental obligations to implement "reproductive rights and reproductive health." The Cairo Programme reaffirms "the basic right of all couples and individuals to decide freely and responsibly the number, spacing and timing of their children and to have the information and means to do so, and the right to attain the highest standard of sexual and reproductive health"; as well as "their right to make decisions concerning reproduction free of discrimination, coercion and violence, as expressed in human rights documents." It also provides an expansive definition of reproductive health which includes access not only to family planning services but also to prenatal care, safe delivery, and breastfeeding; treatment of infertility, reproductive tract infections, breast cancer, and reproductive cancers; treatment and prevention of HIV/AIDS and other sexually transmitted diseases; and "active discouragement of harmful practices such as female genital mutilation." Moreover, reproductive health is defined to include *sexual health,* viewed not only in terms of disease prevention but also in terms of "the enhancement of life and personal relations."

Although Vatican and Muslim fundamentalist pressures have prevented any international recognition of a right to safe, legal abortion as a part of reproductive rights, the Cairo document does achieve a new acknowledgment of "unsafe abortion" as "a major public health concern" and the need to reduce maternal mortality and morbidity from unsafe abortions through access to counseling and treatment of complications (chap. 8). Moreover, for the first time in any international document, "any form of coercion" in family planning programs is condemned, as well as the use of demographic targets and incentives or disincentives attached to specific methods or fertility reduction schemes. Furthermore, all these rights are explicitly extended to adolescents and, though nowhere do the framers specify any right to sexual freedom or sexual orientation, the rights are not restricted to married people or heterosexuals ("all couples and individuals" remains unqualified). Above all, instead of a gender-neutral approach, the Cairo document—for the first time in a United Nations instrument—places reproductive rights firmly in the context of "Gender Equality,

Equity and Empowerment of Women" (chap. 4). Asserting that "the empowerment and autonomy of women and the improvement of their political, social, economic and health status is a highly important end in itself," it eschews the instrumentalist approach that sees women's development as a means to lower fertility. Recognizing at length the need for government action to assure male responsibility and involvement in family planning, child health, child care, housework, and prevention of STDs, it challenges the traditional gender division of labor. In other words, the Cairo document embodies a large part of the international feminist concept of reproductive and sexual rights, and it thus represents a significant victory for women's movements.

But bridging the gap between international legal rhetoric about reproductive rights and the harsh realities faced by most women—especially poor women—will demand much larger transformations. To create the necessary social capital for good-quality, accessible, comprehensive reproductive health services, governments and international organizations must seek a reordering of global economic policies (including structural adjustments), national budgetary priorities, and national health and population policies to deemphasize debt service and militarism in favor of social welfare and primary health care. To create a cultural climate sympathetic to women's reproductive and sexual self-determination, they must combat fundamentalism in all its varieties and adopt affirmative programs that promote both the empowerment and health-awareness of women and an attitude of men toward women and children of respect, non-violence, and responsibility (but not paternalism). The enabling conditions that will make reproductive rights available in practice to the world's women depend, in the end, on women's achieving equality in the arenas of national and international decision making and changing the face of political power and will.

See Also

ABORTION; BIOLOGICAL DETERMINISM; CONTRACEPTION; ETHICS: MEDICAL; FAMILY PLANNING; FEMALE CIRCUMCISION AND GENITAL MUTILATION; MATERNAL HEALTH AND MORBIDITY; POPULATION CONTROL; REPRODUCTIVE HEALTH; SEXUALITY: OVERVIEW

References and Further Reading

Correa, Sonia, and Rosalind Petchesky. 1994. Reproductive and sexual rights: A feminist perspective. In Gita Sen, Adrienne Germain, and Lincoln C. Chen, eds., *Population policies reconsidered: Health, empowerment, and rights.* Cambridge, Mass.: Harvard University Press.

Petchesky, Rosalind Pollack. 1993. Reproductive politics. In Joel Krieger, ed., *The Oxford companion to politics of the world.* New York: Oxford University Press.

United Nations, International Conference on Population and Development. 1994. *Report of the International Conference on Population and Development (Cairo, Egypt, 5–13 September 1994).* New York: United Nations.

Rosalind P. Petchesky

REPRODUCTIVE TECHNOLOGIES

All human societies in all historical periods have developed techniques to prevent and to facilitate conception, and to shape the physiological processes of gestation, labor, birth, and breastfeeding in cultural terms. There is, however, no precedent for the rapid expansion of reproductive technologies in the latter half of the twentieth century—an expansion that has dramatically redefined the parameters of biological reproduction. From the birth of the world's first "test-tube baby" in 1978 to the first cloning of a higher vertebrate from an adult cell in 1997, this period has seen the most intensive human intervention into the reproductive process ever known. The new technologies developed to intervene in human reproduction include, among many others birth control technologies such as intrauterine devices (IUDs) and the birth control pill; assisted conception technologies such as artificial insemination and in-vitro fertilization (IVF); screening technologies such as ultrasound, amniocentesis, and blood testing; reparative technologies such as fetal surgeries performed in utero; labor and birth technologies such as electronic fetal monitoring, synthetic hormones for labor induction and augmentation, and multiple types of anesthesia; and postnatal technologies such as infant surgeries and high-tech treatment of babies in neonatal intensive care units. All these technologies are increasingly affected by developments in biotechnology (such as genetic engineering) which have major implications for the control and management of human fertility.

Like the obstetrical forceps developed by the Chamberlen brothers in the sixteenth century, the new reproductive technologies—often known as NRTs—have double-edged implications for women and their offspring. Those early forceps did save the lives of babies who otherwise might have died, but their overzealous and ill-informed application during childbirth by male midwives and obstetricians often left the mother's body severely damaged and led to increased maternal and fetal morbidity. The NRTs have been fraught with similar contradiction and paradox, often creating as many problems as they solve and causing as much damage as they repair. Maternal mortality as a result of ovarian hyperstimulation and increased congenital abnormality in multiple births are just two examples of the "downside" of IVF. This paradoxical situation is one of several reasons why NRTs have become a focal point for feminist analysis, beginning in the early 1980s.

Reproductive technology has affected every facet of the reproductive process, from pre-conception onward. To some extent, these developments respond to specific impediments to fertility: in-vitro fertilization (IVF), for example, was originally used to assist women with blocked ovarian tubes. Feminist critics, however, have rightly pointed to other, less woman-centered influences shaping the development of these technologies. For example, Robert Edwards, the research scientist who helped to develop IVF, was trained in embryology and foresaw tremendous research potential from the ability to manipulate the human embryo ex vivo (outside the uterus). This potential has been extensively exploited in the rapid expansion of human embryo experimentation in the 1980s and the 1990s.

The encounter between a largely male medical and scientific establishment and women's reproductive capacity is very pointed in the context of IVF: this is often represented as a response to the "desperate" desires of infertile women, but it can as readily be interpreted as a response to the irresistible scientific urge to "unveil" and indeed to redesign "the facts of life." The tremendous value of early embryonic cells—both commercially and in research—has made IVF an important source of human embryonic stem cells. This fact exists in uneasy tension with women's demands for improved reproductive services. As in other historical periods, the neglect of women's reproductive needs is most evident in terms of which kinds of services are developed and prioritized. Although new embryo therapies are used to detect and even to treat genetic disease, other reproductive priorities remain devalued and underfunded. For example, little progress has been made in screening technology for cervical and breast cancer, both diseases of women's reproductive tissue. And while ever more sophisticated technologies are developed to deal with the complications of labor and birth, the normal physiological needs of women in labor remain understudied and unfulfilled. The scientific evidence that exists supports simple technologies like eating and drinking during labor, woman-centered, supportive care, and upright positions for delivery as far more helpful to birthing women than are high tech machines (Davis-Floyd, 1992).

Two major influences continue to shape the development of reproductive technology in ways that are not in women's interests. One is the continuing, and indeed worsening, effects of global inequality which are borne most heavily by women and young children, especially infants. Access to basic contraceptive technology remains out of reach for the majority of the world's female population, despite concerns about population growth, and largely as a result of U.S. anti-abortion policy. Consequently, resource-intensive and largely private fertility care is provided to a predominantly wealthy world élite (not just in western countries, but worldwide). Meanwhile, the enduring tragedies of high maternal and infant mortality resulting from preventable causes (such as malnutrition and lack of a clean water supply), inadequate access to abortion or contraceptives, and limited, nonexistent, or ineffective reproductive health care are the main issues affecting the majority of the world's women. Proper sanitation, adequate nutrition, improved vaccination programs, access to culturally appropriate forms of birth control, access to community midwives backed by adequate transport systems, and—above all—increased literacy and education rates among women remain the most important and life-saving "reproductive technologies."

At the other end of the spectrum, at the cutting edge of twenty-first-century medical science, the second pervasive influence is the resurgence of a new genetic essentialism. Reproductive technology is shifting its focus in the direction of germline gene therapies (therapies that can be genetically transmitted because they modify reproductive cells). Annexed to the project of mapping the human genome, reproductive science and medicine are increasingly aimed at both the elimination of genetic pathology and the effort to re-engineer the genomes of humans and other life forms. In addition to existing means of technologically assisting conception, the effort to alter human genetic characteristics is the most important influence on contemporary reproductive technologies. This effort is driven by enormously competitive economic forces, and by an "if we can do it, we must do it" technocratic mentality, resulting in rapidly escalating and largely unregulated technological innovation.

Although some commentators argue that reproductive technologies such as the freezing of eggs, cloning by nuclear transfer, germline gene therapy, and embryo biopsy will have a radical effect on gender roles and kinship definitions, the majority of evidence predicts the opposite effect: the restabilization of traditional and conservative family ideologies in the face of their potential disruption. Other influences, such as the lesbian and gay movement, the increase in transnational adoption, rising divorce rates, and greater economic independence for women have proven more influential in the redefinition of family and parenthood. Although some uses of reproductive technology have created more parenting options, such as the use of artificial insemination by lesbians, the overwhelming pattern of access to NRTs is defined by the goal of enhancing conventional parenting arrangements among married, heterosexual, middle-class couples.

Feminist concern about reproductive technologies in the twenty-first century will increasingly overlap with the criticisms of biotechnology and genetic engineering raised by environmentalists and the general public. Concern about genetically modified organisms in the food chain and in medical applications will increase, particularly as the human–animal border becomes ever more permeable. The extensive feminist literature on NRTs anticipates with great precision many of the profound social, ethical, and political concerns surrounding new forms of genetic and biological determinism arising out of the attempt to alter the human genome. In addition to the effort to redefine medical and scientific priorities in relation to women's reproductive health worldwide, feminist scholarship will continue to insist upon the primacy of fully informed reproductive decision making, in its widest sense, as a fundamental component of human rights.

See Also

CHILDBIRTH I; CHILDBIRTH II; CYBORG ANTHROPOLOGY; GENETIC SCREENING; GENETICS AND GENETIC TECHNOLOGY; REPRODUCTIVE RIGHTS

References and Further Reading

Casper, Monica J. 1998. *The making of the unborn patient: A social anatomy of fetal surgery.* New Brunswick, N.J.: Rutgers University Press.

Clarke, Adele E. 1998. *Disciplining reproduction: Modernity, American life sciences, and the problem of sex.* Berkeley: University of California Press.

Davis-Floyd, Robbie. 1992. *Birth as an American rite of passage.* Berkeley: University of California Press.

Franklin, Sarah. 1997. *Embodied progress: A cultural account of assisted conception.* New York and London: Routledge.

Franklin, Sarah, and Helene Ragone. 1997. *Reproducing reproduction: Kinship, power, and technological innovation.* Philadelphia: University of Pennsylvania Press.

Ginsburg, Faye, and Rayna Rapp, eds. 1995. *Conceiving the new world order: The global politics of reproduction.* Berkeley: University of California Press.

Haraway, Donna. 1997. *Modest witness@Second millennium. FemaleMan meets OncoMouse™. Feminism and technoscience.* New York: Routledge.

Hartouni, Valerie. 1997. *Cultural conceptions: On reproductive technologies and the remaking of life.* Minneapolis: University of Minnesota Press.

Lay, Mary M., Laura J. Gurak, Clare Gravon, and Cynthia Myntti (eds). 2000. *Body talk: Rhetoric, technology, reproduction.* Madison: University of Wisconsin Press.

Morgan, Lynn M., and Meredith W. Michaels. 2000. *Fetal subjects, feminist positions.* Philadelphia: University of Pennsylvania Press.

Ragone, Helena. 1994. *Surrogate motherhood: Conception in the heart.* Boulder, Colo.: Westview.

Rapp, Rayna. 2000. *Testing women, testing the fetus: The social impact of amniocentesis in America.* New York: Routledge.

Sarah Franklin
Robbie Davis-Floyd

RESEARCH

See LIBRARIES; REFERENCE SOURCES; AND THIRD WORLD WOMEN: SELECTED RESOURCES.

RESEARCH: On-Line

The Internet has been called "the fourth revolution" in communication and the production of knowledge (Harnard, 1992). In the view of many, the Internet has become "the 20th century's most dynamic bequest to the 21st" (Mann and Stewart, 2000). The sheer increase in the number of computers connected to the Internet since its creation in 1969 confirms the view that this communications medium is so powerful that "it has a logic, a momentum, a force of its own. It's damn near unstoppable" (Parr, quoted in Lillington, 1999). But what does the Internet offer women researchers?

As one of the pioneers in writing about gender and technology, Dale Spender (1995) has suggested that the Internet is eminently suited to the conversations and activities of women. Like the telephone before it, the Internet and its "killer application" of electronic mail, or E-mail, have been taken up by women in huge numbers. It is not surprising that millions of women are on-line and that most use various services of the Internet (for example, E-mail, chat rooms, conferencing, World Wide Web, bulletin board services, and mailing lists) on a daily basis. Although there are still wide cultural and geographical divisions in regard to who uses the Internet and toward what ends, there is no doubt that the

Internet is now part of the lives of many women all around the world.

Opportunities for Innovative Research

From the viewpoint of research, the Internet offers a vast array of new ways of gathering information about people and their experiences. The World Wide Web provides women researchers with instant access to all types of information. While much of the Internet is free—users pay only for their local phone call, and/or the services of their local Internet Service Provider (ISP)—the Web also provides easy access to training of all kinds. In recent years, there are also women-specific websites, including <http://www.wow-women.com> and <www.women.com>, and women's resource sites such as <www.wwork.com>.

In addition to providing an instant, global information resource, the Internet has also opened up new opportunities for research on, for, and by women. At the quantitative level, the Internet can make the administration of surveys cheap and easy: a researcher need never generate a hard (paper) copy of a questionnaire, so the costs of printing, paper, and postage can be eliminated. With the use of the most basic technology, questionnaires can be composed and formatted on a computer, and data can be manipulated and stored in the same way. Even more exciting, recipients can be solicited and recruited using a variety of on-line means. For example, researchers can post messages advertising their research and calling for volunteers on mailing lists and bulletin board services. This method encourages specifically focused research. It provides women researchers with ready access to sites that may be for women-only subscribers and on women-focused topics. Finally, questionnaires can be mailed to participants on-line, either through Web sites or as attachments to E-mails.

In the area of qualitative research, there exist even greater opportunities for research innovation and new practices. Because qualitative methodological approaches are often most favored by women researchers across many disciplines, this is a welcome development. Qualitative researchers use multiple methods to collect rich, descriptive, contextually situated data in order to understand human experience or relationships within a system or culture (Mann and Stewart, 2000). In conventional research terms, qualitative research can be understood to refer largely to interview- or text-based research activities in which the researcher is the "human instrument." That is, the researcher is key in all phases of the research, from data-gathering to analysis.

In the context of on-line research, the Internet alters standard practice in a number of important ways. First, it makes possible a number of types of communication.

Internet interaction is sometimes called about "computer-mediated communication" (CMC). Although CMC is usually text based, it can include voice and video communication. Voice is not yet a widely used tool in Internet communication, however, and, in terms of on-line research methods, it is yet to be considered at all. Nevertheless, this is expected to change rapidly.

It is in the area of on-line interviewing that the Internet offers the greatest opportunity. For example, whereas with face-to-face (FTF) interviewing methods there is only one time zone—the here and now—with on-line interviewing, there are two time zones. First, there is "real time" or synchronous CMC (for example, chat). Real time refers to an interchange of messages between two or more users who are logged on at different computer terminals at the same time. Chat can be effectively used to conduct on-line focus groups.

The alternative to real time CMC is "non–real time" or asynchronous CMC (for example, E-mail). Non–real time CMC allows users to type extended messages that are electronically transmitted to recipients who can then read, reply, print, forward, or file them at their leisure. Non–real time CMC can be suitable for researchers who wish to conduct in-depth interviews in a one-on-one situation. It is also useful for longitudinal interviewing, in which the researcher investigates an issue over a specific period of time.

These different methods mean that the first question confronting the qualitative on-line researcher is that of time zones. The researcher has to decide which method is more appropriate for the research topic at hand. There are, of course, benefits and drawbacks associated with each of these methods.

Challenges of On-Line Research

There are myriad challenges in on-line research. Some have to do with disclosure on-line, or rapport and trust between researcher and subject. Questions must be about the type of data a researcher is likely to gather through on-line means, and about whether some topics may be better researched using conventional FTF means.

It is well established that there is a greater propensity for people to disclose personal details in an on-line environment than in an FTF environment. This is usually explained by saying that one's identity is largely protected when one is on-line. As Horn (1998:294) has said, "In cyberspace you have more control over how someone sees you. Everything begins with words. You are who you say you are. And you can make yourself sound really good." Horn later added, however: "You don't have any more guarantees that someone is who they say they are just because you can see them. We are as often fooled by appearances as we are informed by them" (1998: 91).

The issue of on-line identity is difficult because of the "narrow bandwidth" of CMC. Although the concept of bandwidth has a number of technical meanings, it also refers metaphorically to the fact that in Internet communication, the researcher does not have the benefit of hearing her participants' voices—their intonation, accent, and gender identification, for instance. The researcher is also communicating without the embodied aspects of FTF interaction. For example, in CMC one cannot see someone's face or body language. There are no tears, no blushing, and no dirty looks. The absence of factors like these makes the Internet environment an altogether new challenge where research is concerned.

Benefits of On-Line Research

Although the challenges of on-line research include some of the issues noted above—as well as the need for literacy, availability of computer hardware and software, specific on-line skills training, the risk of loss of E-mail contact addresses, and the challenge of ensuring and maintaining cooperation—Mann and Stewart (2000) argue that the benefits far exceed the problems. Among the most important benefits these researchers have noted are researcher access to geographically and otherwise difficult-to-reach participants; the gathering of first-person accounts; access to dangerous or politically sensitive sites; access to specific groups (for example, support, special interest); and time and cost savings in areas such as transcription, travel, room rental, and elimination of transcription bias. Mann and Stewart note such benefits to the participant as ease of communication, participation at times and places that suit everyone, a safe environment, and ease of participation from remote locations. In all these ways, the Internet offers women researchers new and exciting possibilities for undertaking women-oriented research in women-friendly ways.

See Also

COMMUNICATIONS: OVERVIEW; COMPUTING: OVERVIEW; COMPUTING: PARTICIPATORY AND FEMINIST DESIGN; EDUCATION: ON-LINE; INFORMATION REVOLUTION; INFORMATION TECHNOLOGY; NETWORKS, ELECTRONIC; SCIENCE: TECHNOLOGICAL AND SCIENTIFIC RESEARCH; TECHNOLOGY

References and Further Readings

Harnard, S. 1992. Post-Gutenberg galaxy: The Fourth revolution in the means of production of knowledge. *Public-Access Computer Systems Review* 2(1): 39–52.

Horn, S. 1998. *Cyberville: Clicks, culture and the creation of an online town.* New York: Warner.

Mann, C. and Stewart, F. 2000. *Internet communication and qualitative research.* London: Sage.

Maynard, M. and Purvis, J. 1994. Doing feminist research. In M. Maynard and J. Purvis, eds, *Researching women's lives from a feminist perspective.* London: Taylor and Francis.

Lillington, K. 1999. Walk on the wired side, *The Guardian,* 14 January.

Spender, D. 1995. *Nattering on the net: Women, power and cyberspace.* Melbourne: Spinifex.

Fiona Stewart
Chris Mann

RESOURCES

See HOUSEHOLDS: RESOURCES; NATURAL RESOURCES; MONEY.

REVOLUTIONS

What is a revolution? What are its constituent elements? Do revolutions have a gender dimension? Social scientists have disagreed on whether revolutions are purposive or structural in nature: Are they "made" or do they "come about?" There is also disagreement about the dominant features; are they political, social, economic, cultural, or some combination? The political scientist Samuel Huntington defined revolution as "a rapid, fundamental and violent domestic change in the dominant values and myths of a society, in its political institutions, social structure, leadership, government activity, and policies" (1968: 264). The historical sociologist Charles Tilly stresses political factors and defines a revolutionary situation as entailing "(1) the appearance of contenders, or coalitions of contenders, advancing competing claims to control of the state, or some segment of it, (2) commitment to those claims by a significant segment of the citizenry, and (3) the incapacity or unwillingness of rulers to suppress the alternative coalition and/or commitment to its claims" (1993: 49–50).

The revolutionary outcome occurs when the revolutionary coalition successfully takes over control of the state apparatus. The sociologist Theda Skocpol insisted on the structural features of revolutionary causes and outcomes, defining revolutions as "rapid, basic transformations of a society's state and class structure; they are accompanied and in part carried through by class-based revolts from below"

(1979: 4). The definition by John Dunn includes the purposive and violent dimensions of revolution: revolutions are "a form of massive, violent, and rapid social change. They are also attempts to embody a set of values in a new or at least renovated social order" (1972: 12). Perez Zagorin includes the ideational in his definition: "A revolution is an attempt by subordinate groups through the use of violence to bring about (1) a change of government or its policy, (2) a change of regime, or (3) a change of society, whether this attempt is justified by reference to past conditions or to an as yet unattained future ideal" (1982: 17).

Theories of Revolution and Research

The major theories of revolution have linked revolution to the dynamics and contradictions of modernization (including population change and other demographic factors) and to struggles over configurations of state power, covering the period from the French Revolution of 1789 to the eastern European revolutions of 1989. Few studies focus on culture or ideology, although Lynn Hunt (1984) is a notable exception, and the Iranian Revolution sparked a number of studies, principally by Iranian scholars, which emphasize these factors (for example, Farhi, 1990; Moaddel, 1993). There is growing agreement among scholars that revolutions should be studied in terms of the interaction of economic, political, and cultural developments in national, regional, and global contexts (Foran, 1997; Kimmel, 1990; Moghadam, 1989).

The scholarship on revolution is prodigious and rich, but it is deficient in terms of incorporating gender into the analysis. The study of revolution has not yet considered systematically the prominent position assumed by gender—the position of women, family law, the prerogatives of men—in the discourse of revolutionaries and the laws of revolutionary states. Unlike the mainstream literature on revolution, feminist scholarship has been attentive to the theme of women and revolution. Some scholars of the French Revolution have examined how gender was constructed in the political discourse and have discovered the legal disempowerment and exclusion of women based on the "natural fact" of sexual difference. Siân Reynolds (1987) makes the interesting point that the participation of women as mothers and food distributors has a profoundly legitimizing effect on a revolution—at least in its early stages. Mary Ann Tétreault (1994) observes that all twentieth-century revolutionaries retain or re-create private space and family forms, which indicates the importance of family and gender to revolutions and states. Diane Bush and Stephen Mumme (1994) argue that gender as a fundamental feature of social structure underlies the intersection of family, religion, and the state in revolutionary processes as well as in periods of stability. Bush and Mumme do not assume success, as many definitions of revolution do; rather, they conceptualize revolution as a process whereby traditionally subordinate groups attempt to transform the culture and structure of power relations within a society. They stress the need to examine how the revolutionary situation and the revolutionary outcome are related to the social organization of gender. Hanna Papanek (1994) maintains that the construction of the ideal society entails a notion of the ideal woman. In her work on Nicaragua, Maxine Molyneux (1986) distinguishes between women's practical interests and strategic gender interests; she argues that the Nicaraguan revolution served the first set of interests more than the second. Val Moghadam (1997a) has classified revolutions in terms of gender outcomes: revolutions of one set are modernizing and egalitarian, with women's emancipation an explicit goal; revolutions of another set are patriarchal, tying women to the family and stressing gender differences rather than equality. Outcomes for women seem to be determined by the explicit ideology, goals, and social program of the revolution, by the nature of preexisting gender relations, and by the scope of women's involvement in the revolutionary movement.

Roles of Women in Revolutions

Feminists have produced prolific research into the role and position of women in revolutionary France, Russia, China, Vietnam, Cuba, Algeria, Nicaragua, Iran, Afghanistan, and elsewhere (for an early survey, see Rowbotham, 1972; see also Davies, 1983). This body of literature strongly suggests that gender relations constitute an important part of the culture, ideology, and politics of revolutionary societies. Certainly revolutionary states expend considerable effort legislating the social positions of women, revising family law, and defining the prerogatives of men. In the sociology of revolution, however, gender—unlike class or the state or the world system—is not seen as a constitutive category.

A synthetic definition of revolution might be the following: revolutions are attempts to change political and social structures rapidly and profoundly; they involve mass participation; they usually, but not always, entail violence or the use of force; they include notions of the "ideal" society; and they have some cultural reference points. As an integral part of the social structure, as a basic element of production and reproduction, and as a central feature of concepts of the ideal society, gender affects and is affected by revolutionary processes in profound ways. Revolutions always entail constructions of national identity—for example, "Soviet Russia," "Islamic Iran," "revolutionary, popular Nicaragua," "Muslim and socialist Algeria"—within which constructs of gender figure prominently. Theoretically, therefore, gender is at least as important as class in revolutionary transformations or redefinitions of production and (social) reproduction. Although changes in gender relations are especially obvious in revolutionary *outcomes,* so far there is less evidence to support a role for gender in *causality.* In the case of the Iranian Revolution, however, it is plausible to propose that gender intersected with class to constitute a causal factor in the revolt against the Shah and the turn to Islamization, at least for a section of the revolutionary coalition. (That is, the growing visibility of middle-class women and the "westernization" of bourgeois women offended the men of the lower middle class, who sought to recuperate traditional gender roles as part of their revolutionary goals.) For all revolutions, it is possible to posit that gender ideology profoundly *shapes* many actions and decisions, large and small: patterns of revolutionary mobilization, state-building, the establishment of constitution, laws, and policies, household dynamics, and relations within families.

Judith Stacey's (1983) book on the Chinese Revolution and Maxine Molyneux's (1986) writings on the Nicaraguan Revolution reveal the complexities of gendered ideology, revolutionary mobilization, and state structure, and the uneasy coexistence of traditional notions about women's proper place with revolutionary socialist concepts of women's emancipation. Although Molyneux shows how the Sandinista National Liberation Front (FSLN) "politicized traditional roles of women, but did not dissolve them," she rejects the view that socialist revolutions marginalize or deny representation of women's interests. Stacey highlights the interactive process whereby family structure and ideology shaped the Chinese Revolution, and the ideology and structure of the revolution shaped the family as a social institution.

Bush and Mumme (1994) call for attention to the complex, gendered intersection of family, religion, and state in the revolutionary process and in outcomes. In their work on the 1917 Mexican Revolution, they examine the ways in which church, state, and gender ideology influenced the revolutionary situation and resulted in women's second–class citizenship. Despite women's participation in the revolution, the Constitutional Congress excluded them and rejected female suffrage. Bush and Mumme show how gender shaped and was shaped by the Mexican Revolution within the context of Mexico's social structure and the world system.

The "Women's Emancipation" Model

Many feminists have noted that revolutionary movements subordinate women's interests and gender interests to "broader" or "basic" goals of emancipation. For this reason, there has been a veritable indictment of all revolutions and liberation movements as essentially inimical to women's interests (see, for example, Mies, 1986). Nevertheless, it cannot be denied that some revolutionary experiences have been profoundly liberating for women *as women,* especially where traditional gender roles are challenged and where new legislation is enacted toward greater equality and autonomy for women (see, for example, Molyneux, 1986, and Chinchilla, 1993, on Nicaragua, and Lobao, 1990, on El Salvador and other cases). For this reason, two types of revolution—social transformation and national-identity construction—can be distinguished: (1) the "women's emancipation" or modernizing model; and (2) the "woman-in-the-family" or patriarchal model of revolution. These are ideal types, and it should be noted that in each case there may be differential effects on women based on social class, race or ethnicity, and ideological divisions among women themselves. Nevertheless, revolutionary discourses and policies pertaining to women, the family, and citizenship seem to fall into these two categories.

The "women's emancipation" model says that the emancipation of women is an essential part of the revolution or project of social transformation. It constructs Woman as part of the productive forces and the citizenry, to be mobilized for economic and political purposes; she is to be liberated from patriarchal controls expressly for that purpose. Here the discourse is more strongly that of sexual equality than of difference. The first historical example, of such a revolution is the Bolshevik Revolution in Russia, which, especially in its early years, was the avant-garde revolution par excellence, more audacious in its approach to gender than any revolution before or since. Other revolutions that conform to this model—in some cases explicitly—include those of China, Cuba, Vietnam, Democratic Yemen, and Nicaragua (socialist or populist revolutions), and the Kemalist revolution in Turkey (a bourgeois revolution).

In contrast, the "woman-in-the-family" model of revolution excludes women from definitions and constructions of independence, liberation, and liberty, and sometimes expressly designates women as second-class citizens or legal minors. It frequently constructs an ideological linkage between patriarchal values, nationalism, and the religious order. It assigns women the roles of wife and mother, and it associates women not only with family but with tradition, culture, and religion. The historical precursor of the patriarchal model was the French Revolution, which, despite its many progressive features, had an extremely conservative outcome for women. Not for nothing did playwright Olympe de Gouges utter her famous *cri de coeur:* "O my poor sex! O women who have gained nothing from the Revolution!" (Kelly, 1987; Scott, 1996). The French woman's chief responsibility in the Republic was to be the socialization of children in republican virtues. In twentieth-century revolutions that had similarly patriarchal outcomes for women—notably in Mexico, Algeria and Iran—women were relegated to the private sphere despite the crucial roles they had played in the revolutionary movements. In these three cases, men took over the reins of power, assigned women responsibility for family, religion, and tradition, and enacted legislation to codify patriarchal gender relations. Feminist studies in the 1990s on post-communist Russia and eastern and central Europe confirm that the political and economic changes there, too, conform to the patriarchal model of revolution (see Einhorn, 1993; Moghadam, 1993).

The differentiation of revolutions by gender outcomes shows that gender is indeed an integral dimension of the revolutionary process and should be accorded conceptual value by mainstream studies. It also reveals that not all revolutionary outcomes are similar or are entirely contrary or beneficial to women's interests. The "women's emancipation" model of revolution serves (at least some) strategic gender interests, especially through its explicit espousal of gender equality and the full integration of women in public life; it addresses practical gender interests to the extent that its resources allow; and it is in the interests of most strata of the female population—although some groups of women may oppose it because of class and ideological differences. By contrast, the "women-in-the-family" model of revolution, by virtue of its insistence on gender differences and female domesticity, is inimical to the strategic gender interests of women, although it may address some practical gender needs and the specific interests of some groups of women.

See Also

ANARCHISM; EMANCIPATION AND LIBERATION MOVEMENTS; FUNDAMENTALISM AND PUBLIC POLICY; NATION AND NATIONALISM; POLITICAL REPRESENTATION; SOCIAL MOVEMENTS

References and Further Reading

Bush, Diane Mitsch, and Stephen P. Mumme. 1994. Gender and the Mexican Revolution: The intersection of gender, state, church, and family ideology in movement mobilization. In Mary Ann Tétreault, ed., *Women and revolution in Africa, Asia, and the New World.* Columbia: University of South Carolina Press.

Chinchilla, Norma. 1993. Feminism, revolution and democratic transitions in Nicaragua. Program in Women's Studies, California State University at Long Beach.

Davies, Miranda, ed. 1983. *Third world/second sex.* London: Zed.

Dunn, John. 1972. *Modern revolutions.* New York: Cambridge University Press.

Einhorn, Barbara. 1993. *Cinderella goes to market: Citizenship, gender and women's movements in East Central Europe.* London: Verso.

Farhi, Farideh. 1990. *States and urban-based revolutions: Iran and Nicaragua.* Urbana: University of Illinois Press.

Foran, John, ed. 1997. *Theorizing revolutions.* London and New York: Routledge.

Hunt, Lynn. 1984. *Politics, culture and class in the French revolution.* Berkeley: University of California Press.

Huntington, Samuel. 1968. *Political Order in Changing Societies.* New Haven, Conn.: Yale University Press.

Kimmel, Michael S. 1990. *Revolution: A sociological interpretation.* Cambridge, UK: Polity.

Lobao, Linda. 1990. Women in revolutionary movements: Changing patterns of Latin American guerrilla struggles. In Guida West and Rhoda Lois Blumberg, eds., *Women and social protest,* 180–204. New York: Oxford University Press.

Mies, Maria. 1986. *Patriarchy and accumulation on a world scale.* London: Zed.

Moaddel, Mansour. 1993. *Class, politics, and ideology in the Iranian revolution.* New York: Columbia University Press.

Moghadam, Valentine M. 1989. Populist revolution and the Islamic state in Iran. In Terry Boswell, ed., *Revolutions in the world-system,* 147–163. Westport, Conn.: Greenwood.

———. 1997. Gender and revolutions. In John Foran, ed., *Theorizing revolutions.* London and New York: Routledge.

———, ed. 1993b. *Democratic reform and the position of women in transitional economies.* Oxford: Clarendon.

Molyneux, Maxine. 1986. Mobilization without emancipation? Women's interests, state, and revolution. In Richard Fagen, Carmen Diana Deere, and José Luis Corragio, eds., *Transition and development: Problems of third world socialism,* 280–302. New York: Monthly Review Press.

Papanek, Hanna. 1994. The ideal woman and the ideal society: Control and autonomy in the construction of identity. In Valentine M. Moghadam, ed., *Identity Politics and Women: Cultural reassertions and feminisms in international perspective,* 42–75. Boulder, Colo.: Westview.

Reynolds, Siân, ed. 1987. *Women, state and revolution: Essays on power and gender in Europe since 1789.* Amherst: University of Massachusetts Press.

Rowbotham, Sheila. 1972. *Women, resistance, and revolution.* London: Allen Lane.

Skocpol, Theda. 1979. *States and social revolutions: A comparative analysis of France, Russia, and China.* New York: Cambridge University Press.

Stacey, Judith. 1983. *Patriarchy and socialist revolution in China.* Berkeley: University of California Press.

Tétreault, Mary Ann, ed. 1994. *Women and revolution in Africa, Asia, and the new world.* Columbia: University of South Carolina Press.

Tilly, Charles. 1993. *European revolutions, 1492–1992.* Cambridge, Mass.: Basil Blackwell.

Zagorin, Perez. 1982. *Rebels and rulers.* Vol. 1. Cambridge, UK: Cambridge University Press.

Valentine M. Moghadam

RIGHTS

See HUMAN RIGHTS; INDIGENOUS WOMEN'S RIGHTS; JUSTICE AND RIGHTS.

ROMAN CATHOLICISM

See CHRISTIANITY AND FAMILY: RELIGIOUS AND LEGAL SYSTEMS—CATHOLIC AND ORTHODOX.

ROMANCE

The word "romance" denotes both a literary genre and a form of emotional relationship: one can both read and experience romance. These two meanings are interconnected. Cultural ideals of love inform the romantic fiction produced within a society and the ways in which it is interpreted by its readers, most of whom are female: it would have little appeal for women if it did not connect with their emotional experience. Conversely, these narratives may help to construct readers' emotions and to shape their understanding of what it is to be "in love." Within women's studies, more attention has been given to the cultural representation of romance than to women's experience of romantic love, but the two areas of study have been brought together in the 1990s. (Pearce and Stacey, 1994).

Both mass-market romantic fiction and the ideals of romantic love represented within it are products of white, western culture. Romantic fiction series such as Mills and Boon from the United Kingdom and Harlequin from Canada sell in the millions all over the world, and their producers claim that the books speak to a universal feminine concern. Feminists are skeptical of such claims, which they say deny the differences among women from various cultural and national backgrounds. If these romances are being consumed worldwide, it is interesting to learn how and why they are being read: All women everywhere presumably do not make sense of them in the same way. As yet, little research has been done on romance outside Europe, North America, and Australia.

Within western societies, romance is often seen as a specifically feminine preoccupation. Francesca Cancian (1990) attributes this to a "feminized" conception of love which has existed, in varying forms, since the nineteenth century. It has been women's responsibility to watch over the emotional climate of romantic, and especially marital, relationships. Cancian believes that heterosexual love is now becoming more androgynous and egalitarian, but not all feminists share her optimism. Recent sociological research, such as Wendy Langford's British study (Langford, 1999), indicates that many women remain dissatisfied with the lack of romance within heterosexual relationships, and particularly with some men's inability to express love.

Feminists have been critical of romance since at least the beginning of the twentieth century. By the 1970s, they generally agreed that love was the bait that lured women into unequal relationships with men. Hence, they dismissed romantic fiction as a manifestation of patriarchal ideology. Recently, women's studies scholars have taken women's pleasure in romance more seriously, suggesting that it may be a site of limited resistance to patriarchal domination as well as of accommodation to it. For example, Tania Modleski (1984) proposes that part of the appeal of romantic fiction for women may be that it taps into fantasies of revenge: love brings the arrogant male to his knees. It may thus be one of the few ways in which many women can hope to exert power over men. Janice Radway (1984) argues that reading romance is a way in which women can vicariously experience the feeling of being nurtured when their daily lives are spent nurturing others. Ironically, in seeking to escape from the confines of domesticity, they embrace the very ideals of heterosexual romance that put them there in the first place.

Although heterosexual romance has been the focus of these analyses and dominates cultural representations of love, ideals of romantic love affect lesbians as well as heterosexual women. Feminists admit that, whether they are lesbian or heterosexual, being critical of romantic love does not make them immune to it. Many agree that the attraction lies in the excitement of being in love, experienced as a powerful emotion that lifts them above the mundane everyday world. This is also a source of contradictions inherent in the ideal of romantic love, particularly as the basis for long-term relationships.

Being in love is commonly understood as an irrational, uncontrollable and compulsive state, yet this unruly emotion is supposed to provide the basis for a stable long-term commitment (Sarsby, 1983). Literary, psychoanalytic, and social scientific writings suggest that the passion of romantic love thrives only when obstacles are put in its way—that it withers away once lovers are secure with each other. Fairy tales and popular romances typically end at the point where all difficulties have been overcome and mutual love between hero and heroine is affirmed: that they are assumed to live "happily ever after" papers over the contradictions between the two forms of love. Readers of these stories can thus experience the thrill of the chase over and over again, without having to confront the waning of passion or its transformation into a tamer, less exhilarating form of love.

Elaine Hoffman Baruch (1991) suggests that romantic love may die out because the denial it feeds on has given way to easy sexual gratification. Whether a less restrictive sexual morality heralds the decline of romantic love is debatable, although the expectations surrounding it probably are changing. Evidence from sociological studies shows that young women are often cynical about romance, but that it is still central to the ways in which they come to terms with their sexuality (for example, Holland, Ramazonoglu, Sharpe and Thomson, 1998). White weddings are still popular—and profitable—in most western countries (Ingraham, 1999). The effects of recent social changes on the culture of romance remain to be charted.

See Also

MARRIAGE: OVERVIEW; POPULAR CULTURE; ROMANTIC FICTION; SEXUALITY: OVERVIEW

References and Further Readings

Baruch, Elaine Hoffman. 1991. *Women, love and power.* New York: New York University Press.

Cancian, Francesca. 1990. *Love in America.* Cambridge and New York: Cambridge University Press.

Holland, Janet, Caroline Ramazanoglu, Sue Sharpe, and Rachel Thomson. 1998. *The male in the head: Young people, heterosexuality and power.* London: Tuffnell.

Ingraham, Chrys. 1999. *White weddings: Romancing heterosexuality in popular culture.* New York: Routledge.

Langford, Wendy. 1999. *Revolutions of the heart: Gender, power and the delusions of love.* London: Routledge.

Modleski, Tania. 1984. *Loving with a vengeance: Mass produced fantasies for women.* London and New York: Methuen.

Pearce, Lynne, and Jackie Stacey. (eds.). 1994. *Romance revisited.* London: Lawrence and Wishart.

Radway, Janice. 1984. *Reading the romance: Women, patriarchy and popular literature.* Chapel Hill: University of North Carolina Press.

Sarsby, Jacqueline. 1983. *Romantic love and society.* Harmondsworth: Penguin.

Thomson, Rachel, and Sue Scott. 1991. *Learning about sex: Young women and the social construction of sexual identity.* London: Tufnell.

Stevi Jackson

ROMANTIC FICTION

From Chariton's first-century A.D. (C.E.) Greek prose love tales to an international industry with yearly earnings of over $950 million in 1999, romantic fiction represents the doubts and delights surrounding love, fantasy, and desire; it is also a mode of social control for women. It is a genre where women are highly visible as chief editors, writers, readers, and at times executives. The world's most prolific romance fiction writer is England's Barbara Cartland.

Romance fiction is not of one fabric. Within the varieties of romance fiction, the series novel is dominant. Mary Bonnycastle, an early co-owner and chief editor for Canada's Harlequin publishing house, laid the groundwork for Harlequin to become the largest publisher of the series romance novel. Harlequin's acquisition of major competitors—Mills and Boon from Great Britain, and Silhouette Books from the United States,—has resulted in an 80 percent share of the series market. With international distribution and novels translated into more than 20 languages, Harlequin is poised to further its dominance through an agreement with Women.com Network to sell its romance novels on this popular woman-focused Web site.

Romance fiction is distinguished by formulaic subcategories and responsiveness to change. Developed by Great Britain's Mills and Boon around 1919, the series or "formula" romance with its standardized plots, book lengths, and inexperienced women characters is typified by the works of Cartland and the pioneering North American writers of Harlequin romances, such as Janet Dailey and Alice Morgan. In the "Gothics" of the 1950s and 1960s, England's Victoria Holt and Mary Stewart penned tales of women terrorized in sinister mansions. "Historicals" combine romantic motifs with settings in past times while "Regencies" are set in eighteenth-century England. The "bodice-ripper," created by Ceylonese-born Rosemary Rogers in 1974, is characterized by explicit sex and violence.

Romance fiction achieved more depth when *The Thorn Birds,* by Australia's Colleen McCullough was published in 1977, and strong, independent heroines were introduced by Jude Deveraux and LaVyrle Spencer of the United States. Key romance writers are now being published in hardcover in response to the popularity of single-title romances by Danielle Steele and Janet Dailey of the United States, and Barbara Taylor Bradford from Great Britain. African American characters are featured in Black Entertainment's Arabesque Series, while Hispanic characters appear in Kensington Books' Encantoline. Naiad Press specializes in romance fiction for lesbian readers. Once thought to be a fad, the teen romance fiction series, originated in the United States by Scholastic Books in the late 1970s, is an international phenomenon. Its latest incarnation is Dolly Fiction in Australia and Bantam's *Sweet Valley High* series. The latter has sold more than 40 million books and has been translated into 15 languages.

Romances written in the 1990s deal with more than heart and hearth. They wrestle with social issues from incest to spousal abuse. Their women characters are more apt to have career goals and to be single parents in the workforce. Critical responses from women readers have forced these changes in content and scope on publishers (Radway, 1994).

Critical opinions of romance fiction have swung from early condemnation to portraits of a complex and nuanced genre in major studies of adult romance fiction and its readers by Radway (1984) and Thurston (1987), and in Durham's (1998), Finders (1997) Christian-Smith's (1990) research with teenage female readers. These studies find that most romance readers are white, American, and middle class, and many are mothers, although Christian-Smith found teenage readers from working-class, African American, Hispanic, and Asian backgrounds. These readers preferred intelligent and resourceful heroines and sensitive men. Reading romance fiction afforded them time to relax, escape, and acquire a wider store of knowledge. Teen readers escaped home and academic problems while learning to negotiate romantic relationships with boys. Adult women readers gained respite from home and work responsibilities while engaging in a critique of women's relationships with men and of their larger social positions. Radway (1984) suggests that romance fiction reading is a mild form of social protest, but one that forestalls demands for change in the real world. It may desensitize readers to the tolls exacted by rigid gender hierarchies in schools, families, and workplaces. Analyses of romance fiction (Christian-Smith, 1984; Radway, 1984) disclose a traditional universe where women's consent to their social subordination is sought. Teen readers limit their future options when they substitute romance fiction for academic reading materials.

Despite these criticisms, romance fiction is not totally conservative. Reading allows women to exert their rights to a fantasy life where their dreams and pleasures are fulfilled. According to Christian-Smith (1990), the focus on fantasy and pleasure in teen romance novels creates new possibilities in adolescent fiction. For Thurston (1987), romance fiction can chronicle the changing interests and challenges of independent women. It thus provides a vehicle for women to examine their evolving social positions and the circumstances that limit their life possibilities.

See Also

FICTION; PUBLISHING; ROMANCE

References and Further Readings

Christian-Smith, Linda K. 1990. *Becoming a woman through romance.* New York: Routledge.

Durham, Meenakshi. 1998. Dilemmas of desire: Representations of adolescent sexuality in two teen magazines. *Youth and Society* 29: 369–389.

Finders, Margaret. 1997. *Just girls.* New York: Teachers College Press.

Paizis, George. 1998. *Love and the novel: The poetics and politics of romantic fiction.* New York: St. Martin's.

Pearce, Lyane, and Jackie Stacey. 1995. *Romance revisited.* London: Lawrence and Wishart.

Radway, Janice. 1997. *A feeling for books.* Chapel Hill: University of North Carolina Press.

———. 1984. *Reading the romance.* Chapel Hill: University of North Carolina Press.

Thurston, Carol. 1987. *The romance revolution.* Urbana: University of Illinois Press.

Uszkurat, Carol Ann. 1993. Mid twentieth century lesbian romance: Reception and redress. In Gabriele Griffin, ed., *Outwrite Lesbianism and popular culture,* 26–47. London: Pluto.

Linda K. Christian-Smith

ROMANTIC FRIENDSHIP

The Renaissance interest in Platonism encouraged a revival of passionate friendships between men, reflected in works such as Michel de Montaigne's (1533–1592) "On Friendship" (1572–1576, 1578–1580), Baldassare Castiglione's (1478–1529)

The Book of the Courtier (1528), William Painter's (c. 1540–1594) *The Palace of Pleasure* (1566), and Thomas Lodge's (c. 1557–1625) *Euphues Shadowe* (1592). Literary examples of such relationships between women are less numerous in the Renaissance, but they may be found in work such as Lodge's *Rosalynde* (1590), and, in the seventeenth century, in many poems of Katherine Philips (1632–1664). In the eighteenth century such relationships, which came to be called "romantic friendships," became common. Romantic friendship between women was socially condoned, originally because it was not believed to violate the Platonist ideal and later for more complex reasons. But while it is true that love between women was "in style," women's experiences of that love were no less intense or real for their social acceptability.

Eighteenth Century

Such passion in the eighteenth century was not believed seriously to violate any code of behavior, even when it was taken to such extremes that women eloped with each other, as did the Ladies of Llangollen—Eleanor Butler (1739–1829) and Sarah Ponsonby (1755–1831)—in 1778. One relative observed: "[Sarah's] conduct, though it has an appearance of imprudence, is I am sure voide of serious impropriety. There were no gentlemen concerned, nor does it appear to be anything more than a scheme of Romantic Friendship."

The English, during the second half of the eighteenth century, prized sensibility, faithfulness, and devotion in a woman but forbade significant contact with the opposite sex before she was betrothed. It was reasoned, apparently, that women could practice these sentiments with each other so that, when they were ready for marriage, they would have perfected themselves in those areas. It is doubtful that women viewed their own romantic friendships in such a way, but— if we can place any credence in eighteenth-century fiction as a reflection of that society—men did. Because romantic friendship between women ostensibly served men's self-interest, it was permitted and even socially encouraged.

The novels of the period show how women perceived romantic friendship and what ideals they envisioned for love between women. Those ideals generally could not be realized in life because most women did not have the wherewithal to be independent. In fiction, however, romantic friends (having achieved economic security as a part of the plot, which also furnishes them with good reasons for not having a husband around) could retire together, away from the corruption of the man-ruled "great world"; they could devote their lives to cultivating themselves and their gardens and to living generously and productively, and they could share perfect intimacy in perfect equality. The most com-plete fictional blueprint for conducting romantic friendship is Sarah Scott's *A Description of Millennium Hall* (1762), a novel that went through four editions by 1778.

Even the mention of such a relationship in the title of a work must have promoted its sales—which would explain why a 1770 novel that envisions friendship between women as nothing more than an epistolary device was entitled *Female Friendship*. Women readers could identify with the female characters' involvement with each other, since most of them had experienced romantic friendship, at least in their youth. Mrs. Delany's (1700–1788) description of her own first love (in *The Autobiography and Correspondence of Mary Granville, Mrs. Delany* [1861]) is typical of what numerous autobiographies, diaries, letters, and novels of the period contained. As a young woman, she formed a passionate attachment to a clergyman's daughter, whom she admired for her "uncommon genius…intrepid spirit… extraordinary understanding, lively imagination, and humane disposition." They shared "secret talk" and "whispers" together; they wrote to each other every day and met in the field between their fathers' houses at every opportunity. Typical of many youthful romantic friendships, it did not last long (at the age of seventeen, Mrs. Delany was given in marriage to an old man), but it provided fuel for the imagination that idealized the possibilities of what such a relationship might be like without the impingement of cold marital reality. Because of such girlhood intimacies (which often were cut off in an untimely manner), most women would have understood when those attachments were compared with heterosexual love by the female characters in eighteenth-century novels and were considered, as Lucy says in William Hayley's (1745–1820) *The Young Widow* (1789), "infinitely more valuable." They would have had their own frame of reference when, in those novels, women adopted the David and Jonathan story—about a same-sex love that surpasses the love of man for woman—for themselves, and swore that they felt for each other (again, as Lucy says) "a love passing the Love of Men," or proclaimed, as does Anne Hughes, the author of *Henry and Isabella* (1788), that such friendships are "more sweet, interesting, and to complete all, lasting, than any other which we can ever hope to possess; and were a just account of anxiety and satisfaction to be made out, would, it is possible, in the eye of rational estimation, far exceed the so-much boasted pleasure of love."

Romantic Friendship in the United States

By the mid-eighteenth century, romantic friendship was a recognized institution in America, too. In the eyes of an observer such as Moreau de St. Mery, who had recently left

Revolutionary France for North America and must have been familiar with the accusations of lesbianism lodged against Marie Antoinette (1755–1793), the women of her court, and most of the French actresses of the day, women's effusive display of affection for each other seemed sexual. St. Mery, who recorded his observations of his 1793–1798 journey, was shocked by the "unlimited liberty" that young ladies seemed to enjoy and by their ostensible lack of passion toward men. The combination of their independence, heterosexual passionlessness, and intimacy with one another could have meant only one thing to a Frenchman in the 1790s: that "they are not at all strangers to being willing to seek unnatural pleasures with persons of their own sex." It is as doubtful that great masses of middle- and upper-class young ladies gave themselves up to homosexuality as it is that they gave themselves up to heterosexual intercourse before marriage. But the fiction of the period corroborates that St. Mery saw North American women behaving openly as though they were in love with each other. Charles Brockden Brown's *Ormand* (1798), for example, suggests that in the United States romantic friends were much like their English counterparts.

The Female Island

Many of the fictional works about romantic friendship were written by women, and they provide a picture of female intimacy very different from the usual depictions by men. The extreme masculine view, epitomized in Casanova's *Memoirs* (1826–1838), reduced female love to the genital, and, as such, it could be called "trifling." But love between women, at least as it was lived in women's fantasies, was far more consuming than the likes of Casanova could believe.

Women dreamed not of erotic escapades but of a blissful life together. In such a life, a woman would have choices; she would be in command of her own destiny; she would be an adult relating to another adult in a way that a heterosexual relationship with a virtual stranger (often an old, or at least much older, man), arranged by a parent for considerations totally divorced from affection, would not allow her to be. Samuel Richardson (1689–1761) permitted Miss Howe (in *Clarissa* [1747–1748]) to express the yearnings of many a frustrated romantic friend when she remarked to Clarissa: "How charmingly might you and I live together and despise them all."

Nineteenth Century

In the United States and England during the second half of the nineteenth century, as more women began to claim more of the world, the reasons for bonding together against men who wished to deny them a broader sphere became greater. Smith-Rosenberg (1975) has amply demonstrated that deeply felt friendships between women were casually accepted in American society, primarily because women saw themselves, and were seen as, kindred spirits who inhabited a world of interests and sensibilities alien to men. During the second half of the nineteenth century, when women slowly began to enter the world that men had built, their ties to one another became even more important. Particularly when they engaged in reform and betterment work, they were confirmed in their belief that women were spiritually superior to men, their moral perceptions were more highly developed, and their sensibilities were more refined. Thus, if they needed emotional understanding and support, they turned to other women. New England reform movements often were fueled by the sisterhood of kindred spirits who were righting a world men had made wrong. In nineteenth-century North America, close bonds between women were essential both as an outlet for the individual female's sensibilities and as a crucial prop for women's work toward social and personal betterment in man's sullied and insensitive world.

What was the nature of these same-sex bonds? Margaret Fuller (1810–1850), an early feminist, saw same-sex love as far superior to heterosexuality. She wrote in her journal in the 1840s: "It is so true that a woman may be in love with a woman, and a man with a man." Such love, she says, is regulated by the same law that governs love between the sexes, "only it is purely intellectual and spiritual, unprofaned by any mixture of lower instincts, undisturbed by any need of consulting temporal interests."

William Alger, in *The Friendships of Women* (1868), cites one historical example after another of love between women. Typically, the women wrote each other: "I feel so deeply the happiness of being loved by you, that you can never cease to love me"; "I need to know all your thoughts, to follow all your motions, and can find no other occupation so sweet and so dear"; "My heart is so full of you, that, since we parted I have thought of nothing but writing to you"; "I see in your soul as if it were my own."

Twentieth Century

In 1908, it was still possible for a U.S. children's magazine to carry a story in which a teenage girl writes a love poem in honor of her female schoolmate. In the early twentieth century, popular stories in magazines such as *Ladies Home Journal* and *Harpers* often treated the subject without self-consciousness or suggestion that such relationships were "unhealthy" or "immoral," even for several years after French novelists and German sexologists started writing voluminously about lesbianism and were published in the United States.

The United States may have been slower than Europe to be impressed by the taboos against same-sex love, in part because, by virtue of distance, it was not so influenced by the German medical establishment as were countries such as France and Italy and, to a lesser extent, England. Moreover, there was less clear hostility, or rather more ambivalence, toward women's freedom in a land that, in principle, was dedicated to tolerance of individual freedom. Therefore, romantic friendship was possible in the United States well into the second decade of the twentieth century, and even beyond it for women who were born and raised Victorians and remained impervious to the new attitudes.

See Also

FRIENDSHIP; LESBIANISM; SPINSTER

References and Further Reading

Alger, William Rounseville. 1868. *The friendships of women.* Boston: Roberts Brothers.

Faderman, Lillian. 1981. *Surpassing the love of men: Romantic friendship and love between women from the Renaissance to the present.* New York: William Morrow.

Smith-Rosenberg, Carroll. 1975. The female world of love and ritual: Relations between women in nineteenth century america. *Signs: Journal of Women in Culture and Society* 1-1: Autumn, 1–29.

Lillian Faderman

RU 486

Mifepristone is the scientific or generic name for RU 486, an antiprogestin drug that interrupts pregnancy up to nine (Lader, 1995) weeks after conception. Nicknamed the "French abortion pill" and the "morning-after pill," it was originally named RU 486 for Roussel Uclaf, the French manufacturer, a division of Hoechst. It was released in France in 1988 after a tumultuous beginning: initially, protestors succeeded in banning the drug, but it was reinstated after counterprotests by doctors. In 1994, wary of antichoice pressure in the United States, the company assigned its U.S. patent rights without remuneration to the Population Council. Because the drug will not be developed or licensed in the United States by Roussel Uclaf, it is now globally referred to by its generic name, mifepristone.

How Mifepristone Works

When a woman first becomes pregnant, progesterone plays a crucial role. There are specific receptors in uterine cells for progesterone; the hormone helps the new embryo embed in the lining of the uterus, decreases the chance it will be expelled, and promotes placental development. Mifepristone binds to progesterone receptors, preventing the binding of natural progesterone. The developing embryo and placenta then detach from the uterine lining. Through weeks seven to nine after the last ovulation, mifepristone causes early abortion because of diminished progesterone and the bleeding that results from shedding the endometrium, as in menstruation (Lader, 1995). Mifepristone is used in conjunction with a synthetic prostaglandin, misoprostol, which dilates the cervix and induces uterine contractions, expelling the embryo (Pence, 1995).

Mifepristone works much like an intrauterine device (IUD), which also causes expulsion of an early embryo from the uterine lining, and it is also classified as a contraceptive. Because a drug-induced method of dislodging an embryo is less invasive to a woman's body than surgical abortion, mifepristone can be considered a "contraceptive pill," yet some antiabortionists describe it as "chemical warfare on the unborn" (Pence, 1995).

Side effects are similar to heavy menstruation: cramping and bleeding for four days on average, which decreases to spotting, but which may then last several weeks. In 80 percent of women, uterine contractions cause stronger cramping, diarrhea, and vomiting. Some women require mild painkillers. Though current protocols suggest a dose of 600 milligrams, one study found that a dose of mifepristone as low as 10 milligrams, administered as emergency contraception, did not decrease its effectiveness and reduced its side effects (Piaggio, 1999).

Mifepristone has been tested in more than a dozen countries in Europe and in the United States. More than 500,000 women in Europe have used it since 1988, and its efficacy and short-term safety are well documented. It is noninvasive, requires no anesthesia, and poses little risk of infection. Although available in France since 1988, with clinical trials in the United States starting in 1983, its introduction in the United States was delayed until 2000 because of antiabortion protests. Until its legalization by the U.S. Food and Drug Administration (FDA) on 28 September 2000, it had been available only through 17 test sites (Feminist Majority, 2000; Kolata, 2000). Mifepristone has been available in France, Great Britain, Norway, Sweden, Switzerland, and some other countries of the European Union, and Israel. China manufactures its own version (Cook, 1999). Mifepristone was not available in South America or Africa in 1999, although efforts were underway to make it available in South Africa, Russia, and Taiwan.

Social Context

Antiabortion activists have targeted mifepristone, in large part because it makes a woman's choice to terminate her pregnancy a private decision with her doctor. With abortion clinics threatened by firebombing and doctors assassinated, mifepristone makes it untenable for antiabortionists to picket or bomb every doctor's office in a country (Lader, 1995).

In the developing world, mifepristone offers further benefits: doctors and hospital beds are in short supply; abortion and birth control are often unavailable. Every day 40,000 children die hungry because of population growth in regions where there is a lack of food (Baulieu, 1991). Mifepristone relieves these pressures that so affect women's lives, especially if the drug is dispensed and taken at home.

Feminists have championed the drug, which also may be successful in treating diseases that appear to be affected by estrogen and progesterone, including endometriosis, fibroids, breast and ovarian cancers, meningioma, Cushing's syndrome, and the HIV virus (Feminist Majority, 2000). Its antiprogesterone effect of uterine contractions and cervical dilation reduces the number of cesarean births, which stands at one in four in the United States (Lader, 1995). When the drug first became available, the French minister of health hailed the new abortion pill as the "moral property of women," (Feminist Majority, 2000). Eleanor Smeal, president of the Feminist Majority Foundation, stated, "The results are in: Women have responded favorably to RU 486 in every country in which the drug has been made available. Politics—in terms of obstacles to distribution and introduction of RU 486—is all that stands in the way of giving women access to this medical breakthrough" (Feminist Majority, 2000).

See Also

ABORTION; CONTRACEPTION; CONTRACEPTIVES: DEVELOPMENT; PRO-CHOICE MOVEMENT; REPRODUCTIVE PHYSIOLOGY; REPRODUCTIVE RIGHTS

References and Further Reading

Baulieu, Etienne-Emile. 1991. *The "abortion pill": RU-486—a woman's choice.* New York: Simon and Schuster.

Chalker, Rebecca, and Carol Downer. 1992. *A woman's book of choices: Abortion, menstrual extraction, RU-486.* New York: Four Walls, Eight Windows.

Dobie, Sharon A. Roger A. Rosenblatt, Ann Glusker, David Madigan, and L. Gary Hart. 2000. Reproductive health services in rural Washington state: Scope of practice and provision of medical abortions, 1996–1997. *American Journal of Public Health* 90(4): 624.

Feminist Majority; contains assorted press releases cited here. <www.feminist.org>

Fried, Marlene Gerber, and Maureen Paul. 1998. Abortion. In Boston Women's Health Book Collective, eds. *Our bodies, ourselves for the new century,* 388–419. New York: Simon and Schuster.

Kolata, Gina. 2000. U.S. approves abortion pill; drug offers more privacy, and could reshape debate. *New York Times* (29 September): A1, A18.

Lader, Lawrence. 1995. *A private matter: RU-486 and the abortion crisis.*

National Abortion and Reproductive Rights Action League Foundation. Amherst, Mass. and New York: Prometherius. <www.naral.org>

Pence, Gregory E. 1995. RU-486. In Gregory E. Pence, ed., *Classic cases in medical ethics: Accounts of cases that have shaped medical ethics, with philosophical, legal, and historical backgrounds,* 2nd ed. 168–170. New York: McGraw-Hill.

Piaggio, G., H. von Heutan, and D. Grimes. 1999. Comparison of three single doses of mifepristone as emergency contraception: A randomised trial. *The Lancet* 353(9154): 697–702.

Raymond, Janice G., Renate Klein and Lynette J. Dumble. 1991. *RU 486: misconceptions, myths and morals.* Cambridge, Mass.: Institute on Women and Technology.

Reproductive Health and Rights Center, a project of CARAL Pro-Choice Education Fund. <www.choice.org>

Riddle, John M. 1992. *Contraception and abortion from the ancient world to the Renaissance.* Cambridge, Mass.: Harvard University Press.

Spitz, Irving, C. Wayne Bardin, Laurie Berton, and Ann Robbins. 1998. Early pregnancy termination with mifepristone and misoprostol in the United States. *New England Journal of Medicine* 338(18): 1241–1247.

Talbot, Margaret. 1999. The little white bombshell. *New York Times Magazine* 11 July, 1999: 39–43.

Wechsler, Jill. 1998. On a fateful course: FDA finally gets a leader. *Pharmaceutical Executive* 18(12): 32–36.

Winikoff, Beverly, Charlotte Ellertson, Batya Elul, and Irving Siran. 1998. Acceptability and feasibility of early pregnancy termination by mifepristone-misoprostol: Results of a large multicenter trial in the United States. *Archives of Family Medicine* 7: 360–366

Melanie Hahn

RURAL WOMEN

See AGRICULTURE; DEVELOPMENT: CHINESE CASE STUDY—RURAL WOMEN; HOUSEHOLDS AND FAMILIES.

S

SACRED TEXTS

Sacred texts encompass and preserve a wide range of cultural materials, such as divine revelations, the teachings of founders and prophets, and a community's sacred history, all of which provide people with highly valued information about the sacred—information that is evocative, as in myth and story, or legally and ritually binding, as in law codes and prescribed ceremonies. While the content and uses of sacred texts vary greatly from tradition to tradition and even within a single tradition, they are always perceived as the divine word, a truthful and powerful opening into the realm of the sacred. Whether oral or written, sacred texts are the touchstones of a culture; they tell people who they are, presenting them with self-definition and shaping consciousness (Denny and Taylor, 1995; Levering, 1989).

Women and Sacred Language

Given the significance of sacred texts, access to them is a source of power, and many cultures limit that access to men. Sometimes this is accomplished through the maintenance of a sacred language such as Hebrew, Latin, Sanskrit, or Arabic that is taught only to elite men, or by not allowing women to voice sacred words, or, when a sacred text is printed, by not allowing women to touch it, especially when menstruating. Denying women access to a sacred language denies them the right to speak with religious authority or even to interpret their faith for themselves, and it relegates their religious writings to a secondary, non-sacred realm. This has begun to change somewhat in recent years through the use of vernacular languages in religious settings, which has contributed both to a reinterpretation of women's religious status and in some cases to the development of inclusive language that names women as full members of their religious communities.

Most sacred texts, especially compilations that have received canonical status such as the Tanakh, the New Testament, and the Pali Canon, have been composed by men, usually elite men. As a result, an orthodox male view of women tends to dominate such texts, as it often does the few sacred texts written by women. Further, many sacred texts only marginally deal with women, if at all—for instance, Confucius's *Analects* and the *Upanishads*. Equally important is what is chosen for preservation in writing and who decides. For instance, oral sacred texts are often modified when they are finally written down, as in the Christianization of Celtic legends, where goddesses became fairy women and Christian sentiments were inserted.

The influence of sacred texts in shaping gender roles is a worldwide phenomenon. Even in so-called secular societies such as the United States, the ideologies of sacred texts continue to exert an enormous influence on people's lives because they are intrinsic to the culture. In religious societies they are even more influential. The rise of the women's movement in the nineteenth century led to the reading of sacred texts by women, such as *The Woman's Bible* (Stanton, 1895). This effort continues today on an international scale that has expanded the initial concern with gender to concerns about race, sexual orientation, the influence of colonialism, and additional categories of difference (Chakravarti, 1990). Other approaches to the analysis of gender in sacred texts have included the search for compositions by women and questioning the presumption of male authorship (Young, 1993).

Women as Composers of Sacred Texts

Sacred texts composed by women present us with complex and diverse experiences and literary forms. There are the ecstatic poems of mystics such as Mahādevīyakka and Rābi'ah, the theological subtleties of Catherine of Sienna, and the matter-of-fact statements about religion in the tales of tribal women. Sometimes they are the stories women tell one another: the myths about women, their autobiographies, accounts of their religious experiences ranging from drug-induced possession to adventures during a pilgrimage. Most speak with a female-centered voice that is deeply located in women's religious experience. Carol Christ has eloquently written of women's need for the stories of other women, and an informative contemporary collection of women's responses to a woman's story is Judith Kates and Gail Reimer's *Reading Ruth* (1994).

Another important and revealing source of sacred texts by women can be found in folk and fairy tales. In some instances these may provide access to long suppressed practices, because they often contain survivals of earlier extinct religious practices—for instance, pre-Christian practices in Europe or archaic woman-centered practices in China (Young, 1993). For example, the numerous witches and evil old women of the tales may very well refer to women who continued ancient religious practices away from the watchful eyes of the male orthodoxy. Understood in this way, they can be read as deeply subversive texts. In reading such tales, though, particular attention needs to be paid to gender-specific images, and a distinction needs to be made regarding the folklore of women and that of men—the stories women tell one another are different from the stories men tell one another. Briefly, women tell stories that tend to have both female and male characters, while men tend to tell stories only about men (Mills, 1985). Scholars of this genre, even though heavily indebted to the stories collected from women, have tended to show preference for stories told by men, which are defined as being more legitimate, so the tales need to be carefully sifted. This holds true for mythology from around the world.

The creation of and recovery of women's sacred stories and sacred texts is an ongoing process that is changing our definitions of what constitutes a sacred text at the same time that it is empowering women of faith all around the world.

See Also

BIOGRAPHY; CREATION STORIES; LITERATURE: OVERVIEW; MYTH; RELIGION: OVERVIEW

References and Further Readings

Chakravarti, Uma. 1990. Whatever happened to the Vedic *Dasi?* Orientalism, nationalism, and a script for the past. In Kumkum Sangari and Sudesh Vaid, eds., *Recasting women: Essays in Indian colonial history,* 27–87. New Brunswick, N.J.: Rutgers University Press.

Christ, Carol. 1980. *Diving deep and surfacing: Woman writers on spiritual quest.* Boston: Beacon.

Denny, Frederick M., and Rodney L. Taylor, eds. 1995. *The Holy Book in comparative perspective.* Columbia: University of South Carolina Press.

Holdredge, Barbara A. 1998. Sacred literature. In Serinity Young, ed., *Encyclopedia of women and world religion,* Vol. 2, 855–859. New York: Macmillan.

Kates, Judith A., and Gail Twersky Reimer, eds. 1994. *Reading Ruth: Contemporary women reclaim a sacred story.* New York: Ballantine Books.

Levering, Miriam, ed. 1989. *Rethinking scripture: Essays from a comparative perspective.* Albany: State University of New York Press.

Mills, Margaret. 1985. Sex role reversals, sex changes, and transvestite disguise in the oral tradition of a conservative Muslim community in Afghanistan. In Rosan A. Jordan and Susan J. Kalčik, eds., *Women's folklore, women's culture,* 187–213. Philadelphia: University of Pennsylvania Press.

Sheppard, Gerald T. 1987 Canon. In Mircea Eliade, ed., *The encyclopedia of religion,* Vol. 3, 62–69. New York: Macmillan.

Stanton, Elizabeth Cady, and the Revising Committee. [1895] 1974. *The woman's Bible.* Seattle, Wash.: Coalition Task Force on Women and Religion.

Young, Serinity. 1993. *An anthology of sacred texts by and about women.* New York: Crossroad; London: HarperCollins.

Serinity Young

SAFER SEX

In the early 1980s a newly discovered disease, AIDS (acquired immunodeficiency syndrome), began to devastate large segments of the world's population. As the magnitude and seriousness of AIDS was recognized, public health officials and social scientists focused attention on ways to contain and manage it. Medical researchers discovered that AIDS was caused by the human immunodeficiency virus (HIV), which was transmitted when body fluids—blood, semen, and vaginal fluids, for example—were exchanged, especially during sexual contact. Another method of transmittal was exposure to HIV-tainted blood products through the use of shared needles, a form of infection particularly devastating to intravenous drug users.

Among the first groups to be identified as being at high risk for AIDS were gay men, intravenous drug users, and hemophiliacs (who, because of their need for frequent transfusions, were exposed to tainted blood supplies). As awareness of the disease spread, many groups affected by AIDS began to educate themselves about ways to avoid contracting the illness. Out of these educational efforts came the concept of *safer sex:* a series of guidelines to be followed during sex that were supposed to prevent the spread of the disease and preserve and enhance erotic experience. As an example, safer sex guidelines advocated the use of protective devices designed to prevent the spread of body fluids (latex and polyurethane devices such as male condoms, latex gloves, dental dams, saran wrap, and female condoms).

Worldwide Crisis

In December 1999, the World Health Organization (WHO) estimated that 5.6 million people worldwide had been newly infected with HIV that year, of which 2.3 million were women (UNAIDS, 2000). These estimates indicated that AIDS was more prevalent than had previously been thought and that the total number of people in the world living with HIV was close to 33.6 million. Women accounted for 14.8 million cases, or 44 percent of the total. Studies also revealed that women were infected with HIV at rates equal to that of men (Cline and MacKenzie, 1996), and that, worldwide, more than 75 percent of all adult HIV infections resulted from heterosexual intercourse (Quinn, 1996), despite popular belief early in the crisis that the disease attacked only promiscuous gay men and drug users. During unprotected heterosexual intercourse with an HIV-infected partner, women are at least twice as likely as men to become infected (Padian, Shiboski, and Jewell, 1991; Nicolosi, Leite, and Musicco, 1994).

Patton (1989) credits gay men with inventing safer sex. She suggests that the gay male community developed safer sex as a way to remain a positive "sexual" community and to resist messages from the heterosexual world for monogamy and celibacy. These initial steps toward safer sexual activities were eventually adapted and popularized to reach many different groups of people with different sexual practices. Some advocates believe that the groundwork for safer sex was prepared before the AIDS crisis. The need to prevent the spread of other sexually transmitted diseases, for example, helped create an understanding of the importance of manipulating sexual scenarios in order to preserve erotic interest.

Debates About Safer Sex

What exactly do we mean by safer sex? The term is somewhat confusing, in that it implies that sex was safe before the onset of AIDS (Singer, 1993). But was it? Historical accounts of women's sexuality and health in the nineteenth century discuss themes ranging from the challenges of childbirth, the medicalization of women's health issues, the ideological constructions of female sexuality, and the prevalence of dangerous gynecological surgical procedures. These accounts suggest that sexuality, particularly female sexuality, was by definition a high-risk behavior surrounded by threats of death in childbirth, venereal disease, stigmatization, and dangerous medical practices.

For different groups of people, especially women, sex today continues to be associated with violence (rape and sexual battery), illness, physical hardship (reproductive complications), sexually transmitted diseases, and unwanted pregnancies. For gay men, sexually transmitted diseases have posed distinctive risks often unrecognized by many health care professionals. G'dali Braverman, a community activist from the San Francisco Living Well Project, has cited the example of hepatitis as a disease that has been especially devastating to gay men.

Because AIDS is a relatively new communicable disease, knowledge about transmission is still in the process of becoming standardized. AIDS, however, is not merely a new disease. It is an illness that is concentrated in particular communities and has tremendous social significance. For example, homophobia, sexism, and racism have had profound significance in how knowledge about AIDS, HIV, and safer sex has been constructed.

The prevalence of AIDS among women is particularly high in less industrialized countries such as India, Uganda, and Zimbabwe, where sociocultural factors such as poverty, migration, and armed conflicts create environments in which immediate physical survival is of far greater importance than concerns about sexually transmitted diseases. Furthermore, the sexual economy in these countries, especially unsafe sexual encounters along trucking routes, lead to high levels of sexual mixing that are conducive to rapid and widespread transmission of HIV. Instead of further stigmatizing those who engage in sex work, safer sex guidelines in these countries can be implemented through innovative programs. One example is the Indian Health Organization's peer education program for sex workers, which trains and pays prostitutes to teach and distribute condoms to other prostitutes. New devices may also arm women with more options for safer sex. The polyurethane female condom, developed in 1987, is a loose, tube-like device that is used one time. One end of the tube is closed, with an internal moveable ring to be placed on a woman's cervix. The other end is open, and its external ring is placed over the labia. Research in Costa Rica has shown that a majority of both rural and urban women and their partners prefer the female condom to the male condom (Madrigal, Shifter, and Feldblum, 1998).

Certain sexual practices are almost uniformly thought of as high-risk activities. For example, anal intercourse without a latex condom and with internal ejaculation is considered a high-risk activity because of the greater likelihood of HIV transmission through semen mixing with blood in the thin and raw lining of the anus and rectum. At the same time, however, there are gray areas of sexual practice where the question of risk is debated. Opinions about the degree of risk associated with oral sex, for example, vary. As a result, community-based organizations may put out divergent messages about the safety of oral sex without latex barriers, as is the case in the different approaches in Seattle, Washington, and Vancouver, British Columbia (McMillan, 1996). Recent scientific research on the risk associated with oral sex indicates that only three cases of HIV transmission through male homosexual oral sex were documented between 1984 and 1992 (McMillan, 1996). Female-to-female oral sex has also been the subject of many debates (O'Hanlan, 1995).

Such divergent views about safer sex and the content of safer sex messages have been the focus of scholars who study AIDS. Simon Watney (1993), for example, analyzes differences between British and American constructions of safer sex. He characterizes British campaigns as primarily aimed at *safer* sex and risk *reduction*. In contrast, he finds that U.S. messages are unrealistically aimed at *safe* sex and on the *elimination* of risk, both seemingly unattainable goals. In many industrialized countries, however, differentiated risk is now the standard in safer sex messages and representations.

Research suggests that some women, especially Americans living in inner cities, who are intravenous drug users, face potentially serious consequences if they attempt to negotiate for safer sex with their partners. By engaging in discussions of safer sex, these women run the risk of losing a steady partner, intimacy, or economic assistance and, as a result, may face poverty, violence, abandonment, or stigmatization. Safer sex has different meanings to different people, and risk factors vary with each individual. Any list that outlines differentiated risks should encourage individual decision making in order to determine one's acceptable level of risk.

Sex Practices and Risks

The following brief list categorizes a variety of sex practices according to degrees of risk. Note that there are still dis-

agreements about the degree of risk of a number of sex practices.

Practices considered safe or low-risk:

sensual massage
hugging, cuddling, snuggling
masturbation and mutual masturbation
social/dry kissing or tongue kissing on anywhere but genitals and anus
dry humping with clothes on
phone sex
computer sex
fantasy
showering together
flirting
viewing pornography (movies, books, live dancing)

Practices whose safety or risk is debated:

French kissing
anal intercourse with latex condom
vaginal intercourse with latex condom
fisting with a latex glove
oral sex with latex barriers—male condoms, female condoms, dental dams, or Saran Wrap
oral sex on a man without ejaculation
fingering with latex barrier
watersports—contact with urine (not in open cut or wound)

Practices considered possibly unsafe:

oral sex without a latex barrier (especially during menstruation)
fingering without a latex barrier
fisting without a latex barrier
sharing sex toys without latex barriers

Practices considered unsafe:

anal intercourse without a condom
vaginal intercourse without a condom
masturbating with other's body fluid
rimming without a latex barrier
oral sex on a woman during her period
sharing needles or blood while piercing or while shooting drugs

It is within the "Debated" and "Possibly Unsafe" categories that innovations and controversial safer sex ideas are constantly being reformulated. In sum, *there is no standard meaning of safer sex.* As the epidemiology and the meanings of AIDS change, safer sex as a list of practices will inevitably be revised.

See Also

ADULTERY; AIDS AND HIV; BISEXUALITY; CELIBACY: SECULAR; CONFLICT RESOLUTION: MEDIATION AND NEGOTIATION; CONTRACEPTION; LESBIANS: HIV PREVALENCE AND TRANSMISSION; MASTURBATION; SEX EDUCATION

References and Further Reading

Cline, Rebecca, and N. MacKenzie. 1996. Women and AIDS: The lost population. In R. Condit and C. Condit, eds., *Evaluating women's health messages,* 382–401. Thousand Oaks, Calif.: Sage.

Madrigal, J., J. Shifter, and P. J. Feldblum. 1998. Female condom acceptability among sex workers in Costa Rica. *AIDS Education and Prevention* 10(2): 105–113.

McMillan, Dennis. 1996. Everything you always wanted to know about oral sex. *San Francisco Bay Times,* 25 January 1996, Life Section, 2–3.

Nicolosi, A., M. Leite, and M. Musicco. 1994. The efficiency of male-to-female and female-to-male sexual transmission of the human immunodeficiency virus: A study of 730 stable couples. *Epidemiology* 5: 570–575.

O'Hanlan, Katherine. 1995. Do we really need dental dams? *The Advocate* 680: 47–49.

Padian, Nancy, S. Shiboski, and N. Jewell. 1991. Female-to-male transmission of human immunodeficiency virus. *Journal of the American Medical Association* 266: 1664–1667.

Patton, Cindy. 1989. Resistance and the erotic. In Peter Aggleton, Graham Hart, and Peter Davies, eds. *AIDS: Social representations, social practices.* New York: Falmer.

Quinn, T. C. 1996. Global burden of the HIV pandemic. *The Lancet* 3348: 99–106.

Singer, Linda. 1993. *Erotic welfare: Sexual theory and politics in the age of epidemic.* New York: Routledge.

UNAIDS. 2000. *Report on the global HIV/AIDS epidemic.* Geneva, Switzerland: UNAIDS.

Watney, Simon. 1993. Emergent sexual identities and HIV/AIDS. In Peter Aggleton, Peter Davies, and Graham Hart, eds., *AIDS: Facing the second decade.* New York: Falmer.

Winks, Cathy, and Anne Semans. 1994. *The good vibrations guide to sex.* Pittsburgh, Pa.: Cleis.

Lisa Jean Moore

SAINTS

Saints—those illustrious departed individuals recognized by religions for their holiness and virtue—have different roles and meanings in the world's faiths. This article examines sainthood from a feminist perspective.

Women Saints

Feminists tend to believe that patriarchal religions, most notably the Catholic church, have canonized exemplary women as saints largely as a means of encouraging a female ideal of submissiveness to masculine authority. Women who achieved the eternal beatitude of sainthood were usually those who most perfectly adhered to doctrinal faith, often despite brutal persecution by non-Catholics.

However, the Catholic church also used the power to confer sainthood as a way of institutionalizing a few independent female mystics and charismatics who were potentially threatening to male authority. This practice by the church of later conferring sainthood in an attempt to defuse the power of a martyred heretic is exemplified by Joan of Arc (1412–1431), who was burned at the stake as a witch and heretic because of her military success and authority over pagan soldiers. She persisted as a national heroine and was canonized as Saint Joan in 1920.

Some feminist scholars see models for heroic women in hagiography; they find that biographies of saints' lives "chronicle a lifelong process, mediated by visionary experience, which transformed these women from a passive, self-effacing ideal of female goodness into active, energetic, highly individualized women who are taking a forceful role in the world" (quoted in Weigle, 1982: 202).

Women's Relationships with Saints: Afro-Brazilian and Islam Case Studies

Women also make important uses of saint worship to create alternative women-friendly or woman-centered spiritualities within patriarchal and postcolonial syncretic religions such as Islam and the Afro-Brazilian faiths. Rather than aspiring to *be* a saint, women in these religions use saint veneration and rituals to achieve a more immanent relation with the sacred. Practicing polytheism within or alongside a monotheistic religion, women bargaining with or seeking intercession from saints often create a spirituality that is more ambiguous and multifaceted than the good/evil, saint/sinner, God/devil dichotomies established in monotheism.

Just as the medieval Christian church created new saints who incorporated the pagan gods and goddesses that newly converted Europeans refused to forsake completely, the Afro-Brazilian religions also include saints that reflect a need to synthesize Catholicism with older African tribal and Amerindian religions. Whether women establish relationships with saints by ritualistic possession or petition, they seek the advice of the appropriate saints for help with the day-to-day problems the Catholic church tends to ignore. Where the church encourages resignation to suffering, especially for women, Afro-Brazilian saint rituals give women concrete tools for practical solutions.

Islamic women, too, continue to practice saint veneration, despite periodic attempts by the Islamic hierarchy to purge it, because it allows them to have a more intimate communication with a spiritual power that offers concrete help with the "kinds of personal problems in which the high God may seem too remote to be interested" (Smith, 1987: 244). Islamic women use saints' shrines as women's spaces that offer escape from their domestic and reproductive responsibilities and their participation in saint rituals offers them some measure of control over their laws and the men they live with.

See Also

HERESY; MARTYRS; MYSTICISM; NUNS

References and Further Reading

Sered, Susan Starr. 1994. *Priestess, mother, sacred sister: Religions dominated by women.* New York: Oxford University Press.
Smith, Jane I. 1987. Islam. In Arvind Sharma, ed., *Women in world religions,* 235–250. Albany: State University of New York Press.
Warner, Marina. 1981. *Joan of Arc: The image of female heroism.* New York: Knopf.
Weigle, Marta. 1982. *Spiders and spinsters: Women and mythology.* Albuquerque: University of New Mexico Press.

Cathy Peppers
Ivone Gebara

SATI

See SUTTEE.

SCHOOLS: Discipline

See DISCIPLINE IN SCHOOLS.

SCIENCE: Overview

The role of science (including natural, physical, social, and domestic sciences and some aspects of philosophy) in women's studies has been growing in recent years. For sci-

ence viewed as an *institution* that legitimates knowledge, women's studies has been an important voice in flagging the ways in which that institution has traditionally excluded women's voices and knowledge. Feminists have organized for women's inclusion in the conduct of science and have systematically analyzed how the exclusion of women's knowledge has produced a biased way of knowing.

When science is seen as a form of *work,* scholars have analyzed how women have been channeled into certain kinds of scientific careers (for example, anthropology, nutrition and domestic science, and psychology) and away from others (for example, physics, engineering research, and computer science). As with many other branches of women's studies, feminist historians have discovered and celebrated the biographies of those women who have become scientists, whether famous or neglected (Apple, 1993; Bindman et al., 1993; Clewell and Anderson, 1991; Kelly, 1993; Kosheleva, 1983; Martin, 1993; Rossiter, 1982, 1995; Sadli and Dhakidae, 1990). It has also been crucial to reclaim the invisible work done by women and those less powerful, such as immigrants and people of color, who often are the technicians, janitors, and "behind-the-scenes" workers in traditional, modern scientific laboratories.

When science is viewed as a system of beliefs or *worldview,* feminists have challenged many of its premises by developing alternative epistemologies or ways of approaching questions (Tomm, 1989). For example, in proposing approaches to scientific ethics, feminist philosophers of science might emphasize collective responsibility and ecological principles, as opposed to individual genius and the domination of nature. They have also emphasized that the points of view of women in less-developed nations, and of poor women and women of color everywhere, have been traditionally invisible to formal science.

Finally, when science is examined as a kind of *industry,* we can ask not only about patterns of employment and profit, but also on whose behalf the products of industry are created, and whose voices remain silent. Science is little different from many institutions and industries when it comes to patterns of control, employment, and profit. Few women work in very high positions, and this is especially true of women in less-developed nations. Women workers in science and high-technology industries have also often been disproportionately subjected to difficult and dangerous working conditions, such as in the computer chip industry, where many Asian and Mexican women workers have been exposed to toxins and to vision-threatening tasks (Ong, 1987).

In the early days of women's studies, the topic of science was often suspect, particularly the "hard" end of science, such as physics and mathematics. It was difficult to see how science could be a part of women's studies in a positive sense. Much more emphasis in women's studies was placed on the humanities: history, literature, and the understanding of popular culture. The social sciences were in the middle, offering ways to study women's social and cultural roles and to compare across cultures for an understanding of how gender roles differ at different times and places. Feminist psychology, both in its critique of traditional psychotherapy and definitions of mental health, became particularly strong during the 1970s and 1980s. Social scientific research in education was also seen as an ideal venue in which to understand processes of gender socialization. Moreover, a large body of literature questioned the role of traditional methods in social science research and offered an alternative view of feminist methodology.

Critiques and the reclaiming of women's perceptions in the natural and physical sciences and in engineering research have been slower to develop. The links between women's studies and these disciplines, in most locations, have emphasized the life sciences, such as feminist analyses of reproductive physiology, hormone research, and evolution and primatology. However, at the same time, strong professional associations of women in science and engineering have worked around the world for many decades to increase the numbers of women in all areas of science and to better their conditions. A few have begun as well to address the research agendas and problems to be solved in physics, engineering, and computer science, often emphasizing values such as multiple visions of problems, responsible choice of problems to benefit progressive visions, and cooperative work.

Barriers to Women in Science

Both the barriers to women's full participation in science and their achievements have been well documented throughout the world. Barriers include the belief that women are incapable of abstract thought or scientific reasoning; the favoring of men in mentoring and the informal networks of science (AWIS, 1993); the lack of childcare and disproportionate family demands; and, in some belief systems, the equation of women with irrational forces of nature, which is then carried over into modern scientific prejudice (Erinosho, 1994). In many less-developed nations, where resources for scientific education may be scarce for everyone, boys are often the first to be educated (Federal Ministry of Education, Women Education Branch, 1989). Okeke (1989) notes that the problem of underrepresentation of women in science, technology, and medicine is global, although especially serious in Africa and Asia, with the exception of traditionally female-dominated areas such as

nursing. Exceptions to this rule must take into consideration class, ethnicity, and gender, as well as the development and relative poverty of the nation in general. Krishnaraj (1991), for example, notes that although women in India are relatively well represented in medicine and in some branches of science, it is primarily middle-class women who can afford servants who have made it into scientific work; poorer women remain unrepresented. Abir-Am and Outram (1987) note that historically, in the West, family commitments have had a complex influence on both the nature and extent of women's participation in science since the nineteenth century. This often has included a wife nurturing her husband's career at the expense of her own—many feminists have remarked on the phrase "and thanks to my wife (or female secretary), without whom this research could never have been done."

Gender-Based Scientific Research

Women have often been the objects or subjects of scientific research, and from the early days of women's studies, these practices have been subject to scrutiny (see, for example, Weisstein, 1970).

In the social sciences, much gender-relevant research has been, and to some extent continues to be, about sex differences. Women and men were measured and compared on innumerable dimensions: intelligence, aggression, decision-making behavior, talkativeness, personality traits of every description, and perceptual and cognitive abilities. Before the advent of a strong feminist presence in social scientific research, the results of these studies often lined up with expected acculturated gender differences. That is, women were often depicted as passive, not mathematically inclined, talkative, neurotic, incapable of firm decision making, and so forth. These depictions are still prevalent in many social scientific descriptions. However, a strong thrust of feminist research since the early 1970s has been either to debunk this research by a close examination of methodology or to understand the findings in sociohistorical context. This often has meant challenging a putative biological determinism. For example, if girls on the whole do not like science, one may explain this finding with reference to the organization of the brain or with reference to the "chilly climate" for girls and women in the science classroom. Many feminist scholars also question the whole endeavor of a search for sex differences, arguing that the differences between women and men is not as important as the characteristics that overlap. In this approach, neither "women" nor "men" should be seen as monolithic categories, but as complex, culturally and historically determined gender systems with many internal differences and variations.

The methodological critique of life and physical sciences has often meant examining a range of philosophical and even metaphysical questions, such as the notions of objectivity, knowledge itself, and how one certifies truth (Harding, 1986; Keller, 1985). There are here, as elsewhere in women's studies, a range of feminisms, from those who take a traditional approach to scientific knowledge, but who would see greater female participation, to those who would redo science from its foundations on new ethical and epistemological premises. Much of this latter work emphasizes both the exploitation (in a positive sense) of women's experience to enhance the nature of knowledge and a resistance to dualism (Star, 1991). Collins (1986), for example, argues that the dual role of outsider-insider that African American women experience can act as a catalyst for new scientific paradigms.

In the natural sciences women have also been the *object* of scientific research in ways challenged by women's studies researchers. Sex differences have played a role here in many comparisons, stemming back in modern Western science to the eighteenth century and the measurement of male and female skeletons and to the measurement and comparison of male and female brains in the nineteenth century. In reproductive research feminist scholars note the imbalanced emphasis on women's bodies, often with an attendant pathologizing of natural female processes such as menstruation, pregnancy, and menopause. In the study of the natural world, there has often been an overlay of sexist social assumptions onto animal behavior or onto ancient human culture and evolution in traditional scientific research, and feminists have pointed this out (see, for example, Archaeology: overview; Primatology). In a gorilla tribe, a male with many females might traditionally have been described by primatologists as having a "harem" (a term that is also culturally offensive). Feminist primatologists might choose instead to depict the ways in which female gorillas actively select and coordinate a male to serve the group of females, along with questioning the sexist bias in the field (Haraway, 1989).

See Also

ARCHITECTURE; ENGINEERING; SCIENCE, *all entries;* TECHNOLOGY

References and Further Reading

Abir-Am, Pnina G., and Dorinda Outram. 1987. *Uneasy careers and intimate lives: Women in science, 1789–1979.* New Brunswick, N.J.: Rutgers University Press.

American Association for the Advancement of Science. 1993. *Science in Africa: Women leading from strength.* Washington, D.C.: Sub-Saharan Africa Program, American Association for the Advancement of Science.

Apple, Rima D. 1993. *The history of women and science, health, and technology: A bibliographic guide to the professions and the disciplines.* 2nd ed. Madison: University of Wisconsin System, Women's Studies Librarian.

AWIS (Association of Women in Science). 1993. *A hand up: Women mentoring women in science.* Washington, D.C.: Association of Women in Science.

Bindman, Lynn, Alison Brading, and Tilli Tansey. 1993. *Women physiologists.* London: Portland.

Clewell, Beatriz C., and Bernice Anderson. 1991. *Women of color in mathematics, science & engineering: A review of the literature.* Washington, D.C.: Center for Women Policy Studies.

Collins, Patricia Hill. 1986. Learning from the outsider within: The sociological significance of black feminist thought. *Social Problems* 33: 514–32.

Erinosho, Stella Yemisi, ed. 1994. *Perspectives on women in science and technology in Nigeria.* Ibadan: Sam Bookman.

Faruqui, Akhtar M., Mohamed H. A. Hassan, and Gabriella Sandri. 1991. *The role of women in the development of science and technology in the Third World.* Proceedings of a conference organized by the Canadian International Development Agency and the Third World Academy of Sciences, ICTP, Trieste, Italy. Singapore: World Scientific.

Federal Ministry of Education, Women Education Branch. 1989. *Report of the National Workshop on Promoting Science, Technology and Mathematics among Girls and Women in Nigeria.* Lagos: Nigerian Educational Research and Development Council.

Haraway, Donna. 1989. *Primate visions: Gender, race and nature in the world of modern science.* New York: Routledge.

Harding, Sandra. 1986. *The science question in feminism.* Ithaca, NY: Cornell University Press.

Jornadas de historia del pensamiento científico argentino. 1988. Vol. 4: Special issue on the history of women in Argentinean science.

Keller, Evelyn Fox. 1985. *Reflections on gender and science.* New Haven, Conn.: Yale University Press.

Kelly, Farley, ed. 1993. *On the edge of discovery.* Melbourne: Text Publishing.

Kinyanjui, Kabiru. 1988. Secondary school education for girls in Kenya: The need for a more science-based curriculum to enhance women's greater participation in development. Working Paper no. 459. Nairobi: Institute for Development Studies.

Kirkup, Gill, and Laurie Smith Keller, eds. 1992. *Inventing women: Science, technology, and gender.* Cambridge: Polity Press.

Kosheleva, Inna. 1983. *Women in science.* Trans. Frances Longman. Moscow: Progress.

Krishnaraj, Maithreyi. 1991. *Women and science: Selected essays.* Bombay: Himalaya.

Martin, Paula. 1993. *Lives with science: Profiles of senior New Zealand women in science.* Wellington: Museum of New Zealand Te Papa Tongarewa.

Mura, Roberta. 1990. *Profession, mathematicienne: Étude comparative des professeur-e-s universitaires en sciences mathematiques* (Comparative study of male and female mathematicians). Quebec: Groupe de recherche multidisciplinaire feministe, Université Laval.

Ogilvie, Marilyn Bailey. 1986. *Women in science: Antiquity through the nineteenth century.* Cambridge: MIT Press.

Okeke, Eunice A. C. 1989. Promoting science, technology and mathematics (STM) education among girls and women: Review of initiatives. In Federal Ministry of Education, Women Education Branch, *Report of the National Workshop on Promoting Science, Technology and Mathematics among Girls and Women in Nigeria,* 69–78. Lagos: Nigerian Educational Research and Development Council.

Ong, Aihwa. 1987. *Spirits of resistance and capitalist discipline: Factory workers in Malaysia.* Albany: State University of New York Press.

Rossiter, Margaret W. 1982. *Women scientists in America: Struggles and strategies to 1940.* Baltimore: Johns Hopkins University Press.

———. 1995. *Women scientists in America: Before affirmative action, 1940–1972.* Baltimore: Johns Hopkins University Press.

Sadli, Saparinah, and Daniel Dhakidae, eds. 1990. *Perempuan dan ilmu pengetahuan* (Women in Indonesian science). [Jakarta]: Yayasan Ilmu-Ilmu Sosial, Program Pengembangan Karir Wanita.

Star, Susan Leigh. 1991. Power, technologies and the phenomenology of standards: On being allergic to onions. In John Law, ed., *A sociology of monsters? Power, technology and the modern world,* 27–57. Sociological Review Monograph no. 38. Oxford: Basil Blackwell.

Stolte-Heiskanen, Veronica, ed., with Ruza Fürst-Dilic and the European Coordination Centre for Research and Documentation in Social Sciences. 1991. *Women in science: Token women or gender equality?* New York: St. Martin's.

Tomm, Winnie, ed. 1989. *The effects of feminist approaches on research methodologies.* Calgary, Canada: Wilfred Laurier University Press.

UNESCO (United Nations Educational, Scientific, and Cultural Organization). 1995. *The scientific education for girls: Education beyond reproach?* Bristol, PA: UNESCO/Jessica Kingsley Publishers.

Weisstein, Naomi. 1970. "Kinde, Kuche, Kirche" as scientific law: Psychology constructs the female. In Robin Morgan, ed., *Sisterhood is powerful,* 205–20. New York: Random House.

Susan Leigh Star

SCIENCE: Ancient and Medieval

While the participation of women in the scientific professions is a recognized fact in our century, the commonly held belief remains that this is a recent phenomenon. However, historical evidence documents the continuity of the participation of women in the physical and biological sciences as well as in some areas of engineering for well over the past 3,000 years. Throughout the centuries many women overcame economic and social obstacles to acquire education and contribute to the scientific endeavors of their choice (Meschel, 1991).

Women's Paths to Science

The prevailing view in current literature on this subject is that women of the aristocracy and those aided by the so-called craft tradition were most often able to make their mark in the sciences in seventeenth- and eighteenth-century Europe. Being in the aristocracy or having a craft, according to this explanation, allowed women to become scientists for a considerably longer period and in areas outside of Western Europe (Schiebinger, 1989). In a practical sense, career choices for women are determined not only by societal pressures and attitudes but also by the responsibility women take in raising the next generation and caring for aged family members. Throughout recorded history these practical considerations may explain the prevalence of women scientists in the nobility. It is assumed that these women were relatively free of household cares and had access to learned tutors and libraries. A good example is Queen/physician Hatsepshut of the Eighteenth Dynasty in Egypt, who, in addition to her practice in medicine, also organized botanical expeditions to search for hitherto unknown medicinal plants (Herzenberg et al., 1991). An example from Chinese culture is the legendary Se Ling She, wife of the Emperor Huang Te (3000 B.C.), who is said to have invented the process of weaving silk (Meschel, 1992).

In addition to the nobility, we find numerous female scientists among unmarried women, particularly nuns (both Christian and Taoist), a group presumably free of traditional family responsibilities. Medical knowledge of the Middle Ages owes much to such practitioners as Heloise, Elizabeth of Schonau, Herrad of Landsberg, and, the most outstanding of these, Hildegard of Bingen and Trotula of Salerno (Herzenberg et al., 1991). Among the Taoist nuns the alchemist Li Shao Yun's work represented the first attempt at quantitative chemistry in the early 1100s in China (Meschel, 1992).

The craft tradition was also a possible route for women scientists in seventeenth- and eighteenth-century Europe, but it served as such a vehicle well beyond the boundaries of Europe and for many preceding centuries. Many accomplished women scientists in ancient and medieval Near East and China were mothers, daughters, sisters, and wives of scientists. Such relationships must have provided the necessary ingredients for their pursuit of scientific endeavors, such as education, motivation, encouragement, access to laboratory equipment, and economic resources. These women were not merely helpers: many achieved distinction in their own right. A few examples will illustrate the universal role of societal status and craft tradition in the development of women practitioners.

Miriam the Jewess

During the first century A.D., Alexandria was one of the great centers of learning of the ancient world. This city was the home of one of the most accomplished women scientists of antiquity, Maria or Miriam the Jewess. Miriam was the first woman scientist whose writings survived in any form. Although her original works were lost, significant extracts were preserved by Zosimos of Panopolis, an Egyptian alchemist from the third century A.D., who cited Miriam's work extensively in his twenty-eight-volume encyclopedia. Miriam's contribution to science included the design of chemical equipment such as the water bath, the three-armed still, and the reflux oven. The double boiler still bears her name as *Balneum Mariae*. The three-armed still was used for distillation of complex mixtures. Its description, including quantitative measurements, distinguished it from the obscurity and imprecision of most alchemists. Miriam's recognition of the advantages of glass equipment in the laboratory was quite advanced for that time. As an experimental chemist, her contribution included the preparation of a lead-copper sulfide, still called Mary's Black and used as a pigment by artists. Miriam's writings reflect the prevailing attitudes among alchemists of her time and illustrate her Jewish heritage. Little is known about her as a person. She was a student of the alchemist Ostanes and had many followers, and she was reputed to be a good teacher who encouraged her students (Herzenberg et al., 1991; Patai, 1982).

Hypathia of Alexandria

Hypathia of Alexandria (c. A.D. 370–415) is the first woman mathematician whose life and career are known in some detail. She received a thorough education from her father, Theon, a noted mathematician and astronomer. After a period of study and travel in Greece and Italy, she returned to Alexandria and occupied the chair of philosophy at the Neoplatonic Academy. Her interests were broad and included physics, chemistry, and medicine, in addition to mathematics. Pupils—including Synesius of Cyrene, who later became Bishop of Ptolemais—came to study with her from several countries of the Mediterranean world. Some of their correspondence survived, including scientific discussions and diagrams of instruments they designed. Hypathia is credited with inventing several instruments, among them the hydrometer and the astrolabe. Her major contributions were her books in mathematics and astronomy. Unfortunately, Hypathia is best remembered in historical texts by her spectacular death at the hands of a rioting mob. The political or religious motives for her killing are unknown, but she was seized from her chariot, tortured to death, and burned in A.D. 415 (Herzenberg et al., 1991; Kingsley, 1887; Dzielska, 1995).

Teacher Keng

In one of the earliest science books in China (A.D. 975), Wu Shu gives an account of the work of a famous woman alchemist, Teacher Keng or Keng Hsien Seng. The daughter of an eminent scholar, Teacher Keng was described as intelligent, beautiful, and articulate. She is credited with designing a distillation process for vegetable oils. Among other achievements attributed to her was the ability to transform mercury and snow to silver. Her reputed authority and relationship with the emperor suggest that Teacher Keng was a charismatic personality as well as a skilled scientist (Meschel, 1992; Needham, 1980).

Miriam, Hypathia, and Teacher Keng are regarded as recognized authorities in their respective endeavors and are descendants of scholarly families, though not of the nobility.

The Medieval Period

The Medieval period represented an era of extreme attitudes toward women. At one extreme, women were regarded as the instruments of sin and evil, while at the other extreme, they were regarded as saintly and even godlike. Despite these notions, the theoretical subjugation of women was only imperfectly maintained, allowing a quasi state of equality to exist and be taken advantage of (Alic, 1986). The edict forbidding the employment of Jewish physicians in 1267 exemplifies this ambivalent attitude. In all likelihood this edict was observed loosely, for it was renewed every few decades, thus allowing many Jewish women to pursue the study and practice of medicine, particularly in the specialty of ophthalmology (Friedenwald, 1920). To cite another example, while in France women were not allowed to enter medical school until 1897, the edict issued in Paris in 1311 allowed women to practice surgery after passing an examination. Surviving documents provide a fascinating picture of how the possession of necessary and valuable medical skills allowed women to surmount the dual liabilities of being female and Jewish in a male-governed and Christian society. Legal records such as payments, exemptions from taxation, licenses, and title deeds constitute the largest body of evidence of the life and works of these women physicians (Friedenwald, 1920). A good representative of this group is Sarah de Saint Gilles, wife of a doctor, herself a practicing physician who had apprentices and headed a private medical school in Montpellier in the thirteenth century. Another doctor, Sarah of Würzburg, was issued a license by the archbishop of that town and offered protection in the Duchy of Franconia in 1419 in exchange for her medical services. Her practice was so lucrative that she was able to buy an estate from a minor nobleman.

The Trial of Jacobina Felicie

Another case in point is the famous trial of the physician Jacobina Felicie, who maintained a successful practice in Paris in the 1320s. Jacobina was accused of practicing without a license. During the trial seven patients testified on her behalf and described her success in alleviating fevers, kidney problems, and arthritis, previously treated unsuccessfully by licensed male physicians. Jacobina skillfully argued her case and entered an impassioned plea for the training and licensing of female physicians in order to preserve women's modesty and honor. At the conclusion of the trial the charges against Jacobina were withdrawn; however, an injunction was issued to prevent her and other men and women lacking university training from practicing medicine in the Paris area (Hurd-Mead, 1938).

Huang Daopo

Huang Daopo (1271–1368), an inventor in China, was the daughter of farmers who were so poor that they were forced to sell her to another family. After some years of enduring harsh treatment and long hours of daily labor, she ran away. She settled on Hainan Island for thirty years and learned the techniques of cotton weaving. Huang Daopo developed new

equipment to make the preparation of cotton for weaving more effective. Separation of cotton seeds from the fiber became mechanized through her efforts. Her inventiveness resulted in a new type of spinning wheel, able to spin three threads simultaneously. Such technical advancement did not take place elsewhere until the nineteenth century.

These women scientists of Western European and Chinese culture came from "middle class" and poor families, and their intellectual and scientific development was shaped by their heritage of the craft tradition.

Legacy

Women of many social strata and ethnic backgrounds contributed to scientific culture, even in antiquity and the medieval period. In many institutions of secondary and higher education, the erroneous view that women shy away from mathematics and the so-called hard sciences still prevails. Illustrating the continuity of the contribution of women in such varied disciplines as mathematics, crystallography, and astronomy may successfully counter such misconceptions. Discussion of the achievements of women scientists as far back in history as possible may enable a more accurate viewing of these fields as a human endeavor equally appropriate for pursuit by students of both sexes.

See Also

ANCIENT INDIGENOUS CULTURES: WOMEN'S ROLES; ANCIENT NATION-STATES: WOMEN'S ROLES; MATHEMATICS; SCIENCE: EARLY MODERN TO LATE EIGHTEENTH CENTURY; SCIENCE: TRADITIONAL AND INDIGENOUS KNOWLEDGE

References and Further Reading

Alic, M. 1986. *Hypathia's heritage: A history of women in science from antiquity through the nineteenth century.* Boston: Beacon.

Dzielska, M. 1995. *Hypathia of Alexandria.* Cambridge, Mass.: Harvard University Press.

Friedenwald, H. 1920. *Medical Pickwick* 6: 293–94.

Herzenberg, C. L., Meschel, S. V. and Altena, J. A. 1991. *Journal of Chemical Education* 68: 101–5.

Hurd-Mead, K. C. 1938. *A history of women in medicine from the earliest times to the beginning of the nineteenth century.* Haddam, Conn.: Haddam.

Kingsley, C. 1887. *Hypathia; or, new foes with an old face.* New York: Lovell.

Meschel, S. V. 1991. Paper presented at the 9th International Conference of Women Engineers and Scientists, Warwick, England.

———. 1992. *Journal of Chemical Education* 69: 723–30.

Needham, J. 1980. *Science and civilization of China.* London: Cambridge University Press.

Patai, R. 1982. *Ambix* 29: 177–97.

Schiebinger, Londa. 1989. *The mind has no sex? Women in the origins of modern science.* Cambridge, Mass.: Harvard University Press.

Susan V. Meschel

SCIENCE: Early Modern to late Eighteenth Century

The rise of modern science took place in Europe during the seventeenth and eighteenth centuries. The scientific pursuits of early modern women were largely forgotten or undervalued as the leisured activities of a few well-placed "scientific ladies" (Meyer, 1955). Feminist scholarship in the 1980s and the 1990s presents a very different picture of women's part in the scientific revolution (Alic, 1986; Ogilvie, 1986; Schiebinger, 1989; Hunter and Hutton, 1997).

Structural and Legal Barriers to Women

Between 1600 and 1800, women were barred from membership in scientific academies. A few exceptions were made, however: in Italy, physicist Laura Bassi (1711–1788) and mathematician Maria Gaetana Agnesi (1718–1799) were members of the Academy of Sciences in Bologna (Alic, 1986; Schiebinger, 1989). Anna Manzolini (1716–1774), who held the chair of anatomy at the University of Bologna was eventually elected to the Russian Royal Scientific Society (Ogilvie, 1986). However, the French Academy of Sciences did not permit women to be members, nor did the Royal Society of London. Theories of biological determinism claiming that woman is essentially different and inferior to man were reconfigured by eighteenth-century fathers of science, such as Linnaeus and Buffon, whose systems of classification imposed sexual, as well as race politics, on the natural world, and thus served to authorize restrictions on women's intellectual activities (Schiebinger, 1993).

Although ideological barriers frustrated women's contribution to science, some were able to still work. Marie-Anne Lavoisier (1758–1836) worked with her husband Antoine Lavoisier, who is credited with the discovery of oxygen. Mme. Lavoisier also translated Richard Kirwan's 1787 *Essay on Phlogiston* (the competing theory they were working to discredit). Instructed by Jacques Louis David, Mme.

Lavoisier became an accomplished artist and drew the diagrams for her husband's *Elements of Chemistry* (1789). After her husband was guillotined during the Reign of Terror, Mme. Lavoisier continued their research, albeit invisibly, editing her husband's memoirs and manuscripts. Thus, one could say that both Antoine and Marie-Anne Lavoisier founded modern chemistry.

A relatively high number of women managed to practice astronomy, gaining professional training and access to observatories as assistants to their fathers, brothers, or husbands. In Denmark, Sophie Brahe (1556–1643) assisted her brother Tycho Brahe in data collection; in Poland, Elisabetha Koopman Hevelius (1647–1693) assisted her husband, Johannes Hevelius and, after his death, edited his unpublished works. In France, three female astronomers aided the research of Joseph Jérôme Lalande, director of the Paris Observatory and author of *Astronomie des dames* (1790); his niece, Marie Lefrançais de Lalande (1768–1832); Louise Elisabeth du Pierry (b. 1746) (to whom the *Astronomie des dames* was dedicated); and Nicole Lepaute (1723–1788). Lepaute was known as one of the best astronomical computers in France; she made the French calculations and predictions for Halley's comet in 1759, and had a moon crater named in her honor (Alic, 1986). Despite these achievements, neither Lalande nor any other male writers seriously advocated opening the profession to women (Harth, 1992).

In Germany, Maria Winkelmann Kirch (1670–1720), while collaborating with her husband Gottfried Kirch in making observations and preparing calendars, discovered a comet in 1702, and published three astrological tracts between 1709 and 1711. Although Maria Winkelmann Kirch had served the Berlin Academy of Sciences as an expert assistant to her husband, the academy rejected her application after her husband died in 1710. Neither Winkelmann nor her daughters, who were also well-trained astronomers, could obtain access to observatories and telescopes (Schiebinger, 1989).

The most famous female astronomer of the eighteenth century was the British Caroline Hershel (1750–1848). Taught by her brother William to build and to use telescopes, and to study, map, and calculate the movements of the stars, Caroline Hershel made numerous discoveries, including eight comets between 1786 and 1797. She corrected Flamsteed's star catalog and brought out a *Catalogue of Stars* (1798), published by the Royal Society. While she assisted William Hershel in the founding of sidereal astronomy, she summarized her contribution as follows: "I did nothing for my brother but what a well-trained puppy-dog would have done" (Alic, 1986). In 1835, Caroline Hershel became one of the first two women in England to be awarded honorary memberships in the Royal Society, the other being Mary Somerville (Ogilvie, 1986).

Impact on Women of the Rise of Science

The rise of science led to the regulation of women's sciences of herbal medicine and midwifery (Schiebinger, 1989). Recipes were subjected to scrutiny, ridicule, or appropriation by the new sciences. Mrs. Hutton, a pharmacist of Shropshire who extracted digitalis from wild foxglove and experimented with it as a treatment for heart disease, sold the license in 1785 to Dr. William Withering, who is usually credited for its discovery (Alic, 1986).

Midwifery was systematically and successfully challenged by male-dominated obstetrics, becoming subject to the authority of male physicians. However, a number of midwives—Jane Sharpe (fl. 1671) and Elizabeth Cellier (fl. 1678–1688) of England, Catharina Schrader (fl. 1693–1745) of Friesland, and Mme du Coudray (1715–1794) of France—struggled to both defend and reestablish midwifery by advocating such reforms as: midwifery schools, periodic examinations, accurate record keeping, and the publication of instructional pamphlets (Marland, 1993). Maria Donne Dalle (1778–1842) was one of the few women who entered the medical profession itself. Awarded a medical degree from the University of Bologna in 1799, Dalle was appointed director of midwives. Dorothea Leporin Erxleben (1715–1762) earned the first full medical degree awarded by a German university in 1754 (Ogilvie, 1986). French professor of anatomy Marie-Catherine Biheron (1719–1786) was recognized for her wax models, articulating the stages and mechanisms of the birth process (Schiebinger, 1989).

The new science affected women's intellectual lives. A circle of seventeenth-century French women became active Cartesians, taking Descartes's friendships with women, especially Queen Christina of Sweden (1626–1689) and Elisabeth of Bohemia (1618–1680), as encouragements to participate in debates about natural and moral truths. Other women developed circles of learning at various European sites: Mary Astell in London, Elizabeth Brahe in Denmark, and the French *salonnières* (women of the salons). Although the salonnières played an inestimable part in creating networks, in disseminating scientific knowledge, and in determining the careers of male scientists, they were not able to secure women's membership in the Academy of Sciences; they could only wield power as "patrons to young men, not to young women" (Schiebinger, 1989).

The figure of a female learner was deployed in a number of texts made accessible to the lay public. In Bernard

Fontenelle's *Conversations on the Plurality of the Words* (1686) and Francesco Algarotti's *Newtonianismo per le dame* (1737), a male expert patronizingly explains the new science to a receptive woman. Despite obvious asymmetrical power relations, women readers took these texts as authorization to take up scientific pursuits. Fontenelle's *Conversations* was translated into English by Aphra Behn (1640–1689) in 1688, and Algarotti's *Sir Isaac Newton's Philosophy Explained for the Use of the Ladies* was translated by Elizabeth Carter (1717–1806) in 1739. Science was presented in eighteenth-century English periodicals such as *The Female Spectator* (1744–1746) and *Epistles for Ladies* (1749–1750), both edited by Eliza Haywood, and *The Ladies Museum* (1760–1766), edited by Charlotte Lennox (Meyer, 1955).

Early Pioneers

A substantial number of women contributed to the emergence of modern science. Three women merit mention as feminist pioneers because they sought to win for women the freedom to criticize and to produce their own scientific knowledge.

Margaret Cavendish, Duchess of Newcastle (1624–1674) critiqued fundamental assumptions of modern science in her *Observations upon Experimental Philosophy* (1666) and *Description of a New...Blazing World* (1666), attacking both the pretensions of the new science to a monopoly on knowledge and the authority of objective knowledge.

Maria Sibylla Merian (1647–1717) is now recognized as a founder of modern botany and zoology. *Metamorphosis Insectorum Surinamensium* (1705), a study of the insects of Surinam, "revealed to Europeans for the first time the astonishing diversity of the rain forest" (Davis, 1995; Valiant, 1993: 471). Merian traveled to Surinam and undertook this study with her two daughters in 1699 when she was fifty-two years old.

Physicist Émilie, Marchioness du Châtelet (1706–1749) challenged androcentric knowledge with her *Institutions de physique* (1740) and her translation and commentaries on Newton's *Principia,* demonstrating a mastery of mathematics and physics, as well as the courage, to correct Newton. Before her death, du Châtelet was beginning to challenge the gender boundaries that prevented her full recognition as a professional scientist, insisting that women be allowed to legitimately practice (Terrall, 1995).

Accomplishments

It is difficult to accurately assess achievements made within an unjust system. A number of women managed to insinuate themselves into the production of significant research. A short list must suffice to indicate the range of their accomplishments: (1) a system of post-Cartesian vitalism was developed by natural philosopher Anne Finch, Countess of Conway (1631–1679) in *Principles of the Most Ancient and Modern Philosophy* (1690) (Merchant, 1980); (2) vaccination for smallpox was introduced to England by Lady Mary Montagu, who witnessed its successful use by an old woman in Turkey (Alic, 1986); and (3) the termination of the oblique muscle in the eye was discovered by Anna Manzolini, professor of anatomy at the University of Bologna, who was renowned for her skills in molding wax anatomical models and in dissection (Ogilvie, 1986).

Some women were generous patrons of science (Phillips, 1990). Others published scientific textbooks for lay readers: in 1650, German astronomer Maria Cunitz (1610–1664) produced a simplification of Johannes Kepler's tables of planetary motion; in 1680, French astronomer Jeanne Dumée published an explication of Copernican principles; and, in 1666, Marie Meurdrac wrote *Chemistry Made Easy for Ladies*. Italian mathematician Maria Agnesi published *Analytical Institutions for the Use of Italian Youth* (1748) (Ogilvie, 1986).

In Italy, Giuseppa Barbapiccola (fl. 1731) used her translation of Descartes's *Principles of Philosophy* (in 1722) to advocate the education of women in the sciences (Findlen, 1995). Similarly, Maria Angela Ardinghelli of Naples (1728–1825) translated Stephen Hales's *Vegetable Staticks* into Italian in 1756, praising Hales's work, while shrewdly using the footnotes to correct and update their data, thus daring to show her superior powers of experimentation and calculation (Findlen, 1995).

Denied entry into sciences requiring laboratories, some women (as seen in Maria Sibylla Merian) practiced geology, entomology, and botany, which were carried out through field research. Women's knowledge of plants is found in some surprising sources, in Elizabeth Blackwell's illustrations for her *Curious Herbal* (1737–1789), and also in Mary Delany's floral studies, intricately cut in paper or elaborately embroidered on her court dress, now in the British Museum. A number of the Englishwomen accompanying their husbands to various parts of the empire practiced botany and entomology: Lady Anne Monson in South Africa; and Lady Elizabeth Simcoe in Canada. By 1757, American botanist Jane Colden (1724–1766) published a catalog of over three hundred local plants (Ogilvie, 1986). Priscilla Wakefield published her popular *An Introduction to Botany* in 1786, thus signaling the emergence of botany as the appropriate science for nineteenth-century women to practice (Shteir, 1996).

See Also

SCIENCE: OVERVIEW; SCIENCE: NINETEENTH CENTURY; SCIENCE: FEMINISM AND SCIENCE STUDIES

References and Further Readings

Alic, Margaret. 1986. *Hypatia's heritage: A history of women in science from antiquity to the late nineteenth century.* London: Women's Press.

Campbell, Mary Baine. 1999. Outside in: Hooke, Cavendish, and the invisible worlds, and "My travels to the other world," Aphra Behn and Surinam. In *Wonder and Science: Imagining worlds in early modern Europe.* Ithaca, N.Y.: Cornell University Press.

Davis, Natalie Zemon. 1995. Metamorphoses: Maria Sibylla Merian. In *Women on the Margins: Three seventeenth-century lives,* 140–216. Cambridge: Harvard University Press.

Findlen, Paula. 1995. Translating the new science: Women and the circulation of knowledge in enlightenment Italy. Special cluster on gender and early-modern science. *Configurations* 3(2): 167–207.

Harth, Erica. 1992. *Cartesian women: Versions and subversions of rational discourse in the old regime.* Ithaca, N.Y.: Cornell University Press.

Hunter, Lynette, and Sarah Hutton, eds. 1997. *Women, science, and medicine, 1500–1700: Mothers and sisters of the Royal Society.* London: Sutton, 1997.

Keller, Eve. n.d. Mrs. Jane Sharp: Midwifery and the critique of medical knowledge in seventeenth-century England. In Ann B. Shteir, ed., *Women's writing: The Elizabethan to Victorian period.* Special issue of *Women and Science.* 2:2.

Marland, Hilary, ed. 1993. *The art of midwifery: Early modern midwives in Europe.* London: Routledge.

Merchant, Caroline. 1980. *The death of nature: Women, ecology, and the scientific revolution.* San Francisco: Harper and Row.

Meyer, Gerald. 1955. *The scientific lady in England 1650–1760: An account of her rise, with emphasis on the major roles of the telescope and microscope.* Berkeley: University of California Press.

Ogilvie, Marilyn Bailey. 1986. *Women in science: Antiquity through the nineteenth century: A biographical dictionary with annotated bibliography.* Cambridge, Mass.: Massachusetts Institute of Technology Press.

Phillips, Patricia. 1990. *The scientific lady: A social history of woman's scientific interests 1520–1918.* London: Weidenfeld and Nicolson.

Schiebinger, Londa. 1989. *The mind has no sex? Women in the origins of modern science.* Cambridge, Mass.: Harvard University Press.

———. 1993. *Nature's body: Gender in the making of modern science*. Boston: Beacon.

———. 1996. *Cultivating women, cultivating science: Flora's daughters and English botany, 1760–1860*. Baltimore, M.D.: Johns Hopkins Press.

Terrall, Mary. 1995. Gendered spaces, gendered audiences: Inside and outside the Paris Academy of Sciences. Special cluster on gender and early-modern science. *Configurations* 3(2): 207–232.

Valiant, Sharon. 1993. A review essay: Maria Sibylla Merian: Recovering an eighteenth-century legend. *Eighteenth-century studies*. 26(3): 467–479.

Sylvia Bowerbank

SCIENCE: Education

See EDUCATION: SCIENCE.

SCIENCE: Feminism and Science Studies

Feminist social studies of science, like feminist philosophy of science, are part of the growth of scholarship fostering women as the subject of study and focusing on gender as a fundamental factor in the development of knowledge, institutions, culture, and society. Although more recent than feminist studies of literature, for example, feminist theory and research in sociology, history, and anthropology have elucidated the content (knowledge), conduct, and social organization of science.

In these analyses, sociology has contributed in two principal areas. First, the sociology of scientific knowledge, as developed in Europe in the 1970s, showed ways in which social, political, and economic interests of particular groups construct scientific findings and generalizations. This countered the traditional, positivist view that science merely reveals nature, with scientists as neutral agents or mediators. The constructivist view is not synonymous with feminism, however. Sociologists of scientific knowledge have been slower to recognize (according to some feminists) that science and technology reflect and reinforce the interests of patriarchy (Harding, 1983). Second, feminist sociologists have analyzed constraints on the education, participation and rewards of contemporary women in the conduct of scientific work, and the attainment of scientific degrees and careers (Fox, 1996, 1998, 2000).

Women have long worked in science, although not in valued, rewarded, or even visible roles. Historical treatments have recovered contributions of women over time that have been lost, marginalized, misunderstood, or miscredited to others. This includes portraits of women of outstanding, although miscredited, attainments (for example, Sayre's [1975] account of the crystallographer Rosalind Franklin), as well as empirical analyses of the lives and conditions of little-known working scientists (see Rossier, 1982, 1995).

In traditional anthropology, the question has been: How did adult, especially Western, male behavior develop? Technology, the use of tools, and hunting have had extraordinary anthropological significance—constituting what it means to be human and what forms the basis of culture. Women had been thought of mainly in reproductive roles. Feminist anthropology has transformed the frameworks by: (1) determining the variation and flexibility, rather than dichotomy, of man as hunter and woman as plant gatherer; (2) reforming the mystique of meat and meat-eating as a basis for the development of human cooperation, technical skill, and survival; (3) shifting the focus on tools/weapons to include technology used in gathering plants and carrying babies; and (4) renaming female "receptivity" to "choice" in mate selection, with large genetic consequences (see especially Haraway, 1989: chapter 14 on paleoanthropologist Adrienne Zihlman).

These science studies connect also with feminist philosophy of science. In particular, feminist philosophers have critiqued the internal logic and coherence of knowledge, apart from social biases of sex and race in the selection, design, and interpretation of research; the model of the scientist as passive observer of natural fact; and the distinction between subject and object.

See Also

SCIENCE: FEMINIST CRITIQUES; SCIENCE: FEMINIST PHILOSOPHY; SCIENCE: TECHNOLOGICAL AND SCIENTIFIC RESEARCH

References and Further Reading

Fox, Mary Frank. 1996. Women, academia, and careers in science and engineering. In Cinda-Sue Davis, Angela Ginorio, Carol Hollenshead, Barbara Lazarus, and Paula Rayman, eds. *The equity equation: Fostering the advancement of women in the sciences, mathematics, and engineering*, 265–289. San Francisco: Jossey-Bass.

———. 1998. Women in science and engineering: Theory, practice, and policy in programs. *Signs: Journal of Women in Culture and Society* 24 (Autumn): 201–223.

———. 2000. Organizational environments and doctoral degrees awarded to women in science and engineering departments. *Women's Studies Quarterly* (Spring/Summer): 47–61.

Haraway, Donna. 1989. *Primate visions.* New York: Routledge.

Harding, Sandra. 1983. Why has the sex/gender system become visible only now? In Sandra Harding and Merrill B. Hintikka eds. *Discovering reality,* 311–24. Dordrecht: Reidel.

Rossiter, Margaret. 1982. *Women scientists in America: Struggles to 1940.* Baltimore: Johns Hopkins University Press.

Rossiter, Margaret. 1995. *Women scientists in America: Before affirmative action, 1940–1972.* Baltimore, Md.: Johns Hopkins University Press.

Sayre, Ann. 1975. *Rosalind Franklin and DNA.* New York: Norton.

Mary Frank Fox

SCIENCE: Feminist Critiques

Feminist critiques of science are multiple and sometimes contradictory. While they share a consciousness of sexism in science, their analyses differ in extent. The liberal feminist critique, for instance, does not question empiricism; on the contrary, it assumes that bias can be eliminated through stricter adherence to scientific principles. Yet while liberals leave their critique just outside science's door, Marxists and radicals cross the threshold into science proper—critiquing assumptions, theories, and quantitative methodologies. This article will highlight theoretical differences that shape liberal, radical, and Marxist perspectives and will conclude with a brief look at postmodern critiques.

Liberal Critique

In contrast to radical critiques, the liberal position generally affirms the objectivity of the "scientific method." Indeed, it views science as an important means for women to counter biased cultural assumptions. Liberals maintain that sexist or androcentric "science" arises from careless or *politicized* methodologies. They have, for example, criticized studies suggesting biological bases for gender differences in math ability for failing to control for important social influences such as parental encouragement and teacher attitudes.

Observing that much "scientific bias" enters during hypothesis generation, liberals conceive the problem as a manifestation of social inequities, demanding political, not scientific, remedies. For instance, the dearth of research on women's health can be attributed to their low status in society and in medicine. Liberals believe that women's increased participation in science will expand the scope of science but not challenge scientific methodologies.

Radical Critiques

Radical theorists criticize liberals for failing to recognize the ideological commitments of science. While liberals believe that scientific and technological developments spur social changes—for example, assembly-line technology and automation contributed to industrialization—radical theory emphasizes that it also works in reverse: social revolutions provide new categories (for example, gender, class) for interpreting experience. Thus, the historical and social context does not necessarily "pollute" science, but, rather, may provide necessary conditions for scientific discovery.

Radical critiques see Descartes's image of the ahistorical, objective observer as a myth in practice and question it as an ideal. Thus, whereas liberals stress the logic and rationality of science, radicals emphasize the creative aspects of theory formation, hypothesis generation, and data interpretation. Moreover, radical theories question whether scientific knowledge is necessarily best gained through empirical and quantitative methods, arguing that intuition, experience, and qualitative analyses provide alternative routes to knowledge.

Arguing that knowledge is grounded in experience, radical theorists recognize that, in patriarchal cultures, men's experience is defining. Men have developed empirical tools and analytic constructs that shape "reality" in ways that reinforce their self-understanding. The passive voice employed in scientific writing—for example, "it was found"; "it was observed"—obscures the subjectivity of science. Reliance on replicability to identify bias assumes that biases are individual and idiosyncratic. But repeating an experiment may not detect widely shared cultural (for example, sexist) beliefs. Women's oppression provides a powerful incentive to examine the distorting effect of patriarchal concepts. Women's experience affords a perspective—"epistemological privilege"—from which to challenge the unacknowledged social and political commitments of science.

Marxist Feminist Critiques

Marxist feminist critiques share this focus on structural and ideological concerns but stress the economic context in which gender is defined. Specifically, they hold that the deficiencies of Western science flow from the capitalistic imperative of production for profit, rather than for human needs. The organization of science mirrors the larger social structure it helps to support: concentration of financial and political power; workforce stratification by social class, race, and gender; division of intellectual and manual labor; specialization; and lack of accountability to all but those at the top.

Leading Western teaching and research institutions are thus dominated by men who represent corporate interests. The science that emerges reflects and reproduces this system of power. US national health statistics, for instance, rarely incorporate data on social class, since capitalist ideology holds that class fluidity renders the United States a classless society. Significantly, the absence of data hinders critiques that might challenge the distribution of health and disease by social class.

Marxist feminists argue that capitalism represents more than an economic system; it is an *ideology* that organizes the way Western people think and act in areas outside the economic sphere. Thus, industrial metaphors creep into scientific descriptions—cells are factories and the central nervous system a radio transmitter. Metaphors also reflect social and political assumptions about the nature of reality and influence scientific design and analysis. A capitalist society that values production, for instance, views menstruation negatively, as failed (re)production. Similarly, it views menopause as system breakdown: again, a negative interpretation within the industrial metaphor.

Postmodern and Other Critiques

Some Western and non-Western feminists express discomfort with the more radical critiques of science. They warn of romanticizing women's oppression and of philosophical relativism, whereby all methods of gaining knowledge are regarded as equally valid, for women in many non-Western countries employ the objectivity of science as a defense against religious fundamentalism. Thus, liberal theory and positivism—which stress the separation of fact from values, emotion, and opinion—as well as fundamental liberal ideals—such as individual rights—may be essential tools in fighting the prejudices rooted in traditional cultures.

Postmodernists welcome the multiplicity of feminist criticism as evidence that the idea of a single truth or perspective—feminist or otherwise—is itself flawed. Moreover, critiques of science from other socially subordinate groups have sounded strikingly similar chords. African theorists, for instance, have denounced "European" exploitation of the earth in the name of science. Similarly, Native American traditions conceptualize nature as active and alive rather than as inert "resource." Unlike Cartesian dualism, traditional Chinese philosophy does not strictly dichotomize mind and body, as in Western mechanical models. Obvious parallels to feminist critiques indicate that patriarchy should not bear the full burden of causal explanation of scientific ideology, practice, and institutions. Much work is yet needed to integrate these largely separate literatures and to develop more complete explanatory models. Beyond lies the task of developing new, nonexploitative forms of knowledge.

See Also

BIOLOGY; KNOWLEDGE; SCIENCE: FEMINIST PHILOSOPHY; SCIENTIFIC SEXISM AND RACISM; SEXISM

References and Further Reading

Bleier, Ruth, ed. 1986. *Feminist approaches to science.* New York: Pergamon.

Fausto Sterling, A. 1985. *Myths of gender: Biological theories about women and men,* rev. ed. New York: Basic Books.

Garry, Ann, and Marilyn Pearsall, ed. 1990. *Women, knowledge, and reality: Explorations in feminist philosophy.* Boston: Unwin Hyman.

Harding, Sandra, ed. 1993. *The "racial" economy of science: Toward a democratic future.* Bloomington: Indiana University Press.

Hubbard, Ruth. 1990. *The politics of women's biology.* New Brunswick, N.J.: Rutgers University Press.

Keller, E. F. 1983. *A feeling for the organism: The life and work of Barbara McClintock.* New York: W. H. Freeman.

Martin, Emily. 1992. *The woman in the body: A cultural analysis of reproduction.* Boston: Beacon.

Schiebinger, Linda. 1993. *Nature's body: Gender in the making of modern science.* Boston: Beacon.

Elizabeth Fee
Tracy L. Johnson

SCIENCE: Feminist Philosophy

Feminist philosophies of science use the lens of gender to critique traditional philosophies of science and refocus them in order to consider gender as a significant characteristic that interacts with other characteristics such as race, class, and sexual identity in the practice and theory of science. Just as multiple philosophies of science have evolved in connection with different philosophical theories and scientific disciplines, different feminisms, derived from diverse feminist theoretical roots, provide multiple perspectives on traditional philosophies of science. Liberal feminism, socialist feminism, African-American feminism, conservative or essentialist, existentialist, and psychoanalytic feminism, radical and lesbian separatist feminism, and postmodern feminism—each combines gender with other salient factors to focus the lens at a slightly different angle from which to view philosophies of science.

Feminist critiques of epistemologies of science (Fee, 1982, 1986; Harding, 1986; Keller, 1985) have suggested that their theories of knowledge constitute a masculine view of the world. To be trained to be a scientist is to be trained to observe the characteristics of living beings of interest to men in an objective, distant, autonomous fashion that resonates with an androcentric perspective on the world. Depending on the feminist theory in which it is rooted, feminist philosophies of science challenge, to varying degrees, what kinds of things can be known, who can be a knower, and how (through what tests) beliefs are legitimated as knowledge, along with other fundamental aspects of traditional epistemologies of science.

Liberal Feminism

Liberal feminism finds its roots in philosophies of the eighteenth-century Enlightenment and liberal humanism (Jaggar, 1983; Mill (Harriet Taylor), 1970; Mill (John Stuart), 1970; Wollstonecraft, 1975) and suggests that women are suppressed in contemporary society because they suffer unjust discrimination. Liberal feminists seek no special privileges for women and simply demand that everyone receive equal consideration without discrimination on the basis of sex. Liberal feminism shares two fundamental assumptions with the foundations of the traditional method for scientific discovery: (1) both assume that human beings are highly individualistic and obtain knowledge in a rational manner that may be separated from their social conditions; and (2) both accept positivism as the theory of knowledge. These two assumptions lead to the belief in the possibilities of obtaining knowledge that is both objective and value free, concepts that form the cornerstones of the scientific method.

In the last two decades of the twentieth century feminist historians and philosophers of science (Fee, 1982; Haraway, 1990; Harding, 1986) and feminist scientists (Birke, 1986; Bleier, 1984, 1986; Fausto-Sterling, 1992; Keller, 1983, 1985; Rosser, 1990, 1992) have pointed out a source of bias and absence of value neutrality in science, particularly biology. By excluding females as experimental subjects, focusing on problems of primary interest to males, and using faulty experimental designs and interpretations of data based in language or ideas constricted by patriarchal parameters, experimental results in several areas in biology have been demonstrated to be biased or flawed. Feminist critiques (Harding, 1986; Keller, 1985) suggest that these flaws and biases were permitted to become part of the mainstream of scientific thought and were perpetuated in the literature for decades, in some cases (Sayers, 1982) for more than a century, because virtually all of the individuals who were scientists were men. Because most, or all scientists, were male, values held by most males were not distinguishable as biasing; they became synonymous with the "objective" view of the world.

Liberal feminism suggests that now that the bias of gender has been revealed by feminist critiques, scientists can take this into account and correct for this value or bias that had not previously been uncovered. It implies that good scientific research is not conducted differently by men and women and that in principle men can be just as good feminists as women and that women can be just as good scientists as men. Now that feminist critiques have revealed flaws in research due to gender bias, both men and women will use this revelation to design experiments, gather and interpret data, and draw conclusions and theories that are more objective and free from bias, including gender bias (Biology and Gender Study Group, 1989). Liberal feminist critiques do not question the integrity of the scientific method itself or of its supporting corollaries of objectivity and value neutrality. Liberal feminism reaffirms the idea that it is possible to find a perspective from which to observe that is truly impartial, rational, and detached. Lack of objectivity and presence of bias occur because of human failure to follow the scientific method properly and avoid bias due to situation or condition. Liberal feminists argue that it was through attempts to become more value neutral that the possible androcentrism in previous scientific research has been revealed.

In contrast to liberal feminism, other feminist theoretical critiques call into question the fundamental assumptions underlying the scientific method, its corollaries of objectivity and value neutrality, or its implications. They reject individualism for a social construction of knowledge and question positivism and the possibility of objectivity obtained by value neutrality. Many also imply that men and women may conduct scientific research differently, although each theory posits a different cause for the gender distinction.

Socialist Feminism

Socialist feminism serves as the clearest example of a feminist theory that, in contrast to liberal feminism, rejects individualism and positivism as approaches to knowledge. Based on Marxist critiques, which view all knowledge, including scientific knowledge, as socially constructed as a productive activity of human beings, socialist critiques suggest that science cannot be objective and value free because the basic categories of knowledge are shaped by human purposes and values. Defined by the prevailing mode of production, in the twentieth-century United States, scientific knowledge was determined by capitalism and reflected the interests of the dominant class.

Socialist feminism places class and gender on equal ground as factors that determine the position and perspective of a particular individual in society. Socialist feminism asserts that the special position of women within (or as) a class gives them a special standpoint that provides them with a particular worldview that would be more reliable and less distorted than that of men from the same class. Implicit in the acceptance of the social construction of knowledge is the rejection of the standpoint of the neutral, disinterested observer of logical positivism.

Socialist feminism suggests ethical implications for science. Because the prevailing knowledge and science reflect the interests and values of the dominant class and gender, they have an interest in concealing and may in fact not recognize the way they dominate. Women oppressed by both class and gender have an advantageous and more comprehensive view of reality. Because of their oppression, they have an interest in perceiving problems with the status quo and the science and knowledge produced by the dominant class and gender. Simultaneously, their position requires them to understand the science and condition of the dominant group in order to survive. Thus, the standpoint of the oppressed comprehends and includes that of the dominant group, so it is more accurate.

African-American Feminism

Like socialist feminism, African-American or black feminism also rejects individualism and positivism for social construction as an approach to knowledge. It is based on African-American critiques of a Eurocentric approach to knowledge. In addition to the rejection of objectivity and value neutrality associated with positivism, African-American approaches critique dichotomization of knowledge, or at least the identification of science with the first half, and African-American with the latter half, of the following dichotomies: culture/nature; rational/feeling; objective/subjective; quantitative/qualitative; active/passive; focused/diffuse; independent/dependent; mind/body; self/others; knowing/being (Harding, 1986). African-American critiques also question methods that distance the observer from the object of study, thereby denying a facet of the social construction of knowledge.

Whereas Marxism posits class as the organizing principle around which the struggle for power exists, African-American critiques maintain that race is the primary oppression, with the scientific enterprise an extension of white, Eurocentric interests. African-American feminist critiques (Giddings, 1984; hooks, 1981, 1983, 1990; Lorde, 1984) assert that in contemporary society, women suffer oppression due to their gender as well as their race. For African-American women, racism and sexism become intertwining oppressions that provide them with a different perspective than that of either white women or African-American men.

Essentialist, Existentialist, and Psychoanalytic Feminism

Essentialist feminist theory holds that women are different from men because of their biology, specifically their secondary sex characteristics and their reproductive systems. Frequently, essentialist feminism may extend to include gender differences in visuospatial and verbal ability, aggression and other behavior, and other physical and mental traits based on prenatal or pubertal hormone exposure. Existentialist feminism, first elaborated by Simone de Beauvoir (1974), suggests that women's "otherness" and the social construction of gender rest on society's interpretation of biological differences rather than on the actual biological differences themselves. The value that society assigns to biological differences, as opposed to the differences themselves, between males and females has led woman to play the role of the "other" (Tong, 1989). Existentialist feminism would suggest that visuospatial differences between males and females and disparate preferential learning styles between the two sexes might be the result of the differential treatment and reactions that males and females receive based on their biology.

In many ways, psychoanalytic feminism takes a stance similar to that of existentialist feminism. Derived from Freudian theory, psychoanalysis posits that girls and boys develop contrasting gender roles because they experience their sexuality differently and deal differently with the stages of psychosexual development, particularly the resolution of the Oedipus and castration complexes. Rejecting the biological determinism in Freud, feminists such as Dinnerstein (1977) and Chodorow (1978) in particular have used object relations theory to examine the construction of gender and sexuality during the Oedipal stage to determine why it tends to result in male dominance. They conclude that gender difference resulting in male dominance can be traced to the fact that in our society, women, who are the primary caretakers for most infants and children, push boys to be independent, distant, and autonomous from the female caretakers, while girls are permitted to be more dependent, intimate, and less individuated from their mother or female caretakers.

Evelyn Keller (1982, 1983) applied the work of Chodorow and Dinnerstein to suggest how science has become a masculine province. Science is masculine not only in the fact that it is populated mostly by men but also in the choice of experimental topics, use of male subjects for experimentation, interpretation, and theorizing from data, as well as the practice and applications of science undertaken by the scientists. Keller suggests (1982, 1985) that since the scientific method stresses objectivity, rationality, distance, and autonomy of the observer from the object of study (the positivist neutral observer), individuals who feel comfortable with independence, autonomy, and distance will be those most likely to become scientists. Because most caretakers during the Oedipal phase are female, most individuals in our culture who will be comfortable as scientists will be male. The type of science they create will also in turn reflect those same characteristics of independence, distance, and autonomy. It is on this basis that feminists have suggested that the objectivity and rationality of science are synonymous with a male approach to the physical, natural world. Psychoanalytic feminism implies that if both males and females become involved as primary caretakers of children, then gender roles would be less polarized, and science itself might become less reflective of its masculine perspective and become gender free or gender neutral.

Radical Feminism

Radical feminism, in contrast to psychoanalytic feminism and liberal feminism, rejects the possibility of a gender-free science or a science developed from a neutral, objective perspective. Radical feminism maintains that women's oppression is the first, most widespread, and deepest oppression (Jaggar and Rothenberg, 1992). Since men dominate and control most institutions, politics, and knowledge in our society, they reflect a male perspective and are effective in oppressing women. Scientific institutions, practice, and knowledge are particularly male dominated and are especially effective patriarchal tools to control and harm women. Radical feminism rejects most scientific theories, data, and experiments precisely because they not only exclude women but also because they are not women-centered.

The theory that radical feminism proposes is evolving (Tong, 1989) and is not as well developed as some of the other feminist theories for reasons springing fairly directly from the nature of radical feminism itself. Since it is radical, it rejects most of the currently accepted ideas about scientific epistemology—what kinds of things can be known, who can be a knower, and how beliefs are legitimated as knowledge—and methodology—the general structure of how theory finds its application in particular scientific disciplines. Second, radical feminism does not find its basis in a theory such as Marxism, positivism, psychoanalysis, or existentialism, already developed for decades by men. Since radical feminism is based in women's experience, it rejects theories developed by men, proposing instead that theories must be developed by women and based in women's experience (MacKinnon, 1987).

Radical feminism deviates considerably from other feminisms in its view of how beliefs are legitimated as knowledge. A successful strategy that women use to obtain reliable knowledge and correct distortions of patriarchal ideology is the consciousness-raising group (Jaggar, 1983). Using their personal experiences as a basis, women meet together in communal, nonhierarchical groups to examine their experiences to determine what counts as knowledge (MacKinnon, 1987). Lesbian separatism, often seen as an offshoot of radical feminism, would suggest that separation from men is necessary in a patriarchal society for females to understand their experiences and explore the possibility of becoming a scientist.

Postmodern Feminism

Postmodernism dissolves the universal subject as an individual, autonomous, self-constitutive human being, implied by liberal humanism (Rothfield, 1990); postmodern feminism dissolves the possibility that women speak in a unified voice or that they can be universally addressed (Gunew, 1990). Race, class, nationality, sexual orientation, and other factors prevent such unity and universality. Although one woman may share certain characteristics and experiences with other women because of her biological sex, her particular race, class, and sexual differences compared with other women, along with the construction of gender that her country and society give to someone living in her historical period, her experience cannot be universalized for women in general. Since postmodern feminism questions the nature of understanding the subject as defined in the Western world, it also puts the entire edifice of knowledge, including scientific knowledge (Haraway, 1990), into question.

Conclusion

Feminist critiques vary in the extent they call into question fundamental aspects of traditional philosophies of science. Liberal feminism leaves the objectivity and value neutrality of logical positivism intact while pointing out flaws that resulted from gender bias. Socialist and African American feminist critiques point out ethical concerns over class, racial, and gendered interests and their influence in scientific theory and practice. Essentialist, existentialist, and psychoanalytic feminism suggest possible explanations for differences in the numbers of male and female scientists and their work. Radical and postmodern feminism challenge the epistemology of science in terms of the questions asked, who can ask them, and how beliefs are legitimated as knowledge. Diverse feminisms turn the lens of gender in varying angles to reveal new and particular facets of differing philosophies of science.

See Also

BIOLOGY; EPISTEMOLOGY; ESSENTIALISM; ETHICS: FEMINIST; FEMINISM: AFRICAN-AMERICAN; FEMINISM: EXISTENTIAL; FEMINISM: LIBERAL BRITISH AND EUROPEAN; FEMINISM: LIBERAL NORTH AMERICAN; FEMINISM: POSTMODERN; FEMINISM: RADICAL; FEMINISM: SOCIALIST; SCIENCE: FEMINIST CRITIQUES; SOCIAL SCIENCES: FEMINIST METHODS

References and Further Reading

Beauvoir, Simone de. 1974. *The second sex.* Trans. and ed. H. M. Parshley. New York. Vintage.

Biology and Gender Study Group. 1989. The importance of feminist critique for contemporary cell biology. In Nancy Tuan, ed., *Feminism and Science*, 172–87. Bloomington: Indiana University Press.

Birke, Lynda. 1986. *Women, feminism, and biology: The feminist challenge.* New York: Methuen.

Bleier, Ruth. 1984. *Science and gender: A critique of biology and its theories on women.* Elmsford, N.Y.: Pergamon.

———. 1986. Sex differences research: Science or belief? In Ruth Bleir, ed., *Feminist approaches to science*, 147–64. Elmsford, N.Y.: Pergamon.

Chodorow, Nancy. 1978. *The reproduction of mothering: Psychoanalysis and the sociology of gender.* Berkeley: University of California Press.

Dinnerstein, Dorothy. 1977. *The mermaid and the minotaur: Sexual arrangements and human malaise.* New York: Harper Colophon.

Fausto-Sterling, Anne. 1992. *Myths of gender.* New York: Basic Books.

Fee, Elizabeth. 1982. A feminist critique of scientific objectivity. *Science for the people* 14(4): 8.

———. 1986. Critiques of modern science: The relationship of feminism to other radical epistemologies. In Ruth Bleier, ed., *Feminist approaches to science*, 42–56. Elmsford, N.Y.: Pergamon Press.

Giddings, Paula. 1984. *When and where we enter: The impact of black women on race and sex in America.* New York: Morrow.

Gunew, Sneja, ed. 1990. *Feminist knowledge: Critique and construct.* New York: Routledge.

Haraway, Donna. 1990. *Primate visions.* New York: Routledge.

Harding, Sandra. 1986. *The science question in feminism.* Ithaca: Cornell University Press.

hooks, bell. 1981. *Talking back: Thinking feminist, thinking black.* Boston: South End Press.

———. 1983. *Feminist theory from margin to center.* Boston: South End Press.

———. 1990. *Yearning: Race, gender and cultural politics.* Boston: South End Press.

Jaggar, Alison. 1983. *Feminist politics and human nature.* Totowa, N.J.: Rowman and Allanheld.

Jaggar, Alison, and Paula Rothenberg. 1992. *Feminist frameworks.* New York: McGraw-Hill.

Keller, Evelyn. 1982. Feminism and science. *Signs* 7(3): 589–602.

———. 1983. *A feeling for the organism.* San Francisco: Freeman.

———. 1985. *Reflections on gender and science.* New Haven, Conn.: Yale University Press.

Lorde, Audre. 1984. *Sister outsider.* Trumansburg, N.Y.: Crossing Press.

MacKinnon, Catharine. 1987. *Feminism unmodified: Discourses on life and law.* Cambridge, Mass.: Harvard University Press.

Mill, Harriet Taylor. 1970. Enfranchisement of women. In Alice S. Rossi, ed., *Essays on sex equality,* 89–122. Chicago: University of Chicago Press.

Mill, John Stuart. 1970. The subjection of women. In Alice S. Rossi, ed., *Essays on sex equality,* 123–242. Chicago: University of Chicago Press.

Rosser, Sue V. 1990. *Female friendly science.* Elmsford, N.Y.: Pergamon Press.

———. 1992. *Feminism and biology: A dynamic interaction.* New York: Twayne/Macmillan.

Rothfield, Philipa. 1990. Feminism, subjectivity, and sexual difference. In Sneja Gunew, ed., *Feminist knowledge: Critique and construct.* New York: Routledge.

Sayers, Janet. 1982. *Biological politics: Feminist and anti-feminist perspectives.* London: Tavistock.

Tong, Rosemarie. 1989. *Feminist thought: A comprehensive introduction.* Boulder, Colo.: Westview Press.

Wollstonecraft, Mary. 1975. *A vindication of the rights of woman.* Ed. Carol H. Poston. New York: W. W. Norton.

Sue V. Rosser

SCIENCE: Lesbians in Science

See LESBIANS IN SCIENCE.

SCIENCE: Nineteenth Century

As early as the beginning in the fifteenth century, historians and scientists described the contributions of women scientists (Pisan [1405], 1982). In the late 1970s, women authors rediscovered the often ignored achievements of women in science (see Alic, 1986; Ogilvie, 1986; Rossiter, 1982; Schiebinger, 1999). Still, many people think women entered science only in the twentieth century and that Marie Curie is the only woman scientist of note.

In the late 1800s, science was increasingly professionalized and moved from the private or domestic sphere to the public spheres of universities and industry. At that time, men dominated the public sphere and women were relegated to the private sphere. For example, in the nineteenth century, male engineers built sewers and water systems, whereas women were primarily responsible for sanitation within the home and for health education within the community (Benjamin, 1991). It was the rare woman who managed to straddle both worlds—to apply techniques learned in chemistry to improve water quality in the home and city—as, for example, did Ellen Swallow Richards (1842–1911).

Many women were involved in science and scientific careers, especially in the late 1800s, but only a few are ever mentioned in science textbooks. Inclusion in textbooks is especially important because, as Thomas Kuhns (1970) says, textbooks are the primary source of authority from which "scientists and laymen take much of their image of creative scientific activity," and textbooks are the primary "pedagogic vehicles for the perpetuation of normal science" (176). If women scientists are not included in textbooks, then we might assume their contributions were nonexistent or insignificant. Many histories of science are concerned primarily with European and North American people. Thus, many of the women scientists are those from Europe and North America—for example, we do not know much about nineteenth-century Asian or African scientists.

Women in Astronomy

Astronomy is a good place to begin looking at women in science in the nineteenth century. In the late eighteenth century, for example, about 14 percent of astronomers in Germany were women (Schiebinger, 1999). In the early 1800s, people who observed the stars and the planets from their own rooftops or backyards often used telescopes of their own manufacture. By the 1870s, astronomy had moved from the purview of the amateur to the professional working in national or university astronomical observatories. The lives of Caroline Herschel, Maria Mitchell, and the Harvard

Observatory "calculators" illustrate this change in astronomy to that of a profession of college-educated observers in the field (although these observers usually were men). Women's work in astronomy involved data reduction and cataloging. This repetitive, tedious, and exacting work was delegated to women, who typically earned 20 to 25 percent of men's salaries (Rossiter, 1982).

Caroline Herschel (1750–1848) was born in Germany, but did much of her observations of the stars, planets, and comets in the United Kingdom. She worked as housekeeper and astronomical assistant to her brother, William. William was the King's Astronomer and Caroline was the Astronomer's Assistant (a salaried position earning about one-fourth of William's salary). She helped her brother in most of his scientific endeavors, from making telescopes to recording William's observations of the night sky. She used his telescopes when he was out of town, but she did the tedious calculations (precomputer age) of positions and movements of astronomical bodies all the time. She cataloged 860 new stars that William and she had observed, and, in the same year (1787) she compiled the statistics on every star listed in British catalogs. In 1825, Caroline published a catalog of the calculated positions of 2,500 nebulae observed by the then-deceased William. In 1828 Caroline was awarded the Gold Medal of the Royal Astronomical Society for that 1825 catalog, which had required numerous detailed calculations involving stars, planets, and comets.

Caroline Herschel is a prime example of a "woman scientist" of her time. She literally worked only in her home and balanced her astronomical work with her daily housekeeping and family responsibilities. Her achievements were recognized only at the end of her long life when honorary membership to various European scientific societies were worth little to her. She never received fair financial compensation for her work. Caroline was also quintessentially the "scientifically minded" woman of the early nineteenth century, in that she disparaged her contributions to science as those that any well-trained assistant could do. Today, however, we recognize that scientists who observe, perform experiments, and statistically analyze data day after day perform much important scientific work.

Maria Mitchell (1818–1889) was the first American woman astronomer to discover a comet (1847) and, thereby, won a gold medal from the king of Denmark. She was the most famous American woman scientist in the nineteenth century, with quite a number of published scientific articles to her credit. She was the first woman elected to the American Association for the Advancement of Science, to the American Academy of Arts and Sciences, and to the American Philosophical Society of Philadelphia. In addition, she was also one of the few American women professors in science; she became professor of astronomy and director of the astronomical observatory at Vassar College in 1862 (very soon after its establishment). Mitchell was one of the founders of the Association for the Advancement of Women (1873).

Several notable women scientists (Mary Whitney, Christine Ladd-Franklin, and Ellen Swallow Richards, as examples) studied with Mitchell. These women continued Mitchell's advocacy for increased opportunities for higher education for women (many of the US women's colleges were founded in the later half of the nineteenth century) and for equal salaries for men and women (Mitchell was paid about one-third the salary of her male counterparts). Mitchell also argued strongly against the prevalent opinion in the 1870s (and even later) that higher education ruined women's "delicate health (and) small and light brains" (Rossiter, 1982: 13).

Mitchell was typical of women scientists of her time who had moved from the domestic sphere to the public sphere. She was employed at a women's college and carried a teaching load heavier than that of the male faculty, she was unmarried (married women were not permitted as faculty), she was Christian, and she was white.

After the introduction of photography and spectroscopic analysis to astronomy, many thousands of photographic and spectroscopic plates were generated at research and university observatories. The data analysis and calculations required to reduce and classify the data were time-consuming and challenging. Part of the challenge was that careful attention had to be paid to sets of spectra (each set was about one inch long) that were located on photographic plates that could contain information from hundreds of stars. In 1881 Edward Pickering, director of the Harvard College Observatory, hired his domestic worker, Williamina Fleming (1857–1922), to do the data analysis an inefficient male assistant had botched. She worked for Pickering for the next 30 years. She was the first to discover "white dwarf" stars and observed and cataloged 222 variable stars. In 1906 Fleming was elected to the Royal Astronomical Society. Pickering had more than 20 women assistants working with him at a fraction of the salary paid to the male assistants. Some of these college-educated assistants, Annie Jump Cannon, Henrietta Swan Leavitt, and Antonia C. Maury (1866–1952), made important contributions to astronomy.

Annie Cannon (1863–1941) classified more than 350,000 stars into spectral classes that are still used by astronomers today. In 1913, the International Solar Union accepted her classification scheme as standard. Although her work is cited in every introductory astronomy book, her name is not.

Cannon was considered a "computer" at the Harvard College Observatory, someone who did complex mathematical computations, rather than as a scientist. Although she received six honorary degrees (one was the first doctorate Oxford University awarded to a woman), Cannon was nominated but not elected to the National Academy of Sciences. To support younger women scientists, Cannon helped found scholarships for women at Harvard and established an award for the American Astronomical Society to recognize the achievements of women astronomers.

Henrietta Leavitt (1868–1921) was also known as a "computer" at the Harvard College Observatory after she had volunteered there for seven years. She became head of the photographic stellar photometry section. After studying 1,777 variable stars, Leavitt developed the Period/Luminosity Relationship for Cepheid variable stars. This relationship allowed astronomers to calculate distances between widely spaced objects. Fortunately, Leavitt was given credit for her idea and she is frequently mentioned in introductory astronomy textbooks.

Women in Mathematics

In the first half of the nineteenth century, girls from privileged families were often not educated in science or mathematics. Boys and girls from less-privileged families were hardly educated at all in any subject. There was a stereotype, occasionally expressed even today, that female brains were not large enough, "solid" enough, or robust enough to comprehend mathematics and, thus, science. Medical doctors claimed that too much education endangered women's physical health to the point of atrophy of ovaries. Women who wanted to study mathematics, for example, lied about their sex (Sophie Germain), memorized textbooks that they were unable to own (Mary Somerville), or belonged to families wealthy enough to afford tutors (Sonya Kovalevsky).

Sophie Germain (1776–1831) was born in France and studied mathematics primarily on her own, despite her family's protestations. As a woman, she was never permitted the instruction and mathematical discussions with colleagues that would have been accorded a mathematically talented man. Using a male pseudonym, Germain submitted a paper on mathematical analysis to professor Joseph Lagrange at the École Polytéchnique. She also used the same pseudonym to correspond with Karl Gauss, who later sponsored her for an honorary doctorate in mathematics from the University of Göttingen (women were not officially permitted to enter doctoral programs in German universities).

Germain at first worked on number theory, a branch of higher mathematics, and then on the mathematical explanations dealing with resonant vibrations in elastic bodies. In

1816, Germain won the grand prize in a French contest to analyze vibrations of elastic bodies. This prize was established by Napoleon and was worth one kilogram of gold. The competition for this *prix extraordinaire* was opened three times. Germain competed three times (1811, 1813, and 1816) as the sole competitor.

Germain continued her work on the mathematical analysis of elasticity, but her work was privately published. She was not allowed to be a member of The French Academy of Sciences, although, in 1822, Germain was awarded special permission to attend all public sessions of the academy. There were limited tickets available to women to attend public meetings, but these tickets previously went to wives of academy members.

Sonya Kovalévsky (1850–1891) was born in Russia where she was privately tutored in science and mathematics as well as other subjects. She studied mathematics, chemistry, and physics at Heidelberg University in Germany under special dispensation, while her husband studied geology and paleontology. She moved to Berlin to study with a world-famous mathematics professor who accepted her as a private student. Under his sponsorship, in 1874 she earned a special doctorate (*summa cum laude*) from the University of Göttingen based on partial differential equations. Although Kovalévsky had a doctorate in mathematics, there was no university in Europe with a place for her. She and her husband returned to Russia, where she taught elementary school. Ten years later, Kovalévsky became a professor of mathematics at the University of Stockholm (her first year was without salary, then she was granted a five-year salaried position). In 1885 she was also appointed as a professor in physics. Her welcome in Sweden was mixed; the playwright Strindberg said that a "female professor of mathematics is a pernicious and unpleasant phenomenon—even, one might say, a monstrosity …" (Alic, 1986: 170).

In 1888, Kovalévsky won the Prix Bordin, the highest award of the French Academy of Sciences, for her paper on the mathematics involved in rotation. Her submission was one of 15 entries and it was judged so "elegant" that more money was added to the prize. (This award was the equivalent of winning a Nobel Prize in the twentieth century.) In 1889, the Swedish Academy of Science also awarded her a prize for her mathematical work. Despite these awards, Kovalévsky was denied full membership to the Imperial Academy of Science in Russia. She was even excluded from attending the academy's regular meetings.

Mary Fairfax Somerville (1780–1872) was perhaps the most famous woman scientist in the world in the nineteenth century (if one considers the world to be Europe and North America). Somerville was self-educated (her parents thought that one year of formal education was sufficient for girls) and taught herself mathematics using books from her younger brother's tutor. After her first marriage and early widowhood, Somerville became financially independent, so that at age 33 she could devote herself to the study of mathematics and natural sciences. Her second husband was a physician and naturalist who encouraged his wife in her scientific pursuits. Somerville gained her scientific fame as a translator—one who made physical laws familiar and understandable to the general public; yet her work was current enough and detailed enough to be of interest to the scientist.

In 1831, she published a translation and explanation of Laplace's "Mécanique Céleste," which was a critical and financial success. Her *Mechanisms of the Heavens* was a standard textbook in higher mathematics and physics for the rest of the nineteenth century. Her second book, *On the Connexion of the Physical Sciences* (1834), dealt with mathematics, physics, chemistry, and geology. Her third book, 1848, *Physical Geography* (1848), concerned the earth sciences, geology, oceanography, and meteorology. She considered the science of human societies in this text; she criticized slavery and discussed class struggle. She also refuted the "great man" theory of scientific progress. She believed that science progresses more through the work of many scientists than solely through the discovery/theory of an individual.

Many accolades were bestowed on Somerville during her lifetime, although the irony of some of these rewards often escaped the awarding societies. For example, her bust was placed in the Great Hall of the Royal Society, a place she was not allowed to enter. She was elected to honorary membership by many scientific societies in Europe and North America—societies that did not accept women members.

Somerville is an exemplar of the talented but self-trained scientist of the nineteenth century. She was self-educated, not only in science and mathematics but also in Latin and Greek; she had the support and encouragement of her second husband; she and her husband socialized with many of the scientific cognoscenti of Europe; and she was a believer in social, racial, and sexual equality. Despite her numerous awards and financial rewards from her scientific career, Somerville said of herself, "I have perseverance and intelligence but no genius, that spark from heaven is not granted to [my] sex, we are of the earth …" (Alic, 1986: 185).

Other well-known women scientists in nineteenth-century America include Elizabeth Knight Britton (botany), Ellen Swallow Richards (chemistry and home economics),

Alice Fletcher (anthropology), Christine Ladd-Franklin (mathematics and psychology), and Cornelia Clapp (zoology and psychology).

There were many other women scientists in the nineteenth century—most of their achievements and contributions are recorded only in their obituaries. The rise in the "profession" of science often excluded women who had contributed to science. As one example, we can consider the development of botany as a science in North America and Europe. In the early nineteenth century, botany was dominated by women (the culture of educated people at that time determined that botany—rather than geology, physics, chemistry, or zoology—was a suitable field for women as long as the women did not study plant reproduction). By the end of the nineteenth century, the field was "professionalized"—professional botanists needed the proper credentials. These credentials included a doctorate in science, presentations at learned societies, and papers published in prestigious journals. By defining botany in this way, women were excluded. Many women could not attend universities (either in Europe or the United States) to earn their doctoral degrees until the late 1870s (women were permitted into the more prestigious graduate schools in the 1890s). Professional botanists at the U.S. Department of Agriculture who published in government bulletins were excluded because those government bulletins were not prestigious enough. The only woman member of the Botanical Society of America (1893) was Elizabeth Knight Britton (1858–1934), who published nearly 350 scientific papers.

See Also

PLAGIARISM IN SCIENCE; SCIENCE, *all entries*

References and Further Reading

Alic, Margaret. 1986. *Hypatia's heritage: A history of women in science from antiquity to the late nineteenth century.* Boston: Beacon.

Benjamin, Marina, ed. 1991. *Science and sensibility: Gender and scientific enquiry, 1780–1945.* Oxford: Basil Blackwell.

Kuhns, Thomas. 1970. *The structure of scientific revolutions.* 2nd ed. Chicago: University of Chicago Press.

Ogilvie, Marilyn B. 1986. *Women in science: Antiquity through the 19th century.* Boston: MIT Press.

Pisan, Christine de. 1982. *The book of the city of ladies* (1405). Trans. Earl Jeffrey Richards. New York: Persea.

Rossiter, Margaret W. 1982. *Women scientists in America: Struggles and strategies to 1940.* Baltimore, Md.: Johns Hopkins University Press.

Schiebinger, Londa. 1999. *Has feminism changed science?* Cambridge, Mass.: Harvard University Press.

Darlene S. Richardson

SCIENCE:
Technological and Scientific Research

The proportion of women in science and technology is generally low. Women are less apt than men to be tenured or to hold leading positions (Toren, 1991). The higher the position in rank and power, the lower the proportion of women. These career trajectories raise several questions concerning women in science. What are possible barriers to the advancement of women, and what are the possible structural advancements to women's careers?

A career in science refers to the process by which professional positions in science are obtained. The first step is usually a research fellowship or some other way of funding the training toward a doctoral degree. This degree is in most cases a necessary condition for obtaining a tenured position in science. The career opportunities in academia for a person with a doctoral degree are assistant professor, associate professor, and, finally, full professor. These ranks are based on academic qualifications. A similar ranking of positions is found in the institutes of applied research, where the basis for these ranks is a combination of academic qualifications and managerial skills. The proportion of women is especially low in the top positions in academia and applied institutes.

The Underrepresentation of Women in Science as a Universal Phenomenon

Science and technology are generally male-dominated areas. One significant measure of the participation of women in research is the proportion of women with doctoral degrees. Women represent in general between one-quarter and a one-third of the doctoral candidates, but the proportion of women varies between countries. Data from Europe and the United States show that the proportion of women with doctoral degrees varies from 10 percent in the Netherlands to 25 percent in Norway and the United Kingdom. The proportion of women is 30 percent in France and in Germany, 28 percent in Russia, and 36 percent in the United States (Lie et al., 1994). In general, women are more likely to have doctoral degrees in the social sciences or the humanities than in the natural sciences or engineering. Results from the United Kingdom, Germany, and Norway show that the proportion of women with doctoral degrees is highest in the social sciences; lower in the natural sciences; and lowest in mathematics, computer science, and engineering (National Science Foundation, 1995).

A more comprehensive measure of women's participation in research is the proportion of women among scientific and technical human resources. UNESCO (United Nations Educational, Scientific, and Cultural Organization) uses this indicator to compare the proportion of women in different parts of the world. The proportion of women is lowest in the African (20 percent) and Asian countries (25 percent), higher in the European countries (34 percent), somewhat higher in Canada (39 percent), and highest in Russia (55 percent). The higher proportion of women among scientific and technical human resources than among doctoral candidates is a result of the fact that the human resources indicator includes technicians working with research as well as scientists (UNESCO, 1993).

Obtaining a Doctoral Degree

Training for a doctoral degree is usually provided by universities. Preparing a doctoral thesis represents the main part of the training, but most universities also require examinations in specified courses. Universities are characterized by a hierarchical structure, with appointments based on a mentor system. Junior scientists generally are required to hold a nontenured position for several years in order to qualify for a tenured position. The task of the mentor is to socialize the younger scientists to research work and to help integrate the younger staff into the work organization and into the networks between scientists from different universities.

The mentor's role in integrating younger scientists into scientific networks is especially important in relation to women. Women represent a minority in universities and are often on the periphery of collegial interaction. Deprecating attitudes toward women are particularly prevalent in "old boy" networks and may be due to both subtle discrimination and women's reluctance to intrude (Lie and O'Leary, 1990). Increasingly, however, women have been accepted within networks representing their research specialty, although they are found to be less well integrated within their work organization.

Results from a Norwegian study of scientific careers indicate that a good and supportive relationship with a mentor is one of the most important factors enabling women to obtain a doctoral degree (Thagaard, 1994). The relationship to a mentor has different functions. The mentor may have a direct impact on the research work by giving comments and advice on the project design and drafts of the dissertation.

This is just as important for men as it is for women. A second function is to encourage and strengthen professional self-confidence. This may be particularly important for women, because women more often than men experience problems with recognition and credibility in relation to their research work. A third function of the mentor is to give advice concerning career planning and strategy. This may compensate for the fact that women do not receive as much information relevant to the planning of their careers as men do.

The years when scientists qualify for a doctoral degree or a tenured position are likely to coincide with the years when they have small children. Studies of women scientists indicate that childcare responsibilities affect their progress and the choices made during their academic careers (Lie and O'Leary, 1990). The advancement structure of science has generally remained inflexible in response to the fact that the crucial period for ensuring a successful scientific career coincides with childbearing and childrearing age (Stolte-Heiskanen, 1991).

Results from the Norwegian study of scientific careers indicate that flexibility in the number of years that junior scientists work for their doctoral degree—with prolongation for about two years—facilitates the acquisition of a doctoral degree for women (Thagaard, 1994). The need for a prolonged period to work on the doctoral thesis is especially important for women who have responsibilities for childcare. Women scientists, like employed women in general, have the main responsibility for childcare. Moreover, married women tend to subordinate their career to that of their spouse and to have the majority of the household duties. Spending a prolonged period on doctoral work is one way for women scientists to combine family obligations with a scholarly career. The result is that more years can be focused on research without having responsibility for too many other duties at work. A reduction in amount of duties is one important strategy for the advancement of women's careers in science (Cole and Zuckerman, 1987). In the competition for higher positions, however, there can be a problem if women—as a fixed pattern—take more years than men to acquire qualifications for a career in science. Thus, flexibility in the number of years spent on doctoral work for both men and women, combined with the sharing of responsibilities at home, is an important strategy for the advancement of women's careers.

Acquiring Tenured Positions

Career demands in academia and in institutes of applied research pose different challenges for women than for men. Scientific qualifications, as documented by scientists' publications, represent the basis for obtaining tenured positions in academia. The quality of scientific publications is the most important criterion, but the number of publications may also be a factor. Thus, the question of women's careers in science is, among other things, a question of their publication pattern in comparison with that of male scientists.

In general, women tend to have a lower publication rate than their male colleagues. The proportion of women is especially low among scientists with the highest publication rate, whereas the gender difference is almost negligible among those with a medium rate of publications (Thagaard, 1991). Studies that consider the number of citations to publications a relevant criterion for quality find a slight advantage for women concerning the quality of their scientific publishing (Long, 1987). Thus, in relation to a career in science, the issue is the significance for appointments of the particularly high publication rate of some male scientists.

Institutes of applied research base their career trajectories on a combination of scientific qualifications and managerial skills. This "double-tracked" career demand may pose more obstacles for women than for men because of the challenge involved in qualifying scientifically while at the same time pursuing an administrative career. The tasks associated with obtaining funding and managing projects have to be accomplished in order to keep the institutes going. The financial needs may be especially demanding in private institutes and may explain why the proportion of women is lower in privately financed institutes compared with the proportion of women in publicly funded institutes and universities (*Nordic R&D Statistics*, 1991).

There are especially few women in the top positions in research, both in academia and in institutes of applied research. The decline in the proportion of women as the power and prestige of the position increase is an international phenomenon. There are about three times as many women among assistant professors (or equivalents) as among full professors in most European countries and in the United States. Women's share of positions as full professor varies from 2 percent in the Netherlands, to 5 percent in Germany and in the United Kingdom, to 11 percent in France and in Russia, to 14 percent in the United States (Lie et al., 1994).

The generally low proportion of women among full professors can be explained to some extent by the relatively low proportion of women in the generation of scientists who are qualified for higher positions. The higher proportion of women among younger scientists may indicate that there will be more women in top positions in the years to come. However, studies from Europe and the United States indicate that the relatively low number of female scientists with

higher qualifications can only partially explain the situation. Few women in higher positions are also associated with social networks, which implies that men and women have different opportunities within the organization of science. Gender-differentiating processes are especially explicit in relation to recruitment to top positions.

Male Dominance and Its Consequences for Women

Research organizations are male dominated, especially at the top level (Acker, 1992). The implication is that younger scientists are most often recruited by male senior scientists. It is likely that the recruitment to higher positions is characterized by the process of homosocial reproduction, which implies that male senior scientists recruit younger men as their successors. Several studies indicate that women are not given as much encouragement as men for pursuing a career in science (Lie and O'Leary, 1990). There is a tendency for women's competence and achievements to remain invisible, which again leads to lack of scientific credibility and limits access to recognition. A significant minority of women scientists consider lack of encouragement to be the reason for women's marginal position in science (Stolte-Heiskanen, 1991).

Are women scientists being discriminated against by their male colleagues? This question is not easy to answer, because possible discrimination is a subtle process, difficult to verify (Pleck, 1990). One indication of discrimination is the description women give of their situation. Women scientists often admit that sex discrimination exists, but few characterize themselves as victims. This may be due either to lack of discriminatory experiences or to cultural reconstruction of discriminatory actions in order to cope with a conflicting reality. However, it is relevant to assume that simply working in a mostly male environment imposes different pressures on women than on men. The career structure is based on "male norms," and the culture and curriculum prioritize traditionally male values (Acker, 1992). Research on sex stereotypes has shown that science, scientists, and research are perceived as strongly masculine by both men and women, and that successful scientists are described as exhibiting primarily masculine traits. In these respects women are on the periphery of science, both because they represent a minority and because they seek accomplishments and rewards usually sought by men.

The minority position of women may also be associated with sexual harassment. Because women are few in number, their behavior is visible and they are often stereotyped. This is referred to as *tokenism*. It may be a short leap from stereotyping to sexual harassment by such means as ridiculing images of women scientists and using sexist examples. The situation documented as most susceptible to sexual harassment in science is the relationship between a senior male mentor and a female research fellow. Because the young woman is dependent on her mentor for guidance and perhaps also for fulfillment of her project, she finds herself in an extremely difficult position if the mentor flirts with her or starts courting her in combination with supervising her research.

The position of women in science represents a contradictory situation between equal opportunities with men on a formal level and inequality on a more subtle level. The norm of universalism is the formal basis for evaluation of scientific contributions. Directions according to this norm are that scientific contributions should be evaluated on quality, and that personal factors such as gender and age should not influence the evaluation. In reality, women are ranked second or third in competition with men for higher positions more often than can be attributed to their qualifications. This pattern is referred to as the systematics of the accidental. There seem to be invisible barriers to women rising above a certain point, a "glass ceiling" that remains invisible until one reaches its border and which then stops further upward movement. Despite the increase in women in universities and research institutes, the upper positions of the ladder still resist this increase, supporting the idea of such a "glass ceiling," invisible but nevertheless real (Lie et al., 1994).

Future Trends

Opposing male dominance in research is an ongoing development that can be referred to as feminist research. One of the trends in this process is the introduction of feminist programs in many universities around the world (Lie et al., 1994). These programs focus on studies of the position of women, and the goal is to reach an understanding of the conditions for women in society.

Another trend is the introduction of feminist perspectives within different disciplines. These perspectives imply criticism of typical male-dominated points of view and emphasize female interests. In the social sciences, the focus is on traditionally female areas such as family, children, and everyday life. A feminist approach here often implies qualitative methods and epistemological rethinking. In the natural sciences, the traces of feminism are associated with a preference for the application of science in the service of medical and social purposes. Associated with research on women and introduction of feminist issues are the growing networks of female scientists, which contribute to integrating women into the institution of science. Thus, the future position of women in science will probably, to a greater extent than today, be characterized by an improved integration of women and, it is to be hoped, a larger proportion of women at all levels—including the top.

See Also

COMPUTER SCIENCE; EDUCATORS: HIGHER EDUCATION; ENGINEERING; INVENTORS; PHYSICAL SCIENCES; PLAGIARISM IN SCIENCE; PROFESSIONAL SOCIETIES; SCIENCE: EARLY MODERN TO LATE EIGHTEENTH CENTURY; SCIENCE: NINETEENTH CENTURY; SCIENCE: TWENTIETH CENTURY; SCIENCE: FEMINISM AND SOCIAL SCIENCES

References and Further Reading

Acker, Sandra. 1992. New Perspectives on an old problem: The position of women academics in British higher education. *Higher Education* 24: 57–75.

Cole, Jonathan R., and Harriet Zuckerman. 1987. Marriage, motherhood and research performance in science. *Scientific American* 2: 83–89.

Lie, Suzanne, and Virginia O'Leary, eds. 1990. *Storming the power: Academic women around the world.* New York: Nichols/GP Publishing.

Lie, Suzanne, Lynda Mallik, and Duncan Harris, eds. 1994. *The gender gap in higher education.* London: Kogan Page.

Long, John Scott. 1987. Problems and prospects for research on sex differences in the scientific career. In Linda S. Dix, ed., *Women: Their underrepresentation and career differentials in science and engineering.* Washington, D.C.: National Academy Press.

National Science Foundation (NSF). 1995. *Human resources for science & technology: The European region.* Washington, D.C.: NSF.

Nordic R&D statistics. 1991. Oslo: Nordic Industrial Fund.

Pleck, Elizabeth. 1990. The unfulfilled promise: Women and academe. *Sociological Forum* 5(3): 517–524.

Stolte-Heiskanen, Veronica, ed. 1991. *Women in science: Token women or gender equality?* New York: Berg.

Thagaard, Tove. 1991. Research environment, motivation and publication productivity. *Science Studies* 1: 5–18.

———. 1994. Hard work and much patience: Career prospects for women scientists. *Nora* 1: 28–41.

Toren, Nina. 1991. The nexus between family and work roles of academic women in Israel: Reality and representation. *Sex Roles* 24(11/12): 651–667.

United Nations Educational, Scientific, and Cultural Organization (UNESCO). 1993. *Statistical yearbook.* Paris: UNESCO.

Tove Thagaard

SCIENCE:
Traditional and Indigenous Knowledge

The knowledge of indigenous peoples is rooted in culture and in worship of the earth and its life-giving qualities. The more than 6,000 indigenous nations in the world today actively use knowledge derived from ancient and evolving traditions. These traditions have been gathered from careful and systematic observation of nature, the cosmos, and their cycles, and passed on orally from one generation to the next.

The word "science" is derived from the word *sciens/scientia* meaning "to know" and is etymologically linked to sense: hence sensory methods of perceiving and interpreting. Most science that is referred to is Western science, originating from Aristotle and made more comprehensive by Descartes in the seventeenth century. Emerging from philosophies of positivism, or progressivism, science uses objective methods to define cause and effect in the material world. Scientific methods suppose that the observer maintains an objective stance separate from the phenomena under observation. This contrasts with indigenous sciences whose methods of apprehending realities include personal and spiritual identification and participation with the observed. Indigenous knowledge is synthesized via collective perceptual and proprioceptive capacities including access to altered states of consciousness. The senses—touch, taste, smell, hearing, and sight—and extrasensory capacities such as intuition facilitate entry into the "invisible" realms. This universe, governed by subtle energies and scientifically hinted at, though as yet "unproven," remains the subject of debate by orthodox thinkers.

Tart (1972) differentiates between "methods of essential science (observation, theorizing, prediction, communication/consensual validation)" and scientific "paradigms" that act as a super theory governing what will be observed and theorized about (Kuhn, 1979). In the twenty-first century indigenous knowledge and science increasingly intersect as each informs the other in methods, practices, and beliefs. Kuhn's classic work on the structure of scientific revolutions posits the pattern by which scientific paradigms undergo change and provide blueprints for understanding multiple ways of knowing and integrating often divergent phenomena. Among many areas of convergence are medicine, ecology, botany, anthropology, conservation, and consciousness studies.

Definition of Indigenous

The term *indigenous* in relation to human populations has multiple meanings and is widely debated. It refers to "original," as in a place, land, or home. Indigenous peoples, thus, are peoples who live in their original place or homeland, or identify with that homeland in spite of their dislocation or exile. The term is a political word that unifies native peoples. In 1975, it was incorporated into the common lexicon during an historic meeting of the World Council of Indigenous Peoples in Port Albernia, Canada. *Indigenous* is also associated with distinct nations, such as Catalonia, who live under the control or within the boundaries of a state, such as Spain. Synonyms of *indigenous* include Fourth World, Native, First Nations, and Aboriginal, linking political, philosophical, and spiritual identities.

Technically, all peoples today come from indigenous peoples and land. Millennia of natural migrations, forced colonization, displacement, and modern pressures of integration created increasingly complex societies in which many peoples lost their active, conscious connection to their original place and the practices that defined their cultural identities. Instead, their identity is associated with the state in which they were born or the state to which they migrated.

Indigenous peoples maintain and integrate the knowledge of their heritage in a variety of ways. Some Indian tribes of North and South America such as the Haudenosaunee and the Yanomami have a knowledge-base that is intact and active. The traditional Irish in northwestern Ireland are, with independence, recovering knowledge through ceremonies and restoration of the language of their ancestors. Revitalization and renewal movements are actively underway among indigenous peoples throughout North and Central America, and among the Aboriginal peoples in Australia, many parts of Europe, and Eurasia. Revival movements are also growing among the Ainu in Japan and Tibetans, Uygurs, and Manchurians in China who due to colonization, dislocation, or political and religious oppression lost life ways or are safeguarding them for a new era. The early twenty-first century wave of economic globalization and continuing environmental degradation threatens the survival of indigenous peoples, their knowledge, and traditional resources.

Tribal Epistemologies: Ways of Knowing

Indigenous knowledge arises out of communal or tribal life and is rooted in multiple ways of knowing. Ways of knowing and apprehending realities among indigenous peoples have been described as *spiralism*. Spirals shape systems of tribal thought into structures that allow aspects of past experience to combine with the present in order to interpret the future (Ryser, 1998). This mode of thought differs from the dominant global mode of thought called *progressivism*. Progressivism embraces an implicit faith that change will always improve what existed before, and endorses human dominance over the natural world for the benefit of human life. Progressivism also promotes the sanctity of the individual and the validity of rational inquiry and explanation rather than intuitive knowledge. Ways of comprehending reality are filtered through modes of thought. Indigenous knowledge, therefore, comprehends time and space in ways sometimes at odds with the world of progressivism.

Indigenous Knowledge and Women

Traditionally, women around the globe, in rural villages as well as in urban cities, practice and share knowledge and teach indigenous ways of knowing for the benefit of their families, communities, and societies. Many also teach locally, regionally, and internationally. Women are joining together across cultures and training experience to develop a dialogue that includes all ways of knowing.

The archeologist Marija Gimbutas is among a few remarkable indigenous scientists and researchers across centuries and disciplines who are defining, uncovering, and reasserting indigenous knowledge. Gimbutas's exhaustive study of ancient European indigenous societies suggests new interpretations of agricultural and goddess worship societies with profound implications for understanding Europe (Gimbutas, 1989). Adela Breton, whose studies in the nineteenth century among the indigenous peoples of the west coast of Mexico presaged discoveries that went unrecognized until 1970. Deborah Rose is a healer and researcher in the tradition of her Celtic ancestors, and Alisia Araiza is an herbalist in Mexico who carries on the traditions of her great grandmothers. Rosalie Tizya and Pamela Colorado, North American indigenous scholars, work at local and international levels, informed by a strong spiritual foundation and commitment. Tijaart W. Schillhorn van Veen, Constance M. McCorkle, and Evelyn Mathias are pioneers in documenting indigenous veterinary sciences. These scientists have merged a uniquely holistic vision of the interconnectedness of everything, and have brought what in western gendered dichotomous science is often referred to as a "feminine" perspective.

Women thrive as keepers of traditions handed down from their foremothers yet continue to suffer from bigotry and gender bias in the twenty-first century. Women must often labor in secret because states or religions outlaw traditional knowledge and practices, from midwifery and homebirths in many areas of Mexico and the United States

to proscriptions against herbal medicine under Malagasy law in Africa. Poverty, malnutrition, lack of reproductive rights, refugee status, domestic subjugation, and exposure to increased levels of state violence negatively impact women's capacity to serve as resources of traditional knowledge for their communities. Women working as indigenous scientists within academia or not are also surrounded by controversy and marginalization without financial or collegial support or recognition from their peers until much later in life, if ever.

Documentation of Indigenous Science and Knowledge

Indigenous knowledge is typically communicated by way of oral traditions, rituals, and the arts. The earliest forms of indigenous knowledge via the arts may be found in the rock and cave paintings in ancient Europe, Australia, the Americas, and throughout the Western Hemisphere. Here the rhythms of humans and other animals, of life and death, the hunt and cosmic events, were recorded.

Indigenous knowledge has been undergoing systematic documentation and interpretation around the world. Urban indigenous and nonindigenous scientists come together with rural practitioners to develop and define methods of documenting knowledge. One such strategy is called "community determined knowledge." This method requires that the community itself determine its own knowledge base, how the knowledge will be applied, and with whom it will be shared. This is one safeguard designed to protect the rights of indigenous people and the integrity of scientific research. Documenting knowledge ensures its transfer from one generation to the next, enhances decision making, and informs a global network of indigenous peoples.

Examples of documentation include: (1) geographic mapping and ecological and resource management and conservation among peoples of the Arctic; (2) development of regional ethnographic pharmacological and medicinal databases on the use of plant and animal resources for medicine and pest management; (3) oral histories of Indian elders speaking their native language, linked with ethnobotanical and archeological research on village sites among the Northwest American Indians.

One problem with the documentation and sharing of knowledge regarding healing and spiritual ceremonies has been confiscation by people who seek to commercialize such knowledge. This damages indigenous peoples inside and outside of their communities. The "New Age Indian Movement" is one example of the commercialization of indigenous knowledge. Indians and others invent ceremonial practices and attempt to sell these practices for money. In North America efforts to curtail confiscation of sacred knowledge are at various stages of development including negotiating new treaties between indigenous nations to guard against unscrupulous use of cultural property.

Integration of Science and Indigenous Knowledge

Where the positivist western European paradigm stresses specificity and specialty in scientific disciplines many indigenous and traditional scientists are generalists or holists. Debates in the twenty-first century center on questions such as: Is indigenous knowledge science? Is science to be seen as one knowledge system among many, and therefore address the relativity of knowledge and interpretations of reality? (World Conference on Science in 1999; Takashima, Douglas, and Paul de Guchteniere, IKDM. November, 1999).

New practices and disciplines are resulting from the integration of methods, content, and media to form a new syncretic model. Indigenous sciences and knowledge bases are referred to with a prefix of ethno, as in ethnic or culture-based because the defining feature is considered, by science, to be rooted in culture not reason.

While many women are on the ramparts of these changes at the international and national policy levels, there remains persistent lack of inclusion of women in the international arena. Inequity of access persists between the majority of women practicing their knowledge in the fourth world and their impact on corporate and government policies that increasingly affect their lives. In spite of this it must be acknowledged that the majority of women in the world care for their families and their neighbors using the traditions of their grandmothers, and their knowledge and strength survive at great odds.

Public Policy: Indigenous Knowledge, Science, and Biocultural Diversity

Indigenous knowledge is at the center of all major public policy debates in the twenty-first century. Economic globalization centers on indigenous peoples' resource issues because it is estimated by the United Nations that 70 percent of the last remaining natural resources of the earth are located in the lands of indigenous peoples. Indigenous peoples rely on biological diversity for 90 percent of their livelihoods (RAFI, 1998:3). The cultural properties and knowledge of indigenous peoples are increasingly subject to theft, expropriation, and exploitation through copyrights, patents, trademarks, and other legal mechanisms. The concept of knowledge as private property is at odds with indige-

nous societies, which commonly do not regard cultural properties such as knowledge as something to be comodified or commercialized, but sharing of knowledge is a fundamental responsibility.

Debates in the local regional and international arenas focus on a range of issues including: how and whether to exchange knowledge mutually and constructively, the reciprocal integration of indigenous knowledge and Western science, access to knowledge, benefits, and ownership of the knowledge, and the practices and resources, benefits and deficits growing out of these intersections. International states' policy-making bodies such as WHO and UNESCO are undertaking initiatives to apply indigenous knowledge to sustainable development and poverty alleviation. Indigenous nations, and nongovernmental organizations are working in public policy areas of self-determination and applying those principles to international agreements such as the Convention on Biological Diversity (1992). Indigenous scholars and their colleagues ask: Is nature to be manipulated by human beings? If so, how and by whom? Are human beings a part of the whole of nature designated as stewards for the sustenance of biocultural diversity?

See Also

ANCIENT INDIGENOUS CULTURES: WOMEN'S ROLES; KNOWLEDGE; SCIENCE: OVERVIEW; SCIENCE: FEMINIST CRITIQUES; TRADITIONAL HEALING: HERBALISTS

References and Further Reading

Carroll, Jane. 1996. Dr. Pamela Colorado talks to Jane Carroll. In *Revision: A journal of consciousness and transformation* (special issue in indigenous science) 18(3): 6–10.

Center for World Indigenous Studies, Fourth World Development Project. <www.ceis.org>.

CIKARD: Center for Indigenous Knowledge for Agriculture and Rural Development Expert Center for Taxonomic Identification.

Gimbutas, Marija. 1989. *The Language of the Goddess.* New York: Harper and Row.

IK: Indigenous Knowledge and Development: Database, networks, and partnerships facilitated by CIRAN, the Centre for International Research and Advisory Networks. <www.nuffic.nl/ik-pages/index.html>.

Jones, Shirley, ed. 1999. *Simply living: The spirit of the indigenous people.* Novato: New World Library.

Korn, Leslie E. 1999. The rhythms of body and earth in the Mexican jungle. In Miriam Wyman, ed., *Sweeping the earth: Women taking action for a healthy planet.* Charlottetown: Gynergy Books.

Kuhn, Thomas. 1999. *The structure of scientific revolutions.* Chicago: University of Chicago Press.

NAPRALERT: Natural products database. Chicago: University of Illinois.

RAFI, Community Biodiversity Development and Conservation Program. 1998. *Enclosures of the Mind: Intellectual monopolies.* Ottawa, Canada: Rural Advancement Foundation.

Ryser, Rudolph. 1998. Observations on self and knowing. In *Tribal Epistemologies,* ed. Helmut Wautuscher. Brookfield: Ashgate.

Takashima, Douglas, and Paul de Guchteniere. 1999. Report: World Conference in Science, in Indigenous Knowledge and Development Monitor. Amsterdam.

Tart, Charles. States of consciousness and state-specific sciences. 1972. *Science* 176: 1203–1210.

Toledo Maya Cultural Council and Toledo Alcades Association. 1997. *Maya atlas: The struggle to preserve Maya land in southern Belize.* Berkeley: North Atlantic Books.

Townsend, Richard F. ed. 1998. *Ancient West Mexico: Art and archaeology of the unknown past.* London: Thames and Hudson.

Van Veen Schillhorn, Constance M. McCorkle, and Evelyn Mathias. 1996. *Ethnoveterinary research and development.* London: Intermediate Technology Publications.

Leslie Korn

SCIENCE: Twentieth Century

In the twentieth century, women were underrepresented in most disciplines of science in most countries. By the year 2000, in Europe and North America, the overall percentage of women in science and engineering was about 20 to 25 percent of all scientists and engineers. In the United States, for example, psychology was the only science discipline where women earned nearly two-thirds of doctoral degrees. In other countries, such as China and Turkey, women participated in science in greater proportion—nearly one-third of scientists and engineers in China and Turkey were women (Schiebinger, 1999). In all countries, however, women's participation in science and technology decreases with increasing prestige of occupation, position, university, or science academy. That is, women are more often in junior positions than in senior positions, they are more common in non-doctoral than doctoral institutions, and they are underrepresented in prestigious science academies. One example: at the turn of the twenty-first century, in the Chinese Academy of Science, fewer than five percent of its members were women (Schiebinger, 1999).

Many national and international organizations investigated this underrepresentation of women in science and technology, from the standpoint of equity as well as under-utilization of 50 percent of available human talent. The Third World Organization for Women in Science in 1999, sponsored by the United Nations, called for greater participation of women in science and technology, since science has become increasingly important in our lives. Indeed, the conference statement continues, women also should shape the "norms, values, and practices" of science. In order to be inclusive and reflective of reality, both women's and men's perspectives and attitudes must be incorporated in development and utilization of science and technology.

Even though more girls and women studied science in the late twentieth century, they continued to face the barriers to success that women had faced decades earlier. Some of these barriers can be easily quantified—unequal educational opportunities, slower job promotion, unequal remuneration, and unequal access to research space and equipment. A 1999 Swedish study of research grants revealed that women who earned grants were 2.2 times more productive than men who received grants (Wennerås and Wold, 1997). These quantifiable barriers prove that gender bias prevents women from their full participation in science. Other barriers are less easily quantified. Social and cultural stereotypes that girls cannot "do" science are often exclusionary. Lack of family-friendly policies (women predominantly are responsible for childcare) makes it difficult at times for women to pursue their careers in the same timeframe as men. Without many women in powerful and prestigious positions, women may lack networks that informally assist in education and career progression. Women in traditionally defined male domains generally face more sexual harassment.

The following brief biographies of great women scientists recount the many barriers that these women faced in their professions. Ten women have won 11 Nobel prizes in science. The Nobel Prize is awarded in only three categories of science: chemistry, physics, and physiology and medicine. Some of these women Nobel laureates emigrated for greater opportunities in higher education or more opportunities for scientific research in sophisticated laboratories. Some were not fully employed in positions commensurate with their talents and commitment. Most of them were very well educated, with doctoral or medical degrees from prestigious universities. With the exception of Nusslein-Volhard, they earned their doctoral or medical degrees when these post-baccalaureate degrees were rare among women. Few came from families of privilege—most struggled financially through their graduate studies. Most were married with children (exceptions: McClintock, Levi-Montalcini, and Elion) and four were married to scientists with whom they worked. Most were employed, but many of them were in jobs that paid less well and had less prestige than expected (as examples, Goeppert Mayer and McClintock). Five of them won the Nobel prizes in their 50s, two in their 30s, and three in their 70s or very early 80s. The earlier winners of the science Nobel prizes faced many obstacles on their science journeys—lack of educational opportunities, lack of gender equity and pay equity, and, in some cases, nationalism, sexism, and anti-Semitism. Several of the women battled lifelong against debilitating diseases (Marie Curie, Hodgkin, and Cori), while sustaining their research.

It is often too easy to identify the notable women in science as being those women who have won major scientific awards. We know, however, that science is increasingly conducted by groups of people. Discoveries and significant breakthroughs are made by science technicians and science graduate students as well as by directors of science laboratories. Arguments have been made by scientists and historians of science that some scientists have been denied the acclaim to which they are entitled. Some scientists (see Wu and Meittner) contributed much to work that was later deemed Nobel-worthy for someone else. Still other scientists are in fields of science that do not have such well-popularized international prizes as the Nobel awards.

Nobel Prize–Winners in Chemistry

Marie Sklodowska Curie (1867–1934) (nationality: Polish/French) won her second Nobel prize in 1911 at the age of 44 for her chemical isolation of radium and radium components. She was the first person to win two Nobel prizes. She was the first woman scientist to achieve international fame and is forever associated with radioactivity, a term she coined. Even today her image is on postage stamps, banknotes, and coins. She was the first woman to earn a doctorate in science in Europe (1903 at the University of Paris). After the death of her husband and coworker, Pierre, Curie was appointed to the professorship that had been her husband's. She was the first woman to teach at the Sorbonne (1904–1934). In 1914 she founded the Radium Institute, which was a center of international research on radioactivity. With the help of her daughter, Irene, Curie worked with the medical applications of radioactive substances (X radiography).

Irene Joliot-Curie (1897–1956) (nationality: French) age 38, shared the prize in 1935 with her husband, Frederic Joliot, for the synthesis of new radioactive elements by bombarding stable elements with alpha particles, their study of artificial radioactivity, and for their contributions toward the discovery of the neutron. She earned her doctorate in physics from the University of Paris in 1925 and held various positions as a researcher or director of national and university research labs. During World War I she was instrumental in helping military doctors use X radiography to find shrapnel. She was a member of the French Atomic Energy Commission.

Dorothy Crowfoot Hodgkin (1910–1994) (nationality: British) won the prize in 1964 at the age of 54. Working at times with her doctoral supervisor, J. D. Bernal, she deciphered the structure of complex organic molecules using X ray diffraction. She worked out the structures of more than 100 sterols, penicillin, insulin (it took her 34 years), and vitamin B_{12}. She was the first to use an electronic computer for her X ray calculations. Her early work on the structure of penicillin, for example, led the way to the synthesis of penicillin and other antibiotics. She was awarded the Nobel Prize specifically for her work on B_{12}; that work contributed to the artificial production of B_{12} and a "cure" for pernicious anemia. She spent much of her professional life in research labs at Oxford and Cambridge Universities. She earned her doctoral degree from Cambridge University in 1937.

Nobel Prize–Winners in Physics

Marie Sklodowska Curie (1867–1934) shared the prize in 1903 with her husband, Pierre Curie, and Henri Becquerel for the discovery of radioactivity. In 1896, Becquerel discovered what Marie Curie called radioactivity in uranium. Curie codiscovered thorium's radioactivity. The Curies worked together and discovered polonium and radium in 1898 in pitchblende. (See Marie Curie, above.)

Maria Goeppert Mayer (1906–1972) (nationality: German/American) at age 57, shared the prize in 1963 with Johannes Jensen for their independent work on the organization of neutrons and protons in the atomic nucleus. Goeppert Mayer's theory explained why some nuclei were more stable than others. She earned her doctorate in physics at Göttingen University in 1930 where she calculated the probability that an electron would emit two photons as it jumped to a lower orbit (confirmed experimentally more than 30 years later). She did not have a paying job until 1959, when she and her husband became professors at University of

California at San Diego. She had previously conducted research at Johns Hopkins, Columbia University, and the University of Chicago.

Nobel Prize–Winners in Physiology and Medicine

Gerty Radnitz Cori (1896–1957) (nationality: Czech/American) shared the prize in 1947 with her husband, Carl Cori, and Bernardo Houssay for elucidating how glucose is converted into glycogen. At 51 years of age, she was the first American woman Nobel laureate in science. Later studies on enzymes and hormones supplemented their earlier work on diabetes. Gerty Cori earned her M.D. at the German University of Prague in 1920 and soon thereafter emigrated to the United States. She worked as a professor in biochemistry at Washington University of St. Louis, Missouri.

Rosalyn Sussman Yalow (b. 1921) (nationality: American) won the prize in 1977 at age 56 for application of radioactive isotopes to study physiological systems. She worked for many years with a colleague, Solomon Berson, and they developed a new analytic technique—radioimmunoassay—which could diagnose conditions caused by hormonal fluctuations. Her early work centered on peptide hormones. In 1977, the prize in Physiology and Medicine was split, with one-half of the monetary award going to Yalow and one-half shared by Roger Guillemen and Andrew Schally for their work related to production of peptide hormones. Yalow earned her Ph.D. in nuclear physics in 1945 at the University of Illinois and worked for many years at the Veterans Administration Hospital in New York City.

Barbara McClintock (1902–1992) (nationality: American) won the unshared prize in 1983 at age 81 for the work that she had done 35 years earlier on genetic experiments on maize. Her major achievement was proving that chromosomal exchange of genetic material produces new varieties of corn. At the time she first published her work, in the late 1940s, most biologists did not understand the significance or applicability of her research. Decades later, molecular biologists substantiated her findings of transposable genetic elements—that is, DNA can move between chromosome sites. McClintock earned her Ph.D. in biology at Cornell University, New York. From 1941 to 1985 she was a researcher at Cold Spring Harbor Laboratory under the financial support of the Carnegie Institution of Washington.

Rita Levi-Montalcini (b. 1909) (nationality: Italian/American) shared the prize in 1986 with Stanley Cohen, her student. She was 77. The prize was awarded for their work with proteins that control nervous cell growth. Her work has sig-

nificance on diseases such as cancer, Parkinson's, and Alzheimer's. She earned her medical degree in 1936 at the University of Turin, Italy, and moved to the United States in 1947. She was a professor at Washington University of St. Louis, Missouri, from 1947 to 1977.

Gertrude Belle Elion (1918–1999) (nationality: American) shared the prize in 1988 at age 70 with George Hitchings, her research partner of 40 years. They studied structural differences between normal and abnormal cells. Working alone, or with Hitchings, Elion developed 45 patented drugs for diseases, such as leukemia, malaria, and various autoimmune diseases. She also worked on antirejection drugs for kidney transplants. Elion earned a Master's degree in chemistry from New York University in 1941. From 1944 to 1983 she worked as a researcher for Wellcome Research Laboratories.

Christiane Nusslein-Volhard (b. 1942) (nationality: German) shared the prize in 1995 with Eric Wieschaus and Edward Lewis for their work on genes and embryonic development. They bred and mated mutant fruit flies and observed changes in larval or adult forms. This work aids in understanding mammalian genetics, specifically to human birth defects. Lewis began his work in the 1940s at California Institute of Technology and Nusslein-Volhard and Wieschaus collaborated at the European Molecular Biology Laboratory in Heidelberg, Germany, in the 1970s. Nusslein-Volhard works at the Max-Planck Institute for Development Biology, in Tuebingen, Germany.

There are many more women scientists from the twentieth century worthy of mention. Some are familiar to many people—for example, Jane Goodall (b. 1934), foremost expert on chimpanzee behavior, and Rachel Carson (1907–1964), marine biologist and environmentalist. Others are less familiar.

Lise Meitner (1878–1968), physicist, worked with Otto Hahn and Fritz Strassmann on nuclear fission in Germany during the 1930s. In 1938, Meitner emigrated to Sweden, where she was given lab space, but not equipment, support, or colleagues. In 1945, Hahn was awarded the Nobel Prize in Chemistry for that work, whereas Meitner was overlooked, even though it was Meitner who gave the first theoretical explanation of nuclear fission. In 1966, the collaboration of Meitner, Hahn, and Strassmann was recognized with the US Fermi Prize.

Jocelyn Bell Burnell (b. 1943). Some leading astronomers have argued that the Royal Swedish Academy of Sciences overlooked another woman's contributions to a discovery that merited the Nobel prize in physics. Burnell discovered the first four pulsars, or pulsating radio sources (later identified as rapidly rotating neutron stars). Burnell was a graduate student studying radio astronomy at Cambridge University and working with Anthony Hewish. Although Burnell shared the prestigious Michelson Award with Hewish in 1973 for the discovery of pulsars, in 1974 the Nobel Committee awarded the physics prize to Hewish (for pulsars) and Martin Ryle (for observations and inventions associated with radio astrophysics).

Chien-Shiung Wu (1912–1997) was the first woman to be awarded the Comstock Prize from the National Academy of Sciences. This prestigious prize is given every five years. Wu was a physicist who disproved a once widely held belief that identical nuclear particles act alike (conservation of parity). She was also well known for her work on beta decay of atoms. These experiments changed the way physicists thought about the basic structure of the world. Wu was born in China, but emigrated to the United States in 1936 for graduate work at the University of California at Berkley. Wu was a senior research scientist at Columbia University.

Grace Murray Hopper (1906–1992) was a mathematician who became a computer scientist. During World War II, in the US Navy, she programmed Mark I computers to be able to fire weapons. She worked on various computers trying to make computers accessible to laypeople rather than just for scientists or computer programmers. She produced a program that was the precursor to COBOL. She won numerous awards, including the first U.S. National Medal of Technology awarded to an individual.

See Also

PLAGIARISM IN SCIENCE; SCIENCE: OVERVIEW; SCIENCE: ANCIENT AND MEDIEVAL; SCIENCE: EARLY MODERN TO LATE EIGHTEENTH CENTURY; SCIENCE: FEMINIST CRITIQUES; SCIENCE: FEMINIST PHILOSOPHY; SCIENCE: NINETEENTH CENTURY; SCIENCE: TWENTIETH CENTURY

References and Further Reading

Keller, Evelyn Fox. 1993. *A feeling for the organism: Barbara McClintock.* New York: Freeman.

McGrayne, Sharon B. 1993. *Nobel prize women in science: Their lives, struggles, and momentous discoveries.* New York: Birch Lane.

Sayre, Anne. 1978. *Rosalind Franklin and DNA.* New York: W. W. Norton.

Schiebinger, Londa. 1999. *Has feminism changed science?* Cambridge, Mass.: Harvard University Press.

Sime, Ruth Levin. 1997. *Lise Meitner: A life in physics* (California Studies in the History of Science, vol. 13). Los Angeles: University of California Press.

Wennerås, C., and Wold, A. 1997. Nepotism and sexism in peer review. *Nature* 387: 341–343.

4,000 years of women in science. <http://www.astro.ua.edu/4000ws/4000ws.html>

Chinese women scientists. <http://www.friends-partners.org/~china>

African-Americans in science. <http://www.princeton.edu/~mcbrown/display/faces.html>

Women in science and engineering. <http://www.asap.unimelb.edu.au/hstm_women.htm>

Women in many fields. <http://www.distinguishedwomen.com>

Darlene S. Richardson

SCIENCE FICTION

The term "science fiction" refers to a type of speculative writing which blends romance fantasy and rational science to explore the consequences of transformations of the conditions of human existence. Its stock conventions include alien life-forms, alternate worlds, artificial intelligence, time travel, and parallel universes. It is an extremely flexible and broad genre which abuts on, and overlaps with, other types of writing. These include utopian and dystopian writing, "sword and sorcery" fantasy, vampire and Gothic fiction, cyberpunk, and some horror writing.

Although it is possible to identify science-fictional elements in many pre–twentieth-century texts—for example Mary Shelley's *Frankenstein* (1817)—science fiction did not emerge as a discrete genre until the end of the nineteenth century. Charlotte Perkins Gilman's feminist utopia *Herland* (1912) dates from this period. Science fiction quickly became a mass-market industry, supporting clubs, fanzines, comics, and cartoons, translating to film and later television media as well as books.

Like most other areas of popular culture and literature, science fiction is historically a male-dominated genre, and some of its products are sexist and misogynistic. However, women feature strongly as writers of the genre and number among some of its best-selling and most popular exponents.

These include Ursula K. Le Guin, author of science fiction classics *The Left Hand of Darkness* (1969) and *The Dispossessed* (1974), and Anne McCaffrey whose fantasy novels such as *Dragonflight* (1968) and *Dragonquest* (1971) accord women a more prominent place than is usual in mainstream fantasy fiction.

Fantasy differs from science fiction in its often nostalgic preoccupation with a mythical past and in its cast-list of dragons and demons, lords and knights. It approximates to *faery*, an archaic literary term used to designate an imaginary world, as in Spenser's *The Fairie Queene*. The British author Tanith Lee's work uses fantasy inventions such as magic to explore psychological states. In her collection of short stories *Red as Blood* (1983) she reworks fairy tales in disturbing and transgressive ways, representing Snow White as a vampire on a quest for identity and freedom.

The short story is central to science fiction writing. Foremost among contributors to the genre is the North American writer Alice Sheldon, who wrote as James Tiptree Junior. Her work displays a preoccupation with the figure of the alien and with the theme of alienation between human men and women. In her story "The Women Men Don't See" (1973), the male narrator betrays his inability to perceive women as subjects. Interestingly, Sheldon's style was praised by one critic (Silverberg, 1975) as "ineluctably masculine" and the revelation that "he" was a woman came as a surprise to many, if not to feminist, readers.

Women writers have frequently used the genre in order to explore, problematize, and redefine the construction "woman." Marion Zimmer Bradley's *The Shattered Chain* (1976) contrasts women's roles in an Amazonian community to those in a patriarchal society; Le Guin's *The Left Hand of Darkness* depicts a world of bisexual humanoids and seeks to defamiliarize culturally constructed gender differences. Mainstream science fiction by women has a tendency to challenge sexual politics in a way that its realist counterpart does not.

Feminist science fiction makes explicit the critique of gender relations. This critique is at its most radical in Joanna Russ's extraordinary novel *The Female Man* (1975), which dramatizes a lethal sex war and deconstructs the binary opposition man/woman. Other issues explored in feminist science fiction include the dangers and possibilities of new technologies, especially military and reproductive ones; environmental and ecological politics, racism, and male violence against women. Suzette Haden Elgin's *Native Tongue* (1984) explores the concept of gendered language systems, Suzy McKee Charnas's *Motherlines* (1978) explores versions of women's community, while Octavia Butler's *Dawn* (1987)

explores the politics of race and gender in a postholocaust universe.

Utopia has a central place in feminist science fiction, offering the possibility to envision new worlds in which women are no longer subordinated to men. Lesbian writers have made valuable contributions to this genre in providing positive representations of love between women, as in, for example, Sally Gearhart's *The Wanderground* (1979) and Anna Livia's *Bulldozer Rising* (1988).

Many feminist and mainstream fiction writers have on occasion used the conventions of science fiction for the freedom they afford from the constraints of realism. Examples include Angela Carter's *The Passion of New Eve* (1977), Zoë Fairbairns' *Benefits* (1979), and Margaret Atwood's *The Handmaid's Tale* (1986). The novelist Doris Lessing has drawn on and expanded the limits of the genre for the majority of her long writing career.

Historically, there is a close and dynamic relationship between feminist fiction, theory, and politics; this is especially true of feminist science fiction. For example, Marge Piercy's *Woman on the Edge of Time* (1976) was inspired by Shulamith Firestone's radical feminist text *The Dialectic of Sex* (1971), which argued for the technological liberation of women from reproductive sexuality.

Science fiction from the 1990s makes use of the figure of the cyborg—half-human, half-machine. The term has entered feminist theoretical discourse in the work of Donna Haraway (1985) and others to describe the character of feminism in a postmodern era: multiple, hybrid, anti-essentialist, promoting process and coalition, and eschewing a belief in organic wholes and finished utopias. Cyborg feminism substitutes an unorthodox heteroglossia for the dream of a common language. As examples of feminist writing that inscribe "cyborg" identities, Haraway cites *Zami* (1983), the "biomythography" of Audre Lorde, and Cherrie Moraga's Chicana poetics in *Loving in the War Years* (1983).

In 1971 Firestone lamented the absence of a female utopian literary tradition. Following the rediscovery by feminists of early women utopianists (such as Christine de Pisan, whose *City of Ladies*, 1404, may be the first modern utopia of any kind), and the upsurge in utopian and other science fiction writing by women writers, such a literature now exists, occupying an important position in the canons of both mainstream and women's writing.

See Also

ECOFEMINISM; FAIRY TALES; LESBIAN WRITING: OVERVIEW; POPULAR CULTURE; POSTMODERNISM AND DEVELOPMENT; RACISM AND XENOPHOBIA; SHORT STORY

References and Further Reading

Armitt, Lucie. 1991. *Where no man had gone before: Women and science fiction.* London: Routledge.

Bammer, Angelika. 1991. *Partial visions: Feminism and utopianism in the 1970s.* New York and London: Routledge.

Donaworth, Jane. 1997. *Frankenstein's daughters: Women writing science fiction.* Syracuse, N.Y.: Syracuse University Press.

Haraway, Donna. 1985. A manifesto for cyborgs: Science, technology, and socialist feminism in the 1980s. *Socialist Review* 80. Reprinted in *Feminism/postmodernism* (1990), Linda J. Nicholson, ed. New York and London: Routledge.

Russ, Joanna. 1995. *To write like a woman: Essays in feminism and science fiction.* Indianapolis: Indiana University Press.

Silverberg, Robert. 1975. Who is Tiptree, what is he? In *Warm worlds and otherwise:* Introduction. New York: Ballantine.

Sonya Andermahr

SCIENTIFIC ETHICS

See ETHICS: SCIENTIFIC.

SCIENTIFIC SEXISM AND RACISM

Modern Western science has played an important role in promoting sexist and racist ideas, especially in advancing biological determinist theories about the inferiority of women; of racial, ethnic, religious, and cultural minorities; and of non-Western peoples. Scientific sexism is the practice of science in ways that contribute to women's oppression. Historically, three facets of scientific sexism have included: defining science and controlling access to it in ways that exclude or discourage women; developing research agendas and scientific theory that justified women's exclusion from or secondary status in education, employment, politics, religious authority, or other positions of power outside the family; and medical experimentation on women without informed consent.

Scientific racism is the use of science to promote racist ideas and practices, especially hierarchical schemes of racial classification that support notions about racial superiority or inferiority of particular social groups. Historically, and especially in the nineteenth and twentieth centuries, influential scientists pursued research designed to demonstrate or explain a purported racial superiority of Europeans/Euro-Americans relative to peoples of color in the West and non-Western peoples. Despite extensive scientific evidence to the contrary, scientific racism continues to take the form of research that presumes the validity of race as a biological category. Scientific racism has resulted in definitions of science and control of access to science that have excluded or marginalized men and women of color. Scientific racism has also provided authoritative support for social practices such as slavery, racial segregation, genocidal policies toward indigenous peoples, the denial of educational and employment opportunities for people of color; and the maldistribution of the benefits of science and medicine to the detriment of non-European peoples and societies.

Scientific sexism and racism result from the fact that science is a historically and culturally produced enterprise. Despite its self-representation as a value-neutral, universal form of knowledge, sociopolitical interests and values have dramatically shaped scientific questions and interpretations, decisions about which social groups become scientists, and fundamental assumptions of the "scientific method." Until near the end of the twentieth century Western science had been practiced predominantly by Euro-American men who controlled access to education, employment, funding, publication, and the reward structure of science. As late as 1988, for example, only one-seventh of employed scientists and engineers in the United States were Euro-American women, Native Americans, African Americans or Hispanics, while these groups account for two-thirds of the population.

Modern Western science emerged during a historical period in which questions about human variation and social inequality were hotly contested political issues and during the height of Western colonial and imperialist expansion. In the nineteenth century, as the abolitionist and women's rights movements gained momentum, respected scholars produced science that justified slavery, the conquest of indigenous peoples throughout the world, the denial of suffrage and education to women and racial and ethnic minorities, and anti-immigrant prejudice and social policies. In the wake of postcolonial and women's movements and movements of people of color in the second half of the twentieth century, scientific theories that emphasized genetic explanations for social inequality, such as sociobiology, attracted considerable interest and funding. In this regard science has made a significant contribution to the backlash that has accompanied the gains made by progressive social movements globally.

During the twentieth century Western science was often preoccupied with the exploration of anatomical, hormonal, genetic, and molecular differences among "races" and between men and women. Despite increasingly sophisticated scientific tools and changes in the emphasis of research (ranging from research on skull volume and brain size to intelligence, hormones, "reproductive success," and, recently, molecular biology and brain structure), a dominant strain in Western scientific studies of human variation has been one that rationalized the unequal distribution of power and resources between men and women and among racial and ethnic groups. However, there have always been scientific voices that contested overt and tacit forms of scientific sexism and racism, sometimes from those men of color or women who managed to break into the science establishment, but also from influential Euro-American male scientists and scientists outside the West.

At the heart of scientific racism and sexism is an entrenched biological determinism that asserts that complex traits such as intelligence, aggression, nurturance, and achievement and complex phenomena such as race, gender and sexuality are genetically determined. Biological determinist theories often ignore the multiple social, economic, and political forces that shape human variation. A compelling example is that most scientists acknowledge that the racial classifications generally used by scientists, politicians, and the general public have no genetic basis. Despite the lived reality of racism and the salience of racial identity in many societies, so-called racial differences are not scientifically explainable in terms of biology or genetics.

In the late twentieth century science was being closely scrutinized by feminist researchers, postcolonial scholars, and some self-reflexive natural, physical, and social scientists including Lee Baker, Michael Blakey, Susantha Goonatilake, Stephan Jay Gould, Sandra Harding, Donna Haraway, Evelyn Hammonds, Ruth Hubbard, Evelyn Fox Keller, Richard Lewontin, Joseph Needham, Vandana Shiva, Sharon Traweek, and Nancy Tuana. These scholars and others are unmasking scientific sexism and racism by examining who has been privileged to "do" science, how science has inscribed dominant societal values, and how the relative restriction of scientific education and practice to Western Euro-American men has affected what science looks like and how it is done (especially the relationship between the masculinization of science and its reverence for detachment, objectivity, and rationality). While some critics reserve the terms *scientific sexism* and *racism* for the most overtly political aspects of science (for example, Nazi science, eugenics, sterilization abuse, and medical experimentation on groups with limited political power), the new critical attention to science has generated a better understanding of how sexism and racism have structured core assumptions and practices of modern Western science.

See Also

BIOLOGICAL DETERMINISM; EUGENICS; EXPERIMENTS ON WOMEN; GENOCIDE; POST-COLONIALISM: THEORY AND CRITICISM; RACE; RACISM AND XENOPHOBIA; SCIENCE: FEMINIST PHILOSOPHY; SEXISM; SLAVERY

References and Further Readings

Baker, Lee D. 1998. *From savage to negro: Anthropology and the construction of race, 1896–1954.* Berkeley: University of California Press.

Blakey, Michael L. 1999. Scientific racism and the biological concept of race. *Literature and Psychology* (Spring–Summer): 29.

Gould, Stephan Jay. 1981. *The mismeasure of man.* New York: Norton.

Harding, Sandra. 1993. *The "racial" economy of science: Toward a democratic future.* Bloomington: Indiana University Press.

Hubbard, Ruth. 1995. *Profitable promises: Essays on women, science and health.* Monroe, Me.: Common Courage.

Sandra Morgen

SCULPTURE

See FINE ARTS: SCULPTURE AND INSTALLATION.

SECOND-WAVE FEMINISM

See FEMINISM: SECOND-WAVE.

SECTS AND CULTS

Women participate at all levels in religious groups called sects or cults. Because the words *cult* in English and *sect* in Romance languages have taken on pejorative connotations, the term New Religious Movement (NRM) is used to include unconventional or alternative religions. NRMs vary widely in their characteristics, as do women's roles and participation in them.

NRMs often provide scope for women's religious leadership not available in mainstream, highly institutionalized religions. In patriarchal cultures, a religious group founded by a woman with charisma (acknowledged access to revelation) typically will be small and marginal to the dominant culture. Examples of religions focused on the message of a woman are the Shakers (Mother Ann Lee), the Theosophical Society (Helena P. Blavatsky), and the Church of Christ, Scientist (Mary Baker Eddy). In patriarchal cultures, women who found religious groups often rely on men to create institutions and to lead them. Religions based on a woman's religious vision do not necessarily institutionalize women's religious leadership. Charisma enables a woman to carve out for herself a small sphere of relative freedom, as when Pentecostal women report that they are called by God to itinerant preaching or to pastor churches, but the charismatic woman typically does not question patriarchal gender roles.

Alternative religions on the margins of society sometimes provide arenas for experiments in women's religious leadership and for innovations in theology and gender roles. Some of the unconventional religions have been pioneers in conceptualizing the divine as female or neuter, and in their attempts to establish equality of women and men.

Unconventional religions provide space for social experiments in gender roles and sexual relations, but some women join patriarchal new religions, such as the International Society for Krishna Consciousness and the Unification Church, in part because they find security and meaning in traditional gender roles and family relationships. Sexual experimentation in NRMs can involve polygamy, as with the early Mormons and the Branch Davidians, or celibacy and attempted erasure of sexual characteristics, as with Heaven's Gate. Some other NRMs promote an ethic of "free love," as in the Rajneesh and Raelian movements.

Feminist wicca (part of the broad neopagan movement) is important for its innovativeness in worshiping Goddess(es), promoting equality or female dominance in women's leadership, and creating woman-affirming rituals emphasizing the immanence of divinity and the value of female embodiedness. These themes are also found in Jewish and Christian feminist spirituality. A broad feminist spirituality movement cuts across a number of religious traditions.

People in unconventional religions manifest the same range of good and bad behaviors as people in mainstream religions. Thus, women in NRMs may exercise leadership, creativity, and healing power. Women leaders of NRMs have been known to commit crimes and to conspire to hurt others, and women followers have been known to be abused by male leaders and to submit themselves to exploitive leaders.

See Also

CHRISTIANITY: STATUS OF WOMEN IN THE CHURCH; GODDESS; RELIGION: OVERVIEW; SHAKERS; SPIRITUALITY: OVERVIEW; SPIRITUALITY: SEXUALITY; THEOLOGIES: FEMINIST; WICCA; WITCHES: ASIA; WITCHES: WESTERN WORLD

References and Further Reading

Palmer, Susan Jean. 1994. *Moon sisters, Krishna mothers, Rajneesh lovers: Women's roles in new religions.* Syracuse, N.Y.: Syracuse University Press.

Wessinger, Catherine (ed.). 1993. *Women's leadership in marginal religions: Explorations outside the mainstream.* Urbana: University of Illinois Press.

Catherine Wessinger

SEGREGATION

See APARTHEID, SEGREGATION, AND GHETTOIZATION.

SETTLER SOCIETIES

"Settler societies" are those in which European migrants have settled, where their descendants have remained politically dominant over indigenous peoples, and where a heterogeneous social structure has developed in class, ethnic, and racial terms. Settler colonization differs from a more common form of colonialism, in which the appropriation of land, natural resources, and labor involved indirect control by colonial powers through a "thin white line" of primarily male administrators, merchants, soldiers, and missionaries. In settler societies, colonization involves the establishment of a much larger European settler population of both sexes. The history of many of these societies is marked by an ambivalent relationship with the European colonial "sponsors," involving dependency and considerable political and economic autonomy. Settler societies also tend to have higher material standards and liberal democratic states in comparison to conventional colonies.

The legal systems and constitutions of settler societies privilege the dominant ethnic/racial populations at the expense of those groups that did or do not conform in racial, ethnic, and class terms to the idealized image of legitimate settlers or citizens. Typically, the relative prosperity of settler societies has occurred through means of exclusion and exploitation of both indigenous and "alien" peoples within; this has been exercised through a variety of coercive, ideological, legal, administrative, and cooptative mechanisms. Examples include the reserve and pass systems of control over indigenous peoples in South Africa, Canada, and Australia, and the "Natal formula" used to restrict the entry of migrant people of color throughout the British colonies of settlement.

Prior to contact with European settlers, precolonial societies manifested a wide variation in gender-based power relations and gendered rules of inheritance, division of labor, and governance. These ranged from the matrilineal and matrifocal Huron societies of North America to the patrilineal and patrifocal Shona and Ndebele societies of southern Africa. The impact of colonization on gender relations and subordination of indigenous women is most striking in societies organized on a relatively egalitarian basis, in which relations between the sexes were based on the reciprocal exchange of goods and services (Etienne and Leacock, 1980: 9). Both the autonomy and influence of indigenous women were frequently undermined by the almost exclusive access of men to a money economy via wage labor, while women remained the custodians of traditional economies. Missionaries and their wives were also responsible for imposing Christian European sexual, conjugal, and nuclear familial norms through religious indoctrination and the teaching of European homemaking skills and values. The arrival of European women reinforced class and racial distinctions, in part because of the emergence of new sanctions against intermarriage between indigenous women and European men (Van Kirk, 1983; but see Jolly, 1993: 109).

For their part, settler women in the early phases of colonialization were burdened not only with involvement in various forms of agrarian and household production, the arduousness and specific forms of which varied by class, but also with the breeding and ideological tasks of reproducing "the nation." The racial and ethnic diversity of female migrants to settler societies differentiated the experiences of those women who were part of the dominant racial/ethnic group from those who were viewed through the prism of Eurocentric racialized and gendered discourses as inherently incapable of being assimilated to the ideal model of (white) settlers.

The outcome of paternalistic "native" policies and restrictive immigration and citizenship laws has been the disintegration of indigenous and minority families, and the imposition of generations of hardships on indigenous minority communities. Within labor markets stratified by gender, women have become further segmented by race, ethnicity, language, and citizenship statuses. At the end of the twentieth century, minority and indigenous women are overrepresented in occupational enclaves that are low-paying, insecure, hazardous, and unprotected by labor legislation or strong unions. Asymmetrical power and interdependence between racially/ethnically dominant and minority women are also common features of domestic service within private households, a growing occupational niche globally for minority and migrant women.

Women's politics in settler societies have inevitably reflected the power relations, schisms, and conflicts existing between and among ethnically dominant, indigenous, and migrant communities. Historically, the advancement of racially/ethnically dominant women was predicated on assumptions of the inferiority and backwardness of indigenous and minority women. Increasingly at the end of the twentieth century and the beginning of the twenty-first, indigenous peoples are engaging in struggles to regain control of their cultures, identities, territories, and resources through strategies ranging from armed struggle to litigation and constitutional battles. The varied outcomes have included continuous warfare, negotiated land claims and self-government, and renewed or new peace treaties or settlements (for example, the 1840 Treaty of Waitangi signed by Maori chiefs and British colonists in New Zealand/ Aeotearoa; the new peace settlement in Israel/Palestine; and the end to apartheid in South Africa). For their part, subordinated minority groups have sought compensation for historical injustices, resulting in policies offering usually symbolic forms of recognition, such as affirmative action and multiculturalism.

In the context of these (inter)national and interethnic politics, indigenous and minority women perceive their own oppression as vitally connected to the oppression of their own communities, constructed in national, racial, or ethnic terms. Notwithstanding the "masculinized" and patriarchal character of many nationalist and ethnic liberation projects, minority and indigenous women have thus been inclined to participate in political struggles that empower their particular national/ethnic communities and identities, and that distance them from or render them antagonistic to other types of feminist or women's politics. In addition, the dilemma for many indigenous women or other women involved in nationalist (or antiracist) movements is speaking to feminist issues in a context in which feminist ideology has been defined as foreign, exclusionary, or oppressive. Nonetheless, women's and feminist politics have also reflected the particular forms of racial/ethnic heterogeneity characteristic of settler societies in more beneficial ways. Thus, many feminists are increasingly lending support to the most vulnerable groups of women by taking up issues hitherto regarded as irrelevant to feminism—such as racism, nationalism, land claims, and self-government—or broadening their approach to issues—such as reproduction and violence—to take into account the diversity of women's experiences.

See Also

COLONIALISM AND POST-COLONIALISM; DEMOGRAPHICS; ETHNICITY; ETHNOCENTRISM; MIGRATION

References and Further Reading

Devereux, Cecily. 1999. New woman, new world: maternal feminism and the new imperialism in the white settler colonies. *Women's Studies International Forum* 22(2).

Etienne, Mona, and Eleanor Leacock. 1980. *Women and colonization: Anthropological perspectives.* New York: Praeger.

Jolly, Margaret. 1993. Colonizing women: the maternal body and empire. In Sneja Gunew and Anna Yeatman, eds., *Feminism and the politics of difference.* Sydney: Allen and Unwin.

McClintock, Anne. 1995. *Imperial leather: Race, gender, and sexuality in the colonial context.* London: Macmillan.

Stasiulis, Daiva K. 1999. Relational positionalities of nationalisms, racisms, and feminisms. In Caren Kaplan, Norma Alarcón, and Minoo Moallem, eds., *Between woman and nation: Nationalisms, transnational feminisms, and the state.* Durham, N.C., and London: Duke University Press.

Stasiulis, Daiva, and Nira Yuval-Davis, eds. 1995. *Unsettling settler societies: Articulations of gender, race, ethnicity and class.* London: Sage.

Van Kirk, Sylvia. 1983. *Many tender ties: Women in fur trade society, 1670–1870.* 2nd ed. Winnipeg: Watson and Dwyer.

Daiva Stasiulis

SEX: Belief and Customs

Sex is defined as the sum of those differences in the structure and function of the reproductive organs on the basis of which human beings are distinguished as male and female. An unwritten code of regulations, tradition is the transmission of beliefs, rules, customs and rituals by word of mouth, and has, nonetheless, a regulating power that is often stronger than written law. Regulated, reinterpreted and construed by traditions, sex-related practices and beliefs are particularly tenacious.

Sex and Gender

Codes regarding "gender acceptable" attitudes and behaviors, emerging from sex differences, are part of every tradition. Nowhere is what is considered masculine alike to what is considered feminine. Feminist researchers and activists have insisted incisively that these differences have led to a dominion over women. Most traditions build a normativity concerning sex and sexuality where gender is the basic divide. In the historical societies of the West, this normativity is built around a hierarchical model in which males overpower females.

There is a wide variety in the customs, categories and beliefs, however, that relate to sex.

Sex and Pleasure

Most premodern cultures had a sense of the joyful, transitory, unique sense of being here and profoundly enjoying this embodiment. The Aztec called that perception *tlalticpacayotl*. For them sensuous joy was a gift from the Lord to cope with the otherwise painful life on earth. In this tradition, sex was embodied in the Divine. Tlazolteotl—Goddess from the Huastec region—as well as Xochiquetzal were both incarnations and instigators of bodily pleasures. Sexual normativity never included total suppression of erotic satisfaction as an ideal.

Sex-Related Rituals

In most archaic societies, fertility cults made women and women's reproductive capacity central in rituals. For instance, up until 621 B.C., a cult of Asherah (considered the wife of Yahwe) was celebrated in the Jerusalem Temple. The fertility rituals that surrounded her cult included homosexual practices and what has been called sacred prostitution. In Polynesia, although restrictions were placed on sexual behavior, public intercourse was part of religious festivals. Premarital pregnancy only enhanced a girl's attractiveness and sexual activity was strongly encouraged from puberty on. In Mesoamerica, pleasure, sensuousness, and intercourse were sometimes included as sacred rituals in temples. Although normativity regulates these sexual activities, it allows for an enhancement of the transcendent nature of orgasm.

Sexual Identity

Genitals do not always correspond univocally to gender erotic and social roles. Several traditions accept fluidity in sexual identity. Among some Native Americans, cross-gender behavior was accepted and sometimes encouraged. *Berdache* practices allowed a male to live and act as a woman and even to be accepted as a marital partner by a man. In some practices from Brazil, among Amazon peoples, a woman can live and act as a man and can marry a woman.

Broad Differences between East and West

Premodern arrangements varied widely between West and East. In Hinduism and Buddhism, transcendence of human limitations may be achieved through sensual and erotic experiences. Hinduism celebrates sexual pleasure in its own right. *Bhoga* (sexual pleasure) is viewed as one of the two paths that lead to nirvana.

According to early Greek and Roman stoic philosophers, sexual passion distorted a man's reason. Early Christian thinkers like Tertullian and later St. Augustine (c. 300 C.E.) developed and expanded this evaluation. For the Christian West, sex has been both dangerous and disruptive.

Although Judaism did not divinize sex in orgiastic fertility cults like other Near Eastern religions, it has never endorsed permanent sexual asceticism. The Jewish tradition has consistently valued sex for the joy and pleasure of it within marriage.

The Christian Traditions

Christianity has interpreted and understood sex in a constraining way. Inheritors of Platonic dualism, they have emphazised a sexual dominion of male over female and, in general, of mind over body. Women often are identified symbolically with the body and men with the spirit. Permanent virginity is valued. In contrast, pre-Christian traditions, although often displaying a normativity of sexual practices, never considered permanent virginity as an acceptable ideal.

Female Genital Mutilation

The first reference to female genital mutilation, a blood ritual of obscure origins, appears in the writings of Herodotus, Greek historian of the fifth century B.C.E. It is practiced among many Islamic peoples of Africa, but it is known to predate Islam by at least 1,200 years. Although it is found sporadically among other Islamic populations, it cannot be considered an Islamic practice but a practice rooted in more ancient traditions. In analyzing the relationship between sex and tradition, every tradition can appear ambiguous and sometimes contradictory. Its processual, ever-changing nature due to inventiveness across historical periods is at the root of this apparent incongruency. But this characteristic also offers the promise of change if our voices are persistent and strong enough to alter unjust traditions.

See Also

ANCIENT INDIGENOUS CULTURES: WOMEN'S ROLES; GENDER STUDIES; SEXUALITY: OVERVIEW; SEXUALITY: AFRICA; SEXUALITY: HINDU CULTURE; SEXUALITY: PSYCHOLOGY OF SEXUALITY IN CROSS-CULTURAL PERSPECTIVES

References and Further Reading

Blackwood, E. 1984. Sexuality and gender in certain Native American tribes: The case of cross-gender females. *Signs* 10: 27–42.

Bullough, Vern L., and Bonnie Bullough, eds. 1994. Human sexuality: An encyclopedia. New York and London: Garland.

Eilberg Schwartz, H. 1991. People of the body: The problem of the body for the people of the book. *Journal of the History of Sexuality* 2: 1–24.

Gupta, B. 1987. *Sexual archetypes, East and West.* New York: Paragon House.

Gutierrez, R. 1991. *When Jesus came the Corn Mothers went away: Marriage, sexuality and power in New Mexico, 1500–1846.* Stanford, Calif.: Stanford University Press.

Lightfoot-Klein, H. 1989. *Prisoners of ritual: An odyssey into female genital circumcision in Africa.* New York: Haworth.

Lopez, Austin, A. 1988. *The human body and ideology: Concepts of the ancient Nahuas.* Trans. Thelma and Bernard Ortiz de Montellano. Salt Lake City: University of Utah Press.

Marcos, Sylvia. 1992. Indigenous eroticism and colonial morality in Mexico: The confession manuals of New Spain. *Numen* 39(2): 157–174.

Ranke Heineman, V. 1990. *Eunuchs for the kingdom of heaven.* New York: Doubleday.

Roscoe, W. 1991. *The Zuni man-woman.* Albuquerque: University of New Mexico Press.

Sylvia Marcos

SEX AND CULTURE

The relationship between culture and sexual behavior has been the topic of vehement debates since at least the beginning of the twentieth century. Scientists such as Krafft-Ebing and Havelock Ellis established a new field of study, called sexology. They located the study of sexual practices in the biomedical sciences and sought to discover the "essential" nature of sexual behavior (Bland and Doan, 1998). Their work is related to Freud's discussions on sexual drives. In this way they hoped to "proof" that women were naturally passive and men naturally aggressive. Another topic they concerned themselves with was the "medicalization" of homosexuality. They classified same-sex practices as an innate characteristic. Their congenital theories ranged from classifying homosexuality as a relatively harmless anomaly to a mental illness that had to be cured. Their views have been enormously influential. Sex manuals that were based on their theories were widely read. These manuals were intended to teach human beings their proper sexual behavior and the desires that should accompany these practices. Through colonial and imperialist practices, these ideas were spread all over the world, even to never-colonized countries such as Japan. They profoundly changed the wide variety of precolonial sexual practices, the meanings these practices had, and the family and kinship arrangements in which these practices were lived.

The spread of monotheistic religions such as Christianity and Islam also had a profound impact on the cultures they came to dominate. Although in both religious systems women's sexuality is explicitly recognized, it is at the same time a site of patriarchal control. In Christian regions, in particular, the nuclear family became the dominant model. The Brahmanization of Hinduism also meant a strengthening of heterosexual, patriarchal values.

The rise of constructivist theories since the end of the 1960s, and particularly the work of Weeks (1981) and Foucault (1978), has enabled the analysis of historical and cultural factors producing sexual cultures and gender regimes. Sexuality is no longer seen as the outcome of precultural drives—as the product of the body or the psyche—but also, to differing degrees, as the effect of complex discursive practices. The relationship between the body and the psyche, on the one hand, and cultural factors, on the other, is the subject of intense debates. In some approaches, the body almost disappears. Butler (1993), for instance, claims that knowledge about the body is not accessible without the means of discourse. She comes close to implying that embodiment and sexuality are the effects of cultural processes. Other theorists maintain some autonomous space for the body and the psyche, which in their turn can influence the normalizing cultural processes through which they are constructed.

The 1960s sexual revolution in Europe and the United States did not have the same liberatory effects for all people: it mainly meant a loosening of sexual restrictions for heterosexual men. Since the 1970s, feminism and the gay liberation movement have had a major impact not only on the discourses on sexuality but also on sexual practices and on the ways individuals have constructed their identities. On the one hand, the insistence on the sexual rights of women and of lesbian, gay, and transgender people has had a profound liberating effect. On the other hand, these movements also have had a regulatory effect, in which, for instance, role playing such as in butch-femme relations was denounced.

Anthropological research has pointed to the variability not only of gender regimes but also of sexual agency in diverse settings. Although in many urban centers in the South lesbian and gay groups have to counter the strong homophobia of their societies, various same-sex traditional practices have been documented that were fully institution-alized. In certain African societies, for instance, women have the possibility to marry other women, provided they pay the stipulated bride price. These female husbands become the social fathers of the offspring of their wives and profit from the labor power of the members of the compound they have established by their marriage. The Chinese antimarriage sisterhoods that flourished in Guangdong in southern China and lasted until the communist takeover afforded their members a socially recognized space to avoid heterosexual marriage. Sexual relations between the "sworn sisters" of such Golden Orchid societies occurred. In various Asian countries, there are recognized transgender positions for both male- and female-bodied persons. These include the Indonesian *banci* or *waria*. Present-day same-sex relations among women often involve role play between the partners, such as the Thai *toms* (from tomboy) and *dees* (from lady), or the Philippine *pars* and *mars*. In Japan, the female-bodied *onabe* provide entertainment to women. As with the *pars* and the *toms*, they don't see themselves as occupying the gender category "women" nor the category of lesbians. Their female partners don't identify as lesbians either.

In other cultures, as well, there exist cultural niches inhabited by transgendered persons. In Tahiti, both male- and female-bodied persons may occupy the category *mahu*. Certain North American Indian cultures recognize "two-spirit people." These persons typically adhere to the dress codes of and perform the activities assigned to the opposite gender. Their sexual partners may be either men or women but never other *mahu* or two-spirit people, as that would be considered homosexual.

This anthropological material gives rise to renewed debates on the complex relations between sexuality, sexual practice, sexual orientation and identity, gender, and culture. At the same time it provides fuel to those movements that denounce the silence about women's sexual agency and that fight for the sexual rights of women and sexual minorities.

See Also

HETEROSEXISM; LESBIANISM; SEX: BELIEFS AND CUSTOMS; SEXUAL ORIENTATION; SEXUALITY: OVERVIEW; SEXUALITY: PSYCHOLOGY OF SEXUALITY IN CROSS CULTURAL PERSPECTIVES

References and Further Reading

Blackwood, Evelyn, and Saskia E. Wieringa, eds. 1999. *Female desires, same-sex relations and transgender practices across cultures.* New York: Columbia University Press.

Bland, Lucy, and Laura Doan, eds. 1998. *Sexology in culture, labelling bodies and desires.* Cambridge, Mass.: Polity Press.

Butler, Judith. 1993. *Bodies that matter.* New York and London: Routledge.

Foucault, Michel. 1978. *The history of sexuality, volume I: An introduction.* New York: Vintage.

Lancaster, Roger N., and Micaela di Leonardo, eds. 1997. *The gender/sexuality reader: Culture, history, political economy.* New York and London: Routledge.

Weeks, Jeffrey. 1981. *Sex, politics and society: The regulation of sexuality since 1800.* Harlow: Longman House.

Saskia Wieringa

SEX EDUCATION

For the purposes of this article sex education will be defined as education aimed at children and adolescents that takes place within educational institutions, rather than more informal education that may take place in the community, through the media, or within families. Sex education is not the same as learning about sex. Learning about sex, or sexual socialization, is an inevitable and lifelong process, including both knowledge about sex and the acquisition of socially approved masculine and feminine identities and behaviors (Thomson and Scott, 1991). It is not inevitable that sex education will be provided at school; both its aims and the right of access to it are debated within many societies.

The History of Sex Education

Sex education began to appear in the school curricula of economically developed countries such as the United Kingdom and the United States at the end of the nineteenth century, with the emergence of public health as a government function. The spur to introduce sex education into the curriculum came from two sources: from members of the medical profession concerned about rising levels of sexually transmitted disease (STD) and the moral and physical health of the nation; and from early feminists concerned about the sexual exploitation of women and children (Mort, 1987). In more recent years sex education has been promoted internationally by the family planning movement and by development agencies concerned with population growth and, increasingly, the spread of HIV and AIDS. The cause of sex education continues to be championed primarily by these two groups, medics and feminists, although they often employ very different aims and methodologies. The medical agenda in sex education has traditionally stressed the health risks associated with sexual activity, such as STDs and unintended pregnancy. Feminist approaches tend to seek to develop knowledge and assertiveness skills among women to resist sexual exploitation and coercion and to maintain greater control over their personal lives and sexual health.

The Effects of Sex Education

A major international study published in 1985 (Jones et al., 1985) found that countries with developed programs of sex education and contraceptive services freely available to the young had lower levels of teenage pregnancies. They also found that these countries (such as the Netherlands, Sweden, and Denmark) were likely to have more liberal attitudes toward sexuality. The provision and political acceptability of sex education varies across and within cultures. Countries with religious or traditional societal norms have been more reluctant to include sex education in school curricula. However, growing concerns about the threat of HIV and AIDS have persuaded many governments to open public discussion in this area. International moves to address population growth, such as the Cairo World Population Conference in 1994, have also recommended sex education programs for adolescents. Yet sex education continues to be the focus of conflict in some countries—for example, the United States and, increasingly, the United Kingdom—where the religious right targets access to sex education, along with access to abortion, as a focus for activism. In the United States these groups have begun to promote chastity until marriage as an alternative to sex education, arguing that information is corrupting. The programs promoted by these groups tend to either omit information about contraception and safer sex or to stress their unreliability (Stears, 1992).

The Focus of Sex Education

Sex education is influenced by the theories of sexuality on which it is based. Within a medical or biological discourse, reproduction and disease are presented as the "facts" of sexuality, whereas, within a moral or religious discourse, marriage and parenthood are the facts. These discourses have an impact on the content and methodology of school sex education. In the past, sex education tended to take place within a medical or biological framework, teaching the facts of puberty, reproduction, and sexually transmitted disease, sometimes coupled with moral messages about the dangers of sex outside marriage. Medically oriented sex education has been criticized by feminist commentators such as Fine (1988) for educating girls against their own sexual self-interest. By failing to educate girls about their potential for sexual pleasure beyond reproduction, Fine argues, traditional sex education perpetuates the belief that sex is something that a woman gives a man and in which his needs and desires are paramount.

Traditionally sex education has focused on girls and women, equipping them both to protect their own sexual health and behavior and to influence the sexual health and behavior of boys and men. Sex education has paid scant attention to boys, whose sexuality is seen to be less amenable to advice and control (although early STD campaigns did target soldiers). It is only in recent years that sex educators have begun to recognize the importance of educating boys, finding that social norms of masculinity that assume sexual health to be women's responsibility must be addressed before male sexual health can be considered (Holland et al., 1993; Mac an Ghail, 1994). The reproductive focus of traditional sex education has neglected social aspects of sexuality, including emotions, power, and relationships, and has obscured questions of sexual pleasure and sexual identity. Education relevant to and supportive of lesbian and gay sexuality is still absent from the curricula of most countries and in some is legally proscribed (Epstein, 1994).

A Change in Focus

As concerns about adolescent sexual activity and rates of teenage pregnancy and STDs have increased, the medically oriented approach to sex education has become subject to criticism and revision. Information alone is not sufficient to influence sexual behavior. Social factors, such as peer expectations, norms of masculinity and femininity, and power dynamics in sexual relationships are coming to be recognized as of great significance in shaping young people's sexuality (Holland et al., 1992). Strategies for sex education, influenced by feminist, lesbian, and gay health movements, are increasingly acknowledging the importance of these factors both in the content of sex education and in the teaching methodologies employed. Knowledge is seen as one part of the educational project that should be balanced with opportunities to explore and debate attitudes and values and to develop communication and decision-making skills.

Methods such as peer education (where young people educate one another), role play (where pupils practice interpersonal skills), and the use of drama are not only popular with young people but are also showing themselves to be effective in influencing behavior (Kirby et al., 1994). Sex education is also beginning to take young people's opinions more seriously, asking them through research and consultation what they want to learn about and how. The usual response is that it is not more facts that they want but greater understanding of emotions, identity, relationships, and gender differences. They are also interested in talking about the double standards in sexual morality that dominate the hid-

den curriculum of the school. Feminist academics such as Lees (1993) have documented the sexual cultures of young people and the way in which young men dominate sexual language and control young women through their sexual reputations. Sex education is beginning to attempt to help young people understand the pressure they face in conforming to peer expectations (Jewitt, 1994).

The obstacles to sexual health are more complicated than access to information and services, although these are both necessary prerequisites that are still not universally available and in some countries are increasingly insecure. Yet, given the availability of such information, it continues to be social and cultural factors that prevent women from acting in their own sexual self-interest. For sex education to be effective it has to engage with these factors and to equip young people with skills and confidence. Although sex education is not the same as learning about sex, it is at its best when it engages in this process and challenges the assumptions that sex is a man's pleasure and a woman's duty.

See Also

FAMILY PLANNING; HEALTH: OVERVIEW; SAFER SEX; SEX: BELIEFS AND CUSTOMS; SEXUAL ORIENTATION; SEXUALITY: ADOLESCENT SEXUALITY

References and Further Reading

Armstrong, Ewan, and Peter Gordon. 1992. *Sexualities: An advanced training resource.* London: Family Planning Association.

Blake, S., and J. Laxton. 1998. *Strides: A practical guide to sex and relationships education with young men.* London: Family Planning Association.

Clarity Collective. 1983. *Taught not caught: Strategies for sex education.* Cambridge, UK: Learning Development Aids.

Epstein, Debbie. 1994. *Challenging lesbian and gay inequalities in education.* Buckingham, UK: Open University Press.

Epstein, D., and R. Johnson. 1998. *Schooling sexualities.* Buckingham: Open University Press.

Fine, M. 1988. Sexuality, schooling and adolescent females: The missing discourse of desire. *Harvard Educational Review* 58(1): 29–53.

Holland, Janet, Caroline Ramazanoglo, Sue Sharpe, and Rachel Thomson. 1998. *The male in the head: young people, heterosexuality and power.* London: Tufnell.

———. 1992. Pleasure, pressure and power: Some contradictions of gendered sexuality. *Sociological Review* 40(4): 645–74.

———. 1993. *Wimp or gladiator: Contradictions in acquiring masculine sexuality.* London: Tufnell.

Jewitt, Cathy. 1994. *Exploring health sexuality: A guide to sex education in a youth setting.* London: Family Planning Association.

Jones, Elise F., Jacqueline Darroch Forrest, Noreen Goldman, Stanley K. Henshaw, Richard Lincoln, Jeannie I. Rosoff, Charles F. Westoff, and Deirdre Wulf. 1985. Teenage pregnancy in developed countries: Determinants and policy implications. *Family Planning Perspectives* 17(2): 53–56.

Kirby, Douglas, et al. 1994. School-based programs to reduce sexual risk behaviors: A review of effectiveness. *Public Health Reports* 109(3): 339–60.

Lees, Sue. 1993. *Sugar and spice: Sexuality and adolescent girls.* London: Penguin.

Liggins, Sally, Annemarie Wille, Shaun Hawthorne, and Leigh Rampton. 1994. *Affirming diversity: An educational resource on gay, lesbian and bisexual orientations.* Auckland, New Zealand: Family Planning Association.

Mac an Ghail, Mairtin. 1994. *The making of men: Masculinities, sexualities and schooling.* Buckingham, U.K.: Open University Press.

Mort, Frank. 1987. *Dangerous sexuality: Medico-moral politics in England since 1830.* London: Routledge and Kegan Paul.

Stears, J. T., ed. 1992. *Sexuality and the curriculum: The politics and practices of sexuality education.* New York: Teachers' College Press.

Thomson, Rachel, and Sue Scott. 1991. *Learning about sex: Young women and the social construction of sexuality.* London: Tufnell.

Rachel Thomson

SEX-GENDER DISTINCTION

See FEMINISM: POSTMODERN; AND GENDER.

SEX RESEARCH

See SEXOLOGY AND SEX RESEARCH.

SEX, SAFER

See SAFER SEX.

SEX SELECTION

Sex selection is a term used to describe a variety of scientific methods used at the preconception as well as the antenatal stage to beget a child of a desired sex, essentially by allowing for the rejection or elimination of a progeny of an unwanted sex. The most popular among tests used for sex selection are amniocentesis, chorion-villi-biopsy, and sex preselection aided by fetoscopy, needling, or sonography. Although the medical purpose of these tests is to identify genetic disorder in the fetus, in several cultures such tests are used especially to identify the existence of a female fetus. Owing to a legacy of preference for sons and neglect of daughters, these tests have gained in popularity in the late twentieth century among Asian communities, especially among the Indians, the Chinese, and the Koreans, as a means of femicide.

The most devastating influence of these tests has been experienced in India, where women have been a "declining sex" from the beginning of the twentieth century. In 1901, there were 972 women per 1,000 men in India; in the 1991 census of India, however, there were only 929 women per 1,000 men. Similar trends are found in China, Taiwan, Korea, and Hong Kong. This alarming phenomenon has spurred women's rights activists to vigorously challenge the demographic, sociocultural, medico-legal, and philosophical aspects of these tests.

Scientists, doctors, researchers, and academics in Europe, the United States, Australia, and South Asia belonging to the Feminist International Network for Resistance to Reproductive and Genetic Engineering (FINRRAGE) pursued the debate in their respective professional bodies, but organized expression in terms of campaign-building against physicians' abuse of advanced scientific techniques of sex determination (SD) and sex preselection (SP) was found by women's and health groups only in Korea and India. They highlighted the commercial interest of medical professionals, who capitalized on patriarchal prejudice against women and girls in the society. After a decade-long battle the governments of India and Korea each passed legislation prohibiting the use of sex selection tests for selective abortion of female fetuses. In the United Kingdom, the government appointed a medical ethics committee to regularize sex selection tests in the medical market flourishing under the attractive name of the "Gender Centre."

Doctors providing these services have protested against the state taking any action to regulate their activities. They justify their business using a conventional economics argument based on the law of supply and demand. They refuse to see any long-term connection between their services and gender discrimination. Feminists have taken strong objection to any suggestion that a laissez-faire philosophy is acceptable in the medical market, where tests are conducted on women's bodies.

The population-control lobbies in India and China have found in the sex selection tests a twofold means to achieve their goal for population stabilization: (1) If couples manage to get a child of their desired sex, they will not procreate further. The sex-selection tests are therefore considered by the Chinese government to be a useful measure with which to attain their target of the one-child family. (2) If couples choose to abort female fetuses, there will be fewer women, and if the number of women decreases, there will be less procreation. Such arguments were used in Nazi Germany to justify forced sterilization of the Jews. Feminists and human-rights organizations have decried such a fatalistic approach, which victimizes the victim, and have demanded a paradigmatic shift in the thinking of the scientific and medical fraternity, the intellectual elite enamored of the ideology of Social Darwinism, and social policy makers.

Development of women that ensures the basic right to survive to the mass of Asian women spread all over the globe, in terms of education, employment, and health, is the only solution for the enhancement of women's sense of self-esteem and self-worth. It will provide an autonomous space in which women can decide whether or not to produce children, and if so, the number of children and the interval between births.

See Also

ABORTION; EUGENICS; EXPERIMENTS ON WOMEN; FAMILY PLANNING; FEMICIDE; GENDER CONSTRUCTIONS IN THE FAMILY; GENOCIDE; INFANTICIDE; MEDICAL CONTROL OF WOMEN; PATRIARCHY: FEMINIST THEORY; REPRODUCTIVE RIGHTS

References and Further Reading

Bin Park Chai and Cho Nam-Hoon. 1995. Consequences of son preference in a low-fertility society: Imbalance of the sex ratio at birth in Korea. *Population and Development Review* 21(1: March): 59–84.

Chhachhi, Amrita, and C. Satyamala. 1983. Sex-determination tests: A technology which will eliminate women. *Medico Friends Circle Bulletin*, no. 95: 3–5.

Holmes, Helen, and Betty Hoskins. 1984. Pre-natal and pre-conception sex-choice technologies: A path to femicide. Paper presented at the International Interdisciplinary Congress on Women, the Netherlands.

Jesani, Amar. 1988. Banning sex-determination tests: Scope and limits of Maharashtra legislation. *Radical Journal of Health* 2(4): 88–90, 98.

Kulkarni, Sanjeev. 1986. *Pre-natal SD tests and female foeticide in Bombay City: A study.* Bombay: Foundation for Research in Community Health.

Patel, Vibhuti. 1984. Amniocentesis: Misuse of modern technology. *Socialist Health Review* 1(2): 69–71.

Ravindra, R. P. 1986. *The scarcer half: A report on amniocentesis and other SD techniques, SP techniques and new reproductive technologies.* Bombay: Centre for Education and Development.

Vibhuti Patel

SEX WORK

Sex work is labor performed for remuneration that involves some kind of performance of sexuality. The legal definition is usually sex exchanged for money or other consideration, but without any specific definition of sex, and the term *other consideration* could mean anything of value, including food or a place to sleep. Sex work includes prostitution, the provision of direct sexual services to multiple partners, in succession, including vaginal and anal intercourse, fellatio and cunnilingus, and manual stimulation of the client. It also includes posing in various stages of dress or undress for still pictures or live for a client who pays for the pose, erotic dancing, talking dirty, and performing sexual acts before a movie or video camera. It can involve various forms of domination and submission, with or without bondage, and with or without any direct genital contact. Sex workers and clients can contact each other on the street, in bars, in hotels, in brothels, on front porches or patios, in massage parlors, over the phone as a result of ads in a newspaper or magazine, and over the Internet. The sexual labor can take place in cars, alleyways, doorways and hallways, massage parlors or spas, brothels, rooming houses, apartments, hotel rooms, private booths of exotic dance theaters, on a stage, before a camera, or over the phone. Sex workers can work independently or for managers. And whether they are independent or their work is controlled by someone else, the work may be completely voluntary, ambivalent, or forced.

If these descriptions make sex work sound easy to recognize, it is important to understand that the use of sex to earn a living, or to survive, can be much more ambiguous. For example, there are people—women, men, transgendered persons—who perform sex work invisibly to outsiders, and other people who observers think are performing sex work but who do not, themselves, define it as such. To some extent, it has to do with the use of euphemisms—such as massage, escort, hospitality, entertainment—to mask prostitution from the police, but it can also be the result of the participants establishing a boundary between what they are doing and prostitution. An example would be a woman who lives in the vicinity of a truck stop who has long-term relationships with a number of long-distance truck drivers. Each man stays with her when he is in the area, receiving emotional support, food, a place to sleep, and sex, and contributing towards her expenses. Many epidemiologists doing research identify that as "prostitution" or "sex work," but neither the woman or the men are likely to do so.

Almost everywhere, some or all aspects of sex work are illegal. The most restrictive system is in the United States, where all aspects of prostitution are illegal. The only exception is the closed brothel system in Nevada's rural counties, where approximately 300 women work legally (under tight restrictions on their movement and mandatory registration and health checks), while an estimated 150,000 to 1.5 million prostitutes work illegally nationwide. The pornography industry in the United States is tolerated without any state regulation of working conditions (for example, occupational safety and health regulations), although many cities have enacted zoning ordinances. In many countries the act of engaging in prostitution is decriminalized, but most activities required for the act to take place are illegal, including talking about it (soliciting), housing it (running or residing in a house of prostitution), or organizing or earning money from it (pimping, pandering, procuring, or promoting prostitution). Many countries bar anyone with a history of prostitution from crossing their borders, sometimes at the same time that they grant temporary work permits or artists' visas to migrants to work in bars, dance halls, and clubs with sexual entertainment.

The modern sex workers' rights movement began in the United States in 1973 when Margo St. James, a former prostitute, formed COYOTE (Call Off Your Old Tired Ethics), one of the first organizations formed by prostitutes to discuss prostitution. By the turn of the twenty-first century, the sex workers' rights movement had become international, with sex workers forming organizations in countries as different as India, Ecuador, Germany, Australia, and Senegal, with the common demands of safe working conditions, an end to police harassment, and the right to have families. Since the mid-1980s, many governments have encouraged and funded sex workers to form projects designed to reduce the incidence of HIV infection and other sexually transmitted diseases, which has made it easier for sex workers to speak out about how the laws against prostitution increase their vulnerability to disease and violence. Three states in Australia have decriminalized various aspects of prostitution and developed some occupational safety and health regulations for brothels, the Netherlands has legalized brothels and will be developing occupational safety and health regulations, and Germany is considering similar changes. However, even when countries reform the laws, they often leave

significant populations of sex workers illegal, including street-based workers and most immigrants.

A majority of people who engage in sex work, worldwide, have made a conscious decision to do so. Sometimes they don't know beforehand the conditions in which they will work, including the number of hours or clients to be seen a day, or how restricted their movements will be outside of the place of work. Nonetheless, even when they know there is a risk of abuse, many say it is worth the risk because the amount of money they can earn and use to support their families is so much greater than in other kinds of work.

As long as any aspects of prostitution are illegal, it is difficult to say where the line falls between voluntary and involuntary sex work. Even when the work is not prohibited outright, it is rarely recognized as work, and sex workers have difficulty getting the laws governing employee-management relationships enforced, or the laws against rape, physical assault, theft, and extortion. Until those laws and practices are changed so that they support those who work in the sex industry—instead of scapegoating them, giving them permanent police records, and making their work dangerous—it will be impossible to tell where the line is.

See Also

CENSORSHIP; EROTICA; HIV AND AIDS; LAW AND SEX; MISTRESS; PORNOGRAPHY AND VIOLENCE; PROSTITUTION; SEX AND CULTURE; SEX: BELIEFS AND CUSTOMS; SEXUAL SLAVERY; SEXUAL VIOLENCE

References and Further Reading

Alexander, Priscilla. 1995. Sex workers fight against AIDS: An international perspective. In Beth E. Schneider and Nancy Stoller, eds., *Women resisting AIDS: Strategies of empowerment.* Philadelphia: Temple University Press.

———. 1996. Bathhouses and brothels: Symbolic sites in discourse and practice. In Ephen Glenn Colter, Wayne Hoffman, Eva Pendleton, Alison Redick, and David Serlin, eds., *Policing public sex.* Boston: South End.

———. 1997. Sex Industry. In Jeanne Mager Stellman, ed., *Encyclopedia of occupational health and safety.* Geneva: International Labour Office.

———. 1997. Making a living: Women who go out. In E. Maxine Ankrah and Lynel Long, eds., *Women's experiences with AIDS.* New York: Columbia University Press.

———. 1998. Sex work and health: A question of safety in the workplace. *Journal of American Medical Women's Association* 53(2): 77–82.

Delacoste, Frederique, and Priscilla Alexander, eds. 1998. *Sex work: Writings by women in the sex industry.* San Francisco: Cleis (originally published 1987).

Elias, James E., Vern L. Bullough, Veronica Elias, and Gwen Brewer, eds. 1998. *Prostitution: On whores, hustlers, and johns.* New York: Prometheus.

Kempadoo, Kamala, and Jo Doezema, eds. 1998. *Global sex workers: Rights, resistance, and redefinition.* London: Routledge.

Langley, Erika. 1997. *The lusty lady: Photographs and texts.* Zurich: Scalo.

McKeganey, Neil, and Marina Barnard. 1996. *Working the streets: Sex workers and their clients.* London: Open University Press.

Nagle, Jill, ed. 1997. *Whores and other feminists.* New York: Routledge.

Overs, Cheryl, and Paulo Longo. 1997. *Making sex work safe.* London: Network of Sex Work Projects and AHRTAG.

Perkins, Roberta. 1991. *Working girls: Prostitutes, their life and social control.* Canberra: Australian Institute of Criminology.

Pheterson, Gail, ed. 1989. *A vindication of the rights of whores.* Seattle: Seal Press. Translations: *Nosotros, Las Putas.* Madrid: Talasa Ediciones, 1992.

———. 1996. *The prostitution prism.* Amsterdam: University of Amsterdam Press.

Roberts, Nickie. 1992. *Whores in history: Prostitution in western society.* London: Harper Collins.

Scambler, Graham, and Annette Scambler, eds. 1997. *Rethinking prostitution: Purchasing sex in the 1990s.* London: Routledge

Sleightholme, Carolyn, and Indrani Sinha. 1996. *Guilty without trial: Women in the sex trade in Calcutta.* Calcutta: Stree. New Brunswick, N.J.: Rutgers University Press.

Truong, Thanh-Dam. 1990. *Sex, money and morality: Prostitution and tourism in South-east Asia.* London: Zed.

Vanwesenbeeck, Ine. 1994. *Prostitutes' well-being and risk.* Amsterdam: VU University Press.

Weitzer, Ronald, ed. 1999. *Sex for sale: Prostitution, pornography, and the sex industry.* New York: Routledge.

White, Luise. 1990. *The comforts of home: Prostitution in colonial Nairobi.* Chicago: The University of Chicago Press.

Priscilla Alexander

SEXISM

Sexism signifies both a worldview or perspective that sees social life in stereotypically binary and gendered ways. It also refers to behavior that treats males and females in these stereotypical ways. There is no invariable relationship between sexist attitudes and sexist behavior, for people can hold sexist attitudes yet not necessarily behave in sexist ways, and people with nonsexist or even antisexist worldviews can engage in starkly sexist behavior. Sexism is not an exclusively male preserve, although the "institutional sexism" widely embedded in organizational practices systematically benefits males at the expense of females. Sexist conduct can range from "chivalrous" behavior toward women, through assigning different, and differently valued, characteristics and rewards on the basis of gender, to acts of extreme sexual and other forms of violence such as serial sexual murder or mass rape and murder during war. The two ends of this continuum of sexisms have been characterized (Wise and Stanley, 1985) as "the dripping tap" and the "sledgehammer," along with the argument that feminist analysis should not focus exclusively on the "sledgehammer" end, for doing so removes from analytic sight the fact that a continuum is involved and also encourages the view that sexism and sexual harassers are atypical features of social life rather than a fundamental part of society's gendered fabric, as the pervasive existence of institutional sexism indicates.

See Also

ANDROCENTRISM; SEXUAL HARASSMENT

Reference and Further Reading

Wise, Sue, and Liz Stanley. 1985. *Georgie Porgie: Sexual harassment in everyday life.* London: Pandora.

Liz Stanley
Sue Wise

SEXISM, SCIENTIFIC

See SCIENTIFIC RACISM AND SEXISM.

SEXOLOGY AND SEX RESEARCH

Although human sexuality has been a prime focus of art, literature, religion, and philosophy in every culture, the scientific (social science as well as medical science) study of human sexual experience and behavior is only about 150 years old. *Sexology* is the name given to multidisciplinary research on erotic experience, sexual conduct, and gender identity. Sexologist researchers usually work in, for example, departments of medicine, history, or psychology, using those methods and theories to examine sexual subjects. Sexologist clinicians are usually mental health specialists who treat individuals and couples with sexual problems.

Feminists have criticized sexology as a repressive political force, arguing that "sexology came into being as a mode of regulation, a means of controlling through classifying, distinguishing 'normal' sexuality from 'pathological' forms" (Scott and Jackson, 1996: 9). Because norms for sexual conduct have served to socialize and oppress women's lives, feminists are keenly interested in sexologists as expert authorities on human sexuality. How has sexology helped women? How has it interfered with women's sexual understanding, pleasure, and self-determination? How much of sex research uncritically incorporates cultural assumptions about gender and sexuality?

Not only have feminist scholars critiqued sexology, but feminist nonacademic writings on sexuality have greatly affected the content and conduct of sex research and clinical practice by exploring women's sexual lives, struggles, and desires (Irvine, 1990; McLaren, 1999).

Women's Sexual Rights

Growing out of nineteenth-century European psychiatry and biology, early sex research endorsed a double standard of morality regarding the right to erotic experience. By contrast, early feminist writers in Sweden, Britain, Germany, and the United States, such as Ellen Key, Marie Stopes, Helene Stöcker, and Margaret Sanger, promoted not only reproductive rights for women but also women's right to sexual education and pleasure.

As middle-class companionate marriage replaced the traditional patriarchal family form in the industrialized world, women's sexual rights became more widely acknowledged. These changes were instituted more as a result of political and social change than because of sex research. However, sex research surveys such as those in the United States by Alfred Kinsey in the mid–twentieth century stimulated public awareness of the range of women's sexual activity and values. By the 1960s sex research followed social change. The physiological research of William Masters and Virginia Johnson was explicitly designed to describe parallels in arousal and orgasmic capacities between men and women that would support women's entitlement to sexual pleasure and orgasm.

Political feminist writings in the 1970s by US authors such as Shere Hite, Anne Koedt, and Susan Brownmiller greatly affected sexological theory and research. They raised awareness of the prevalence and impact of rape and child sexual abuse. They diagnosed the extent and multiple social sources of women's sexual shame and inhibition. They analyzed how sexological as well as popular definitions of normal sexual response and activity were male-centered and coitus-centered, minimizing clitoral and whole-body pleasures. The new field of sex therapy was very affected by such views, and sexologists have denounced all forms of sexual abuse including female genital mutilation as interfering with women's birthright to sexual pleasure and self-determination.

Gradually, over the second half of the twentieth century, spurred first by the feminist movement and then by the AIDS crisis, social science sex research has eliminated all negativity towards Lesbian sexual preferences. Clinical and medical sex researchers have been slower to challenge prejudicial sexual norms in society.

Feminist Criticisms of Sexology

Feminists have criticized how sexology minimizes the role of social factors in shaping sexual attitudes and experiences (Tiefer, 1995). Critics have examined sexology's tendency to medicalize sexual problems, viewing them as derangements of biology or psychological development rather than the outcome of patriarchal social arrangements. The continuing strength of the medical model in sexology is shown by the current tidal wave of interest in pharmacological approaches to sexual problems, which some feminists argue will again bypass issues of power in personal life.

Conflicts among Feminists Concerning Sexology

There is no single feminist vision or methodology when it comes to sex research or clinical practice, and in fact, there have been important disagreements. One concerns the use of pornography in research and sexual treatment. Some feminists believe that exploring physiological and subjective responses using erotic stimuli empowers women; other feminists argue that pornography is degrading and harmful to women and that positive responses merely reflect eroticized domination.

Another conflict concerns research design and results analysis. Some feminists belief that qualitative methods will better allow women's own views of sexuality to emerge; other researchers argue that valid and reliable statistical methods will promote women's interests most strongly.

A third conflict concerns method and philosophy of sex-therapy methods. Some feminists argue that sex research and therapy serve to preserve conventional heterosexual relationships and phallocentric sexual scripts. Others see sex therapy as promoting egalitarianism in relationships and sexual life.

Despite their small numbers, however, feminists have had a substantial impact on sexology and sex research in Europe, North America, and the United Kingdom. Sex research in other parts of the world is thus far much more limited and often dominated by physicians, excluding feminist models and insights about power in ideology and personal relations.

See Also

SEX AND CULTURE; SEX EDUCATION

References and Further Readings

Bland, Lucy, and Laura Doan, eds. *Sexology in culture: Labelling bodies and desires.* Chicago: University of Chicago Press.

Daniluk, Judith C. 1998. *Women's sexuality across the life span.* New York: Guilford.

Irvine, Janice. 1990. *Disorders of desire: Sex and gender in modern American sexology.* Philadelphia, Penn.: Temple University Press.

McCormick, Naomi B. 1994. Feminism and sexology. In Vern L. Bullough and Bonnie Bullough, eds., *Human sexuality: An encyclopedia.* New York: Garland.

———. 1994. *Sexual salvation: Affirming women's sexual rights and pleasures.* Westport, Conn.: Praeger.

McLaren, Angus. 1999. *Twentieth-century sexuality: A history.* Oxford: Blackwell.

Scott, Sue, and Stevi Jackson. 1996. Sexual skirmishes and feminist factions: Twenty-five years of debate on women and sexuality. In Stevi Jackson and Sue Scott, eds., *Feminism and sexuality: A reader,* 1–31. New York: Columbia University Press.

Tiefer, Leonore. 1995. *Sex is not a natural Act and other essays.* Boulder, Colo.: Westview.

Leonore Tiefer

SEXUAL DIFFERENCE

Because of the biological differences between the sexes, sexual difference is often envisioned as a universal and inherently "natural" category that distinguishes men and women. For instance, hormonal factors or women's childbearing capacity are sometimes invoked as determinants of their identity and as evidence of an "essential femaleness." Biological laws are then used to explain why women are less aggressive, make better parents and homemakers, or why they are fit for different occupations than men. Many believe that this way of defining human nature is fundamental to patriarchal societies that have a vested interest in keeping the original sexual division of labor and the traditional norms of femininity and masculinity intact. The appeal to a fixed natural order not only constrains women to specific roles and limits their range of alternatives but, by fixing the meaning of femininity, also forecloses the possibility of change.

Feminist responses to the male-centered organization of social life vary according to the importance they assign to

biological determination in the acquisition of gender identity. Liberal feminists argue that women, like men, are endowed with a capacity for rationality and autonomy that they could freely exercise, were it not for the stereotyped gender roles society imposes on them. They reject the idea that a person's biological sex is constitutive of his/her gender (the behavior patterns and psychological traits that are associated with femininity or masculinity), and emphasize individual choice and freedom, irrespective of biological differences. By contrast, most cultural feminists believe that gendered subjectivity is biologically structured. They identify and celebrate psychological traits such as emotionality and nurturance as essentially female, and criticize liberal feminism for upholding male values (rationality, autonomy) as universal human values. Radical feminists also advocate the development of a female (counter)culture, but they consider sexual difference to be socially produced. Their constant identification of power with maleness, however, makes them succumb to essentialism. Other perspectives that reject the notion of a biologically grounded gendered identity but that nonetheless tend to amplify differences between men and women are that of psychoanalytic feminists (for whom sexual differentiation is produced by pregiven and universal psychosexual structures, such the castration and the Oedipus complexes) and of some cultural feminists who value the (socially constructed) attributes of care and responsibility that have historically been associated with women.

Because of their reliance on fixed and cross-cultural categories as determinants of identity, these various feminist approaches have failed to account for the culturally and historically changing meanings given to biological difference. In the 1970s, women of color and lesbians began to challenge "hegemonic" white feminism's use of gender as an immutable and universal analytical category to which all other types of differences (class, race, sexual orientation, nationality, and so on) are subordinated. Along with socialist feminists (Jaggar, 1988; Rubin, 1975), they exposed the received constructions of the "feminine" and "masculine" as historically and culturally specific prescriptive statements, which constantly shape and reshape our perceptions of the male and female subjects. In these accounts, sexual difference is not a social pregiven but a construction, whose meaning depends on its interplay with other axes of domination as well as on the range and social power of existing discourses (medical, psychiatric, and so on). Even the conceptualization of men and women's biological differences in terms of a binary opposition is shown to be a recent phenomenon, as scientific representations of the body before the late eighteenth century depicted the male and female anatomies in terms of their physiological similarities and not of their differences (the uterus and ovaries were seen as exactly equivalent to the penis and testicles). It is only in the early nineteenth century that women's reproductive system came to occupy a predominant place in medical representations as well as in people's conception of women's "natural" and social functions.

Whereas most contemporary feminists believe that a distinct theory of gender need not be antithetical to an analysis of differences among women, postmodernists argue that any appeal to the category "woman" will necessarily exclude differences between and within women. They point out that Western thought is constituted by a series of hierarchical binary oppositions (man/woman, subject/other, and so on), in which each term is reciprocally but asymmetrically defined by the other. Thus, for the masculine side to acquire meaning, it needs to negate the feminine instance. The feminist attempt to reverse this opposition is denounced by postmodernists for reproducing the binary mode of thinking, which is endemic to patriarchal thought. According to postmodern feminists, women's efforts to appropriate the ideals of self-identity and autonomy from which they have traditionally been excluded ineluctably replicate the eradication of differences (within and between women) which characterizes the formation of identity. Because they see representations, including feminist ones, as constituting—rather than reflecting—reality, postmodernists have helped draw attention to the situatedness of feminist assumptions and to the exclusions and oversimplifications that might result from their sisters' focus on sexual difference.

Another way of distinguishing between these various feminist conceptions of the nature and sources of sexual difference is to divide them into two broad categories; the first category wants to uphold and emphasize the dualism male/female either as a way of empowering women or as an important analytical tool to understand history and culture; the other wants to deconstruct the category "Woman" and minimize the meaning of sex distinction, either because of its irrelevance to human nature or because of the exclusions it (necessarily) entails.

See Also

BIOLOGICAL DETERMINISM; FEMININITY; FEMINISM: OVERVIEW; GENDER; IDENTITY POLITICS; MASCULINITY; PATRIARCHY; PEDAGOGY: FEMINIST I; PEDAGOGY: FEMINIST II

References and Further Reading

Jaggar, Alison M. 1988. *Feminist politics and human nature.* Lanham, Md.: Rowman and Littlefield.

Mohanty, Chandra. 1991. *Third world women and the politics of feminism.* Indianapolis: Indiana University Press.

Nicholson, Linda J., ed. 1990. *Feminism/postmodernism.* New York and London: Routledge.

Rhode, Deborah L. 1990. *Theoretical perspectives on sexual difference.* New Haven, Conn. and London: Yale University Press.

Rubin, Gayle. 1975. The Traffic in Women: Notes on the "Political Economy" of Sex. In Rayna Rapp Reiter, ed., *Toward an anthropology of women,* 157–210. New York: Monthly Review Press.

Carine M. Mardorossian

SEXUAL HARASSMENT

The term *sexual harassment* was coined in the United States, by women. Catharine MacKinnon, a feminist legal scholar whose work was instrumental in getting sexual harassment legally recognized as discrimination, has traced the history of the term to the Working Women United Institute of New York City in 1976 (MacKinnon, 1979). This label is known in translation around the world to describe unwanted sexually oriented behavior, typically in a work context (Bernstein, 1994; Riger, 1991). Although the behavior undoubtedly occurs all over the world, as a legal concept sexual harassment is largely an American construct (Bernstein, 1994). The scarcity of research materials on sexual harassment law in non-Western cultures further attests to this.

Sexual harassment is recognized legally as discrimination in France (Goette, 1997), Canada, Taiwan, and Spain (Webb, 1994). It is illegal in Australia (Graycar and Morgan, 1990), Germany, Ireland, and Sweden through judicial interpretation rather than by statute (Webb, 1994). In most countries of the European union, sexual harassment cannot be the basis for criminal prosecution or private civil actions; however, there is growing acceptance of the idea of harassment as discrimination, evidenced through recent judicial interpretation in Scotland, Ireland, Denmark, and Portugal (Bernstein, 1994).

In a hearing to determine whether sexual harassment could be considered discrimination under the Anti-Discrimination Act 1977 of New South Wales, Australia, a person is sexually harassed if "he or she is subjected to unsolicited and unwelcome sexual conduct by a person who stands in a position of power in relation to him or her" (Graycar and Morgan, 1990: 356–357). According to similar guidelines issued by both the Equal Employment Opportunity Commission (EEOC) in the United States and England's National Council for Civil Liberties, this behavior includes unwelcome sexual advances, requests for sexual favors, and other verbal or nonverbal conduct of a sexual nature, when submission to or rejection of this behavior affects an individual's employment status, interferes with work performance, or creates an offensive or hostile work environment (Benn, 1985; EEOC, 1992). Although they do not carry the force of law, the EEOC guidelines have served as a basis for numerous judicial decisions regarding sexual harassment. Under US law, sexual harassment is not a crime but a civil rights violation, recognized as a form of sex discrimination under Title VII of the Civil Rights Act of 1964 (Childers, 1993).

This trend was followed by the US Supreme Court in *Meritor Savings Bank v. Vinson* (477 US 57) in 1986, in which the court relied on the EEOC guidelines to recognize explicitly the hostile environment claim as actionable sex discrimination (Childers, 1993). The precedent established by this case, the first sexual harassment cause to be addressed by the highest court in the United States, requires that the sexual attention to be both clearly unwelcome and so severe that the employee can prove she has suffered psychologically as a result (Bennett-Alexander, 1991; DeCosse, 1992). Decisions of US lower courts in recent years expanded the definition of hostile environment harassment to include sexually explicit pinups of women and sexual jokes and remarks (Bennett-Alexander, 1991). The definition of *hostile environment* was further refined by the Supreme Court in the 1993 decision in *Harris v. Forklift Systems* (114 S. Ct. 367), in which the Court held that workers need not prove that the harassment caused irreparable psychological harm.

Several surveys of North American workers and students show that not only are women more likely than men to experience sexual harassment but also that about 40 percent of women workers have reported experiencing sexual harassment (Riger, 1991). Although this proportion is consistent across several unrelated studies, the actual incidence of sexual harassment is unknown and may be unknowable. Even if governments or institutions did keep statistics on sexual harassment reports, evidence suggests that fewer than 5 percent of victims report the harassment to any authority. Among other research problems, it is difficult to develop operational definitions of sexual harassment, partly because of its nature as a process rather than a single event (Fitzgerald and Shullman, 1993).

In addition, women and men frequently have different perceptions of whether behaviors are offensive, hostile, or intimidating, and may react differently to behaviors of the opposite sex (Guild and Jennings, 1997). Women's responses to sexual harassment range from avoidance tactics, such as ignoring the harasser or feigning noninvolvement and quitting or transferring positions, to defusion, such as attempting to minimize the harassment, to negotiation and confrontation, such as asking the harasser to stop and threatening formal action (Gruber, 1989). Any individual woman's response to harassment is shaped by numerous factors, including but not limited to the success of previous responses to the harasser; her knowledge of responses other women have given to sexual harassment; the degree to which harassment, discrimination, and other forms of unprofessional behavior are tolerated in her workplace; and how likely it seems that a more assertive response will increase the tension or antagonism already present in the workplace (Gruber, 1989). Of course, cultural context is also a significant influence. Pryor et al. (1997) found, for example, a substantially different understanding of the concept of sexual harassment among the Brazilian participants in their research, compared to Americans, Australians, and Germans.

Most research on sexual harassment is on nonrepresentative groups of women; women in blue-collar and nontraditional female jobs are both underrepresented in social research and more at risk. Recent publicity of unchecked sexual harassment in the US military has prompted more stringent scrutiny of this work environment, and more rigorous enforcement of sexual harassment policies in the armed forces. There also is very little research on sexual harassment of racial and ethnic minority women, who also may be more vulnerable to harassment (Fitzgerald and Shullman, 1993). Neither the courts nor social researchers have attended to how such factors as a woman's race, class, and sexual orientation impact her experience of harassment (DeCosse, 1992).

Most US legal cases involving sexual harassment deal with harassment of women in their roles as workers, although harassment of women as students is also well documented. Studies of academic women suggest that nearly half of all women college students in the US experience some form of sexual harassment (Fitzgerald and Shullman, 1993). In recognition of this problem, universities have begun developing policies on sexual harassment that define preventive and corrective actions. These policies typically define sexual harassment in terms consistent with the EEOC guidelines and detail procedures for pursuing a formal action.

Sexual harassment is typically understood within one of three explanatory frameworks: (1) it is viewed as an outgrowth or exaggeration of natural or biological sexual attraction; (2) it is understood as the misuse of organizational authority; or (3) it is a particular manifestation of sociocultural gender relations, a way for men to dominate or control women. Legal definitions, often the basis for institutional policies prohibiting sexual harassment, are based on the organizational definition of sexual harassment as an abuse of power, not an abuse of sexuality.

Catharine MacKinnon offers a broader definition of sexual harassment as the unwanted imposition of sexual attention on someone who is not in a position to refuse it; she points out that women are frequently unable to safely refuse male attention (MacKinnon, 1979). She has argued that legalistic analyses separate sexual harassment from other forms of sexism and sex discrimination, resulting in a view of sexual harassment as the misuse of institutionally conferred power. These definitions ignore the question of whether sex itself is a power structure. MacKinnon argues that abuses of power are recognized in employer-employee and teacher-student relationships because courts of law recognize them as hierarchies; only when sexuality comes into the context of another hierarchy is it considered an abuse of power. Women and men are not considered a hierarchy, socially, legally, or politically. Many feminist scholars have shown that in patriarchal societies the primary difference between women and men is not biological but social: the difference is male power, which often is expressed and enacted sexually. From a feminist analytical framework, sexual harassment is not fundamentally sexual behavior but the use of sexuality to enact power. It cannot be eradicated until it is understood in the larger context of gender hierarchy.

Note: Research assistance of Judy Luck and April Styer is gratefully acknowledged.

See Also

ANTIDISCRIMINATION; DISCRIMINATION; EDUCATORS: HIGHER EDUCATION; LAW: FEMINIST CRITIQUES; POWER; SEXISM; STREET HARASSMENT; WORK: OCCUPATIONAL EXPERIENCES

References and Further Readings

Benn, Melissa. 1985. Isn't sexual harassment really about masculinity? *Spare Rib* 156: 6–8.

Bennett-Alexander, Dawn D. 1991. Hostile environment sexual harassment: A clearer view. *Labor Law Journal* 42: 131–143.

Bernstein, Anita. 1994. Law, culture, and harassment. *University of Pennsylvania Law Review* 142: 1227–1311.

Childers, Jolynn. 1993. Is there a place for a reasonable woman in the law? A discussion of recent developments in hostile environment sexual harassment. *Duke Law Journal* 42: 854–904.

DeCosse, Sarah. 1992. Simply unbelievable: Reasonable women and hostile environment sexual harassment. *Law and Inequality* 10: 285–309.

Fitzgerald, Louise F., and Sandra L. Shullman. 1993. Sexual harassment: A research analysis and agenda for the 1990s. *Journal of Vocational Behavior* 42: 5–27.

Goette, Caroline. 1997. Sexual harassment in the workplace in France and in the United States. *NLA Review* Spring: 22–25.

Graycar, Regina, and Jenny Morgan. 1990. *The hidden gender of law.* Leichhardt, New South Wales, Australia: The Federation Press.

Gruber, James E. 1989. How women handle sexual harassment: A literature review. *Sociology and Social Research* 74: 3–9.

Guild, Thomas E., and Sandra A. Jennings. 1997. *Sexual harassment: Stereotypes complicate public policy.* Paper presented at annual meeting of the Society for the Study of Social Problems.

MacKinnon, Catharine A. 1979. *Sexual harassment of working women: A case of sex discrimination.* New Haven, Conn.: Yale University Press.

———. 1987. *Feminism unmodified: Discourses on life and law.* Cambridge, Mass.: Harvard University Press.

Pryor, John B., Eros R. DeSouza, Julie Fitness, Caludio Hutz, Martin Kumpf, Karin Lubbert, Outi Pesonen, and Maureen Wang Erber. 1997. Gender differences in the interpretation of social-sexual behavior: A cross-cultural perspective on sexual harassment. *Journal of Cross-Cultural Psychology* 28: 509–534.

Riger, Stephanie. 1991. Gender dilemmas in sexual harassment policies and procedures. *American Psychologist* 46: 497–505.

United States Equal Employment Opportunity. 1992. *Facts about sexual harassment.* Washington, DC: US Equal Employment Opportunity Commission.

Webb, Susan L. 1994. *Shock waves: The global impact of sexual harassment.* New York: MasterMedia Limited.

Elizabeth Arveda Kissling

SEXUAL ORIENTATION

The term *sexual orientation* refers to the relationship between gender and sexual desire, that is, men are generally considered to be "programmed" for attraction to women, and women to men. When same-sex programming occurs, that desire is called homosexual or lesbian or gay. Some researchers suggest that this programming is determined biologically, probably before birth (Bailey, 1993; LeVay and Hamer, 1994). Some believe that it occurs after birth in response to social or cultural factors rather than biological ones (Solomon, 1975). Others argue that biological or social factors may influence the tendency toward homosexuality (Small, 1993).

Still others maintain that sexual orientation is about how an individual interacts with the world, and that it has more significant psychological and emotional components than physical (Card, 1992; Weille, 1993). When bonding between two people of the same sex takes place at the psychological and emotional levels, the relationship is called a *friendship*. When that bonding includes physical and erotic attraction, the relationship is called *lesbian* or *homosexual*.

Recent theories and challenges have been clouded by the political assumption that if it can be proven that sexual orientation is biological and determined before birth then prejudice against homosexuals will evaporate. Others maintain that biological determinism is dangerous and could lead to selective abortion, internment, or euthanasia. Many critics of biological determinism note that sexual desire can and does fluctuate during a person's lifetime, not necessarily fixing permanently on the same or the opposite sex.

Sexual orientation as a psychological term is Western in its derivation. In many cultures outside of European-based countries, sexual orientation is a function of age, class, opportunity, and other factors, and these can fluctuate.

See Also

BIOLOGICAL DETERMINISM; BISEXUALITY; HETEROPHOBIA AND HOMOPHOBIA; HETEROSEXUALITY; IDENTITY POLITICS; LESBIANISM; SEXUALITY: OVERVIEW; TRANSGENDER

References and Further Reading

Bailey, J. Michael. 1993. Familial aggregation of female sexual orientation. *American Journal of Psychiatry* 5(2): 272.

Bower, Bruce. 1992. Genetic clues to female homosexuality. *Science News.* 142(8): 117.

Card, Claudia. 1992. Lesbianism and choice. *Journal of Homosexuality* 23(3): 39.

LeVay, Simon, and Dean Hamer. 1994. Evidence for a biological influence in male homosexuality. *Scientific American* 270(5): 44.

Small, Meredith F. 1993. The gay debate: Is homosexuality a matter of choice or chance? *American Health* 12(2): 70.

Solomon, Barbara. 1975. Taking the Bullshit by the Horn. In Nancy Myron and Charlotte Bunch, eds., *Lesbianism and the women's movement,* 91–103. Baltimore: Diana Press.

Weille, Katherine Lee. 1993. Reworking development theory: The case of lesbian identity formation. *Clinical Social Work Journal* 21(2): 151.

Judith McDaniel

SEXUAL SLAVERY

Feminist activists and theorists have used the term *sexual slavery* to include all those situations in which women and children are sexually used by men in conditions of slavery. These situations range from child sexual abuse in the family home, through forced marriage, to trafficking of women into prostitution.

History of the Concept

Feminist campaigns against sexual slavery have a long history. As soon as the Anti-Slavery Convention came into force in 1927, feminists pointed out that the specific form of slavery that women alone suffered, sexual slavery, was entirely omitted. Feminists worked in the 1920s and 1930s in the British Commonwealth League against what they called "sexual slavery." This included the ways in which women were bought and sold between male relatives in marriage, the imprisoning of women and girls in brothels, child marriage, and the traffic in women for prostitution. Men, it was pointed out, had freed themselves from being sold and "Women are now intent on doing the same for their fellow women, though in their case sale, barter or inheritance is slavery disguised as family custom" (Jeffreys, 1997: 14).

Nina Boyle, of the Save the Children Fund, expressed rage in 1931 that the League of Nations Convention was restricted to men on the basis of the principle that "none may own nor dispose of the person of a man, and more particularly of the person of a wage-earner" (Boyle, 1931: 136). Women did not have the right not to be slaves because "a woman is not entitled to be a 'person'" (Boyle, 1931: 137). In the late 1990s feminists were campaigning internationally once again to end the same abuses. Save the Children has joined with Anti-Slavery International to form the Forum on the Rights of Girls and Women in Marriage to investigate how early marriage, nonconsensual marriage, and rape within marriage affect girls and women (Ouattara, Sen, and Thomson, 1998).

Female Sexual Slavery and Prostitution

The term *sexual slavery* was applied to prostitution by Kathleen Barry, founder of the international Coalition Against Trafficking in Women (CATW), in her influential 1979 book *Female Sexual Slavery*. Her definition of female sexual slavery situates prostitution within a range of experiences in which women live subject to men and with no ability to leave. These include marital rape, father-daughter and brother-sister incest, wife beating, pornography, brideprice, the selling of daughters, purdah, and genital mutilation as well as prostitution. Female sexual slavery is present in all situations where women or girls cannot change the conditions of their existence; where regardless of how they got into those conditions, e.g., social pressure, economic hardship, misplaced trust or the longing for affection, they cannot get out; and where they are subject to sexual violence and exploitation (Barry, 1979: 40).

In her most recent book, *The Prostitution of Sexuality* (1995), Barry explains that the use of the term *sexual slavery* in the earlier work suggested that "forced" prostitution could be separated from so-called free prostitution. She now considers, as do many feminists in the international campaign to end men's abusive prostitution behavior, that the distinction between forced and free prostitution is a false one (see also Raymond, 1998). Feminist antiprostitution campaigners argue that prostitution is a form of violence against women that arises from women's subordination and that prostitution abusers exploit women's inferior social status, economic disadvantage, and the victimization they have suffered in childhood and from other men. In such a context, "freely chosen" prostitution is not a useful concept.

Military Sexual Slavery

The most common use of the term *sexual slavery* in feminist debate relates to the rape of women in combat situations from the "comfort women" from Korea, Taiwan, Philippines, the Netherlands, and Indonesia who were rounded up to service Japanese soldiers in World War II, to the women raped and forced to service combatants in Bosnia, Kosovo, and East Timor. Military sexual slavery is a matter of urgent concern for feminist legal theorists because of the need to seek justice for the "comfort women" who have survived. These women are old and need recompense. The abuse of women in rape camps in Bosnia has increased the pressure to find a way to punish and discourage such violations through international law.

Feminists in Korea, the Philippines, and Japan became aware of the sexual violence conducted by the Japanese military toward the comfort women in the late 1980s and

encouraged the survivors to speak out about their experiences and demand compensation from the Japanese government (Matsui, 1999). Nelia Sancho of the Philippines says the sexual slavery of the comfort women is unique because it "is the only case of government-institutionalized sexual slavery in the world's history of war" (Sancho, 1997: 145).

It may be that the history of men's sexual violence in warfare offers no other example of such institutionalized abuse, but there are so many well-documented instances of widespread—and in some cases systematic—rape and sexual violence in men's wars that it is hard not to see sexual slavery as endemic to warfare. Feminist theorists of war have argued that soldiers need to have their aggressive masculinity enhanced if they are to be effective in killing those with whom they have no quarrel. Masculinity is constructed out of a contrast with that which is seen as womanly and the most effective way of asserting this distinction lies in the sexual use, particularly the aggressive sexual use, of women (Enloe, 1983). Thus in Brownmiller's foundational account of rape from 1975, *Against Our Will*, we find descriptions of wholesale rape of women from medieval knights through to World Wars I and II, the Vietnam War, and the war that followed Bangladesh's secession from Pakistan in the 1970s (Brownmiller, 1975).

Feminist commentators have suggested that the rape camps set up in Bosnia and Kosovo form part of a strategy of genocide against Bosnian Muslims or other ethnicities (Stiglmayer, 1994). Women have been deliberately impregnated so as to destroy the culture and future of the enemy. In Bosnia and Kosovo, too, as in other theaters of war, rape has undoubtedly been employed as a tactic to create terror and humiliate and "unman" the enemy through the rape of "his" women.

Sexual Slavery versus Prostitution: A False Distinction?

What feminist commentators have not necessarily agreed about is the relationship between this sexual slavery of wartime and the ordinary sexual violence of pornography, prostitution, and the sexual exploitation of everyday. The creation of distinctions between exceptional sexual violence that is the result of force and that which can be regarded as the chosen and free sexual exploitation of the sex industry is identified by antiprostitution feminist theorists as giving a false legitimacy to those everyday practices. At the same time as feminist activists are seeking to get sexual slavery condemned in international law, there are moves worldwide to legalize prostitution on the grounds that this form of men's sexual practice is chosen by women and should be seen as legitimate work for women (Kempadoo and Doezema, 1998). This conflict of ideas is most visible internationally over the issue of the trafficking in women and children for prostitution. The global traffic in women grows exponentially and there is little argument among human rights workers that many trafficked women and girls are being held in slaverylike conditions through force, deceit, or debt slavery in many countries in Asia, Africa, the Americas, Europe, and Australasia.

Some women involved in international nongovernment organizations are seeking to weaken or replace the 1949 Convention on the Traffic in Persons that outlaws licensed brothels and penalizes pimps and procurers, on the grounds that prostitution should be seen as a legitimate destination. Trafficking, they say, should be seen as nongender specific, as requiring the use of force, and involving the trafficking in any persons for any purpose with no special concern about prostitution (Klap, Klerk, and Smith, 1995). The International Labour Organization has entered the debate with the publication of a report in 1998, *The Sex Sector,* which calls for the recognition of the important role of prostitution in the economies of Southeast Asia (Lim, 1998).

The existence of a clear distinction between "free" prostitution and trafficking, or "forced" sexual slavery, is queried by feminist theorists and activists with experience in campaigning against sexual violence and pornography. Catherine MacKinnon, the respected radical feminist legal theorist, resists the clear distinction between sexual slavery in Bosnia and everyday prostitution, for instance. She stresses the connections:

> In the camps, it is at once mass rape and serial rape in a way that is indistinguishable from prostitution. Prostitution is that part of everyday nonwar life that is closest to what we see done to women in this war. The daily life of prostituted women consists of serial rape, war or no war. The brothel-like arrangement of the rape/death camps parallels the brothels of so-called peacetime: captive women impounded to be passed from man to man in order to be raped (MacKinnon, 1994: 191).

She explains that the men who organized and took their pleasures from the military prostitution of these women were trained by the use of women in brothels before the war. They had a model. They were also geared up by the proliferation of pornography, which occurred in Yugoslavia in the 1990s. Sexual slavery, then, can be narrowly defined as the exceptional situation in which the mass rape of women occurs in conditions of institutionalized slavery, such as wartime, or seen as the extreme form of the broader condition of women in which some men exact sexual servicing through the exploitation of women's subordinate status, whether in marriage, in childhood, or in prostitution.

See Also

PROSTITUTION; RAPE; SEXUAL VIOLENCE; SLAVERY; TRAFFICKING; VIOLENCE AND PEACE: OVERVIEW; WAR

Reference and Further Reading

Barry, Kathleen. 1979. *Female sexual slavery.* Englewood Cliffs, N.J.: Prentice Hall.

———. 1995. *The prostitution of sexuality.* New York: NYU Press.

Boyle, Nina. 1931. What is slavery? An appeal to women. In *The Shield* 7, 3rd series.

Brownmiller, Susan. 1975. *Against our will: men, women and rape,* London: Secker and Warburg.

Coalition Against Trafficking in Women website: <www.uri.edu /artsci/wms/hughes/catw>.

Enloe, Cynthia. 1983. *Does khaki become you? The militarisation of women's lives.* London: Pluto Press.

Jeffreys, Sheila. 1997. *The idea of prostitution.* Melbourne: Spinifex.

Kempadoo, Kamala, and Jo Doezema, eds. 1998. *Global sex workers: Rights, resistance and redefinition.* New York: Routledge.

Klap, Marieke, Yvonne Klerk, and Jacqueline Smith, eds. 1995. *Combatting traffic in persons.* SIM Special No 17. Utrecht: Studie—en Informatiecentrum Mensenrechten.

Lim, Lin Lean, ed. 1998. *The sex sector: The economic and social bases of prostitution in Southeast Asia.* Geneva: International Labour Office.

MacKinnon, Catharine A. 1994. Rape, genocide, and women's human rights. In Alexandra Stiglmayer, ed., *Mass rape: The war against women in Bosnia-Herzegovina.* Lincoln: University of Nebraska Press.

Matsui, Yayori. 1999. *Women in the New Asia.* Melbourne: Spinifex.

Ouattara, Mariam, Purna Sen, and Marilyn Thomson. 1998. Forced marriage, forced sex: The perils of childhood for girls. In Caroline Sweetman, ed., *Violence against women.* Oxford: Oxfam.

Raymond, Janice. 1998. *Legitimating prostitution as sex work: UN Labor Organization (ILO) calls for recognition of the sex industry.* Amherst, Mass.: Coalition Against Trafficking in Women.

Sancho, Nelia. 1997. The "comfort women" system during World War II: Asian women as targets of mass rape and sexual slavery by Japan. In Ronit Lentin, ed., *Gender and catastrophe.* London and New York: Zed.

Stiglmayer, Alexandra, ed. 1994. *Mass rape: The war against women in Bosnia-Herzegovina.* Lincoln: University of Nebraska Press.

Sheila Jeffreys

SEXUAL VIOLENCE

Sexual violence refers to child sexual abuse, rape, and the sexual harassment of women and children. Some would include certain medical and religious practices, such as clitoridectomy, involving genital mutilation. Sexual violence is an issue that has long been shrouded in secrecy and it is only recently that women all over the world have begun to successfully speak out about it. A landmark in this struggle is the recognition of violence against women as a fundamental barrier to women's equality by the United Nations and the Council of Europe. This article outlines how the recognition of sexual violence developed in the West and summarizes different theoretical explanations and strategies to address it.

Historical Background

The growth of cities in the nineteenth century, growing disparity between the rich and the poor, and the resultant rise in prostitution and sexual exploitation of women led to an increasing identification of public disorder with sexual danger and male sexuality. In the 1880s in Britain, following the publicizing of the sale of young working-class women into prostitution, widespread protests spread throughout the West and calls for greater state regulation of prostitution coincided with demands for the extension of legal reproductive, marriage, divorce, and custody rights for women. Campaigns to protect women from exploitation together with the rise of the "social purity" movement led to the increased politicization of the role of sexual violence in the subordination of women. The media moral panic surrounding the Jack the Ripper murders in the East End of London in the 1880s amplified the terror of male violence and its association with homicide, as eloquently described by Judith Walkowitz (1992).

Second-Wave Feminist Campaigns: Challenging Myths

With the emergence of second-wave women's liberation movements, feminists in the 1970s attempted to dispel myths about the nature, the incidence, the perpetrators, and the causes of sexual violence, all of which absolved men of

responsibility. A vast array of myths were challenged, including the myth that sexual violence was an expression of sexual desire (rather than of sexual power and violence) and the myth that rape was due to an irresistible biological "urge" of male sexuality (or was a question of misunderstood sexual negotiation) rather than a violent sexual assault.

Providing the Evidence

Campaigns across the world focused around three main approaches. First, women conducted empirical research to document the extent of sexual male violence. The very low incidence of rape reflected in official statistics was refuted by victimization surveys which indicated that rape and sexual violence were not rare events but common experiences, not typically carried out by strangers or by unbalanced psychopaths but far more often by men acquainted or intimate with their victims; rapists were likely to be brothers, fathers, husbands, lovers, uncles, and friends. Research findings confirmed that violence against women is a key concern for the majority of women.

Providing Services and Challenging the Law

Second, feminists campaigned to provide services—refuges, rape crisis centers, survivors' groups, and help lines—for women and children subjected to violence. Third, feminists campaigned for legal changes to bring the perpetrators of sexual violence to justice. In the United Kingdom and the United States, the inadequacies of the adversarial system of law have been documented (Allison and Wrightsman, 1993; Lees, 1996). It is estimated that fewer than 5 percent of reported rapes result in a conviction. Yet there is no monitoring of the courts and any improvements tend to be neutralized by resistance against implementing reforms.

Explanations for Sexual Violence

Feminists have been divided over the meaning and importance of sexual violence in explaining women's subordination. One of the main disputes has centered on whether sexual violence should be seen in terms of sexuality or of violence and on the relationship of violence to normative male sexuality. Feminist activists argued that it was vital that rape, for example, should be seen as an act of violence rather than as an act of sexual desire, as was often the case in trials. MacKinnon's (1989) analysis agrees that violence is crucial but that many forms of sexuality are abusive to women, and that pornography, rape, and sexual harassment should not be reduced to a single category of violence against women, which diverts attention away from the abusive nature of heterosexual relations. According to her viewpoint, feminism is a theory of how the eroticization of dominance and submission create gender.

Whereas socialist feminists regard women's subordination to be a result of economic factors, radical feminists (Brownmiller, 1975; Millett, 1972) argue that patriarchy is a social and political system in which men control and have power over women and which ultimately rests on force. Others such as Jukes (1993) argued from a psychoanalytic perspective that male misogyny was rooted in the Oedipus crisis and in resentment emanating from the need to break away from early dependency on the mother when male identity develops.

Finally, feminists have campaigned to politicize the use of sexual violence and its links with militarism, male domination, and colonial exploitation. Publicity was first given to war rapes in the 1990s Bosnian war, where growing evidence that rape had been strategically used as a military tool of "ethnic cleansing" by the Serbs led to international outrage. The growth of pornography, prostitution and sex tourism, and the sale of brides from the developing world to the West suggests that sexual violence is a problem which will not easily be solved.

See Also

ABUSE; DOMESTIC VIOLENCE; FEMALE CIRCUMCISION AND GENITAL MUTILATION; MISOGYNY; PORNOGRAPHY AND VIOLENCE; PROSTITUTION; RAPE; SEXUAL HARASSMENT; SEXUAL SLAVERY; VIOLENCE: MEDIA

References and Further Reading

Allison, Julie, and Lawrence Wrightsman. 1993. *Rape, the misunderstood crime.* London: Sage.

Brownmiller, Susan. 1975. *Against our will: Men, women, and rape.* New York: Simon and Schuster.

Kelly, Liz. 1988. *Surviving sexual violence.* Cambridge: Polity Press.

Jukes, Adam. 1993. *Why men hate women.* London: Free Association Books.

Lees, Sue. 1996. *Carnal knowledge: Rape on trial.* London: Hamish Hamilton.

MacKinnon, Catharine. 1989. *Toward a feminist theory of the state.* Cambridge, Mass.: Harvard University Press.

Millett, Kate. 1972. *Sexual politics.* London: Abacus.

Walkowitz, Judith. 1992. *City of dreadful delights: Narratives of sexual danger in late Victorian London.* London: Virago.

Sue Lees

SEXUALITY: Overview

Sexuality is an integral component of women's self-definition throughout the lifespan, including biological femaleness, sexual orientation, gender roles, intimacy, erotic activities, physical sensations, emotions, memories, thoughts, and meanings. Many sexologists agree that women's sexual response and what activates it are unique to each woman, complex, multidimensional, and sometimes paradoxical; that these can shift focus and intensity with circumstances, conditions, and belief systems. Factors such as age and development, health and vigor, hormone balance, self-esteem, being in love, partner gender, partner empathy, physical stimulation, memories, safety, and economic security may all play significant parts. Similarly, women's perception of sexual satisfaction may range widely, including tension release, physical orgasm, emotional bonding, spiritual connection, or any combination of these. Many sexologists also agree that it is possible for a woman to identify as a sexual being even if she is celibate (without a partner) or abstinent (engaging in no overt sexual behaviors).

Women report that sexual desire, arousal, and satisfaction can be powerful and transformative sources of energy, able to connect women with themselves, their partners, and with a power beyond themselves, such as nature or a universal spirit. Medical evidence points to a correlation between sexual health and overall health (Northrup, 1995). But sexual response is not unanimously interpreted by women as positive. What can move women to ecstasy can also move women to inhibition, pain, fear, rage, and despair. Negative sexual response may depend on factors such as lack of information, partner insensitivity, past abuse, homophobia, or limiting norms, such as religious injunctions to procreate and the Freudian notion that orgasms through clitoral stimulation are immature.

Historical and Cultural Influences on Women's Sexual Response

The development and expression of women's sexual response are so entwined with culture that it is impossible to articulate these fully without acknowledging historical, geographical, religious, ethnic, and racial influences. The earliest evidences of women as sexual beings derive from Goddess cultures, dating from Paleolithic times until about 3000 years ago. Artifacts from every continent reveal a belief that the human body—especially woman's body—is inseparable from the soul, and that the physical senses, when aligned with the natural world, are channels for divine revelation. They also reveal a belief that a harmonious flow of sexual energy may be the most powerful creative force in the universe, as evidenced in images of "sacred marriage"—the union of sexual and spiritual pleasure and of female and male essence.

The advent of cultural dualism over the last three thousand years, along with patriarchy and the increasing industrialization of most societies, refocused human belief systems on a global scale and separated sex from the sacred (Eisler, 1987). The subsequent history of women's sexuality reflects a shift from celebrating women's power to controlling it. Male ownership of women became institutionalized first within the patriarchal religions and ultimately within the legal, economic, and medical systems of all major cultures. For instance, the Goddess, birth mother of all life, devolved into the Virgin Mary, an asexual vessel, whose task was no longer to create but only to intercede with the Creator. The sacred marriage became a vehicle for female bondage and reproduction of male heirs. Other illustrations of the cultural control of women's sexual power include the use of chastity belts in sixteenth century Islam and England, witch burning in seventeenth century Europe and America, and footbinding in nineteenth century China.

In cultures where women's sexual power was severely controlled, women's sexual response was often characterized by manipulation—seduction of powerful men, infidelity to arranged or abusive marriages, withholding sexual favors, and competition with other women. Nonetheless, there have also been women throughout history whose work and lives illustrate the positive power of sexual energy. Some functioned from within repressive institutions, such as the sixteenth century Spanish saint, Teresa of Avila, who bridged the Church's separation of body and soul by embracing Christ as a lover and bridegroom. Others worked from without, such as eighteenth-century English feminist Mary Wollstonecraft, who championed sexual relationships beyond the often oppressive boundaries of wedlock.

Defining Sexual Norms for Twentieth-Century Women

The development of sex as a science has affected sexual norms for twentieth-century European and American women. In England and the United States, the earliest women doctors were sex-education pioneers who strove to counter Victorian—and Freudian—stereotypes that reified motherhood and normalized sexual repression, shame, ignorance, and submission to men. In the early part of the century, Elizabeth Blackwell wrote of the health benefits of women's orgasms and Marie Stopes's explicit manual, *Married Love,* was a best-seller. The first surveys of sexual behavior were also conducted by women doctors, who recorded experiences that were physically orgasmic and emotionally and spiritually satisfying.

Clelia Mosher surveyed 47 wives from 1892 to 1912 (MaHood and Weinberg, 1980) and Katharine Bement Davis surveyed 2,200 women, including unmarried women and lesbians (Davis, 1929). From the 1930s on, however, the bias of scientific sex surveys almost universally supported the dominant paradigm that women's sexual energy (or sex "drive") is inferior to men's. While the largest of these surveys—by Kinsey, et al. (1953) and Laumann, et al. (1994)—generated important national conversation about sexual taboos such as homosexuality and masturbation, the emphasis on activities rather than meanings, and the quantitative methodology necessarily omitted much that is integral to women's sexual response.

The discipline of sex therapy has further codified contemporary norms of women's sexual response for Western women. Of major significance was the publication of William Masters and Virginia Johnson's *Human Sexual Response* (1966) and *Human Sexual Inadequacy* (1970) and Helen Singer Kaplan's *New Sex Therapy* (1974) and *Disorders of Sexual Desire* (1979). These studies proposed a categorical sexual response cycle consisting of desire, arousal, and orgasm, which set a medical tone for clinical approaches to sexual function and dysfunction for the rest of the twentieth century. Consequently, sexual function for women is now most widely defined as a goal-oriented, often heterosexual set of activities such as intercourse, cunnilingus, and fellatio, which stimulates physiologic reactions such as vaginal lubrication and orgasmic contractions occurring at intervals of .08 second. Sexual dysfunction for women is most widely defined in terms of intercourse-related disorders: inhibited desire for intercourse or activities leading to intercourse, dyspareunia (pain on intercourse), and vaginismus (vaginal spasms that prevent successful intercourse).

In less industrialized countries, sexual science has had little impact on cultural beliefs which are still characterized by menstruation taboos, reproductive imperatives, and male domination. The resultant sexual control of women varies from culture to culture: in Africa, ritual genital mutilation of girls; In India, dowry burnings and low status of mothers; in the Middle East, virginity rites and forced marriage; in China, abortion of girl babies; in Thailand and Vietnam, child prostitution. Moreover, widespread poverty and malnutrition has left women in these countries especially vulnerable to HIV/AIDS. Despite these negatives however, reports reveal that many individual women in these cultures have enjoyed loving and satisfying sexual relationships.

From the Sexual Revolution and Sexual Self-Help to Female Ejaculation

The sexual revolution of the 1960s and 1970s arguably gave more license for men to have multiple partners than for women to explore new avenues of sexual response. However, it did produce two major events with the potential to free sexual expression for women worldwide. In 1962 the birth-control pill was introduced, which (whatever its side effects would later prove) allowed users to experience intercourse without fear of unwanted pregnancy. In 1973, the landmark U.S. Supreme Court decision of *Roe v. Wade* granted U.S. women the constitutional right to safe, medical abortions, and by implication the right to control their own reproductive choices. This decision has been continually challenged by religious and right-wing groups who wish to reinstate the reproductive imperative for women, and hundreds of legislative bills have refined its applications.

The combination of women's liberation, gay/lesbian liberation, and the women's health movement during this era provided popular permission for some women to explore non-traditional relationship options such as lesbian and bisexual unions, cohabitation, open marriage, group sex, and masturbation—sexual relationship with one's self. There was concomitant permission to experiment with non-traditional sexual activities such as fantasies and sadomasochism (S/M), along with use of sex toys for clitoral stimulation, and pleasure enhancing drugs. Information about women's sexual response became available through women's sexuality boutiques, erotic films by and for women, and publications such as *Off Our Backs*. The 1964 release of Betty Friedan's *Feminine Mystique* was the first in a succession of influential books by authors such as Kate Millett (*Sexual Politics*, 1970), Germaine Greer (*The Female Eunuch*, 1970), Nancy Friday (*My Secret Garden*, 1973), Andrea Dworkin (*Woman Hating*, 1974), and Betty Dodson (*Liberating Masturbation*, 1974), along with the classic guide to women's sexuality and health, *Our Bodies, Ourselves*, first published in 1971. Sociologist Shere Hite's survey revealed that women often preferred clitoral stimulation to intercourse (*The Hite Report*, 1976). Sex therapist Lonnie Barbach's "preorgasmic" women's groups generated a succession of self-help alternatives to the medical dysfunction model (*For Yourself*, 1975). Beverly Whipple's 1981 laboratory research on female orgasm confirmed a Grafenberg Spot (G Spot) on the anterior vaginal wall and the possibility of female ejaculation, sparking controversy between women who felt validated, traditionalists who denied the validity of the research, and feminists, who saw the research as another way of limiting women's sexual response to intercourse.

Although this was an era of sexual liberation for many women in the United States and beyond, the Pill, medical abortions, and other changes were not readily available or affordable to women of color, poor women, and third world women. Also, not all white middle-class women wanted changes. For most of the world's women, traditional constructions of sexual response remained the norm.

From Conservative Values to the Medicalization of Women's Sexual Response

By the early 1980s, worldwide conservatism and an epidemic of sexually transmitted diseases (STDs), herpes, chlamydia, and AIDS, ended the sexual expansiveness of the 1960s and 1970s. Attention turned from the pursuit of pleasure to recovery from addictions and sexual abuse. Global concern for sexual safety fueled a debate between Pro-Choice activists, who argued for the right to choose voluntary reproduction and comprehensive sexuality education in the schools, and Right-to-Life activists, who argued for sex within marriage only, bans on legal abortion, and abstinence only sex education.

The media increasingly influenced attitudes about sexual response, reflecting both liberal and conservative views on talk-show radio and television, in newspapers, and in popular magazines. The prevailing picture of women was sexualized, and therefore far from the Victorian stereotype. At the same time, women were still most often depicted as sex objects, whose role was to please men. By the late 1990s, the Internet had the capacity to transmit information about sexuality and erotica worldwide, yet much Internet communication reflected the performance aspects of sexual response and the role of women as sex objects.

In 1998, release of the drug Viagra to enhance male erections created a multi-billion-dollar industry. By the year 2000, medical focus had turned to women's sexual dysfunctions with Viagra trials for women and production of hormone creams and gels to retard menopausal vaginal atrophy and enhance lubrication. While some critics regarded this medical focus as sexually empowering to aging women, others saw it as still another instance of controlling and pathologizing women by limiting their sexual response to intercourse.

Issues Affecting Women's Sexual Response in the Twenty-First Century

By the beginning of the twenty-first century, international issues focused less on aspects of pleasure and power than on negative aspects of women's sexual response: worldwide epidemics of gender imbalances, poverty, teen pregnancy, HIV/AIDS, domestic violence, incest, and sexual harassment; female genital mutilation in Africa, and female sexual slavery in Latin America, Southeast Asia, Europe, Japan, and the United States, and the commercialization of sex from pornography to the exploitation of women's sexuality through advertising.

In affluent Western countries, particularly the United States, a new equality emerged in female-male relationships as a result of the women's movement changing economic and political structures. Yet the dominant sexual discourse continued to be the medical model, which shaped the understanding of sexual response as performance issues separate from the rest of life. The prevailing dysfunction for women continued to be seen as inhibited desire for sexual intercourse. A few feminist sexologists created more nuanced definitions of women's sexual response which include emotional and spiritual meanings such as connection, intimacy, and transformation (Daniluk, 1998, Ellison, 2000, Ogden, 1999, Tiefer, 1995). As a result, the sexual paradigm is presently expanding beyond moral and medical constructs to affirm women's sexual agency, empathic partnership, broadened perspectives on sexual satisfaction, and the notion of sexual response as a life force integral to women's personal power.

Organizations that provide ongoing information about women's sexual response include The Sexuality Information and Educational Council of the United States (SIECUS), the Society for the Scientific Study of Sexuality (SSSS), The American Association for Sex Education, Counseling, and Therapy (AASECT), and the World Association of Sexology (WAS).

See Also

ABUSE; LESBIAN SEXUALITY; PORNOGRAPHY; REPRODUCTION: OVERVIEW; SEX AND CULTURE; SEXUALITY: ADOLESCENT SEXUALITY; SEXUALITY: PSYCHOLOGY OF SEXUALITY IN CROSS-CULTURAL PERSPECTIVES; SEXUALITY: PSYCHOLOGY OF SEXUALITY IN THE UNITED STATES; TRANSGENDER

References and Further Reading

Arditti, Rita. 1997. Mothers and disappearing daughters: sex determination tests in India. In Jetter, Alexis, Annelise Orleck, and Diana Taylor, eds., *The Politics of motherhood: Activist voices from left to right.* Hanover, N.H.: University Press of New England, Dartmouth College.

Barbach, Lonnie. 1975. *For yourself.* New York: Signet.

Boston Women's Health Book Collective. 1998. *Our bodies, ourselves for the new century.* New York: Touchstone.

Daniluk, Judith. 1998. *Women's sexuality across the lifespan.* New York: Guilford.

Davis, Katharine Bement. 1929. *Factors in the sex life of twenty-two hundred women.* New York: Harper Brothers.

Eisler, Riano. 1987. *The chalice and the blade: Our history, our future.* San Francisco: Harper and Row.

Ellison, Carol. 2000. *Women's sexualities.* Oakland Calif.: New Harbinger.

Hite, Shere. 1976. *The Hite report.* New York: Macmillan.

Kaplan, Helen Singer. 1974. *The new sex therapy.* New York: Brunner/Mazel.

Kaplan, Helen Singer. 1979. *Disorders of desire.* New York: Brunner/Mazel.

Kinsey, Alfred C., Wardell Pomeroy, Clyde Martin, and Paul Gebhard. 1953. *Sexual behavior in the human female.* Philadelphia: W.B. Saunders.

Laumann, Edward O, John Gagnon, and Robert Michaels. 1994. *The social organization of sexuality: Sexual practices in the United States.* Chicago: University of Chicago Press.

MaHood, John and Katherine Weinburg, eds. 1980. *The mosher survey: Sexual attitudes of 45 Victorian women.* New York: Arno.

Masters, William H. and Virginia Johnson. 1966. *Human sexual response.* Boston: Little, Brown.

———. 1970. *Human sexual inadequacy.* Boston: Little, Brown.

Mikell, Gwendolyn, ed. 1997. *African feminism: The politics of survival in sub-Saharan Africa.* Philadelphia: University of Pennsylvania Press.

Mohanty, Chandra Talpade, Ann Russo, and Lourdes Torres, eds. 1991. *Third World women and the politics of feminism.* Bloomington: Indiana University Press.

Moore, Tracy, ed. 1995. *Lesbiot: Israeli lesbians talk about sexuality, feminism, Judaism and their lives.* London: Cassell.

Northrup, Christiane. 1995. *Women's bodies, women's wisdom.* New York: Bantam.

Ogden, Gina. 1999. *Women who love sex: An inquiry into the expanding spirit of women's erotic experience* rev. ed. Cambridge, Mass.: Womanspirit.

Tiefer, Leonore. 1995. *Sex is not a natural act and other essays.* Boulder, Colo.: Westview.

Gina Ogden

SEXUALITY: Adolescent Sexuality

Adolescents are expected to cope with overwhelming complexities of normative developmental transitions and conflicting social demands. Cultural norms cross-culturally seem to reinforce reproduction as a female function and sexuality as a male physiological necessity. There has been a great deal of research evidence on the importance of male sexuality (Heiman and Verhulst, 1982), but female reproduction and sexuality are neglected areas. Aulagnon (1995) reported that the Beijing conference in 1995 recognized women's rights to control and decide their sexual health without coercion and violence. This empowers adolescents to take control of their bodies, which leads to the control of their health.

Female sexuality and reproduction denote vague, distorted meanings by society and underline limited choices and restrictions for adolescents. Rubin (1984) explains that these are social constructs shaped by male orders where power prevails in a political way. They incorporate changes that include primary and secondary reproduction characteristics. The *primary reproduction characteristics* involve the growth of sex organs. For girls, sex organs become mature to make fertility possible (the menarche). For boys, the spermarche is the first ejaculation of seminal fluid containing sperm (Thornburg and Aras, 1986). The *secondary reproduction characteristics* are apparent in the development of the body shape, and facial and pubic hair. Whereas the sequence of both the primary and secondary reproduction characteristics are similar biologically for most adolescents, there are great variations in the sociocultural expectations for girls.

Adolescence comes from the word "adolescere," which means to grow to maturity. Adolescence is a period of transition from childhood to adulthood and an important period in the life span. Puberty is the sudden, rapid growth relative to physical and sexual maturity. A continuous adjustment is involved in relation to internal, biological development and to external, cultural expectations. Unfortunately, many aspects of maturational changes remain unclarified to adolescents in addition to conflicting sociocultural expectations. These factors aggravate women's subordination and oppression, and affect health. McDonough and Harrison (1978) stress that oppression and abuse have a negative impact on women's sexuality and reproduction by keeping them "just as mothers and wives." Both these roles are vital to society, yet they are undervalued and unpaid. Female adolescents also are kept ignorant about their reproductive rights (Winter, 1988). Preventing females from knowing and controlling their bodies consolidates patriarchal powers.

This article will examine the double standards imposed by society on adolescent female reproduction and sexuality, with a specific focus on the menarche and early pregnancy. It addresses the perceptions conveyed to adolescents by stressing that men should sow their wild oats, whereas women should save themselves for marriage.

Both sexuality and reproduction are important to the understanding and analysis of the adolescents' needs. Most cultures manage sexual behaviour in order to regulate fertility and its economical benefits (Paige and Paige, 1981). Adolescents encounter many problems associated with the lack of knowledge about sexuality, reproduction, menarche, transmitted diseases, early pregnancy, and abortion. The riskiness of engaging in sexual intercourse and becoming a mother at an early age and how these risks affect identity formation and health during the growth spurt in puberty are hardly discussed (Miller and Moore, 1990). Patriarchal systems seem to create confusion and taboos about sexuality and reproduction that maintain power and inequality rather than honesty and openness. Sexuality becomes a critical concern at the onset of puberty; adolescents start their womanhood defined by their reproductive role and sexual functions. They do not receive adequate education on how to channel their sexual drives. Very often, the dilemma for most teenagers is how to deal with the overpowering sex drives within the prevailing social attitudes and sanctions imposed, especially those on girls. To some female adolescents, sex is a frightening experience, yet it is reinforced by the media, myths, nocturnal dreams, and fantasies.

Feminist research contends the examination of gender differences and how social institutions models have been created by patriarchy to help maintain oppressive practices on female adolescents' reproductive rights. Miller (1988) explains that the cultural climate that defines male and female sexuality uses an array of symbolic representations to control development. Lees (1993) argues that the use of derogatory language to stigmatize and oppress is used against female adolescents to confuse them about their reproductive and sexual rights. Boys' self-esteem is enhanced by the number of conquests they have, whereas for females, honor and reputation must be protected. The control of women seems to be reinforced, however, through the construction of a discourse that equates beauty with passivity in sexuality. The question of an individual's honor and dignity is linked to sexual matters in many countries, especially in the Middle East. "Ayb" is the shame brought in by being too open about sexual matters. The growth of sexual characteristics and the attainment of reproduction maturity are associated with adolescents' perceptions and reactions to them (Guernina, 1994). The concept of "charaf" relates to moral principles concerning sexual matters that might be kept secret, such as menarche and accidental pregnancy.

The Menarche

Female adolescents receive contradictory messages about the menarche. They are expected to enter maturation; at the same time, they are controlled by the sociocultural system that often alienates them. The secrecy and lack of information on the menarche makes it appear undesirable and dirty in some countries. Deaney (1988) states: "We purchase socially approved statements about childbirth, marriage or death but no cards to say best wishes on becoming a woman.... We hide the fact of the menarche" (107). Adolescents seem to view menstruation negatively and consider it as dirty and painful in some cultures. Among many Brazilian tribes, a girl is punished, starved, and confined in a hammock under the roof of a hut (Laws, 1990). In other cultures, adolescents perceive the menarche positively because of the adequate preparation for it. As Mead (1974) discovered, adolescents in Samoa Islands celebrate puberty with a rite of passage. Among the Kung hunters in Botswana, menstruation is celebrated by a woman who stays with the adolescent and holds her during urination and defecation. During her menstruation, she is not allowed to touch hunting implements or be near her husband. This event assures adolescents that their new adulthood is welcomed.

In many countries, virginity is seen as sacred and adolescent girls are killed if they lose it before marriage, as they are seen as dishonoring the family (Mernissi, 1975). It has been stressed by Dreyer (1982) that adolescents who engage in premarital sexuality suffer from serious adjustment difficulties. There are so many contradictions and opposing messages about female adolescent sexuality and reproduction. On the one hand, adolescents encounter the growth spur; on the other hand, they are left without any relevant clarification on how to manage their sexuality responsibly (Gordon and Gilgun, 1987). The confusion about women's sexuality are an example with respect to gender and sexuality issues. Contrasting images to describe women's sexuality are linked to life, death, Mother Earth, virgin, Mary, Eve, and witch. These recreate in adolescent girls a subjugation through reproduction and sexuality (Mitchell, 1966). For many adolescents, decisions about sexuality are important in defining their values. Gilligan (1982) describes the struggles and difficulties that adolescents girls face in the process of sexual development.

Expectations concerning female adolescents' sexuality and behavior vary across cultures. Inconsistent social guidance makes the transition from childhood to adolescence confusing. As a result, female adolescents encounter considerable exploitation and abuse because of poor preparation for this stage of their lives. The lack of social and emotional support in addition to inadequate information have contributed to high rates of unwanted pregnancy, abortion, sexually transmitted diseases, and lack of contraceptive use.

Adolescent Pregnancy

Feminist research shows that each year about 70 percent of unmarried female adolescents become pregnant worldwide. Unprotected sex occurs, followed by unplanned pregnancy, which is more damaging for girls than boys (Miller and Moore, 1990).

The late twentieth century put the female adolescent at great risk by closing opportunities for the continuation of education and difficult transition to adulthood and healthy development. Adolescent pregnancy has negative consequences on education, identity formation, and causes reliance on public assistance (Lansdale, Gunn, and Paikoff, 1991).

Research has often neglected in-depth studies and relevant statistics that the consequence of rape often results in unwanted pregnancy, which often ends with an abortion. Trussell (1988) specifies that an American girl has about one chance in six of becoming pregnant before her 17th birthday.

In some cultures—for example, Latin American and Islamic countries—rape is blamed on the woman and results in social rejection. It is considered to be an attack on family honor (Mernissi, 1975).

Many teenage pregnancies are unplanned, unwanted, and tend to disrupt adolescent developmental tasks such as identity formation, career, or school plans (Kuziel-Perri and Snarey 1991). Many adolescent girls are ill-prepared to take on the psychological, social, and emotional responsibilities of bringing up children and looking after them.

Schorr (1988) found that the reasons given by teenage girls for getting pregnant are related to not knowing how to use contraceptives or to their nonavailability when needed. There is a raft of psychological factors that push adolescents to have sexual intercourse, such as loneliness, alienation, depression, and poverty. These lead the adolescent girl to search for an outlet or an escape, so she grants sexual favors to obtain friendship and commitment.

The French phrase, *tomber enceinte*, describes being pregnant as a mere accident, literally as "falling into a trap." A similar attitude may explain the high rate of death among pregnant teenagers in countries such as Bangladesh, India, and Pakistan. In south Asia, each year 300,000 women die and many more suffer serious illnesses and permanent disabilities as a result of pregnancies (Ungar and Crawford, 1992). Early pregnancy in adolescence is risky socially—and physically—especially in countries where sex is a taboo. Women's role is seen as reproductive, and there is little understanding of human rights legislation that would allow women to plan their lives and to learn about all aspects of reproductive health and sexuality. The social, economical, and psychological consequences of pregnancy can be disruptive to the development of adolescents.

Adolescents' Sexuality and Reproduction Management

Preventative measures to understand the causes of early pregnancy are needed. It is important to identify the cultural and socioeconomic factors that put adolescents on the road to maternal death. Adolescents need to find appropriate ways to come to terms with adolescent sexual behaviour problems. Educational programs are needed to clarify issues around sexuality and reproduction so that adolescents can make informed, responsible choices.

Providing knowledge on sexual and reproductive development is necessary to improve skills for risk management. Evaluation designs are needed to benefit adolescents who are at risk. Reproduction, sexuality, and health in adolescence require further empirical research, looking specifically at the special needs of adolescent mothers, community-based reproduction, and sexuality clinics.

See Also

ADOLESCENCE; AIDS AND HIV; GIRL STUDIES; GYNECOLOGY; MENSTRUATION; REPRODUCTIVE HEALTH; REPRODUCTIVE RIGHTS; SEX EDUCATION; SEXUALITY: OVERVIEW; VIRGINITY

References and Further Reading

Aulagnon, M. 1995. La conférence à Bejing. *Le monde* (18 Sept.): 1.

Chase Lansdale, P., and Brooks Gunn, and R. Paikoff. 1991. Research and programs for adolescent mothers: Missing links and future promises. *Family Relations* 40: 1–8.

Deaney, J., M. Lupton, and E. Toth. 1988. *The curse: A cultural history of menstruation.* Rev. ed. University of Illinois Press.

Dreyer, P. 1982. Sexuality during adolescence. In B. Wolman, ed., *Handbook of developmental psychology,* 26. Englewood Cliffs, N.J.: Prentice Hall.

Gilligan, C. 1982. *In a different voice: Psychology theory and women's development.* Cambridge, Mass.: Harvard University Press.

Gordon, S., and J. Gilgun. 1987. Adolescent sexuality. In V. Van Hasselt and M. Hersen, eds., *Handbook of adolescent psychology,* 15. New York: Pergamon.

Guernina, Z. 1994. *Human development: Adolescent studies in Algeria.* London: Avebury.

Heiman, J., and J. Verhulst. 1982. Gender and sexual functioning. In I. Al Issa, ed., *Gender and psychopathology,* 20. New York: Academic Press.

Kuziel-Perri, and J. Snarey. 1991. Adolescent repeat pregnancies: An evaluation study of a comprehensive service program for pregnant and parenting black adolescents. *Family Relations* 40: 381–385.

Laws, S. 1990. *Issues of blood.* London: Macmillan.

Lees, S. 1993. *Sugar and spice: Sexuality and adolescent girls.* London: Penguin.

McDonough, R., and R. Harrison. 1978. Patriarchy and relation of production. In A. Kahn and A. Wolfe, eds., *Feminism and materialism.* London: Routledge.

Mead, M. 1974. Adolescence. In *Youth and culture: A human development approach.* London: Brooks and Cole.

Mernissi, F. 1975. *Beyond the veil.* London: John Wiley.

Miller, A. 1988. *The drama of being a child.* London: Virago.

Miller, B., and K. Moore. 1990. Adolescent sexual behaviour, pregnancy and parenting: Research through the 1980s. *Journal of Marriage and the Family* 52: 1025–1044.

Mitchell, J. 1966. Women: The longest revolution. *New Left Review* 40: 11–37.

Paige, K., and J. Paige. 1981. The politics of reproductive rituals. Berkeley: University of California Press.

Rubin, G. 1984. Thinking sex: Notes for a radical theory of the politics of sexuality. In C. S. Vance, ed., *Pleasure and danger: Exploring female sexuality.* London: Routledge and Kegan Paul.

Schorr, L. 1988. *Within our reach: Breaking the cycle of disadvantage and despair.* London: Anchor.

Thornburg, H., and Z. Aras. 1986. Physical characteristics of developing adolescents. *Journal of Adolescent Research* 1: 47–78.

Trussell, J. 1988. Teenage pregnancy in the United States. *Family Planning Perspectives* 20: 262–272.

Unger, R., and M. Crawford. 1992. *Women and gender.* London: McGraw Hill.

Winter, L. 1988. The role of sexual self concept in the use of contraceptives. *Family Planning Perspectives* 20: 123–127.

Zoubida Guernina

SEXUALITY: Africa

In African tradition, sexuality encompasses the whole spectrum of activities pertaining to conception, childbirth, childhood, adolescence, adulthood, senescence, and death. Well-established rites of passage, courtship, marriage, and behavioral codes, as well as relationships to the not-yet born, the clan, and the dead, must be understood before contemporary African sexuality can be defined.

Although at the start of the twenty-first century, there is an emerging African feminist analysis, defining a cultural understanding of sexuality presents a major challenge to social scientists and feminists. An analysis of African sexuality must occur in the context of African traditional social structure prior to the infiltration of Western missionaries, colonization, and the introduction of European values. Sexual activity occurred within a socially sanctioned environment in which each age group and individual within the tribe, clan, community or family played well defined roles (Mugo, 1982).

Sexuality as well as sexual activity were, thus, part of social organization (Mbiti, 1969). Individual as well as communal responsibilities were clearly delineated. A breach of the sexual code of conduct by an individual or group would lead to a chain reaction sometimes affecting the entire community (Mboya, 1986). Misfortunes such as miscarriage, the death of a child, or infertility were attributed to individual impropriety (Ochola, 1980; Ominde, 1968). So, too, were natural disasters.

Sexuality was an important vehicle for socialization. Sexual activity was, thus, a collective responsibility. For example, specific punitive measures were applied to a man or woman who did not fulfil sexual obligations in a married situation, particularly relating to sexual denial or lack of restraint at given times and in the prescribed manner. Traditionally, sexuality among African peoples was influenced by the belief system, kinship, rites of passage, social coherence, and male dominance.

The Belief System

All social subsystems originated from a belief system under the supernatural control of a deity. Many societal provisions were, therefore, beyond reproach. The belief system operated through a set of rituals and ceremonies to celebrate, commemorate, or cleanse. There was little distinction between sacred and secular beliefs. They governed marriage, childbirth, circumcision, and funeral ceremonies as well as farming, harvesting, and livestock rearing. The symbols for various aspects of the belief system included celestial bodies—sun, moon, and stars—as well as rivers, lakes, forests, and mountains and the female symbol of fertility. Men played a bigger role than women during rituals and ceremonies. Women served and ensured the comfort of all, a role perceived as valueless. A few powerful women such as herbalists, rainmakers, and fortune tellers were held in high esteem by the entire community. Such women were no longer considered or referred to as women but were referred to by these positions, thereby assuming a different and revered position than ordinary women or men in those societies.

Sexuality, Kinship, and Socialization

Sexuality served the complex institution of marriage. Marriage was a duty and the point of convergence of all the members of a community: the departed, the living, and those yet to be born (Mbiti, 1969; Wambue, 1979). It was a rhythm of life in which everyone participated. It was equally important to have many children to name after parents, grandparents, and important ancestors in order to immortalize them. An individual with no descendants was considered to have abrogated this sacred obligation and was deemed to be forever dead, even during their lifetime (Mbiti, 1969). Kinship was one of the strongest forces in African traditional societies. It was established through marriage. It governed sexuality by specifying marital rules, customs, and practices within a community. In those societies, the scope of relatives was wide, because to blood relatives was added those relatives through marriage. The kinship system also included vertical "communication" between the living, their departed kin, and those yet to be born, making the three groups merely components of a single living entity. In essence, one lived eternally within the family and community.

Rites of Passage

Within African traditional societies, rites of passage marked "coming of age" for both sexes and an initiation into their proper roles and purposes in the family, community, and society at large. This developmental stage marked the end of a prolonged socialization process, which commenced at birth. For the boys, these stages included circumcision (Kenyatta, 1965), engraving, and scarification, extraction of teeth, as well as performing feats showing courage and commitment such as killing a lion singlehandedly. For women, they involved scarification and engraving and, in some tribes, female circumcision. Training of girls in acceptable sexual practices and positions was carried out by old women—aunts and grandparents. Sexual pleasure was rarely addressed. Recognizing the requirements of body, mind, and spirit, it was believed that recreational sex could sap the couples' energy and carry ill omens. Men were therefore forbidden from having sexual intercourse on the eve of any social or sacred event such as interclan war, a wrestling festival, or a hunting expedition. As part of sexual training, social adolescents (boys and girls) were allowed to make genital-genital contact without male penetration (Ahlberg, 1991;

Njau, 1992). If a girl conceived outside marriage, she was sent away to stay with distant relatives to conceal the shame that would befall her family and community. If the efforts to marry the pair failed, she would usually not be able to get a young man to marry and would eventually be married off to an elder polygamous man (Mbiti, 1969). Proverbs reflect the double standard by exhorting such "heroic" men but ridiculing the girl for shaming her family.

Social Coherence

In African traditional society, marriage was predominantly exogamous. It was an elaborate and tedious process of negotiations between the two families, which could take as long as two years. After a prospective bride had been identified either by the boy himself or members of his clan, comprehensive investigations were commenced regarding her virginity, honesty, loyalty, physical strength, generosity with food, and ability to prepare traditional brew. The family's wealth and social status were also assessed. The girl's clan would carry out similar investigations on the boy. Only when both sides were satisfied did negotiations for marriage begin. Exogamy was intended to prevent incest, which seemed to have a much broader and significant meaning in African than in Western societies. For instance, whole tribes could not intermarry because they were "related." Thus, the societies achieved a greater genetic diversity than was necessary to merely reduce genetic defects. Second, marrying the enemy reduced interclan wars. The few tribes that practiced exogamy feared "genetic contamination" by "inferior" communities or assimilation by bigger and stronger ones. Both exogamous and endogamous communities practiced wife inheritance but for different reasons. In exogamous communities, widows were inherited to prevent them from marrying enemies and bearing for them sons who would then be used to fight their mother's clan. Endogamous clans practiced widow inheritance to preserve the purity of their clan by preventing assimilation. A widow was deemed to belong to her late husband's clan. She was inherited by brothers or male cousins of the deceased.

Thus, marriage transcended death as fertility, legitimacy, and sexual rights were communal, not individual, affairs. A childless woman was allowed to bring her (usually younger) sister to her husband to bear children on her behalf. She would then treat these children as her own. Where the man was suspected to be infertile, the wife was advised (usually by women from her parent community) to discreetly have sexual relations with her brothers-in-law in order to conceive and bear children. These were considered her husband's children. A woman whose husband died childless was allowed

to take a lover to father his children. Women were blamed for childless marriages and suspected of misconduct. (Actually, one of the most common causes of female infertility is tubal blockage following salpingitis [Okumu, 1990]; this probably was always the case.) Illegal abortions also accounted for high rates of infections and mortality. So fundamental is childbearing to African social order that disabled, chronically sick women and women with mental disorders were given significant regard in expressing their sexual rights in relation to their reproductive aspirations.

Polygamy was practiced to rapidly increase the number of sons within the community and to maintain maternal and child-health by prolonging interpregnancy intervals. Following delivery, sexual contact between the couple was prohibited until the child carried food from the mother's hut and served it to the father. It was the assumption that a woman had no sexual desires besides procreation.

Many traditional sexual practices were clearly discriminatory, erroneous, and punitive toward women. To advance meaningful participation in the women's continental and global movement and to define gender-balanced, holistic African sexuality, contemporary writers such as Ahlberg (1991), and Njau (1992) have analyzed, compiled, and disseminated crucial information on traditional and contemporary African societies' sexuality, human rights, and social justice.

See Also

ANCIENT INDIGENOUS CULTURES: WOMEN'S ROLES; FAMILY: RELIGIONS AND LEGAL SYSTEMS—EAST AFRICA; FAMILY: RELIGIOUS AND LEGAL SYSTEMS—WEST AFRICA; FEMALE CIRCUMCISION AND GENITAL MUTILATION; HOUSEHOLDS AND FAMILIES: SOUTHERN AFRICA; HOUSEHOLDS AND FAMILIES: SUB-SAHARAN AFRICA; IMAGES OF WOMEN: AFRICA; MARRIAGE: REGIONAL TRADITIONS AND PRACTICES; SEX: BELIEFS AND CUSTOMS

References and Further Reading

Ahlberg, B. M. 1991. *Woman, sexually and the changing social order.* Philadelphia: Gorder and Breath.

Kenyatta J. 1965. *Facing Mount Kenya.* New York: Vintage.

Mbiti J. S. 1969. *African religious and philosophy.* Nairobi: Heineman.

Mboya P. 1986. *Luo customs and their culture.* Trans. J. A. Achieng. Gendia Mission. (Unpublished manuscript.)

Mugo, E. N. 1982. *Kikuyu people: A brief outline of their customs and traditions.* Nairobi: Kenya Literature Bureau.

Njau, P. N. 1992. Traditional sex education in Africa: The case of Kenya. Paper presented at the African Conference, held at Safari park Hotel, Nairobi.

Ominde, S. H. 1952. *The Luo girl from infancy to marriage.* London: Macmillan.

Otieno-Ochieng, N. A. 1968. *Luo social systems with a special analysis of marriage ritual.* Nairobi: Equator Publishers.

Wambeu, D. N. 1979. *Kikuyu customary marriage with particular reference to present.* LLb. thesis, U.O.N.

Worthman, C.M., and J.N.M. Wheting, 1987.

Social change in adolescent sexual behavior, mate selection, and pre-marital pregnancy in a Kikuyu community. *Ethnos* 15(2): 14–167.

Mary Okuma

SEXUALITY: Bisexual

See BISEXUALITY.

SEXUALITY: HINDU CULTURE

The roots of Hindu beliefs about sexuality are buried under centuries of colonial rule that have superimposed different meanings upon the original Indian outlook. India is composed of myriad social, linguistic, and religious cultures that all follow their own customs. Generalization about Hindu culture is impossible, but we can trace some core beliefs by reference to the written text of the Kama Sutra, to beliefs regarding creation, to the spiritual direction of Tantra, and to the Indian medical system, Ayurveda.

Kamasutra

The text known as the Kama Sutra is said to have been composed sometime between the second and fifth century. It attempts to define the relationship between a man and a woman. Kama is the Hindu god of love; the word *kama* means "pleasure," a meaning that encompasses any pleasure that can be experienced through the senses.

Kama, or pleasure, including sexual pleasure, is one of the three great aims of Hindu life; it should be pursued in harmony with *dharma* and *artha. Dharma* broadly means duty, while *artha* means wealth. The Kama Sutra brings these ideas together in its instruction upon the techniques of love making; the text emphasizes that women's pleasure must come before men's.

Beliefs Regarding Creation

Through the centuries of Indian cultural change one idea has been fundamental, though sometimes dormant: sexuality in men and animals celebrates the presence of a creative divinity. One of the oldest Upanishads, the Brihadaranyaka, celebrates the sexual union as a sacrificial act of creation:

Woman is the sacrificial fire,
the lips of her *yoni* (vulva) the fuel,
the hairs around them the smoke,
and the vagina itself the flame.
The act of penetration is the lightening,
the feeling of pleasures are the sparks.
In this fire the gods offer up semen-seeds,
and from this offering man is born.
(Sinha, 1992)

The Hindu belief that sexuality is intrinsically divine is also ritualized in the worship of the *Lingam and yoni,* a symbolic representation of Siva—the Hindu god of destruction and creation—and his consort Parvati.

The sculped image of the lingum (the phallus) usually stands erect in a shallow, circular basin that represents the yoni (the vulva). As an icon, it reflects the notion of creativity, including sexuality, through which all life is created. This image is an object of worship in homes all over India, and each Monday, millions of men and women tend their family shrines by pouring milk over the lingam, which spills into the yoni and then flows out over a spout on its side.

The central role of sexuality in Indian spiritual life is also demonstrated in the flourishing erotic art within the temples of India. Most Indian temples have sculpture relating to sexuality and depicting sexual intercourse; the temple site of Khajuraho, with its thousands of erotic scuptures, is perhaps the most famous.

Tantra

The philosophical and religious system of Tantra involves rituals in which sex plays a fundamental part. In this system sexual excitement is created but is never discharged: the intent of Tantric practice is to turn sexual energy back inward and transform it into an experience of religious bliss.

Ayurveda

Indian medical thought is based on Ayurveda, a holistic system that emphasizes the relationships between body, mind, and soul, and sees *dis-ease* as an imbalance in the system.

Sexuality plays a major role in Ayuvedic thought. For instance, excessive loss of semen is believed to take a heavy toll on the body; consequently, controlling loss of semen plays an important role in male sexuality. It is further believed that the male absorbs the female's secretion during sexual intercourse and hence that female satisfaction is beneficial to his development. Further, Ayurveda specifies times in which sexual intercourse should not occur; biological cycles are viewed as being properly tied to particular lunar cycles. Certain Hindu beliefs also sanctify women's right to insist on sexual intercourse at certain times (Meyer, 1971). This gives a societal sanction for women to refuse or demand sexual intercourse.

Despite the profusion of sexual images and allusions in Hindu religion and literature there is little talk about sex in the day-to-day culture of India. Some observers maintain that sexuality in Hindu culture is repressed. Women, on the whole, are said to have little autonomy or pleasure in matters related to sex. Many Indians view the beliefs rooted in Ayurveda as superstitious and wrong. Sexuality in Hindu culture is thus a complex interplay of various levels of thoughts, beliefs, and attitudes.

See Also

BIGAMY; CELIBACY; GODDESS; HINDUISM; MARRIAGE: REGIONAL TRADITIONS AND PRACTICES; SACRED TEXTS; SEX AND CULTURE; SPIRITUALITY: SEXUALITY; TRADITIONAL HEALING: INDIA

References and Further Reading

Frawley, David. 1989. *Ayurvedic healing.* Delhi: Motilal Banara-sidas.

Meyer, Johann Jakob. 1971. *Sexual life in ancient India,* 17. Delhi: Motilal Banarasidas.

Punja, Shobita. 1992. *Divine ecstasy: The story of Khajuraho.* New Delhi and New York: Viking.

Rawson, Philip. 1973. *The Indian culture of ecstasy: Tantra.* London: Thames and Hudson. London.

Sinha, Indira. 1992. *The love teachings of kamasutra,* 10: Bookwise.

Karkar, Sudhir. 1989. *Intimate relations: Exploring Indian sexuality.* Chicago: University of Chicago Press.

Sur, A. K. 1992. *Sex and marriage in India.* Columbia, Mo.: Allied.

Mira Savara

SEXUALITY: Lesbian

See LESBIAN SEXUALITY.

SEXUALITY: Psychology of Sexuality in Cross-Cultural Perspectives

Feminist psychological research shows that sexual inequality is a common feature among women across cultures, manifested by ambivalence between cultural norms and male power. Frankenhaueuser et al. (1991) report that women constitute half of the world's population, perform two-thirds of work hours, receive one-tenth of the world's income, and own less than one-hundredth of the world's property. The marked contrasts of inequalities have aggravated gender categorization and preoccupation with sexuality based on habituation and social conditioning. Most people who congratulate the parents of a newborn ask first about the baby's sex before they inquire about the mother's health. Most cultures seem to welcome the birth of a boy. The cultural trappings of gender categorization aim at the retention of a male monopoly, which is reflected in the multiplicity of meanings of gender.

Gender is often confused with *sex* and *sexuality.* These terms are the product of historical and cultural construction. They have been defined as biological categories to aggravate women's seclusion and oppression. Feminist research defines *gender* as a sociocultural category often characterized by assumptions made about males and females on the basis of sex. It encompasses culturally determined cognitions, attitudes, and belief systems at the cultural and historical levels. Stoller (1968) defines *gender* as the amount of masculinity or femininity found in persons. Sex is operationalized as a biologically based variable grounded in reproductive processes. Dworkin (1974) defines *sex* in terms of the endocrinological male versus female hormones. Sexuality is perceived as being governed by sex roles and is determined by variables such as life events and an individual's psychological processes. Plummer (1981) contends that sexuality does not exist, but culture builds a construction of what it is to be sexual. Gender, sexuality, and sex are clusters of expectations of behaviors that define male or female identity in most cultures.

Feminism, in the context of this article, is defined as the principle by which women are entitled to political and social rights equal to those of men. It denounces gender dimensions dominated by patriarchal systems that oppress women's identity.

This article attempts to apply a historical, cross-cultural, psychological perspective to women's sexuality. It stresses that women's gender, sexuality, and sex need to be understood in their historical and cultural contextual diversity within a feminist framework rather than through a monocultural, male-dominated approach.

Historical Perspectives on Gender, Sexuality, and Sex

Throughout history, women have been portrayed in contradictory, conflicting symbols—myths that degrade their sexuality and gender identity. These negative positions have clouded the psychological experiences of women's worth.

Historically, in Judaism, Christianity, and Islam, Eve is viewed as the sinful woman who seduced Adam. She is perceived as the source of human confrontation with mortality. This has aggravated the widespread fear in many cultures about the destructive powers of women's sexuality. The Virgin Mary restored the balance by symbolizing chastity, obedience, and service. Toward the eleventh century, courtly love—whereby females were served and adored—was deemed necessary. In the Victorian period, the emphasis on the purity and chastity of married women was balanced by the exploitation of women through prostitution (Foucault, 1978). Feminist theories have analyzed these traditional approaches and introduced women's voices to define themselves. Women's sexuality is not innate; it is learned and expressed through conditioning. Bern and Bern (1970) emphasize that historically women have developed personal behavior that fit cultural stereotypes. This process, called sex typing, has traditionally encouraged women to be submissive and men to be dominant. As a result, sex-role socialization takes the form of oppressing women and limiting their potential.

The feminist movement has led to a revision of thinking about gender roles and women's sexuality. It recognizes the impact of sociocultural, political roles on gender socialization as a major source of women's oppression. Women are not born weak, but they are taught to be passive, submissive, and supportive, whereas men are taught to be strong and dominant. Historically and cross-culturally, great cultural diversity exists in defining gender, sexuality, and sex.

Cross-Cultural Perspectives on Gender, Sexuality, and Sex

Cross-cultural studies examine gender, sexuality, and sex outside the limited views of monocultural approaches. Early cross-cultural psychological reports on sexuality were ethnographic in nature. Westermarch (1891) found that incest is central to family life in many cultures. Malinowski (1929) reported on the sexual practices of the Trobriand Islanders, where fathers are not the authority figure. He repeated the mistake of many western anthropologists by classifying other cultures as savage and their sexuality as barbaric. In 1930 Margaret Mead focused on the importance of gender roles by observing that men and women have different value systems in expressing their sexuality. Among the Mundugumor, both males and females are expected to behave in ways that we think of as aggressive and masculine. The Arapesh expect males and females to behave in feminine ways: cooperative and maternal. Women's oppression is a male invention that supports patriarchy and an economic hierarchy that is beneficial to men at the exploita-

tion of women's sexuality by restraining women's identity inside restricted walls. In many cultures, routine daily duties are performed behind kitchen walls by women preparing food and making sure that all members of the family are cared for. In the bedroom, women are expected to endure sexual harassment silently and to give pleasure. In the street and at work women are seen as a waste of space and are constantly humiliated and unjustly treated. Cross-cultural research shows that stereotyped roles are widespread. Ford and Beach (1951) report the incidence of cultural variance on sexuality: kissing is never done in many cultures and is seen as dirty and sinful. The Thonga of Africa consider Europeans dirty, and they express their horror when they see couples kissing: "Look at them, they are eating each other's saliva and dirt" (49).

However, there are many variations on attitudes to sexuality across cultures. Christensen (1973) refers to the *etic* (universal) and *emic* (specific) aspects of sexual behavior in nine different cultures through courtship; marriage varies from one culture to another. In the Middle East boys and girls are prohibited from embracing and holding hands in public but are allowed to do so with the same sex.

In Bangladesh, as Lindenbaum (1977) reports, gender, sex, and sexuality are associated with the right and left sides. Men are associated with the right side, which is seen as the strongest, and women with the left side, the weakest. Women who are respected by their husbands should eat and lie in bed on the left side of their husbands rather than on the right. Every culture has its regulations that define the conditions under which virginity, marriage, pregnancy, and childrearing take place.

Families across cultures differ in gender-role typing by the ways in which they organize socialization for their children according to their gender. Boys and girls are observed and treated differently. Boys are dressed in blue and girls in pink. The findings from cross-cultural studies by Williams and Best (1990) found a consensus across cultures that men are seen as adventurous and robust, whereas women are seen as dreamy and sentimental.

Although the above studies are not widely representative of all cultures, they are the starting point in challenging the patriarchal forces that still prevail in many countries. These have been fueled by feminist ideas that have changed the values and beliefs surrounding sexuality. The declaration by Ross and Rapp (1981) stresses that the personal is political: "the seemingly most intimate details of private existence are structured by larger social relations" (51).

Cross-cultural psychologists often focus on the individual's role and tend to neglect society's role (Guernina,

1994). They describe women as unable to adjust to their gender roles and sexuality but do not provide any clarification of the impact of the sociocultural systems on women's lives. A relevant example is the work of Mandelbaum (1988), who focused on cross-cultural study in Northern India, Bangladesh, and Pakistan. Interesting examples are given of women's oppression by men but without any clarification of the role of society.

In the three cultures studied, women's behavior and sexuality—for example, the importance for women to avoid eye contact with men, to speak and laugh quietly, and to preserve honorable behavior (an unmarried, pregnant woman is likely to be killed by her father to protect the family's honor)—are clearly defined by patriarchal systems.

Davis and Whitten (1987) note that the nature of cross-cultural research on sexuality has been a function of how attitudes are formed on patterns of women's sexual behavior, which reflects the value system and social structures of different cultures.

Conclusion

Historical and cross-cultural perspectives are important in clarifying the concepts of gender, sex, and sexuality. As it has been shown, these three important concepts have been shaped by cultural norms that tend to limit women's ability to perceive their role and their sexual identity. This stresses that sex is not the hidden force behind history. It is the discursive use of sex that enables some people to be dominated by others. Men have defined what counts as sexuality for themselves, which, by excluding women, has left women with few sexual role models. Moreover, women encounter conflicting double standards of expectations in many countries where permissiveness is a male activity and abstinence a woman's "expression." Guernina (1993) shows that the implications of traditional sex-role socialization and discrimination at all levels of the social community are complex and multidetermined.

See Also

ANTHROPOLOGY; GENDER; GENDER CONSTRUCTIONS IN THE FAMILY; PSYCHOLOGY: OVERVIEW; SEX AND CULTURE; SEXUALITY: OVERVIEW; SEXUALITY IN HINDU CULTURE; SEXUALITY: PSYCHOLOGY OF SEXUALITY IN THE UNITED STATES

References and Further Reading

Bern, S., and D. Bern. 1970. Training the woman to know her place. The power of a non-conscious ideology. In M. Gaskoff, ed., *Roles woman play: Readings towards women's liberation.* Belmont, Calif.: Brooks Cole.

Christensen, H. 1973. Attitudes towards marital infidelity: a nine-culture sampling of university student opinion. *Journal of Comparative Family Studies* 4: 197–214.

Davis, D., and R. Whitten. 1987. The cross-cultural study of human sexuality. *Annual Review of Anthropology* 16: 69–98.

Dworkin, A. 1974. *Woman hating.* New York: Dutton.

Ford, C., and F. Beach. 1951. *Patterns of sexual behaviour.* New York: Harper.

Foucault, M. 1978. *The history of sexuality.* New York: Pantheon.

Frankenhaueuser, M., U. Lundberg, and M. Cherney. 1991. *Women, work and health: Stress and opportunities.* New York: Plenum.

Guernina, Z. 1993. *The use of hypnosis as a therapeutic tool for adolescents' sexual problems: A transcultural approach in hypnosis connecting disciplines.* Vienna: Medizinisch Pharmazeutische.

———. 1994. *Human development.* London: Avebury.

Lindenbaum, S. 1977. *The last course: Nutrition and anthropology in Asia.* New York: Humanities.

Malinowski, B. 1929. *The sexual life of savages.* Boston: Beacon.

Mead, M. 1930. *Growing up in New Guinea.* London: Morrow.

Plummer, K. 1981. *The making of the modern homosexual.* North Pomfret, Vt.: Hutchinson.

Ross, E., and R. Rapp. 1981. Sex and society. A research note from social history and anthropology. *Comparative Studies in Society and History* 23: 51–72.

Stoller, R. 1968. *Sex and gender.* New York: Aronson.

Westermarck, E. 1891. *The history of human marriage.* New York: Macmillan.

Williams, J., and D. Best. 1990. *Sex and psyche: Gender and self viewed cross-culturally.* Thousand Oaks, Calif.: Sage.

Zoubida Guernina

SEXUALITY:
Psychology of Sexuality in the United States

The psychology of sexuality relates to the human cognitive and emotional response to personal and interpersonal sexual behaviors. From the beginning of recorded time, human beings have created ideas, laws, customs, fantasies, and art around sexual acts. In other words, although mating is universal in the animal kingdom, the psychology of sexuality—the feelings and behaviors of human beings concerning sex—is a uniquely human trait.

Eighteenth and Nineteenth Centuries

In the eighteenth and nineteenth centuries there was significant variance in sexual tolerance among different countries, levels of society, and religious groups. In the United States, however, the Puritan ethic prevailed. Sex outside of marriage in the form of adultery or premarital sex was condemned, and family solidarity was exalted (Bullough, 1976).

Twentieth-Century Sexuality

In the twentieth century sexuality began to be investigated in a more objective manner. The works of Sigmund Freud, Havelock Ellis, Abraham Maslow, Margaret Sanger, Katherine Davis, Marie Stopes, and Alfred C. Kinsey and others paved the way for a more tolerant approach to the subject of sexual behavior. Sigmund Freud termed the sex drive *libido* and saw sex as one of the two major forces motivating human behavior. Havelock Ellis, a physician in Victorian England, believed that women as well as men were sexual creatures and that sexual deviations from the norm were generally harmless. Abraham Maslow believed that sex was a basic human drive and that the healthier the person the more closely sex and love were fused. The result of the *Kinsey Reports* (Kinsey et al., 1948; Kinsey et al., 1953) was alarm and confusion. A *Life* magazine article in August 1948 called the initial Kinsey study "a celebration of licentiousness." For the first time in the history of the United States there was documentation of actual sexual behavior that differed significantly from the commonly held perceptions of sexual behavior.

In the 1960s and 1970s the United States witnessed several changes that led to a revolution in sexual attitudes and behaviors. The major factors in this shift were the availability of birth control pills, the reemergence of feminism in a modern form, and a greater openness in discussion of sexuality. This greater openness was due in part to the availability of the extensive research findings of the new sex therapists, most notably William Masters and Virginia Johnson (Masters and Johnson, 1966, 1970) and Helen Singer Kaplan (Kaplan, 1979). With evidence from this clinical research, the average American began to more clearly understand the anatomy and physiology of the sexual response. Armed with this information, more women began to expect sexual pleasure and reproductive freedom in their sexual relationships.

The last twenty-five years of the twentieth century saw the emergence of literature of significance for various population groups. Writers emphasized the "truth about sexual pleasure" from a male perspective (Zilbergeld, 1992), a female perspective (Barbach, 1975), a gay and lesbian perspective (Greene and Herck, 1994), and a heterosexual perspective (Masters and Johnson, 1976). Each of these researchers and writers gleaned information from their clinical practices that traced the disappointments, discouragement, and dysfunctions of their patients and presented information of a self-help nature to the general population.

This information was widely disseminated and became the basis for many popular news and journal articles, as well as the content for television and radio talk shows. It was clear that sexuality had broadened from an issue of fertility to an issue of pleasure and emotional intimacy. The literature of male sexuality stressed topics decidedly psychological in nature—becoming a better listener, dealing with conflict, becoming a good lover for a partner, improving intimacy in a relationship, and clarifying the nature of performance versus pleasure. The psychology of sexual behavior was also emphasized in the writing concerning female sexuality. Significant topics were those related to knowing the female body, learning self-pleasuring, practicing sexual assertiveness, and enhancing intimacy in a relationship apart from the sexual act itself. The literature of homosexual partnering delved into such subjects as building permanent relationships, improving communication, empowering relationships, dealing with fertility, and parenting and family issues. Of particular significance in the homosexual community was the response to the AIDS epidemic in the general population. The homosexual community took a leadership role in educating the population about safe-sex techniques.

The 1980s and 1990s witnessed the proliferation of information concerning those whose sexual arousal patterns are not the norm. These more unusual patterns are labeled the "paraphilias," and significant information exists concerning individuals who fit this pattern of expression of fantasy and behavior. Paraphilias are adult arousal patterns such as exhibitionism, voyeurism, frotteurism (rubbing), pedophilia, and fetishes. Psychologist John Money is a prolific researcher and writer in this field whose work describes the inception of these behaviors, and he outlines the paths or "lovemaps" that are the bases of these sexual patterns (Money, 1986).

The professional writing concerning the psychology of sexuality in the 1990s stressed the role of intimacy and loving relationships, equality in relationships, and the expectation of consensuality in relationships. There has been division among professionals about the role of sexually explicit material in the healthy sexuality of adults. Consensus remains, however, that in the new millennium, sexuality education for children, adolescents, and adults will continue to be vital so that each person can substantially create a psychology of their individual sexuality that is effective for their health and happiness.

See Also

PSYCHIATRY; PSYCHOLOGY: OVERVIEW; SEX: BELIEFS AND CUSTOMS; SEXOLOGY AND SEX RESEARCH; SEXUALITY: OVERVIEW; SEXUALITY: PSYCHOLOGY OF SEXUALITY IN CROSS-CULTURAL PERSPECTIVES

References and Further Readings

Barbach, Lonnie. 1975. *For yourself: The fulfillment of female sexuality.* New York: New American Library.

Bullough, Vernon L. 1976. *Sexual variance in society and history.* New York: Wiley.

Greene, Beverly, and Gregory M. Herck. 1994. *Lesbian and gay psychology.* Thousand Oaks, Calif.: Sage.

Kaplan, Helen Singer. 1979. *Disorders of sexual desire.* New York: Brunner/Mazel.

Kinsey, Alfred C., Wardell B. Pomeroy, and Clyde E. Martin. 1948. *Sexual Behavior in the Human Male.* Philadelphia: Saunders.

Kinsey, Alfred C., Wardell B. Pomeroy, Clyde E. Martin, and Paul H. Gebhard. 1953. *Sexual Behavior in the Human Female.* Boston: Little, Brown.

Masters, W. H., and V. E. Johnson. 1966. *Human sexual response.* Boston: Little, Brown.

———. 1970. *Human sexual inadequacy.* Boston: Little, Brown.

———. 1976. *The pleasure bond.* New York: Bantam.

Money, John. 1986. *Lovemaps.* New York: Irvington Press.

Zilbergeld, Bernie. 1992. *The new male sexuality.* New York: Bantam.

Mary Ann Watson

SEXUALITY: Spirituality

See SPIRITUALITY: SEXUALITY.

SHAKERS

Many religions led by women have been more concerned with improvement of life circumstances and the world of today rather than with rewards in the afterlife. Certainly feminist spirituality groups today are usually focused on the empowering of women, broad-based social change, and protection of the environment. Life here and now should be enjoyed and death not feared but considered a part of a cyclical process.

The Shakers (or Believers in Christ's Second Appearing), as they developed under the leadership of Mother Ann Lee in England and then in North America after she and eight followers immigrated in 1774, shared some of the this-world orientation. They believed in the unity of the spiritual and the earthly, with neat communities, pacifism, a God with an androgynous nature, and a theology of equivalence, with women and men working in the same community but living in separate sections of the household. During the time that Lee was the leader and center of the community (until her death in 1784), the group suffered a great deal of harassment, much of it directed toward Lee, who was accused by civil authorities of being a British agent, and, by other people, of being a witch. The ecstatic (or "free") worship practiced by the Believers, Lee's leadership position and charismatic personality, her critique of male-centered theology, and her teachings on celibacy were unconventional enough to be frightening to many who were more comfortable with patriarchal conventions.

After Lee's death, leadership was taken by men, and the new Shaker communities became more patriarchal. However, the continued need for a set of leaders for the women meant that compared with most other women in the eighteenth and nineteenth centuries, the Shaker women had access to some leadership possibilities, more options for travel (to organize new groups), access to some of their own profits, personal security, and in-house support from other women.

See Also

CHRISTIANITY: STATUS OF WOMEN IN THE CHURCH; THEOLOGIES: FEMINIST

References and Further Reading

Procter-Smith, Marjorie. 1985. *Women in Shaker community and worship: A feminist analysis of the uses of religious symbols.* Lewiston, N.Y.: The Edwin Mellen Press.

Sered, Susan Starr. 1994. *Priestess, Mother, sacred sister: Religions dominated by women.* New York: Oxford University Press.

Cheris Kramarae

SHAKTI

In Hindu cosmology Shakti is the supreme cosmic energy, personified as female, that animates the universe, deities, and the souls of people. As the supreme creator, sustainer, and destroyer of the cosmos, Shakti is still worshipped in India today as a figure of divine power and wisdom, continuing an apparently universal tradition of Mother Goddess worship dating to several millennia B.C.

As Shakti-Kali, she is worshipped as the benign and fearful Mother. Portrayed alternatively as a female figure with legs apart and a plant issuing from her womb, and as standing over her dead consort, Shiva, devouring his body, she is responsible for both the creation and the dissolution of the cosmos. Embodying the ancient wisdom that life cannot exist without death, Shakti is venerated as the Mother who gives birth and nurtures life, as well as the Mother to whom one's soul returns blissfully in death. Shakti's female energy in the Tantric tradition includes a sexual expression, where sexual union can be equated with attainment of a powerful spiritual union with the cosmic All. Such a vision of divine female energy encourages the honor and respect of women and girls, although the power of Shakti is held to be latent in every person.

Shakti is also worshipped as the image of female wisdom and enlightenment, an idea that was embraced by other wisdom traditions such as Gnostic Christianity, which worshipped Shakti under such names as Sophia (wisdom), Pneuma (breath/spirit), or Anima (feminine soul). As the source of all creative energy and wisdom, Shakti is said to have invented Sanskrit and is the goddess of all creative arts, particularly poetry and music, of learning, and of science. Shakti understood as wisdom reflects the active presence of God's involvement in the world, an affirmation of God's nearness to the people, especially in their struggles for liberation.

Many women in India find inspiration in Shakti as a symbol of feminine power and energy that enables them to break the traditional submissive, self-sacrificing stereotype, calling attention to the injustice of women's abuse and generally subordinate status in secular life. However, as Jawahara K. Saidhulla (1992) points out, "the land that worships strong mother images burns women for dowry and debases them in many ways." The contradictions between Shakti worship and the realities of women's lives will need to be resolved before this aspect of Hinduism represents a true spirituality of empowerment for women.

See Also

DEATH; GODDESS; HINDUISM; HOLY SPIRIT; MOTHER EARTH

References and Further Reading

Madtha, William. 1980. Shakti, the feminine aspect of God in Indian tradition. *Journal of Dharma* 4(Jan.–Mar.): 175.

Mookerjee, Ajit. 1988. *Kali: The feminine force.* London: Thomas and Hudson.

Saidulla, Jawahara K. 1992. Shakti—The power of the Mother: The violent nurturer in Indian mythology and commercial cinema. *Canadian Women's Studies* 13(Fall): 37–41.

Margaret Shanthi Stevens

SHINTO

Shinto, "the way of the gods," is the indigenous religion of Japan. The first use of the term was about 720 C.E., in *Nihon Syoki* (*Chronicle of Japan*), one of Japan's earliest surviving writings. At that time it referred to conventional rituals and beliefs expressing a reaction against Buddhism. Later, Shinto interacted with Buddhism, Confucianism, and Taoism, becoming the state religion and an important component of Japanese identity.

Ancient Period

Shinto developed at the time of the *ritsu-ryo*—a governing system based on a combination of criminal codes (*ritsu*) and admininstrative codes (*ryo*), enforced from the late eighth century to the early ninth century. Before this, in general, each great family or community had performed its own religious ceremonies, *jingi-saishi* ("god rites").

The basic purpose of *jingi-saishi* was to entertain the gods. In these community rites, women had status equal to men, or even had a dominant, official status. Both men and women could perform the ceremonies, and no gender distinction was made regarding most duties, such as cooking, setting up, and serving. However, hard manual work was done by men; also, shamans were involved in the rites, and usually a female shaman communicated with the gods and a male shaman would interpret her words. Little or no notice was taken of the gods' gender. Shinto is an animistic religion: the gods (*kami*) were nature deities, invisible spirits residing in, for example, sacred trees or ancestor gods associated with the land where members of the community had originally lived. The nature gods are described in *Nihon Syoki* and in *Kojiki* (*Record of Ancient Matters*, 712).

Under the *ritsu-ryo* system, which modeled itself on the patriarchal bureaucracy of Tang China, women lost the status they had held in the *jingi* rites. Thereafter, the "bureaucratic" or priestly ceremonial positions were typically monopolized by men. Men also officiated at family rites, since the family was patriarchal.

However, the patriarchal system at that time was not thoroughgoing; thus although women were not admitted to the official Shinto priesthood, they continued to play an important role at the scenes of rites. Notably, some of the most important shrines—*jinja*—were believed to have been founded by a female shaman; one example is Kitano-ten-mangu, the shrine of the celestial god Kitano. Also, Amat-erasu-omikame ("Person Who Makes the Heavens Shine"), chief of the pantheon and the ancestor of the imperial family, was known as a female *kami*.

Medieval Period

The religious doctrines of the *jingi* rite were still immature at the time of the *ritsu-ryo* system, but they gradually developed further after the middle of the eighth century, as Shinto began to accept and incorporate elements of Buddhism. In this process, the deities took on personality and gender, and many Shinto beliefs came to have something in common with Buddhist ideas. For example, the concepts of yin and yang were associated, respectively, with the male and the female; and some native *kami* were considered manifestations or temporary manifestations of the Indian buddhas and bodhisattvas—this amalgamation of *kami* and buddhas was called *shinbutsu-syugo*. The most valued virtues of the *kami* were honesty, purity, and mercy. Iznaki and Izanami, the first couple among the *kami*, who had given birth to the islands that make up Japan, rose in status, and love stories of the *kami* were created and widely circulated; these stories suggest that tenderness, compassion, and femininity were highly regarded. The guardian deity residing in water such as a spring or a ferry crossing was female, a manifestation of the goddess Benzaiten (Sarasvati) and the god of love and art. It was also believed that female gods guarded mountains and guided dead men to *jodo*—heaven, which was identified with high mountains.

On the other hand, female gods had to yield to male gods. A concept of women as unclean and nearer to death meant that women and goddesses had lower status than men and gods. In the *jingi* rites, although menstruation and childbirth were taboo, they were regarded as merely situational declines from vitality. After *shinbutsu-syugo,* Shinto took on the Buddhist tendency to despise women—Buddha does not redeem women—and so women were considered soiled; the blood of menstruation and childbirth became evidence of their sinfulness. These ideas were intensified by the emphasis of Shinto on purity. Adherents of Shinto criticized Buddhist funeral rites; to remain pure, Shinto insisted on getting rid of the uncleanliness of death—an idea that offered a convenient rationale for excluding women from holy places. Of course, this concept conflicted with the idea of goddesses residing in mountains and water; to resolve that conflict, female deities were said to be jealous of women.

Until the late medieval period, male priests nearly monopolized the management of shrines. However, there were two types of female priests (*miko*). *Jinja miko* were shrine virgins who could take part in rites under the supervision of men; these women and girls had sanctity rather than authority. *Aruki miko* were female religious practitioners; they traveled around to perform magic or to entertain—activities that were facilitated by the increased social mobility of this period.

Edo Period

Early in the seventeenth century, the Tokugawa government organized all the *jinja* and priests under the supervision of the Yoshida family, significantly restricting the activity of female priests. Women were not considered capable of learning the Yoshida rites or of acquiring official status; and in the newly standardized rites, the importance of the *jinja-miko* was diminished. In fact, though, women still played a part in shrine rites and sometimes even retained their former status, because the *jinja* continued to be managed by a hereditaty priestly family, the Syake.

At this time, Shinto had close rapport with neo-Confucianism, and some schools of thought emerged that tried to harmonize Shinto, neo-Confucianism, and Buddhism. The Confucianist influence tended to reinforce Shinto's concept of women as less valuable than men.

Early in the eighteenth century, *kokugaku,* or national learning, developed; representative figures included Komo no Mabuchi (1697–1769) and Motoori Norinaga (1730–1801). *Kokugaku* was critical of Confucianism and Buddhism and urged a return to the sources of Japanese identity. Komo looked for the essence of Shinto in ancient manly, ingenuous bravery; but Motoori associated the "ancient way" with human truth and with femininity, which respected emotion more than logic.

Meiji Period and Later

The nineteenth-century Meiji government, which was zealously nationalistic, reconstructed Shinto as Japan's state religion. The traditional Shinto priesthood was discontinued, leaving women totally alienated from the *jinja* priesthood. Women were allowed to engage only in "shadow" work, helping the male clergy in its private capacity.

Modern Shinto hardly discussed women and sex, for several reasons. First, the Meiji government considered Kokka Shinto—state Shinto—less a religion than a national morality, and the government controlled all doctrinal disputes. Second, the influence of western science and rationalism had led to a devaluing of sexual desire and similar worldly concerns. Third, the restructuring of Shinto had not changed its concept of the female as more sexual and therefore less clean than the male. Thus until World War II patriarchy was established as a moral standard and had a strong impact on social values; and Shinto supported the ideology of patriarchy and modernity.

The Postwar Period

After World War II, it was necessary to fill vacancies among the clergy, since many men had been killed during the war. Jinja Honcho, the Association of Shinto Shrines, therefore permitted widows of priests to hold the same positions their husbands had filled. This was only provisional, though, and women in such positions were expected to designate men as their successors. Today, women are no more than 10 percent of the clergy, and their role is mainly to provide assistance.

Recently, there has been a tendency for women to participate more, and more eagerly, in the management of the *jinja* organization, as a result of egalitarianism and also of demographics—the male population has decreased. But problems of women's orthodoxy and identity remain and are often overlooked or given little attention.

See Also

ANCIENT INDIGENOUS CULTURES: WOMEN'S ROLES; ANCIENT NATION-STATES: WOMEN'S ROLES; BUDDHISM; CONFUCIANISM; GODDESS; RELIGION: OVERVIEW

References and Further Reading

Erhart, H. Byron. 1982. *Japanese religion: Unity and diversity.* Belmont, Calif.: Wadsworth.

Littleton, C. Scott. 1996. Shinto. In C. Scott Littleton, ed., *Eastern wisdom: An illustrated guide to the religions and philosophies of the East.* New York: Holt.

Ono, Sokyo. 1962. *Shinto: The kami way.* Tokyo and Rutland, Vt.: Tuttle. (Paperback edition, 1994.)

Varley, Paul. 1998. Shinto. In Edward Craig, ed., *Routledge encyclopedia of philosophy,* Vol. 8. London and New York: Routledge.

Mori Mizue

SHORT STORY

The term *short story* is a seemingly obvious description for fictional writing that is shorter than a novel. Short stories can be as short as the 150-word fables written by Suniti Namjoshi in *Feminist Fables,* or as long as the 22,000-word stories in Isak Dinesen's collection *Seven Gothic Tales.* There are no strict rules for how long a piece of writing should be but publishers' printing costs can dictate the word count of stories, particularly when writers are invited to submit material to an editor commissioned to put together a collection. For this reason 3,000–3,500 words for short fiction has become the norm. Fictional works that go beyond 7,500 words (in adult fiction) are referred to as *novellas,* while the term *novel* describes stories longer than 40,000 words.

The short story as a Western literary genre was developed in the nineteenth century. Chekhov, along with Edgar Allan Poe, has been credited with the "founding" of the short story form. It is relevant to ask how limited this definition might be. For instance, oral storytelling has a tradition that only in more recent times is finding publishing form. Aboriginal Dreamtime, Native American, African and Caribbean cultures, and many white working-class communities have passed stories down from one generation to another. This longer history, in which women have played a major part, is now striving toward a wider audience within the limitations of the publishing market.

Short stories call for an economic use of words and suggestion. There is not enough space to develop multiple characters, complex interrelationships, in-depth examination of complex issues or plots of soap opera proportions. It is often (wrongly) assumed that short story writing is the first step, the nursery slope for beginners, in establishing a career as an author. The length of the short story form might seem an advantage but it can also be a test. How to convey stirring events, passionate feelings, subtle meaning in a few words?

In 1842 Edgar Allan Poe pronounced that the short story should aim for "a single effect," "a unity of expression." Most modern writers of the genre accept this as a general rule and adhere to it.

A second "rule" is that a short story should deal with a "moment of crisis." The word *crisis* here can include a moment of change, or realization. In the following extract from Katherine Mansfield's "The Dill Pickle" a couple are meeting after some years of separation:

"Ah no. You hate the cold ..."
"Loathe it." She shuddered. "And the worst of it is that the older one grows ..."
He interrupted her. "Excuse me," and tapped on the table for the waitress. "Please bring some coffee and cream." To her: "You sure you won't eat anything? Some fruit perhaps. The fruit here is very good."
"No thanks. Nothing."
"Then that's settled." And smiling just a hint too broadly he took up the orange again.

"You were saying—the older one grows—"

"The colder," she laughed. But she was thinking how well she remembered that trick of his—the trick of interrupting her—and how it used to exasperate her six years ago. She used to feel then as though he, quite suddenly, in the middle of what she was saying, put his hand over her lips, turned from her, attended to something different, and then took his hand away, and with just the same slightly too broad smile, gave her his attention again...Now we are ready. That is settled (1981: 168).

What is learned need not be dramatic. It is possible that none of the characters (unlike the example above) learn anything, that the "moment of realization" belongs to the reader—the author colluding with the reader in revealing the character's *lack* of understanding or progress.

All aspects of fictional writing—character, plot, dialogue, description, theme, and so on—can be employed in the short story and the narrative can be told from any point of view. In a novel there could be pages and pages of description concerning just one character; in a short story a paragraph or even a few sentences might have to suffice. This does not mean that the theme, the essence, has to be stated quickly or explicitly. On the contrary, the theme could emerge slowly or be left implied.

A collection of stories may be framed by a particular setting or overall theme. The same character might appear in a series of stories. A specific *type* of story or genre might be the aim—for example, a science fiction collection that focuses on crime solving by a futuristic private eye or a collection of autobiographical stories told from the author's point of view, centered around her childhood years in a particular location.

Women writers, such as Suniti Namjoshi and Angela Carter, have worked extensively with the short story form, using fables and fairy tales as their basic ingredients. Fables are centuries old and were devised to carry a moral lesson, such as Aesop's Fables. Suniti Namjoshi's eloquent and knowledgable "Blue Donkey" stories draw on this classic tradition of having beasts or mythical birds able to speak and act like humans but the "Blue Donkey" provides ironic comment rather than a moral lesson.

Angela Carter has rewritten fairy tales from the point of view of the heroine. In her collection *The Bloody Chamber* she examines the messages about adolescent sexuality in stories like "Beauty and the Beast" and "Snow White," overturning the sexual mythology of "simple" fairy stories.

Both writers have moved away from "realism" in the sense that the worlds they describe are not the world as we know it, yet these stories convey their own sense of logic.

Joanna Russ's science fiction stories are set in other worlds altogether. Alyx, in *The Adventures Of Alyx,* is the central character around whom each story revolves, and on each occasion she is in a different situation in a different location.

A strong tradition in the short story form is the tale with a twist in the end. This could be a subtle suggestion left hanging in the air or a powerful punchline carefully placed with exactly the right amount of emphasis and impact. Tail twisters bring stories to a full stop but an elliptical ending is a story that trails off. It doesn't literally have to show the three dots at the end...but it does mean leaving open the question of what happened next, what the outcome of a described situation might be, or what solution was found to resolve dilemmas encountered. This enigmatic type of ending encourages the reader to work out the ramifications according to her own ways of thinking and, though seemingly unsatisfactory, allows the story to live on in the reader's mind.

Down a well-worn path that is signposted to the future of the short story, a woman writer hurries along, an irreverent gleam in her eye ...

See Also

FAIRY TALES; FICTION; LITERATURE, *all entries*

References and Further Reading

Carter, Angela. 1981. *The bloody chamber.* London: Penguin.

Dinesen, Isak (also known as Karen Blixen). 1988. *Seven gothic tales.* London: Penguin.

Mansfield, Katherine. 1981. The dill pickle. *The collected stories of Katherine Mansfield.* London: Penguin.

Namjoshi, Suniti. 1988. *The blue donkey fables.* London: Women's Press.

Russ, Joanna. 1985. *The adventures of Alyx.* London: Women's Press.

Pearlie McNeill

SILENCE

Feminist approaches to "silence" address the multiple ways in which women's voices are suppressed or "silenced," as well as how women resist such repression, within various contexts of unequal social relations (that is, across gender, nation, race, class, sexuality). Marsha Houston and Cheris Kramarae (1991) assert that silencing tactics operate in everyday practices to isolate and disempower people. They also serve broader forms of social and political control.

As Carmen Luke (1994) states, a substantial body of feminist research documents women's exclusions from the public sphere, speech, and writing. Houston and Kramarae (1991) describe various ways in which women are silenced: by ridicule and labeling; interruption; exclusion from ownership and production of media forms so that, for example, newspapers and history books do not include much of women's commentary or experiences; enforced illiteracy and denial of schooling; classroom structures that reflect and legitimate "masculine" knowledge; and racist practices, such as when white people in the United States imposed severe penalties on enslaved Africans who spoke in their indigenous language.

Imposed silence for women has been abundant and profound. Since women's oppositional voices are implicitly and explicitly suppressed, empowerment through "voicing" women's experiences has been a key concept in feminist circles. Feminists suggest that women must resist silence through "voice," as in "naming" one's identity, for example. Usually, this practice of giving "voice" is put in opposition to "silence" (Luke, 1994).

According to Houston and Kramarae (1991), while most silence is imposed, some silences are chosen, desirable, and productive. For some religious groups, silence is a valued expression of spirituality. For many Native Americans, silence functions as a method of communication. Silence, then, is not inherently oppressive. Rather, silences are constructed within specific contexts, and their cultural function depends on how the silence is constructed and interpreted, between and among whom, and to what effect.

Silence As Resistance

An understanding of silence as an *absence* of voice obscures the ways in which women have actively deployed "silence" to resist oppression. For example, enslaved Africans used silence as a form of resistance, to make themselves appear docile and ignorant to appease their white oppressors (Houston and Kramarae, 1991). Carmen Luke (1994) refers to critical anthropologists who acknowledge that "silence" among the people they study, particularly women and men of color, can be a refusal to participate in the research, and is a technique used to resist the historical legacies of colonialism. In these ways, silence indicates dissent and is a tool for survival.

Some feminists, drawing largely on Lacanian psychoanalysis, claim that language is inherently male biased, and thus silence is a space of resistance to and escape from patriarchal regulations. According to this perspective, since language is "masculine" or "male," women who use it are alienated from their true selves and thus remain "mute." Women are positioned "outside" of "masculine" language,

in the "feminine" space of the unconscious, the "unspoken" and "unspeakable," that is, in "silence." Thus, women's speech has been muted, devalued, and indecipherable within patriarchal interpretive models. Women necessarily live a contradiction: To be silent is to remain outside of history and culture. Yet, for women to speak or write is to be estranged from the truly "feminine" self, to remain suppressed and contained within the language and culture of patriarchy. From this view, the method of escape is to inhabit the space of the "unspeakable" that is "feminine" and express, through other modes, that which exceeds linguistic codification. This is the emancipatory space of "silence." Many feminists attempt to locate, recover, or "make present" the displaced sites and forms of women's knowledge, such as that which is expressed through poetic language (Kaplan, 1983; Luke, 1994).

Silence As Alternative Communication

By extension, many feminists assert that there is, in fact, no such thing as "silence." Rather, what has traditionally been interpreted as silence is actually an "other" way of knowing and expressing that exists outside of culturally legitimated methods. People in subjugated subcultures, to communicate amid the threat of violence and/or other retaliation, often develop alternative codes and symbols that only they can interpret. Such messages often go unnoticed, or are dismissed, by outsiders who lack the conceptual tools to "read" the code. For example, many lesbians actively appropriate particular styles of dress, body decoration, and/or body language in order to be identifiable to one another. Yet, such markers of visibility often go unnoticed by people outside the community. Thus, it is exactly that which is perceived to be "meaningless" within "legitimate" culture that can travel and allow "others" to make meaning, to communicate.

bell hooks (1989) suggests that for black women in the United States the goal is not necessarily to emerge from silence, since black women have been very expressive. Rather, since when they speak, black women are often dismissed, it is crucial to produce speech that is compelling, demands to be heard, and is allowed to circulate. hooks explains that she learned that it is important to speak, but she also learned to talk in a way that itself is a perceived "silence." Thus, she learned to produce a culturally encoded speech that would not be perceived as "defiant" by those in power. For hooks, this "secret voice" is expressed through poetry. She describes this expressive "silence" as a necessary survival strategy, a way to speak and be heard, to maintain spaces of sanity and safety that are always threatened in a racist, patriarchal, and exploitive social climate. Similarly,

Gloria Anzaldua (1990) explains that, for many women, writing, painting, and performing are not aesthetic exercises but political acts that strategically deploy aesthetic practices to interrupt cultural norms and subvert the status quo.

Thus, women employ traditionally devalued and indecipherable, or "silent," expression to communicate, organize, and protest. Marjorie Agosin (1987) describes a significant way in which Chilean women took advantage of prescribed roles and devalued activities, located outside of "legitimate" expression, to initiate social reform. Chilean women used "feminine" activities such as sewing and embroidering to create political *arpilleras* (pictorial tapestries) that denounced the oppressive Pinochet government. The production and circulation of *arpilleras* were symbolic acts of protest that have, indeed, had a significant impact on the social and political climate in Chile. Since sewing was perceived as a benignly feminine "craft" that did not threaten political expression, women gained entry into the public sphere even when public protest was strictly forbidden. Through the *arpilleras* Chilean women have "voiced" their protest in an effective and powerful way.

Silence As Passivity

Yet, even while "silence" may be a form of resistance, it can also be viewed as passivity. Marsha Houston and Cheris Kramarae (1991) suggest that silence may function to perpetuate subjugation, since "silent" people often continue to be mistreated, are perceived to be incompetent, and remain disconnected from support systems. The type of resistance instigated through silence may be a controlled resistance since this is exactly the expressive space that patriarchy itself constructs and *allows* for women. Thus, silence functions as an adaptation, a controlled release, that ultimately perpetuates the oppressive system.

Silence, Speech, and Language

"Silence," then, is not always the most effective political strategy through which to realize social change. Some feminists argue that language is not inherently oppressive to women, but economic and cultural factors position women and men differently in relation to speech, language, and knowledge (Kaplan, 1983; Luke, 1994). Ann Kaplan (1983) argues that to view language as necessarily and totally patriarchal is dangerous because it puts forth essential differences between men and women, obscures differences among women, and limits women's options to *either* domination *or* silence. At best, silence is a temporary defense against patriarchal authority. But Kaplan rejects "silence," or "feminine expression," as a viably sustainable political strategy. She

asserts that women must acknowledge oppressive operations of language, and recognize them as effects of cultural power relations rather than as functions essential to language itself. Feminists, Kaplan argues, must appropriate language as a useful and necessary tool in the struggle for social change.

Yet, if women are to use language as a tool by which to disrupt "silence" even if languages are not inherently oppressive, then it must be acknowledged that to adopt any language is necessarily to assume elements of the culture, ideologies, and ways of understanding the world that are embedded within it (Anzaldua, 1990). Some of these imposed cultural values and hierarchies may conflict with those with which people already identify. In order to resist or subvert the oppressive culture that accompanies it, many people who are forced to speak in standard English engage in "linguistic code-switching," which disrupts the linguistic rules. This transformed language is often not approved by, nor is it understandable through, dominant cultural apparatuses. In other words, it functions subversively and productively for its creators, yet it is perceived as illegitimate, imperfect, and/or noncommunicative by those in power.

Gloria Anzaldua (1990) draws on Audre Lorde's (1984) notion that one cannot use the master's tools to dismantle the master's house, to problematize the appropriation of any "master language." Anzaldua asserts that it is possible to internalize the cultural values associated with a language and, even unwittingly, collaborate in self-subjugation. Yet, Ann Kaplan (1983) argues that it is not possible, but necessary, for women to use the "master's tools," albeit in a subversive way. To do otherwise may be "resistant" but not oppositional. bell hooks (1989) states that, even while she understands and values surreptitious "voicing" tactics, it is, in the end, destructive to withhold or hide speech in secrecy or silence. Ultimately, it is necessary to strike an informed and cautious balance that acknowledges the fine line between appropriation of and domination by the "master's tools."

In a related vein, unequal social relations *between* women are also constructed and maintained through linguistic practices. Intersections of "difference" among women cause some women to be inadequate "decoders" of other women's expressions. Women can, and do, silence and resist one another. bell hooks (1989) explains that for her, an African American woman, very direct speech is a subcultural norm and is useful and preferred to other more compliant or submissive styles. Yet, white women often misinterpret her direct and blunt expression as angry and hostile, and they disparagingly refer to her as "confrontational." hooks states that to label her "confrontational" and assert a white, middle-class behavior as a "standard" against which others are measured is yet another form of silencing. Thus, women must learn to decipher multiple forms of expression.

To completely reject "silence as resistance" in favor of prescribed and constrictive discourses may also function to silence women. This view accepts "speech" and "silence" as opposites and oversimplifies the complex negotiations of meaning, resistance, and empowerment that women must perform. Audre Lorde's (1984) assertion that women are not protected by silence is founded in broad and flexible notions of "speech" and "silence." Silence, she maintains, is born of very real fears, yet ultimately it supports a destructive invisibility and, therefore, must be rejected. Yet, possible modes of appropriate and effective "voicing" are multiple. Women are both within and outside of dominant discourses, both speaking and mute. Taken collectively, feminist approaches to "silence" suggest it is necessary to interpret the "silences" within that which is "spoken" and the "utterances" within "silence," and to struggle within the contradictory spaces that women inhabit, spaces of tension both between and outside of "speech" and "silence."

See Also

AUTOBIOGRAPHY; COMMUNICATIONS: SPEECH; HISTORY; LANGUAGE; LITERACY; NAMING; POETRY; PSYCHOANALYSIS

References and Further Readings

Agosin, Marjorie. 1987. *Scraps of life: Chilean "arpilleras": Chilean women and the Pinochet dictatorship.* Trans. Cola Franzen. Trenton, N.J.: Red Sea Press.

Anzaldua, Gloria. 1990. Haciendo caras, una entrada. In Gloria Anzaldua, ed., *Making face, making soul: Creative and critical perspectives by feminists of color,* xvi–xxvii. San Francisco: Aunt Lute.

hooks, bell. 1989. *Talking back: Thinking feminist, thinking black.* Boston: South End Press.

Houston, Marsha, and Cheris Kramarae. 1991. Speaking from silences: Methods of silencing and of resistance. *Discourse and Society* 2 (4: special issue on silence): 387–399.

Kaplan, E. Ann. 1983. Silence as female resistance in Marguerite Duras's *Natalie Granger.* In *Women and film: Both sides of the camera.* New York: Methuen.

Kingston, Maxine Hong. 1975. *The woman warrior: Memoirs of a girlhood among ghosts.* New York: Random House.

Lorde, Audre. 1984. *Sister outsider.* New York: Crossing Press.

Luke, Carmen. 1994. Women in the academy: The politics of speech and silence. *British Journal of Sociology of Education* 15(2): 211–230.

Rich, Adrienne. 1979. *On lies, secrets, and silence.* New York: W. W. Norton.

Williams, Linda. 1988. A jury of their peers: Marlene Gorris's *A question of silence.* In E. Ann Kaplan, ed., *Postmodernism and its discontents,* 107–115. London: Verso.

Lori Reed

SIMULTANEOUS OPPRESSIONS

Women are not born into neat little social groups through which they live the rest of their lives. Socially constructed factors such as sexism, disablism, racism, heterosexism, ageism, social class, and other ingredients will have a major impact on the lifestyle, opportunities, and barriers that women are confronted with. In the past there has been a tendency to deal with each individual oppression separately; consequently, people who may belong to two or more social groups, such as disabled women and black women, have been marginalized and isolated by the pressure groups that purport to represent their interests. Disabled women (Keith, 1994; Morris, 1996) and black women (Carby, 1982; Joseph and Lewis, 1981) have written extensively about the difficulties of identifying with more than one pressure group movement, with their politics not really being adequately addressed anywhere, and being forced to create an identity that sits comfortably with their multifaceted lives. Likewise, in Britain there has been a growing debate about the identities and allegiances of black disabled people (Begum, 1995; Stuart, 1992)—in particular, the position of black disabled women. We live in a society that has to label people's experiences before it can begin to acknowledge and deal with any issues or concerns that may emerge from those experiences. Consequently, in relation to black disabled women, terms such as *double disadvantage, triple jeopardy,* and so on have become popular shorthand expressions for describing the experience of simultaneous oppressions. Unfortunately, these descriptive labels have been unhelpful because they have endorsed a hierarchical approach rather than providing a useful analysis. More important, notions of double disadvantage and triple jeopardy have obstructed an understanding of multiple oppressions because the equations $1 + 1 = 2$ or $1 + 1 + 1 = 3$ do not work. Racism and disablism as two different forms of oppression cannot simply be added together to create a third. If a mathematical equation is to be used to describe the reality of multiple oppressions, then a number of questions need to be considered. For example, can the experience of racism be paralleled with the experience of disablism, sexism, or heterosexism? Do two (or more) oppressions have an equal impact on the equation?

Black disabled women's experience of disablism cannot be compared with the experience of white disabled women. Although there will be common ground, there will also be distinct differences.

Black disabled women's lives are made up of many components. Simultaneous oppressions occur with the interconnection of race, disability, and gender, to name at least three forms of oppression that shape the lives of black disabled women. Simultaneous oppressions affect the lifestyles, politics, and concerns of black disabled women in many different ways. Four of these key areas are: identification, prioritization, survival strategies, and empowerment.

- Identification: Which social group black disabled women identify with is a source of much debate. One may choose to identify with other disabled women who are not black but who may share a common experience of disablism; alternatively, one may choose to spend time and energy with other black nondisabled people. Because one's identity falls between two categories, one may prefer to meet primarily with other black disabled women. How one identifies as a black disabled woman must be something the individual determines, not others.
- Prioritization: It is virtually impossible to deal with the reality of racism, disablism, and sexism all at once. Most people will prioritize what is affecting their life at any give time. In the Western world our battle cry is one of antidiscrimination legislation and equality for all disabled people; whereas in other parts of the world the priorities are much more fundamental—freedom from war and famine, for example. In the latter case, black disabled women are unlikely to be sharing experiences in the same way, but instead using their energy to feed themselves and find safety.
- Survival strategies: Everyone develops survival strategies to cope with everyday life. Black disabled women, in addition to prioritizing which oppression is of most concern to them at a given point in time, will also develop survival strategies to deal with the reality of simultaneous oppressions. This may mean internalizing the oppressions they encounter to avoid the harsh pain and distress they may cause, or it might present a much simpler way of going about their daily life. Other black disabled women who may be more conscious of their identity and simultaneous oppressions may use them as a source of energy with which they can build alliances and network with a wide range of individuals and groups. At an individual level, black disabled women may be fighting for a positive self-identity and the opportunity to live their life to the full; at a collective level, the fight for recognition of simultaneous oppressions will go on.
- Empowerment: Black disabled women are not monolithic structures or empty vessels that pacify us or render us subject to the debate and concerns of other people. Through using our personal energy, peer support, networking, training, and advocacy, black disabled women can be empowered. It is vital that through the process of empowerment and politicization black disabled women can provide an analysis of oppression that has the potential to be all-encompassing and the most threatening. For in reality the major systems of oppression interconnect, and it is the almagamation of these oppressions that creates the matrix of black disabled women's lives.

See Also

ANTIDISCRIMINATION; DISABILITY AND FEMINISM; DISABILITY: HEALTH AND SEXUALITY; EMPOWERMENT; FEMINISM: AFRICAN-AMERICAN; FEMINISM: BLACK BRITISH; NETWORKING; RACISM AND XENOPHOBIA; SEXISM

References and Further Reading

Begum, N. 1995. *Beyond samosas and reggae: Guidelines for developing services for black disabled people.* London: King's Fund.
Carby, H. 1982. White woman listen: Black feminism and the boundaries of sisterhood. In Centre for Contemporary Studies, *The empire strikes back.* London: Hutchinson.
Joseph, G., and J. Lewis. 1981. *Common differences.* London: South End Press.
Keith, L., ed. 1994. *Musn't grumble: Writing by disabled women.* London: Women's Press.
Morris, J., ed. 1996. *Encounters with strangers: Feminism and disability.* London: Women's Press.
Stuart, O. 1992. Race and disability: Just a double oppression? *Disability, Handicap and Society* 7(2).

Nasa Begum

SINGLE PEOPLE

Marriage is still the most prevalent way of organizing intimate social relations. Family is considered the bedrock of societal organization. Though attitudes to diverse family forms have become more liberal, the majority of young people wish to marry and have children. Single people have to construct their lives in the context of the ideological emphasis on the family.

Singleness is most prevalent in Europe and the United States and has increased over the last decades. In 1992, 26.5 percent were unmarried in the United States. It is useful not simply to equate "single" with "unmarried." Though a majority of people do marry, at any given time in Western societies a large proportion live without a present married partner (45.2 percent in the United States in 1992). Single people are more likely to live in metropolitan areas; the greater cultural diversity makes a range of lifestyles more possible. In most countries lesbians and homosexuals are not legally able to marry.

Single men benefit from the higher social status conferred to men. Single women have a lower status, but they are more likely to have skills and possibilities to develop networks of social relations that buffer them against some of the difficulties associated with singleness. In single women's experience, there is still a societal inclination to wonder if there is something "wrong" with women who have not married (Gordon, 1994). Single men are more likely to be considered homosexual, and thus suspect.

Single parents (the majority of whom are single mothers) are likely to experience hardships. There are differences in their economic position in different countries. For example, in Britain, single mothers are encouraged to remain at home, whereas in the Nordic countries they are more likely to be encouraged to enter the labor market (Maclean, 1991).

Singleness is due both to pushes and pulls (Stein, 1981). Increasingly diversified patterns of social relationships and family forms have facilitated being single. For women, improved educational opportunities and improved access to the labor market have provided financial independence. But singleness is also a result of structural and cultural problems. In the United States, singleness has been more prevalent among African-Americans, which indicates a flexible adaptation to hardships caused by poverty. With the crises in welfare states beginning in the 1980s, some increased singleness is because of difficulties in forming and maintaining two-parent families because of problems caused by unemployment and poverty. There has been renewed emphasis on the value of the family, but basic support systems for families have deteriorated.

Although the position of single people has in many ways improved, marital status is still significant. Many people still live in familist societies dominated by ideologies emphasizing "the family," where "marriage casts a long shadow over everybody" (Chandler, 1991), and negative stereotypes about single people exist. Although it can be argued that single people still are marginalized (Gordon, 1994), they form a diverse, often adaptable group of people. Unless they suffer from severe poverty, they are likely to value their independence and, although some would hope to establish marriagelike relations in the future, others wish to remain single.

See Also

DIVORCE; FAMILY STRUCTURES; MARRIAGE: OVERVIEW; SPINSTER

References and Further Reading

Chandler, Joan. 1991. *Women without husbands: An exploration of the margins of marriage.* London: Macmillan.

Gordon, Tuula. 1994. *Single women: On the margins.* London: Macmillan; New York: New York University Press.

Maclean, Mavis. 1991. *Surviving divorce: Women's resources after separation.* London: Macmillan.

Stein, Peter, ed. 1981. *Single life: Unmarried adults in social context.* New York: St. Martin's Press.

Tranzen, Trisha. 1996. *Spinsters and lesbians: Independent womanhood in the U.S.* New York: New York University Press.

Tuula Gordon

SINGLE-SEX EDUCATION

See EDUCATION: SINGLE-SEX AND COEDUCATION.

SISTER

The term *sister* refers to the kinship designation of a female sibling and the social and legal relations common to the role. Full biological sisters share parentage and ancestry, whereas half sisters have only one parent in common. The term is at times generalized to include all women, as in the usage of "sisterhood," or to address Roman Catholic, Anglican, Orthodox, or Tibetan Buddhist female members of a religious order, assigning nonrelated persons fictive kinship designation.

Although some societies define social relations between brothers and sisters, few societies impose obligations on sisters. For example, in the matrilineal society of Buganda, brothers held veto power over their sister's choice of marriage partners (Sacks, 1979: 213). In addition, if a woman divorced, the woman's brother was obliged to return to her in-laws the bridewealth payment made upon marriage. Such arrangements are common in matrilineal societies where a woman's brother's authority over her and her offspring supersedes that of her husband. Yet, among sisters, relations are relatively more equal, if equally powerless. Among Muslims in Egypt and other societies, where both married and unmarried women are expected to be sequestered in the household, a woman's brother may act in place of her father in punishing her for any perceived transgression of local custom, sometimes taking her life in the case of sexual experimentation before marriage or with someone other than her husband after marriage (Atiya, 1994).

Karen Sacks (1979) defines a sister as simultaneously a decisionmaker and a female member of a community, and states that where a woman is defined by her role as sister she is an "adult among adults," whereas a woman defined by her role as wife is commonly a dependent. In addition, Sacks theorizes that precapitalist societies more often than capitalist states stressed the "adult" relation of sister over the subordinate relation of wife. As states strengthen, the power of women seems to weaken concurrently, and increasing complexity often marks a changeover from higher status as sisters to lower status as wives.

Elder sisters often take on a mothering role to younger siblings and, therefore, are socialized into becoming mothers themselves, while investing in the care of younger siblings. Thus, birth order is often an indicator of future prospects and opportunities for both sisters and brothers, with the most resources going to aid the youngest siblings. But at other times, an elder position is advantageous, as among the Tongan people of Oceania in the nineteenth century. They elevated sisters, and especially eldest sisters of chiefly lineage, over both brothers and wives. The sisterly role was invested with rights called *fahu*, meaning "above the law," which extended over her brother's children and over his household in general. When her brother died, it was she, not her brother's wife, who divided the household property, taking a sizable share for herself (Gailey, 1987). Similar practices are found among the Dahomey of West Africa, where unmarried women of the ruling class retained more power as sisters than they would have held as wives. Such societies emphasize the family of orientation over the family of procreation that the individual forms as an adult (Sacks, 1979).

See Also

KINSHIP; SISTERHOOD

References and Further Reading

Atiya, Nayra. 1994. *Khul-Khaal: Five Egyptian women tell their stories.* Syracuse, N.Y.: Syracuse University Press.

Gailey, Christine Ward. 1987. *Kinship to kingship.* Austin: University of Texas Press.

Sacks, Karen. 1979. *Sisters and wives.* Urbana and Chicago: University of Illinois Press.

Maria Ramona Hart

SISTERHOOD

Sisterhood, a term often associated with radical feminists, describes the bonds that exist among women. In its broadest sense it can be used to mean that which all women have in common—the common feelings that bind all women irrespective of differences. The commonality of feelings arises from women's shared experiences of domination and oppression in patriarchal society and the way in which women are defined negatively, as that which is not man.

Sisterhood can more positively be seen as the support and nurturance that women can give one another: mutual support built on a special relationship that gives women strength in their daily lives. This type of mutual support, often based on kinship networks, has provided women with the basis for constructing their own lives in patriarchal society (see Delamont, 1980).

However, the notion of all women—sisters—uniting against patriarchy is likely to result in a denial of difference. Hazel Carby (1982), for example, has argued that the concept of sisterhood renders black women invisible and denies the extent to which white women are implicated in racism. Thus there is a pretense as to homogeneity of experience concealed by the word *sisterhood* that does not in fact exist. Nevertheless, the concept is powerful in enabling women to recognize their commonalities despite differences.

See Also

CONSCIOUSNESS-RAISING; OTHER; SISTER

References and Further Reading

Carby, Hazel V. 1982. White women listen! Black feminism and the boundaries of sisterhood. In Centre for Contemporary Cultural Studies, ed., *The empire strikes back: Race and racism in '70s Britain.* London: Hutchinson.

Delamont, Sarah. 1980. *A sociology for women.* London: Routledge & Kegan Paul.

Pamela Abbott

SLAVERY

Slavery, as defined by the Slavery Convention of 1926, is "the status or condition of a person over whom any or all of the powers attaching to the rights of ownership are exercised" and a slave is a "person who is wholly or partly owned by another person or organization" (Stearman, 1999: 4). Thoughts on slavery typically turn to the transatlantic slave trade of past centuries. However, at the end of the twentieth century there are thought to be approximately 27 million people in slavery and slavelike conditions (Bales, 1999: 8). Many of the abuses that constitute slavery involve people working in the informal sector, such as some domestic servants and prostitutes, while others are held as bonded laborers. Other abuses take place within the framework of marriage, traditionally considered to be in the private domain, where women and girls continue to be given no choice about their lives, or the exploitation of their bodies.

Transatlantic Slave Trade

According to Reynolds (1985: 57), approximately 7,525,600 slaves were imported into the Americas and the Atlantic basin between 1451 and 1810. The precise figures for the gender ratio is not known, although it is suggested that during this period more men than women were transported. However, Bush (1990: 36) highlights modern research into the occupational distribution of sugar plantations that indicates "that planters may have exaggerated the adverse sex ratio to play down the exploitation of women slaves as field hands." Bush also points out that owing to women's inferior status to all men, white and black, they were subjected to sexual and economic exploitation. From the viewpoint of the European, women slaves were ideal for hard field work because of their "perceived 'drudge' status in polygynous marriages" (33). The work on the plantations echoed the traditional "women's work" of hoeing, digging, and domestic work, while the men were often given jobs as skilled craftsmen and were viewed with higher status than women. Despite the important contribution of female slaves to the operation of plantations, their purchase price was invariably lower than that for males.

Legal Framework

The abolition of the transatlantic slave trade began in the early 1800s. As more countries banned the trading of slaves, laws were drawn up to enforce its abolition. In 1926 the Slavery Convention of the League of Nations was set up to "prevent and suppress the slave trade" and to lead to its eventual abolition. To strengthen the legislation against slavery, the Universal Declaration of Human Rights (1948) states:

Article 1: All human beings are born free and equal in dignity and rights.
Article 4: No one shall be held in slavery or servitude; slavery and the slave trade shall be prohibited in all their forms.

Article 23 (1): Everyone has the right to the free choice of employment, to just and favorable conditions of work and to protection against unemployment.

By 1956 two more conventions had been introduced to enforce the prohibition of slavery. In 1949 the Convention for the Suppression of the Traffic in Persons and the Exploitation of the Prostitution of Others was introduced. Following this in 1956 was the United Nations Convention on the Abolition of Slavery, the Slave Trade and Institutions and Practices Similar to Slavery. This convention aimed to abolish not only the trading in slaves but also other slavery-like practices, such as debt bondage, serfdom, and practices and institutions that contravened the rights of women and children, particularly girls.

Women in Slavery

These legal frameworks plainly state that slavery and slavery-like practices are illegal, yet evidence proves that millions of men, women, boys, and girls are still being held in servitude. However, women and girls are particularly vulnerable. Within many societies around the world, women and girls are viewed as subordinate to men and boys. Owing to this inferior status, women and girls are often forced into many situations without a choice or are subjected to more forms of violence, including rape.

Marriage As a Form of Slavery

Marriage, for many, is a consenting relationship between two people, but for thousands of women and girls, marriage is forced on them, without their consent or their choice of whom, where, or when they marry. There are many forms of marriage that can be considered slavelike. Although forced marriage has deleterious effects on women, it can result in serious health problems for the immature minds and bodies of young girls who are forced into early marriage or dedicated to a shrine.

Servile forms of marriage are defined as "any institution whereby a woman, without the right to refuse, is promised or given in marriage, on payment of a consideration in money or in kind, or may be transferred to another person or, on death of her husband, may be inherited by another person" (Montgomery in Sawyer, 1986: 9). A woman who is forced into marriage often finds that her reproductive and productive powers—her womb and her work—stay under the control of her husband and usually at a very young age (Taylor, 1993: 11). This enslavement can be further worsened if the husband dies and the female is "inherited" by the deceased husband's brother. However, it must be noted that inheritance of a brother's wife, levirate marriage, is classified as servile, while other specific circumstances that include the exchange of money are not necessarily made without the woman's choice. Furthermore, nonconsensual marriage, while a violation of human rights, does not always lead to slavery.

Early marriage, although researched for its health implications, has yet to be fully researched as a form of slavery. Anti-Slavery International (1994) states that on an average 50 percent of African girls are married by the time they are 18 years old. Marrying with parental consent may reduce the age of child marriage, resulting in girls marrying without their own consent. Ghana, for instance, has no minimum age limit for marriage with parental consent. Research carried out in Calcutta found that of the sample size chosen, half the girls were married by the time they were 15 years old, the youngest being 7 (Ouattara, Sen, and Thomson, 1998). Reasons for early marriage include exchanging the girl for a bride-price, marrying the girl off before she loses her virginity or starts menstruating, honoring pledges between two communities, repaying a debt, or easing the burden of one extra child to feed.

Problems relating to child marriage vary, but may include low birthweight, malnutrition and anemia for the mother and child, and protracted labors resulting in vesico and recto-vaginal fistulas that render the girl incontinent and a social outcast in many societies. Furthermore, in many of these marriages the girls are faced with violence and painful forced sex (even before the onset of menstruation), extensive domestic duties that are performed while caring for children, and lack of schooling, further weakening her children's chances of education.

Ritual Slavery

In some instances the symbols associated with marriage are used to exploit women and girls. Cases in Ghana and India have revealed that young girls are dedicated to a shrine or god. In India girls from poor families are given to the local gods to guarantee a happy future. The girl (*devadasi*) must move into the temple and care for the "saint" she is married to. She can do no other work, nor can she leave the village or marry anyone else, but she is under the control of the men who look after the temple. For centuries the girls have been used as prostitutes by these men, who pocket the profits (Bales, 1999: 199). In Ghana, among the Ewe ethnic group, a virgin girl is dedicated to a fetish priest's deity to atone crimes her forefathers have carried out. The girl becomes a *trokosi*. She must tend the priest's fields, carry out his domestic chores, and bear his children. Some girls remain in the shrine until they are middle aged and then leave, while others die as *trokosi*. If a girl dies while in the shrine, the family must dedicate another virgin.

Chattel Slavery

Chattel slavery is the buying and selling of people. This form of slavery is closest to the traditional form of slave trading. Although chattel slavery affects only a small proportion of people, compared to other forms of slavery, it still occurs in some countries, such as Mauritania and Sudan. In recent years reports of chattel slavery in Sudan have become increasingly common. These slaves (mostly from the Dinka ethnic group) are kidnapped during violent raids on villages, usually by government-armed militias from the Rezeigat and Meseriya communities. Once captured, the raiders view the slaves as their property, capable of being exchanged, bartered, or used to carry out forced labor in agriculture, cattleherding, or domestic servitude. This situation is worse for girls and women—they are often kept as concubines of their captors, although there are also reports of male sexual exploitation. Additionally, women slaves find that their children inherit their slave status, making it harder for them than for men to leave their slave-holder.

Debt Bondage

Debt bondage occurs when a person's labor is demanded as a means of repayment of a loan. The United Nations Working Group on Contemporary Forms of Slavery estimated that there were 20 million bonded laborers in the world in 1998. In its original form debt bondage flourished in the caste system of the Indian subcontinent. There are approximately 10 million people trapped in debt bondage in India, with the majority from the *dalit* (untouchable) and *adivasi* (indigenous) communities.

Debt bondage often occurs through the need for lump sums of cash. Some parents pass on their debt to their children, while others exchange their children's labor for money to feed the family. However, debts are rarely paid off, despite the fact that the work done by the laborer invariably exceeds the original loan. The laborers find themselves ignorant of how much they must repay because of cheating landlords.

New forms of debt bondage are appearing as women are increasingly moved around the world to areas of demand. In many cases the women and girls think they are going to earn a good living but are taken abroad and often forced into prostitution or domestic servitude. They usually owe their traffickers money for airfares and other expenses and are forced into a life of debt that in many cases is impossible to leave (see Bales, 1999).

New Forms of Slavery

The population booms of the twentieth century contributed to what Bales (1999) described as the "new forms of slavery." In the past slaves were viewed as long-term investments, and they were expensive to buy. People are now cheaper to buy because of higher population and increased vulnerability and are therefore deemed more "disposable" (Bales, 1999). The impact of these new forms of slavery is felt not only in developing countries but through out the world. In London and Paris enslaved domestic workers have been found and freed, and in New York, Seattle, and Los Angeles, Thai and Philippine women have been found working as sex slaves in brothels (Bales, 1999). The pressures of globalization and the accompanying demand for ever-cheaper products, services, and sexual gratification add impetus to this trend.

See Also

ANCIENT NATION STATES: WOMEN'S ROLES; CHILD LABOR; DOMESTIC LABOR; DOWRY AND BRIDEPRICE; EMANCIPATION AND LIBERATION MOVEMENTS; FAMILY: POWER RELATIONS AND POWER STRUCTURES; MARRIAGE: REGIONAL TRADITIONS AND PRACTICES; PROSTITUTION; SEXUAL SLAVERY; TRAFFICKING

References and Further Readings

Anti-Slavery International. 1994. Committee on the Rights of the Child: Role of the family in the promotion of the rights of the child. General Discussion Day, 10 October. Submission by Anti-Slavery International.
———. 1998. *Debt bondage.* London: Anti-Slavery International.
Anti-Slavery International and International Working Group for Indigenous Affairs. 1997. *Enslaved peoples in the 1990s.* Document No. 83. Copenhagen, Denmark.
Bales, K. 1999. *Disposable people: New slavery in the global economy.* Berkeley: University of California Press.
Bush, B. 1990. *Slave women in Caribbean society 1650–1838.* London: James Currey.
Ouattara, M., P. Sen, and M. Thomson. 1998. Forced marriage, forced sex: the perils of childhood for girls. *Gender and Development* 6(3): 27–33. London: An OXFAM Publication.
Reynolds, E. 1985. *Stand the storm: A history of the Atlantic slave trade.* London: Allison and Busby.
Sawyer, R. 1986. *Slavery in the twentieth century.* London: Routledge and Kegan Paul.
Stearman, K. 1999. *Talking points: Slavery today.* West Sussex, UK: Wayland.
Taylor, D. 1993. *Servile marriage: A definition, a survey and the start of a campaign.* Oxford: Unpublished.
Verney, P. 1997. *Slavery in Sudan.* London: Sudan Update and Anti-Slavery International.

Carron Somerset

SLAVERY, SEXUAL

See SEXUAL SLAVERY.

SLOGANS: "The Personal Is the Political"

A slogan in wide feminist use by the later 1960s and a central theme of feminist analysis and action, "the personal is the political" is the recognition of the politics of the everyday and an accompanying rejection of the masculinist view that "politics"—and thus what is important—lies solely with governments, economies, armies, and so forth. This feminist politics of the everyday sees complex interlinkings between "the public" and "the private" and rejects the conventional view of these as binary oppositions. An entire range of "everyday life" has thus become available for analytic scrutiny and political analysis, including domestic labor, childcare, orgasms and their absence, sexuality, domestic violence, rape, abortion. Many of these concerns have resulted in feminist campaigns and alternative feminist organizations: important here are the refuge movement, rape crisis, "a woman's right to choose," and so on. By the 1980s such slogans became associated specifically with radical feminism and came under increasing criticism, particularly from Marxist/socialist feminists. "The personal is the political" was portrayed by such critics, erroneously as the above account indicates, as confining feminist political engagement to the realm of the personal only, as a kind of psychological reductionism. "The personal is the political" must count as one of the most influential of feminist ideas, because it reconceptualizes politics from a woman-centered perspective that is central to feminism worldwide.

See Also

FEMINISM: SECOND-WAVE NORTH AMERICAN; FEMINISM: RADICAL; GLOBAL FEMINISM; WOMAN-CENTEREDNESS

References and Further Reading

Morgan, Robin, ed. 1984. *Sisterhood is global.* Harmondsworth, UK: Penguin.

Rowbotham, Sheila. 1992. *Women in movement.* London: Routledge.

Liz Stanley
Sue Wise

SOAP OPERAS

"Soap opera" or "soap" refers to a serialized radio or television drama featuring domestic and romantic relationships, interconnected stories, and sentimental or melodramatic plots. Named after the soap companies that originally sponsored them, soap operas appeared in the United States during the 1930s as radio programming and moved to television in the late 1940s. Soap operas now enjoy a global viewership, largely made up of women.

Melodrama, sentimental fiction, and folk tales have all influenced the development of the soap opera. Perhaps the most distinguishing feature of the soap opera is its continuing plot of interconnected stories. While individual story lines may find resolution, the larger soap opera doesn't possess a definite ending. Soap operas appear in a weekly or daily serialized form and can continue running for decades. Latin and Anglo-American programs are exported throughout the world. Examples include *Eastenders* and *Coronation Street* in Great Britain; *Days of Our Lives, Guiding Light,* and *Dynasty* in the United States; and *Neighbors* in Australia. The closely related *telenovelas* of Central and South America share many characteristics with soaps but differ in their adherence to a finite number of episodes. Examples include *The Rich Also Cry* and *The Next Victim* from Brazil, and *Cristal* from Venezuela.

With their emphasis on romantic relationships, family ties, emotions, and homelife, soaps traditionally have been viewed as dealing with women's concerns, fantasies, and interests. Male heroes generally demonstrate sensitivity as well as strength. Female characters often possess the privileges of class, power, and physical beauty. More recent soaps feature women in prestigious jobs such as doctor or business executive. Individual story lines may confront issues that hold particular ramifications for women, such as rape, divorce, and adultery. When a story line portrays a country's specific political or historical concerns, it often does so in terms of how these events affect characters' personal lives.

Given the popularity of soap operas, feminists have questioned their effects on viewing audiences. One criticism of soap operas is that they tend to perpetuate traditional stereotypes of women: that women are subordinate to men, that women must use their beauty and sexuality to reach their goals, that relationships with men define women, and that women properly belong in the domestic sphere of home and family life. Western soaps, whose characters largely belong to the white upper and middle classes, receive criticism for perpetuating race and class stereotypes. Often, soap opera plots center on the physical and emotional victimization of women for suspense. Some critics view this focus as a way to increase women's fears for their own physical safety and as a means to support the larger culture's domination of women. Because of their powerful ties to commercialism, soaps also tend to manipulate women's concern with physical beauty in order to sell products, further encouraging destructive views of the female body. The soap opera's connections to escapist and fantasy genres have also drawn criticism; if a woman can escape dissatisfaction with her own life through the fantasy of the soaps, she is less likely to effect social change.

Others examine how soap operas celebrate women's ways of interacting, knowing, and coping with larger structures of oppression. Carol Traynor Williams, for example, points out links between soap operas and oral discourse, showing how such actions as storytelling and gossip become ways of making meaning and building community for women. She points out the pitfalls of class elitism and condescension that mark some academic studies of soap opera viewers, pitfalls that have also been noted in studies of women and romance novels (Williams 1992). Similar critics have observed how the use of multiple story lines, inclusion of differing personal perspectives, and exploration of different sides of contemporary social issues celebrate the multiplicity of women's experiences and opinions. Soap operas thus can resist static, circumscribed definitions of womanhood.

See Also

ADVERTISING; BEAUTY CONTESTS AND PAGEANTS; COMMUNICATIONS: OVERVIEW; CULTURE: WOMEN AS CONSUMERS OF CULTURE; DRAMA; FAIRY TALES; IMAGES OF WOMEN: OVERVIEW; MEDIA: OVERVIEW; ROMANCE FICTION; TELEVISION

References and Further Reading

Barker, Chris. 1997. *Global television: An introduction, communication and human values series.* Robert A. White and Michael Traber, eds. Oxford: Blackwell.

Blumenthal, Dannielle. 1997. *Women and soap opera: A cultural feminist perspective.* Westport, Conn.: Praeger.

Brown, Mary Ellen. 1994. *Soap opera and women's talk: The pleasure of resistance.* Thousand Oaks, Calif.: Sage.

Brunsdon, Charlotte. 2000. *The feminist, the housewife, and the soap opera.* Oxford: Oxford University Press.

Nochimson, Martha. 1992. *No end to her: Soap opera and the female subject.* Berkeley: University of California Press.

O'Donnell, Hugh. 1999. *Good times, bad times: Soap operas and society in western Europe.* London: Leicester University Press.

Williams, Carol Traynor. 1992. *"It's time for my story": Soap opera sources, structure, and response.* In J. Fred MacDonald, ed., *Media and Society Series.* Westport, Conn.: Praeger.

Catherine Swender

SOCIAL CONSTRUCTIONISM

See BIOLOGICAL DETERMINISM; ESSENTIALISM: GENDER; NATURE-NURTURE DEBATE.

SOCIAL MOVEMENTS

Social movements are collective attempts to promote or resist change at the local, national, regional, or international levels. Women have been active participants in many social movements throughout history and, to an even greater extent, in the late twentieth century. Women's participation in these movements often is an attempt to create alternative political spaces where their views and voices can be heard. They work to resist or change the existing political, social, or economic order as well as the unequal, gendered divisions of power, labor, economics, and violence that women face in their lives. Women have been involved in social movements at many levels and in many areas, in response to changes in their lives.

Social movements are generally fluid groups of people working toward a common goal. They often lack a cohesive structure or a single leader. Some of the first social movements included socialist, nationalist, and anticolonial movements in the mid-1800s. Twentieth-century examples of social movements are the environmental, peace, women's, civil rights, and fundamentalist Christian movements. These movements draw strength from many highly organized organizations or interest groups, which can mobilize their memberships and the broader public for specific actions.

Interest groups—or, as some call them, social movement organizations—are more formally organized groups, with a membership, usually some form of organizational structure or hierarchy, and, often, an identifiable leader. Interest groups often form around a specific action or set of identities. The environment movement includes organiza-

tions such as Greenpeace or the World Wildlife Federation (WWF), and it is these groups that provide the organizational base and mobilize people for action to protect the environment.

There are numerous explanations for the reasons for social movements. A large number of analysts suggest that people join social movements when there are political opportunities or openings for action. They join together to take advantage of these and then create new opportunities for action. Social movements (or what Tarrow calls "contentious politics") emerge "when ordinary citizens, sometimes encouraged by counter elites or leaders, respond to opportunities that lower the costs of collective action, reveal potential allies, show where elites and authorities are most vulnerable, and trigger social networks and collective identities into action around common themes" (Tarrow, 1998: 20). This approach focuses on changes to political structures that make them more susceptible to collective action.

Others suggest that, while this perspective gives some insights on how some people organize primarily in northern democracies, this approach fails to explain the rise of many of the "new" social movements in the north (such as gay and lesbian rights, antifree-trade and women's movements), movements in other parts of the world, or more global movements. They argue instead that changes in the structures of the political economy—such as restructuring policies undertaken by states to minimize their involvement in the economy, and moves to make their economies and societies more hospitable to global trade and finance—provoke social movements into action. These broad societal changes mobilize people as the effects become more personal and make the lives of individuals more difficult. Social movements arise, in this perspective, because people within a particular community, or across the world, resist the changes to their world and want to create alternatives to what is around them.

Most feminist theory on social movements adapts the latter approach to explain why social movements emerge. Women's movements have been formed in response to the changing economic structures; they have also responded to the rise of nationalisms, the devastation of the environment, the incidence of violence against women, and the challenges of new biomedical technologies for women's reproductive health, among other changes. Women have worked within social movements to bring about change within the existing political order, such as the state, and also to transform civil society including the family, education, and the media (Peterson and Runyan, 1999). Women have worked not only within autonomous women's movements but also with labor organizations, in environmental organizations, in peace movements, and within nationalist movements.

There is considerable tension among scholars and activists about whether there is a single global women's movement or many women's movements across the world. Some have suggested that the struggle against women's oppression is a unifying factor for all women's movements, despite the differences in location, context, or issues of concern (Morgan, 1984). Increasingly, feminists, led in large part by postmodern feminists, recognize that women have different experiences of oppression as a result of their economic, political, personal, or cultural situations. These differences mean that women organize around the changes in their lives in different ways. Their understanding of and resistance to the changes in their lives are within their own context; their solutions are created to address their own situations. Women may choose to work together across these differences, as some are doing in transnational coalitions, but in doing this they are making a conscious and strategic decision to address common problems with potentially differing and localized strategies for action (Grewal and Kaplan, 1994).

Given the diversities of women's experiences across the world, it is not surprising that women's movements also have different motivations and tensions. Not all groups of women who organize themselves in response to changes in their lives accept that women are oppressed or that greater equality for women is necessary. Some women's movements, including many of the "new right" in Canada, the United States, and Britain, or "right to life" movements working in the area of reproductive policies, want to keep the unequal divisions of power and resources in order to maintain women's and men's traditional places in societies. A similar call for a return to traditional roles and responsibilities is seen in many of the Islamic and Christian fundamentalist movements.

Among women's movements across the world, there also is considerable resistance to feminism. As the collection *The Challenge of Local Feminisms* illustrates, many women in Chile, Bangladesh, Namibia, Kenya, China, Peru, Russia, and Eastern Europe regard feminism with considerable skepticism. Basu suggests this is a result in part of the disregard many Christian, Islamic, and Hindu leaders have for feminism, because of its threat to their values, as well as a widespread belief that feminism is from the West and especially for middle-class women (Basu, 1995: 6–7).

Women's movements have been strengthened by international gatherings like the 1995 Beijing Women's Conference. These gatherings provide an opportunity for individual women, groups, networks, and coalitions to gather to share information and strategies, identify areas for action, and celebrate successes. Over thirty thousand women gathered in Beijing and many more worked in their local communities to celebrate the Beijing conference as evidence of the strength and diversity of women's movements across the world.

Local, national, regional, and international groups provide the organizational strength and mobilization for women's work in social movements. At the local level, there are groups such as those organizing to support a local battered women's shelter or the Self-Employed Women's Association in India. In many countries, there are national women's groups, such as the National Organization of Women in the United States or the Women's National Coalition in South Africa, which provide a crosscountry organizational structure for women's groups. Some women's groups work together with other groups across their geographical region. For example, Latin American and Caribbean feminists have met together since the early 1980s to strengthen their capacity to work for change in their region (Stienstra, 1994). Women in the European Union (EU) have increasingly organized themselves regionally in groups such as Network Women in Development Europe (WIDE) (Moghadam, 1996). As well, often separate, international women's groups exist to push for change in international organizations, to organize women, and share strategies across national boundaries, and to respond to global issues. Some international women's groups include the International Women's Tribune Centre, Development Alternatives for Women for a New Era (DAWN), Women's Environment and Development Organization (WEDO), Women Living Under Muslim Laws/International Solidarity Network (WLUML), and the Women's International League for Peace and Freedom (WILPF).

See Also

DAWN MOVEMENT; GLOBAL FEMINISM; INTERNATIONAL ORGANIZATIONS AND AGENCIES; NONGOVERNMENTAL ORGANIZATIONS (NGOS); POLITICAL PARTICIPATION; POLITICS AND THE STATE: OVERVIEW

References and Further Reading

Basu, Amrita, ed. 1995. *The challenge of local feminisms: Women's movements in global perspective.* Boulder, Col.: Westview.

Grewal, Inderpal, and Caren Kaplan, eds. 1994. *Scattered hegemonies: Postmodernity and transnational feminist practices.* Minneapolis: University of Minnesota Press.

McAdam, Doug, John D. McCarthy, and Mayer N. Zald, eds. 1996. *Comparative perspectives on social movements: Political opportunities, mobilizing structures, and cultural framings.* Cambridge, U.K.: Cambridge University Press.

Moghadam, Valentine M. 1996. Feminist networks north and south. *Journal of International Communication* 3(1): 111–126.

Morgan, Robin, ed. 1984. *Sisterhood is global: The international women's movement anthology.* Garden City, N.Y.: Anchor.

Peterson, V. Spike and Anne Sisson Runyan. 1999. *Global gender issues.* 2nd ed. Boulder, Colo.: Westview.

Stienstra, Deborah. 1994. *Women's movements and international organizations.* London: Macmillan.

Tarrow, Sidney. 1998. *Power in movement: Social movements and contentious politics.* Cambridge: Cambridge University Press.

Deborah Stienstra

SOCIAL SCIENCES: Feminist Critiques

See HUMANITIES AND SOCIAL SCIENCES: FEMINIST CRITIQUES.

SOCIAL SCIENCES: Feminist Methods

The term *feminist methods* first appeared in the mid-1970s, when feminist scholars asserted that the social sciences were a product of sex-biased society and that scientific methods did not protect the social sciences from this type of bias. In fact, feminists challenged the very idea that scientific methods were objective. Rather, they saw these methods as intrinsically rooted in a male vantage point, designed to buttress existing power arrangements. Feminists argued that because social science is a human product, it invariably reflects social values. Only a social movement could challenge social science.

Origins and Definition of Problems

These problems were documented in every field, including psychology, anthropology, sociology, economics, and political science, among others. For example, economics hitherto had no method for calculating the worth of housework because there was no recognition of its economic value, either in society at large or among economists (Ferber and Nelson, 1993). In psychological experiments, the kinds of tasks on which subjects (usually males) were tested mirrored activities valued in the dominant, male culture. Studies that produced no statistical differences between men and women were not published, leading to an exaggerated sense of difference rather than overlap among women and men (Sherif, 1979). Similarly, in anthropology there was an assumption that males had evolved throughout history, developing new skills that in turn affected human biology (Hrdy, 1981). Females, it was assumed, had always done the same thing—

borne and raised children—and this consistency undermined any evolutionary change among women. In political science, feminists pointed out that the predominant definition of politics excludes the kinds of activities that many women prefer or engage in (Elshtain, 1979). These assumptions produce research that in turn reinforces these assumptions.

Evidence for sexist bias in scientific methods included selecting subject matter relevant to males, using male-only samples, relying on concepts rooted in male experience, identifying women in terms of their relationships to men, and writing up results in an androcentric manner (Reinharz, 1988). In response to these pathbreaking insights, feminist scholars attempted to develop alternative methods for doing research. Many of these alternative approaches were explicitly labeled "feminist methods." In each social science, research using methods that challenged previous approaches started from the following premises: that women are an integral component of a social system, performing valuable work that most often is expropriated by others, enduring oppression or second-class status, and not necessarily having the same interests as men or as the family as a unit. As British sociologist Helen Roberts wrote, "feminism is in the first place an attempt to insist upon the experience and very existence of women" (1981: 15). Feminist social scientists have been attempting to devise research methods to get at that experience.

Initial Approaches to Feminist Methods

To explore this entirely unfamiliar territory, new feminist methods were needed to replace the old biased methods. The two initial approaches were the articulation by women researchers of their own experiences (Smith, 1987) and interviews by feminists of other women (Oakley, 1981). In each case, the purpose was to hear a new set of "voices" that had been ignored or silenced. An enormous array of studies appeared in which personal experiences of incest, motherhood, harassment, denial of promotion, abortion, miscarriage, rape, battering, work, and more were analyzed in detail. Hidden forces of social control and other cultural contexts were explored as explanatory ideas. Special attention was paid to language and to silences. Sometimes groups were assembled to discuss the intimate phenomena of women's lives, and these direct statements were studied in a way that linked feminist methods with *consciousness-raising* (MacKinnon, 1983).

The analysis of personal experiences, whether through reflexive studies or in-depth interviews, allied feminist methods strongly at first with qualitative research methods. This alliance was reinforced by the notion that feminist methods opposed conventional research, which was overwhelmingly quantitative (Jayaratne, 1983). In stereotypical terms, qualitative research was soft, open, "attentive," subjective, and narrative; quantitative research was hard, disinterested, objective, cold, and numerical.

New Developments in Feminist Methods

By the late 1990s, however, this alliance had broken down, and feminist research methods have come to include both quantitative and qualitative research strategies (Burt and Code, 1995). This is a welcome change because allying feminist research with only a small array of methodological approaches makes it impossible to study those phenomena that require other approaches. Feminist methods may, in addition to in-depth interviewing, include women studying men or conducting surveys or reanalyzing demographic data. The new definition of feminist methods, therefore, is to examine carefully the assumptions underlying the use of any method and to modify or employ it for feminist aims.

Because feminists have learned how important it is to gain power in society for the sake of making and protecting social policy, feminist researchers are needed who can conduct the kind of research that will assist women in gaining and retaining power for the sake of social reform. Thus, to create change in wage scales for the sake of rewarding comparable work equitably, massive sophisticated quantitative studies are needed. To illustrate that domestic violence is not confined to a single class, large data sets are needed.

Although some feminist philosophers continue to ask if a particular method should be considered a separate, uniquely feminist research method, in general this question is no longer debated. Rather, there are three new foci of concern. The first is to clarify feminist principles and then apply them to the broadest possible array of methods in the social sciences, including the particular research project at hand. Examples of research methods debated and refashioned by feminists include interviewing, ethnography, survey research, experimental research, cross-cultural research, oral history, content analysis, case studies, action research, and multiple methods research, among others (Reinharz, 1992). This approach allows feminist research to remain open, dynamic, and amenable to change. It redefines feminist research as a set of perspectives rather than as a unique research method.

The second focus is to explore in depth the conflicting voices of different feminists and feminisms as they utilize various methods. There is no single feminist voice and thus no single feminist perspective even on a particular method (Collins, 1991). This concern has led to a new focus on multicultural research teams and a commitment to end racism and other forms of discrimination that also pervade research designs. This new focus pays special attention to ethical problems that arise while research is conducted. Some examples are the problem of exploiting research subjects for one's own career, the problem of not accepting people's interpretations of their experiences ("false consciousness"), and the distribution of rewards within research teams.

And, finally, the third focus is to remain creative as researchers struggle to understand human psychology as well as the economy, polity, and society as a whole. Remaining creative sometimes means devising new research methods in response to new insights about women's experience.

Feminist research methods thus stand at the intersection of the women's movement and the social sciences, linking activism and the academy. Because the work of feminist researchers since the 1970s has been effective in changing some of the norms regarding mainstream research, it is likely that feminist researchers will continue to explore areas where change is needed. Books and articles are published regularly on this topic, and university seminars are offered in various countries.

See Also

ANTHROPOLOGY; ECONOMICS: FEMINIST CRITIQUES; HUMANITIES AND SOCIAL SCIENCES: FEMINIST CRITIQUES; KNOWLEDGE; LANGUAGE; PSYCHOLOGY: OVERVIEW; SCIENCE: FEMINIST CRITIQUES; SOCIOLOGY

References and Further Reading

Burt, Sandra, and Lorraine Code, eds. 1995. *Changing methods: Feminists transforming practice.* Ontario: Broadview.

Belenky, Mary Field, Blythe McVicker Clinchy, Nancy Rule Goldberger, and Mill Mattuck Tarule. 1986. *Women's ways of knowing: The development of self, voice and mind.* New York: Basic Books.

Collins, Patricia Hill. 1991. Learning from the outsider within. In Mary Margaret Fonow and Judith A. Cook, eds., *Beyond methodology: Feminist scholarship as lived research.* Bloomington: Indiana University Press.

Elshtain, Jean Bethke. 1979. Methodological sophistication and conceptual confusion: A critique of mainstream political science. In Julia A. Sherman and Evelyn Torton Beck, eds., *The prism of sex: Essays in the sociology of knowledge.* Madison: University of Wisconsin Press.

Ferber, Marianne A., and Julie A. Nelson, eds. 1993. *Beyond economic man: Feminist theory and economics.* Chicago: University of Chicago Press.

Fonovu, Mary Margaret, and Judith A. Cook, eds. 1991. *Beyond methodology: Feminist scholarship as lived research.* Bloomington: Indiana University Press.

Harding, Sandra. 1987. Is there a feminist method? In Sandra Harding, ed., *Feminism and methodology: Social science issues*. Bloomington: Indiana University Press.

Hrdy, Sarah. 1981. *The woman that never evolved*. Cambridge, Mass.: Harvard University Press.

Jayaratne, Toby. 1983. The value of quantitative methodology for feminist research. In Gloria Bowles and Renate Klein, eds., *Theories of women's studies*. Boston: Routledge and Kegan Paul.

MacKinnon, Catharine. 1983. Feminism, Marxism, method and the state: An agenda for theory. In Elizabeth Abel and Emily K. Abel, eds., *The signs reader*. Chicago: University of Chicago Press.

Oakley, Ann. 1981. Interviewing women: A contradiction in terms. In Helen Roberts, ed., *Doing feminist research*. London: Routledge and Kegan Paul.

Reinharz, Shulamit. 1988. Feminist distrust: Problems of content and context in sociological research. In David Berg and Ken Smith, eds., *The self in social inquiry*. Beverly Hills, Calif.: Sage.

————. 1992. *Feminist methods in social research*. New York: Oxford University Press.

————. 1994. Toward an ethnography of "Voice" and "Silence." In Edison J. Trickett, Roderick J. Watts, and Dina Birman, eds., *Human diversity: Perspectives on people in context*. San Francisco: Jossey-Bass.

Roberts, Helen. 1981. *Doing feminist research*. London: Routledge and Kegan Paul.

Sherif, Carolyn Wood. 1979. Bias in psychology. In Julia A. Sherman and Evelyn Torton Beck, eds., *The prism of sex: Essays in the sociology of knowledge*. Madison: University of Wisconsin Press.

Smith, Dorothy E. 1987. *The everyday world as problematic: A feminist sociology*. Toronto: University of Toronto Press.

Shulamit Reinharz

SOCIALISM

Socialism Before the Twentieth Century

Though its origins are obscure, the word *socialism* was commonly used throughout Europe beginning in the 1840s to designate the belief in community ownership and administration of financial resources, land, and other property. Socialism can best be understood in contrast to individualism, in which society is understood to serve the interests of the individual with no government regulation of economic life. Social critics of individualism proposed new ideas for societies based on community, harmony, and altruism, which defined the doctrine of socialism. The essence of socialist theory is the principle of human *equality*—an egalitarianism that strives to eradicate oppression. The defining concept of socialism, however, is the belief that humans can only realize their full potential and achieve emancipation in community. Charles Fourier, Robert Owen, Saint-Simon, and Karl Marx were key thinkers who developed this central theme of community and emancipation. Although Owen and Fourier elaborated socialist utopias of small-scale communities that established the principles equality and collectivism, the ideas of Saint-Simon and Marx shaped nearly all socialist tendencies. Saint-Simon is recognized as having proposed what became the theory of industrial society, and his consideration of the nature of solidarity outlined the theory of communities working in cooperation. Utopian socialist writings and experiments in the 1830s and 1840s criticized capitalism by championing a new concept of the individual and new possibilities of social life. These critiques focused on the conflict between the individual and society under capitalism and promoted alternative communities that would unify the personal and social needs of people. Some of these socialist views regarded the bourgeois family as naturally "good," while others advocated free love as a way of undermining the bourgeois ideal of the patriarchal family. Followers of Saint-Simon extended his ideas of communal society to fantastic extremes so that his importance and lasting impact is now undervalued. The body of writings by Marx and Engels in the thirty years after *The Communist Manifesto* (1848) makes up the core of work from which later Marxist socialists drew.

Marxist Socialism

The German philosopher Karl Marx outlined a theory of human development that unfolds in a series of economic stages. Capitalism was viewed as a "necessary evil" within a two-stage process that would achieve socialism. The first was the victory of the middle classes over the aristocracy, removing feudal ties and developing successful capitalist production and political rights for all in society. This democratic revolution in which capitalists own the means of production was oppressive to the working people (proletariat) and under certain conditions they would develop the consciousness of themselves as a single class of humanity willing to struggle to overthrow the capitalists/bourgeoisie and take over the ownership of the means of production. This two-stage approach applied best to the social and economic conditions mid-nineteenth century England. At the time of the Russian Revolution in 1917, Russia appeared ready for only the first stage of the revolutionary process; the transition from feudal to capitalist society. The revolutions envisioned by Marx and Engels, and later Marxists, meant a complete transformation of society abolishing private property and by ending the political and social privileges of the ruling classes. Whether these aims could be achieved by peaceful means remained undecided. The question of peaceful reform or violent revolution caused major conflicts within the many socialist movements until 1914.

In nineteenth-century Europe, working-class parties, particularly those influenced by Marxism, strongly supported cooperation between workers of different countries—strength in unity. The Communist Manifesto ends with the slogan: "Working men of all countries, unite!" Theoretically, socialism was expected to be an international phenomenon, particularly as capitalism developed into a full imperialist system. In response to this, there was an attempt, in which Marx himself played a leading part, to form an international socialist movement in the 1860s. This is known as the *First International,* followed in 1889 by a second attempt, the *Second International.* It was in the latter that socialist women participated in large numbers, and in which leaders like Clara Zetkin discussed the establishment of a Socialist Women's International.

Impact of World War I and II

By the outbreak of World War I in 1914, socialism had become the most significant political force throughout Europe, with socialist movements building mass political parties and developing working-class cultures. Some socialists doubted that capitalist society was developing in the ways predicted by Marx, with the emergence of white-collar workers who did not generally identify with manual workers or socialist parties. Socialist parties found that they were having to organize in political systems that they were simultaneously attempting to destroy. Ideas regarding party organization and leadership became important under such conditions. Revolutionary socialists like Rosa Luxemburg, however, believed that after seeking to export capital surpluses through imperialism, capitalist systems would break down and there would be a revolutionary spontaneity in the masses, so that party hierarchical leadership would be unnecessary and harmful.

The war of 1914 brought revolution to Russia and signaled the collapse of international socialism. Following the Bolshevik victory in 1917 the Third (Communist) International was formed, with Lenin's writings used to claim a special understanding of revolutionary tactics. The dominance of the Russian party over all communist parties was in place. After Lenin's death in 1924 Joseph Stalin assumed control of the international, and Stalinist orthodoxy

rejected of socialist leaders and ideals and operated on the basis of noncooperation with socialists in favor of communist predominance. Communists then proceeded to split socialist parties and trade unions throughout the world. Contrary to the predictions of Marx that socialism would be victorious in industrialized countries as a result of capitalist crises, socialism had emerged in less developed countries and in agrarian societies, with the Soviet Union and China becoming models for many new states embarking on industrialization.

After World War II socialism of varying types emerged. With Soviet-style regimes in Europe, the victory of Maoist communism in China in 1949, and independence in India in 1947, the balance of power in the world changed. Socialism evolved throughout the so-called Third World—in African, Asian, Arab, and Caribbean countries—further expanding socialist ideas within specific cultural contexts. The context of these socialist developments steered economic development within nationalist rather than nineteenth-century universalist and internationalist frameworks. For example, African socialism viewed capitalism and private property as less central to African experiences than the aftereffects of colonial oppression, division, and alienation. Socialist parties within Western Europe underwent key changes including giving up violent revolutionary ideas; developing people's parties rather than class parties; recognizing gradual economic transformation toward mixed economies; and opposing totalitarianism. Trends away from utopian thought were reinforced by the recognition that industrialization imposed specific conditions that required limited choices of action. The breadth and coherence of socialist ideas cannot be reduced to means or ends, yet some analysts argue that the means promoted by socialist beliefs have diminished the ends.

Impact on Feminist Analyses and Actions

With the spread of industrialization across Europe and North America during the nineteenth century, women of the new urban working classes started demanding their rights, primarily as workers. Socialist political movements explicitly stated that women's liberation was an *integral* part of the *communal* revolutionary project.

Socialist thinking, whether utopian socialism, scientific socialism anarchism, or bolshevism, considered links between economic exploitation and sexual oppression. Socialist theorizing treated questions regarding gender as a sexual division of labor and discussed women's work outside and inside the home, in production and in reproduction. Utopian and Marxist socialism had greatest influence on ideas concerned with overcoming the oppression of women and creating more egalitarian societies. Although Marx and Engels saw the emancipation of women subsumed in the larger struggle for proletarian emancipation, it can be argued that Engels produced the first materialist analysis of women's oppression (1884).

The replacement of feudal states with democratic class societies and principles of popular sovereignty highlighted the oppression of working people apparent under capitalist industrialization. Since socialism sought to eliminate oppression for all working people, feminist activism in socialist circles had first to ensure the inclusion of women workers. This activism expressed itself in the struggles for trade union representation for women before proceeding to articulate women's specific needs within a socialist framework. In this context, work—domestic and public, productive and reproductive, paid and unpaid, valued and undervalued—was to become, for feminists, a key issue in both their analyses and activism.

Early socialist theories explicitly addressed women's needs and included a feminine perspective. Saint-Simon wrote of women's emancipation as an integral part of the emancipation of the "useful class." Fourier focused consistently on overcoming women's oppression, arguing that social progress could be measured by women's progress envisioning communities based on feminine principles, so that rather than expecting women to conform to a male-defined world, women would be able to make their communities in their own images. In Britain and the Americas the work of Anne Wheeler and William Thomson, *Appeal on Behalf of Women* (1825), was widely discussed, creating a foundation for feminist thinking. In France, Utopian Socialist women included Claire Demar, Flora Tristan, and Suzanne Voilquin. Tristan wrote the influential *The Workers' Union* (1843), with its links to the ideas of workers' model communities proposed by Owen and Fourier. Tristan's ideas were taken up by a group of socialist feminists in Paris during the 1848 revolution. The value accorded to the feminine in French writing is an enduring contribution of socialist feminism.

Women's concerns were central to a new morality and, unlike later Marxist arguments, economic change was not viewed as sufficient to *change* the existing order. The key differences between the utopian and Marxist socialists was their belief in reform and persuasion, rather than force and conflict, and their creation of communities based on their principles. Marx and Engels were impressed by Fourier's critique of marriage and symbolic equation between women's liberation and social principles (Coole, 1988). Utopian socialism provided later socialist thought with ways of overcoming the oppression of women and achieving women's liberation. Yet

when Alexandra Kollantai wrote about sexuality, Lenin and other Bolsheviks regarded this as divisive.

At the turn of the century, various socialist voices warned the suffragists that their goal was limited and doomed to disappointment. Auguste Bebel, leader of the Social Democratic Party (SPD) in Germany, published the first edition of *Women under Socialism* in 1879 (widely available in 1883). In arguing against liberal aims, Bebel believed that "countless women would still experience marriage as a form of sex slavery; that the vote would do nothing to abolish prostitution and nothing to abolish the economic dependence of wives" (Rossi, 1973: 496). Bebel argued that women must organize and struggle for their own liberation, and women's organizers in the SPD women's movement, Clara Zetkin and Lily Braun, did just that. Both were ardent socialists yet were divided over the feminist content of their politics. Zetkin established separate local structures for women with national "agitators" under the communication umbrella of the SPD's women's magazine, yet the chief means of gaining party acceptance of this scheme was her focus on the irreconcilable divide between bourgeois feminism and proletarian women. Her declaration that the SPD would not countenance bourgeois feminism brought Zetkin into direct conflict with ideas such as Braun's on a woman's rights to abortion and contraception. Zetkin's strategy of separating feminists from socialists did mean the rapid establishment of a large and fairly autonomous women's movement, but it also meant that feminists such as Lily Braun were pushed out of the socialist women's movement. Because feminism was viewed as reformism, Zetkin was able to defeat supporters who wished to cooperate with bourgeois feminists. The split between the feminist and socialist women activists clearly highlighted wider conflicts over the role of the party and on the nature of socialism. These conflicts were to be even more clearly reflected in debates on the "woman question" after the Russian revolution of 1917–1918 (Buckley, 1989), and arose again for feminists in varied forms after 1989, with the collapse of "state socialism" in Central and Eastern Europe and the former Soviet Union (Renne, 1997; Posodskaya, 1994).

The ideas of some anarchists, particularly those of Emma Goldman (1869–1940), deserve mention, not least because her distrust of state intervention echoes that of many socialist thinkers, including Marx, when considering aspects of popular sovereignty and face-to-face democracy. In *Socialism: Caught in the Political Trap* Goldman notes the dangers of "scientific" socialism because it does not recognize the power of the middle classes (Shulman, 1996). She points out that since the majority of workers have become poorer, Marx was correct but that the rise of an "aristocracy" among the working class who have higher wages and savings or property meant that they had lost sympathy with revolutionary aims. Having escaped Czarist repression in Russia, Goldman became a revolutionary agitator and key anarchist thinker in the United States. Being deported with 248 other "undesirables" to Russia in the Red Scare of 1919 enabled her to experience the Russian developments firsthand and to write about her disillusionment from a socialist perspective. Goldman believed that the "triumph of the state meant the defeat of the Revolution" (Rossi, 1973: 508).

The doctrines of anarchism, much like the works of Marx and Engels, generally paid no special attention to women's liberation, yet Goldman's writings provide a radical feminist stance on many issues (including female sexuality and the family as fundamental to women's oppression). She was well aware that victories at court or at the polls would be useless "without a woman's claiming unrestricted freedom over her body." Goldman recognizes in *The Traffic in Women* (1910) that all women are treated as sex objects, whether a woman sells herself to one man—in or out of marriage—or to many men (Shulman, 1996). Until the state protects the rights and welfare for women, Goldman warned, it could not be a trustworthy vehicle for feminists. In her fiery speeches against capitalism, the state, and the family, "Red Emma" spoke of, among other things, free love, prostitution, contraception, war resistance, and workers' rights. All of these things mattered to women and to feminism, but in her day, by her own admission, she was denounced by other feminists as "an enemy of women's freedom" and as "a man's woman" (Shulman, 1996: 4).

The prominent leader of the Russian Social Democrats, Alexandra Kollantai, wrote *The Social Bases of the Woman Question* (1908), repeating much of Zetkin's belief in separating feminists (viewed as "bourgeois") from socialist women. Her later work was concerned more directly with women's situation and addressed inequality between the sexes and a new proletarian morality. Lenin brought Kollantai into his government after the October Revolution as Commissar for Social Welfare. With the success of the Bolshevik revolution, women such as Kollantai, Krupskaya, Inessa Armand, Zinaida Lilina, Ludmilla Stael, and others worked to implement socialist policies for women against a background of famine and civil war. The Bolsheviks needed women's support and participation to overthrow the old order, and the primary concern was to reduce working women's oppression so that they might realize their interests. Writing by Inessa Armand and Alexandra Kollantai, the first two directors of the *Zhenotdel* (Revolutionary Women's Committee), shared with Bebel, Engels, and Marx the belief that women's liberation was only possible under socialism. Like Lenin they realized there would be nothing "automatic" in this.

Change could not come merely from new economic structures or legislation, but changes had to take place within the family, in domestic labor, maternity, child rearing, and sexual relations. In the Bolshevik analyses of the socialization of housework and childcare tasks, the economic benefits of women's participation in the public sphere were overestimated, and the high costs (economic and psychological) of making available public utilities for meals, laundry, and child care, were radically underestimated. As the gendered nature of domestic work was not analyzed, the psychological costs for women were not considered, and this gendered dichotomy in work was to prove a heavy burden for women in the Soviet-type societies. Both Armand and Kollantai viewed the reorganization of domestic labor and child rearing as fundamental to the transformation of the family. When these thinkers broadened their analyses to the dynamics of sexual relations, Lenin and other revolutionaries disapproved of it as "bourgeois self-indulgence." Although the "communist sexual puritan" element of Bolshevik thinking echoes the Puritanism of the Owenites in Britain, such views are wholly contradictory to the French Utopian Socialist theories advocating sexual revolution. Certain strands of twentieth-century feminist thinking were also divided, in various respects, in their analysis of sexual divisions of labor—between a materialist and idealist framework or a structural and cultural framework.

Impact of Socialist Theories on Feminist Debates

For Zetkin, Kollantai, and other revolutionaries, the aims of the "bourgeois feminists" were insufficient because they left capitalism intact. In the years after the Russian revolution, the value of separate women's organizations were questioned and said to be counterproductive. This question of separate women's organizations has remained a central point of contention in socialist politics and feminist politics throughout the world.

Gender roles and socialization were not systematically analyzed in revolutionary writings, allowing the ill-founded belief that women would be released from their domestic burden without men assuming any new domestic roles. The wider effects of male-female relations and the means by which women were subordinated to men were nowhere thoroughly analyzed.

Socialist-feminist thinking raised questions concerning conceptions of socialism after 1989 when many elements of the underlying political practices of the systems in Central and Eastern Europe were discredited. In the wake of changes in Central and Eastern European societies in 1989, the names of various parties and groups were changed from Communist to Socialist or Social Democrat or Left and so on.

There has been deep reluctance on the part of many socialist parties and organizations to countenance autonomous women's movements or indeed to see that women's oppression raises particular questions for women as social beings. This problem is something to which later Marxist and socialist feminists returned in the later twentieth century. Feminists also returned to the roots of socialist developments in Third World countries, which had different antecedents and contended with different forces, particularly colonialism (Jayawardena, 1986). Socialist feminist activists internationally have continued to discuss the thoughts of women from Central and Eastern Europe who have rejected so-called socialist values. Many of these dialogues consider the rejection of both the legacies of their old regimes and the opportunities offered by market-oriented democracies for various women's situations. Debates concerning feminist thinking in the "liberalizing" atmosphere of Central and Eastern European countries have gained an urgency, as have notions of the "dictatorship of the market" within globalizing economic conditions. Debates around feminism, socialism, and socialist internationalism or transnationalism (Alexander and Mohanty) are very much present within Women's Studies today.

See Also

ANARCHISM; COMMUNISM; FEMINISM: ANARCHIST; FEMINISM: MARXIST; FEMINISM: SOCIALIST; MARXISM; REVOLUTIONS; UTOPIANISM

References and Further Reading

Alexander, Jacqui, and Chandra Talpade Mohanty. 1997. *Feminist genealogies, colonial legacies, democratic futures.* New York and London: Routledge.

Buckley, Mary. 1989. *Women and ideology in the Soviet Union.* London: Harvester.

Coole, Diana. 1988/1994. *Women in political theory from ancient misogyny to contemporary feminism.* Hemel Hemstead, U.K.: Harvester Wheatsheaf.

Jayawardena, Kumari. 1986. *Feminism and nationalism in the third world.* London and New Jersey: Zed.

Kollantai, Alexandra. 1977. *Selected writings.* Trans. A. Holt. London: Allison and Busby.

Kruks, Sonia, Rayna Rapp, and Marilyn B. Young, eds. 1989. *Promissory notes: Women in the transition to socialism.* New York: Monthly Review Press.

Luxemburg, Rosa. 1971. *Selected political writings.* Ed. D. Howard. New York and London: Monthly Review Press.

Posadskaya, Anastasia, ed. 1994. *Women in Russia: A new era in Russian feminism* New York and London: Verso.

Renne, Tanya. 1997. *Ana's land: Sisterhood in Eastern Europe.* Boulder, Colo., and Oxford: Westview.

Rossi, Alice, ed. 1973. *The feminist papers from Adams to Beauvoir.* New York and London: Columbia University Press.

Shulman, Alix Kates, ed. 1996. *Red Emma speaks: An Emma Goldman reader.* Amherst, N.Y.: Prauetheus Books.

Vogel, Lise. 1983. *Marxism and the oppression of women: Toward a unitary theory.* London: Pluto.

Chris Corrin

SOCIALIST FEMINISM

See FEMINISM: SOCIALIST.

SOCIALIZATION FOR COMPLEMENTARITY

Environmental Pressures

Complementarity within a social group is the phenomenon of individuals mutually supplying each other with what any one individual alone would lack. In order to understand how persons are socialized for complementarity in human societies, one must examine the societal frame in an ecosystem. Societies that are referred to as "hunting and gathering societies" are often labeled the most egalitarian. These societies often have a very low subsistence level. Such groups are called, somewhat disparagingly, "digging stick cultures," and include some Native Californian groups. Among such groups are included buffalo hunting peoples in the North American plains and some fishing tribes in the Pacific Northwest. Societies characterized as having an unstable resource base often rely on socialization for complementarity. Food is plentiful at times and scarce at other times during the seasonal year. Storage of food may also be a problem. Therefore, individual effort, and at times, collectivities in the form of communal buffalo drives formed the basis of food-getting enterprises. During such hunting drives, both men and women were important. Children were often involved in the endeavor and learned early that both genders were vital for the continuity of the people. Individual autonomy was valued but the good of the group was also part of the training and responsibility of the members. To fully comprehend egalitarianism it is imperative to examine any ethnographic accounts of complementarity that focus on behavior based on the ideas of personhood and other cultural values that undergird a specific society.

The Case of the Lakota

The Lakota, often called Sioux, who formerly inhabited the great plains of North America illustrate how notions of persons, gender, and complementarity are maintained. The Lakota originally based their livelihood upon the migration of bison herds, which followed a seasonal pattern. In summer, effective political and economic units were formed to control individual access to this resource. At other times of the year, individual effort in hunting other animals prevailed. Females helped in the equally important task of butchering and processing meat and hides and were seen as equal participants in this major event. Provisioning for the winter involved female participation in the storage of dried meat and collections of wild fruits and vegetables. In the summer plentiful food resources allowed the Lakota to form into larger groups and enact rituals such as the sacred sun dance, and corollary rites of intensification which included children's naming ceremonies, adoption rituals (Hunka), puberty rituals (such as the vision quests for boys and the coming "into womanhood" *isnati* ceremonies for girls), and marriage events. After these heightened social events—which stressed the four dominant cultural values of generosity, bravery, fortitude, and wisdom—the Lakota dispersed into smaller units, called *tiospaye* (ti = household, ospaye = part of), or in anthropological terminology, an "extended family."

Socialized Complementarity among the Lakota

Individual families could join or leave larger kinship units as they wished. Personal circumstances and choice prevailed. Both men and women made the decision. These household units were flexible and allowed for friction alleviation and smooth social functioning within the extended family unit. Leadership was attained through exceptional skills and were gender-based. Male skills in warfare, hunting, and ritual knowledge were assessed on individual striving and achievement. In a hunting society leaders usually had no more privileges or goods than their followers. They could be replaced at any time for transgressing notions of sharing or for failing to excel in hunting or warfare activities. Decision making for the group was through band opinion with both genders contributing their opinions. Interest in being seen as a strong leader, a competent hunter, or active ritualist motivated males to participate in the sun dance. Concern for household chores by women produced ritualized male sexual continence (for example, the sun dance) to avoid frequent pregnancies. Women's prestige was attained through excellence in tanning and decorating skins, tipi making, and porcupine quill embroidery, and by being chosen by group opinion to play principal roles in sacred rituals. There were sodalities for outstanding warriors to which young males aspired and could enter through individual achievement. In women's societies, esteem and honor could be achieved by excellence in Quilling or tipi making. Personal autonomy and achievement underlay these achieved roles. Role modeling and praise—in honoring and giving away ceremonies—served to motivate children. Children were referred to as "*wakan yeza*"—translated as "like the sacred"—and child training was based on the emulation of adults and on group-centered welfare. Thus, the adage "that my people may live" was an important one. The *tiospaye* (extended family) had a vested interest in socializing individuals to live by the four cardinal virtues of the group. Since the kinship structure was based on bilateral descent, both fathers' and mothers' kinship units had equal concern and force in raising children to fulfill the expected normative behavior.

Each *tiospaye* instilled the underlying value structure of the group. Generosity, bravery, fortitude, and wisdom were modeled strongly in the socialization of children, the "sacred beings." These values proved adaptive in the early reservation period and are still evoked in contemporary situations to maintain complementarity in the present. However, colonialism, coerced culture change, legal repression of belief systems and languages, plus superimposed educational and religious systems have disrupted the cultural balance of many indigenous societies in Native North America.

See Also

FOOD, HUNGER, AND FAMINE; HOUSEHOLDS AND FAMILIES: NATIVE NORTH AMERICA; HUNTING; SOCIALIZATION FOR INEQUALITY

References and Further Reading

Delorie, Ella C. 1945. *Speaking of Indians*. New York: Freedom Press.

DeMallie, Raymond. 1981. Male and female in traditional Lakota culture. In Patricia Albers and Beatrice Medicine, eds., *The hidden half—Studies of Plains Indian women*, 237–265. Lanham: UP of America.

Leacock, Eleanor. 1978. Women's status in egalitarian society: Implications for social evolution. *Current Anthropology* 19: 247–75.

Beatrice Medicine

SOCIALIZATION FOR INEQUALITY

Learning and Unlearning Inequalities

Inequalities are socially constructed—that is, they are learned and taught, including those inequalities in power, authority, access to resources, and sense of self-worth that are based on differences in gender. In any one society or group, specific kinds of inequalities are systematically learned and taught from generation to generation so that, in effect, the moral basis of a society—its sense of justice—embodies and perpetuates these inequalities.

To understand how these inequalities are perpetuated requires studying the processes by which they are communicated, defined here as *socialization for inequality*. Socialization for inequality passes on many kinds of inequalities—based on race, class, gender, religious affiliation, ethnicity, among others—that continue to characterize groups and societies.

But since ideas about social inequalities are learned, they can also be unlearned. That is why ideas and practices that sustain inequalities need to be understood in concrete, empirical terms— and not only in the abstract—since it is in these concrete terms that such practices can best be contradicted, challenged, and subverted, whereas an outright challenge to a society's abstract sense of justice may be more difficult.

Gender Inequality

Gender differences are often socially constructed from biological sex distinctions and are one of the great fault lines of societies—those marks of difference among categories of persons that govern the allocation of power, authority, and resources. Gender differences operate within a larger context of other socially constructed distinctions—class, race, ethnicity, religion, and nationality—that give them their specific dynamics in a given time and place. Within this context, gender differences have been recognized as a major source of inequalities, in power, authority, and access to resources that define a given society, group, or family unit.

Formation and Consequences

Beginning in the late twentieth century, considerable research has been carried out on inequalities based on gender differences, although central concepts and types of data used by researchers and activists in different societies and cultures may have distinct differences. This distinction is based on the relative levels of poverty or economic well-being that characterize these societies. Researchers in more affluent societies have focused their attention on psychosocial variables in the formation of socially constructed gender differences; in societies (and groups within societies) where poverty is widespread, more attention has been given to the consequences of gender-based inequalities in meeting survival needs. Since these tangible consequences play a critical role in socializing new generations, an adequate understanding of socialization for inequality requires an analytical framework that links formation theories with an understanding of how consequences are both used in and result from socialization.

Researchers in wealthier nations tracing the development of gender-based inequalities have most often used psychological or sociological concepts such as gender roles, or have focused on language, religious traditions, and the history of a culture, particularly its symbolic aspects. This research is part of a concrete efforts to change gender biases, and gender-based socialization for inequality is its central and explicit focus.

Studies of the consequences of inequalities in resource allocations between males and females usually reflect broader concern over widespread social inequalities of various kinds, especially in poorer nations and in minority populations in affluent societies. These studies have dealt with differences between males and females with respect to mortality (death and survival rates), morbidity (impact of disease), nutrition (who gets how much and what kind of food), educational participation (who goes to school), and educational attainment (who reaches what levels of education). In effect, they document differences in the allocation of resources in a particular group on the basis of gender differences. These studies, which became widespread in the 1970s and 1980s—often in conjunction with policies and programs affecting economic development and population growth—are frequently linked to practical efforts to change the documented inequalities through programs of education or compensatory allocation of resources (affirmative action).

Division of Labor

A great deal of empirical research (both ethnographic and statistical) of gender-based inequalities has also been carried out on the division of labor between males and females and on women's participation in the paid labor force. This research is obviously also related to the issue of socialization for inequality, since these studies demonstrate the extent of specific differences in the work done by women and men as well as how this work is rewarded. Because education and training for future work are crucial parts of the socialization process, differences in how work and its rewards are regarded are a vital part of socialization for inequality. Research on the division of labor attempts to change support in a situation that might be characterized as "to each less than she needs, from each more than she can do" (Papanek, 1990).

Sociocultural Entitlements to Resource Shares

Concepts that could bridge the gap between these different approaches to the systematic study of socialization for gender-based inequality have received enough attention. In the case of the demonstrated concrete consequences of unequal allocations of medical care, education, or nutrition between males and females, it is crucial to understand how such differences develop so that more effective steps can be taken to unlearn the ideas and practices that produce them. On the assumption that the unequal allocation of resources is not accidental but represents systematic differences in a given society or group, the ideas that underlie inequalities are generally inferred from the outcomes caused by such biased practices rather than studied directly. That is why systematic ethnographic observations of allocational behaviors and direct study of the pattern of ideas and practices associated with them are needed to support such conclusions.

Where the internal workings of the domestic group (household or family) are the main focus of inquiry, three distinct aspects of intrahousehold resource allocation need to be examined in any study of the process of socialization for inequality:

1. the measurable consequences of an allocational pattern in terms of differences in nutritional status, morbidity, mortality, and skill acquisition among household members;
2. the psychological consequences for individuals, in terms of how they feel about themselves and others, and how they behave on that basis (assertiveness);
3. the moral basis of the group and society reflected in norms that directly and indirectly govern resource-sharing.

Although they have not been well documented, commonplace statements about allocational behaviors abound in many societies and can be found both in domestic groups and in the larger social setting. One idea, often heard within domestic groups, is that "men need more [or better] food than women," an idea often accompanied by the statement "because men work harder." Examples from rural areas in North India show that girls are not given so-called heat-producing foods like butter, milk, and meat because such foods are believed to hasten the onset of puberty in girls. Early

menarche is considered undesirable, but these practices also make girls less well nourished than boys and reinforce other kinds of perceived inequalities among growing children.

Implicit Consensus

Adults invoking these explanations do not need to justify a preferential action each time that it occurs, although an action based on a different principle might need to be carefully explained as a deviation from common practices. Because these behaviors and casual comments are taken for granted and express the consensus of a group, they are rarely discussed explicitly, so that a systematic search for the ideas that govern these entitlements is necessary for understanding how allocational differences are enforced and perpetuated.

The phrase "sociocultural entitlements to resource shares" (Papanek, 1990) is a useful way to describe these ideas as well as the patterns of action by which they are carried out. The concept makes it easier to develop an analytical framework for the study of socialization for inequality that focuses on the allocation of scarce resources.

Types of Entitlements

The term *resources,* as used here, covers a wide range of concrete items (food, clothing, housing, health care, schooling) but also such behaviors as respect from others and encouragement of self-esteem. These latter behaviors can be thought of as "love"—in the sense of nurturance, care, and concern for other members of the group, especially with respect to children (for examples from India, see Miller, 1981; Trawick, 1990). Loving care may even offset some kinds of concrete deprivation, but beyond a certain point it is no substitute for adequate food, schooling or medical care.

In addition to its most common usage as a right mandated by law, the term "entitlement" has been used in the context of political and economic analysis (see Sen, 1981, 1990) as a right associated with an individual's position in a group or the group's position in a society, within a socially shared concept of distributional justice. The term has also been used in the social-psychological analysis of interpersonal behavior in its relation to ideas of justice (see Lerner and Mikula, 1994) and with respect to behavioral entitlements and disentitlements in Colombian *machista* families (Restrepo-Ramirez, 1995). In all these contexts, persons "feel entitled" to behave in a particular way and to expect specific actions from others on the basis of their acknowledged position within a group and with reference to ideas of justice. The concept of sociocultural entitlements to resource shares incorporates both these nonlegal meanings. It emphasizes that the process of resource allocation is governed not only by explicit relations of power and authority within a group or society but also by ideas and practices that maintain the legitimacy of specific resource allocations to particular categories of persons.

The notion of male entitlement to larger shares of food affects teaching and learning about gender-based inequalities in many ways. Where good food is scarce, those who receive bigger and better portions of it are demonstrably more valuable members of the group or family; they may also survive longer and be in better health. Allocational behaviors reflect the values of certain categories of individuals and are usually linked to the power and authority such individuals hold in the group.

Value of Work

Statements like "men need more food because they work harder" convey an explicit message that the work of men is more highly valued than that of women. Small children may see their mother busy working around the home while the father's labor may be less readily observed. Yet the allocational practice—and its explanation—introduce children to the contrary idea that men's work is more highly valued than women's because men themselves are more valuable members of the domestic group. This is an example of socialization for inequality through sociocultural entitlements at an early age. Both the practice and its stated justification have a significant didactic impact: they convey several linked messages of inequality, especially to children, but also confirm the situation for the adults who do the teaching.

An example of how affirmative-action projects that involve sociocultural entitlements can undermine these ideas is shown in a new program in the Indian state of Haryana. A government agency invests a small amount of money in a savings scheme in the name of a newborn girl. The account reaches maturity when the girl becomes 18, the legal age for marriage, but is forfeited if she marries earlier. In a society with a strong preference for male children, higher mortality among female children than male, and widespread early marriage, this scheme is intended to demonstrate concrete support both for the value of a female child and for postponing marriage to the legal age. It also meets parental anxieties about dowry payments and the costs of educating a child who will then move into (and work for) another household.

Domestic Hierarchies

Hierarchically organized domestic groups are usually the most likely arenas for systematic socialization for inequality, including unequal resource allocations. Extended multi-generational patrilineal families, where sons, their wives, and their children continue to reside with the parents of the sons, remain an ideal in many societies, especially in Asia, and affect commonplace ideas and behaviors. The ideas may outlast the practice and it is often unclear how widely this pattern is being observed today, how prevalent it may have been in the recent past, or in which status groups (such as castes) it is most often found (for India, see Kolenda, 1987; Forbes, 1996; and Jeffery and Jeffery, 1996).

Multigenerational domestic groups of this kind are highly differentiated internally—that is, there are differences in power and authority among members of the group, based on gender, age, and whether they were born into the group or married into it (Dube, 1997; Miller, 1993). Newcomers, whether children or in-marrying brides, must be socialized into the group's ideas and ways of doing things. Powerful pressures within and beyond the domestic group result in effective socialization for inequality, teaching newly married women to identify their own interests with those of the patrilineage of their husbands rather than with those of their fathers, let alone their personal wishes, especially where single women have few alternative options. Life-cycle events that deprive women of the support of a household, such as reproductive failure (Cain, 1988), may be catastrophic, and women's continued dependence, even on an oppressive domestic group, can be necessary for survival.

Riding the Escalator

Typically, some members of the group advance in status as they grow older, riding up the escalator of the domestic hierarchy. For example, mothers-in-law in patrilineal families initially marry into the group as young brides of sons of the house and only gradually move up the ladder to positions of authority over the wives of their sons. Having suffered inequality themselves, the older women may be unwilling to give up the gains they can make by controlling other women (and sometimes men) and sharing the prevailing attitudes of men. They retain their status within the group by exercising control over other women, since the mother-in-law controls the behavior and labor of her sons' wives living in the same household.

The slowly evolving power and authority over others by some members of a group is a key factor in the complex pattern of socialization for inequality. The older women may be said to undergo a process of *secondary* socialization for inequality when they socialize their daughters and present proof that they have deeply internalized the standards that mandate the inequality of females.

Complicity of the Disadvantaged

While there are always some women (and men) who are strong enough to resist and break the generational cycle of inequality, the complicity of the disadvantaged is a major barrier to achieving change. That is also why it is crucial to understand the social and psychological pressures that bring this about, as well as the conflicts that may accompany the imposition of a painful practice. For example, mothers are often expected to do things to daughters— or at least allow them to be done—that alter their bodily integrity and appearance (such as genital mutilation, extreme thinness, corseting, seclusion, and veiling). Commonly the mothers themselves have undergone these practices; yet in spite of their own remembered pain, they impose them on daughters. Why? Part of the answer may be that the society offers no alternatives to women beyond marriage, and making a good marriage requires proof of adequate socialization for inequality, including adherence to practices that alter women's bodies and, with it, their demeanor.

Although the pattern here called escalator hierarchies has been described in many domestic groups as well as by ethnographic and sociological studies of small groups and institutions in different societies, it has rarely been the explicit focus of research on socialization for inequality. Such a focus is crucial because the nonperception of disadvantages of a deprived group helps to perpetuate those disadvantages (Kynch and Sen, 1983). Ideas about inequality are often taught by the very persons who are disadvantaged by them and who thereby become complicit in their perpetuation (for examples of resistance, see Mazumdar, 1999).

Kinship Systems, Entry, and Exit in Family Formation

Another factor in the persistence of gender-based discrimination and socialization for inequality is the extent to which women are prevented from making their own choices of mates and leaving intolerable situations by the termination of a marriage. The ease of entry into a marriage and the possibilities of exit are closely related to the complicity of the disadvantaged and its impact on socialization for inequality. In societies where women have some control over the choice of a mate and where divorce is possible not only by male edict but also by the woman's choice, women are less dependent on a single domestic group as their sole alternative for survival and are likely to be socialized to a less-stringent future of inequality. Older women's control over younger women is much weaker in some Southeast Asian societies, where kinship is bilateral (that is, where a married couple retains ties to both sets of parents and can reside with either or independently), when compared to others in South Asia, where kinship is patrilineal. Yet even where there seems to be ample alternatives, as in Western Europe and the United States, socialization for inequality is one of the forces keeping some women in abusive marriages.

See Also

AFFIRMATIVE ACTION; DISCRIMINATION; EQUALITY; FAMILY: POWER RELATIONS AND POWER STRUCTURES

References and Further Readings

Agarwal, Bina. 1994. *A field of one's own: Gender and land rights in South Asia.* Cambridge, U.K.: Cambridge University Press.

Cain, Mead. 1988. The material consequences of reproductive failure in rural South Asia. In Daisy Dwyer and Judith Bruce, eds., *A home divided: Women and income in the Third World,* 20–38. Stanford, Calif.: Stanford University Press.

Dube, Leela. 1997. *Women and kinship: Comparative perspectives on gender in South and Southeast Asia.* Tokyo: UNU Press.

Forbes, Geraldine. 1996. *Women in modern India.* New York: Cambridge University Press.

Jeffery, Patricia, and Roger Jeffery. 1996. *Don't marry me to a plowman: Women's everyday lives in rural North India.* Boulder, Colo.: Westview.

Kolenda, Pauline. 1987. *Regional differences in family structure in India.* Jaipur: Rawat.

Kynch, Jocelyn, and Amartya Sen. 1983. Indian women: Wellbeing and survival. *Cambridge Journal of Economics* 7: 363–380.

Lerner, Melvin J., and Gerold Mikula. 1994. *Entitlement and the affectional bond: Justice in close relationships.* New York: Plenum.

Mazumdar, Vina. 1999. A heritage of heresy within tradition. *Indian Journal of Gender Studies* 6(2): 291–309.

Miller, Barbara D. 1981. *The endangered sex: Neglect of female children in rural North India.* Ithaca, N.Y.: Cornell University Press.

———, ed. 1993. *Sex and gender hierarchies.* Cambridge: Cambridge University Press.

Papanek, Hanna. 1990. To each less than she needs, from each more than she can do: Allocations, entitlements, and value. In Irene Tinker, ed., *Persistent inequalities,* 162–181. New York: Oxford University Press.

Restrepo-Ramirez, Dalia. 1995. Gender entitlements in Colombian families. Ph.D. diss., University of Guelph, Canada.

Sen, Amartya. 1981. *An essay on entitlement and deprivation.* Oxford, UK: Clarendon.

———. 1990. Gender and cooperative conflicts. In Irene Tinker, ed., *Persistent inequalities,* 123–149. New York: Oxford University Press.

Trawick, Margaret. 1990. *Notes on love in a Tamil family.* Berkeley, Calif.: University of California Press.

Hanna Papanek

SOCIETY OF FRIENDS

See QUAKERS.

SOCIOECONOMIC STATUS

See CLASS.

SOCIOLOGY

Sociology: Some Problems of Definitions

Sociology, like most other disciplines, is often presented in textbooks in the form of a definition, typically by describing the subject in contrast to other disciplines. The most widely used definition of sociology for many years was some variant of "the study of society," although it is now more common to find the discipline described in terms of broad sociological theories or perspectives: functionalism, Marxism, interactionism, and ethnomethodology. There are a number of important things to keep in mind about trying to understand a discipline by using "a definition" as a starting point.

All disciplines are highly complex and contain internal divisions and separations, so that no definition can do justice to the reality: the way a subject is taught can be very different from what is published in specialist journals, and what appears in these is often rather different from books about it. Definitions are "canonical" statements—they usually advance a mainstream opinion, and many other discipline members, including many feminists, are likely to disagree with it. Definitional statements are typically given in textbooks, and these are formulated at the end of the process during which the ideas of a discipline are produced, rather than at the beginning. That research or theorizing is first carried out, then the original researchers publish the results in journal articles, then these people write about it in research monographs (books concerned with a single research theme), and only later does it appear in textbooks.

An important result of this division of labor, which occurs in all disciplines, is that textbooks can be seriously "out of sync" with what is happening in a discipline, par-

ticularly so during a period of rapid intellectual change. Feminist thinking is an important site of fermenting ideas and rapid intellectual change, but how feminist ideas and Women's Studies are presented in textbooks can be a particular problem. For instance, textbooks often cover the least threatening aspects of these—usually describing gender patterns—rather than presenting feminist theoretical innovation or new epistemological or methodological thinking.

Sociology and National Contexts

In addition to defining sociology by the similarities and differences emphasized in the research, teaching, and publications of the discipline, it is also useful to keep in mind that "a discipline" can sometimes take different forms within particular national contexts. How sociology is practiced in the United Kingdom, for example, is very different from how it is practiced in France, and both are different than the sociology practiced in the United States, Brazil, India, or Russia. Although often highly general statements are made in textbooks—along the lines of "physics says ..." or "sociology suggests ..."—these mask important differences in the form that such disciplines take in different contexts, often producing "facts" and "principles" that differ by location.

Epistemology, Perspectives, and Methodology

It is also useful to distinguish between epistemology, theory or conceptual perspectives and methodology within sociology and to look at the range of variants in each, so that this "model" can be used to look at the discipline either comparatively or within a particular national context.

Epistemology

Epistemology can best be described as "a theory of knowledge." It is a body of related ideas specifying what "knowledge" is seen to be; how it differs from "opinion"; who the knowledge producers are; the role of gatekeepers in keeping some people out of the field by determining standards and conditions of entry; and how and by whom competing claims to knowledge are adjudicated. The different and competing epistemological positions within sociology are frequently characterized as "realist versus idealist," where the realist position is one that insists that there is a world of material and external facts that exists independently of any knower, and the idealist a position is one that argues that interpretation is all, and that "reality" does not exist outside of interpretation. The problem with this characterization is that it is a simplifying binary constructed by those holding the realist position who stereotype those disagreeing with it.

An epistemological distinction between positivism or foundationalism on the one hand, and interpretivism on the other would be a more accurate one. Proponents of a "more realist" *and* of a "more idealist" position can be positivists or interpretivists: positivists if they are looking for certain facts, interpretivists if such facts are seen to be the product of interpretation and negotiation within grounded contexts. Emile Durkheim, one of the founders of the discipline, theorized social facts as external and constraining (that is, he was a positivist)—but also theorized that this is how people understand and construct them (that is, he was also an interpretivist).

Perhaps most feminist research and writing within sociology is aligned with one variant or another of a broadly realist and foundationalist position; however, work at the level of epistemology itself is much more strongly interpretivist in character. From very early in this present feminist renaissance within the discipline, feminist sociologists have been concerned with analyzing these different ways of conceiving "knowledge" and with challenging the "scientific" basis for making that determination. This led them to criticize realism, empiricism, positivism, and foundationalism for codifying as "objectively true" a highly partial view of the world produced from the perspective of men. This earlier strain in feminist sociology has recently been given new impetus from the growing influence of postmodernist and deconstructionist ideas.

Perspectives. The broad perspectives or conceptual approaches within sociology are usually presented as either emphasizing structural description or social action.

The structural approaches are those that look for explanations of social phenomena at the level of "social structures"—patterned regularities that persist over generations and that systematically differentiate "types of people," affecting their lives in a multiplicity of ways. These structures are seen as a determiner of social life, and theory here is typically concerned with "the social system" as a whole—a kind of society or culture characterized by one or more of these structures: thus "capitalist patriarchy" or "colonialism" are structural terms. Action approaches certainly do not deny that such systematically patterned regularities and inequalities exist, and much social action theory and research is concerned with looking for explanations of these. The difference is that the type of explanations sought within social action approaches focuses on particular grounded social contexts and how collections of people behave within these—and understand their behavior and that of others.

All the epistemological variants outlined above are found within both broad perspectives. In addition, although "perspective" within the discipline is often presented in textbooks in terms of theoretical approaches—typically, functionalism, Marxism, interactionism, ethnomethodology—it is important to remember two things. The first is that proponents of *all* these theories can adopt either structuralist or social action "slants": some Marxists, for example, are strongly oriented to frameworks of social action, whereas many ethnomethodologists are strongly oriented toward structural frameworks. The second is that other theoretical approaches exist in addition to these, but are typically ignored, seen as unimportant, and thus "silenced." The obvious example here is feminism, which exists as a theoretical position within the discipline (as well as at the level of epistemology and methodology) but is frequently absent from even recent textbooks providing "overviews" of the various theories within sociology.

Methodology. The word *methodology* can be used in at least two senses: to describe general understandings of "how to proceed in finding out" about something and in the more narrow sense of method as a specific technique.

In the first sense, methodology involves the aims, concepts, and forms of *explanation* of "finding out" about some aspect of social life: it specifies the procedural aspects of how research (both substantive and theoretical) is conducted. In its early writings, feminism sought causal explanations for women's oppression: why it occurs, and why it occurs in what some claim is an invariant pattern in the social structure of human societies. Feminism also sought purposive explanations: how to discern women's oppression through the behaviors that produce this oppression, either those enacted by men or those internalized by women. More recently, there has been a greater concern with generating statistically probable and inductive explanations for particular aspects of inequalities in grounded contexts.

A wide range of research techniques use methods that are frequently designated as either "quantitative" or "qualitative." As with other binary oppositions this distinction is oversimplistic; for example, all methods involve counting in some form or another, and all methods use language in some way or another. Epistemological stance and methodological (in the broad procedural sense) assumption have been more important to feminism than the specific choice of method; thus feminists have often used conventional, positivist survey methods, but in a very different way from their mainstream use.

Subject Areas within Sociology

Sometimes an academic discipline is described by the "subject areas" within it that are research topics taught to newcomers. Within sociology, for example, these subject areas include stratification and inequalities, the family, work and employment, politics and the state, education, crime and deviance, religion and belief systems, and organizations and bureaucracy.

The emphasis and importance given to any of these subject areas tends to differ considerably in different national contexts. The definitional approach also fails to explain why theoretical and other differences exist within these; such an explanation would require knowledge of the epistemological, perspectival, and methodological aspects of the discipline outlined here. From the viewpoint of feminist analysis, more can be understood about the organization, practice, and sexual divisions of labor in sociology by looking first at these aspects that help clarify "what is going on" within particular subject areas.

With these provisos in mind, such an approach can give a useful guide to grounded concerns within sociology. Overall, feminist ideas have had little impact in some subject areas of sociology; however, feminist work has fundamentally changed many aspects of other subject areas in the mainstream of many national sociologies. These include work, deviance, and family and household; areas of high contestation include stratification (particularly class analysis); and areas least impacted by feminism include politics, mainstream epistemology, and the higher status areas of theory.

Sociology "On the Ground"

Another useful way of characterizing sociology from a feminist analytic perspective is as a discipline "on the ground" within the academy.

A relatively "open" discipline. Sociology is a relatively "open" discipline in two related ways. First, is the existence of different ways of thinking about, investigating, and understanding society is central to all aspects of its operations. This makes it particularly welcoming for newcomers, because there is no single "line" that they have to accept. Second, it has no "specialist" subject matter unavailable to ordinary observation—everyone knows something about society and how it works. This makes it very different from some other disciplines, which have high "barriers to entry" demanding that newcomers have a good deal of prior specialist knowledge. This is one of the things that has attracted feminists to sociology: it takes seriously "the everyday" and "ordinary."

Polarized reactions. Sociology is a very popular discipline. People often want to study sociology, rather than feel they must. To a large extent this is because many people are both curious about and critical of the society and the world

they live in. And *many* people want to study it: unlike many academic disciplines, in many countries sociology is taught at all levels of the educational system, not just within universities. However, the very things that make sociology so popular with some people also make it unpopular with others.

More than any other academic discipline, sociology has been the target of media stereotyping and routine critical remarks, generally along the lines of "loony lefties." To have an inquiring and critical mind means not just accepting the status quo—whether government policies, marital relations, distributions of wealth, or sexual divisions of labor in a society—but investigating why this is so, and with what effects on what people. These questions make the discipline unpopular with those who have most to lose. Critical curiosity is the basis of "the sociological imagination"—wanting to know more and not accepting everything at face value—and this is certainly the central reason why feminists have been attracted to sociology, for the field has many of the same critically inquiring attributes of feminism itself.

A complex organizational structure. Because of its popularity and the many locations in which it is taught, sociology has a complex organizational structure. To understand this requires taking into account:

- Different activities of teaching, research, and publication
- Different levels of epistemology, perspectives, and methodology
- Different subject areas in research and theory

These have been already noted; and to them should be added the different educational locations where sociology is taught:

- School sector
- Continuing and adult education (primarily for "mature students")
- Vocational studies (to gain knowledge for pleasure rather than a qualification)
- Colleges and universities

Gender patterns and sexual divisions of labor. Within *all* of these educational locations, there are overlapping and mutually reinforcing gender patterns and sexual divisions of labor, where men are systematically found in the highest, most secure, and best-paid locations, and women in the lowest, least secure, and worst paid; and this pattern is made more complex, rather than being overturned, by "racial" divisions (white men, black men, white women, black women, is the typical pattern):

- In organizational activity (administrative, teaching, research, secretarial, "support," student)
- In hierarchical position (for example, in teaching: casual, temporary or sessional, permanent, tenured; and lecturer, senior lecturer or "professor," and full professor/head of department)
- In academic status, regarding, for example: the prestige or academic standing of the institution; teaching versus research and publication; kind of research—theoretical or empirical; the standing of publications produced

It is an interesting paradox that although feminist ideas are becoming increasingly important in all areas of sociology, and particularly its publishing, women remain concentrated in the lower-status organizational positions of the discipline.

See Also

ANTHROPOLOGY; ECONOMICS: FEMINIST CRITIQUES; EPISTEMOLOGY; HUMANITIES AND SOCIAL SCIENCES: FEMINIST CRITIQUES; SOCIAL SCIENCES: FEMINIST METHODS

References and Further Reading

Collins, Patricia Hill. 1999. *Black feminist thought.* 2nd ed. London: Allen and Unwin.

Millman, Marcia, and Rosabeth Moss Kanter, eds. 1975. *Another voice: Feminist perspectives of social life and social science.* New York: Anchor.

Riley, Martha, ed. 1988. *Sociological lives.* Newbury Park, Calif.: Sage.

Reinharz, Shulamit. 1992. *Feminist methods in social research.* New York: Oxford University Press.

Roberts, Helen. 1981. Some of the boys won't play anymore: The impact of feminism on sociology. In Dale Spender, ed., *Men's studies modified,* 73–81. Oxford: Pergamon.

Smith, Dorothy. 1987. *The everyday world as problematic: A feminist sociology.* Boston: Northeastern University Press.

Stanley, Liz. 1992. The impact of feminism on sociology in the last 20 years. In Cheris Kramarae and Dale Spender, eds., *The knowledge explosion: Generations of feminist scholarship,* 254–69. New York: Teachers College Press.

———, ed. 1996. *Borderlands: Feminist essays on academic borders, territories and knowledge.* London: Sage.

Liz Stanley

SOUTH

See THIRD WORLD.

SPACE

Women in Space Travel

When the former Soviet Union launched *Sputnik* in 1957, it fueled the cold war "space race" that eventually resulted in "man's" historic walk on the moon in 1969. The Soviet space program has since emphasized long-duration missions and habitation in semipermanent space stations. The Russian station *MIR* has been in orbit since 1986, and other space agencies (United States, Japan, Europe, and Canada) are collaborating to plan, finance, and eventually build the international space station *Freedom.* Also since *Sputnik,* space missions have grown from one- and two-person rocket flights to elaborate shuttle missions of longer duration. From the earliest space activities, women have participated in these space programs in a variety of capacities.

On 16 June 1963, Russian cosmonaut Valentina Tereshkova became the first woman in space. The first American woman to journey to space was Dr. Sally Ride on 4 April 1983. The first woman to walk in space was cosmonaut Svetlana Savistkaya in 1984. Notable women in the US space program since then include: Dr. Mae Jemison, the first African American woman astronaut; Lt. Col. Eileen Collins, the first woman to pilot a spacecraft; Dr. Judith Resnick and teacher Christa McAuliffe, both of whom died in the 1986 *Challenger* explosion; and Dr. Shannon Lucid, a biochemist, who spent a record 188 days aboard *MIR* in 1996, more than any other woman and any other US astronaut. A colleague at the National Aeronautics and Space Agency (NASA) called her a "space superwoman" (Borenstein, 1996). In addition, there are thousands of women working at NASA in the United States and at other international space agencies as engineers, electronics designers, astronomers, physicians, life scientists, technicians, managers, and support personnel. Women have made up 9 percent of the 214 astronauts selected in the US space program since 1959. Yet throughout the history of space flight, masculinist assumptions have undergirded long-term geopolitical goals, assumptions about crew behavior, scientific research, life-support systems, shuttle design, and even space suit design (Hughes, 1984). Women have not always had access to space travel and related activities.

Long-Term Space Travel

A shift in international priorities regarding space flight and increased emphasis on long-term missions and habitation has made the role of women in space both more important and more challenging. These developments mean that astronauts may be in space for longer periods of time, with significant consequences. Human bodies are radically changed by the space environment, astronauts must maintain proper social relationships in extreme conditions, and activities such as sex and reproduction pose important questions. Space stations may become twenty-first century "spaces" for gender and sexual experimentation.

The major causes of physiological problems are microgravity and radiation, from which the space shuttle and space suits can only minimally protect astronauts (David, 1992; Fowler, 1991; Monga and Gorwill, 1990; Smith, 1990). Almost all of the body's functions and processes may be affected. Motion sickness, muscle atrophy, bone loss, and other problems have all been recorded during space flights (Fowler, 1991). Because much of this data is based on flights in which mostly men served as crew members, its relevance to female bodies is questionable. Related to these physiological changes are a host of psychological problems, including loneliness, boredom, and homesickness (Smith, 1990). Furthermore, anxiety, sleep disturbances, territorial behavior, withdrawal, and depression are possible responses to the stresses resulting from prolonged confinement and isolation (Chandler, 1989). Impaired cognition, motivation, and performance may result in lowered morale, mission failure, and even death. Add to this the social and political implications of mixed-gender, mixed-race, and mixed-nation crews.

Along with the formidable technical challenges, there are important cultural and political issues of particular relevance to feminism. Female bodies are judged by a standard in which male bodies are accepted as the norm, a process that extends to the masculine (and Western) context of space travel. The masculine perception of space flight creates an institutional and ideological framework that not only excludes women but also treats their gender, bodies, sexualities, and reproductive capacities as a problem. At NASA, humans in general are considered "messy hardware," and women's bodies are the "messiest" of all. Female bodies thus become an obstacle to overcome for space agencies that insist women fit into existing space programs and engineering practices.

Sexuality in Space

Sexuality in space, discussed in exclusively heterosexist terms within space agencies, is often explicitly linked to reproduction. This implies that men and women, confined to a small environment for long periods of time, will inevitably have sexual intercourse. This view precludes the possibility of alternate sexualities, as well as of heterosexual relations without reproduction. It is not known whether contraceptive methods on Earth would be effective in space because of changes in human bodies and the demands of the space environment. Unfortunately, there has been little research on female or male reproductive health. Solutions to the "problem" of female fertility include sending only men to space (which raises discrimination and equality issues), sending only postmenopausal women to space, or making research on contraception a priority.

Research on reproductive health would be invaluable because space pregnancy is likely to be dangerous. Childbirth may be a traumatic experience in space due to physiological changes and complications related to the environment. Pregnant women may have different needs from other crew members for nutrition, oxygen, water, and physical spaces, all of which may be in short supply on long-term missions. Space pregnancies may also threaten crew social dynamics. In addition, embryos and fetuses may be impaired during space flight. On Earth, physical movement is known to be necessary for fetal development. Weightlessness could severely impact fetal growth and development. Further, fetuses that develop in a space environment may be unable physiologically to return to Earth if and when they are born. Who, then, would be responsible for these "space babies"? Historically, women have been made to be responsible for their children, and there is little evidence to suggest that space would be any different.

Now in the twenty-first century, women's continued participation in space flight is certain to grow. Women, as much as men, are captivated by the possibilities beyond Earth's atmosphere. Both orbiting the galaxy and stationed on Earth, the roles that women fill will undoubtedly shape the future of human presence in space. It is essential that issues discussed here—including equal access to space careers, gender biases in research and planning, sexuality and reproductive health and body politics—continue to be publicly debated.

See Also

BODY; CHILDBIRTH; CONTRACEPTION; GENDER; HETEROSEXISM; PREGNANCY AND BIRTH; REPRODUCTION: OVERVIEW; SCIENCE: TWENTIETH CENTURY

References and Further Reading

Borenstein, Seth. 1996. Back on earth, M & Ms and adulation. *San Jose Mercury News,* 27 September.

Chandler, Janice Vanston. 1989. Health problems in the extraterrestrial environment. *Orthopedic Nursing* 8(5): 51–64.

David, Leonard. 1992. Artificial gravity and space travel. *Bioscience* 42(3): 155–159.

Fowler, Joseph F., Jr. 1991. Physiological changes during spaceflight. *Cutis* 48: 291–295.

Hughes, Kathleen A. 1984. NASA's wardrobe for spacewalks isn't suitable to these astronauts. *Wall Street Journal*, 26 September.

Monga, Manju, and R. Hugh Gorwill. 1990. Effects of altitude, flight, and space travel on reproduction. *Seminars in Reproductive Endocrinology* 8(1): 89–93.

Smith, Jeanette. 1990. Long periods in space flight may take physiological, psychological toll among crew. *Journal of the American Medical Association* 263(3): 347, 351.

Monica J. Casper
Lisa Jean Moore

SPECIAL EDUCATION

See EDUCATION: SPECIAL NEEDS.

SPECTATORSHIP

See COMMUNICATIONS: AUDIENCE ANALYSIS; CULTURE: WOMEN AS CONSUMERS; *and* GAZE.

SPEECH

See COMMUNICATIONS: SPEECH; CONVERSATION; AND LANGUAGE.

SPINSTER

The term *spinster* refers to a woman who is not married. The expression dates from a time when a woman considered "unmarriageable" (perhaps because of her age, her physical appearance, or her social status) was expected to stay occupied at the spinning wheel. Considered pejorative, the term *spinster* was superseded by the term *unmarried woman*. Even this implies marriage as a yardstick against which women's life-courses are measured. Therefore *single* is a term increasingly used.

Many spinsters lived with their families of origin. Others were in pitiful circumstances in poorhouses. The social condition of unmarried women has varied on the basis of social class and ethnic grouping. Gradually, industrialization created the opportunity for working-class women to take jobs in factories. Over time, professions opened up to upper- and middle-class women. Some women confined to families were able to obtain access to the public sphere by engaging in philanthropic activities. Their work laid the foundation for the welfare state by promoting the idea of collective responsibility for each citizen. For white middle-class women the Victorian idea of different spheres for women and men provided opportunities. Lee Chambers-Schiller (1984) discusses the "cult of single blessedness," which enabled spinsters to devote themselves to public causes. Women's homoerotic friendships were able to flourish.

Increasing participation of single women in the workforce gradually eroded the idea of spinsters as social surplus, a burden to themselves, to those around them, and to society. Nonetheless, with the development of sexology, sexuality became an important definition of "normal" women. Unmarried women were seen as unnatural. Single women became suspect as deprived old maids or potential lesbians. Proportions of single women declined from the beginning of the century until the 1950s. Beginning around the 1960s, however, increased educational opportunities and expanding labor markets enabled unmarried women to live independently, and the numbers of single women gradually increased to the point that 23 percent of women in the United States were single in 1993.

Single women are increasingly likely to live in diverse living arrangements—ranging from one-person households to communal living—though some live with their families of origin, caring for elderly relatives. Geographic and social mobility and the development of social services have reduced the need for families to have one daughter remain unmarried in order to care for them (Allen, 1989).

Single women are a heterogeneous group with diverse lifestyles that diverge from the typical path to marriage. Alongside the negative stereotype of an "old maid" who has not been able to "get" a man and is single against her will, a new stereotype has developed of a "city single" who does not "want" a man and is single through choice (Gordon, 1994).

Singleness among women is more typical in the West but has increased elsewhere as well. This may be due to modernization (for example, in Japan) or to a breakdown of social patterns, which causes difficulties in forming families (as has happened in Russia). Though most people require intimate social contact, this need not be arranged through marriage. Single women develop diverse social networks of relatives and friends. However, a divide generally exists between married and unmarried people. Single women associate mostly with other single women (Gordon, 1994).

See Also

FRIENDSHIP; MOTHERHOOD; SINGLE PEOPLE

References and Further Readings

Allen, Katherine. 1989. *Single women/family ties: Life histories of older women*. London: Sage.

Anderson, Michael. 1984. The social position of spinsters in mid-Victorian Britain. *Journal of Family History* (Winter): 377–393.

Chambers-Schiller, Lee. 1984. *Libery, a better husband: Single women in America, the generations of 1780–1840.* New Haven, Conn.: Yale University Press.

Gordon, Tuula. 1994. *Single women: On the margins?* London: Macmillan, and New York: New York University Press.

Jeffreys, Sheila. 1985. *Spinster and her enemies: Feminism and sexuality 1880–1930.* London: Pandora.

Tuula Gordon

SPIRITUALITY: Overview

Concept of Spirituality

Spirituality is a mode of being, of living one's life according to one's worldview, which gives a meaning to one's existence. It is the inner core of a human being, made up of all of that individual's experiences and encounters in life. Out of that core come the motivation, inspiration, and commitment that make one live and make decisions in one's own unique way.

Spirituality is not a simple concept. It is used to describe different realities that may have converging elements. In Christian theology and practice the traditional understanding of spirituality is the application of the tenets of religion to daily life—in one's personal life of prayer and asceticism, for example. Each religious congregation has its own distinctive way of living its particular vision and tenets—so that one can speak of a Benedictine spirituality, a Franciscan spirituality, a Carmelite spirituality, a Jesuit spirituality, and so on.

However, it cannot be denied that there can be a spirituality without affiliation to any organized religion. In this respect, spirituality differs from religiosity, which is the adherence to the beliefs of a particular religion and the devoted observance of its rituals, practices, and ethical principles.

This core of one's being is influenced in part by one's genetic heritage and environment but is largely shaped by gut-level experiences and major choices in life. It is also this center that is the focus of one's experience of transcendence—for theists, "of God." It is where one is challenged by new and unpredictable experiences that might totally contradict the accumulated experiences that have shaped this core throughout the years. This is the level at which the phenomenon of conversion is realized. It is likewise the locus of personal disintegration, depending on one's response to this shattering experience. Meditation, prayer, and asceticism can enable one to integrate these experiences into one's inner core or, perhaps, to revise this core, totally or in part, as happens in crisis moments of a person's life.

Forms of Spirituality

One general way of categorizing spirituality is into its Eastern and Western forms. These categories are not mutually exclusive; elements of each can be found in the other. However, there are marked tendencies and features that do make a distinction possible.

Western spirituality, which is largely influenced by Christianity, is centered in the concepts of sin and redemption. It tends to be dualistic and to focus on dichotomies: between spirit and matter, body and soul, sacred and profane, heaven and earth, and so on. Its understanding of salvation is abstract and otherworldly. Its form of prayer is oral and mental, and it is discursive in its meditative practice. It emphasizes striving for perfection, asceticism, abnegation, self-control. It fosters obedience to external authority and duty and puts a high premium on "good deeds." It is patriarchal, with a predominantly male image of God.

Eastern spirituality takes a cosmic rather than a personal view of God. It is holistic, emphasizing the oneness of body and soul, matter and spirit, and seeing the whole of the universe as interwoven. Life's contradictions are seen not as mutually canceling but as two poles of one reality, one giving meaning to the other. Eastern spirituality is more creation-centered: it is ecological and cosmic, concerned with the environment and conscious of one's interconnectedness with all beings. It gives priority to contemplation, silence, and intuitive prayer. It pays attention to bodily posture in prayer and emphasizes the role of the guru or spiritual teacher. It is less pragmatic than Western spirituality, and, though not denigrating "doing," it focuses more on "being" and "becoming." Because Eastern spirituality does not personalize God, it goes beyond the father–mother image. Salvation is understood as the experience of enlightenment and oneness with the infinite.

In contemporary times, theologians, especially from the Third World, have shown interest in the spirituality of indigenous peoples—among Native Americans, Aboriginal Australians, Africans, and various ethnic groups in Asia. Denise Lardner Carmody (1996) classifies indigenous religions as "oral religious traditions" because they "do not have scriptures, literate sources of guidance, or a linear sense of history." One common characteristic in the spirituality of these religions is the shamanic experience or the centrality of ecstasy as a religious experience. Also important are sacred rituals, dancing, chanting, interpretation of dreams, and healing. There is greater use of the imagination, in contrast to the focus on reason, will, and understanding of other world religions, especially Western religions. Third World theologians have also noted the woman-friendliness of these religions, which may prefer women as shamans or priests, as celebrants of rituals, and as the main spiritual leaders of the community. There is also a regard for the sacredness of nature, which appeals to Westerners' heightened ecological concerns. Filipino theologians quote a tribal woman saying: "Sometimes we wonder why Christians have to preach about God. For us, God's presence is clear in all creation. Why don't we allow creation to make God known to us?" (Filipino EATWOT Theologians, 1995).

The Emerging Women Spirituality

The feminist movement has given women a new awareness of their situation in society and a new understanding of themselves as human beings. Women have realized that mainstream consciousness, and therefore mainstream spirituality, especially when it is influenced by institutionalized religion whether in the West or in the East, is predominantly patriarchal. It is lived by both men and women, but to the benefit of men and the detriment of women.

Gut-level experiences are those that shape one's spirituality. Among women's many experiences, it is their experience as women that touches them most on both personal and social levels. For centuries, women in different cultures and traditions have been conditioned to be docile, passive, subservient, long-suffering, and self-abnegating—to see their worth and significance not in self-fulfillment but in relation to and in service of the significant males in their lives. This conditioning has given rise to discrimination against women and to their subordination, exploitation, and oppression; at the extreme, it has made them victims of various forms of gender violence and trafficking in women.

Women experience everyday oppression: the limiting experiences of housewives confined to the home; the despair of battered wives who cannot separate from their husbands because of emotional, psychological, and economic dependence; the exploitation, discrimination, and sexual harassment of women workers, both in rural areas as invisible contributors to agricultural production and in factories as low-wage earners who are the last to be hired and the first to be fired. A continual insult to womanhood is seen in the mass media, in advertisements, and in pornography.

But aside from these regular, day-to-day experiences, each woman has her own private hell, which she experiences at crisis points in her life, and from which she emerges either with inner liberation or with bitterness and resentment, crushed and wounded in the depths of her being.

Because of the oppressive consequences of a patriarchal, male-centered religion, women feel a need to redefine spirituality in a way that is enhancing to them. When women reflect on their experiences, they may develop a new spiritual consciousness that enhances their power and augments their energy. It is a spirituality that creates a new woman's culture and that gives a vision of wholeness, not only personally but also socially.

The Goddess Spirituality

One search for this women's spirituality goes back to the ancient worship of the Great Goddess. Women anthropologists and other feminist researchers have investigated ancient and medieval religious and witchcraft traditions. They have theorized that before the patriarchal God, there was a prepatriarchal era in which the Goddess was worshipped—an era characterized by peace, cultural development, egalitarianism, and enhancement of life. Although the most common form of the Goddess was the Goddess of Fertility, she also represented all-encompassing power over life and death.

There has been a revival of rituals and symbols of this ancient worship of the Goddess, although new symbols and rituals are also being developed by emerging religious groups of women who see in Goddess worship the discovery of a feminine ground of being. This form of spirituality also often goes back to the idea of the womb of the earth as a haven of security and a source of life. From this idea developed an ecofeminist spirituality that is sensitive to and concerned about preserving nature and safeguarding the environment. There is a sense of righteous indignation at the rape of the earth, the pollution of the air, and the destruction of the fruits of the sea—the same sense of righteous anger felt at the rape of a woman. From this anger has emerged a creation-centered spirituality rather than one focused on sin and redemption, a spirituality that begins not with an original sin but with an original blessing—the innate goodness and beauty of creation.

The Emerging Spirituality among Christian Women

Among Christian women, this emerging spirituality has grown side by side with theological understanding. The contextualized theology that results is a reflection of individuals' spirituality that is shaped by personal and social experiences.

This is not a new phenomenon. The history of salvation in the Judeo-Christian tradition begins with the experience of liberation, the Exodus, by the people of God. The understanding of salvation that emerged from that experience was a total and concrete one worked out by a God of history. It was total because it was an experience of the whole person, body and soul, in the context of a social milieu. It was concrete in the sense that it was a liberation from the concrete evil of Egyptian bondage and the enjoyment of the concrete blessing of the Promised Land and the covenant with Jahweh. Throughout the ages that followed, this was the understanding of salvation in the experience of Israel. In the subsequent spread of Christianity and especially in its hellenization, Christian concepts were influenced by Platonic dualism, resulting in theological dichotomies of body and soul, heaven and earth, spirit and matter, and so on. Salvation began to be taught as the salvation of the soul from sin, hell, and death in order to go to heaven. This teaching brought about a moral theology based on the suspicion that "the body is bad," resulting in a spirituality that was narrow, prudish, focused on avoiding "sins of the flesh," and plagued by a sense of guilt.

After the Second Vatican Council, theology regained some equilibrium, transcending dualisms and dichotomies and calling instead for integral salvation and integral evangelization. A further development was the emergence in Latin America of a theology of liberation, which contextualized theology in the situation and struggles of the peoples of that region and made liberating action imperative for Christians. Feminist theology accepts some insights of liberation theology but contributes its own gender perspective. The development of such a theology has further contributed to the growth of a holistic approach to spirituality.

One of the most visible forms of this emerging spirituality among Christian women is the women-church movement, which began in the United States but which has spread to other parts of the world. Women-church is not a schismatic group but, rather, consists of ecumenical communities of women who hold onto the original inspiration of the Gospels but seek spiritual nourishment and support by coming together regularly, celebrating creative and alternative forms of worship, and trying to live in more egalitarian and democratic ways than they find in the patriarchal church. Women-church is committed to sociopolitical transformation and expresses solidarity with the oppression, needs, and anguish of peoples all over the world.

Characteristics of the Emerging Women's Spirituality

Whether through a return to Goddess worship or a rethinking of Christian theology, the struggle of women for full humanity has given rise to a spirituality that is uniquely female. This spirituality exhibits the following characteristics:

1. It is self-affirming: In contrast to the self-denying characteristics of traditional spirituality, the emerging women's spirituality enables women to affirm themselves, to value their strengths, to nourish their self-esteem, and to strive for self-fulfillment as the only genuine basis of helping others. In so doing, women rid themselves of crippling feelings of guilt and allow themselves to bloom.

2. It is empowering: Women have realized that they have within them a wellspring of limitless possibilities for growth and development—an inner source of power and strength. Realization of their situation and renewed self-esteem have enabled women to tap this inner source, allowing them to rise from their victim status not only to the status of survivors but to that of agents of change capable of empowering others to bring about societal changes toward a more humane world.

3. It is integral: Women living this spirituality transcend the dichotomies and dualisms of traditional patriarchal spirituality. Matter and spirit, the sacred and the profane, contemplation and action are all necessary elements of life. Women flow with their positive and negative experiences, living life fully and intensely.

4. It is liberating: Women who have gained spiritual self-knowledge and acceptance experience an inner liberation from fear, guilt, bitterness, and resentment. These women are still fearful, but they have learned to distinguish between substantiated and unsubstantiated fear and to act in spite of justified fears. They have transcended neurotic guilt and self-flagellation whenever anything untoward happens to them or their families. They have been freed from worrying about other people's opinions of them. These women have decided to eliminate bitterness and resentment from their hearts, to set themselves free for creative actions.

5. It is contemplative: Women see the importance of moments of silence, reflection, and contemplation. These silences allow them to gain a better perspective, to evaluate life events from a distance, to keep in touch with their inner spiritual core, and to retain their sense of humor amid difficulties. The result is an attitude of "committed carefreeness."

6. It is healing: Women trying to live this way are healed from their psychic wounds. Having gotten in touch with themselves and having gained self-esteem, these women can transcend their traumas and regain their

spiritual health and vigor. Because of the integrity of matter and spirit, these women may find that even their physical ailments are alleviated. Like wounded healers, they are able likewise to heal others with compassion and empathy.

7. It is Easterly: Women's spirituality is exuberant rather than austere, active rather than passive, joyful rather than mournful. It feasts more than it fasts. It is not cold asceticism but a glorious celebration of life. It does not remain with the sadness of Good Friday but goes on to the triumph of Easter Sunday.

8. It is a continuous process: Women's spirituality is not achieved once and for all, nor is it a smooth, progressive path. It has its peaks and abysses, its agonies and ecstasies. Women can regress but can also take quantum leaps. They are on a path that is open to possibilities of life and freedom and therefore to increasing opportunities to be truly, intensely, and wholly alive.

This emerging women's spirituality can be summarized in a phrase: It is a passionate and compassionate spirituality.

See Also

EDUCATION: RELIGIOUS STUDIES; GODDESS; RELIGION: OVERVIEW; THEOLOGIES: FEMINIST; WOMANCULTURE; WOMANIST THEOLOGY; WOMANSPIRIT; WOMEN-CHURCH

References and Further Reading

Carmody, Denise Lardner, and John Tully Carmody. 1996. *Mysticism.* Oxford: Oxford University Press.

Dorr, Donald. 1985. *Spirituality-justice.* Quezon City, Philippines: Claretian Publications.

Filipino Ecumenical Association of Third World Theologies (EATWOT) Theologians. 1995. *Dugo Duga ng Buhay: A Philippine experience in spirituality.* Manila: EATWOT and FIDES.

King, Ursula. 1993. *Women and spirituality.* 2nd ed. London: Macmillan.

Mananzan, Sr. Mary John. 1989. Emerging spirituality of women. In Sr. Mary John Mananzan, ed., *Essays on women.* Manila: Institute of Women's Studies.

Neu, Diann L., and Mary E. Hunt. 1993. *Women-church handbook.* Silver Spring, Md.: Waterworks Press.

Schulenberg, Andrea. 1993. *Feministische spiritualitat.* Cologne: Verlag W. Kohlhaer.

Statement of the Asian Women's Consultation. 1985. (Unpublished manuscript.)

Stone, Merlin. 1976. *The paradise papers.* London: Virago.

Sr. Mary John Mananzan

SPIRITUALITY: Sexuality

The complex history of women's sexuality in a context of androcentric spirituality is recorded in ancient writings from the fourth millennium B.C. until the present era. The ambivalence of the male-normative tradition toward human sexuality has had negative consequences for the world as a whole and for women in particular.

The experience of female sexuality and spirituality has moved through three primary modalities. The first was awakening: women rejected stereotypical patriarchal paradigms—wife, mother, whore—and began to reflect on their own understanding of sexuality. The next was separation: women stood apart to critique their cultural context, exposing the demonization of their sexuality. In the third approach, acclamation, women reclaimed their sexuality and spirituality as women.

Terminology

Sex refers to biological differentiation, while *gender* is related to cultural conditioning. Derived from the prevailing perception of male and female cultural roles, gender is a constantly changing cultural product. *Sexuality* refers to biological- and gender-related roles.

Spirituality comes from the Latin term *spiritualitas,* originally associated with the dualism between spirit and body. Early Christian writings describe the dichotomy as the tension between one's fleshly (female-identified) and spiritual (male-identified) desires. The term also describes the interplay between the natural and supernatural worlds.

Patriarchy and Women's Sexuality

Mesopotamian and Hebrew influences. Researchers have established that from the earliest male-recorded history, women experienced marginalization. They were excluded from writing their community stories and from recounting their experiences, such as the "Great Mother Goddess" cults.

Early Mesopotamian writings show that for over 2,500 years B.C. males increased their control over women's sexuality. This was legitimated by class and property laws.

With the expansion of Hebrew monotheism, fertility goddesses came under attack. The Hebrew Scriptures externalize men's condemnation through their roles as producers and tillers of the earth and internalize women's condemnation through their bodies and life-giving powers. Women's identity took shape in a spirituality of guilt, bodily rejection, and submissiveness.

Greco-Roman influences. Sexuality and spirituality are described by historians of the Greco-Roman culture as male

1883

and elitist. Good order and control were the ideal of a good state and the essence of male spirituality in the Greek and Roman cultures. Male sexuality was seen in terms of maintaining appropriate power relationships. Objectified as possessions, owned by and subservient to men, women were also reduced to the status of passive spectators at public and private religious rituals in Roman society.

Christian influences. The prevailing scientific opinion in the early Christian era was that males were the fetuses at their full potential, while females were the result of a failure in the fertilization process. This medical theory had been elaborated in the fourth century B.C. by Aristotle. Women's spirituality was repudiated by their definition as "incomplete" beings.

As Christianity became the dominant religion of the Western world, women were denounced as sources of temptation, and regulations (such as the Christian church's utilization of celibacy as a means of control) were enforced.

The medieval period was one in which female sexuality was denigrated and women who exercised spiritual leadership were denounced as witches. It is generally accepted that more than a million women were executed during the Inquisition in fifteenth-century Europe. Medieval fears of women's sexuality and anxiety about menstrual blood caused major religious traditions to proscribe women as unclean, thus excluding menstruating women from the religious rituals of their communities. Menstrual blood was also believed to be capable of killing plants, giving dogs rabies, and causing disease. The sexual arousal of celibate clergy and the emasculation of males in general were also attributed to women's deviancy. This fear of women's potency is not confined to Western religions but exists across cultures and in medical and scientific literature as well as religious writings.

Some women transcended the misogynism of their religious tradition. Hildegard of Bingen (1098–1179), a gifted and creative writer in the fields of science, medicine, and theology, accepted the prevailing patriarchal views regarding women, but her vast expanse of works represent women as strong and gifted contributors to their church and society.

The Birth of Feminism: An Awakening

Women's awakening began in the nineteenth and twentieth centuries. With the industrial revolution, women became able to challenge the control of economic and gender dependency, an experience that raised their consciousness about their social circumstances.

The two waves of feminism (1870s and 1970s) moved women from a sense of shame to a celebration of their womanhood. Writers such as Virginia Woolf (*A Room of One's Own,* 1929) and Simone de Beauvoir (*The Second Sex,* 1972)

challenged the religious and social repression of women. The reduction of women's sexual choice to procreation or a life of virginity was questioned. In social and church groups, women took initiatives on behalf of themselves and other voiceless people to claim their identity as sexual and spiritual beings. Groups of Christian women formed communities to educate and help the poor, the ill, and the needy, directing spirituality toward service.

As many men of the nineteenth century increasingly questioned their religious belief systems, women became the backbone of the Christian churches. By their majority presence, women affected the writing of contemporary prayer manuals and devotional services. The feminization of religion began to form and the prevailing popular spirituality was largely defined by women.

Other Voices

Women oppressed within their cultural and religious contexts found ways to express themselves. Mystical spirituality had been an avenue for gifted women, like the seventeenth-century Mexican nun Sor Juana Ines de la Cruz, a renowned poet and scholar. She produced some of the earliest liberating women's literature in Latin America, expressing women's spirituality and sexuality through the themes of human and divine love.

There was also a sexual and spiritual outlet in science fiction and magic realism. Social critiques that, if recognized, would be denied publication were presented in coded language. In violent and abusive situations where women were prevented from speaking, women's experience is voiced through alternative media. Mary Shelley's *Frankenstein* (1831) and Toni Morrison's *The Bluest Eye* (1972) are diverse examples of this.

Women's sexuality and spirituality have also been expressed in arts and crafts. An example of this is seen in African American women's quilt-making. Although it was usually white women who wrote about quilting, African American women also passed on their own spirituality: "A woman made utility quilts as fast as she could so her family wouldn't freeze, and she made them as beautiful as she could so her heart wouldn't break. Women's thoughts, feelings, their very lives were inextricably bound into the designs just as surely as the cloth layers were bound with thread" (hooks, 1990: 117).

New Directions

Two strands of feminism occurred in women's secular and religious writings. There were those who wrote in reaction against male domination, and there were women whose concern was to claim their own voices. And alongside these were the emancipatory woman-centered writings from all parts of the globe.

Separation: "reaction against." Women scholars such as Mary Daly, Rosemary Radford Ruether, Phyllis Trible, Elizabeth Schussler Fiorenza, and Elizabeth Johnson have exposed a tradition of Christian misogyny from theological and scriptural perspectives, reinforcing the critique of male-nomative spirituality and questioning roles and relationships in civic and ecclesiastical communities. Jewish feminist scholars like Judith Plaskow, Judith Wegner, and Judith Hauptman analyzed Jewish religious texts, critiquing the view of women's sexuality as "abnormal, anomalous, dangerous, dirty, and polluting" (Davidman and Tenenbaum, 1994: 44), acclaiming religious feeling and the presence of God in everyday life as integral to women's spirituality.

New groups of women—lesbian, post-Christian—arose to express their autonomy. Women's control over their own bodies epitomized their spirituality and sexuality.

Asian women similarly critiqued their societies. In Japan, analysis of legislation and customs of the Meiji era (1868–1912) led to a rejection of the dictate that women accept the role of "repositories of the past" (*Signs,* 1984: 786). The "ideal" of diffident and nurturing Japanese women was disclaimed, exposing myths about women's place in society. Elsewhere, women are questioning clitoridectomy, which is destructive not simply of women's bodies, but of their whole sense of womanliness. They are also questioning why women are collaborating in these maiming practices.

In the Middle East, some women have denounced fundamentalist imposition of the Islamic religion as oppressive. Educated Arab women reacting against male-imposed purdah requirements see not only facial veiling but also a "veiling of the mind" through the abusive ways in which religion can maintain subordination. The patriarchal world of Islamic culture becomes the medium through which women understand religion and their community status. Contemporary Middle Eastern feminists are working to reintegrate women's sexuality into their spirituality.

Acclamation: A woman-centered approach. As some work to free women's sexuality and spirituality, others are creating alternative contexts where silenced women can find their own voices and experience being heard by others.

Women working from different cultural and sexual orientations bring more expansive insights to women's experience of sexuality, generating new understandings of women's sexuality and spirituality and working "to develop a healthy theology of the body and to demystify the cult of virginity" (Mananzan, 1995: 31). New perspectives on feminist sexuality and spirituality demonstrate that a full chorus of women's voices must be heard if the range of women's sexuality and spirituality is to be appreciated.

Conclusion

Social sciences and medical and scientific research at the end of the twentieth century have helped women to understand their bodies and affirm their sexuality. Theological scholarship has opened to the realization that women's relationship with God is not as negative as was previously depicted. Solidarity across religious traditions and in secular feminist scholarship enables further understanding about women's place in the world of creation.

The acclaiming process of women's sexuality comes from a dialogue that is interdisciplinary, international, ecumenical, interreligious, and cross-cultural, moving toward an interdependent way of relating in the world. Consciousness-raising activities lead to a greater understanding of sexuality and of the embodiment of female spirituality and affirming that there can be no single spirituality or sexuality. Women's sexuality is dynamic and diverse, open to desire and affirming of bodiliness. Theirs is a spirituality that is liberating, not simply for women, but for the created world.

See Also

BODY; MISOGYNY; SEXUALITY: OVERVIEW; SPIRITUALITY: OVERVIEW; VIRGINITY

References and Further Reading

Behr-Sigel, Elizabeth. 1991. *The ministry of women in the early church.* Trans. Stephen Bigham. Redondo Beach, Calif.: Oakwood.

Brown, Peter. 1988. *The body and society.* New York: Columbia University Press.

Davidman, Lynn, and Shelley Tenenbaum, eds. 1994. *Feminist perspectives on Jewish studies.* New Haven, Conn.: Yale University Press.

Duby, Georges, and Michelle Perot, gen. eds. 1994. *A history of women in the West,* Vols. 1–5. Cambridge, Mass.: Harvard University Press.

Feminist Review. 1982. Special issue on sexuality, no. 11.

Hinsdale, Mary Ann, and Phyllis H. Kaminski, eds. 1994. *Women and theology.* Annual Publication of the College of Theology Society, Vol. 40. New York: Orbis.

hooks, bell. 1990. *Yearning: Race, gender and cultural politics.* Boston, Mass.: South End.

Lerner, Gerda. 1993. *The creation of feminist consciousness.* London: Oxford University Press.

Mananzan, Sr. Mary John. 1995. Feminist theology in Asia: A ten years' overview. *Feminist Theology*, no. 10 (September).

Schneiders, Sandra. 1993. Feminist spirituality. In Michael Downey, ed., *The new dictionary of Catholic spirituality*, 394–406. Collegeville, Minn.: Michael Glazier.

Signs. 1984. Special issue on feminist sexuality debates, no. 10.

Stuart, Elizabeth, Alison Webster, and Gerard Loughlin, eds. 1995. *Theology and sexuality: Journal of the Institute for the Study of Christianity and Sexuality.* Sheffield, UK: Institute for the Study of Christianity and Sexuality.

Torjeses, Karen J. 1993. *When women were priests: Women's leadership in the church and the scandal of their subordination in the rise of Christianity.* New York: Harper San Francisco.

Maryanne Confoy

SPORT

In western popular culture successful sportswomen have been regarded as freaks of nature, a perspective that overlooks the social reality of dedication and sacrifice necessary to be successful. Feminists, sociologists, historians, biomedical experts, and psychologists have analyzed such phenomena recently with growing sophistication (Costa and Guthrie, 1994). Throughout the modern industrialized world privileged women have taken part in sport and during the past hundred years have created women's sporting organizations and physical education for girls (Hargreaves, 1994). For poor and working women within the industrial world with little or no leisure time, sport must be recognized as an exclusive luxury. Some professions like trapeze artists provide a meager marginal living. For women in less industrialized cultures work may include considerable physical demands quite separate from leisure, which may not exist at all or not include opportunities for organized sport. For those living in Somalia, Bangladesh, or Ethiopia such possibilities are remote luxuries (Cohen, 1993). In spite of this it is often said that sport is a universal phenomenon and that women take part for the love of it.

A growing number of women are writing about sport and extending programs throughout the world to enable all women to benefit in a way that transcends culture and promotes well-being. Women are participating in sport for health (Melpomene Institute, 1990) and recreation, to lose weight, get fit, for self-defense, for social reasons, to get out of the home, to compete, as part of a sense of self and identity, to prove something to themselves and others. Women

also provide, administrate, coach, teach, and theorize. A few work in the media. On the global level television transmits images of the Olympics and international sporting events that overlook female involvement in favor of male activity, presented as the ultimate in human endeavor, apart from some rare women track and field athletes, tennis players, gymnasts, ice-skaters, divers, and marathon runners. This is organized, highly competitive, elite sport. The form of sport seen on TV is only one form of sport, culturally Western and imbued with values of competition, efficiency, rationality, technical expertise, training, measurement, and timing—it is concerned with the fastest, highest, and longest. Some women strive for such goals. Others say that sports have become corrupted by politics and drug-taking and have lost the element of play.

The Influence of Western Practices

Western practices, partly through England's games-playing heritage, in an organized, rule-bound form, with muscular Christian codes of conduct, informed the establishment of modern sport. Games were taken around the world by merchants, missionaries, soldiers, teachers, and industrialists as part of the colonial process. Thus, for example, the Christian beliefs of western women missionaries in Malaysia influenced their portrayal of sport as wholesome and encouraged them to use it to try to eradicate prostitution, concubinage, opium smoking, and gambling (Brownfoot, 1990, cited in Cohen, 1993). The codes of conduct also were copied by those wishing to emulate what they saw as ideals of western culture dating back to classical antiquity. Pierre de Coubertin's concept of the modern Olympics was based on his view of the superiority of practices of athleticism in British Victorian boys' public schools. His view of women as not fitted for athletic pursuit, but for decoration, applause, and to present the winners with laurel leaves is a view that was endorsed by nineteenth- and early twentieth-century sporting organizations whose remnants live on today in spite of female activism. Science also supported women's sporting constraint in promoting limited energy theories of the body that developed into caring medical ideologies mostly around the protection of reproductive organs and the necessity of childbearing for the perpetuation of certain social/racial groups in power (Hargreaves, 1994). Although part of preparation for health and military defense in, for example, the former Soviet Union, Cuba, and China, and tied in with ideas of strong nationhood and motherhood as in Hitler's Germany, sport tends often to be thought of as a world apart from social and political influences. Today various cultures are shaping their own distinct social constructions of sport to reflect multiple or diverse heritages based on indigenous traditions and religious beliefs.

The Influence of Feminism on Sport

Hargreaves (1994) reports that sportswomen have not been enthusiastic feminists and feminist intervention in sport has lagged behind other attempts by feminists to politicize areas of culture. Perhaps this is because sport has been seen as the last bastion of male domination because of the conservative social construction of sports, their sex-segregated institutionalization historically, and the idea that male strength is necessary for sport. Sports organizers and participants are slowly realizing that organized sport perpetuates institutionalized sexism. Women's involvement in high administrative posts such as the International Olympic Committee is very low and many women physical educators see promoted posts taken by men. Few women coach or have positions of power within sport. Females tend to participate in sports less than males in all age groups, and even though sporting structures rarely cater for mixed-sex competition, their performance levels are often compared unfavorably with males. The popular explanation for this is physiological weakness, while sports feminists tend to favor cultural explanations.

Hargreaves (1994) and Cohen (1993) illustrate the way the subject of women in sport tends to be tackled. Cohen exemplifies a multidisciplinary approach to sports study with reference to political, economic, herstorical, psychological, physiological, and sociological perspectives. In her cultural analysis, Hargreaves (1994) covers many corresponding issues.

The main issues within women in sports research have been related to broader feminist debates (Boutilier and San Giovanni, 1983), in spite of Hargreaves' (1994) observation earlier. Sex-appropriate sports as institutionalized segregationally since the nineteenth century, such as field hockey, gymnastics, tennis, swimming, and diving, were rejected in the 1970s as the only sports in which women could participate. Women wanted to use male sporting facilities, play their games, and achieve equality. Some rejected the male standard, while others developed women's versions of men's games such as football and rugby. Some radical feminists have argued for sports played according to a feminist ethos rather than the highly competitive, aggressive ethos of most male sports: inclusive, cooperative, supportive softball for example (Birrell and Richter, 1994). Others have criticized the way that heterosexuality is constantly restated as the norm against which lesbians are prejudiciously judged and have opened up new areas for research (Clarke and Hum-

berstone, 1997). For some women, regardless of sexual orientation, playing male sports in an aggressive style can be a liberating experience normally denied them in everyday life. Women of color have pointed out their neglect in spite of the high visibility of women of African origin in track and field events particularly. Myths of racial physiological superiority can be perpetuated by black and white alike in the sporting context, for many see Africa as a sleeping lioness abrim with sporting talent, and sport is one road to the dream of a Western lifestyle. Muslim women, meanwhile, are viewed as both heroines and infidels for abandoning traditional dress codes and running in shorts in public.

The Women's International Sports Coalition seeks gender equity in sport (Brackenridge, 1992, cited in Cohen, 1993). Its difference from liberal feminist initiatives may be that it has cultural feminist persuasions to do with elevating women's ways of working, challenging the male standard, and countering the institutionalized abuse of athletes. Liberal feminists are often sportswomen wanting to do what male sporting structures denied them. The global coalition is for women, working with women. The love of sport ideology lives on in this ethos. Democratization of women's sport has been limited by association with privilege. It needs to be vigilant to avoid neocolonialism. With the coming of television and consumer capitalism for the masses there is the popular conception that sporting choice has expanded. Women's participation has increased, not in traditional team sports or individual sports, but in activities like aerobics and jogging. Some argue this has broadened choice and led to new sensitivities (Bloch, 1987). Others argue that the slim female body image of advertising is related to women's involvement in new activities, not for the love of sport but for the purpose of improving body shape and glamor. Meanwhile, such television spectacles as *Gladiators* have a large audience in the United Kingdom. Screened at prime time on Saturday evenings, glamorous, muscular men and women, sometimes well-known sporting stars, dress in revealing "gladiatorial" garb to confront each other in contests of strength, speed, and stamina. Rail (1990) shows how the voyeurism present in the sport dynamic is rarely examined.

Nationalism in sport and the involvement of big business run counter to the "sport is good for you" ideology. Media and promoters of sport, theorists who want to challenge the male hegemony, rarely consider the casualties. The ethic of care may have been a good one for women that should now be extended to men. Overtraining can cause failures of the immune system, making athletes susceptible to viral infections, and combinations of overtraining, eating disorders, and amenorrhea may lead to osteoporosis, making young women's one density as low and prone to stress fractures as women twice their age. Osteoporosis can affect men too, but medical practitioners still expect clients to be older women. The damaging effects of sport are not only physical but may also be psychological, in that it presents an aggressive television spectacle that rarely features women. Consequently, even some male commentators now seek a transformation of sport as it presently exists.

Have women reached their full sporting potential? As yet not all women have the freedom to take up sport or choose something preferable. There are many gender realities to be understood in sport. Study has only just begun.

See Also

EDUCATION: PHYSICAL; EXERCISE AND FITNESS; HEALTH: OVERVIEW; SPORTS AND DISCRIMINATION

References and Other Readings

Birrell, Susan, and Diana Richter. 1994. Is a diamond forever? In Susan Birrell, and Cheryl Cole, eds., *Women, sport, and culture*. Champaign, Ill.: Human Kinetics.

Bloch, Charlotte. 1987. Everyday life, sensuality and body culture. *Women's Studies International Forum* 10(4): 433–442.

Boutilier, Mary, and Lucinda San Giovanni. 1983. *The sporting woman*. Champaign, Ill.: Human Kinetics.

Breckenridge, Celia. 1992. Women's international sports coalition. In Proceedings of the First Meeting of the Women's International Sports Coalition. Unpublished manuscript. Sheffield, UK.

Brownfoot, Janice N. 1990. Emancipation, exercise and imperialism: Girls and the games ethic in colonial Malaya. *International Journal of the History of Sport* 7(1): 61–84.

Clarke, Gill, and B. Humberstone, eds. 1997. *Researching women and sport*. Basingstoke: Macmillan.

Cohen, Gretah, ed. 1993. *Women in sport: Issues and controversies*. Newbury Park, Calif.: Sage.

Costa, Margaret, and Sharon Guthrie. 1994. *Women and sport: Interdisciplinary perspectives*. Champaign, Ill.: Human Kinetics.

Hargreaves, Jennifer. 1994. *Sporting females: Critical issues in the history and sociology of women's sports*. London: Routledge.

Melpomene Institute for Women's Health Research. 1990. *The bodywise woman*. Champaign, Ill.: Human Kinetics.

Rail, Genevieve. 1990. Medium is model: Postmodernity and mediated sport. Unpublished paper presented at the XIIth World Congress of Sociology, Madrid, Spain, 9–13 July.

Joyce Sherlock

SPORTS AND DISCRIMINATION

Discrimination has plagued the field of women's sports for centuries. Women were barred from participating in the Olympics, for instance, from ancient times until the late 1800s and were slow to catch up when finally admitted in some events.

With the dawn of the third millennium, that picture is changing. At the Sydney 2000 games, women participated in 44 percent of all Olympic events. Women's sports analysts predict more changes ahead with several social and economic factors acting as catalysts for gender equity.

A general, global movement toward capitalism will promote a marketplace for women's sports. International corporations will encourage women's participation and court the female market.

Governments around the world will continue to exploit the achievements of women athletes in order to advance nationalistic political agendas. National pride and ideology break through the gender barrier as nations promote their sports heroes, both men and women. Such goals will render outmoded most sexist ideas about the "inferiority" of female athletes.

Increased exposure of women in sports through television, the Internet, and other mass communications systems will break down stereotypes and provide role models for girls. Women will increase participation in such nontraditional sports as wrestling, boxing, and weight-lifting. More sports will be coeducational. The number of women in team sports will grow.

A new image of the strong, healthy woman will emerge as the paradigm, where once women were discouraged from participating in sports for fear that vigorous exercise would drain energy from their reproductive organs and lead to infertility. At the turn of the twentieth century, American doctors determined that exercise would indeed enable women to more easily propagate and began to promote physical activity. Women were ostensibly free to pursue athletic endeavors, but for many more decades they would be underrepresented on the fields of sport.

For many women, exercise still constituted scrubbing clothes against a washboard or walking to market—physically taxing, but hardly in the realm of Olympic events. Women's place continued to be in the home, not on the tennis court or the soccer field.

Because of its physical demands, sports has traditionally been a field dominated by men and ripe for gender discrimination. Mixed-gender competition is rare—it is most often found in mixed doubles tennis, beach volleyball, and some sailing and equestrian events. Some sports favor the participation of women, including figure skating, gymnastics, softball, and field hockey—considered more "ladylike" than contact sports. But women have made inroads even in more physically challenging games. In 1977, Lucy Harris became the first woman drafted by the National Basketball Association, by the New Orleans Jazz. Although she never played for the team, she joined the Women's Professional Basketball League as a member of the Houston Angels. Lynette Woodard became the first woman to play on an all-male professional basketball team in 1986, and scored seven points in her debut with the Harlem Globetrotters. Women have climbed into the boxing ring against male opponents and have sat behind the wheel in auto racing. Girls have won the right to compete with and against boys on high school wrestling teams. In 1974, the National Women's Football League was formed to support women in professional football; however, 20 years later, there were only 328 girls playing high school football out of 955,000 total players. Two girls were stand-out placekickers.

In many venues—such as the Olympics—sports transcends culture and unites peoples of different countries. The march of nations during opening ceremonies of the Olympic Games is a colorful demonstration of peace and unity. Yet, many countries in Africa and the Middle East bar women from competition for religious and cultural reasons. In Islamic countries, a strict reading of the Qu'ran forbids women from exposing any part of their body, preventing them from donning proper athletic garb. Other restrictions prohibit women from participating in sports in a public arena.

After the Barcelona Olympics in 1992, female athletes formed Atlanta Plus, which called for a ban of all-male teams, but the International Olympic Committee did not comply, even while taking action against racial discrimination. South Africa, for example, was barred from Olympic competition until it abolished apartheid. No such reform has been taken on behalf of female athletes. The Women's Sports Foundation (WSF) continues to press for reform and an end to gender discrimination, believing it violates the Olympic Games charter.

Many countries actively promote women in sports. Scandanavia has long fostered an ethic of gender equity. In China, the government subsidizes both male and female athletes, and women are given equal pay, equal time, and equal recognition to their male counterparts. Countries such as Australia, New Zealand, and Germany have established club systems that provide equal opportunities for girls and women. The United States does not officially fund Olympic athletes but promotes private contributions, while focusing on high school and college involvement.

In 1972, a revolution in women's sports in America began with the passage of Title IX of the Education Amendments Act, which barred discrimination in any educational program funded by the federal government. Although mostly positive, Title IX proved in some ways a mixed blessing. Among its benefits have been increased participation in school sports by girls, which studies have shown leads to greater self-esteem, improved health, delayed sexual activity, and higher academic performance. In 1971, the year before passage of Title IX, 1 in 27 girls participated in high school sports. By 1997, that figure had increased to one in three.

At the same time, opportunities for women in coaching positions have decreased as men begin to find such jobs more desirable with their increased funding, support, and acceptance. In 1996, there were 1,003 more head coaching jobs for women's teams than in the previous decade, but women held only 333 more jobs than 10 years before, while men held 670 more. Even the U.S. women's soccer team, which won fame for beating the Chinese team in the 1999 Women's World Cup, was coached by a man.

Although it is the law of the land in the United States, violations of Title IX often must be fought in the courts by individual athletes. One landmark case was *Cohen v. Brown University*, filed in 1992 when women gymnasts and volleyball players sued the college for downgrading its teams to club status. In November of 1996, the U.S. Court of Appeals for the First Circuit upheld a district court decision finding Brown's athletic program in violation of Title IX.

Monitored by organizations such as the WSF—founded in 1974 by tennis legend Billie Jean King and enjoying international representation—and the National Association for Girls and Women in Sport—founded in 1899—Title IX continues to foster opportunities for female athletes and coaches.

Sexism in sports is a reflection of the larger picture of sexism throughout world cultures. In many Muslim nations, women are restricted from much sporting activity and are barred from sports altogether under repressive Taliban rule in Afghanistan. Women enjoy the strongest support systems in such countries as Australia, Canada, the United States, Finland, Norway, and other Scandanavian states, and Sri Lanka. As progress toward social equity continues, it will also be made in the field of athletics. Where women have made advances politically—particularly in developed nations—those advances will foster enlightenment in sports opportunities. With the gradual evolution of women from their traditional roles as sex objects and caregivers to broader and more fully realized roles, they will be accepted into sports as they have been in other fields.

See Also

ABILITY; DISCRIMINATION; EQUAL OPPORTUNITIES; EXERCISE AND FITNESS; SPORT

References and Further Reading

Cahn, Susan K. 1994. *Coming on strong: Gender and sexuality in twentieth-century women's sport.* New York: Maxwell Macmillan.

Condon, Robert J. 1991. *Great women athletes of the twentieth century.* Jefferson, N.C.: McFarland.

Dowling, Colette. 2000. *The frailty myth.* New York: Random House.

Sparhawk, Ruth. 1989. *American women in sport, 1887–1987: A 100-year chronology.* Metuchen, N.J.: Scarecrow.

Stradwick, Leslie. 1999. *Athetes (women in profile).* New York: Crabtree.

Turco, Mary. 1999. *Crashing the net: The U.S. women's Olympic ice hockey team and the road to gold.* New York: HarperCollins.

Zimmerman, Jean, and Gil Reavill. 1998. *Raising our athletic daughters: How sports can build self-esteem and save girls' lives.* New York: Doubleday.

Barbara Yost

STATE

See GOVERNMENT *and* POLITICS AND THE STATE: OVERVIEW.

STEPFAMILIES

A stepfamily is formed when two adults, one or both of whom already have a child from a previous relationship, form a new household. Stepfamilies are not the same as a nuclear, adoptive, or foster family. Stepfamilies may follow death, separation, or divorce of partner, or single parenthood. It is estimated that 33 percent of the U.S. population is in steprelationships (1989), and over 2.5 million children and young people in stepfamilies in the United Kingdom (1993), many of whom are members of two stepfamilies when both parents repartner. Stepcouples often have a child of their own (52 percent in the United Kingdom), which can create renewed tensions for adults and children. Helplines report a high proportion of calls on this issue, often coinciding with a change of residence for stepchildren.

Research on stepfamilies developed significantly at the end of the twentieth century, primarily seeking differences between two-parent-, lone-parent-, and stepfamilies. The focus of this research is now on attempting to understand how adults and children cope with such family transitions and what can be done to minimize the disruption and stress. The information below is based primarily from research in the United States, the United Kingdom, and Australia. There has been some research in Scandinavia, but little from the rest of Europe.

Difficulties often arise initially and may continue over property, general finances, and child support; contact with nonresident parent and extended family; discipline; time available to maintain relationships and pursue normal activities; establishing same-sex and different-sex relationships, for example, stepfather/stepson and stepdaughter, stepmother/stepdaughter and stepson. Stepparent relationships are often easier when parent/child relationships are good, especially with the nonresident parent. It has been suggested that it takes around two years to establish new routines and good working relationships between stepfamily members.

There are at least 72 permutations by which stepfamilies may be formed. Differences within these stepfamily types may be greater than differences to two-parent or lone-parent families. Research has identified that most adults and children do adjust to the transition to stepfamilies. Some have problems linked with marital conflict in the first home, stress, and disruption, as well as low income, and health problems for adults and children, poor educational achievement for some children, and young people leaving home early may also be seen. Although child physical and sexual abuse is often cited, the research evidence does not show unequivocally that this is greater in stepfamilies than any other types of families; indeed, in the United Kingdom, it appears to happen less often than in other family types.

Stepmothers and second wives are subject to numerous myths, fantasies, and stereotypes, often cast as both intruder into the original family and rescuer of motherless children. Whether in classical mythology, plays, novels, folktales, or fairy stories, the stepmother appears as a hated and hateful figure, aggressive where the ideal woman is passive, with attributes of jealousy, greed, or vanity, often used to epitomize witches or evil forces, a symbol of harshness and absence of affection. Stepmothers are equally caught in the cultural message to women as mothers—and therefore also to stepmothers—that whatever befalls children is the mother's responsibility. Mothers and stepmothers often are seen as a mediating influence by which fathers may or may not maintain a relationship with their children, whether actively encouraging and facilitating contact or withholding or discouraging. For many stepmothers, the guilt of not loving a stepchild and the desire to be seen as a perfect stepmother intensifies the difficulty in establishing an appropriate relationship with her stepchild and mediating between father and child.

Sexuality frequently occurs in the forefront of such myths. Clearly, the birth of a child to the stepcouple gives explicit testimony to the sexual relationship between parent and stepparent. The second wife may be caricatured as a much younger woman seducing the father and tempting any adolescent stepsons, just as a stepdaughter may be seen as a seductress of the stepfather.

The majority of stepchildren will live primarily in stepfather households, as most children remain with their mother after divorce or separation. Stepfathers rarely have an agreed legal role or status and many seek to achieve this through stepparent adoption, which gives full parental rights and responsibilities as any other adoptive parent. They may, however, be held financially liable for stepchildren, which adds to the ambiguity of the role and accountability of a stepfather. Many stepfathers are also fathers separated from their children. Research has identified three forms of absent fathering/parenting styles: no contact, parallel (contact with child but no communication with ex-spouse), and communicative (with both child and ex-spouse). The attempt to accommodate steprelationships into absent parenting, however, often results in the demise of the father's relationships with his children.

See Also

DIVORCE; MARRIAGE: REMARRIAGE; FAMILY: POWER RELATIONS AND POWER STRUCTURES; FAMILY STRUCTURES

Reference and Further Reading

Bray, James H., and John Kelly. 1999. *Stepfamilies: Love, Marriage, and parenting in the first decade.* New York: Broadway Books.

Erica De'Ath

STEREOTYPES

Categorization, ingroup preference, and stereotyping are automatic cognitive behaviors. These cognitive shortcuts occur regardless of people's feelings toward other groups or their desire to protect their own status, and unless checked they produce unintended sex bias. The visibility and cultural importance of sex make it a standard basis of categorization.

This categorization, an instance of the general tendency to categorize others into ingroups and outgroups, is an automatic, nonconscious process. Accompanying categorization is the exaggeration of between-sex differences and minimization of within-sex differences.

Sex-based categorization leads to sex stereotyping. Sex stereotypes are unconscious thought habits that link personal attributes to sex, even among people who consciously reject the stereotypes. The distinction between descriptive and prescriptive stereotypes illuminates the role of stereotyping in sex-based employment outcomes. Descriptive stereotypes characterize how group members are and thereby influence how we perceive others and interpret their behavior. Descriptive stereotypes distort observers' impressions of the behavior of members of stereotyped groups by predisposing them toward interpretations that conform to stereotypes and blinding them to disconfirming possibilities.

Prescriptive sex stereotypes are normative beliefs about what the sexes are supposed to be, based usually on descriptive stereotypes. They function as standards against which observers evaluate women's and men's behavior. Both descriptive and prescriptive stereotypes influence what we remember about others and the inferences we draw about their behavior. Thus, stereotypes serve as "implicit theories, biasing . . . the perception, interpretation, encoding, retention, and recall of information about other[s]" (Krieger, 1995: 1188).

Stereotyping is tenacious because people seek, prefer, and remember information that supports their stereotypes and ignore, discount, and forget information that challenges them. In addition, stereotyping is cognitively adaptive: we process information that conforms to our descriptive stereotypes more quickly than inconsistent information and are more likely to stereotype when under time pressure. Moreover, anything that focuses observers' attention on sex activates sex stereotyping. Although the propensity to categorize is universal, holding a position of power may prompt people to invest extra effort into categorizing others. In addition, power affects people's motivation to obtain accurate information about others; since it is more costly for the powerless to be wrong about the powerful than the reverse, the powerful are more likely to stereotype than the powerless.

Sex stereotyping introduces bias into our expectations, perceptions, recollections, interpretations, and evaluations of others' behavior. Descriptive stereotypes affect our expectations of others and the attributions we make for their success and failure. Because descriptive sex stereotypes assume that men do well at stereotypically male tasks and women at stereotypically female tasks, we attribute these successes to internal propensities and view them as predicting future success. In contrast, we attribute unexpected success at sex-atypical tasks and failure at sex-typical tasks to unstable, situational factors that do not predict future performance. Thus, evaluators tend to credit the situation, not the person for succeeding at a sex-atypical task. Employers can minimize sex bias stemming from these cognitive processes. Sex-integrated groups and those whose members are interdependent are less subject to cognitive sex biases. These biases can also be suppressed when decisionmakers who use objective data on all the evaluation dimensions are held accountable for their decisions.

See Also

ABILITY; DISCRIMINATION; EQUAL OPPORTUNITIES; SOCIALIZATION FOR INEQUALITY

References and Further Reading

Brewer, Marilyn B., and Rupert J. Brown. 1998. Intergroup relations. In D. T. Gilbert, S. T. Fiske, and G. Lindzey, eds., *Handbook of social psychology*, 554–594. New York: McGraw-Hill.

Fiske, Susan T. 1998. Stereotyping, prejudice and discrimination. In D. T. Gilbert, S. T. Fiske, and G. Lindzey, eds., *Handbook of social psychology*, 357–411. New York: McGraw-Hill.

Greenwald, Anthony, and Mahzarin Banaji. 1999. Implicit association test. <http://www.yale.edu/implicit/>

Heilman, M. E. 1995. Sex stereotypes and their effects in the workplace: What we know and what we don't know. *Journal of Social Issues* 10: 3–26.

Krieger, Linda Hamilton. 1995. The contents of our categories: A cognitive bias approach to discrimination and equal employment opportunity. *Stanford Law Review* 47: 1161–1248.

Reskin, Barbara F. 2000. The proximate causes of employment discrimination. *Contemporary Sociology* 29(March): 319–328.

Sedikides, Constantine, John Schopler, and Chester A. Insko, eds. *Intergroup cognition and intergroup behavior*. Mahwah, N.J.: Erlbaum.

Barbara Reskin

STERILIZATION

As of 1995, sterilization was the world's most widespread form of birth control, accounting for over one-third of contraceptive practices worldwide and almost half in developing countries. By 1992 an estimated 140 million women of reproductive age had been sterilized, as compared to 42 million men.

The surgical process for sterilization involves the cutting or burning of the fallopian tubes to prevent the passage of eggs from the woman's ovaries to her uterus, permanently preventing pregnancy. Male sterilization, or vasectomy, involves the surgical removal of part or all of the vas deferens to prevent semen from reaching the testicles. This so-called Band-Aid surgery, a procedure requiring a high degree of technical competence in industrialized countries, can be debilitating to women and men in less industrialized countries who often suffer persistent postoperative pain in the pelvis and lower back as well as recurring infections. Sterilization may bring on early menopausal symptoms, with risks of osteoporosis and heart disease. Another side effect is heavy menstrual flow, which may lead to a need for hysterectomy. Reversal of surgical sterilization is considered experimental and is expensive as well as having limited success.

Invasive Methods

Hormonal methods of "intermittent sterilization" have been introduced that are not considered permanent. Among these highly invasive, professionally controlled methods are Norplant, a series of sticklike insertions in the arm, Depoprovera, known as "the shot," the contraceptive vaccine, and Quinacrine. Hartmann (1995) reports that in the 1970s Quinacrine pellets, a sterilization device, were inserted into the top of a woman's womb where they dissolved and caused low-level inflammation. This caused scar tissue to develop at the ends of the fallopian tubes, preventing the passage of the egg into the uterus. Quinacrine risks included a possible link to cancer, ectopic pregnancy, uterine complications leading to hysterectomy, and vaginal irritation.

A woman who smokes should not use any systemic, invasive methods, and neither should a woman with any of the following conditions: liver disease, jaundice, history of blood clots, circulation or heart problems, stroke, breast cancer, possible pregnancy, breastfeeding, high blood pressure, diabetes, high cholesterol, migraine headaches, epilepsy, mental depression, gallbladder or kidney disease. Many systemic sterilization products have no antidote, and professionals often brush off as "mere nonmedical inconveniences" many side effects that women experience as debilitating.

Chemical Sterilization

Like surgical sterilization, chemical sterilization takes out of women's hands the control of their lives and bodies. Throughout history women have struggled to wrest control of their reproduction decisions from the machinery of church and state. Correa and Reichmann (1994) explain that for millions of women sterilization has been a desperate response to poverty, gender constraints, and the absolute lack of enabling conditions favoring reproductive choice. Recent technology has lent itself to massive and insidious state control of women's reproduction in the guise of population control policies.

Policies and Legislation of Sterilization

Sterilization use and abuse raises issues of personal freedom and human rights. Historically, certain groups of people have been subject to forced sterilization, among them the disabled; those designated as racially, ethnically, or socially inferior; or those who for any reason are seen as threatening to the ruling class. In recent history, sterilization has amounted to genocide for many peoples, including indigenous women in the United States, African Brazilian women, Indo-Fijians, indigenous Kanaks, and aboriginal women in the Northern Territory of Australia. As many as 45,000 people were sterilized in the United States between 1907 and 1945 (Ferringer et al., 1992). Until a law was passed in 1975 prohibiting hysterectomies for sterilization purposes, elective hysterectomies were performed on poor women in New York City to train medical residents.

Sterilization legislation has presented a racial, ethnic, and class paradox for women—for example, in South Africa under apartheid, where the white population was given tax breaks to have larger families while coerced sterilization was forced on the black population. In the postslavery United States as well, white women's access to sterilization was also subject to control, with legal and medical stipulations that the woman had to be of a certain age, have borne a certain number of children, and have their husband's permission. The state imposed no rules on male sterilization. Ross (1993) shows how birth control by hysterectomy was widely used and black women had to "adapt themselves to limited choice." Ross notes that Fannie Lou Hamer, prevented legislation that would have poor women sterilized from being passed. Ross quotes Hamer as saying that 6 out of 10 African American women were sterilized and that "often the women were not told that they had been sterilized until they were released from the hospital."

In the 1970s, sterilization as public policy became epidemic worldwide, largely because of the launching of global population control policies by the United States and the exporting of the International Planned Parenthood Federation. Correa and Reichmann (1994) state, "In the 1970s sterilization was offered in many developing countries, as a part of the population control strategy not as a service to meet emerging needs of people." Whereas men could choose to be sterilized, women needed permission. Correa also shows how international family planning initiatives encountered religious, military, and nationalist resistance movements who excluded sterilization and abortion as interfering with their own pronatalist goals.

Hartmann (1995) reports that in India fines and imprisonment threatened couples who failed to be sterilized after having three children. In less industrialized countries desperately seeking to meet demographic goals, men were not exempt. In July 1971 alone, 62,913 men in Kerala State in India were given vasectomies at one camp. In the mid-1970s, China pushed individual and community incentives for sterilization (this was prior to its one-child policy of the 1980s, which resulted in 20 million people being sterilized in 1983). In 1974, a US government report acknowledged that by 1968, more than 35 percent of Puerto Rican women of childbearing age had been sterilized, decreasing the birth rate of Puerto Rico from 5.2 in 1950 to 2.7 in 1977. (Now women in Puerto Rico who want to be sterilized have to wait two to three years.) Despite the advent of a pronatalist government in Brazil in 1970, Brazil's population-control policies became implemented through private family planning organizations. Brazil now has one of the highest rates of sterilization in the world (44 percent of contraceptive users). Another 41 percent of contraceptive users are on the pill. Correa (1995) indicates that the contraceptive mix in Brazil reflects lack of information in addition to poor quality of care and lack of contraceptive options, as family planning programs have maximized profit. In the United States in the 1970s, mothers (who were not informed of the permanent nature of the surgery) of young black girls were coerced into giving permission for the sterilization of their children.

According to the *Women in the World Atlas* (1986), sterilization abuse is known to have occurred since 1970 in India, Bangladesh, the United States, Mexico, Guatemala, El Salvador, Puerto Rico, Colombia, Brazil, Bolivia, and Malaysia. They show how governments wield population-control policies with little regard for women's rights and health. They also indicate how and where coercive sterilization, especially of poorer women and women from ethnic minority groups, is used to reduce population growth.

See Also

ABORTION; ETHICS: MEDICAL; EUGENICS; EXPERIMENTS ON WOMEN; FAMILY PLANNING; FERTILITY AND FERTILITY TREATMENT; NORPLANT; REPRODUCTIVE RIGHTS; REPRODUCTIVE TECHNOLOGIES

References and Further Reading

Asetoyer, C., and N. Lewry. 1994. *The impact of Norplant in the Native American community: A review of the use and effects of Depo-Provera on Native American women within Indian Health Service and other federal agencies.* Asetoyer and Ellen H. Chen, Native American Women's Health Education Resource Center, South Dakota.

Correa, S. and R. Reichmann. 1994. *Population and reproductive rights: Feminist perspectives from the south.* London, Zed Books.

Haas, A., and S. Puretz. *The woman's guide to hysterectomy.* Berkeley, Calif.: Celestial Arts, 1995.

Hartmann, B. 1995. *Reproductive rights and wrongs.* Boston: South End.

Koblinsky, M., J. Timyan, and J. Gay. *The health of women: A global perspective.* Calif.: Westview.

Newman, E. *Smothered by invention: Technology in women's lives,* ed. W. Faulkner and E. Arnold. London: Pluto.

Petschesky, R. 1979. *Reproduction, Ethics, and Public Policy: The Federal Sterilization Regulations,* Hastings Center Report, October 1979.

Rodriguez-Trias, H. 1994. *Puerto Rico, Where Sterilization of Women Became "La Operacion." Political Environments* (1, Spring):

Ross, L. 1993. *Theorizing black feminism: African American woman and abortion,* ed. S. James and E. Busia. Routledge Press.

Charon Asetoya

STREET HARASSMENT

The term *street harassment* refers to a variety of behaviors that some men direct toward women in public places. These behaviors include comments about a woman's appearance, whistles, leers, name-calling, pinches, and so on. The existence of labels for this behavior in many languages and countries indicates how commonly such harassment is part of women's lives. In India, it is called *Eve-teasing,* a term that makes harassment sound like a game. Syrian women often use the colloquial Arabic word *taltish,* which implies a quick way to say something, as if thrown on the recipient. The term *street harassment* has been chosen by some feminists because it links these behaviors to harassment in the workplace, now prohibited by law in many societies.

Street harassment occurs all over the world, often in similar forms and with comparable social functions. Some women regard comments about their attractiveness as casual compliments, while others find all street remarks annoying and intrusive. Whether intended to be flattering or inflammatory, street harassment serves multiple social functions simultaneously; it is a means of social control, reinforcing spatial boundaries and marking women as trespassers in public places that "belong" to men. It teaches women that their place is the private world of the home.

Street harassment provides daily reminders to women of their status, subject to unwanted evaluation as sexual/aesthetic objects in ways that men are not. Women are dehumanized by such objectifying behavior. This objectification is not only offensive to women, but it also negatively affects both their personal dignity and public regard by others.

Often, these status reminders are threatening to women, emphasizing their vulnerability to violence and sexual assault. Street harassment contributes to an environment that reinforces fears of rape and other acts of sexual terrorism: a term usefully defined by Carole Sheffield as a system by which males frighten, control, and dominate females (Sheffield, 1987). Women around the world have developed numerous strategies for coping with street harassment. Some women report talking back to harassers, when they feel it is safe for them to do so. Others ignore or pretend to ignore it, hoping the perpetrators will desist when they do not receive a response.

Cynthia Grant Bowman, a feminist legal scholar in the United States, has proposed possible legal remedies for the damage to women's liberty, equality, and self-dignity represented by street harassment (Bowman, 1993). By discussing their experiences, women have discovered that it is not a personal problem but a political issue, part of a seemingly international *system* of sexual terrorism, and have begun their work to change the system.

See Also

SEXISM; SEXUAL HARASSMENT; SEXUAL VIOLENCE

References and Further Readings

Bowman, Cynthia Grant. 1993. Street harassment and the informal ghettoization of women. *Harvard Law Review* 106(3): 517–580.

Hadleigh-West, Maggie. 1998. *War zone.* Northampton, Mass.: Media Education Foundation.

Kissling, Elizabeth Arveda. 1991. Street harassment: The language of sexual terrorism. *Discourse & Society* 2(4): 451–460.

Sheffield, Carole J. 1987. Sexual terrorism: The social control of women. In Beth Hess and Myra Marx Ferree, eds., *Analyzing gender: A handbook of social science research,* 177–189. Newbury Park, N.J.: Sage.

Elizabeth Arveda Kissling

STRENGTH, PHYSICAL

See PHYSICAL STRENGTH.

STRESS

Stress is a significant threat to the overall mental, physical, and spiritual wellness of women. The body's reaction to general external trauma (whether real or perceived) is a qualitative alert that stressors exist. Some obvious signs of stress may be irritability, fatigue, restlessness, depression, and feelings of being overwhelmed, even by a minor task. Globally, women face the life stressors of parenting, working in and outside the home, poverty, marriage, divorce, infertility, sexual abuse, sexual harassment, pregnancy, violence, caring for the elderly, loss of loved ones, and many others. Consequently, an interesting picture emerges on the subject of stress and women.

The gender differences in the mental disorder rates (particularly depression and anxiety) in North American women are linked to the many roles women play simultaneously that induce stress. In a 1992 study of family caregivers in Quebec, the sexual division of labor and its reinforcement through social policy and socialization recognize women as the caregivers for the elderly. A 1997 study examining quality of experiences in the roles of mother, wife, and employee and the effect of stress in the parent-care role on women's psychological well-being found that regardless of the role considered, parent-care stress was related to depression. Indeed, everyday life stressors encountered through multiplicity of roles and responsibilities may impair immunologic functions, facilitate chemical imbalance, and affect overall physical and mental health.

The norms regarding appropriate gender-role behavior are in flux throughout the world. Although women may not object to the role of nurturer or caregiver, the degree of commitment required and the amount of energy expended to fulfill unrealistic expectations go to the heart of women's complaints. The role of caregiver remains extremely demanding and yet elusive.

Research clearly indicates that even when women work outside of the home, their traditional role at home remains intact. Because caregiving in its absolute sense is undervalued, women may find themselves nurturing in an environment in which their efforts are underestimated, dismissed as an obligation, or viewed as nonessential to the whole process of anchoring and establishing stability. Women may not be in environments that support the growth of their individuality, and the biases of gender-role behavior may provide an avenue for disregarding and disrespecting women. Gender-role bias often follows women into the workplace, where salary inequity and sex discrimination are still pervasive and sources of continued stress.

When other factors, such as domestic violence, are superimposed on societal inequities, women are further exposed to emotional and physical harm or even death. In fact, violence against women is on the rise worldwide: in the year 1993, 28 percent of women in Australia, 75 percent of women in Japan, 66.7 percent of women in Sierra Leone, and 55.1 percent of women in the United States reported that they had experienced physical abuse by their partner. The increase in substance abuse, chemical dependency, and stress-related diseases such as ulcers, headaches, and hypertension are also indicators that all is not well.

Why are women more vulnerable to stress? In a recent study of pregnant women living in Hawaii who are Filipino, Hawaiian, and Japanese, it was apparent that one theme consistently connected these women to one another: the conflicts in their significant relationships. This point is global: women's identities are intricately linked and intrinsically constructed around the significant relationships in their lives. When women take most of the responsibility for establishing the foundation for the success of these relationships, this constitutes an obvious cycle of insurmountable stressors. It can become a situation of continuous output, in many instances without revitalization or reward, either in kind or monetary.

The more basic question "Why do women care?" was conceptualized by Ungerson (1983), who distinguished between caring *for* and caring *about* a person. Often, women mistakenly interchange the two. Although stress and stressors are not peculiar to women, the expectations placed on women by society at many levels, coupled with lack of support, are, at best, unrealistic and extremely taxing. The stressors borne by women increase exponentially when their deeds are undervalued and disrespected. The expectations placed on women may be so demanding that some women may assume greater roles of responsibility to gain a stronger sense of self-worth as their efforts are continually minimized. As the primary nurturer, the woman becomes the common denominator bearing the burden of those she cares about and for whom she cares.

Women throughout the world find support from other women who are coalescing to form structures of empowerment and confronting the multiplicity of biases that perpetuate misinformation. Structures of empowerment for women generally operate through individual empowerment, community empowerment, and organizational empowerment. Kar and others (1999) define this multilevel empowerment model as follows: Self-empowerment is the belief in self-efficacy, awareness and knowledge of the problems' source and the solutions and personal competency for proactive actions to deal with the problems adversely affecting their quality of life. Community empowerment focuses on the enhancement of a community resource base including leadership development, communication systems, community support and network needed to mobilize community assets and resources to address common concerns. Organizational empowerment aims at the creation or enhancement of a power base and resources of community base organizations (CBOs), including voluntary organizations, unions, associations and cooperatives to better protect, promote and advocate priorities of the powerless. They conclude that empowerment at all these levels interact in ways that can fundamentally change the quality of life with many implications for policy and health promotion. In a world when stress and life are inextricably linked it is to women's advantage that they become active partners for overall health promotion.

See Also

ANGER; CAREGIVERS; DEPRESSION; EATING DISORDERS; EMPOWERMENT; FAMILY: POWER RELATIONS AND POWER STRUCTURES; PREMENSTRUAL SYNDROME (PMS); WORK: EQUAL PAY AND CONDITIONS

References and Further Reading

Affonso, D. D., L. J. Mayberry, J. Shibuya, J. Kunimoto, K. Y. Graham, and S. Sheptak. 1993. Themes of stressors for childbearing women on the island of Hawaii. *Family Community Health* 16: 9–19.

Coker, A. L., P. H. Smith, R. E. McKeown, and M. J. King. 2000. Frequency and correlates of intimate partner violence by type: Physical, sexual, and psychological battering. *American Journal of Public Health* 90(4): 553–9.

Coker, A. L., and D. L. Richter. 1998. Violence against women in Sierra Leone: Frequency and correlates of intimate partner violence and forced sexual intercourse. *African Journal of Reproductive Health* 2(1): 61–72.

Gordon, S. 1991. Fear of caring: The feminist paradox. *American Journal of Nursing* 91: 44–46, 48.

Hegarty, K. and G. Roberts. 1998. How common is domestic violence against women? The definition of partner abuse in prevalence studies. *Australia and New Zealand Journal of Public Health* 22(1): 49–54.

Kar, S. B., C. A. Pascual, and K. L. Chickering. 1999. Empowerment of women for health promotion: A metanalysis. *Social Science & Medicine* 49: 1431–1460.

Martire, L. M., M. A. Stephens, and A. A. Atienza. 1997. The interplay of work and caregiving: Relationships between role satisfaction, role involvement, and caregivers' well-being. *J Gerontol B Psychol Sci Soc Sci* 52(5): S279–89.

Stephens, M. A., and A. L. Townsend. 1997. Stress of parent care: Positive and negative effects of women's other roles. *Psychol Aging.* 12(2): 376–86.

Ungerson, C. 1983. Why do women care? In J. Finch and D. Groves, *A labor of love: Women, work and caring,* London: Routledge and Kegan Paul.

Jean A. King
Audrey Gomes

SUBCULTURES

See GIRL'S SUBCULTURES *and* YOUTH CULTURE.

SUBSTANCE ABUSE

See DRUG AND ALCOHOL ABUSE.

SUFFRAGE

The term *suffrage* refers to a series of organized campaigns for women's rights that were prominent in the late nineteenth and early twentieth centuries. Although the term is most frequently associated with organizations within the English-speaking world, notably Great Britain and the United States, the suffrage movement was explicitly international. Suffrage organizations existed in several European countries, including Hungary, Czechoslovakia, and Germany, as well as in India, South Africa, and Canada.

The extent of internationalism within the suffrage movement was displayed by the International Woman Suffrage Alliance (IWSA), a body formed in 1902 to promote women's issues on a worldwide scale. By 1914 the IWSA had members in 26 different countries. Biennial congresses brought the membership together, while the IWSA paper *Jus Suffragii* provided a more regular form of contact through its English and French editions and recorded the breadth of activity that constituted international suffrage work.

Positions Embraced by Suffrage

Suffrage embraced a variety of theoretical positions. Millicent Garret Fawcett, the British suffrage campaigner and vice president of the IWSA, wrote in 1912 that the movement's origins lay in the increased demands for the liberty of the individual that followed the French Revolution. She cited Mary Wollstonecraft and the Marquis de Condorcet as the first to attempt to extend the new rights of man to women. The earliest organized suffrage agitations similarly were based on claims for individual political liberty. Within the United States, women seeking the vote initially linked their campaign to broader alliances: during the American Civil War, for example, they worked through the Loyal League (1863–1864), collecting signatures in support of the emancipation of slaves. An Equal Rights Association founded after the war linked black and female emancipation even more directly. But both British and US women discovered that working for the political freedom of others would not help them gain their own objectives. Woman suffragists supported the campaigns that led to the 1832 Reform Act in Britain and the Fourteenth Amendment enfranchising male blacks in the United States (9 July 1868). Yet both these pieces of legislation, by explicitly defining voters as men ("male persons" in Britain) reinforced the barriers against female enfranchisement. Indeed, in Britain this effectively removed the right to vote at local elections that some women had enjoyed as ratepayers (Bolt, 1993; Pankhurst, [1931] 1977).

Against such setbacks, organized suffrage groups developed in Britain and the United States. In both countries they followed established ways of campaigning that had proved successful in achieving other legal reforms such as the Married Women's Property Act: petitioning, occasional public meetings, and the quiet individual lobbying of prominent public figures. At this stage, suffrage was still just one of many separate concerns attracting feminist attention and did not appear to require different tactics. Vindication of this stance came to British activists when the municipal franchise was extended to women in 1869, an advance that fueled hopes that the parliamentary vote would soon follow. Legislation enfranchising women in Wyoming in 1870 was similarly felt to justify the tactics of American suffragists, although the lack of national campaigning for women's emancipation became increasingly irritating among more radical American suffragists.

Some British women began to feel that their constitutional campaigns had reached a similar impasse. By the 1890s suffrage victories elsewhere could be cited as examples of what could be achieved given sufficient political will. Millicent Garrett Fawcett (1924) claimed that one of the most positive effects of the enfranchisement of women in New Zealand (1893) and the Australian states (1893–1909) was that it demolished the argument that women's suffrage was an untried experiment while simultaneously casting doubt on Britain's claim to be a leader of world democracy. Such advances, while offering encouragement, also highlighted what some women came to view as the failure of constitutional campaigning.

Dissatisfaction with earlier campaigning methods crystallized in Britain in 1903 with the formation of the Woman's Social and Political Union (WSPU). Originally envisaged as a branch of the Independent Labour Party dedicated to suffrage propaganda, the first indication that it was to be something more came in October 1905. Christabel Pankhurst and Annie Kenny, two young WSPU members who were disillusioned with the lack of impact that their group was achieving in the public arena, attempted a new tactic, hitherto unused by franchise campaigners, and borrowed from the socialist movement. They carried out a sustained interruption of cabinet minister Sir Edward Grey's speech during a public meeting in Manchester. This activity, which they continued outside, led to their arrest and, following their refusal to pay a fine, their imprisonment. The WSPU was now transformed into a militant society whose members were prepared to take direct action in order to achieve the franchise.

The Role of Militancy

Militancy brought international publicity to the suffrage campaign. The WSPU relocated its headquarters from Manchester to London. From its offices in Clements Inn the founder, Emmeline Pankhurst, and a close circle of associates, including her daughters Sylvia and Christabel, Annie Kenney, and WSPU treasurer, Emmeline Pethick-Lawrence, ran a campaign that was to keep the union in the public eye until the outbreak of World War I. The women became known as suffragettes, a name that Christabel happily adopted from the *Daily Mail*, originally pronouncing it with a hard *g* to stress that these women intended to "get" the vote. Stone-throwing, heckling at public meetings, selling newspapers in the streets, and organizing "monster" demonstrations hundreds of thousands strong were seen as newsworthy when undertaken by women. As the campaign escalated, new and often violent methods were constantly sought to maintain a high level of public pressure. Arson, bombing, and the firing of mailboxes characterized the later period of WSPU militancy, and the movement gained its first martyr in June 1913 when Emily Wilding Davison died when attempting to grab the reins of the king's horse at the Derby. Violence was often used against suffragettes. Many women imprisoned during the campaign were subjected to the horrors of forcible feeding when they attempted to gain the status of political prisoners through hunger strikes. Susan Kingsley Kent (1990) has also revealed how many public demonstrations by suffragettes resulted in sexual violence being used against them by men unable to stomach such "unfeminine" actions. But nonviolent tactics were continued, among them the successful publicity stunt of "prayers for prisoners," which involved planned interruptions of church services by women praying for suffragettes on hunger strikes. Such tactics attracted as much publicity as violent militancy and represented an important part of the WSPU campaign. Similarly, the use of imagery and color afforded the WSPU campaign a level of novel impact unprecedented within popular politics.

The question of militancy as an appropriate tactic split the international suffrage movement, with some fearing that militant actions would undo the results of decades of patient campaigning. In 1906 the Copenhagen Congress of the IWSA considered an application for membership from the WSPU that was opposed by vice president Millicent Garrett Fawcett, a staunch constitutional suffragist and president of the other major British suffrage society, the National Union of Woman's Suffrage Societies (NUWSS), on the grounds of the Pankhursts' attitude toward militancy. Consequently, suffragettes remained outside the official international suffrage body, although the WSPU's journals *Votes for Women* and *The Suffragette* consistently reported on gains by suffrage campaigns in other countries.

Historians such as Sandra Stanley Holton (1986) have begun to question the validity of erecting a solid divide between militant and constitutional suffrage campaigns. In support of their arguments they cite many examples of individuals who held simultaneous membership in militant and nonmilitant societies. Indeed, suffrage was more than a simple campaign for the vote, it being argued that women possessed certain special qualities unique to their sex, qualities that were desperately required by the modern state. This resulted in suffrage campaigns moving beyond equal rights demands as the women involved in them sought to redefine the sphere they wished to enter rather than simply achieve entry on the same terms as men. Hence, many issues other than the vote came to be taken up within suffrage, among them the problem of venereal disease, the white slave trade, and working conditions for female shopworkers.

Other suffrage campaigners saw the vote as an essential way of politicizing women and allowing them to participate fully in public life. One unique feature of the suffrage campaign was its ability to attract women of all classes. For feminists this was an essential part of a woman-centered campaign. Many socialist women, however, viewed this development of an autonomous cross-class women's movement as posing a direct threat to the strength of the class-based socialist movement. As a result, socialism increasingly moved to take suffrage on board. The Socialist Second International adopted the necessity to campaign for women's suffrage at its Paris Congress in 1900, and its member parties rapidly fell into line. From 1911, following a suggestion by the German socialist Clara Zetkin, an international women's day was held, which underlined the socialist commitment to female suffrage. Despite this public commitment, many socialists feared that the vote for women, if awarded on the same property-owning terms as for men, would result in an increased majority for parties representing middle-class interests. Even so, some women socialists continued to push for closer links between suffrage and socialist groups, believing that suffrage could benefit socialism if newly enfranchised women saw socialist parties as representing their interests. One notable success for these women was the decision by the British NUWSS to campaign for the Labor Party from 1912. This allowed many suffragists access to trade unions and won many unionists to suffrage (Liddington and Norris, 1978).

The Effect of World War I

The outbreak of World War I effectively ended franchise campaigning on an international level, although not suffrage work in its broader sense. The war brought an immediate end to suffrage militancy. The WSPU committed itself to the anti-German cause in Britain, and some suffrage campaigners saw the war as an opportunity to further demonstrate the unique qualities of women in public life. A different reaction was demonstrated when the IWSA was instrumental in setting up women's peace conferences in The Hague in 1915, testimony to the enduring internationalism of suffrage.

The aftermath of World War I saw women achieve the vote in many of the IWSA's more active centers. Britain achieved limited female suffrage in 1918; postwar revolution in Russia and Germany secured it in those countries, fulfilling the promise of the Socialist Second International. Other countries followed, although the process was not automatic: in France, for example, women were not enfranchised until 1945.

The achievement of the franchise, however, did not effectively end all suffrage campaigning. Groups such as the Women's Party in the United States, or the Women's Freedom League (WFL) and the National Union of Equal Citizenship in Britain, which developed as or from suffrage organizations, continued to fight for women's rights for many years. Indeed, the WFL, which survived until the 1960s, provided a direct bridge between the first and second waves of feminism, while emphasizing the rich diversity of issues that were encompassed within the international suffrage campaign.

See Also

References and Further Reading

Bolt, Christine. 1993. *The women's movement in the United States
and Britain from the 1790s to the 1920s*. New York: Harvester
Wheatsheaf.

Caine, Barbara. 1997. *English feminism 1780–1980*. Oxford:
Oxford University Press.

Fawcett, Millicent Garrett. 1912. *Women's suffrage: A short history
of a great movement*. London: T. C. and E. C. Jack.

———. 1924. *What I remember*. London: T. Fisher Unwin.

Holton, Sandra Stanley. 1986. *Feminism and democracy: Women's
suffrage and reform policy in Britain 1900–1918*. Cambridge,
U.K.: Cambridge University Press.

———. 1996. *Suffrage days: Stories from the women's suffrage
movement*. London: Routledge.

Kent, Susan Kingsley. 1990. *Sex and suffrage in Britain 1860–1914*.
London: Routledge.

Liddington, Jill, and Jill Norris. 1978. *One hand tied behind us:
The rise of the women's suffrage movement*. London: Virago.

Pankhurst, Christabel. 1959. *Unshackled: the story of how we won
the vote*. Ed. Lord Pethick-Lawrence. London: Hutchinson.

Pankhurst, Sylvia. 1977 [1931]. *The suffragette movement*. London:
Virago.

Krista Cowman

SUICIDE

Suicide is defined as the act of taking one's own life. Suicides are voluntary, intended, and self-inflicted acts. Emile Durkheim was the first to systematically study suicide and distinguished three different types, depending on what motivates the act of self-destructiveness. The first type is *altruistic,* in which the motivation is to sacrifice oneself for the good of others. Examples of this would be a mother who throws herself in front of a car in order to push her child out of harm's way or more ritualistic suicides like hari-kiri (Japan), which saves one's family from shame, or sati or suttee (India), which honors a dead husband. The second is *anomic,* in which the motivation comes from a loss of meaning in life. Loneliness, isolation, or estrangement from the values and norms of one's culture often characterizes this. The third is *egoistic,* in which the motivation stems from a

deep sense of personal failure. An individual may feel totally responsible for not living up to the expectations of one's family, society, or one's self.

Following Durkheim's work, an additional form of suicide was identified, in which the individual deliberately and knowingly placed himself in a position to be killed by others. This form of suicide has been, most often, reserved for men and has been seen as glorious. Even though the man would publicly state his rejection of life—by finding a means of death the society viewed as honorable—the act was considered courageous. In contrast, a woman whose life situation was unbearable would meet with cultural disapproval from her self-inflicted suicide. Although these types of suicide were most common in warrior societies such as the tribal societies of Amazonia in South America or the Muslim societies in southeast Asia, it is not uncommon to find this typecasting of motives or meanings in other societies. For example, in attempting to understand suicidal behavior, it often is said that "she dies for love and he for glory." From a cultural perspective, women who commit suicide are seen as succumbing to internal problems or emotional weakness, whereas men's suicides are described as acts of strength that connote independence and fighting against external problems. These cultural notions of "noble" suicides seem to serve the interests of male-dominated societies (Andriolo, 1998).

Suicides are reported in most countries worldwide and pose a serious public health problem. There is, however, a wide variance in the incidence of suicide throughout the world. For example, Latvia leads all nations in suicides, with 42.5 occurrences per 100,000 people (World Health Organization; WHO, 1995). In the United States and Canada, there are about 11.4 suicides per 100,000 people (Centers for Disease Control and Prevention, 2000). Guatemala and the Philippines rank lowest, with suicide rates at 0.5 per 100,000 people. These statistics are not completely reliable, however, due to the variable national abilities to report statistics as well as the lack of uniform methods for reporting on cause of death.

In most countries, more men than women succeed in suicide. In the United States, about four times more men than women commit suicide (Centers for Disease Control and Prevention, 2000). In India, where the suicide rate is 4 per 100,000, the ratio is equal throughout the country and greater for women than men in areas where there are higher educational levels (3:1) (Tousignant et al., 1998). When statistics for women are considered, there are 4.5 female suicides per 100,000 people in the United States. In South Africa, there are 5.0 suicides per 100,000 for white, female

South Africans. New Zealand has the third highest international female suicide rate (WHO, 1995).

Age appears to have an influence on suicide. The highest suicides rates for women in the United States occur in the over-55 age group. Similarly, suicide is the third leading cause of death among young people between the ages of 15 and 24 years, with two young women in 100,000 succeeding in the act of suicide. Suicide is rare under the age of 12, although intentional suicides as early as age 4 have been reported. The young and the middle-aged-to-elderly appear to be at the greatest risk.

The major risk factors for suicide have been found to be depression, alcohol and drug use, and recent loss, for example, separation, divorce, or loss of job. Among young people, aggressive or disruptive behaviors also are a major risk factor for suicide. Although more men than women succeed in committing suicide, women attempt suicide four times more often than men do. Eighty percent of people who commit suicide are known to have suffered from depression. As the lifetime risk of major depression for women is estimated to be between 7 percent and 25 percent—a rate that is twice the estimate for men—it follows that women would be more prone to suicidal behavior (Range and Leach, 1998).

The difference in the death rate from suicide is often attributed to the means women use. Women more often use drugs to commit suicide, a method that allows for medical intervention. Men tend to use more immediately lethal means, such as firearms. Twenty-five percent of all suicides involve alcohol, and it is estimated that 15 percent of all alcoholics will commit suicide. For young people who often have difficulties with impulsive behavior and depression, it is known that these two combined behaviors may increase the probability of suicide.

Women are also at risk for suicide because of their position in society, conflicted or abusive relationships, lower education levels, and cultural harassment. In India, for example, it is common for women to be blamed both for their own suicides and for their husband's suicides. Women's suicides are seen to be a result of their own sins and the suicides of their husbands are seen as the woman's failure to protect the man from harm. As the sociocultural expectations of women change, there often is an increase in the suicidal behaviors among women.

Suicide can be prevented. At least 80 percent of the people who commit suicide in the United States have mentioned their intentions to someone else. These people appear to be asking for help. It has been demonstrated that many people who think about killing themselves do not actually want to die. Similarly, among lethal suicide attempts, the majority of victims have made prior attempts. It is estimated that there are about 36 attempts for every suicide. Unfortunately, less than one-half of people attempting suicide seek professional help, so the underlying factors that place people at risk for suicide—such as depression and substance abuse—are not addressed. The risk of suicide does not increase if it is talked about. In fact, it makes the suicide less likely. Because of the isolation and futility that many suicidal individuals feel, attempts to reach out to them may be appropriate and effective methods of suicide prevention. It should be noted, however, that if someone is determined to commit suicide, she will. The individual is ultimately responsible for both the preservation and the termination of her own life.

See Also

ADOLESCENCE; AGING; DEPRESSION; DEPRESSION: CASE STUDY—CHINESE MEDICINE; HEALTH: OVERVIEW; MENTAL HEALTH I; MENTAL HEALTH II

References and Further Reading

Andriolo, K. R. (1998). Gender and the cultural construction of good and bad suicides. *Suicide and Life-Threatening Behavior* 28: 37–49.

Centers for Disease Control and Prevention (CDC). *Suicide in the United States* [on-line document]. Retrieved April 4, 2000 from the World Wide Web: <http://www.cdc.gov/ncipc/factsheets/suifacts.htm>

Range, L. M., and M. M. Leach. (1998). Gender, culture, and suicidal behavior. *Suicide and Life-Threatening Behavior* 28: 24–36.

Tousignant, M., S. Seshadi, and A. Raj. (1998). Gender and suicide in India: A multiperspective approach. *Suicide and Life-Threatening Behavior* 28: 50–62.

World Health Organization. (1995). *World Health Statistics Annual 1991–1995.* New York: Oxford University Press.

Joan E. Huebl

SURGERY

Surgery was not unknown in the ancient and medieval world, but premodern practitioners were extremely reluctant to invade the body cavity. Most procedures consisted of venting abscesses, setting bones, splinting fractures, soothing hemorrhoids, repairing rectal fistulas, and very occasionally excising tumors of the breast. The Greeks were also successful in treating certain kinds of head wounds through trephination, or perforating and draining the skull. Caesarean sections, though not unknown, were usually fatal to mothers, despite the legend of Julius Caesar's vaunted live birth. The prevailing theory of disease, which attributed sickness to a vague imbalance in body fluids and dictated treatment of the whole body rather than particular parts, was also a deterrent to conducting surgery. By the end of the eighteenth century, the young and audacious exhibited growing eagerness to open the abdomen—more accessible than other areas of the body—but high mortality rates from hemorrhage, shock, and infection continued to discourage such attempts at European medical centers, except in the most extraordinary of circumstances. When French pathologists in the early nineteenth century developed an understanding of localized infection, however, they animated the notion that removing specific diseased organs could effect cure. New technology such as the stethoscope and the thermometer, and innovative diagnostic techniques such as auscultation, percussion, and palpation, also trained practitioners' attention on abnormal internal structures. The new knowledge of the body gleaned from this clinical and diagnostic innovation yielded novel approaches to treatment that encouraged specialization. Once the medical profession perceived internal pathology as local, "the body became a surgical object *in potentia*." Practice logically followed (Lawrence, 1992). Modern surgery was thus primarily an invention of nineteenth-century Western medicine.

Gynecological Surgery

It is perhaps not coincidental that medical theorists became interested in treating internal lesions of the body just as "the science of woman"—gynecology—emerged as a separate specialty. Greek tradition held that male and female bodies were essentially the same. Superior structure and the presence of greater heat explained why men's genitals were visible *outside* the body; otherwise, they were said to be analogous in every way to women's hidden organs. Male and female differences, in other words, lay not in biology. In the late 1700s, however, this belief was challenged by a novel paradigm of divergence. The new gynecology was *not* inevitable, however, and it is only with historical hindsight that its emergence is understood. Neither the argument that specialties followed naturally from research in pathological anatomy, nor that they represented a division of labor modeled on industrial capitalism has satisfied scholars. The emergence of gynecological surgery is a cultural as well as a medical story, its development grounded in a new, historically contingent conception of womanhood.

For centuries doctors encountered women suffering from huge ovarian cysts and other types of abdominal tumors, their distended abdomens, excruciating pain, and emaciated bodies indicating unspeakable suffering. During the early stage of gynecological specialization, the physician's role was still largely palliative, because without anaesthesia and antisepsis, surgery terrified patients and was justly regarded by practitioners as a last resort. The physician who attempted it required brute strength, manual dexterity, speed, and a strong stomach. Surgeons performed harrowing procedures on semiconscious persons whose senses had been dulled by alcohol and whose bodies were held down by strong male assistants. The surgeon, one commentator remarked, needed to be willing "to cut like an executioner" (Pernick, 1985). In the nineteenth-century United States, surgeons' metaphors led them to compare their work to the conquest of the frontier, where "darkness was giving way to light and civilization was taming the 'primary terrors' of pain and suffering" (Lawrence, 1992).

Until the very end of the nineteenth century, most physicians regarded specialization as a form of quackery, so gynecologists separated themselves from generalists only gradually. Within the specialty itself there was much fluidity as debates raged between "radical" and "conservative" proponents of surgery. Many who became surgical gynecologists were initially attracted to operating rather than to the treatment of women, and never confined themselves only to female patients. But other than the diseased appendix (the first appendectomy occurred in London in 1848), it was the female reproductive system, hidden but accessible behind the abdominal wall and subject to myriad types of infection, that became the experimental arena upon which surgical techniques were invented and improved, especially after midcentury, when the use of anesthesia and antisepsis contributed to lower mortality rates and made surgery a viable option for middle-class, white women.

Pain management was essential to making gynecological surgery an option for all women, because nineteenth-century theories of womanhood were race- and class-based, and white, middle-class women were represented as extremely delicate. Indeed, it was in the southern United States in the 1840s that J. Marion Sims perfected the repair of vesico-vaginal fistula, operating over forty times without anesthesia on eleven slave women suffering from the condition. Female slaves offered a ready-made patient population, and nineteenth-century theories regarding the lesser sensitivity of black women to pain gave Sims added incentive.

Before the 1850s most practitioners confined themselves to the repeated tapping and draining of fluid-filled sacs, removal of labial growths, minor plastic procedures in the form of perineal repairs, and curretting and topical treatments for a variety of inflammatory indications. Sponge tents and pessaries inserted at the mouth of the cervix were also favorite devices for treating uterine displacements. Real suffering led a few bold practitioners to try more radical solutions. As early as 1809, Ephraim McDowell performed the first successful ovariotomy (removal of the ovaries) on a willing patient, Jane Crawford, who survived the surgery and lived in good health until her seventy-eighth year. But the dangers of the operation were readily apparent; McDowell attempted it only twelve more times, with eight recoveries, and four deaths. After McDowell, a few in the United States and abroad tried ovariotomy with varying degrees of success.

Physicians in Europe and the United States greeted the work of pioneer ovariotomists with a mixture of respect and suspicion. In the medical world, surgery always had dramatic appeal. Until the mid-1870s, practitioners operated primarily on ovarian cysts that were relatively easy to diagnose because of their size. By the 1880s and 1890s surgeons experimented with new methods as they became more confident of success. Therapeutic debates turned less on the legitimacy of the operation *per se,* than on the efficacy of various techniques, including the use of the clamp or the ligature; vaginal versus abdominal routes to extirpation; the effectiveness and necessity of Listerism (named after the Scottish surgeon Joseph Lister, who developed a system of antisepsis, especially the use of the controversial carbolic acid spray); the length of incisions; proper management of the pedicle (the stump of an organ left attached to the abdominal lining after excision); the validity of drainage; and various methods of cleansing the peritoneal cavity. Removal of fibroid tumors, extirpation of ovaries and tubes, and eventually hysterectomy were perfected, with mortality rates dramatically reduced. New methods of arresting bleeding also stimulated the improvement and increased use of Caesarean section, which, until the end of the nineteenth century, was almost always fatal to the mother. Several approaches to plastic repair and treatment of uterine prolapse were devised and discarded during this period as well. Surgeons also pioneered in making use of new pathological research in surgical diagnosis.

In the 1870s, the British surgeon Spencer Wells, along with Alfred Hegar of Germany and Robert Battey of the United States, began to remove ovaries for indications no more precise than acute menstrual difficulties and dysmenorrhoea (painful menstruation). There ensued an enthusiasm for surgical solutions that virtually guaranteed that removal of the ovaries and tubes would be performed too frequently for a range of vague mental and physical symptoms. This development has provoked the disdain of some contemporary feminist scholars who take such procedures as proof of the profound misogyny embedded in Victorian culture. But the craze for surgical solutions was not driven solely by practitioners. Many doctors understood that pressure from patients also played a role in their notions of what was acceptable treatment. "Pelvic operations on women," admitted one practitioner, "has become a fad. It is fashionable, and the woman who cannot show an abdominotomy line is looked upon as not belonging to the correct set." (MacLean, 1894). Marie Zakrzewska, who founded and ran the New England Hospital for Women and Children, was unsympathetic with women's desires for operation and often found their motivations suspect. She feared many married women requested ovariotomies as a means of birth control, remarking that "material comfort, indulgence in luxurious living, dislike to work & self abnegation are the motives which prompt women to seek operations." In the late twentieth century, cosmetic surgery for women has generated similar ambivalence regarding the motives of both patients and practitioners.

Although women physicians such as Elizabeth Blackwell were outspokenly opposed to gynecological surgery, female surgeons such as Mary Dixon Jones of Brooklyn, who in 1888 performed the first total hysterectomy for fibroid tumors in the United States, practiced it with enthusiasm. Eventually, surgery in doubtful cases of organic disease troubled not only hostile critics but leading practitioners of the new specialty. By the end of the 1890s surgeons had pulled back from what some historians have called the "transgressive" stage in the evolution of the specialty.

Mastectomy

Surgeons not only revolutionized treatment of a variety of female ailments, they also altered traditional understandings of body parts and their disease in a manner that led to the desirability of surgical solutions. The invention of the radical mastectomy is a case in point. While French pathologists dominated medical theory in the first half of the nineteenth century, the center of innovative scientific research gradually shifted to Germany after 1850, and German pathological researchers, led by Rudolph Virchow, increasingly argued that breast cancer began as a local disease. German surgeons Richard von Volkmann and Lothar Heidenhain began to experiment with removal of both the breast and surrounding tissue. The English surgeon Charles Moore recommended similar therapeutic procedures. But it was an American who studied in Germany, William Stewart Halsted, who in the 1890s perfected the surgery that came to dominate the treatment of breast cancer for much of the twentieth century. Though surgeons in Canada and Western Europe performed radical mastectomies less often than their colleagues in the United States, the theory behind the operation—that breast cancer originated in local cell tissue and spread in slow and orderly fashion through the lymph nodes which carried it to other parts of the body—prevailed. If caught in time, patients could be "cured." In the first half of the twentieth century, critics of this view, primarily from outside the United States, argued that survival rates were no better with radical than with more modest procedures, but American surgeons were reluctant to accept their evidence until they performed their own random clinical trials. In the 1960s and 1970s, the women's health movement in the United States pressured surgeons to take patient preferences into account. Meanwhile new pathology research pointed to some breast cancers as systemic rather than local in origin. As a result, in the 1980s and 1990s, surgeons gradually abandoned the radical mastectomy and recognized the limits of surgery in the treatment of cancer.

The Future of Surgery

Today, doctors, especially in the United States, are guilty of overmedicalizing the normal reproductive events of women's lives. Next to Caesarean section, hysterectomy is the second most common surgical procedure in that country. Ninety percent of hysterectomies are performed for nonmalignant conditions similar to those experienced by the nineteenth-century patients we have already described. Moreover, some contemporary gynecologists still advocate the operation as a cancer-prevention measure for women who have completed childbearing.

The problem is not inherent in the technology itself, and doctors are only partially to blame for its overuse. Much like the present, nineteenth-century surgeons functioned within a larger health care system where women's voices were not heard equally, either as patients or as practitioners. Social conceptions of femininity perpetuated this discrimination, while constructions of masculinity, coupled with a masculine professional ethos integral to medicine, indeed to the entire sex/gender system, gave doctors, most of whom were men, the authority to dominate discussions about female illness. This is not to say that doctors always used their power irresponsibly. Many women welcomed the relief medical technology made possible. Certainly some wanted surgery, as do many today who suffer the ill effects of bleeding fibroids and premenstrual and perimenopausal pain. Indeed, surgical procedures often improve health. In the end the question becomes one of power—who has it when invasive medical procedures are being invoked, and to what ends such techniques are used.

See Also

CANCER; EXPERIMENTS ON WOMEN; GYNECOLOGY; HEALTH: OVERVIEW; MEDICAL CONTROL OF WOMEN; MEDICINE: INTERNAL I; MEDICINE: INTERNAL II

References and Further Reading

Dally, Ann. 1991. *Women under the knife: A history of surgery.* New York: Routledge.

Haiken, Elizabeth. 1997. *Venus envy: A history of cosmetic surgery.* Baltimore: Johns Hopkins University Press.

Laqueur, Thomas. 1990. *Making sex: Body and gender from the Greeks to Freud.* Cambridge, Mass.: Harvard University Press.

Lawrence, Christopher. 1992. Democratic, divine, and heroic: The history and historiography of surgery. In Lawrence, ed., *Medical theory, surgical practice: Studies in the history of surgery.* London: Routledge.

Leopold, Ellen. 1999. *A darker ribbon: Breast cancer, women, and their doctors in the twentieth century.* Boston: Beacon.

MacLean D. 1894. Sexual mutilation of women. *California Medical Journal* 15: 382–384.

McGregor, Deborah Kuhn. 1998. *From midwives to medicine: The birth of American gynecology.* New Brunswick, N.J.: Rutgers University Press.

Morantz-Sanchez, Regina. 1999. *Conduct unbecoming a woman: Medicine on trial in turn-of-the-century Brooklyn.* New York: Oxford University Press.

Moscucci, Ornella. 1990. *The science of woman: Gynaecology and gender in England, 1800–1929.* Cambridge: Cambridge University Press.

Pernick, Martin. 1985. *A calculus of suffering: Pain, practitioners and anesthesia in nineteenth century America.* New York: Columbia University Press.

Russett, Cynthia Eagle. 1989. *Sexual science: The Victorian construction of womanhood.* Cambridge, Mass.: Harvard University Press.

Yarnall, M. 1891. Too much surgery. *Texas Health Journal* 3: 351–352.

Regina Markell Morantz-Sanchez

SURGERY: Case Study—Contemporary Issues in the United States

Surgeries specifically for women are among those most frequently performed in the United States. Every year there are nearly 1 million cesarean sections (surgical deliveries); 2 million episiotomies (surgical enlargement of the vulva during childbirth); 600,000 or more hysterectomies (removal of the uterus); and 500,000 oophorectomies (removal of the ovaries). A quarter of the 1 million cardiac catheterizations are done on women. For both sexes, there are 420,000 open reductions of fractures; 600,000 cholecystectomies (removal of the gallbladder); and 410,000 coronary artery bypass grafts. Some of these operations have been found not to produce the promised results, and some are performed for dubious indications. On the other hand, some do relieve pain and other symptoms, prolong life, and restore function.

Concerns about surgery on women include why surgery is wanted, whose needs it is meant to meet, what the risks are, how well-trained the surgeon is, and what short- and long-term effects may occur. The answers can have lifelong ramifications; but in an emergency—for example, in the presence of internal bleeding from a ruptured aneurysm—there is little time to consider these questions, and in childbirth, a physiologic but intense setting, it is extremely hard for a woman to weigh information before agreeing to, say, a cesarean section.

Surgeries

One example of an emergency recommendation is coronary artery bypass grafting, which is known to relieve angina but not to prolong life except in the case of severe blockage of more than two arteries. Angioplasty, a far less invasive procedure with a much shorter convalescence, can be an alternative.

Other operations that may be urgent involve childbirth. The United States has the world's highest rate of cesarean sections: 21 percent of births in 1998. Perhaps 12 percent of these are true emergencies arising during pregnancy or labor, such as a hemorrhaging placenta previa or prolapsed umbilical cord. Others, however, are performed after a cascade of tests and interventions have interfered with normal labor and in some cases produced the "emergency": immobilization for continuous fetal monitoring, for example, can produce "failure to progress." The risk of death from cesarean section is four times that of a vaginal delivery. Fearing lawsuits if babies do not meet the parents' expectations, doctors may practice defensive medicine; and parents, fearing harm to the baby, may allow interventions without insisting on explanations.

With elective surgery, by contrast, patients can consider their own motivation; evaluate information from various sources such as health-care providers, libraries, the Internet, and other women; consider the credentials of the surgeon and the facility; and learn about indications, methods, risks, benefits, and convalescence for the procedure.

Elective cesarean section is an example. In many places a cesarean is the "standard of care" for all breech presentations, "elderly gravidas," and women who are unwilling to labor, including those who have had a cesarean before. Sometimes, women who might deliver vaginally after an earlier cesarean are not offered this option. What options are offered is more a matter of the local climate or a physician's style than of medical documentation of outcomes.

Among other elective surgeries are photorefractive keratotomy (PRK) and laser in situ keratomileusis (LASIK), to reshape the surface of the eye's cornea and do away with the need for eyeglasses. Though there may be good reasons, related to an individual's lifestyle, to perform this surgery, its cosmetic benefits are advertised more than its risks.

Purely cosmetic surgery can be a difficult decision. Very few other issues produce such a struggle within women who wish to alter their appearance and yet think of themselves as feminists. Pressure to conform to a bland, youthful, white, western ideal is exploited as plastic surgery becomes more widely available and competition for patients increases. Using such aids as computer "rebuilding" of a photograph, cosmetic surgeons may persuade the patient that she can become what she dreams of, while the very real risks, pain, and prolonged recovery time are minimized.

For at least two decades, breast cancer has been recognized as a systemic disease. Numerous studies have shown that radical mastectomy does not prolong life, and that even axillary lymph node dissection benefits only a few specific women. Yet surgeons still do not always give a balanced picture of all options available for breast cancer, including oral therapy. On the other hand, many surgeons are reluctant to discuss prophylactic mastectomy with women at high risk of breast cancer, such as those with positive BRCA-1 and -2 gene mutations.

Some hysterectomies are performed for weak indications, yet annually, 600,000 to 700,000 American women undergo this sugery. By age 60, one-third of all American women will have had a hysterectomy, and 90 percent of these are elective. Among the risks of hysterectomy are hemorrhage, infection, collapse of the pelvic floor, hormonal changes, and changes in the sexual response cycle. Vaginal hysterectomy promises a shorter healing time, but even with new laparoscopic techniques, it too is major surgery. There are some distinct reasons to have a hysterectomy, among them invasive cancer of the vagina, cervix, uterus, fallopian tubes, or ovaries; intractable pelvic infections, bleeding, or endometriosis; and obstetric emergencies such as uterine rupture. Some of these situations are emergencies, but others call for rigorous appraisal.

Assisted reproductive techniques (ARTs) may involve surgery, and these too raise issues, social as well as medical. Some experts believe that ART consumes health-care resources that might be used for more basic needs. ART pregnancies, often multiple, may require intense surveillance, demand complex ethical decisions about "selective reduction" of embryos, and result in premature birth of two or more tiny babies prone to lifelong disabilities. ART has become an enormous business, in which many people get paid: egg and sperm donors and banks, surrogates, lawyers, finders, health care professionals, and institutions. The burden is not only financial; women's lives can become a treadmill of tests, procedures, and reporting.

Urinary incontinence, another problem for which there is a surgical "cure," affects 13 million Americans, 85 percent of them women. Surgery helps correct just one type: stress incontinence, in which a woman leaks urine uncontrollably and painlessly when she coughs, laughs, jumps, or just stands up from a chair. Urgency, overflow, and mixed incontinence are much more likely to respond to biofeedback, exercises, and medication. Up to one-sixth of women develop increased problems with voiding (urination) after surgery, and many have no symptom relief. The emerging subspecialty of urogynecology offers women a range of options in dealing with incontinence of all kinds.

Arthritic men tend to have more knee-replacement operations to restore function, though arthritic women have more symptoms and are more miserable and disabled. Female athletes, too, are less likely to be offered reconstructive knee surgery. Their training and injury patterns differ from those of male athletes, and the tendency to treat them as smaller men is not appropriate. Only 3 percent of orthopedic surgeons in America are women; among them, however, are many who have been athletes themselves and who have started sports-medicine clinics for women.

The Profession of Surgery

Some issues have to do with the profession of surgery itself. Surgical specialties are now open to women, but many women patients report that visits to these surgeons have been disappointing. Expecting to find the "feminine" values of listening and mediating, they find instead brusque, dismissive, and patronizing surgeons. In fields such as obstetrics and gynecology, where well over half the doctors in training are now women, it has been found that many of these women doctors relate to patients much as males do.

Training is a related issue. Surgical patients are often advised to request that no students or residents be present; on the other hand, a patient is also told that it is important to find a surgeon who has often seen and done the procedure. There is also the opposite danger: a surgeon may have done a procedure so often that it has become routine, and therefore may be less vigilant for problems or warning signals.

Constraints imposed by modern medical economics reduce the time all doctors have for discussion and answering questions. Sometimes the "raw facts" are presented by a film, reading material, or conversation with a helper; the doctor enters the discussion when individualized questions are asked.

As surgical technology becomes more complicated, the question arises: how well do surgical facilities train professionals and acquire and maintain technology? In general, the more times a hospital does any procedure, the safer it is, but here again, a hospital and staff may become blasé. High-volume facilities specializing in just one kind of surgery—such as heart, eyes, or orthopedics—are becoming more prevalent and have obvious advantages. But if a patient at such a facility unexpectedly needs another kind of doctor, that help may be delayed or hard to obtain at all. In general, the smaller and less specialized a facility, the more personalized the care, so each patient must weigh various factors if she has a choice of sites for surgery.

See Also

COSMETIC SURGERY; GYNECOLOGY; OBSTETRICS; REPRODUCTIVE TECHNOLOGIES; SURGERY

References and Further Reading

Birkmeyer, John D. 2000. High-risk surgery—Follow the crowd. *Journal of the American Medical Association* 283 (9, March 1): 1191–1193.

Boston Women's Health Book Collective. 1998. *Our bodies, ourselves for the new century.* New York: Touchstone.

Dally, Ann. 1992. *Women under the knife: A history of surgery.* New York: Routledge.

Davis, Kathy. 1995. *Reshaping the female body: The dilemma of cosmetic surgery.* New York, Routledge.

Hoffman, Eileen. 1995. *Our health, our lives: A revolutionary approach to total health care for women.* New York: Simon and Schuster.

Macho, James, and Greg Cable. 1994. *Everyone's guide to outpatient surgery.* Kansas City, Mo.: Somerville House.

McCabe, John. 1997. *Surgery electives: What to know before the doctor operates—A guide for those considering elective surgery.* Santa Monica, Calif.: Carmania.

Olson, Kaye. 1998. *Surgery and recovery.* Traverse City, Mich.: Rhodes and Easton.

Rothman, David J. 2000. Medical professionalism—Focusing on the real issues. *New England Journal of Medicine* 342(17, April 27): 11284–11286.

Sachs, Benjamin, and Cindy Kobelin. 1999. The risks of lowering the cesarean delivery rate. *New England Journal of Medicine* 340(1, January 7): 54–57.

Anne Wigglesworth

SURROGACY

So-called surrogacy involves the conception of a child specifically for the purposes of giving it away to another. It can take place in three ways: through commercial surrogacy agencies; through using reproductive technology such as in vitro fertilization; or outside established institutions in personal arrangements that are never made public.

The term *surrogate* is misleading because it implies that the woman carrying the child for another is not a real mother but rather just a "substitute" mother. Other terms reinforce this impression, gradually dropping the term mother altogether: *gestational mother, host mother, host womb, gestational carrier, endocrinological environments, surrogate uteruses, therapeutic modalities* (Rowland, 1992).

Issues of Exploitation and Loss

Problems with surrogacy revolve around the issue of exploitation: financial, physical, and emotional. Commercial surrogacy primarily operates in the United States. (It has been banned in Australia and in Germany a US surrogacy agency was stopped from operating after public protest.) Many women who contract as the carrier in commercial surrogacy arrangements are poor, and they may have resorted to surrogacy as a short-term strategy of financial survival. All too often, however, they end up with even more serious financial problems because of their involvement. Some of the women employed as surrogates in the United States are accused of welfare fraud, and others have difficulty with the Internal Revenue Service (Kane, 1990). Some surrogacy agencies see the employment of poor women in the industry as desirable because there is less chance they will refuse to relinquish the child (Corea, 1985).

Surrogacy also involves the physical exploitation of women, as the woman yields control to the contracting man, the commissioning couple, or those to whom she has agreed to relinquish the child. If she is undergoing in vitro fertilization (IVF) procedures, she faces the dangers involved in the techniques itself, including the possible links with cancer from the use of fertility drugs (Rowland, 1992; Fishel and Jackson, 1989).

The emotional exploitation of women in surrogacy involves the manipulation of the identity of woman as supposedly selfless, self-sacrificing, and self-denying. Papers written by "surrogates" themselves and numerous interviews with women undergoing this procedure show the enormous emphasis on the woman's need to gain approval from those around her through doing a "altruistic act" (Klein, 1989). IVF surrogacy is often called "altruistic" or "compassionate family" surrogacy in order to present it as merely part of the construction of a normal family. Altruistic or IVF surrogacy involves using IVF technology: a woman agrees to carry a child from an egg belonging to a sister (or friend), and after the delivery she is expected to to relinquish the child to the woman from whom the egg has come. Doctors have called this arrangement a "superior form of surrogacy" (Rowland, 1992). Ironically, the possibility of exploitation in the case of intrafamily surrogacy is especially powerful: once the birth mother has agreed to bear a child for her sister (or friend), the relationship dynamics of the situation make it even more difficult for her to refuse to relinquish the child should she so desire. In a basic contradiction, it is notable that if a woman uses IVF with donated eggs, she is referred to not as a *surrogate,* but as the *mother.*

Apart from the effect on the woman carrying the child, "surrogates" themselves have written of the tragic effect of the loss of a child through surrogacy on his or her remaining sisters and brothers, documenting their insecurity, fear, grief, and anger. As one child said, "Mommy, if I'm a bad girl, are you going to give me away too?" (Klein, 1989: 158).

The Commodification of Babies and Motherhood

To date, no studies have taken into account the effect on a child of being the product of an arrangement necessitating relinquishment by his or her birth mother. The adoption literature has clearly indicated the grief and pain that many adoptees, and also their relinquishing mothers, feel; in these situations women were usually socially coerced into relinquishing. Yet in surrogacy, children are deliberately conceived as a commodity for transfer to those who commissioned the arrangement. The commodification of children in the process is made clear even in popular media discussions of surrogacy: "Its first product is due for delivery today. Twelve others are on the way and an additional 20 have been ordered. The 'company' is Surrogate Mothers Ltd, and the 'product' is babies."

Apart from the child becoming a commodity and the woman merely a body part to be used by others, surrogacy is changing the definitions of *mother.* This is particularly true with technologically assisted surrogacy through IVF. Doctors argue that a woman carrying a child which is not from her egg will not develop a relationship with that growing fetus during pregnancy. There is a masculine contention that just as paternity has been defined as where the sperm comes from, maternity can be defined as where the egg comes from. But each person is first mothered in the womb. A child when it is born has lived on, within, and through its birth mother's body. During this process the two have formed a relationship. Others may ultimately raise the child, but for better or worse, this is a child's first relationship.

Surrogacy negates this relationship created by the pregnancy experience, a negation that has been enforced by US law—for example in the case of Anna Johnson, an African American woman who carried a child for Mark and Christina Calvert (both white) using their egg and sperm. During the pregnancy Johnson attempted to be released from her contract to relinquish the child, but a court determined that the child was not Johnson's to keep; it ruled that Johnson was merely a "foster parent" during the pregnancy (Goodman, 1990).

The increased demand for babies in Western countries brings concern about international trafficking: the countries of Guatemala and Sri Lanka, for example, are known to support "gestation houses" where women either agree to go to have children for Western couples or may be trafficked into pregnancy schemes. A 1982 report prepared for the United Nations Working Group on Slavery stated that evidence of organized "baby farms" in Sri Lanka was in the hands of that government and that child trafficking between Switzerland and Sri Lanka, as well as between Sri Lanka and Australia existed without government interference (Raymond, 1993).

Feminist Debate

Libertarian feminists have taken a position that surrogacy is procreative liberty: they maintain that a woman can choose whether or not to be involved; that her body is her property to be rented or used at will; and that autonomy and informed consent can operate to ensure the elimination of exploitation (Andrews, 1989). Radical feminists, particularly those in the international network *Feminist International Network of Resistance to Reproductive and Genetic Engineering (FINRRAGE)*, argue that surrogacy turns the body into a commodity: women are their bodies, they maintain, and women will only become powerful through a holistic approach to body identification. FINRRAGE condemns the fact that the international operation of patriarchal power institutionalizes reproductive exploitation as it does sexual exploitation and contends that the lived lives of women are

evidence of the fact that surrogacy is a damaging process for the women and children involved.

Surrogacy is part of a reproductive technology agenda that is involved in artificially constructing and changing human relationships. In the mix of IVF and surrogacy enabled a 62-year-old woman to give birth to an IVF child using a donated egg in Italy; in a daughter gave birth to a child after carrying her mother's embryo; and in a grandmother in South Africa gave birth to triplets for her daughter. Many see surrogacy as part of a social and emotional experiment, fuelled by commercial interests and a medical fraternity involved in a variety of forms of human reproductive experimentation.

See Also

ADOPTION; CHILDBIRTH; ETHICS: MEDICAL; FAMILY PLANNING: MOTHERHOOD; PREGNANCY AND BIRTH; REPRODUCTIVE PHYSIOLOGY; REPRODUCTIVE RIGHTS; REPRODUCTIVE TECHNOLOGIES

References and Further Reading

Andrews, Lori B. 1989. Alternative modes of reproduction. In Sherrill Cohen and Nadine Taub, eds., *Reproductive laws for the 1990s.* Clifton, N.J.: Humana.

Corea, Gena. 1985. *The mother machine.* New York: Harper and Row.

Fishel, S., and Jackson, P. 1989. Follicular stimulation for high tech pregnancies: Are we playing it safe? *British Medical Journal* 299 (29 July): 309–11.

Goodman, Ellen. 1990. The product of a rented womb. *San Francisco Chronicle,* October 25, p. A25.

Kane, Elizabeth. 1990. *Birth mother.* Melbourne: Pan MacMillan.

Klein, Renate, ed. 1989. *Infertility: Women speak out about their experiences with infertility.* London: Pandora.

Raymond, Janice. 1993. *Women as wombs.* San Francisco: Harper.

Rowland, Robyn. 1992. *Living laboratories: Women and reproductive technology.* Bloomington and Indianapolis: Indiana University Press.

Robyn Rowland

SUTTEE (SATI)

Sati, also known as suttee, is the custom of a Hindu widow being cremated on the funeral pyre of her dead husband, as an indication of her devotion to him. The word is also used to refer to women who have died in such a way. The literal meaning of the word *sati* is "virtuous woman," but it has come to signify widow immolation because joining a husband in death is regarded as the ultimate proof of a woman's virtue.

Sati is the culmination of a series of cultural practices imposed upon the widow, especially among the upper-caste Hindus of India. Because a woman's existence is defined through her husband among these castes, on his death the widow is regarded as ceasing to have a social function and thus enters a state of social death. Traditionally she could not remarry: therefore her particular situation as widow was enforced by social and cultural norms that were not voluntarily accepted. However, the culture prized the "voluntary" sati who "chose" to immolate herself on the funeral pyre of her husband. Thereafter, a sati was highly revered and even worshiped. The sati brought enormous merit to herself and her husband, wiping out both her own and her husband's sins.

There is a great deal of controversy about how and when the practice of sati originated. In the course of the movement to ban the practice, spearheaded by Rammohun Roy, a humanist social reformer in the 1820s, traditionalists opposing a ban tried to prove its antiquity. Those advocating its abolition tried to prove its recent appearance in order to seek textual legitimization for their reformist position.

Sati was finally banned in 1829. Earlier, there had been moves to regulate it, for example, by Emperor Akbar (1556–1605). There was also a local critique of the practice long before the colonial government decided to ban it.

It is important to note that sati has never been widespread, but because it has tremendous symbolic value, is ideologically powerful, and has resurfaced in the late twentieth century, the women's movement has mobilized public opinion to ban its propagation. Feminists argue that this is necessary because the idealization of sati has continued, despite the ban on the practice, and that the survival of the ideology of sati has created the conditions for its reappearance.

A notable aspect of sati in the past, one that lingers today among some groups, was that its practice was presented as "voluntary." However, in practice it was often forced upon the widow. In any case, the voluntary aspect of widow immolation was based on the ideological belief that a miraculous power entered into certain widows, making them immune to pain and the fire in which they burned. It is the existence of this power (Sat, which means "true" or "good"), upon which the argument rests that sati is voluntary, that lifts it beyond suicide or ritualized murder and converts it into a supremely holy act (Sangari and Vaid, 1996). Feminist scholars continue to argue against the notion of a voluntary sati. They argue that the textual and social sanctions for sati and the degrading conditions under which widows are forced to live create the context for women to immolate themselves.

See Also

CASTE; DEATH; FEMICIDE; HINDUISM; HOUSEHOLDS AND FAMILIES: SOUTH ASIA; SEXUALITY: HINDU CULTURE; WIDOWHOOD

References and Further Readings

Kumkum, Sangari, and Vaid Sudesh. 1996. Institutions, beliefs and ideologies: Widow immolation in contemporary Rajasthan. In Kumari Jayawardena and Malathi de Alwis, eds., *Embodied violence: Communalising women's sexuality in South Asia,* 240–296. Delhi: Kali for Women.

Uma Chakravarti

T

TABOO

Taboo is a term used for something that is forbidden. It can be applied to an action, a place, an object, a food, or a living thing such as a person. Originally, it described the relationship between human beings and the sacred, but this early interpretation has undergone changes; today, *taboo* refers to social as well as religious customs and practices. For example, in virtually every culture, one of the earliest known taboos is a prohibition against incest—sexual relations between close blood relatives. Taboos often have to do with women, placing boundaries on their behavior and activities.

Taboos Regarding Women

In many cultures, taboos that apply to women are related to menstruation. For example, at one time in certain cultures menstruating women were confined in some way, for instance in a separate hut or in a place marked off in a room. A menstruating women might not be permitted to cook food or draw water; and she might also be forbidden to tend plants or to go near fruit-bearing trees, for fear that the plants would wither and the fruit would rot. Many such practices have changed in the course of time, but the notion that menstruation is unclean has persisted.

Possibly, in primeval times the flow of blood during menstruation, although visible, was not understood and thus was feared. In menstruation—unlike the bloodshed of war or injury—women do not seem to lose anything by bleeding; this may have evoked awe and a sense that some special energy was present, which had to be controlled or avoided. As a result, physical contact with a menstruating woman could become taboo; the woman's mobility could be restricted; and she might be forbidden to participate in religious rituals, since she would be defiling the sacred. Even-

tually, such prohibitions can be extended to apply to women at all times, not just while they are menstruating.

Actual taboos reflect such beliefs. For example, in some agricultural communities, a woman is not allowed to cut the first handful of ripe rice or to enter the threshing floor, and women may be forbidden to take any part in rituals or ceremonies connected with harvesting or threshing. In some cultures, women are forbidden to take part in building a house or in the rituals related to construction. Often, women are not permitted to prepare food that will be offered to the gods: to do so would be to incur the displeasure of the gods and thereby to bring adversity. In some fishing communities, women do not mend nets, do not go out on boats to fish, and indeed do not even go near the fishing boats; otherwise, it is believed, misfortune may befall the community. A woman's involvement in activities related to fishing is sometimes believed to determine the catch not just for the day on which it takes place but perhaps for the entire year. In certain societies, when a well is being dug a woman cannot make the first cut in the sod or draw the first bucket of water, for fear that the well will dry up.

Not all taboos affecting women are related to menstruation. There are many taboos related to childbirth, a time at which the idea of defilement is often important. Also, widows, unmarried women, and childless women are sometimes considered to be bearers of misfortune; they may be relegated to the background during ceremonies and festive occasions, or they may not be allowed to be present at all.

Taboo and Religion

Taboos connected with menstruation, pregnancy, and women's sexuality are deeply entrenched in many (or, arguably, all) religions. The idea that a woman is unclean and therefore unworthy to offer sacrifices is widespread, although it is applied with varying degrees of rigidity. A menstruating woman may not be permitted to enter a place of worship, such as a temple or mosque. In India, a menstruating woman cannot enter the *puja* (worship) room in her home or light the lamp of the house at dusk.

All the major religions of the world have at some time debarred women from the priesthood. The theology on which this prohibition is based varies but often includes the concept of women as impure. At some times, women have not even been allowed to read or study religious scriptures, and the authority to teach and preach has been vested entirely in males. In some religions, this practice originated in or has been reinforced by scriptural passages that are discriminatory toward women. Some texts forbid women to read sacred texts, or to speak at all, in places of worship or on public occasions. Often, scripture has been interpreted as identifying women with sin and identifying men with the divine, or purity. Women's sexuality has been widely perceived as endangering men's aspiration to holiness. Such ideologies have, for centuries, effectively subdued women and kept them in a subordinate position designated by men.

Taboos and Women's Consciousness

It is reasonable to suppose that in early times, segregating women during menstruation may have been intended not only to isolate uncleanliness but also to protect the woman herself. However, as noted above, the concept of seclusion became more general and was applied to women when they were not menstruating; perhaps as a consequence, the sense of soiling and defilement associated with blood came to be associated with women, so that a woman's person or body as such was considered impure and unclean. This emphasis on purity and holiness set against uncleanliness had the effect of reducing a woman to an inferior, not only in men's eyes but in her own eyes as well. Women began to believe that they were impure and that this state was divinely ordained.

By legitimizing the exclusion of women from important social activities or by placing women at the periphery, taboos have contributed to women's marginalization in society. This has worked to deny women access to decision making and to prevent them from sharing power or authority with men. Because menstruation and childbirth are central to a woman's sexuality and to her role in procreation, taboos relating to them reduce her worth in a culture, and her sense of self-worth.

In most parts of the modern world, the situation with regard to taboos has changed or is changing. Women's scholarship in the social sciences and religion has focused on women's cultural status; these factors, together with the growth of the women's movement, have equipped women to challenge negative norms and concepts related to gender and female sexuality and in some contexts to substitute more positive ideas. Modern thought tends to perceive taboos, for the most part, as irrational; this is particularly true of taboos related to women's defilement and impurity. To a considerable extent, there is a new sense of women's spirituality, creativity, and wholeness. For instance, some religions now accept women in the priesthood, and in virtually all religions women now claim the right to study scripture and interpret it from their own point of view. Some women agriculturalists, to take another example, became conscious of their identity as a group and did away with exclusionary ritualistic practices. On the whole, undermining taboos contributes to women's understanding of themselves as full human beings.

See Also

CHILDBIRTH; CURSE; INCEST; MENARCHE; MENSTRUATION; RELIGION: OVERVIEW; SACRED TEXTS; SPIRITUALITY: SEXUALITY

References and Further Reading

Countryman, L. William. 1989. *Dirt, greed, and sex.* London: SCM.

Kelly, Joan. 1984. *Women, history, and theory: Essays.* Chicago, Ill.: University of Chicago Press.

Audrey Rebera

TEACHERS AND TEACHING
See EDUCATORS *and* PEDAGOGY.

TECHNOLOGY

Technology touches on people's work, bodies, health, living arrangements, and communication processes. It is both commodity and infrastructure for all these and other aspects of human life. Feminist analyses have focused on several areas: understanding the impact of new domestic technologies on women's traditional roles; how technology in less-developed nations (the "South") has affected women's lives and the gendered division of labor; the role of technology (including the role of automation) in the area of women and work; information technology and the invention and reproduction of social forms; the built environment; and medical and reproductive technologies and their effects on women's health. In addition, there are forms of "social technology" that have received extensive scrutiny from feminists; these include intelligence testing and gender-biased vocational tracking.

In women's studies, there has often been tension between resisting the negative impacts of high technology and advocating equal access to its benefits. For instance, in studies of less-developed nations, some argue that the pursuit of high-tech solutions has disempowered women, especially those in traditional marriages and in rural areas, making them even more marginal. Often these scholars and activists advocate low-tech or "appropriate technology" solutions, a turning away from high-tech blandishments. By contrast, other authors argue that the low-tech solution relegates women to ancillary economic status, and that only equal access to the most advanced technological opportunities will resolve problems of marginalization (Mitter, 1994). Similarly, in the area of reproductive technology, one group contends that access to advanced procedures such as in vitro fertilization provides maximum freedom of choice; others emphasize the possible dangers, experimental nature, and invasiveness of such procedures (Cowan, 1992). In the area of information technology, some women's studies scholars celebrate the Internet and the World Wide Web as exciting ways to expand global community; others see the potential for surveillance and alienation from natural rhythms.

The complexity of these arguments points to the ways in which technology is woven into the fabric of daily life (Kramarae, 1988). As with feminist studies in the humanities and the fine arts, there has been a movement to reclaim and redefine certain traditionally female skills, such as sewing and homemaking, as forms of technology. There has also been important work to reclaim women inventors, both formal and ad hoc, and to understand some aspects of traditional, heavily female occupations as highly sophisticated in often unrecognized technological knowledge.

Domestic Technology

Because women have had disproportionately more responsibility for domestic labor in nearly every country on earth, domestic technology is important for women's studies. In the West, the introduction of "time-saving devices" into the kitchen and laundry began in the nineteenth century and rose sharply through the mid-twentieth century. Cowan's classic study, *More Work for Mother* (1983), is a good exam-

ple of how multifaceted such technological advances can be. Cowan shows that while each device alone would in fact save time (for example, a dishwasher does speed the cleaning of dishes), standards and the number of tasks also rose during this period. Laundry had to be cleaner than before, floors more highly polished after floor polishers were available, and so on. The result was an actual decrease in women's free time that—combined with the increasing isolation of many women in suburban developments—formed the setting for the stereotypical American housewife of the 1950s depicted in Friedan's *Feminine Mystique* (1963).

Technology and Development

In less-developed nations, the intertwining of technology, women's issues, and the general politics of development is complex. A number of different approaches have been taken to the use of technology to empower women in these areas, including overall integration schemes (getting more women to use technology and employing more women in technological positions); appropriate technology initiatives; and income-generating schemes using medium- or low-technology "alternatives." Each of these approaches has strengths and weaknesses. Stamp (1990) reviews those issues. Because less-developed countries (the "South") are often a testing ground for new, potentially dangerous technologies, as well as a development site for utilizing cheap labor in such technologies and a dumping ground for toxic wastes generated by technologically driven processes in developed countries (the "North"), technology has broad ramifications for work and ecology (Shiva, 1993, 1994). At the same time, technological occupations may be an important source of upward mobility for girls and women, as well as for the economy as a whole (Erinosho, 1994; Leigh, 1991).

The Workplace

Women employed in the high-technology sector have often had difficulty rising above a so-called glass ceiling (for example, Gabor, 1994) and have been disproportionately confined to lower echelons of employment. In some industries, such as computer manufacturing, this can mean doing difficult and dangerous work. In clerical labor, processes of automation and electronic surveillance have often disproportionately affected women workers—for example, clerical data-entry workers (a largely female occupation), whose productivity is monitored even to the point of counting the number of keystrokes and controlling toilet breaks. With corporate restructuring and increasing reliance on job fragmenting, electronic methods of cross-national data sharing, and reserve labor pools, the impact of technologies is becoming global (Greenbaum, 1995). Women, who have always formed a large proportion of the part-time labor force and have been more vulnerable to corporate layoffs, are affected by technologies in this way. At the same time, many women have found new industries, such as the software industry of the 1980s, good avenues for entrée and upward mobility, whereas more established industries were harder to break into.

One aspect of technology, work, and flexible labor has been the much-touted "electronic cottage." When the option for people to work from their homes via computer ("telecommuting") first became feasible on a wide scale in the 1980s, many companies hailed it as the answer to women's dilemmas in choosing between public and private life. Women could have children, stay home to take care of them, and at the same time earn a good salary, long-distance. Most feminist scholars have now challenged this vision, pointing out that it rendered the work of child care trivial and isolated women from informal networking—and thus from promotion opportunities in the workplace (Calabrese, 1994).

Information Technology and Communication

With the advent of large-scale information technology networks such as the Internet (the Net) and the World Wide Web, a plethora of material has been produced examining the role of women on-line. Again, there is a range of opinions about how these technologies will affect women as participants. Some theorists, noting that most participants on the Net are male (although recently the numbers seem to be shifting), have emphasized a reappearance of old, sexist social forms, including electronic sexual harassment and domination. Others celebrate the possibility of gender anonymity and the chance for women to organize and exchange information on-line across geographic and cultural borders. Feminists all over the world, notably in Latin America, have used the Net as a tool for organizing and informing. Many in women's studies play with the opportunities afforded by the Net to blur the distinctions between real and imaginary, encouraging radical playfulness for girls and women—for example, the Australian magazine *Geekgirl* (http://www.next .com.au/spyfood/geekgirl/). The feminist theorist Donna Haraway (1991) popularized the term *cyborg* to talk about the ways in which the positive, radical, playful aspects of high technology mingle with its negative aspects in all our lives, in every conceivable configuration. According to Haraway, we are all a little bit machine and a little bit human these days, and the nature and meaning of that mixture keep changing rapidly.

See Also

ALTERNATIVE TECHNOLOGY: CASE STUDY—AFRICA; ARCHITECTURE; EDUCATION: TECHNOLOGY; ENGINEERING; INFORMATION TECHNOLOGY; SCIENCE: OVERVIEW

References and Further Reading

Apple, Rima D. 1993. *The history of women and science, health, and technology: A bibliographic guide to the professions and the disciplines.* 2nd ed. Madison: University of Wisconsin Library System, Women's Studies Librarian.

Bindocci, Cynthia Gay. 1993. *Women and technology: An annotated bibliography.* New York: Garland.

Bourque, Susan C., and Kay B. Warren. 1987. Technology, gender, and development. *Daedalus* 116: 173–197.

Calabrese, Andrew. 1994. Home-based telework and the politics of private woman and public man: A critical appraisal. In Urs Gattiker, ed., *Technological innovation and human resources.* Vol. 4, *Women and technology,* 161–199. Berlin: Walter de Gruyter.

Camera Obscura. 1992. Nos. 28–29. Special issue on feminism and medical images.

Canadian Women's Studies. 13(2). Special issue on feminism and technology.

Cockburn, Cynthia, and Susan Ormrod. 1993. *Gender and technology in the making.* London: Sage.

Cowan, Ruth Schwartz. 1992. Genetic technology and reproductive choice: An ethics for autonomy. In Daniel J. Kevles and Leroy Hood, eds., *The code of codes: Scientific and social issues in the human genome project,* 244–263. Cambridge, Mass.: Harvard University Press.

———. 1983. *More work for mother: The ironies of household technology from the open hearth to the microwave.* New York: Basic Books.

Donini, Elisabetta. 1994. Feminisms, contextualisation, and diversity: A critical perspective and development. *Women's Studies International Forum* 17: 249–256.

Erinosho, Stella Yemisi, ed. 1994. *Perspectives on women in science and technology in Nigeria.* Ibadan: Sam Bookman.

Faruqui, Akhtar M., Mohamed H. A. Hassan, and Gabriella Sandri. 1991. *The role of women in the development of science and technology in the third world.* Proceedings of a conference organized by the Canadian International Development Agency and the Third World Academy of Sciences, ICTP, Trieste, Italy. Singapore: World Scientific.

Federal Ministry of Education, Women Education Branch. 1989. *Report of the National Workshop on Promoting Science, Technology and Mathematics among Girls and Women in Nigeria.* Lagos: Nigerian Educational Research and Development Council.

Friedan, Betty. 1963. *The feminine mystique.* New York: Dell.

Gabor, Andrea. 1994. Cracking the glass ceiling in R&D. *Research Technology Management* 37: 14–19.

Greenbaum, Joan. 1995. *Windows on the workplace.* New York: Monthly Review.

Haraway, Donna. 1991. A cyborg manifesto: Science, technology and socialist-feminism in the late twentieth century. In *Simians, cyborgs and women: The reinvention of nature,* 149–81. London: Free Association.

Hynes, H. Patricia, ed. 1989. *Reconstructing Babylon: Essays on women and technology.* London: Earthscan.

Kirkup, Gill, and Laurie Smith Keller, eds. 1992. *Inventing women: Science, technology, and gender.* Cambridge, Eng.: Polity.

Koenig, Dolores. 1986. Alternative views of "the energy problem": Why Malian villagers have other priorities. *Human organization* 45: 170–176.

Kramarae, Cheris, ed. 1988. *Technology and women's voices: Keeping in touch.* New York: Routledge and Kegan Paul.

Leigh, Sue Doyle. 1991. Increasing women's participation in technical fields: A pilot project in Africa. *International Labour Review* 130: 427–444.

Miller, Laura. 1995. Women and children first: Gender and the setting of the electronic frontier. In James Brook and Iain Boal, eds., *Resisting the virtual life: The culture and politics of information.* San Francisco: City Lights.

Mitter, Swasti. 1994. What women demand of technology. *New Left Review* 205: 100–110.

Okeke, Eunice A. C. 1989. Promoting science, technology and mathematics (STM) education among girls and women: Review of initiatives. In Federal Ministry of Education, Women Education Branch, *Report of the National Workshop on Promoting Science, Technology and Mathematics among Girls and Women in Nigeria,* 69–78. Lagos: Nigerian Educational Research and Development Council.

Osborn, Mary. 1994. One step forward, two back? (Only four female scientists on new European Science and Technology Assembly). *Nature* 372: 720.

Shiva, Vandana. 1993. Women's indigenous knowledge and biodiversity conservation. In Maria Mies and Vandana Shiva, eds., *Ecofeminism.* London: Zed.

———, ed. 1994. *Close to home: Women reconnect ecology, health and development.* London: Earthscan.

Stamp, Patricia. 1990. *Technology, gender and power in Africa.* Technical Study 63e. Ottowa: International Development Research Centre.

Terlon, C. 1990. Attitudes des adolescent(e)s à l'égard de la technologie: Une enquete internationale (International survey of adolescents' attitudes toward technology). *Revue française de pédagogie* 90: 51–60.

Wagner, Ina. 1994. Connecting communities of practice: Feminism, science, and technology. *Women's Studies International Forum* 17: 257–265.

Wajcman, Judy. 1991. *Feminism confronts technology.* University Park: Pennsylvania State University Press.

Whalen, Irene. 1990. Development of agricultural technology for women—Some ILCA experiences in the Ethiopian highlands. *Sage* 7: 28–32.

Susan Leigh Star

TECHNOLOGY: Alternative

See ALTERNATIVE TECHNOLOGY.

TECHNOLOGY: Domestic

See DOMESTIC TECHNOLOGY.

TECHNOLOGY: Education

See EDUCATION: TECHNOLOGY.

TECHNOLOGY: Research

See SCIENCE AND TECHNOLOGICAL RESEARCH.

TECHNOLOGY: Women and Development

Technology, a product of science, developed out of the human need and desire to live comfortably and compatibly with our social and physical environment (Martins, 1969: 269). Although there is a strong interaction between science and technology (for the progress of science depends in part on the progress of technology, and vice versa), they differ in significant ways. While the object of science is the progress of knowledge, the object of technology seems to be the transformation of a given reality (the latter being predominantly the product of culture).

Merete Lie (1991) broadly defined technology to include tools and machinery and the knowledge connected to their development and use. Technology has over the years been largely associated with heavy, greasy, noisy machines: objects that have definite male connotations. Lie noted that "technology is a gender symbol of specific importance because of its connection to the sexual division of labor...a symbol of maleness and a source of male identity." Sklorz-Weiner (1991) wrote that technology, like no other area, represented the culture of a society that is structured by men. Thus, it is often seen as a "male system" that "requires a behavior that women are not prepared for while at the same time female structures, abilities, and attitudes do not fit."

Studies (Chodorow, 1978; Cockburn, 1983; Sorensen and Berg, 1987) have shown that women and men in technological professions differ not in ability but in attitudes or socialization. For example, Chodorow (1978) argued that boys and girls are socialized to different patterns, resulting in separately learned, different abilities and attitudes, which in turn lead to different positions in society. Rosaldo (1974) hypothesized that culture is made by men and that women do not participate in the production of public structures. Women are therefore often stereotyped and ghettoized in sex-typed jobs. This stereotyping has also affected how scholars have analyzed the relationship among gender, technology, and development. Rathgeber (1991) found that the literature on women, technology, and development tended to focus on problems of utilization, with relatively little consideration of women's roles as producers of technology.

Writing on the impact of technology on women's lives in the less developed countries (LDCs, the "South" or the third world) describes a unique experience. Women in the LDCs are subjected to double subordination: first, as members of peripheral economies and, second, for being culturally treated as socially inferior to men. Technology is thus not only a symbol of maleness and a source of male identity, but also a symbol of power and dominance, and as such must be guarded and defended (Lie, 1991). Technology appropriated for demonstrating superiority and as a tool of power ascribes positions of dependency across nations and particularly across gender groups. For example, women of the "South" are seen as victims of technology transferred from the "North" (the developed countries) in the context of global capital transactions.

Gender Issues and Development

Traditional concepts of development programs and policies were based for a long time on the assumption that industrialization and modernization would promote economic growth and thereby reduce poverty in the third world countries. With the use of macrogrowth theories and techno-economic models of development, the degree of success or failure of development programs and policies was measured by means of increases in indexes of modernization, (for example, gross national product or gross domestic product, per capita income, literacy rates, life expectancy, and fertility rates).

The global economic crisis of the 1980s led to a reappraisal of development goals and policies. This is because, rather than improved quality of life for the masses, the third world continues to manifest poverty, famine, malnutrition, unemployment, inequality, disease, mortality, environmental destruction, political repression, violence, war, and rural stagnation. Many people now call for a more humane development strategy to help narrow disparities in income levels and offer distributional equity both within and between nations, and among men and women of different races, classes, and ethnic origins.

More important, the traditional view of development has been criticized for giving credence and emphasis to policies that are predominantly profit-centered rather than to programs that are people-centered. Also, the experience in the third world nations has been that industrialization projects tend to rely on foreign investment, commercialization, and manufacturing for export rather than for local consumption (Sen and Crown, 1987), with the result that third world nations remain dependent. Another major flaw in traditional development efforts in the third world is the failure to recognize women's contribution to development processes or the effect of development processes on women and the implications of development for gender relations.

In most indigenous African societies, for example, women's and men's spheres of activities were rather complementary, although this does not necessarily imply equality between the sexes. The introduction of industrial capitalism in Africa has had a negative impact on gender relations. Although capitalism exploits the labor of the (male or female) wage earner, women have been doubly deprived because the system of administration under the new capitalist mode not only ignored women as producers but also denied women access to western education (Obbo, 1980). Men, who were given technical education, gained dominance in the new production systems (Boserup, 1970). A complex mix developed among the indexes of change: patriarchy, colonialization, capitalism, foreign religions, and the process of industrialization and technological development.

Postindependence, the materialistic culture inherent in the new industrial mode continues to hurt women. The change from agrarian rural economy to urban industrial society altered gender roles and the definitions of women's work. In many cases, economic policies such as the structural adjustment program (SAP) in Africa have further resulted in a "femininization of poverty" because they are permeated by the culture of male dominance (Gladwin, 1991).

The new vision of development has led to a search for alternative development based on the historical experience and the cultural context of particular societies. It is now seen in terms of satisfaction of basic minimum needs, better and more humane societies, and freedom from exploitation of any type. Worldwide, there is much more attention to finding appropriate means of integrating women in the development process, because women are now seen as key actors in economic systems. Estimates by the International Labor Organization (ILO) in 1985 indicated that women constituted 41 percent of the total labor force in developed countries and 32 percent in the developing nations (even though this figure was found to undercount these women's productive activities).

Women in developing countries play a greater role in the sectors of the economy poorly measured by national statistics, including the urban informal sector, low-resource farming and marketing, and unpaid family productive labor. According to Blumberg (1989), if women's unpaid household labor were given economic value, it would add an estimated $4 trillion, or about one-third, to the world's annual economic product. In fact, women in rural Africa have stronger provider obligations than women in the United States, western Europe, and the other industrial capitalist countries. Women in third world countries play a major role as producers and reproducers. They manage natural resources (soil, water, forests, and energy), predominate in rural agricultural production, provide the raw materials used in the commercial sectors, and dominate informal marketing and trade.

The "basic needs" strategy adopted in 1976 by the World Employment Conference of the ILO, in recognition of the central role of women in national development, recommended greater access for women to income-generating activities, enabling them to contribute more efficiently to the economic survival of their families and nations.

A series of efforts have since been made to strengthen the technological and scientific capacity of women in developing countries. In 1979, one of the resolutions of the United Nations Conference on Science and Technology for Development (UNCSTD) was the recognition of women in national and international development agendas, so that women can participate in the decision-making processes related to science and technology, including planning and setting priorities for research and development, and in the choice, acquisition, adaptation, innovation, and application of science and technology for development (Ahooja-Patel, 1988). Thus, "gender" has become a major variable in debates over policies regarding technology. How do we bridge the gender gap, which has been exaggerated by modern development efforts, with a view to making men and women cooperate rather than compete in the process of harnessing resources from the natural environment for their survival needs?

Women and Technological Change

Technology is now a household word, and *development* is almost always equated with technological development. National communities and private individuals use technology to transform modes of thought and patterns of living. Advanced technologies, such as biotechnology and computer-aided technologies, have altered labor relations and skill requirements, and have been an impetus for the development of innovative work organization. For example, Mitter (1995) found that recent developments in biotechnology led to the introduction of genetically engineered herbicide-resistant plant varieties, leading in turn to a replacement of manual weeding systems by chemical herbicides. Also, the use of robotic technologies is responsible for the rapid emergence of new management practices and sometimes a massive reduction in the number of blue-collar workers on an assembly line.

Introduction of a dominant technology may weaken the fabric of societal value systems and ideological beliefs; thus, it must be accompanied by a thorough understanding of its sociocultural impact. Technology is not value-free or value-neutral; neither is it gender-neutral, because every society has a gender-based division of labor. Technology has different effects on men and women within and across classes and ethnic and racial groups.

Variations exist among the LDCs with respect to the impact of modern technology on women's roles; but generally, in many of these countries the effects on women have been negative—much more so than is true for their counterparts elsewhere (Tadesse, 1982: 78). To reduce drudgery and to increase women's earning potential, a series of technical innovations have been introduced under new "gender and development" initiatives, either as "hardware technology" (machinery, tools, equipment, chemical technology, biotechnology, among others) or as "software technology" (that is, economic, social, political, cultural, institutional, and administrative factors necessary for the adoption of specific hardware technology).

Changes in technological capabilities take different forms across sectors (agricultural and informal and formal labor markets) and have various implications for women's lives and life opportunities.

Agricultural Sector

Women play important roles in both subsistence and commercial agriculture, although many such roles have not been given adequate recognition and remain unpaid family labor. Traditional agriculture had a distinct sexual division of labor. Baumann (1928), who studied division of labor by sex in hoe culture in eastern, central, and southern Africa, observed that while men's work on the farm lasted only a few months, women's work lasted through the agricultural year. Women's tasks included growing root crops, vegetables, and spices; men cultivated fruit trees and some perennial crops. A study in Uganda done in the 1950s found that women were responsible for agricultural production, while men essentially reared livestock. Among the Junkun-speaking people of Nigeria, Meek (1931) found that the heavy work of clearing bush and felling trees was done by men; women took part in year-round farm tasks such as planting, harvesting, and transporting farm produce. In 1970 Boserup described Africa overall as a region of female farming. The special role of women in Latin American agricultural development has also been well documented (Deere and Leon, 1987). Since the resource base is insufficient for agriculture to be a male occupation, and as wage income becomes an increasingly significant component of household income, agricultural production becomes increasingly an extension of women's domestic work. In countries like Mexico, Colombia, Brazil, Nicaragua, and the Dominican Republic, women are continuously employed as seasonal wage workers in carrying out laborious tasks involved in export agriculture (for example, strawberries, peanuts, flowers, coffee, cotton, and tobacco).

The incorporation of women into commercial agriculture does not necessarily make them socially visible. The agricultural sector is now split into two sectors: mechanized, visible, globally planned and controlled, state-subsidized production for profits and markets; and feminized, less visible, sometimes invisible, decentered self-provisioning through subsistence farming (Shiva, 1989). Women in the third world are generally discriminated against in the agricultural wage-labor force. According to Deere and Leon (1987), wages are only potentially equal for tasks paid as piecework, which are labor-intensive.

Another major implication of commercial agriculture is that women are often dispossessed of land by virtue of the increasing concentration of land in the hands of a few elites. Women have title to only 1 percent of the world's agricultural land, and the percentage is higher in countries where food is scarce. Despite improved technology and increased mechanization (that is, high levels of chemical and biological technology) brought by reforms related to the "green revolution" in southeast Asia and India, these regions still remain predominantly malnourished (Lappe and Collins, 1986). Under these reforms, these regions witnessed increased erosion, desertification, and the dispossession of women from the use of land. Muntemba (1989: 2), writing on women and the environment in Africa, remarked that

"the process has been one of dewomanization and patrilinealization of control and access of agricultural land and consequent marginalization of women."

Most agricultural schemes thus have increased women's workload and reduced their decision-making power. The position of women within the distributional mechanisms of peasant households and within the agrarian system as a whole—that is, the whole rural production system—continues to deteriorate. Most technical innovations are directed at men and strengthen the dominant position of the male as head of the household (Palmer, 1978). Ladipo (1994) found that the positive productive effect of maize-shelling technology for rural women in the Isoya Agricultural Project in some Ife villages in Nigeria resulted in many social problems at home. Husbands became envious of their wives' sudden prosperity, brought about by the new improved technology. Many husbands abandoned their familial obligations and stopped paying children's school fees and household maintenance allowances. The economic prosperity from maize-shelling technology was short-lived, as women found themselves responsible for household and child maintenance.

The introduction of mini–combine harvesters in western Malaysia in 1974 displaced 2,000 workers, including women (Agarwal, 1981). In Bangladesh, Indonesia, and India the introduction of rice mills resulted in a loss of paid employment for women who traditionally dehusk and hand-pound rice (Collier, 1974).

Informal and Formal Sectors

The nonagricultural rural sector and the informal and formal urban sectors of the labor market have all witnessed a series of technical innovations. While other innovations have been directed at reducing household drudgery—cooking, washing, and general maintenance—often technical innovation aimed at women's work is either unaffordable or unadaptable for use by women. In a study in Nigeria, Aina (1994) looked at technological assimilation in female-owned small enterprises. She found that many of the improved technologies introduced to rural women under the government-sponsored Better Life Program (BLP) met with failure. For example, traditional soap makers in Inisa, Osun state, abandoned the soap-slicing machine donated by the BLP. They discovered that the soap slicer was not cost-effective, as the soap bars produced did not fit into their pricing system. Moreover, the women complained that the manual operation of the soap slicer often resulted in backaches and fatigue, because the pushing system exerted too much pressure on the wrist, back, and chest. Similarly, female potters in Isua-Akoko, Ondo state, launched attacks on improved ovens supplied to local potters under the BLP. The potters found the ovens too small to accommodate large-size pots, while the heat produced was too low for proper baking. Half of the pots cracked before they were fully baked.

The broad looms introduced to cloth weavers in Nigeria in most BLP multipurpose centers also caused problems. In Owo, Ondo state, many trainees who graduated from local BLP vocational centers could not afford to establish businesses, while weavers with small looms tended to attract more apprentices; although broad looms are cost effective, apprentices still prefer the small looms, which are quite affordable though less efficient.

In developing countries, the transfer of technology has often lowered the quality of life and caused more economic and social problems for women and their families than it has eased (Ahooja-Patel, 1988). Developers may fail to take into account the interaction between technology and its social and economic environment. For example, much harm is done to African women by lack of understanding of the women's role on the part of regional planners, international experts, and even national planners, whose training and points of reference are often based on the status of women in Europe, the Middle East, and south Asia (Dhamija, 1984). Therefore, new technologies are often directed at men; when women are allowed to participate in using such a technology, they are "unequal partners." In many cases, women are totally displaced as a result of technological changes.

Stevens (1981) wrote about discrimination against women in Senegal who traditionally engaged in fish processing. The government introduced ovens for smoking the fish but handed these ovens over to men, because it was thought that women prefer to work in the open air. When women collectively tried to build their own ovens, the government planned equivalent assistance for fishermen; women thus were permanently kept as cheap labor, rather than becoming owners.

In Ivory Coast, men have suddenly taken control of the cloth industry, displacing women who were traditionally responsible for spinning cotton. Water pumps and wells in African communities have often fallen into disrepair because instructions for their use and maintenance were given to men, instead of to the women who were traditionally responsible for the water supply (Ahooja-Patel, 1988). Ivory Coast women also rejected pedal-operated maize mills because the mills required sitting astride, a position that was considered "improper" and violated a cultural taboo (Ahmed, 1983).

This trend is also evident in formal-sector jobs. The use of computers in office jobs leads to "deskilling" and replaces many secretaries and typists (traditionally women) with computer programmers and data-entry operators (mostly men). Women in traditionally male professions are often stigmatized and discriminated against (Aina, 1994). Few women in Nigeria make it to the top of their professions, because sociocultural norms demand that they combine three roles—worker, wife, and mother (Soriyan and Aina, 1991).

The general pattern has been that technological changes displaced women: men took over activities traditionally done by women; or activities became subdivided, with men taking over skilled technological tasks while women were relegated to less skilled, menial tasks.

Other basic problems include lack of access to technology, training, and credit; failure to consult female users about the choice or design of technology; and the fact that women are rarely part of training or retraining plans. Women's lack of access is closely related to continuing social inequality and is likely to persist as long as gender-related discrimination continues, no matter how many resources are poured into technology transfer (Ahooja-Patel, 1988).

Cultural biases in developing countries continue to inhibit women's access to new technologies. For example, because of a general familial preference for educating boys, female children have less education and training, particularly in technical skills; the few women with a western education are trained in arts and humanities. Social institutions like purdah continue to prevent women from taking full advantage of innovations, because women cannot work in public (since that would require contact with unrelated males).

Male union leaders have been unsupportive of agitation for improved work conditions for women because the labor market itself is seen as an exclusive preserve of men. There are few union policies guiding the choice or use of technology; when such policies are formulated, under pressure, they are likely to be made by men who lack proper knowledge of women's suffering. For example, the ideology of rural extension services is "separate but parallel" development. Hence, while men are taught how to use new agricultural skills and how to manage new machinery, women are often left with the "old tricks." Even when new technology is accessible to women, it is often unaffordable or unpracticable.

To put gender properly into a model of technological change focusing on employment, productivity, and income distribution, we must incorporate sociological and economic aspects of intra- and extrahousehold relations. Specific historical contexts for technological change become very important. The capacity of women to become independent producers depends on a number of factors, including access to productive resources and public provision of credit, technical skill, and basic social infrastructures.

The economic crises that erupted in the 1980s and early 1990s, with their double impact on developing countries, adversely affected women's productive roles. In fact, the structural adjustment and stabilization policies (SAPs) that followed these crises not only halted and disrupted the scanty progress made in the 1960s and early 1970s but, more important, left women's issues out of the focus of development (Aina and Soetan, 1991). Under SAPs, women, like men, continue to face increased unemployment; for those who are self-employed, new technologies have become unaffordable. However, in a country such as Nigeria, both governmental and nongovernmental organizations are making efforts to assist women in ameliorating the effects of SAPs on their productive activities. Intervention programs such as BLP now make available to women agricultural inputs (high-yielding varieties of seed, fertilizers, and machinery) and credit facilities. Yet efforts aimed at women remain limited. Only a few women are targeted, while many of the feminine occupations remain unexamined.

Use and Development of Appropriate Technologies: Proposal for the Future

Successful transfer of technology across cultures requires a thorough understanding of the receiving culture and the implications for local conditions. The basic social units—for example, the family—and the general pattern of social and gender relations must be well understood. For example, the misconception of the "household" as a homogeneous unit, and "women" as a homogeneous group, has often distorted the analysis of the impact of new technologies on women. Household relationships are heterogeneous, particularly since intrahousehold relations become rather competitive when new industrial-capitalist relations are emerging (Aina, 1994). Both men and women in a household seek individual access to power and property, but in a typical polygynous setting the woman continues to be responsible for the survival of her children. Empirical evidence supports the view that intervention programs aimed at men as heads of families do not necessarily trickle down to other family members, because of subtle competition for goods of productive value. Furthermore, women as a social group are not homogeneous. Thus, among rural women alone, Ahooja-Patel (1988) identified different social groups, including women from landless households, tenant households, and female-headed households. Each intervention program must properly understand and explicate its own minimum criteria. Also, technological change is more effective when sociocultural as well as economic dimensions are considered. It is therefore important for women to be consulted at each stage: selection, design, and development.

To adopt a new technology, attention must be paid to availability, practicality, and profitability; infrastructural facilities for market linkages and other support systems must be available and affordable; and there must be local sources of raw materials. Governments must provide both infrastructure and funds for research and development institutions. Extension workers (both men and women) must be available to inform women about current innovations and to give advice on procurement, maintenance, and repair.

To assess a new innovation, a multidimensional approach must be encouraged—that is, the assessments of such experts as engineers, sociologists, economists, and management experts—with a view to finding solutions to the inherent gender conflicts that often accompany technological innovation and dissemination.

See Also

AGRICULTURE; AUTOMATION; DEVELOPMENT: OVERVIEW; DIVISION OF LABOR; ECONOMIC STATUS: COMPARATIVE ANALYSIS; INDUSTRIALIZATION; MODERNIZATION; POSTMODERNISM AND DEVELOPMENT

References and Further Reading

Agarwal, B. 1981. Women and technical change in agriculture: The Asian and African experience. *ILO World Employment Program Working Paper*. Geneva: International Labor Organization.

Ahmed, I. 1983. Technology and rural women. *International Labor Review* 122(4).

Ahooja-Patel, Krishna. 1988. Recent trends in women and technological development. *Development and South-South Cooperation* 4(7, December).

Aina, O. I. 1994. *Technology and female-owned small enterprises in Nigeria*. Research report submitted to the Carnegie Corporation of New York.

———. 1995. Women in the Nigerian urban labor force: Trends and issues. In Simi Afonja and Bisi Aina, eds., *Nigerian women in social change*, 90–115. Ife, Nigeria: Obafemi Aurolowo University Press.

———., and R. O. Soetan. 1991. *SAP, gender and technology: The African experience*. Lagos, Nigeria: Paper presented at International Conference of the West African Technology Policy Studies Network. (9–10 December).

Baumann, H. 1928. The division of work according to sex in African hoe culture. *Africa* 1(3): 289–319.

Blumberg, R. L. 1989. Making the case for the gender variable: Women and the wealth and well-being of nations. *Technical Reports in Gender and Development*. Office of Women in Development, USAID.

Boserup, Ester. 1970. *Women's role in economic development.* London: Allen and Unwin.

Chodorow, N. 1978. *The reproduction of mothering: Psychoanalysis and the sociology of gender.* Berkeley: University of California Press.

Cockburn, C. 1983. *Brothers: Male dominance and technological change.* London: Pluto.

Collier, W. 1974. Choice of technique in rice milling: A comment. *Bulletin of Indonesian Economic Studies* (March).

Deere, C. D., and M. Leon, eds. 1987. *Feminist perspectives on Latin American agricultural development.* Boulder, Col.: Westview.

Dey, J. 1975. Role of women in third world countries. Master's thesis, University of Reading, U.K.

Dhamija, J. 1984. Income-generating activities for rural women in Africa: Some successes and failures. *Proceedings of the seminar on rural development and women in Africa* (Dakar, Senegal, 15–19 June): 75–78.

Gladwin, C. H., ed. 1991. *Structural adjustment and African women farmers.* Gainesville: University of Florida Press.

Ladipo, C. H., ed. 1994. Unexpected gender issues in the introduction of a maize sheller. In Simi Afonja and Bisi Aina, eds., *Nigerian women in social change,* 79–89. Ife, Nigeria: Obafemi Awolowo University Press.

Lappe, Frances, and J. Collins. 1986. *World hunger myths.* New York: Grove.

Lie, Merete. 1991. *Technology and gender: Identity and symbolism.* Tampere, Finland: Paper presented at the Fourth Conference on Women, Work, and Computerization (30 June–2 July).

Martins, B. 1969. *The social responsibility of the scientist.* London: Collier-Macmillan.

Meek, C. K. 1931. *A Sudanese kingdom.* London: Kegan Paul.

Mitter, Swasti. 1995. Who benefits? Measuring the differential impact of new technologies. In Gender Working Group, United Nations Commission on Science and Technology for Development, eds., *Missing links: Gender equity in science and technology for development,* 219–242. Ottawa: International Development Research Center in association with Intermediate Technology Publications and Unifem.

Muntemba, S. 1989. Women and environment in Africa: Towards a conceptualization. In *Women's role in natural resource management in Africa,* 1–5. IDRC manuscript report 238a (October).

Obbo, C. 1980. *African women: Their struggle for economic independence.* London: Zed.

Palmer, I. 1978. *Women and green revolutions.* Paper presented to the Conference on the Continuing Subordination of Women and the Development Process, Sussex, U.K., Institute of Development Studies.

Rathgeber, Eva M. 1991. *Some preliminary thoughts on technology, gender, and structural adjustment policies.* Lagos, Nigeria: Paper presented at International Conference on Structural Adjustment and Technology Policy in Africa (9–10 December).

Rosaldo, M. 1974. Woman, culture, and society: A theoretical overview. In M. Rosaldo and L. Lamphere, eds., *Women, culture and society.* Stanford, Calif.: Stanford University Press.

Sen, Gita, and Caren Crown. 1987. *Development, crises and alternative visions: Third world women's perspectives.* New York: Monthly Review.

Shiva, V. 1989. *Staying alive: Women, ecology and development.* London: Zed.

Sklorz-Weiner, M. 1991. *Gender and technology: A psychological view.* Tampere, Finland: Paper presented at the fourth Conference on Women, Work, and Computerization (30 June–2 July).

Sorensen, K., and A. J. Berg. 1987. Genderization of technology among Norwegian engineering students. *Acta Sociological* 30(2).

Soriyan, Bimbo, and Bisi Aina. 1991. *Women's work and challenges of computerization: The Nigerian case.* Tampere, Finland: Paper presented at the Fourth Conference on Women, Work, and Computerization (30 June–2 July).

Stevens, Y. 1981. *Technologies for rural women's activities: Problems and prospects in Sierra Leone.* ILO World Employment Program Working Paper. Geneva: International Labor Organization. (Mimeographed.)

Tadesse, Z. 1982. Women and technology in peripheral countries: An overview. In P. M. D'Onofrio-Flores and S. M. Pfafflin, eds., *Scientific-technological change and the role of women in development.* Boulder, Col.: Westview.

Olabisi Aina
Bimbo Soriyan

TEENAGERS

See ADOLESCENCE *and* YOUTH CULTURE.

TELEVISION

Television plays a significant role in many women's everyday lives because it is a media technology located in the home and interwoven with family and community life. The economics of commercial television have fostered a close relationship between women and television: advertisers target women as an audience in an attempt to sell them household goods and beauty and health products. Genres such as the soap opera and the *telenovela* have attracted millions of women as loyal fans—and the attention of many feminist critics. Audience researchers have explored what women think about television's stories and representations of gender. Women have also made important creative contributions as television writers, producers, and actors. Recent technologies such as videocassette recorders (VCRs), cable, and satellite distribution have created new problems for women (for example, they can make it more difficult for mothers to monitor their children's viewing of explicit sex and violence) as well as new possibilities (for example, they can make television programs with special appeal to women more available). The increasing availability and affordability of lightweight, simple-to-use, broadcast-quality video cameras hold enormous promise for increasing women's participation in television production around the globe and for creating new ways of telling stories about women's lives. The opportunities for women's television continue to be tempered, however, by the large amounts of capital involved in the production of television programming and the control of distribution by multinational corporations and centralized institutions, often government-owned, government-controlled, or linked to government.

Women's Underrepresentation On-Screen

Women have tended to be scarcer than men on the television screen and, when they do appear, have often been relegated to playing seducers, victims, or marginal dramatic roles, such as the mother or wife of a male lead. In the 1970s George Gerbner, referring to television's tendency to trivialize or ignore women's contributions to society, called this process symbolic annihilation (Tuchman et al., 1978). This same tendency holds true for prime-time commercial television and for public service broadcasting in the United States and Europe, where men vastly outnumber women as experts on nonfiction programs and as newscasters. Underrepresentation and stereotyping of women on television have been documented through quantitative studies of television content around the globe.

Feminist Criticism and Perspectives

Feminist debate about television content has undergone a shift. In the 1970s in the United States, research was driven by a confidence that television would be improved by showing more women in positions of authority, increasing the portrayal of middle-class professionals, and reducing the stereotypical portrayals of dumb blonds and dizzy housewives. In the 1990s feminist critics were less certain about what positive images of women would look like and more

reluctant to prescribe remedies for television's negative portrayals. Feminist criticism should not be limited to encouraging portrayals of more white women in middle-class professions—a goal that to some extent has already been achieved in the United States, where mothers on television routinely have middle-class careers, but working-class women, women of color, lesbians, and elderly women continue to be symbolically annihilated.

Feminist researchers have turned to new questions regarding women in front of the television set rather than on the screen. If television is so negative in its portrayal of women, why do so many women enjoy watching it? How do we account for the variability of interpretations of different characters? Increasingly, feminist critics have recognized that the meaning generated by television programs is not fixed but is dependent on the interaction of the viewer and the program and contingent on a wide range of cultural and individual factors (Brown, 1990). Television programs are often ambiguous and contradictory, and they seem to change points of view from moment to moment. Women have a spectrum of reactions to television characters—reactions that include psychological identification but can also reflect rejection or ridicule (D'Acci, 1994).

Soap Operas, *Telenovelas,* and Their Audiences

In the United States the television soap opera has been the type of program with the greatest number of women characters and the most faithful and enthusiastic women fans. "Soap operas" or "soaps" are hour- or half-hour-long programs broadcast on network television Monday through Friday between 10:00 A.M. and 3:00 P.M. While soap operas have been one of the most denigrated forms of programming—often ridiculed for their lack of realism, their implausible and overblown story lines, and their stereotyped characters—they are now one of the most widely imitated (Allen, 1995). Native-language soap operas are produced in Europe, South America, and Asia and have been encouraged by the spread of satellite television. Soap operas in the United States resemble *telenovelas*—melodramatic serialized stories with romantic heroines that have gained wide followings among men and women throughout Central and South America, as well as in Italy, France, Spain, Portugal, Russia, Japan, and Korea. However, U.S. soap operas have stories that never end—in some instances characters have remained on a show for decades. The *telenovela* typically runs for about 100 episodes, following the passionate romance of a heroine in a specific cultural, social, and sometimes historical setting.

Soaps are concerned with familial relationships, interpersonal communications, and sexuality, areas that are usually excluded from action-adventure genres or treated superficially or comically in prime-time television. Women's interest in soap opera stories is, perhaps, socially motivated by the responsibility assigned to women to support men and children psychologically and emotionally. Just as the nineteenth-century domestic melodrama expressed a new interest in family life, brought on by the industrial revolution, the soap can be seen as addressing family conflicts created by increasing investments in personal life in the twentieth century.

Women Targeted by Advertisers

Television producers deliberately attempt to manipulate women as an audience, both to ensure a loyal following and to provide a favorable environment for advertisers' messages, which also often focus on women's responsibility for the psychological and physical well-being of other family members. Feminist critics have faulted television—especially commercials—for manipulating women through idealizations of a slim body and a European face or through guilt-inducing messages about women's responsibility for family members and for housework. Television has targeted women in the audience as the primary shoppers for the family. In the 1950s it displayed commodities that could be bought—thus spurring consumption of refrigerators, home furnishings, and such appliances as washers and dryers—and portrayed a new, glamorous housewife. No longer a drudge, she could do light housekeeping without sacrificing her physical attractiveness or her ability to care for her family's emotional needs (Spigel, 1992).

Cable channels now target women specifically as audience members; a notable example is *Lifetime* television in the United States, which has offered a combination of original programs, television movies devoted to social issues, talk shows, and rerun network series 24 hours a day.

Family Patterns

A common theme in research on television audiences in North America and western Europe has been the way nuclear families negotiate differing preferences for television content. In many families, fathers dominate the selection of television programming by holding on to the remote control device. A term in popular parlance, *football widows,* refers to the absorption of adult men in sporting events over the weekend and, increasingly, in the evenings.

In many western countries the multiplication of television sets within a single household has lessened some of the gender conflict over selecting programming while widening the gap between men's and women's experiences of viewing. It is increasingly common for the members of a household

to watch individually, using television sets at several points throughout the living space, thus lessening conflict over control between male and female members.

Remote controls and VCRs have provided new insights into the ways in which women use communication technologies. Are these viewed as domestic appliances like the dishwasher and the washing machine and therefore women's domain? Or are they technical gadgets of the hobbyist and therefore the kinds of technological toys men tend to dominate? In a study based on working-class families in London, David Morley (1986) found that men and women held differential power over the television set. Women did not usually control the remote, often deferred to other family members in selecting programs, enjoyed talking while the set was on, and enjoyed television the most when they were alone and could watch their preferred shows without interference. In another study in the United Kingdom, Ann Gray (1992) found that some women refused to learn to use the VCR timer so as not to be given an additional household chore by children and husbands. The denigration of the women's preferred genres (often soaps and melodramas) and the existing tendency for men to control communication technologies in the household limited women's use of the VCR.

Women in the Ascendant:
Performers, Writers, Producers, and Directors

In the late 1940s and 1950s most of the women working in television in the United States worked on soap operas. Irna Phillips and Agnes Nixon, for example, were extremely influential in turning daytime soap operas in the direction of social issues. Amid the more familiar stories of family feuds, maternal love, and betrayals, Phillips and Nixon planted innovative plotlines intended to educate the audience about social issues such as illness, wife battering, abortion, interracial marriage, and adoption. Lucille Ball and her husband, Desi Arnaz, were pioneers of the modern situation comedy. Their phenomenally successful program of the 1950s, *I Love Lucy,* relied on Ball's considerable talents as a physical comedienne, doing slapstick and vaudeville routines.

In the past three decades women have begun to appear much more frequently as television newscasters (on all but the most prestigious prime-time network news slots) and as stars of dramas and situation comedies. Significantly, two of the most powerful actor-producers in U.S. television have been Oprah Winfrey and Roseanne Barr. Winfrey's successful talk show, *Oprah!*—devoted largely to women's issues—and her Chicago-based television production company gave her considerable clout and the ability to produce her own series, including a black feminist drama, *Women of Brewster*

Place, based on a novel by Gloria Naylor. Barr parleyed her success as a stand-up comic and then as the star of the popular situation comedy *Roseanne* into an unprecedented degree of creative control over her television program, a formidable fortune, and the development of several new series. *Roseanne* broke many television taboos by discussing sexuality, body image, menstruation, and masturbation from a frankly feminist perspective in the context of a situation comedy about working-class life (Newcomb, 1994). Some women, such as Linda Bloodworth-Thomason and Marcy Carsey, have gone directly into producing without first achieving recognition through on-screen performances. Within the U.S. television industry, however, women remain clustered in nontechnical positions, such as performer, screenwriter, or producer.

Videocassette distribution has greatly increased the availability of the work of independent video artists and filmmakers. Distribution companies such as Women Make Movies (based in New York) rent and sell experimental art videos and feminist documentaries, many of which are produced by lesbians and women of color. Paper Tiger Television (also based in New York), through a community-based television studio, has produced television essays on many feminist themes. In the United Kingdom, Channel Four television regularly produces feminist work in a wide variety of genres.

The failure of most commercial television programs to view women's problems in anything other than entirely individual terms restricts the progressive potential of most women's genres such as the soap opera, made-for-TV movie, situation comedy, and talk show. When television programs take up a topic such as abortion or violence against women, the situation is treated as a unique problem whose solution can be found in individual actions. This failure to relate women's problems to a shared social context is what most seriously limits the television world.

See Also

COMMUNICATIONS: AUDIENCE ANALYSIS; CULTURE: WOMEN AS CONSUMERS OF CULTURE; IMAGES OF WOMEN: OVERVIEW; LEISURE; MEDIA: OVERVIEW; MEDIA, *all entries;* SOAP OPERAS

References and Further Reading

Allen, Robert C. 1995. *To be continued: Soap operas around the world.* London: Routledge.

Ang, Ien. 1985. *Watching "Dallas": Soap opera and the melodramatic imagination.* London: Methuen.

Angerer, Marie-Luise, and Johanna Dorer. 1994. *Gender und Medien.* Vienna: Braumüller.

Brown, Mary Ellen. 1990. *Television and women's culture: The politics of the popular.* London: Sage.

D'Acci, Julie. 1994. *Defining women: Television and the case of "Cagney and Lacey."* Chapel Hill: University of North Carolina Press.

Gray, Ann. 1992. *Video playtime: The gendering of a leisure technology.* London: Routledge.

Morley, Dave. 1986. *Family television: Cultural power and domestic leisure.* London: Comedia.

Newcomb, Horace. 1994. *Television: The critical view.* 5th ed. New York: Oxford.

Spigel, Lynn. 1992. *Make room for TV: Television and the family ideal in postwar America.* Chicago: University of Chicago Press.

Tuchman, Gaye, Arlene Kaplan Daniels, and James Benet, eds. 1978. *Hearth and home: Images of women in the mass media.* New York: Oxford University Press.

Zoonen, Liesbet van. 1994. *Feminist media studies.* London: Sage.

Ellen Seiter

TELEWORKING

From the time of the first energy crises of the 1970s, how and where we work has been increasingly questioned by a growing number of people from academics to corporate personnel officers to seekers of alternative lifestyles. Of the considerable range of new and flexible work options, one of the most innovative approaches, and one that has perhaps fired public imagination the most, is telework. Electronic cottages spreading across the vista and freeway spaghetti junctions replaced by umbilical fiber-optic networks are powerful visions indeed, suggesting radical change in the familiar fabric of family, work, and social structures.

What, then, is telework? How does it function? What does it involve? Can it be useful for me and my company? These and other questions are being voiced in countries as far-flung as the United States, Japan, Finland, and Australia, to name but a few, proving that the appeal of telework transcends both cultural and national boundaries.

The Definitional Framework

While opinion remains at times sharply divided over the precise parameters of telework, the gradual accumulation of expertise in the field during the 1990s and the constant application of new configurations of this work arrangement have led to a certain consensus concerning its core concepts. Of these, paramount would have to be the central idea of eradicating unnecessary work-related travel, most usually through the use of information and communications technology (ICT). Hence, the definition coined by Jack Nilles, widely recognized as the father of telework: "sending the work to the workers instead of the workers to work" (JALA Associates, 1990).

Other important variables that appear frequently are contractual status (full-time employee, subcontractor, self-employed or free agent); the level of ICT applications (high tech, low tech, no tech, and more recently, networked or stand-alone); place of work (home-based, alternative office–based, mobile); and telework frequency (full-time, regular part-time, occasional, or "ad hoc").

A recent trend has been to focus on the impact rather than the precise specifications of what is now a highly diverse work arrangement. One example of this approach is the definition proposed at the Second International Telework Workshop in 1997, a conference bringing together researchers and practitioners from around the globe: "Telework is a portfolio of flexible work arrangements, which offers business flexibility, personal flexibility and public policy flexibility."

A further note is required regarding the sometimes confusing interchangeable use of the terms *telecommuting* and *telework*. Current practice is to use *telework* to refer to all forms of work where ICT substitutes for work-related travel and *telecommuting* to refer solely to the corporate employee subset of telework. Accordingly, a telecommuter is always a teleworker, but the reverse does not always hold true.

Historical Development

The terms *telecommuting* and *telework* were first coined in the United States in 1973, and it is from this period that mainstream interest in telework can be said to date, although there are earlier examples of networked or "virtual" companies. At the risk of oversimplification, it is possible to divide the development of telework into several distinct phases according to predominant drivers.

The jump in energy costs triggered by the "oil shocks" of 1973 and 1979 was the main catalyst for reassessing how workers got to work, with some farsighted people advocating the expedience of using electronic instead of bitumen highways. Telework at this stage, therefore, was largely relegated to the status of an emergency, energy-saving measure.

In the 1980s the penetration of the personal computer and the rapid increase in the number of women employees set the scene for the next push toward telework, especially in North America. Technical progress and lower acquisition costs ensured that personal computers were increasingly

found in offices and homes. The widespread availability of such technological tools changed how much work was done and also highlighted the inconsistency of forcing workers to commute to the office every day to use the very same machine they might well have at home. It also led to expectations of better, faster, cheaper telecommunications just around the corner and perhaps overly optimistic predictions for the spread of information work and, by extension, telework.

As the number of women in paid employment rose and their positions became more senior, corporate management was loath to lose such a highly and expensively trained staff because of family commitments, especially childbirth and child care. It was hoped that a more flexible approach to workstyles would help organizations retain more women, and that women themselves would also benefit from such a work arrangement. This issue will be discussed in more detail below, in the section on teleworking and gender, but suffice it to say that telework at this stage was largely viewed as a human resources measure, especially for women, made increasingly feasible by advances in new technology and telecommunications.

From the late 1980s, environmental concerns were once again becoming of major import around the globe. *Conservation* became a key word, finding political voice in the proliferation of Green parties in North America as well as Europe, Australia, and Japan. Telework was seen to dovetail with these concerns by keeping more cars off the road, thereby helping improve air quality. Regulation XV (1987, South Coast Air Quality Management District, Los Angeles) was one, if not the first, example of such mandatory trip-reduction ordinances, not to mention the U.S. Federal Clean Air Act (1970, amended in 1990 and 1997).

Lackluster economic performance was another key factor in this period. By removing "location" from the job equation, telework was seen as a way of revolutionizing job opportunities in traditionally isolated or disadvantaged communities. On the corporate front, the realization that restructuring did more damage than good led to a greater focus on work quality and workers' motivation and morale, areas where telework has been an effective tool. This new awareness, coupled with ICT progress, led to expanded interest in telework as a management strategy.

Risk management is an aspect of telework that emerged after the devastating earthquakes experienced in Los Angeles (1994) and Kobe (1995), as well as the bombing of the World Trade Center in New York (1993) and the sarin poison gas attack in the Tokyo subway (1995). How to maximize workers' safety as well as maintain business functions is a question neither individual firms nor governments can afford to ignore. The fact that telework often makes travel unnecessary has obvious benefits in this area. While by no means universal, telework is figuring more in corporate and government contingency plans.

Underlying all these changes is the growing consensus that the nature of work has changed and will continue to change even more. In the 1990s, a surge in networked telecommunications—whether intranets, extranets, or the Internet—added momentum to the drive toward new work and business arrangements. The rise of the independent SOHO entrepreneur, much touted in the popular press, has expanded telework applications, which until the early 1990s were predominantly confined to the corporate domain and aimed at employees or outsourcing.

Teleworking and Gender

The issue of telework and gender is a complex one that is frequently colored by whether this work arrangement is perceived as inherently benign or base. This, however, is a somewhat false dichotomy, given that any work arrangement is of itself neutral. It is only in the implementation that virtuous or vicious practice comes into play. In any event, a considerable body of research has been conducted on both the enabling and the marginalizing aspects of telework for women, as well as its impact on the work-life balance.

In the corporate setting, with more women occupying more responsible positions, the retention of female employees in the face of the "biological imperative" and other family-care demands has emerged as a key management issue. For women themselves, not only do family-induced absences from the workplace damage career prospects, but hiring practices or technological changes often make the return to a former position impracticable. Telework has been seen as one way of offering a more flexible work environment, although it was quickly discovered that telework was not a substitute for child care and that "one hand on the keyboard and one hand on the cradle" was neither feasible nor desirable. Interestingly, the stereotype of the female home-based worker does not hold true in the corporate environment, where men are just as likely to participate in in-house telework programs as their female counterparts.

Outside the corporate setting, concern is frequently voiced about the marginalizing potential of telework. From this perspective, telework is seen as a way of locking women into low-paid, low-skilled work, a typical example being data entry. Having no access to a central workplace may well deprive such workers of opportunities to upgrade their skills; their isolated position also places them at a considerable disadvantage in finding work and negotiating pay scales and general work conditions. In recognition of these dangers,

on-line training systems and worker networks are springing up in the major industrialized countries. Another often cited example, the call center, poses a different kind of problem. (See, for example, the studies by Huws and her colleagues.) The flatter organizational structures commonly found in call centers offer little possibility of promotion beyond the supervisory level. So, while these facilities offer *job* opportunities, they very rarely offer *career* opportunities. Elsewhere there is still very little recourse for the offshore teleworker should a work supplier resort to exploitive practices. Nevertheless, it must be noted that abusive telework practices are part of the larger issue of ensuring equitable work practices in general in the face of the ongoing erosion of traditional employment. Proactive measures on the part of policy authorities and trade unions are crucial.

Another complicating factor is the equivocation to be found among female teleworkers themselves. While a principled demand and concerted push for job equity, worker protection, and best practice are most certainly not to be taken lightly, for many women their current reality can often be summed up as "any job is better than none." Interviews with home-based teleworkers engaged in low-skilled, low-pay work reveal what is almost an eagerness to be engaged in something other than punching the cash register at the local supermarket—often their only other option. In isolated areas, frequently even this option does not exist. Drawing the line between enabling and marginalizing impacts is not as straightforward as it might initially seem.

In a nutshell, one of the key gender issues in telework is whether it is applied to expand work opportunities, especially employment and career opportunities, for women, or whether it represents merely a newfangled, high-tech opportunity for exploitation: an "electronic sweatshop." As already mentioned, however, this is ultimately a question that needs to be considered against the larger backdrop of unremitting workplace change and the overall erosion of job security.

See Also

COMPUTING: OVERVIEW; CYBERSPACE AND VIRTUAL REALITY; INFORMATION TECHNOLOGY; NETWORKS: ELECTRONIC; PART-TIME AND CASUAL WORK; WORK: PATTERNS

References and Further Reading

Christensen, Kathleen. 1988. *Women and home-based work: The unspoken contract.* New York: Holt.

———, ed. 1988. *The new era of home-based work: Directions and policies.* Boulder, Col.: Westview.

European Foundation for the Improvement of Living and Work Conditions. 1997. *Social implications of teleworking: Sum-*

mary. Dublin: European Foundation for the Improvement of Living and Work Conditions.

Handy, Charles. 1991. *The age of unreason.* Oxford: Blackwell.

Huws, Ursula, ed. 1995. *Action program for the protection of home-workers: Ten case-studies from around the world.* International Labor Office.

Huws, U., and A. Denbigh. 1999. *Virtually there: The evolution of call centres.* Newport, U.K.: Mitel.

Huws, U., N. Jagger, and S. O'Regan. 1999. *Teleworking and globalisation.* IES Report 358. Grantham, U.K.: Grantham.

Huws, Ursula, Werner B. Korte, and Simon Robinson. 1990. *Telework: Towards the elusive office.* Chichester, U.K.: Wiley.

Huws, U., S. Podro, E. Gunnarsson, T. Weijers, K. Arvanitaki, and V. Trova. 1996. *Teleworking and gender.* IES Report 317. Grantham, U.K.: Grantham.

Jackson, Paul, and Jos M. M. van der Wielen, eds. 1998. *Teleworking: International perspectives.* London: Routledge.

JALA Associates. 1990. *The California Telecommuting Pilot Project final report, June 1990.* State of California: Department of General Services.

Kinsman, Francis. 1987. *The telecommuters.* Chichester, U.K.: Wiley.

Korte, Werner B., Simon Robinson, and Wolfgang J. Steinle, eds. 1988. *Telework: Present situation and future development of a new form of work organization.* Amsterdam: Elsevier Science.

Nilles, Jack. 1998. *Managing telework: Strategies for managing the virtual workforce.* New York: Wiley.

Wendy A. Spinks

TERRORISM

Women are directly affected by terrorism in two situations: where women are the terrorists, and where terrorist attacks single out women or are designed especially to intimidate women and their male allies on issues that are intrinsically feminist in nature.

Defining Terrorism

Terrorism has often been defined as the use of criminal violence to force political or social change. It frequently involves perpetrating violence to threaten a population and make a state or society ungovernable.

However, any definition of terrorism is imprecise. For example, until recently terrorism was almost always defined as involving violence or the threat of violence—that is, bod-

ily harm—but the continued expansion of the Internet and the World Wide Web will probably lead to definitions of terrorism that do not include bodily harm. Also, definitions in which political or social change is the purpose of terrorism might fail to include some terrorists, such as those who would use terror simply for personal gain or cyberterrorists who seem to enjoy causing mayhem for its own sake.

Whatever the method or definition, the immediate goal or result of terrorism was succinctly explained by the founder of the Soviet Union, Lenin (Vladimir Ilyich Ulyanov): "The purpose of terrorism is to produce terror." Components of terrorism include the use of violence (often indiscriminate violence) to frighten a population, to strike terror into their hearts; actions that indiscriminately kill people without regard to the precise victim, such as a mass bombing; targeted assassination; planting bombs and other destructive devices with little or no regard for who is actually harmed; and actions directed at a few individuals but also designed to intimidate others in the community who have not been harmed. During wartime, terrorism can occur when armies direct their wrath not at enemy soldiers but at civilians, or when actors who are not in uniform and are not under any traditional command structure attack either soldiers or civilians.

Not all terrorists fit neatly into categories. Furthermore, the designation of someone as a terrorist can be highly political and is often subjective. One person's terrorist is another's freedom fighter. For example, during World War II the resistance movements in Poland, Greece, Yugoslavia, and France participated in violence against German civilians and military authorities and local collaborationists. The Nazis and their puppet regimes saw members of the resistance as terrorists, and their actions were terrorist in nature, designed to undermine the governing of the country by the invading Nazis. But even among people who would label this "terrorism," almost no one today would deny that it was a necessary evil.

Defining terrorism, then, inevitably involves distinguishing legitimate and illegitimate terrorism. An analysis of the motivations and goals of terrorists and the political regimes in which they operate may lead us to the conclude that some terrorism is a legitimate response to oppression. When all routes to change are closed, and when the existing regime violently suppresses dissidents, minorities, or even the majority of the population, then those who resist with violence might be considered freedom fighters rather than terrorists—though to be fair, we must admit that it is unlikely that the targets of such terrorism would agree.

Scholars and critics also identify what has been called "state terrorism," in which a government uses terror to intimidate the population to make it more governable and tractable. "State terror" can be accomplished through private or extralegal actors who terrorize populations in violation of the law but are not prosecuted or even investigated. Often such terrorists are members of the police or army but are out of uniform and acting outside their official roles. In the southern United States, for instance, many members of the Ku Klux Klan were also public officials and even law enforcement officers. Similarly, during the 1960s and 1970s Argentina suffered from such terrorism, as thousands of citizens, many of whom were utterly apolitical, disappeared at the hands of private actors who were often under the unofficial control of government and military officials; many of these actors held military or civilian jobs. (Significantly, large, peaceful demonstrations by Argentinian women—including some mothers of those who had disappeared—helped end this terrorism and bring down the regime that allowed it.) State terrorism is also conducted by members of the army, militia, police, or "secret police" in their official capacity; the Gestapo in Nazi German and the KGB in the Soviet Union are examples of state-run instruments of terrorism.

Women as Terrorists

Historically, women have rarely been involved in military conflicts as combatants. However, even in ancient times women acted outside a strictly military context to fight an enemy through methods that might be deemed terroristic. For example, the biblical Judith assassinated an enemy general, Holofernes, cutting his head off while he slept. In Russia in the early twentieth century, many women were involved in revolutionary terrorist activities, including such assassinations. At least twenty-seven women were involved in terrorist attacks in Russia between 1902 and 1911. A. Bitsenko, trained as a schoolteacher, assassinated General Sakharov in 1905. In 1906 another young teacher, Zinaida Konopliannikova, assassinated General Min; and Mariia Spiridonova shot and killed General Luzhenovkii. Both were executed. Mariia Benevskaia, the daughter of an army officer, lost a hand while making a bomb to kill a political official. Dora Brilliant made the bombs that killed Grand Duke Sergei. The most famous female revolutionary of this period, Rosa Luxemburg (1871–1919), was a key member of the German Spartacus League, which advocated violence and terrorism as a prelude to a communist revolution. However, there is no evidence that Luxemburg actually practiced violence or terrorism, and she died at the hands of the Frei Korps, a protofascist organization that relied on terrorism to suppress its opponents. During World War II, many women participated in anti-Nazi resistance activities including planting bombs and killing Nazis and collaborationists. Most modern scholars would not consider these women terrorists.

Women have also been involved in "state terror." For example, although the Gestapo in Nazi German and the KGB in the Soviet Union were predominately male, these organizations had women members who took part in their terrorism.

Since World War II the rise of terrorism as a political strategy has led to a similar rise in women terrorists. Many of these women have had prominent roles. Gabriele Krocher-Tiedemann worked with the terrorist "Carlos" in kidnapping diplomats at a meeting in Vienna of the Organization of Petroleum Exporting Countries (OPEC). In the early 1970s in the United States, the founders of the Weatherman Faction of Students for a Democratic Society included Bernadine Dohrn, and in the mid-1970s a number of women held leadership positions in the Symbionese Liberation Army. Silvia Baraldini, an Italian leftist, was involved in the terrorist murder of four people, including two policemen, in New York City. She spent twenty years in prison in the United States before being deported to Italy, where she was incarcerated for another eight years. In South Africa during apartheid, Winnie Mandela was involved in planning, if not actually implementing, numerous acts of violence against the white regime. After the collapse of that regime, she was convicted of kidnapping and assault for her role in terrorizing some black South Africans who did not accept her leadership. Kim Hyon Hui, a North Korean agent, planted the bomb that killed 115 people on Korean Air Lines Flight 858 in 1987. Her goal was to sabotage South Korea's hosting of the 1988 Olympic Games.

Women have been particularly active in two modern European terrorist organizations, the Red Brigade in Italy and the Red Army Faction in Germany. Susanna Ronconi, Giulia Borelli, and Silveria Russo were the best-known women leaders of the Prima Linea, also called the Italian Red Army Brigade. Of the 19 leaders in the Brigade's history, seven (nearly 40 percent) were women. Ulrike Meinhof was one of the founders of the Red Army Faction in Germany, initially called the Baader-Meinhof Gang; the majority of its members were women, and in 1978 Germany was seeking to arrest 16 members, 11 of whom were women. In the 1970s the Red Army Faction killed more than 25 people, wounded more than 90, and kidnapped over 150. Two other women in the Red Army Faction, Susanne Albrecht and Inge Viett, were involved in the murder of at least three Germans, including a banker who was a friend of the Albrecht family; another woman, Silke Maier-Witt, also had a significant role in the organization.

According to Human Rights Watch, the Shining Path, a Maoist organization determined to disrupt all government in Peru, "is unique among armed insurgencies for the high number of women in its ranks, particularly in leadership positions." (Human Rights Watch, 1995: 78). Four of the six leaders of Shining Path have been women, and its women members are often involved in assassination attacks on local leaders, national political representatives, the police, and the military. Indeed, Shining Path women are often called on to deliver a coup de grâce by shooting soldiers and police officers in the head point-blank. The female leadership of Shining Path has not affected its willingness to attack other women. Between 1985 and 1992, Shining Path murdered at least ten feminists and grassroots leaders as well as scores of other women working in community organizations.

Worldwide, women have been involved in terrorism in the name of national liberation. Like all indiscriminate terrorists, these women have planted bombs or set off explosions that killed bystanders, civilians, and children. Women in the African National Congress, the Basque separatist movement, and the Palestinian Liberation Organization (PLO) have planted bombs, plotted assassinations, and been arrested, jailed, and occasionally killed while being captured. A Palestinian, Abir Al-Wheidi was involved in a drive-by shooting of a Jewish settler, and Lamia Maarouf drove a car used in the kidnapping and murdering of an Israeli soldier. (Both were later released from Israeli prisons as part of agreements between the PLO and Israel in 1995.) The Palestinian terrorist Leila Khaled, who hijacked and blew up a TWA plane in August 1969, "became a sex symbol for her violence; she shattered a million and one taboos overnight; and she revolutionized the thinking of hundreds of other angry young women around the world" (MacDonald, 1992: 91).

The Irish Republican Army (IRA) has had numerous women members who were involved with terrorism (MacDonald, 1992). Marion Price and her sister were arrested for planting bombs in London in 1973 that wounded 180 people. Marie Drumm was an active terrorist before she in turn was shot by Protestant terrorists in 1969; and Mairead Farrell was involved in several bombings before she was shot by security forces while resisting arrest in 1988. In 1983 Anna Moore was sentenced to life imprisonment for bombing a pub; twelve British soldiers and five local civilians had been killed in that bombing.

In the United States, some women opposed to abortion have used terrorism. Federal authorities alleged that Shelley Shannon firebombed or otherwise damaged nine women's health clinics and other buildings and shot one male physician in a two-year period in the early 1990s. She was convicted of several of these charges.

Finally, women, like men, may commit acts of terrorism for no apparent reason. The first reports of the "Love Bug" computer virus—which had a far-reaching impact in the year 2000—alleged that a woman was responsible, suggesting that the suspected cyberterrorists included at least one female; the man who was eventually considered the perpetrator may have worked with a woman accomplice.

Terrorism Directed Against Women

Most terrorism has not been directed at women per se. The overwhelming majority of assassinations, for instance, have been directed at men, because historically men have held power. The assassination of Indira Gandhi in 1984 by Sikh extremists and the unsuccessful attempts by the IRA to murder Queen Elizabeth II of Great Britain are unusual examples of terrorist assaults on women leaders.

However, some terrorists have targeted women, using rape and other sexual violence. Often rape has been a tool of state terror, directed at women by the police, the army, and paramilitary organizations trying to suppress dissent and control populations. Just as male prisoners sometimes face torture aimed at their sex organs, women prisoners are sometimes sexually mutilated or systematically raped. Rape has often been a tool of terror because it effectively attacks males as well as the female victims: not only the raped women but also their male colleagues, friends, and relatives—who are unable to protect them—are demoralized and traumatized.

In the United States during the Reconstruction period that followed the Civil War—and later—members of the Ku Klux Klan often sexually abused freedwomen in order to terrorize black communities. Sometimes Klansmen raped black women, but they also resorted to sexual mutilation and humiliation, including stripping and whipping black women. Whatever the methods, the goal was to strike terror into the community and to discourage black males from participating in politics or independent economic activities.

During World War II the Japanese army raped and murdered women as a way of terrorizing and subjugating civilian populations. In 1937 the Japanese army murdered more than 369,000 people in Nanking; in this episode—which has come to be called the "rape of Nanking"—Japanese soldiers also raped an estimated 80,000 Chinese women and girls and then killed or mutilated many of them. Later in the war, the Japanese seized about 200,000 women, mostly from Korea, to be used as sexual slaves, euphemistically called "comfort women." In addition to victimizing the women directly involved, this sexual slavery demoralized the civilian population in the conquered regions.

In patriarchal societies, such as the Muslim communities of Bosnia, rape is an especially effective form of terrorism, because victims of rape are often ostracized by their own communities. Rape was also used as a tool by all sides in the Yugoslav civil wars of the 1990s. Some rapes were purposeful attempts to impregnate women of the "wrong" ethnic group in order to humiliate them and disrupt their families. Rape, or the threat of rape, has been used to drive women and their families out of villages as a strategy of ethnic cleansing. In Rwanda, rape has been part of the tactics of ethnic cleansing by terrorists and soldiers on both sides.

In Peru, rape has been used as a weapon by both terrorists and their opponents. The Shining Path guerilla movement, which is dominated by women, expressly prohibits its male members from committing rape and has been accused of few rapes. It is more likely simply to kill women deemed "the enemy." However, Shining Path has raped some women. In retaliation, policemen and soldiers in Peru have often raped women suspected of involvement in Shining Path.

Terrorism has also been directed at people and institutions that are more central to the lives of women than men. In Peru, Shining Path has gone out of its way to destroy grassroots organizations and institutions, like soup kitchens, run by women or serving women; it sees the destruction of these female-centered institutions as central to undermining Peruvian society. Palestinian terrorists have on occasion directed bombs at schools and other institutions housing young children; while not a direct attack on women, such assaults on children disrupt families and probably affect the daily lives of women to a greater degree than men.

In the United States, some opponents of abortion have resorted to terrorism in an attempt to suppress women and their interests, wounding or murdering doctors, nurses, bodyguards, and others and bombing women's clinics. Some of these terrorists, like Paul Hill, have ambushed and murdered doctors and nurses; others have bombed clinics, shattering glass and sometimes shattering lives. Paul Bray, a preacher in Maryland, spent four years in prison for bombing ten women's clinics. In Spokane, Washington, four men known as the "Phineas priests" bombed Planned Parenthood clinics as part of a reign of terror based on the theology of the Christian Identity Church. In 1996, they were arrested by the FBI.

Although they are more difficult to document, various terroristic hate crimes have been perpetrated against lesbians in the United States. These acts, like antiabortion violence, suggest that in the U.S. context terrorism against women is tied to the "culture wars" of the decades from 1960 to the twenty-first century. In this sense, such modern terrorism resembles the earlier terrorism perpetrated by the Ku Klux Klan: the effect is to prevent minorities and women from participating in society as fully equal citizens.

Conclusion

Historically, more men than women have been terrorists and victims of terrorism, but in the last few decades women have been increasingly involved in terrorism as both perpetrators and victims. Both trends may, in part, be a function of the increasing liberation of women from traditional roles and circumstances throughout the world. Liberation from tradition has enabled more women to be involved in terrorism; at the same time, male anger at the liberation of women from historic patterns of oppression may have led to new assaults on women. Women's involvement in terrorism may also increase as cyberterrorism increases, since gender is often irrelevant in cyberspace.

Research by the Italian scholars Luisella de Cataldo Neuburger and Tiziana Valentini on the Red Brigade in Italy and the Red Army Faction in Germany in the 1970s and 1980s showed that women terrorists were far less likely than their male counterparts to renounce terrorist activities or to cooperate with authorities in suppressing terrorism. This research suggests that in the twenty-first century women terrorists may be even more active than men, and even more committed to their causes.

See Also

ETHNIC CLEANSING; GENOCIDE; RAPE; VIOLENCE, *specific entries*

References and Further Reading

Clay, Fay, and Sabra N. Love. 1999. *NOW* v. *Schiedler:* Protecting women's access to reproductive health services. *Albany Law Review* 62: 967–997.

Galvin, Deborah M. 1983. The female terrorist: A socio-psychological perspective. *Behavioral Sciences and the Law* 1: 19–32.

Hedges, Stephen J., David Bowermaster, and Susan Headden. 1994. Abortion: Who's behind the violence. *U.S. News and World Report* 117(19: 14 November): 50.

Hicks, George. 1995. *The comfort women: Sex slaves of the Japanese imperial forces.* New York: Norton.

Human Rights Watch. 1995. *Human Rights Watch global report on women's human rights.* New York: Author.

Hsu, Yvonne Park. 1993. "Comfort women" from Korea: Japan's World War II sex slaves and the legitimacy of their claim for reparations. *Pacific Rim Law and Policy Journal* 2: 97–129.

Knight, Amy. 1979. Female terrorists in the Russian Socialist Revolutionary Party. *Russian Review* 38: 139–159.

MacDonald, Eileen. 1992. *Shoot the women first*. New York: Random House.

Marshall, David C. 1985. Political asylum: Time for change—The potential effectiveness of reforms to prevent terrorist attacks in America. *Dickinson Law Review* 99: 1017–1033.

Merari, Ariel, ed. 1985. *On terrorism and combating terrorism.* Westport, Conn.: Greenwood.

Neuburger, Luisella de Cataldo, and Tiziana Valentini. 1996. *Women and terrorism.* New York: St. Martin's.

Stephens, Beth. 1999. Humanitarian law and gender violence: An end to centuries of neglect. *Hofstra Law and Policy Symposium* 3: 87–109.

Totsuko, Etsuro. 1999. Commentary on a victory for "comfort women": Japan's judicial recognition of military sexual slavery. *Pacific Rim Law and Policy Journal* 8: 47–61.

Yin, James, and Shi Young. 1996. *The rape of Nanking.* Chicago: Innovative.

Women's Rights Project. 1992. *Untold terror: Violence against women in Peru's armed conflict.* New York: Human Rights Watch.

Byrgen Finkelman

TEXTILES

The term *textiles* is defined as "woven fabric," but popular use of the term often refers also to nonwoven products such as felt. The most common textiles are those that are part of our everyday lives in the form of furnishings or clothing. However, the subject of textiles also spans fine art practice, which includes tapestry and embroidery. There is a large body of literature on a variety of textile issues, but only a minority of sources focus specifically on the female aspects of textiles, and even fewer take a feminist perspective.

Textile Manufacture and Economic Context

According to Chapkis and Enloe, "Women are at the cutting edge of one of the most globalized of all industries—textiles" (1983: 1). Yet it is generally agreed that although women are integral to the production process, they are often the lowest paid and of the lowest status. In *Of Common Cloth: Women in the Global Textile Industry* it is made clear that "cheap labour…is a euphemism for women's labour." (Chapkis and Enloe, 1983: 1). Therefore, the process of production is often indistinguishable from the hierarchical divisions of labor, which are not only gendered but further segregated by economic status.

Most countries have, or have had, an indigenous textile industry, which may vary in size or type of production. For many countries, textile manufacture was or is fundamental to the economic structure, a fact that has affected the employment status of women. Consequently, the role of women within the culture of industrial production is an issue of women's rights, as the global industry usually competes on the basis of labor costs. Factory manufacture is a large part of textile production, but an even less visible sector is connected to "outwork" or "piecework," that is, women who work from home. For these homeworkers, legal regulations may not apply, and because these women are usually paid per piece (that is, per completed component), they often receive only a percentage of a minimum factory wage. Therefore, exploitation is a consequence. An example of this is hand knitting.

Sociocultural Implications and Gender

Disciplines such as anthropology, art history, and the history of design have contributed to various perspectives on the societal place of textiles, often under headings such as "decorative art" and "folk art." This locates those textiles that are concerned with hand and craft production. Domestic production plays a large part in a history of textiles and is often entrenched within a cultural tradition. For example, books on textiles from Peru are categorized in terms of heritage and cultural traditions. The fact that the maker is most often female appears to uphold the general view that the applied, decorative, and folk arts are aligned to being female and hence are "feminine" activities. A number of women writers discuss how woven art is traditionally associated with nature rather than culture, a division that, in design terms, "has placed [women] in fields where manual dexterity, a feel for natural materials…take precedence" (Anscombe, 1984: 12). Feminist writers since the 1970s have often rejected the study of textiles because it is thought to perpetuate stereotypes, and they argue that activities such as knitting serve to internalize further an "acceptable" female occupation or hobby within a male-dominated society. In 1984, Roszika Parker published an important text titled *The Subversive Stitch,* which looks at how embroidery has come to mean "feminine." In the 1980s and 1990s, the women's studies perspective broadened the feminist debate to include this large part of women's history and its contribution to a social structure.

Pattern, Design, and Designers

Identifying female designers in the world of textile design can be difficult, if only because it is considered a woman-dominated area. Though growing in quantity in recent years, the literature is patchy. For example, two Russian artists of the early twentieth century, Varvara Stepanova and Lyubov Popova, were reevaluated in the 1990s as making an important contribution to the avant-garde modernist movement. A European example is the Irish-born Eileen Gray, who was invisible within the modern movement because she was categorized under decorative arts. She has recently been elevated into the mainstream. A feminist perspective questions how the object or subject of textiles can be given credibility and empowerment if it achieves recognition through a male value system and hierarchy. However, the contradiction is that some female textile designers, such as Anni Albers of the Bauhaus, (1919–1933), have received *more* attention because they are women. Many sources on the history of textiles are not driven by feminism or feminist theory, so although many cited designs and designers are female, gender and sexual politics are excluded. Because textiles are predominantly women-made, it is useful to question if the product as a whole is gender specific. If female makers are equated with a feminine product, then textiles contribute to the realms of our lives that are female strongholds, such as the domestic interior. Feminist history has an important contribution to make; for example, *A View from the Interior: Feminism, Women and Design* (Attfield and Kirkham, 1989) seeks to examine the relationship between female, feminine, and feminist.

Ironically, evidence suggests that when women are involved with more traditional areas in textiles, their role is often better documented by feminist writers. Yet rigorous study of the contribution of women to contemporary textile fields such as fiber technology and fabric manipulation (considered to be at the forefront of innovation) is largely unexplored.

Fine Art Practice and Fiber Art

The well-documented artwork *The Dinner Party* (by Judy Chicago, 1979) has become famous because it encapsulated the feminist issues of women and art of that era. It has been described as "a glossary of the so-called 'lesser arts'—tatting, lace, weaving, making ceramic household vessels, embroidering" (Rickey, 1987: 73). When textiles shift into the realm of art, theoretical debates emanating from art history and criticism begin to be applied. An ongoing debate focuses on the relationship between "art textiles" and "high art" (Colchester, 1991). This is pertinent because fiber art was a burgeoning discipline in the last two decades of the twentieth century. The work of Caroline Broadhead, in the United Kingdom, is an example of how the boundaries between art, design, and textiles are being pushed out and blurred. However, it was in the 1970s that North America and Scandinavia witnessed the birth of the fiber art movement. Two artists who typify the variety and practice of the 1980s and 1990s are Marian Schoettle (United States), who used concepts of intimacy and clothing as the basis for much of her work, and Mitsuo Toyazaki (Japan), who transformed synthetic fibers into "unnatural" environments. The profile of such art is becoming increasingly accepted; accordingly, women artists working with so-called female material are becoming elevated.

See Also

CRAFTS; ECONOMY: HISTORY OF WOMEN'S PARTICIPATION; FINE ARTS: OVERVIEW; FINE ARTS: SCULPTURE AND INSTALLATION; INDUSTRIALIZATION; QUILTING; WORK: PATTERNS

References and Further Reading

Anscombe, Isabelle. 1984. *A woman's touch: Women in design from 1860 to the present day.* London: Virago.

Attfield, Judy, and Pat Kirkham. 1989. *A View from the interior: Feminism, women and design.* London: Women's Press.

Braddock, Sarah, and Marie O'Hanlon. 1998. *Technotextiles.* London: Thames and Hudson.

Chapkis, Wendy, and Cynthia Enloe, eds. 1983. *Of common cloth: Women in the global textile industry.* Washington, D.C.: Transnational Institute.

Colchester, Chloe. 1991. *The new textiles: Trends and traditions.* London: Thames and Hudson.

Parker, Roszika. 1984. *The subversive stitch: Embroidery and the making of the feminine.* London: Women's Press.

Rickey, Carrie. 1981. Judy Chicago: The dinner party. In *Art Forum Journal* (Jan.): 73.

Lee Wright

THEATER: Overview

Theater is a performing art that is collaborative, requiring performers, an audience, theatrical space, and a text. Unlike the visual or literary arts, theater is a living art form. It does not exist outside the lived moment of the performance except in the memories of those who saw it. Historically this characteristic of theater has been both its glory and its downfall. Theater has often been criticized as being insubstantial, ephemeral, and impermanent. Conversely, others celebrate its transient, time-bound qualities and consider the lived moment of performance to be a unique and often unsettling, provocative experience.

The Greek philosopher Plato held that theater should be banned from his ideal kingdom. In his view theatrical performance—acting—encouraged citizens to be something other than what they actually were. For Plato imitation, or mimesis, is formative, and those who imitate others in the theater will tend to become what they imitate. In particular Plato warns against imitating women, slaves, workers, villains, or madmen. The dangers of mimesis are multiple, both for actors and spectators, threatening to undermine one's identity in ways that are antithetical to the maintenance of an enlightened city-state.

Aristotle's Rebuttal

Plato's pupil, Aristotle, wrote what could be considered a rebuttal to his teacher's views on theater in his famous work *The Poetics*. Considered the founding document of western dramatic theory and criticism, *The Poetics* provides a detailed analysis of the elements that go into making a tragedy. It is noteworthy that Aristotle counters Plato's antimimetic stance with a celebration of the theatrical event. For Aristotle imitation is natural to humankind; we learn through imitation. By imitating nature, Aristotle tells us, the artist works in a manner that parallels nature. As a seed slowly grows into a tree over a period of time, so too an artwork evolves over time, potentially becoming an excellent example of imitation. Theater, then, according to Aristotle, is an art form that celebrates the notion of change, flux, and process; theater imitates nature and the actions of human beings, which are not single, stationary events but activities taking place over time.

Western theater has maintained this Aristotelian model over the centuries despite the various permutations of the definition of "nature" (in both Renaissance and neoclassical thought) and the shift in sensibilities during the Romantic period, which focused the idea of imitation on the emotional life of the artist. One of the dominant concerns with the concept of mimesis that has influenced all the periods following Aristotle's pronouncements is how to judge the relative success of the artwork. The critical apparatus that developed was to focus on how true the artistic copy was in relation to its original.

So for Aristotle, and the many artists and critics that followed him, art was to be judged successful according to the truth it posited about its original model. Art as "truth," art conceived as holding up a mirror to nature, has permeated western cultural thought. Women in theater have questioned the notion of mimetic representation as an upholding of some essential, neutral "truth," since historically women were excluded from its genesis and its development. Such questioning has happened on several fronts: by examining the ways in which women have been positioned and represented in theatrical storytelling, by looking at the access (or lack of access) that women have had to the means of theatrical activity and stagecraft, by considering the manner in which western culture has historically viewed artists who are also women, and by taking into account the problematic nature of the actress as a public female figure.

Classical Greek Theater

The myths and storytelling of the classical Greeks, whose culture is generally identified as the initiator of western theater, were an important source for both maintaining and justifying the position of women in Greek society. For example, in the third part of Aeschylus's trilogy, *The Oresteia*, Orestes, who has killed his mother Clytemnestra, is put on trial for this murder by the goddess Athena. In the first example of a trial by jury in the West, Orestes is exonerated of matricide. The argument used in his defense is that the mother is not the "true" parent; only the father has that privilege. Thus the law of the father is maintained over that of the mother.

The literal absence of real women from the Greek stage—a theatrical "convention" that lasted for centuries in other cultures in the West—supported the general view that woman's "natural" place was inside, in a private world of hearth and home. Theater is a public art form, and only men had access to the public realm.

In addition to enforcing the gender alignment of private and public, theater also added to the nature-culture binary. Men, as cultural creators, have access to the arts while women, associated with nature, do not. Such social and cultural assumptions have had a great impact on the fate of women who became actresses. When women began to play their own roles for the first time, they had to contend with the idea of a symbolic female, the consequence of centuries of aesthetic representation by male writers and performers.

The symbolic female was promulgated by male actors cross-dressing as female characters. While theatrical costumes for male characters aligned themselves to the biological body of the actor under the costume, this was not the case when men played women's roles. Not only were female characters identified by their clothing; the clothes *stood* for the woman—a fact that emerges with particular clarity in some of the Greek comedies of Aristophanes, in which male characters dress as women to further the plot. The women in the play are doubly defined by the theatrical convention of actors playing female roles and the onstage cross-dressing required by the narrative. The symbolic nature of the female was perhaps heightened by another costume convention of this period: male actors playing male roles in comedies wore a phallus as part of their costume. The costume phallus, which played a versatile role itself by often changing shape, engendered countless sight gags. So women are passively defined and contained by the clothes they wear, while men are actively defined by their costume-sign, the phallus.

Women Portraying Women at Last

When women took the stage the first time, the audience had to acknowledge real women, not simply their symbolic or aesthetic representation. The effect of this clash—the flesh-and-blood actress colliding with a dominant tradition of male-generated female characters—had the effect of suggesting that actresses are not creators of theatrical roles but are merely women who *play themselves*. After all, according to standard male wisdom, weren't women, in general—with their practiced deceit, fickleness, changeability, falseness, and use of makeup—natural actresses already? Such prejudice against the actress's creative role, the belief that women had no access to mimesis, was maintained by the conviction, espoused by Goethe among others, that in theatrical performance male actors portray women more artistically and more effectively than do real women.

Despite the controversies about women playing their own roles on the stage and the belief that actresses were assumed to be prostitutes (the only female category that was accorded a public persona), women were gradually accepted on the stage in continental Europe in the early Renaissance. Some of the first professional actresses were part of the *commedia dell'arte* tradition that developed in Italy. In 1588, precisely the time when *commedia dell'arte* was at its height in popularity, the Catholic church launched an offensive against actresses by issuing a new edict (it remained in force until 1797) that banned the appearance of women on the stage in the Papal States. The effect of this edict on the traveling *commedia* companies was that they had to use boys or young men in their female roles when playing in or near Rome.

The English Renaissance, whose active, popular transvestite stage combined with a reactionary, puritanical antitheatrical prejudice, played out a range of controversial gender issues that ended with the closing of all public theaters in 1642, when the monarchy was dethroned and Oliver Cromwell established as the head of state. When the theaters reopened in 1660, King Charles II, newly restored to the throne and accustomed to seeing women perform in France during his exile, allowed women on the stage. The arrival of the actress on the English stage brought significant social changes. The previously safeguarded territories of women in the private realm of the home and men in the public world no longer applied. The new theater, as well as the actress within it, actively contested this dichotomy.

The Social Mobility of Actresses

Access to the stage often elicited social mobility. Many of the first English actresses were lower-class working girls who were able to elevate their class position through their work in the theater. It was common practice during the Restoration for well-to-do gentlemen and aristocrats to "keep" an actress, and not unusual for an actress to marry into the gentry. But, more important, acting was a profession that could potentially bring autonomy and independence, and the period witnessed a growing demand for actresses.

"Breeches roles," in which women cross-dressed as men, became wildly popular. Where previously boy actors played women's roles dressed as men (many Shakespearean comedies provide examples: Viola in *Twelfth Night* and Rosalind in *As You Like It*), now actresses play female characters who dress as men as part of the plot. Accounts estimate that between 1660 and 1700 nearly one-third of all new plays written in Great Britain contained "breeches" parts. And if much of this popularity was attributable to the male costume sexualizing the female body in new ways, by showing the legs and thighs, it is also the case that more than this was involved, since women dressed as men onstage worked against such simple assimilation of cross-dressing by demonstrating that gender was socially constructed.

From the middle to the end of the nineteenth century, the actress, always a popular target for moral diatribes and idealized elevation (both, arguably, aspects of male desire), was evoked as an ambivalent, equivocal image by various novelists. The literary fascination with the actress found its source on the stage itself, where middle-class women were turning for the first time for professional fulfillment. In addition, commercially successful actresses were combining their performing talents with management in order to have more say about their material. The desire to have artistic control over their creative work has recently led women to perform autobiographical material. This performance work questions the Aristotelian notion of mimetic "truth" (how can it be mimesis if a woman performs her *own* story?) and, more important, explores the significance of the female body by asserting its subjectivity, an assertion that counters a history that has denied women's presence. Such autobiographical work, which often articulates women's sexuality, sexual preference, and issues of class and race, has been an important source for much recent feminist theory that evokes the female body as a political site.

See Also

THEATER: 1500–1900; THEATER; WOMEN IN THEATER

References and Further Reading

Barish, Jonas. 1981. *The anti-theatrical prejudice.* Berkeley: University of California Press.

Case, Sue-Ellen. 1988. *Feminism and theatre.* New York and London: Methuen.

Davis, Tracy C. 1991. *Actresses as working women: Their social identity in Victorian culture.* London and New York: Routledge.

Dolan, Jill. 1993. *Presence and desire: Essays on gender, sexuality, performance.* Ann Arbor: University of Michigan Press.

Ferris, Lesley. 1990. *Acting women: Images of women in theatre.* London: Macmillan.

Ferris, Lesley, ed. 1993. *Crossing the stage: Controversies on cross-dressing.* London: Routledge.

Gilder, Rosamund. 1960. *Enter the actress: The first women in the theater.* New York: Theater Art.

Hart, Lynda, and Peggy Phelan, eds. 1993. *Acting out: Feminist performance.* Ann Arbor: University of Michigan Press.

Wandor, Michelene. 1986. *Carry on understudies: Theatre and sexual politics.* London and New York: Routledge and Kegan Paul.

Zeitlin, Froma I. 1985. Playing the other: Theatre, theatricality, and the feminine in Greek drama. *Representations* 2 (Summer) 63–94.

Lesley Ferris

THEATER: 1500–1900

Women contributed to theater in this period by finding and consolidating a place for themselves in a male-dominated industry. In the 1500s few cultures permitted women to act or even sit in the audience, and when they began to appear onstage in greater numbers, they had to negotiate many problems of working in a male environment. Over the centuries, women actors and playwrights contributed toward making theater that spoke to and about women, while women patrons and managers battled for the commercial and financial power to let this happen. By increasing the profile of women in the theater, these pioneers had a pro-found effect on the development of theater as an art and as a form of social expression.

Women As Actors

Very few cultures allowed women to appear onstage in the sixteenth century. There were female actors in China, but they were permitted to perform only in all-female troupes. Italy, which had mixed groups of traveling players, produced one of the first prominent female actors in Europe: Isabella Andreini (1562–1604). In England, Shakespeare's plays were originally staged by all-male casts.

Women's first involvement as actors in theater in Europe was at private performances, especially at court. France and Flanders were among the first countries to accept this practice: women performed in court dramas in Brussels, and a touring group of Frenchwomen caused outrage when they appeared in London in 1629.

Societies often considered it immoral for women to perform onstage because a close connection was made between acting and prostitution. In China some troupes were made up entirely of prostitutes, and acting was considered an essential skill for a prostitute. When professional actresses began to emerge in England (from around 1660), the public was often more interested in their sensuality than their acting skills. For example, Nell Gwyn (1642–1667), one of the most famous actresses of the time, is often best remembered for her affair with Charles II.

Yet even in this climate, a number of women actors made important contributions because the characters they created helped to shape the plays in which they appeared. Elizabeth Barry (1658–1713) helped to develop Thomas Otway's plays in this way, and Anne Bracegirdle (1671–1748) presented lively interpretations of Congreve's female roles. Later, Sarah Siddons (1755–1831) became one of the greatest tragic actresses in England in her time, and she is particularly remembered for her representation of Shakespeare's Lady Macbeth.

In the nineteenth century, a number of women rose to international stardom, thereby gaining the power to direct their own careers. Pioneers were the French actress Rachel (1820–1858) and the Italian Adelaide Ristori (1822–1906), who toured abroad after becoming popular at home. Later the Italian actress Eleonora Duse (1858–1924) and the Frenchwoman Sarah Bernhardt (1844–1923) toured throughout the world with great success. Each was an influential pioneer of acting techniques: Bernhardt developed a highly romantic style that transformed the plays in which she performed; Duse helped to make popular a more "realistic" rendering of character.

The first star born in the United States was Charlotte Cushman (1816–1876), whose notable roles included both female and male parts such as Lady Macbeth, Romeo, and Hamlet. However, in both Great Britain and the United States, the most popular forms of theater tended to exploit actresses' sexuality: the U.S. entertainer Adah Isaacs Menken (1835–1868) won fame by feigning nudity in a tight, flesh-colored costume in *Mazeppa*.

By the end of the nineteenth century, acting was becoming a more respectable profession, and Dame Ellen Terry was one of the first theater workers in Great Britain to be given a state honor. A number of actors, including Elizabeth Robins, Janet Achurch, and Mrs. Patrick Campbell, prioritized women's experience in their work, paving the way for the politically feminist theater of the twentieth century.

Women As Managers

In the sixteenth and seventeenth centuries, there were no women theater managers in the modern sense of being responsible for administration and selecting plays to produce, since women had little social or economic power in any public sphere. Not surprisingly, the first women who could be said to manage theaters were wealthy noblewomen like Queen Anne, the Danish wife of James I of England, and Henrietta Maria, the French wife of Charles I, who commissioned plays and sponsored drama at the English court.

Women's involvement in theater management in its modern sense began with taking administrative responsibilities for small theater groups, often working in partnership with a spouse. For example, Maddalena Battaglia jointly ran a troupe in eighteenth-century Italy with her husband, Carlo. Some women became involved in management as part of a theatrical family and assumed control of the group on the death of a spouse; that was the situation of Sarah Baker, who managed England's Canterbury Circuit for 30 years. The most successful female theater manager of the nineteenth century in the United States was Mrs. John Drew (1820–1897), who took over the management of the Arch Street Theater in Philadelphia from her husband and ran it from 1861 to 1892.

By the nineteenth century, several actresses felt that male actor-managers were reluctant to give them prominent roles, and took up managing to showcase their own talents. In England, the way was led by Eliza Vestris (1797–1856), who managed three important London theaters—the Olympic (1830–1839), Covent Garden (1839–1842), and the Lyceum (1847–1855). Her lead was followed by Marie Effie Wilton (1839–1921), who took over the Queen's Theatre in London in order to lose her image as a sex symbol and as the queen of burlesque, and to take her career in a more respectable direction. Her innovations—furnishing the auditorium with curtains, carpets, and plush seats—set a new trend in England and gave the theater a more respectable, middle-class ambience than it had previously enjoyed. Sarah Thorne, manager of the Margate Theatre Royal from 1667 to 1899, also helped to establish acting as a serious profession by founding a stage school.

In addition, Sarah Bernhardt furthered her career by managing the Théâtre de l'Ambigu (1890), the Théâtre de la Renaissance (1893), and finally the Théâtre Sarah Bernhardt (1898). Eleonora Duse also tried managing, as leader of the Compagnia Drammatica della Città di Roma troupe (1891–1895).

Although women managers never outnumbered their male counterparts, several women had attained prominent and influential positions by the end of the nineteenth century: Dorothy Leighton, Elizabeth Robins, Olga Nethersole, Millicent Bandmann-Palmer, and Adelaide Stoll all ran prominent commercial theaters in England, and Mary Moore was the power behind Wyndham's theatrical management company.

Women continued to contribute to theater as patrons and managers. Lady Augusta Isabella Gregory (1852–1932) founded the Irish Literary Theatre (1899–1901), which would later become the Abbey Theatre, Dublin. Annie Horniman (1860–1937) financed an experimental season run by Florence Farr at the Avenue Theatre in London, going on to fund the Abbey Theatre and to establish England's first provincial repertory theater, the Gaiety in Manchester.

Women Playwrights

The early history of women playwrights is obscure. Many early plays by women were produced anonymously because most cultures considered the poem and the novel to be more suitable genres for women writers. Moreover, very little is known about sixteenth-century women playwrights. Several plays by women from the seventeenth century, however, do exist. The nun Sor Juana Inés de la Cruz (1651–1695) was one of the most important Mexican playwrights of her time. She composed *El divino narciso* (The Divine Narcissus, 1680), *Amor es más laberinto* (Love Is a Greater Labyrinth, 1668), and *Los empeños de una casa* (The Obligations of a House-hold, 1680). Great Britain had a number of important women playwrights, chiefly Aphra Behn (1640–1689), whose plays include *The Forced Marriage* (1670), *The Rover* (1677 and 1681), *The City Heiress* (1682), and *The Lucky Chance* (1686). She and five of her contemporaries—Mary Pix (1666–1709), Catherine Trotter (1679–1749), Mary de la Rivière Manley (1663–1724), Susanna Centlivre (1667–1723), and Mary Davys (1674–1732)—are estimated to have written between a third and a half of all the plays performed in London from 1695 to 1706 (Ferris, 1990).

Women playwrights from the eighteenth century include Italy's Elisabetta Caminer (1751–1796), who gained success with *L'onesto colpevole* (The Honest Criminal), and England's Elizabeth Inchbald (1753–1821) and Eliza Haywood (1693–1756).

The novel became the dominant genre for women writers in the nineteenth century; however, there were some notable playwrights, including Anna Cora Ogden Mowatt (1819–1870) from the United States, whose work included *Fashion* (1845) and *Armaud* (1847). A number of playwrights at the end of the century produced work that directly addressed women's experience and political interests. In England these included Elizabeth Baker, Florence Bell, Cicely Hamilton, Emily Morse Symonds (George Paston), Margaret Nevinson, Elizabeth Robins, Christabel Marshal (Christopher St. John), and Githa Sowerby. Among their counterparts in the United States were Rachel Crothers, Susan Glaspell, and Sophie Treadwell.

Women's Roles

Since there were no women actors in most cultures in the sixteenth century, women's parts were written to be performed by men and boys. This gender crossing had a profound effect on the roles created for women both at this time and for centuries beyond (Jardine, 1989; Ferris, 1990). Roles for women were often stereotypes or parodies of women. These stereotypes included the silent woman (as in Jonson's *Epicoene, or the Silent Woman,* 1609), the pure heroine (as in the Spanish *capa y espada*—"cape and sword"—comedies, with plots such as the farce of keeping unmarried women away from men), or the repentant whore (such as Marguerite in Dumas's *La Dame aux camélias,* or *The Lady of the Camélias*). Clever women like Kate in Shakespeare's *The Taming of the Shrew* (1594) were shown submitting to male authority, and strong women such as Blanca in Middleton's *Women Beware Women* (1657) or the duchess in Webster's *Duchess of Malfi* (1614) were often portrayed as dangerous.

Stereotypes changed little when women began to act, and the presence of women onstage actually sexualized these roles. Plots became more sexually explicit, and even Aphra Behn's comedies involved scenes with seminude actresses (Howe, 1992). Women began to play men's parts in so-called breeches roles, which had great erotic potential, not least because the trousers revealed the shape of actresses' legs. This trend continued into the nineteenth century, when popular theater, such as the music hall, was considered bawdy.

In contrast, the plays of Ibsen in the late nineteenth century were important for providing actresses with complex parts, such as Nora in *A Doll's House* (1879), which enabled women to use their acting skills seriously to portray female characters in ways that did not conform to stereotypes.

In the 1890s, however, a stereotype of the "new woman" emerged, as the move toward women's emancipation was satirized in Grundy's *The New Woman,* Jones's *The Case of Rebellious Susan,* and Pinero's *The Amazons.* In response, women like Baker, Hamilton, and Sowerby wrote plays that questioned women's traditional positions, developing radical new conceptions of women's roles.

See Also

DRAMA; LESBIAN DRAMA; PERFORMANCE TEXTS; THEATER: OVERVIEW; THEATER: MODERN AND CONTEMPORARY; THEATER: WOMEN IN THEATER

References and Further Reading

Davis, Tracy C. 1991. *Actresses as working women: Their social identity in Victorian culture.* London and New York: Routledge.

Ferris, Lesley. 1990. *Acting women: Images of women in theatre.* Basingstoke, U.K.: Macmillan.

Gardner, Viv, and Susan Rutherford, eds. 1992. *The new woman and her sisters: Feminism and theatre 1850–1914.* Hemel Hempstead, U.K.: Harvester Wheatsheaf.

Goodman, Lizbeth, ed. 1998. *The Routledge reader in gender and performance.* London and New York: Routledge.

Howe, Elizabeth. 1992. *The first English actresses: Women and drama 1660–1700.* Cambridge: Cambridge University Press.

Jardine, Lisa. 1989. *Still harping on daughters: Women and drama in the age of Shakespeare.* 2nd ed. Hemel Hempstead, U.K.: Harvester.

Salmon, E., ed. 1977. *Bernhardt and the theatre of her time.* Westport, Conn., and London: Greenwood.

Scullion, Adrienne. 1996. *Female playwrights of the nineteenth century.* London: Everyman.

Stokes, John, Michael R. Booth, and Susan Bassnett. 1996. *Three tragic actresses: Siddons, Rachel, Ristori.* Cambridge: Cambridge University Press.

Jane de Gay

THEATER: Modern and Contemporary

While women's contribution to theater internationally since 1880 has been greater than at any other time, theater has still been dominated by a male hegemony of managers, directors, playwrights, and actors. Women have sought to develop strategies to counter this imbalance, including both assimilation into and separation from the mainstream.

1880–1920

Performance was the predominant area of women's involvement in theater. Ibsen and theatrical naturalism produced more progressive roles for women and increased debate of the "woman question." In countries where women traditionally had been excluded from the stage, such as Japan and Korea, these plays provided some of the first opportunities for female performance. Elsewhere, the international prominence of "star" actress-managers such as Sarah Bernhardt (France, 1844–1923) and Eleonora Duse (Italy, 1859–1924) signaled to many women the emancipatory benefits of a stage career. Actresses likened to or influenced by Duse and Bernhardt include Mariia Ermolova (Russia, 1853–1928), Marika Kotopouli (Greece, 1887–1954), Sado Yakko (Japan, n.d.), and the "Jewish Duse," Esther Kaminska (Poland, 1862–1930). All-female cross-dressing casts were another feature of this period, whether performing gaucho plays such as *Juan Moreira* in Argentina or satirical operetta as staged by the British group Lila Clay's Lady Minstrels, or as part of the Japanese Takarazuka company (founded 1914), which specialized in western-style revues. Women also began to engage more actively in other aspects of theater production. In Russia, Lyubov Popova (1889–1924), Natalia Goncharova (1881–1962), and Aleksandra Ekster (1884–1949) made significant contributions in costume and set design. Theater direction or management attracted numerous actresses: for example, the African-American Henrietta Vinton Davis (United States, 1860–1941) produced and starred in three plays by black dramatists; Johanne Dybwad (Norway, 1876–1950) also directed from 1906; and Japan's first modern actress, Matsui Sumako (1886–1919), established her own company, Art Theater, with a male colleague in 1913.

Most notable, however, was the increase in women playwrights, many of whom again had begun their professional careers as performers. In Europe and North America, the central emphasis of women's writing tended to be on redressing the absence of a female perspective on the nineteenth-century stage. Plays such as Gabriela Preissová's *The Housewife Slave* (1889), Cicely Hamilton's *Diana of Dobson's* (1908), and Rachel Crother's *He and She* (1911) investigated women's experience in both the domestic sphere and the workplace. This notion of "women's voice" led inexorably to overtly political texts. The political stance was particularly notable in Britain, where the establishment of the Actresses' Franchise League in 1908 in support of women's suffrage was associated with the development of propaganda

plays such as Elizabeth Robin's *Votes for Women* (1907) and Cicely Hamilton and Christopher St. John's *How the Vote Was Won* (1909). Women's political concerns also included issues of race, as in *Rachel* (1916), written by the African-American Angelina Weld Grimké (1880–1958). Finally, avowedly feminist theater groups such as the Pioneer Players (established by Edy Craig in London in 1911) began providing important opportunities for female theater practitioners of all kinds.

1920–1968

In Europe and North America, women's involvement in theater changed following World War I. The commercial theater continued to support a limited number of women writers, among them Clare Boothe Luce (1903–1987), Clemence Dane (1888–1965), Dorothy L. Sayers (1893–1957), and Dodie Smith (1896–1990); such as producers Auriol Lee (1880–1941) and Nancy Price (1880–1970); and pioneering managers such as Lilian Baylis (1874–1937) at London's Old Vic and Sadler's Wells theaters. Others were engaged in the aesthetic movements of the 1920s and early 1930s, promoting radical theater work, such as the dadaist Emmy Hennings (Germany, 1885–1948); the expressionist writer Sophie Treadwell (United States, 1891–1970), best known for *Machinal* (1928); Marita Bonner (United States, 1899–1971), supposedly the first black woman to use surrealism, in her play *The Purple Flower* (1926); and the Pulitzer Prize–winner Susan Glaspell (US, 1876–1948), cofounder of the Provincetown Players, participant in the Federal Theater Project, and author of several noted experimental plays. The focus in the women's movement fragmented, and many women's political engagement was with the socialist and anti-Nazi movements.

Significantly, only a few women emerged as major contributors to theater in postrevolutionary Russia. The most prominent of these, the dramatist and poet Marina Tsvetaeva (1892–1941), wrote "safe" neoclassical tragedies and romantic-escapist costume dramas. In both Europe and the United States women were involved in the agitprop and workers' theater movements. Although it is virtually impossible to disentangle names from what was essentially a collective process in which amateurs and professionals worked together, documentary evidence clearly shows women participating in the movement. Two women figure prominently in the development of the concept of a people's theater: Joan Littlewood (United Kingdom, b. 1914), who joined the Theatre of Action, Manchester, in 1934 and then formed the influential Theatre Workshop group; and Hallie Flanagan (United States, 1890–1969), who directed the

Federal Theater Project, which was responsible for establishing a black theater section and for the development of the "living newspaper" (dramatizations of current news stories) in the United States. Other women involved in left-wing theater include the actress and cofounder of the Berliner Ensemble Helene Weigel (Austria, 1901–1971); the actress-manager Margarita Xirgu (Spain, 1888–1969), who was forced into exile in Buenos Aires at the end of the Spanish Civil War); and the dramatists Marieluise Fleisser (Germany, 1901–1974), Lillian Hellman (United States, 1905–1984), and Stanislawa Przybyszewska (Poland, 1901–1935), author of the anti-Stalinist plays *The Danton Case* and *Thermidor*. Hellman was responsible for one of two infamous "lesbian" plays of the 1930s, *The Children's Hour*, the other being Christa Winsloe's (Germany, n.d.) *Mädchen in Uniform* (1930) produced and directed by Leontine Sagan. African-American theater women wrote, produced, and directed plays that dealt with western black experience—the best known of which was Lorraine Hansberry's (1930–1965) *Raisin in the Sun* (1956). Women of color in colonial and postcolonial societies, however, saw many of their indigenous theater forms suppressed by the dominant European culture or commodified as "native entertainment."

1968–1994

The second wave of feminism in Europe, the United States, and Australia in the 1960s introduced a new generation of women committed to radical forms of theater that challenged patriarchal hegemony. The women's liberation movement led to street theater (the London and San Francisco Women's Street Theaters), all-women companies (the British and Melbourne Women's Theater Groups, La Maddalena in Rome, the Women's Project and Women's Experimental Theater Group in the United States, Akne Theater in Poland), mixed-gender groups with feminist politics (Charablanc—Northern Ireland; Monstrous Regiment—United Kingdom), mixed groups with socialist feminist politics (Le Théâtre du Soleil—France; Red Ladder—United Kingdom), ethnic groups (Spiderwoman—Native American; Sistren—Jamaica), and groups based on sexual orientation (Siren, Split Britches).

The majority of these groups worked collectively, seeking to replace the hierarchical structures that characterize traditional theater practice. Attempts to move into mainstream theater have been limited. Between 1987 and 1992, a mere 7.9 percent of the plays staged in major theaters in New York (including Broadway) were written by women. In December 1995, only one female author appeared on the listings for London's West End: Agatha Christie (United Kingdom, 1890–1976), with the record-breaking 43-year run of her *The Mousetrap* (1952). Nevertheless, several women writers have made effective if sporadic inroads into this area, with works earning both critical and commercial success. Some of these texts have specifically feminist themes: for example, Wendy Wasserstein's *The Heidi Chronicles* (1988), which had a two-year run on Broadway, and the African-American Endesha Ida Mae Holland's *From the Mississippi Delta* (1988), which was nominated for a Pulitzer Prize. Other writers have tackled broader issues: Timberlake Wertenbaker's *Our Country's Good* (1988) explored the purpose of theater, and Caryl Churchill's *Serious Money* (1987) was a savage satire on contemporary capitalism; both found success in London's West End.

Perhaps the most fundamental reason for the comparative invisibility of women playwrights in the mainstream is described by Bai Fengxi, the first major female dramatist of the People's Republic of China: "When I take up my pen and start to write a play, I deliberately work against an accepted concept in life, a challenge which naturally arouses confrontation and counter-challenge." Bai Fengxi sees herself as writing directly for her "sisters": "I write about their fate. I speak on their behalf" (quoted in France and Corso, 1993). This notion unites the work of women dramatists throughout the world despite differences of culture: a brief list might include Zulu Sofola (Nigeria), Griselda Gamboro (Argentina), Kerstin Specht (Germany), Efua Sutherland (Ghana), Tripurari Sharma (India), Fatima Dike (South Africa), Sandra Shotlander (Australia), Megan Terry (United States), and Koharu Kisaragi (Japan). Many of these writers also explore innovative techniques, as in Caryl Churchill's challenge to conventions of dramatic narrative in *Top Girls* (United Kingdom, 1982); or Hélène Cixous's attempt to define an *écriture féminine* in *Portrait of Dora* (France, 1976).

Women's writing also has a significant impact on other aspects of theater production. Female dramatists often use predominantly female casts, thus providing more and varied roles for the actress (who has traditionally been constrained by male writers to stereotypical images). There has been an increase in women directors, some emerging directly from feminist theater groups (such as the Jamaican Honor Maria Ford Smith), others gaining from the recognition of women's talents within theater as a whole: for example, Nuria Espert (Spain), Ruth Berghaus (Germany), and Nancy Meckler (United States). Frequently, the women's movement has fostered creative partnerships between theater practitioners: the writer Hélène Cixous and director Ariane Mnouchkine (France), dramatist Griselda Gambaro and designer Graciela Galan (Argentina), and director Deborah Warner and actress Fiona Shaw (United Kingdom).

Commitment to developing a women's theater has not diminished since the early 1990s, but it has changed. The two most significant strands are performance art and interculturalism. Jean Forte claims that "women have virtually taken over the post-modernist genre of performance art" (quoted in Chinoy and Jenkins, 1987), as it affords them ultimate control of the representation of the self and the body. Performance art is a prominent part of the intercultural movement exemplified by the Magdalena Project, founded in 1986. Magdalena seeks to find an international women's theater language independent of literary text, draws on women's theater from all over the world, and uses dance, drama, music, and storytelling to liberate a "transcultural female consciousness" (Bassnett, 1989). Many of the dramatic practices found in the Magdalena workshops and performances originate in the postcolonialist countries that have, since the 1970s, sought to revivify indigenous theater forms. Women such as Penina Muhando Mlama and Amandina Lihamba in Tanzania are often at the center of these "theater for development" projects, working at the grassroots level (recently with an emphasis on AIDS education), as well as recording and chronicling the work.

See Also

DRAMA; PERFOMANCE ART; THEATER: OVERVIEW; THEATER: WOMEN IN THEATER

References and Further Reading

Bassnett, Susan, ed. 1989. *Magdalena: International women's experimental theatre.* Oxford, U.K.: Berg.

Berney, K. A., ed. 1994. *Contemporary women dramatists.* London, Detroit, Mich and Washington, D.C.: St. James.

Case, Sue-Ellen. 1988. *Feminism and theatre.* Houndmills, U.K.: Macmillan.

Chinoy, Helen Krich, and Linda Walsh Jenkins, eds. 1987. *Women in American theatre.* New York: Theater Communications Group.

France, Anna Kay, and P. J. Corso, eds. 1993. *International women playwrights: Voices of identity and transformation—Proceedings of the First International Women Playwrights Conference, October 18–23, 1988.* Metuchen, N.J.: Scarecrow.

Ferris, Lesley. 1990. *Acting women: Images of women in theatre.* Basingstoke, U.K.: Macmillan.

Gardner, Viv, and Susan Rutherford, eds. 1992. *The new woman and her sisters: Feminism and theatre 1850–1914.* Hemel Hempstead, U.K.: Harvester Wheatsheaf.

Goodman, Lizbeth. 1993. *Contemporary feminist theatres: To each her own.* London: Routledge.

Mlama, Penina Muhando. 1991. *Culture and development: The popular theatre in Africa.* Uppsala: Nordiska Afrikainstitutet.

Viv Gardner
Susan Rutherford

THEATER: Women in Theater

Despite restrictions against women entering the theatrical profession, they became involved in all aspects of theater as soon as it was possible for them to do so. In particular the role of the actress offered women professional work that could give them financial independence. At the same time, however, the actress had to endure long and strenuous working days and social ostracism.

One of the earliest and most celebrated comic actresses on the European continent was the versatile Italian Isabella Andreini (1562–1604) who, with her husband, Francesco, cofounded the popular and renowned *commedia dell'arte* company, the Gelosi. Her popularity overode Christian custom that forbade members of the acting profession from being buried in consecrated ground, and she was buried inside a church.

Caroline Neuber (1697–1760), the first actress-manager in Germany, is considered responsible for reforming the moribund state of theater in her country by demanding discipline and focusing on the rehearsal process. Eliza Vestris, known as Mme. Vestris (1797–1856), a popular actress known for her breeches roles, instituted reform in management and design and in 1832 introduced the box set to London audiences.

Sarah Thorne (1837–1899) was an actress-manager responsible for establishing the Theatre Royal, Margate, and thus helped to create a significant provincial theater movement in Britain. Laura Keene (1826–1873) was the first actress to manage an American theater company, and her long-run production in 1858 of *Our American Cousin* helped establish New York City as the theatrical capital of the United States.

Annie Horniman (1860–1937), a theater manager and patron whose interest in the new Irish theater movement led her to Dublin, built and equipped the now famous Abbey Theatre in 1903. In 1905 Vera Komisarjevskaya (1864–1910), a leading Russian actress, left the stability of conventional theater contracts to found her own theater dedicated to theatrical innovation.

In 1926 the prominent American actress Eva Le Gallienne founded the Civic Repertory Theater in New York as an attempt to break away from the strictures of commercial Broadway management. Perhaps the closest example of a national theater in the United States came about with the appointment by President F. D. Roosevelt of Hallie Flanagan (1890–1969) as the director of the short-lived Federal Theater Project. Between 1935 and 1939 Flanagan oversaw more than 1,000 productions across the country. She promoted and encouraged a variety of experimental theatrical forms, and was responsible for developing the "living newspaper."

Flanagan, like others before and after her, demonstrated the importance of the political nature of theater. In Great Britain in 1908, for example, actresses formed the Actresses' Franchise League (AFL) in order to use their art to further their commitment to the suffrage campaign. In Washington, D.C., in 1916 a production of *Rachel* by Angelina Weld Grimké (1880–1958), presented by the National Association for the Advancement of Colored People (NAACP), caused much controversy with its examination of the psychological impact of racism. Much later in both the United States and the United Kingdom, live theater performance became an important element of the women's movement in the 1970s and 1980s. With a focus on the collaborative nature of theater, many companies formed as collectives. These include the Women's Theatre Group (United Kingdom), Monstrous Regiment (United Kingdom), Sistren (Jamaica), Melbourne Women's Theater Group (Australia), At the Foot of the Mountain (United States), Spiderwoman Theater (United States), Split Britches (United States), Nightwood Theatre (Canada), and Maenad Theatre (Canada).

Women playwrights have significantly affected the course of western theater. Hrotsvitha, a nun in Saxony during the late tenth century, wrote six plays that are the only extant theater scripts between the fall of the Roman Empire and the liturgical drama of the medieval period. Aphra Behn (1640–1689), considered the first professional woman writer in England, was one of the leading Restoration playwrights, excelling in comedy.

There are playwrights, actresses, directors, and designers too numerous to discuss in this short article. However, it is important to at least name some of the notable and successful women while keeping in mind the majority of anonymous women who worked as chorus girls, supernumeraries, ingenues, character actresses, and so on. Among the actresses who helped define and delineate some of the best of the western theater canon are: Elizabeth Barry (1658–1713), Sarah Siddons (1755–1831), Rachel (1820–1858), Sarah Bernhardt (1845–1923), Ellen Terry (1847–1928), and Eleonora Duse (1858–1924). Others known for their performance in music halls and vaudeville include Vesta Tilley (1864–1952), Yvette Guilbert (1866–1944), Marie Lloyd (1870–1922), and Josephine Baker (1906–1975).

More recent innovators are solo performers who often use autobiographical material: Gcina Mhlophe (South Africa), Graciella Serra (Argentina), Bobby Baker (United Kingdom), Robbie Macauley (United States), Rachel Rosenthal (United States), Holly Hughes (United States), and Carmen Samayoa (Guatemala).

The ongoing Magdalena Project sponsored the first International Festival of Women's Experimental Theatre, which took place in Cardiff, Wales, in 1986. This event, followed by a series of conferences, workshops, and performances, enhanced cross-cultural understanding between women in theater, as does the International Women's Playwright Conference held, for example, in Buffalo, New York (1988); Toronto, Canada (1991); and Adelaide, Australia (1994).

See Also

DRAMA; THEATER: 1500–1900; THEATER: OVERVIEW

References and Further Reading

Bassnett, Susan, ed. 1989. *Magdalena: International women's theatre.* Oxford, U.K., and New York: Berg.

Chinoy, Helen Krich, and Linda Walsh Jenkins, eds. 1987. *Women in American theater.* New York: Theater Communications Group.

Gardner, Viv, and Susan Rutherford, eds. 1992. *The new woman and her sisters: Feminism and theatre 1850–1914.* New York and London: Harvester Wheatsheaf.

Goodman, Lizbeth. 1993. *Contemporary feminist theatres: To each her own.* London and New York: Routledge.

Howe, Elizabeth. 1992. *The first English actresses: Women and drama 1660–1700.* Cambridge: Cambridge University Press.

Miller, Jeanne-Marie. 1982. Black women playwrights from Grimké to Shange. In Gloria Hull, Patricia Bell Scott, and Barbara Smith, eds., *But some of us are brave,* 280–296. Old Westbury, N.Y.: Feminist Press.

Lesley Ferris

THEOLOGIES: Feminist

Feminist theologies are spoken, enacted, and written by those who wish to interpret their religious traditions from the perspective of advocacy for the full humanity of women together with men. These reflections on the meaning of faith, in particular religious communities, are frequently called *feminist* because they join other feminist disciplines in searching out ways of making sense of women's lives in patriarchal cultures and religions. Recognizing discrepancies between the ways that religions describe their reality and their actual experience of being women, many scholars have sought to develop theories of reinterpretation that would enable religious traditions to teach justice and integrity for women and men and for all creation.

Feminism has many different forms and is expressed in many different ways. From the point of view of an Anglo-American Christian feminist theologian, it represents a search for liberation from all forms of dehumanization by those who advocate full human personhood for all of every race, class, sex, sexual orientation, ability, or age. Both women and men can do feminist theology if they are willing to share in the work of critique of patriarchal religious structures and of advocacy for all women as full participants in their faiths, communities, and societies.

There is so much ferment of freedom among women in religion around the world today that it is impossible to describe all the various theologies that are emerging. The word *theology* literally means "God-talk" or "thinking about God," as God is known in and through our lives (Ruether, 1983). Although it has its origins in classical Greece as a description of cultic proclamation and critical reflection, since the fifth century C.E. theology has been particularly associated with Christian articulation of the tradition of the communities of faith. There are more Christian and Jewish feminist resources because publication of critiques within these traditions emerged earlier than in other religions. The current development of feminist theologies began in the early 1970s in North America, as part of the second wave of the international women's movement.

Others make use of the term, but it is not necessarily a part of their tradition. For instance, theology is marginal to Jewish religious expression, which is praxis oriented (Plaskow, "Jewish Feminist Theologies," in Russell and Clarkson, 1996). In some forms of Buddhism, in people's religions like shamanism in Korea, and in some forms of feminist spirituality there is no one God that is the center of thought and ritual. Feminists who worship the Goddess or practice neo-paganism do not speak of theology at all but use the word "thealogy," to emphasize the Goddess as their focus (Plaskow and Christ, 1989).

Diverse Perspectives

The plurality of feminist theologies is so broad that it is possible to talk about them only in generalizations about meth-

ods and issues that cut across race, nationality, language, religion, and academic tradition. There is no such thing as theology in the singular except as one person speaks out of her or his own faith tradition at a particular time and place. In a feminist perspective theologies emerge from a plurality of contexts and, therefore, are only particular approximations of truth, not "the truth."

There is a pluralism of theology or religious reflection and practice in each religion and in each variation of that religion. World religions are those that have taken root in different cultural areas. Yet even Judaism, Hinduism, Buddhism, Confucianism, Taosim, Christianity, and Islam have many variations within their traditions, according to their religious history and development in different cultures (Sharma, 1987). The variation increases endlessly as we also think of the work that feminists are doing within people's religions of a particular area, such as Native American and African tribal religions (Young, 1993). In order to speak of this great variety and to emphasize links with feminist neo-paganism and the worship of the Goddess, *women's spirituality* is often the preferred term rather than *theologies*.

Feminist theologies are diverse not only because of religious belief and context but also because the term *theologies* is used to refer to a variety of disciplines previously considered separate, such as the study of sacred scriptures, of history, doctrine, ethics, and cultic and community practices and nurture. They also take on a different perspective when they are linked to various other academic disciplines.

Perhaps the most important variation in theologies concerns the perspective that feminists have on diverse experiences of multiple oppressions. Because each theology is written from the perspective of women struggling to gain full human liberation, each must begin with a particular struggle for freedom and articulate what that means for the community of struggle that the theology represents. For women in the midst of political conflicts and wars such as those in Bosnia, Rwanda, Guatemala, and Palestine, the focus on what this means for their own oppression and liberation is crucial (Eck and Jain, 1987). For women caught in traditional cultures that restrict the roles of women, the focus is on family structures and customs that need change. For women writing out of struggles to change the leadership and liturgical patterns of a religion, the focus is on the tradition of the religious institutions.

Those who see a most basic need to be social change of oppressions—racism, classism, heterosexism, and the like—focus on analysis of the relationship of a particular religious tradition to preserving or critiquing the status quo (Williams, 1993). These feminist theologies sometimes have their own names as well, such as Womanist, or African

American, theologies and *mujerista,* or Hispanic-American, theologies (Isasi-Diaz, 1993).

What holds all these theologies together is the commitment to advocate for the full humanity of women in a particular religious, social, cultural, and political context. Feminist theologians ask whether their particular religious tradition promotes justice and human well-being from the perspective of women and of all oppressed groups. They are often deeply loyal to their own religious faith but oppose forms of universalism that maintain that one particular religion can include all. They often reject forms of religious exclusion that require people to qualify for membership by being of a certain race, gender, sexual orientation, and so on.

Types and Methods

Types of interpretation vary according to the position the interpreters hold with respect to their particular sacred texts and communal traditions. Some writers are willing to reject their religious traditions, perceiving them as "harmful to women's health." Usually these writers move beyond the texts to other traditions or to no tradition because they have found the texts to be so embedded with patriarchy that there seems to be no way to redeem them (Plaskow and Christ, 1989). Others take up the task of retrieval of the traditions. Like other feminists, they are suspicious of the patriarchal formation of those traditions, but they seek to retrieve the liberating themes within them or within their particular culture (Oduyoye and Kanyoro, 1992). A third group of scholars seek to reconstruct their traditions so that they are transformed into traditions that are connected with the religious faith yet are life giving for women (Ruether, 1983).

The methods vary with the particular subdiscipline of the scholar, but feminist theologies are praxis oriented. Even the most abstract writings are part of the political struggle against the oppression of women, and their theoretical analysis is a service of advocacy for women. Most of the feminist interpretations include at least four aspects of action and reflection, although they often emphasize research in only one of the areas.

The first aspect of the method of action and reflection is to work with the concrete experiences of women struggling for full human dignity together with men. These experiences are reflected on critically from within the community of faith that is engaged in the struggle, and they provide the basis for a hermeneutics of suspicion and questions for other aspects of the methodology (Fabella and Oduyoye, 1988).

The second aspect of the method of action and reflection is to use various social, political, economic, historical, and psychological tools to do social critical analysis of the contradictions and sources of oppression discovered in reflection on the experiences of women, particularly those most oppressed in any particular society (Isasi-Diaz, 1993).

The third aspect of feminist theological methodology is represented by the careful analysis of the particular religious tradition and its teachings and practices in light of the questions raised by experience and social analysis. This careful study and analysis of the tradition does not stand alone but is embedded in a methodology that uses the questions and perspectives of advocacy for women to discover new insights and interpretations of the faith of the particular religious community (Wadud-Muhsin, 1992).

The final aspect of a feminist theological methodology is action for transformation. This action can take the form of a reconstruction of a tradition to liberate women's lives in the religious community (Gross, 1993). It also takes the form of joint action for change of religious and cultural institutions that are life denying for women. This action, in turn, contributes to the struggle for full human worth and dignity of women together with men and produces new insights that can be analyzed and used as resources for questioning religious traditions.

Themes and Issues

This style of theological action and reflection usually raises many questions about the authority of those who are questioning the sacred texts and teachings of their religion (Plaskow, 1990). For this reason, an important aspect of the work is the clarification of the authority of women's experience and the importance of inclusion of that experience in religious interpretation. Such a method is itself controversial because it places value on cross-disciplinary study of the tradition from the perspectives of experience, social science, and the impact on the lives of women already marginalized by poverty, race, and political circumstances. Yet it makes the claim that all these aspects must be studied because our understanding of reality is socially constructed and must be looked at in a holistic way.

The themes most often dealt with derive from sacred teachings, but also from the issues of women's lives, their bodies, health, art, families, and nation, and the struggles to preserve nature and the environment on which they depend for the lives of their families (King, 1995). In each area the work of feminist theologies is to identify the needs of women who are most marginalized and oppressed and to see how the resources of religion and culture can contribute to full human dignity for all.

See Also

RELIGION: OVERVIEW; WOMANIST THEOLOGY

References and Further Reading

Eck, Diana L., and Devaki Jain. 1987. *Speaking of faith: Global perspectives on women, religion, and social change.* Philadelphia: New Society.

Fabella, Virginia, and Mercy Oduyoye. 1988. *With passion and compassion: Third world women doing theology.* Maryknoll, N.Y.: Orbis.

Gross, Rita M. 1993. *Buddhism after patriarchy: A feminist history, analysis, and reconstruction of Buddhism.* Albany: State University of New York.

Isasi-Diaz, Ada Marie. 1993. *En la lucha (In the struggle): A Hispanic women's liberation theology.* Minneapolis: Fortress.

King, Ursula, ed. 1995. *Religion and gender.* Oxford: Blackwell.

Oduyoye, Mercy Amba, and Musimbi R. A. Kanyoro. 1992. *The will to arise: Women, tradition, and the church in Africa.* Maryknoll, N.Y.: Orbis.

Plaskow, Judith. 1990. *Standing again at Sinai: Judaism from a feminist perspective.* San Francisco: Harper and Row.

———, and Carol P. Christ, eds. 1989. *Weaving the visions: New patterns in feminist spirituality.* San Francisco: Harper and Row.

Ruether, Rosemary Radford. 1983. *Sexism as God-talk: Toward a feminist theology.* Boston: Beacon.

Russell, Letty M., and J. Shannon Clarkson, eds. 1996. *Dictionary of feminist theologies.* Louisville, Ky.: Westminster/John Knox.

Sharma, Arvind. 1987. *Women in world religions.* Albany: State University of New York.

Wadud-Muhsin, Amina. 1992. *Qur'an and woman.* Kuala Lumpur: Penerbit Fajar Bakti Sdn. Bhd.

Williams, Delores S. 1993. *Sisters in the wilderness: The challenge of womanist God-talk.* Maryknoll, N.Y.: Orbis.

Young, Serinity, ed. 1993. *An anthology of sacred texts by and about women.* New York: Crossroad.

Letty Mandeville Russell

THERAPY

See MENTAL HEALTH I; MENTAL HEALTH II; *and* PSYCHOLOGY: PSYCHOPATHOLOGY AND PSYCHOTHERAPY.

THIRD WORLD

The term *third world* is part of a classification of nations as first, second, or third world or that corresponds to the United Nations system of classifying countries as developed market (first), nonmarket-socialist (second), and developing market (third) economies. Africa, Asia, the Caribbean, Latin America, and the Middle East tend to be included in the third world. In recent years the World Bank has identified a "fourth world," consisting of third world countries that are particularly poor (for example, Bangladesh or Tanzania); the term *fourth world* is also used to denote indigenous people.

As argued by Berger (1993), the concept of a third world reflects two mutually contradictory ideologies, one being a political alliance between ex-colonies in Asia and Africa committed to national liberation, and the other a movement led by western capitalism to manage and control third world countries seen to be in need of economic development. There is considerable literature regarding women in the third world; here the emphasis is primarily on economic development (and especially on the importance of women's incorporation into the development process).

The use of the term *third* (or *fourth*) is problematic on two main counts: first is the Eurocentric reference to "developed" market economies as first (that is, better); second is the sweeping generalization *third world* implied by the term, because it ignores the vast differences among third world countries and the women and men within them.

See Also

DEVELOPMENT: OVERVIEW; ECONOMICS: FEMINIST CRITIQUES; ECONOMY: GLOBAL RESTRUCTURING

References and Further Reading

Berger, Mark T. 1993. Global liberalization? Rethinking the "third world" after the cold war. *Journal of Pacific Studies* 17: 4–37.

Cora Vellekoop Baldock

THIRD WORLD WOMEN:
Selected Resources

Interest in the study of women in developing countries and areas increased during the last two decades of the twentieth century—especially after the United Nations Fourth World Conference on Women, held in Beijing, China, in 1995. Integrating awareness of gender issues within international development projects and within developing countries has been growing as well since the early 1970s.

Until approximately 1980, many organizations and governments that collected statistics too frequently did not even measure factors of great importance to women's lives. More frequently, statistics on important life matters were not disaggregated by sex.

The impact of gender issues in the developing world is felt in such arenas as health care, ecology, education, law, banking, and national economic planning. Obvious improvements in communication technologies, along with the work of the United Nations and its allied agencies, make it far more feasible to be aware of what is happening in the developing world, but one must also be aware of history and context.

As women's studies programs and scholars become more international in scope, the demand for information on women and gender issues in the developing world grows. The following is a highly selective, annotated listing of research resources about women in developing countries and areas.

For more extensive research purposes, see Beth Stafford, *Women in international development: A research guide to reference sources in the social sciences,* to be published by Libraries Unlimited in 2001.

Selected On-Line Resources:
Major Sources Focusing on Women and Gender Issues

1. WomenWatch: the United Nations Gateway on the Advancement and Empowerment of Women <Http://www.un.org/womenwatch>. This is a joint project of the United Nations Division for the Advancement of Women (DAW), the U.N. Development Fund for Women (UNIFEM), and the U.N. International Research and Training Institute for the Advancement of women (INSTRAW). It provides access to a variety of types of information on women and gender issues, including worldwide statistics. Major divisions of this Web page include the U.N. Working for Women (U.N. entities and intergovernmental and treaty bodies); U.N. Global Conferences and Women (conferences and follow-up); Women of the World (regional and country plans of action); News and Views (events at the United Nations and elsewhere; and Global Forum (selected nongovernmental organizations' Web sites).

Within each division is access to an estimated several hundred documents issued by the United Nations and numerous of its regional (for example, the Economic Commission for Africa) and other entities. Many full-text documents are available via these means.

2. Contemporary Women's Issues (CWI). Provides full-text access to journals, hard-to-find newsletters, reports, pamphlets, and more regarding a broad array of gender-related issues (for example, economic development, human rights, law, health, and violence). CWI has excellent international coverage of English-language titles from more than

150 countries, comprising more than 30,000 items. It covers publications from 1988 to the present and is updated weekly. Most materials are activist oriented.

3. Women's Resources International. This bibliographical resource combines 10 databases from a variety of sources. In particular the POPLINE Subset on Women emphasizes the health and social concerns of women in the developing world. Most materials cited are in the social sciences. One database, Women's Health and Development, is based on the holdings of the World Health Organization (WHO) library in Switzerland. Some databases cover from 1964 and the 1970s to the present, for a total of more than 232,000 references.

Major Resources That Include Materials
on Women and Gender Issues

1. Bibliography of Asian Studies (BAS). Sponsored by the Association for Asian Studies and housed at the University of Michigan in Ann Arbor, this resource covers western-language monographs, articles, and book chapters on all areas in Asia that have been published since 1971. The database can be searched by subject, by journal title, or by individual country. It covers 32 countries in east asia, southeast Asia, and south Asia.

2. ABSEES Online (American Bibliography of Slavic and East European Studies). A bibliographic database of journal articles, books, book chapters, book reviews, dissertations, and selected government publications published in the United States and Canada about east-central Europe and the former Soviet Union. Can be searched by subject heading as well as by author, title, publisher, and date of publication. Also has full-record keyword searching. It includes more than 36,000 records of materials published since 1990 and is maintained by the University of Illinois Library in Urbana-Champaign.

3. African Studies Centre. This bibliographic database reflects the library collection of the Afrika Studie Centrum (African Studies Centre) in Leiden, the Netherlands, a government-funded agency. It includes titles of monographs, journal articles, and chapters in edited books acquired since 1988. Most entries include professional abstracts. The collection is especially strong in the social sciences and covers both north and sub-Saharan Africa.

4. HAPI Online (Hispanic-American Periodicals Index). HAPI Online and the annual printed AHispanic-American Periodicals Index@ are produced by the University of California, Los Angeles Latin American Center. This bibliographical database makes available mostly scholarly information about Central and South America, Mexico, the Caribbean, the United States–Mexico border area, and His-

panics in the United States. It includes journal articles, book reviews, documents, original literary works, and other materials, regardless of country of publication. Emphasis is on the social sciences and humanities materials published in the western world since 1970. The growth of feminist scholarship in the field is clearly apparent. Keyword searching by author, title, subject, or journal title and combined keywords from more than one discipline is done easily. Searching can be delimited by date of publication, language, or articles about U.S. Hispanics. This database includes materials in English, Spanish, Portuguese, French, Italian, and German, and foreign-language materials can be searched with English keywords. Many articles are available from HAPI via document delivery.

5. Latin America Database. A news and information service produced at the University of New Mexico, this database consists of three news bulletins covering politics, economics, human rights, indigenous issues, and other issues that are not covered in the English-language mainstream press. They are SourceMex on Mexico, NotiCen on Central America and the Caribbean, and NotiSur on South America. Articles are by journalists experienced in writing about the region. The fully searchable on-line archive is updated weekly.

Printed Resources

What follows is a brief sampling, by no means complete, of selected types of existing resources on women in the developing world, which are available in printed format. These examples are representative of the various sorts of printed resources available.

Global focus:
Stromquist, Nelly P. 1998. *Women in the third world: An encyclopedia of contemporary issues.* New York: Garland.

This is a major reference tool for the study of women in the developing world. Articles range from feminist epistemology and research methods to women and literacy to women's participation in science and technology. It has a subject index and includes five appendixes of statements, such as the Beijing Declaration.

Seager, Joni. 1997. *The state of women in the world atlas.* London: Penguin.

This excellent work illustrates graphically, in the form of political maps of the world, the state of women in regard to 12 different life factors such as domestic violence and population policies, and gains and losses since the mid-1980s.

As an example, there is a map of the global sex trade shows—which are the main source countries of sex tourists, with their main destinations, and more. Each map is supplemented by a brief essay on its individual topic. There is also a world table on life indicators and a subject index.

Regional focus:
Rolfes, Irene. 1992. *Women in the Caribbean: A bibliography, 1986–1990.* Leiden, The Netherlands: Royal Institute of Linguistics and Anthropology (KITLV).

This is a bibliography of more than 1,500 monographs, book chapters, unpublished dissertations, conference papers, masters' theses, journal articles, and more about women in the Caribbean islands, Belize, Guyana, Suriname, and French Guyana. Items are not annotated. An index provides access to materials via authors, editors, organizations, subjects, and geographic locations.

National focus:
Ardayfio-Schandorf, Elizabeth. 1990. *Women in Ghana: An annotated bibliography.* Accra: Woeli.

This annotated bibliography includes books, journal articles, conference papers, book chapters, reports, and unpublished papers on women in Ghana. Each item includes subject descriptors as well as full citations. Nine major sections on such topics as Law and Politics, Health and Nutrition, and Agriculture and Environment define the organization of this work. Author and subject indexes complete the work.

Cultural, ethnic, or religious focus:
Meghdessian, Samira Rafidi. 1980. *The status of the Arab woman: A select bibliography.* London: Mansell.

This guide, produced under the auspices of the Institute for Women's Studies in the Arab World in Beirut, Lebanon, provides access to research materials on the economic, religious, legal and social status of twentieth-century Arab women. It includes more than 1,600 titles about all Arab countries in the Middle East and north Africa. One can find materials about women in the Arab world generally or by individual country. There are author and subject indexes.

Statistical focus:
Economic and Social Commission for Asia and the Pacific. 1997. *Women in Fiji: A country profile.* New York: United Nations.

Part of a series on 19 Asian and Pacific countries analyzing available statistical data and information on women and men in the family, at work, and in public life. Each profile is prepared by an expert from each country, with an introductory overview and analysis for each indicator measured. It has multiple tables, figures, and annex tables on such indicators as average income of paid workers in the informal agricultural sector by sex.

See Also

INFORMATION REVOLUTION; INFORMATION TECHNOLOGY; LIBRARIES; NETWORKS: ELECTRONIC; PUBLISHING; *and* PUBLISHING: FEMINIST PUBLISHING IN THE THIRD WORLD

Beth Stafford

THIRD-WAVE FEMINISM

See FEMINISM: THIRD-WAVE.

TORTURE

Consider these three scenarios:

Emanuel, a middle-ranking cadre of a rebel group, is arrested and put in prison. The state authorities want information on the whereabouts of his leader and the group's plans to sabotage the impending visit of a foreign dignitary. In custody, he is chained, beaten badly, burned with cigarettes, stabbed, and forced to eat feces. The purpose of inflicting such pain on Emanuel is to get him to speak and provide information that he may have about his leader and the sabotage plans.

The rebel leaders capture Maria, Emanuel's wife. She is not a member of the rebel group but is suspected to have some papers the officials want. The leaders want to make sure that these papers do not fall in the hands of officials, in the event that Emanuel breaks down. Emanuel dreads the prospect of his wife in captivity with the rebel group. He knows how the leaders and cadres of the group treat women in such circumstances. In captivity she is sexually abused and raped repeatedly by the leaders and other members of the group.

Jane lives with her husband, who beats her up every day. If she does or says something he does not like, he beats her. If she does nothing at all, he still beats her. He beats her until she is on the floor, hardly able to get up. If she does, he knocks her down again. She thinks having a child will make him more responsible toward his family. The beating continues even when she is pregnant. He beats and kicks her pregnant belly, until one day she miscarries. She is never able to predict when the next blow will come or how severe it will be. She is in a perpetual state of terror and lives in constant fear of him.

Definitions of Torture

Torture, as defined in international treaties and conventions (such as the Declaration on the Protection of All Persons from Being Subjected to Torture and Other Cruel, Inhuman, or Degrading Treatment or Punishment; the Convention Against Torture and Other Cruel, Inhuman, or Degrading Treatment or Punishment; or the Convention for the Prevention of Torture and Inhuman or Degrading Treatment or Punishment), has three main elements:

- Intentional infliction of severe mental or physical pain or suffering
- By a public official or on his behalf
- For the purpose of obtaining information or to punish a person

Scenario one clearly meets all the elements of torture as defined above. Torture is inflicted on Emanuel intentionally by officials of the prison to obtain information about the activities of the rebel group. Strictly speaking, scenario two does not meet the elements of torture, neither for Emanuel nor for Maria, despite the fact that both are being tortured. Knowing that his wife is in the custody of the rebel group is torturous for Emanuel, but that torture is not inflicted by state officials. Maria is tortured for the purpose of obtaining papers, but again by rebel leaders and not by state officials. Scenario three does not meet any of the elements of torture as listed above.

A critical review of the definition of torture from the experiences of people all over the world, and particularly those of women, reveals its inadequacies in its understanding of the crime of torture. The essence of the crime of torture is the infliction of an extreme sense of terror and powerlessness on a person. The acts of inflicting pain or suffering, such as physical violence or injury, exposures to extreme violence, or witnessing grotesque death, are only means of torture. In any such act, the salient characteristic of the event is its power to inspire helplessness and terror (Herman, 1997: 34).

Torture is used not just to hurt physically but also to humiliate the victim. Rape and pain inflicted on the genitals are therefore the most commonly used forms of torture. Yet rape and other forms of sexual violence directed at women have been considered only as "inhuman treatment," whereas inflicting pain on men's genitals was considered torture. This is a reflection of the general and universal discriminatory attitude on the issue of sexual and domestic violence against women in day-to-day life. For women to speak about sexual violence is to invite public humiliation, ridicule, and disbelief. Fear and shame silence women, and their silence gives a license to the practice of sexual violence (Herman, 1997: 28), which is then reflected in the lawmaking process and reinforced in the law-implementing process. *Jean Akayasu* v. *Prosecutor*, a case decided in 1998 by the International Criminal Tribunal for Rwanda (ICTR), is among the few cases that made a comparison of rape to torture. "Like torture, rape is used for such purposes as intimidation, degradation, humiliation, discrimination, punishment, control or destruction of a person.... Rape is violation of personal dignity, and...in fact constitutes torture when inflicted by or at the instigation of or with the consent or acquiescence of a public official or other person acting in an official capacity" (1999).

Another serious gap in the understanding and definition of the crime of torture stems from the fact that Maria's rape in scenario two would not constitute torture. Human rights law as stated in the conventions has led to an exclusive focus on violations of civil and political rights by state actors, and a refusal to acknowledge violations by nonstate actors.

Many nonstate rebel or opposition groups around the world, whether or not engaged in international or internal war, increasingly use torture in pursuit of their political ends. Torture is used as a means of attaining political power and intimidating nonconforming populations. Human rights organizations have contributed to this state of affairs by not documenting violations by nonstate actors. As a result, such groups have freely engaged in all kind of violations with no accountability. Thus, despite the fact that Maria was held captive and tortured by the rebel leaders to obtain papers they suspected she had, the injuries she suffered are not considered torture. If Maria survives the torture, she might have recourse to charge the rebel leaders with torture under their national law. However, by virtue of being parties to international treaties and conventions, many countries have definitions in their national laws similar to the international law for crimes such as torture and therefore still exclude torture by nonstate actors. Moreover, scenarios one and two describe the relationship between Emanuel and the state, and under such circumstances Emanuel and his family cannot reasonably expect to have a fair trial under the national legal system.

The real issue of inquiry from a gender perspective is whether scenario three—that is, domestic violence—is or can be considered torture. If we analyze domestic violence using the three elements of the crime of torture, domestic violence does not "obviously" meet those criteria. More specifically, it does not seem to meet two of them. State officials or other persons acting on behalf of the state are not the perpetrators intentionally inflicting the torture, nor is the act necessarily for the purpose of obtaining information. The question that therefore arises from the inadequacies of the understanding of torture as discussed above is whether the framework provided by the elements of the crime in international conventions is adequate.

Torture is not only the criminal act per se; it encompasses the objective and the impact: that is, terror, intimidation, and ultimate submission of the victim. As in torture, in domestic violence the sense of terror is instilled by use of escalating physical brutality such as beating, kicking, slashing, burning, and so on. In addition, domestic violence often accompanies sexual abuse in many forms, including insertion of objects into the woman's vagina, forced oral sex, anal sex, sex with others, with animals, and so on. Sometimes women are terrorized not by overt brutality but by other means that destroy the sense of autonomy and of control of bodily functions. Purely psychological means of threat to kill, mutilate, or torture the woman or others she cares about sometimes have greater traumatic impact on the victim than physical brutality itself (Copelon, 1994: 123). In fact, it was discovered that the psychological syndrome seen in survivors of rape, domestic battery, and incest was essentially the same as the syndrome seen in the survivors of war, and that the most common posttraumatic disorders are the result not of trauma suffered by men in war but of trauma suffered by women in civilian life (Herman, 1997: 34).

Torture is understood as an intentional act. Batterers often argue that their acts are done not intentionally but impulsively. The mental element required to prove any violent acts requires only that the perpetrator knew or should have known that the act would cause the harm. From that perspective the added intentional requirement is not necessary either in torture or in domestic violence. Furthermore, there is an inadequacy in restricting the crime of torture only to state officials or persons acting on their behalf as possible perpetrators. The understanding of "state official," however, can be stretched to encompass the categories of perpetrators who meet the essence of what the "state official" embodies. That is, torture is also an extreme exercise of domination by those in authority or power to force submission of those over whom they have power. The element of state official involvement can therefore include those in authority or a position of power who abuse their authority or power. Domestic violence is a means of keeping women in subordinate status and a terrorist effort at domination. Batterers, therefore, fall squarely in the category of someone in a position of power in relation to the victims.

The most common distinction between torture and domestic violence or other inhuman treatment is that torture has a specific purpose—to obtain information or to punish. If torture is increasingly understood as a means of terrorizing and an act of domination, however, the element of purpose becomes redundant. Rhonda Copelon claims that the notion of torture as an act in pursuit of confession or information, unlike domestic violence, is mistaken: "Whether precipitated by rage, jealousy, or a real or feared loss of control, domestic violence has its own interrogation—questions, accusations, insults and orders: Where were you today? Who were you with? Who visited you? What do you mean you want to go out to work? Why is the coffee cold? the house a mess? this item moved? What the confession is to torture, the explanation, the accounting-for-oneself, the apology, the begging is to domestic violence" (1994: 131). Whereas one may start by wondering if this analogy is far-fetched, on closer examination one cannot but agree with it. Still, domestic violence can happen without any questioning. It is therefore strategic to stay with the redundancy of the "purpose element," rather than argue that domestic violence, too, encompasses "purpose." Women are battered because of the batterer's loss of esteem, power, or control in his public sphere and sometimes for no reason at all. It is still torture.

Torture is an egregious form of violation of fundamental rights, that is, the right to freedom from fear and terror. International law is inadequate to deal with situations of torture that women around the world experience routinely. International law claims to deal with crimes that are extraordinary experiences, and violence against women is so routine that hundreds of thousands of women experience it daily. But that fact makes it an extraordinary criminal act, which deserves the serious attention of the international community. Until such time as violence against women is accorded the same seriousness as crimes such as torture for the purpose of charging and prosecution, these crimes will remain egregious in form and content and will continue to be relegated to the category of "private problem," not deserving public attention.

See Also

DOMESTIC VIOLENCE; INTERNATIONAL ORGANIZATIONS AND AGENCIES; RAPE; SEXUAL VIOLENCE; VIOLENCE AND PEACE: OVERVIEW

References and Further Reading

Copelon, Rhonda. 1994. Intimate terror: Understanding domestic violence as torture. In Rebecca J. Cook, ed., *Human rights of women: National and international perspectives*, 116–152. Philadelphia: University of Pennsylvania Press.

Fitzpatrick, Joan. 1994. The use of international human rights norms to combat violence against women. In Rebecca J. Cook, ed., *Human rights of women: National and international perspectives*. Philadelphia: University of Pennsylvania Press.

Herman, Judith. 1997. *Trauma and recovery.* New York: Basic Books.

Pope, Nicole. 1999. Torture. In Roy Gutman and David Rieff, eds., *Crimes of war: What the public should know,* 352. New York: Norton.

Prosecutor vs. Jean-Paul Akayesu. 1999. Case No. ICTR-96-4-T. *Judgment by Trial Chamber of the United Nations ad hoc International Criminal Tribunal for Rwanda.*

Roth, Kenneth. 1994. Domestic violence as an international human rights issue. In Rebecca J. Cook, ed., *Human rights of women: National and international perspectives*. Philadelphia: University of Pennsylvania Press.

United Nations Convention Against Torture and Other Cruel, Inhuman, or Degrading Treatment or Punishment. 1987. Entered in force on 26 June 1987 in accordance with Article 27(1) of UN General Assembly resolution 39/46 of 10 December 1984.

Vahida Nainar

TOURISM

History of Western Tourism

The word *tourist* first occurred in the English language in the late eighteenth century, as a synonym for traveler. Since then tourism has come to refer to traveling for recreation as opposed, for example, to traveling for business or exploration. Tourism is not a new activity, although large-scale tourism is a fairly recent phenomenon. In the second century C.E., wealthy Romans took holiday excursions, called *peregrinatio,* to Riviera resort towns, Delphi, Troy, and Egypt (Feifer, 1985). For most people throughout history, however, a motive other than pleasure—for example, commerce, family visits, or religion—was required for travel.

A *pilgrimage*—a word derived from *peregrinatio*—is a journey to a sacred site. For millennia, pilgrims all over the world have traveled to shrines for numerous reasons, including supplication, fulfillment of vows, healing, penance, and, to some extent, what we call tourism. In A.D. 385, the wealthy Roman widow Aula traveled with servants and guides to the Holy Land to visit places mentioned in the Bible. Elgeria, a devout woman from northwestern Spain, went alone to Jerusalem and the Near East at about that same time. Her letters (Wilkinson, 1981) provide a fascinating description of her three-year-long journey.

Pilgrimage grew in popularity in the Middle Ages with the construction of impressive cathedrals, the availability of numerous sacred relics, and active marketing campaigns. A network of hospices, improved roads and bridges, travel handbooks, and desirable souvenirs supported this mass phenomenon. Pilgrimage was a sacred journey, but many people undertook it because it provided a socially sanctioned escape from normal life and an opportunity for adventure. Chaucer's *Canterbury Tales* vividly describes a number of pilgrims, including the Wife of Bath.

Medieval women were not forbidden to go on pilgrimage, but they were not encouraged. Pilgrimage was morally ambiguous, because it afforded a unique opportunity to evade community surveillance. A number of pious women were not dissuaded by this ambiguity, however. Friar Felix Faber, a fifteenth-century Italian pilgrim, encountered six elderly European matrons on pilgrimage in the Holy Land. Margery Kempe, a fifteenth-century Englishwoman of intense religious fervor, left her husband and children behind and traveled alone to Palestine. Before she died, she dictated a colorful account of her experiences.

By the fifteenth century, large groups of pilgrim-tourists traveled overland or by sea from England, France, and Germany to the Spanish shrine of St. James the Greater at Santiago de Compostela. More than 500,000 pilgrims visited Santiago annually. Rome had over 1,000 inns and hostels; entertainment included visiting ruins, going to Passion plays, and buying souvenirs. All-inclusive tours from Venice to the Holy Land also were available. Foreign travel—including pilgrimage—remained an exceptional event, however, because it was quite expensive, amounting to a year's customary income for the rich and the bourgeoisie.

As a result of the Reformation, pilgrimage began waning in the sixteenth century, but the Renaissance spirit of exploration and adventure was waxing. A typical British tourist to "the continent" was a young unmarried male, recently graduated from Oxford or Cambridge, and travel abroad was believed to be preparation for government service. Elizabethan tourists brought back new ideas in commerce and statesmanship, as well as new methods of gardening and cooking. By the eighteenth century, taking the "grand tour" had gained considerable popularity in England, and young men just graduated from a university went to the continent with servants, lots of luggage, and often ineffective chaperones. The "continental finishing school" was supposed to provide them with grace, ease, and refinement. At the turn of the nineteenth century, they were joined by the English Romantic tourist, "that rare hybrid of rakish flamboyance and pastoral innocence" (Feifer, 1985: 135). Percy Bysshe Shelley, Mary Shelley, and Lord Byron set the mood of emotional intensity, excess, and social exile. The adventurous Lady Caroline Craven, who wore the opulent attire of a Turkish man, and the formidable Lady Hester Stanhope traveled where no Englishwomen had gone before—but they did not travel together.

By the mid–nineteenth century, the grand tour had come to include the whole family. The upwardly mobile in the United States and England often used the grand tour to attempt to gain access to a higher social class than they could at home. Another social class also began traveling at this time. Because of the industrial revolution, many workers were now free to leave the land and take vacations. Better highways and coaches made travel faster and more comfortable, and the railroad revolutionized and helped democratize travel.

In 1841 the Englishman Thomas Cook invented the modern tourist industry; soon he began organizing all-inclusive tours to the Rhineland, Switzerland, and Italy, and by 1869 there were Cook's Tours to the Holy Land and Egypt. A trip abroad was a bold step for the Victorian woman, but many were eager to take one under the safe guidance of a Cook's tour, with the result that women "Cookites" soon significantly outnumbered men. Guidebooks filled with advice and cautions were published; large-scale hotels and restaurants were developed; and a range of travel goods was produced, including miniature sewing kits, portable baths, and hot water bottles.

By the twentieth century, tourism had become increasingly popular. The wealthy, as always, demanded luxury: fine passenger ships, elegant railway cars, and exclusive hotels. The middle and working classes demanded, and got, good value for money. Then came the Great Depression and the world wars. But tourism rebounded, assisted by the development of commercial airlines.

Tourism was the world's biggest growth industry in 1967. People of all classes and all ages wanted to take vacations—to "get away from it all," to experience "something different." In response, tourist attractions sprang up everywhere, along with a burgeoning network of travel agents eager to offer all-inclusive package tours. One result of these package tours was the preselection (and even artificial creation) of what was worth seeing, often resulting in a fabricated world glimpsed from a safe distance.

A new kind of tourist began to develop, one Maxine Feifer (1985) calls the "postmodern tourist." This traveler is quite independent and recognizes the difference between the glossy tourist brochure and reality. Although the postmodern tourist wants to participate in world culture rather than see it from a distance, she or he is also aware of the social, political, cultural, and economic implications of tourism.

Theoretical Issues

By the mid–nineteenth century, *tourist* began to acquire a negative connotation and to stand in contrast to *traveler*. *Traveler* exemplified independence and originality; *tourist* embodied caution, pampering, and traveling en masse. Today that negative image remains: few people want to be called tourists, preferring instead to be called travelers.

Tourism involves a series of temporary relationships with other people and, often, other cultures. The degree of engagement and its impact vary enormously, depending on the tourist and the kind of tourism. Categories include sun-and-sand, ecological, "extreme" adventure, family recreation, cultural, and humanitarian-service-project tourism—to name just a few. Most tourists (including those who prefer to be called travelers) participate in several kinds of tourism.

A number of critiques of tourism have been written. Nelson Graburn (1989) suggests that tourism is a journey from the profane into the sacred, a quest for an experience of renewal. Other writers have presented a less benign view. Jeremy Boissevian (1996) writes that tourists seek a change from their ordinary, alienated lives, which may include a temporary shedding of identity and behavioral norms. In the process government agencies and private enterprise, often without input from or permission of the locals, commoditize local cultural resources (for example, rituals, historic sites, art forms), turning them into objects divested of deeper meaning.

Dean MacCannell examines the impact of tourism on remote regions of the world, which has resulted in the construction of hotels, restaurants, and transportation systems as well as in "restorations of ancient shrines, development of local handicrafts for sale to tourists, and rituals performed for tourists" (1992: 1). He states that "tourism is an ideological framing of history, nature, and tradition" (1992: 1). In ethnic tourism, people's lives become the attraction in a relationship based on hierarchy, inequality, and manipulation.

The object of the tourist's gaze, however, is not helpless: tourists may be covertly or overtly critiqued, ridiculed, misled, or abused by the people they come to see.

Tourism is a complex interaction between the tourist's culture and that of the people with whom the tourist interacts. Although tourism inevitably results in cultural change, this change is not always negative. For example, a tourist may gain a deeper appreciation of cultural or ecological diversity. Tourism may promote enhanced self-awareness and solidarity among those being visited. This, in turn, may lead to either authentic revitalization or staged authenticity. The opposite also may occur: inhabitants of isolated destinations may be eager to change their traditional lifestyle and emulate that of the tourist, thus destroying the very thing that brought tourists to them.

Though gender issues are a reality of tourism, they are extremely complex, involving not only intercultural perceptions and expectations but also intracultural ones. Tourists of either sex may offend local dress and behavior codes, through ignorance or arrogance, and members of the host country may behave in ways that puzzle, denigrate, or even threaten tourists. Sometimes these actions and reactions are based on gender; sometimes they are based on the inequalities of other power relationships (for example, colonialism or military occupation). In addition, complex negotiations of traditional female roles may be required in order to meet the service needs of tourists.

On the Greek island of Skyros, topless sunbathers outraged the villagers. Soon Skyrians developed a defensive strategy: they directed would-be nudists to a secluded beach, which they called the "Nudist Beach." Eventually, the Skyrians grew accustomed to seeing foreigners in provocative attire. The presence of tourists initially resulted in Skyrian girls' being more strictly chaperoned; gradually, however, girls and older women have gained more freedom of movement than ever before as a result of tourism (Zarkia, 1996). In Malta, where women make up more than one-third of the official workforce, tourism has accentuated domestic and moral pressures on women. A number of women work as chambermaids in hotels, but such employment was initially thought to put their moral purity (and that of their families) at risk. By using parish priests to help supervise young working women, acceptable social control was provided. (Black, 1996).

Impact of Tourism: Some Examples

In the latter part of the nineteenth century, the Fred Harvey Company, in conjunction with the Atchison, Topeka, and Santa Fe Railroad, opened the American Southwest to mass tourism. At the same time it fostered a coherent, persistent, and inaccurate view of Native Americans as "'living ruins' from the childhood of civilization" (Dilworth, 1996: 79). Although its principle activity was operating restaurants and dining cars, the Fred Harvey Company also bought and sold Indian-made objects. Through extensive promotion, the company developed a national market for Indian art. Two women artisans, the Navajo weaver Elle and the Hopi-Tewa potter Nampeyo, became celebrated tourist attractions for the Harvey Company. Other women also benefited from Harvey-sponsored tourism. By the end of World War II, some 100,000 "Harvey Girls" had worked for the Harvey Company as waitresses and tour guides. They were immigrants, widows, from cites and from farms—women eager to earn their own money, have an adventure, and, sometimes, find a husband.

According to Michal Smith's study of the impact of tourism on rural women in 12 southeastern states in the United States (1989), service-sector jobs in tourism grew rapidly but were exploitive. Employment as food servers, maids, and retail clerks offered women only minimal wages, marginal benefits, and virtually no advancement. The government's encouragement of tourism resulted in destruction of the environment and local culture, raised the cost of living, and strained the communities' infrastructures. The economic rewards gained by tourist industries did not trickle down to the service providers.

The Greek island Skyros was opened for tourism in 1973; by 1994, mass tourism had changed practically every aspect of social life, including reorganizing the use of land and its value (Zarkia, 1996). The poor had owned previously undesirable land by the beach, which they now exploited for tourism, giving them access to financial resources and power. They were the first to take in guests, build restaurants, and convert tiny workplaces into souvenir shops. Approximately half the guest houses are owned by women, many of whom have converted their dowry houses into income-producing resources. However, this traditional matrilinial transmission is now perceived to threaten male status and men are beginning to object. As a result, economic opportunities for women based on tourism have led to undesirable inheritance conflicts. The value of women's property has risen, but their power has not.

At first Skyros residents treated tourists as honored strangers and guests, for whom the women of the house felt a moral obligation. But tourism soon produced a radical change in this relationship. In the late 1960s, for example, one elderly woman offered a tourist a glass of water and, after an exchange of conversation, invited him to stay with her as a houseguest. When he left, he insisted on paying, much to her confusion and despite her protests. Over the next few years, he sent more tourists to stay with her, who also insisted on paying. Gradually she changed from being a host to being a service provider. Although she was able to earn much-needed money, she also had to provide services to clients that she would not have provided for guests. A relationship based on cultural values had changed to one based on money.

Tourists may be drawn to a particular community because of its reputation for "sun, sea, sand, and sex." Sex tourism occurs not only in third world countries but also in Europe, the United States, and Australia: tourists seek out the brothel districts in Amsterdam, Hamburg—and the state of Nevada—as well as in the Philippines, Sri Lanka, Pakistan, and Thailand. Rather than being a cause of prostitution (including child prostitution), tourism is now thought to be a contributing and perpetuating factor. Underlying causes include indigenous cultural mores, including the "institutionalized exploitation of women within patriarchal societies" (Hall, 1992), and the impact of colonialism, military activity, and economic upheaval. Because a number of developing countries rely economically on sex tourism, significant change can occur only if economic, power, and gender relationships are radically transformed. It should be remembered, however, that the "sexually predatory" tourist is not always a man looking for a female prostitute; sometimes it is a man looking for a male prostitute, or a woman looking for a sexual liaison. Nor is the predator always the tourist.

See Also

CULTURE: OVERVIEW; TRAVEL WRITING

References and Further Reading

Black, Annabel. 1996. Negotiating the tourist gaze: The example of Malta. In Jeremy Boissevain, ed., *Coping with tourists: European reaction to mass tourism*, 112–142. Providence, R.I.: Berghahn.

Boissevain, Jeremy, ed. 1996. *Coping with tourists: European reactions to mass tourism*. Providence, R.I.: Berghahn.

Dilworth, Leah. 1996. *Imagining Indians in the Southwest: Persistent visions of a primitive past*. Washington, D.C.: Smithsonian Institution.

Feifer, Maxine. 1985. *Tourism in history: From imperial Rome to the present*. New York: Stein and Day.

Graburn, Nelson. 1989. Tourism: The sacred journey. In V. Smith, ed., *Hosts and guests: The anthropology of tourism*, 2nd ed., 21–36. Philadelphia: University of Pennsylvania Press.

Hall, C. Michael. 1992. Sex tourism in southeast Asia. In David Harrison, ed., *Tourism and the less developed countries*, 64–74. London: Belhaven.

MacCannell, Dean. 1992. *Empty meeting grounds: The tourist papers*. New York and London: Routledge.

Smith, Michal. 1989. *Behind the glitter: The impact of tourism on rural women in the southeast*. Lexington, Ky.: Southeast Women's Employment Coalition.

Wilkinson, John. 1981. *Egeria's travels to the Holy Land*. Rev ed. Warminster, England: Aris and Phillips.

Zarkia, Cornélia. 1996. Philoxenia: Receiving tourists—but not guests—on a Greek island. In Jeremy Boissevain, ed., *Coping with tourists: European reaction to mass tourism*, 143–173. Providence, R.I.: Berghahn.

Elyn Aviva

TOXICOLOGY

Toxicology is the study of harmful effects of chemicals or radiation on biological (living) systems; it is the science of poisons. Poisons (toxicants) are chemical, physical, or biological substances that are harmful to biological systems. Toxicants naturally produced or derived from biological sources are termed *toxins;* organisms producing toxins include bacteria and plants. Toxicants not naturally produced are called *xenobiotics;* examples include pesticides, food additives, industrial chemicals, environmental pollutants, and household poisons. As a discipline, toxicology includes the identification of toxic substances and determining how they disrupt biological systems. Thus, toxicology requires an understanding of biological mechanisms. Toxicology provides essential information for protecting humans, other organisms, and the environment from harmful effects of chemicals and radiation. Along with other sciences, toxicology provides knowledge for safer use of chemicals, for example, in food, medicine, industry, and agriculture. Toxicologists provide a valuable service to society and the environment.

Toxicology is not a new field. From earliest times, humans have been aware of such natural poisons as snake venom and poisonous plants and minerals, such as arsenic and lead, and have used toxins for both destructive and beneficial purposes. Poisons were used in hunting to obtain food for survival; they have also been used for executions, suicides, and political assassinations. In fact, homicides and suicides by poisoning were quite common in Europe for centuries.

The practice of using poisonous substances for executions was common in other cultures as well. As early as 1500 B.C.E. in ancient Egypt, Papyrus identified vegetable and mineral poisons and described the harmful effects of opium, hemlock, lead, copper, and antimony. In 400 B.C.E., Xenophon wrote that the use of poisons was so widespread that it was common practice for a cupbearer to taste wine before presenting it to the nobility. A famous victim of poisoning was the Greek philosopher Socrates, who reportedly was condemned to commit suicide in 399 B.C.E. by drinking hemlock. Hypocrates, a contemporary of Socrates, believed, as did other Greek physicians, that environmental factors caused disease. A popular medical practice at the time was to purge the body by drugs or diet to restore health; purging was the treatment of choice for accidental poisoning. Today, the idea of cleansing the body of xenobiotics in order to restore health is reminiscent of these earlier practices. In 185–135 B.C.E., the personal physician to the king of Bithynia reportedly studied poisonous plants and animals and their antidotes by experimenting on condemned criminals. In 50 C.E., Discordes wrote *Materia Medica*, classifying all known poisons according to their origin: animal, plant, or mineral. His writings remained the definitive work on poisons for the next 15 centuries.

Concurrently, the Chinese were also contributing to the field of toxicology. The Chinese emperor Shen Nung, considered the father of Chinese medicine and agriculture, is credited with writing a 40-volume text listing poisons and antidotes in 2735 B.C.E. In addition to producing the most complete list of drugs and poisons, the early Chinese contributed to the field of toxicology by using the concept of circulating blood to provide a new understanding of how poisons spread throughout the body. Nung is also credited with the elucidation of the principle of yin and yang, two opposing forces responsible for creating balance, including ebb and flow, male and female, life and death. Health was considered to result from balance among forces and elements, a concept that still has proponents today. The milestones described represent just a few of the many examples of the understanding that existed in early history of the power of toxicants.

Modern history is full of examples of the growing sophistication and development of the field of toxicology. In the 1500s, Paracelsus, considered the "father of toxicology," established the foundation of toxicology by describing the concept of dose response. He wrote in his *Third Defense* of the importance of dose in determining toxic versus therapeutic effects. Paracelsus is best remembered for positing the following thesis:

- All substances are poisons.
- There is none that is not poison.
- The right dose differentiates a poison from a remedy.

Others expanded his thesis to include concepts such as no-effect level, threshold, extrapolation, and dose-response relationships, ideas that remain an integral part of the present structure of toxicology. Paracelsus's other contributions include the concept of target organ toxicity, the use of animal experimentation to study the effects of chemicals, and the use of inorganic salts in medicine. Following Paracelsus's principles, the Italian-born Frenchman M.-J.-B. Orfila formally incorporated analytical techniques into toxicology in the late 1700s. He recognized toxicology as an independent science, and in 1814 wrote a treatise describing a systematic correlation between chemical and biological characteristics of certain poisons. He also devised methods for detecting poisons and pointed out the necessity of chemical analysis for legal proof of poisoning, the beginning of forensic toxicology. Thus, by 1800, toxicology had evolved from a field concerned only with cataloging poisons and antidotes to one concerned with identifying and quantifying human risk from exposures. By the late 1800s, Claude Bernard further developed the field by investigating the mechanisms by which toxic effects were produced.

Women in Toxicology

Little documentation exists of women's roles in the history of toxicology. This omission was symptomatic of society in general at that time and is reflected in the histories of other disciplines as well. Unfortunately, the few stories that were told placed women in a negative light. For example, lore has it that during the Middle Ages, Catherine de Médicis used her knowledge of poisons to advise wives on how to eliminate their husbands, a "skill" she perfected through experimentation. Under the guise of helping the sick and poor, Catherine tested toxic concoctions, carefully noting the rapidity of the toxic response (onset of action), the effectiveness of the compound (potency), the degree of response of the different parts of the body (specificity, site of action), and the complaints of the victim (clinical signs and symptoms). Catherine's experiments culminated in the establishment of a commercial poisoning service in France operated by Catherine Deshayes, known as "La Voisine," who was executed by Louis XIV after being convicted of numerous poisonings.

Although few positive examples exist, the most significant woman associated with the field of toxicology, Rachel Carson, is world-famous and is considered the "mother of the environmental movement." In 1962 Carson wrote the controversial book *Silent Spring*, describing the devastating effects of pesticides (especially DDT) on flora and fauna of North America. Her work focused public attention on the harmful effects of toxic chemicals on the environment. *Silent Spring* was an angry book designed to stun the reader and stir the public and scientific communities to action. Carson did not advocate abandoning all chemical pesticides; rather she attacked their widespread indiscriminate use. She preferred an ecological approach to pesticide use, emphasizing a biological understanding of nature and natural systems, use of biological agents, and methods of agriculture that worked in harmony with nature. Her writings catalyzed the formation of the Environmental Protection Agency (EPA) in 1970 by the United States government.

Today, the scope of modern toxicology has expanded, and its impact on women's health issues continues to be significant. For example, all medicines, food additives, and agricultural and industrial products are studied for toxic effects. If toxicities are discovered, the compound is carefully scrutinized to determine whether its beneficial effects are greater than its detrimental effects in the dose range that would occur in the environment. This process of risk assessment is influenced by both scientific data and the public's perception of risk. Thus, the intense concern of women regarding the consequences of toxic exposures for their health and the health of their children has spurred development of the field to include regulatory practices.

Occupational and environmental exposures are key targets of women's interest groups, which recognize that toxic responses are often sex-specific; how the body metabolizes and eliminates toxic substances often differs between sexes. In addition, such toxicants as caffeine, alcohol, nicotine, drugs, pesticides, and hormones can easily be transported by mother's milk to infants; many compounds, in fact, concentrate in human milk. In females, toxicants may concentrate in the ovary, affecting unfertilized oocytes. Since the total number of oocytes is fixed at birth, any toxic insult to unfertilized eggs during a woman's reproductive life may be a permanent, irreparable event. Finally, women are keenly aware that a fetus is extremely sensitive to toxic substances: even small amounts of some chemicals, such as thalidomide or mercury, or estrogenic compounds like diethylstilbestrol, can cause birth defects or increased susceptibility to cancer later in life. Thus, toxicological data ultimately must be viewed in terms of the differences in exposure effects between men and women, and the unique sensitivity of the developing fetus. Women's intense interest in the consequences of toxic exposures can be credited with lifting the field of toxicology to the level of prominence it holds today.

See Also

CANCER; ENDOCRINE DISRUPTION; POLLUTION; POLLUTION: CHEMICAL

References and Further Reading

Briggs, Shirley. 1992. *Basic guide to pesticides: Their characteristics and hazards.* Washington, D.C.: Taylor and Francis.

Carson, Rachel. 1962 (1994). *Silent spring.* Boston: Houghton Mifflin.

Rudd, Robert L. 1977. *Environmental toxicology.* Detroit: Gale.

Whorton, James C. *Before silent spring: Pesticides and public health in pre-DDT America.* Princeton, N.J.: Princeton University Press.

Retha Newbold

TRADE UNIONS

See UNION MOVEMENTS.

TRADITIONAL HEALING:
Aboriginal Australia

Before the nineteenth century, when British colonization and ongoing wars between British settlers and Aboriginals initiated changes that had a devastating impact on Aboriginal healing traditions, the lives of women and their families revolved around a comprehensive knowledge of the complex interdependent relationships between the land, plants and animals, and the *jukurrpa* ("dreamtime"). Aboriginal cosmologies centered on this idea of a dream-based reality throughout the cycles of the "walkabout," which took up to a generation to complete. Tribes or troops undertook a hunting-and-gathering journey to sites of water worship and plants, which nourished the families in body and spirit.

Like those of the indigenous peoples of Africa, Europe, and the Americas, ancient carvings such as those found at Uluru (Ayers Rock) near Alice Springs and woodcarvings called *cheringa* detail the customs and rituals of healing, and record the nomadic journey for future generations.

Among Aboriginal peoples, women are revered and autonomous and are charged with the knowledge of healing with plants such as the sacred *emu* (fuschia) administered for colds, flu, pain, and wounds. According to the

feminist author Diane Bell (1982), Aboriginal woman regard the qualities of "health, happiness and harmony" as uniquely intertwined with ceremonies, part of "women's law" (for women only) celebrating the land and women as nurturers of country, people, and relationships. As healing is linked to the land, so are the autonomy, esteem, and identities of Aboriginal women. Colonial policies and practices aimed at separating Aboriginal people from their land contributed to a breakdown in Aboriginal societies, leading to what has been called "intergenerational community trauma" and to grief in response to the effects of colonization and development (Korn, 2000). The loss of traditional rituals, of the land, and of native plants has led some to "self-medication" by chemical and other substances. The traditional plant kava *(Piper methysticum),* combined with alcohol and gasoline, makes a suicidal mixture used by both female and male Aboriginal young people. Because good health has traditionally been seen as dependent on good relationships, men and women have responded to the high rates of substance abuse among Aboriginal youth by taking their children "back to the bush" to initiate them in traditional ways. As the collective esteem of women has been diminished, the whole social fabric has suffered.

Not until the latter part of the twentieth century did Australian law recognize Aboriginal people as human. This initiated a slow process of healing, called "reconciliation," which attempts to allow Aboriginal people to restore and revitalize their traditions.

In response to efforts at reconciliation as part of indigenous peoples' efforts globally to ensure the future of their cultures and medicine ways, a report (Frankel, 1998) was issued on indigenous cultural and intellectual property. This report makes strong statements calling for the creation of a center for traditional medicine at Wujul Wujul to preserve, enhance, and restore the traditional healing practices of Aboriginal peoples in Australia.

See Also

HEALERS; SCIENCE: TRADITIONAL AND INDIGENOUS KNOWLEDGE

References and Further Reading

Bell, Diane. 1982. Women's changing role in health maintenance in a central Australian community. In Janice Reid, ed., *Body, land, and spirit: Health and healing in Aboriginal society,* 197–224. Australia: University of Queensland Press.

Frankel, Michael, and Terri Janke. 1998. *Our culture, our future: Report on Australian indigenous cultural and intellectual prop-*

erty rights. Canberra: Michael Frankel and Company, Solicitors, commissioned by the Australian Institute of Aboriginal and Torres Strait Islander Studies.

Korn, Leslie. 2000. Community trauma and development. *Fourth World Journal* (Spring). <www.cwis.org>

Leslie Korn

TRADITIONAL HEALING: Africa I

Taken as a group, African therapeutic traditions have five distinctive characteristics:

1. They are *empirical* therapies based on careful, though not necessarily "experimental," observation of sickness and remedies.
2. They are *ritualized* therapies entailing deliberately heightened affect on the part of the healer in a symbolic framework that involves singing and dancing with metaphoric uses of natural and cultural objects.
3. They are *collective* therapeutic rites conducted by associations of formerly afflicted persons who have become healers.
4. They involve *divination*—the systematic scrutiny of life events within the rubric of distinctive etiologies and epistemologies or orders of ideas.
5. They are based on concepts of *wellness* that promote health in daily life.

These empirical therapies include midwifery, bonesetting, trephination, and specific interventions for such ailments as lactation deficiency, menstrual disorders, fever, rheumatism, intestinal disorders, and parasites, among others (Feierman, 1992).

In the last forty years of the twentieth century, western biomedicine was adopted by most African governments as the official, publicly funded health care service (Nyamwaya, 1992). Women's health issues include some of the highest rates of maternal mortality and infant mortality in the world, and these are sometimes adversely affected by biomedicine. For example, STDs (sexually transmitted diseases) and HIV (human immunodeficiency virus) are rampant throughout Africa; yet available, funded contraception rarely includes barrier methods that can prevent transmission. Provider-dependent approaches, such as female sterilization, the intrauterine device (IUD), and injectable hormones and implants, which are the most widely available methods of contraception may be harmful to women and do not prevent the spread of STDs and HIV (Visvanathan, 1998).

Illness is explained in many ways in Africa, including biomedical explanations. Yet it is also believed that changes in the weather, bad food, and poisonous substances can cause illness, as can a person's thoughts. Social causes of illness may include a breach of taboo, effects of a curse, or a dishonored oath. Spiritual factors include God's punishment for individual or communal sins, or affliction by ancestor spirits.

Throughout Africa, healers may be either women or men. Women tend to be midwives, but both women and men serve as herbalists and diviners. A few of the distinct regional healing traditions are discussed here.

Kenya

Women healers in Kenya among the Pokot and Samia tribes often serve as traditional birth attendants (TBAs), called *kamaecho* and *omwibusia*, respectively. TBAs, who may have received some training in western medical procedures, combine the work of an obstetrician-gynecologist with that of an herbalist. They examine and advise the pregnant woman on exercise, diet, and appropriate medicines and also help the mother during labor and continue to support her after delivery. Most TBAs are identified and trained on a hereditary basis, and they are the most highly respected branch of indigenous healers today. In Kenya, 75 percent of women rely on TBAs when they are pregnant. Problems with TBAs include the lack of instruments for monitoring the mother's blood pressure and fetal condition, as well as the issue of infection from contaminated materials and instruments.

In Kenya, incisions, scarifications, and excisions are common. These procedures, which include female genital mutilation and surgery, pose risks of infection, hemorrhage, and shock, as well as the very serious possibility of exposure to HIV from shared razor blades or knives when these rituals are performed en masse (Nyamwaya, 1992).

East Central Africa:
Zaire, Tanzania, Mozambique, Zimbabwe

According to traditional beliefs, anything that makes an individual or community weak or dysfunctional places that person or society in a state of danger. Menstruation is considered such a time of danger; a menstruating woman is not supposed to perform some of her normal activities, such as salting the soup, because her condition is believed to make other people susceptible to illness. Newborns are also considered to be in a state of danger in that they are seen as susceptible to sickness. During these times of danger, taboos are believed to protect people.

There are two types of practitioners in east central Africa: those who diagnose only by divination and serve as spirit mediums, and those who provide medicines and do not divine. Only rarely do practitioners practice healing exclusively; usually they also farm, as others do. One becomes a healer through apprenticeship to a practicing family member or an outsider. Sometimes illness precedes the acquisition of healing powers. Often a healer receives treatments in a dream in which ancestral spirits augment the healer's medical skills.

Both women and men may be healers. Herbal remedies for women's health, used in eastern Zambia and south central Tanzania, include the herb *Crossopterysx febriguga,* an abortifacient; it contains alkaloid compounds that promote menstrual discharge, including the termination of pregnancy (Waite, 1992).

Botswana

Among the Kalahari !Kung, there is believed to be a specific spiritual, healing energy in the body called *num,* possessed by both women and men, and strengthened by particular movements, notably *kia* in the drum dance. *Kia* involves shaking the body all over without moving one's feet, and it is believed that this movement raises energy in the body.

Diet affects spiritual energy, so a healer in training observes food taboos, especially the prohibition on consuming certain meats. Women may be healers, but it is considered difficult for a woman in her childbearing years to raise her *num* fully because each pregnancy interrupts the course of perfecting *num.*

South Africa

Sangomas, traditional healers in South Africa, may be women or men. They are revered and beloved in their communities and are instantly recognizable by their distinctive skirts and red and white beads, worn bandolier style from each shoulder to the opposite hip as well as on the wrists and around the neck. Becoming a *sangoma* involves a lengthy apprenticeship in divination; in the medicinal properties, uses, and preparation of herbs; and in performing rituals, dance, and songs. Diagnosis of patients' ills is made solely by divination; the patient does not describe symptoms to the *sangoma* as she or he might to a physician. *Muti,* medicine, may be given as herbs over which the patient steams her or his body, or may be rubbed into the skin at points of incision, usually at the joints. *Sangomas* make a prosperous living, and the ritual dancing and divination ceremonies held at their houses are popular celebrations throughout their communities (Arden, 1999).

See Also

HEALERS; SCIENCE: TRADITIONAL AND INDIGENOUS KNOWLEDGE; TABOO

References and Further Reading

Arden, Nicky. 1999. *African spirits speak: A white woman's journey into the healing tradition of the Sangoma.* Rochester, Vt.: Inner Traditions International.

Feierman, Steven, and John M. Janzen, eds. 1992. *The social basis of health and healing in Africa.* Berkeley: University of California Press.

Green, Edward C. 1989. Mystical black power: The calling to diviner-mediumship in southern Africa. In Carol Shepherd McClain, ed., *Women as healers: Cross-cultural perspectives.* New Brunswick, N.J.: Rutgers University Press.

Katz, Richard. 1982. *Boiling energy: Community healing among the Kalahari !Kung.* Cambridge: Harvard University Press.

Lewis, I. M., Ahmed Al-Safi, and Sayyid Hurreiz. 1991. *Women's medicine: The Zar-Bori cult in Africa and beyond.*

McCallum, Taffy Gould. 1992. *White woman witchdoctor: Tales from the African life of Rae Graham.* Tulsa, Okla.: Council Oaks.

Nyamwaya, David. 1992. *African indigenous medicine: An anthropological perspective for policy makers and primary health care managers.* Nairobi: African Medical and Research Foundation.

Patton, Adell, Jr. 1996. *Physicians, colonial racism, and diaspora in west Africa.* Tallahassee, Fla.: University Press of Florida.

Sindiga, Isaac, Chacha Nyaigotti-Chacha, and Mary Peter Kanunah, eds. 1995. *Traditional medicine in Africa.* Nairobi: East African Education Publications.

Visvanathan, Nalini. 1998. The global politics of women and health. In *Our bodies, ourselves for the new century.* New York: Simon and Schuster.

Waite, Gloria M. 1992. *A history of traditional medicine and health care in precolonial east-central Africa.* Lewiston, N.Y.: Edwin Mellen .

Organizations

Inter-African Committee on Traditional Health Practices Affecting Women. c/o ECA/ATRCW, P.O. Box 3001, Addis Ababa, Ethiopia (25-11) 515793; or Inter-African Committee, 147 rue de Lausanne, CH-1202 Geneva, Switzerland. (41-22) 732-0821.

ISIS-WICCE, P.O. Box 4934, Kampala, Uganda (256 41) 2660007, 266008. E-mail: *isis@starcom.co.ug.*

Women's Action Group, P.O. Box 135, Ivory House, 5th Floor, 95 Robert Mugabe Road, Harare, Zimbabwe. (263) 4702986.

Women's Global Network for Reproductive Rights, Uganda Chapter, Plot I 2/4, City-House, William Street, Kampala, Uganda.

Women's Health Project, P.O. Box 1038, Johannesburg 2000, South Africa. (27-11) 489-9917. Produces *Women's Health News*. E-mail: <womenhp@sn.apc.org>

Melanie Hahn

TRADITIONAL HEALING: Africa II

Among the more than one thousand tribes and linguistic groups in the fifty-two states of Africa, traditional healing remains as important today as it did among the earliest peoples of five thousand to thirty thousand years ago, who left their shamanic imprints on the cave rocks of the Tassilli Plateau in what is now called Algeria. There, women actively shared in the rituals of the "Neolithic trinity," which melded the cult of the great goddess, the cult of cattle, and the rituals surrounding use of the hallucinogenic mushrooms that sprang from the cattle dung (McKenna, 1988). In modern times, as then, women hold primary status as herbalists and healers who can obtain intimate knowledge that helps both body and spirit. Ancient women learned from observation—of other animals, such as the chimpanzees that forage among the fuchsia leaves (*Aspilla*) for an antibiotic; of the cosmos and its elements, earth, fire, water, air, and minerals. The Dagara people of Burkina Faso, for example, organize this felt and experienced knowledge into a cosmology symbolized by the wheel or circle representing the cycles of the earth and the cosmos.

Among traditional peoples, healing is a community event, whether undertaken on behalf of an individual or for community harmony. The science and art of trial and error may be orally transmitted from generation to generation, as is the practice among the !Kung of the Kalahari. The oral-only language of the !Kung expresses healing ceremonies as women clap rhythmically for communal dance-into-trance states that generate *num chxi* for health and community healing (Katz, 1982). The healing methods catalogued by the Mano include herbal medicine, enemas, snuffs, infusions, juices, baths, and bloodletting.

Contact with nonindigenous religions, beginning in the eighth century with Islam and with Christian colonization in the eighteenth century and then globalization in the twenty-first century often affected the practice of traditional healing. Outside intervention changes healing in both positive and negative ways and thus profoundly influences the lives of women who rely on it for their health, their families' health, and their way of life. Often, externally initiated contact with traditional societies by more metropolitan societies leads to the creation of syncretic practices, as in some western African peoples' use of iboga (*Tabernanthe iboga*), a root used traditionally to treat impotence, infertility, and fatigue, which in larger quantities produces dreamlike states. With the influence of Christianity, iboga (or ibogaine) was used with the sacraments to enlarge on rituals that led to the development of the Bwiti religion. The Fang people then adapted its use to unify peoples suffering from the traumas inflicted by colonialism. In the United States, Dr. Deborah Mash is researching ibogaine's efficacy for the treatment of drug addiction and posttraumatic stress disorder.

The legacies of colonial governments often include laws forbidding the practice of healing, as in Madagascar, where laws prohibiting the practice of traditional medicine have remained in place (Bodeker, 1997). Yet despite these obstacles, women thrive as the dominant cultivators, vendors, herbalists, and conservationists, healing their families as well as livestock.

The use of traditional healing for treatment of AIDS is a public health priority in many African counties, with consultants from the World Health Organization (WHO) seeking advice from local women who can address both prevention and treatment. The Organization of African Unity (OAU) has called for the protection of cultural property rights, including ownership of traditional healing and plants (1996), and the indigenous women's working group on biodiversity, meeting in Nairobi in May 2000, called for more active participation by women as strategists and policy makers in laws affecting women's medicine.

See Also

HEALERS; SCIENCE: TRADITIONAL AND INDIGENOUS KNOWLEDGE; TRADITIONAL HEALING: AFRICA I

References and Further Reading

Bodeker, Gerard. 1997. Women and herbal medicine in Africa. *Journal of Alternative and Complementary Medicine* 3(4): 323–325.

Katz, Richard. 1982. *Boiling energy: Community healing among the Kalahari !Kung*. Cambridge, Mass.: Harvard University Press.

Kokwaro, John. 1995. Ethnobotany in Africa. In Richard Shultes and Siri von Reis, eds., *Ethnobotany: Evolution of a discipline*, 218–225. Portland, Ore.: Timber.

McKenna, Terrence. 1988. Hallucinogenic mushrooms and evolution. *Revision: The Journal of Consciousness and Change* 10(4: Spring): 51–57.

Sindiga, Isaac, Chacha Nyaigotti-Chacha, et al. 1995. *Traditional medicine in Africa.* Nairobi: East African Education Publications.

Leslie Korn

TRADITIONAL HEALING: Central and South America and the Caribbean

Traditional healing, also called "indigenous medicine" or "ethnomedicine," is a system of healing practices unique to the people of a given region and based on their social, cultural, and religious beliefs regarding physical and social well-being and the causation of disease. These terms are distinguished from biomedicine and "western" or "modern" medicine, misleading terms in that this latter system extends beyond the West and has its own tradition, based on pathogenic causes for illnesses, supported by microbiology, and practiced by physicians (Bastien, 1992). In Latin America, traditional healing is based on the Hippocratic-Galenic humoral theory of the balance of hot, cold, wet, and dry; the Andean topographic-hydraulic theory of the centripetal and centrifugal flow of fluids between the body and the environment; and "folk" traditions. In the Caribbean, illness is understood through syncretic Afro-Christian beliefs to be caused by malevolent spirits or as chastisement by God for disobedience (Wedenoja, 1989). These disparate influences have ramified into a variety of healing traditions, of which a few are examined here. Patients generally have a choice between indigenous and biomedical systems; but dialogue between healers and physicians, an objective of the World Health Organization, is just beginning.

Women's Health Issues and Women Healers

Biomedicine has brought benefits and dangers to Latin American women. Biomedical treatments, such as inoculations, are efficacious when ritual cures are not. Yet in rural areas, doctors are often inaccessible and their fees prohibitive. Women describe discomfort with educated, wealthy, usually male physicians who practice in white, sterile offices and who use medical terminology and unfamiliar instruments (Bastien, 1992). This distrust extends to prescription drugs manufactured by multinational corporations. Drug companies have circumvented regulatory barriers in many countries and promote products with impunity, often with-out advising women of side effects. The high-dose birth control pill was first tested on women in Puerto Rico and later in El Salvador, with severe health consequences. Drug companies routinely dump banned and unmarketable drugs on "southern"—or third world—countries (Visvanathan, 1998). Such risks have led many Latin American women to rely on traditional, often female healers, who are accessible, more affordable, familiar with lay terms, and likely to practice in a familiar environment.

Women Healers and Health in Ecuador and Colombia

The Saraguro Indians are a Quichua- and Spanish-speaking tribe in Ecuador, where, despite the availability of both healers and biomedical treatment modalities provided free of charge, mothers are the primary health care providers. Mothers supervise diet as a preventive health measure, balancing hot (corn, beans, plantains, beef) and cold (potatoes, rice, milk, eggs) foods in the home—considered a sanctuary from illness in the outside world. Aspects of biomedicine, such as germs, pharmaceuticals, and some notions of disease causation, have been integrated into health care, but Saraguros consider their mothers' emotional support and experience in curing to be superior to those of physicians, whom they consider inadequately trained and supplied.

Women in Cali, Colombia, face the church's dictum to maximize fertility and its opposition to birth control and abortion; a nationalist agenda that asserts that population increase will enhance the country's development; a Latin cultural heritage that promotes large families and rewards men who father many children with prestige; and the self-sacrificing Virgin Mary as the primary role model for women (Browner, 1985). Within this context is the coexistent belief that women should remedy menstrual delay, *atrazo,* to maintain health. Caleñas thus take herbal remedies to cure *atrazo,* diagnose pregnancy, or cause early abortion. Because it is difficult to distinguish a late period from early pregnancy, unwanted pregnancies may be surreptitiously terminated through the use of remedies; women find this an effective and culturally acceptable way to practice fertility control.

Mexican *Curanderas*

Curanderismo is a mix of Spanish medicine of the Conquest mixed with Aztec *wewepahtli* ("greatest medicine") and traditional healing methods brought by African slaves. A *curandera* may be female or male; may be an herbalist, masseuse, midwife, counselor, trance medium, or chiropractor; or may practice all these forms of healing to treat the whole person physically, mentally, and spiritually. Curanderas recognize and treat physical diseases, such as *bilis* (rage); *empacho* (blocked stomach or digestive tract); or *mal aire* (bad air: cold symptoms, earaches, or facial paralysis); emotional diseases, such as *envidia* (envy), *mal puesto* (hex or curse), *mal ojo* (illness caused by staring), and *mal suerte* (bad luck); and spiritual diseases, for example *susto* (soul loss) and *espanto* (fright from seeing a ghost or being startled awake). Mexican grandmothers traditionally passed healing knowledge to their daughters.

Balm in Jamaica

The Balm healer, usually a woman, works as a spirit medium to diagnose without having the patient describe symptoms. She heals with herbs and religious services. Balm is considered a "spiritual science," illness a spiritual issue, and the healer's abilities God-given. Balm is distinguished from "temporal science," which can be learned and practiced by both physicians and *obeahmen* (sorcerers). Since illness is understood to originate with *duppies* (ghosts), fallen angels, demons, the devil, and ancestors, and since a visit to the doctor is expensive and involves long travel and a wait, the Balm healer is often the initial health care provider in her community.

Women healers enjoy power and influence otherwise denied women in their communities (Perrone et al., 1989). As global development and dialogue with physicians increase, women healers will probably incorporate efficacious aspects of biomedicine into their healing practices.

See Also

HEALERS; HEALTH CARE: CENTRAL AND SOUTH AMERICA AND THE CARIBBEAN; HEALTH CHALLENGES; HERBALISM; HOUSEHOLDS AND FAMILIES: CARIBBEAN; HOUSEHOLDS AND FAMILIES: CENTRAL AND SOUTH AMERICA; PHARMACEUTICALS

References and Further Readings

Avila, Elena. 1999. *Woman who glows in the dark: A Curandera reveals traditional Aztec secrets of physical and spiritual health.* New York: Tarcher/Putnam.

Bastien, Joseph W. 1992. *Drum and stethoscope: Integrating ethnomedicine and biomedicine.* Bloomington: Indiana University.

Browner, C. H. 1985. Traditional techniques for diagnosis, treatment, and control of pregnancy in Cali, Colombia. In Lucile Newman, ed., *Women's medicine: A cross-cultural study of indigenous fertility regulation.* New Brunswick, N.J.: Rutgers University.

CIDHAL, apdo, Postal 579; Calle des Flores No. 12; Col. Acapantzingo; Cuernavaca, Morelos, Mexico <www.laneta.apc.org/cidhal/index.html>.

Cowan, Eliot. 1995. *Plant spirit medicine.* Newberg, Ore.: Swan Raven.

Finerman, RuthBeth. 1989. The forgotten healers: Women as family healers in an Andean Indian community. In Carol Sheperd McClain, ed., *Women as healers: Cross-cultural perspectives.* New Brunswick, N.J.: Rutgers University.

ISIS Internaciónal, Esmerelda 636, 20 piso; Casilla 2067, Cor. Central; Santiago, Chile; (56-2) 638-2219. E-mail: isis@reuna.cl.

Levinson, David, and Laura Gaccione. 1997. *Health and illness: A cross-cultural encyclopedia.* Santa Barbara, Calif.: ABC-Clio.

Perrone, Bobette H., Henrietta Stockel, and Victoria Krueger. 1989. *Medicine women, Curanderas and women doctors.* Norman: University of Oklahoma Press.

Visvanathan, Nalini. 1998. The global politics of women and health. In Boston Women's Health Book Collective, *Our bodies, ourselves for the new century.* New York: Simon and Schuster.

Wedenoja, William. 1989. Mothering and the practice of "Balm" in Jamaica. In Carol Sheperd McClain, ed., *Women as Healers: Cross-cultural perspective,* 76–97. New Brunswick, N.J.: Rutgers University Press.

Melanie Hahn

TRADITIONAL HEALING:
East and Southeast Asia

East and southeast Asia together represent an area in transition, where traditional healing, often called "indigenous medicine," is prevalent, but where biomedicine, brought from western nations, is also increasingly available, especially for women's health concerns.

The changing economic situation profoundly affects women's health. Tourism is an important source of income, and often women work as prostitutes, performers in sex shows, or waitresses. Sex tours are offered to travelers from the United States and Europe and to the U.S. military. Women enter these fields out of economic necessity and because there is no comparable alternative: for example, a Thai sex worker earns an astronomical livelihood compared with what she could earn in her rural village (Visvanathan, 1998). But with these jobs, incidence of sexually transmitted diseases (STDs) and of human immunodeficiency virus

(HIV) is increasing. The availability of abortion varies from one country to another: abortion is legal in Vietnam and Singapore, illegal in Indonesia and the Philippines.

Yet nearly every country boasts a vibrant healing tradition, several of which are examined here. Women often play powerful roles as healers in their communities.

Chinese Medicine

Chinese medicine is based on Taoism, which posits the unity of all life, with a universal force of energy running through everything, called *chi*. Yin and *yang*, the balance of opposites, are believed to constitute *chi*. Yin is feminine, passive, cold, small, and the quality of night. *Yang* is masculine, active, hot, large, and the quality of daytime. Health is the balance between these two, and because everything in the universe consists of *yin* and *yang*, the goal is to resonate in balance with the universe. Treatment consists of sending energy to those organs with deficient *chi* and diverting it from those that have too much. Massage, herbs, diet, and acupuncture are techniques that can be used to rebalance *chi* (Levinson, 1997).

Chinese healers can be female or male. They diagnose by taking twelve pulses in the patient's wrists, each corresponding to one of the twelve "spheres of influence," (which in turn roughly correspond to the organ systems in biomedicine). An encyclopedia compiled in the sixteenth century, *Pen T'sao Kang-mu*, lists substances and plants attributed to Shen Nung, China's legendary farming god, and said to be useful for healing. For example, women after childbirth are advised to take a remedy of sliced deer antler combined with dried seahorses and herbs (Levinson and Gaccione, 1997).

Korean *Mansin*

Most Korean shamans (*mansin*) are women, and their clientele is primarily female. The few male shamans perform wearing women's clothing, including silky pantaloons under their slips. Korea is Confucian, and gender roles are separate but complementary. The *mansin* is the ritual specialist of Korean women, especially housewives, who share certain values: children should respect their elders; elders should be benevolent and understanding; the living should honor the ancestors with appropriate rituals; sons should be born who will inherit the family's lands and sustain the family's ancestors; and parents, having successfully married off their children and seen them established in life, should live to become elderly. Often, however, these dreams do not unfold according to plan, and the *mansin* provides explanations and also therapies. The *mansin* is marginal and shares the status of such women as actresses, female entertainers, and prosti-

tutes; yet she is free to say things that traditional housewives cannot, and for this she earns a prosperous livelihood. Further, she is considered chosen or "god-descended."

The *mansin* heals with a divination tray bearing a mound of rice, a handful of brass coins, and the brass bell rattle she uses to summon her visions. The client places a bill under the pile of grain on the tray. The *mansin* shakes her rattle and receives from the gods a message for each member of the client's family. She also performs healing rituals (*uhwan kut*) for both female and male patients, but even then women play key ritual roles (Kendall, 1985).

Nat Kadaw in Burma

These shamans or spirit mediums are almost always women. One becomes a shaman by marrying, in a real ceremony, the spirit (*nat*) that possessed one and may affect one for good or evil. Most healing activity is concerned with propitiating *nat*. Because *nat* cause illness, especially diseases of the eye, choking feelings, diarrhea, dysentery, fright, and mental illness, a shaman is frequently consulted. The shaman performs her role when possessed by her *nat* husband, who then reveals the identity of the *nat* who caused her client to be ill. Women are considered more susceptible to supernaturally caused diseases than men. Ghosts (*tasei, thaye*) may also cause one to become ill, and may be the cause of plague or cholera. Supernatural beings are propitiated by food offerings.

Thailand

In contrast to those countries in which women hold the power of traditional healing, healers in Thailand are all male. Women may have knowledge of herbs but are frequently illiterate and are not permitted in their "impure" state to chant incantations even if they are able to write prescriptions. Thailand is also a country with a booming sex trade and a high rate of HIV and AIDS infection.

Philippines

Women healers in the Philippines have a strong tradition. In the 1990s they began to organize politically and to gain power from the Filipino government. In one method of diagnosis, the healer (who may be either female or male) burns the mineral alum (*tawas*) with a cross-shaped dried palm leaf from Palm Sunday leaves (*palaspas*). The healer utters prayers while the leaves burn, and the liquefied alum takes a shape that is then read by the healer. Then ashes are applied in the form of crosses over the forehead, chest, throat, navel, palms, backs of the knees, and soles of the feet, to open the energy centers. Rice may be used over a basin of water as a diagnostic variation.

In 1992 Women Healers of the Philippines organized a conference that called for elder healers (*babaylan*) to teach indigenous rituals such as sweat/smudging (*paagsusuob*) and dancing (*pagsasayaw*). They called for protection of indigenous plants and for dialogue with physicians.

Conclusion

As Asia industrializes, the challenge is to integrate rituals that are socially relevant and sometimes efficacious with biomedicine, which is usually efficacious but does not always improve women's lives.

See Also

HEALTH CARE: EAST ASIA; HEALTH CARE: SOUTHEAST ASIA

References and Further Reading

Address speaks of the concerns of women traditional healers in the Philippines. 1994. In Lakshmi Menon, ed., *Organizing strategies in women's health—An information and action handbook*. Manila: Isis International.

Brun, Viggo, and Trond Schumacher. 1987. *Traditional herbal medicine in northern Thailand*. Bangkok: White Lotus.

Cargill, Marie E. 1998. *Well women: Healing the female body through traditional Chinese medicine*. South Hadley, Mass.: Bergin and Garvey.

Jones, Heidi, Susheela Singh, and Deirdre Wulf. 1997. Health professionals' perceptions about induced abortion in south central and southeast Asia. *International Family Planning Perspectives* 23(2).

Kaptchuk, Ted J. 1983. *The web that has no weaver: Understanding Chinese medicine*. New York: Conodon and Weed.

Kendall, Laurel. 1989. Old ghosts and ungrateful children: A Korean shaman's story. In Carol Shepherd McClain, ed., *Women as healers: Cross-cultural perspectives*. Old Westbury, N.Y.: Feminist Press.

———. 1985. *Shamans, housewives, and other restless spirits: Women in Korean ritual life*. Honolulu: University of Hawaii Press.

Kleinman, Arthur, Peter Kunstadter, E. Russell Alexander, and James L. Gate. 1978. *Culture and healing in Asian societies: Anthropological, psychiatric and public health studies*. Boston: Hall.

Kristof, Nicholas D. 1998. As Asian economies shrink, women are squeezed out. *New York Times* (National Edition) 147(51): 185.

Laderman, Carol. 1991. *Taming the wind of desire: Psychology, medicine, and aesthetics in Malay shamanistic performance*. Berkeley: University of California Press.

———. 1983. *Wives and midwives: Childbirth and nutrition in rural Malaysia*. Berkeley: University of California Press.

Levinson, David, and Laura Gaccione. 1997. *Health and illness: A cross-cultural encyclopedia*. Santa Barbara, Calif.: ABC-Clio.

Matilac, Rosalie. 1996. *Indigenous healing*. Quezon City, Philippines: ISIS International.

McNamara, Sheila. 1996. *Traditional Chinese medicine*. New York: Basic Books.

Nordstrom, Carolyn. 1989. It's all in a name: Local level female healers in Sri Lanka. In Carol Shepherd McClain, ed., *Women as healers: Cross-cultural perspectives*. Old Westbury, N.Y.: Feminist Press.

Williams, Tom. 1995. *Chinese medicine: Acupuncture, herbal remedies, nutrition, qigong and meditation for total health*.

Visvanathan, Nalini. 1998. The global politics of women and health. In Boston Women's Health Book Collective, *Our bodies, ourselves for the new century*. New York: Simon and Schuster.

Melanie Hahn

TRADITIONAL HEALING: Herbalists

Herbalism, the use of plants for health and healing, is probably as old as humanity. In hunting-gathering societies, herbalists tend to be women, and this connection between women and herbs continues today. Throughout much of the world, especially in countries where women's wisdom has traditionally been honored, herbalism remains, as ever, the treatment of choice for many acute and most chronic health problems; and in some places where it has not always been practiced extensively, such as the United States, it is undergoing a renaissance. Herbal medicine is a complex and daunting study; yet it is also the medicine of the people, and often it is so simple that children can safely apply it.

The Wise Woman Tradition

The earliest known herbalism is the "wise woman" way of our prehistoric foremothers—our ancient female ancestors, primarily in Africa. This women's herbalism is still used and respected in many places, especially in Asia, the Middle East, and India. Wise women view herbs not only as medicines but also as intrinsically important foodstuffs and also, in effect, as spiritual allies. Psychoactive plants are both teachers and healers and are used, under the guidance of the herbalist or shaman, by all members of the community.

Wise woman herbalism is characterized by compassion, connection, community, and honoring the earth. The nourishing herbal infusions, mineral-rich vinegars, and edible herbs favored by wise women are generally considered safe, even in quantity, for all women, including those who are pregnant or lactating. Favorite herbs include nourishing tonics such as nettle, red clover, oatstraw, comfrey leaf, linden, dandelion, seaweed, and burdock.

The Heroic Tradition

In Europe, and then in the Americas, wise women herbalists and midwives became a target of the Inquisition, the Roman Catholic tribunal of the fourteenth century and later that suppressed heresy. The women, who were often tortured and murdered, were replaced with male "heroes." These "heroic" practitioners used herbs to drive out the devils of illness from the hated body, so they favored plants that caused catharsis and purging. (They also favored bloodletting.)

The heroic tradition, despising all things female, licensed only men as healers and persecuted anyone who practiced without a license. Some women healers escaped to the Americas, learned Native American herbal medicine, and began a tradition of serving their communities that lasted for generations; but these community herbalists would eventually be vilified and replaced by school-trained male physicians from England.

The heroic tradition is still popular in Europe, and in Latin and black communities throughout the Americas. This medicine is characterized by domination, mentation, isolation, and distrust of the earth. (Earth is regarded as "female" and therefore is considered sinful and dirty.) Favorite herbs include powerful stimulants and sedatives such as cayenne, lobelia, valerian, ephedra, goldenseal, cascara sagrada, turkey rhubarb, and aloes. Most plants used by heroic herbalists are dangerous to women, especially pregnant or lactating women.

The Scientific Tradition

Where the practice of medicine becomes dominated by linear, "either-or" thinking, the scientific tradition replaces the heroic tradition. In this tradition too, wise woman herbalists are vilified, but as quacks rather than as witches. A quest for powerful drugs brings plants to the laboratory, where active ingredients are extracted, concentrated, isolated, standardized, sanitized, and ultimately synthesized.

Plants are considered raw materials: until a plant is processed, its effects are thought to be crude, inexact, and unpredictable.

Approximately 85 percent of the hundreds of thousands of drugs currently used are derived directly or indirectly from plants; examples are foxglove (digitalis compounds), Pacific yew (a cancer drug), wild yam (used in cortisone and birth control pills), and chinchona (quinine). Drugs and druglike herbs may cause severe side effects and should not be self-administered by pregnant or lactating women.

See Also

HEALERS; HOLISTIC HEALTH, *I and II;* NATURE: PHILOSOPHY AND SPIRITUALITY; SCIENCE: TRADITIONAL AND INDIGENOUS KNOWLEDGE

References and Further Reading

Achterberg, Jeanne. 1990. *Woman as healer: A panoramic survey of the healing activities of women from Prehistoric times to the present.* Boston, Mass.: Shambala.

Benedetti, Maria Dolores. 1998. *Earth and spirit: Medicinal plants and healing lore from Puerto Rico.* Orocovis: Verde Luz.

Bennett, Jennifer. 1991. *Lilies of the hearth: The historical relationship between women and plants.* Willowdale, Ontario: Firefly.

Brooke, Elisabeth. 1997. *Medicine women: A pictorial history of women healers.* Wheaton, Ill., and Madras, India: Quest.

Chamberlain, Mary. 1981. *Old wives' tales: Their history, remedies, and spells.* London: Virago.

Christopher, John R. 1976. *School of natural healing: The reference volume on heroic herbal therapy for the teacher, student, or practitioner.* Springville, Utah: Christopher.

Griggs, Barbara. 1997. *Green pharmacy: The history and evolution of western medicine.* Rochester, Vt.: Healing Arts.

McClain, Carol Shepherd. 1989. *Women as healers: Cross-cultural perspectives.* New Brunswick, N. J., and London: Rutgers University Press.

Vogel, Virgil J. 1970. *American Indian medicine.* London and Norman: University of Oklahoma Press.

Weed, Susun S. 1989. *Healing wise: The second wise woman herbal.* Woodstock, N. Y.: Ash Tree.

Wichtl, Max. 1994. *Herbal drugs and phytopharmaceuticals: A handbook for practice on a scientific basis.* Ed. and trans. Norman Grainger Bisset. Stuttgart: Medpharm Verlag; and Boca Raton, Ann Arbor, London, and Tokyo: CRC.

Women healers: Portraits of herbalists, physicians, and midwives. 1995. Rochester, Vt.: Healing Arts.

Susun S. Weed

TRADITIONAL HEALING: India

A few centuries ago, there were no doctors, clinics, or hospitals. Health was in the hands of the people. There was a fund of knowledge about the medicinal properties of common herbs among elders of all communities. Traditional home therapies, using locally available herbs and common spices, were integral to the lives of common people. For more complex ailments, however, one took the advice of specialist healers such as bonesetters, birth attendants, or snakebite healers.

Herbal remedies were an important part of traditional medicine. Many other systems of medicine coexisted with traditional techniques, such as ayurveda, siddha, unani, yoga, and folk, also based on herbs and minerals. Each system had its own method of diagnosis and treatments that were passed from one generation to another. Some of them, such as ayurveda and unani, were even institutionalized.

The birth of modern medicine pushed aside this vast reservoir of traditional knowledge. Allopathy—a product of the industrial age—with its quick action therapies, rapidly took hold. In a changed paradigm, traditional health practices were dismissed as irrational, unscientific, and superstitious. Health became commoditized into something one had to "buy." The health care models adopted by the colonial and subsequent independent governments never integrated traditional medicine.

In the indigenous systems, unlike modern medicine, treatment was not simply through medicines; rather, it was a spiritual experience and process. There was a relationship of mutual faith and respect between the patient and the healer. It was a complete relationship, not only between two humans but between humans and nature.

Generally speaking, however, whether in allopathy or traditional healing systems, women's ailments, other than those related directly to pregnancy and child care, were given little importance. The primary health care system in India saw women's health only in the context of maternity and child welfare, while reproductive tract infections, a major area of concern, traditionally have received little official attention. Within the family, too, women's health is of the lowest priority. Even the traditional healing systems could not escape the inherent patriarchial bias of Indian society, whereby women either found it difficult to discuss their gynecological complaints openly, or faced difficulty in obtaining treatment.

But, in spite of a patriarchial bias, there exists a wide variety of treatments, particularly concerning women's health, in herbal and folk medicine, which could emerge in the twenty-first century as an effective alternative to modern medicine, which is becoming increasingly expensive, hazardous, technological, and far from the control of people.

Tribal peoples in Banda, a rather "backward" district of Uttar Pradesh, practice a completely indigenous massage technique to relieve menstrual cramps and back pain, by application of pressure to certain points on the palms of the hands and soles of the feet. Women of rural Andhra Pradesh know of twenty to thirty herbs that can cure vaginal infections and urinary tract infections. With indigenous methods of diagnosis, they can identify the type of infection from the nature of the discharge. In many villages all over India, women still use a traditional dai (birth attendant) who conducts even complex deliveries using simple skills and traditional knowledge. In Orissa, Dongria Konds use their own herbal recipes for contraception.

These are only a few illustrations of treatments that exist in spite of the growing onslaught of deforestation, modern technologies, and medical practices. There is an urgent need to explore and document this knowledge system, which is on the verge of extinction, and to integrate traditional healing systems into the overall health options of all, especially women.

See Also

ANCIENT INDIGENOUS CULTURES: WOMEN'S ROLE; DISEASE; FAMILY LAW: CASE STUDY—INDIA; HEALING; HINDUISM; SEXUALITY IN HINDU CULTURE; TRADITIONAL HEALING: HERBALISTS

References and Further Reading

Achterberg, Jeanne. 1990. *Woman as healer: A panoramic survey of the healing activities of women from prehistoric times to the present.* Boston: Shambala.
Women healers: Portraits of herbalists, physicians, and midwives. Rochester, Vt.: Healing Arts.

N. B. Sarojini

TRADITIONAL HEALING: Native North America

Great cultural diversity existed in the precontact world of aboriginal North America; this variation is especially true in spirituality and healing. However, one major theme emerges. Native peoples had a holistic view of the world in which natural and social realms were equally balanced. Individual beings—creatures who are "two-legged, four-legged, who fly in the air, or swim in the water," as the

Lakota philosopher Black Elk stated—were all equally reflected in a "primitive" image of sacred thought and deed. Many native societies viewed these creatures as being surrounded by a sacred aura or power, called *wakan* (Lakota), *manitou* (Chippewa), or *orenda* (Iroquoian), for example. This invisible force encompassed all things. The power could be tapped for various reasons—benevolent in most cases, but malevolent in others—and was a source for healing.

Much ethnographic literature has discussed "medicine men" or "shamans" who were, in most cases, male. Native women as spiritual leaders or agents of healing—both mental and physical—have been neglected by researchers. But women's activity in the spiritual and healing arts has been fundamental to many cultures of native North America. This article will concentrate on a specific group, the Lakota (formerly called Sioux), to explore just one example among many.

The Lakota ritual belief system—based upon values of generosity, bravery, fortitude, and wisdom—was brought to them by a young woman. This culture heroine is known as the White Buffalo Calf Woman. She brought the sacred pipe and the seven rites that formed the ritual realm. This included the sun dance, vision quest, and girls' puberty ceremony. The rites were enacted as a part of daily life and women had an honored place in this ceremonial life. The culmination of the ritual cycle was the sacred sun dance. Honored older women offered the pipe in the four-day event, which occurred in the summer, and young virgin women acted as the honorary cutters of the sacred tree that united earth and cosmos.

Lakota women, like women of other indigenous nations, were skilled in the use of plants. The efficacious properties of plants were used to treat the ordinary diseases and ailments that beset every group. In most cases, curing skills were learned as part of feminine socialization. Girls accompanied the older females of their kin groups and memorized plants' medicinal uses. Useful plants were dried and formed a part of every household's medicine bag. Besides learning to identify medicinal plants, novice healers were exposed to the cultural rules surrounding the use of plants as medicine—for example, rules guiding the proper way to approach a plant, depending on the wind; rules about propagating new plants; and rules for being in the proper physical state (that is, nonmenstruating) to practice medicine.

Essentially, most women had this indigenous knowledge, but some were recognized as being more skilled. These women were called *winyan wapiya* (women "fixers"). They were experts and often had apprentices in their kin groups who evidenced interest and aptitude. Thus, continuity of healing arts was ensured.

Other avenues for curing included dreams or supernaturally sanctioned events. Recurrent dreams of certain plants indicated a healer's propensity toward a specialization; for example, effective midwives may have found their calling through dreams related to the treatment of women's disorders. Lakota women, unlike Lakota men, did not go on vision quests to receive occupational options, so dreaming was a recognized means to curing. In all cases, the *wakan* power was called upon for efficacious curing. Some women were seen as powerful purveyors of "love magic." These acts were secret negotiations between the client and practitioner and might be seen as unethical. The client was expected to pay the practitioner, whereas legitimate forms of medicine in this egalitarian society were nonremunerative, practiced strictly out of a commitment to contributing to the health and welfare of the group.

As wisdom was seen as a corollary of aging, elderly and respected women served as counselors for both genders. These women were seen as exemplars of Lakota life.

Careful perusal of ethnographic accounts indicates that every North American aboriginal society had women in spiritual and healing domains, but ultimately colonization, Christianization, and the denigration of native lifestyles eroded feminine curing systems. In the case of the Lakotas, as farmers and ranchers moved into the Plains areas, gathering places were restricted, traditional knowledge was eroded, and reliance on western medical practices followed. The building of dams on rivers completely demolished Lakota gathering places. Aboriginal women today face another debilitating challenge. The "new age" movement and the cultural appropriation of indigenous belief systems often usurp and corrupt these views and do immeasurable harm to indigenous self-concepts.

See Also

HEALING; HOUSEHOLDS AND FAMILIES: NATIVE NORTH AMERICA; SPIRITUALITY: OVERVIEW

References and Further Reading

Jones, D. Sanapia. 1970. *Comanche medicine woman.* New York: Holt, Rinehart, and Winston.

Medicine, Bea. 1980. American Indian women: Spirituality and status. *Bread and roses* 2(3: Fall): 15–18.

———. 1987. Indian women and the renaissance of traditional religion. In Raymond J. DeMallie and Douglas R. Parks, eds., *Sioux Indian religion,* 159–171. Norman: University of Oklahoma Press.

———. 1998. Native American religions. In Wilma Mankiller, Gwendolyn Mink, et al., eds., *The reader's companion to U.S. women's history*, 403–405. New York: Houghton Mifflin.

Tijerina-Jim, Aleticia. 1993. Three Native American women speak about the significance of ceremony. *Women and Therapy* 14(1–2): 33–40.

Walker, James R. 1980. *Lakota belief and ritual.* Ed. Raymond J. DeMallie and Elaine A. Jahner. Lincoln: University of Nebraska Press.

Wallace, Anthony F. C. 1969. *The death and rebirth of the Seneca.* New York: Knopf.

Beatrice Medicine

TRAFFICKING

Trafficking in Women: What Is It?

A common definition specifies that a woman is trafficked if she is lured by coercion or deceit into traveling from her place of residence to a location foreign to her. However, experts as well as those who work with these women do not necessarily agree that coercion or deceit must be present. Many discussions of trafficking also include the situation that a woman finds herself in on arrival. She may be forced to work under conditions which are exploitative and from which she cannot escape without serious consequences. During the 1990s, some groups working on the issue of trafficking in women began to include working conditions in their analyses of the problem, regardless of whether the woman traveled.

A useful and explicit definition of trafficking in women is that of Marjan Wijers and Lin Lap-Chew (1997), who explicitly distinguish between the aspect of recruitment ("trafficking in women") and the living and working conditions to which women are subjected ("forced labor and slavery-like practices"). This is a necessary distinction because "on the one hand, women can be recruited and transported under conditions of coercion but not end up in a forced labor/slavery-like situation. On the other hand, women may find themselves in forced labor/slavery-like situations without having been trafficked" (37). The term *trafficking* is sometimes used, in an unclear way, to refer to both of these aspects. Both are important problems to examine and combat.

The phenomenon of trafficking in women is large in scope and global in nature. Although the issue of trafficking in children is often separated from trafficking in women, it has been estimated that "from one to two million women and children are trafficked each year" (Mirkinson, 1994: 2). Women tend to be trafficked from "underdeveloped" to "more developed" countries, as well as within countries where exploitative working conditions may await them. Many countries may be classified as both countries of origin and countries of destination. Trafficking is not static, however; traffickers shift routes and destinations in order to avoid various government regulations.

What Exploitative Working Conditions Are Included in Discussions of Trafficking?

Although the term *trafficking in women* has been used traditionally to refer to situations of prostitution, over the past decade definitions have broadened to include other types of work and services that exist in the informal economy. Women can be trafficked and subjected to slaverylike practices within many areas: prostitution, entertainment, domestic labor, marriage, and sweatshop labor, to name a few.

These activities have two things in common. First, they are overwhelmingly performed by women and have traditionally been considered "women's work." Second, they all exist in the informal economy. Because women working in these areas are rarely protected by labor laws and regulations, forced labor and abysmal working conditions are common. Employers may take advantage of the illegal nature of the work, the illegal status of the worker, or the lack of workers' rights in the informal economy in order to enslave these women.

In discussions of trafficking and slaverylike conditions, it is rare to find much elaboration on issues other than domestic work, the commercial marriage market, and sex work. Domestic or household workers do necessary chores in private homes. The demand for these workers is especially high in "developed" countries and in cases where members of the household work in the formal sector every day. Household workers do not enjoy the same rights as other workers. Even if they are working in their country of origin, they often have limited rights to form organizations or to receive social security benefits, equitable salary, leisure, training, privacy, and maternity leave. Household workers may have no written contract and can be easily fired because of their invisibility. Mental, physical, and sexual abuse by their employers is common.

Women usually become domestic workers in foreign countries through employment agencies or acquaintances. Some methods of recruitment are honest and well intended, while others are "characterized by deceit, cheating, overcharge, false promises and debt bondage" (Wijers and Lap-Chew, 1997: 78). If the woman has traveled overseas for domestic work, her rights are even more limited, whatever her status. Household workers continue to fight for independent legal status and rights as workers.

In the "mail-order bride" system, international agencies mainly market women from "developing" countries as potential brides to men in industrialized nations. These agencies cater to the desires of the men and treat these women as commodities. They tend to rely on racist or female stereotypes to sell wives, and they perform background checks only on the women. Potential wives may be desperately looking for a way out of poverty or believe that men from "more developed" countries will treat them better than men in their own country.

Some of these marriages are successful, but the potential for exploitation is alarming. The wife's status as a legal resident depends on her marriage. In the case of a divorce, she may face deportation. She is also in a strange country, may have no other acquaintances, and may not speak the native language. Abuse is frequent, with rape and battering more common than in traditional marriages. Some men sell their new wives into prostitution or "marry" them in order to receive free domestic service. (For other servile marriage practices, see Wijers and Lap-Chew, 1997: 62–65; for a narrative of mail-order brides, see Draper [1998]).

Although the current literature concerning trafficking and exploitative working conditions within household work and the commercial marriage market tends to be fairly straightforward, sex work is more controversial.

What Views Exist on Trafficking in Women for Sex Work?

For women's groups, nongovernmental organizations, and government, questions of the morality of prostitution may shape their decisions concerning what approach should be taken to address trafficking and slaverylike practices within sex work. Activists fall into four general categories: abolitionists, antitrafficking activists, pro-rights activists, and what one author refers to as activists with a "socialist-oriented" perspective (Joshi, 1997: 36).

Abolitionists base their views on the belief that prostitution, by nature, is violence against women. From this view it follows that prostitution and being recruited for prostitution are forced activities. The issue of whether the woman has consented to sex work or to being recruited into sex work is deemed irrelevant.

Antitrafficking activists' opposition to trafficking in women is based on their definition of the issue. These activists may be combating coercive and deceitful recruitment and working conditions. Or, if they define trafficking as illicit transport or travel, then they may be looking only at the illegality of the migration, not at whether a woman consented to it. Finally, if trafficking is defined as prostitution, then they may be taking an abolitionist stance.

Next, pro-rights activists espouse a "liberal view," holding that the decriminalization of sex work is the best way to protect women's rights (Joshi, 1997: 37). These activists look at the problem from the perspective of the women themselves. They claim that sex workers should get the same rights as other workers.

Finally, the socialist-oriented approach arises from the concern that women's economic impoverishment may leave them with little choice but to agree to sex work. If a woman consents to sex work when she really has no other options for a livelihood, then the terms *free* and *forced* tend to lose their meaning.

How Are These Approaches and Views Reflected in Law?

These approaches are reflected in law in three broad ways, calling for criminalization, legalization, or decriminalization. Those countries using the criminalization approach either attempt to abolish the entire system of prostitution or simply prohibit outward indications of prostitution such as soliciting.

The legalization approach is based on the assumption that there is a public need for prostitution, but that the health of customers needs to be safeguarded. Thus, sex work is deemed legal but is highly regulated. This approach, like criminalization, is frowned on by sex workers themselves, who feel that it caters to the public while further stigmatizing sex workers through licensing and mandatory checkups.

Increasingly, groups are beginning to call for the decriminalization or deregulation of sex work. In this view, all laws and regulations that are unique to prostitution should be abolished. Sex workers should be guaranteed the same rights that workers in the formal sector enjoy, such as social security, pensions, and labor codes that would protect them from exploitative working conditions.

Those who espouse this view see it as an attractive policy for two main reasons. First, sex workers would no longer be arbitrarily arrested. Next, it removes stigmatizing laws and empowers sex workers to demand better working conditions. Sex workers, whether consenting or coerced, tend to favor deregulation. It would make potential abuses by traffickers, customers, pimps, and brothel owners easier for these workers to address.

The demand for domestic workers, sexual services, and foreign wives will not soon fade. This demand will be filled regardless of governmental policy on issues of "trafficking" and exploitative working conditions. Only when policies and laws are shaped with trafficked and exploited women in mind will women be empowered to fight the abuses they may face.

See Also

References and Further Reading

Altink, Sietske. 1995. *Stolen lives: Trading women into sex and slavery.* London: Scarlet.

Barry, Kathleen. 1979. *Female sexual slavery.* New York: New York University Press.

Doezma, Jo and ASI. Redefining prostitution as sex work on the international agenda: <www.walnet.org/csis/papers/redefining.html>.

Draper, Robert. 1998. Death takes a honeymoon. *GQ* (June): 228–235; 281–284.

Joshi, Madhu D. 1997. *Women and children in prostitution: Human rights perspective.* New Delhi: Uppal.

Leuchtag, Alice. 1995. Merchants of flesh: International prostitution and the war on women's rights. *Humanist* (March/April): 11–16.

Mirkinson, Judith. 1994. Red light, green light: The global trafficking of women. *Breakthrough* (Spring): 1–7.

Skrobanek, Siriporn, Nattaya Boonpakdi, and Chutima Janthakeero. 1997. *The traffic in women: Human realities of the international sex trade.* London: Zed.

Trafficking of women and girls into forced prostitution and coerced marriage. In Sarah Lai and Regan Ralph, eds., *The Human Rights Watch global report on women's human rights*, 196–273. New York: Human Rights Watch.

Wijers, Marjan, and Lin Lap-Chew. 1997. *Trafficking in women: Forced labour and slavery-like practices in marriage, domestic labour, and prostitution.* Utrecht: Foundation Against Trafficking in Women.

Kristina E. Gleeson

TRAINING, VOCATIONAL

See EDUCATION: VOCATIONAL.

TRANSGENDER

The term *transgender* or *trans* came into use in the mid-1990s as part of a move toward common discourse for a broad range of gender minorities such as transsexuals, transvestites, crossdressers, persons of ambiguous gender or with ambiguous genitalia, and others whose concerns were not addressed in gay and lesbian studies or politics, or, until the end of the millennium, by queer theory.

From a theoretical or political perspective, in western industrialized nations most transgendered activists and theoreticians hold that gender construction is social, interactive, and performative, and primarily serves the needs of established power structures. This theoretical position, however, no more frees transgendereds from the tyranny of social gender than it does feminists in the population at large, whose major efforts have been directed toward the more achievable goal of establishing a modicum of gender equality rather than directly attacking the epistemic structures of gender itself.

Basic Definitions within Transgender Discourse

Berdache, Mujerado, Mah'u: A few of many terms used by various cultures to designate persons who do not belong to either of the usual socially "legible" genders as these are generally understood in western industrialized cultures. The roles are sometimes freely chosen, or they may come to the individual in a dream or vision. Such persons may perform sacred tasks, be teachers of specific knowledges, or possess other special status in their social group.

Cross-dresser: A person who wears clothing that is a social marker for the "opposite" gender.

Intersex: A person with ambiguous genitalia or with both male and female genitalia in any proportion.

m2f, f2m: Male-to-female, female-to-male; usually in reference to transsexuals.

Passing: Creating a socially legible persona that is different from one's given persona and usually more acceptable to the dominant social group.

Becoming invisible: This term also appears in discourses on race and ethnicity with approximately the same meaning.

She-male: Transsexual. Most frequently seen in discourses on pornography; occasionally pejorative.

Transvestite: A person who experiences pleasure, usually of a sexual nature, from crossdressing.

Transsexual: A person who experiences the need to perform the social roles appropriate to the "opposite" gender. Depending on the extent of the need, this may involve crossdressing, hormonal therapy, or body modification in order to conform to customary social expectations (see "passing"). In some instances, transsexuality extends to a desire to possess the genitalia of the gender of choice, although some transsexuals desire genital modification in order to possess a socially legible body rather than for sexual performance.

Theorizing about the etiology of transsexuality was a growth industry into the 1980s but, as with similar efforts in regard to homosexuality, was ultimately fruitless. The common medicolegal definition involves such subjective terms as feeling that one was "born into the wrong body." Not all transsexuals experience the "wrong body" paradigm, nor do all transsexuals accept as unproblematic the binary concept of two and only two sexes and genders.

Because of its high visibility in the media, because of the ways it has been attacked by certain factions within academia and parts of the lesbian population, and possibly because of its direct engagement with heated social issues such as human genitalia, transsexuality is the most emotionally fraught of the categories within transgender.

Because the mass media has usually emphasized the freakishness of trans issues in order to maximize the value of trans as consumable spectacle, transgendereds most visible to the public have tended to be the minority of m2f transsexuals who practice stereotypically gendered behavior. In contradistinction, the greater transsexual population—less visible in the media—is far more diverse. Some transsexuals do essentialize sex and gender, employing terms such as "born into the wrong body." But a growing mass of evidence links this self-presentation to the individual's perceived need to successfully negotiate a medicolegal system that itself essentializes sex and gender. When such constraints are absent or in abeyance, most transsexuals evince far more complex personal presentations, much as does the non-transgendered population in general.

Transsexual categories

Preop: Transsexual who elects genital surgery but has not yet had it. Some gender reassignment programs require that transsexuals who choose genital surgery spend a period of time living in the social role appropriate to their gender of choice before undergoing surgery, as a hedge against rash decisions. Apart from that, raising sufficient funds for surgery may take years; thus, the preop period may be quite extensive.

Postop: Transsexual who has completed genital surgery.

No-op: A transsexual who does not choose genital reassignment. Not to be confused with a cross-dresser. In a slightly reductionist explanation, cross-dressing is primarily about appearance, whereas no-op transsexuality is primarily about identity.

History

Though in a general sense there always have been destabilizing instances in most sociocultural constructions and representations of sex, gender, sexuality, and embodiment, the term *transgender* is of recent origin and largely unknown outside a few western industrialized nations, although the hege-

mony of the United States in the establishment of transnational capitalism and its associated forms of "meaning production" is rapidly changing this situation.

To follow the historical narrative of transgender, a useful point of origin is the coinage of the precursor term *transvestite* by Magnus Hirschfeld in 1910. The term included virtually everything that would now be identified by one or the other of the broad variety of subterms within transgender discourse: in early twentieth-century sexology, transvestism, homosexuality, and intersexuality were broadly interrelated or conflated.

Devising elaborate schema of sexual classification was a favorite pursuit of many biologists, psychologists, criminologists, and other specialists in human behavior from the Victorian era through Kinsey, until modern genetics described the structure of DNA in the 1950s and introduced another kind of representation. A critical early turning point in this classificatory endeavor remains the introduction of the endocrinological model of sex difference, beginning around 1910, which permanently upset older Victorian notions of men and women. It is during the period in which the endocrinological model held sway, from 1910 into the 1950s, that most of the medical interventions still in use to manage gendered embodiment were deployed.

After World War II, a new sociopolitical environment crystallized in the United States and Europe, in which sexual identity politics and minority social movements moved to center stage as agents of cultural change and political rallying points. Additionally, Stryker points out how a new (postmodern, for lack of a better term) episteme began to take shape after concentration camps, atomic weapons, computers, and television changed the terrain of signification, and how transsexuality perhaps becomes the paradigmatic form of gendered embodiment for these conditions.

In 1949–1954, the word *transsexual* entered the discourse of popular culture, largely owing to the media attention focused on Christine Jorgenson, who was widely reported to have undergone the first male-to-female "sex change." (In actuality, there were several prior to Jorgenson, but their accounts tend to be more simplistic and sensational and to introduce elements of magical realism. The earliest example of this genre, from 1929, is "Man into Woman," the story of the m2f Lili Elbe.) During this period, the sexologist Alfred Kinsey not only conducted research with but also actively encouraged networking between what were then called "sex variants." Thus, in a literal Foucauldian way, sexological discourse provided the basis for new social formations predicated on minoritized identity, as exemplified by (for example) James-Virginia Prince, a transvestite psychotherapist and activist in identity politics.

During 1966, three events constituted major points in Trans discourse. First, with the opening of the Johns Hopkins University Gender Clinic, surgical gender reassignment or "sex change" became possible in the United States. Second, Harry Benjamin's *The Transsexual Phenomenon* was published. Although plagued with essentialism, this book marked the first attempt at a reasoned and sympathetic exploration of transsexuality for a lay audience. Third, a pivotal event that became known as the Compton's Cafeteria riot occurred in San Francisco's Tenderloin district. For the first known time, trans patrons fought back against police harrassment—an event trans historians refer to as the "Transgender Stonewall," three years before the Stonewall riot in New York City (which also was led by transgendered persons).

Out of this transgender militancy came an efflorescence of peer-run, politically progressive social programs: for example, the National Transsexual Counseling Unit, the Stanford Gender Dysphoria Program, and the Center for Special Problems, all in San Francisco. The consolidation of the Benjamin Standards and the creation and official pathologization of GID (gender identity disorder, replacing the slightly older and less pathological term gender dysphoria syndrome) was completed in 1979–1980. These medical-pathological classifications drove the proliferation of transgender categories that emerged from this moment, and that were based on physical interventions such as surgery. This situation, although fraught with the potential for its own essentialism and reification, was nevertheless a significant advance in at least clarifying and formalizing the uneasy relationship between trans discourses and gatekeepers of more mainstream discourses; and it became the background against which other gender-related social formations defined themselves.

The AIDS pandemic pulled transgendereds back into coalition with other sexual minority groups, and led to the conceptual shift known as "queer." Among transgender communities of color, the real mobilization and beginnings of new organizations and institutions and new sources of funding began in 1989, in the second wave of response to AIDS. This move reached middle-class white transgendereds in 1991–1992; and from it emerged such "queer" transgender groups as Transgender Nation San Francisco, Transsexual Menace, and the Intersex Society of North America, each with its own politics and purposes.

Beginning in the 1970s, transsexuality was "discovered" by academe, and scholarly texts appeared that claimed to be critical studies of trans. For reasons yet to be understood, this first crop (for example, Janice Raymond, *The Transsexual Empire;* Catherine Millot, *Horsexe;* and, later, Bernice

Hausman, *Changing Sex*) almost without exception evinced casual bigotry, essentialism, and (in the case of Millot) a tendency to exploit trans's potential freakishness, sometimes in the guise of dispassionate criticism.

In 1991, *The Empire Strikes Back: A Posttranssexual Manifesto,* written by the present author as response to one of the more bigoted studies, constituted the point at which trans issues entered mainstream academic and intellectual discourse, and the conduit in critical discourse where transgender issues once again engaged mainstream cultural processes. In the wake of the *Posttranssexual Manifesto* came a spate of trans critical work (for example, Kate Bornstein, *Gender Outlaw* and *My Gender Workbook;* Leslie Feinberg, *Transgender Liberation;* Markisha Greaney, *How to Guarantee Rejection by the University of Your Choice*), and the founding of what has come to be called transgender studies. From that point to the present, trans theorists have been engaged in creating a peer-driven discourse; and it has become progressively less fashionable for non-trans academics to publish books claiming to "explain," invent critical discourses about, or otherwise speak for transgender and transgendered theoreticians—just as with subaltern discourse and the point at which, in an earlier age, white critics realized they could not claim to speak authoritatively as or for theoreticians of color.

In 1993, the trans presence at the March on Washington brought trans politics back into national lesbian-gay-bisexual (LGB) discourse—the first time trans issues were raised in a serious manner since the late 1960s, when LGB political debates and decisions marginalized and later silenced trans issues. Increasingly, the abbreviation LGB became LGBT.

In 1994, Susan Stryker's "My Words to Victor Frankenstein Above the Village of Chamounix" became the first article by an openly trans author to be published in a peer-reviewed academic journal. In 1998, Stryker edited a special issue of *Gay and Lesbian Quarterly* devoted entirely to transgender studies. At the Queer Studies Conference in Iowa in 1994, the Transgender Academic Network was established, growing into a series of electronic mail lists, which are still in active use.

In the mid-1990s, the murder of Brandon Teena–Teena Brandon called greater attention to trans issues, both in the LGBT community and more broadly. It helped spur the growth of politically active trans organizations, as did controversies over the Michigan Womyn's Music Festival (MWMF). MWMF, which from its inception had maintained a policy of admitting only "womyn-born womyn," came under polite attack from a militant trans group, at first consisting solely of m2f, but later joined by f2m, transsexuals. The group set up its own camp, Camp Trans, across the road from the MWMF entrance, distributing pamphlets and holding consciousness-raising classes.

Among a host of other things, the episode of MWMF and Camp Trans served to make visible to nearly all the participants that workable definitions of sex and gender remain partial, situated, and socially emergent. It also produced heightened awareness of the deep emotions, old wounds, and unresolved conflicts surrounding struggles over meaning, conflicts that impinge on the task of elucidating working definitions and building consensus—even at the heart of both Lesbian and Trans discourses.

Recently mass media have evinced a heightened fascination with trans for reasons other than its freakishness. Trans and transgendered people (or nontransgendered actors impersonating transgendered people) have begun to appear in movies, on talk shows, and in sly fashion ads. In short, there is some evidence that at the millennium transgender is being mainstreamed. That is to say, like other social formations that have evinced potential to destabilize existing power structures, transgender is being rearticulated to perpetuate masculinist fantasies of escape from embodiment through commodity consumption, while ignoring the legal and economic plight of real transgender lives. Perhaps in spite of itself, however, this problematic media attention—plus the role of the Internet, the Web, and other new communication technologies—has fostered serious transgender discourse within the academy and, to a certain extent, with a larger public; and it has encouraged transgendered individuals and groups to speak out for their own self-determination.

See Also

HETEROPHOBIA AND HOMOPHOBIA; IDENTITY POLITICS; SEXUAL DIFFERENCE; SEXUAL ORIENTATION; SEXUALITY: OVERVIEW

References and Further Reading

Bolin, Anne. 1994. Transcending and transgendering: Male-to-female transsexuals, dichotomy, and diversity. In Gilbert Herdt, ed., *Third Sex, Third Gender: Beyond Sexual Dimorphism in Culture and History,* 447–485. New York: Zone.

Bornstein, Kate. 1994. *Gender outlaw: On men, women, and the rest of us.* New York: Routledge.

Bullough, Bonnie, Vern Bullough, and James Elias, eds. 1997. *Gender blending.* Amherst, N.Y.: Prometheus.

Butler, Judith. 1990. *Gender trouble: Feminism and the subversion of identity.* New York: Routledge.

Califia, Pat. 1997. *Sex changes: The politics of transgenderism.* San Francisco: Cleis.

Feinberg, Leslie. 1996. *Transgender warriors: Making history from Joan of Arc to RuPaul.* Boston: Beacon.

Hausman, Bernice. 1995. *Changing sex: Transsexualism, technology, and the idea of gender.* Durham, N.C.: Duke University Press.

Israel, Gianna, and Donald E. Tarver, eds. 1997. *Transgender care: Recommended guidelines, practical information, and personal accounts.* Philadelphia: Temple University Press.

Sandy Stone

TRAVEL WRITING

There was a distinct revival of interest in women's travel writing at the end of the twentieth century, especially after the English publisher Virago reissued a series of British women's travel texts written in the nineteenth and early twentieth centuries. Many of these travel texts had not been reprinted since their original publication, and they surprised many late twentieth-century readers by the range of possible forms of behavior that were available to Victorian women travelers. Rather than the shy, retiring stereotype of the middle-class British feminine woman, there emerged a vision of individuals who defied conventions and traveled in conditions that would challenge most women from the turn of the twenty-first century.

Women travelers have conventionally been viewed as curious eccentrics, oddities who transgressed the boundaries of behavior judged acceptable for women to maintain their femininity. Victorian notions of femininity determined that women should center their lives largely on the private sphere of the home. When middle-class women went outside the home or when they were in the company of men, it was common for them to be chaperoned—to have an older female companion who would protect their "honor." Women who traveled, particularly those who traveled alone, were judged to be "adventuresses," a term that has strong sexual connotations.

Women have written about their travels since at least the fourteenth century, beginning with the English mystic Margery Kempe (c. 1373–c. 1440). She traveled to the major Christian shrines—Jerusalem, Santiago de Compostela, and Rome—as well as traveling extensively to holy sites in Great Britain. There were a fair number of women travelers in the eighteenth century, for example, Celia Fiennes (1682–1712), Mary Wollstonecraft (1759–1797), and Lady Mary Wortley Montagu (1689–1762); these women were drawn mainly from the aristocracy. It was only in the nineteenth century that a greater number of women traveled, and the majority of these were from the middle classes. They traveled on missionary work, for exploration, to write reports for newspapers, to accompany their husbands, to collect botanical specimens, or simply for the sake of traveling.

Many of them wrote strikingly original texts. For example, Mary Kingsley (1862–1900) wrote an account of her travels, *Travels in West Africa* (1965; orig. 1897), that is witty and idiosyncratic, stressing the problems she encountered and the humorous ways she managed to solve them. For example, unlike many male travelers, she focused on the mistakes she made and the accidents she had, pointing out how ridiculous she looked to the inhabitants of the region: "Going through a clump of *shenja*, I slipped, slid and finally fell plump through the roof of an unprotected hut. What the unfortunate inhabitants were doing I don't know, but I am pretty sure they were not expecting me to drop in, and a scene of great confusion occurred" (79). She represented herself as an indomitable spirit while not transgressing the image of herself as feminine. Characterizing her account as a "well-intentioned word-swamp," she struggled to find a form of expression that was appropriate to recounting her adventures while not offending her reading public.

Other women travel writers, such as Alexandra David-Neel (1868–1969), chose other methods to deal with the constraints of writing about other countries. In her book *My Journey to Lhasa* (1983; orig. 1927), David-Neel adopted a straightforwardly heroic masculine adventurer role model in describing her attempt to be the first western woman to reach the "forbidden city" of Lhasa, Tibet, in a narrative that is full of suspense and intrigue. In contrast, writers such as Nina Mazuchelli (1832–1914) stressed the efforts that they made to retain their femininity and preserve British decorum while in foreign countries. Thus, what is most notable about women's travel writing is the great variety of strategies that individual authors adopted in order to navigate in the complex networks of socially acceptable behavior.

Most of the critics who have written on this subject have been interested primarily in women who traveled to countries that were subject to British imperial rule, because of interest in colonial and postcolonial discourse and theory (Blunt, 1994; Mills, 1991). However, some of them, like Shirley Foster (1990), have been concerned with women who traveled to Europe and to the United States. Some of the critics have taken a rather straightforwardly biographical approach to these writings, but many of the critics in the 1990s subjected them to close textual analysis to see whether these women wrote within the same textual confines as did their male counterparts, or whether in fact women travel writers developed a different voice to describe their travels.

Some critics see women's travel writing as necessarily different textually from men's writing; so, for example, it is asserted that women travelers write about the domestic environment and about details of dress and customs more than men do. Some critics, such as Catherine Stevenson (1982, 1985), also see women as necessarily critical of the colonial powers; she views this critique as a displacement of their potential feminism. While in many cases that is true, it cannot be assumed that women are any less racist or less involved in colonialism simply because they are female.

Women travel writers, particularly within the colonial setting, experienced a range of pressures on their writings; they were pulled in different directions by their allegiance or resistance to colonial or imperial rule and by their need to present or challenge an acceptable feminine persona for their reading public. The writings of women travelers challenge readers to rethink stereotyped views about women in earlier periods; we cannot simply see these women travelers as eccentric and abnormal. In some sense, they force us to reconsider the way that women managed to carve out spaces for themselves within a social system that repressed women's freedoms.

See Also

DIARIES AND JOURNALS; LITERATURE: OVERVIEW; TOURISM

References and Further Reading

Birkett, Dea. 1989. *Spinsters abroad: Victorian lady explorers.* Oxford: Oxford University Press.

Blunt, Alison. 1994. *Travel, gender and imperialism.* New York: Guilford.

Foster, Shirley. 1990. *Across new worlds: nineteenth-century women travellers and their writings.* Hemel Hempstead, U.K.: Harvester Wheatsheaf.

Midgley, Clare, ed. 1998. *Gender imperialism.* Manchester, U.K.: Manchester University Press.

Mills, Sara. 1991. *Discourses of difference: Women's travel writing and colonialism.* London: Routledge.

Montagu, Lady Mary Wortley. 1767. *Letters of lady Mary Wortley Montagu.* London: De Hondt.

Pratt, Mary Louise. 1992. *Imperial eyes: Travel writing and transculturation.* London: Routledge.

Robinson, Jane. 1990. *Wayward women: A guide to women travellers.* Oxford: Oxford University Press.

Stevenson, Catherine. 1982. *Victorian women travel writers in Africa.* Boston: Twayne.

Wollstonecraft, Mary. 1987. *Letters written during a short residence in Sweden.* Harmondsworth, U.K.: Penguin (originally published 1796).

Sara Mills

U

UNDEREMPLOYMENT

Underemployment may be regarded as a form of disguised unemployment. A narrow definition of underemployment would relate primarily to hours worked in the wage economy. Even that definition creates conceptual problems, however. For example, should all persons working less than the normal hours of wage labor, usually taken as full-time work, be regarded as underemployed? This approach endorses the "male breadwinner" model of participation as the "normal" mode and thus renders invisible the domestic labor provided by women to facilitate male employment.

An alternative approach is to define underemployment with respect to preferences, so that persons may be regarded as underemployed if they would prefer to engage in more hours of wage work. This approach allows for nonwage work to be taken into account but again takes the domestic division of labor as given. Underemployment may also relate to the predictability of work, so that those who are not guaranteed a reasonable amount of work could be regarded as underemployed. This definition applies to many areas of female employment, such as home-working or part-time and temporary work on variable-hours contracts.

A still broader definition of underemployment might include those employed below their skill level or potential, and those whose jobs provide inadequate income. Many women face discrimination in their access to education and training and are employed in jobs that do not use the skills and qualifications they have acquired. Moreover, many cannot earn sufficient income to cover their subsistence needs. However, under this broader approach, many men will also be considered underemployed. No precise definition of underemployment can be given, but the recognition of the existence of underemployment allows for a richer analysis of the meaning of full employment on the one hand, and of unemployment on the other.

See Also

PART-TIME AND CASUAL WORK; UNEMPLOYMENT

References and Further Reading

Livingstone, D.W. 1998. *The education-jobs gap: Underemployment or economic democracy.* New York: Perseus Book Group.

Jill Rubery

UNEMPLOYMENT

Gender and the Definition of the Unemployed

Unemployment is a concept usually applied to persons who are without, but are available for, wage work. Participation in nonwage work is not taken directly into account, unless it renders the person unavailable for wage work. Women's greater involvement in nonwage work lies at the center of debates over the appropriate definition of unemployment as applied to women. For women, the alternative to wage employment is still regarded in many societies—even those with high female participation in the workforce—as participation in nonwage work (domestic work, work related to the informal economy, and volunteer work), instead of the male alternative of seeking reentry into wage employment. Thus many of the female "unemployed" become the "hidden" unemployed, as they move between wage employment and nonwage work rather than between wage employment and unemployment. As women have increased their share of wage employment over recent years, this difference between women's and men's relationship to these classifications of economic activity has increasingly rendered official unemployment statistics inappropriate as a measure of persons available for wage work.

Most new jobs, over recent decades, have been taken by those regarded as outside the labor market and not part of the unemployed population (see CEC, 1993). This has generally led not to any major reassessment of the official means by which unemployment is assessed, but rather to policy statements to the effect that increased labor demand will not have a major effect on the unemployed. From this approach, not only are women outside the labor force and not to be counted as unemployed—for official statistical purposes or for benefit payment purposes—but the policies of creation of wage employment aimed at reducing hidden unemployment are often regarded as having missed the real target of reducing *measured* unemployment—that is, male unemployment. Some evidence of a change in perspective can be found in the recent emphasis within the European Union on relative employment rates rather than on measured unemployment rates. This places greater value on increasing the employment rate across the population and not simply on integrating those classified as unemployed into wage work.

The actual definition used to measure unemployment has a major impact on the share of women included in the unemployment count. OECD (Organization for Economic Cooperation and Development) countries tend to have two main series of unemployment statistics: one relates to national systems of defining unemployment, often linked to benefit systems; the other relates to OECD and ILO (International Labor Organization) definitions of unemployment, which focus on an individual's involvement in looking for work over the past month. These two approaches result in quite different levels of unemployment, but, more important, quite different compositions of the defined unemployed labor forces. The ILO/OECD definitions tend to include higher shares of women because they do not depend on eligibility for benefits. Most countries, but not all, still effectively discriminate against women in access to unemployment benefits (Meulders et al., 1993) because access is often linked to evidence of past labor market behavior corresponding to that of a male breadwinner—that is, continuous full-time wage employment. These eligibility conditions often exclude women, who may take breaks from wage employment, work part-time, or earn wages too low to qualify.

These problems are exacerbated if household income is taken into account in determining access to benefits. In some countries, such as the United Kingdom, women may effectively be induced into unemployment by the benefit system; wives of unemployed men find it uneconomic to continue in wage work because they lose entitlement or tax benefits equal to all that they earn once their earnings rise above a very low level (McLaughlin, 1994). Thus women suffer double jeopardy: they have reduced access to unemployment benefits because of their lower probability of a full-time continuous career path and their lower earnings levels, and they may face extremely high rates of tax on their earnings if their partners are employed.

Even the ILO/OECD definitions may not provide an adequate definition of female unemployment if more women undertake nonwage or informal-sector work when they are without wage employment. Under these conditions, they may be less active in seeking wage work and less likely to perceive themselves as without work (Dex, 1985), even though they may still be available for wage work. Women are more likely than men to seek work through informal networks and thus are less actively engaged in the formal job hunt. Moreover, to be regarded as unemployed, it is often necessary to prove availability for work, but those with childcare responsibilities are unlikely to make alternative childcare arrangements before finding a job.

Although the high entry rates into wage employment from nonemployment provide evidence of continued hidden unemployment, it must also be recognized that women have shown a greater tendency to register as unemployed over recent years, and in many countries women's unemployment rate exceeds men's. Women's measured unemployment has risen alongside their measured employment rates. This suggests a continuation of problems for women in gaining access to employment, but also a reduced tendency for women to retire from the wage labor force when they have difficulty obtaining employment. Women's unemployment in rural areas has reached particularly high levels (EC, 1994a). In urban areas, women may be less likely to be put permanently out of work by local economic restructuring. Women are much less geographically mobile than men and thus are more likely to remain unemployed if they lose their jobs in a depressed local labor market with a limited range of employing organizations.

As a consequence of the definitional problems relating to unemployment, women are often excluded both from unemployment benefits and from programs designed to help the unemployed back into wage work. Many programs intended to help women back into work are training schemes, but these focus on the women's lack of skills and not on the perhaps discriminatory hiring policies of employers. Such programs thus may not be enough to help women back into work.

Underemployment and Gender

Another problem with the classification of women's economic activity relates to the question of whether women are more prone to underemployment as well as unemployment. The concept of underemployment is by no means clear-cut. To define underemployment implies a norm of what constitutes full employment for the individual. Norms relating to full or full-time employment in the wage labor market have been defined with respect to a male breadwinner who is deemed not to have domestic responsibilities. It is therefore not appropriate to determine that women who work less than a standard full-time week are underemployed, because that would be to ignore the vast amount of nonwage work that is undertaken by women to facilitate the full-time work of their partners and adult children. However, the normal amount of wage and nonwage work to be carried out by an individual is clearly culturally determined and is not related solely to gender factors. Thus, the level of nonwage work may vary between societies as well as between men and women. In some societies women may still be constrained by social expectations of high levels of nonwage work from taking more than a very part-time wage job, or perhaps working for limited hours in the informal sector, for example as a homeworker. In other societies, the constraints on participation may not be expectations—for example, of home cooking—but simply the absence of child-care facilities or the lack of employment opportunities other than part-time or informal-sector jobs offering very short hours. Many surveys have pointed to the satisfaction of women with part-time jobs in countries where this is the established norm (Hakim, 1991), but these surveys can be criticized on two counts. First, the expressed levels of satisfaction may reflect an accurate perception of opportunities in a country with limited support for working mothers; second, the surveys often fail to ask detailed questions about desired hours. Where these questions are asked, evidence suggests that a significant number of women in part-time jobs would in fact like to work longer hours (Marsh, 1991), although not necessarily full-time. Thus, there is evidence of underemployment among those working part-time.

There is also considerable evidence of women being underemployed throughout the economy if we take into account not only hours of work but also quality of jobs. Even allowing for the clear undervaluation of women's jobs within the economy, it is evident that women are underemployed relative to their economic potential. Women are likely to be employed in low-productivity firms and sectors—for example, in the small-firm service sector and in the informal economy. Here women may be asked to exercise considerable skills, but their low economic rewards in part reflect the fact that these firms may be relatively inefficient and use out-of-date or limited capital equipment. The fact that women are often available at wage levels that would be unlikely to cover their full subsistence costs may act as a significant subsidy to these firms and perhaps helps to disguise the extent to which the economy falls below full employment.

Redefining Full Employment

The increasing entry of women into employment over recent years has challenged the accepted definitions of unemployment. In the Beveridge Report, which introduced the notion of full employment to Britain, full employment was explicitly defined with respect to men and clearly referred to the provision of full-time stable jobs: "Full employment... means having always more vacant jobs than unemployed men, not slightly fewer jobs. It means that the jobs are at fair wages, of such a kind, and so located that the unemployed men can reasonably be expected to take them" (Beveridge, 1944: 18).

The development of more flexible employment forms, coupled with the entry of women into the economy, has caused problems in developing a modern definition of either full employment or unemployment. Should the unemployed be forced or encouraged to take part-time jobs? Should those who are available only for part-time work be counted among the unemployed, and if so, is there an hours threshold below which they should not be included? Should those employed part-time who wish to have full-time jobs be counted as unemployed (as they are, for example, in Italy)? Should the benefit system make up the shortfall between income needs and part-time work, or does that just subsidize low-paying employers? How much part-time work should the unemployed be allowed to undertake and still retain access to unemployment benefits?

These questions appear difficult enough to resolve even before we consider gender factors. The problems multiply once the extremely varied household circumstances and the gender of the unemployed are taken into account. The implicit object in discussions of the unemployed in Europe is the unemployed male. There is claimed to be a decline in the demand for low-skilled labor, but in practice there has perhaps been more of a switch toward low-skilled labor in services away from manufacturing. Many of the persons employed in services are women, and in some countries these jobs are mostly part-time. Despite the increasing integration of women into the wage economy, in many countries jobs are still effectively designed *either* for male breadwinners *or* for second-income earners. The increasing importance of the latter type of jobs in the economy raises the likelihood of a mismatch between the jobs available to the unemployed and the aspirations and needs of those unemployed, both male and female, who have sole or main responsibility for their own or their family's living costs. In the United Kingdom, these patterns are resulting in an increasing divide between work-rich and work-poor households, because the only persons who can take low-paid part-time jobs tend to be found in households where there is already one income earner (Gregg, 1993).

The level of female unemployment depends both upon the participation rate of women in the labor market and on the demand for female labor. Participation rates within and between countries still can vary more for women than for men. Thus, the prospects for unemployment among women are still driven by these two variables. In the post–World War II period, the demand for female labor has been relatively buoyant and has thus tended to provide some protection for women against rising unemployment accompanying rising participation rates. There must be more doubts about future prospects for women's employment, however. Women's participation rates have tended to retain an upward trend even in the face of general recession and job loss. Even though some women may retire temporarily from the labor market when faced with unemployment, their exit has been more than offset by entry of other women from inactivity—possibly to safeguard family incomes when overtime and general employment opportunities for men decline.

The buoyant demand for female labor has been the consequence of continued gender segregation (Rubery, 1988). Employers do not select disinterestedly between male and female labor, and in some job areas they consider women more appropriate, both because the skills required have become associated with female labor and because they regard women as better or more stable employees under current pay and working conditions. However, the job areas that have been the major source of expansion of female employment in the past—for example, service work in the private and public sectors, and clerical work—may in the future be subject to the same process of rationalization and reduction resulting from the introduction of new technologies that damaged men's employment prospects in the 1980s and 1990s. It is significant that in the 1990s, for the first time, there was evidence of a contraction of clerical work, which

had been a major area of growth in the past; and drops in employment in sectors such as banking and the public sector also heralded major cutbacks in female-dominated areas, particularly in intermediate-level jobs for women (EC, 1994b). Thus, female unemployment may be expected to rise, bolstered by both the downturn in relative employment demand and the seemingly unstoppable trend for women to seek participation in the wage economy.

See Also

ANTIDISCRIMINATION; DISCRIMINATION; ECONOMY: INFORMAL; ECONOMY: WELFARE AND THE ECONOMY; UNDEREMPLOYMENT; VOLUNTEERISM; WORK: FEMINIST THEORIES; WORK: OCCUPATIONAL EXPERIENCES

References and Further Reading

Beveridge, William. 1944. *Report on full employment in a free society.* White Paper. London: Her Majesty's Stationery Office.

CEC (Commission of the European Communities). 1993. *Growth, competitiveness and employment: The challenges and ways forward into the 21st century.* White Paper. Luxembourg: European Commission.

Dex, S. 1985. *The sexual division of work: Conceptual revolutions in the social sciences.* Brighton, U.K.: Wheatsheaf.

EC (European Commission). 1994a. The economic role and situation of women in rural areas (by Dr. Mary Braithwaite). *Green Europe,* no. 1. Luxembourg: European Commission.

———. 1994b. *Employment in Europe.* Luxembourg: European Commission.

Gregg, P. 1993. Why job creation alone will not solve unemployment. In E. Balls and P. Gregg, *Work and welfare: Tackling the jobs deficit.* Commission on Social Justice issue paper no. 3. London Institute for Public Policy Research.

Hakim, C. 1991. Grateful slaves and self-made women: Fact and fantasy in women's work orientations. *European Sociological Review* 7(2): 101–21.

Marsh, C. 1991. *Hours of work of women and men in Britain.* Equal Opportunities Commission Research Series. London: Her Majesty's Stationery Office.

McLaughlin, E. 1994. *Flexibility in work and benefits.* Commission on Social Justice issue paper no. 11. London: Institute for Public Policy Research.

Meulders, D., R. Plasman, and V. Vander Stricht. 1993. *Position of women on the labour market in the European Community.* Aldershot, U.K.: Dartmouth.

Rubery, Jill, ed. 1988. *Women and recession.* London: Routledge and Kegan Paul.

Jill Rubery

UNION MOVEMENTS

"Bread and Roses," the anthem celebrating a stike by textile workers in Lawrence, Massachusetts, in 1912, succinctly captures the economic and social aspirations long associated with women's union activity. Women organized into unions for "bread"—economic security through demands for a living wage sufficient to sustain life—and "roses," dignity and shorter work time, with the possibility of a meaningful life beyond the workplace. "Our lives should not be sweated from birth until life closes; hearts starve as well as bodies; give us bread, but give us roses!"

The phenomenon of workers' combining for self-help and improved working conditions, mutual protection, and economic advancement can be traced back to antiquity. But a labor movement in the contemporary sense, suggesting large, formal, membership organizations of wage-earners that engage in collective bargaining and representation of their members, is essentially a product of the industrial revolution. For women, as for male workers, the particular form of union organization and activity engaged in tended to parallel the organization and growth of the industry in which workers were employed. National and local labor laws have shaped unions throughout their history, first by banning collective action by workers as a conspiracy against commerce, and later by reluctantly permitting limited and highly regulated concerted activity. In the North American model, unions are certified by a government agency to be the exclusive bargaining agents for all employees within a designated bargaining unit. In the European model, workers have both enterprise-level employee councils, and unions at a regional and national level for collective bargaining purposes. In both systems, unions seek to represent both men and women workers as broadly as possible.

History

The earliest unions—precursors of the mass organizations that exist today—were benevolent societies, mutual aid associations, and craft guilds. These organizations were small, localized, and—for the most part—short-lived. Reflecting the highly gendered division of labor and women's confinement within the paid labor market to a few crafts and occupations, women workers in the nineteenth century tended to form their own local craft organizations. Unions such as the United Tailoresses' Society of New York (circa 1831), the Female Union Society of Tailoresses and Seamstresses of Baltimore (circa 1833), and the Female Boot and Shoe Binders Society (circa 1836) were some of the earliest examples of women's labor societies. Occasionally, women workers

joined with men in a common craft organization, such as the United Men and Women's Trading Society (1835, Baltimore). But with few enduring labor organizations (male or female) in the nineteenth century, women's unions were a tiny minority within a very small and precarious labor movement. Employers' and governments' hostility, long hours, and the tremendous employment turnover, combined with the restriction of women's paid labor mostly to young, unmarried women, made it impossible to sustain these associations for any length of time.

Labor unions everywhere have had to struggle against hostile employers, restrictive labor laws, and state action aimed at weakening labor's collective power. Women's union activity, however, had to contend in addition with the hostility of male workers, who saw female workers as unskilled labor and a source of lower-paid competition. The American Federation of Labor's founding president, Samuel Gompers, reflected the view of the federation and its male workers when, in an editorial in the *American Federationist* in the summer of 1917 titled "Don't Sacrifice Womanhood," he urged labor to take a stand against "laying tasks on women they are not able to bare [sic]" (Foner, 1982: 248). Gompers argued that "it is wrong to permit any of the female sex of our country to be forced to work, as we believe that men should be provided with a fair wage in order to keep his female relatives from going to work."

Unions and Women's Rights

Unions at their finest have assisted women workers in combating such prejudice and promoting women's equality and rights in the workplace and within society as a whole. Unions, for example, were among the first organizations to call for equal pay for equal work. As well, unions have been in the vanguard of the movement for shorter work time, paid vacations, pensions, health care, maternity leave, and family care leave. But as democratic organizations adopting policies reflecting the majority view of their members, they have throughout their history also displayed a wide variety of contradictory policies and attitudes toward women workers and toward women in unions. As a result, the women's movement often takes an ambivalent and occasionally even hostile stance toward unions, arguing that, all too often, unions have acted as male job trusts rather than organizations promoting equality and justice for all workers. Unions have sometimes sought to protect women workers, demanding gender-specific protective legislation. But whether intentional or not, this selective protection has often resulted in women's exclusion from certain jobs, industries, and whole sectors of the economy. Similarly, the demand for a "family wage," made by male unionists, rarely took into consideration the needs of female household heads or single women. And even where unions encouraged women workers to organize and form unions, male workers often excluded women from full membership in existing unions, offering women instead special membership status as "auxiliaries," and denying them the full complement of benefits and privileges extended to male members.

An important exception to the exclusionary policy of many early craft unions was the large national labor federation, the Knights of Labor, which voted in 1881 to admit women as full members. The Knights proved to be an important training ground for many women union leaders, including one of the most famous union organizers and agitators, Mary Harris Jones, known as Mother Jones. In spite of their inclusive policy, the Knights declined toward the end of the nineteenth century and were replaced by the more exclusionary national union of craft and trades, the American Federation of Labor (AFL). Most AFL unions either directly excluded women from membership or relegated female members to a separate and inferior status.

In face of the AFL's hostility, and in an effort to promote organizing working women and educating them on the benefits of unions and to assist them in gaining support, recognition, and—eventually—acceptance within the male labor movement, women middle-class reformers, socialists, and working women formed the Women's Trade Union League (WTUL) in 1903. Although the WTUL was modestly successful in bringing the plight of women workers to greater public attention, and in prompting occasional support for working women from the AFL, most women workers remained excluded from union membership well into the twentieth century. The development of a competing union federation, the Congress of Industrial Organizations (CIO), during the Great Depression and the wartime entry of women into war work temporarily broke many barriers to women in both the workplace and the labor movement.

By the time the two competing federations merged in 1955 to form the AFL/CIO, many of the wartime gains by women in industrial and union leadership had been rolled back. But with a new wave of women's activism in the 1960s, the Coalition of Union Women was formed in 1974. This organization—within the AFL-CIO but otherwise in the tradition of the WTUL—is committed to organizing women, promoting affirmative action in the workplace, and increasing women's participation in unions.

Women in Unions

At the start of the twenty-first century, with women's participation in the paid labor force at record levels, account-ing for just under 50 percent of the U.S. workforce, women constitute over one-third of the membership of the U.S. labor movement, and a majority of new members joining unions. Underscoring this trend, public opinion polls over the last decade of the twentieth century consistently reported that women outpolled men in their receptivity to unions. Many unions, including organizations in the traditional male blue-collar sector, are eager to organize women and are revising their policies, constitutions, and practices in an effort to encourage greater participation by women at all levels of the organization. The AFL/CIO revised its constitution in 1995 to create a new senior officer position, executive vice president. Linda Chavez Thompson, a Latina public-sector unionist from Texas, was elected to this position. In addition, the executive council of the federation was expanded to improve the representation of women and minorities in the federation's leadership body.

Women's support of unions and their interest in collective bargaining are easy to understand. Unionization has proved to be an effective action that women workers can take to close the gender wage gap. On average, women covered by collective agreements earn 40 percent more than women workers without the benefits of unionization. As well, women union members are much more likely than nonunion women workers to have company-paid pensions, health insurance, vacations, and other benefits negotiated with employers. Women's growing weight within the labor movement, however, cannot be attributed solely to their increased receptivity to unionization; we also must take into account the decline in unionization among male workers.

Although unions and many other national and international institutions have condemned unequal pay and gender discrimination in the workplace, in both developing and advanced industrial economies women's paid labor is still characterized by wage discrimination and job segregation. In 1996, for example, for every 10 working women in the United States, 8.6 were employed in the less-unionized service sector. Not surprisingly, unions with the highest percentage of women, and those most likely to have women in leadership roles, are in these sectors—education, health care, and clerical occupations.

Unions in the Future

Women's participation and leadership within unions at the start of the twenty-first century is as varied as the international labor movement itself. In advanced industrial countries with mass, institutionalized labor movements, the continued increase in women's workforce participation has prompted unions to develop organizing campaigns, special departments, and policies to encourage women to join and actively participate in unions. Inside unions, women have organized to increase the proportion of women in union leadership at all levels and to draw greater attention to issues of concern to working women, such as pay discrimination, job segregation, harassment, and balancing the demands of work and family. In a number of European countries, as well as in Canada, Australia, and New Zealand, women have been elected presidents of national union federations. Women tend to be leaders in unions in the public sector, especially education, and in unions for traditional female occupations, including health care, nursing, hospitality, clerical work, and apparel. Overall, however, even in unions and federations where women are in leadership, women are rarely found in union leadership in the same proportion as women's total membership within the union.

In developing countries, the situation also is complex. In countries that have high levels of women's workforce participation and institutionalized unions, women often join existing unions. As in advanced industrial countries, these women have sought to increase women's presence and influence within the labor movement and to encourage organizing efforts in the sectors of the economy in which women workers are concentrated, such as the many free-trade manufacturing centers set up by various countries—the export processing zones (EPZs)—which typically attract young women workers from the countryside. Workers in EPZs experience long hours and low pay and are an important target for organizing and regulatory action by the international labor movement and human and labor rights organizations.

In poorer countries, where the vast majority of women's employment is in the informal sector of home-based, small enterprises, or is dependent or casual employment as street vendors, artisans, or tenant farmers, women have formed their own organizations, such as the Self Employed Women's Association in India and the Self Employed Women's Union in South Africa. Forming networks and international alliances of homeworkers, such as HomeNet, and street vendors, such as StreetNet, women in the informal sector in developing and advanced industrial countries have been in the forefront of organizing both men and women in this important but often ignored economic sector. Some of these organizations are unions, affiliated with local and national labor federations; in other instances, they are proto-unions, operating as nongovernmental organizations but similar to the benevolent and mutual aid associations that were the precursors of many of today's unions.

The labor movement is a social movement that seeks to build a community of interest among workers. It is well understood that the community of workers must include women. When unions forge a community in the workplace, they provide both a collective vehicle for exercising rights and an organization for struggling for more rights. As well, unions provide a collective voice for the interests and concerns of workers, providing a powerful check to the power of management in the workplace.

Unions at the start of the twenty-first century face major challenges and are undergoing extensive change in response to a new economic environment fostered by trade liberalization, deregulation, privatization, and rapid technological change, which has tended to strengthen the power of capital over labor. Millions of women workers in the United States and internationally have decided that unions are a valuable institution for advancing their rights as workers in this changing world.

See Also

CAPITALISM; CLASS; FAMILY WAGE; NONGOVERNMENTAL ORGANIZATIONS (NGOS); POLITICAL LEADERSHIP; POLITICAL PARTICIPATION; POLITICAL REPRESENTATION; WORK: EQUAL PAY AND CONDITIONS; WORK: OCCUPATIONAL SEGREGATION; WORK: PATTERNS

References and Further Reading

Cobble, Dorothy Sue, ed. 1993. *Women and unions: Forging a partnership.* Ithaca, N.Y.: ILR.

Foner, Philip S. 1982. *Women and the American labor movement: From the first trade unions to the present.* New York: Free Press.

International Labour Organization. 1999. The role of trade unions in promoting gender equality and protecting vulnerable women workers: First report of the ISO-ICFTU Survey. <www.ilo.org>

Kenneally, James J. 1978. *Women and American trade unions.* St. Albans, Vt.: Eden.

Kessler-Harris, Alice. 1982. *Out to work: A history of wage-earning women in the United States.* New York: Oxford University Press.

Milkman, Ruth, ed. 1985. *Women, work, and protest: A century of U.S. women's labor history.* Boston: Routledge and Kegan Paul.

O'Farrell, Brigid, and Joyce Kornbluh, eds. 1996. *Rocking the boat: Union women's voices, 1915–1975.* New Brunswick, N.J.: Rutgers University Press, 1996.

Leckie, Shirley. 1996. Labor unions. *Women's History* (Summer). <www.thehistorynet.com>

Elaine Bernard

UNITED NATIONS

See INTERNATIONAL ORGANIZATIONS AND AGENCIES and GLOBAL HEALTH MOVEMENT.

UNIVERSALISM

Universalism is identified in recent thought as a tendency to see knowledge as unanchored both temporally and contextually and also as yielding totally generalized statements about the social world. For example, notions of "humanity," "the subject," or "the self" appear to be universal, even though they are actually based on "descriptions" that draw on particular western and twentieth-century characteristics; contrary concepts are positioned as "other" to these presumed norms. Feminism has determinedly opposed universalism, calling it a "totalizing discourse" or "master (literally) narrative" that actually derives from a set of values and perspectives in which male is the normative case. It is therefore paradoxical that feminism has itself come under fire from deconstructionists for apparently totalizing and universalizing elements within feminist precepts, particularly regarding the category "women." "Women," as a shared category, is fundamental to the definition of feminism because feminism is an analysis of "women" and its subordinate relationship to its superordinate binary category, "men." However, some deconstructionist theorists have equated feminist claims about *categories* ("women" and "men" as generalized social groupings) with those about category *members* (actual individual women and men who may or may not conform to category "norms"); a related argument holds that feminist analysis treats differences between category members as absolutes, rather than as a complex set of positions between the two "ends" of binaries such as women-men. In arguing this, however, these deconstructionists have produced a meta-narrative (a grand narrative or theory) that treats "feminism" as an absolute, not allowing for any internal variation or any difference between the category of "feminism" and individual feminists' views and behaviors. This is ironic, for by doing so, deconstructionists have worked and theorized in exactly the ways for which they castigate feminists.

See Also

ESSENTIALISM; POSTMODERN FEMINISM

References and Further Reading

Fuss, Diana. 1990. *Essentially speaking.* London: Routledge.
Stanley, Liz, and Sue Wise. 1993. *Breaking out again.* London: Routledge.

Liz Stanley

UNIVERSITIES

See EDUCATION: HIGHER EDUCATION and EDUCATORS: HIGHER EDUCATION.

UTOPIANISM

A long tradition of women's writing—much of which has been made newly visible in the past twenty years—might loosely be described as utopian, in that it involves the imagination of societies less oppressive to women (Albinski, 1988; Sargent, 1988). Feminist utopianism in this sense exploded in the 1970s and 1980s with new novels by Marge Piercy, Ursula Le Guin, Joanna Russ, Suzy McKee Charnas, and others, and the revival of work by earlier writers such as Charlotte Perkins Gilman. The flowering of feminist literary utopianism coincided with the upsurge of the women's movement. Some commentators, such as Angelika Bammer (1991), argue that feminism itself is essentially utopian, a view that many readers might initially find surprising or even offensive. The contested definitions of utopia studies over the last two decades of the twentieth century years are essential to how the relationship between utopianism and feminism is understood.

The term derives from Thomas More's *Utopia,* written in Latin in 1516. It is a pun, combining the Greek meanings "good place" (*eutopos*) and "no place" (*outopos*): the good society that is nowhere. The double meaning has carried into the colloquial and somewhat pejorative meaning of "utopia" as a perfect state of society whose attainment is impossible, and of "utopian" as unrealistic. Contemporary scholarly uses are more various. J. C. Davis (1981) distinguishes utopias from other forms of ideal society such as paradisical myths, golden ages, and millennial dreams and sees utopia as emerging in the early modern period, with More's text. Krishan Kumar (1991) confines the term to a literary genre of fictional descriptions of ideal societies, again beginning with More. Lyman Tower Sargent essentially agrees with Kumar but includes both positive images (eutopias) and negative ones (dystopias) under the general heading of utopia.

Sargent also recognizes a wider category of utopianism that includes intentional communities and elements of political culture. The overlapping fields of literary studies, communal studies, and political and social theory are all represented in the interdisciplinary field of utopian studies, together with history, art, architecture, film, myth, and religion. The wide scope of utopianism leads some writers to argue for a definition of utopia that goes well beyond the literary form. Crucially, Ernst Bloch (1986) argues that there is an innate utopian impulse in human beings that is expressed in a multitude of ways. The social utopia and its fictional description constitute only a small fraction of these expressions. Not only are they diffused throughout art, architecture, music, and literature, but they are also present in more mundane practices like dress. Wherever people imagine themselves or their lives transformed—through the perfect outfit, the perfect body, or the perfect house or garden, not just the perfect society—we have an expression of the utopian impulse. Ruth Levitas (1990) reviews earlier definitions of utopia and, following Bloch, argues for a broad analytic definition in which utopia is the expression of the desire for a better way of living. In this sense, there is no pejorative meaning attached to the description of feminism in general as "utopian." Broad definitions have the advantage of facilitating exploration of historical changes in the form, content, location (both temporal and spatial), and function of utopianism. They are also arguably less ethnocentric than those that tie the idea of utopia to a specifically western literary genre.

The question of function, or what utopia is for, is a vexed one. For many writers, utopia has, or should have, an instrumental function in relation to social change as well as an expressive one. Sometimes this is construed positively: utopia is that which effects transformation. Sometimes it is seen negatively (as in orthodox Marxist tradition), so that utopianism is seen as preventing change. There is also a strong current of anti-utopianism that sees utopia as leading to totalitarianism through attempts to impose on society a blueprint of impossible perfection (the prototype is Aldous Huxley's *Brave New World*). It is now generally recognized by scholars that utopian fiction, though intended to represent societies significantly better than that inhabited by the author, does not necessarily lay claim to perfection. While these societies are fictional and therefore by definition nonexistent, their possibility is an open question. But in some ways the question of possibility is irrelevant, since it assumes that utopias are imagined with a view to their literal realization. Both literary utopias (and other forms of social dreaming), however, are better understood as spaces for exploration of how things might be otherwise. They retain the critical function in insisting on the possibility of alternatives to the present, but not the didactic one of prescribing what that should be. Moylan (1986) uses the term *critical utopias* for the (mainly feminist) utopias of the 1970s, while Sargisson (1996), who discusses Hélène Cixous and Luce Irigaray as well as feminist literary texts, distinguishes between open and closed forms and definitions of utopianism.

Postmodernism, critical theory, and poststructuralist feminism have all pointed to a far less literal understanding of utopian fiction. Once utopianism is understood as an experimental space, the boundary between utopian fiction and other fictions, especially science fiction, becomes blurred. Thus, Lefanu (1988) argues that feminist science fiction, which also has a long history but blossomed in the 1970s and 1980s, is essentially a space for imagining the deconstruction of gender. In the late 1990s, science fiction remained an important space for the projection of alternative visions, both in literature and in film. However, the dominant mode of these was dystopian rather than utopian. And while this holds open the possibility of criticism, it is rather less conducive to the exploration of positive alternatives to the world in which we live.

See Also

MARXISM; UTOPIAN WRITING

References and Further Reading

Albinski, Nan Bowman. 1988. *Women's utopias in British and American fiction.* New York: Routledge.

Bammer, Angelika. 1991. *Partial visions.* London: Routledge.

Bloch, Ernst. 1986. *The principle of hope.* Oxford: Blackwell. (Originally published as *Das Prinzip Hoffnung,* 1955–1959.)

Davis, J. C. 1981. *Utopia and the ideal society.* Cambridge: Cambridge University Press.

Kumar, Krishan. 1991. *Utopianism.* Milton Keynes: Open University Press.

Lefanu, Sarah. 1988. *In the chinks of the world machine: Feminism and science fiction.* London: Women's Press.

Levitas, Ruth. 1990. *The concept of utopia.* Hemel Hempsted, U.K.: Philip Allan.

Moylan, Tom. 1986. *Demand the impossible.* London: Methuen.

Sargent, Lyman Tower. 1988. *British and American utopian literature 1516–1985: An annotated, chronological bibliography.* New York and London: Garland.

Sargisson, Lucy. 1996. *Contemporary feminist utopianism.* London: Routledge.

Ruth Levitas

UTOPIAN WRITING

Utopian writing refers to literary treatments of ideal worlds or ideal communities. The word *utopia* is a Greek pun, which means both "no place" ("utopia") and "good place" ("eutopia"). Lyman Tower Sargent divides utopian writing into three categories: the "eutopia," or positive vision; the "dystopia," or negative vision of an undesirable society; and the satirical utopia. Utopian writing can take the form of novels, plays, poetry, or short stories; political, religious, and social commentary is united with typical literary elements such as plot and characterization. A feminist utopia is distinguished by its content rather than its form. Such utopias offer a challenge to the existing patriarchal order, and also to class and race oppression. Utopian writing, therefore, offers an opportunity for women writers both to criticize the existing order and to speculate about more positive alternatives.

Notable examples within the utopian tradition include Plato's *Republic* (c. 378), Thomas More's *Utopia* (1516), and Jonathan Swift's *Gulliver's Travels* (1726). Women writers have made significant contributions to the utopian literary tradition, especially in the portrayal of all-female ideal communities. The most notable female utopian writer of the medieval period was the Italian Christine de Pisan, who, in *Le Livre de la Cité des Dames* (*The Book of the City of Ladies*, 1405), imagined a world inhabited by exemplary women from all ages. To envision a city made up of virtuous and high-achieving heroines was to underline the worth and importance of women. In the early modern period, Margaret Cavendish's *New Blazing World* (1666) created a world of almost limitless opulence, ruled over by a charismatic woman who has risen to absolute power. Sarah Scott's *A Description of Millenium Hall* (1762) also showed an all-female community inhabited by independent women; a group of male visitors marveled at their virtue and ingenuity. In the nineteenth century, Mary E. Bradley Lane's *Mizora: A Prophecy* (1880–1881) presented an all-female parthenogentic society. The most famous utopian novel written by a woman is Charlotte Perkins Gilman's *Herland* (1915), which, like Scott's *Millenium Hall* was an all-female utopia. In *Herland,* male tourists on the Eve of World War I stumble on a society made up of women and are astonished at its superior social organization.

In the late twentieth century, science fiction and fantasy writing allow women writers to speculate about alternatives to current gender roles. Many current women writers working in science fiction, fiction, and utopian genres create worlds marked by biological androgyny as a means of ensuring greater freedom for all human individuals. In Ursula K. LeGuin's *The Left Hand of Darkness* (1969), gender differences are eliminated altogether in the utopian world of Gether. Reproduction takes place when people go through a state called kemmer. Each individual becomes either a man or a woman depending on mood and circum-

stance. In this way, all sex-role stereotyping and gender discrimination is removed.

Utopian writing also has been a means of engaging with racial and religious difference, as in the work of Shari Tepper (who unites all the citizens of her country under one religion), Marge Piercy, Melissa Scott, and Suzy McKee Charnas. Women writing in the utopian genre have been intrigued by the link between women's lives and socioeconomic circumstances. For example, Joanna Russ's *The Female Man* (1975) chronicles the very different lives of four women raised in completely different worlds and social settings; all four women portrayed are biologically identical. Women writers also have been active in the subgenre of dystopian writing, which shows a nightmarish world in order to describe an undesirable future or warn against a disturbing social trend. Margaret Atwood's *The Handmaid's Tale* (1975) is an important example of this kind, because it envisions a late-twentieth-century fundamentalist world in which the few fertile women left in an environmentally ravaged society are used for their capacity to breed and are kept under strict control.

Women writers use the genre of utopian writing to test new possibilities for women's lives, and to challenge the current status quo, especially with regard to gender normatives.

See Also

PATRIARCHY: FEMINIST THEORY; SCIENCE FICTION; UTOPIANISM

References and Further Reading

Albinski, Nan Bowman. 1988. *Women's utopias in British and American fiction.* New York: Routledge.

Barr, Marleen, and Nicolas B. Smith, eds. 1983. *Women and utopia: Critical interpretations.* Lanham, Md.: University Press of America.

Donaworth, Jane, and Carol Kolmerton. 1984. *Utopian and science fiction by women: Worlds of difference.* Syracuse, N.Y.: Syracuse University Press.

Pfaelzer, Jean. 1988. The changing of the avant-garde: The feminist utopia. *Science Fiction Studies* (15: Nov.): 282–294.

Quilter, Laura. Website: Feminist Science Fiction, Fantasy and Utopia <http://www.wenet.net/~lquilter/femsf>.

Silbergleid, Robin. 1997. Women, utopia, and narrative: Toward a postmodern feminist citizenship. *Hypatia: A Journal of Feminist Philosophy* 12(4: Fall): 156–177.

Stinson, Pamela Talley. 1997. *Uncovering a female tradition: Female utopias before Herland.* Ph.D. thesis, University of Oklahoma.

Carrie Hintz

V

VEGETARIANISM

Vegetarianism, a diet of grains, vegetables, fruits, nuts, and seeds, with or without eggs and dairy products, rejects animal bodies as a source of food. Motivations for vegetarianism vary from ethical objections to the slaughter of animals to expectations of improved personal health. In developed countries, vegetarianism is often also a rejection of a form of animal-based agriculture (factory farming), which is regarded by many as particularly cruel and environmentally devastating.

The last quarter of the twentieth century saw an increased interest in vegetarianism, partly in response to the anti–Vietnam War movement and partly in response to a high-tech, fast-food pattern of modern life. Other influences have included Frances Moore Lappé's *Diet for a Small Planet* (1971), Peter Singer's *Animal Liberation* (1976), and John Robbins's *Diet for a New America* (1987), the Hindu concept of *ahisma* (nonviolence), and the 1990s straightedge music scene, which actively promotes veganism (a totally vegetarian diet). Those feminists who are motivated by a feminist-vegetarian theory that recognizes the interconnected oppression of women and animals also have become vegetarians.

Historical Context

The practice of vegetarianism has a long history. It is associated with many of the world's religions, and progressive individuals have often advocated vegetarianism as one aspect of social change. The dietary history of most cultures consists primarily of complete protein dishes made from vegetables and grains.

Nineteenth-century advocates of white superiority endorsed meat as "civilized" food. Many believed that meat eating contributed to the western world's dominance. Multi-national fast-food corporations in the latter part of the twentieth century have fulfilled this colonialist view of meat eating, as they seek to expand their clientele. Because the environmental costs of producing animal protein (deforestation, water and air pollution) are borne by the state, not the corporation, new markets in developing countries are continually being established.

The Feminist-Vegetarian Analysis

Many feminist-vegetarians perceive opposition to vegetarianism in patriarchal cultures as one aspect of the sexual politics of meat, in which meat eating is associated with virility and seen as symbolic of masculinity; vegetarianism, by contrast, is seen as feminine (Adams, 2000).

Lori Gruen and Greta Gaard, two U.S.-based ecofeminist theorists, give their version of the feminist vegetarian viewpoint: "Our dietary choices are made on the basis of both rights and responsibilities: our right to a healthy diet, and our responsibilities based on our relationships to all life on earth. These relationships—to other humans, other animals, the earth, and our immediate cultural, economic, and political environments—shape the context in which our dietary choices are made" (Gaard and Gruen, 1995: 238).

Feminist health concerns, like feminist politics, intersect with vegetarianism. Vegetarians maintain that because of the length of time it takes to digest meat, toxins are released into the body. Therefore, on a pure vegetarian diet the risk of death by heart attack is reduced significantly, as is the risk of breast and ovarian cancer. By contrast, a diet high in animal fats lowers the age of menstruation, which increases the incidence of cancer of the breast and reproductive organs while also lowering the age of fertility, thus contributing to the risk of pregnancy for young teenagers. A diet with meat as the central source of protein is associated with some aspects of dysmenorrhea as well as increased risks of cancer, heart disease, obesity, diabetes, hypertension, and osteoporosis. Numerous health advantages are associated with appropriately planned vegetarian diets (see Gaard and Gruen, 1995, for summary).

Ecofeminist analysis reveals the environmental costs of animal-based agriculture, especially as it is conducted in developed countries. Wastes from the livestock industry make animal-based agricultural suppliers major industrial polluters. This type of agriculture is associated with the desertification of land and the loss of topsoil as well as habitat. It contributes to the greenhouse effect and uses an inordinate amount of fossil fuels and other raw materials (see Adams, 1994, 1997, for a fuller discussion). Five hundred calories of food energy from one pound of steak requires twenty thousand calories of fossil fuel. The same land that can be used to produce flesh for 250 days would provide sustenance for 2,200 days if cultivated with soybeans.

Feminist-vegetarians reject a patriarchal world that objectifies women, animals, and the earth; they simultaneously announce connections with animals, while defining themselves as subjects with the right to act and make moral decisions. In doing so, they also define animals as subjects rather than as consumable objects. Feminism, they argue, transforms relationships with all of nature.

See Also

ANIMAL RIGHTS; COOKING; FOOD AND CULTURE; GREEN MOVEMENT; HEALTH: OVERVIEW; MULTINATIONAL CORPORATIONS; NATURE

References and Further Reading

Adams, Carol J. 1997. "Mad cow" disease and the animal industrial complex: An ecofeminist analysis. *Organization and Environment* 10(1: Mar.): 26–51.

———. 1994. *Neither man nor beast: Feminism and the defense of animals.* New York: Continuum.

———. 2000. *The sexual politics of meat: A feminist-vegetarian critical theory.* 10th anniversary ed. New York: Continuum; Oxford: Polity.

Gaard, Greta, ed. 1993. *Ecofeminism: Women, animals, nature.* Philadelphia: Temple University Press.

Gaard, Greta, and Lori Gruen. 1995. Comment on George's "Should feminists be vegetarians?" *Signs* 21(1): 230–241.

Lappé, Frances Moore. 1971. *Diet for a small planet.* New York: Ballantine.

Leneman, Leah. 1997. The awakened instinct: Vegetarianism and the women's suffrage movement in Britain. *Women's History Review* 5(2): 271–287.

Robbins, John. 1987. *Diet for a new America.* Walpole, N.H.: Stillpoint.

Singer, Peter. 1976. *Animal liberation.* New York: New York Review.

Worldwatch Press. Briefing on the global trends in meat consumption. 2 July 1998. <www.worldwatch.org/alerts/pr980704.html>

Carol J. Adams

VEILING

A veil is a garment designed for covering parts of the body, head, or face, as women generally do in some parts of north Africa and the Middle East. In Asia and Europe, women used to put on a head veil for church services, and they still commonly wear a bridal veil in wedding ceremonies. The religious veil is part of the garb of nuns and sisters in the Roman Catholic church, although it is no longer worn by all Catholic nuns.

In the ancient Orient, the veil was a sign of the dignity of women. The Old Testament book of Genesis recounts that Rebecca covered herself with her veil at the approach of Isaac, whose bride she was to be, in order to command his respect (Gen. 24:65). In contrast, an adulteress sentenced to stoning by Mosaic law was stripped of her veil to expose her shame. The veil also symbolized the mystery of fertility and life. On the wedding night the bridal veil was used to cover the bride, thus giving rise to the term *nuptials,* from the Latin *nuptiae* and *nubere,* to cover oneself.

Some traditional Muslim countries such as Saudi Arabia, Pakistan, and Iran enforce the veil (*purdah*) on women in public, although this practice was abolished in Turkey and Egypt after the 1930s. Purdah aims to separate women from men when they are of marriageable age. Islamic teaching enjoins women to appear veiled everywhere, except within the family circle and before those male kin whom they are not allowed to marry. This custom is aimed at protecting them from being molested outside the home.

In Christianity, the veil is associated with reverence and purity. St. Paul exhorts women in 1 Cor. 11:5–6 to wear a veil on their heads in church. The *velatio virginis* is a significant rite in the liturgy of the "consecration of virgins," which goes back to the earliest centuries (Tertullian). Like the bridal veil, it came to signify the spiritual marriage between Christ and the consecrated religious. The expression "taking the veil" has been synonymous with making religious profession in the Roman Catholic church since the ninth century. The veil is still an important part of the religious dress of many religious institutes of women today.

Nowadays the veiling of women in public in Islamic countries appears socially restrictive and favors traditional female invisibility decried by feminists. However, although fewer and fewer women veil themselves in universities and workplaces with men, a revivalist trend is evident in countries like Saudi Arabia. Women have returned to wearing a long high-necked dress and cowl (*chador*) to counteract unwelcome western ideas and foreign cultural influence. The veil has become a symbol for upholding national values. On the other hand, feminists encourage women to become highly visible in public, with or without the veil, and to overcome patriarchal control, which stifles their gifts for peacemaking and social concern.

See Also

DRESS; FUNDAMENTALISM: RELIGIOUS; ISLAM; MARRIAGE: REGIONAL TRADITIONS AND PRACTICES; NUNS; VIRGINITY

References and Further Reading

Dwyer, Claire. 1999. Veiled meanings: Young British Muslim women and the negotiation of difference (1). *Gender, Place and Culture: A Journal of Feminist Geography* 6(Mar.): 5.

Fandy, Mamoun. 1998. Political science without clothes: The politics of dress on contesting the spatiality of the state in Egypt. *Arab Studies Quarterly* 20(2: Spring).

Jomiers, Jacques. 1989. *How to understand Islam.* London: SCM.

Lozano, John. 1986. *Discipleship: Towards an understanding of religious life.* Chicago: Claret.

Muslim veil gaining acceptance. <www.bergen.com/bne /veilme19990711.htm>

Nafisi, Azar. 1999. The veiled threat cover story. *New Republic* 220(22 Feb.): 24.

Nanda, Bihram Naryan, and Mohammed Talib. 1992. In search of meaning: Sociological exploration into the biography of a Muslim woman. *Islam and the Modern Age Quarterly* 23: 71–113.

The practices of Islam. *Encarta 2000* (encyclopedia on CD-ROM).

Sadat, Jehan. 1987. *A woman of Egypt.* New York: Simon and Schuster.

Women dress code in Islam. <www.org/dress.htm>

Sr. Irene Dabalus

VIDEO

There is widespread recognition that video is one of the most important developments in communications technology in recent history. Video was developed during the early part of the twentieth century as an outgrowth of the invention of cinema and radio. Basic video technology consists of a system of electronic sound and image reproduction, recording, and playback. The imaging process is optical-video transduction, through which the camera changes incoming light into electronic information that communicates the color and brightness of an image. This signal is then recorded in an analog or digital process on videotape, on videodisk, or directly into a computer hard drive. Synchronous sound is recorded through a microphone. The video editing process consists of the selection and sequencing of video images to create a final program, a process that may also include the addition of sound, special effects, and graphics. The uses of video are distinct, based on their contexts of production, distribution, and exhibition. The same principles of video technology, however, form the basis for all of its many variations of use.

The most prominent forms of distribution for video programs are television broadcast, cablecast, and closed-circuit video screening. The broadcasting of videotapes occurs almost solely within the industrial system of television. Television is distributed by combining the video signal with radio waves and broadcasting this information by radio tower and satellite. Television also uses cablecasting, which relays the video signal through underground cables directly to receivers. Closed-circuit screenings occur in specific locales, in which videotape is played by a videocassette recorder (VCR) onto a video monitor. Closed-circuit screenings may occur in private or public places, for individuals or groups. Increasingly, video images are also making their way into interactive CD-ROM formats and the World Wide Web. These media represent new forms of distribution for video, which will inevitably have an effect on the form and content of the video created for these purposes.

Video has had a significant impact on women's lives worldwide, increasing women's technological capacity for artistic and political expression and creating new networks of communication. Television, the industry that developed from video technology, was established as one of the most influential communications systems worldwide by the late 1950s. Ownership of and access to video technology lay mainly in the hands of the television industry and the state until the 1960s, when portable and affordable video cameras and recording equipment became available on the consumer market. Portable video, because of its instant-replay capability and its cheapness relative to film, quickly became popularly accepted as a new form of visual expression. At that point, the production of video became diversified by its use by political activists, artists, educators, and other individuals and groups.

Video plays an important role in public life. The capacity to create videotapes reflects and produces social power because of the communicative qualities of video, its ability to reach large audiences, and the enormous cultural and political significance of television. With the recognition that the democratization of the public sphere requires the diversification of media production, widespread access to video has become a political issue for oppressed groups around the world. Women remain in the minority of those producing videotapes, in both the commercial and the nonprofit sectors. Women around the world, however, are struggling to gain access to video as a means to maintain control over their own images, as well as to exchange information among themselves or with other communities. Video offers an important venue to create representations that accurately portray women's lives, that convey imaginative interpretations of women's stories, and that communicate unique political and social perspectives. Despite the economic, political, and cultural obstacles to accessing video technology, it has become an important component in women's artistic expression, intellectual inquiry, and political activism worldwide.

Alongside its use as the basis for the television industry, video is a tool for microcommunication and, as such, has vast implications for women's culture and politics on a grassroots level. Independent production and distribution occur outside of the economic and political context of the television industry. The freedom of independent video production relative to television programs results in more diverse content, form, and uses. Its presence in women's lives ranges from participating in a grassroots oral history videotape to be screened in community organizations to videotaping a child's birthday party to interacting with video art presented in metropolitan museums to viewing documentaries on women's history broadcast on national television.

The forms of independent video production include home video, video art, and documentary, narrative, and experimental hybrid-genre videos. "Home video" consists of using video as a tool for documenting everyday life. While this form of video production is mainly for personal enjoyment, it has a social implication, popularizing video production as individual, and not corporate, expression. Video art production is the use of video by artists to create videotapes, sculptural installations, or performances with video that reflect a variety of aesthetic and social concerns. Video

art has amplified the definition of art internationally and is at the vanguard of technologically based fine art. Other forms of independent productions include activist documentaries and narrative dramas.

In all cases, video is an important means for the representation of women's lives. Indeed, much of independent video production by women is based solidly on a critique of the forms and systems of the mainstream media, and a commitment to creating an aesthetic and political alternative. The production and distribution of videotapes by women's organizations and individual women have created local, national, and international forums for the discussion of women's lives. Women have used video in all its forms as an alternative means of information gathering and distribution, with the intended effect of supporting women's culture and political movements. When broadcast, independently produced videotapes by women about women's issues may reach millions of viewers, with the possible effect of influencing their opinions and political participation. Video art screenings and video installations in museums and galleries offer an alternative to traditional static art forms, and often offer a critique of a male-dominated art world and aesthetic language. The use of video on a grassroots level increases women's capacity for self-representation and communication. Feminist grassroots efforts have used video to create new means for community building, popular education, artistic expression, and access to production. Videotapes produced by grassroots groups have been used to document injustices, to offer alternative political analysis, and to communicate new models of women's organizing and mutual aid.

Independent producers have had to become extremely creative and resourceful to fund their video productions. Projects are usually funded by amalgamations of individual contributions, government and private foundations, and occasional support from national television industries. Independent videotapes may also be produced under the auspices of governmental or nongovernmental organizations, such as social service agencies, schools, universities, and cultural associations, or they may be produced and supported by relatively autonomous individuals.

An economic and cultural infrastructure for the support of independent video production has been slowly developing in many countries. In some cases, national public television systems have been central to the development of noncommercial video programming. For example, National Television of Niger, which was founded in 1978, supports educational programming with a focus on national development. It has provided the opportunity for women, such as Aissatou Adamou, to produce work that includes ethnographic, cultural, and social themes concerning women and children. The National Video Movement, in Cuba, has also supported women producers. Gloria Rolando has produced numerous documentaries on Afro-Caribbean culture in this context.

Many nonprofit, nongovernmental organizations have been created around the world to support independent video production. In many cases, the creation of these organizations has been the result of intensive political organizing with the aim of creating access to the media for women, minorities, and indigenous groups. Thus, several media organizations are successful coalitions and represent innovative approaches to community organizing and mutual support. Videazimut, for example, is an international coalition of video producers and organizations promoting media development and democracy. Headquartered in Quebec, the group has members in over forty countries. The group works on policy advocacy, media training, and women's advancement through conferences, workshops, and newsletters.

Many groups have been organized around the world with the sole purpose of supporting women's independent video production. Based in New York City, Communication for Change collaborates with women's organizations internationally to create participatory training workshops in video production, enabling women to represent their own concerns and reality. With an emphasis on communication as process, not product, women use interviews, testimony, and dialogue with their communities as the basis for creating videos for self-empowerment, development, and advocacy. These workshops have resulted in the formation of lasting media components of these organizations' programs. In Brazil, the Lilith Video Collective was formed by a group of independent video producers to create videotapes directly related to the immediate political and material needs of women. These videos organize women around a variety of feminist issues, including labor, domestic violence, and the rights of sex workers.

There is an increasing interest in the use of video in media literacy programs for girls by schools and community organizations. Media literacy is the critical analysis of the mass media and the development of media production skills. Many educational theorists and media activists advocate for the inclusion of media literacy as a core component of public schooling for children. Organizations and schools have developed extensive curricula on video production for children and young people, with an emphasis on empowerment through self-representation. The lesbian video maker Sadie Benning, based in the United States, began making videotapes as a teenager. Her moving personal narratives attest to the need for girls and young women to share their experiences through video production.

Feminist theorists have created a large body of work concerning the representation of women in film and video, and this work is both reflected in and generated by women's independent video production. Formal innovations reflecting feminist concerns with the politics of representation have occurred across all genres and contexts of production. These innovations reflect strategies unique to different historical and cultural locations of producers. The theoretical preoccupations of feminist video makers have included the desire to create representations that emphasize women's power and self-determination. The development of alternative narrative forms that are appropriate to different cultural contexts and a concern for creating pluralistic, complex views of women and women's communities have also been important. A feminist analysis of television is also present in the work of independent women video makers. The lack of representation of women of color and indigenous women on television, the tendency toward the sexualizing of women, and the use of women as narrative devices are just a few of the critical points to which women have responded with their own videotapes.

In all contexts, women work to create new strategies of representation that are appropriate to representing unique histories. In the documentary realm, video makers such as Julia Barco in Mexico have worked to present issues that urgently affect women, and to help organize women to better their situation. In her videotape *Ondas de Cambio/Waves of Change,* Barco collaboratively documented the grassroots efforts of a women's health collective, which started a radio program to create dialogue with rural women. The videotapes of Video SEWA, the video unit of the Self-Employed Women's Association, a trade union in Ahmedabad, India, also uses a collaborative documentary approach that involves the participants in the construction of their own images. These videotapes document organizing initiatives and activism, as well as profile members of SEWA. In 1998, these videotapes reached 19,150 viewers via closed-circuit screenings in community centers.

In the fine arts, video art and performance video have evolved around an exploration of the conceptual and material representational possibilities of the medium. This has strongly reflected the feminist critique of the sexist and racist representational strategies of the mainstream media, as well as critiques of fine art for failing to include women's concerns. Mona Hatoum, a Lebanese video artist based in England, has addressed issues of colonialism and diaspora. Through the layering of images, text, and sound, her videotapes and video installations require the viewer to shift subjective positions that mirror a process of travel and displacement. Her focus on aesthetic and cultural fragmentation reflects the concerns of the postmodern movement in international art as well as an engagement with postcolonial theory.

Feminist videomakers have also theorized about and practiced alternative modes of production. In the mainstream industry, production is carried out in a hierarchical system, led by a producer and a director. In independent feminist video production, a collective, nonhierarchical process and all-women crews are often used. In addition, many videotapes are produced in collaboration with grassroots communities, allowing communities to participate in the structuring of their own representation. In these collaborations, the process of production itself is used as a means of consciousness raising among women. Individual women may also assume all production roles in independent video, as is often the case in video art, reflecting the conception of the artist as individual author characteristic of the contemporary production of art objects.

Venues for independent video include museums, galleries, community organizations, schools, universities, and festivals. Many feminist media arts administrators and activists work to expand the audience for independent women's video. There are many organizations that are devoted to distribution and exhibition. Most of these supply videotapes for closed-circuit screenings by educational and cultural institutions. Women Make Movies, in New York, distributes films and videos by women from around the world. The Bildwechsel, in Hamburg, Germany, houses an extensive archive of works by women and engages in regular screenings of women's work, with a focus on work by lesbians. There are numerous festivals as well, many of which have an equal focus on video as well as film. Women in the Director's Chair, in Chicago, has successfully run an international women's film and video festival for twenty years. FESPACO, the Pan-African Festival of Cinema and Television of Ouagadougou, Burkina Faso, has become a central forum for women video makers in Africa. In addition, festivals in Creteil, Berlin, Havana, and Hong Kong all have a strong focus on video and have had strong representation by women video makers.

See Also

CULTURE: WOMEN AS CONSUMERS OF CULTURE; CULTURE: WOMEN AS PRODUCERS OF CULTURE; FILM; FILM THEORY; IMAGES OF WOMEN: OVERVIEW; MEDIA: ALTERNATIVE; MEDIA: GRASSROOTS; PHOTOGRAPHY; REPRESENTATION; TELEVISION

References and Further Reading

Archer, Michael, Guy Brett, and Catherine de Zegher. 1997. *Mona Hatoum.* London: Phaidon.

Armes, Roy. 1988. *On video.* London and New York: Routledge.

Attile, Martina, and Maureen Blackwood. 1987. Black women and representation: Notes from the workshops held in London, 1984. In Charlotte Brunsdon, ed., *Films for Women,* 202–208. London: BFI.

Burton, Julianne. 1990. *The social documentary in Latin America.* Pittsburgh: University of Pittsburgh Press.

Dowmunt, Tony, ed. 1993. *Channels of resistance: Global television and local empowerment.* London: British Film Institute.

Ellerson, Beti. 2000. *Sisters of the screen: Women of Africa on film, video and television.* Trenton and Asmara: Africa World.

Fifer, Sally Jo, and Dong Hall, eds. 1991. *Illuminating video: An essential guide to video art.* San Francisco: Aperture in association with Bay Area Video Coalition.

Gever, Martha. 1983. Video politics: Early feminist projects. *Afterimage* II(1/2): 25–27.

MacBride, Sean. 1988. *Many voices, one world: Communication and society, today and tomorrow. A report by the International Commission for the Study of Communication Problems.* London: Kogan Page; New York: Unipub; Paris: UNESCO; in association with World Association for Christian Communication.

Parmar, Pratibha, John Greyson, and Martha Gever, eds. 1993. *Queer looks: Perspectives on lesbian and gay film and video.* New York: Routledge.

Schneider, Cynthia, and Brian Wallis, eds. 1988. *Global television.* New York: Wedge.

Williams, Raymond. 1974. *Television: Technology and cultural form.* New York: Schocken.

Dalida Maria Benfield

VIOLENCE AND PEACE: Overview

Political Violence and Sexuality

The issues of violence, which cut across national, racial, and ethnic boundaries and are therefore international, include abuse, armament, battery, capital punishment, crime, femicide, infanticide, militarization, murder, pornography, prison, rape, refugees, sexual harassment, sexual mutilation, sexual slavery, street harassment, terrorism, torture, and war. Peace is the alternative to these various form of violence— more specifically, peace in the form of nonviolence and social change, conflict resolution (mediation and negotiation), disarmament, peace activism, peace education, women's human rights, international peace organizations, and various resistance and peace movements.

Sexuality and sexual relations are central to an analysis of the political and national struggles occurring in the world. Recent sociological, anthropological, and political studies dealing with aggression, violence, war, and the role of women clearly indicate this connection. Aspects of nationalism and how they relate to sexuality and to women's traditional roles in society are also part of this tangle.

Among the problems associated with masculinity are aggressiveness and violence, which are directly linked with political and personal exploitation of nature and women. Exploitation takes various forms, including exhausting and misusing the world's resources; oppressing other races, sexes, or ages; invading and dominating other countries or continents; and running the arms race. The consequences of such values are death, destruction, and more violence and death. It is a vicious circle that keeps repeating itself, as if human beings were incapable of breaking the circle: war creating and emboldening codes of heroism and masculinity, and masculinity creating war. Only a different vision, different values, a change in power relationships, and a change in the social construction of identities—to be grounded no longer in dominance and submission but in harmonized acceptance of differences—can bring about harmony and a future of life and hope, instead of wars and nuclear holocaust.

Many studies by women and men in the 1980s and 1990s find a link between sexuality and national and international conflicts. Jean-William Lapierre and Anne-Marie de Vilaine (1981) see a connection between masculine predominance and the importance of war. According to them, most civilizations are based on conquest and war. They argue that in so-called modern societies, politics, industry, and business are always a kind of war where people (mostly men, and sometimes women imitating men's behavior) must be energetic and aggressive to be powerful. Miranda Davies (1983, 1987) comments that many women in the third world realize that when needed, they may join guerrilla movements, participate in the economy, enter politics, and organize trade unions, but at the end of the day they are still seen as women, second-class citizens inferior to men, bearers of children, and domestic servants. Zarana Papic (1992) and Helke Sander (1992) have remarked that women's condition drastically worsened in the former Yugoslavia because of the war. This holds true for most places experiencing similar "postmodern" wars.

Nationalism

Nationalism is a difficult notion, about which much is written and about which much can be found to be conflicting. In both East and West, in old and new concepts of the term,

nationalism is a complex component of revolutionary discourse. It can move among all the various facets of political power. For example, nationalism in one extreme form can be fascism. Thérèse Vial-Mannessier summarized Maria-Antonietta Macciocchi's analysis (1974–1975) of fascist ideology in Italy from and throughout the feminine universe. She argues that a collective irrational is at work in all human groups. Conscious and unconscious forces led the masses to fascism, from a transcendence of the individual ego into total allegiance to the Italian nation. At first victims of this racism, women adhered to it through a masochism ready for all possible sacrifices.

While nationalism has been necessary for the young Arab states gaining their autonomy from colonialism, it nevertheless, like fascism, reclaimed many of the most patriarchal values of Islamic traditionalism. Mai Ghousoub analyzed the political rights of women, nominally granted by national states, as in practice a dead letter, since there are military dictatorships in which suffrage has no meaning. Helke Sander (1992) noticed how in the former Yugoslavia the strongest and most dominant parties expressed extreme forms of nationalistic ideology, and their nationalism rejected the national identities of others. Civil society is the first victim of this totalitarian domineering nationalistic ideology. According to Sander, the former Yugoslavia, which used to be, like Lebanon, a country where various ethnic, cultural, and religious groups lived in tolerance and relative autonomy and harmony compared with their neighbors, became a hellish country in which human rights were threatened, especially women's rights, as women are looked at almost exclusively as reproductive bodies to bring into the world bodies to kill and be killed because the nation wants it this way. Sander sees as incredible irrationality at work a rational manipulation aiming at leading people to accept the dominant exclusive nationalistic ideology with its horrible consequences of cruelty and hatred for the "other." Rada Ivekovic argues that radical nationalism is a mechanism of binary oppositions which, in the long term, invariably leads to war. Because women are less anguished about their internal frontiers and the limits of their bodies, they are more peaceful concerning outside (political) frontiers, and all this has to do with identity and the way the subject (the one who acts) is built. Women are biologically and socially more open to the acceptance of the "other" in themselves (the sexual act and pregnancy).

Feminism Meets Nationalism

In the Middle East and elsewhere, nationalism and feminism have never mixed very well. Women were used in national liberation struggles—as in Algeria, Iran, and Palestine—only to be sent back to their kitchens after "independence" had been gained. Rather than dismissing nationalism as a corrupting force, we need to redefine it. For example, in the case of Lebanon and the former Yugoslavia, countries with a mosaic of ethnic groups and religions, what political entity could help bring them unity? If nationalism meant belief in one's country as an entity to be loved for itself, left to develop and flourish outside of selfish interests; if it meant love for the earth without ownership and possession, like the ideal of love between two persons, that is, respect for the other, and help in allowing him or her to develop and flourish without jealousy and domination; if all the various parties trying to dominate small pieces of territory were to unite under this love, then we could move toward a solution. This is where feminism and nationalism blend.

Is it utopian to think that feminism and nationalism can ever mix? How can we know, since sexuality has never been conceptualized as being at the center of the problem, and sexual relations were never truly incorporated into revolutionary struggle? If women were to demand their rights and a transformation of values and roles in the family at the beginning of national struggles, and if national struggles were conceived with aims that would not perpetuate domination and ownership, then we would move toward a different concept of revolution from that witnessed so far. And is not utopia the exploration of the possible?

Masculinity and War

How is sexuality articulated and mixed in violence and wars? In societies that take pride in the leader—or chief, or hero—in which the macho man embodies all the masculine values of conquest, domination, competition, fighting, and boasting, in which to succeed means to get what one wants, even through lying and perfidy, in such societies war transforms the hero into the man with the gun, the militia man. The man with the gun has a military role and an economic-social function. He uses weapons of war to destroy and seize control of one region or of another group. He participates in looting to benefit his clientele of family and to extend the range of his influence. Given the extension of his influence, he builds a system of wealth distribution and gains even more power. Material goods and gains are obtained through his arsenal. It is a "primitive" system and a destructive vicious circle rather than a self-preserving one. The more men desire omnipotence and control, the more weapons are used. The means of conquest are given a value in proportion to their success.

The gun, the machine gun, the cannon—all, arguably, masculine sexual symbols that are extensions of the phallus—are used to conquer and destroy. For Adam Farrar, there is a kind of *jouissance*—pleasure in a sexual sense—in war. It is at some terrible level, for men, the closest thing to what childbirth is for women, an initiation into the power of life and death. Elisabeth Badinter (1986) makes a connection between the experience of childbirth and war. But there is a fundamental difference between creating life in the act of childbirth and destroying it in war. Relating the two within a human concept is not a valid explanation. Even if the two experiences could be brought together, they would divide rather than unite man and woman.

It is often said that the meaning and importance given to a military weapon and to the sexual weapon are equal. Man uses his penis as he uses his gun: to conquer, control, and possess. The macho society must be revealed and condemned, because in the present system one tries to obtain material goods and territory not in order to enjoy them or out of need but to enlarge one's domain and authority. Similarly, sexual relations are often built not on pleasure, tenderness, or love, but on reproduction, the preservation of a girl's virginity (so-called family honor), the confinement and control of women to increase in male prestige, and the overestimation of the penis. Lapierre and Vilaine (1981) hold that this phenomenon exists in almost all civilizations, hunting followed by war being at the root of women's oppression. Bob Connell sees a relationship between masculinity, violence, and war. He says that it is not by chance that the majority of soldiers are men. But this should be attributed not to biology, which would absolve men of responsibility—men's violence being associated with human "destiny"—but rather to social and cultural factors. For Connell, it becomes a matter of urgency to analyze and understand how masculinity is entangled in all that threatens the survival of humanity.

Susan Brownmiller (1976) has noted that rape is a conscious tactic of warfare. Michel Foucault has written powerfully on the connection between death, sex, violence, and male sexuality. Wilhelm Reich (1972; orig. 1932) has analyzed repressed sexuality as based on authoritarian family patterns and as being at the root of sadistic murders, perversions, psychological problems, and social and political conflicts. René Girard (1972) sees a relationship between violence and religion, which is rooted in sexuality, expressed in various human groups that often need a scapegoat to avoid violence that would lead them to annihilation. Finally, Issa Makhlouf (1988), in his impressive analysis of the Lebanese tragedy, which he sees as a collective fascination with death and destruction, describes Lebanese males as having gone mad and drunk with killing.

Fascination with War

Throughout the ages, men have been fascinated with war. At some very deep level, it has been for them a way to prove their existence, an expression, according to Adam Farrar, of "male desire." Desire closely linked to sexuality and the death instinct has been much written about by famous authors (Freud and Lacan, to name only two) and lesser-known ones. Sexuality connected with war, oppression, power, and aggressiveness has been analyzed by a great many authors, ranging from Reich, Bataille, Foucault, Laborit, and Girard to more recent works by men making the connection between masculinity and war (Connell, Farrar, and Poole, among others), to the whole body of feminist writing (Reardon, Michel, Dworkin, Stiehn, Carroll, Benn, Barnes, Morgan, Ivekovic, Sander, Elshtain, Bunch, Barry, Enloe, Woolf, Brownmiller, Badinter, Houston, Chodorow, Showalter, and Higonnet, among others). How these issues can be articulated in today's societies and what avenues can be found for nonviolence and peace as a positive force have been the concern of a number of other writers, such as Vilaine, Waring, Morgan, Charara, Ben Ghadifa, Brock-Utne, Michel, Ennaifer, Lerman, Corm, Duvignaud, Lapierre, Muller, and Mendel.

The difference between the male theorists—for example, Lacan, Freud, and Bataille—and the feminists—for example, Brownmiller, Dworkin, Michel, and Reardon—is that the connection between sexuality and violence made by the men does not lead them to want to change men, women, objectification, or dominant-submissive sexuality; in fact they celebrate it. The women, along with a recent body of Australian male theorists—Connell, Farrar, and Poole—want to change these conditions of female oppression and male domination.

Actions for Peace

Are there any solutions to violence and war? Have they been expressed theoretically? And have any been tried? In some modern recent wars, like those in Lebanon and the former Yugoslavia, disarming all the various fighting factions as a way—immediate and efficient—to remedy the conflict seemed obvious but not sufficient to get at the roots of the problems. Disarmament on an international level and a moratorium on the sale of weapons worldwide could equally bring immediate unforeseen results.

In many geographic areas plagued by war, solutions such as peace marches, hunger strikes, sit-ins, petitions, appeals to international and national peace organizations, conferences, and talks between the various communities have been tried. They have brought some relief and hope. Significant marches have been organized. One, for the handicapped of Lebanon, was organized and carried out by Laure Moghaïzel, a woman lawyer and activist in the nonviolence and human rights movements, during the summer of 1987. Asked what she meant by nonviolence, Moghaïzel replied that she was not a pacifist because she was revolting against injustices and violence, but she was nonviolent. Nonviolence meant a movement wanting peace and making itself known through an opposition, a struggle expressing activity and dynamism, a political action refusing to exercise violence. She explained how the origins of the movement lay with Gandhi and Martin Luther King. They were ready to suffer, but martyrdom was not the aim of nonviolence. Their objective consisted in eliminating violence through nonviolence. With dialogue and persuasion, they hoped to modify the actions of human beings.

These are some of the positive actions at work for peace. They may appear weak, simple, and utopian in the face of the destructive and violent forces of politics and of history. But history has also shown that the actions of Gandhi and Martin Luther King did have an impact on society and on the world. The theoretical framework for change lies in a blend of nationalism, feminism, and nonviolent active struggles.

If nationalism could unite all the various factions under a common aim and belief in the existence and the survival of a country, it could move toward a real solution. But if nationalism remains at a sexist stage and does not move beyond ownership and possession as final goals, the hellish cycle will repeat itself and the violence will start all over again. The work must begin at the most personal levels: with changes in attitudes and behavior toward one's mate, one's family, one's sexuality, and ultimately toward one's community and society. From such a personal beginning, at least some of the internal conflicts might work toward resolution.

According to many, what needs to be formulated is a radical change, a whole system to be rethought and reconceptualized. Betty Reardon (1985), for example, has said that the new world order ought to be one of reconciliation and even forgiveness, by understanding that no human being is totally incapable of the most reprehensible or the most noble acts. And this is where the philosophy of nonviolence really lies, in coming to terms with and accepting the other in ourselves, be it masculine or feminine, or any other traits we project on enemies or criminals, heroes or saints. People's attitudes must undergo profound transformations—radical changes in the way they perceive power and love. Aggression and submission, which are seen at the core of relations between men and women, must change, because they are the primary cause of all forcible exploitation and account for perhaps the most significant common characteristic of sexism and the war system: rape.

Ivekovic observes that rape is a way for the rapist to capture what constitutes strength and power in women: "mixedness." She comments that in today's Balkan wars, as in many other conflicts, women exercise less violence and express more compassion, desire to help, and desire to understand the other side. The notions of mixedness, hybridity, and creolization have been developed by Ivekovic, who says that, symbolically, women—more than men—represent a space of mixedness, meeting, and it is this feminine principle that women create through mixing that is being attacked by those who want to purify their origins, "liberate" themselves from and negate the other. In her analysis, she argues that identification, for men, means exclusion of the other, since they identify with the "same"; for women, it implies a paradox, since they have to identify with the "different," or the other; nationalism for women signifies not exclusion of the other (sex), but coexistence with him, since identification with the father figure itself means mixing, inclusion. Nationalism, for women, does not mean (symbolic) self-breeding by the same, since identification is made with the father figure and not with the mother. It means symbolic breeding in and with the other. Nationalism needs founding myths, and these myths usually say something about "the birth of a nation," about "one's" culture as more ancient, better, "male," and "heroic." The sexual dimension allows (and structures) a very important form of thought, and also one of the mechanisms for the symbolic construction of power: the dominant group holds the power to represent God the Father or the father of the nation. Ivekovic says that Luce Irigaray's research on syntax, in particular, shows that generally women do not place themselves at the center of the space opened up by their speech. They tend to ask questions rather than state affirmations. Their subject is hesitant, open to interaction with the other, oriented toward the other, and waiting for it (him).

The idea of mixing, or blending, leading to hybridity, plurality, or creolization, is a notion at the center of an action or theory for peace; it is the kind of *métissage* Lionnet (1989) describes as "a dialogical hybrid that fuses together heterogeneous elements." It is Andrée Chedid's "wish to graft all [her] various roots and sensitivities" (1985). It allows one to see problems from many angles, to identify or distance oneself when necessary. Multiculturality is positive. It allows one to be assertive and autonomous, rejecting traditional as well as neocolonialist values and struggling in the world for more human values in both East and West—finding out how difficult this is in both.

See Also

ABUSE; BATTERY; CRIME AND PUNISHMENT; FEMICIDE; NATION AND NATIONALISM; NONVIOLENCE; PEACE MOVEMENTS, SPECIFIC REGIONS; PHALLOCENTRISM; RAPE; SEXUAL VIOLENCE; WAR

References and Further Reading

Accad, Evelyne. 1990. *Sexuality and war: Literary masks of the Middle East.* New York: New York University Press.

Badinter, Elisabeth. 1986. *L'un est l'autre: Des relations entre hommes et femmes.* Paris: Éditions Odile Jacob.

Brownmiller, Susan. 1976. *Against our will: Men, women and rape.* New York: Bantam.

Chedid, Andrée. 1985. *La maison sans racines.* Paris: Flammarion. English ed., *House without roots.* 1989. London: Serpent's Tail.

Davies, Miranda, ed. 1983, 1987. *Third world, second sex: Women's struggles and national liberation. Third world women speak out.* 2 vols. London: Zed.

Elshtain, Jean Bethke. 1987. *Women and war.* New York: Basic Books.

Enloe, Cynthia. 1983. *Does khaki become you? The militarization of women's lives.* London: Pluto.

Gadant, Monique, ed. 1986. *Women of the Mediterranean.* London: Zed.

Girard, René. 1972. *La violence et le sacré.* Paris: Grasset.

Laborit, Henri. 1970. *L'agressivité détournée.* Paris: UGE.

Lapierre, Jean-William, and Anne-Marie de Vilaine. 1981. Femmes: Une oppression millenaire. *Alternatives non-violentes: Femmes et violences* 40: 21–25.

Lionnet, Françoise. 1989. *Autobiographical voices: Race, gender, self-portraiture.* Ithaca, N.Y.: Cornell University Press.

Macciocchi, Maria-Antonietta. 1974–1975. *Eléments pour une analyse du fascisme,* Vol. 1. Paris: Vincennes.

Makhlouf, Issa. 1988. *Beyrouth ou la fascination de la mort.* Paris: La Passion.

Michel, Andrée. 1995. *Surarmement, pouvoirs, démocratie.* Paris: L'Harmattan.

Morgan, Robin. 1990. *The demon lover: On the sexuality of terrorism.* New York: Norton.

———. 1992. *The world of a woman.* New York: Norton.

Papic, Zarana. 1992. Ex-citoyennes dans l'Ex-Yougoslavie. *Yougoslavie, logiques de l'exclusion/peuples Méditerranéens* 61(Oct.–Dec.): 207.

Patton, Paul, and Ross Poole, eds. 1985. *War masculinity.* Sydney: Intervention.

Reardon, Betty. 1985. *Sexism and the war system.* New York: Teachers College and Columbia University Press.

Reich, Wilheim. 1972. *L'irruption de la morale sexuelle.* Paris: Payot (originally published 1932).

Sander, Helke. 1992. Une guerre de mâles à l'extrême. *Yougoslavie, logiques de l'exclusion/peuples Méditerranéens* 61(Oct.–Dec.): 201.

Scarry, Elaine. 1985. *The body in pain: The making and unmaking of the world.* New York: Oxford University Press.

Woolf, Virginia. 1966. *Three guineas.* London: Harcourt Brace Jovanovich.

Evelyne Accad

VIOLENCE, DOMESTIC

See DOMESTIC VIOLENCE.

VIOLENCE, SEXUAL

See SEXUAL VIOLENCE *and* RAPE.

VIOLENCE: Australia, New Zealand, and the Pacific Islands

Violence against women in the Oceania region (Australia, New Zealand, and the Pacific islands of Micronesia, Melanesia, Polynesia, and Papua New Guinea) is widespread and often reinforced by cultural and societal factors. Such violence is often underreported, and only a few nations have adequate laws and programs in place to address gender violence. Nonetheless, certain states have undertaken significant measures to deal with the issue.

Violence against women takes several forms, including sexual assault and physical violence (such as domestic abuse). Sexual assaults are generally unreported in the region, and societal factors often make it difficult for women to come forward without incurring a stigma against themselves and their families. This situation is true even for the more developed states of Australia and New Zealand. In Australia, some 18 percent of all women have experienced sexual violence during their lifetimes, and 45 percent of the victims report more than one incident. However, only about half of the women who experienced sexual assaults reported the incidents. Unlike domestic violence, sexual crimes are more likely to be committed by strangers than by people the victims know. Class and economic status exert a considerable influence over sexual assault. In New Zealand, there were higher levels of sexual assault among the native peoples, including the Maori and other Pacific peoples, than among the European population. Maori women are also more likely to be repeat victims of gender violence than are their European counterparts (New Zealand Ministry of Justice, 1999). When the statistics are adjusted for income differentials, however, there is a significant decline in the differences in sexual assault rates.

Economic Factors

The correlation between poverty and violence exists at several levels in the region. To begin with, there is extraordinary stress created by the abject poverty of the native populations on many islands of Melanesia, including Papua New Guinea, Fiji, the Republic of the Solomons, and Vanuatu. The populations of many of these areas exist on incomes below the level considered necessary for adequate nutrition, health, and education. Many of the households are headed or supported by women. Research into prostitution has shown economic deprivation to be a causative factor. Many Pacific communities in the subsistence sector still live effectively and healthily without cash, but the monetary demands of church, government, and education and the growing attraction of a "western" lifestyle resulting from multimedia (especially television) and advertising are changing established lifestyle patterns and putting enormous stress on cultures and societies with few resources to cope with such transitions. Environmental degradation caused by coastal destruction, logging, unsustainable development, and the loss of biodiversity, when combined with growing urbanization and population problems, also greatly disrupts family and cultural patterns. In Melanesia, women have traditionally been the agriculturalists, and the loss of this capability has further deprived them of livelihood and increased their dependence on men. The result of such societal disruptions has been dramatic increases in sexual assaults and domestic violence. There have also been dramatic increases in the suicide rate among both men and women. For example, Indo-Fijian women in some rural areas have much higher suicide rates than international averages, because of harsh marriage practices and sexual harassment (Haynes, 1984). Even in the more affluent communities, heightened parental expectations have led to increased suicide rates among teenagers who do not pass the secondary or university entrance examinations.

Sexual Crimes and Physical Violence

In response to sexual crimes, women's groups have set in motion a variety of strategies and actions. For instance, in

Australia and New Zealand, there have been direct lobbying efforts aimed at changing laws and increasing penalties. In 1995, the Fiji Women's Rights Movement was responsible for presenting legislation to the parliament on sexual assault, aggravated sexual assault, and child sexual abuse. Meanwhile, in New Caledonia, the Kanak Pro-Independence Movement initiated efforts not only to enact legislation but also to overturn cultural practices that devalue women and promote physical violence against them. Often police forces are underequipped or ill trained to investigate sexual crimes, and there is a chronic lack of materials needed to collect physical evidence. Many national police forces also lack efficient procedures for investigating sexual crimes. Often nations in the region do not have even rudimentary sexual harassment laws, and this lack has perpetuated gender stereotypes, as well as devaluing women in society. In many areas of the region, women's groups have concentrated on efforts to get victims of crimes to report them, and to compel police to enforce the law and arrest perpetrators of sexual violence. Because of poverty and the lack of adequate educational facilities and programs, many women in the Pacific islands remain unaware of their rights under the law or how to report gender crimes.

Murder in the region is committed almost exclusively by males, and women are most often the victims. For example, a police survey showed that between 1992 and 1995, there were 35 murders in Fiji (out of a population of 750,000) and 26 of the victims were females. The police considered almost all the murders to be related to domestic violence. In New Zealand, police believe that the main cause of murder between 1988 and 1994 was domestic disputes. Between 1993 and 1998, 42.8 percent of murders and 36.8 percent of manslaughter cases were domestic (New Zealand Ministry of Justice, 1999).

Domestic Violence

In general terms, the number of incidents of domestic violence in the region is considered to be very high, especially in Melanesia. Such crimes are unreported, underrecorded, and underprosecuted. The advent of women's crisis centers in some countries has brought the issue to public notice, and the number of women attending these centers is rapidly increasing. In Melanesia, there are estimates that one in four women suffers from domestic violence. On the small island states of the region, funding for programs to prevent domestic violence and provide shelters for victims is limited or nonexistent. Governments often take little responsibility for such resources or for problems in obtaining access to the limited sites. Hence, for most of the Pacific

states, the burden of care falls to nongovernmental organizations and the church. Governments accept, and often encourage, the role these groups play, but resources remain limited and many international groups must rely on sporadic funding. On Fiji, efforts by the Women's Crisis Center to improve conditions through legislation have had only limited success. One positive note has been new policies that force police to attend seminars on domestic violence and obtain special training to handle these kinds of incidents. Various private groups were instrumental in securing approval for these initiatives. The program can serve as a model to overcome the general reluctance among police forces in these island states to intervene in domestic disputes. Although French law prevails in French Polynesia, enforcement of statutes against gender-based crimes is sporadic (Aldrich and Connell, 1992). Sexual crimes and domestic violence occur at a much higher rate in these territories than in France, but little effort has been made to ensure greater enforcement.

Both Australia and New Zealand have generally done a better job in implementing strategies to deal with domestic violence. This is the result of deep government involvement in seeking solutions. For instance, in Australia, the portfolio for the minister for women's interests includes the elimination of domestic violence. The government has also established a Domestic Violence Prevention Unit, which coordinates state and federal efforts to address the issue. The first refuge for battered women was established in Australia in 1974, and by 1999 there were 150 centers across the nation. These sites are funded by the Women's Refuge Program through monies from the federal Department of Community Services and Health and state community services boards. In New Zealand, the Police Family Violence Policy of 1993 mandates that except under extraordinary circumstances, males suspected of domestic violence are to be immediately arrested. The law also allows victims to seek protection orders that prevent the attacker from gaining access to them. By 1998, the number of applications for such protection orders averaged around 7,000 per year and covered some 11,000 people (New Zealand Ministry of Justice, 1999).

Under pressure from women's groups, there has been a dramatic increase in prosecutions for violations of these orders. The Domestic Violence Act of 1995 increased the range of activities that are considered a violation of these restraining orders, and it expanded the reasons that such protective orders could be granted. As a result, the number of cases of individuals violating these orders increased by 145 percent from 1996 to 1998, and the number of prosecutions during the same period increased by 224 percent, while convictions increased by 278 percent (New Zealand Ministry of Justice, 1999). Behaviors that fall under these new laws include psychological abuse.

The Pacific region presents a dichotomy to the world. On the one hand, several nations, including Australia and New Zealand, have very progressive policies in place to combat gender violence. Yet the problem is acute in other nations in the region, and many governments seem unwilling to undertake significant reform efforts. In the end, meaningful strides in the prevention of gender violence can come about in the Pacific only through continued pressure from international nongovernmental organizations and domestic women's groups.

See Also

ENVIRONMENT: PACIFIC ISLANDS; HOUSEHOLDS AND FAMILIES: MELANESIA AND ABORIGINAL AUSTRALIA; HOUSEHOLDS AND FAMILIES: MICRONESIA AND POLYNESIA; LAW ENFORCEMENT; POVERTY; RAPE; SEXUAL VIOLENCE; VIOLENCE AND PEACE: OVERVIEW

References and Further Reading

Aldrich, Robert, and John Connell. 1992. *France's overseas empire*. New York: Cambridge University Press.

Australian Bureau of Statistics. 1996. *Women's safety, Australia*. Canberra: Australian Bureau of Statistics.

Haynes, Ruth H. 1984. Suicide in Fiji: A preliminary study. *British Journal of Psychiatry*: 433–438.

——— 1987. Suicide and social response in Fiji: A historical survey. *British Journal of Psychiatry*: 21–26.

Linniken, Jocelyn, and Lin Poyer, eds. 1990. *Cultural identity and ethnicity in the Pacific*. Honolulu: University of Hawaii Press.

New Zealand Ministry of Justice. 1999. *Responses to crime: Annual review 1999*. Wellington: Ministry of Justice.

O'Brien, Denise, and Sharon W. Tiffany, eds. 1984. *Rethinking women's roles: Perspectives from the Pacific*. Berkeley: University of California Press.

Ruth E. Lechte

VIOLENCE: Caribbean

The Caribbean region includes a number of nation-states with various forms of government, from stable democracies to one of the last communist dictatorships in the world. Narrowly defined, the region includes only the islands in the Caribbean Sea. More broadly, it includes, especially in the modern era, states bordering on the sea—such as Guyana, Suriname, and Belize—that are culturally and historically connected to the islands. The nations all have a colonial past that included slave-based plantation economies from the sixteenth to the nineteenth centuries. Some are still part of the British and French empires, and a few islands are owned by the United States. Because of the complex colonial heritage of the Caribbean region, as well as the many different governments and legal systems, it is difficult to make generalizations about violence and women. Most of the modern Caribbean nations trace their roots to Spanish discovery and settlement in the fifteenth and sixteenth centuries, but subsequent intervention by France, the Netherlands, Denmark, and England led to a variety of cultures, languages, religions, and legal traditions. The most pervasive influence on the region since the beginning of the twentieth century has been its proximity to the United States, which has dominated it economically and militarily. In addition, the presence of large numbers of Soviet, Russian, and eastern European troops and advisers has affected the culture of the largest nation in the region, Cuba.

Conquest and Slavery

The heritage of women in the Caribbean begins with the violence of Spanish colonization and slavery. Although little is known about violence against European women or their female descendants before the modern era, scholars know a great deal about colonial violence against native women and slave women.

In the fifteenth and sixteenth centuries Spain conquered and occupied most of the Caribbean, brutally subduing and enslaving the native population. Carib Indian women faced the usual sexual exploitation that accompanied the conquest and enslavement of Indians throughout the hemisphere in this period. Some of the conquistadors took Indian women as concubines, or even wives, while others more callously exploited them for sexual gratification. By the mid-sixteenth century most of the Carib Indians had died out from a combination of direct violence, overwork in mines and fields, and diseases carried to the New World by Europeans. This drastic reduction of the native population led the Spanish to bring African slaves to their Caribbean colonies, starting around 1517. The Spanish, and later the French and Dutch, imported far more slave men than women to the region, leading to severe gender imbalances. Such a disproportion naturally placed sexual pressures on slave women and created sexual tension within slave communities. Until the nineteenth century, with the exception of Barbados and the Leeward Islands (both British colonies), male slaves continuously outnumbered females in both importations and total population. Starting in the mid-eighteenth century, importers began to shift toward a gender balance, but the preference for men remained. In an analysis of 272 shipments of slaves to the British West Indies between 1791 and 1798, Hilary Beckles found that 183 men were imported for every 100 women. Yet by 1833, when Britain ended slavery in its New World colonies, only Trinidad and Demerara had a male majority—which was slight—while Barbados, Saint Kitts, Jamaica, Nevis, and Saint Vincent all had a female majority. The rise in the proportion of female slaves throughout the Caribbean may reflect a diminution in violence and in the mistreatment of slave women. Especially after the United States and Great Britain banned the African trade in 1808, slave women became more valuable for their reproductive potential, and therefore their survival became more important.

While probably suffering less direct physical abuse and a lower likelihood of execution than male slaves, women slaves were nevertheless brutally punished throughout the region. The last execution for witchcraft in the English New World colonies involved a slave woman burned at the stake for attempting to poison her master. Whippings—a hundred lashes—were not unheard of for slave women; and some women (though less commonly than men) were forced to work in chains and with a steel collar around the neck, which prevented them from even lying down. Women slaves were often flogged while nude, perhaps giving an added sexual dimension to the punishment. One overseer ordered a male slave to defecate into the mouth of a female slave who had stolen sugarcane, the same punishment meted out to men. However, this overseer did not order that punishment for one of his female slaves with whom he had a sexual liaison (Beckles, 1999: 52).

As this case indicates, sexual liaisons with masters and overseers could gain the exploited slave women special privileges. Indeed, in the Spanish, French, and British colonies the slaves most likely to be emancipated were the paramours of their owners or overseers. But throughout the region slave women faced sexual exploitation, abuse, and violence. There was no such crime as rape of a slave woman—by another slave, a free black, or a white man. Prostitution was illegal, but in Jamaica and Barbados, at least, there is no indication that these laws were enforced against slave prostitutes or their masters. The level of violence associated with slave prostitution is unclear. Reports to the British Parliament suggest that many slave women practiced prostitution on their own time, and one English abolitionist claimed that elite slaves and slave midwives "were frequently the suppliers of young girls to urban clients" (Beckles, 1999: 27).

Violence in the Modern Era

The heritage of slavery left many nations in the Caribbean with cultures of violence. For example, the nation of Haiti emerged out of the only successful slave rebellion in the New World, a rebellion marked by barbarities on all sides of what became a series of multisided revolutions and civil wars. Slave rebels often raped the daughters of French and Creoles, while forcing their parents to watch, perhaps in revenge for decades of sexual abuse of slave women. Slave women were treated similarly by French and Creole soldiers during the wars.

From the end of slavery until the modern era there is surprisingly little documentation of violence against women for this region. Even for the modern era huge gaps exist. In 1998, a report by the United Nations concluded: "Inadequate data makes it difficult to get an accurate picture of the extent of violence against women in all its manifestations in the Caribbean region" (Clarke, 1998: 6).

The data that do exist suggest that violence against women in the modern Caribbean has been both political and economic. In some parts of the region, violence is used to force women into prostitution and to keep them in that role. In Haiti various repressive regimes have used rape as a tool of political oppression, aimed at women who protest the political structure or at the wives and daughters of men involved in the political reform movement (Brasieleiro, 1997: 26).

The underreporting of rape is an enormous problem in this region: it is estimated that only one rape victim in eight actually reports the crime. In 1991, for example, a study found that in Dominica, less than 14 percent of all rape victims reported the crime. There is also a huge gap between reporting of rape and prosecution or conviction. In 1985 there were 142 reported rapes in Trinidad and Tobago, but they led to no convictions; in 1989 there were 239 reported rapes and only ten convictions. Similarly, in Barbados there were 64 reported rapes in 1989 but no convictions. The huge underreporting of rape and the even larger disparities between reports and convictions are explained in part by lack of police training and by police forces' insensitivity to the problem.

The problems that make rape difficult to prosecute are even more apparent in domestic violence, which may be the most common and most dangerous form of violence against women in this region. Both rape and domestic violence are undergirded by a complicated set of social factors, including a "tendency to treat violence against women as a private matter" (Clarke, 1998: 11), a lack of clear statutes proscribing domestic violence, cultural notions that rape victims have enticed men to rape them, social stress brought about by economic pressures and poverty, and a culture of violence. Some scholars trace this culture of violence directly to slavery and other forms of forced labor. Statistics on overall violence against women are scarce, but studies in Jamaica suggest that one woman in five has been assaulted by a man—and this number excludes cases of domestic violence.

Most nations in the region have at least criminalized domestic violence, although several, including Jamaica, Guyana, and Antigua, did not pass such legislation until after 1995, when an international conference on the status of women highlighted the problem. As of May 2000, Dominica and Grenada had still not passed any legislation criminalizing domestic violence.

The laws, however, have had little effect on domestic violence, which seems pervasive in the region. A study by the United Nations in 1998 found that between a quarter and a half of all married women in Latin America and the Caribbean were victims of domestic violence. The problem is probably greatest in the poorest nations of the Caribbean. Indifference on the part of the police and prosecutors leads most women to suffer in silence. Women's tendency to remain silent is reinforced by a history of subjugation within the family—a subjugation that many women have internalized. Those who have been beaten by their husbands often declare, "I think I help to cause it," or "It is better to hit and get rid of feelings than to keep them inside" (Clarke, 1998: 6). Poverty, joblessness, and the economic dependence of women also lead to underreporting of domestic violence—as does a reluctance to arrest or prosecute. For example, in 1997 Jamaican men had an unemployment rate of 13.5 percent, which in itself is high enough to cause great social tension and lead to violence; women, meanwhile, had an unemployment rate of 64.7 percent, a condition that would make it particularly difficult for most women to report domestic violence. Patriarchal traditions loom large in this problem. As one police officer noted, "If we encourage wives to take their husbands to Court then what will happen to the family?" (Clarke, 1998: 7). Studies in Guyana, for instance, have shown that domestic violence is endemic among the large East Indian population, with 44 percent of all wives suffering physical abuse, even after twenty years of marriage; but according to one of these studies, the reporting rate for cases of domestic violence was only 5.9 percent.

Most abuse, then, is not reported, not only for these reasons but perhaps also because reporting seems to have little affect. One study found that in only 10.6 percent of reported cases did the police arrest the offender; in a third

of the cases the offender received a warning. Without a serious response from the law enforcement system—which might include counseling as well as legal sanctions—reporting this apparently common crime seems at best a waste of time and at worst tends to increase the danger for the abused wife. Reflective of the police forces' attitude was a statement by one officer that "we do not take husband and wife disputes seriously because families must have their ups and downs" (Clarke, 1998: 7). Given this attitude, it is not surprising that health agencies in the Bahamas and Suriname, for example, report one and a half times as many instances of wife abuse as were reported to the police, and that low rates of arrest are common in so many places. In Saint Vincent and the Grenadines during one period, only 15 percent of all reports of domestic abuse led to convictions. It is worth repeating, moreover, that reported cases are only a tiny fraction of the domestic abuse being committed: in Barbados, to cite just one figure, it is estimated that a third to a half of all adult women are battered. Domestic violence often leads to death. In the late 1990s an average of 90 women a year were murdered in Jamaica, and it was estimated that 40 to 70 percent of these deaths were the result of domestic violence.

Starting in the 1980s women throughout the region began to organize to protest against gender-based violence, to seek legal reform, and to provide institutionalized aid for victims. Rape hotlines and women's shelters are now found in many Caribbean nations, although they are usually in cities and serve only a limited population. Laws remain weak throughout the region, and only in a few places, like Jamaica and Barbados, are women attorneys available to fight for better enforcement and new legislation.

See Also

ABUSE; DOMESTIC VIOLENCE; HOUSEHOLDS AND FAMILIES: CARIBBEAN; INDIGENOUS WOMEN'S RIGHTS; RAPE; SLAVERY; VIOLENCE AND PEACE: OVERVIEW

References and Further Reading

Beckles, Hilary McD. 1999. *Centering women: Gender discourses in Caribbean slave society.* Kingston, Jamaica: Ian Ranel.

Barnes, Corinne. 2000. Women—Caribbean: Despite laws, violence against women continues. *Inter Press Service* (May 21).

Brasiliero, Ana Maria. 1997. *Women against violence—Breaking the silence: Reflecting on experience in Latin America and the Caribbean.* New York: United Nations Development Fund for Women.

Clarke, Roberta. 1998. *Violence against women in the Caribbean: State and non-state responses.* New York: United Nations Development Fund for Women.

Lewis, Marlene. 1998. Population—Jamaica: Violence against women on rise in Caribbean. *Inter Press Service* (20 January).

Byrgen Finkelman

VIOLENCE: Central and Eastern Europe

Violence in central and eastern Europe has been an acute social and political problem since the fall of the Berlin Wall in 1989. At the end of the cold war the former communist regimes went through turbulent transformations on the path to western-style political democracies. This radical change happened most obviously in those countries with multinational, multiethnic, and multicultural structures that were dissolved and formed into new states, such as the former Yugoslavia, resulting in ethnic and genocidal war and extreme gender violence. State ethnic violence also occurred to a lesser degree in the former Soviet Union.

Gender and Ethnic Violence

Milder forms of both gender and ethnic violence were present in other countries of the eastern bloc as well. The continuing existence of ethnic and gender violence in postcommunist regimes is seen by many as reflecting political and social structures that are conducive to highly charged ethnic-racial and sexual policies and violence. The most prevalent concept in postcommunist state building has been the patriarchal nation-state, so the ideology of state and ethnic nationalism based on patriarchal principles has become the most dominant force in rebuilding. Various forms of ethnic nationalism, national separatism, gender and racist exclusion, or minimalizing of old and new minority groups are often closely connected to discriminatory and violent policies against women and their civil and social rights, which were protected under the old communist order.

Although some postcommunist states with a more or less ethnically homogeneous population, like Poland, did not practice extreme ethnic or sexual violence, all of them violated women's essential human rights, especially the right to abortion, suggesting that the colonization of women's bodies had been central to postcommunist nation building. Because men have gained decisive political and reproductive control over women, these societies are often called "male democracies" or "new patriarchies."

The near absence of women from politics in postcommunist transitions demonstrates the damaging effects of the patriarchal communist legacy, which gave women the right to work, education, divorce, and abortion but prevented them from becoming active politically and thus in control of their own destiny. The nations' new legislatures were masculinized, and eastern European gender relations have become predominantly sexualized (Enloe, 1993). The acute economic crisis, which limits women's other opportunities, has also led to their increased sexual abuse (often violent) in, for example, prostitution, sex trafficking, pornography, and beauty contests.

The connection between ethnic and gender violence is most clearly seen in the case of the former Yugoslavia. Yugoslavia's multiethnic and multicultural structure became the most dramatic example of lethal nationalism. The first postcommunist elections in 1990 in Yugoslavia's republics-states resulted in the victory of parties with more or less open nationalistic and patriarchal agendas that excluded other ethnic groups. With Serbia being the dominant nation, its ethnic nationalism prevented a peaceful integration and played the crucial part in causing the war, first in Slovenia and then in Croatia, Bosnia, and Herzegovina. Croatian ethnic nationalism also played its part, with its racialized project of a "pure" Croatian nation-state. The genocidal brutality of ethnic war in the former Yugoslavia shows how ethnic hatreds are promoting "enemy-otherness" through the fluid lines of religion, culture, ethnicity, and gender, thus reflecting the contemporary redefinition of racial hostility (Eisenstein, 1996).

Ethnic Nationalism

Ethnic nationalism is based on hostile "identity-difference" politics in which women are simultaneously mythologized as the nation's "deepest essence" and used in their "natural" role as breeders. The war in the former Yugoslavia can be interpreted not solely as a result of a people's tribal mentality, but also as a result of the postcommunist strategy of defining new ethnic and subethnic borders between males in power and all others in a given political entity. The nationalistic abuse of women sheds light on the institution of ethnic nationhood as a fraternal order in which women-insiders are seen as a commodity and dominated, and women-outsiders are a target of violence. The reproductive use and abuse of women and their bodies in "pure nation building" results in two interdependent forms of violence against them: highly restricted abortion or no abortion for insiders, and rape for outsiders.

The issue of rape as a systematic, historical, and political (private and public) strategy against women has been obvious in the war in Bosnia and Herzegovina. There is evidence of mass rape committed by Serb military men as a conscious instrument of war for the purpose of ethnic cleansing, destruction of culture, and genocide against Muslims. Also, there is evidence that all sides in this war used rape as a form of revenge, punishment, and humiliation of the enemy. This war, happening in "civilized" Europe, showed once more that women's bodies are an instrument of war strategy, a symbolic and actual battlefield of men's ritual conquering of the other, and women as the universal other. Bosnian women activists and Croatian and Serbian feminists, with the help of international feminist networks, alerted media and politicians to rape as a lethal tool of war, ethnic cleansing, and genocide. In 1992 they demanded a change in Section IV of the Geneva Convention (1949) that would include rape as a war crime and a crime against humanity; it was officially designated a crime against humanity in 1993. While they do not deny that all sides have committed rape, Bosnian women activists insist that the Serbs' rape of Muslim women was a particular form of genocide-rape. Both Croatian and Serbian feminists are against all political and media manipulation of rape victims, the abuse of data (by ascribing genocidal rape only to the enemy), and further nationalist abuse of women in order to spread ethnic hatred. For the feminists, militarism, nationalism, and sexism go hand in hand, and war rape is only the tip of the iceberg of structural violence against women in patriarchal societies. Feminists have also pointed out other forms of abuse of women: the obstruction of humanitarian aid convoys, the condition of women refugees, rape by army veterans, and prostitution and sexual trafficking on United Nations army bases.

New Women's Groups

Although feminism in the former Yugoslavia had some influence even from the late 1970s, with feminist groups formed in Zagreb, Belgrade, and Ljubljana, only in facing the disastrous war and state nationalist and militarist ideologies did feminism become more activist and influential. Since the beginnings of pluralism and the country's disintegration in 1990, numerous new autonomous women's groups have been formed. Here are some examples.

Slovenia: Women for Politics, Modra, Cassandra, Women's Centre, Women's Counseling (Ljubljana), Women's Initiative (Koper).

Croatia: Women's Lobby, Kareta, Autonomous Women's House, Women's Infotheque, Women of Antiwar Campaign, Centre for Women War Victims, Women's Human Rights Group, Independent Alliance of Women, Women's Studies Centre, Rosa House Project (Zagreb); Women's Initiative (Osijek); Women's Group, Vida Tućan Project (Split); Women's Peace Workshop (Rijeka).

Bosnia and Herzegovina: MAK Bosnian Woman (Sarajevo), Medica (Zenica), Women Intellectuals, Amica (Tuzla).

Serbia: SOS Hotline, Women's Party, Women's Parliament, Women in Black Against War, Women's Studies Centre, Autonomous Women's Centre Against Sexual Violence, Centre for Girls, Women's House, Arkadia—Lesbian and Gay Association (Belgrade); Women's Centre Isidora (Pančevo); SOS Hotline (Kraljevo and Niš); League of Albanian Women, Humanitarian Women's Organisation, Albanian Women's Health Group, Women's Law Group, Media Project for Women, Women Creators and Teachers Group (Prishtina, Kosovo).

Macedonia: Women's Organisations Alliance (Skopje), Gipsy Women's Organisation (Kumanovo).

These groups are independent nongovernmental organizations based on feminist principles, making women's resistance to war and militant nationalist patriarchy visible. They struggle for the survival of multiethnic and multicultural civic identities, against racist, nationalist, and all other sexist ideologies.

See Also

ARMAMENT AND MILITARIZATION; ETHNIC CLEANSING; FEMINISM: EASTERN EUROPE; GENOCIDE; NATION AND NATIONALISM; POLITICS AND THE STATE: EASTERN EUROPE; RAPE; SEXUAL VIOLENCE; WAR

References and Further Reading

Coulson, Meg. 1993. Looking behind the violent breakup of Yugoslavia. *Feminist Review* 45: 86–101.

Eisenstein, Zillah. 1996. *Hatreds in the 21st century: Globalism, nationalism, and feminism.* New York: Routledge.

Enloe, Cynthia. 1993. *The morning after: Sexual politics at the end of the cold war.* Berkeley: University of California Press.

Kesić, Vesna. 1994. Žene su žrtve rata… (Women are victims of war …) *Zbornik.* Zagreb: Centar za žene žrtve rata.

Stiglmayer, Alexandra, ed. 1994. *Mass rape: The war against women in Bosnia-Herzegovina.* Lincoln: University of Nebraska Press.

United Nations Commission on Human Rights. 1993. *Rape and abuse of women and children in the territory of the former Yugoslavia.* Report on the 49th session.

Zajović, Stasa. 1995. The abuse of women on nationalist and militarist basis. In *Women for peace.* Belgrade: Women in Black.

Zarana Papic

VIOLENCE:
Central and South America

Violence against women in Central and South America reflects global trends, influenced by specific regional history and conditions. These regional factors include colonization, war, migration, and neoliberalism. As in other regions, gender-based violence was integral to the European conquest of Latin America, setting a pernicious pattern in which indigenous women have been, disproportionately, targets of rape as a weapon of war. Nonindigenous women have also been abused during armed conflicts, including more than seventy military interventions by the United States. In the 1970s, under the military regimes of the "southern cone" countries, thousands of women's children and other relatives disappeared and were murdered; and women political prisoners were systematically subjected to sexual torture. In the 1980s, violence against women was a widespread counterinsurgency strategy in Central America. In the 1990s, women in the heavily militarized state of Chiapas, Mexico, were subjected to sexual harassment, rape, forced prostitution, and compulsory servitude in military camps.

Women who were active in regional struggles for liberation and democracy during the 1970s and 1980s gradually developed an autonomous movement that grew to challenge violence against women. However, the defeat and co-optation of liberation struggles in the 1990s undermined progressive politics, including the fight against gender violence. In Nicaragua in 1990, for example, the electoral defeat of the Sandinistas refortified the Roman Catholic church and its oppressive gender policies. The church hierarchy is a powerful institution in all Latin American countries, and it is often seen as reinforcing gender violence by encouraging reconciliation in cases of domestic violence and denying women's reproductive rights. The end of armed conflicts also created new political spaces in which women have mobilized to pursue antiviolence agendas. For instance, Guatemalan women demanded legislative reforms in the context of the peace accords of 1996.

Roots of Gender Violence

As the most marginalized sector of Latin American societies, indigenous women are effectively denied access to most public services—such as education, medical care, police protection, telephone service, and transportation—that could prevent or redress violence. In fact, public services are themselves a site of violence against indigenous women. For example, in numerous Central and South American countries, poor and indigenous women seeking professional health care have been forcibly sterilized. Many rural indigenous women do not speak fluent Spanish, the language of public education, the mass media, and the courts. Even within the women's movement, persistent racism means that programs to combat violence against women usually do not include components designed by indigenous women and therefore do not adequately address the problem as it affects them.

War and economic ruin have led to the displacement and migration of millions of Latin Americans. Displaced women are particularly vulnerable to abuse by soldiers, bandits, and "coyotes"—guides offering transportation to the United States. In Latin America, as elsewhere, refugee communities have a high level of domestic violence. Displacement shatters the environment that enables women to meet their families' needs, and violence against them is often a reaction to their failure to perform this primary social role. Refugee women, who are unfamiliar with or fearful of local authorities, have little legal recourse. Those displaced inside their own national borders, like the hundreds of thousands of Colombian and Guatemalan peasants dislocated from their land by political violence, lack legal status as refugees and are therefore denied services or protection by international authorities.

Economic Links

A study by the Inter-American Development Bank in Nicaragua in 1996 found strong links between women's economic dependence on men and physical abuse—a correlation that also exists elsewhere. However, employment of women does not necessarily provide sufficient leverage to challenge domestic violence. Many women in Central and South America report that their male relatives use violence or the threat of violence to take their earnings from them. Also, for thousands of women, the workplace itself is a site of abuse. In fact, the sector most emblematic of Latin America's role in the global economy is also the most notorious for abuse of women. Export manufacturing sweatshops—called *maquiladoras* or *maquilas*—hire mainly women who are paid less, work longer, and are subjected to worse conditions than men. Many of these women are migrants who have left behind social networks that could provide protection from violence. Documented examples of violence against women in *maquilas* include humiliation, sexual harassment, intimidation, sexual assault, beatings, strip searches, forced pregnancy tests, and violence against union organizers.

The proliferation of *maquilas* is one aspect of neoliberal economic restructuring that swept through Latin America at the end of the twentieth century. Neoliberal policies, including privatization and "structural adjustment programs" (SAPs), have induced rapid changes in traditional social structures throughout the region, increasing urbanization, migration, and women's employment—and, it is commonly held, intensifying poverty. Violence against women has been one manifestation of men's attempts to reassert traditional authority and cope with economic crises. Privatization of hospitals and schools and the displacement of peasant farmers by agribusiness have meant life-threatening deprivation for poor women and girls, who are less likely than boys and men to receive costly medical care, schooling, or scarce food.

Nearly every country in Central and South America has instituted SAPs, which have had the effect of drastically cutting public services that could help prevent gender violence, including education, drug treatment, job training, and women's leadership development programs. The SAPs have also slashed resources that supported survivors of violence and provided alternatives to abusive situations, such as counseling, shelters, health care, and subsidized housing. In poor communities, birthrates rise as women have less and less access to education, information, and reproductive health care; this increases women's vulnerability to male violence because women with more children are more dependent on men's wages.

Centuries of economic exploitation by industrialized countries (often referred to as the "North") have made development a major concern in Latin America, particularly in poverty-stricken Central America. However, neoliberal development strategies, which rely on macroeconomic indicators such as exports and gross national product, tend to disregard the impact of gender violence on society. In 1998, for example, after hurricane Mitch, one of the worst natural disasters ever recorded in Central America, development strategies were narrowly focused on industrial reconstruction. Crises in poor communities—including documented increases in domestic violence associated with the trauma of the storm—were neglected. Latin America has spearheaded potentially egalitarian development strategies, notably agrarian reform. But the discriminatory implementation of these programs has concentrated land resources in the hands of men, thereby reinforcing women's subordination, the root cause of violence against women.

Another economic factor in violence against women has been sex trafficking. As economic opportunities for women in Central and South America shrank and the AIDS epidemic shifted sex tourism away from Asia, sex trafficking increased throughout the region. For instance, Brazil's sex tourism industry involves an estimated 500,000 girls under age 14; thousands more serve as prostitutes in remote mining camps under conditions of virtual slavery. Guatemala City has also become a center of international sex trafficking, with girls from all over Central America smuggled in and forced to work as prostitutes.

Challenging Violence

The Latin American women's movement is recognized internationally for its advances in combating violence against women. Latin America was the first region in the world where all countries ratified the Convention on the Elimination of All Forms of Discrimination Against Women and the first to formulate a legal instrument explicitly designed to eradicate gender violence: the Convention for the Prevention, Punishment, and Eradication of Violence Against Women. The worldwide observance of November 25, the International Day Against Violence Against Women, is a Latin American initiative.

Until the 1990s, most countries in Central and South America lacked any legislation covering domestic violence; by the end of the decade, women's organizing had led to new laws in nearly every country. However, neoliberal policies had concurrently undercut governments' capacity to meet their legal obligations. Also, many of these laws continued to discriminate agains women in various ways: they trivialized gender violence by making it a civil rather than a criminal offense, neglected prevention and rehabilitation as keys to eradicating violence, exonerated rapists who offered to marry their victims, and denied redress to non-wage-earning women by recognizing "injury" only when a victim was rendered unfit for paid employment. Too often, even progressive laws have been hamstrung by a lack of political will to implement them.

Regional campaigns to establish women's shelters, improve health care for survivors of abuse, conduct research, and develop gender training programs for public servants have been undertaken by groups like the Latin American and Caribbean Women's Network Against Domestic and Sexual Violence and the Latin American and Caribbean Committee for the Defense of the Rights of Women (CLADEM). Hundreds of other organizations across Latin America work locally to challenge gender violence.

For example, MADRE, an international women's human rights organization, supports local women's initiatives against violence in Chiapas, Mexico, Guatemala, and Nicaragua. These programs recognize the indivisibility of human rights by addressing the range of violence in women's lives, whether on the job, in the streets, or at home. In Chiapas, MADRE's partner, K'inal Antzetik ("Women's Home" in the indigenous language, Tzotzil), offers reproductive health workshops, medical care, and psychological counseling for women survivors of domestic and military violence. This program establishes a dialogue to connect the struggle of indigenous people in Chiapas and the rights of indigenous women within their communities. In Guatemala City, MADRE supports the Women's Group for the Betterment of the Family (GRUFEPROMEFAM), which holds consciousness-raising workshops for survivors of gender violence, conducts public awareness campaigns, lobbies for legislative reform, and provides women *maquila* workers with the legal training and social support they need to challenge workplace abuses.

On Nicaragua's North Atlantic coast, Wangky Luhpia ("Child of the River" in Miskitu) offers drug treatment and leadership development programs that address violence against women. The regional university trains government officials and local leaders in incorporating a gender perspective into public policy.

Today, Central and South American activists' most fundamental challenges are those shared by women globally: to transform social attitudes that reproduce male violence and to oppose all policies that violate women's human rights.

See Also

DOMESTIC VIOLENCE; INDIGENOUS WOMEN'S RIGHTS; RAPE; TORTURE; VIOLENCE: CARIBBEAN

References and Further Reading

Brasileiro, Ana Maria, ed. 1997. *Women against violence: Breaking the silence.* New York: UNIFEM.

Cook, Rebecca J., ed. 1994. *Human rights of women: National and international perspectives.* Philadelphia: University of Pennsylvania Press.

Davies, Miranda, ed. 1994. *Women and violence: Realities and responses worldwide.* London and Atlantic Highlands: Zed.

Kamal, Rachel, and Anya Hoffman, eds. 1999. *The maquiladora reader: Cross-border organizing since NAFTA.* Philadelphia, Pa.: American Friends Service Committee.

Rosen, Fred, and Diedre McFadyen, eds. 1995. *Free trade and economic restructuring in Latin America: A NACLA reader.* New York: Monthly Review.

Yifat Susskind

VIOLENCE:
Commonwealth of Independent States

Before the Soviet period (1917–1991), the treatment of violence against women in different regions of the present-day Commonwealth of Independent States was determined by a diversity of religious and national customs. Muscovite and Kievan civil law, as well as church courts, protected the honor of physically assaulted and raped women in medieval Russia. All women, regardless of their social status, were able to appeal to the court. Even a married woman could petition for divorce and receive a compensatory sum if her husband forced her to have intercourse with him or if he beat her. Usually the punishment and fines for the "dishonor" depended on the social status of the litigant (Clements et al., 1991).

The law of the southern Slavs dictated a more severe punishment: a rapist's nose was cut off or he was sold into slavery if the victim was a betrothed maiden. Women received a more severe punishment than men for adultery or for their husband's murder: they were taken naked around the village, stoned, or buried alive (covered with earth up to the neck) until they died. Fathers and husbands were allowed to discipline and control their wives, female children, and daughters-in-law. The Russian Orthodox rules prescribed in the Domostroi (Household Book), written at the time of Czar Ivan IV, describe how wives should be treated: men should avoid beatings that might result in deafness, blindness, or broken bones, or that would prevent a woman from doing physical work around the house or in the fields (Sperling, 1990).

Status of Women

Women's subordinate position was reflected in a variety of patriarchal customs, traditions, and proverbs. For example, at a traditional seventeenth-century wedding, a whip with the special name *durak* ("fool"), was hung over the newlyweds' bed as a symbol of the husband's authority. The practice of *snokhachestvo* (sexual relations between father-in-law and daughter-in-law) was widespread in peasant communities. Even now the following proverbs are often used: "To beat means to love" and "A chicken is not a bird and a *baba* [a married woman] is not a person."

Among Tadjiks and Uzbeks, the Shari'a (Muslim laws) had great influence over women's lives. The situation of Kazakh and Kyrgyz women largely depended on traditions that included some Islamic elements. The payment of a bride-price (*kalym*) made a wife the property of the husband's family. According to levirate tradition, a widow could not bring up her children alone. Usually she was made the wife of one of her husband's close relatives if her relatives did not return the bride-price. If the senior brother already had a wife, then the widow became his junior wife.

Although most of the regions were characterized by a patriarchal honor-and-shame ethic for women, in the Asian and Caucasian regions seclusion was practiced, as well as veiling or physical mutilation for the protection of the woman's honor. Even now in the Caucasus republics there are cases in which brothers murder a raped sister with the aim of lifting the "disgrace" from their family. According to physicians' testimonies, victims of rape, by "hooligans" or violent mobs, were provided with abortions. Because of the hardships of the post-1905 years, mass-scale women's migration from villages and the growth of prostitution and infanticide were observed.

After the revolution, the Bolsheviks attempted to transform the woman's role, but opposition to women's emancipation was great. For example, in the republics of central Asia men harassed and raped unveiled Muslim women and murdered hundreds of women activists in defense of forced marriages and traditional polygamy (Massell, 1974). Between 1917 and 1922 issues of sexual violence became taboo, as Marxist theory stated that rape would not exist in the socialist state. During World Wars I and II rape was a frequent occurrence in the near-front areas. According to the testimony of the writer Elena Glinka (1989), the Russians practiced mass rape (lasting for several days) of imprisoned women in Stalinist camps.

After 1933 Stalin prohibited the publication of criminal statistics, and for many years they were not made public. In 1987 women reported 16,800 rapes countrywide, with 10,900 in the Russian Federation. In 1993 women were victims of more than 330,000 reported crimes, of which 14,000 were rape. According to the Ministry of Social Security, 15,000 women were killed by their husbands or partners in 1994. Another 54,000 women were seriously injured by their partners (Morvant, 1995). The research and statistics of the independent Association of Crisis Centers indicate that the official figures dramatically underreport the actual occurrence of rape, which could be 30 to 50 times higher.

After the disintegration of the Soviet Union in 1991, the national and religious revival of the republics was associated with political self-determination. In reality, a renaissance of patriarchy was taking place as well as a re-Islamization in Asia and a restoration of the former model of discrimination against women. Many traditions banned during the Soviet period were revived. Cases are not infrequent in Uzbekistan of women's suicide (self-immolation) when they cannot tolerate humiliation in the family. Military conflicts in the territory of the former Soviet Union included murders, rapes, and pogroms. Because of severe unemployment at home, some women from different parts of Russia have tried to earn money abroad as providers of sex services. Prostitution and sexism in the mass media in general have escalated in recent years.

New Criminal Code

From 1991, under the New Criminal Code, the maximum punishment for a rapist is 15 years imprisonment. Aggravating circumstances, such as rape of a minor or gang rape, could subject the rapist to the death penalty. Comprehensive legal regulations, though severe, make it difficult for victims to obtain justice. There are no laws dealing specifically with domestic violence or rape within a marriage or partnership. As of mid-2000, however, the State Duma was in the process of drafting a law on domestic violence. An article that might be used in cases of sexual harassment does exist, but in reality it is extremely difficult to produce evidence, especially within the sphere of private relationships and in the environment of mass unemployment of women.

The public attitude toward victims of rape and domestic violence tends to be that women "ask for" rape; that provocative dress or particular behavior serves as an incitement for an abuser. Moreover, young as well as mature women who have previously engaged in promiscuous sexual intercourse are discriminated against in rape cases.

Since World War II, Soviet lawyers have treated rape as a sexual abnormality. Rape now is regarded as a crime connected with sexuality and contrary to the norms of accepted sexual practice. Lawyers are still taught to use a victimization defense, emphasizing a person's predisposition to become a crime victim. A booklet on defending oneself from criminals issued by the Russian Ministry of Internal Affairs in 1993 recommends that women behave "in a modest way, with a feeling of self-dignity, so as to avoid infringement of one's honor." Officially supported family criminology suggests that the reasons for family violence include disputes over possessions, power, sexual freedom, and changes in family traditions. Some sociologists think that female emancipation creates conflict situations.

The feminist approach is promoted by several crisis centers for women within the independent women's movement. In some cities shelters have been set up for battered women with children. Contemporary violence against women in the Commonwealth of Independent States has its roots in national origins as well as patriarchal values, anarchy, impunity in the legal sphere, and women's poverty.

See Also

FEMINISM: COMMONWEALTH OF INDEPENDENT STATES

References and Further Reading

Clements, Barbara Evans, Barbara Alpern Engel, and Christine D. Worobec, eds. 1991. *Russia's women: Accommodation, resistance, transformation.* Berkeley: University of California Press.

Glinka, E. 1989. Kolymskyi tramvay sredney tiazhosti (Kolyma's tram). *Neva* 6 (Moscow).

Issraelyan, Y. and T. Zabelina, eds. 1999. *Russian women's crisis centers: Achievements and ideas.* Moscow: Press-Solo.

Juviler, P. 1977. Women and sex in Soviet law. In D. Atkinson, A. Dallin, and G. W. Lapidus, eds. *Women in Russia,* 243–265. Stanford, Calif.: Stanford University Press.

Khodyreva, N. 1996. *Sexism and sexual abuse in Russia: Women in a violent world. Feminist analyses and resistance across Europe,* 27–40. Ed. Chr. Corrin. Edinburgh: Edinburgh University Press.

Levin, Eve. 1989. *Sex and society in the world of the Orthodox Slavs, 900–1700.* Ithaca, N.Y.: Cornell University Press.

Massell, Gregory. 1974. *The surrogate proletariat: Moslem women and revolutionary strategies in Soviet central Asia, 1919–1929.* Princeton, N.J.: Princeton University Press.

Morvant, Penny. 1995. Bearing the "double burden" in Russia. *Transition* 8(Sept.): 7–8.

Russia: Neither jobs nor justice. 1995. *Human Rights Watch Report* 7(5).

Sperling, Valerie. 1990. Rape and domestic violence in the U.S.S.R. *Response to Violence Against Women and Children* 13(3): 16–22.

Waters, Rob. 1995. A hotline movement grows in Russia. *Ms.* (Nov.–Dec.): 19–21.

Women's safety in the family, at work, on the street. 1998. *Vestnic of Independent Women's Forum* 7A (Moscow).

Natalia V. Khodyreva

VIOLENCE: East Asia (China) I

For the purposes of this article, *violence* will be defined as ill-treatment or unequal treatment of women in their private or sexual life. In China, responses to such violence, and attempts to prevent it, take various forms: (1) laws that punish perpetrators of violence against women; (2) government regulations protecting women's rights; (3) appeals by women to local news media and to magazines, often in the form of letters describing their physical and mental suffering; and (4) the work of local women's associations. In "old China" before 1949, there were antiviolence movements in which many women were active, but these no longer exist; in the "new China," the most useful and most powerful avenue of antiviolence is the People's Laws.

The Chinese government and people maintain, in general, that only a small number of women are victims of violence in modern China, because women were liberated both economically and politically when the new China was founded in 1949, and because of the reforms that have taken place in the past two decades. Today, most women go out to work, and women have the right to take part in national affairs and in administration and management. The People's Republic of China seeks to guarantee women's basic rights and interests primarily through legislation; its constitution established equal rights for women, and a number of laws and decrees have been adopted to protect women in various ways. However, for certain historical reasons, "Women still have a lot of catching up to do until they really equal their male counterparts" (*China Daily,* 1994)—and this can be seen in the fact that some women are still subject to sexual violence and mistreatment in their families. Such abuses are believed to have their origin in the feudal idea that men are superior to women. They are illegal under contemporary Chinese law, but China ended its feudal system only half a century ago, and feudal influences are still deeply rooted in some people's minds. Moreover, Chinese women value the quality of reserve, or reticence, with regard to their private life; as a result, some women are reluctant to reveal unfair treatment or ill-treatment, especially in sexual matters; often, women will appeal to a court of law only if they find their abuse unendurable.

Forms of Violence

Specific forms of violence against girls and women include female infanticide; rape, both within and outside marriage; and prostitution.

Female infanticide occurs because some families prefer sons to daughters. Thus some female fetuses are aborted, and some female babies and children are abandoned or fatally ill-treated. In certain rural areas, a woman who gives birth to a daughter (rather than a son) may be looked down on, abused, or deserted; the birth of a girl is blamed on the mother, as if the father had nothing to do with it. A notorious case took place in 1993, when a 3-year-old girl was maltreated so severely, by her own mother, that she died (*Southern Daily,* 1993). The mother's defense was that she had borne four daughters and was compelled to kill the fourth because she could no longer withstand her husband's retalitative violence; but a people's court convicted her and sentenced her to death. The court recognized that the husband was the source of this tragedy but explained that the woman should have appealed to the law, letting the legal system punish him. In a fairly typical case, a newborn girl was abandoned on a bench in a hospital; the mother's family had rejected the infant and forced the young mother to abandon her. Another young woman aborted three female fetuses, but she herself was nevertheless "deserted at last" (*Guangzhou Daily,* 1993; this woman eventually obtained a divorce and an independent life).

One form of sexual violence occurs because some women feel only "sexual duty," and "no pleasure in sex" (*Yangcheng Evening,* 1993); that is, these women's sexual life is not for their own pleasure or fulfillment but is rather a matter of meeting their obligations. It is believed that this occurs mostly among less educated people in rural areas; one study, for example, involved 20,000 people in Jiangsu Province. A woman who has not given birth after several years of marriage may become a victim of sexual abuse in the form of violent intercourse with her husband, along with psychological abuse: she will be forced to see doctors and to take medicines and is blamed for infertility even if the husband is the infertile partner. (Men in China seldom undergo fertility tests.) The media report that sexual violence is frequent within marriage and among couples premaritally. One representative case involved a wife who went to the security police to accuse her husband of raping her (*Yangcheng Evening,* 1994): she said that he was too forceful and took no account of her fragility, and that she could no longer stand it; finally, she obtained a divorce. In another case that can serve as an example, when a woman refused to marry a man she had been seeing, he took revenge by raping her.

Prostitution apparently became more commonplace in the 1980s and 1990s, especially in southern China. Some girls were sold by men and forced to become prostitutes; only by going to the police could they be freed. (In some areas, there are still incidents of women and girls being kidnapped for sale.) Some young girls and women were attracted by wealth and illegally cohabited with rich men. One case, which sounds sensational but is probably not unique, involved a woman aged 23 who had been a concubine for five years, had undergone eight abortions, and had developed several gynecological disorders. She eventually went to live with a rich married man in Hong Kong who supported her but made so many sexual demands that from time to time she would escape by having herself admitted to a hospital.

Dealing with Violence

It is generally argued that the way to freedom in general, and freedom from violence in particular, is for women to become better educated and to learn more about the law. Chinese women should not be afraid to report violence or sexual abuse; the Chinese legal system will prosecute and punish people who ill-treat women, girls, and infants. Unfortunately, however, many women are unwilling to expose problems of sexual or family life, and if they themselves do not report this abuse, it cannot easily become known to the public or to the law enforcement agencies.

It is possible that violence against women is related to discrimination against women: although Chinese women overall are liberated and have equal rights, a good education, and work, they still face some discrimination in employment (as regards hiring, wages, and promotion) and in housing. To improve women's position in society and in the family, both men's and women's education may need to be bettered, in turn improving civilization and culture and eliminating feudal ideas.

See Also

ABUSE; DOMESTIC VIOLENCE; HOUSEHOLDS AND FAMILIES: EAST ASIA: INFANTICIDE; VIOLENCE: EAST ASIA (CHINA) II

References and Further Reading

Analysis of family sexual ill-treatment. 1994. *Yangcheng Evening* (10 October): 7.

Look, tears are running down the face of "Moon." 1993. *Yangcheng Evening* (3 March): 2.

"Men and woman are equal" should not just be a slogan. 1993. *Southern Daily* (27 April): 5.

What happens to women who give birth to female babies? 1993. *Guangzhou Daily* (12 May): 13.

Women's liberation. 1994. *China Daily* (1 October): 4.

Annie Cheng Jinglan

Violence: East Asia (China) II

The Legal Protection of Women

One-quarter of the world's women live in China. Since the revolution of 1949, the Chinese government has voiced unequivocal support for the right of women to enjoy lives free of domestic and social violence and has promoted the notion of equal access to political decision making, to education, to the courts, and to employment. These efforts culminated in the passage of the Women's Law of 1992, the first law that systematically and comprehensively defined the rights of women in key sectors of Chinese public life (politics, culture, education, labor, and the economy) as well as private life (marriage, the family, and the individual).

Despite governmental efforts to protect women from domestic violence, crime, and discrimination, China is confronting powerful forces of tradition and of economic change that undermine the implementation of the strongly worded law. Legal rulings have succeeded only in softening the impact on women of a rigid feudal culture undergoing severe economic transformation. In the future, China will need to extend reform into the daily lives of its women.

Cultural Violence

In China, cultural values and practices often stand between women and the protections offered by the law. In rural China, where poverty and feudalism still prevail, mercenary or arbitrary marriages, characterized by ill treatment and abuse, are not uncommon. Chinese culture so values a family's reputation that throughout the country women who are the victims of domestic violence are expected to endure their abuse quietly to protect that reputation. Wife beating is the most prevalent form of domestic abuse and is apparently on the rise. In response to this situation, services have been established to encourage women to free themselves from spousal violence, including counseling, hot lines, medical services, temporary shelters, child care, family life education, housing and financial assistance, and legal aid. China has recently introduced family courts to adjudicate cases of domestic violence, as well as the complex social and economic issues concerning a woman's right to divorce, to gain custody of children, and to divide property.

However, to protect women's rights, such institutions must be viable and respected options. Courts must work for women when they seek legal protections, and Chinese culture must encourage women to do so. In this context, women in urban China fare much better than those in rural China, because cities provide more accessible and modern legal networks and information sources (such as television and radio). In addition, cities provide better education and economic opportunities. Both encourage independence and are significant factors in a woman's ability to understand and seek the legal protections that counteract strong cultural forces and to protect herself from an abusive marriage or other violence. Women in urban areas enjoy a literacy rate of nearly 98 percent, compared with only 63 percent for women in the countryside. However, even in urban areas, where equal access to education is protected, women are more likely than men to cut short their education to fulfill

economic and familial obligations, in part because a preference for sons still figures as a significant source of discrimination against women in general.

State-Sanctioned Violence

As part of its modernization efforts, which include increased affluence and universal health care and education, China has imposed a one-child policy on families, which is intended to limit the destructive effects of overpopulation. This policy restricts families in urban areas to one child and families from rural areas to two children. However, the one-child policy points out the connection in China between state-condoned violence in the name of modernization and the domestic violence that contradicts the stated desire to leave behind certain feudal cultural practices. Through this policy, the government intervenes in the domestic sphere by regulating and restricting the number of children a married couple may have—at times, forcibly. As a matter of law, the one-child policy violates a woman's right to physical autonomy and personal security. Although the State Family Planning Commission of China claims that coercion is not permitted in the implementation of the policy, there are widespread reports of officials' exerting informal pressures on women, such as psychological intimidation, continuous harassment, threats of job loss, and even violence. Despite such reports, the law has never prosecuted an official for using violence against women, but those who have protected women from the imposition of the policy have been illegally detained, imprisoned, and tortured.

Moreover, the cultural preference for sons turns the state's one-child policy against daughters, encouraging female infanticide and sex-selective abortions of female fetuses. As a result, approximately 500,000 more male children than female children are born each year in China—a figure far greater than the statistical norm. Recent surveys suggest that 12 percent of all female fetuses were aborted or unaccounted for after ultrasound screening determined the sex of the unborn child. Ultrasound has now been outlawed.

Economic Violence

The massive liberalization of the Chinese economy—which is moving from a state-run command economy to an entrepreneurial free-market economy—has introduced new forms of social violence against women. Changes in the economy have produced greater wealth for China as a whole but have also caused an increase in domestic violence in those families hit by economic hardship, which often takes the form of job insecurity in the new economy. Economic reform has also given rise to other types of social violence, including rape, trafficking, and kidnapping of women, as well as forced prostitution among laid-off women workers unable to find new jobs. Legal protections have not successfully blocked the illegal activities made possible by economic reform.

Because women have experienced more of the negative effects of reform than men, including unemployment and an inability to regain employment, the Chinese government has begun providing special retraining programs to curb the systemic discrimination against women. But in an atmosphere of competitive employment and cultural discrimination, the workplace is an area where women also confront violence and harassment and where a willingness to endure such treatment in order to protect one's job can supersede recourse to the law.

The Future for Chinese Women

China has received international respect for its efforts to overcome the sources of abuse against women. By acknowledging the problem of violence—one result of reform—China has set out to change it. But in the effort to change, the drive toward modernization cannot compromise the cause of human rights. Currently, China is increasing the actual participation of women in political life, something it sees as essential to pushing the nation toward greater domestic and social equality. China must evolve so that the writ of law and the lives of women are linked to ensure a woman's physical and personal integrity as a citizen in civil society.

See Also

HOUSEHOLDS AND FAMILIES: EAST ASIA; VIOLENCE: EAST ASIA (CHINA) I

Reference and Further Reading

Starr, John Bryan. 2000. *Understanding China: A guide to China's economy, history, and political structure.* New York: Hill and Wang.
United Nations Economic and Social Council. 1996. Commission on Human Rights, Fifty-Second Session (5 February).
United Nations Press Release. 1999 Wom/1092 (1 February).

Editorial Staff

VIOLENCE: Media

Women are often the object of violence portrayed by various media outlets. Because many people have the conviction that violence is unacceptable, and given the fact that immense commercial powers support media violence, the relationship between women, media, and violence demands

attention. For instance, does the broadcast of violence against women stimulate violence in reality? Does the broadcast of violence in general stimulate the practice of violence in reality, and are women the first victims of the general increase in media violence? To what degree is the augmentation of media violence responsible for a decrease in the quality of living, especially for women? Is the fact that there is so much violence in the media a case of unequal distribution of resources, because in general women do not like the violence? What are the criteria for evaluating media productions in order to prevent media-provoked violence against women? How can the media contribute to preventing violence against women? What are the criteria for fair portrayal in cases of news media reports about violence against women?

The supposition that it is hurting women has led many researchers and activists to oppose the increase of violence in the media. They are concerned that violence in the media could inspire more violence, that images of violence against women humiliate women, and that these violent portrayals hurt women vicariously.

Media and Violence

The scientific and social discussion about the connection between violence and the media had long been inconclusive; no direct correlation between violence in the media and the behavior of the audience could be proved. Public concern about the negative influence of media violence continued to increase, however.

In September 1999 a report prepared by the Majority Staff of the U.S. Senate Committee on the Judiciary on "Children, Violence, and the Media" was released. The report boldly states: "The effect of media violence . . . is no longer open to debate. Countless studies have shown that a steady diet of television, movie, music, video game, and Internet violence plays a significant role in the disheartening number of violent acts committed by America's youth." Despite the lack of conclusive scientific evidence linking the media to increased violence, then, it is generally recognized that the cultural climate is influenced negatively by aggressiveness portrayed in various forms of media.

The Cultural Cultivation Paradigm

The true impact of the media lies in its influence on audiences as they cultivate their worldviews, attitudes, opinions, aspirations, and anticipations. Violence in the media potentially promotes widespread feelings of vulnerability and fear, often at the expense of women and minorities, in the interest of corporate control and profit. Most portrayals of violence reflect the aggressiveness of individual perpetrators, without much empathy for the victims. Gebner (who developed the "cultivation" paradigm) calls this phenomenon "happy violence." Structural aspects of violence or state violence are seldom an ingredient; rather, power struggles between individuals or small groups with a few protagonists are more common elements of violent plots.

Minorities, the lower classes, and women pay the highest price for violence on television; this finding corresponds to existing patterns of domination and exploitation in society. Black women, for instance, are often used either as a symbol of danger or as an icon of emancipation and achievement. This kind of stereotyping, when consumed by an unquestioning audience, can potentially lead to a distorted worldview.

Fair Portrayal Approach

The issue of media violence provokes divergent reactions between women and men. Women are less likely than men to watch violent programs and films. Those who do watch may not enjoy what they see. Margaret Gallagher (1995), in a paper written for the United Nations' Division for the Advancement of Women, claims that women are made "uncomfortable, anxious, or frightened by depictions of violence" in the media. Scenes of media violence against women may be especially painful for women who have been victims of sexual violence.

Female Victims: Some Figures

- The victims we see on television are, in most cases, victims of violence. They outnumber victims of other kinds of disasters.
- The way female victims are constructed in the media reflects traditional patterns of gender construction (Michielsens and ten Boom, 1996): a female victim generally is pictured in a "clean" way, as young, happy, and beautiful; women victims do not have names and are killed or hurt not in the center of an action but often as bystanders. Female victims of violence are the norm in the media; in reality, however, men are more frequently victims of violence than women. This distortion reinforces the traditional portrayal of women as vulnerable.
- For every white male victim of violence there are 17 white female victims. For every white male victim there are 22 minority female victims. For every 10 female aggressors there are 16 female victims. Minority women are twice as likely to be victims as they are to be aggressors. Villains are disproportionately male, lower class, young, and Latino (Stossel, 1997).

Resolutions

Various international bodies have been active in trying the stop the portrayal of violence against women in the media. Most proposed resolutions link the unfair general portrayal of women with the portrayal of violent acts and with the appearance of real violence against women.

At the Third European Ministerial Conference on equality between women and men (Rome, 21–22 October 1993) the media were urged to take the lead in countering violence against women. Because media profoundly affect the socialization of men and women, they were called on to stop gender stereotyping. Stereotypes of women are believed to be one of the basic causes of violence against women. The European Parliament, in September 1997, formulated a resolution based on the list of European Human Rights Resolutions and Acts and a report by the Committee on Women's Rights, calling on governments, nongovernmental organizations, the media, and the advertising industry to respect women and the rights of women in the media. In addition to fair portrayal, a decrease of women-related violence in the media was also called for.

At the Fourth World Conference on Women (United Nations Conference, held in Beijing from 4 to 15 September 1995), ample attention was paid to the problem of violence against women. The media were identified as part of the problem. The conference's conclusions stipulated that images of violence against women, in particular those that depict rape, sexual slavery, the use of women and girls as sex objects, and pornography, are factors contributing to the prevalence of such violence. In March 1998, a follow-up resolution of the Beijing conference was published, stating strategic objectives in the fight against media portrayals of violence against women.

Globalization

Although globalization reduces the difference between the media in different regions, and although violence is one of the "cultural" ingredients that are easiest to export, the fight for fair portrayal of women differs greatly from country to country. An eight-country study of television violence in Asia conducted by the Asian Mass Communication Research and Information Centre classified 59 percent of the programs studied as "violent," with particularly high levels reported in India, Thailand, and the Philippines. In India, women were found to have a strong dislike for television films that depict violence; they said they just waited for the violent scenes to be over so that they could enjoy the next violence-free scene.

Several researchers indicate that gender violence in the media is pervasive in most Asian countries. Popular entertainments—particularly films—portray violence against both women and men in a graphic manner. Violence against women in films takes the shape of rape, spousal violence, and public humiliation of fallen women. In Singapore, where censorship is a regular practice, violence in television drama is omnipresent, particularly in Chinese programs and Tamil drama. In Thailand, gender violence in the media has been a serious problem since the 1960s, but few studies on violence against women in the media have been conducted. Thai studies on media coverage of rape cases show that the narratives tend to emphasize rape scenes and the acts of violence in great detail. This dramatization effectively reinforces sexual control of women.

Empowerment

All recommendations start from a self-regulatory approach. Media producers are urged to make their own responsible rules and follow them. Government interference with free speech and free expression is seen as politically unacceptable. In some countries (such as Canada, 1990) or in some organizations (public broadcasting companies in Europe, 1995) the recommendations are taken seriously. Media watchers, media monitors, and media literacy projects are initiatives of consumers and audiences, often supported by organizations or research bodies, to empower the public with regard to media violence. Women (as a group vulnerable to violence and fear, and as often the prime educators of children exposed to media violence) are especially addressed in these initiatives. Finally, the Cultural Environment Movement, a coalition for equity and fairness in media, initiated by George Gebner, has made media violence a major political issue.

See Also

CULTURAL STUDIES; CULTURE: WOMEN AS CONSUMERS OF CULTURE; MEDIA: OVERVIEW; MEDIA: MAINSTREAM; VIOLENCE AND PEACE: OVERVIEW

References and Further Reading

Gallagher, Margaret. 1995. *Lipstick imperialism and the new world order: Women and media at the close of the twentieth century.* Paper prepared for the Division for the Advancement of Women, Department for Policy Coordination and Sustainable Development, United Nations.

Gerbner, George, et al. 1993. Growing up with television: The cultivation perspective. In *Media effects: Advances in theory and research.* Hillsdale, N.J.: Erlbaum.

Gerbner, George, et al. 1994. *Television violence profile.* No. 16, *Current data on violence on TV.* Philadelphia: University of Pennsylvania.

Global Media Monitoring Project. 1995. *Women's participation in the news.* Toronto: National Watch on Images of Women in the Media (Media Watch).

Isi International–Manila. 1998. *The state of women and media: Focus on violence against women.* United Nations Development Fund for Women.

Media: The TV habit. 1993. *Marketing to Women* 6(5): 6–7.

Meyers, Marian. 1997. *News coverage of violence against women: Engendering blame.* Thousand Oaks, Calif.: Sage.

Michielsens, Magda, and Annemarie ten Boom. 1996. Illustrating human suffering: Women as victims on the news. In Nevena Dakovi et al., eds., *Gender and media,* 188–199. Ankara: Mediation.

Platform for action and the Beijing declaration. 1996. New York: United Nations Department of Public Information.

Potter, W. James. 1999. *On media violence.* Thousand Oaks, Calif., and London: Sage.

Stossel, Scott. 1997. The man who counts the killings. *Atlantic Monthly* 279(5: May): 86–104.

Magda Michielsens

VIOLENCE: Middle East and the Arab World (Lebanon)

In many ways, violence against women in Lebanon does not differ from violence against women in other parts of the world. The reasons for this violence and its impact on women and their children also do not differ. Yet Lebanese society's customs, traditions, attitudes, and laws do affect the problem and its consequences in a particular way. And because of extended wars in the area, the Lebanese situation is of particular interest to people studying violence against women.

Violence against women in Lebanon was not publicly addressed as an issue until 1993, when a campaign was launched by a few concerned individuals to create awareness of the problem and support for combating it. Yet when this group asked for a permit to form an association for the defense of women against violence, the Lebanese government refused to grant it, claiming that no one had the right to interfere in other people's family affairs. This group, however, did find a way of continuing its campaign through other organizations such as the Human Rights League and the Women's Rights League, as well as the Middle East Council of Churches. One of the results of this effort was that the official Lebanese delegation to the Women's Conference in Beijing in 1995 included combating domestic violence against women on its agenda.

Physical Violence

Lebanese women are still subject to violence regardless of their social class, religion, culture, or level of education. Violence takes several forms. Beating is one of them—beating children, wives, or even aged parents. An Arab proverb reflects some male Arabs' attitude toward women: "A woman is like a rug: the more you beat her the better she becomes." A woman may be beaten with a whip or a strap, trampled on, have an object thrown at her or be threatened with a weapon, injured, disfigured, or even killed. Some men imprison their wives in the house, refusing to allow them to leave or see even their closest relatives.

Another form of physical violence against women is rape. Because talking about rape is taboo, very few cases are reported or publicized. And when a husband forces his wife to sleep with him against her will, it is not considered rape. According to the Muslim Shari'a (laws), a wife's first duty is to satisfy her husband's sexual appetite, and if she refuses, he has every right to beat her (Qur'an, Surah IV, Women, verse 34). With the increase in poverty, especially after the 15-year Lebanese war (1975–1990), many men have forced their wives or daughters to practice prostitution, even if their daughters are under age. Incest, too, is not uncommon, although girls are more emboldened to complain to a friend, teacher, mother, or doctor and to request help in dealing with or escaping incest.

An even more severe form of physical violence in some conservative Muslim societies is killing a girl in what is called an honor crime. A male member of her family has the duty and the right to kill a girl if she goes out with a boy or marries someone against her father's wish or is believed not to be a virgin on her wedding night. Thanks to the efforts of women lawyer activists, the laws have changed in Lebanon since 1997, but people's attitudes are slow to change. A brother killed his sister because she was thought not to be a virgin on her wedding night, in spite of her swearing that she had never had sexual relations with anyone before her marriage. An autopsy carried out on her body found that she had an elastic hymen and therefore did not bleed when her husband penetrated her.

The laws in Lebanon do punish the person responsible for rape, sexual harassment, and incest if these activities are made public. But both the woman and the man are punished for prostitution, even if it is the man who encouraged or instigated it. Unfortunately, violence against a wife or daughter is not punishable by law unless the woman can obtain a medical report stating that she was incapacitated for seven days. Even then, if she retracts her complaint her husband or father is not punished. If a woman is injured by a man who is not her father or husband, a retraction does not stop the court from punishing him.

Psychological Violence

In Lebanon, women are subject to psychological violence even more often than to physical violence. Very often this form of violence is not recognized and, consequently, is not punished by the law. This is because psychological violence is a result of customs, traditions, and upbringing. From birth, boys are brought up to feel strong, independent, and superior, while in many families a girl is ordered to serve her brother, and the brother is given full right to order his sister about and to punish her if she disobeys him. Ironically, the girl is held totally responsible for any wrong done and at the same time is considered to be an inferior being.

In very strongly patriarchal societies, such as that in Lebanon and those in most of the Middle East, a man usually looks down on women, considering them inferior in all respects, and does not hesitate to show his disrespect for a wife or sister, even in front of strangers. He might mock her ignorance or her taste in clothing, point out her inferiority to other women he knows, and brag about his sexual exploits and the number of his mistresses. Therefore, a woman may lose even the little bit of self-confidence that was left after her upbringing and may become more and more inclined to believe her husband and blame herself for not being pleasing or acceptable to him or others.

Legal Violence

Added to the physical and psychological violence against women is what might be called legal violence. The Lebanese government had reservations about Article 16 of the United Nations declaration concerning personal status—principles that declare equality between men and women in matters of marriage, divorce, inheritance, guardianship, penalty, compensation, and so on. This was in spite of the fact that the Lebanese constitution proclaims that all Lebanese are equal before the law. In 1997, more than a dozen nongovernmental organizations joined to form the Lebanese Council to Resist Violence Against Women and are working on a civil law for the protection of women to be presented to the government.

Lebanon might be unique in that it has 18 personal status laws, one for each of the 18 different religions and religious sects in the country. These ecclesiastical laws were formulated in 1952 and show little awareness of any progress or change that has taken place over the years in family relations or women's status. Since these laws were written by men and also are implemented by men (the ecclesiastical courts in Lebanon do not include women), many of these laws strongly discriminate against women, some more than others, according to the sect or religion to which a woman belongs. The Catholic and Maronite churches do not grant a divorce, but a man can become a Muslim and marry another woman, since Islam accepts polygamy, whereas his wife has no such right. She thus remains tied to a husband who leaves her for another wife. This, of course, is also true for all Muslim women who are subjected to polygamy, although even bigamy is rare in Lebanon. A new phenomenon has appeared among the Shi'a Muslims in Lebanon who are influenced by Iran: contemporary marriages contracted for a limited number of months, days, or even hours, which leave the man with no obligations whatsoever toward the woman after the contract expires. It is true that in principle, a woman contracts such a marriage out of her own free will; nevertheless, she is still the victim of a form of legal violence, which she often accepts owing to her limited knowledge and sexual options.

Although Islam allows divorce, it is only the man who has the right to divorce his wife, unless her right to divorce is clearly stipulated in the marriage contract. But most men and religious clerics who draw up the contracts refuse to mention this point. In Islam the man signs his marriage contract himself, whereas the woman is obligated to entrust a male guardian to sign it for her. If she is kept ignorant of its contents, she cannot express either her satisfaction or discontent with the contract. Unless the Muslim marriage contract mentions an amount of alimony in the case of divorce, no law obliges the man to pay anything. While most marriages contracted today in Lebanon mention an amount of support to be paid, the figure is often only symbolic and leaves the woman virtually penniless when divorced. If a Muslim woman leaves her home against her husband's wish, he can divorce her, and she forgoes her right to alimony, even if an amount is stated in the marriage contract.

In the Christian churches that allow divorce, matters are just as unfair, for they do not give the woman the right to any alimony unless she is the victim of "severe damage." It is up to the religious courts presided over by men to determine what qualifies as severe damage as well as to estimate what is due the woman. In most cases the divorcée is paid an amount so small that it will not support her. This is one reason why many women remain with a violent man, since most Lebanese women are economically dependent on their husbands. In the Armenian Apostolic church, the husband has full right to the money the bride is given as dowry, and in the case of a divorce she can retain only one-third of it.

Also, in the case of a divorce, the father is the sole guardian of a girl after the age of 9, and a boy after the age of 7, no matter to what religion they belong. This is the general law, but because decisions about guardianship of the children are left to the discretion of the ecclesiastical judge, some have ruled that the child should be given to the father after the age of 2. In the Armenian Apostolic church, it is the husband who decides the guardianship of the children. Maintaining a relationship with their children is another significant reason women choose to stay with a violent husband.

Another form of legal violence against women is found in the laws of inheritance. If a husband dies leaving no children, his widow inherits only one-half of their assets, even though she may have worked all her life side by side with him either in the home or outside it; the other half goes to his family. According to the Muslim Shari'a, a boy inherits twice as much as a girl. If a Sunni or Druze man dies leaving only daughters, most of the inheritance goes to a next-of-kin male relative.

Women in Lebanon are not only victims of the laws. Their society blames women for everything that goes wrong: it is the wife's or daughter's impudence, stubbornness, and defiance that cause her husband, father, or brother to beat her; it is her loose behavior and her power of seduction that tempt men to harass or rape her. If she goes to the police for help, in most cases all she will get are jeers and sexual harassment. Even if an adult female runs away from home to escape the violence of a father or brother, the police force her back to what they consider her appropriate place of residence until she gets married. If a wife complains of her husband's violence to her mother, the response most likely will be to be quiet so as not to disgrace the family.

The attitude of the whole society of Lebanon must be changed if there is any hope of alleviating the plight of women who are victims of violence. In all of Lebanon there are few shelters for women who have been abused. Only in 1998 did an emergency hot line become available in Beirut, and several more were established in 1999. Because women fear society's criticism and because so little help or support is available to them, most of the violence perpetrated against women goes unreported. Even their own families are kept ignorant of their suffering. This is why there are no statistics regarding the number of victims of violence in Lebanon.

See Also

FAMILY: RELIGIOUS AND LEGAL SYSTEMS: ISLAMIC
TRADITIONS; FEMICIDE; FEMINISM: MIDDLE EAST;

HOUSEHOLDS AND FAMILIES: MIDDLE EAST AND NORTH AFRICA; VIRGINITY

References and Further Reading

Battered women in Lebanon. 1994. *Al-Raida* 11 (65/55). Beirut, Lebanon: Institute for Women's Studies in the Arab World.

Women's rights are human rights. 1996. *Al-Raida* 13 (74/75). Beirut, Lebanon: Institute for Women's Studies in the Arab World.

Nazik Saba Yared

VIOLENCE: North America

Violence against women is a pervasive social problem around the world and in North America, although there have been growing efforts to pass legislation to curb brutality and to increase punishments for those convicted of violent acts toward women. Accurate measurement is difficult because of the stigma associated with reporting the crime and the varying definitions and terms used from study to study. Violence against women takes many forms and is given many labels, such as "domestic violence" or "intimate partner violence," rape, sexual harassment, and assault. Victimization by an intimate partner accounted for about 21 percent of the violence experienced by women between 1992 and 1996 (U.S. Department of Justice, 1998). Violence against women crosses all socioeconomic, racial, religious, class, disability status, sexual orientation, and age groups. Significantly, violence against women appears to be the result of environmental factors, and those who commit violence toward women are four times more likely than the general population to have grown up in a violent household. It is estimated that some 3.3 million children in North America have witnessed violence toward their mother.

In the United States, the number of women who have been murdered by spouses exceeds the number of U.S. soldiers killed during the Vietnam War, and each year an average of 1,400 more women are killed. Approximately 1,800 murders in one year were attributed to intimate partners, and nearly three out of four of these had a female victim (Supplementary Homicide Reports, 1996). Among the other impacts of violence directed toward women are enormous societal costs. At least 6 percent of all pregnant women in the United States are battered by their partners each year (Centers for Disease Control and Prevention, 1994). The result is an increased number of miscarriages and stillbirths and an increased likelihood of preterm and low-birthweight babies. Finally, women who are the victims of violence are far more likely to commit suicide than the general population.

Types of Violence

In North America, violence against women is common in several forms. In general, such violence can be broadly divided into three categories: sexual assault, domestic violence, and sexual harassment. Although overall crime rates in North America, including crimes against women, have declined, sexual assaults continue to occur with high levels of frequency and, in some cases, specific crime categories have increased. On average, some 132,000 women in the United States report that they have been the victim of rape or attempted rape. Many scholars and public officials in North America contend that two to six times that number of women are victimized but do not report these crimes. Overall, this raises the number to over one million sexual assaults per year. Also on the increase are instances of date rape and the use of narcotic drugs, such as rohypnol—the "date-rape drug"—to render victims unconscious. One bright note in the issue of sexual assault has been the increasing use of DNA to "fingerprint" criminals and secure convictions. Also, the passage in 1994 of the Violence Against Women Act, which provided $1.8 billion, greatly expanded efforts in the United States to implement programs to prevent violence against women.

In North America, violence against women in the context of the family is referred to by a number of terms, including domestic violence, wife abuse, battering of women, and interpersonal violence. For the purposes of this article, *domestic violence* refers to a pattern of assaultive and coercive behaviors, including physical, sexual, and psychological attacks, as well as economic coercion, that adults or adolescents use against their intimate partners (Schechter and Ganley, 1994). Domestic violence is the leading cause of injury to women between the ages of 15 and 44, and estimates are that two to four million women suffer such abuse each year. Domestic violence causes more injuries than violent robberies and automobile crashes combined. Women are 10 times more likely to be victimized by a family member than a stranger. Moreover, violence by a family member is more dangerous than by a stranger, and women are more likely to be murdered when endeavoring to quit an abusive relationship.

Awareness of sexual harassment has grown dramatically since Clarence Thomas's confirmation hearings in the 1990s. Numerous programs to promote awareness have been implemented by government institutions and private interest groups. Yet between 1988 and 1998 sexual attacks and harassment doubled. Furthermore, harassment also has expanded, including attempts to block access to abortion clinics, and efforts to redress past discrimination such as affirmative action have faced a backlash that has overturned such programs in California and Texas. Since 1993, several abortion providers and staffers have been killed and numerous staff members have been injured by antiabortion extremists. In addition, attacks on clinics have temporarily prevented access to clinics.

Historical Context

The first laws against wife battering anywhere in the world were enacted by the Puritans of colonial Massachusetts. Between 1640 and 1680, the number of cases dwindled. Until the 1900s, there were only a few statutes that limited the severity of abuse directed toward female spouses—most notably the "rule of thumb," which limited sticks to a diameter no greater than that of the husband's thumb (Fleming, 1979). From the 1800s through the early 1900s, husbands were entitled to discipline their wives and family. During the 1970s, the women's movement in the United States began to agitate for increased protection for women in the home and workplace. The first shelters to house victims of domestic violence or rape were opened in the 1970s. Since then, some 1,700 shelters have been opened. However, the United States still has three times more shelters for animals than it does for women and their children.

Awareness of the problem led to increased research on the causes of violence toward women. One of the pioneer researchers was Lenore Walker, who identified the cycle of battery that victims experienced in domestic violence. The cycle included a tension-building stage, an acute battery incident, and then a contrite, loving stage. Identifying the cycle was significant in understanding how battered women became victimized, how they underwent a training in "learned helplessness," and what factors made it so difficult for them to escape the violent situation.

Conceptualization

In explaining violence toward women, and domestic violence in particular, a number of models have been proposed: psychiatric, social-situational, patriarchal, and exchange theory. The psychiatric model (Strauss, 1980) focuses on the abuser's personality traits, mental illness, and psychopathology. In other words, it suggests that the abuser is abnormal. Research suggests, however, that less than 10 percent of family violence is attributable to the psychiatric model. Moreover, the problem of domestic violence is more common than once thought (efforts to promote reporting of violence have had success). Still, it should be noted that

cutbacks in state and federal programs targeting mental health have caused reductions in the funds available for medication and treatment of disorders that often prompt violence against women.

The social-situational model attributes violence to stress, such as that caused by low income, unemployment, or illness. Statistics demonstrating that severe spouse abuse is twice as likely to occur in families when the male is unemployed seem to bear out this theory. This model also suggests that violence is learned in society and at home. Although not suggesting that everyone exposed to violence will repeat it, the model does suggest that those exposed to violence are at a greater risk of being violent. The effort to overcome these societal factors has spawned more programs to increase awareness and to forestall violence at an early age.

Going beyond analysis of the individual and the family, the patriarchal model (Dobash and Dobash, 1979) attributes violence against women to the economic and social structures that directly or indirectly support a patriarchal society. It suggests that this patriarchal culture leads to the subordination of women. This model uses a historical and structural analysis in understanding violence against women.

Exchange theory argues that people choose violence when the benefits of violence outweigh the costs. In other words, people will use less violence when the costs associated with violence outweigh the rewards. These costs may include police intervention, criminal prosecutions, discipline at the workplace, and other forms of societal disapproval.

Responses

In addition to strengthened legislation that increases the penalties for violence against women, national and state governments and private interest groups have undertaken a variety of programs to combat the problem. Colleges and universities in Canada and the United States have begun incorporating classes on violence prevention in orientation courses. In addition, the proliferation of women's studies programs has increased research into the causes of such violence and into methods to prevent the various forms of physical oppression. Meanwhile, private groups such as the U.S. National Organization for Women (NOW) have sponsored programs in elementary and high schools to educate young people on issues of violence and sexual harassment.

One of the most successful strategies for violence prevention has been the establishment of hot lines and crisis numbers for women to call to report incidents of violence and, just as important, to seek aid in recovery and access to providers of counseling. The U.S. government raised the amount of grants allocated to prevent violence against women from $26 million in 1995 to more than $172 million by 1998.

See Also

DOMESTIC VIOLENCE; HOUSEHOLDS AND FAMILIES: NORTH AMERICA; RAPE; SEXUAL HARASSMENT; SEXUAL VIOLENCE; SLAVERY; VIOLENCE AND PEACE: OVERVIEW

References and Further Reading

Dobash, R. E., and R. Dobash. 1979. *Violence against wives.* New York: Free Press.

Fleming, J. B. 1979. *Stopping wife abuse.* Garden City, N.Y.: Anchor.

Gelles, R. J., and C. P. Cornell. 1990. *Intimate violence in families.* 2nd ed. Newbury Park, Calif.: Sage.

Hesse, Lori. 1989. Crimes of gender. *World Watch* (March–April): 12–21.

Schechter, S., and A. Ganley. 1994. *Domestic violence: A national curriculum for family preservation practitioners.* San Francisco: Family Violence Fund.

Straus, M. 1980. A sociological perspective on the causes of family violence. In M. R. Green, ed., *Violence and the family.* Boulder, Col.: Westview.

Walker, L. 1979. *The battered woman.* New York: Harper and Row.

Yllo, K., and M. Bogard, eds. 1988. *Feminist perspectives on wife abuse.* Newbury Park, Calif.: Sage.

Suja George

VIOLENCE: South Asia

Violence in south Asia can, perhaps, be explained only in the context of uneven and combined development in the region experienced in the precolonial, colonial, and postcolonial periods. A history of invasions, the coexistence of moribund feudal customs, and traditions of phallocentrism and femicide created by *manu, mullah, missionary,* and *bhikhkhu* have combined with the hedonistic influence of technologically advanced capitalist societies to shape the nature and extent of violence in south Asia. The unprecedented concentration and centralization of economic and political power in the hands of a microscopic minority has created a mind-set in which power disputes are settled over women's bodies. In the past two decades women's rights organizations have made collective efforts to highlight this fact. As a result, increasing numbers of women have refused to remain mute victims of violence and have individually or collectively fought against violence in their personal and public spheres.

Violence in the Name of Religion, Culture, and Tradition

Critics contend that the most striking feature of systemic violence in south Asia has been the adverse sex ratio—that is, the number of women per 1,000 men. Since the beginning of the twentieth century there has been a perpetual proportionate decrease of south Asian women as compared with their male counterparts. Various methods of annihilation of women include antenatal sex determination tests leading to selective abortion of female fetuses; female infanticide; depriving girl children of nourishing food and health care while at the same time overburdening them with drudgery; child marriage and child motherhood; repeated pregnancy; dowry murders; and wife battery. In today's complex world, not being allowed to attain functional literacy also poses a major threat to women's survival. Glorification of the Hindu rite of voluntary *suttee* (after the burning of a young, educated widow from a middle-class family in 1987 in front of a thousands-strong hysterical crowd) has put tremendous pressure on widows to lead a life of self-negation and has been a terrible blow to the progressive work of nineteenth-century social reformers. Islamic punishments are playing havoc with Muslim women's lives in Bangladesh, India, and Pakistan. The legend of Draupadi is used by the vested interests in Nepal to induct young girls and women into prostitution. Chauvinist forces in Sri Lanka, of Tamil Hindu and Sinhala Buddhist varieties, use innocent girls as cannon fodder for a self-destructive war. It has been charged that patriarchs of the church who make the nuns do the most backbreaking menial chores in their institutional structures maintain a conspiracy of silence when those nuns are brutally attacked or murdered. In the name of the goddesses Yellamma and Basavi, the dedication of Dalit women for the sex trade, that is, temple prostitution, gets customary approval in southern India. Traditionally polyandrous tribes have become major suppliers of sex workers, where husbands and fathers operate as pimps and control cash. In the rural and tribal areas, witch-hunting of assertive single women (widows, divorcees, and deserted and unmarried women) has taken barbarous forms with the sharpening of the dualism between tradition and modernity against a background of the erosion of basic means of survival, that is, food and fuel, fodder and water.

Violence by the State Apparatus

Postcolonialism in south Asia is marked by a highly volatile political situation. The partition of India left a painful legacy of mass rape of "enemy women" (who might be the citizens of neighboring countries, members of minority communities, assertive ethnic minorities, oppressed nationalities, or subjugated caste groups). Even a common body launched by the governments of the region (which includes Bangladesh, Bhutan, India, the Maldives, Nepal, Pakistan, and Sri Lanka), called the South Asian Association for Regional Cooperation (SAARC), has not done anything about atrocities committed on women by the military and paramilitary forces of the member countries. The government-controlled media in the subcontinent are seen as preoccupied with jingoistic proclamations that provide a rationalization for increasing militarization. Against this background, the sheer geographical size of India creates a psychosis of fear among neighboring countries, whose cynics perceive India as an Orwellian Big Brother. The "threat from foreign elements" has become a convenient tool in the hands of the hegemonic forces to legitimize their oppression of the toiling masses. Regrettably, civil liberties groups have not gone beyond routinely publicizing gory details of state-sponsored violence. In the absence of a concrete action plan at a grassroots level, too much of this kind of publicity generates paralysis and benumbs the senses.

In this grim situation, individual artists, women's organizations, and cultural groups with the courage of conviction may be the only forces that are striving to build an atmosphere of trust and solidarity. Pioneering work in this direction was done by the Gandhian women in the refugee camps after the partition of India between 1947 and 1956 to rehabitate women who had been raped (many of whom were pregnant) and who had lost or were rejected by their family members. In the early 1970s, during and after the Bangladesh war, many western feminists worked in the refugee camps to provide moral, material, and medical support to Bangladeshi women survivors of rape, living testimony of sexual violence perpetrated by Yahya Khan's army. Medics influenced by the Gandhian philosophy undertook a similar type of work in the northeastern frontier zone among tribal women brutalized by the Indian military and paramilitary forces. Their firsthand experience of the state's repressive machinery motivated them to address the medical problems in a broader political perspective, and they launched the Medico Friend Circle (MFC). In 1987 the Women's Center in Bombay condemned atrocities against Sri Lankan women by the Indian Peacekeeping Forces (IPKF). Since the early 1990s, women's groups in Delhi have been making efforts to reach out to women who have survived attacks by the Indian army as well as the extremist violence in Kashmir. Many human rights lawyers have provided free legal aid to people who have been mistreated by the police and army. Women researchers from the College of Social Work in Bombay, the Asian Women's Research and Action Network (AWRAN) in Colombo and Tokyo, and the Feminist International Network for Resistance to Reproductive and Genetic Engineering (FINRRAGE) in Dhaka and Hamburg have compiled detailed documentation of trafficking of women and girls from Bangladesh and Nepal to India, and from India and Sri Lanka to the Gulf countries, with the collusion of community and religious leaders and the border security forces of the supplying and receiving countries. Human Rights Watch (Asia) (1995) has given recommendations to the Nepali and Indian governments to protect the victims of trafficking.

Violence in Civil Society

The increasing assertiveness, educational achievements, and economic independence of women have made south Asian men extremely insecure. Evidently, this male anxiety finds its release in domestic violence, obsession with pornographic literature and movies, and sexual abuse of women and children (both boys and girls). Media barons are getting rich by exploiting the electronic media to meet the demand for soft porn for bored housewives and teenagers and XX and XXX movies for "experienced" men. The majority of women workers and employees are in the informal sector, where the law of the jungle prevails. In the absence of protection by labor laws, women have to put up with an excessive workload, long working hours, and hazardous work conditions. The most helpless among them are migrant workers. More and more working women are reporting sexual harassment in the workplace. The criminalization of politics in south Asia has made ordinary women more vulnerable to violence. Parliamentary democracy in India has allowed women's groups to combat violence in a militant manner without facing much repression from the state, whereas women's rights activists in the rest of the south Asian countries have faced considerable resistance at the hands of their authoritarian rulers. During the last two decades, targeting poor south Asian women for forced sterilization, harmful contraceptives, and antifertility vaccines has been described as the ugliest aspect of violence against women perpetrated by proponents of population control with the enthusiastic support of the state. Elitist women's groups are also accused of using poor Indian, Pakistani, and Bangladeshi women as guinea pigs for population control.

New Initiatives

The collaboration of women activists, lawyers, trained social workers, educationalists, medical experts, and psychologists has created an atmosphere in which violence is handled with great care and understanding. Women's groups are consulted in the process of carrying out a series of legal reforms and prison reforms. Mass communication institutes and staff training programs on human rights for politicians, police, and civil servants have included "violence against women" in their syllabi. Decision makers are showing greater interest in social psychology and therapies (multicultural get-togethers; sharing of experiences; singing and dance sessions; role-playing; speak-out sessions; encouraging debates and group discussions in a noncompetitive atmosphere; reading prose and reciting poems; culture-specific symbols and imagery; drawing; painting; overcoming addiction to a hedonistic lifestyle; body workshops) used by women's groups to support and energize the survivors of violence.

See Also

DOWRY AND BRIDEPRICE; FEMICIDE; FEMINISM: SOUTH ASIA; HOUSEHOLDS AND FAMILIES: SOUTH ASIA; POLITICS AND THE STATE: SOUTH ASIA; PROSTITUTION; SUTTEE

References and Further Reading

Asian and Pacific Women's Resource and Action Series. 1989. (See section on "Violence Against Women"). Kuala Lumpur: Asian and Pacific Development Centre.

Ghadially, Rehana, ed. 1988. *Women in Indian society.* London: Sage. (See section III "On Violence").

Goonatilke, Hema, and Savitri Goonesekere. 1988. Industrialization and women workers in Sri Lanka: Working conditions inside and outside the investment promotion zone. In Noeleen Hayzer, ed., *Daughters in industry: Work, skills and consciousness of women workers in Asia.* Kuala Lumpur: Asian and Pacific Development Centre.

Human Rights Watch (Asia). 1995. *Rape for profit: Trafficking of Nepali girls and women to India's brothels.* New York: Human Rights Watch (Asia).

Jahan, Roushan. 1988. Hidden wounds, visible scars: Violence against women in Bangladesh. In Bina Agarwal, ed., *Structures of patriarchy: State, community and household in modernizing Asia.* Delhi: Kali for Women.

Jahangir, Asma. 1989. How far are penal laws effective in protecting women? *Women living under Muslim laws* (Dossier 3): 33–36.

Lawyers Collective (Bombay). 1987. Special issue: "Violence" (March).

Matsui, Yayori. 1989. *Women's Asia.* London and Atlantic Highlands, N.J.: Zed.

Mumtaz, Khawar, and Farida Shaheed. 1987. *Women of Pakistan: Two steps forward, one step back?* London and Atlantic Highlands, N.J.: Zed.

Sadgopal, Mira, ed. 1995. *Na shariram nadhi* (My body is mine). Bombay: Sabala and Kranti.

Voice of Women Newsletters (Colombo). 1985–1986.

Vibhuti Patel

VIOLENCE: Southeast Asia

From what little is known, we see that the nations of southeast Asia—Vietnam, Laos, Cambodia, Thailand, Myanmar (Burma), Singapore, Malaysia, and Indonesia—offer striking contrasts in history and political organization that lead to markedly different responses to violence against women. Politically, the region includes one of the few remaining communist dictatorships (Vietnam), a western-style democracy (Malaysia), a repressive dictatorship (Myanmar), and one of the oldest monarchies in the world (Thailand).

"Comfort Women" in World War II

There is virtually no documentation of violence against women in this region before the modern period. During World War II, Japan occupied much of the region and forcibly recruited thousands of women to serve as "comfort women"—sex slaves—for Japanese soldiers. Most of the comfort women were Korean, but many women in Singapore, Malaya (now Malaysia), and Indonesia were also forced into sexual servitude. Most comfort women in southeast Asia were ethnic Chinese or Malay, although some were Dutch nationals, captured on Indonesian islands. Most of the comfort women were forced to perform a dozen or more times a day and were beaten or otherwise abused if they did not. Some were mutilated, "including having their breasts cut off with swords, or being killed by being shot through their private parts" (Bhalla, 1994). The Japanese government refused to acknowledge this history until 1994, and then only when it was faced with official Japanese documents from the period.

Cambodia

Events of the recent past, including the war in Vietnam and subsequent conflicts in Cambodia, have led to rampant violence and cultural breakdowns, which have in turn led to a steep rise in domestic violence. Like World War II, the twenty-five years of war in Indochina, followed by nearly twenty more in Cambodia, have left that nation in social disarray and have led to violence against women. The wars and the Pol Pot regime, with its "killing fields," vastly reduced the population and led to a huge gender imbalance.

By 1993 two-thirds of Cambodia's population was female, because so many men had been killed in combat. Thus in the 1980s and 1990s the indiscriminate violence of war, and the Pol Pot regime, affected women more adversely than men because there were simply more women to be harmed.

Since the end of the wars, domestic violence has been on the rise. Most observers see the plight of women as worse in Cambodia than any other nation in the region. A study reported in 1996 found that one in six adult Cambodian women were victims of physical abuse, with one in twelve suffering head injuries. The study found that three of four people interviewed (75 percent) knew one or more families harmed by domestic violence. This contrasts sharply with Malaysia, where only 9 percent of people interviewed knew anyone who had encountered domestic violence. Divorce in Cambodia is difficult, and courts prefer mediation, often endangering women in abusive marriages. The chaos caused by years of war may have only exacerbated existing social norms. Speaking on International Women's Day, the Cambodian minister of Women's Affairs, Mu Sochua, pointed out, "It is custom and tradition that allows men to think that women can be beaten, can be sold, can be bought" and causes women to "believe that it is their destiny." This culture, she argued, was what really needed to change in Cambodia (Hunt, 2000: 1).

Vietnam

Communist Vietnam has long criminalized domestic abuse, but according to the sociologist Le Thi Quy, domestic abuse is "everywhere, absolutely everywhere" in Vietnam. In the suburb of Hanoi she interviewed thirty women, and "all 30 had been beaten by their husbands." In 1995 Quy became the first scholar in Vietnam to translate the term "domestic violence" and use it in her research. The Vietnamese government, however, hampers even identifying the problem, or its victims, because of the view that any discussion of social problems will be used as propaganda against the regime. Thus there are no women's shelters in Vietnam, and only two telephone hotlines—one in Ho Chi Minh City, the other in Hanoi. Quy argues that wife-beating is common, that it is accepted throughout the country, and that it is on the rise. In 1992 men killing their wives accounted for 14 percent of all homicides in Vietnam; in 1997 they accounted for 20 percent. A wealthy physician received only "a light prison term" after he murdered his wife by "slitting her throat with a scalpel" (McDonald, 2000).

Malaysia

Although evidence suggests that Malaysia is far less violent than countries in Indochina, 40 percent of women in Malaysia report some form of physical abuse. This figure contrasts sharply with the rate of affirmative responses—only 9 percent—when Malaysians are asked whether they know of a woman who has been a victim of abuse; the implication is that wife-beating is not socially acceptable and remains hidden. All observers seem to agree that "wife battering is rooted in the hierarchical family structure" (Women's International Network News, 1994).

Despite cultural traditions allowing men to abuse their wives, women in Malaysia are fighting back. They are talking about the issue and pushing for legislation to provide greater protection for abused women through strictly enforced "interim protection orders." Malaysia's Domestic Violence Act of 1994, passed after ten years of lobbying, was the first of its kind in southeast Asia and was copied by Singapore and Korea. More important, perhaps, is the fact that it is one of the few such acts passed by a predominantly Muslim country and has thus been studied by other Islamic nations.

Singapore

Singapore, like Malaysia, seems to be taking the problem of domestic violence seriously and perhaps is making strides toward its elimination. As a tiny nation, really a city-state, noted for its harsh and uncompromising criminal justice system, Singapore may be able to accomplish what larger nations cannot—or the problem may be better hidden in Singapore. In 1995 Singapore reported 73 cases of family violence against women leading to serious injury. This number dropped to 40 in 1996, 39 in 1997, and only 17 in the first half of 1998. Singapore claims that the decrease is a result of its "firm handling of crimes in general," but a report sponsored by the United Nations expressed the fear that "the criminal justice perspective in Singapore may discourage women from reporting domestic violence and thus may increase their risk of violence in the home" (UN Commission on Human Rights, 1999).

Indonesia

Indonesia is a Muslim nation that has refused even to ratify the declarations of three major conferences sponsored by the United Nations to discuss violence against women: the Vienna Declaration (1993), the Declaration on the Elimination of Violence Against Women (1994), and the Beijing Declaration and Platform for Action (1995). There are few statistics for Indonesia, and even a deputy in its State Ministry of Human Rights Affairs has admitted that a cultural and political preference for "family values and harmony often prevents recognition of real problems going on within the family" (*Jakarta Post*, 2000).

Apparently, the Indonesian government not only ignores violence in families but also turns a blind eye to rape and sexual abuse by its soldiers, who at the time of this writing were fighting a guerilla war in East Timor. Women there had been repeatedly raped by Indonesian soldiers; in addition, Timorese women were forced to serve as sex slaves for soldiers, much like the Japanese army's "comfort women" in World War II. Some soldiers had set up brothels, or taken over existing brothels, for military use; and officers on duty in the area had forced Timorese women to act as their "local wives." In 1998 a woman activist, Odilia Victor, was living in the Australian embassy because of her involvement with the Timor Women's Popular Organization. Soldiers had captured and tortured one of her cousins, declaring that they also planned to capture Victor and rape her.

Myanmar

Since 1988, when it was taken over by the State Law and Order Restoration Council (SLORC), the military government in Burma, or Myanmar, has become the most repressive regime in the region; observers report that human rights are "grossly and persistently" violated. The military rulers use rape as a means of social control and use torture for women deemed dangerous to the regime. "Rape is one common form of torture perpetrated by SLORC against women. The women in Burma have been raped at their homes, often in front of their husbands or other members of their families or relatives" (Sajor, 1998: 287, 288). Women are often raped by soldiers after their husbands have been commandeered to work as laborers for the army. Refugees who have escaped to Thailand report that women are forced to work in army camps during the day, are beaten if they do not finish their work, and are then forced to sleep with soldiers at night. In addition, random rape by soldiers, on or off duty, appears to be common, with few soldiers being punished. There are apparently no statistics and no other information about spousal abuse or other types of violence against women in Burma.

Thailand

Perhaps the most complex situation with regard to women and violence is found in Thailand. This nation, which was never colonized by any European power, is a constitutional monarchy with a strong economy. However, rapid economic development and urban growth have left many Thais in rural poverty and in urban slums, where women and young girls are vulnerable to a thriving "sex trade" that is legal and supported by a large tourist industry.

The Thai constitution of 1997 provides for the protection of women from domestic violence—a provision found in few other countries—but implementation has been slow. Since 1997, statistics indicate a rise in rape, domestic abuse, and sexual harassment; however, many experts believe that this is a result of greater willingness of victims to report crimes against them, and thus that the increase actually bodes well for the future of women in Thailand. Still, abuse is high: an estimated one in five wives are beaten by their husbands at least once in their marriage, and the World Organization Against Torture reports that in Bangkok's slums half of all married women are regularly beaten by their husbands. Until very recently, most Thai officials considered domestic abuse a family matter, not the concern of the police or law enforcement; and most courts are unsympathetic to complaints by battered women. Moeover, the constitutional protection against domestic violence excludes marital rape, which is not considered a crime in Thailand. The police often ignore complaints of female victims, and there are only thirty-six female police officers in the country who have training in dealing with domestic violence or rape.

While not unique to Thailand, prostitution, including child prostitution, is perhaps a greater problem there than elsewhere. Rural families often sell the labor of their daughters to "businessmen" and "industrialists" who in fact take these young girls to work in brothels. Almost all international observers express concern about widespread trafficking in women and young girls in parts of Thailand. The Suppression of Prostitution Act of 1996 is largely unenforced, as is the Act Concerning Measures of Prevention and Suppression of the Trafficking in Women and Children of 1997. On the other hand, the very fact that such laws have been enacted suggests the beginning of cultural changes which may ultimately lead to greater respect for women in Thailand, as well as greater protection for them.

Laos

Laos evidently provides the brightest spot in this region as regards violence and women. According to Women's International Network News (1994), "There is no pattern of widespread domestic violence against women" in the country. Reports of "sexual harassment and rape are rare," and when rape is reported, rapists are usually prosecuted. The national Family Code guarantees equality for women in marriage and inheritance. The greatest danger to women in Laos seems to come from "recruiters for brothels and sweatshops in Thailand and elsewhere" who entice women from this relatively poor nation with promises of high salaries and wealth.

Conclusion

An overall assessment of violence against women in southeast Asia is not easy to make. There are bright spots, like Laos; and there are nations moving toward a new understanding of violence and women, like Malaysia, Singapore, and Thailand. But throughout the region cultural notions of patriarchy remain strong, and wife-beating is apparently deeply embedded in some cultural norms. In addition, sexual exploitation, prostitution, and trafficking in women and girls remain a problem in much of the region. This is exacerbated by high rates of poverty, even in nations with relatively strong economies, and by large numbers of refugees fleeing war or repressive regimes.

See also

ABUSE; DOMESTIC VIOLENCE; TRAFFICKING; SEX WORK; RAPE; VIOLENCE: EAST ASIA (CHINA), *I and II*

References and Further Reading

Associated Press. 1996. Study shows rampant abuse in Cambodia. *Telegraph Herald* (Dubuque, Iowa, 26 August).

Bhalla, S. Tsering. 1994. Comfort women book is both poignant and horrific. *Straits Times* (Singapore, 21 December), Life section: 1.

"Distorted notions" behind violence against women. 2000. *Jakarta Post* (12 July).

Hunt, Luke. 2000. Asia marks International Women's Day with calls for justice. *Agence France Presse* (8 March).

Lim, Beverley. 2000. Protecting victims of domestic violence. *New Straits Times* (7 February).

McDonald, Mark. 2000. Domestic violence reaches epidemic level in Vietnam. *Portland Oregonian* (18 June).

Peters, Gretchen. 2000. Women speak out about sexual abuse in Thailand. *South China Morning Post* (3 July).

Sajor, India Lourdes. 1998. *Common grounds: Violence against women in war and armed conflict situations.* Quezon City, Philippines: Asian Center for Women's Human Rights.

United Nations Commission on Human Rights. 1999. *Integration of the human rights of women and the gender perspective* (10 March).

Women's International Network News. 1996. *Country reports on human rights practices for 1994: Laos* 21(2, Spring): 22.

———. *Wife abuse law finally passed in Malaysia* 20(4, Autumn): 36.

World Organization Against Torture. 1999. *Violence against women in Thailand.* Report Prepared for the Committee on the Elimination of Discrimination Against Women.

Byrgen Finkelman

VIOLENCE:
Sub-Saharan and Southern Africa

The United Nations Declaration on the Elimination of Violence Against Women (1994) describes such violence as "a manifestation of historically unequal power relations between men and women, which have led to domination over and discrimination against women by men and to the prevention of the full advancement of women." Violence and abuse can be physical, sexual, psychological, economic, and political; overt examples include femicide and infanticide, battery, rape, sexual torture, slavery and trafficking, incest, child marriage, and sexual harassment. Violence is also expressed as sexism and misogyny in the media, and in cultural practices that wear down women's and girls' autonomy and self-esteem and direct women's energy toward maintaining male dominance.

Statistics on Violence

Violence against women is endemic in many parts of southern Africa, particularly South Africa, which has the world's highest rate of rapes per capita. In townships throughout South Africa, girls are afraid to go to school lest they be abducted and jackrolled (gang-raped). In 1996, it was estimated that one in three women in South Africa had been raped, and that one in two would be raped at some time in her life. In a survey in the Khayelitsha township of Cape Town, 30 percent of the women reported that their first sexual intercourse had been a result of force.

The problem of rape in southern Africa is compounded by the fact that in some cultures—for example, Botswana, Namibia, Zimbabwe, Zambia, and Mozambique—rape was traditionally considered a crime against a lineage rather than against a woman or girl. Consequently, fathers and guardians sought "damages" or reparations for the decrease in the woman's or girl's value.

Wife beating and femicide have long been a part of southern African societies, but today they have reached huge proportions. In Zimbabwe, wife battery has been found to occur in 32 to 42 percent of rural households. It has been estimated that 60 percent of all women murdered in Zimbabwe are killed by husbands or boyfriends; in South Africa, the proportion is 50 percent. The weapons of choice are fists, knives, axes, and paraffin, and the "trigger" can be something as innocuous as a woman asking a man for household money.

The South African Department of Justice has estimated that one woman in four is a victim of domestic abuse. In

1998, a study of pregnant women in Cape Town found that 60 percent had been beaten by their partners, and it was likely that many more had been beaten but would not disclose the fact. Generally speaking, violence against women and girls is difficult to measure because it often goes unreported. A woman's fear of reprisal is a major deterrent. Women are also socialized to be ashamed of being a victim of rape, incest, or domestic violence. Moreover, they are deterred by the fear that police will be unsympathetic and that the perpetrator will get off with a light sentence. In Botswana, 70 percent of reported cases are closed before prosecution, and of the 30 percent that do go to trial, less than half result in a conviction. Even when there is a conviction, the jail sentence is often shockingly brief. In Zambia and Zimbabwe, women's groups complain that a man can receive a stiffer sentence for stealing a goat.

Another problem is violence against domestic workers. In South Africa, many women domestic workers are sexually harassed and abused by their employers. An abused worker often stays with her employer because she has children to feed and cannot afford to leave, and in some cases the woman is also being abused at home by a jealous partner.

Incest, child abuse, and sexual abuse involving girls are on the rise throughout southern Africa. Organizations such as the Musasa Project, a shelter and advocacy program for abused women, have extended their work to include child sexual abuse—which, like rape, is especially dangerous to the victim because of the astronomical rates of HIV and AIDS in Africa.

Contributing Factors

Many factors contribute to violence against women in this region; often, such factors work in combination and are mutually reinforcing.

European imperialism and capitalism: Although gender violence existed before colonialism, most observers agree that it escalated during the colonial period. Women's traditional sources of power and status were undermined by European colonial administrators and missionaries, who often aided and abetted existing patriarchies. Female chiefs were ignored; female (and male) priests and spirit mediums were treated as criminals and scapegoats; and colonial policies for controlling venereal diseases taught whole societies to associate the female body with infection and shame—in Zimbabwe, the colloquial expression for a sexually transmitted disease remains "woman's disease."

Slavery also undermined women's and girls' status and security, and southern Africa was affected by both the Atlantic and the Indian Ocean slave trade. Slave trading was accompanied by war, raiding, and militarization, processes in which women were particularly vulnerable—as the enemy's women, as a commodity, and as the victor's booty. In matrilineal societies the proliferation of slave wives, who were by definition kinless, gradually eroded the authority of women. Among the BaKongo of Angola, slave wives did not have the higher status of "sister," and so this society was increasingly populated with dependent wives rather than entitled sisters.

Other factors related to the subordination of African women under colonialism were wars of pacification; the Mefecane, a period of military turmoil and dislocation of the 1820s; racially exploitative capitalism; and the mobilization of African men as migrant workers, with African women relegated to often unpaid rural work. As colonized societies became more materialistic and cash-based, women's labor was valued less and women became more dependent. In societies like South Africa and colonial Zimbabwe (southern Rhodesia) African men were required to carry a pass to move from place to place. African women were not generally issued passes until the 1950s (South African women successfully fought against their issuance), but women in colonial Zimbabwe could not enter a town without a husband's or father's permission. Women who migrated to urban areas were labeled as prostitutes.

Throughout southern Africa, colonial governments established "customary laws" that made African women legal minors, dependent on men for a right to a domicile; these laws perpetuated women's traditional subordination to African men in a modern context. Another aspect of patriarchy stemming from colonialism is the dichotomy between "public" and "private" violence against women. Under colonialism, marriage transactions were increasingly seen as commercial; wives were increasinsly dependent on men's wages and isolated from kinship and other social networks.

Under apartheid in South Africa women suffered like everyone else but also as women. It is argued in general that the brutality of apartheid bred brutality in its victims; and in particular that apartheid emasculated men, who then tried to reestablish their manhood by making women submissive and beating those who resisted.

Patriarchy: It is important to recognize that gender violence in southern Africa has deep precolonial roots. Although there were significant contexts of female power, the general position of women was subordinate. Child pledging and forced marriages were common, as were the capturing of women in war and female pawnship. Wife abduction was practiced, and women were objects of exchange and insurance. These practices are inherently violent in that they treat a female as a will-less object, and they were accompanied by outright violence when the female refused to comply.

Even after independence, many "customary laws" remained. In Zimbabwe, Mozambique, Namibia, and Angola, women claim to have fought two "colonialisms"— European colonizers and African patriarchies. Patriarchy persists today: throughout southern Africa, cultures and institutions uphold and reinforce male authority and superiority, and violence against women and girls is a direct consequence. The patriarchal value system gives men a sense that they are entitled to control women and fails to address gender violence as a national priority.

African women are infantalized within customary marriage and largely disenfranchised. An important source of violence is the bride payment—a gift from the groom's family to compensate the bride's family for her productivity. With the rise of the cash economy, this became a commercial transaction reflecting the value placed on a particular woman's sexuality and her expected contribution to the groom and his lineage; thus a man often feels that he has purchased his wife and she must obey him. He may also feel that he has bought the right to do what he pleases with her, including physically chastising or "correcting" her, and this is increasingly understood as the right to batter her. With the breakdown of social institutions and extended family networks, particularly in the townships of South Africa, women often feel that they have no recourse.

Ironically, the establishment of women's rights after independence has also contributed to violence. For example, Zimbabwe gained its independence in 1980 and passed the Legal Age of Majority Act in 1982, giving adult women citizenship status; the new nation also addressed women's rights on other fronts. For many men, including those in power, it seemed that things had gone too far too fast. In 1983, local authorities instituted Operation Clean-Up, directed against "undesirable" women, who were rounded up and detained. Actually, these women's only crime was that they had challenged traditional gender boundaries: they had been seen alone at night by the police or the Zimbabwe African National Union's Youth Brigade and could not produce proof of marriage. In the same year, the government of Mozambique conducted Operation Production, ostensibly to transform idleness in towns and cities into work on state farms; but one actual target, as in Zimbabwe, was women who failed to produce a marriage certificate. More recently, the supreme court of Zimbabwe decided that, under customary law, a woman could not inherit land—an example of the opportunistic use of customary law to reverse advances in women's rights. The backlash against women's rights also takes the form of attacks by men in the street on women wearing miniskirts and other clothing considered too revealing; during these attacks the woman is stripped and assaulted.

War and militarism: Warfare has intensified women's subordination and increased tolerance of gender violence. War is a persistent feature of southern Africa, which has been a battlefield of imperialism, anticolonialism, the cold war, liberation, nationalism, and protracted civil wars. Although women may be combatants, military institutions are archetypically male and contribute enormously to antisocial violence in general and gender violence in particular.

In almost all respects, women have been especially vulnerable in these wars. Rape continues to be a weapon of political terror and part of an ideology of male dominance. Tens of thousands of women and girls were raped during anticolonial wars, and even more during postcolonial civil wars. Mothers were forced to watch while their daughters were gang-raped. Girls were kidnapped for the sexual amusement of soldiers.

During Namibia's struggle with South Africa for independence, rape was used by the South African forces against the local population as an antiguerrilla strategy. Within South Africa, particularly from the mid-1980s to the elections of 1994, violence was rampant. After the Soweto uprising, there was a rapid increase in youth violence along with militant activism. Testifying before the Truth and Reconciliation Commission in South Africa, women described episodes of gang rape and sexual torture. Often, women were targeted because they were thought to be informants, but many were simply victims of the prevailing culture of male violence. Moreover, women are victimized not only by the enemy but also by their own countrymen; during Zimbabwe's struggle for liberation, for instance, women were compelled to supply sexual services to Zimbabwean soldiers.

Worldwide, women (like children) suffer disproportionately from war. Internationally, for example, 80 percent of war refugees are women; and as refugees, women and girls are once again vulnerable to sexual violence, often being forced to negotiate their passage to security.

Nor does violence stop with the end of war—prolonged warfare creates a permissive atmosphere for violence. In most African civil conflicts, the combatants remain within or return to communities, and they may or may not have been rehabilitated; moreover, these communities themselves are often unrehabilitated "war cultures" (a term used by the South African antiviolence activist Mmatshilo Motsei).

The high level of sexual violence during warfare has increased the already high rate of HIV infection among women and children, particularly girls. South Africa, for instance, has one of the highest rates of HIV transmission in the world, and—not coincidentally—it also has one of the highest rates of gender violence. AIDS has proved uncontainable during times of military conflict.

Reactions and Constraints

Almost every country in sub-Saharan and southern Africa has signed the Convention for the Elimination of Discrimination Against Women (CEDAW), although some have signed with reservations based on incompatibility with their traditional customs, and all are a long way away from eradicating discrimination and violence against women. Government and nongovernmental organizations (NGOs) have begun to tackle the huge problem in South Africa. This nation underwent a kind of purification ritual with the Truth and Reconciliation Commission, which—significantly—held special "gender hearings" so that abuse of women, and women's pain and suffering, would be brought out into the open. South African NGOs committed to eliminating gender violence include People Opposing Woman Abuse (POWA) and the Agisanang Domestic Abuse Prevention and Treatment project (ADAPT); they engage entire communities in the battle against violence, which is seen as a sickness to be healed.

Zimbabwe has well-organized antipatriarchal women's and human rights organizations, and Zimbabwean women are actively seeking power and a voice in the state. In Mozambique, a campaign called All Against Violence includes governmental and nongovernmental women's organizations and mental health groups, which are studying the dimensions of violence against women and making policy recommendations. One strategy of NGOs in Mozambique is to make the "private" public—to break through the silence and secrecy surrounding gender violence. The government of Mozambique supports these efforts, though it is facing budget constraints. In Zambia, the Women's Lobby Group and the YWCA met with the president and enlisted his support in fighting violence against women.

However, globalization of markets has meant that weapons continue to be supplied to southern African nations. These arms are recycled from conflict to conflict and can be purchased cheap on the streets of Mozambique and Angola. Women have a very long way to go in these countries, and it is imperative that they begin to claim more power and more voice in the reconstruction process.

Conclusion

In conclusion, it is worth noting that the rationale for violence against women is similar to the rationale of colonialism: "they" (women, colonial peoples) are deemed inferior, are incapable of managing their own affairs, and are by nature childlike and dependent; "we" (men, colonizers) are superior and are born to rule, protect, and make decisions for "them." As protectors, "we" are entitled to benefit and profit; "they" must submit and show gratitude—otherwise, "we" will resort to violence. Male domination, like colonial domination, is perpetuated through violence. Women in sub-Saharan and southern Africa, like women elsewhere, realize this and are demanding their human rights.

See Also

ABUSE; AIDS AND HIV: CASE STUDY—AFRICA; COLONIALISM AND POSTCOLONIALISM; RAPE; VIOLENCE: NORTH AFRICA

References and Further Reading

Armstrong, Alice, and Welshman Ncube. 1987. *Women and law in southern Africa.* Harare: Zimbabwe Publishing House.

Davies, Miranda. 1994. *Women and violence: Realities and responses worldwide.* London and New Jersey: Zed.

Getecha, Ciru, and Jesimen Chipika, eds. 1995. *Zimbabwe women's voices.* Harare: Zimbabwe Women's Resource Center and Network.

Green, December. 1999. *Gender violence in Africa: African women's responses.* New York: St. Martin's.

Made, Patricia, and Isabella Matambanadzo. 1996. *Beyond Beijing: Strategies and visions towards women's equality.* Harare: SADC Press Trust, Gender and Media Development Project.

McFadden, Pat, ed. 1998. *Southern Africa in transition: A gendered perspective.* Harare: SAPES.

Turshen, Meredeth, and Clothide Twagiramariya. 1998. *What women do in wartime.* New York and London: Zed.

Tomasevski, Katarina. 1993. *Women and human rights.* London and New Jersey: Zed.

Lynette Jackson

VIOLENCE: Western Europe

Defining Violence

Violence can take many forms and includes behaviors legally defined as crime and others that are not. *Violence* is usually defined as including physical, sexual, and emotional *abuses,* which can be the result of compelling women to act in particular ways or of constraining their actions. For example, women may be compelled to take part in undesired sexual activities or restrained from seeking medical attention when injured. When the woman knows the perpetrator, economic aspects may also be involved; for example, men may refuse to share their wages with their wives and children, or they may forcibly take from their wives state benefit payments meant to support the family. Women's definition of violence both includes crimes identified by the criminal justice and legal systems and is more extensive (Hanmer and Saunders, 1984, 1993). In women's definition of violence a number of terms can be used interchangeably or as descriptive of actions that incorporate violence, such as *abuse, harassment,* and *threats.* Their definition includes situations where women cannot stop the initiation of behaviors and, once they begin, women cannot control the interaction or its cessation. Thus, what one woman may find violent, abusive, harassing, or threatening is not necessarily perceived as such by another.

Recognizing Violence

In Europe the recognition of violence against women began in the early 1970s. The special events that created a climate where violence against women became socially visible arose from women's liberation movements. These movements in Europe began at different times, and recognition of the first type of violence against women varied. In Britain and the Netherlands the initial focus was on home-based violence from husbands, cohabitees, and boyfriends, and in France the focus was on rape. By 1974 there was a network of refuges (shelters) in the United Kingdom, a refuge was opened in Amsterdam, and public protests were being held on rape. The family was conceptualized as a major site of women's oppression by women's liberationists, many of whom later came to identify as radical feminists. Knowledge of these new issues was taken into Europe through the International Tribunal on Crimes Against Women held in Brussels in March 1976 (Russell and Van de Ven, 1976). Witnesses spoke of their violent experiences, with testimony on rape from Denmark, France, the Netherlands, Norway, and Portugal; on violence from known men (woman battering) from England, Scotland, and the Netherlands; on forced incarceration in mental hospitals and in marriage from Ireland; on assault from Belgium; on brutal treatment in prison from Spain and Greece; and on violence against women in general from Italy. Women in Denmark testified on the harm caused by pornography. This conference served to extend women's knowledge of specific types of violence and to facilitate the taking up of previously unknown issues by women in other European countries.

Recognition of different types of violence continued to develop through women's disclosures to one another. Women who contacted rape crisis centers prompted a focus on incest and other forms of sexual assault and the development of new services. The concept of victim, with its implied passivity, was rejected by women who "discovered" yet another form of violence against women in favor of the more dynamic word *survivor.* Around the same time equal opportunity legislation began to recognize sexual harassment at work. Reclaim-the-night marches raised issues of women's safety and of pornography. The homicide of women by men and the refusal of the courts to recognize the relevance of repeated violence against wives in their killing of men led to further campaigns.

Explanations

The first research studies and theoretical papers on violence against women shifted the analysis from an individual problem caused by the personal failure of the victim to structural explanations of male domination and patriarchal social relations in the family and society (Dobash and Dobash, 1979). This work followed an analysis begun by the women's liberation movement elaborating key insights. The family was conceived as the locus of male dominance and female subordination, with violence the outcome of unequal relations. Further, violence and its threat were conceived as the underpinning of all hierarchical systems, such as social class, race, imperialism, and gender. The state is an important source of the power of men over women in families, because it defines the family as located in the private rather than in the public domain. The argument is that legitimated violence and its threat are regulated and exercised by the state and the state can exercise its power through what it does and what it does not do. By not intervening in any serious way in the exercise of violence and threat by individual men against individual women, the state gives legitimacy to the maintenance of hierarchical relations between women and men in families and in society generally.

There were a number of areas of disagreement between those who did not accept violence against women as a serious social problem and those who did: in particular, the extent of the problem, the responsibility of the victim for her plight, and whether violence against women was more evident in some social groups. Research into these issues followed the lead of the women's liberation movement.

Although the incidence (the number of violent acts per head of population) and prevalence (the number of victims per head of population) of violence against women is not accurately known, certain findings are replicated by research studies and by criminal justice statistics (Mooney, 1993). Notably, violence against women is largely perpetrated by men whom women know, and the closer the relationship the more likely there is to be violence and the repetition of violence. Stranger assault is much less frequent and much less likely to be repeated on the same woman. Women may be subjected to violence as children, as adults, and as seniors. Although some women have a more or less continual personal history of living with violence, younger women are more likely to be victimized. The significance of age is associated with the greater dependency of women on men when their children are very young. There are numerous methodological problems with incidence and prevalence studies, but the overall conclusion is that violence and violent crime against women are major social problems in western Europe.

With attention directed to sexual violence and to male power, the question arose about the relationship between heterosexuality as a sexual practice and as a system of social relations and violence. Is heterosexuality violence, or is violence an aberration or the extreme end of heterosexuality? One solution is to define all violence as sexual, in recognition of its largely heterosexual location, while another is to elaborate the forms that violence may take and to explore women's violence against men and against one another. This is both an empirical and a theoretical response to issues of individual agency, differences between women, the concepts of power and subordination, social domination, and oppression.

There are important differences between women created and maintained by the state; for example, a woman who enters a European country to marry a European national may not be able to leave him for a year or longer, no matter how he treats her, unless she is prepared to be returned to her country of origin (European Women's Lobby, 1993). Agencies respond differently to women from different ethnic communities, which creates differences in how women experience violence and its resolution (Mama, 1989).

It is now 30 years since women in Europe first attempted to change patterns of social responses to women experiencing violence from men known to them. We must conclude that societal resistance to change is very great because despite the progress made, women's safety from the violence of men remains a major social problem throughout Europe. However, there are now measures to counter violence against women, however rudimentary, in all European countries. Issues of policy, provision, and state agency intervention on behalf of women are being raised at the local, national, and European level (Council of Europe, 1990, 1991; d'Ancona, 1984).

See Also

ABUSE; CRIME AND PUNISHMENT; HETEROSEXUALITY; HOUSEHOLDS AND FAMILIES: WESTERN EUROPE; INCEST; POLITICS AND THE STATE: WESTERN EUROPE; PORNOGRAPHY AND VIOLENCE; RAPE; VIOLENCE AND PEACE: OVERVIEW; WOMEN'S MOVEMENT: MODERN INTERNATIONAL MOVEMENT

References and Further Reading

Council of Europe. 1990. Legal Affairs, recommendation No. R (90) 2 of the Committee of Ministers on social measures concerning violence within the family, adopted by the Committee on 15 January 1990.

Council of Europe. 1991. Solemn declaration of the Committee of Ministers of the Member States of the Council of Europe.

d'Ancona, Hedy. 1984. *Report drawn up on behalf of the Committee on Women's Rights on Violence Against Women.* European Parliament Reports, PE Doc. A 2-44/86, No. AY-CO-86-069-EN-C, Office for Official Publications of the European Communities: L-2985 Luxembourg.

Dobash, R. E., and R. P. Dobash. 1979. *Violence against wives.* New York: Free Press.

European Women's Lobby. 1993. *Confronting the fortress: Black and migrant women in the European Community.* Luxembourg: European Parliament.

Hanmer, Jalna, and Sheila Saunders. 1984. *Well-founded fear: A community study of violence to women.* London: Hutchinson.

———. 1993. *Women, violence and crime prevention.* Aldershot, U.K.: Gower.

Mama, Amina. 1989. *The hidden struggle: Statutory and voluntary sector responses to violence against black women in the home.* London: Runnymede Trust.

Mooney, Jayne. 1993. *The hidden figure: The North London domestic survey.* London: Islington Council.

Russell, Diana, and Nicole Van de Van, eds. 1976. *Crimes against women: Proceedings of the international tribunal.* Millbrae, Calif.: Les Femmes.

Jalna Hanmer

VIRGINITY

The term *virginity* denotes the state of physical integrity and total sexual abstinence expected generally of women before marriage. In Christian usage the word is synonymous with *celibacy* when referring to the vow of consecration of those who remain unmarried and practice total continence in following Christ in a religious community.

The value of virginity differs from culture to culture. Ancient Rome held the vestal virgins in honor for their lives of service to the gods. In the Jewish tradition, however, virginity was a curse, except for women prior to their wedding. Jews were obliged to marry and have children for the people of Jahweh. The same marriage ideal holds true for Islamic society and religion, where virginity as a state of life is virtually unknown. In fact, marriage is regarded to be already half religion and parenthood to be the condition for attaining full personhood.

Christian church history, however, shows several trends in the development of virginity. In the New Testament Jesus Christ gave it validity as a state of life alongside marriage, freeing it from the stigmatization of Jewish society. As a biblical inspiration in the early church it rests on Jesus's words in Matthew 19:12, counseling nonmarriage "for the sake of the Kingdom of heaven."

After the Christian persecutions in the first centuries, when dying for the faith was no longer possible, virginity became an alternative to martyrdom. Young women and widows dedicated themselves fully to Christ as virgins. Monastic communities introduced the "consecration of virgins" in the liturgy for females to symbolize their nuptials with the Lord.

As the church absorbed Greek culture, Hellenistic influences led to an alienation of virginity from its biblical inspiration. The writings of the church fathers and succeeding monastic practices stressed preserving bodily sexual integrity more for its own sake than for greater love and service. As the striving for "angelic purity" grew, a negative asceticism emerged, waging war against the flesh, suppressing carnal desires, and putting enmity between sexuality and virginity. Without its biblical context, virginity soon became a cult, pursued for its own sake and praised for its superiority over marriage.

This view of "consecrated virginity" distorted the meaning of women's total humanity. Women were either highly honored as persons untainted by sex or maligned as seducers causing men's downfall. The opposition between virginity and sexuality meant negating the goodness of the body as God's beautiful creation.

In the context of feminism today women have discovered a new meaning for consecrated virginity. When they choose this state of life, they believe in the goodness of the body, claim the right to say yes or no to its use, and determine when and whether to have sex. They oppose a stereotyped role of women as married women, liberating themselves from laws oppressive to women in a sexist religion and society.

See Also

CELIBACY: RELIGIOUS; CELIBACY: SECULAR; CHASTITY

References and Further Reading

Dowell, Susan. 1993. A feminist critique. *The Way Supplement* 77: 76–86.

Jomier, Jacques. 1989. *How to understand Islam.* London: SCM.

Malone, Susan. 1993. The unfinished agenda of the church: A critical look at the history of celibacy. *The Way Supplement* 77: 66–75.

Ridick, Joyce. 1984. *Treasures in earthen vessels: The vows.* Middlegreen, U.K.: St. Paul.

Sr. Irene Dabalus

VIRTUAL REALITY

See CYBERSPACE AND VIRTUAL REALITY.

VOCATIONAL EDUCATION

See EDUCATION: VOCATIONAL.

VODOU

Vodou is one of the most renowned of the syncretic and pluralistic Afro-Caribbean religions. A religion of the African diaspora, Vodou is a synthesis of elements from African tribal religions, Native American religions, and Catholicism, composed by Haitian slaves. Vodou united Africans from different tribes and provided the inspiration for the slave revolt that ended French colonial rule in Haiti (1791–1804), which in turn inspired other major slave revolts in the Caribbean and the Americas.

The most widely known feature of Vodou is the ritual of spirit possession, in which participants, especially priestesses and priests, are "ridden by" the spirits, who are thereby available to address the problems of the people in powerful and direct ways. The spirits themselves, represented as conflations of African deities and heroes, Catholic saints, and spirit beings from Native American religions, reflect the pluralistic cultures where Vodou is practiced; in the Caribbean and in Central and South America, many people practice Vodou alongside Catholicism. Women, in particular, turn to Vodou for help with problems that the Catholic Church does not address to their satisfaction, such as domestic problems, which many women feel that priests, as celibate men, cannot understand.

Researchers have documented a historical shift from male to female dominance in the practice of Vodou as a result of shifting demographics in Haiti from primarily rural to urban living, a trend also found in the Haitian expatriate community in New York, where Vodou is a religion led by women. Karen Brown's (1989) understanding of the Vodou worldview and moral vision suggests further reasons why

Vodou resonates so effectively with women's experiences. It is a religion that sacralizes women's primary concern with caring for others and women's understanding of morality in contextual, interpersonal terms. "All Vodou is about healing and that healing work is aimed at relations between people as well as those between the 'living' and the spirits" (226–227). In contrast to a European-based cultural opposition between individual and group concerns, "the moral wisdom of Vodou lies in teaching that it is precisely in responsive and responsible relation to others that one has the clearest and most steady sense of self" (233).

The essential work of Vodou in healing relations between the "living" and the spirits and Vodou's historical function as a survival tool for Haitian slaves are both reflected in the related African-American folk religion Hoodoo. The Hoodoo practice of doing "conjure work" with herbs, roots, spells, and storytelling provided concrete remedies for a people facing the racism of American culture without legal resources, both during slavery and in post-slavery times. While Charles Chesnutt became the first African-American writer to draw on Hoodoo for creative authority in *The Conjure Woman* (1899), it was Zora Neale Hurston (1901–1960) who became the first African-American authority on black folklore.

Hurston's work as the first African-American anthropologist, including an apprenticeship to a Vodou doctor in New Orleans and travels to Jamaica and Haiti recorded in *Tell My Horse* (1938), helped correct the outsider's perception of Vodou as mere pagan savagery and superstition. Her recovery of folk traditions of Hoodoo and conjure work also inspired her own influential body of literary writing, establishing a spiritual authority for later African-American women writers such as Alice Walker. Walker's own journey to "conjure" Hurston from historical neglect, chronicled in "Looking for Zora," embodies the traditional power of Vodou to make connections between generations of women and to let one reassert oneself and one's heritage in the face of injustice. Haitian Vodou and African-American Hoodoo continue to inspire women writers such as Maryse Condé and Gloria Naylor.

See Also

HOUSEHOLDS AND FAMILIES: CARIBBEAN; SAINTS; TRADITIONAL HEALING: NATIVE NORTH AMERICA

References and Further Reading

Brown, Karen McCarthy. 1989. Women's leadership in Haitian Vodou. In Judith Plaskow and Carol Christ, eds., *Weaving the visions: Patterns in feminist spirituality,* 226–234. San Francisco: Harper and Row.

Clark, Vèvè A. 1984. Marassa: Images of women from the other Americas. *Woman of Power* 1(1): 58–61.

Hemenway, Robert E. 1977. *Zora Neale Hurston: A literary biography.* Urbana: University of Illinois Press.

Hurston, Zora Neale. 1990. *Tell my horse: Voodoo and life in Haiti and Jamaica.* New York: Harper and Row (originally published 1938).

Sered, Susan Starr. 1994. *Priestess, mother, sacred sister: Religions dominated by women.* New York: Oxford University Press.

Walker, Alice. 1983. Looking for Zora. In *In search of our mothers' gardens,* 93–116. San Diego, Calif.: Harcourt Brace Jovanovich.

Cathy Peppers

VOLUNTEERISM

Volunteerism may be defined as any activities involving volunteers, that is, people who on a regular basis willingly contribute unpaid services to a group or organization. Volunteer work is as varied as paid work. Although some volunteers may dedicate all their time to such activities, it is more common for volunteers to contribute their unpaid services for five hours or less per week. The sum total of volunteer activities is large: in some countries their number runs to the millions, and the economic value of volunteer work is considerable. However, there are marked differences between countries as to the use of volunteers. For example, in Denmark there have been volunteers in sporting and church activities, and in political and social clubs, but until recently a virtual absence of any volunteers in welfare, which is the domain of paid professionals (Boolsen and Holt, 1988). In the United States, welfare services are also mainly delivered by paid workers, but volunteers are heavily involved in fund-raising, while in Australia volunteers play a limited role in fund-raising but carry a major responsibility for direct service delivery in health and welfare (Baldock, 1990). In Japan, neighborhood organizations including all inhabitants of a locally defined area rather than a specified group of volunteers may organize social activities, garbage collection, consumer cooperatives, and care of the old and infirm (Thränhardt, 1990).

Volunteerism has special application to capitalist countries, in which a sharp distinction tends to be made between paid and unpaid work. Historically in western industrialized countries, volunteerism is associated with the development of charitable work carried out by upper-class "ladies." In nonindustrialized countries such charitable support has generally been part of traditional family or community networks of mutual aid, rather than formal voluntary organizations to assist the poor. Volunteerism is a feminist issue, in that the majority of volunteers who engage in regular volunteer work, especially in the area of welfare services, are women.

A Controversial Concept

The concept of volunteerism is a controversial one: some left-wing writers, for example, have described volunteerism as middle-class patronizing welfare on the cheap. The notion of volunteerism is also rejected by many feminists. Their sentiments were exemplified in a resolution, passed at the 1974 conference of the National Organization for Women (NOW) in the United States, which stated that women should engage only in social action and lobby work that would help to bring about social change. Delivery of services to clients within traditional voluntary agencies was seen as exploitation of women, designed to keep them in a subordinate position (Kaminer, 1984). Paradoxically, many feminist organizations, although ideologically opposed to the idea, use women as volunteers.

Whatever the nature and scope of the organizations using volunteers, there is a sexual division of labor. Although men participate extensively in volunteer work, it is generally in addition to their paid work and their activities tend to be restricted to fund-raising and administrative or executive work, with only limited involvement in day-to-day service delivery. The exception is stereotyped male activities such as volunteer firefighting and rescue services, which are dominated by men. On the other hand, women by and large fulfill the routine everyday tasks required of their organization. For example, it is well established that men act as coaches, managers, and financial backers of sporting clubs, while women chauffeur, feed, clothe, and rally for the players. Most men engage in such volunteer activities after (paid) working hours or during working hours in an ex officio capacity, while many women combine volunteer work with the role of housewife and mother, at most picking up some part-time paid work at the same time. Women, then, tend to spend more hours in volunteer work, do such work on a more regular, day-to-day (or week-to-week) basis, and do more mundane volunteer work than men.

Volunteerism and Class

Much of the literature on volunteer work tends to be preoccupied with issues of class. The assumption is a logical extension of the historical development of charity work and of the notion that only middle-class women can afford to spend time and resources to engage in such unpaid work. It is apparent, however, that such an assumption is based on an inappropriate use of the concept of social class in reference to women. Female volunteers whose husbands are in middle-class occupations may themselves be in (part-time) working-class jobs with low pay. Others may have no independent income and require their husband's approval for any expenses incurred as volunteers. Also, low-income female single parents increasingly make an active contribution as volunteers in women's shelters, women's health centers, learning centers, and other community action groups. References to social class, then, should be based on a woman's own life chances and resources rather than those of her partner, and it should not be assumed that all female volunteers are "middle class."

For an understanding of volunteerism it is important to distinguish between the experiences of individual women who volunteer and the structural arrangements that allow unpaid volunteer work to exist as an activity most commonly assigned to women. As to the experiences of individual women, it is apparent that there is a range of issues that need to be taken into account (Baldock, 1990; Daniels, 1988; Kaminer, 1984). Many women volunteer as young mothers for activities associated with their children (sport, cafeteria service, and so on), while some older women take up volunteer work when their children leave home or after the death of their spouse. Generally, women volunteer for three reasons: the need for self-development as an alternative to paid work (either because they find it more rewarding than paid work or because it provides them with skills that help in finding paid work) and the desire to contribute to the community at large. It appears that some women see the opportunity to engage in volunteer work as a break from "compulsory altruism" (Land and Rose, 1985). They choose to do volunteer work, sometimes against the wishes of their husbands, as an activity that takes them away from what they see as the private sphere and toward a community service in the public domain.

Feminist Approach to Volunteerism

An analysis of structural factors explaining the existence of volunteer work, and the role of women in it, requires scrutiny of broader economic, political, and cultural forces responsible for the predominance of women in unpaid work. Feminists have theorized about the contribution women make through their unpaid domestic labor, their involvement in informal care, and their unpaid work in family enterprises. Few feminists, however, have attempted a full theoretical analysis of volunteerism, and major theoreticians of women's paid and unpaid work have ignored volunteer work (Baldock, 1998). It could be argued that the invisibility of volunteerism in feminist accounts of unpaid work is due to the strong socialist-feminist flavor of such accounts, which leads them to deny the significance of what they see as middle-class charity.

Feminists trying to explain women's role in volunteering generally see it as "part of the gender tasks that women do by virtue of their position as wives and mothers" (Daniels, 1988: xxvii) and suggest that most women negotiate volunteer tasks around family responsibilities. Among those who have theorized about women's role in volunteerism, three attempts are worth noting. An early example was Mueller (1975), writing from a rational choice model, who maintained that one of the specific reasons women volunteer is that they want to improve their marketability for some future employment. In other words, they volunteer time for training, thereby exemplifying free choice in a rational exchange of costs and benefits. This view was strongly criticized by Hartmann, who argued that a free choice model does not apply in the case of female volunteers because "women have so few options that we are reduced to working for nothing in order to keep from getting thrown on the scrap heap of a society that does not want us" (1975: 775). A third perspective, developed by Baldock (1990, 1994), provides a more specific linkage between the nature of capitalism and patriarchy. Baldock, focusing on volunteers in welfare and with specific reference to Australia, argued that female volunteers involved in everyday service delivery, like their counterparts in paid work, are part of a secondary labor market, carrying out menial tasks subject to the control of paid staff and male volunteer leaders. Also, like their counterparts in paid work, female service volunteers form flexible and expandable pools of labor, available to take up volunteer work when governments try to reduce expenditures by increased reliance on the nongovernment voluntary sector to carry out welfare services.

In a number of western countries, there has indeed been a deliberate effort in recent years to cut the costs of government by contracting out essential welfare services to the nongovernment welfare sector. This has led to an increased demand for the services of volunteers, together with an emphasis on volunteer training and professionalism. The outcome has been an awareness among female volunteers of the value of their contribution. Baldock (1994) suggests that if pressure continues on the voluntary sector to perform crucial welfare services, and if at the same time professionalism remains emphasized as an incentive for responsible service, the result will be an increased demand by women for financial remuneration and entry into paid work. Where such work is not available, women may reject repetitive service work and channel their skills and experience into more meaningful volunteer tasks. "Thus, the 'good works' that women once did that kept the social structure intact may become the activism that challenges the status quo" (Berk, 1988: 300).

See Also

CHARITY; CLASS; DOMESTIC LABOR; ECONOMICS: FEMINIST CRITIQUES; ECONOMIC STATUS: COMPARATIVE ANALYSIS; ECONOMY: HISTORY OF WOMEN'S PARTICIPATION; ECONOMY: INFORMAL; ECONOMY: WELFARE AND THE ECONOMY; UNEMPLOYMENT; WORK: FEMINIST THEORIES; WORK: OCCUPATIONAL SEGREGATION; WORK: PATTERNS

References and Further Reading

Baldock, Cora Vellekoop. 1998. Feminist discourses of unwaged work: The case of volunteerism. *Australian Feminist Studies* 13(27): 19–34.

——. 1990. *Volunteers in welfare.* Sydney: Allen and Unwin.

——. 1994. Working without wages in Australian welfare. In Esther Ngan-ling Chow and Catherine White Berheide, eds. *Women, the family and policy: A global perspective,* 99–115. Albany: State University of New York Press.

Berk, Sarah Fenstermaker. 1988. Women's unpaid labor: Home and community. In Ann Helton Stromberg and Shirley Harkess, eds. *Women working: Theories and facts in perspective,* 287–302. Mountain View, Calif.: Mayfield.

Boolsen, M. Watt, and H. Holt. 1988. *Voluntary action in Denmark and Britain.* Copenhagen: Danish National Institute of Social Research.

Daniels, Arlene Kaplan. 1988. *Invisible careers: Women civic leaders from the volunteer world.* Chicago: University of Chicago Press.

Hartmann, Heidi H. 1975. Comment on Marnie W. Mueller's "The economic determinants of volunteer work by women." *Signs* 1(3): 773–776.

Kaminer, Wendy. 1984. *Women volunteering.* Garden City, N.Y.: Anchor.

Land, Hilary, and Hilary Rose. 1985. Compulsory altruism for some or an altruistic society for all? In P. Bean, J. Ferris, and D. Whynes, eds. *In defence of welfare.* London: Tavistock.

Mueller, Marnie W. 1975. The economic determinants of volunteer work by women. *Signs* 1(2): 325–328.

Thränhardt, Anna Maria. 1990. Traditional neighborhood associations in industrial society: The case of Japan. In Helmut K. Anheier and Wolfgang Seibel, eds. *The third sector: Comparative studies of nonprofit organizations,* 347–360. Berlin: de Gruyter.

Cora Vellekoop Baldock

VOODOO
See VODOU.

VOTING
See FEMINISM: MILITANT *and* SUFFRAGE.

WAR

Women have been history's designated noncombatants. Thus, the story of women and war would seem to be a story of how women have either directly or indirectly been war's victims despite their status as those who mourned or cheered or stalwartly persevered, rather than fought. As with all historical truisms, however, the story of the female noncombatant is not a simple one. There are the inevitable exceptions to the rule—with mythic examples of Amazons and Joan of Arc saints lurking in the background. World War II partisans and resistance fighters, anticolonial guerrillas, Soviet women tactical fighter pilots in World War II, American women loading ordinance or, now, piloting Navy fighter aircraft—all come to mind most immediately. But these exceptions remain exceptions, and that is why we take note of them. Nevertheless, there is a story to be told about women and war in modernity, and it is rather more complex than the story of noncombatants and those we note as exceptions. In order to bring conceptual clarity to the tale, it will be necessary to step back, briefly, to look at antique and medieval antecedents to women and modern warfare.

Antique and Medieval Exemplars:
Trojan Women, Spartan Mothers, and the Madonna

Myth aside, women were very much part of the war story of antiquity. For the Greeks, war was a natural state and the basis of society. The Greek city-state was a community of warriors. The funeral oration of Pericles enshrines the warrior who, as the true Athenian, has died to protect the city. The Greek citizen army was the expression of the *polis*; indeed, the creation of such armies served as a catalyst to create and to sustain the polis as a civic form (Elshtain, 1987). How did women figure in this ancient story of war? As non-combatants, to be sure, but the female noncombatant comes in several varieties. No more than the "soldier" is she quite a generic figure. Noncombatant roles and identities are profoundly shaped by particular historical matrices and forces. Two forceful and prototypical collective female representations from Greek antiquity help to drive home this point. The central theme is that warrioring is a male affair. A woman may seek private vengeance (for example, when Clytemnestra murders her husband, Agamemnon), but it is the maternal Hecuba, mourning the death of her son and grandson, who figures more prominently in subsequent stories of women and war. The tears and mourning of women dominate: they suffer from war, but they, too, regard it as both inevitable and an arena of male combat and honor.

A fiercer noncombatant alternative is that embodied in the Spartan mother. The Spartan mother does not give way to tears and lamentations: she is the goad who urges her son to return with his shield or on it. In volume 3 of his *Moralia*, Plutarch reproduces tales, anecdotes, and epigrams that constructed the Spartan woman as a mother who rears her sons to be sacrificed on the altar of civic need. Such a martial mother, for example, is pleased to hear that her son died "in a manner worthy of herself, his country, and his ancestors than if he had lived for all time a coward" (Plutarch, 1931: 459). Sons who failed to measure up were reviled. One woman, whose son was the sole survivor of a disastrous battle, killed him with a tile, in Plutarch's account, the appropriate punishment for his obvious cowardice. To expressions of sympathy Spartan women responded with words that bespeak an unshakable civic identity. Plutarch recounts a woman, as she buried her son, telling a would-be sympathizer that she has had "good luck," not bad: "I bore him that he might die for Sparta, and this is the very thing that has come to pass for me" (463). This story of the determined

Spartan mother, a civic militant, devoted above all else to *polis* or *la patrie* is one enduring feature in the western story of women and war.

But there are other figures that rise to dominance with the triumph of Christianity in the West. The warrior's task becomes a more ambivalent one, at least theologically and theoretically speaking. The woman's mission is powerfully shaped by the image of the Madonna, the mater dolorosa, suffering the loss of her son rather than cheering him to glory. Unlike the stern Spartan mother, the suffering mother is cast in the role of a victim of war. She may support the war of her country, but she mourns rather than exults over the deaths of sons. Over the long sweep of western history, the mourning mother is one who may, in her own way, be mobilized for combat, that is to say, become available in the early modern era as a civic republican mother whose duty is to buttress and to sustain the call to arms. But this Spartan mother figure is now haunted by the more pacific figure of the mother as beautiful soul, who embodies verities and virtues at odds with the clamor and killing of war. This is the mother who laments and protects and regrets and mourns. Finding in the paths of peace the most desirable way of being, she exalts a pacific alternative. Ironically, of course, she does so from a stance that has historically been civically denuded. Absent from the ranks of warriors and leaders, she had to exert her influence in other ways and through other forms, often religious, sometimes sentimental. No doubt the anthropologist would also remind us of the fact that the imperative to protect the childbearers is a deep exigency of the human race. That is, there are some good evolutionary reasons to keep women out of the thick of things. But with modern war much of this was to change. To be sure, women remained noncombatants, overwhelmingly so, but they could now be attacked not just by marauding bands and occupying forces but by long-range weapons of siege warfare and, in our own century, by bombs dropped on cities. Even as warfare grew more total, women's involvement in war fragmented into multiple possibilities—all of them, however, making contact, one way or another, with antique and medieval models.

Renaissance and Early Modern Warfare

With Spartan mothers and beautiful souls framing the story, the historical development of warfare in the Renaissance and early modern periods contains few surprises. Women play their multiple parts. But they are still peripheral to the main story. For example, the historian J. R. Hale's entry for "women" in his *Artists and Warfare in the Renaissance* (1990) reads "(see Atrocities, Baggage Train, Camp Followers,

Encampment Scenes, Sex, Wives)" (277). Following up on these hints, one encounters a few specifics of an old tale: women as victims of war (atrocities), as sufferers of their men's wars (wives), and as the disreputable but ever-present provisioners of material supplies and sex (baggage train, camp followers, encampment scenes, sex). These latter do not occupy an honorable place in the iconography and dominant narratives of the western way of war. From the rape of the Sabine women to modern use of rape as a weapon of war in the Balkans, the dark underside of women and war is a persistent counterpoint but, like the rare female combatant, is regarded by most military historians more as the exception than the rule. This assessment should not be used to gloss over the pervasive presence of women in war or at least in the general field over which the drama of war is played.

Depictions of caravans by Renaissance artists routinely feature women as dispensers of drink, medicines, food, and solace of both a maternal and a carnal nature. Wives followed husbands in campaigns, and wherever there were soldiers there were camp followers. With the coming of state-dominated, conscripted, disciplined standing armies, the loose congeries that characterized premodern warfare—a ragtag agglomeration of fighting men, speculators, provisioners, wives, prostitutes, and animals—gave way to a far more restrictive enterprise. Wives were kept out of it. Sex never could be, of course, but attempts were made to restrict "fraternization" and to discourage lingering or long-term relationships with off-base women, whether domestic or foreign. Women in war were there to serve the men, one way or another, but they were overshadowed by the prototypical figures already discussed.

The Modern State, Women, and War

Once one arrives at the nation-state in its modern form, one finds congealed the notion of the woman as a collective noncombatant, and by the late eighteenth century strong distinctions between men and women in regard to violence were the prevailing norm. Male violence had been moralized into fighting the "just war"—and observing the rules of war—but female violence lay outside the boundary of normal expectation. When the latter occurred, it was seen as disruptive and personal whereas male violence in time of war could be orderly and rule-governed. At the same time, very sharp cleavages emerged between personal life and public life, between family and state. Women were the guardians of the family; men were the protectors of the state. Through the lens of these constructions, men saw edifying tales of courage, duty, honor, and glory as they engaged in heroic acts of protection and defense and daring. Women saw edifying stories of nobility, sacrifice, duty, and quiet immortality as they engaged in nonheroic defensive acts of protection and care. To be sure, the emergence of total war in the modern era threw irritants into this picture—scenes of leveled cities, refugees clogging highways, starvation, and disease. But the force of received understandings never lost its resonance. To this day, the phrase "the deaths of innocent women and children" springs to the lips of observers when they want to describe the authentic horror of wartime destruction. Women, then, remain noncombatants, outside the circle of collective violence, even as the history of twentieth-century warfare places them at the epicenter of war's destruction—quite literally in the case of the terror bombing of German cities in World War II and the dropping of the atomic bombs on Hiroshima and Nagasaki. Moreover, women bring themselves more forcefully into the picture not as they were in the premodern era but as irregulars and partisans, as bomb-throwers and assassins, as provocateurs and spies, and, finally, as combatants in uniform, subject to military requirements and discipline.

Women and Modern War

The story of women mobilized for modern war predates World War I. Much of the U.S. Civil War—particularly for women of the Confederacy—is a story of stolid suffering and indefatigable patriotism, all necessary to pursue the war effort. Indeed, General Sherman's notorious insistence that in order for the forces of the Union to pursue the war to a successful conclusion, it would be necessary to "make the women of Georgia howl." The point was to break the will of the South, and it was necessary to demoralize southern women, Spartan mothers of their time, in order to undermine the war effort overall. Southern women cursed the foe, agitated on the home front, and "rushed out of their homes" to champion the Confederate cause by stimulating enlistments (one historian notes that "the cowards were between two fires,... the Federals at the front...the women in the rear"), creating relief and soldiers' aid societies, providing individual and collective examples of martial enthusiasm and religious faith in the southern cause, and receiving the "enemy" with hatred and invective (Simkins and Patton, 1936: 17). Northern women were pressed into patriotic service too, of course, but the drama was most visible on the southern side for it was their "homeland" that was invaded and occupied. Perhaps the most famous Spartan mother on the northern side was one Mrs. Bixby, who received a letter from President Abraham Lincoln that became a classic: he wrote to this mother of five slain soldier sons of "the solemn

pride that must be yours to have laid so costly a sacrifice upon the altar of freedom."

When the opening salvos of World War I were fired, women no less than men were swept up in patriotic fervor. In Great Britain, women formed long lines to sign up for the Women's Emergency Corps. Relief committees were set up all over the country. Young women could be seen shaming young men not in uniform by handing out white feathers as a symbol of their cowardice. Spartan mothers sprang up everywhere, trouncing pacifism and faintheartedness. One Mrs. F. S. Hallowes, in her book *Mothers of Men and Militarism* (1918), noted women's equally "passionate love of mother-country.... Though we loathe slaughter we find that after men have done their best to kill and wound, women are ever ready to mend the broken bodies, soothe the dying, and weep over nameless graves." The suffragists in England and the United States, where these efforts were most visible and highly developed, gave themselves over to the war effort—with a few notable exceptions. The newspaper of the Women's Social and Political Union in Britain was renamed *Brittania* and dedicated to king and country. The National American Women's Suffrage Association in the United States prepared itself for U.S. entry into the war as early as 1914 by proclaiming a readiness to serve in a variety of detailed capacities in the event of war. Among the departments of work the association declared its willingness to undertake were employment bureaus for women's war work, increase of the food supply, the Red Cross, and integrating "eight millions of aliens" into the American way of life. Politically active women of the Triple Entente powers often justified the war on liberal internationalist grounds: the world will be safe only when democracy defeats autocracy.

Although women were separated from combat, they did serve in a variety of capacities, most notably as field nurses, a job created as honorable and necessary in the nineteenth century. This put many women closer to the point of actual combat but simultaneously reaffirmed the view of women as healers, not fighters. Women also served as couriers, and the occasional notorious spy turned up (Mata-Hari being the most infamous and glamorous). At the same time, the war also occasioned an outburst of antiwar activity by women. To such activists, opposition to war was a logical continuance of the suffrage campaign, which to their minds meant humanizing governments by extending the vote to women. For example, in the United States, a Women's Peace Party was formed. At its height some 40,000 women were involved. The Women's Peace Party was one section of the Women's International Committee for Permanent Peace, later to become the Women's International League for Peace and Freedom. After the war, women were pressed for the Kellogg-Briand Pact of 1928, declaring war illegal, and served as members of the National Committee on the Cause and Cure of War, which collected 10 million signatures on a disarmament petition in 1932.

Women rose to the surface in yet more dramatic ways in World War II. Nobody knows how many women participated actively in resistance movements in Nazi-occupied Europe. Saywell (1985) claims that "tens of thousands" of women were involved in the French Resistance alone, as "couriers, spies, saboteurs and armed fighters." In France, "in the tradition of Joan of Arc, women led partisan units into battle.... During the liberation of Paris women fought in the streets with men." Some women members of the armed services, recalling events many years later, remain vexed by restrictions on what they could and could not do—for example, women pilots for Britain's Air Transport Auxiliary—as others detail wartime camaraderie and equality with men. French Resistance fighters and Soviet women regulars thought of themselves as "comrades...soldiers...just the same as the [men]" (67, 146).

One of the least-told tales of World War II is that of Soviet women in combat. Soviet women formed the only regular female combat forces during the war, serving as snipers, machine gunners, artillery women, and tank women. Their peak strength was reached at the end of 1943, at which time it was estimated at 800,000 to 1,000,000, or some 8 percent of the total number of military personnel. Soviet women also formed three air regiments and participated in minesweeping actions. According to a recent historian, the women's "instruction, equipment, and ultimate assignment were identical to those of their male counterparts. There is nothing in the designation of the regiments that were later formed out of the 122nd [the women's air group]—the 586th Fighter Regiment, the 587th Bomber Regiment, and the 588th Air Regiment—to indicate that these were female units" (Noggle, 1994: 9). Ground crews attached to these regiments included large numbers of women as well. In the aftermath of the war, 92 women combatants received the title Hero of the Soviet Union, and about one-third of these were airwomen. It should be noted that women who served in this capacity were volunteers but, unlike their U.S. counterparts—the WASPS, or Women Airforce Service Pilots—they were not restricted to noncombatant activity. One of these Soviet bomber pilots, when asked to recount her wartime experience, uses classic language of force, familiar to all soldiers in all wars: "They were destroying us and we were destroying them.... That is the

logic of war.... I killed many men, but I stayed alive. War requires the ability to kill, among other skills. But I don't think you should equate killing with cruelty. I think the risks we took and the sacrifices we made for each other made us kinder rather than cruel" (Cottam, 1980; Saywell, 1985). Despite this quite rare experiment—given the numbers of women involved and the tasks to which they were assigned—after the war the Soviet Union returned to the standard model, with women designated as noncombatants. At the time of the demise of the Soviet Union as a geopolitical entity, women played a marginal role in its army, primarily in secretarial capacities.

Far more important in World War II were those women called on to manage the home front. Some women were direct victims of the war—women in bombed-out Germany, occupied France, and eastern Europe—but nearly all women in the combatant nations found their lives touched by this most extensive of all modern wars. Women entered factory war work to make up for the "manpower shortage" with so many men off to combat. Women had to make do through shortages and deprivations of all kinds.

Meeting adversity head-on signified what the home front helpmeet was all about. Mothers who sacrificed their sons to the war were honored in all combatant nations. In the United States, for example, women who lost a son received a "gold star" from their government and were officially designated "gold star mothers." Dramatic imagery of "mother-home-homeland" was part of the rhetoric and propaganda of all nations as ancient myths and memories mingled with modern realities. Perhaps the most dramatic instance was Stalin's call to his people to fight the fascist invader: not in the name of communism but for "Holy Mother Russia." There was little doubt in Stalin's mind, it seems, about what icon carried the most patriotic clout.

Women and War since World War II

The story of women and war in the second half of the twentieth century is not a single story, but many. Europe, worn out by war, turned to commerce and cold war politics under the nuclear umbrella of the United States. It was difficult to generate any enthusiasm for war, and the question of women's role in combat was not an urgent one. More exigent by far, for many women, was fear of nuclear war. Crisscrossing with forms of feminist protest, large numbers of women protested nuclear dangers, often in flamboyant and dramatic ways—by creating "Women's Peace Camps" in Great Britain and the United States, for example. As noted, women in the Soviet Union were demobilized and political circumstances did not permit their political mobilization, either to support war or to protest it. In the United States, feminism cut a number of ways—both for and against war and women's participation in it. This latter story, together with the participation of women in anticolonial struggles and, more recently, nationalistic upheavals, is an important and interesting development in the saga of women and war.

The story of women's deepening involvement in the armed services of the world's one remaining superpower is a tangled tale of competing forms of feminist (and antifeminist) politics. The United States had a higher proportion of women in its armed forces in 1999 than did any other industrial nation, around 12 percent of an overall force of nearly two million. This rise in the number of female soldiers is extraordinary. By the middle of 1948, the figure for women was down to approximately 8,000—about 0.25 percent of the total, given postwar demobilization. The Persian Gulf War of 1991 not only put more women in uniform closer to combat than ever before in the history of the United States but also was a definitive signal that the United States was willing to put more women officially in war danger zones than any other major industrial country.

Israel, for example, often thought of as a country with "women soldiers," exempts all married women from the military and reserves, and women in the Israeli Defense Forces have no combat duties on land or sea. It should be noted that U.S. society at the turn of the twenty-first century was divided on the matter. Although 74 percent of women and 71 percent of men favored sending women on combat missions, 64 percent overall rejected sending mothers of young children into the war zone (NBC/Wall Street Journal poll). But mothers of children as young as 6 weeks were called up and deployed in the Gulf. This action prompted a debate concerning the welfare of children, especially infants, and what baneful effects might result if they were torn from the primary parent. (The estimate is that some 17,500 children were left without a custodial parent during the Gulf War.) But that debate was short-circuited in the general fervor concerning "our men and women in the Gulf."

The figures on actual participation are lopsided in favor of men. Women were 9 percent of the overall force in Operation Desert Storm. Women served as supply pilots, mechanics, police officers, ordinance workers, and the usual array of clerical, nursing, and support workers. Several women were taken prisoner and lived to tell the tale, in language familiar to all students of war. For example, Major Rhonda Cornum, a surgeon and helicopter pilot, discussed her own views of being in war: "Being killed doing an honorable thing like defending my country wasn't the worst end I could envision." She did not want to be a coward, she said, and she feared that her own daughter would think she "was a wimp if I stayed home" (Copeland, 1992). Perhaps, after the humiliation and distress occasioned by the Vietnam debacle, the people of the United States were prepared to hear upbeat tales of heroism from women who were fighting the enemy rather than mending mangled and broken bodies in often unbearable circumstances—the stories Vietnam-era nurses brought back with them.

Although women's participation in the Persian Gulf War was, in actual numbers, quite small by comparison with that of the men deployed and put in harm's way, enthusiasm for eliminating nearly extinct "combat exclusion" rules waxed in 1992 and 1993. The result was that the U.S. Navy began integrating women into its combat fleet in March 1994. Although women made up less than 10 percent of the 5,500-member crew of the aircraft carrier *Eisenhower,* they paved the way for further infusion of women into the combat fleet. The Air Force and Navy also opened the door for female combat pilots—another first—in 1994. At the end of the twentieth century women were not yet permitted to serve as ground combat troops or in the special forces. These final limitations, based on mission philosophy and necessary physical ability, especially upper body strength, are unacceptable to those most committed to seeing women in every combat role.

Will the twenty-first century see the curtain close on the male-female, combatant-noncombatant issue so strenuously interwoven with the way modern nations have made war, so earnestly reincoded from generation to generation, so clearly etched into the legal codes of nations and the ethical codes of peoples? That is unlikely. Even in the United States, embarked as it is on a nearly unprecedented experiment in this regard, ambivalence runs deep. Although some female officers see combat slots as a way to move up the ranks to officer positions, only 10 percent of military women overall consider ineligibility for combat roles a "very important" issue and only "one in nine would volunteer for such duty" ("Door Opens," 1991). For the vast majority of women in the U.S. all-volunteer force, the risks of combat far outweigh any potential benefits. Undoubtedly this has been the view held by the overwhelming majority of young men historically, too. The difference, of course, is that they have had little or no choice in the matter.

There have always been those who declared that war would one day, perhaps soon, become obsolete, in part because human beings would simply cease to be able to bear the destruction that war trailed in its wake. That seems not to have deterred the human race, and there is little likelihood that it will be a determent in the early twenty-first century. In fact, if anything, there are now doctrines generating a gender politics that would eradicate societies' traditional ways of trying to limit war's damage—by erecting a barrier between combatants and noncombatants. If women are no longer designated noncombatants, a designation that did not spare them altogether but did have a discernible effect in taming war's fury, what new barriers might arise? Perhaps a distinction between "civilians" and "war fighters," whatever the gender. This, of course, lacks the texture and depth of the centuries-old division by gender. It will probably not yield iconography, myth, story, and song to the same extent, but it may one day operate as well as the old gender divide. It is very difficult to say.

What is easier to conjure with is the fact that in the matter of women and war a vast array of options, many of them unattractive, will continue to present themselves. Women were not spared in the mass killings by machete in Rwanda. Women were not killed in as large numbers as men in the war raging in the Balkans, but, whether as noncombatants being shelled in cities or as victims singled out for brutalization, they have had war forced upon them in the most horrendous ways. Palestinian women have long been in the fight for full-fledged statehood for their people. In the successor microstates to the Soviet Union, women, so far as one can tell, are no less nationalistic or chauvinistic than men, whether in the name of defense or offense. Ironically, it is in the postindustrial western democracies that, at one and the same time, a highly developed "peace politics" generated by religious women and one strand of feminism clashes with a "realpolitik" sustained by yet another strand of feminism. Although at one point citizen and soldier were tightly tethered in western history, this is no longer the case. But we continue to honor soldiers who behave honorably. The difference is that we can expect women to number among them in a way we could not in the past. Whether this is progress or not is a judgment to make, but it is definitely a change. How significant the change is remains to be seen. One is struck, looking back on this long history, by the ways in which symbols and themes recur, and the number of combatants in the armies of nation-states remains minuscule compared with the number who continue to carry out those daily tasks of sustenance, care, and perseverance with which women have always been associated.

See Also

ARMAMENT AND MILITARIZATION; MILITARY; PEACEKEEPING; VIOLENCE AND PEACE: OVERVIEW

References and Further Reading

Copeland, Peter. 1992. *She went to war: The Rhonda Cornum story.* Novato, Calif.: Presidio.

Cottam, K. Jean. 1980. Soviet women in combat in World War II: The ground forces and the navy. *International Journal of Women's Studies* 3(14): 345–357.

Elshtain, Jean Bethke. 1987. *Women and war.* New York: Basic Books.

Hale, J. R. 1990. *Artists and warfare in the Renaissance.* New Haven, Conn.: Yale University Press.

Hallowes, F. S. 1918. *Mothers of men and militarism.* London: Headley/Bishopsgate.

NBC/Wall Street Journal poll. *Public Perspective* 2(3: Mar.–Apr.): 87.

Noggle, Anne. 1994. *A dance with death: Soviet airwomen in World War II.* College Station, Tex.: Texas A & M University Press.

Plutarch. 1931. *Moralia.* Vol. 3. Trans. Frank Cole Babbitt. Cambridge, Mass.: Harvard University Press.

Saywell, Shelley. 1985. *Women in war.* New York: Viking.

Simkins, Francis Butler, and James Welch Patton. 1936. *The women of the Confederacy.* Richmond: Garrett and Massie.

Door opens for women, but not all the way. 1991. *USA Today* (28 July): 11A.

Jean Bethke Elshtain

WATER

Water is the lifeblood of the planet. In the same way that it covers most of the Earth, water makes up the the greatest percentage of all living matter. The liquid oxide of hydrogen, it is a vital solvent that bathes us at both a cellular and an organismal level and that connects all living things. Water is the element that mixes with both earth and air. It descends from clouds as rain; forms streams, lakes, and seas; and regulates our climate because of its ability to retain heat. It is the giver of green, of growth, of crops, of abundance, of life.

Lao Tsu wrote in the *Tao Te Ching:* "Water always seeks the lowest level, and enters the most despised places, yet gives life to the ten thousand things."

Water shares much imagery with the feminine: giving birth (the concept of a primal body of water from which everything is derived is prevalent in many coastal cultures), nourishing (water is often equated with blood), sustaining (life could not exist without it), supportive (buoying up), healing (cleansing and refreshing), soothing (offering comfort and relief), and yielding.

In many cultures, bodies of water, especially rivers, are associated with the feminine or with goddesses. In India, many rivers are considered "women without husbands." Offerings are made to river deities out of gratitude for abundance. A large class of inferior female divinities are the water nymphs. Associated with springs, rivers, fountains, and lakes, the nymphs or naiads are usually represented as beautiful, young, lighthearted, and beneficent. More wily and seductive are the fabled mermaids, female spirits of the sea, with the upper body of a woman and the tail of a fish. Mermaids are considered magical and often are said to seduce sailors with their singing.

In most cultures throughout history—and in many still today—women have been the main procurers of water. Because women are primarily responsible for domestic chores, family sanitation and hygiene, and caring for the sick, they, more than men, have been designated "water carriers" (collectors, transporters, haulers, storers, and distributors) and often spend more than half of their day traveling to and from a water source. Research has shown that women who carry water all of their lives often become disfigured or suffer serious health problems.

As women do the unforgiving work of society, water does the often slow but constant reworking of the planet, by erosion and deposition. It is water that shapes the physical landscape on both small and large scales, as it simultaneously nourishes living matter (also from the *Tao:* "Though yielding, water can wear down a stone and find its way in where tools could not").

In her poem "A River of Women," from her collection *Holy Water,* Pat Mora writes, "The River of women penetrates boulders, climbs / crags jagged as hate, / weaves through clawing thorns / to depths parched, shriveled / offers ripples of hope."

See Also

EARTH; ECOFEMINISM; ENVIRONMENT: OVERVIEW; NATURAL RESOURCES; NATURE

References and Further Reading

Feldhaus, Anne. 1995. *Water and womanhood: Religious meanings of rivers in Maharashtra.* New York: Oxford University Press.

Mora, Pat. 1995. *Agua santa, holy water.* Boston: Beacon.

Women and water. Domestic shallow well water supplies: The family handpump scenario. 1989. In *Proceedings of Regional Seminar,* Manila, 29 August–1 September. Asian Development Bank and UN Developmental Program.

Women's issues in water and sanitation. Attempts to address an age-old challenge. 1987. In *Proceedings Series.* Ottawa: IDRC.

Lynne Fessenden

WEDDINGS

Within patriarchal societies, weddings are highly organized rituals that signal readiness for membership in marriage as an organizing practice for the institution of heterosexuality. Their history varies cross-culturally according to religion, region, and social order. In cultures where women have few civil rights in relation to men, weddings symbolize a woman's exchange value in patriarchal or patrilineal property relations. Weddings are highly ritualized practices laden with symbolism that demonstrates the worth of the bride and of the pending marriage.

In societies in which women experience higher levels of equity with men, weddings carry fewer markers of "woman as property," and these are frequently reframed to fit today's social norms. For example, whereas fathers formerly "gave away" the bride to the groom in what was considered bride exchange or property exchange, this ritual has been modified to some degree to incorporate different interpretations of the celebration of the marriage and of new kinship arrangements. Frequently, both parents or a sibling will perform the "giving away," and it is done with great sentimentality that marks the ritual as a rite of passage to womanhood and independence. Additionally, the practice of taking the groom's family name, long taken for granted, has become more optional, particularly among women in the professional-managerial class.

In advanced capitalist societies, the wedding has become highly consumption-oriented. The average wedding in the United States, for example, costs nearly $20,000, and the wedding industry averages $32 billion in revenues each year. Symbolically, such weddings have become spectacles of accumulation that provide the couple's community with evidence of their promise as members of their upwardly mobile social class.

Billed in contemporary capitalism as the "most important day in a woman's life," the consumption-oriented wedding, at the extreme, is supported by nothing less than a wedding-industrial complex, rife with ideological baggage and antifeminist backlash. As depicted in contemporary popular culture in western societies, the wedding represents a Disney-like "happily ever after" experience that reinforces racial, gender, sexuality, and class hierarchies. The "tradition" of the white wedding gown, rooted in recent British history from Queen Victoria to Princess Diana, has been marketed so successfully that women in India, Pakistan, Japan, and various parts of Africa are shedding their traditional wedding attire for the white gown or, in some instances, wearing both white and traditional dress alternately during the wedding.

With the exception of royal marriages, weddings have evolved from simple ceremonies for bride exchange and establishment of kinship bonds into what some observers see as symbolic expressions of wealth and accumulation. From this point of view, the ideology of romance is invoked to create an illusion of desire and well-being that secures the interests of the powerful. Weddings have become a site for enacting the rules for social differentiation while placing less emphasis on the investment of the state and religious institutions in preserving a patriarchal social order.

See Also

MARRIAGE: REGIONAL TRADITIONS AND PRACTICES

References and Further Reading

Ingraham, Chrys. 1999. *White weddings: Romancing heterosexuality in popular culture.* New York: Routledge.

Chrys Ingraham

WELFARE

One of the striking phenomena of the past hundred years has been the expansion of the welfare state in industrialized countries. Definitions of the welfare state diverge concerning the scope of provision of benefits and services, but a common denominator is state responsibility for the well-being of its citizens. In the view of Lois Bryson, a welfare state can be defined as a nation that "has at least a minimum level of institutionalized provisions for meeting the basic economic and social requirements of its citizens" (1992: 36). Both the nature of the social minimum and the scope of state responsibility have been issues of political dispute, and the outcomes of these disputes account for the shifting boundaries of welfare states. The questions of whether state policies enhance women's welfare and the nature of women's relationships to the welfare state are highly contested issues in feminist analysis. One body of writings portrays the state as an instrument of repression that regulates women's lives.

Other feminists emphasize contradictions in both the outcomes of state policies and women's relationship to the state. Still others stress the emancipatory potential of state policies for women. A more recent discussion has focused on women as collective actors in the making and restructuring of welfare states.

State Policies and Women's Welfare

Radical and neo-Marxist feminists have viewed the state as a force maintaining male domination in society. For radical feminists, the state is a form of public patriarchy. In the eyes of neo-Marxist feminists, the state serves the interests of capitalists, and patriarchy is inseparable from capitalism. These views share a conception of the state as an instrument of women's oppression, and social welfare policies are no exception. Elizabeth Wilson writes, "Social welfare policies amount to no less than the state organization of domestic life. Women encounter state repression within the very bosom of the family" (quoted in Pascall, 1986: 34). One argument of these feminists is that a major function of the welfare state is social control. The rise of a welfare state bureaucracy and male-dominated professions has usurped women's authority in the domestic sphere—and transferred control to men. Furthermore, welfare state policies reinforce women's dependency on men and reproduce the traditional social division of labor between the sexes in the family and society. Feminist literature has documented how income maintenance and tax policies have reinforced the position of married women as dependents of their husbands (Bryson, 1992; Gordon, 1990; Pascall, 1986).

A basic objection to this view of the state and state policies is that women's welfare has changed over time and varies in different national contexts. To capture these variations, an entirely negative view of the state has given way to a position that does not rule out state measures having positive effects—both unintended or by design—for women's well-being. Gradually, many feminists have moved from assuming that state intervention sustains the sexual division of labor and gender hierarchies to considering the ways in which such intervention might alter these conditions. Nonetheless, much feminist scholarship is characterized by an ambivalence toward the state, and the contradictory consequences of policies for women are stressed. Carole Pateman underscores the patriarchal nature of the welfare state. Most social rights are based on typical male activities—primarily paid labor but also soldiering. To gain these rights, women must deny their identities and capacities as women and mothers by engaging in male tasks, which disadvantage women in relation to men. Simultaneously the patriarchal welfare state, through social benefits, can eliminate women's economic dependence on individual men (Pateman, 1988: 250–252). Contradictions also emerge in Helga Hernes's writings on the Scandinavian state form and its impact on women. On the one hand, she describes it as a "tutelary state for women" because corporatist arrangements of negotiation deny women access to the political process. On the other hand, Hernes also depicts it as a "women-friendly state" or a potentially women-friendly state—a state that would "enable women to have a natural relationship to the children, their work, and public life" (Hernes, 1987: 15, 35, 135–137). Among the features contributing to a women-friendly state are the mobilization of women through the state and the public sector, decentralization of the welfare state to the local level, and the ideologies of equality and universalism.

A third perspective has attached more weight to the possible emancipatory effects of state policies. The argument that social entitlements can reduce market inequalities has been recast to explore how social rights can undermine gender inequalities. Ann Orloff points out that welfare states must be assessed in terms of two criteria: (1) whether policies allow women to form and maintain an autonomous household, and (2) whether they promote women's access to paid work (1993: 318–319). In another vein, Diane Sainsbury (1996) argues that the bases of entitlement—the principles of eligibility—are crucial to whether welfare policies buttress women's dependency or enhance their autonomy. More specifically, married women's dependency is reinforced when benefits are "familialized." In social insurance schemes where the family is the unit of benefit and the beneficiary is the head of the family, married women have no social rights. Entitlements based on need also usually have the family as the unit of benefit. Eligibility for means-tested benefits is calculated according to the resources of all members of the household. Likewise, married women's dependency is embedded in social provision when they are beneficiaries, but their entitlements stem from their husband's rights. By contrast, benefits based on citizenship or residence are individual rights and negate the importance of family relationships in determining social entitlements. Nor does this basis of entitlement favor paid work in relation to domestic labor. Social rights based on people's status in the labor market also have the potential to enhance women's autonomy, especially when these rights are complemented with employment-enabling policies.

Women's Relationships to the Welfare State

Women's relationship to the welfare state has been conceptualized in several ways. Feminists who have viewed the state as an instrument of oppression underline that women are primarily objects of policy. They are "policy takers," or recipients, and their relationship to the welfare state has been largely analyzed in terms of dependency and social control. Other analytical perspectives, utilizing the categories of "claims" and "status," conceptualize women as claimants and actors. These perspectives also highlight the complexities and multiplicity in women's relationships to the state. Generalizing on the basis of the Scandinavian experience, Helga Hernes (1987: 37–38) concentrates on women's relationships as citizens, employees, and clients of the state. Decisive to women's status as citizens is the extent to which they influence issues and hold positions of power; their status as employees is shaped by the fact that the state is their major employer, and women as clients are more numerous because of their role as mothers and as a larger proportion of the elderly and sick. Other Scandinavian feminists have distinguished an additional category, that is, women as consumers of public services, specifically to differentiate women in this position from clients. They argue that this is of fundamental significance to women's welfare because a strong public service sector lessens the likelihood of women's becoming solely dependent on the state as a client. Finally, women's relationships to the welfare state in their capacity as mothers have been studied (for example, Koven and Michel, 1993; Sainsbury, 1996). These studies serve as a corrective to the assumption that welfare state policies are directed only to workers.

Helga Hernes's conception of women's citizenship in welfare states assigns importance to both social rights and political rights, and it has prompted a rethinking of women as political actors. Her discussion of women as citizens focuses, however, on formal influence and positions of power. Indirectly, it plays down women's activism outside the formal political process and state institutions, as well as women's struggles prior to winning the vote or gaining substantial representation in elected office.

Increasing attention has been devoted to women's activism in the making of welfare states (Gordon, 1990: 23; Orloff, 1993: 321–323). Historical research has shed light on how maternalist politics—campaigns to promote maternal and child welfare–shaped programs benefiting women and children even before women had the right to vote in the United States, France, Britain, and Germany (Koven and Michel, 1993). This research reveals the possibility of influence even when women lack positions of institutional power in the political process. In their monumental study, *Women and Politics Worldwide*, Barbara Nelson and Najma Chowdhury argue for a redefinition of politics to include public activism in everyday life in order to investigate women's influence on policies affecting their welfare and their families across nations (Nelson and Chowdhury, 1994: 16–18, 32–36).

Gendering the Analysis of the Welfare State

Feminists have criticized mainstream analysis of the welfare state because it has ignored gender. First, feminists have noted that mainstream scholarship, by focusing on class inequalities, has glossed over disparities in the social rights of the sexes. To rectify this defect, feminist researchers have detailed existing inequalities between women and men in social provision. Second, feminists have objected to the pivotal position of paid work in mainstream analytical frameworks and the neglect of unpaid labor. Frameworks of this sort block an examination of how social rights are gendered. Third, mainstream researchers have defined the private and public spheres as the market and state, respectively, a definition that deemphasizes the family. Fourth, in a similar fashion, ideology in mainstream analysis has centered on relations between state and market without considering gender and familial ideologies. Fifth, feminists have complained that the political agents in mainstream explanations of welfare state development have been restricted to social classes and that this has obfuscated women's role in the making of welfare states.

Nor has attention been devoted to how race and ethnicity intersect with gender. The feminist critique indicates what is missing and how to gender welfare state analysis. The research agenda suggested by this critique consists of analyzing the nexus between family, state, and market relations. It is necessary to examine the extent to which paid work is accorded higher status in social provision and how social provision reinforces the existing gendered division of labor where women do unpaid work (Orloff, 1993). Equally important is an examination of the dynamics between the public and private spheres and its effects on women's welfare (Pascall, 1986), paying specific attention to the public-private division of responsibility for the costs of children and care work. The research agenda also calls for incorporating the influence of gender and familial ideologies on state policies and their impact on women's welfare (Nelson and Chowdhury, 1994: 19–20; Sainsbury, 1996).

An additional point on the agenda is a more careful consideration of women's agency in the making of welfare states. Last, feminists have stressed the necessity of an analysis of welfare policies that includes how race and ethnicity intersect with gender (Bryson, 1990; Gordon, 1990; Williams, 1989).

Feminists have pursued three approaches to bring gender into the analysis of welfare states. One strategy has been to analyze core mainstream concepts to illuminate how they are gendered and their possible different implications for women and men. A second has been to attempt to build gender into existing mainstream analytical constructs (Orloff, 1993). A third course has been to devise new frameworks where gender is central (Lewis, 1992; Sainsbury, 1996). Despite dissimilar paths of inquiry, recent feminist scholarship has led to a gendering of comparative welfare state analysis. This, in turn, has provided the beginnings for an understanding of not only the differing consequences of policy variations for women's welfare across nations but also of women as collective actors in the making of welfare states.

See Also

ECONOMY: WELFARE AND THE ECONOMY

References and Further Reading

Bryson, Lois. 1992. *Welfare and the state: Who benefits?* London: Macmillan.

Gordon, Linda, ed. 1990. *Women, the state and welfare.* Madison: University of Wisconsin Press.

Hernes, Helga. 1987. *Welfare state and women power.* Oslo: Norwegian University Press.

Koven, Seth, and Sonya Michel, eds. 1993. *Mothers of a new world: Maternalist politics and the origins of welfare states.* New York: Routledge.

Lewis, Jane. 1992. Gender and the development of welfare regimes. *Journal of European Social Policy* 2: 159–173.

Nelson, Barbara J., and Najma Chowdhury, eds. 1994. *Women and politics worldwide.* New Haven, Conn.: Yale University Press.

O'Connor, Julia S., Ann Orloff, and Sheila Shaver. 1999. *States, markets, families: Gender, liberalism and social policy in Australia, Canada, Great Britain and the United States.* Cambridge: Cambridge University Press.

Orloff, Ann. 1993. Gender and the social rights of citizenship: The comparative analysis of gender relations and welfare states. *American Sociological Review* 58: 303–328.

Pascall, Gillian. 1986, 1997. *Social policy: A feminist analysis.* London: Routledge.

Pateman, Carole. 1988. The patriarchal welfare state. In Amy Gutmann, ed., *Democracy and the welfare state,* 231–260. Princeton, N.J.: Princeton University Press.

Sainsbury, Diane. 1996. *Gender, equality and welfare states.* Cambridge: Cambridge University Press.

Williams, Fiona. 1989. *Social policy: A critical introduction.* Cambridge: Polity.

Diane Sainsbury

WHITENESS

See BLACKNESS AND WHITENESS *and* RACE.

WICCA

Wicca is an earth-based religion that derives its celebrations from the seasons. It can be practiced alone as a "solitary" or in groups called "circles," "groves," or "covens." Wiccans recognize divinity in the form of Goddess; most, though not all, also recognize God, but the Wiccan God is radically different from the God of patriarchal religions. Wicca is a religion of embodiment: Goddess *is* the earth and its creatures (including humans), the stars, and the processes of life, and God is the one who dances life's spirals. Wicca is thus a religion of cycles, of change; birth, life, death, and rebirth are all sacred, and Goddess and God appear in many forms. Goddess is Maiden, Woman, and Crone, mirroring the phases of the moon and the stages of a woman's life; God may be Young God and Old God, Holly King and Oak King, reflecting the changing seasons and the life cycle. It is important to emphasize that these aspects of divinity are seen as polarities within a whole rather than as mutually exclusive dualities.

Because all matter is sacred, Wiccans find the sacred in all aspects of their lives; for example, recycling becomes a religious activity and not just a civic duty. All acts of love and pleasure are seen as rituals to celebrate divinity, and so sex in all its forms is sacred as well, which means that Wiccans are more accepting of gays, lesbians, bisexuals, transsexuals, transgender, and intersex than most. In Wicca, all practitioners are clergy; no one mediates the divine for anyone else, and all speak with equal authority, though elders are treasured for their experience. While some Wiccan traditions include three levels of initiation, most are egalitarian in their organization and practice. Wicca is an eclectic religion, and practices and beliefs can vary widely from group to group, but there are two ethical statements to which most followers would adhere: "An' it harm none, do what you will" (also known as the Wiccan Rede), and "Whatever you send out returns to you multiplied" (which means that practitioners are highly unlikely to cast harmful spells). Wiccan practice emphasizes personal responsibility and the use of one's will, not just in the practice of *magick* (a term used to distinguish the forms and practices of Wiccans and other Pagans from stage magic) but in all aspects of one's life.

History

There are many branches of Wiccan practice today, reflecting its origins and growth. Some Wiccans derive their faith from family traditions going back many generations, while others happily invent new traditions inspired by older practices. But all would agree that the contemporary rise of Wicca can be traced to Gerald Gardner, a retired English civil servant who formed his practice in the 1930s from a variety of sources, including ceremonial magick, the Order of the Golden Dawn, and Masonic ritual. Gardner claimed that he was reviving an ancient, indigenous European religion; Doreen Valiente, Gardner's most influential high priestess, has written many books that describe with greater accuracy the development of Gardnerian Wicca. Her liturgical writings for Gardner's covens serve as the basis and inspiration for many of the best-loved Wiccan rituals.

In the 1960s several of Gardner's initiates traveled to the United States to introduce the Craft to that country. More recently, Gardnerians and other Wiccans have been initiating individuals and starting groups in Germany, Norway, Denmark, Finland, Sweden, France, and the Netherlands. Word soon spread of this new religion, inspired by ancient practices, which included the Divine Feminine and encouraged individual religious responsibility. Various practitioners of family traditions were also inspired to speak about their religions for the first time, and it was in this way that Wicca became known to spiritual feminists in the United States, Canada, Australia, and elsewhere who were seeking alternatives to the patriarchal religions that used exclusively male imagery for the divine and that ignored and even devalued women's experiences.

Wicca and Feminism

Z. Budapest developed the first woman-only Wiccan tradition in the early 1970s. Often referred to as Dianic Wicca, this form of the Craft does not use God imagery and emphasizes political action as well as spiritual expression. Diane Stein was another initiator of women-centered Wicca; both women are known for their writings. Starhawk is probably the best-known Wiccan today, feminist or other. Her introduction to the Craft came from the Faery Tradition via Victor and Cora Anderson, but she added to that tradition much that she learned from the feminist movement. Starhawk's form of Wicca is now often referred to as Reclaiming Tradition, after the Reclaiming Collective that she helped to found, and is taught in many countries. The Reclaiming Tradition is not separatist, but it is undeniably feminist in its insistence on gender equity, social change, and the need to replace "power over"—the essence of hierarchies, and thus of patriarchy—with "power from within," which encourages empowerment.

Clearly, feminism has brought politics to Wicca. Many of the more traditional, or formalist, Wiccans have become uncomfortable with what they see as the feminist takeover of the Craft, claiming that women-only rituals that omit God can hardly be said to be Wiccan in nature, since they ignore the gender polarity that formalists claim is at the center of Wiccan practice. For their part, many feminist Wiccans decry what they see as a heterosexist emphasis on male-female union at the heart of formalist Wiccan ritual and beliefs. They also point to Gardner's sexist practice of insisting that the high priestess be young and beautiful and claim that since Gardner invented to suit his own purposes, so may they, and such invention in no way invalidates practice. All would agree that such discussions can enhance Wicca in the long run and that Wicca will continue in its many forms to emphasize the ethics of individual worship, causing no harm, and celebrating cycles.

See Also

GODDESS; MOTHER EARTH; SPIRITUALITY: SEXUALITY; WITCHES: WESTERN WORLD; WOMANSPIRIT

References and Further Reading

Adler, Margot. 1986. *Drawing down the moon.* Boston: Beacon.

Budapest, Zsuzsanna E. 1989. *The holy book of women's mysteries.* Oakland, Calif.: Wingbow/Bookpeople.

Crowley, Vivianne. 1996. *Wicca: The old religion in the new millennium.* San Francisco: HarperCollins.

Guiley, Rosemary Ellen. 1999. *The encyclopedia of witches and witchcraft.* 2nd ed. New York: Facts on File.

Hutton, Ronald. 2000. *The triumph of the moon: A history of modern pagan witchcraft.* Oxford: Oxford University Press.

Starhawk. 1999. *The spiral dance.* 20th anniversary ed. San Francisco: Harper and Row.

Stein, Diane. 1990. *Casting the circle.* Freedom, Calif.: Crossing.

Valiente, Doreen. 1989. *The rebirth of witchcraft.* Custer, Wash.: Phoenix.

Marilyn R. Pukkila

WIDOWHOOD

The term *widowhood* refers to the death of the spouse, the dissolution of the marital bond, and the renegotiation of social obligations and rights. Widowhood has different consequences for men and women, including social, economic, sexual, legal, and emotional. In the West, bereavement and other stresses associated with the death of a wife seem to increase the risk of mortality for men. Women, however, tend to become widows more often than men and to survive their widowhood longer.

Widowers have fewer restrictions and have more possibilities of establishing a new relationship (Lopata, 1979). Widows often are deprived of social status, economical standing, and even fundamental human rights, as are their dependent children. It is common for them to be separated from the rest of society, isolated, marked by special clothes, and subjected to degrading practices. Many cultures require the widow to shave her head (Orthodox Jewish and strict Brahman), to forgo washing (Nigeria), or to drink only water that has been used to wash her husband's body (Owen, 1996). In India, widowhood can be the most terrible thing that can happen to a woman; she is considered an inauspicious carrier of bad luck. The suicide of widows has been encouraged and glorified in India and China. *Sati* or *suttee*—widow burning—in Hindu groups required that the widow throw herself on the funerary pyre of her husband. Although illegal today, *sati* has recently been revived, raising serious concerns (Narasimham, 1990).

Most religions have rules regarding the remarriage and the chastity of widows. In addition, widows may be held responsible for the care of the soul of their husbands.

In some African and Middle Eastern societies, through a custom known as levirate, a widow is required to marry the brother of her deceased husband so that she may continue to belong to the husband's lineage. The practice of sororate, in which a widower marries his deceased wife's sister, is reported in very few societies.

In many societies, strict controls and regulations exist for widows' chastity. In some Hindu castes and certain African ethnic groups, if a widow shows any interest in the opposite sex, she is seen as a prostitute or a witch and is severely punished (Owen, 1996). This is related to property and inheritance rules. Widows seem to encounter fewer social and economic penalties in societies where access to property is equally shared and where women have achieved autonomy and high status before their widowhood. Widowhood can also have positive consequences for women in terms of personal freedom and independence, particularly when the widow has her own property or no property at all. In India, among the landless, women have more autonomy as widows.

Most western countries have programs and policies designed specifically to protect widows and orphans; in industrializing countries, where pensions are available to only a privileged few, those monies that are available are grossly inadequate or are even seized by the in-laws. A widow's access to pensions often depends on her husband's occupation and social standing. For example, in Israel, where widows are subject to a combination of modern laws and ancient leviratic customs, preference can be given to army or police widows.

Many widows have begun to organize, both locally and on an international level, to address the breaches in human rights for widows all over the world and to begin to alleviate the financial, emotional, and physical suffering that comes with widowhood.

See Also

DEATH; MARRIAGE: OVERVIEW *and* REMARRIAGE; SUTTEE (SATI)

References and Further Reading

Lopata, Helena Znaniecka. 1979. *Women as widows: Support systems.* New York: Elsevier.

Narasimhan, Sakuntala. 1990. *Sati: Widow burning in India.* New York: Anchor.

Owen, Margaret. 1996. *A world of widows.* Atlantic Highlands, N.J.: Zed.

Potash, Betty. 1986. *Widows in African societies: Choices and constraints.* Stanford, Calif.: Stanford University Press.

Patricia Tovar

WIFE

The term *wife* refers to a woman who has undergone a marriage ritual, linking her to a man (or men) who will be her husband, and whose status has jural, sexual, and social rights and obligations that are socially and juridically enforced. Upon marriage, a woman's primary role identification shifts from that of daughter to wife, and the ceremony often marks the formation of a new household. Many societies assign domestic responsibilities to wives as a correlation of their customary obligation to care for infants and young children, and these responsibilities often reduce their status. Elizabeth Croll (1985) relates that the word in Chinese for "wife," *neiran,* means "inside person," a clear reflection of women's household duties. Other societies emphasize other "wifely duties." Ancient Hebraic tradition required a wife to produce a male heir; to do so would ensure her status and help guarantee that her husband would not divorce her, as he could a barren wife.

Matrilocal societies, in which women remain with their matrilineal descent group after marriage, tend to confer more authority upon women than do patrilocal societies (such as traditional China and India), where a woman leaves to live with her in-laws. Part of the reason for her greater authority is that a wife is not at the mercy of her husband's family, as she is in patrilocal systems, in which she is often perceived as an interloper.

Social sanctions are sometimes used against a man who mistreats his wife or insults a woman. Among the Pokot of east Africa, women shame an offending man by ridiculing him, exposing his genitals, grabbing him and urinating or defecating upon him. Fear of such sanctions is often enough to keep men in line (Edgerton and Conant, 1964). However, many other societies offer no such outlet to wives and, in addition, often permit men unequal access to divorce or separation. In traditional Chinese society, a man could divorce his wife, but a woman so divorced was shamed. In India, a wife's role is one of implicit obedience, because she, as a subordinate, both female and typically much younger than her husband, is obliged to respect the wishes of her husband in this gender and age-graded society.

Inheritance and marriage payments also often determine a wife's position in the household. Although some observers have interpreted bride-price as the purchase of a woman, bride-price is more correctly the compensation a groom pays to the bride's father for her absence as well as the fee a man pays for rights to her future children. A woman so regarded is honored and the match thought well made, but above all else, the payment is a kind of collateral in the marriage, which is then not easily dismantled.

Bride-price is the norm throughout Africa and Oceania and is the most common form of marriage payment, although it is not associated with high status for wives. A related type of "transaction" is bride service, a period of service to the bride's parents performed by the groom. In this case, the man's labor pays for rights to the woman, but the transaction is continually negotiated during the period of coresidence in the bride's natal household.

Dowry, a woman's inheritance acquired at the time of marriage, is different from bride wealth in several respects. First, property remains within the stem family rather than being transferred to in-laws; it has been theorized that this stipulation is a woman's insurance that she will be able to care for her future children and that the capital will serve to attract a mate of similar economic standing. Second, where dowry is common, in nation-states such as those in Europe and in India, great emphasis is placed upon the chastity of the bride. It has been proposed that bridal virginity serves to ensure that children will belong to the patrilineage. Where material resources are scarce, as in western Sicily, bridal chastity may even be an important element of family patrimony, perhaps supplanting the transfer of property. In other words, the bride is, in essence, the "property" being trans-acted (Schneider, 1971).

See Also

References and Further Reading

Croll, Elizabeth. 1985. The sexual division of labor in rural China. In Lourdes Beneria, ed., *Women and development: The sexual division of labor in rural societies.* New York: Praeger.

Edgerton, Robert, and Francis Conant. 1964. Kilipat: The "shaming party" among the Pokot of east Africa. *Southwestern Journal of Anthropology* 20: 404–419.

Schneider, Jane. 1971. Of vigilance and virgins. *Ethnology* 9: 1–24.

Maria Ramona Hart

WIFE-BEATING

See BATTERY *and* DOMESTIC VIOLENCE.

WITCHES: Asia

The persecution of women as witches in Christian Europe is well known, and women have also been identified with witches in Asian communities influenced by Christianity, for example the Philippines (Lieban, 1967). But this identification is not confined to areas influenced by Christianity; it is widespread across Asia among peoples historically called tribal and now often referred to as indigenous. In these regions, there are also specific situations in which both women and men are considered witches.

Background: Analyses of Witchcraft

In traditional anthropology, the phenomenon of witches was related to maintaining social stability. Later, witchcraft and witch-hunting came to be seen as a symptom of social change; thus, for example, spirit cults associated with witchcraft in southeast Asia could be considered women's rebellion against male authority (Wijeyewardene, 1970). Feminist analysis has further changed the approach to witches and witchcraft, introducing questions of sex, the body, and the self (Purkiss, 1996), and this feminist perspective can be extended to gender relations and changes in gender relations.

From the feminist viewpoint, witch-hunting and denunciation of women as witches are related to attempts to declare certain forms of women's knowledge, mainly ritual knowledge, evil. As in other analyses, this can be seen as rebellion by women who are not allowed to possess such knowledge; or it can be seen as an attempt by the male denouncers to change an established order in which women alone had authority, or women and men had joint authority, to an order based on male authority—witch-hunting, then, can be a rebellion by men.

In the anthropological literature, spirits and witches have been analyzed as peripheral, marginal, or nonstructural (Lewis, 1996; Douglas, 1966); but witchcraft was once central—it was driven to the periphery, or underground, by persecution and defeat. The association of women with witches is, then, part of a "demonization" of women. Demonization takes many forms: it can be physical, for example, as when the female body is considered unclean or women's sexual attractiveness is considered destructive; and it can be spiritual, as when women are considered incapable of knowing, or unfit to know, sacred texts.

Here we will look at denunciation of women as witches and as keepers of demons among several indigenous peoples in India (Austro-Asiatic speakers of the Jharkhand region), China (Tibeto-Burman speakers of Yunnan), and southeast Asia (Thai speakers).

The Extent of Witchcraft

In the Jharkhand region of India, especially among the Santhal and other Austro-Asiatic peoples like the Munda and the Ho, witch-hunting was widespread enough in the eighteenth and nineteenth centuries to be frequently commented on by British colonial officials (such as Colonel Dalton and W. G. Archer) and European missionaries (such as Paul Bodding and J. Hoffman). Although witchcraft took place on a smaller scale in the twentieth century, it was evidently still not uncommon. As late as the 1990s, there were still reports of women being killed as witches. During the 1990s in several districts of Jharkhand, Bihar, there were evidently hundreds of such killings. In one district of India, Malda, police figures indicate that at least 46 people were killed as witches in the period 1950–1980—and these were, of course, only those cases that came to the notice of the police.

In China before communism, "suicide for love" was sometimes associated with witchcraft. Lijiang, the region of the Naxi, was notorious as the "suicide capital of the world"; large numbers of young people—but many more women than men—committed suicide rather than accept the arranged marriages that were imposed by the Confucian system. These suicides were widely noted and analyzed (Rock, 1947; Yang Fuquan, 1993); and underlying them was the denunciation of many of the young women, or of their female relatives, as *chao pu xi,* "keepers of evil demons."

Among the Dai in Yunnan and other Thai communities like the Thai Yuan in northern Thailand, mainly women were declared to be *pippa,* harborers of evil spirits—*phii ka.* These women and their families formed separate villages of *pippa* and their descendants. The present author found at least six *pippa* villages in Xishuangbanna: Man Ying, Man Gue, Man Jingdai, Man Nungdiem, and Man Jingiun— and there are similar *pippa* villages in other countries where the Dai live. During the 1870s and 1880s, missionaries reported that hundreds of people in northern Thailand were accused of harboring *phii ka* and were being driven out of their villages (Ganjanapan, 1984: 325).

Even from these brief examples, we can conclude that denunciations of women as witches or keepers of evil spirits, and the accompanying violence, took place on a large scale. These are not isolated or random incidents; thus they need to be explained in terms of underlying conflicts and social changes.

Witchcraft and Subordination:
Women as Witches; Men as Witch-Finders

The Santhal myth of the origin of witchcraft ascribes it to a gender struggle between men and women, in the family and in Santhal society. The men asked the god Maran Buru to teach them how to keep their women in order; the women got the men drunk, dressed up in men's clothes, and thus tricked Maran Buru into teaching them instead—and what he taught them resembled witchcraft. When he realized that he had been tricked, he made the men "expert in the art of witchfinding" (Archer, 1974: 292–293). The idea that women had some power that was then stolen from them by men, and carefully guarded by the men, appears in many myths. In all these myths, there is a change in the social order, a change that establishes male authority. Myth, of course, is not history, but it does raise the question why so much mythology envisions a chaotic era when women ruled.

Among the Dai and the Naxi, and in some other cases, there is evidence that women officiants in rituals were displaced by men. This change is paralleled by a change in religious methods: shamans, typically women, practice ecstatic methods to placate the spirits; by contrast, exorcists, typically men, use such methods to expel spirits. This difference has important social connotations. Male exorcists—*dongba* among the Naxi, *po mo* or *mau tham* among the Dai, and *ojha* among the Santhal—are protagonists in the struggle to control and devalue women, spiritually and socially. Women's ritualistic knowledge is defined as dangerous to society; nonhuman malevolent spirits are believed to have

women as their human mediums; and so women are potentially evil and must be controlled by the threat of denunciation. Denunciation as a witch or a keeper of evil spirits (*dain, pippa, chao pu xi*) can entail social ostracism, expulsion, or even death.

This concept of women is accompanied by another step in controlling them: an emphasis on female sexuality as dangerous—among the Dai and the Naxi, for instance, condemned women were invariably described as beautiful and alluring. In Indo-Aryan myths, women's sexuality seems to be equated with their being more libidinous than men, and thus with their becoming witches (Doniger, 1976).

Any special ability outside accepted female roles—such as literacy or ritualistic knowledge—might also be a reason for denunciation. In Bastar, India, the wife of a priest is afraid even to be nearby when her husband is chanting prayers, lest she be accused of trying to learn them in order to become a witch. Among the Warli of western India, "education for bhagathood (priesthood) is forbidden to women because they become witches and misuse the knowledge" (Dalmia, 1988: 46).

A related point is men's domination of systems of symbolism. This is explained, at least partly, by the fact that men had more leisure, so that priests who required full-time training (such as the Naxi *dongba,* the Santhal *ojha,* and the *lamas,* who completely retire from production), have invariably been men. Men have not always monopolized symbolism—the rituals of Santhal women as witches, of Naxi women as *phaw* (shamans), and of Dai women as worshipers in matriculs all involved symbols—but when men established their authority generally, they also came to dominate symbol systems. The connection between the ritualistic, political, and economic sphere in these societies should also be noted. Denunciation and spiritual devaluation of women were crucial in enforcing new social norms and structures.

Witchcraft and Land

Concepts of witchcraft often reflect an attack on women's households and land. The new household spirits were patrilineal, and women (such as the Naxi) might be forbidden to make offerings to them or even, in some cases (such as the Santhal) to know of them. However, Mosuo women make offerings to ancestors and Dai women to matriculs; and even in patrilineal systems women had certain limited rights in land. Witch-hunting was a form of internal, or class, struggle which sought to remove land rights from women and confer them solely on men.

Briefly, there are two kinds of land rights: one is a life interest, a right to manage land and its produce; the other is a right to share in the produce. The right that came most under attack was the widow's life interest in her husband's land. In the first phase of this attack, the widow has rights equal to her husband's; in the next phase she has rights over a plot of land sufficient for her own self-maintenance; in the third phase, even this right is abrogated, and the widow is maintained by her husband's male heirs. For Santhal women, to take one example, phase three is similar to the position of widows in Hindu society, although the Santhal women can gather and sell forest products.

We can expect that in contexts where women have greater land rights, there will be a more intense internal struggle and thus more widespread witch-hunting. Such witch-hunting amounts to an attack on the existing status of women with regard to social authority in general and land rights in particular. It is unnecessary in contexts where patriarchy is already well established and women's status is low—only where women have rights and authority is it necessary to attack them as the source of all evil. This may explain why both women and men can be witches among the Munda in India (who are closely related to the Santhal) and some Dai regions in China, where patrilinealism is firmly established.

Witchcraft and Gender Roles

Witch-hunting has also been used to force women into new gender roles, because deviant behavior can be punished by denunciation. One example is found among the Oraon, Dravidian speakers from the same Jharkhand region as the Santhal: married Oraon women continue to maintain relations with their birth family, and this creates conflicts with the husband's family; also, women traditionally have some autonomy regarding money. Consequently, "a powerful mode of making women align is . . . [an] elaborate and public discourse on the limits of socially acceptable autonomous and moral behavior, the witchcraft-*bisahi* complex" (Bleie, 1985: 157).

Witchcraft is also associated with stamping out other practices, such as healing by women. The suppression of women healers and dealers in magical potions may be linked to women's loss of control over their own bodies, particularly in childbearing.

Conclusion

In feminist analysis, denunciation of women as witches is related to an important question: How did gender relations change, leading at some point to patriarchy? In other words, if male domination was not always the rule, how did it come to be the rule? With regard to Asia, and perhaps other parts of the world, one possible answer is that men's social dominance was established, or partly established, by categorizing women with ritual knowledge as witches and keepers of

demons, and then persecuting these women. Barbara Bender has argued that "social differentiation hinges, in the first instance, on differential access to social knowledge" (1989: 92)—a difference, we conclude, enforced through denunciation of "witches."

Some evidence for this conclusion can be found in religious texts. For instance, in Hindu texts we can see the results of a process whereby women are excluded from knowing the scriptures—the Vedas. The earliest Vedas, such as the Rig-Veda (which dates from the time of the Aryan spread into south Asia), may suggest the nature of the process itself. Feminist archaeology, although still nascent, could provide other clues. Perhaps even more important is evidence from anthropological fieldwork and ethnographic accounts of indigenous cultures that female-dominated religions were replaced by male-dominated religions. These struggles over ritual and the transformation of belief systems preceded changes in labor, production, marriage, and other social arrangements.

Note: This article is based on work cowritten with Dev Nathan.

See Also

ANCIENT INDIGENOUS CULTURES: WOMEN'S ROLES; DEMONIZATION; WITCHES: WESTERN WORLD

References and Further Reading

Archer, W. G. 1974. *The hill of flutes: Love, life, and poetry in tribal India.* London: Allen and Unwin.

Bender, Barbara. 1989. The roots of inequality. In D. Miller, M. Rowlands, and C. Tilley, eds., *Domination and resistance.* London: Unwin Hyman.

Bleie, Tone. 1985. *The cultural construction and the social organization of gender: The case of Oraon marriage and witchcraft.* Bergen: Ch [Christiane] Michelson Institute.

Dalmia, Yashodara. 1988. *The painted world of the Warlis: Art and ritual of the Warli tribes of Maharashtra.* New Delhi: Lalit Kala Akademi.

Doniger, Wendy. 1976. *The origins of evil in Hindu mythology.* Berkeley: University of California Press.

Douglas, Mary. 1966. *Purity and danger.* London and New York: Routledge.

Ganjanapan, Anan. 1984. The idiom of phii ka: Peasant conception of class differentiation in northern Thailand. *Mankind* 14(4): Special issue 3.

Kelkar, G., and Dev Nathan. 1991. *Gender and tribe: Women, land, and forests in Jharkhand.* New Delhi: Kali for Women; and London: Zed.

Lewis, I. M. 1975. *Ecstatic religion*. Harmondsworth, U.K.: Penguin.

——— . 1996. *Religion in context: Cults and charisma*. Cambridge: Cambridge University Press.

Lieban, R. W. 1967. *Cebuano sorcery: Malign magic in the Philippines*. Berkeley and Los Angeles: University of California Press.

Nathan, D., G. Kelkar, and Yu Xiaogang. 1998. Women as witches and keepers of demons: Cross-cultural analysis of struggles to change gender relations. *Economic and Political Weekly* (31 October).

Purkiss, Diane. 1996. *The witch in history: Early modern and twentieth century representations*. London and New York: Routledge.

Rock, J. F. 1947. *The ancient Na-Khi kingdom of southwest China*, Vol. 1. Cambridge, Mass.: Harvard-Yenching Institute, Harvard University Press.

Wijeyewardene, Gehan. 1970. The still point and the turning point: Towards the structure of northern Thai religion. *Mankind* 7(4): 247–255.

Yang Fuquan. 1993. *Naxi suicide for love*. Taipei: Zhuhai. (In Chinese.)

Govind Kelkar

WITCHES: Western World

Dictionaries define witches as ugly old crones or as seductive, bewitching temptresses. They are supposed to possess malignant, "supernatural" powers. Popular imagination still fancies them with their conical-shaped hats (once the sign of their wisdom) riding on broomsticks or chanting around bubbling cauldrons (once the symbol of the origins of life). Witches are thought to have a special relationship with the devil and other evil spirits, from whom they receive magical powers.

The term *witch* comes from the Indo-European root *wic,* meaning "to bend or shape." A witch, then, is a "shaper," one who bends energy and shapes consciousness, one who has the gift of evoking power from within. From time immemorial, tribes and rural villages counted on the services of its wisest elders (variously called shamans, healers, herbalists, *curanderos/as,* midwives, counselors, and so on) to mediate the sacred and to penetrate the powers of life and death (Starhawk, 1989).

Contemporary witches define themselves as followers of *wicca,* or what they call the Old Religion, a prepatriarchal worldview that sees the divine as immanent and all that lives as sacred. This Old Religion, or "paganism," practiced by *paganae,* or rural peoples, was based in the pre-Christian folklore and mythology of ancient Europe. Like other earth-based, tribal traditions, this nature religion regarded the earth as the living body of the ancient Mother Goddess, from whom all life comes and to whom all return. Many witchcraft traditions also worship a god, related to the ancient horned lord of animals, who in Christianity was elevated to the devil. Many modern witches also see themselves as heirs to the ancient mystery traditions of Egypt, Crete, and Eleusis (Gadon, 1989).

"Women's Holocaust"

Between one million and nine million victims, 85 percent of whom were women, are said to have been hanged, burned, or drowned between the fifteenth and seventeenth centuries in what has become known as the "women's holocaust." Today, the history of the "burning times," that largely unknown 300-year period of brutal persecution and death leveled against women healers by a paranoid and threatened church, is being reclaimed by a new generation of women (*Burning Times,* 1990).

During the "burning times," traditions based in rural life that had endured for thousands of years in Europe were wiped out, branded as heresy by the Inquisition. These traditions were based on life's experiences, on the changes of the seasons, and on people's relationship to the land; they had little to do with belief or doctrine. The church was determined to destroy the remnants of this pre-Christian nature religion.

Older women were the primary targets of the witch-craze. Many were widows or spinsters and thus outside the control of the patriarchal family. These wise women were the village healers, midwives, counselors, and teachers. Although most were poor, the power they wielded as respected physicians had political and theological implications. They were versed in anatomy and nutrition; they not only could ease the pains of childbirth (and thus interfere with what they considered God's curse on Eve), but they also knew the secrets of birth control and abortion.

The church feared the use of such knowledge in women's hands. According to church authority, a witch's ability to heal, to "perform miracles," or "do magic," had to be acquired through diabolical agency. Women could not be allowed to heal of their own power because they would escape church control. Therefore, ecclesiastical judges ruled that such power had to come from the devil, and even though a witch might do good deeds, she must die because she had made a pact with Satan, the rival of the Christian God. Those responsible for the witch burnings were in large measure an aspiring elite of professional men who wanted exclusive control over the body of knowledge held by these village wise women. Feminist historians show how the suppression of witches as midwives and healers coincides with the creation of the male medical profession (Daly, 1978).

Witches were accused of atrocities that were clearly male-projected sexual fantasies. It was believed that at the Sabbat witches kissed the devil in homage and engaged in promiscuous sexual orgies. Since their obscene acts were performed with God's enemy, inquisitors felt justified in condemning, torturing, and slaughtering women. Since witchcraft was defined as a *crimen exceptum,* ordinary legal proceedings were waived. To extort confessions, women would be stripped, shaved, and frequently raped. Torture instruments included eye-gougers, branding irons, spine-rollers, forehead tourniquets, thumbscrews, racks, iron boots for crushing legs, heating chairs, and choking "pears." The torturers cut off hands and ears, imposed artificial sleeplessness, unendurable thirst, and "squassation," which completely dislocated hands, feet, elbows, limbs, and shoulders (Daly, 1978). Furthermore, under torture, witches were forced to name and accuse sisters, friends, and neighbors of supposedly assisting at the Sabbat, a midnight assembly of witches and sorceresses.

Children as young as 7 were often used as legal witnesses. Those accused of accompanying their mothers to the Sabbat were flogged in front of the fire where their parent perished. Many of these children would not only remember seeing their mothers burned but would also bear the burden of knowing they had been used to condemn them to death.

The most authoritative manual on interrogating witches was written in 1486 by two Dominicans, Heinrich Kramer and James Sprenger. Called *Malleus Maleficarum* (The Hammer of Witches), the handbook worked as a self-fulfilling prophecy because *maleficarum* is the female form of the word *evildoer.* Because it was published in the early period of the witch-craze, it set the stage for the next two centuries for focusing the hunt almost exclusively on women. Kramer and Sprenger argued that witches turned men into beasts, copulated with devils, and stirred up hail-storms and tempests. They posed the question, "Why is it that women are chiefly addicted to evil superstitions?" The answer: "Women are more credulous, they are naturally more impressionable, have slippery tongues, are feebler in both mind and body, are more carnal than men to the extent of having insatiable lust, have weak memories, are liars by nature." The Dominicans were given Vatican support in their campaign to extend the witch-craze to the Rhine in a papal bull of Innocent VIII.

Fostered by the invention of the printing press, *Malleus Maleficarum* circulated widely. Witch-hunts spread from the mountainous areas of Italy and Germany to all Europe. In works of art, engravings, and other handbooks on demonology, women of the sixteenth and seventeenth centuries were depicted as disorderly and insolent, beating and tricking their husbands, drinking wine, and lustfully dragging them off to bed. Representations of the witches' Sabbat portray orgies with the devil, represented by a goat, and naked women brewing poisonous potions from dismembered snakes and toads, said to be used in the killing of men and cattle.

By the early eighteenth century the witch-craze phenomenon had spent itself. (The last witch trials took place in Puritan Massachusetts between 1647 and 1700.) The Enlightenment, with its stress on reason and the scientific method, replaced Christian belief in the devil, evil spirits, and a magical universe. Scientists could fathom the laws of nature, reducing them to mathematical formulas. The living world became viewed as a machine, something made of nonliving, atomized parts that could ultimately be known and controlled.

By the end of the "burning times," a whole way of life had been destroyed. It took the church more than two centuries to turn paganism into devil worship and folk religion into heresy. The old organic view of life, which saw sacred presence in all existence, became obsolete.

The Old Religion went underground and for four hundred years became the most secret of religions. Only recently has it reemerged as women meet in small groups to celebrate the solstices and equinoxes of the full moon. During these rituals women again connect with the mysteries within their bodies that are in rhythm with the movement of the living body of the earth.

Starhawk, a modern witch, psychologist, and political activist, calls on women to name themselves "witch" in order to reclaim the right to be powerful, independent women on the edge of social change, to reclaim women's heritage as spiritual leaders, healers, and midwives.

See Also

FEMICIDE; GODDESS; HEALERS; HERESY; MIDWIVES; MISOGYNY; MYSTICISM; WICCA; WOMEN: TERMS FOR WOMEN

References and Further Reading

Adler, Margot. 1986. *Drawing down the moon: Witches, druids, goddess-worshippers, and other pagans in America today.* Boston: Beacon.

Barstow, Anne Llewellyn. 1994. *Witchcraze: A new history of the European witch hunts.* San Francisco: HarperCollins.

The Burning Times. 1990. Video. Narr. Donna Reed. Canadian Film Board.

Daly, Mary. 1978. European witchburnings: Purifying the body of Christ. In *Gyne/ecology: The metaethics of radical feminism,* 178–222. Boston: Beacon.

Ehrenreich, Barbara, and Deidre English. 1973. *Witches, midwives, and nurses: A history of women healers.* New York: Feminist Press.

Gadon, Elinor W. 1989. The way of the Goddess: An earth-based spirituality. In *The once and future Goddess,* 233–256. San Francisco: HarperSanFrancisco.

Karlsen, Carol F. 1987. *The devil in the shape of a woman: Witchcraft in colonial New England.* New York: Norton.

Merchant, Carolyn. 1980. Nature as disorder: Women and witches. In *The death of nature,* 127–148. San Francisco: Harper and Row.

Starhawk. 1989. Witchcraft as Goddess religion. In *The spiral dance,* 15–30. San Francisco: Harper. Also in *Truth or dare,* 6–8, San Francisco: HarperSanFrancisco.

Mary Judith Ress

WOMAN-CENTEREDNESS

One of feminism's most powerful challenges to foundationalist constructions of knowledge has been the insistence that there is a "politics of location," and that *who* looks and *where* people look from will influence *what* they see—and also of course what they do not see. *Woman-centeredness* has been interpreted as meaning women's difference from men and a separate women's culture. However, the stronger meaning is one that rejects seeing the world in apparently objective but actually masculinist terms and instead addresses from where and on whom the feminist "gaze" is directed. Feminism is concerned with the production of knowledge by women, with the condition of women and with men's part in bringing about conditions of inequality (the denial of social and legal rights), with exploitation (economic injustice and the extraction of surplus profit from women's labors), and with oppression (force and the threat of force) that characterize women's lives worldwide, however the specific content of these may differ historically and geographically. Thus, woman-centeredness is an epistemological concept that marks the transition from feminism as the critique of old knowledge to feminism as the producer of new knowledge. Woman-centeredness, like the term *women* itself, has been subject to criticism for what is seen as a false universalism; however, newer work on feminist epistemol-

ogy recognizes forms of feminist knowledge relating to the different locations of feminist knowers and to the very different material conditions in which women's lives are lived.

See Also

EPISTEMOLOGY; GAZE; UNIVERSALISM

References and Further Reading

Hypatia. 1992. 7(4). Special issue: Lesbian philosophy.
Lennon, Kathleen, and Margaret Whitford, eds. 1994. *Knowing the difference: Feminist perspectives on epistemology.* London: Routledge.

Liz Stanley

WOMANCULTURE

In the United States in the 1970s, *womanculture* was a term coined to refer to women's ways of seeing, thinking, and acting that make them different from men. It is an attempt to provide a corrective to a mainstream culture that feminists have identified as "malestream" or masculinist.

Associated mainly with cultural feminists, womanculture asserts that women's ways are superior to men's. For cultural feminists, women are essentially more loving and peaceful than men, because they bear the responsibility of caring for children. Mary Daly, a U.S. philosopher, believes that female energy is inherently life-affirming (1990). The U.S. poet Adrienne Rich (1981) writes that goddess worship among aboriginal peoples shows the importance that this female principle held before the coming of patriarchy.

Unfortunately, in this view, because men hold the power in patriarchal society, women's superior values have few opportunities for expression outside the home. From this perspective, the reasons why nations wage wars that cause death and destruction can be found in the control men have over the major institutions of society. Womanculture would replace values that lead to conflict with feminist values.

On the one hand, then, womanculture is seen as a means of recovering a lost culture; on the other, it is seen as the shaping of an alternative lifestyle.

Womanculture asserts the need for a space, both physical and social, in which an alternative women's culture might develop. In the industrial West, womanculture can be seen in women's literature, music, art, theater, bookstores, publishing, coffee houses, and other woman-centered businesses. In these settings, women have the opportunity to get together and form bonds with one another, free from the presence of men. It is in such places that the often unarticulated thoughts of women—ideas and perspectives arising from their particular experiences as women—are given voice. As caregivers for children, the sick, and the elderly, women are believed to cherish nurturance rather than aggression, and cooperation and mutual respect rather than competition or combativeness.

In a culture dominated by heterosexism—that is, one that favors opposite-sex over same-sex relationships—lesbians have found the creation of women-identified environments necessary for their well-being. Here, they can define an identity of their own and, like heterosexual women, can work independently from men in the formation of new values.

The term *womanculture* is derived from the more formal *women's culture,* a concept introduced by U.S. feminist historians of the 1970s to describe the bonds of womanhood among white middle-class females in England and the United States during the late eighteenth and nineteenth centuries. Because the society of that period restricted this group of women to their homes, feminist historians writing about these women focused on their lives within the household, a territory they labeled "women's sphere." Looking into women's culture, historians learned not only that this confinement stifled women but, more important, that women did not readily accept their confinement and devised practices to resist it. Despite their restriction to "women's sphere," they were not merely passive victims of men's rules. In this respect, comparisons have been made between women's culture and slave culture.

Developing World

In the developing world, the existence of women-centered networks, along with rituals and practices in which women are the principal actors, suggests a thriving women's culture. Shirley Ardener (1975), an anthropologist, describes the militancy of Bakweri women of western Cameroon. Employing the technique of *titi ikoli,* for example, these women would assemble in large numbers and, through the use of obscenity, shaming, and mockery, cause an offending man to submit. Ardener cites the observations of other anthropologists who have documented similar instances in other parts of Africa, and concludes that these female-instigated practices are widespread in the continent.

Activist women in the developing world recognize the significance of women-centered rituals and traditions, particularly as these concern village, grassroots, and working-class women. In Argentina, the Madres of the Plaza de Mayo demonstrated faithfully in a square every Thursday afternoon beginning in April 1977 to protest the death or disappearance of their children.

As the nations of the world become incorporated into one economic order in the twenty-first century, women's culture is acknowledged as vital for the survival of many communities. The Egyptian feminist Nawal El Saadawi (1998) and the Nobel Prize winner Rigoberta Menchú (1998) call attention to "North–South" relations of power that underpin globalization processes, and the resulting gendering of politics and poverty. The U.S. political economist Saskia Sassen (1998) writes about the distinct utility of women's labor for the global economy.

The voluntary migration, in unprecedented numbers, of women from developing countries seeking employment as overseas contract workers in industrialized regions is creating diasporic female societies that are now the subject of feminist inquiry. Filipino women, hired mainly as domestic helpers, constitute the largest diaspora. Though perhaps not enunciated in the lexicon of womanculture, these studies necessarily reveal the ways in which women work together to define themselves as a collectivity. Situated thus in the context of economic and cultural internationalization, womanculture has departed from its original, more narrowly conceived meaning.

See Also

FEMINISM: CULTURAL; GODDESS; HETEROSEXISM; MIDWIVES; PATRIARCHY: DEVELOPMENT; VIOLENCE AND PEACE: OVERVIEW; WOMAN-CENTEREDNESS; WOMANISM; WOMANSPIRIT; WOMEN'S CENTERS

References and Further Readings

Ardener, Shirley, ed. 1975. *Perceiving women.* New York: Wiley.

Cott, Nancy. 1977. *The bonds of womanhood: "Women's sphere" in New England, 1780–1835.* New Haven, Conn.: Yale University Press.

Daly, Mary. 1990. *Gyn/Ecology.* Boston: Beacon. (Originally published 1978.)

Dubois, Ellen, et al. 1980. Politics and culture in women's history: A symposium. *Feminist Studies* 6(1): 26–64.

El Saadawi, Nawal. 1998. *The Nawal El Saadawi reader.* London: Zed.

Hoagland, Sarah Lucia. 1988. *Lesbian ethics: Toward new values.* Palo Alto, Calif.: Institute of Lesbian Studies.

Menchú, Rigoberta. 1998. *Crossing borders.* London: Verso.

Rich, Adrienne. 1981. *Of woman born: Motherhood as experience and institution.* New York: Norton. (Originally published 1976.)

Sassen, Saskia. 1998. *Globalization and its discontents.* New York: New Press.

Delia Aguilar

WOMANISM

Embraced as an alternative to feminism, which many women of color perceive as alienating, womanism embodies both race and gender identities in understanding and theorizing about the experiences of black women. The term *womanist,* a designation for one who practices womanism, is often preferred over the term *black feminist* to further signal the rejection of feminism's white, middle-class perspective.

Womanist was first coined by Alice Walker in her collection of essays *In Search of Our Mothers' Gardens: Womanist Prose* (1983). In Walker's definition of a womanist, provided in the introduction, the term refers to the folk expression used by black mothers who would admonish daughters for "acting womanish"—which Walker describes as "outrageous, audacious, courageous or willful behavior. Wanting to know more and in greater depth than is considered good for one." Such behavior, according to Walker, indicates that one is in charge and "serious"—an attitude shown in the work of many womanists who address the serious nature of the intersection of race and gender oppression in the lives of women of color.

In response to the exclusionary nature of feminism, womanism, according to Walker, specifically addresses the solidarity of humanity, in that a womanist is "committed to survival and wholeness of entire people male and female and not a separatist." The definition not only captures the strength of black women in the midst of adversity but also celebrates an ability to love and express love (even for self) in spite of struggle and the difficulties it brings.

The Nigerian womanist Mary E. Kolawole (1997), in her work on African women in literature, defines womanism as the "totality of feminine self expression, self retrieval and self assertion in positive cultural ways." She states that an African womanist ideology is "central to self recovery of the African woman." Quite often, black women academics embrace the term *womanist* over *feminist,* and, perhaps because of Walker's reference to loving "the Spirit," several theology scholars use *womanist* to distinguish themselves from white female theologians.

For other black female scholars, *womanist* does not connote the same level of commitment as *feminist.* The cultural

critic bell hooks notes this distinction in her essay on black women and feminism (1989: 181): "For me the term womanist is not sufficiently linked to a tradition of radical political commitment to struggle and change." The reason for Walker's stated preference for *womanist,* however, is that it speaks directly to the commitment to struggle as seen in "the spirit of the women (like Sojourner) the word calls to mind" (in Triechler et al., 1985).

See Also

WOMANCULTURE; WOMANIST THEOLOGY

References and Further Reading

Cannon, Katie G. 1996. *Katie's canon: Womanism and the soul of the black community.* New York and London: Continuum.

hooks, bell. 1989. *Talking back: Thinking feminist, thinking black.* Toronto: Between the Lines.

Kolawole, Mary E. 1997. *Womanism and African consciousness.* Lawrenceville, N.J.: Africa World.

Treichlar, Paula A., Cheris Kramarae, and Beth Stafford, eds. 1985. *For alma mater: Theory and practice in feminist scholarship.* Urbana: University of Illinois Press.

Walker, Alice. 1983. *In search of our mothers' gardens: Womanist prose.*

Note: Scholarly publications with a womanist emphasis can be found in *Womanist Theory and Research,* an interdisciplinary journal supporting the feminist research of women of color and published by the Institute for African American Studies at the University of Georgia.

Karla D. Scott

WOMANIST THEOLOGY

Womanist theology is critical reflection on black women's positive sense of themselves as black women in relationship with God. As human beings reflecting God's self, black women through womanist theology create a way of reasoning about themselves in relation to black humanity and the search for freedom, justice, and a decent quality of life. In this way, womanist theology provides the ontological essence of black womanhood—that is, it offers the foundation for who black woman are as creatures formed in God's image and in God's power. Womanism is a philosophy that incarnates black women's full sense of being and significance in the world as they stand with their community: unabashedly black, female, and deeply spiritual.

The term *womanist* was coined by Alice Walker (1983) in her book *In Search of Our Mothers' Gardens: Womanist Prose* to signal the unparalleled experience that black women have in the societies in which they live. Walker's concept takes seriously the ways black women daily deal with and defiantly expend energy on multiple oppressive structures. Likewise, Walker's definition speaks to black women's allegiance to the overall African-American community, which is a source of both nurture and suffering. Walker's womanist framework advocates unity, allegiance, and a bias toward those values that bring promise and renewal to the black community. Finally, Walker claims womanism as a distinctive exercise for gathering and narrating areas of knowledge about the lives of black women.

Building on Walker's definition of womanism, womanist theology carefully assesses the negative experiences of black women, confronting both the racism of white feminists and white male theologians and the sexism of black and white, as well as other males of color who are theologians. Womanist theology, however, moves beyond the negative aspect of racism in feminist theology by providing its own critique of racism and by joining feminist sisters. It also goes beyond the negative aspect of sexism in black theology by providing its own critique of gender discrimination and joining black men, to lead them to be holistic.

The goals of womanist theology are to examine the social construction of black womanhood in relation to the African-American women's community, to unearth the ethnographic sources within the African-American community to reconstruct knowledge and overcome subordination, and to decolonize the African mind in order to affirm African heritage. Thus, the tasks of womanist theology are to claim history; to declare authority for black women, men, and children; to learn from the experience of our forebears; to admit shortcomings and errors; and to improve the quality of life.

The sources of womanist theology are informed by biblical, theological, historical, and economic conditions. Moreover, womanist theology searches for particular voices, actions, opinions, struggles, and faith of African-American women, thereby shaping a distinctive perspective that takes seriously their experience and traditions in response to the emancipation and redeeming activity of God. Therefore, its sources are not limited just to traditional church doctrines and written texts. Womanist theology embraces African-American fiction, poetry, narratives, prayers, and people's narratives such as those of nineteenth-century black women leaders, poor and working-class black women in Pentecostal churches, and African-American women under slavery. Other vital sources include the personal stories of black women suffering domestic violence and psychological trauma, the empowering dimensions of African and African-American religiosity, and womanist ethnographic approaches to excavating the life stories of poor women of African descent.

The methodology of womanist theology is holistic in its worldview because womanists approach all that they do with inclusive vision. Womanist theologians write about the black woman's story and experience in the total relationship with God. They imply a holistic relationship in the positive sacred–human connections at the location of gender, race, class, sexual orientation, and ecology. The method of womanist theology validates the interconnection of past, present, and future. The whole experience of black women in the past lives of African women and in the present lives of African-American women struggling for a liberating quality of life fuses to create a dynamic multivocal account of black women's experience. Womanist theology uses the manifold theological ways, the many disciplines of analyses, and the diverse dimensions of African-American women in order to foster liberation.

Anthropological methodology also encourages womanist theologians to embrace the cultural, symbolic, and ritual diversity dispersed throughout the religious lives of women of color on this earth. In this sense, the methodology of womanist theology is holistic.

Consequently, womanist theologians advance a new philosophy of holistic survival and liberation. They bring to the center the experiences and knowledge of those marginalized by a complex layering and overlapping of race, gender, and class experiences of all groups, inclusive of those with privilege and power. Womanist theologians, in a word, retrieve sources from the past, sort and evaluate materials, and thereby construct new philosophies that effect change in the space and time occupied by black women. A womanist anthropology of survival and liberation is a new framework for the twenty-first century.

History of Womanist Theology

Womanist theology began when three African women, (along with seventeen African men) were stolen from their native land by European slavers and brought to Jamestown, Virginia, in 1619. The anguish, grief, and endurance of these women gave rise to descendants who resisted the debilitating system of slavery. The three women who were originally snatched from Africa planted the seeds for future womanist theology. The daughters to whom these original three gave birth, during the days of enslavement, were subject to rape by any man in the oppressive system. Many African and African-American women refused and resisted the system by running away and taking part in slave revolts. Harriet Tubman, a well-known activist, was a Christian freedom fighter. In a similar fashion, the life of Fannie Lou Hamer, a Christian civil rights leader of the 1960s, and the lives of other women who resisted and struggled with oppressive slavery lay the groundwork for future womanist faith and thought about God's liberation. With all unnamed women, these women who stood at the forefront of survival and freedom to resist are the ones who watered and nurtured the seeds of womanist theology. Their experience of resistance against discrimination and oppression and their assertion of their positive relation to God laid the foundation for womanist theology before its visible rise.

Womanist theology more directly emerged from the black civil rights movement of the 1950s and 1960s and from the feminist movement of the 1970s. One success of the white feminist movement was the increased presence of women in professional positions as well as theological seminaries. African-American women did not benefit as white women did in professional jobs, nor did as large a number begin seminary. Moreover, black women realized that racism still existed in the feminist movement and that sexism still persisted in the civil rights and black power movements. Even in seminaries, African-American women experienced black men's resistance to their receiving ordination and denial of black women's calling by God.

In 1985 Katie G. Cannon used the term *womanist* in her article "The Emergence of Black Feminist Consciousness." In that essay Cannon identified womanism as a new category to describe the work that black women did in the church. In 1987 Delores S. Williams, using Alice Walker's definition of womanism as a theoretical backdrop to outline a black women's theology, coined the term *womanist theology* in her article "Womanist Theology: Black Women's Voices."

In 1988 Katie G. Cannon's *Black Womanist Ethics* described womanist liberation ethics and argued that the intention of such an ethic was to educate black women about the importance of using the life experiences of grassroots people and their narratives to usher in the reign of justice. Her sources included her family biography, black folk culture, and biblical interpretation. She also used African-American women's literature as a source, arguing that such texts provided the finest set of data for understanding the ethical principles black women have established and advocated in American society past and present.

Also in 1988 Renita J. Weems published *Just a Sister Away: A Womanist Vision of Women's Relationships in the Bible.* This book attempted to locate black women in God's new human community. In so doing, Weems investigated the ways women relate to other women in biblical texts. For instance, using the story of the Egyptian woman Hagar and the Hebrew woman Sarai, Weems highlighted issues such as monetary abuse, human bondage, ethnic conflict, and adversarial social relations. The story of the Hebrew Ruth and Moabite Naomi presented an example of devoted friendship and loyalty among women.

In 1989 Jacquelyn Grant published *White Women's Christ and Black Women's Jesus: Feminist Christology and Womanist Response,* which deciphered the significance of Jesus for women in the African-American church. Grant claimed that black women in the United States lived with three layers of structural oppression relating to race, gender, and class. She underscored the fact that an unusually large number of African-American women made up the poor and working-class population. As a result, womanist philosophy and its expression must be based on the everyday reality and struggle for survival in the lives of poor black women.

The volume of womanist literature is both substantial and comprehensive. For instance, Delores S. Williams's *Sisters in the Wilderness: The Challenge of Womanist God-Talk* (1993); Emilie M. Townes's books *Breaking the Fine Rain of Death* (1999) and *In a Blaze of Glory: Womanist Spirituality as Social Witness* (1995); Kelly Brown Douglas's *The Black Christ* (1994) and *Sexuality and the Black Church: A Womanist Perspective* (1999); and Karen Baker-Fletcher's *Sisters of Dust, Sisters of Spirit: Womanist Wordings on God and Creation* (1998)—all point to a discipline that is not only in the making but is radically challenging the way all theology is articulated. Indeed, womanist theology is the work of African-American women creating and articulating the essence of black womanhood in relationship to God.

See Also

CHRISTIANITY: FEMINIST CHRISTOLOGY; EMPOWERMENT; FEMINISM: AFRICAN-AMERICAN; HOLISTIC HEALTH, *I and II*; RELIGION: OVERVIEW; SISTERHOOD; SPIRITUALITY: OVERVIEW; WOMANISM; WOMANSPIRIT

References and Further Reading

Baker-Fletcher, Karen. 1998. *Sisters of dust, sisters of spirit: Womanist wordings on God and creation.* Minneapolis: Fortress.

Cannon, Katie G. 1985. The emergence of black feminist consciousness. In Letty M. Russell, ed., *Feminist interpretations of the Bible,* 30–40. Louisville, K.Y.: Westminister.

———. 1988. *Black womanist ethics.* Atlanta: Scholars.

Douglas, Kelly Brown. 1994. *The black Christ.* Maryknoll, N.Y.: Orbis.

———. 1999. *Sexuality and the black church: A womanist perspective.* Maryknoll, N.Y.: Orbis.

Grant, Jacquelyn. 1989. *White women's Christ and black women's Jesus: Feminist Christology and womanist response.* Atlanta: Scholars.

Terrell, JoAnne Marie. 1998. *Power in the blood?* Maryknoll, N.Y.: Orbis.

Thomas, Linda E. 1999. Womanist theology, epistemology, and a new anthropological paradigm. *CrossCurrents* 48 (Winter–Spring): 448–499.

Townes, Emilie M. 1999. *Breaking the fine rain of death.* New York: Continuum.

———. 1995. *In a blaze of glory: Womanist spirituality as social witness.* Nashville: Abingdon.

———. 1993. *Womanist justice, womanist hope.* Atlanta: Scholars.

Walker, Alice. 1983. *In search of our mothers' gardens: Womanist prose.* New York: Harcourt Brace Jovanovich.

Weems, Renita J. 1988. *Just a sister away: A womanist vision of women's relationships in the Bible.* San Diego: LuraMedia.

Williams, Delores S. 1993a. Womanist theology: Black women's voices. In Gayraud S. Wilmore and James H. Cone, eds., *Black theology: A documentary history, 1966–1999,* 423. Maryknoll, N.Y.: Orbis.

———. 1993b. *Sisters in the wilderness: The challenge of womanist God-talk.* Maryknoll, N.Y.: Orbis.

Linda E. Thomas

WOMANSPIRIT

The womanspirit movement, also called the women's or feminist spirituality movement, is a wide-ranging grassroots movement of women who accept the authority of women's experience, celebrate the body, affirm the human place in the web of life, and increasingly invoke the divine power as Goddess. The womanspirit movement surfaced in the 1970s in the wake of the second wave of the feminist movement. It numbers hundreds of thousands in North America, Europe, Australia, and New Zealand.

The womanspirit movement is designated by the anthropologist Susan Starr Sered in *Priestess, Mother, Sacred Sister* (1994) as one of a handful of religions worldwide created and led by women. It overlaps with the Goddess movement, feminist witchcraft or Wicca, feminist neopaganism, and ecofeminism. It differs from related movements within Christianity and Judaism in its repudiation of ties to inher-

ited religious communities. Unlike the New Age movement it rejects, with gurus and authoritative teachings, the womanspirit movement affirms a feminist and ecological political agenda. The womanspirit movement has no recognized leaders, no creed, no single organizational structure, and no membership lists.

WomanSpirit magazine, published quarterly by Ruth and Jean Mountaingrove from 1974 to 1984, documented and fostered the emerging movement. Women expressed their alienation from traditional religions, wrote of mystical experiences in nature, and shared emerging rituals. The archaeologist Marija Gimbutas's *Gods and Goddesses of Old Europe* (1974) proposed the theory that neolithic "old Europe" (6500–3500 B.C.E.) was a highly developed, peaceful, egalitarian civilization that worshiped the Goddess as the symbol of birth, death, and regeneration in nature. Hungarian-born Zsuzsanna Budapest published *The Feminist Book of Lights and Shadows* in 1975, urging women to reclaim the ancient religion of the Goddess, which she called Dianic witchcraft (for women only). Merlin Stone's *When God Was a Woman* (1976) popularized the thesis that "in the beginning, God was a woman." In New York, Ntozake Shange's long-running play, *for colored girls who have considered suicide when the rainbow is enuf,* ended with the words "i found god in myself / and i loved her fiercely." In 1978 more than 500 women (and some men) came together in Santa Cruz, California, to celebrate "The Great Goddess Re-Emerging." The keynote address by Carol P. Christ, "Why Women Need the Goddess," became a touchstone. In 1979 Starhawk's *The Spiral Dance* articulated a vision of feminist witchcraft (for women and men) as the rebirth of pre-Christian worship of the Goddess and the Horned God. In the 1980s and 1990s many books and articles, both scholarly and popular, uncovered the history of the Goddess; connected the rise of patriarchy, warfare, and hierarchy with religions that celebrated male gods; and argued that the revival of earth-based Goddess religion could help to promote equality and planetary survival. In 1997 Carol P. Christ published *Rebirth of the Goddess,* the first "thea-logy" (from *thea,* Goddess) of the movement.

Most come to the movement through reading, attending conferences and workshops, and participating in rituals. Celebrations are commonly held on the full or new moon, the equinoxes and solstices, and on 2 February (Brigid's day), 1 May, 1 August, and 31 October (Halloween). This ritual calendar, which is claimed to be pre-Christian, is adapted from the neopagan or witchcraft movement as reconstructed by the Englishman Gerald Gardner. Other rituals celebrate the cycles of the female body, including menstruation, pregnancy and birth, abortion, and menopause. The home altar, which usually includes images of the Goddess, stones, feathers, chalices filled with water, and other sacred objects, is popular. Divination is practiced using tarot cards, amulets, pendulums, and so on. Some practice nontraditional forms of healing, including visualization, energy and breath work, and the laying on of hands. For those who identify as witches, casting spells and trancework are important. Many are vegetarians.

The womanspirit movement, like the consciousness-raising groups of the 1970s, was originally for women only. It was thought that women would be more comfortable expressing their intimate thoughts and feelings in groups of women because women traditionally defer to men, and men are taught to dominate. Many of the early leaders of the movement, including Z. Budapest and Ruth and Jean Mountaingrove, were lesbian and separatist, but the movement also included heterosexual and bisexual women. Starhawk incorporates men and male gods in some of her groups, though she also recognizes the need for groups for women only.

Members of the womanspirit movement agree in rejecting the image of a judgmental, authoritarian, dominating, white male God who sits on a throne in heaven. Religion is not about reward and punishment or life after death. The focus is on finite life in the body on this earth. All beings are connected in the web of life and share a common destiny. Some envision the earth as the body of the Goddess. Others prefer nonanthropomorphic imagery, invoking the spirits of all living things.

The womanspirit movement has been labeled ahistorical and apolitical by materialist feminists. Spiritual feminists counter that religion influences politics and that creating a new religion is a political act. Spiritual feminists have been involved in many political protests, including those against the military at Greenham Common, Great Britain; against the nuclear power plant in Diablo Canyon, California; and for women's reproductive choice. The womanspirit movement's understanding of Goddess history (which is not monolithic, as critics sometimes imply) and Marija Gimbuta's theories are a subject of lively academic controversy.

See Also

ECOFEMINISM; GODDESS; WICCA

References and Further Reading

Budapest, Zsuzsanna. 1989. *The holy book of women's mysteries.* Oakland, Calif.: Wingbow.

Christ, Carol P. 1997. *Rebirth of the Goddess: Finding meaning in feminist spirituality.* New York: Addison-Wesley.

Eller, Cynthia. 1995. *Living in the lap of the Goddess: The feminist spirituality movement in America.* Boston: Beacon.

Gimbutas, Marija. 1974. *Gods and goddesses of old Europe.* Berkeley: University of California Press.

Iglehart, Hallie Austen. 1983. *Womanspirit: A guide to women's wisdom.* San Francisco: Harper and Row.

Sered, Susan Starr. 1994. *Priestess, mother, sacred sister: Religions dominated by women.* New York: Oxford University Press.

Starhawk (Miriam Simos). 1979. *The spiral dance: A rebirth of the ancient religion of the great Goddess.* San Francisco: Harper and Row (2nd ed., 1989).

Stone, Merlin. 1976. *When God was a woman.* New York: Dial.

WomanSpirit magazine. 1974–1984. 2000 King Mountain Trail, Sunny Valley, Ore. 97467.

Carol P. Christ

WOMEN'S CENTERS

In 1972 in Lancaster, Pennsylvania, a group of women gathered for the beginning of a weekly meeting of kindred spirits at the city's women's center. The center was one of a constellation of projects that were part of the Lancaster women's liberation movement. The center was among the first for the state along with a Pittsburgh center and was designed to provide services to women. It offered women a place to meet, explore their lives, and consider future possibilities for change. The women at the Lancaster center were not alone in their desire to explore other possibilities for their future. At the time of the development of centers in the United States, women in western Europe were also assembling to address similar concerns and issues.

The women in Lancaster gathered for the beginning of their consciousness-raising sessions. The members of the group were diverse. The sessions were to be held weekly and open to any woman interested in self-exploration and achieving a sense of her own abilities and independence; all women were welcomed without conditions placed on their membership. The ages of the women typically ranged from 22 to what might be considered today as middle-aged (45 to 55). Consciousness-raising was the process through which the women were attempting to understand their circumstances. For some of the women, that meant they also wanted to understand their relationships to friends, family, and present and future employers. They were reframing themselves in their lives. The complexities of values that are familial, extrafamilial, personal, and interpersonal were areas of exploration. The women felt the limiting nature of definitions imposed on them. They wanted dominion over themselves.

At the group meeting described here, the women introduced themselves. They offered explanations of their participation and their goals. One of the young women said she was in the process of becoming—a description she had offered some weeks earlier to a group of women meeting for a similar purpose at a women's college.

Some of the women were in relationships they felt were constraining. Their lives were prescribed by family tradition, by religion, and legally through marriage. Although not all of the women were in relationships, those who were would be described as physically, mentally, or emotionally abused. Some of the women wanted to gain the confidence they believed it would take to pursue college, train as artisans, or simply obtain employment that would allow them to be heads of their households. The women, in ways that were important to themselves, wanted to change, to be independent, to be free.

The women were doing what Belenky et al., in *Women's Ways of Knowing: The Developing Self, Voice and Mind* (published 14 years later, in 1986), described as conceiving of the self. Doing so is difficult particularly when "the source of self-knowledge is lodged in the other—not in the self" (31). The women were choosing to be proactive in their identity development and to build futures that defied present and continued subjugation. They were attempting to build identities bolstered against trepidation.

History of Women's Centers

The Lancaster women's liberation movement was one among other similar movements across the country. "In the 1970s, applying feminist principles, women created hundreds of autonomous services and organizing projects throughout the United States" (Schechter, 1982). The women's centers that were organized were part of that national development along with women's shelters. The centers were provided as places organized by women for women. Initially the centers had broad missions, which also made them places for women to meet and pursue their personal and career interests. The work of the women at the centers might include organizing civil and political action toward gaining civil and domestic rights and economic independence (see Gilman, 1989, on women's economic independence).

Feminist women's centers, like Women's Center South in Pittsburgh, sometimes offered a safe place for women in crisis. This women's center, with a kitchen, a place to sleep, a reading room, and an information center, had some in the house 24 hours a day. In an 11 month period in 1975, "the center logged 191 women sheltered, 86 children, and 839 visitors arriving to talk, create, nap, plan work, or just be themselves. Incoming phone calls climbed to an astronomical 4961." Two other Pennsylvania shelters, Women Against Abuse in Philadelphia and the Domestic Violence Service Center in Wilkes-Barre, also evolved from women's centers. (Schecter, 1982: 57).

During late 1974, a multiracial group of women in Boston's South End began meeting to plan a shelter for neighborhood women and their children. They were concerned about the complete lack of bilingual services for Latin women in crisis and the absence of any Latina controlled organization in the city of Boston.

Schechter (1982: 58) explains that until the 1970s, being slapped by one's husband was considered a mild form of chastisement and was acceptable. In some states, women had very few rights in addition to those her husband was willing to accord her. When she chose to leave an abusive relationship, she was even denied welfare. Consequently, if she wanted to leave and take her children with her, she could anticipate a life of poverty not only for herself but for her family as well.

From the 1970s to the turn of the twenty-first century, the centers have been part of the longest sustained effort against domestic violence in the United States. As a result, the national consciousness has been raised regarding the cause of battered women. Judith Herman, in her work *Trauma and Recovery* (1992, 1997), pointed out the similarities between delayed stress syndrome and the trauma of the battered woman. In 1982, Susan Schecter's *Women and Male Violence*, a training text for practitioners and support staff at the centers around the country, was published. Schectner was also the coauthor of *When Love Goes Wrong* (1993) and *Guidelines for Mental Health Practitioners in Domestic Violence Cases*, published by the National Coalition Against Domestic Violence (1987).

Public interest in battered women became part of the national culture of caring seeded by women's centers, women's liberation, and the battered women's movements. These social action groups continued to be prominently featured in the media into the middle to late 1970s, when the Vietnam War overshadowed them. The visibility and prominence gained by the antiwar protests overshadowed the work of the centers and drew off concern and focus from liberating women to ending of the war.

Notwithstanding the distracted media, women's centers have played a distinctive role in the history of establishing women's independence. They invited women across socioeconomic, racial, and educational lines to come together. In short, they invited border crossings. By the 1980s, however, the women's liberation movement, and the centers, were quiet. In the twenty-first century, women's centers are institutionalized as areas of medical and social services.

See Also

BATTERY; BOOKSHOPS; DOMESTIC VIOLENCE; WOMAN-CENTEREDNESS; WOMEN'S MOVEMENT: UNITED STATES

References and Further Reading

Belenky, M. F., B. M. Clinchy, N. R. Goldberger, and J. M. Tarule. 1986. *Women's ways of knowing: The development of self, voice, and mind.* New York: Basic Books.

Davis, A. Y. 1983. *Women, race, and class.* New York: Vintage.

Gilman, C. P. 1989. *The yellow wallpaper and other writings by Charlotte Perkins Gilman.* New York: Bantam.

Herman, J. 1992, 1997. *Trauma and recovery: The aftermath of violence from domestic abuse to political terror.* New York: Basic Books.

Jones, A., and S. Schechter. 1993. *When love goes wrong: What to do when you can't do anything right.* New York: Harper Perennial.

Schechter, S. 1982. *Women and male violence: Visions and struggles of the battered women's movement.* Boston: South End.

Barbara Curry

WOMEN'S LANGUAGE

See ÉCRITURE FÉMININE.

WOMEN'S LIBERATION

See LIBERATION *and* WOMEN'S MOVEMENT.

WOMEN'S MOVEMENT:
Early International Movement

Individual feminists began to write critiques of western society's treatment of women by the early fifteenth century, but it was not until the democratic revolutions of the late eighteenth century that women began to band together in movements to improve their own situation. During the French Revolution of 1789–1795, feminists in the United States, France, Britain, and the German states wrote a number of treatises arguing for women's rights, and the Parisian Society of Revolutionary Republican Women demanded equal female political participation with men. But in 1793, the revolutionary French government forbade women any political involvement, from petitioning parliament to forming clubs and associations. Discouraged by this opposition from their natural allies (conservative men automatically excluded women from the body politic), feminists remained silent for over a generation. By 1830, however, new conditions gave rise to an early international women's movement that stretched across the Atlantic, uniting sympathizers from the United States to Russia and Sweden. Isolated among their compatriots, early feminists reached out to their counterparts in other lands. In the middle decades of the nineteenth century, hundreds of people in the western world formed an international community dedicated to changing women's status in society.

Early international feminism arose from three radical movements of the day: socialism, antislavery, and the German free religion movement, which sought to form interdenominational congregations challenging the frozen political situation east of the Rhine. All of these movements initially welcomed female participation as essential to their goals of reforming society. Numerous women activists joined socialist communities promulgating the ideas of Robert Owen, Charles Fourier, and the Count de Saint-Simon; the British and American abolitionist societies; and the German free congregations, often because these groups seemed to promise them equal rights. But in each instance, male members severely limited the extent of female involvement, refusing women equality even within these radical fringe movements. Antislavery societies divided rather than allow women to be delegates and officers, socialists paid them lower wages and ridiculed their attempts to enter politics, and the free congregations tried to oust female teachers from their new kindergartens. These rebuffs inspired a number of activists to form international feminist connections, which rapidly developed into a loose-knit movement. The Frenchwomen Jeanne Deroin, Pauline Roland, and Jenny d'Héricourt; the Germans Louise Otto, Mathilde Franziska Anneke, and Louise Aston; the Englishwomen Anne Knight, Harriet Taylor Mill, Bessie Rayner Parkes, and Barbara Leigh Smith Bodichon; the Americans Lucretia Mott, Elizabeth Cady Stanton, and Paulina Wright Davies; the international feminist Ernestine Rose; and the Swedish novelist Fredrika Bremer formed the core of this early feminist movement. These women knew and learned from one another, corresponded and visited, and read the same books and articles, distributing them among themselves. They connected through the 15 or more feminist journals they founded between 1830 and 1860, the extensive correspondence networks that linked female activists throughout the western community, and the U.S. women's rights conventions, held almost every year in the 1850s. Coming to the fore during the revolutionary year of 1848, when women's movements formed in the United States, France, and Germany, they forged further connections when conservative repression defeated the revolutions in Europe. French and German feminists emigrated to England and the United States, where they contacted allies in their new homes, fostering more cross-fertilization.

This early international women's movement promoted a wide range of feminist demands. Its advocates wanted full political equality—not just the vote, but the right to hold political office, to serve on juries, to do everything in political life that men did. But in addition to equal rights with men, they also insisted on "women's rights," which they defined as including protection from marital rape and the right to divorce and gain custody of their children, as well as access to education and the professions. They criticized prostitution as the direct result of an unjust economic system that forced women into only a few degrading and poorly paid jobs. They argued that many "respectable" marriages were legal prostitution, in which a woman with no other options sold herself to a single man. At the height of the Victorian era, they consistently spoke in public for "a cause which is still in its rotten-egg stage (I mean its advocates are apt to have rotten eggs and dirtier words thrown at them)," as the English feminist Barbara Leigh Smith Bodichon wrote after visiting Lucretia Mott (Anderson, 2000: 10). Utterly rejecting the traditional view that women's subordination was natural, God-given, and universal, they invented feminist strategies still useful today: creating new names of their own, asserting that the deity was female as well as male, teaching their sons as well as their daughters to sew and cook. They believed that women were both different from and equal to men and insisted that society could not function rightly unless the "female half of humanity" played its full part. If women are equal, then we deserve to vote because men do, Ernestine Rose often declared, and if we are different, then we deserve to vote because men cannot represent us.

In the 1860s, this early women's movement collapsed and its proponents were remembered primarily in numerous caricatures that depicted them as grotesque females aping male behavior. Fearful of losing their spontaneity, these early feminists never created the organizations or institutions that might have enabled their international movement to survive in an era of increasing nationalism. Too radical for their own time, they looked to the future to fulfill their dreams. In two hundred years, the German feminist Louise Otto wrote in 1866, women would "smile good-humoredly" at the problems of the current age (Anderson; 2000: 205). Some of their hopes have been fulfilled, such as their demand for a "reformed dress" that discarded corsets and crinolines in favor of shorter skirts and trousers. Others remain to be realized.

See Also

FEMINISM: EIGHTEENTH CENTURY; FEMINISM: NINETEENTH CENTURY; PUBLISHING: FEMINIST PUBLISHING IN THE WESTERN WORLD; SOCIALISM; WOMEN'S MOVEMENT: MODERN INTERNATIONAL; WOMEN'S MOVEMENT: UNITED STATES

References and Further Reading

Anderson, Bonnie S. 2000. *Joyous greetings: The first international women's movement, 1830–1860.* New York: Oxford University Press.

McFadden, Margaret H. 1999. *Golden gables of sympathy: The transatlantic sources of nineteenth-century feminism.* Lexington, Ky.: University Press of Kentucky.

Offen, Karen. 2000. *European feminisms: A political history.* Stanford, Calif.: Stanford University Press.

Bonnie S. Anderson

WOMEN'S MOVEMENT:
Modern International Movement

Beginning among elite feminists of the West, the modern international women's movement has expanded over the past century to encompass women of all classes from the entire planet. This progress has been neither smooth nor uniform but, instead, reflects historical developments during the twentieth century.

Early Efforts

After the early international women's movement ended in 1860, European feminists made two attempts to form new alliances. The Swiss feminist Marie Goegg organized the International Association of Women in 1868. Petitioning governments for the vote and improved education for girls, the group met in a congress in 1870 but collapsed the next year under the conservative repression that followed the defeat of the revolutionary Paris Commune. In 1878, French feminists convened the International Women's Rights Congress in Paris. Primarily male and representing France, the 220 delegates refused to support women's suffrage or any proposal that could be seen as socialist. The congress met only once.

A more lasting organization, the International Council of Women (ICW), came into being ten years later, in 1888. Originating from the European trips of the U.S. feminists Elizabeth Cady Stanton and Susan B. Anthony in the early 1880s, the U.S.-sponsored ICW was a federation of national councils created in the 1890s and 1900s. Initially composed of European and neo-European nations (like the United States, Canada, and Australia), the ICW came to include South American and Asian groups, but it remained conservative, elitist, and Eurocentric. Led by the Scottish Lady Aberdeen from 1893 to 1936, the ICW saw women's "first mission" as "her home" and refused to take any stand on controversial topics, from pacifism to the vote (Rupp, 1998: 20). The ICW's refusal to support women's voting rights led to the creation of the International Woman Suffrage Alliance, later the International Alliance of Women (IAW), in 1904. Meeting every other year, the IAW added issues of labor, prostitution, peace, and equal rights to its suffrage agenda before World War I. Similar in its original membership to the ICW, the IAW admitted China in 1913, followed by India, Japan, Palestine, and a number of Latin American nations in the 1920s.

During these decades and for much of the twentieth century, feminists divided between "bourgeois" associations like the ICW and IAW, composed of middle- and upper-class women, and socialist groups which included working-class members, but whose first allegiance was to socialist or communist political parties. The German feminist Clara Zetkin organized the Socialist Women's International in 1907 to fight for the vote, equal pay, and maternity insurance. Designating 8 March as International Women's Day, this European group met sporadically in the years before 1914.

World War I and After

World War I (1914–1918) disrupted international feminist development. Two rival associations—Zetkin's International Conference of Socialist Women and the much larger International Women's Congress under the leadership of the Dutch doctor Aletta Jacobs—met in Europe during the spring of 1915 to call for peace. They could not end the war, but at these meetings feminists forged international bonds that lasted for decades. After the war, new political configurations shaped international feminism. The victory of the Communist Party in the Soviet Union and its subsequent edict that separate women's organizations were no longer necessary led feminists like Zetkin to subordinate women's issues to those of the state. In nonwestern nations such as Egypt, India, China, and Japan, women's movements coalesced, negotiating their way between the rival claims of an anti-imperialist nationalism and a feminism that seemed to be associated with western colonialism. In response to the racism of the older women's groups, the International Council of Women of the Darker Races was formed in 1920 by African-American women and representatives from the Caribbean and the Pacific. The Inter-American Commission of Women convened in 1928, and the All-Asian Women's Conference met in 1931. Providing opportunities for elite women to meet and debate, these new organizations fostered the development of feminism outside of European and neo-European nations. By the 1930s, international feminism was forming a female critique of imperialism, racism, and war.

A unique group, the Women's International League for Peace and Freedom (WILPF), formed in Geneva in 1919. Emerging from the International Women's Congress, 1915, WILPF claimed 50,000 members by 1926 and sought to combine pacifism with opposition to imperialism and fascism. The contradictions inherent in this approach became apparent in the 1930s, as Nazism triumphed in Germany. Could fascism be stopped without war? Like WILPF, a popular-front organization of 1934, the World Committee of Women against War and Fascism, foundered on this dilemma. "Now that women start to slide down from the peak of achievement," the feminist pacifist Rosika Schwimmer declared in 1935, they should gather the documents of their earlier "marvelous epoch" (Rupp, 1998: 8). World War II (1939–1945) brought international women's movements to a standstill as international connections ceased for the duration of the war. In the 1940s and 1950s, older women's organizations survived through the doldrums of an era of resurgent domesticity in the West, while the new United Nations provided little support for feminism. Although the U.S. delegate, Eleanor Roosevelt, called for attention to women's issues and helped establish the UN Commission on the Status of Women in 1946, international resolutions proved ineffectual. The International Labour Organization ratified equal pay for equal work in 1951, but its declaration remained a dead letter for decades.

Late 1960s and Early 1970s

The entire situation changed dramatically in the late 1960s and early 1970s as a new women's liberation movement arose in the United States and spread rapidly to western Europe. Created by activist women who asserted that neither democracy nor socialism had brought them equality or justice, this new feminism challenged the status quo. Raising a wide range of issues, from rape laws to job segregation, feminists combined grassroots organizing for women with intellectual analyses of male dominance. Women's liberation rapidly went international, pressuring the United Nations to designate 1975 as International Women's Year, to hold a world conference in Mexico City that June, and subsequently to proclaim 1976–1985 the United Nations Decade for Women.

The meeting in Mexico included representatives of 133 governments, as well as 6,000 women who attended as delegates of nongovernmental organizations (NGOs). Deep differences among participants emerged: many governmental delegations were composed solely of men, and the United Nations itself remained a bastion of male privilege; the final World Plan of Action failed to mention women or sexism and instead focused on combating colonialism. Problems also arose at the world conference in Copenhagen in 1980, as discussion of clitoridectomy (female genital mutilation) divided delegates. Westerners condemned the practice as backward and barbaric; Muslim Middle Eastern and African women felt compelled to defend it as part of their traditions and religion.

Overcoming Division

But progress overcame such divisions. The conference in Copenhagen allowed for education and dialogue as well as dissension and resulted in the passage of the Convention on the Elimination of All Forms of Discrimination against Women (CEDAW), which set national targets and strategies for full female participation in government, society, and economic development. Nations began to create women's commissions and organizations, as well as gathering data about the female condition. Regional feminist alliances, like the Asian Women's Association, met and influenced policy. Western feminists became more aware of their own biases and supported nonwesterners' leadership of struggles against genital mutilation, child marriage, and female infanticide within their own societies. Issues developed in nonwestern cultures—for example, Indian ecofeminism or Islamic critiques of the exploitation of women's bodies in advertising—circulated widely. The global exchange of information as well as periodic world conferences brought increasing numbers of women together in the late 1980s and 1990s.

Fifteen thousand NGO representatives attended the meeting in Nairobi in 1985, and 35,000 participated in the Fourth World Conference on Women at Beijing in 1995. "My dear brothers and sisters, we have made it," declared Secretary-General Gertrude Mongella at the conference's conclusion, "We have managed to transcend socioeconomic disparities and diversities; we have kept aflame our common vision and goal of equality, development, and peace" (Bulbeck, 1998: 69). The contemporary international women's movement has been able to bring its presence to bear on a number of issues around the world. "Rape warfare" in the Balkans and elsewhere has been condemned internationally, and rape itself has been legally classified as a war crime rather than being accepted as an inevitable part of armed conflict. The Cairo International Conference on Population of 1994 concluded that women's education was a key factor in controlling population growth and urged nations to provide more schooling for girls. UNIFEM, the United Nations' monetary fund for women's development, provides resources for thousands of grassroots projects and groups. Women's studies has become a global enterprise, as feminists around the world criticize curricula, publications, and biases that perpetuate discrimination. "Beijing was a catalyst for a whole lot of things," the Zimbabwean Joana Foster, a leader of Women in Law and Development in Africa, told the Beijing Plus Five meeting in New York City in 2000. "Look at somewhere like Namibia, which now has 44 percent women in the local government system" (*New York Times,* 6 June 2000: 12A). Although much remains to be done, the modern international women's movement seems to have reached a critical mass in pushing for improvements in women's status around the globe.

See Also

FEMINISM: NINETEENTH CENTURY; FEMINISM: SECOND WAVE, *various regions*; FEMINISM: THIRD WAVE; WOMEN'S MOVEMENT: EARLY INTERNATIONAL MOVEMENT; WOMEN'S MOVEMENT: UNITED STATES

References and Further Reading

Ashworthy, Georgina, ed. 1995. *A diplomacy of the oppressed: New directions in international feminism.* London: Zed.

Basu, Amrita, ed. 1995. *The challenge of local feminisms: Women's movements in global perspective.* Boulder, Col.: Westview.

Berkovich, Nitza. 1999. *From motherhood to citizenship: Women's rights and international organizations.* Baltimore: Johns Hopkins University Press.

Bulbeck, Chilla. 1998. *Reorienting western feminisms: Women's diversity in a postcolonial world.* Cambridge: Cambridge University Press.

Daley, Caroline, and Melanie Nolan, eds. 1994. *Suffrage and beyond: International feminist perspectives.* New York: New York University Press.

Jayawardene, Kumari. 1986. *Feminism and nationalism in the third world.* London: Zed.

Moghadam, Valentine M., ed. 1994. *Identity politics and women: Cultural reassertions and feminism in international perspective.* Boulder, Col.: Westview.

Morgan, Robin. 1996. *Sisterhood is global: The international women's movement anthology.* Reprint with a new preface. New York: Feminist Press at the City University of New York.

Pettman, Jan Jindy. 1996. *Worlding women: A feminist international politics.* Sydney: Allen and Unwin.

Rupp, Leila J. 1998. *Worlds of women: The making of an international women's movement.* Princeton, N.J.: Princeton University Press.

Stienstra, Deborah. 1994. *Women's movements and international organizations.* New York: St. Martin's.

United Nations. 1996. *The United Nations and the advancement of women, 1945–1996.* New York: Department of Public Information, United Nations.

Bonnie S. Anderson

WOMEN'S MOVEMENT: United States

The history of women organizing in the United States is long and rich with successes and has survived periods of backlash and fragmentation. Several aspects of the movement illustrate its importance to American society. It is enduring, rooted in the abolition movement of the 1800s and continuing in a variety of forms into contemporary times. It is organized, drawing on networks of activists and organizations from the first attempts at suffrage to current critiques of gender inequality. The movement is also in flux, continuing to define and redefine the concept of feminism as a means for working to change social institutions and cultural norms. Finally, the women's movement is dynamic, constantly changing, and spilling over into other movements, keeping feminism alive for more than 150 years.

The movement emerged and reemerged during periods when the political environment was conducive to social change. Two periods in particular served as the starting point for "waves" of women's activism: the early nineteenth century and the 1960s and 1970s. These waves are characterized by times of unity, when women of different backgrounds united on common issue, and times of fragmentation, when feminists searched for ways to acknowledge differences and work on a variety of issues, including those pertaining to race, class, ethnicity, and sexual identity.

Early Feminism

Industrialization, rapid social change, and a public discussion on individuals' rights set the stage for the emergence of the first wave of feminism in the 1800s. The country was expanding, industrialization was changing how Americans thought about work and the family, and social reformers were interested in helping the "unfortunate" in society.

Many women were drawn to issues of social reform and, despite a lack of public roles, rights, and responsibilities, were instrumental in organizing and participating in the abolition movement to end slavery. In 1837, women organized the first Anti-Slavery Convention of American Women without the assistance of men. Although women such as Sarah and Angelina Grimké were active participants in the movement, they were largely denied the right to speak on the issues at conventions and were often attacked in public when they attempted to address the wrongs of slavery. This unequal treatment and silencing helped women connect their lack of individual rights to the issue of slavery and led to the organizing of the first women's rights convention (Flexner, 1971). Organized by the abolitionists Lucretia Mott and Elizabeth Cady Stanton, the Seneca Falls Women's Rights Convention, held 14 July 1848, focused on multiple issues including education rights, property reforms, and women's restricted roles within the family. Drawing 300 women and men, the convention resulted in a Declaration of Sentiments and a series of resolutions. The resolutions included the right of women to determine their own lives, seek employment, enjoy equality within marriage, and find freedom from oppressive legal and religious dictates. After much deliberation, the attendees also decided to address the controversial issue of women's suffrage.

It is a misconception that the first wave of U.S. feminism was concerned only with obtaining women's right to vote. Early feminists addressed a variety of women's concerns including fair custody arrangements, the right to own property as an individual after marriage, and freedom from restricted dress. The campaign to change women's dress was called the Bloomer movement after Amelia Bloomer, who advocated a more "rational" dress in her women's rights journal of the 1850s, *The Lily.* The movement was one of the first to inspire a hostile backlash, and, consequently, feminists dropped the issue after a few public actions.

While the Bloomer movement was short-lived and did not significantly divide the movement, issues of temperance, suffrage, and race posed challenges to feminists' attempts at a unified movement. Some women and men supported the efforts of the temperance movement in the late 1800s, reasoning that drunken behavior and alcoholism put dependent women and children at risk within the family. Other feminists avoided the issue, finding it too controversial and seeing it as detracting from the movement's other goals.

Suffrage also divided the movement. In 1868, the movement split into two different organizations, each pursuing different strategies. The National Woman Suffrage Association (NWSA), started by two well-known leaders, Elizabeth Cady Stanton and Susan B. Anthony, pursued a broad range of issues and endorsed more radical tactics. In 1872, for example, Anthony was arrested and tried for attempting to vote for Ulysses S. Grant in the presidential election. Stanton caused a controversy when she critiqued organized religion and wrote the *Women's Bible*. Stanton and Cady's journal, *The Revolution*, took a hard line on women's issues, running the slogan "Men, their rights and nothing more; women, their rights and nothing less" in every issue.

Stanton and Anthony believed that the courts were the fastest avenue to suffrage and pursued cases up to the Supreme Court. This strategy ran aground when, in 1875, the Supreme Court ruled that suffrage was not a privilege granted by the Fourteenth Amendment, which guarantees the rights of men. The association suffered another defeat when the Court also refused to add women to the Fifteenth Amendment, which prohibits the denial of suffrage due to race.

Adopting a different strategy was the American Woman Suffrage Association (AWSA), founded by Lucy Stone. The AWSA focused solely on suffrage issues and also had a publication, the *Woman's Journal*, which was more conservative than the *Revolution*. Stone and her primarily middle- and upper-class followers believed that working state by state was the best strategy for winning national suffrage. The AWSA had success working with western states, and Wyoming was the first to grant women suffrage.

Race also became a divisive issue when activists, fearing that black men would get the vote before white women, began to use racist arguments for women's suffrage. Some activists, such as Stanton, stated that white women should be given the vote to offset the votes of African, Chinese, and "ignorant" immigrant men. This argument served to drive a wedge between blacks and whites who were organizing together to win the vote (Deckard, 1979).

By 1890, the focus of both groups had narrowed to suffrage and the two organizations merged, creating the National American Woman Suffrage Association (NAWSA). In 1900, Carrie Chapman Catt and Anna Howard Shaw took over the presidency from Anthony and a second generation of women began to work for suffrage. Once again strategy and ideology divided the movement when, in 1919, a radical group called the Congressional Union formed. Led by Alice Paul, Congressional Union members engaged in radical tactics to draw public attention, such as hunger strikes, pickets, and getting arrested. The union, later renamed the National Women's Party (NWP), brought new attention to suffrage, and with the efforts of the NAWSA, the groups finally achieved their goal. The Nineteenth Amendment, introduced by feminists every year since 1848, passed on 26 August 1920.

During the years that followed suffrage, the movement was less active but did not disappear or die (Rupp and Taylor, 1987). Feminism stayed alive through the efforts of the NWP, the charisma of Alice Paul, and women in the Communist and Socialist Workers Parties. The NWP turned its focus to passing the Equal Rights Amendment (ERA). However, with the end of World War II and the increased social pressure for women to return to domestic roles after doing war-related work, feminism became "quaint" and little progress was made. Changes in women's lives during this period set the stage for a reawakening of the movement. In the 1950s, despite the traditional images of women in TV shows such as *Father Knows Best* and the *Donna Reed Show*, more and more middle-class white women were entering the labor force, and single motherhood and divorce rates were beginning to rise. The strain between societal expectations of domesticity and women's experiences in education and the workforce led to the reemergence of the movement in the 1960s and 1970s.

Contemporary Feminism

Just as in the early wave of the movement, the contemporary movement embraced a variety of strategies and goals, enjoyed periods of unity and division, and emerged in a time of social change. The 1960s and 1970s saw the passage of several pieces of legislation and policies that contributed to a dialogue on women's rights. The legislation included Title VII of the Civil Rights Act of 1965, the Equal Pay Act of 1963, and the establishment of the Equal Employment Opportunity Commission (EEOC). The reemergence of feminist activism was marked by two events instrumental in the formation of the movement's two "branches." First was the formation of the National Organization for Women (NOW), an organization that would come to symbolize liberal feminism and the women's rights branch (Freeman, 1975). Second was the break from the civil rights and other New Left movements by younger women dissatisfied with the lack of attention to gender issues (Evans, 1979). These women would come to form the women's liberation branch of the movement and largely embrace ideas of radical and socialist feminism.

The membership of the women's rights branch of the movement was composed of predominantly older, middle-class, professional women. For example, NOW was founded in 1966 by a group of professional women discouraged by the lack of enforcement by the EEOC. To address women's subordination, NOW created its own Bill of Rights that included working for the ERA, equal education for women, and maternity leave and child care policies. One of the primary founders of NOW was Betty Friedan, author of *The Feminine Mystique,* a book that brought many women to feminism, particularly suburban homemakers stymied by domestic roles. The women's rights branch focused on change through legislation and placement of women in positions of power as the vehicle to equality. Therefore many of the women's rights organizations came to resemble the institutions that feminists targeted for change and developed a professionalized and hierarchical structure.

The ideas of liberal feminism reflected the overall strategies and ideologies of the women's rights branch. Liberal feminism advocates gaining equality through women's access to power. Therefore, men and women will become equal when they are in comparable positions in society. Besides NOW, organizations such as Women's Equity Action League, the Feminist Majority, and the National Women's Political Caucus are examples of women's rights groups.

Drawing on younger, college-age students, the women's liberation branch encompassed different ideologies and organizational structures. Women coming into women's liberation did so after repeated attempts in the early 1960s to encourage civil rights, student rights, and antiwar leaders to acknowledge gender discrimination within their movements. These women, such as the civil rights activists Casey Hayden and Mary King, were repeatedly told by a predominantly male leadership that women's issues were secondary to other causes. Hayden and King were two of the first women to articulate their grievances, in 1965, in a paper entitled "Sex and Caste: A Kind of Memo." Their attempts to raise issues of sexism were ridiculed and disregarded and led women to organize separately.

The women's liberation branch endorsed the ideology that change comes through personal and systematic transformations. To accomplish personal transformation, the Redstockings, a radical feminist group, began to organize consciousness-raising groups (Brownmiller, 1999). *Consciousness-raising* (CR) is a process by which women share personal experiences and beliefs as a means to illuminate patriarchal control and oppression. In CR groups, women discussed a variety of issues from sexuality to housework, connecting them to gender inequality, thus giving rise to the feminist slogan "The personal is political." CR groups, as well as other women's liberation groups, differed from women's rights organizations. Women's liberation groups tended to be collectivist versus hierarchical, and without established leaders, organizational positions, and structure.

Two feminist ideologies came to dominate women's liberation groups. One was radical feminism, centering on the belief that women are subordinate because of societal systems maintaining male superiority. Therefore, when women enter into male systems of power, they accomplish little for equal rights. Radical feminists believe that societal transformation comes from a complete transformation of society, something that begins on a personal level. A similar feminist ideology is socialist feminism. Socialist feminists turn to capitalism as the reason for gender inequality and argue for an economic and societal transformation. Radical feminist groups include The Feminists, WITCH (Women's International Terrorist Conspiracy from Hell), and the Redstockings. An example of a socialist feminist organization is the Chicago Women's Liberation Union, which emerged in the 1970s.

The different feminist ideologies and organizational structures of the two branches corresponded with their goals. The women's rights branch took on more "mainstream" issues of employment discrimination and worked to end sex-segregated want ads and age discrimination in occupations such as that of airline flight attendant. The women's liberation branch often focused on cultural issues and staged a takeover of *Ladies' Home Journal* in 1969 and a highly publicized protest of the Miss America Contest in 1968.

Actions from both branches brought media and public attention to feminism. From the years 1972 to 1982, the movement was in its heyday. Women's liberation groups continued to draw women into feminism and caused cultural shock waves with their critiques of femininity, gender roles, and heterosexuality. Women's rights groups won legislative ground with the passage of Title IX, ending sex discrimination in publicly funded education, and *Roe* v. *Wade,* a Supreme Court decision that allowed for legalized abortion.

Although these years were times of success for feminists, it was also a time of conflict and fragmentation. Lesbians, working-class women, and women of color all voiced dissatisfaction with the predominantly white, middle-class women in the movement. NOW in particular had difficult times because of dissension over lesbians in the organization. In the late 1960s, NOW's president, Betty Friedan, labeled lesbians a "lavender menace," forcing many lesbians to leave the organization. At the Second Congress to Unite Women, 20 lesbians protested and took over the stage wearing lavender T-shirts identifying themselves as the "Lavender Menace." In a show of support, women from the audience joined the protesters. These conflicts caused some lesbian feminists to organize separately in the 1970s, and in 1973 they held a national conference. NOW eventually changed its position and began to work for lesbian rights. Working-class women have also struggled to remain in the movement. Believing that their work and family lives were not being addressed, they created separate organizations. For example, the Coalition of Labor Union Women was formed in 1974, when 3,000 women met to address sexism in the unions and also women's inequality in society.

Women of color have also worked with and separated from the movement. Black women in particular have a long history of activism. The National Association of Colored Women, started in the 1890s, was the first black organization in the United States. Black women, along with Chicano and Asian-American women, often found that their racial, ethnic, and class-based experiences were ignored and consequently created organizations to address their issues. In the 1970s and 1980s a variety of organizations were started including Black Women in Sisterhood for Action, the Mexican American Women's National Association, and the Pan Pacific and Southeast Asian Women's Association of the U.S.A.

As time passed, many of the women's liberationist and women's rights activists came together and were united in an effort to pass the ERA. As feminists pushed for ERA, a constitutional amendment prohibiting sex discrimination, counterforces organized to stop their progress. One major countermovement group was Phyllis Schafly's organization STOP ERA. Lacking the needed number of state ratifications, the amendment was declared defeated in 1982. Despite this defeat, feminists have continued to work for its passage.

With the defeat of the ERA and the election of a conservative president, Ronald Reagan, feminism faced a period of backlash in the 1980s (Faludi, 1991). Many of the gains of the past decade were eroded and media pundits labeled the movement dead and the 1980s the "postfeminist era." Among the setbacks were a lack of compliance with Title IX, increased cases of work-related sexual harassment, increased restrictions on abortion and related services, and an escalation of antiabortion violence, including clinic bombings and murders.

Although suffering from some setbacks, feminism continues to thrive into contemporary times. Women's studies programs in universities and colleges, which arose from the women's liberation branch, continue to grow, along with feminist scholarship in a variety of disciplines. The 1990s saw the passage of the Gender Equity in Education Act and other women-friendly legislation. Young women continue to identify as feminists and organize around issues specific to their generation. Feminism has also found a home on the Internet, and cyberfeminism, using information technologies, works to empower and mobilize women. In addition, the influences of feminism and women's movement activism can be seen in a variety of movements including antirape, ecofeminism, women's health, environmental, and peace.

American women's activism, through the Internet and international conferences, has also influenced the global feminist community. Cyberfeminists in Australia, Europe, and the United States work collaboratively on feminist actions and art projects. In 1995, the United Nations Fourth Conference on Women and NGO Forum in Beijing, China, brought together approximately 35,000 women from around the world to work on a variety of issues and to learn from one another.

In sum, the American women's movement has a long history of activists coming together and separating. While some initial victories have been reversed or challenged, feminists still organize and continue to work for women's equality (Whittier, 1995). Activists draw on their feminist history and work in informal CR groups and formal organizations, and through new technologies. Women activists seek to change cultural practices, to legislate their equality, and to educate society about gender equality.

See Also

FEMINISM: *related entries* (AFRICAN-AMERICAN; ASIAN-AMERICAN; CHICANA; FIRST-WAVE; NORTH AMERICAN; POSTMODERN; RADICAL; SECOND-WAVE NORTH AMERICAN; THIRD WAVE)

References and Further Reading

Anderson, Bonnie. S. 2000. *Joyous greetings: The first international women's movement, 1830–1860.* New York: Oxford University Press.

Brownmiller, Susan. 1999. *In our time: Memoir of a revolution.* New York: Random House.

Carden, Maren Lockwood. 1974. *The new feminist movement.* New York: Russell Sage Foundation.

Davis, Flora. 1991. *Moving the mountain: The women's movement in America.* New York: Simon and Schuster.

Deckard, Barbara Sinclair. 1979. *The women's movement: Political, socioeconomic, and psychological issues.* New York: Harper and Row.

DuPlessis, Rachel Blau, and Ann Snitow. 1998. *Feminist memoir project: Voices from women's liberation.* New York: Three Rivers.

Evans, Sarah. 1979. *Personal politics: The roots of women's liberation in the civil rights movement and new left.* New York: Knopf.

Faludi, Susan. 1991. *Backlash: The undeclared war on women.* New York: Anchor.

Flexner, Eleanor. 1971. *A century of struggle.* New York: Atheneum.

Freeman, Jo. 1975. *The politics of women's liberation.* New York: Longman.

Hole, Judith, and Ellen Levine. 1971. *Rebirth of feminism.* New York: Quadrangle.

Rosen, Ruth. 2000. *The world split open: How the modern women's movement changed America.* New York: Viking.

Rupp, Leila J., and Verta Taylor. 1987. *Survival in the doldrums: The American women's rights movement, 1945 to 1960s.* New York: Oxford University Press.

Whittier, Nancy. 1995. *Feminist generations.* Philadelphia: Temple University Press.

Jo Reger

WOMEN'S STUDIES: Overview

In India, young women who have taken women's studies courses perform street theater in the poor districts to dramatize the fierce determination of a young girl resisting the deeply embedded structural and cultural forces that dismiss, marginalize, and subordinate her. In South Africa, a young woman argues in a hushed but insistent voice for the necessity of women's studies in a country where the euphoria of triumphing over a white supremacist state sometimes masks the periodic violence against black women. In central and eastern Europe, women's nongovernmental organizations (NGOs) shelter emerging feminist scholars who seek to untangle gender politics from the earlier constraints of a communist legacy. In the West Indies, scholars in a women's development center look for alternative socioeconomic development models that won't leave women and girls in poverty. In the United States, lesbian and bisexual students

turn hungrily to women's studies to analyze the origins of the homophobia that haunts their lives.

Women's studies has circled the globe since its emergence from the women's movement in the United States and Europe in the late 1960s. A mercurial creation, women's studies continues to change over time, geography, and political context, but some tenets are foundational, and many issues form points of connections between women's studies scholars around the world. High among them is the insistence that women describe what the world looks like from where they stand—be it a field, factory, house, office, or studio. With this priority, women's studies continues to serve as a bellwether of women's status.

Definitions

Although the emergence of women's studies in each country needs to be understood in its local and historical contexts, women's studies scholars share some fundamental working assumptions wherever they are located. Women's studies is the academic arm of the women's movement, and it sometimes follows, sometimes leads, and sometimes debates with the larger political, cultural, and economic organized efforts to improve women's lives. As a discipline, it assumes that women matter, that they have shared—but differently experienced—a history of subordination, and that they have always helped shape and sustain culture and society. The principal category of analysis in women's studies is the concept of gender, understood as a pervasive social construction that reflects and determines differentials of power and opportunity. Most women's studies practitioners perceive gender as operating in a complex matrix with race, class, national identity, ethnicity, religion, sexual identity, and other key markers. They seek to produce new knowledge and to provide a framework through which to analyze all existing knowledge. Their goal is to help people uncover the ideological dynamics of their lives and then become actively engaged in social, political, and personal transformations. Women's studies practitioners aspire through scholarship and teaching to imagine alternatives to present systems of inequality and to solve societal problems that threaten the well-being of all humanity.

Women's studies is almost everywhere. It is found in separate women's studies courses, programs, and majors at the undergraduate and graduate levels or as a special area of focus within specific disciplines. It is in campus-based and community-based research centers that either focus on women alone or study women and gender as part of a larger agenda. It is found in women's centers that provide special support to women through services, education, or training.

It is found in adult education, government-sponsored programs, and community-based education.

Women's studies recasts the understanding of the past, records the present more accurately, and opens up new possibilities for the future. Because of the knowledge base that women's studies has uncovered and developed, it will be difficult to erase women from humanity's history ever again. Women have been creating, working, caring, building, writing, and guiding through the ages, but this reality has for the most part been omitted from or devalued or misrepresented in history books. Women's studies makes it less likely that such distortions can be perpetuated. The research, books, journals, publishing houses, archives, centers, programs, infrastructures, and institutional locations of power that women's studies has amassed in four short decades are formidable—and in many cases permanent. Women's studies has therefore helped restore continuity historically, reveal intersections geographically, and invoke women's astonishing diversity as a resource for the planet.

Origins and Evolutions

Each country where women's studies has taken hold has its own particular historical context. In many instances, there were parallel and sometimes intersecting causes that led to the simultaneous creation of women's studies in different pockets around the globe. But it was in the United States that women's studies took hold early, and grew rapidly, and therefore influenced the shape of women's studies to follow. The United States and western Europe defined the first major wave of women's studies globally. Later, U.S. and western European women's studies was influenced by the emergence of different kinds of women's studies programs, especially those in developing nations.

Perhaps because of the flexibility of American institutions, women's studies expanded and institutionalized more quickly in the United States than anywhere else in the world. Like almost every women's studies program in almost every country, women's studies in the United States was an outgrowth of an emerging, divergent women's movement that itself was spawned by other political movements. Disparate women's studies courses offered in the mid-1960s coalesced into formal academic programs in 1969. By 1973, there were 78 undergraduate women's studies programs; by 1976, when the National Women's Studies Association was founded, there were 276. By 2000, there were 680 undergraduate and 111 graduate women's studies programs in the United States.

Not far behind, Japan, Australia, Taiwan, India, New Zealand, South Korea, and the West Indies initiated women's studies courses and programs in the 1970s. These programs sought to redefine or adapt the emerging new field

in terms of the particular circumstances, histories, and politics of their own nations. In the 1980s a string of new nations followed suit, and women's studies programs and women's research centers were seen in the Philippines, Thailand, South Africa, Puerto Rico, the Dominican Republic, the Commonwealth of Independent States (Belarus, Russia, and Ukraine), and the People's Republic of China. In the 1990s, women's studies became visible in still other nations, such as Malaysia, Vietnam, the Czech Republic, Slovakia, and Uganda.

A series of international women's conferences quickened the development of women's studies around the world and broadened the focus from U.S., or western, concerns to global ones. A series of conferences begun in the 1980s and held every three years in different countries brought together women's studies practitioners, researchers, and policy makers. These meetings helped cast a new kind of international dialogue, enlarging, deepening, and complicating existing theoretical notions and educational structures.

Even more influential has been the series of international conferences on women that the United Nations (UN) has sponsored since 1975, when it announced its Decade for Women. The conferences have been held in Mexico City (1975), Copenhagen (1980), Nairobi (1985), and Beijing (1995), with a smaller follow-up conference in New York City in 2000 to assess progress. The most dynamic part of the conferences has been the NGO Forum wrapped around each of the more formal UN sessions. In each forum, a huge number of activists on women's and girls' behalf gather. The result is that, for example, women's studies groups who come to the conference only to discuss education leave having reconsidered the relation of education to larger transformations of social justice.

By the time the Copenhagen conference was held in 1980, any illusion that a monolithic women's movement existed had been dispelled. Participants were energized, but also newly aware of the deep fissures between national movements that would need to be addressed before women could collaborate internationally on common concerns. Women in western countries slowly began to see women's issues with new eyes and to construct a worldview that acknowledged that theirs was merely one vantage point among many. Although differences became apparent at the NGO Forums, ultimately they have actually helped a global women's movement coalesce. The women's agenda hammered out over the years has become more focused and the tie among women's organizations even stronger. The UN Platform for Action that emanated from the Beijing conference identified 12 areas of critical concern, all of which are threaded throughout women's studies: poverty, education and training, health, violence, armed conflict, the economy, power and decision making, mechanisms to advance women, human rights, the media, the environment, and the girl child. The future direction of women's studies will be determined by how effectively practitioners tap the generative possibilities in the dynamic tensions that distinguish this worldwide movement.

Women's Studies Programs Worldwide

In the first decade of women's studies, any attempt to chart programs and projects would have produced a spotty map. Not so today. Women's studies exists in hundreds of countries, thousands of colleges and universities, and even more independent organizations and government-sponsored offices. It has proliferated in the number of courses, academic programs, and degrees offered and in the ways it has been institutionalized. More professors are appointed to teach women's studies as part of their field, and research on women and gender issues seems to have no end. Yet some programs are fragile, faculties are sometimes marginalized, and resistance to the message of equality, social transformation, and economic parity can be fierce. Nonetheless, the overall picture is a testament to women's commitment and collective power. The future looks promising. This is good news for everyone, since women's studies has proved to be one location where alternative visions are cultivated for how we allocate our natural and economic resources, organize our communities, and preserve our cultural and ethical values.

United States. Having begun to offer women's studies courses in the late 1960s, the United States was the first country to establish women's studies programs formally in universities and colleges and soon had the most expansive, entrenched programs in the world. In addition to self-standing women's studies programs, U.S. educational institutions initiated what they called the curriculum transformation movement, faculty development incentives to integrate new scholarship on women and gender into traditional courses. Women's studies is also supported by a network of women's presses; feminist journals, both discipline-specific and interdisciplinary; women's caucuses within professional scholarly associations; and women-centered professional associations. Hardly a mainstream university press in the United States fails to promote publications on women and gender, and hardly an academic discipline remains unaffected. With private and government funding, there have also been organized efforts to reach out to primary and secondary teachers as well as influence how they are initially prepared for the classroom. Women's studies in the United States has proved resilient and intellectually flexible.

That said, many of the programs are small, their faculty overworked, and their budgets modest. There continue to be debates about the relationship between theory and practice, with growing criticism that some programs have abandoned their engagement in social change and focus too much on theory, without translating its implications to a broader public. Among the top agenda items for women's studies in the United States are globalizing women's studies; continuing to investigate the relationship of gender to diversity; renewing a commitment to put women's studies theory in the service of social justice movements; integrating feminism, science studies, and technology; and investing in curriculum and faculty development with a special emphasis on interdisciplinary frameworks.

Europe and the Commonwealth of Independent States. Most western European countries date the inception of women's studies to the women's movement of the late 1960s and 1970s. Although there is variation among European countries in location, focus, and funding of women's studies projects, women's studies can be found in all western European countries and is supported by a variety of cross-national women's studies organizations. Women's studies research is sustained by a strong network of research centers, women's studies associations, journals, and new technology sites. The development of women's studies in western Europe reflects both a north-south and an east-west economic divide. In addition, political, social, and cultural influences and the structures of educational institutions have given distinctive national imprints to women's studies in the region. Nonetheless, the region's women studies initiatives share some commonalities that have been heightened by the formation of the European Union.

As is the case around the globe, some women's studies activities in Europe are located outside academia by choice or by necessity, and others are embedded in the structures of academic institutions. For example, in Spain women's studies is strongest outside the academy, because of its alliance with groups who resisted the Franco regime, whereas in the Netherlands, the Ministry of Education provided the financial support that led to the appointment of women's studies teachers and coordinators in almost all universities. Despite the fact that women make up almost half the undergraduate population, it is still not possible to take an undergraduate degree in women's studies in many countries in western Europe. Postgraduate programs have historically been the most institutionalized. It is still rare for women's studies departments to have a dedicated women's studies staff, which means that many of the faculty work both in women's studies and in their home disciplines. Thus, although women's studies courses are offered in almost all countries in the region, most are integrated into existing disciplines, with few institutions offering courses at both the undergraduate and the graduate level and even fewer offering degrees or diplomas in women's studies.

For the emerging women's studies programs in central and eastern Europe as well as in the Commonwealth of Independent States, western Europe along with the United States is providing key leadership. The enormous political, social, economic, and cultural shifts that occurred in those regions after 1989 opened up new explorations of gender in an entirely new context. Built on the resources of a women's movement that predated 1989, a degree from the Program on Gender and Culture at the Central European University in Budapest and women's studies specializations at Charles University in Prague have been established. Women's organizations are an important leavening force in eastern and central Europe and are critical to the growth of women's studies.

Women's studies programs in this region are reexamining the role of gender in communist ideology, in postsocialist transition movements, and in the future of the new democratic Europe. Free markets have opened up some opportunities, but it is not clear what impact they will have on women's lives. Many people in eastern and central Europe, as in other parts of the world, are suspicious about western feminism and what some see as its colonizing practices. The goal among some feminist leaders is to foster a two-way exchange about feminisms instead of being trapped in bipolar oppositions.

In the Commonwealth of Independent States, the perestroika of 1985–1991 opened up exchange with western feminists for the first time. In Russia, unlike central and eastern Europe, there is not a strong women's movement or women's organizations to catalyze the construction of women's studies in higher education. Nonetheless, by 1989, Russia had established the Center for Gender Studies, which came amid some new publications and several cross-cultural conferences. Predictably, there is great variation among the republics in terms of women's studies; Russia has the strongest women's studies activities. Wars in parts of the commonwealth have hampered the development of women's studies. One of the central concerns of feminists in the region is whether the policy directives that women's studies generates will be sufficient in the face of economic instability and political uncertainty.

Caribbean islands and Latin America. The Caribbean islands share a history of colonization by European nations. The English Caribbean has the most institutionalized women's studies programs in the region. Its Center for Gen-

der and Development, established at the University of West Indies in 1977, focuses primarily on population, the environment, and alternative socioeconomic development models. In the Spanish Caribbean, women's studies began outside academia through NGOs. The Gender Studies Center in Puerto Rico offers the only master's degree in women's studies in the Caribbean. The French-Dutch Caribbean Islands have only modest initiatives to develop women's studies, in part because the government has resisted supporting them.

In most of Latin America, the 1970s stand out for military regimes and not for women's studies. The UN Women's Conference in Mexico in 1975 sparked significant grassroots organizing on behalf of women. A strong heterogeneous women's movement was spawned through efforts to restore democracy, elevate human rights, and meet the needs of families and communities. It in turn helped create women's studies, especially when democratic institutions were restored in the early 1980s. Most women's research and activist projects occurred outside academia and were supported financially not by the government but by outside international agencies.

The first women's studies program in academia was the Nucleus of Study and Research on Women and Gender, created in 1981 in Rio de Janeiro. By 1994, 50 nuclei belonged to a national network in Brazil. A similar proliferation of programs occurred in other countries. At the UN conference in Nairobi in 1985, 11 Latin American countries participated in the International Women's Studies Section. A decade later, 17 Latin American countries had women's studies programs in their universities.

Asia. The women's movement in south Asia has a long and complex history dating to British and French colonization of the region, but it became visible on a large scale only in the late 1970s and eventually found expression in women's studies, with perhaps the earliest program in the region being the research center for women's studies at SNDT Women's University in Bombay in 1974. The women's movement was influenced by a combination of factors: critiques of underdevelopment, the black power movement in the United States, world anger over neocolonialism, and feminist voices from western Europe and North America. The south Asian agenda for women's studies coalesces around the problems that all women in this region share, principally the ways poverty and widespread female illiteracy make it extremely difficult for them to obtain education and knowledge. The women's movements here are also deeply affected by interventionist governments that are alternately welfarist and coercive. Although India has the most extensive women's studies network in south Asia, all the countries have some form of women's studies education, research, and activism.

In India, a government report, *Towards Equality* (1975), galvanized an incipient feminist movement into action by revealing the extent of social and economic injustice the majority of Indian women suffered. Within a few years, a national conference on women's studies was held, which led to the formation of the Indian Association of Women's Studies, involving 18 universities, 10 colleges, and 15 research institutes. Parliament has been a partner in women's studies, passing laws such as the National Policy on Education (1986), which prescribes that the national education system provide "education for women's equality." Since the mid-1980s, the government of India has also funded women's studies centers and cells in a number of colleges and universities. In Nepal and Bhutan, women's studies research has similarly been supported by governmental initiatives. In addition to the government, NGOs, especially women's groups, have been critical partners.

Pakistan's women's rights activists have been deeply involved in debates about knowledge and empowerment. The Women's Action Forum has a notable global project titled "Women Living under Muslim Law."

Feminist NGOs throughout south Asia stand out for their efforts to promote regional cooperation and solidarity. Several successful comparative research projects have focused on war, women, violence, human rights, and citizenship.

Like women's studies practitioners throughout the world, some in south Asia ponder the relevance of women's studies in the academy to the lives of most women, especially those who do not speak or read English. Yet others worry that too many women's studies courses are optional and ancillary and frequently dependent on a specific professor rather than being tied to a program of study.

Japan and Korea developed women's studies programs and projects at roughly the same time during the late 1970s, and these are now some of the strongest in the region. Influenced in part by Japanese women who had studied in the United States and Europe and the UN women's conferences, the Women's Studies Society was founded in 1977, followed two years later by the Association of Women's Studies in Japan. Today 25 percent of universities and junior colleges in Japan have women's studies, and 13 universities have institutes on gender and women studies. Japanese feminists have been focused on the changing gender roles and double binds of women, women's roles in the family and marketplace, and sexual discrimination in the workplace. Korea dates the emergence of its women's studies to this same decade, attributing some of the impetus in the 1970s to the govern-

ment's decision to liberalize its policies, which opened the country up to foreign influences. Ewha Women's University established the Korean Women's Institute in 1977, after which 9 other universities followed suit with courses and institutes.

Although women's studies began in 1972 in Taiwan, martial law restricted the development of an open women's studies movement until a Gender and Social Studies Program began in 1985. The issues dominating the program's agenda include minority and indigenous women, student movements, the environment, and women's labor. By 1987 the People's Republic of China had also established its first Center for Women's Studies, influenced by the UN conferences on women. Its research focuses on labor issues, internal migrant women, and the fact that multinational corporations are not protecting women workers.

Slower to develop than in the rest of Asia, women's studies in southeast Asia has expanded only recently, provoked in part by the UN conferences on women. Gender equity and social justice dominate its concerns, but lack of funding, uneven commitment by the government, and a stress on utilitarian agendas with a narrow focus on women and development driven by government and international agencies stifle more expansive development and outreach. Countries in southeast Asia are also ambivalent, as are many third world countries, about western feminism.

The Philippines began offering women's studies as early as 1981, opting both to mainstream women's studies and to create autonomous units, much like the United States and the Netherlands. In 1987, the universities organized themselves into a consortium, the Women's Studies Association of the Philippines, which includes 65 colleges. In Malaysia, there was no formal women's studies unit until 1994. Programs are frequently funded by outside agencies such as the United Nations Educational, Scientific, and Cultural Organization (UNESCO) or international investment interests. In Indonesia, women's studies appeared in the 1980s, but its most active research is not funded by the university. In Thailand there are 10 institutes doing a range of women's activities and small women's studies centers funded by foreign agencies.

The newest women's studies activities are found in Vietnam, where they are connected to mass organizations such as the Vietnam Women's Union and the Peasants' Union. The Center for Women's Studies began in 1987, followed by a number of new centers that tend to focus on practical policy matters such as family planning, urban issues, and foreign investments. The research agenda is driven by national government policy and international donor agencies.

Australia and New Zeland. Like the United States and western Europe, New Zealand and Australia had women's studies programs in place by the early 1970s. New Zealand's first women's studies courses were offered in 1974. Within two years, there were 46 women's studies courses, and the number tripled two years later. New Zealand founded its Women's Studies Association in 1976, the same year the United States founded its association. Though highly popular with students, women's studies programs are often underresourced and marginal.

In Australia, women's studies began in 1973, and the first program was institutionalized two years later. By 1986, five universities offered majors in women's studies, and by 1993, 30 of the 43 higher education institutions offered women's studies topics (in contrast to western Europe, where undergraduate women's studies is not offered). The Australian Women's Studies Association was established in 1989. Though progress in improving women's status has stalled recently, women's studies is making a new connection with indigenous people and seeking to be a more multicultural. As in many other countries, there are uneasy alliances between academic and grassroots feminists.

Africa. Women's studies in Africa has emerged in relation to African studies, especially in its postcolonial context; international and local women's activism; and the development industry. In academia, as African women produce their own scholarship, they have critiqued both western universities' domination of knowledge production in women's studies and the male domination of African scholarship.

Spurred in part by the UN's declaration of its Decade for Women in 1975, feminist scholars began to focus on African women's collective protests in the 1960s and 1970s and their participation in national liberation movements. By 1977, they had formed the Association of African Women for Research and Development, which was soon followed by study groups and then a steady, if limited, number of other research centers. Women's studies courses were first taught in 1979 at Ahmadu Bello University and have slowly spread to other institutions.

Critiques in the 1970s that examined women's involvement in economic development generated an exciting stream of research about women's roles in families, communities, and the larger economy. Since servicing international development agencies continues to dominate African political economies, it will remain a critical site for women's studies engagement.

A more regional focus is cultivated in some regions, such as southern Africa, where there are strong cultural and economic ties, migratory patterns, cultural exchanges, and linguistic fusions. Gender equity there as in other African nations is not always seen as important as national, antiracist, or anticolonial struggles. Nonetheless, in 1989 the University of Natal in Durban, South Africa, offered the first women's studies graduate degree. The University of Western Cape followed with a graduate degree in 1995. Several other institutions offer courses, but no others offer a degree yet. Often the centers are underresourced, and the faculty teaches women's studies on top of other duties.

Structural Forms and Institutional Locations

A quick review of the global map of women's studies reveals a wide variety of structural approaches with four central components: research, teaching, women's support services, and social activism and outreach. Although some countries manage to weave all four components together in one unit, more typically there is either development of one aspect at the expense of another or a strategic decision to separate the four. In some cases, university structures are so resistant to women's studies that self-sustaining organizations need to be established outside the academy. In other cases, universities have nurtured and sheltered the development of women's studies in a wide range of institutional forms.

Every nation has identified research and the generation of new knowledge as critical to women's studies. Most have established strong research centers. The focus of the research is hotly debated as feminists struggle to define their relationship to the practical needs of women and of nations. Third world countries seem to have the strongest history of welding the development of their women's studies programs with urgent economic and political needs. Africa, Latin America, and southeast Asia have invented useful models worth investigating. Because women's studies grew out of the women's movement for equity and justice, its future strength depends on its ability to negotiate and renegotiate the role it will play in eliminating gender inequities and forging policies that empower and protect women. How effectively women's studies can align education to action will determine just how transformative this new interdisciplinary field will be.

In terms of institutional locations, western Europe has its strongest institutionalization at the graduate level, while India, the United States, and Japan are distinguished principally by their undergraduate offerings. However, each country has sought to achieve a better balance between undergraduate and graduate programs. Every country seems to debate the merits of autonomous versus integrative women's studies. The Netherlands, Australia, and the United States seem to be the most successful in seeking to do both simultaneously, sustaining independent women's studies programs with a designated faculty and integrating women's studies into the curriculum of every discipline. Whichever the approach, all university programs tend to be under-resourced and their faculties overworked.

Where a women's studies program is located is often determined by its funding. In some nations, such as the Netherlands, the Nordic countries, and India, the government allocates significant resources to women's studies programs. In many developing nations, such as those in southeast Asia, Africa, and South Asia, outside foreign agencies including UNESCO, the United Nations Development Fund for Women, the U.S. Agency for International Development, and the Canadian International Development Agency provide funding for various kinds of women's studies work. Although it has access to some government monies, women's studies in the United States is funded primarily by private foundations, especially the Ford Foundation. It and several other private foundations have also begun to support the development of women's studies internationally, with a special interest in cross-fertilization among programs.

Emerging Themes

As women's studies has developed over more than three decades, it has at its core everywhere an analysis of power. It is particularly interested in examining the specific ways in which some groups are advantaged and others disadvantaged. In addition to examining gender as a worldwide mechanism for social stratification and differentiation, women's studies programs investigate racial stratification in North America, Africa, and Latin America; class stratification in Europe, Oceania, and South America; and religious differences in south Asia, north Africa, and the United States. Economic development undergirds women's studies in each country, but the framing of that notion varies widely, especially between "north" and "south." Exploration of sexual difference, a hallmark of women's studies in the United States, has also begun to appear in Canada, Oceania, western Europe, and some developing nations.

As the women's movement and women's studies begin to effect social transformations, they have been subject to increasing backlash from conservative forces that resist such changes. The United States has witnessed a particularly aggressive backlash, first in the mid-1980s and then again in the mid-1990s. Similar political forces have hampered women's studies progress in some parts of Europe, some countries in Latin America, and in Mideast, with Afghanistan being a shocking example. The rise of religious fundamentalism, whether Christian, Muslim, or other religions, often threatens women's studies worldwide, as do the violence and warfare seem, for example, in central Africa, the Balkans, and parts of southeast Asia.

Although North America and western Europe had a head start on the development of robust women's studies programs, programs now emerging in other parts of the globe are challenging the United States and western Europe to reexamine their categories, restore their connections to grassroots women's organizations, and assess women's roles in the West as contributing to the shameful global imbalances in resource allocations. Postcolonial studies offers an exciting new dimension for women's studies, and the series of UN conferences on women provides a new context for understanding the issues, both the points of connection and the points of profound disagreement. Finally, women's studies around the globe is beginning to reframe its work, both locally and globally. Instead of providing a more equitable and just world *for* women, it seeks to establish a more equitable and just world *through* women. It is clear from the Forward Looking Strategies generated by the Beijing UN conference on women in 1995 that the women's agenda in the twenty-first century, both in the movement and in women's studies, is to transform the world not just for women's sake but for everyone's sake. As the U.S. Congresswoman Bella Abzug argued in the early 1980s, every issue is a women's issue. The development of a women's studies movement globally promises to help everyone understand more precisely just what that might mean.

See Also

EDUCATION: HIGHER EDUCATION; GENDER; GENDER STUDIES; WOMEN'S STUDIES: BACKLASH; WOMEN'S STUDIES: FUNDING; WOMEN'S STUDIES, *regional entries;* WOMEN'S STUDIES: RESEARCH CENTERS AND INSTITUTES

References and Further Reading

Bird, Elizabeth. 1996. Women's studies in European higher education. *European Journal of Women's Studies* 3(3): 151–165.

Bonnin, D. 1995. *National report on women's studies in South Africa.* Durban, Natal, South Africa: University of Natal.

Boxer, Marilyn Jacoby. 1998. *When women ask the questions: Creating women's studies in America.* Baltimore: Johns Hopkins University Press.

Committee on Women's Studies in South and South-East Asia, eds. 1994. *Women's studies, women's lives: Theory and practice in south and southeast Asia.* New Delhi: Kali for Women.

Moraga, Cherrie, and Gloria Anzaldua. 1981. *This bridge called my back: Writings by radical women of color.* Latham, N.Y.: Kitchen Table/Women of Color.

Musil, Caryn McTighe, ed. 1992. *The courage to question: Women's studies and student learning.* Washington, D.C.: Association of American Colleges and Universities.

Pearson, Carol S., Donna L. Shavlik, and Judith G. Touchton, eds. 1989. *Educating the majority: Women challenge tradition in higher education.* New York: Macmillan.

Women's Studies International Forum. 10(5). Special issue: Women's studies in Australia.

Caryn McTighe Musil

WOMEN'S STUDIES: Australia

Since its official inception in 1973, academic women's studies has spread rapidly and become an institutionalized academic discipline (or interdiscipline). Academic women's studies has maintained a largely productive relationship with the wider women's movement. Its major specifically indigenous contribution to international women's studies scholarship has been to prompt debate concerning "official feminism" (Eisenstein, 1990) or the role of femocrats in reshaping public policies to the advantage of women. The major challenge over the next decade will be to enrich and diversify women's studies beyond its largely white, Anglo-centric, middle-class, and increasingly middle-aged voice. This challenge faces the Australian women's movement at a time when femocracy is in retreat in public service around Australia, and when women's studies programs in universities are reconstituting themselves as gender studies or cultural studies in response to budget cuts and students' changing interests. The women's movement shares with other leftist movements a lack of success in responding to the globalization of economic rationalism and a reduced commitment to the welfare state on the part of the Australian government.

The Institutional Development of Women's Studies

The first named "women's studies" course was introduced in 1973 at Flinders University, a radical course that saw the women's movement as its validating reference group. The first interdisciplinary course was offered in 1974 at Sydney University. The first independently located program was introduced at the Australian National University in 1975,

along with the first named and tenurable lectureship. In 1986 five Australian universities taught women's studies majors. The first full-fledged university department was formed at Adelaide University in 1992. By mid-decade, there were 30 tenured faculty positions designated as women's studies (Magarey et al., 1994). By the end of the century, almost every university in Australia offered at least some subjects in women's or gender studies. Twenty-two of Australia's thirty-three universities offered a collectively identified set of subjects in either women's studies or gender studies or had a prominent women's or gender studies research center. But there are no stand-alone departments of women's studies, and as of this writing there is now only one named professor of women's studies, at Adelaide University.

Relations between Academic Women's Studies and the Women's Movement

As women's studies courses developed, journals like *Hecate* (founded in 1975) and *Australian Feminist Studies* (1985) emerged alongside the women's movement newsletters and journals like *Refractory Girl* (founded in 1973). However, by 1976, "Women's Studies" was dropped from the subtitle of *Refractory Girl*, the editors believing university women's studies had been taken over by "conservative" methodologies and "reactionary" content (Sheridan, 1993: 42). To a considerable extent, hostile relations have been supplanted by more cooperative exchanges, although feminist academics are still accused of being "bourgeois" (overpaid and nonradical) theoreticians of the inaccessible and abstract. Thus from the 1970s, feminist graduates affected many scholarly and political debates—for example, Robyn Rowland and Renate Klein's work on reproductive technologies also influenced Australia's ethical guidelines for in vitro fertilization and surrogacy; Dale Spender's work on gender and schooling has informed educational policies addressing formal and informal classroom curricula; Bettina Cass's analyses of welfare policy have been incorporated into Australian social security payments to primary carers; Jocelynne Scutt and Regina Graycar have contributed to changes in family law, domestic violence, and sexual assault law. These cross-fertilizations have increased as women's studies graduates join the workforce as policy makers and journalists, and to a much lesser extent as private businesswomen.

South Australian women were the first in the modern world to win the right to stand for parliament, which they won in 1894. With the burgeoning of women's liberation, women found a political voice as *femocrats,* a term offered to the international feminist lexicon and describing women who were appointed to senior levels in government bureaucracies specifically because of their feminist knowledge and whose role was to improve the status of women (Eisenstein, 1991: 12). Femocrats initially drew on and expanded community initiatives like women's health centers, refuges, rape crisis centers, and working women's centers. However, they have also been forced to deal with issues concerning the appropriate location and role of femocrats in the bureaucracy. "Official feminism" has not gone unchallenged in Australia. Debates concerning the uses and misuses of the state by feminists are tackled by Hester Eisenstein, Marian Sawer, and Anna Yeatman.

Debates in Women's Studies: Past, Present and Future

Possibly the most widely known Australian feminist writer is Germaine Greer, whose book *The Female Eunuch* (1971) applied its libertarian message to women's subordination. Two other influential early texts were Anne Summers's *Damned Whores and God's Police* (1975) and Miriam Dixson's *The Real Matilda* (1976). Miriam Dixson identified the homophobia of mateship, attributing Australian male fear and hatred of women to a convict and Catholic history. Summers claimed that Australian women had always been divided into two groups, "bad" whores and "good" God's police, whose role was to marry and civilize Australian men and control and divert bad women. The distinction, according to Summers, was for the benefit of men and not women; thus all women are prostitutes to the extent that they exchange sexual services for economic returns, whether inside or outside marriage.

In the 1970s women's studies courses were dominated by either radical feminists or Marxist feminists (important contributions in this area being offered by Ann Game and Rosemary Pringle). By the 1980s feminist theory turned away from material events in the world to their discursive meanings (Barrett, 1992). This was accompanied by a turn away from a clear if simple politics of intervention. A grafting of feminism and postcolonialism superseded the rational female subject, the heroine of 1970s feminism, for the postcolonial subject, fractured along contradictory lines of race, gender, and class. A grafting of psychoanalysis and feminism fractured the female interior to explore the ways women desire and collude in their subordination. Grafting French feminism and Australian feminism, the feminist philosophers Genevieve Lloyd, Moira Gatens, and, particularly, Elizabeth Grosz have produced a "feminist antihumanism" that identifies the body as a social construct, thus avoiding oppositions like mind-body, natural-social, sex-gender, emotion-reason, and by implication malefemale (Sullivan, 1994: 8).

Academic feminism has seen a shift away from the social science disciplines toward the "sexy" areas of cultural studies, representation, psychoanalysis, and postmodernism—see, for example, the edited collection by Barbara Caine and Rosemary Pringle (1995), *Transitions: New Australian Feminisms.* However, many older students, particularly those in the workforce, remain committed to "bread and butter" issues. Those theorists who continue to work in the realm of "things" now pay more attention to representations, especially the ways in which women and men are gendered in their daily practices—for example, sexual harassment at work. This shift in academic preoccupations is a response to a number of factors, including the stalling of women's improved status despite the destruction of formal barriers and the rise of economic rationalism, which makes political intervention to improve the collective lot of women appear increasingly hopeless.

One promise of postmodernism's fractured subject is a pathway to feminist theory's dialogue with the women previously "othered" or ignored by a largely Anglo feminist academia. In the emerging texts, which seek to mainstream women's studies, both race and gender are addressed. Examples are Patricia Grimshaw et al. (1994), *Creating a Nation,* in history, and Chilla Bulbeck (1997), *Social Sciences in Australia,* in the social sciences. The interface between postcolonialism and women's studies has focused attention on disrupting the category of "woman" (presumptively a white English-speaking middle-class woman). The first Aboriginal lecturer in women's studies was appointed in 1999 and Aboriginal women are completing honors degrees in women's studies. A major textbook for women's studies includes three contributions from non-Anglo feminist academics (of the 13 chapters; Hughes, 1997). Thus the 2 percent of the Australian population who are Aboriginal or Torres Strait Islander and the 25 percent who have at least one parent born overseas or who were themselves born overseas are finding their issues and voices represented in the intersections of race and gender or in discussions of indigenous and multicultural political, legal, and historical issues. However, despite white Australian feminists' increasing attention to the intersections of race and gender, Aboriginal women writers remain suspicious of white feminism's capacity to overcome its "missionizing" past or of the relevance of feminism to their race-based struggles (Huggins, 1994). While white feminist scholars are increasingly excited by the potential of postcolonialism to infuse diversity into their theories and materials, to some of the previously "othered" postcolonialism threatens yet another form of appropriation, this time of their culture. The way forward requires both ongoing dialogue and the appointment of senior women's stud-ies academics from beyond the Anglo-Celtic fold.

See Also

FEMINISM: AUSTRALIA AND NEW ZEALAND; FEMOCRAT; IMAGES OF WOMEN: AUSTRALIA AND NEW ZEALAND; LITERATURE: AUSTRALIA, NEW ZEALAND, AND THE PACIFIC ISLANDS; WOMEN'S STUDIES: OVERVIEW

References and Further Reading

Barrett, Michèle. 1992. Words and things: Materialism and method in contemporary feminist analysis. In Michèle Barrett and Anne Phillips, eds., *Destabilizing theory: Contemporary feminist debates*, 201–219. Cambridge: Polity.

Bulbeck, Chilla. 1997. *Social sciences in Australia*. Sydney: Harcourt Brace Jovanovich.

Caine, Barbara, and Moira Gatens, eds. *Australian feminism: A companion*. Melbourne: Oxford University Press.

Caine, Barbara, and Rosemary Pringle, eds. 1995. *Transitions: New Australian feminisms*. New York: St. Martin's.

Eisenstein, Hester. 1990. Femocrats, official feminism and the uses of power. In Sophie Watson, ed., *Playing the state: Australian feminist interventions*, 87–104. London: Verso.

———. 1991. *Gender shock: Practising feminism on two continents*. Sydney: Allen and Unwin.

Grimshaw, Patricia, et al. 1994. *Creating a nation*. New York: Viking Penguin.

Gunew, Sneja, ed. 1990. *Feminist knowledge: Critique and construct*. London: Routledge.

Huggins, Jackie. 1994. A contemporary view of Aboriginal women's relationship to the white women's movement. In Norma Grieve and Ailsa Burns, eds., *Australian women: Contemporary feminist thought*, 70–79. Melbourne: Oxford University Press. See other articles in this collection, as well as earlier collections: Norma Grieve and Patricia Grimshaw, eds. (1981), *Australian women: Feminist perspectives*, and Norma Grieve and Ailsa Burns, eds. (1986), *Australian women: New feminist perspectives*.

Hughes, Kate Pritchard, ed. 1997. *Contemporary Australian feminism 2*. Melbourne: Longman.

Magarey, Susan, et al. 1994. Women's studies in Australia. In Norma Grieve and Ailsa Burns, eds., *Australian women: Contemporary feminist thought*, 285–295. Melbourne: Oxford University Press.

Sheridan, Susan. 1993. Women's studies. In Refractory Girl, ed., *Refractory voices: Feminist perspectives from Refractory Girl*. Sydney: Refractory Girl Feminist Journal.

Sullivan, Barbara. 1994. Contemporary Australian feminism: A critical review. In Geoff Stokes, ed., *Studies in Australian political thought*. Sydney: University of New South Wales Press.

Chilla Bulbeck

WOMEN'S STUDIES: Backlash

Backlash refers to a negative reaction against a perceived threat to the social order. Though other views are of course possible, this article will consider backlash from the perspective of woman's studies itself. In that view, backlash is one measure of the success of women's studies in challenging the structures and assumptions of academia. In the United States in the late 1980s and early 1990s, attacks on women's studies, ethnic studies, curriculum revision, and efforts to improve campus climates for women and minorities reached a crescendo. Women's studies was often attacked in the *political correctness* debates or the *culture wars*. At international meetings in the 1990s, U.S. feminists learned that opponents of feminism and women's studies abroad had adopted some terms of the U.S. debates, especially *political correctness* and arguments against affirmative action, to maintain the status quo in their own countries.

Opponents of change in higher education in the United States appropriated the term *political correctness*, or *p.c.*, from the New Left movements of the 1960s and 1970s. These movements used *p.c.* as an ironic, self-critical guard against their own ideological rigidity. Those defending the status quo in more recent debates have used *p.c.* as an epithet in media and campus campaigns to discredit and demonize liberal academics and the reforms they advocate. Specifically, they accuse women's studies of diluting the curriculum by attempting to include the works and experiences of women or people of color; overstating the problems of sexual harassment and date rape on campus; and creating a climate inimical to free speech. Because the conservative reaction seems out of proportion to actual or proposed changes, it represents a backlash.

Several books popularized the conservative attack on higher education, with the help of extensive print and broadcast media coverage. These books included Allan Bloom's *The Closing of the American Mind: How Higher Education Has Failed Democracy and Impoverished the Souls of Today's Students* (1986); Roger Kimball's *Tenured Radicals: How Politics Corrupted Our Higher Education* (1990); and Dinesh D'Souza's *Illiberal Education: The Politics of Race and Class on Campus* (1991). Two communications professors who analyzed print media coverage of the p.c. debates found that in 1988, 101 articles appeared in approximately 500 general interest magazines and newspapers. By 1991, the number of articles had grown to approximately 4,000, representing a 600 percent increase over the previous year (Whitney and Wartella, 1992).

Cultural and Political Contexts

The backlash against women's studies and multiculturalism represents resistance to a process of institutional change that began in the United States in the late 1960s. In response to the civil rights movement and the legal victories it won, colleges and universities began to grant access to previously underrepresented groups. Among them, women, who began attending college in greater numbers in the 1960s, translated the lessons and demands of the women's liberation movement into higher education. At the same time that affirmative action programs increased access to higher education and awarded faculty and administrative jobs to minorities and women, new ethnic studies and women's studies programs began to grow in response to students' demands for a more relevant curriculum.

The growth of women's studies programs and women's research centers through the 1980s and 1990s was all the more remarkable given the hostile ideological and economic climate they faced in the academy during the Reagan and Bush administrations. The academic p.c. debates reached their height at the end of a decade and a half marked by major reductions in federal, state, and foundation funding for higher education and a retreat from assumptions about educational equity that once bolstered affirmative action. Heated debates about the "canon" masked growing anxiety about competition for scarce resources in academia. Increases in hate crimes and sexual violence reflected rising tensions on campus.

In 1984, William Bennett, chairman of the National Endowment for the Humanities (NEH) in Ronald Reagan's administration, introduced the conceptual framework for the backlash. Bennett claimed that curriculum reformers were denying students a timeless intellectual and moral legacy by replacing "classic texts" of western civilization with works of less quality and significance. Bennett charged that reformers of the 1960s, now entrenched as university professors, were threatening the very fabric of American society in the name of a more inclusive curriculum.

Oppositional Networks

William Bennett was one of the most visible critics in an interlocking network of conservative political appointees, think tanks, foundations, and activist organizations deter-

mined (arguably) to institutionalize conservative values throughout society. Bennett's successor at the NEH, Lynne Cheney, shared his views and had particular animus toward women's studies. In the 1980s and early 1990s, using the NEH as their political platform, Bennett and Cheney each wrote several policy-oriented reports decrying the state of the humanities and calling for a return to the "classics" in liberal arts education. Bennett helped found the Madison Center for Educational Affairs (MCEA), which generates conservative ideas and tactics for influencing higher education. Among such tactics were projects geared toward recruiting students and minorities to conservative points of view. The MCEA's student journalism program, for example, sponsors and funds the Collegiate Network of 70 conservative newspapers on campuses across the country.

Organizations such as the National Association of Scholars (NAS), founded in 1987, strategically presented their objectives in more neutral language. Thus, they attracted a range of supporters motivated less by ideology than a genuine concern for higher education. However, NAS's funding sources and conservative intellectual founders link the organization to conservative networks. Corporate and business family foundations such as the John M. Olin Foundation, the Coors Foundation, the Lynde and Harry Bradley Foundation, the Smith-Richardson Foundation, and the Sarah Scaife Foundation poured hundreds of thousands of dollars into nurturing conservative think tanks, right-wing intellectuals, and right-wing campus organizations and publications.

Challenges to Women's Studies

In addition to being included in generalized attacks on political correctness by the aforementioned institutions and individuals, women's studies has its own specialized cadre of critics. The small group of women scholars and writers who have attacked women's studies consider themselves women's advocates who want only to moderate some of feminism's excesses. Characteristic of those taking this approach—considered disingenuous by some observers—is Christina Hoff Sommers, author of *Who Stole Feminism? How Women Have Betrayed Women* (1994). Sommers argues that women's studies is dominated by a group of unscholarly, man-hating feminists who have an investment in portraying women as victims. In her book Sommers tries to debunk a number of high-profile feminist research projects with public-policy impact, such as a work on how schools shortchange girls, conducted by the Wellesley College Center for Research on Women and the American Association of University Women. By citing incidents and statements out of context and challenging the empirical validity of such studies with statistics that have then been challenged by her critics, Sommers (along with other writers using similar tactics) threatens to turn what could be a legitimate debate into a numbers game.

Sommers is a board member of the Women's Freedom Network (WFN), a group founded in 1993, according to its literature, "by a group of women who are seeking alternatives to extremist, ideological feminism and to antifeminist traditionalism." While this goal sounds reasonable enough, the group hardly represents the diversity of opinion within the strong, vital, multifaceted women's studies movement that has been in existence for 25 years. It seems, for the most part, to represent the conservative ideologues in the political correctness debates. The only committed gender studies scholars on the group's board of directors (as of this writing) were Jean Bethke Elshtain (University of Chicago) and Elizabeth Fox Genovese (Emory University); other members included Jeane Kirkpatrick, of the American Enterprise Institute, and Mona Charen, both conservatives.

In the elections of November 1994, Republicans gained majorities in the United States Senate and the House of Representatives, where the conservative activist Newt Gingrich presided as Speaker. The House Republicans' "Contract with America," which influenced state and local policy, proposed to cut education funding at all levels, as well as to defund the NEH and the National Endowment for the Arts. In January 1995, Bennett and Cheney appeared at a House Appropriations Subcommittee hearing and called for an end to federal funding for the endowments.

In June 1995, the Republican presidential candidate, California's Governor Pete Wilson issued an executive order to end racial and gender preferences that exceeded federal or state affirmative action requirements in the California community college system—the country's largest higher education system. Federal cuts in student loans, which disproportionately affect working-class students and students of color, were proposed. In 1996 voters in California passed a referendum that effectively eliminated affirmative action in the state. Such wavering state and federal commitments to affirmative action seemed certain to affect the modest gains women and people of color had made in the academy in the past two decades. In addition, the proposed cuts and policy changes were aimed at new scholarships, programs, and constituencies most likely to foster critical thinking and challenge the status quo.

Thus, debates that seemed at first to be purely academic—attacks on women's studies, curriculum transformation, and affirmative action for minority students, staff, administrators, and teachers on campus—have helped legitimize what some critics see as a radical national policy shift to the right.

International Perspectives

The fate of women's studies programs and funding patterns of foundations in the United States can often affect the maintenance of existing women's studies programs and the creation of new programs abroad. While women's studies has not been institutionalized as extensively in other countries as in the United States, it has taken firm root on every continent. This progress has occurred despite resistance that portrayed women's studies as a bourgeois western import, including the contention in some places, such as South Africa, that women's studies was only for privileged white women. International conferences, such as the United Nations Nongovernmental Organization Forums in Copenhagen in 1980, in Nairobi 1985, and in Beijing in 1995, helped break down many such barriers, fostering international collaboration and renewed commitments to organizing in women's home countries.

Women's studies has been established in a number of countries undergoing serious political and economic crises, such as in the former Soviet Union, where women's studies is growing in Russia, Lithuania, and Ukraine. Even in Croatia there is a new women's studies course at the University of Zagreb. One of the strengths of women's studies in countries undergoing transitions is that, by necessity, women's studies research has been linked more closely with public-policy interventions and the need to bring women into political life.

By the early 1990s, academics seeking to implement gender studies and affirmative action in South African universities had encountered arguments against political correctness and affirmative action that originated in the United States. Nevertheless, contact with women's studies supporters in the United States and around the world has enabled women's studies advocates in countries like Russia and South Africa to learn from earlier experiences of backlash.

While each country's situation is unique, feminists and women's studies advocates have a common imperative in dealing with backlash: to counter distortions and keep hold of the terms of the debate.

See Also

References and Further Reading

Berman, Paul, ed. 1992. *Debating p.c.: The controversy over political correctness on college campuses*. New York: Dell.

Bloom, Allan. 1986. *The closing of the American mind*. New York: Simon and Schuster.

Chamberlain, Mariam, and Florence Howe, eds. 1994. Women's studies: A world view. *Women's Studies Quarterly* 22(3–4: Fall–Winter).

D'Souza, Dinesh. 1991. *Illiberal education: The politics of race and sex on campus*. New York: Free Press.

Faludi, Susan. 1991. *Backlash*. New York: Crown.

Kimball, Roger. 1990. *Tenured radicals: How politics corrupted our higher education*. New York: HarperCollins.

Messer-Davidow, Ellen. 1993. Manufacturing the attack on liberalized higher education. *Social Text* 36(Fall): 40–80.

Minnich, Elizabeth. 1990. *Transforming knowledge*. Philadelphia: Temple University Press.

Schultz, Debra. 1993. *To reclaim a legacy of diversity: Analyzing the "political correctness" debates in higher education*. New York: National Council for Research on Women.

Sommers, Christina Hoff. 1994. *Who stole feminism? How women have betrayed women*. New York: Simon and Schuster.

Whitney, Charles D., and Ellen Wartella. 1992. Media coverage of the "political correctness" debates. *Journal of communications* 42(2): 83–94.

Debra Schultz

WOMEN'S STUDIES: Caribbean

This article traces the history and present situation of women's studies in the Caribbean: its origin, main activities, and subject matter. Although emphasis will be given to women's and gender studies in educational institutions, the nonacademic contributions by nongovernmental organizations (NGOs) to the development of women's studies in the region will also be addressed.

The Caribbean, a geographical region made up of some 20 islands of different sizes, takes its name from the Caribbean Sea, which borders the Atlantic Ocean and which is common to a group of islands known as the Antilles. These islands lie to the north of South America, to the east of Central America, and to the west of Africa. *Caribe* was the name of the natives who occupied a wide expanse of American soil and whose physical characteristics were as varied as the vast geographic territory they inhabited. Besides its geographic diversity, the Caribbean is characterized by its rich ethnic, linguistic, and cultural diversity, largely the product of multiple colonization by different countries: Spain, England, France, the Netherlands, and the United States. From the early sixteenth century, when Spain began its conquest and colonization of the American continent, to the late twentieth century, the Caribbean has had one of the longest and most varied histories of colonial conquest, a history of colonization that has been the region's common denominator and the determining factor in its socioeconomic development.

The history and situation of women's studies in the Caribbean have been influenced by two main groups. On the one hand, the English Caribbean islands (British colonies where English is the dominant language) pioneered different projects on women's and gender-related studies, and these became the most institutionalized programs in the region. On the other hand, the Spanish Caribbean countries (colonized by Spain, where Spanish is the dominant language) had a late start in this type of program, and their institutionalization was slow to materialize. Finally, there is a third group of countries—the French- and Dutch-speaking islands—where modest women's studies and gender studies initiatives were developed. It bears noting, however, that in this region, as in the rest of the world, women's studies dawned outside the institutional context, promoted mostly by individuals or organizations on the fringe of institutions of higher learning.

The English Caribbean

The most effective women's studies initiative in the English Caribbean came about in 1977, when the Women and Development Unit (WAND) was set up at the University of the West Indies (UWI), a regional university with campuses in Jamaica, Barbados, and Trinidad-Tobago. WAND paved the way for several academic projects on women's, gender, and development studies. As a result of WAND's work, women and development studies groups were established in 1982 at UWI's three main campuses. In 1986, the University of the West Indies and the Institute of Social Studies, The Hague, founded the Project of Cooperation in Teaching and Research in Women and Development Studies. Finally, in 1993, the initiative took shape when the Centre for Gender and Development Studies (CGDS) was opened. This center has a regional viewpoint and operates from the three campuses of the University of the West Indies. The center incorporated the Women and Development Unit as its support, staff development, and outreach operations arm. The Women's Studies Unit of the University of Guyana (UG)—which originated from that university's extramural studies in 1987—also belongs to the English Caribbean center's network. In 1994, the unit achieved formal status within the College of Social Sciences at UG. WAND runs its own operations from the Extra Mural Centre of UWI in Barbados, totally independent of the CGDS. It focuses on advocacy, training, and communications, and has been the home base of Development Alternatives with Women for a New Era (DAWN).

CGDS's local centers develop projects in coordination with one another, but autonomously with regard to teaching, research, and outreach. All the centers offer regularly scheduled bachelor of arts courses at introductory or advanced levels on women's and gender subjects. The number of courses varies from campus to campus. There are plans to offer a graduate program in Women and Development Studies through the Consortium Graduate School at Mona, Jamaica. The centers also offer nondegree programs in women and development studies, addressed mainly to NGOs and governmental organizations that work with women's and gender subjects. The most frequent research and outreach topics have to do with literature, health, development, education, agriculture, and domestic unity. The outreach phase is developed through workshops, seminars, and conferences. The publications address such subjects as gender and development, agriculture, and women's studies, all from a Caribbean perspective.

On the other hand, although DAWN is not actually a women's studies center, it carried out academic research and it operated from the WAND at UWI's Barbados campus. DAWN, founded in 1984, operated as a network of feminist activist researchers and policy makers primarily from developing countries. It has regional representatives in Asia, Latin America, the Caribbean, and the Pacific. Its work focuses mainly on studying alternative socioeconomic development models. Among the subjects of its studies are the impact of the debt, food, and energy crises on women; reproductive rights and population; environment; and alternative economic frameworks. It publishes a newsletter, *DAWN Informs,* in English and Spanish, as well as special issues on its research work.

The Spanish Caribbean

The first formal initiatives in the Spanish Caribbean within institutions of higher learning occurred in Puerto Rico in 1981 and in the Dominican Republic in 1986. In Puerto Rico, a rather short-lived Women's Center was organized early on at the University of Puerto Rico, Aguadilla, campus. Two projects were later organized in 1986: the Women's Resources and Service Center, within the Center for Social Research, and the Women's Studies Project (*PRO MUJER*), both at the University of Puerto Rico, Río Piedras and Cayey campuses, respectively. In the Dominican Republic, the Women's Studies Program of the Social Research Team (*Equipo de Investigación Social,* EQUIS) at the Santo Domingo Technological Institute (*Instituto Tecnológico de Santo Domingo,* INTEC) was organized in 1986. In 1992 it became INTEC's Gender Studies Center. There are also several projects in both countries, still at a very early stage. In the Dominican Republic, at the *Universidad Madre y Maestra* in Santiago, a women's studies group was organized in 1990. In Puerto Rico, two private universities—Inter American University and Sacred Heart University—initiated women's and gender studies in the 1990s.

In Puerto Rico and the Dominican Republic, academic research on women's and gender subjects began outside the university walls. In Puerto Rico the movement originated in the 1970s at the Center for Studies on Puerto Rican Reality (*Centro de Estudios de la Realidad Puertorriqueña,* CEREP), which researched women's participation in history. In the Dominican Republic, the Research Center for Feminine Action (*Centro de Investigación para la Acción Femenina,* CIPAF), an NGO founded in 1980, sponsored research, education, and documentation activities on women's subjects.

In Cuba in the 1960s, the Federation of Cuban Women (*Federación de Mujeres Cubanas*), a government group, began intensive activity in research, advocacy, and policy making regarding women's subjects. However, it was not until 1991 that the University of Havana set up a formal academic program on women's studies, known as Women's Seminar (*Cátedra de la Mujer*), an interdisciplinary effort that sponsors research, university courses, and community education activities. In 1994 *Casa de las Américas,* an important nonacademic government center for the dissemination of culture, also launched a women's studies program offering short courses and international symposia.

INTEC's Gender Studies Center in the Dominican Republic, with its undergraduate and graduate courses, is the most institutionalized effort in the Spanish Caribbean. As of this writing, INTEC offered the only master's degree in gender studies in the Caribbean region. In 1993 it began publication of its review, *Género y Sociedad* (Gender and Society). In Puerto Rico there were no regular academic programs on women's studies.

The development of the centers in Puerto Rico and Cuba has focused on research and publications. In Puerto Rico, CERES began to publish the results of its research work in 1986 and *PRO MUJER* began to do so in 1989. From 1988 to 1994, *PRO MUJER* published a quarterly newsletter, *Tejemeneje,* on women's subjects. The main subjects addressed in Puerto Rico are health, curricula, science, history, domestic violence, and sexual harassment; in the Dominican Republic, migration, work, curricula, domestic violence, and development; and in Cuba, health, employment, social communication, and education. As in the English Caribbean, all Spanish Caribbean centers organize seminars, symposia, and conferences for the university community as well as for the general public.

The French and Dutch Caribbean

The French and Dutch Caribbean islands (former and present French and Dutch colonies) currently undertake little activity in the area of women's and gender studies within educational institutions. At the time of this writing, only Surinam had a study group for women's studies, at Anton de Kom University. On the other hand, in Haiti, which is part of the French Caribbean, there is an NGO—*Centre National et International de Documentation et d'Information des Femmes en Haiti*—that occasionally publishes a newspaper, and undertakes networking and advocacy activities on women's and gender subjects.

Conclusion

Women's and gender studies in the Caribbean are as diverse as the area's geographic, linguistic, and cultural context. Programs in the English Caribbean and the Dominican Republic appear more stable and institutionalized, since they offer regular undergraduate and graduate courses. It also bears noting that in contrast to the Spanish Caribbean centers, the English Caribbean centers have managed to develop an organization and vision with a regional English-Caribbean character. The political realities of the Spanish Caribbean seem to deter more regional interaction between the Spanish-speaking islands. All have in common, however, their interdisciplinary character and the fact that they work from within academia, teaching and doing research and taking up issues of social interest for the community at large. The diverse activities generated by these women's studies centers have had different impacts on the academic and nonacademic world. The programs, however, face some degree of resistance from the government sphere, which is usually slow to accept changes and public-policy recommendations. For example, proposals for change and alternative materials from a gender perspective for elementary-school curricula—developed by most centers throughout the Caribbean—have found little acceptance in government education systems.

In this sense, nonacademic spaces that facilitate encounters among all Caribbean countries have promoted communication and networking throughout the region. Since 1985 the Caribbean Association for Feminist Research and Action (CAFRA), an organization based in Trinidad-Tobago, has been a case in point. CAFRA is a feminist umbrella regional organization comprising a complex diversity of Caribbean organizations and individuals who work with women's and gender subjects. Other academic organizations, such as the Association of Caribbean Historians and the Caribbean Studies Association, have also contributed to the discipline by strengthening academicians' networking in the region.

The contribution made by NGOs and other non-academic sectors to strengthening women's and gender studies has been and will be important for the development of these disciplines. It must be borne in mind that women's studies began to take shape on the fringe of academia or, as Lynn Bolles (1993) has accurately written, that it was *"an area of study born of political struggle."* The great challenge faced by most programs in women's and gender studies in the Caribbean will be the level of institutionalization they achieve and their persistence in overcoming the typical and traditional resistance of the academic context. In most cases, their development has been possible because of the financial backing of international and nonacademic agencies, which has somewhat retarded the recognition and legitimation of the programs on the part of university administrators. The groundwork having been laid, they must still consolidate their program with the necessary institutional support and respect for imagination and creativity. Therein lies their strength and continuity.

See Also

DAWN MOVEMENT; FEMINISM: CARIBBEAN; NONGOVERNMENTAL ORGANIZATIONS (NGOS); POLITICS AND THE STATE: CARIBBEAN; WOMEN'S STUDIES: OVERVIEW

References and Further Reading

Azize Vargas, Yamila. 1994. Estudios de la mujer en Puerto Rico: Marginalidad e institucionalización. In *Estudios de la mujer en América Latina*. Argentina: UNESCO.

Bolles, Lynn. 1993. Doing it for themselves: Women's research and action in the Commonwealth Caribbean. In Edna Acosta and Christine Bose, eds., *Researching women in Latin America and the Caribbean*. Boulder, Col.: Westview.

CAFRA Journal. Caribbean Association for Feminist Research and Action. Published quarterly. Address: P.O. Bag 442, Tunapuna, Trinidad and Tobago, West Indies.

Casa de las Américas, Programa de Estudios de la Mujer. Newsletter. Address: 3ra y G, El Vedado, La Habana, Cuba.

CIPAF Brochure. Centro de Investigación para la Acción Femenina. Address: P.O. Box 1744, Santo Domingo, República Dominicana.

DAWN Informs. Newsletter. Published regularly in Spanish and English.

ENFOFANM. Newsletter of Centre National et International de Documentation et d'Information des Femmes en Haiti. Address: 253 Ave. John Brown, Boite Postale 1093, Port-au-Prince, Haiti.

Género y Sociedad. Journal of Centro de Estudios del Género, INTEC. Published regularly. Address: Box 342-9, Santo Domingo, República Dominicana.

Mohammed, Patricia, and Catherine Shepard, eds. 1988. *Gender in Caribbean development.* Mona, St. Augustine, Cave Hill: University of the West Indies.

Reddock, Rhoda E. 1991. New developments in research on women: The Commonwealth Caribbean experience. In *Women's studies international: Nairobi and beyond.* New York: Feminist Press.

———. 1993. Women's studies at the University of West Indies: A decade of feminist education? Mimeographed copy provided by author.

Rivera, Marcia. 1991. El Caribe, los movimientos de mujeres y los estudios del género. Mimeographed copy provided by author.

Within and Without. Newsletter of the Women's Studies Unit, Faculty of Social Sciences. University of Guyana. Published three times per year. Address: P.O. Box 101110, Georgetown, Guyana.

Yamila Azize Vargas

WOMEN'S STUDIES:
Central and Eastern Europe

The field of women's studies has expanded enormously in central and eastern Europe since the political, social, economic, and cultural transitions brought about by the collapse of communism in 1989. Although each country in this region has its own history of feminist thought going back far earlier than the twentieth century, only after 1989 did women's studies begin entering academia as an important discipline and political discourse as an integral part of the mechanisms of change.

A growing number of universities, including the Central European University in Budapest and Charles University in Prague, offer courses in women's studies leading toward a degree or as an area of specialization. A growing awareness of women's studies or gender studies is evident not only in the increase in the number of academic institutions offering women's studies courses, but also in the growing degree of comfort of the mass media with using the word *gender* in their rhetoric, an important sign of deeper cultural change, given that the concept of gender and even the word *gender* do not exist in Slavic languages and Hungarian.

This emerging interest needs to be attributed first and foremost to women's organizations that have worked hard to accommodate women's studies and the novel concept of gender into multiple layers of social, political, cultural, and economic life and into public consciousness. In addition, since the opening of borders, information about the study of women in other parts of the world is now available, most of it from western Europe and the United States. The introduction of free-market economies in central and eastern Europe since 1989 has also played a large role in the proliferation of women's studies. Finally, the European Union (EU) has played a role in bringing gender and women's interests to the forefront of the agendas of central and eastern European countries, especially the Czech Republic, Slovenia, Hungary, and Poland, which as of this writing had yet to make their legal systems fully compatible with the EU gender guidelines.

Women's studies in this region must come to terms with the legacies of the communist era's gender politics, which saw women's identity primarily as mothers and workers and therefore focused on issues of social welfare, employment, and the role of women's reproductive functions, without fully reaching out into such areas as queer theory, gay and lesbian studies, science and technology, women and health, the arts and popular culture, feminist literary criticism, and issues of gender and environmental protection. Differences among women in sexuality, class, ethnicity, race, gender identity, abilities and handicaps, and other individual features need to be recognized.

The Role of Women's Organizations

Women's organizations in the many countries of central and eastern Europe differ significantly in their agendas, which are tailored to a specific country's needs, in official affiliations, and in the range of services they offer to the general public. In addition to building public awareness of cultural mechanisms of gender construction, these organizations work to influence the political discourse directly by lobbying on behalf of women and cooperating with public policy makers. They offer advice to individual women, hot line and referral services, and educational and retraining programs. The involvement of women's organizations that combine grassroots activities with action in governmental agencies and nongovernmental organizations (NGOs) legitimizes the field of women's and gender studies in central and eastern Europe.

Most of the women's organizations are involved in both activist and academic or theoretical work. Women who are professors affiliated with a university may also be committed to activist work in the center. One institution promoting studies of women and gender in the Czech Republic is the Gender Studies Foundation in Prague, which was founded in 1991 as an NGO. It began as a private book collection of a famous feminist sociologist and activist, Jirina Šiklová, and only later came to be supported financially by the New York–based organization Network of East-West Women. In 1992, the women's organization Frauen Anstiftung from Hamburg, Germany, began funding this center, which allowed for a significant increase of the multilingual library collection and archive available for the use of scholars and the general public.

The center organizes lectures on the theme of gender in culture and society and workshops on gender and childhood, rape, sex, women and religion, and pornography. The foundation prepares seminars and offers free language courses for women in Czech and English. In addition, the center offers consultations, advice, and research assistance and works with other centers and with university professors who prepare seminars and study programs (*Alty a Soprany,* 1994: 42) There are about 30 women's organizations in the Czech Republic, but the Gender Studies Foundation in Prague has perhaps most importantly influenced the introduction of studies of women, gender, and feminism into academia and the consciousness of the general public. The foundation has attracted more than a thousand visitors a year and wide media attention.

Another influential women's organization in the Czech Republic is Pro-Fem (or the Central European Center for Women's Projects), which offers mostly advice and consultation services for individuals and organizations on how to raise funds for and manage a successful women's organization, foundation, or center. La Strada is a network organization in central and eastern Europe sponsored by the EU that works to prevent the trafficking in women. Some of the many other existing women's groups are the Association of Women Entrepreneurs and Managers; Democratic Alternative, which strives to promote plurality among women's organizations; a cultural-social NGO called the Czech Association of Women; Movement for Equal Status of Women in the Czech Lands and Moravia; Club Jantar, bringing together women affected by breast cancer; the Rosa Foun-

dation, helping divorced women; the ecological association Southern Mothers; a fine arts group, Koza Nostra; and an association of lesbian women and gay activists, L-Club Lambda.

Communist Legacies

The status of postsocialist transition movements and the place gender has taken in this process have been common topics of many studies that draw largely on communist ideologies. Although communism claimed gender equality as one of its goals, the system has been shown by many women's studies scholars to be patriarchal, discriminatory, and contradictory when it comes to women's rights.

The collapse of communism ended the concept that there is one common social identity of women. This collective social identity was based on the role of women as mothers and workers, a concept that gave rise to solidarity and the belief in sisterhood among women. The celebration of motherhood was charged with patriotic notions of nation building, protecting and holding the communist nation in the state of equality for all. The role of woman as a worker, or rather the "proper" management of her maternal role with her role as worker, was also emphasized. As a gesture of respect to women's full engagement at work, many routines were established, such as a "women's day" at work, when women were given flowers and small presents such as soaps or detergents to underscore their identity as mothers, wives, and workers. This distribution of roles for women latently conveyed a gendered difference between public and private spheres. Whereas the home, the private sphere, was gendered feminine because of women's reproductive functions, the law of patriarchy ruled the public sphere. Thus women were "allowed" to be "equal" partners with men at work while being reminded of their additional role of taking care of the home. The fact that a wide network of day care and school care allowed women to pursue their "career" as a worker only made it more difficult to reveal the unspoken gender distributions of the totalitarian regime.

An illusion of equality and emancipation of women was based on the belief that being a good worker, wife, and mother could get a woman to the same place on the social ladder as men, but this also created severe discriminatory practices. The unification of women under communism erased differences, so that women with disabilities, single mothers, lesbians, or single women who did not want to have children could not live up to what communism cherished as the model of a good and true woman. Such a model of womanhood relied on women's reproductive functions and the "appropriate" management of their double duties.

Women's gender identities as defined by sexual preference, ethnicity, race, religion, and other individual differences were consciously displaced by totalitarian regimes in central and eastern Europe.

Mapping the Territory of Women's Studies and Gender Studies

This patriarchal gender "equity," social "justice," and view of womanhood have been widely criticized (Funk and Mueller, 1993; Haney, 1997; Watson, 1993; Wolchik, 1995). Many scholars have discussed the communist gender order in relation to its discriminatory access to citizenship rights and the impact of this phenomenon on democratization processes (Einhorn, 1993; Ferge, 1996). The role of women's reproductive function in gendering the public-private dichotomy has been analyzed (Grapard, 1997; Havelkova, 1993). This phenomenon translated into the transition processes and the development of civil society and has been defined as the masculinization of public domain.

The masculinization has meant a severe marginalization of women in representational practices and decision-making acts. In addition, it implies that women have limited ability to create spaces of political culture. Several authors have theorized about and called for women's democratic citizenship (for example, Regulska, 1997, 1998; Regulska and Graham, 1997). Were women really marginalized in communist representational practices? Just as it has been difficult to discern forms of gender discrimination in the supposedly equal distribution of roles between women and men, one cannot simply claim without further elaboration that current underrepresentation springs from the totalitarian regime. Women's presence in positions of power was more visible under communism than is the case today. Their number in the communist parliament seemed to be equal to the number of men, as the Czech sociologist Jirina Šiklová points out. She claims that one needs to explain the difference between the totalitarian system and a parliamentary democracy to avoid any misunderstanding by claiming that women had better sociopolitical status under communism.

> Although there were elections and parliament under communism, everything was only a "game," a formality. To be a representative was not anything to be proud of, it did not mean having any real political influence. It was an expression of conformity. Communist parties in every socialist country used to have quota that determined how many workers, peasants, women, intelligencia there have to be in the parliament while these people were selected in advance by the only ruling party. (*Alty a Soprany*, 1994: 8)

The illusion of having political influence in patriarchal communist structures while having no real impact and the masculinization of the public sphere are among the factors causing women's disbelief in politics, leading to their underrepresentation.

Replacement of the state-governed economy by free market economies has also raised many questions with regard to women's employment and their new position in the labor market. Women face multiple layers of social, economic, and political injustice and often become the victims of the difficulties that the transitional processes have brought about. The free market has brought competition and an extreme emphasis on the individual and his or her individual rights. Considering the collective self-representation of women under communism, one can understand that the current position of women in the labor market and their access to employment are extremely difficult. Generally, middle-aged and elderly people (who have spent most of their lives under communism) find it hard to keep up with the market competition and the rise of individualism. They experience the societal pressures of the transition severely, just like every individual with special needs or a disability that prevents him or her from becoming a competitive entity of the market economy. Unemployment, which is more severe for women than it is for men, is growing in many countries of the region (Fodor, 1997).

Whereas communism provided a wide social safety net against unemployment, as well as extensive social welfare and free health care, the current market economies of central and eastern Europe make their citizens more directly accountable for their destinies. This creates a challenge for women in particular. The market economies have also enabled women to venture into jobs that were previously considered the domain only of men.

Another large area of interest is the body politic. Women's studies scholars have pointed out the use of women's bodies for inscription of various communist ideologies: homogenization, patriotism, neopatriarchal pressure, and conservatism (Berry, 1995; Enloe, 1993; Kligman, 1995). Such studies point to the ways in which women's bodies were understood through reproductive functions and used to produce discriminatory discourses regarding social control, citizenship, and abortion. Related to this was the association of women's bodies with the birth of a nation, the symbolism of the mother as the nation. This symbolism has been used in the rhetoric of nationalism of the mother as the nation, ethnic cleansing, war propaganda, racism, and other expressions of xenophobia (Verdery, 1994).

The study of politics is closely tied to studies of women's status and forms of violence against them and resistance movements before and after 1989, especially in relation to the war in the Balkans. This literature has examined the physical, psychological, and emotional experiences of women who have been subject to some form of violence: sexual assault, abuse, rape, domestic violence, sex work, or the trafficking in women. In addition, legal protection and forms of prevention have also been addressed. Both theoretical work and activist work have been done in this area by scholars, women's centers (for example, the Zagreb Action for War Rape Crisis Center in Croatia), NGOs, and women's grassroots movements (Corrin, 1996).

The aversion to feminism and feminist theories in central and eastern Europe is one of the biggest areas of women's studies. The status of feminism has been a lively topic for scholars in both the East—the countries that have experienced totalitarianism—and the West: western Europe and the United States. These comparative studies point out that there are deep cultural, political, social, economic, historical, and epistemological differences between eastern and western views on the development of women's movements and studies in the region. The lack of ack-nowledgment of these differences in knowl-edge-making practices has led to numerous misunder-standings and stereotyping. Western feminist writings about women from central and eastern Europe are often criticized for their ethnocentric inability to recognize or acknowledge the complex web of differences that cir-cumscribe their places of articulation in relation to their object of study.

Women of the East are often viewed as victims of the communist regime as well as of democratization processes, devoid of any agency for self-organizing or for promoting women's rights. They are objectified, pitied, and regarded as needing help by the more experienced and well-versed feminists of the West. This compassion toward the "poor East" has been attacked for presupposing that the West sets the standard for feminist thinking. Efforts at establishing a cross-cultural rapport that would articulate and benefit from differences have become problematic.

The uneasy status of feminism in this region has also sprung from the fact that it is often the most radical forms and misrepresentations of feminism that are brought to the East by the mass media. The general population tends to see feminism as an ideology or dogma that needs to be exter-minated after the history of communism. It is unfortunate that there are more articles that deal with the negative inter-ference of western feminisms and their colonizing practices and tendencies toward the East than there are articles that try to foster a two-way exchange about different feminisms on both sides of this artificial divide.

Toward New Areas

Women's studies and gender studies in central and eastern Europe have only barely ventured into some areas, such as queer, gay, and lesbian studies; science and technology; and ecofeminism and environmental degradation. The arts and popular culture, cultural studies, and literary studies and criticism have gained some attention by scholars, but not appropriate visibility in women's studies scholarship on cen-tral and eastern Europe.

Among the few gay studies dealing with sexual orien-tation, sexual rights, rights of self-representation, socio-cultural challenges such as the pressure of coming out, rights of bodily integrity, and discrimination are those by Busheikin and Trnka (1993) and Funk and Mueller (1993).

In the area of the arts and popular culture, only a little work has been done on the place of gender in media, com-munications, theater, film, and cinema studies: see Falkowska (1995) on the representation of women in Polish postsocialist films, Iordanova (1996–1997) on women in the Balkan cinema, Attwood (1995) on post-Soviet cinema and discourses of gender, Goscilo (1993) on post-Soviet culture and the construction of womanhood, or Indruchova (1995) on gender stereotyping in Czech billboard advertising. Feminist literary criticism is not a well-developed area of gender studies and women's studies, even though there are a num-ber of women writers and poets whose work engages issues of gender, such as Dubravka Ugresic, Slavenka Drakulic, Eva Hauserová, and Iva Pekárková. Recent feminist literary crit-icism has studied women's narratives in Croatian and Ser-bian literatures (Lukic, 1996) the role of the erotic in Polish women's poetry (Peretz, 1993), and the masculine sexual pol-itics in Milan Kundera's *The Book of Laughter and Forgetting* (Popovicova, 1998). Almost no attention has been given to women in science and technology and the relation between gender and environment protection. The conference "Women and the Environment in Central and Eastern Europe: Stories and Ways of Working for a Change" by Kon-takt Oost Europa is a pivotal step in this direction.

This article gives only a bird's-eye view of women's issues, studies, and activities, which differ greatly among the countries in central and eastern Europe. Trying to charac-terize the most representative events in the recent history of women's studies in this region—and the role of women's organizations in shaping and legitimizing them—necessi-tated locating the discourses of gender in relation to com-munism. The communist gender contract created a limited view of woman's identity that erased differences, a view that still affects much of current women's scholarship. The con-struction of woman's identity needs to be understood as a multiple and nondiscriminatory process that has to engage notions of race, class, sexuality, ethnicity, physical ability, and so on. It is important that studies on women explore and analyze new areas so that the process of acknowledging and embracing differences among women can be fully implemented in central and eastern Europe.

See Also

COMMUNISM; DEMOCRATIZATION; FEMINISM: EASTERN EUROPE; POLITICS AND THE STATE: EASTERN EUROPE; WOMEN'S STUDIES: OVERVIEW; WOMEN'S STUDIES: COMMONWEALTH OF INDEPENDENT STATES; WOMEN'S STUDIES: RESEARCH CENTERS AND INSTITUTES

References and Further Reading

Alty a Soprany (kapesni atlas zenskych iniciativ). 1994. Prague: Gender Studies Center.

Attwood, Lynne. 1995. Men, machine guns, and the Mafia: Post-Soviet cinema as a discourse on gender. *Women's Studies International Forum* 18(5–6): 513–521.

Berry, Ellen E. 1995. *Postcommunism and the body politics.* New York: New York University Press.

Busheikin, L., and S. Trnka, eds. 1993. *Bodies of bread and butter: Reconfiguring women's lives in post-Communist Czech Republic.* Prague: Prague Gender Studies Center.

Corrin, C., ed. 1996. *Women in a violent world. Feminist analyses and resistance across Europe.* Edinburgh: Edinburgh University Press.

Drakulic, Slavenka. 1998. What we learned from western feminists. *Transitions* 5(1): 42–47.

Einhorn, Barbara. 1993. *Cinderella goes to the market: Citizenship, gender and women's movements in east central Europe.* London: Verso.

Enloe, Cynthia. 1993. *The morning after. Sexual politics at the end of the cold war.* Berkeley: University of California Press.

Falkowska, Janina. 1995. A case of mixed identities: The representation of women in post-socialist Polish films. *Canadian Woman Studies/Les Cahiers de la Femme* 16(1): 35–37.

Ferge, Zsuzsa. 1996. Social citizenship in the new democracies. The difficulties in reviving citizens' rights in Hungary. *International Journal of Urban and Regional Research* 20(1): 99–115.

Fodor, Eva. 1997. Gender in transition: Unemployment in Hungary, Poland, and Slovakia. *East European Politics and Society* 11: 470–500.

Funk, N., and M. Mueller, eds. 1993. *Gender politics and post-communism: Reflections from eastern Europe and the former Soviet Union.* New York: Routledge.

Goscilo, Helena. 1993. Demostroika or perestroika? The construction of womanhood in Soviet culture and glasnost. In T. Lahusen and G. Kuperman, eds., *Late Soviet culture. From perestroika to novostroika,* 233–255. Durham, N.C.: Duke University Press.

Grapard, Ulla. 1997. Theoretical issues of gender in the transition from socialist regimes. *Journal of Economic Issues* 31(3): 665–686.

Haney, Lynne. 1997. But we are still mothers: Gender and the construction of need in post-socialist Hungary. *Social Politics* 4(2): 208–244.

Havelkova, Hana. 1993. "Patriarchy" in the Czech society. *Hypatia* 8(4): 89–96.

Indruchova, Libora. 1995. The construction of femininity in contemporary billboard advertising in the Czech Republic. *Sociologicky Casopis* 31(1): 85–104.

Iordanova, Dina. 1996–1997. Women in new Balkan cinema: Surviving on the margins. *Film Criticism* 21: 24–39.

Kligman, Gail. 1995. Political demography: The banning of abortion in Ceausescu's Romania. In F.D. Ginsburg and R. Rapp, eds., *Conceiving the new world order: The global politics of reproduction,* 234–256. Berkeley: University of California Press.

———. 1998. *The politics of duplicity: Reproduction, social control and power in Ceausescu's Romania.* Berkeley: University of California Press.

Kontakt OostEuropa, East-West. *Women and the environment in central and eastern Europe: Stories and ways of working for a change.* Tenth East-West Consultation, Lipnik nad Becvou, Czech Republic.

Lipovska, Olga. 1994. Sisters of stepsisters. *Women's Studies International Forum* 17(2–3): 273–276.

Lukic, Jasmina. 1996. Women-centered narratives in contemporary Serbian and Croatian literatures. *Engendering Slavic Literatures,* 223–243.

Peretz, Maya. 1993. The power of the erotic in Polish women's poetry. In *Heart of the nation: Polish literature and culture. Selected essays from the 50th Anniversary International Congress of the Polish Institute of Arts and Sciences of America,* 29–48. East European Monographs 3. New York: Columbia University Press.

Popovicova, Iva. 1998. Gender and the Kundera paradigm: Truth-telling in *The book of laughter and forgetting. One Eye Open* 132–151.

Regulska, Joanna. 1998. The "political" and its meaning for women: Transition politics in Poland. In J. Pickles and A. Smith, eds., *Theorizing transition: The political economy of post-communist transformations,* 309–329. London: Routledge.

———. 1997. Politics, political and gender in central and eastern Europe: A relation in the making. In D. Knezevic and D. Koraljka, eds., *Governments without women or the long march*, 81–89. Zagreb: Zenska Infoteka.

———, and A. Graham. 1997. Where the political meets women: Creating local political space. *Anthropology of East Europe Review* 15(1): 4–12.

Verdery, Katherine. 1994. From parent-state to family patriarchs: Gender and nation in contemporary eastern Europe. *East European Politics and Societies* 8(2): 225–255.

Watson, Peggy. 1993. Eastern Europe's silent revolution: Gender. *Sociology* 27(3): 471–487.

Wolchik, Sharon L. 1995. Gender issues during transition. In J.P. Hardt and R. Kaufman, eds., *Joint Economic Committee, Congress of the United States. East central European Economies in Transition*, 147–170. New York: Sharpe.

Iva Popovicova

WOMEN'S STUDIES:
Central and South America

Women's studies in Latin American universities began during the early 1980s in the midst of complex political, cultural, and economic conditions which, paradoxically, favored the emergence of this field but in which it subsequently became an object of much public and academic debate.

During the 1970s, academic conditions in Latin America were not propitious to women's studies programs. Many countries, particularly those of the "southern cone," were governed by military regimes. Countless teachers, professors, and researchers were in exile. Some had willingly left their university posts to set up private research centers or nongovernmental organizations where they tried to develop centers of research, training, and community outreach. Others had simply been fired from their university positions.

In order to understand the problems that academics faced during the 1970s, it is important to explain some of the historical background of how universities had been founded.

Historical Context

In the beginning, universities were established with the purpose of educating the elite—a population that has historically been the dominant group. In 2000, the majority of universities continued to operate and function under the traditional structure. Even though, conceptually, universities became more democratic in the 1960s, they are in reality still characterized by compartmentalized disciplines; this tends to isolate the institutions from society at large.

Meanwhile, the more progressive intellectual groups seized the 1960s as an opportune time to call attention to the social problems that surrounded Latin America. These groups—which espoused dependence theory, with its emphasis on anti-imperialist and class struggles, and development theory—argued that the problems could be overcome by applying these theories. However, many scholars have contended that both concepts, because of their patriarchal and economic-centered focuses, have made invisible the subordination of women, as well as women's lack of economic, cultural, and social participation throughout history.

Additionally, studying discrimination against women was not considered a legitimate course for an academic setting. Only occasionally did it manage to filter into the university sphere, presented as a mobilization issue and a political debate. Even in 2000, universities were more accepting of the International Women's Day celebrations and associated activities than they were of the creation of regular academic degrees and seminars in women's studies.

During this time, enrollment of Latin American women in secondary schools and universities increased greatly as a consequence of the expansion of the middle class that began in the 1940s. This extraordinary enrollment in higher education produced a large number of women professionals. Because of their high levels of education, these women had built up expectations of becoming autonomous and contributors to society, but their hopes could not be realized in the patriarchal atmosphere of the time. Among this group of women were some who would later become leaders in the women's rights movements at the grassroots level and in academic arenas.

On the political front, the failure of some revolutionary movements of the 1960s and 1970s gave rise to new movements and to new social and political voices. These activities brought to the forefront some previously hidden tensions and power struggles such as those involving youth groups, ecologists, grassroots Christian communities, and women. The crisis of institutions and the downfall of traditional political protocols made way for women's presence in the public sphere. Women assumed a leading role in various causes, such as a return to democracy, human rights, and family and community care.

This is how a vast and heterogeneous women's movement came to be. It was a movement that not only questioned and debated with traditional institutions but also confronted the very definition of politics, cultural models, ethical values, and, at its core, the power of interpersonal relationships (Luna, 1990).

This movement influenced the birth of organizations such as Centra de Estudios de la Mujer (CEM, Argentina), Fundación Carlos Chagas (Brazil), GRECMU (Uruguay), Casa de la Mujer La Morada and CEM (Chile), and Centro Flora Tristan and Manuela Ramos (Peru). These grassroots women's organizations—some formed as self-help groups and others as nongovernmental organizations—played a crucial role in comprehending and articulating the needs of women. Of particular importance, these groups helped create an awareness of women's social conditions that ultimately influenced the writing of congressional bills leading to legislative changes in democratic governments. Made up primarily of professional women who were previously university professors and researchers, feminists in exile, and mothers who fought against civil violence, the women's nongovernmental organizations developed a wealth of intellectual resources that generated knowledge and innovations, including new institutional practices. Despite its extraordinary diversity, this movement addressed problems that were common to all women.

In the early 1980s, some of the countries of the region regained their democratic institutions and were able to breathe in a stimulating and open climate of research and new social themes. The center of discussion in Latin America shifted toward democracy. This change in perception meant a change in political culture, as well as scientific paradigms that revealed the human condition as a whole and gave it a new dimension at the institutional level (Lechner, 1993).

This framework allowed for the emergence of previously unspoken and unheard of differences among Latin American societies (in gender, race, and ethnicity, for instance). Hence, the framework went beyond traditional interpretations, motivating new conceptual and political answers about social equality and recognizing and validating diversity.

In this intellectual climate of the 1980s, women activists and researchers, many of whom had still not returned to academia, began to criticize sexist concepts in different scientific fields in order to expose what they saw as biased approaches. These women demanded equality not just in the home but also in social and political arenas, as a true expression of democracy. In fact, the Chilean feminists, who were struggling with a dictatorship, expressed their sentiment with the slogan "Democracy in the nation and in the home."

Other key events were the start of the United Nations Women's Decade celebration, which took place in Mexico in 1975, and increased support from international organizations for projects and programs launched by women's organizations.

Women's Studies in Academia

In Latin America (unlike Europe or the United States), the emergence of women's studies was not limited to the universities. In the early 1980s, feminist researchers who had formed nongovernmental organizations were the main founders of this field. They conducted their scientific research with subsidies from agencies and international support.

For example, there were conferences sponsored by UNESCO. In 1981, the first Latin American Seminar on Women's Studies was held in Brazil. Four years later, the Colegio de Mexico's Interdisciplinary Program of Women's Studies organized a second meeting, which was attended by representatives from 13 countries. Of these representatives, 9 belonged to nongovernmental organizations. In 1986, Argentina's Women's Studies Center (CEM) initiated a new seminar, held at the University of Buenos Aires, which was attended by 18 participants, only 7 of whom belonged to universities.

The first initiative to establish a women's studies program at the university level took place in 1981 at the Pontifica Universidad Catolica de Rio de Janeiro, and the program was called the Nucleus of Study and Research on Women and Gender (NEM). This manner of implementation grew rapidly in Brazil, and by the end of the decade the country had 20 "nuclei." In 1994, approximately 50 nuclei were members of a national network.

The Interdisciplinary Women's Studies Program (PIEM) in the Colegio de Mexico was formed in 1983. It is one of the most developed and prestigious programs in the area of research.

In 1985, 11 Latin American countries participated in the International Women's Studies Section of the United Nations' portion of the Women's Decade conference in Nairobi.

In 1987, the first interdisciplinary graduate program with specialization in women's studies was set up at the University of Buenos Aires. The purpose of this two-and-a-half-year program was to offer higher levels of education in addition to training in the areas of research and teaching. This program also included the formation and implementation of gender-sensitive programs and policies. Upon successful completion of the program, the student is granted a certificate as a specialist in women's studies.

In Costa Rica, two programs were born in 1987: the interdisciplinary women's studies center (CIEM) at the National University of Meredia and the Interdisciplinary

Gender Studies Program (PRIEG) at the University of Costa Rica. In 1993, these two institutions jointly organized a master's degree program in women's studies that in 2000 was one of three existing programs at this level in Latin America. The third was created in 1993 at the National University of Rosario in Argentina.

The proliferation of projects and the need for an exchange of experiences fueled the formation of women's studies networks. The first was started in 1983 and included researchers and activists. The Latin American and Caribbean University Programs of Women's Studies network, initiated by academics from Argentina, Colombia, Costa Rica, Mexico, Puerto Rico, and the Dominican Republic, began in 1989. It was presented in several conferences and undertook the dissemination of information about its members' activities. Because of a lack of funds, this program lasted only two years.

Halfway through the 1990s, 15 countries had established university women's studies programs. These included Argentina, Brazil, Colombia, Chile, Mexico, Peru, Uruguay, and Venezuela, as well as countries grouped together in the Central American University Confederation (CSUCA): Costa Rica, Nicaragua, Honduras, Guatemala, El Salvador, and Panama. Among the programs, there are significant differences with regard to curriculum and accreditation (from master's degrees and graduate studies to electives and extracurricular courses).

Generally speaking, the programs all try to include teaching, research, community outreach, and academic publishing. The emphasis is different at each university. For example, PIEM in Mexico principally aims toward research, documentation, and publication. It has funding for research grants for both master's degrees and doctoral dissertations. Also, PIEM has a special documentation unit for Mexico and Latin America, as well as a current directory of researchers in women's studies. It has also published numerous books.

In Brazil, research takes preeminence over teaching. On the other hand, Costa Rica has an important documentation center in its Women's Information Program (PIM). The interdisciplinary graduate program with a specialization in women's studies at the University of Buenos Aires concentrates on graduate-level teaching and community outreach programs.

Then and Now

Women's studies in Latin America has undergone two stages of development. The first took place at the end of the 1970s in the form of "recovery." Its goal was to challenge the practice of silencing, stereotyping, and discriminating against women that was prevalent in theory and social research. The projects were influenced by agendas of activists who were involved in political and civic work concerning critical issues for women, such as participation in the labor market, violence, education, and legal rights.

By the middle of the 1980s, the primary research topics had to do with daily family life, language, social participation, culture and politics of women in different social sectors, sexuality, mental health, and abortion and reproductive rights. In the 1990s, research was directed more toward the study of social and cultural constructs of gender differences and their relation to other forms of social stratification.

The biggest success for women's studies in Latin America has been the broad diffusion of the notion of "gender." In 2000, gender was part of the conceptual baggage of both university and nonuniversity researchers, particularly those in social sciences and humanities. It also appears in cultural discourse in the broadest sense, including the opinions of politicians and social leaders. The proliferation of programs is both a cause and a consequence of women's continuous growth in knowledge.

Despite all this progress, some important obstacles remain. Women's studies has evolved in academic circles without consideration of the most efficient strategies for its development. Women's studies is usually incorporated into a program or specific area. On the one hand, this strategy facilitates the quick dissemination of knowledge without the need for constant justification from academia. On the other hand, women's studies runs the risk of becoming a feminist ghetto, separated from the rest of the disciplines, whose patriarchal premises may remain intact. The debate continues. Should universities create multi- or interdisciplinary programs exclusively devoted to women's studies? Should they make gender a central analytical category in all disciplines in order to comprehend existing modes of thinking, thereby changing existing paradigms?

Generally, the university programs are sustained with financial support from other sources and with the strong dedication of the women who created and direct these programs. Only in a few cases do the programs receive economic support from the universities. The majority face unending problems of subsistence.

Another concern is the relationship between women's studies and the feminist movement. Should research respond specifically to activists' demands, even at the cost of lowering academic standards? May the need to make women's studies a legitimate field imply the risk of falling into the trap of bureaucracy in academia? The tension between feminist activists and academics affects both groups equally. For some, it seems necessary to have distinct boundaries on the roles of academics within and for the women's movement—since academics have some distance from political and practical urgencies. For others, it seems imperative to maintain "anger as the catalyst . . . for radical protest" (Malverde, 1994). This is the base for empowerment, and it is the origin of new demands on the university. Although building a common agenda is not easy, the continuation of dialogue and interaction can make a valuable contribution.

In the 1990s, several journals began publication in the academic institutions of the region, such as *Etudos Feministas (Feminist Studies,* CIEC/ECO/UFRS) in Brazil and *Debate Feminista (Feminist Debate)* in Mexico. In addition, brochures and pamphlets continue to proliferate, however irregular and limited they may be. The publication of research is still very restricted because of limited financial support from universities and commercial publishers.

Another huge obstacle is a lack of awareness of discrimination against women in society at large, and in scientific study by the majority of professors and teachers. Other obstacles are academics' resistance to interdisciplinary work and their propensity to defend their own fields, power, and prestige.

Between 1980 and 2000, women's studies became a reality in the majority of the region's universities. Nevertheless, because the programs are still relatively small, coexisting with the region's scientific and financial projects, they are always at risk of being cut. Women's studies has a long way to go before it ceases to be a compensatory strategy restricted to universities and is instituted at all levels of education. An exception to this scenario is the Programa Nacional de Promoción de la Igualdad de Oportunidades para la Mujer (National Program of Opportunity and Equality for Women), which is carried out by the education sector of the Ministry of Education and Culture in Argentina. It has been undertaking the systematic task of communication between people working in university research, women's studies, and educational reform throughout the country and at all levels. A similar initiative was begun at the Ministry of Education in Chile.

See Also

DEVELOPMENT: CENTRAL AND SOUTH AMERICA AND THE CARIBBEAN; EDUCATION: CENTRAL AND SOUTH AMERICA AND THE CARIBBEAN; FEMINISM: CARIBBEAN; FEMINISM: CENTRAL AND SOUTH AMERICA; WOMEN'S STUDIES: CARIBBEAN

References and Further Reading

Lechner, N. 1993. La igualdad como oportunidad para la democracia (Equality as an opportunity for democracy). *Politicas de igualdad de oportunidad.* Chile: SERNAM.

Luna, L. 1989–1990. Género y movimientos sociales en América Latina (Gender and social movements in Latin America). *Boletín Americanista* (Universidad de Barcelona) 39–40.

Malverde, I. 1994. Mujeres y varones conviviendo en equidad: Aportes de la Universidad para el cambio social. *Seminario Regional de Universidades y Ministerios de Educacion: Los Aportes de los Estudios de la Mujer a la Reforma Educativa Conference.* Argentina: PRIOM.

Gloria Bonder

WOMEN'S STUDIES:
Commonwealth of Independent States

Women's studies does not exist in the Commonwealth of Independent States (CIS) as it does in the West. For more than 70 years, until 1991, the CIS existed as a union of federative republics within the USSR. Until the 1970s there was no serious research done on women because Soviet ideology claimed that the so-called woman's question had been solved. Suppressed for ideological reasons, feminist and gender-related writings from the West could have little influence in the USSR. Under perestroika (1985–1991), however, many problems related to women's studies were raised for the first time, and the first serious intellectual exchanges with western feminists began to occur.

Since the breakup of the USSR in 1991, CIS countries have been passing through a complicated transition period to a new type of society. In the midst of that transition, women's concerns are often left unaddressed. Today research on women is no longer restricted by communist ideological barriers. Instead, a patriarchal mentality, severe economic difficulties, and political instability have become serious obstacles to the flourishing of women's research and its practical use for women.

Women's studies appeared in western Europe and North America as a result of a strong feminist movement in the 1960s and 1970s. The Soviet Union was a different case, because feminism was prohibited there. Ideology in the USSR controlled all spheres of Soviet life, including science and research. All research on women had to be ideologically verified—that is, research on women had to be consistent with or at least not contradictory of Marxist-Leninist ideology (*The Woman Question,* 1975).

The "Woman Question" after the Revolution

The main thrust of Marxist thought on the woman question was that women were oppressed under capitalism at work and at home and only a socialist revolution could free them. The socialist revolution of October 1917 proclaimed equal rights for women and men. By 1917 Marxists had developed preliminary thoughts on the emancipation of women, the meaning of equality, and the nature of family. The young Bolshevik state began with a commitment to these ideas and to the liberation of women.

From 1917 to 1930 the woman question provoked a lively debate about domestic labor, maternity pay, civil marriage, divorce, women's organizations, equality, and sexuality (Buckley, 1989: 18–102). In some ways, it was an attempt to extend Marxist theorizing on the woman's question begun by I. Armand and A. Kollontai, two famous Russian women revolutionaries. Kollontai's writings are widely known by western feminists (Clements, 1979; Holt, 1977), but Soviet readers had no chance to be acquainted with them because of censorship.

In the 1930s Joseph Stalin declared the "woman question" solved, which blocked any comprehensive analysis of gender roles. For more than 20 years serious discussion about women's issues was silenced. Even statistical data on women remained unpublished. Theoretical arguments of the 1920s about domestic labor, motherhood, marriage, and sexuality were quashed. In spite of such suppression, Soviet propaganda regularly proclaimed that women enjoyed equal rights. Heroic literature spoke of women workers who overfulfilled production quotas. From 1924 to 1953, when Stalin was in power, however, the reality was that no research was done on women's issues (Lapidus, 1978: 95–122).

After Stalin's death and during Nikita Khrushchev's time (1953–1964), there was an attempt to inspire political activity by women in the USSR, because representation of women in governmental bodies was so low. Official leaders at least acknowledged that equality between men and women had not yet been achieved. The task of promoting women's participation in politics was to be resolved by the Zhensovety (Women's Councils), guided by communist officials. Unfortunately, the Soviet government was motivated solely by appearances and satisfied with superficial changes such as appointing a single woman to a position of power and prestige. No comprehensive changes that might have affected the majority of women were adopted.

Under Leonid Brezhnev (1964–1983), Soviet propaganda accepted so-called nonantagonistic contradictions, or those problems and issues that could be overcome by communist processes. This gave legitimacy to researchers who were examining inequality between the sexes. In the late 1960s and early 1970s, then, for the first time in Soviet history, women's issues became the subject of research.

The serious economic and demographic problems the USSR was facing forced policy makers to invest in detailed analysis of women's lives. Because women constituted 51 percent of the labor force, the Soviet economy could not develop without using women's labor. Social science institutions were encouraged to make recommendations to improve the economic situation and the falling birthrates. The initiative boosted the sociological research on women, a discipline that had previously been banned. The sociological research done at that time showed women as less qualified, performing more unskilled manual jobs as compared with men. Researchers also identified for the first time how poor working conditions endangered women's health.

The Second Wave

Despite some new attention to women's issues, when women's studies began in the West in the 1970s, the Soviet Union was still a closed society. The second wave of feminism was labeled by Soviet ideologists as "bourgeois." They declared that the woman question should not be separated from the other problems of Soviet society and there was no need for an independent women's movement. Soviet scholars condemned the antifamily tendencies of western feminism and were critical of the western feminist scholars who focused on Soviet women's dependent position in politics, the workplace, and the home (Atkinson et al., 1978; Jancar, 1978; Lapidus, 1978). However, in spite of the strict control of feminist ideas by the government, a group of women in Leningrad prepared a samizdat, an unofficial publication, titled *Women in Russia* (Women in Eastern Europe Group, 1980), which contained a bitter criticism of the Soviet political system, Soviet institutions, and Soviet men. The main subject of discussion was the quality of social services, standards of living, and the lack of care in maternity homes and abortion clinics, crèches, and pioneer camps.

Anxious after the appearance of the first feminist magazine in the USSR, the Soviet government banned its distribution. Some time later, in spite of government pressure, another two feminist magazines, *Rossianka* (Russian woman) and *Maria,* were published by a group of women who had split off from *Women in Russia.* Based on Russian Orthodoxy, they were strikingly different from the antireligious orientation of early western feminism (Holt, 1985).

In 1980 religious feminist groups protested the Soviet government's sending troops to Afghanistan. This action could not be unpunished. The leaders of samizdat publication were expelled from the USSR but continued their work in the West. A number of books were published by them there, including Tatiana Mamonova's *Russian Women's Studies,* essays on sexism and Soviet culture, which contained such chapters as women in history, Russian classical writers, attitudes toward women, women in art and science, and sex and the contemporary scene (Mamonova, 1989).

In 1985, when Mikhail Gorbachev became general secretary of the Communist Party of the USSR, he had the same policy toward women as previous leaders, which was based on the combination of mother and worker as roles for women. Subsequently, the opportunities for part-time work were increased, women were promoted to decision-making posts according to the quotas, and Women's Councils were revived.

Women and Perestroika

In 1987 a new political policy, known as perestroika (reconstruction, restructuring), began in the USSR. The concept of perestroika was a radical political and socioeconomic transformation of society. Perestroika came with glasnost (publicity or openness).

The adoption of glasnost dramatically changed the nature of discussion about women's lives. Women's status was among the first topics to be affected by democratization and glasnost. Many stereotypes of the former social prosperity of Soviet women were broken. For the first time such topics as the USSR's record in the number of abortions, poor contraceptive development, prostitution, and many other related areas were debated. Discussions about previously taboo subjects revealed how insufficient the research on women was. The academic community finally put onto the agenda the need for a special scientific council on women's problems.

A small group of researchers on women's issues was created through the initiative of female scholars from the Institute of Philosophy. As a result, a series of articles about American feminism was published in the philosophical magazine in 1988. A year later the first Center for Gender Studies was established in the USSR. It was based at the Institute for Social and Economic Problems of Population of the Moscow Academy of Sciences.

The same year, three scholars at this center published an article titled "How We Resolve the Woman's Question" in the Soviet magazine *Kommunist* (Communist). The article argued that patriarchal relations in Soviet society should be replaced by egalitarian ones, based on mutual complementarity of the sexes, which could be realized only in an environment of free choice (Rimashevskaya, 1992). For the first time Soviet scholars used the term *patriarchy* in reference to Soviet society. An egalitarian society and women's choices also were new concepts, even in academia, where the initiative was supported by only a few scholars.

Since its founding the Center for Gender Studies has prepared various publications and newsletters. Two books, *Woman in a Changing World* and *Women and Social Policy,* were published in 1992. Both publications identified women and their transition to the market economy as a problem that had both theoretical and practical significance. Both publications examined Soviet laws on family, maternity, and childhood adopted in 1990–1991. According to the specialists, these protectionist laws, which expanded maternity leave without special provisions to integrate women into a market economy, had not improved women's status but rather had undermined it.

Women and Social Policy also raised the problem of women's employment. The authors concluded that in conditions of economic crisis, women were the first to lose their jobs and were victims of indirect discrimination. For the first time Soviet scholars had begun to use the term *discrimination* with regard to women's status in the USSR. The book also contained a chapter on gender, with an explanation of this new term in academia and the suggestion that gender analysis should become part of the methodology in the social sciences. Other sections of the book discussed the role of men in a changing society and the psychological problems of boys and girls.

Feminism since the 1990s

More frequent contacts with their western counterparts involved in women's issues dramatized for Soviet women the practical need for women's studies in the USSR. In 1990 the Soviet American Women's Summit took place in the United States. Shortly afterward, in October 1991, eight Soviet women researchers were invited to the United States by the University of Wisconsin Women's Studies Consortium to learn about the American experience in establishing women's studies programs. Many joint projects were planned during this visit.

A month later the UNESCO (United Nations Educational, Scientific, and Cultural Organization) conference "Gender Studies: Issues and Comparative Perspectives" was held in Moscow. About 100 participants from the USSR republics and from abroad attended. The conference objectives were to advance the teaching of women's studies in higher education; to enhance women's perspectives in planning, policy making, and implementation through training programs in gender studies; and to promote networking through the exchange of information among national, regional, and international women's studies programs.

Thematic conference working groups were dedicated to family, household, and demographic changes; women in economic life; and teaching and training in gender studies. The fact that the UNESCO conference took place in Moscow played an important role in promoting women's studies in the Soviet Union. In addition, a series of conference papers presented by western scholars on gender and the development of women's studies in various countries was published in the magazine *Sociological Studies,* thus introducing this new field to Soviet readers.

During the Soviet period the network of women's organizations was subordinated to the Communist Party. Not until perestroika did the first informal women's organizations surface that were differently oriented. About 200 women representing various women's groups gathered in March 1991 in Dubna, Moscow region, for the first Independent Women's Forum. They discussed three major topics: women and politics, women and the market economy, and the role of women in modern culture.

The second Women's Independent Forum was held in Dubna in November 1992. By then the Soviet Union had been dissolved, and the conference drew principally Russian women, along with some representatives of former USSR republics, as well as foreign guests. The motto of the forum was "From Problems to Strategy," with the aim of addressing the problem of women's declining status in society. One central concern was the small number of seats that women were elected to during the first democratic elections in 1990. Because of some of the strategies developed at the forum, and after it, women obtained many more seats in the Russian parliament during the elections of December 1993.

Another forum section that generated attention was called "Feminism and the Women's Movement." Many women were eager to learn about feminism, although feminism had received negative coverage in the media, largely because critics knew so little about it.

The first book in Russian about western feminism appeared in 1992. The Moscow editorial house called Progress translated and published *Feminism: The Essential Historical Writings,* with introduction and commentaries by M. Schner. For the first time, essays, fiction, and memoirs of the major writers of the first wave of feminism such as Abigail Adams, Mary Wollstonecraft, George Sand, John Stuart Mill, Emma Goldman, Virginia Woolf, and many others were presented in Russian. The other book published on feminism that same year was a compilation of modern western feminist writings on science, history, anthropology, and philosophy, prepared by specialists from the Institute of Scientific Information of the Russian Academy of Science.

The first feminist magazine in Russia, *Preobrazhenie* (Transfiguration), also appeared in 1992. It was the initiative of a feminist club of the same name. A second feminist magazine, *Zhenskoe Chtenie* (Women's Reading), was published by the Saint Petersburg Women's Center. Still another feminist-oriented magazine, *Vi y mi* (You and We), is published by Americans in the Russian language and contains much material about women's experiences in both the United States and Russia. The programs of the women's radio show *Nadezhda* (Hope) have also become very popular among women because they discuss real problems women are now facing in Russia and the CIS.

Women's studies courses have been introduced in several Russian universities: Russian People's Friendship University in Moscow, Russian Humanitarian University (Moscow), Moscow State University, and the University of Saint Petersburg at the University of Tver (Moscow region). Many women's organizations and groups invite women's studies lecturers to give talks.

There is a special urgency about all this fervent feminist activity, for after the disintegration of the Soviet Union, the daily life of the majority of women in the CIS became a matter of survival and of political, social, and emotional disasters. There are many common traits in the situation of women in all the republics of CIS, although each of them has its own peculiarities. Women's status is obviously declining throughout the republics. Women are the first to be fired; the feminization of poverty is escalating. In the newly liberated republics, "reformers" are directing women to return to their "purely womanly mission" as housewives. In the new market economy, women are portrayed as "consumer objects" by the male-dominated media, which has a demoralizing effect not only on women themselves but on the society as a whole. In such conditions it is extremely difficult to develop women's studies, and there is almost no economic support for it.

Among all the CIS republics, Russia has the most developed research and teaching on women. After the breakup of the USSR, Russia became the inheritor of all the main institutions that deal with women. Overall, information about research on women in the CIS is sparse and scattered. A women's studies center has been established in Kiev, Ukraine. There are also a number of groups and individuals working on women's issues in Belarus, Moldova, and the non-CIS republics in the Baltic States.

The women in the Caucasus republics (Georgia, Azerbaijan, and Armenia) are facing all the difficulties of war in their region. As a result, women's organizing efforts have focused primarily on establishing peace in this area. The war itself makes impossible any serious research on women, although there are plans to establish women's studies programs in the Transcaucasian republics. Because of the strong revival of Islamic traditions in the Central Asian States (Uzbekistan, Tajikistan, Kyrgyzstan, Kazakhstan, Turkmenistan), the development of women's studies in this region may prove problematic if women are oppressed as an integral part of a religious expression.

In such conditions of economic crisis, skyrocketing inflation, increasing prices, and political instability in the CIS republics, the development of women's studies programs has been very difficult. Shaped by this historical context, most women's studies efforts are turning to practical projects, directed to support women. Sometimes with the help of their western partners, varieties of women's groups have organized all kinds of professional training for women in order to integrate them into the market and to enable them to become genuinely equal members of society. Because of the initiative of women of the CIS, many international and domestic conferences and seminars now take place in the region, in which women can discuss various pressing topics: women's participation in politics, the problems of survival, economic and environmental issues, women and violence.

The question remains whether the policy directions generated by women's studies research and teaching will be sufficient in the face of the economic instability and political uncertainty that have emerged after a legacy of suppression.

See Also

FEMINISM: COMMONWEALTH OF INDEPENDENT STATES; POLITICS AND THE STATE: COMMONWEALTH OF INDEPENDENT STATES; WOMEN'S STUDIES: OVERVIEW; WOMEN'S STUDIES: RESEARCH CENTERS AND INSTITUTES

References and Further Reading

Atkinson, Dorothy, Alexander Dallin, and Gail Warshofsky Lapidus, eds. 1978. *Women in Russia.* Hassocks, England: Harvester.

Buckley, Mary. 1989. *Women and ideology in the Soviet Union.* London: Harvester Wheatsheaf.

Clements, Barbara Evans. 1979. *Bolshevick feminist.* Bloomington: Indiana University Press.

Holt, Alix. 1977. *Alexandra Kollontai: Selected writings.* New York: Norton.

———. 1985. The first Soviet feminists. In Barbara Holland, ed., *Soviet sisterhood.* London: Fourth Estate.

Jancar, Barbara Wolfe. 1978. *Women under communism.* Baltimore: Johns Hopkins University Press.

Lapidus, Gail Warshofsky. 1978. *Women in Soviet society: Equality, development and social change.* Berkeley: University of California Press.

Mamonova, Tatiana. 1989. *Russian women's studies.* Oxford: Pergamon Press.

Rimashevskaya, Natalia. 1992. The new women's studies. In Mary Buckley, ed., *Perestroika and Soviet women.* Cambridge: Cambridge University Press.

The woman question: Selections from the writings of Karl Marx, Friedrich Engels, V. I. Lenin, and Joseph Stalin. 1975. New York: International.

Women in Eastern Europe Group. (Translation.) 1980. *Women in Russia: First feminist "samizdat."* London: Sheba.

Irina Akimushkina

WOMEN'S STUDIES: East Asia

Among the major east Asian nations, women's studies has grown dramatically in importance and diversity since the first colleges and universities initiated programs in the field in the 1970s. Many individual women's studies programs have benefited greatly from interaction with existent programs in western academic settings and the exchange of information through nongovernmental organizations. While the scope and focus of women's studies programs vary significantly from nation to nation, most east Asian centers have concentrated on efforts to redefine women's place in society and culture and to educate women for participation in both the political and the economic sphere. The United Nations Fourth World Conference on Women in Beijing in 1995 helped publicize many women's issues in the region and gave impetus to many existing programs.

Women's studies programs serve a variety of functions in the region. At one level, they exist to provide academic study of issues and concerns to women both regionally and globally. In addition, women's studies provides a mechanism for discourse between the women of east Asia and their counterparts throughout the world by sponsoring conferences and producing journals and other information for public use. On another level, these programs serve as the focal points for organizing campaigns and initiatives to address the main problems facing women in the region. There are some common themes among the east Asian nations, including the need for greater political participation and awareness and greater protections for gender-based crime, including sexual assault and domestic violence. However, the women of each nation also have distinctive or specific issues. For instance, the onerous birth control policy in China has placed high burdens on women and female children in the nation.

In the often traditional and gender-discriminatory societies of east Asian nations, women's studies centers provide a means of liberation and academic freedom that serves to promote the otherwise often muted concerns of the women of these nations. They also serve as a vehicle to coordinate regional and international efforts to address problems confronted by women in the region. In this regard, the women's studies centers have had a major impact in improving the lives of ordinary women in east Asia.

Women's Studies in Japan

In the region, Japan has the most highly developed system of women's studies programs and one of the oldest continuing traditions of feminist research. Japanese women were prominent in the peace movement of the 1970s, and their activism was spurred on by the development of feminist and women's studies at the university level. Women's studies was formally initiated in Japan in the late 1970s. Many scholars and graduate students who had the opportunity of studying in the United States and in Europe rebelled at the experience of discrimination in Japan. They started to question deeply held assumptions about women's place and role in society and began to use feminist arguments against traditional forms of gender discrimination. Discussions took place in the classroom and in private homes as women began to organize themselves into groups. These groups were supported by women who worked at home and in the paid workforce.

While there had been some studies on women and women's history prior to this time, they had not focused on the status of women or their independence in Japanese society. Instead they had reflected an academic emphasis on traditional values and gender roles. The first major organized groups to emerge from the efforts to broaden the study of women in Japan were the Women's Studies Society of Japan (WSSJ) and the Association of Women's Studies in Japan (AWSJ), which were organized in 1977 and 1979, respectively. Both organizations endeavored to address four main topics that were central to efforts to advance gender equality during that time period. The first and main issue was the changing role of married women, especially in light of both the increased desire and the economic pressure they felt to work outside the home, and the societal constraints on women workers. The second issue was the double-bound pressure on women ("no-win" if you do, "no-win" if you

don't) to modernize, and the societal backlash against women who did. The third issue was related to the first and encompassed the impact of the changing roles of both married and unmarried women, in the family and in the marketplace. The fourth issue was sexual discrimination in the workplace. This issue became especially contentious when more women moved into the labor market. Specific institutions that were at the forefront of the women's studies movement included Tokyo Women's College, Nihon Women's University, and Ochanomizu Women's University. By the 1990s, these older institutions that helped start women's studies housed various institutes and centers for women's studies and gender studies.

The establishment of women's studies was strengthened by the influence of International Women's Year in 1975. The early programs were multidisciplinary in nature and incorporated courses from political science, history, economics, and sociology. The newly coined word *Jyosei-gaku* was used for this emerging area of interdisciplinary study, and further support was provided by feminist bookstores such as Crayon House and Shokado Women's Bookstore in Tokyo and Osaka.

In addition to the development of academic centers and programs, women's studies was supported by private organizations that promoted and coordinated efforts across colleges and universities. One of the oldest women's studies groups in Japan is the Women's Studies Society of Japan (WSSJ), located in Osaka. It produces the academic journal *Annual Report of Women's Studies* and the monthly newsletter *Voice of Women*. Several other women's studies journals are also published. By 1998, the number of women's studies courses in colleges and universities had risen to 570. In addition, some 30 percent of universities and junior colleges had women's studies and related courses. By 1995, 13 universities had established institutes on gender and women's studies. In 1996, Jyousai International University in Chiba Prefecture established a graduate women's studies program. This was in addition to the Aichi Shukutoku University (in Aichi Prefecture) Institute for Gender and Women's Studies that had been established in 1994 as the first institute for women's studies in a coeducational university in Japan. Subsequently, 18 other gender and women's studies institutes were established nationwide.

Besides courses at the college and university level, various national and local government adult education programs and NGO educational activities started to include women's studies in the curriculum. Over the years, these courses have proved to be among the most popular in adult education. For example, the National Women's Education

Center, which is run by the Ministry of Education, has gender and women's studies courses every summer for three days. More than 3,000 participants from all over Japan enroll in the courses each year.

Although the number of institutes and colleges that have women's studies is increasing, the social norm of patriarchy and the custom of male supremacy still remain in Japan. What the women's studies institutes have been most successful in achieving is the promotion of dialogue over gender patterns and the establishment of methods to increase educational opportunities and political awareness among Japanese women. During the 1990s several new laws were passed, including the basic law for gender equality, an anti–child pornography law, and the revised equal employment law.

Women's Studies in Taiwan

Women's studies were initiated in Taiwan concurrently with the effort to establish such programs in other industrialized nations, although the first actual program on the island began in 1972. It was undertaken as a scholarly enterprise by individual women academics rather than as a popular movement. Initially the new program was called the study of women or research on women. However, women students who studied in the United States in the 1970s and were impressed by the women's liberation movement began to use the term *women's studies*. They also began to push for a much more comprehensive and radical approach to gender issues.

In the 1970s the Taiwanese government strictly controlled social activities. Freedom of speech and thought were severely restricted. Some women activists were arrested for their radical stand on women's issues. But in the 1980s, the liberal social movement started. In the late 1980s, the government permitted plural political parties. The women's movement became very active and efforts focused on gender consciousness-raising. Specifically, women's groups began to focus on the changing relationships in the family, especially the relations between wife and husband. One result of this effort was that the New Awakening Society for Women was organized. The monthly journal *New Awakening of Women* began publication to disseminate information on gender relations and increase the awareness of feminism. The journal introduced many Taiwanese to the writings of Virginia Woolf, Simone de Beauvoir, and other European feminist writers. Located near Taiwan University's national campus, the society's office offered students there alternative perspectives on women's issues. Another major Taiwanese center of higher learning, Shinfa University, also established gender and social studies programs.

In 1985, the executive committee of Taiwan University was asked to assess the changing role and attitude of women in Taiwan. The main issues were women's labor, the changes in family relationships, student movements, environmental protection movements, and the status of minority and indigenous women. Within many universities, there was a broad debate over the relationship between academic research and the women's movement. At Taiwan University, the initial preference was to separate the two, but the women's research program is now connected to the population research center of the university. In the 1990s, topics for seminars and conferences in universities have included "gender and women," "sexuality and gender," and "women in Taiwan: past, present, and future." However, a major problem for women's advocates remains: there is still tension between the movement activists and the women's studies scholars. This difficulty is related to perceptions of the role of women in society and to the political stance toward mainland China. In 1999, a new political regime took office and Hsui-Lien Annette Lu, a woman who had been active in the feminist movement (1970s–1980s), became vice president.

Women's Studies in Korea

At the end of the twentieth century, 10 universities had women's studies courses and institutes in South Korea. Since the late 1970s, government policy has been relatively open to the study of international relations. One result was the establishment of the governmental institute for women's development. However, despite the early openness, there has been relatively little progress toward true gender equality in South Korea. An increasing number of female scholars protest to the general society and to the government that there should be greater participation of women in politics and especially in decision-making circles. The women's movement has worked to ensure greater equality of pay and working conditions and to address the broader societal inequities in South Korea. Women's studies scholars participated in the investigations and revelations of the Japanese Army's use of Korean women during World War II as "comfort women" (sexual slaves). They also were involved in the efforts to bring the matter before international courts. In doing so, they helped highlight the impact of militarization on societies and the potentially devastating effect on women. Women activists have openly criticized the government for the sexual abuse of women in detention. And they have spoken out against the continuing U.S. military presence in the nation, which has resulted in a number of notorious sex crimes against Korean women and girls.

Support for the development of women's studies led to the creation of a number of programs and centers in the

1970s. The Korean Women's Institute was established in 1977 in Ewha Women's University. Its main objectives were to raise the consciousness of scholars, students, and staff in the academy and at the local community level. Areas of study included women's history, the study of women from a feminist perspective, and the development of a support program for women and children. Sookmung Women's University, Pusan National University, Pusan Sookmyund Women's University, Pusan National University, Pusan Women's University, Hyosung University, Seoul Women's University, and Mokpo National University also have women's studies institutes. The main goals of these programs continue to be the promotion of awareness of inequalities and the development of resource centers for women, both at the academic level and for general societal use.

In the late 1990s great progress was achieved in legal reformation in the areas of equal employment and gender equality. President Kim Dejun made efforts to include women in decision-making roles, and women's studies have therefore gained support nationwide.

Women's Studies in China (People's Republic of China)

The control exerted by the central government in Beijing delayed the development of women's studies in China until after similar programs had been well established in other east Asian nations. In 1987, the Center for Women's Studies of Zheng-Zhou University was established. A seminar on Chinese women and their social participation and development was organized. Women researchers and scholars from across the nation and from abroad met and exchanged information. Since 1995, following the United Nations Fourth World Conference on Women in Beijing, the center has been in a delicate position politically for its liberal and open attitude toward NGOs from all over the world.

Representatives of women's studies programs from many nations attended the Beijing conference, as did numerous NGOs and advocates of feminism and women's rights. While the Chinese regime tolerated some open discussion of gender issues at the conference, any sought-after relaxation of censorship or governmental interference in the exchange of ideas was short lived. While issues such as China's one-child-per-couple birth control policy, gender equality in the workplace, sexual harassment, gender crimes, and the patriarchal nature of Chinese society were discussed and debated at the conference, such debate has since been tempered.

Nonetheless, even while restrictions on intellectual discourse remain, the nation is gradually building a substantial infrastructure to support women's studies. In 1990, the Cen-

ter for Women's Studies in Beijing University was established, and that same year it held its first academic seminar on women's issues. A report on the findings of the conference was later published. The People's University also introduced women's studies courses, taught by feminist scholars. The government sponsored the establishment of the Chinese Women's Federation, which has its institute for women's issues and a number of branch offices all over China (the Beijing Institute of Women is located in the office of the Chinese Women's Federation).

Demographic data on China are collected by the government and used as a basis for formulating policy on women. The Women's Federation offices in Shanghai and Guangzhou have established research institutes that collaborate with the local universities to provide information and statistics to the government. These institutions of higher learning also engage in transnational women's studies. For instance, the Guangzhou Women's Federation is engaged in research with international organizations on migrant women workers. This research focuses particular attention on discrimination and the exploitation of women's labor.

As a result of China's open economic policy, discrimination against women workers is increasing and their maternal leave is not being protected by some of the multinational companies. This problem is especially acute in factories in the large southern cities. Women have tended to suffer to a greater extent than men in areas of economic transformation, as the few protections that exist within the legal system are increasingly ignored. Speech and information continue to be controlled by the central government. This became apparent during the UN's conference in 1995, when indigenous Chinese women were censored and excluded from participation in the conference if they were perceived to hold anti-institutional views.

Although they have no university-based women's studies institutes or courses, women in Hong Kong are very active in the organization of women workers and activists. In 2000, there continued to be a strong movement to change family law and challenge existing norms. Feminism is on the increase in the area, especially as a result of the influence of young scholars who studied in Great Britain and the United States. However, with the Chinese takeover, freedom of expression has begun to erode. One of the major women's advocacy groups is called Feminism and the Advancement of Women. In addition, migrant women's organizations actively support and supply information services. Some 80 percent of women migrant workers in Hong Kong are from the Philippines and are domestic workers. Many of them are supported by Christian churches. Voting practices remain an obstacle to the advancement of women's causes: in Hong

Kong, each individual has one vote, but the head of an organization or institution, usually male, is granted an additional vote.

Macao

Macao also lacks any form of academic institute of women's studies. Migrant women workers and battered women's shelters in Macao are organized by the Good Shepherd Sister's House. However, Beijing has begun to increase its control over church-sponsored activities. Meanwhile, the issue of violence against women is studied and discussed at Macao's Adult Education Organization. Both Hong Kong and Macao are increasingly subject to Chinese social law and policies, although their economies remained directed toward the West. Women's rights advocates in Hong Kong and Macao are concerned about how their lives will be affected as China plays an increasing role in the governments of both of the former colonies.

Mongolia

In 1998 the first women's studies exchange program was held in Ulan Bator, cosponsored by the Liberal Women's Brain Pool (an NGO), Tsetseguun College, and the Association of Japanese Women's Studies. At the four-day seminar the history, demography, and present-day issues of Mongolian women were discussed by 100 women and men. A women's studies program was planned to begin in the near future.

See Also

EDUCATION: EAST ASIA; FEMINISM, *regional articles*; INTERNATIONAL ORGANIZATIONS AND AGENCIES; WOMEN'S STUDIES: OVERVIEW; WOMEN'S STUDIES: RESEARCH CENTERS AND INSTITUTES

References and Further Reading

Agarwal, Bina, ed. 1988. *Structures of patriarchy: The state, the community, and the household.* Atlantic Highlands, N.J.: Zed.

Committee on Women's Studies in Asia. 1995. *Changing lives: Life stories of Asian pioneers in women's studies.* New York: Feminist Press at the City University of New York.

Evans, Harriet. 1997. *Women and sexuality in China: Female sexuality and gender since 1949.* New York: Continuum.

Human Rights in China (HRIC). 1995. *Caught between tradition and the state: Violations of the human rights of Chinese women.* The Hague: HRIC.

Ramusack, Barbara, and Sharon Sievers. 1999. *Women in Asia: Restoring women to history.* Bloomington: Indiana University Press.

Richardson, Diane, and Victoria Robinson, eds. 1993. *Thinking feminist: Key concepts in women's studies.* New York: Guilford Press.

Yayori, Matsui. 1989. *Women's Asia.* London: Zed.

Junko Kuninobu

WOMEN'S STUDIES: Funding

Women's studies as a formal area of teaching and research emerged in the late 1960s as feminist scholars on U.S. campuses, reflecting the concerns of the women's movement, began to question the portrayal of women and their underrepresentation in the college curriculum. Research and writing about women, though not unknown before that time, had not been conceptualized or organized as an academic program.

The first two women's studies programs came into being in 1969 at Cornell University in New York and at San Diego State University in California. From then on, women's studies courses and programs spread rapidly. By the end of 1971 more than 600 women's studies courses existed in colleges and universities throughout the United States. Neither university support nor outside funding was initially available, and progress was dependent on the voluntary efforts and commitment of the scholars themselves.

For mutual support and exchange of information, these early pioneers formed informal networks and organized women's caucuses within their respective disciplines and professional associations. In 1969 women's caucuses were formed in the American Sociological Association, the Modern Language Association, the American Historical Association, the American Political Science Association, and the American Psychological Association. By the end of 1971, at least 50 such groups of academic women had been formed in the United States, including both autonomous caucuses and advisory committees appointed by and operating under the aegis of their parent association. Both kinds of groups were funded largely by membership dues and in-kind contributions. Advisory committees received some funding for operating and research expenses, but the amounts were minimal. During the period 1969–1971, the total amount appropriated to all the committees did not exceed $50,000 (Klotzburger, 1973).

Early Funding

Beginning in 1972, external funding for women's studies was forthcoming from a few foundations, primarily the Ford

Foundation. Ford support was initially provided in the form of faculty fellowships for research on the role of women in society and doctoral dissertation fellowships in women's studies broadly construed. Over a three-year period, 1972–1975, the foundation appropriated more than $1 million for these awards. In addition to providing financial support, this program also gave recognition to women's studies as a legitimate field of academic endeavor. Later, fellowship support became increasingly available from other foundations, such as the Rockefeller Foundation and the Andrew Mellon Foundation, as well as from government agencies, such as the National Endowment for the Humanities.

In the United States, private foundations played a major role in the development of women's studies; in other countries, the main sources of support were governmental. Following the conclusion of its fellowship program, the Ford Foundation provided strategic support throughout the 1970s, 1980s, and 1990s. Beginning in 1974, the foundation initiated a new program of support to establish a national system of centers for research on women on campus to provide institutional resources for ongoing efforts and to facilitate large-scale and interdisciplinary work. Since that time, more than two dozen colleges and universities have received Ford grants to develop campus-based research centers on women. Additional centers were formed, both on and off campus, with financial support from a variety of other funding sources: home institutions, government, corporations, private donors, bequests, philanthropic organizations, and contractual projects. By 1999 there were more than 80 centers operating under diverse institutional arrangements across the United States. To sustain these centers further and promote collaboration among them, the Ford Foundation also funded the National Council for Research on Women as an association of the centers and related organizations.

Other essential elements in the development of women's studies benefited from early support from the Ford Foundation. These included an enabling grant to help establish the National Women's Studies Association as a professional association of faculty members, program administrators, and women's studies practitioners; support for *Signs*, a major new scholarly journal in women's studies; and support to the Feminist Press for the development of curricular materials and educational projects in the United States and worldwide. During the 1980s and 1990s, Ford Foundation support of women's studies was concentrated in three main areas: (1) the integration of women's studies, including minority women's studies, into the mainstream liberal arts curriculum; (2) the strengthening of links between women's studies and international and area studies; and (3) the advancement of women's studies in developing countries. Overall, Ford Foundation grants for support of women's studies total well over $30 million to date. This represents perhaps two-thirds of the total in dollars spent by all foundations on women's studies programs (Chamberlain and Bernstein, 1992).

Government Funding

Government funding of women's studies in the United States began with the passage of the Women's Educational Equity Act in 1974. The act authorized a broad range of activities, including the development, evaluation, and dissemination of curricula, textbooks, and other educational material. College-level women's studies received some attention under the program, but support was directed largely to primary and secondary education and to projects concerned with training of educational personnel, guidance and counseling activities, and other aspects of educational equity in higher education. A more important source of government funding for women's studies is the Fund for the Improvement of Postsecondary Education (FIPSE), which was established in 1972. Beginning in 1973, FIPSE provided crucial support for women's studies programs as part of its overall activities to improve the educational experiences of women. Curricular reform was high on its agenda, and its efforts in this area made significant contributions to the integration of feminist research and perspectives into the mainstream curriculum in such fields as literature, history, and even mathematics. Another government agency that has provided substantial funding for women's studies is the National Endowment for the Humanities (NEH). The NEH has supported both research and curriculum development. For example, the NEH funded one of the earliest and most influential curriculum integration efforts, a four-year cross-disciplinary project conducted by the women's studies program at the University of Arizona. This program, initiated in 1981, was the forerunner of the curriculum integration movement and served to demonstrate the dimensions of the task involved.

In addition to funding from federal sources, government funding in the United States came from state and local agencies, such as arts councils and departments of education. During the 1980s, under conservative administrations in Washington, D.C., federal support declined and increased reliance was placed on other funding sources. Women's funds were established to encourage financial contributions for programs on behalf of women. In 1999 there were 95 such funds, large and small, throughout the United States. Although these funds, by and about women, tend to support primarily community projects and leadership development, funding is sometimes available for research or conferences. One fund, the Women's Studies Endowment, located in Washington, D.C., was founded by women's studies alumnae, students, faculty, and friends to foster feminist scholarship and investment.

Funding in Western Countries outside the United States

Outside the United States, in other western countries, private foundations have played a lesser role in the development of women's studies. Indeed, one might say that they have played an insignificant role, not surprisingly, given the fact that foundations are not common in those countries. In Australia, Canada, and some European countries, notably the Netherlands and the Scandinavian countries, major funding has come from the government. In Australia, all women's studies courses have been developed within the state university system and the emergence of "femocrats" (declared feminists within the bureaucracy) has helped to provide government funding for various projects. In Canada, the Social Sciences and Humanities Council of Canada has been the main source of funding for research. In 1992 alone, women's studies scholars received more than $4 million in research grants (Tancred, 1994). Endowed chairs in women's studies have been established in five universities with federal matching funds. By way of comparison, endowed chairs in women's studies are a rarity in the United States. There are probably not much more than a dozen nationwide, all of them privately funded (Chamberlain, 1988).

In the Netherlands, as in Canada, women's studies has received generous government support including both research support through the Dutch Committee for Emancipation Research and funding for university positions through the Ministry of Education and Science. In 1992 there were 300 university posts, including 14 chairs, in women's studies in the Netherlands (Brouns, 1992). The Dutch government has also subsidized European-wide and other international programs in women's studies. In the Nordic countries, government support has been provided through national research councils. State funding has made possible the establishment of more than 20 university centers for women's studies and feminist research, but there have been few tenured positions, and grants have often been of short duration. In the United Kingdom, France, and other countries in Europe, governmental support for women's studies has not been forthcoming to any significant degree. Fortunately, some possibilities of support are offered through participation in pan-European programs and networks. The European Network for Women's Studies (ENWS) was funded by the Council of Europe for the purpose of stimulating research in women's studies, incorporating the results of that research into postgraduate courses, and applying the results to policy making. Toward these ends, ENWS conducted conferences, workshops, and training programs. Another organization, Women's International Studies Europe (WISE), is an association of individual members initiated with support from the European Union (EU). Its activities include publication of a European journal of women's studies.

Funding in Developing Countries

Among developing countries, India is clearly outstanding in women's studies. Indeed, Indian feminists are among the world leaders in the field. They have benefited from a high level of support from both Indian funding sources, primarily government agencies, and international donor organizations. The main Indian funding sources are the University Grants Commission (UGC) and the Indian Council of Social Science Research (ICSSR). The UGC has provided funds to establish women's studies research centers in various universities as well as support for conferences, seminars, and research projects. The ICSSR supports research and research organizations in the social sciences and has sponsored numerous programs and projects in women's studies. Foreign funding agencies that have supported women's programs include the Canadian International Development Agency (CIDA), international agencies such as UNESCO (United Nations Educational, Scientific, and Cultural Organization), and UNIFEM (United Nations Development Fund for Women), and the Ford Foundation (Vyas and Signh, 1993). The Ford Foundation, through its field offices, has supported women's studies in a number of other developing countries in Asia, Latin America, and Africa, including, more recently, South Africa.

UNESCO has been actively involved in support of women's studies since 1980, when it convened a committee of experts on the subject in connection with the United Nations Decade for Women. The committee recommended that the organization cooperate in the creation and development of women's studies programs and research in various parts of the world. This recommendation was incorporated into the UNESCO Plan 1984–1989 and was carried forward in a series of regional seminars. These included a seminar in Rio de Janeiro on "Development of Women's Studies Programmes in Latin America and the Caribbean" (1981); a seminar in Tunisia on "Multidisciplinary Research on Women in the Arab World" (1982); and a regional meeting in New Delhi in 1982 on "Women's Studies and Social Sciences in Asia." A global meeting was held at the Institute of Social Studies, The Hague, in 1985 with additional funding from the Ministry of Development Cooperation, Netherlands.

Political and economic changes during the 1990s opened up new channels of international communication among women's groups, and it was not long before women's studies began to appear in the former Soviet states and eastern Europe and in Asian countries. The Fourth United Nations World Conference on Women, which took place in Beijing in 1995, was also a spur to further funding, particularly in Asia. There are now centers for research on women in Russia, Ukraine, Poland, Hungary, Lithuania, and the Czech Republic, as well as in China and Vietnam. University-level women's studies courses and programs are still rare, but they are making a start in a few places, notably Poland and China. In addition to the funding sources already active in women's studies, new sources of funding have emerged in these areas. Most notable among them is the Open Society Institute of the Soros Foundation, which operates primarily in central and eastern Europe, the former Soviet Union, and Mongolia. In 1999 the institute published a directory of women's studies and gender studies programs that included more than 150 entries in 28 countries throughout the region.

See Also

CURRICULUM TRANSFORMATION MOVEMENT; WOMEN'S STUDIES: OVERVIEW; WOMEN'S STUDIES; *regional articles*

References and Further Reading

Brouns, Margo. 1992. The Dutch development: Women's studies in the Netherlands. *Women's Studies Quarterly* 20(3–4): 44–57.

Chamberlain, Mariam K., ed. 1988. *Women in academe.* New York: Russell Sage Foundation.

Chamberlain, Mariam K., and Alison R. Bernstein. 1992. Philanthropy and the emergence of women's studies. *Teachers College Record* 93(3): 556–568.

Guy-Sheftall, Beverly, with Susan Heath. 1995. *Women's studies: A retrospective.* Report to the Ford Foundation.

Klotzburger, Kay. 1973. Political action by academic women. In Alice S. Rossi and Ann Calderwood, eds., *Academic women on the move,* 359–392. New York: Russell Sage Foundation.

Open Society Institute. 1999. Network Women's Program, *Gender studies and women's studies directory.* Budapest.

Tancred, Peta. 1994. Into the third decade of Canadian women's studies: A glass half empty or half full. *Women's Studies Quarterly* 22(3–4): 12–25.

Vyas, Anju, and Sunita Singh. 1993. *Women's studies in India.* New Delhi: Sage.

Mariam Chamberlain
Alison Bernstein

WOMEN'S STUDIES:
Middle East and North Africa

The emergence of women's studies as an academic discipline in the Middle East and north Africa is a relatively recent phenomenon that can be traced back to the early 1970s. It is important to note, however, that there are significant discrepancies between the countries that make up this geographical entity, which is itself not clearly delimited. In the present context, the Middle East and north Africa (MENA) region refers to the Arab Middle East and Iran, as well as Algeria, Morocco, and Tunisia. Despite the existence of common denominators between most of these countries—namely religion, language, and culture—they differ in more than one respect, be it at the level of the prevailing political and economic systems, income, or the emphasis placed on norms and traditions. These differences get clearly reflected in the women's issues and the status of women in each of these countries.

Historical Overview of the Feminist Movement

The feminist movement in the MENA region has evolved against a background of political instability, economic dependency, and Islamic fundamentalism (Abdo, 1998). At the political level, the region has witnessed decolonization struggles (as in Algeria), regional conflicts (such as the 50-year-old Palestinian–Israeli conflict; the 1967 Arab–Israeli war; the Iran–Iraq war; the Iraqi invasion of Kuwait), and civil strife (as in Lebanon, Yemen, Intifadah). In addition, the emergence of transnational corporations coupled with the globalization process has increased the region's economic dependency on the western world; at the same time, the emergence of Muslim fundamentalist movements has threatened women's gains achieved through the westernization or modernization process.

The discourse on women in the Arab Middle East began as early as the nineteenth century when intellectuals such as Rifa'ah al Tahtawi, Qasim Amin, and Ahmad Faris al-Chidyaq focused their discussion on "the compatibility of Islam with women's emancipation" (Kandiyoty, 1996). They perceived their action as a nationalist defense of Islam, which had been identified by western Orientalist scholars as the cause of Arab women's oppression. The intellectuals' primary objective was to prove that a symbiosis between western indices of modernization and gender roles within the Islamic family structure is possible. This nationalist discourse succeeded in ensuring women's rights to public space, enabling them to pursue public activities such as joining schools and labor markets, but it insisted on maintaining what Mervat Hatem called "the asymmetrical definitions of gender roles and relations within the family."

According to Hatem, the national liberation discourse, which followed the nationalist discourse, emphasized women's role in fighting for political and economic decolonization. Women were expected to get involved in the decolonization struggle without challenging the established order regarding gender roles. The maintenance of the status quo was intended to ensure the preservation of traditional culture, of which women were the custodians. This vision of women's involvement in the decolonization process was a source of great tension within the ranks of the Algerian and Palestinian women fighters.

After the 1970s, a new discourse, more intellectual in nature, emerged in the MENA region. Its proponents, mainly women social scientists, saw in development a cure for gender inequality. As a result, their "women in development" studies centered on issues related to poverty, access to resources, and education.

Despite the emphasis since the mid-nineteenth century on women's need for more public space—space which they have obtained—women are still subject to male leadership, and the "asymmetrical definitions of gender roles and relations within the family" prevail.

Survey of the Various Academic Institutions Offering Women's Studies Programs and Women's Research Centers

The MENA region is characterized by significant educational discrepancies among women. In some countries, such as Lebanon, equal educational opportunities were provided to men and women in the last quarter of the nineteenth century; in others, such as Morocco, the illiteracy rate among women was very high—the figure in Morocco was 67.3 percent in 1997 (UNDP, 1999).

The first women's college in the Middle East—the American Junior College for Women—was founded by the Presbyterian mission in Beirut, Lebanon, in 1924. This college, now a coeducational university—the Lebanese American University—has educated Middle Eastern women for half a century. The year it became coeducational (1973–1974),

it established the Institute for Women's Studies in the Arab World (IWSAW), the pioneer program in the region. Like many other institutes, IWSAW does not grant degrees in women's studies, but courses related to women's issues are offered through various divisions, particularly the humanities and social sciences. Four universities grant degrees in women's studies:

- *University of Jordan:* The only university in the country that grants degrees in women's studies. The program is independent and does not fall under the auspices of the university's faculties of humanities or sciences. The master's program was launched during the academic year 1999–2000 in cooperation with the Women Studies Center at Britain's York University.
- *Sana'a University (Yemen):* The Empirical Research and Women's Center at Sana'a University offers a master's degree in women's studies focusing on empirical research to increase awareness about women's issues and help Yemeni women improve their status. Other activities of the center include organizing lectures, hosting national and international conferences, establishing a documentation center, and publishing a journal. The center also links with other scholars and universities to contribute to the international dialogue on gender issues.
- *Birzeit University (Palestine):* The Institute of Women's Studies at Beirzeit University offers a minor in women's studies as well as a master's program in gender, law, and development. To empower women, the institute conducts research and organizes conferences, training programs, seminars, and workshops as part of its gender intervention programs, intended to help Palestinians change their own reality.
- *American University of Cairo (Egypt):* The minor in gender studies at AUC offers students the opportunity to become aware of the gender relations that affect society. The Advisory Committee on Gender Studies has the university's approval to establish the Institute for Gender and Women Studies and Research.

The paucity of women's studies programs in this part of the world, where—despite high illiteracy rates in some countries—the gender gap in enrollment at the secondary and tertiary levels closed faster than in any country in the developing world between 1970 and 1991 (UNDP, 1995), could be attributed to many reasons. Among the most important is an inability to attract enough students to join such programs, making them economically nonviable. Perceived as "feminist" studies, they do not seem to be of great interest to most male students, or to many female students.

Further, the limited number of jobs available for this kind of specialization, particularly in developing countries, may contribute to the slow growth of these programs.

Finally, the difficulties encountered in securing funds for such ventures create obstacles. Once funds are secured, the need to abide by a scale of priorities determined by the donors often conflicts with the goals of the program's founders.

Major Research Centers

Funding is a great concern for the various research centers dealing with women's issues in the MENA region. Lack of funding notwithstanding, all programs seem to be essentially engaged with local issues that they try to address using a pragmatic approach.

IWSAW (Lebanon). The Institute for Women's Studies in the Arab World at the Lebanese American University serves as a data bank and resource center on Arab women. It conducts academic research on women in the Arab world, organizes conferences and seminars, and engages in action programs designed for women. The institute also facilitates networking and communication among individuals, groups, and institutions concerned with Arab women. To increase knowledge of social, economic, and legal conditions of women in the Arab world, the institute publishes a quarterly magazine, *Al-Raida,* and has a documentation center that contains an extensive collection of books (more than 5,000 as of this writing), periodicals (approximately 200), and unpublished papers in Arabic, French, and English related to women's issues in the MENA region.

Arab Center for Strategic Studies: Women and Family Affairs Department (Syria). The Women and Family Affairs Department, which is part of the Arab Center for Strategic Studies, aims to encourage women to participate actively in the public sphere, by raising their awareness about their political and legal rights and by eliminating all forms of discrimination and prejudice against women. The department concerns itself with studying women's contributions in the fields of politics, development, production, and decision making, and the obstacles that might impede these contributions. The department also evaluates women's access to health, education, and other social services. In addition, it conducts studies, organizes conferences, prepares training programs, and cooperates with other Arab and international research institutes.

Women's Studies Center (Palestine). The Women's Studies Center initiates programs to respond to Palestinian women's social and economic needs. It focuses on raising women's awareness about their right to enhance their role in the public sphere. The center is composed of several units: a women's training unit, a women's educational unit, and a primary research unit, in addition to a library in women's affairs.

CAWTAR (Tunisia). The Center of Arab Women for Training and Research is an independent institution with international status and a regional reach. It is sponsored by the Arab League, the Tunisian government, Arab Gulf Program for UN Development Organizations (AGFUND), UN Population Fund (FNUAP), Economic and Social Commission for Western Asia (ESCWA), the European Union, and the International Union of Family Planning. Its primary objectives are to be a reference center on the questions related to gender issues in the Arab region, thus reinforcing the capabilities of governments and NGOs to integrate gender into their development policies and programs; and to be an information center that disseminates quantitative and qualitative data related to Arab women.

CREDIF (Tunisia). The Center for Studies, Research, Documentation, and Information is an arm of the Ministry of Women and Family Affairs. Its activities include conducting research and studies as well as establishing a data bank on women and their status in Tunisian society. The center is also involved in gathering documentation related to women's rights as well as networking and developing research tools to improve women's conditions. These activities were recently expanded through the establishment of an observatory that monitors developments in women's conditions and the development of a training program on gender and development for Tunisian and African women.

Women's Center (Iran). The center was created to facilitate and encourage research on the past, present, and future of Iranian women. It also holds organized seminars and conferences on women's issues. Among the most important goals of the center is to be a forum for scholars and feminists to publish their research and to further "the development of theoretical and practical knowledge that will lead to a better understanding of the condition of women in Iran and other Muslim societies."

Assessment of the Role Played by Nongovernmental Organizations in Promoting Women's Issues

During the last two decades, women's NGOs of the MENA region have played an important role in promoting women's issues in an attempt to create a society in which women can participate, along with men, in policy formulation and decision making. These NGOs operate in various sectors of society, including education, health, women's rights, and work. Their activities and roles differ from one country to another, however, depending on the nature of the political and socioeconomic infrastructure prevailing in each country.

Some women's NGOs that concern themselves with benevolent activities and welfare services adopt a rather traditional perspective on women's role in society. Other newer NGOs are heavily influenced by global changes in women's status. These organizations work toward the elimination of all forms of discrimination against women as well as on achieving women's rights. They are often politically oriented and active.

The recent rise in advocacy NGOs is indicative of their awareness of gender issues. Despite this rise, however, women's participation in NGOs is still low, mainly because of the nature of the civil society. In fact, the dichotomy between the public and private spheres is still prevalent in most parts of the Arab world. Women have always been confined to the private sphere, whereas men are active in the public sphere. Since civil society is part of this public sphere, which women have only recently joined, women's contributions in this area are limited.

The activities of nongovernmental organizations include alleviating poverty resulting from structural adjustment programs, and its added burden on women, by supporting poor and needy families. NGOs work to reduce illiteracy rates among women, thereby enabling them to obtain adequate education and training. This is achieved through decreasing the disparity between the sexes in the rate of school enrollment at various levels and providing equal access to available education opportunities. They strive to provide basic health services for women, such as preventive health care and health orientation. They help women participate in the labor force by providing job opportunities, thus decreasing unemployment among women. Various NGOs fight for the legal rights of women and increase women's awareness of these rights. In this respect, concerted efforts among women's NGOs are undertaken to study the status of women within the law, highlighting discrimination and calling for its elimination. Some NGOs work to protect women against violence by raising their self-confidence. Numerous NGOs work on eliminating various forms of violence against women, such as female genital mutilation, rape, and marriage of girls below legal age. Others help women to make use of available opportunities and to acquire the skills and capabilities necessary to face challenges and overcome obstacles. NGOs also work to improve the negative image of women in the media. To this end, many NGOs attempt to use the media to promote women's issues. Many

NGOs help women partake in decision making by offering them new outlooks on social relationships based on democracy and equality. Despite their official status as NGOs, many women's groups in the MENA region undertake research and documentation projects of the same nature as those carried out by women's centers and research institutes. Among these groups, the Women and Memory Forum in Egypt collects and documents the life stories of Egyption women from written records and oral sources. The purpose of this endeavor is to counteract processes of exclusion and marginalization and to challenge present cultural stereotypes and representation of women. The group considers its work a step toward creating a gender-sensitive history that will help to empower women. Another such group, also in Egypt, is Nour, which started in 1993 as a publishing house for women in the Arab world with the purpose of enabling women's voices to be heard. Its main objectives are to encourage Arab women to write and publish their work and to ensure the dissemination of good writing on women's issues to Arab audiences. Nour has been split into two different entities—one involved with research, and the other with publishing. The Lebanese Association of Women Researchers, "Bahittat," is a similar group. "Bahithat" is a nongovernmental association that brings together women researchers from various disciplines with the purpose of promoting cultural and scientific exchange. Among its main objectives is to encourage young Lebanese women researchers by providing them with a platform to present and discuss their various research projects. The association publishes an annual book, *Bahithat,* which tackles specific issues related to women in the Arab world and to which scholars from various Arab countries contribute. In addition, it holds monthly meetings to discuss research proposals submitted by one of its members or academicians from various universities in Lebanon.

The Future Prospects of Women's Studies in the Middle East and North Africa

In the last few decades, various academic institutes and independent NGOs that concern themselves with women's issues have multiplied in the MENA region. The emergence of independent NGOs constitutes a new development. The involvement of these organizations in academic research and studies and the publication of journals on women's issues implies a lasting trend that addresses real needs. Such a trend is indicative of a different feminist consciousness and modes of analysis offered by a new generation of Arab women. Times have changed. "Before the last few decades, women in our Muslim societies were not allowed a future. They only grew old" (Mernissi, 1987). The Arab women of today are more self-confident and can skillfully use their social science expertise to develop critical analyses of their societies and women's position within them.

Women's studies in the MENA region have been characterized by their pragmatic approach in addressing specific local women's issues. Although their contribution to feminist theory has been minimal, they have attempted to adapt the western feminist discourse to the sociocultural circumstances of the region. This adaptation will be successful only to the extent that women's studies has a positive impact not only on women but also on their relationships with their male partners and their status in society.

Despite the process of globalization, there is an urgent need to devise programs and policies that fit this complex part of the world. The advances in communication technologies and the creation of Arab women networks through the Internet such as Nisswa and Development (NAD) and NISSAA will undoubtedly help in ironing out regional differences.

See Also

DEVELOPMENT: MIDDLE EAST AND THE ARAB REGION; EDUCATION: MIDDLE EAST AND NORTH AFRICA; FEMINISM: MIDDLE EAST; FEMINISM: NORTH AFRICA; WOMEN'S STUDIES: OVERVIEW

References and Further Reading

Abdo, N. 1998. Women's studies programs: The Middle East in context. In C. Nelson and S. Altorki, eds., *Arab regional women's studies workshop* 20(3): 20–40. Cairo:American University of Cairo Press.

Afkhami, M., and E. Friedl. 1997. *Muslim women and the politics of participation: Implementing the Beijing platform.* Syracuse, N.Y.: Syracuse University Press.

Badran, M. 1993. Independent women: More than a century of feminism in Egypt. In J. Tucker, ed., *Arab women: Old boundaries, new frontiers.* Bloomington: Indiana University Press.

CAWTAR and ESCWA. 1997. *Arab women 1995: Trends, statistics, and indicators.*

CREDIF. 1996. *Collective catalogue of the documentation on women.* Vol. 3.

ESCWA. 1999. *Indices on the situation of Arab women: A critical review.* United Nations.

Hadraoui, Tania, and Monckachi Myian. 1991. *Etudes féminines, répertoire et bibliographie.* Collection Femmes Maghreb dirigée par Fatima Mernissi. United Nations University: Editions Le Fennec.

Johnson, P. 1997. *Social support: Gender and social policy in Palestine.* Women's Studies: Birzeit University, Palestine.

Kandiyoti, D. 1996. Contemporary feminist scholarship and Middle East studies. In *Gendering the Middle East,* 1–28. London: Tauris.

Khatib, H. 1984. *History of the feminist movement and its relation to the Arab world 1800–1975.* Dar al Hadathah.

Mernissi, F. 1987. *Beyond the veil: Male-female dynamics in modern Muslim society.* Bloomington: Indiana University Press.

Obiora, L. 1997. Feminism, globalization and culture: After Beijing. *Indiana Journal of Global Legal Studies* 4(2:Spring): 1–29.

Roded, R. 1999. *Women in Islam and the Middle East.* London and New York: Tavris.

Saadawi, N. 1980. *The hidden face of Eve.* London: Zed.

United Nations. 1999. *World survey on role of women in development, globalization, gender and work.* New York: United Nations.

United Nations Development Programme (UNDP). 1995, 1999. *Human development report.* Oxford: Oxford University Press.

UNICEF, USAID, and Social Fund. 1995. *Report of the Egyptian NGOs for the forum on women—Beijing 1995.*

Mona Khalaf

WOMEN'S STUDIES: New Zealand

Many of the issues discussed by participants in women's studies in Aoteroa/New Zealand (NZ) would probably sound familiar to their counterparts elsewhere. However, to assume that problems, solutions, and strategies are universal is as misleading as the notion that a category called "women" always applies to all females regardless of the way any political economy may affect an individual. In New Zealand, for example, until the 1970s women were generally absent from accounts of the country's development, but the indigenous Maori women were invisible because of both gender and ethnicity. Maori migration from east Polynesia probably began about 800 C.E. (Davidson, 1981); British annexation occurred in 1840, but it was not until 1987 that the Maori language was given equal official status with English (Evans, 1994: 138). The Maori term *Aotearoa* (land of the long white cloud) is sometimes added to New Zealand to indicate the presence of both Maori and Pakeha (NZ European) in a bicultural society. Another feature is New Zealand's small population: only approximately 3.5 million people (of whom about 13 percent are Maori) in a country comparable in size to Japan or the British Isles.

In the nineteenth century, despite New Zealand's far-flung Pacific location, the Women's Christian Temperance Union led a vigorous suffrage campaign, which succeeded in 1893 with a world's first: the passing of a *national* electoral act enabling women to vote (Grimshaw, 1972). Women were not legally entitled to run for election to Parliament until 1919, and it was 1933 before the first woman member was voted in (Evans, 1993: 14) Sixty-one years later, only fourteen of the ninety-seven parliamentarians were women. Two were Maori, one of whom leads the Alliance, while a Pakeha woman is leader of the Labour Party (as of the 1999 election, these political groupings formed a coalition government). Yet New Zealand's most pervasive myths represented the nation as a model of racial harmony with opportunities open to all in an egalitarian society. In the past two decades, more accurate analyses, by feminists and others, have questioned these claims.

Resourceful Women Then and Now

In the late 1960s and 1970s the sheer numbers of the "baby boomers" of the postwar generation galvanized the NZ women's movement. They were impatient with formal organizations and used imported ideas and language to express their flamboyant kind of liberation. Television arrived in New Zealand in 1960 and reached the more youthful members of the population during their growing-up years. Their activities were validated in quite a new way for a place seemingly on the edge of the world, as they saw and heard some of their own challenges being aired simultaneously by their peers overseas. The "new woman" of the 1970s had a solid, if largely unrecorded, history behind her of resourceful organizers rising to public and private occasions, for, as reformers and educators, New Zealand women of all ethnic backgrounds have always worked together at different times in groups of various sizes and interests to improve the female lot (Coney, 1993; Evans, 1993; Macdonald et al., 1991; Te Awekotuku, 1991). As ideas were canvassed up and down the country, groups rose and fell, coalesced or parted company, arranged large and small gatherings, brought out publications—*Broadsheet,* a feminist magazine established in 1972, still appears regularly—and began to document their foremothers' lives. All this was a propitious foundation for the introduction of women's studies programs in 1974 by Waikato University in Hamilton and by the Auckland Workers' Education Association. Rosemary Seymour, from Waikato University, initiated the Women's Studies Association (WSA) in 1976 with a ready-made national membership based on an informal network drawn from those who

had answered her appeal for material on women. The response, she said, was "a deluge indicative of the vital interest women showed in something previously denied them, their own heritage." In 1978 there were 46 women's studies courses in New Zealand, and by 1980 the number had almost trebled (Roth and McCurdy, 1993).

Aims and Antiracism

In 1978 the WSA held its first conference and its first annual general meeting. What might be called the "man question" arose right away, as the rather complex draft constitution presented at the first conference proposed that men should be equal members. The draft was rejected, and the next year a simpler version was adopted, which accepted men as associate members only. Since then the "man question" has arisen from time to time, with debates over men's status as student-tutor-contributor to WSA publications (as a rule, men remain associates). WSA's statement of aims begins: "The Association is a feminist organisation formed to promote radical social change through the medium of women's studies."

The aims appear in the WSA publications, which consist of a quarterly newsletter used on occasion to start or finish a discussion; the *Conference Papers,* which record workshops as well as papers; and a twice-yearly *Journal,* established in 1984. A lively lesbian caucus has provided an extra dimension to conference debates, and it was one of these caucuses that first put forward resolutions about practicing biculturalism as well as theorizing about it. The analysis of racism has been a continuing concern: the conference of 1981, for example, took a brief leave from its proceedings to march in support of the antiapartheid protests that greeted a South African rugby team touring the country. In 1982 a separate Maori gathering accompanied the WSA conference, and in 1986 antiracism was the subject of one workshop. The resolutions, the questions, and the answers continued in the newsletter, bringing about an amendment to the constitution at the 1987 conference to include: "particular responsibility to address...oppressions (of the Maori) among our work and our activities" (Roth and McCurdy, 1993). One result is that the three conferences of 1990, 1993, and 1994 were bicultural with Maori and Pakeha women organizing programs in tandem.

No conferences took place in 1991 and 1992, largely because there was insufficient womanpower available. Right-wing economic policies regarded by many as Draconian are internationally familiar and mean that New Zealanders, especially women, are less likely to have spare time and money. The rationalizing and romanticizing of voluntary work into one of the philosophical tenets of community education has also affected the majority of volunteers (women), who often accept the notion of unpaid work or token pay for something they believe in. The WSA, with a membership that fluctuates around the 400 mark, is one of many organizations sustained by volunteers, who circulate the various chores associated with editing, correspondence, and managing conferences.

When women's studies began, voluntary organizations sponsored many of the programs. Since there was little commitment to them by salaried power brokers, they have withered away like the funding of nonvocational community education. And, despite Waikato University's example, the other NZ universities were slow to recognize women's studies as a separate interdisciplinary subject. Not until 1991 did Auckland, the large university, follow four of the other five and set up its own women's studies, which continues to have relatively marginal academic status but high popularity among students—a combination that causes the staff to be overextended and underresourced.

Both the *Conference Papers* and the *Journal* provide an interesting record of developments in New Zealand's feminist thought and research, while a high proportion of contributors to and authors of feminist texts are WSA members. (The number of such publications rose significantly in 1993 as part of the suffrage centennial celebrations.)

Although the educational establishment has largely ignored women's studies—and women, especially Maori, still experience discrimination (Middleton and Jones, 1992)—for more than 20 years WSA members have enriched the intellectual and political life of New Zealand, especially with regard to women.

See Also

FEMINISM: AUSTRALIA AND NEW ZEALAND; IMAGES OF WOMEN: AUSTRALIA AND NEW ZEALAND; POLITICS AND THE STATE: AUSTRALIA, NEW ZEALAND, AND THE PACIFIC ISLANDS

References and Further Reading

Coney, Sandra. 1993. *Standing in the sunshine*. Auckland: Penguin.

Davidson, Janet M. 1981. The Polynesian Foundation. In W. H. Oliver and B. R. Williams, eds., *The Oxford History of New Zealand*, 3–27. Wellington: Oxford University Press.

Evans, Jane, ed. 1993. *New Zealand official yearbook 1993/Te Pukapuka Houanga Whaimana o Aotearoa*. Department of Statistics/Te Tari Tatau.

———, ed. 1994. *New Zealand official yearbook 1994/Te Pukapuka Houanga Whaimana o Aotearoa*. Wellington: Statistics New Zealand.

Grimshaw, Patricia. 1972. *Women's suffrage in New Zealand*. Auckland: Auckland University Press/Oxford University Press.

Macdonald, Charlotte, Merimeri Penfold, and Bridget Williams, eds. 1991. *The book of New Zealand women/Do Kui Ma Te Kaupapa*. Wellington: Bridget Williams.

Middleton, Sue, and Alison Jones, eds. 1992. *Women and education in Aotearoa 2*. Wellington: Bridget Williams.

Rosier, Pat. 1992. *Been around for quite a while*. Auckland: New Women's Press.

Roth, Margot, and Claire-Louise McCurdy. 1993. In Anne Else, ed., *Women together/Nga Ropu Wahine o te Motu*, 366–369. Wellington: Historical Branch, Department of Internal Affairs/Daphne Brasell Associates.

Te Awekotuku, Ngahuia. 1991. *Mana Wahine Maori. Selected writings on Maori women's art, culture and politics*. Auckland: New Women's Press.

Margot Roth

WOMEN'S STUDIES:
Research Centers and Institutes

The landscape of women's studies as we know it in the twenty-first century includes not only teaching programs but also a broad array of research centers and institutes. Some are affiliated with college and university women's studies programs, and others are autonomous. In either case, they serve as resources not only for women's studies but also for the women's movement at large.

Origins and Growth

Organized centers for research on women in the United States emerged around 1970, about the same time as women's studies programs, similarly impelled by concerns of the women's movement. It is interesting to note, however, that the earliest centers were more policy-oriented than curriculum-oriented. Campus-based women's studies centers date from about 1974, at a further stage in the development of women's studies. There were several precursors to women's studies research centers in the United States, basically providing institutional facilities for research by and about women. One is the Schlesinger Library on the History of Women in America, which was established in 1943 at Radcliffe College and which has played a vital role in the expanding field of women's history and information access since then. The second facility is the Bunting Institute, also at Radcliffe College, which was established in 1960 as a center for independent scholarship by women. Although the institute was not designed necessarily for research specifically relating to women or girls, an increasing proportion of Bunting Fellows over the years have been those active in women's studies. A third precursor was formed in 1964 as the Center for Continuing Education for Women and is now the Center for Education of Women at the University of Michigan. Its founding purpose was to help adult women whose education had been interrupted to return to college and complete degrees. In that connection, it conducted research on women's lives, changing needs, and aspirations. The present-day center offers an enlarged program of service, advocacy, and research for the educational advancement of women.

The rapid growth of the women's movement during the 1970s created special needs for research, on the one hand, to inform public policy and advocacy on behalf of women and, on the other, to provide curriculum material for burgeoning women's studies programs. Among pathbreaking centers was the Center for the American Woman and Politics, a unit of the Eagleton Institute of Politics at Rutgers University. The center was founded in 1971 to conduct research, develop educational programs, and provide information services relating to women's participation in the political process. Another of the early entries into the field was the Center for Women Policy Studies, founded in 1972 in Washington, D.C. An independent nonprofit organization, it initiated programs combining research, advocacy, policy development, and public education addressing educational equity, economic opportunities for women, violence against women, and reproductive rights and health. Both of these centers were funded by the Ford Foundation. Also funded by the Ford Foundation during this early period was the Institute for Women's Studies in the Arab World at Beirut University College (now the Lebanese American University). The objectives of the institute, established in 1973, are to serve as a data bank and resource center for information pertaining to women and children, to assess the impact of change on the role of women, to serve as a catalyst for policy makers, and to enhance the university curriculum.

As part of its overall program for the advancement of women, in 1974 the Ford Foundation launched a systematic program of grants for support of research centers nationwide. The first two centers in the series were the Center for Research on Women at Wellesley College and the Institute for Research on Women and Gender at Stanford University. These centers provided the models for the rapid expansion of research centers that followed. The Wellesley Center is one of the largest in the United States, housing its own staff of scholars engaged in work on a wide range of projects con-

cerned with issues such as employment, family and child care, adolescent girls' development, and curriculum revision. The Stanford Institute is a campus resource for faculty members and visiting scholars for interdisciplinary research encompassing employment, education, law, literature, art, health, poverty, and families. Between 1974 and 1981, 12 new centers were established, including 3 that were intended to provide regional resources in women's studies. For example, the Southwest Institute for Research on Women (SIROW) at the University of Arizona serves scholars primarily in four states: Arizona, Colorado, New Mexico, and Utah. It promotes collaborative, interdisciplinary research focused on southwestern problems or populations, identifies and disseminates research in the Southwest, maintains a clearinghouse of the work of scholars in the region, and links researchers with community organizations and policy makers. Other centers were established for the northwestern and southern regions.

The National Council for Research on Women

In 1981 representatives from 28 university-based research centers, national policy organizations, and educational coalitions met in New York to exchange information about research programs and educational and public service activities and data needs, and to explore the possibility of establishing a working alliance to share resources and to maintain channels of communication on programs relating to women and girls. This working alliance was formally incorporated as the National Council for Research on Women in 1982 and since that time has grown to more than 80 member institutions. These include campus-based centers, independent organizations, and research units of national nonprofit organizations.

The council acts as a networking and information resource for its member centers. It also works to strengthen ties between them and related organizations. Since 1987 the council has also opened affiliate membership to other organizations and individuals. There are now some 3,000 affiliate members, including women's studies programs, professional women's groups, scholars, and practitioners. In addition, the council maintains contact with centers for research on women throughout the world and regularly publishes a directory of such centers. In 1999, the directory listed 354 centers in 77 countries, including newly established centers in eastern Europe, Vietnam, and China. The council's constituencies include the academic community, government, media, business, public-policy and nonprofit institutions, and the general public. Through these networks and affiliates it is estimated that the council serves more than 10,000 scholars and practitioners worldwide.

At the core of the council's activities are the U.S.-based research centers that are members of the working alliance. Of these, 55 are campus-based, most but not all affiliated with women's studies programs; 11 are Washington-based, most but not all autonomous policy research and advocacy groups; and the rest are diverse centers in New York and various other parts of the country. Their research, ranging from theoretical to action-driven, is fully described in the council's directory, *The Common Catalog*. This directory also provides information about publications, projects, and available resources of member centers and is widely disseminated to publicize the work of the centers and to provide ready access to potential users.

Regular communication among the member centers is maintained through the council's periodic newsletter, *Women's Research Network News,* and through annual meetings of center directors. The annual meetings focus on important topics of shared concern, such as fund-raising strategies, media outreach, and setting research priorities. Intensive workshops are held to strengthen center staffs and administrative skills in these areas. The council also links centers in collaborative projects. One example is the multi-campus program to integrate minority women's studies into the mainstream curriculum, a four-year project that culminated in the publication of a volume titled *Women of Color and the Multicultural Curriculum,* published by the Feminist Press in 1994. Also in collaboration with member centers the council has produced a series of research reports, among them: *Risk, Resilience and Resistance: Current Research on Adolescent Girls* and *Sexual Harassment: Research and Resources.* The council is also linked to member centers via e-mail and fax broadcasting and is experimenting with the use of other advanced telecommunications to expand interactive processes for collaboration with member centers in the production of information resources and to make council resources more widely available to user communities.

One of the functions of the council is to promote visibility for feminist research and analysis and build stronger links between research, policy, action, and the media. Toward this end, in 1994 the council inaugurated a new publication, *Issues Quarterly,* which is designed to synthesize information based on research and other resource material about pressing topics affecting the lives of women and girls and to make that information available to wider audiences. Each issue focuses on a particular topic, such as teen-on-teen sexual harassment and problems of immigrant women and children.

Basic to the entire enterprise of the council is the necessity to maintain adequate funding levels for research. In 1991 the council sponsored the Funding Women Project in collaboration with Woman and Philanthropy, the national association of grant makers concerned with women's issues, and the Women's Funding Network (formerly the National Network of Women's Funds). The goals of the project were to examine existing funding patterns, identify obstacles to funding equity for women and girls, and develop an agenda for improving philanthropy with respect to women. Two reports have emanated from this project. *Who Benefits, Who Decides?* is a special report, issued in 1995, that presents the findings and recommendations of the project. The other report is the featured topic for the second edition of *Issues Quarterly* with the title "Philanthropy: Do 'Universal' Dollars Reach Women and Girls?" Although research centers have been successful in diversifying funding sources over the years, private foundations remain the critical element in most cases. Government agencies provide support for special projects, campus-based centers receive varying degrees of academic subsidies, and individual and corporate donors are becoming increasingly visible.

Global Spread of Research Centers

In contrast to the United States, women's studies programs in Europe are typically not found in the curriculum of higher education institutions. With some exceptions, notably in the United Kingdom, the Netherlands, and the Scandinavian countries, research centers serve as the main base for women's studies. They also serve as a resource for social activism. They have not for the most part had the benefit of local or national philanthropic support for their endeavors. Nor, with the notable exception of the Netherlands and the Scandinavian countries, has government support been forthcoming to any significant extent. Some support has been provided by pan-European organizations like the European Union and the Council of Europe, and these have made possible the formation of two networks: Women's International Studies Europe (WISE) and the European Network of Women's Studies (ENWS), the former an individual membership network and the latter a forum for cooperation among representatives of educational institutions concerned with women's studies. Research centers in Europe have also participated in these networks.

Among developing countries, centers for research on women are most advanced in India, where there are more than 20 women's studies research centers within the university system and at least 6 others that are autonomous or affiliated with nonuniversity institutes. Research focusing on women began with the investigations of the Committee on the Status of Women in India during the period 1971–1974 and expanded rapidly during the ensuing United Nations (UN) Decade for Women. The main emphasis, particularly during the early years, was research related to women's role in national development. Teaching programs at the university level were initiated in the early 1980s and are now established at some 30 institutions. As a result, research about women has been broadened to encompass other subjects that relate to women's studies courses, including not only the social sciences but other fields such as history and literature. India was able to move ahead rapidly because, unlike most European countries, it had the benefit of multiple sources of funding—the national government, private foundations, and international donor agencies. There is no separate network of research centers, but they are among the members of the Indian Association for Women's Studies, which came into existence in 1982.

Research centers focusing on women in development constitute an extensive network across various regions of the world. The Institute of Social Studies in The Hague has played an important supporting role, providing resources and training. One of the most influential groups in this field is the international network of researchers, activists, and policy makers known as DAWN (Development Alternatives with Women for a New Era). The Secretariat for DAWN, which began in 1984, moved from India to Brazil to the Caribbean (as of this writing it was in Fiji). DAWN is best known for its landmark volume, *Development, Crises, and Alternative Visions: Third World Perspectives*. In the Caribbean, DAWN collaborates with CAFRA, the Caribbean Association for Feminist Research and Action, a network of researchers and women's organizations. Its main projects have covered topics such as women and the law, women's history and creative expression, and women in Caribbean agriculture.

The most recent research centers to be formed are those in what are known as "countries in transition," including those in eastern Europe and the former Soviet Union and Asian countries in transition from controlled to free market economies. During the 1990s, new centers were formed in Russia, Ukraine, Poland, Lithuania, Hungary, and the Czech Republic. Among these new centers is the Moscow Center for Gender Studies, which states as its mission introducing gender perspectives into academic and social life, combating growing tendencies toward sexism in social policy making, and contributing to the rise of civil society in Russia by playing a coordinating role in the independent women's movement. In Asia, several new centers have been formed in Vietnam and China.

Another set of research centers around the world consists of units within national machineries for the advancement of women or in international development organizations. An example of the former is the Australian Government Office of the Status of Women in the Department of the Prime Minister and Cabinet. Within the United Nations system the principal centers for research are INSTRAW (UN International Research and Training Institute for the Advancement of Women) and UNIFEM (UN Development Fund for Women). The UN Statistical Office compiles and publishes data relating to the world's women, with country-by-country data ranging from marriage patterns and childbearing to labor force participation, educational attainment, and public life and leadership. Among regional centers perhaps the best-known is the Asian and Pacific Development Centre in Kuala Lumpur, which has an active Gender and Development Programme (GAD). GAD conducts research studies as well as conferences and projects and publishes books and other material for the advancement of women.

The Fourth UN World Conference on Women, held in Beijing in September 1995, provided the impetus for further expansion of research centers around the globe. The Platform for Action adopted by more than 180 participating governments refers to the need to strengthen national capacities to carry out women's studies and gender research and recommends working with centers for women's studies and research organizations to develop methodologies for measuring progress. At the Forum of Nongovernmental Organizations, which was held in conjunction with the official conference, a workshop on centers for research on women was organized by the National Council for Research on Women in collaboration with Women's Studies International, a network formed by the Feminist Press at the City University of New York during the UN Decade for Women. Nearly 50 representatives of research centers participated, including some newly organized or in the planning stage. Clearly, centers for research on women worldwide have not yet reached their peak in numbers or influence.

See Also

DAWN MOVEMENT; INTERNATIONAL ORGANIZATIONS AND AGENCIES; LIBRARIES; NETWORKING; WOMEN'S CENTERS; WOMEN'S STUDIES: OVERVIEW; WOMEN'S STUDIES: FUNDING; WOMEN'S STUDIES, *regional articles*

References and Further Reading

Chamberlain, Mariam K., ed. 1988. *Women in academe.* New York: Russell Sage Foundation.

Gender studies and women's studies directory: Resources in the countries of central and eastern Europe, the former Soviet Union and Mongolia. 1999. Budapest: Open Society Institute–Network Women's Program.

International Centers for Research on Women. 1999. New York: National Council for Research on Women.

Rao, Aruna, ed. 1991. *Women's studies international: Nairobi and beyond.* New York: Feminist Press at City University of New York.

Tinker, Irene. 1990. *Persistent inequalities: Women and world development.* New York: Oxford University Press.

Vyas, Anju, and Sunita Singh. 1993. *Women's studies in India.* New Delhi: Sage.

Women's studies: A world view. 1994. *Women's Studies Quarterly* 22 (3–4: Fall–Winter).

Mariam Chamberlain
Mary Ellen Capek

WOMEN'S STUDIES: South Asia

Women's studies in south Asia emerged in relationship to women's movements in the region. These movements have a long and complex history, going back to colonial times. They acquired a self-conscious edge and clear political resonance from the late 1960s onward. The trajectory of the women's movements, and the specific political contexts in which they emerged in the different countries of the region, informed the beginnings of women's studies in explicit ways.

In spite of regional differences and priorities, it is possible to speak of a south Asian agenda for women's studies. All the countries of the region live with essentially the same set of problems: poverty and widespread female illiteracy complicate the question of female education and knowledge. Interventionist states that are alternately welfarist and coercive determine the fate of this education, both in its primary stages and at the level of the university. As donors, planners, and ideologues with their own distinctive visions of development and gender justice (or injustice), south Asian states play an important role in the making (or unmaking) of women's studies.

India

In India, the contemporary women's movement burst onto the historical stage in the late 1970s. A combination of factors created an enabling historical conjuncture for feminist radicalism. Critiques of underdevelopment, the black power movement in the United States of America, feminist voices from western Europe and North America, the third world's anger over neocolonialism—all these produced a worldview that seethed with discontent (Desai and Patel, 1988: viii–ix). In 1975, a committee constituted by the government of India published a report, *Towards Equality,* on the status of women in the country. This report served to galvanize an incipient feminism into action, even as it shocked a complacent civil society into admitting that a majority of women in India suffered immense social and economic injustice. A tragic and cruel instance of custodial rape that captured the public imagination in the early 1980s rendered this emergent feminism purposive and determined.

By the early 1980s several women's groups had been formed across the country. As these groups struggled to define their political agenda, a group of women (and a few men) responded to the anxieties of history somewhat differently. A national conference on women's studies was held at Mumbai (formerly Bombay) in April 1981 and attended by a medley of people—trade unionists, political and social activists, and government functionaries. These women and men acknowledged the centrality of knowledge in social transformation and articulated the need for a new knowledge domain that would explore, study, analyze, and make sense of women's experiences and lives in theoretically distinctive ways. This new knowledge was to be informed by two ideals: a commitment to securing equality for women and an affirmation of women's right to independent action.

A resolution was passed at the conference to constitute an Indian Association of Women's Studies (IAWS) to initiate, support, and further research, debate, and communication on women and development. The IAWS was to function primarily as an intellectual and political forum: coordinating knowledge with action, information with public use. It would challenge chauvinism and prejudice, call into question existing conceptual biases, and offer new and enabling perspectives on women's lives. The founding group of the IAWS comprised several women and men who were also involved in the making and implementation of government policy. Thus, from its inception, the IAWS was well placed to mediate and arbitrate between an emergent women's movement and a state that historically had played an interventionist role in matters of social and economic change.

Initially the state responded favorably. In fact, even earlier, the state had undertaken certain initiatives: in 1976, for example, the state-sponsored Indian Council for Social Science Research had commissioned a study on the problems of poor, rural, and other "invisible" women. A research center for women's studies had been set up in the SNDT Women's University, Mumbai, in 1974. Now, acting on the conference resolution of 1981, the Universities Grants Commission (UGC), a government-run agency, urged colleges and universities in the country to incorporate women's studies courses into the general curriculum. From the middle and late 1980s, women's studies centers and cells, funded by the government of India, were constituted in several colleges and universities across the country.

Meanwhile, the IAWS persisted in its founding objectives. Throughout the 1980s, it organized workshops that reviewed developments in the field, outlined themes for research, discussed questions of method, and reflected critically on the content and objectives of women's studies. The IAWS efforts in this regard have endured: it continues to organize regional and national seminars and workshops on a variety of themes, works hard to make interdisciplinary research a reality, and conducts national conferences, every two years, to debate, in a focused fashion, persistent concerns of women's movements. In turn, these conferences help to identify and frame political and public issues that movements adopt subsequently.

The progress of women's studies in India has not been wholly dependent on the largesse of government. Nor is governmental policy always central to the agenda of the IAWS. As one of its founding members aptly put it, the job of the state was to listen, not to lead. However, this does not mean that the IAWS is indifferent to state initiatives. In several instances, its members have sought to interpret their own demands in the light of state directives (Research Center for Women's Studies, 1989: 34, 39). But since the government's initiatives with respect to women's studies are seldom imaginative or engaging, the IAWS has looked to other sites to carry out its agenda: nongovernmental organizations and women's groups with which it shares common and crisscrossing objectives. In this sense, women's studies in India happens at several sites. There are feminist newsletters, magazines, and journals, both in English and in several Indian languages. Nongovernmental organizations that work on gender-related issues conduct informal education sessions, for both their volunteer helpers and the general public, and disseminate vital information on law, rights, health-related concerns, history, and economics. Feminist campaign networks, committed to specific struggles, often build archives comprising publications related to their area of concern. For instance, there are ongoing struggles that have to do with women's reproductive health and sexuality, law and gender, violence and healing. Statistical data and sociological information on these subjects generated during the course of these struggles are subsequently organized into information modules that women's groups across the country can access and use. These various instances of knowledge creation and communication take place both in English and in several Indian languages.

Another important space where extremely rich, diverse, and fruitful exchanges of ideas and information take place

is the National Conference of Women's Movements. This conference happens once every three or four years and brings together women from varied backgrounds: peasant and working-class women, middle-class intellectuals, women from India's indigenous communities, political activists, performers, writers. Ideas generated at a national conference are not always encrypted into written and finished texts, yet they serve as points of departure for subsequent research or activism.

Pakistan

In Pakistan, too, women's activism served as a catalyst for the emergence of women's studies. Women's rights activists and feminists in Pakistan were (and continue to be) fiercely involved in debates concerning knowledge and empowerment, since in societies living under Islamic law, scriptural and religious legal texts are central to negotiations of justice and equality. The Women's Action Forum (WAF) and its remarkable work on a global project titled *Women Living under Muslim Law* has to be acknowledged in this context. The WAF has also been instrumental in networking with women's groups in India, Bangladesh, and Sri Lanka on issues such as violence. These studies are both historical and contemporary—they have to do with the experiences of women during the partition of India, and they also connect with the continuing violence in all the countries of the region caused by civil war, fundamentalist militancy, and cross-border conflicts.

Other Countries

In Bangladesh and Sri Lanka, countries where women's movements emerged in the context of civil war and nationalist struggles, women's studies exists at two distinctive levels: self-conscious intellectual activity, carried out in universities, and research and documentation, undertaken by nongovernmental organizations. In Nepal and Bhutan, governmental initiatives have been central to research and study with respect to women's lives and their histories.

Feminist nongovernmental organizations in the various countries of south Asia have been instrumental in promoting regional cooperation and solidarity. India, Pakistan, and Sri Lanka have linked up quite effectively on several comparative research projects with respect to war, women, violence, human rights, and citizenship.

Questions of Method and Problems of Relevance

Two sets of questions are often raised and debated with respect to women's studies in India. These questions are pertinent to the development and future of women's studies in south Asia as a whole.

The first set of questions has to do with the identity of women's studies. Is it a discipline, an integral and coherent body of knowledge with definite founding premises and methods of analysis? Or is it a program of study and research that may be adopted within other clearly demarcated disciplines? One often-articulated definition argues for women's studies as a multidisciplinary program of scholarly engagement that considers gender a pertinent category of analysis (Committee on Women's Studies in South and Southeast Asia, 1994: 3–4). Women's studies may thus be deployed within existing disciplines to suggest fresh and provocative perspectives on known, routine, and obvious realities. It is further argued that this "mainstreaming" of women's studies prevents it from being confined to an academic ghetto, a state of existence that can render futile even the best and most sophisticated attempts at research and intellectual expression.

Those who are uneasy with what appears to them an all-too easy passage for women's studies into other disciplines point to the lack of seriousness that attends its adoption as an area of study or research. They argue that in many colleges and universities, women's studies courses are offered as optional or ancillary subjects. Further, such courses exist in a piecemeal fashion and depend for their effectiveness on the individual teacher, who, in turn, has to contend with hostile and indifferent colleagues and a hierarchical educational system. The original pedagogical impulse of women's studies, aligning education to action, becomes problematic in a context where neither the teachers nor the students seem to be able to leave behind their class and caste biases to interact productively with women's movements (Research Center for Women's Studies, 1989: 41–45). But these critics also admit that securing disciplinary autonomy for women's studies is not really a productive alternative. To many, the only option seems to be to struggle to establish an ever-widening constituency of both male and female students who, on their own initiative, would pursue research and teaching careers that are sensitive to gender concerns, in a political as well as an epistemological sense.

The second set of questions centers on the relationship of women's studies to women's movements and feminist ideologies. Is this relationship an essential and fundamental principle that underwrites the women's studies project? Or is it one that is contingent on the individual learner's political preferences? Many believe firmly that women's studies is constitutively and explicitly committed to the politics of women's empowerment and liberation. Yet they also see it as a political project in its own right whose research challenges the patriarchal political establishment and the vested interests that underwrite its existence.

Others pose the problem somewhat differently. They ask if doing women's studies implies that one commits oneself to action. This has been a sensitive question in women's studies circles and with women's movements in India. Often an unstable and imagined fault line emerges between self-confessed "academics" and equally self-confessed "activists." Activists sometimes insist that the rigors of academic argument are not really relevant to everyday struggles or even sustained campaigns and that intellectual work is really a waste of time and scarce resources. Academics have responded to these criticisms in one or the other of the following three ways. First, research and writing are politically important acts in their own right, since they produce histories, genealogies, interpretations, and analyses that activists could put to profitable use. Second, those who perform intellectual labor are not all that alienated from political struggles on the ground; in fact, several well-known feminist scholars and thinkers have been and continue to be associated with several mass struggles. Conversely, several activists pursue research themselves and utilize their learning in their political work. There are also activist groups that interact with universities, either with women's studies centers and cells, or with individual departments for particular sorts of work. Third, even at a purely epistemological level, the charges of irrelevance are not just, since research and interpretative methodologies favored by those who do women's studies bear the impress of "the field"—they rely on collaborative and participatory methods of information gathering and interpretation.

Yet the question of relevance haunts women's studies. Even those who have been involved with the project since its inception sometimes despair of rescuing it from the stranglehold of what they term *academic neutrality*. They argue that the problem is both epistemological and political: for what is required is "a subjective concern about the oppressed, combined with a dispassionate analysis." Thus, one needs to explore a new mode of analysis, "sensitive, innovative, and enormously perceptive," that would generate "a sense of commitment to translate convictions into action." In turn, this commitment needs to be sustained and nurtured by a supportive web of activities—feminist counseling, campus activism, neighborhood support groups (Krishnaraj, 1987).

There are other questions raised by activists for which academics have no easy answers. Since most women's studies research is carried out in English, how will it reach those who need this knowledge? Many women activists do not read or write English and are literate in only one or two of the Indian languages. Likewise, interested students who are unfamiliar with and tentative in their use of English cannot access the knowledge core of women's studies.

The IAWS, of course, is not entirely unaware of these problems. Limited resources, the absence of a sufficient number of bilingual intellectuals in women's studies and in the women's movements who can actually enable a transference of knowledge from English to Indian languages, and the problems posed by the sheer logistics of translation into several Indian languages have made it quite difficult for this concern to be addressed adequately. Women's studies centers in some universities—for example, the center at the University of Pune, western India—have begun to offer courses in the local language. The initial responses have been modest but encouraging. Since the courses are also offered to part-time students, women workers and homemakers have enrolled in the course and enjoyed going back to school. A nongovernmental organization in the south Indian city of Hyderabad has begun to offer summer courses in women's studies to enable interested persons to learn and pursue research on their own. While most of the reading material is in English, actual classroom sessions are conducted in local languages.

The IAWS has sought to render its concerns more representative and universal through other means. For one, it has taken its agenda to those parts of India, such as the northeastern states, whose problems seldom attract the attention of mainstream political and civil societies in India. The northeastern states are populated by India's indigenous peoples. They possess a history that is vastly different from the rest of the country. Since colonial times, these regions have witnessed incessant civil strife and struggles for national self-determination. This history has come to frame the question of women in distinctive ways. The IAWS agenda has been to record testimonies of displacement due to war, encourage studies of indigenous resistance and assimilation into nonindigenous social and cultural orders, and engage in a constructive critique of culture.

Women's studies in south Asia dates only from the early 1980s, yet in some respects its impact has been striking in certain knowledge domains. The articulation of patriarchy within different social and political structures and historical expressions of female subjectivity are concerns that have been expressed as part of an emergent feminist historiography. In economics, studies done by women economists and sociologists on the household, female participation in social labor, and the nature of women's work have resulted in a more nuanced and flexible definition of labor. This in turn led to a reconsideration of certain questions with regard to women's work in the official census of India for 1991. Research undertaken by feminist lawyers and activists, revealing the patriarchal biases inherent in some laws, prompted attempts to rewrite law, as with the law on sexual assault, and helped to start debates on the need for substantive rather than formal rights for women. In the field of health and demography, studies undertaken by women's groups on the harmful effects of injectible contraceptives have inspired a widespread questioning of government policies on family planning. Reviews of the official population policy have pointed to the very narrow definition of female well-being. Literary studies has been enriched enormously: texts have been read and reread to uncover gendered semantic underworlds. Women's literary struggles, the figure of the feminine in both the visual and the verbal arts, the problems posed by complex and ambiguous feminist-female subjectivities—all these mark the lines of force that indicate this knowledge domain.

Since the mid-1990s the rise of the Hindu right has provoked scholarly work on religions, religious sensibilities, and gender. Women's movements and nongovernmental organizations have produced sharp, critical studies of the media and their representations of gender, female sexuality, gender in the context of caste, and folk culture—the list is varied. Women's studies has generated a distinctive politics of knowledge. Research sometimes creates its own discursive terrain, leading to what one theorist has termed "citadel research," with no obvious social and political anchorage. More importantly, women's movements and groups get caught in a rush of hurried documentation and research, which yield extremely superficial information on complex social and emotional processes. In some instances, fashionable and high-powered research, supported by global funding, becomes an easy and facile substitute for political activity.

Yet, the founding moment of the women's studies project endures. Small groups of eager students and committed and persistent teachers in several centers across the region continue their everyday exchanges, anxious to link up with women's groups and campaigns. In these cross-currents of dialogue, debate, and polemic, the future of women's studies remains secure and alive.

See Also

EDUCATION: SOUTH ASIA; FEMINISM: SOUTH ASIA; NONGOVERNMENTAL ORGANIZATIONS (NGOS); POLITICS AND THE STATE: SOUTH ASIA, *I and II;* VIOLENCE: SOUTH ASIA; WOMEN'S STUDIES: OVERVIEW.

References and Further Reading

Committee on Women's Studies in South and Southeast Asia, eds. 1994. *Women's studies, women's lives—Theory and practice in south and southeast Asia.* New Delhi: Kali for Women.

Desai, Neera, and Vibhuthi Patel. 1988. *Critical review of women's studies researches, 1975–1988*. Research Centre for Women's Studies. Mumbai (Bombay): SNDT Women's University.

Jayawardene, Kumari, and Malathi de Alwis, eds. 1996. *Embodied violence: Communalising women's sexuality in south Asia*. New Delhi: Kali for Women.

Kapur, Rathna, ed. 1996. *Feminist terrains in legal domains: Interdisciplinary essays on women and law in India*. New Delhi: Kali for Women.

Krishnaraj, Maithreyi. 1987. *A discussion paper for ICSSR—Regional workshop on women's studies, Pune*. Research Centre for Women's Studies. Mumbai: SNDT Women's University.

Kumar, Radha. 1993. *The history of doing: An illustrated account of movements for women's rights and feminism in India*. New Delhi: Kali for Women.

Research Center for Women's Studies. 1989. *Planning women's studies in Indian universities. Report of the proceedings of the national-level workshop of UGC-sponsored women's studies centers*. Mumbai: SNDT University.

Sangari, Kumkum, and Sudesh Vaid, eds. 1990. *Recasting women—Essays in Indian colonial history*. New Brunswick, N.J.: Rutgers University Press.

Saradomani, K. 1992. *Finding the household—Conceptual and methodological issues*. London: Sage.

Tharu, Susie, and K. Lalitha, eds. 1991. *Women writing in India*. Vol. 1, *600 B.C. to the early twentieth century*. Mumbai: Oxford University Press.

———. 1995. *Women writing in India*. Vol. 2, *The twentieth century*. Mumbai: Oxford University Press.

Towards equality. 1975. Report of the Government of India Committee on the Status of Women in India.

V. Geetha

WOMEN'S STUDIES: Southeast Asia

Recent years have seen extensive efforts by concerned local academics and other activists in a number of countries in southeast Asia to introduce women's studies into universities and other tertiary-level institutions. According to Norani Othman in Malaysia, they regard it as a significant project in the celebration of a new awareness about women, which has drawn much strength from the United Nations (UN) Decade for Women (1975–1985) and the UN women's conferences. Churairat Chandhamrong, like many others in the region, understands women's studies as both a body of inter-disciplinary knowledge about the intertwined and complex relationships between life, society, and environment and an activity whose goal in changing cultural beliefs, values, and social institutions is gender equity and social justice.

The development of women's studies in the region, however, has confronted a number of problems: these have included varying levels of commitment from governments, lack of funding, and a stress on utilitarian agendas in research on women and gender. Much of this work is narrowly policy-oriented. There has also been some ambivalence about women's studies itself. Not only critics but also supporters have continuing worries about what they see as the "western" origins and orientations of feminism and women's studies.

Indonesia

The establishment of women's studies centers in Indonesia was a phenomenon of the mid-1980s. A number of institutions had previously undertaken research into gender relations (including Bogor and Universitas Indonesia). As part of its participation in the UN Decade for Women, the Indonesian government made a commitment to establish women's studies centers (*pusat studi wanita*) at all government universities. The minister of women's affairs, who was elevated to a cabinet position in 1983 (also in response to the Decade for Women), was actively involved in the development of many of the women's studies centers. These are generally oriented to research rather than teaching, with contributions from faculty members from a variety of disciplines.

A number of factors have shaped the direction of women's studies in Indonesia: the close relations with government policy; the limited funds available from national and international sources, which tie these centers to research focusing almost exclusively on "women in development"; and the general conditions of academic life. Low levels of academic pay mean that almost all academic research is separately funded. These centers produce sociological or economic studies that are almost exclusively empirical.

Research agendas thus have been driven largely by government and international donor agency agendas. But it is considered that this eschewing of more theoretically oriented feminism has allowed Indonesian women's studies centers to remain relevant both to policy makers and to political activists. These centers, along with women's nongovernmental organizations (NGOs), have been instrumental in introducing the language and ideals of what is seen to be western liberal feminism into government policy and even to some extent into the mass media. Women's studies academics played a significant role in supporting student activists campaigning for

Suharto's downfall and as advocates for the victims of the racially motivated rapes in Jakarta during May 1998.

Malaysia

Women's studies in Malaysia grew out of concerned scholarship in the 1960s and 1970s dealing with issues of poverty and social change. While academics have lobbied actively for women's studies, it is felt that the government has shown little commitment to these efforts. Thus, the governing bodies of two senior universities, the University of Malaya (Universiti Malaya) and the National University (Universiti Kebangsaan Malaysia UKM), have both been reluctant to provide funding for a gender or women's studies unit or program. It was only in 1994 that the multidisciplinary Rancangan Pengajian Gender (Gender Studies Program), offering undergraduate courses, was established in the Faculty of Arts and Social Sciences, Universiti Malaya. Funded mainly by CIDA (the Canadian development agency), the program came about through the energetic efforts of Professor Nik Safiah Karim (dean of the faculty as well as chairman of the National Council of Women in Development, NACWID) and Professor Rokiah Talib (of the Department of Anthropology and Sociology).

Elsewhere, Universiti Sains Malaysia (the "younger" science university in Penang) has a fourth-year course on women and society, while the National University (UKM) currently offers a few undergraduate courses dealing with women and gender. A growing number of postgraduate and honors students, however, have been pursuing research studies covering issues of women and gender. Further efforts to develop programs await the outcomes of policies corporatizing the universities.

Despite these difficulties, other academic activities promoting scholarship and teaching on issues of women and gender have developed. In 1978 Universiti Sains Malaysia (USM) set up a research unit on women and children in development, KANITA (United Kajian Anita), which in 1991 was succeeded by Unit Pengajian Anita dan Sumber Manusia (UPWSM, Women's and Human Resources Studies Unit). KANITA received much of its funding from organizations outside Malaysia, like UNESCO (United Nations Educational, Scientific, and Cultural Organization). The Agricultural University (Universiti Pertanian Malaysia, UPM) had established a Women's Studies Unit (Pusat Pengajian Anita) by the mid-1980s. Basically a service and extension unit researching women in development, it also offers some undergraduate courses. The Population Studies Unit at Universiti Malaya has served as a platform to promote women's and gender studies, both directly through its postgraduate training programs and indirectly through research programs relating to women, particularly in Malaysia and the southeast Asian region.

Most government-funded or -sponsored research is policy-oriented, focusing on aspects of women's participation in national development policies and women in development. The government agency HAWA, within the prime minister's department, carries out national-level programs and projects for the advancement of women's status and development.

The Philippines

From 1981 several universities in the Philippines offered teaching, research, advocacy, and outreach programs in women's studies. They adopted two approaches: mainstreaming (that is, the integration of women's studies into existing disciplines) and autonomous (that is, creating separate women's studies programs).

Certificate courses in women's studies were introduced in 1981 at Silliman University (Visayas) and in 1985 at St. Scholastica's College (Manila), which set up an undergraduate course in 1986. The Women's Resource and Research Center (WRRC), which now functions as a service institution with public access, opened in 1987 at Mariam College (Manila). In 1986–1987 the Philippine Women's University established a Development Institute for Women in Asia, which conducts training seminars. In 1988 the University of the Philippines College of Social Work and Community Development (UP Diliman Manila) offered a master's degree in women and development, and Ateneo de Manila University (Manila) also commenced a course on gender studies. The focus on teaching has now broadened to include curriculum development in the pretertiary education system and in-service and preservice teacher training and outreach programs. The latter have focused on peasant women, workers, and the urban poor.

In 1987 all contributing universities organized themselves into a Women's Studies Consortium (WSC), which later became the Women's Studies Association of the Philippines (WSAP). With approximately 300 individual members from 65 colleges and universities WSAP has been successful in collectively facilitating and maintaining new and continuing programs and activities, including research.

Local and international factors such as the antidictatorship struggle of the 1970s and 1980s, the prevalence of poverty, the emergence of women's studies in North America and elsewhere, and the UN Decade for Women produced a women's studies philosophy that is nationalist and democratic (De Dios and Rodriguez, 1991). Theoretical trends have shifted from the early structural-functionalist focus on women's status and roles to Marxist and socialist feminist analyses in the 1980s and early 1990s and, in the late 1990s, to feminist postmodernism and poststructuralism. There is, however, considerable variation in viewpoints among academics, advocates, and practitioners, and at times feminism has been represented as too western, antimale, and middle-class. Many women in development (WID) courses make little effort to challenge male dominance or sexual divisions of labor.

Singapore

Singapore does not have a women's studies program as such, but there has been a course on gender begun in the sociology department at the National University in 1987 by Dr. Aline Wong and Dr. Vivienne Wee. This course evolved from a graduate course to a very popular third-year option. The attraction of the course has derived in part from interest by students in Singapore's only feminist organization, the Association of Women for Action and Research (AWARE). This organization has had a very public face in the person of the nominated member of parliament Dr. Khanwaljit Soin. While students view feminism as a western and radical phenomenon, they are very receptive to the kinds of issues raised by AWARE, such as demands for equal medical benefits for female civil servants. The level of student interest in gender issues is underscored by the increasing number of research projects undertaken by honors-year students on gender-related issues.

Moreover, almost all the social science departments have at least one scholar who has the interest and capacity to undertake the supervision of research work pertinent to women's issues. Most of this research centers on in-depth and qualitative material. Given the dearth of women's voices in almost all disciplines in Singapore, says Nirmala PuruShotam, the value of this research cannot be overstated. The rich ethnographies provide a powerful basis for the development of concepts and theories unclouded by methodologies that would otherwise be informed by male-only voices. In her view, the lack of unified women's studies programs has not prevented the development of a multidisciplinary field of studies giving voice to issues relating to women and men from perspectives that powerfully enlarge women's vision as scholars and Singaporeans generally.

Thailand

Women's studies in Thailand is a recent phenomenon, having developed in the mid-1980s in major government-run universities. According to the National Commission on Women's Affairs, set up in 1989, there are at least 10 institutes of higher learning engaging in research, curriculum development, training, and academic services relating to women's studies. These include Chulalongkorn University's women's and youth studies in the Institute of Social Research, which is research-oriented; Thammasat University's Project for Women's and Youth Studies, founded in 1986; Chiangmai University's Women's Studies Center under the Faculty of Social Sciences, begun in 1986; the Center for Women's Research and Development, Songklanagarin University at Hadyai (in the south); the women's studies program at Payap University (a private university in Chiangmai), founded in 1986; and the women's studies program at Rajapat Institute at Chiangmai (a state teacher college, begun in 1988). Thammasat also provides an information center. Chiangmai planned to offer a master of arts degree in 2001. The faculty of education there also set up another study center, in 1990, dealing with Lanna women, which focuses on training and promoting the political roles of grassroots women, conducting research on women workers, and developing women's studies courses within the school curriculum. In 1991 Srinagarintharawiroth University at Songkla (in the south) set up a special program on research and women's studies for rural development, focusing its activities on research and integrating gender issues into existing courses. Mae Jo Agricultural Technology Institute (in Chiangmai) in 1989 informally started a Study Project on Women and the Development of Agricultural Extension, conducting research and providing training. In 1994 Naraesuan University (in the north) informally set up a women's studies program, concentrating on providing vocational training for rural women and integrating gender issues into existing courses. There is also a nongovernmental Center for Gender Research and Development in Don Muang. In 1987 a Women in Development Consortium, backed by CIDA, linked three universities, Thammasat, Chulalongkorn, and Khon Kaen, with York University in Canada. The Thai studies project at York University also supported a publication series. The Asian Institute of Technology, Bangkok, set up a Center for Gender and Development Studies in 1991, offering a graduate program in 1998.

Women's studies centers mostly have been set up by small groups of concerned people, often financed by foreign agencies, although the program at Thammasat University was set up by a woman rector and funded by the university. Overall, however, the development of women's studies curricula is felt to be slow, mainly consisting of the integration of gender issues into existing courses.

Vietnam

The history of women's studies in Vietnam has been tied closely to the establishment of centers and other research groups. These have a close relationship with mass organizations, the Vietnam Women's Union, youth organizations, the Labour Confederation, and the Peasants' Union.

The Center for Women's Studies (CWS, part of the National Center for Social Sciences and Humanities, Hanoi), was founded by Professor Le-Thi in 1987 and became the Center for Family and Women's Studies (CFWS) in 1992. The center carries out research into gender issues and employment within the rural and market economies, on new technologies and the new market-oriented socioeconomic policies, women's education, and education for family life. It also promotes a participatory approach to gender-responsive policy planning teaching and organizes short-term training.

Other centers include the Research Center for Gender-Family-Environment in Development, founded in 1993 by Professor Le-Thi Nham Tuyer, which has carried out research on family planning, abortion, and reproductive health and has organized training courses; the Center for Training and Women's Studies in the Teacher (Training) College No. 1, founded in 1993 by Professor Dang Thanh Le, which is mainly interested in "social evils" and also provides scholarships for poor students; and the Center for Women's Studies in Ho Chi Minh City, set up in 1992 by Professor Bui Thi Kim Quy, which has organized training and carried out research on women and urban employment, prostitution in the city, and women workers in foreign-investment enterprises and the export-processing zone in Tan Thinh. Two centers, one in the Ministry of Labor, War Invalids, and Social Affairs, founded in 1994, and the research section on Women in the Vietnam Women's Union, established in 1980, look at policy issues. Recently, a number of NGOs have developed in Hanoi, including the Center for the Improvement of Women's Ability and Empowerment (led by Dr. Vuong Thi Hanh), the Center for Reproductive and Family Health (directed by Dr. Nguyen Thi Hoai Duc), and the Center for Women's Studies, part of the Hanoi National University (directed by Dr. Nguyen Bich Ha). In 1992 the Open University, Ho Chi Minh City, established a faculty of women's studies, headed by Professor Thai Thi Ngoc Du, which conducts research and runs a four-year joint program in social work and women's studies.

The research agenda of Vietnamese women's studies centers is largely driven by national government policy and, lately, by international donor agencies. Research programs are mainly directed at social policy issues and closely linked to "family."

Conclusion

Much of the body of work produced by centers and projects in these countries has been extremely rigorous, well researched, and innovative. But the conditions of intellectual production in many of the countries may be seen to discourage more adventurous feminist-womanist scholarship with a local face. There is clearly a strong emphasis on utilitarian agendas. This reflects several factors: the force of concerned activists' agendas from which much of the original impetus for women's studies developed; the role of the state as patron in commissioning and shaping research; and the growth of the consulting industry, which responds to priorities often set by external agencies. Krishna Sen's suggestion that less theoretically oriented agendas also allow Indonesian women's studies centers to remain "relevant" points to some of the tensions between academics and activists.

Both opponents and supporters of feminism and women's studies in the region have expressed considerable ambivalence about the western origins of women's studies. Some "womanists," disowning the term *feminist*, argue against the view of women as victims, which they see as an inappropriate western model of male–female relations. In their view, this model ignores the vast differences in women's experiences in the region and globally. They acknowledge the difficulties for local scholars in escaping western intellectual and cultural domination and in developing alternative ways of knowing and acting. But many feel nonetheless that accusations of being "western" can be used too easily to discredit feminist claims for social justice. The histories of such claims across the region point to the ways in which the development of women's studies programs can be seen as only the latest chapter in a long engagement with the politics of women's rights in southeast Asia.

Acknowledgments

Material on Indonesia was supplied by Dr. Krishna Sen, School of Communication, Murdoch University; on Malaysia by Dr. Norani Othman, Anthropology and Sociology, National University of Malaysia; on the Philippines by Dr. Anne-Marie Hilsdon, Curtin University, drawing on Sylvia H. Guerrero's unpublished paper, "The State of the Art of Women's Studies in the Philippines"; on Thailand by Professor Churairat Chandhamrong, Sociology and Anthropology, Thammasat University; on Singapore by Dr. Nirmala PuruShotam; and on Vietnam by Professor Le-Thi, National Center for Social Sciences and Humanities.

See Also

FEMINISM: SOUTHEAST ASIA; POLITICS AND THE STATE: SOUTHEAST ASIA; WOMEN'S STUDIES: OVERVIEW

References and Further Reading

Committee on Women's Studies in Asia. 1994. *Women's studies, women's lives: Theory and practice in south and southeast Asia.* New Delhi: Kali for Women.

DeDios, A., and L. Rodriguez. 1991. *Women's studies consortium report (Philippines).* Manila.

Illo, J. 1999. *Women and gender relations in the Philippines.* Quezon City: Women's Studies Association of the Philippines.

Karim, Wazir. 1993. Gender studies in southeast Asia. *Journal of Southeast Asian Social Science* 12 (1): 98–112.

Mohamad, Maznah, and Wong Soak Koon, eds. 1994. Special issue: Feminism: Malaysian critique and experience. *Kajian Malaysia: Journal of Malaysian Studies* 12 (1–2: June–Dec.).

Ong, Aihwa, and Michael G. Peletz, eds. 1995. *Bewitching women, pious men: Gender and body politics in southeast Asia.* Berkeley: University of California Press.

Sears, L. ed. 1996. *Fantasizing the feminine in Indonesia.* Durham, N.C.: Duke University Press.

Sen, K., and M. Stivens, eds. 1998. *Gender and power in affluent Asia.* London: Routledge.

Tantiwiramanond, Darunee. 1997. Changing gender relations in southeast Asia and the contribution of women's organizations. *Southeast Asia Studies Bulletin* (Oct.).

Van Esterik, P., ed. 1996. *Women of southeast Asia.* 2nd rev. ed. DeKalb: Northern Illinois University Center for Southeast Asian Studies.

Maila Stivens

WOMEN'S STUDIES: Southern Africa

Various postcolonial theorists argue that the institutional and political developments in feminism in third world contexts are very different from those in the West. In her article "Can the Subaltern Speak?" Gayatri Spivak (1990) examines the ways that western theories extinguish the distinctiveness of third world women. Focusing on the practice of widow sacrifice in India, Spivak shows how the perceptions of many third world women may be silenced both by male-centered perspectives and by feminist discourses that address gender relations in a western context. In a similar vein Chandra Mohanty (1991) describes how western feminist theory constructs a homogeneous third world "woman," yet ignores the distinctiveness of women's gendered identities and feminist politics in particular third world contexts. Mohanty also offers guidelines for considering how certain feminist theories can address specific women's experiences. In particular, she stresses that gender intersects with other axes of power and sets forth ideas about methodological, theoretical, and academic processes that might lead to a better understanding.

These broad theoretical and political issues raised by postcolonial feminists are of obvious relevance to the southern African region, a constellation of countries that have battled against various forms of colonial domination. Angola and Mozambique are former colonies of Portugal, while countries such as Botswana, Lesotho, Malawi, South Africa, Swaziland, and Zambia endured many years of British colonial domination and distinctive patterns of internal colonization. In these countries, and especially in South Africa, with its iniquitous system of apartheid, white minorities with entrenched national identities have subjugated black majority groups. In the face of these forms of racial and colonial exploitation (and associated patterns of cultural and intellectual dependency), what are the peculiar difficulties with which southern African feminists have battled? How have colonialism, neocolonialism, and racism affected local developments in feminist studies, theory, and politics? How have the diverse forms of oppression in which southern African women are situated affected gender politics?

These questions require detailed attention to specific trends. It is possible, however, to survey general patterns affecting the region that influence both existing and future developments in women's studies and feminist politics. The different countries in southern Africa have developed strong cultural and economic ties with one another. Colonial systems of migratory labor, resource exploitation, and political control, as well as patterns of white settlement concentrated in the south, have gone a long way toward entrenching these connections. Centuries-old forms of migration, cultural exchange, and linguistic fusion also unite countries in the region. Therefore, a regional perspective on past and evolving developments in feminism is politically and culturally important. A regional approach does not mean ignoring the particularities of individual countries or naturalizing the dominance of areas that, for various historical reasons, have become more culturally and politically powerful than others. This article will address the need for a regional perspective on questions asked about women's studies and feminist theory, while remaining alert to the cautions raised. The case study of one country, South Africa, illustrates a particular response within women's studies to the problems posed by women's struggles and feminist theory in the region. It is not meant to suggest that

South African patterns are more important than others or that South Africa presents the ideal model that other countries should aspire to.

The Area "Defined" As Women's Studies

Internationally there is no one common understanding or definition about what constitutes gender studies and gender training (Kasente, 1996; see, for example, Bonnin, 1995; and Rao et al., 1991). For the purposes of this paper we focus mainly on courses taught at the tertiary level.

The Status of Women in Southern Africa

It is clear that South African women, legislatively speaking, have rights and a status that far outweigh those of women in other southern African countries. The South African constitution includes a bill of rights that outlaws discrimination on the basis of gender, sex, and sexual orientation. To strengthen this constitutional right as well as to monitor and promote the spirit of gender equality, the Commission for Gender Equality (CGE) was established. South Africa also has an Office on the Status of Women whose primary goal is to ensure that state policies and programs adhere to the constitutional principles of gender equality. There are also various other gender-equality initiatives government has sponsored. Unfortunately, other countries in southern Africa have not seen fit to follow the example set by South Africa in terms of gender equality. Some controversial legal decisions have negatively affected women's rights in Zimbabwe, for example. Regarding South Africa, De La Rey and Kottler (1999: 122) comment that overall, "moves towards gender equality have mostly been in legislative change, the creation of gender structures and policy documentation—the real challenge still lies in turning these steps into real changes in the daily lives of the majority of women." This statement holds true for all the other countries in southern Africa.

Feminist Women's Movements in Southern Africa: A Contradiction in Terms?

Before discussion of a history of women's studies in southern Africa, it is important to contextualize the discussion. The following digression into the nature of women's movements is an attempt to do so. One issue that distinguishes gender politics in southern Africa is its intersection with other political relationships. Where it has often seemed impossible in the West to speak about the distinct category "woman," the gendered identities in southern Africa have always been intertwined with their racial locations, class, or positions in imperial and neoimperial processes. Some of the theory and politics emerging from southern Africa therefore must struggle to address interconnected forms of oppression. In many of the regions of southern Africa national, antiracist, and anticolonial struggles have seemed more pressing than the gender dynamics that affected relationships between men and women within subordinated groups.

A survey of the way women have been involved in political struggles is therefore revealing. During the 1960s and 1970s, the high points of emerging feminist activism in the West, many southern African women were centrally involved in political struggles. This political involvement, however, was often broadly antiracist, anticapitalist, or anticolonial. Women's movements did not overtly focus on women's sense of their struggles as distinct from men's or as directed against gender oppression. In fact, women's movements were explicitly affiliated with movements led by men. In the liberation movements of Angola, Mozambique, Namibia, South Africa, and Zimbabwe, women were directly involved in guerrilla warfare.

This pattern of women's induction into political activism is very different from the initiation of most women in the West. There, ideas about a "women's movement" or "women's politics" have automatically implied women's mobilization in the face of patriarchal domination. This distinct history of women's movements in southern Africa also poses questions about how to assess them, and, in terms of this article, how to view and assess the impact (if any) that these movements have had on women's studies programs at a tertiary level.

Certain observers have drawn attention to the fact that South African women have organized on the basis of motherhood (see Charman et al., 1991; Hassim, 1991; Hassim and Walker, 1993; Horn, 1991; Wells, 1991). Wells, like others, uses the term *motherism* and argues that it is not feminism. Fouché (1994) challenges Wells's argument and suggests that motherist movements, which confront patriarchy along with all other forms of oppression, will most likely lead to a meaningful, appropriate feminism. Fester (1997) supports Fouché's notion and emphasizes that "women's resistance arises out of their particular historical contexts and that motherism and working shoulder to shoulder with our menfolk can be seen as a form of South African feminism."

For some observers, southern African women may appear antifeminist or unaware of gender politics. For these observers, western models of separatist opposition or an exclusive focus on gender may seem to offer ideals that southern African women should aspire to. This view, however, ignores the extent to which women may connect a gendered awareness and nascent feminism with opposition to other forms of domination. In other words, while their involvement in broad political processes may not be explicitly or primarily gendered or feminist (in the western understanding of feminism), their sense of agency may also signal awareness of patriarchal oppression. Illustrating this trend in Zimbabwe, one study found that women in rural areas had evidently used the changes in the gender ideologies that took place during the war to renegotiate relationships within their households. A history of women's movements in southern Africa cannot overlook such findings, or the points made by Fester.

Another point that cannot be overlooked in relation to southern African feminism and gender studies is the issue of race. Mainly as a result of institutionalized apartheid, race has been one of the categories that feminists have had to grapple with, and there is general recognition that gender and race are intrinsically linked. De La Rey (1997: 8) made this point succinctly when she stated that "any South African feminism that ignores the centrality of race will run the risk of making it invisible, and it will be a limited feminism." The same holds true for women and gender studies programs.

Women's Studies:
Past, Present, and Future Developments

Talking about a "history" commonly assumes the period under discussion is a lengthy one. Not so with women's studies in southern Africa. This is not to say that an overview or history of women's studies in southern Africa has not been attempted previously. Hassim and Walker (1993) wrote an article titled "Women's Studies and the Women's Movement in South Africa." Bonnin (1995) was responsible for the "National Report on Women's Studies in South Africa." Another work that reflects on teaching gender at a tertiary institution in South Africa is the article by Shefer, Potgieter, and Strebel (1999) titled "Teaching Gender in Psychology at a South African University." Regarding the broader African continent, Mama (1996) provided useful and critical insight into the domain with her article entitled "Women's Studies and Studies of Women in Africa during the 1990s."

The formal institutional introduction of a degree in women's studies took place in 1989 when the University of Natal at Durban, South Africa, introduced a graduate degree in women's studies. A year later another campus of the same university also introduced a graduate degree as well as an interdisciplinary undergraduate course. In 1995 the University of Western Cape (UWC) introduced a graduate degree in women's and gender studies. The degree programs offered by these two universities are currently the longest running

and thus the most developed programs in the country, and the universities are the only ones that have produced graduates with degrees in women's studies. The University of Cape Town has for a number of years had an African Gender Institute (AGI), which conducts research, does training and advocacy work, and since the year 2000, offers formal studies (degrees) in women's studies. The University of Cape Town has also appointed the first-ever African chair in women and gender studies. Other universities, such as the distance-learning university, the University of South Africa (UNISA), have women's studies centers and some teaching programs but do not offer degrees in the area. This is the case with other universities in the southern African region, such as the University of Namibia, Eduardo Mondlane (Mozambique), and the University of Zimbabwe.

A common question that academics in southern Africa (as elsewhere) feel compelled to address and one they are commonly asked, especially when the "history" is under discussion, concerns the relationship between the women's movement and women's studies. In South Africa the question has been posed in different spaces, structures, and times. Bonnin (1995) states that many organizationally based women, in response to her request to interview them about women's studies in South Africa, responded in the vein of "women's studies, what has that got to do with us?" In addition, the relationship of women's studies and academic feminism with the women's movement in South Africa and with the national liberation movement has never been an easy one (Kadalie, 1995). She correctly points out that women's studies developed in spite of and also because of the opposition of comrades in the liberation struggle to feminism. A number of writers have attempted to capture the history of the relationship between the women's movement and women's studies. Hassim and Walker (1993), while not totally negating a relationship between women's studies courses and broader political women's structures and organizations, are quite adamant that no strong independent women's movement can claim to be the birth mother of women's studies in South Africa. In South Africa in the 1970s and early 1980s white women, because of race, location, political allegiance, and interest, were involved in almost exclusively white organizations such as the National Union of South African Students (NUSAS) and Rape Crisis. Bonnin (1995: 7) claims that "you can't underestimate the influence of this kind of feminist politics on the development of women's studies courses." Our interpretation is that individual women who had links with these organizations might have had an influence on certain women's studies courses, but we do not think that these organizations per se had any direct link to politics.

University politics at historically black universities such as the University of Western Cape (UWC) and the University of Durban-Westville (UDW) was intrinsically linked to national politics, which meant challenging and fighting the apartheid regime. Many women academics who were teaching at these universities clearly state that their feminism can be traced to their involvement in politically aligned women's organizations (Potgieter and De La Rey, 1997). The embryonic stage of their feminist teaching was conceived outside the university but developed within the context of an academic teaching and research environment.

What is the present relationship between women's studies and women's organizations? Bonnin (1995) states that "at present there is very little contact between women's studies and women's organisations, some women's studies courses give voice to women's organisations (and struggles) but don't in any way relate to them.... They do not relate in terms of course content and they do not relate to the priorities that women's organisations set." An examination of the women's and gender studies programs at the University of Western Cape and the University of Natal reveals that some points in Bonnin's report no longer hold true. For example, if one scrutinizes the courses taught, it is clear that gender issues are pertinent to southern African society and are critical components of curricula. The issues of gender and development and of gender and transformation are a case in point. In addition, issues facing women on the African continent—such as female genital mutilation—are covered in courses, seminars, and students' research.

For a long time women in southern Africa have argued that men and issues pertaining to men need to be factored into the struggles women are embarking on, as well as into courses. This view is reflected in the interest students have shown in a course offered at the University of Western Cape titled "Teaching Men." The course is taught by an African male, and it challenges notions of masculinity that are oppressive and discriminatory toward women and men.

In South Africa a number of women's organizations were started after the first democratic election in 1994. These include organizations that are involved in training and other activities related to the empowerment of women. Although women's studies departments have not signed formal agreements with these organizations, working alliances do exist. However, in the early 1990s certain women's studies departments affiliated with the National Women's Coalition, which was an umbrella organization of various women's organizations (Bonnin, 1995). Some of the students at the University of Western Cape are women who work for these organizations on a full-time basis and pursue part-time studies. Where these students are positioned in terms of their work and interests in itself influences curriculum and the development of courses. One of the shortcomings of the curriculum and the courses offered is that they are determined by individual teachers' interests and not by clearly assessed needs and interests of stakeholders. This situation may exist in part because university managements have not provided the necessary human and monetary support for programs. Teachers thus teach in home departments and volunteer their services to the women's and gender studies programs. Given that gender is a government priority and that it is a program that may increase graduate student numbers, it is most likely that universities will do the "politically correct" thing and provide more resources for these programs.

Although certain developments in southern Africa might suggest a bleak scenario for women's studies and feminist politics, many progressive developments have emerged in the region. One of these is evident in new forms of context-sensitive research, where there is a strong emphasis, driven by many postcolonial and poststructuralist feminists, on carefully locating gender struggles. Emphasis is placed on how particular groups of women experience the conditions of their lives and devise strategies of survival. For this research, feminism is not the preserve of the western-educated feminist academic. Instead, it may define a diverse range of theoretical and political positions in which different women empower themselves in relation to oppressive gendered institutions.

Another important concern for feminist teachers (and others) has been to locate their own feminist assumptions at the same time that they interpret others. Contributions to *SAFERE,* the southern African feminist review developed by Pat Mcfadden and published in Harare, and *AGENDA,* a South African feminist journal, are particularly interesting in this respect. For many contributors, writing about gendered experiences is often a self-reflective process of understanding themselves, their own locations and responses. It does not entail dogmatically instructing others or assuming that the writer has reached a stage of absolute feminist self-awareness.

Many universities are introducing courses in women's studies. In addition, government departments are creating posts linked to gender positions with titles such as gender training officer. It can be assumed that women currently studying for degrees in women's studies will eventually hold these or similar positions. Gouws (1996) argues that the institutionalization of gender could shape women's issues outside government and contribute to the creation of a new kind of woman, the "femocrat" inside government. It remains to be seen how gender studies courses would position themselves in relation to this argument and, equally important, how graduates of women's studies programs would face this challenge. The president of South Africa, Thabo Mbeki, raised the issue of an African renaissance, and it has led to many debates about what actually constitutes an African renaissance. The late president of Mozambique, Samora Machel, stated, in relation to the African renaissance and women's studies, that "the liberation of women is a fundamental necessity for the revolution, the guarantee of its continuity and a precondition for its victory" (quoted in Urdang, 1984: 9). Many believe that the empowerment of women in southern Africa and the rest of Africa is a fundamental necessity for the success of an African renaissance, the guarantee of its continuity, and a precondition for its victory. Should women's studies courses and research in southern Africa continue to create space for an African feminism, they would indeed be contributing to achieving the goal of an African renaissance.

See Also

APARTHEID, SEGREGATION, AND GHETTOIZATION; COLONIALISM AND POSTCOLONIALISM; DEVELOPMENT: SUB-SAHARAN AND SOUTHERN AFRICA; EDUCATION: SOUTHERN AFRICA; FEMINISM: SOUTH AFRICA; FEMINISM: SUB-SAHARAN AFRICA; GENDER STUDIES; IMAGES OF WOMEN: AFRICA; POLITICS AND THE STATE: SOUTHERN AFRICA; RACE; WOMANISM

References and Further Reading

Bonnin, D. 1995. National report on women's studies in South Africa. University of Natal, Durban.

Charman, A., C. De Swardt, and M. Simons. 1991. The politics of gender: Negotiating liberation. *Transformation* 15.

De La Rey, C. 1997. South African feminism, race and racism. *Agenda* 32: 6–10.

———, and A. Kottler. 1999. Societal transformation: Gender, feminism and psychology in South Africa. *Feminism and Psychology* 9(2): 119–126.

Fester, G. 1997. Women's organisations in the Western Cape: Vehicles for gender struggle or instruments of subordination? *Agenda* 34: 45–61.

Fouché, F. 1994. Overcoming the sisterhood myth. *Transformation* 23.

Gouws, A. 1996. The rise of the femocrat? *Agenda* 30: 31–43.

Hassim, S. 1991. Gender, social location and feminist politics in South Africa. *Transformation* 15.

———, and C. Walker. 1993. Women's studies and the women's movement in South Africa: Defining a relationship. *Women's Studies International Forum* 15: 5.

Horn, P. 1991. Post-apartheid South Africa: What about women's emancipation? *Transformation* 15.

Kadalie, R. 1995a. The F-word. *Agenda* 25: 73–81.

———. 1995b. Women's studies in South Africa: University of the Western Cape as a case study. Unpublished paper.

Kasente, D. H. 1996. Gender studies and gender training in Africa. *Development in Practice* 6(1): 50–54.

Mama, A. 1996. Women's studies and studies of women in Africa during the 1990s. CODESRIA Working Paper 5/96.

Mohanty, C., A. Russo, and Lourdes Torres, eds. 1991. *Third world women and the politics of feminism.* Bloomington: Indiana University Press.

Potgieter, C., and C. De La Rey. 1997. Gender and race: Whereto psychology in South Africa. *Feminism and Psychology* 7(1): 138–142.

Rao, A., M. B. Anderson, and C. Overholt, eds. 1991. *Gender analysis in development planning: A case book.* West Hartford, Conn.: Kumarian.

Shefer, T., C. Potgieter, and A. Strebel. 1999. Teaching gender in psychology at a South African university. *Feminism and Psychology* 9(2): 127–143.

Spivak, G. 1990. Can the subaltern speak? Speculations on widow sacrifice. *WEDGE* 7(8) (Winter/Spring): 120–130.

Urdang, S. 1984. The last transition? Women and development in Mozambique. *Review of African Political Economy* 27–28: 8–32.

Wells, J. 1991. The rise and fall of motherism as a force in black women's resistance. Paper read at Women and Gender in Southern Africa conference, University of Natal, Durban.

Cheryl Ann Potgeiter

WOMEN'S STUDIES: Sub-Saharan Africa

Women's studies in sub-Saharan Africa can be understood as developing under three main rubrics. The first of these is a feminist trajectory of scholarship generated by international and local women's activism in and beyond sub-Saharan African contexts. The second rubric is that of African studies, and traces a path through colonial and postcolonial engagements over the study and conceptualization of Africa, and of African women in particular. Third, there are the research and information gathering activities in and around the development industry over the last half of the twentieth century.

African Women as Objects of Study

African women have long been objects of study, but as the contemporary reviews acknowledge, the terms on which the study has been done have largely been dictated by the assumptions of others: African women's scholarship is only now emerging into the international arena.

Earlier, colonial studies of sub-Saharan Africa and Africans tended to echo imperial policies that often disregarded African women entirely, occasionally regarding them either as an unwanted presence, or as objects of curiosity. Denise Paulme's collection *Women of Tropical Africa* (1963) marked the emergence of contemporary studies of African women.

Thereafter, African women were increasingly targeted as objects of study within the frameworks of changing international development discourses. During the 1950s and 1960s, the development industry took shape. The prevailing modernist approaches to development relied on the introduction of capitalist labor relations premised on a gender division that treated men as waged laborers and women as housewives (Rogers, 1980). The international economic crisis in the 1970s led to a new questioning of the dominant paradigms. Ester Boserup's book (1970) highlighted the importance of recognizing women's role in development, attributing the apparent failure of economic development plans to the exclusion of women's work, particularly in African farming systems, by planners. Her work had particular impact in the aftermath of the large-scale famines that characterized the crisis in many parts of Africa, giving rise to a new interest in "integrating women into development"—or WID, as it soon became known. The interest in WID generated far-reaching interest in studies of women and their roles in the household, community, labor market, and economy. The declaration of the UN Decade for Women in 1975 also sparked an international upsurge of interest by scholars and development agencies in African women's lives and activities.

Feminist Scholars' Approach

Feminist scholars took a different approach, initially focusing their attention on African women's collective protests during the 1960s and 1970s, and documenting their participation in national liberation movements worldwide. By the early 1980s a series of books had appeared documenting women's participation in independence struggles in Nigeria (Mba, 1982), South Africa (Walker, 1982), Guinea Bissau, and Mozambique (Urdang, 1989) and these radically altered the representation of African women. There was now ample evidence that women all over Africa not only were occupied with a variety of productive activities that the development industry had initially overlooked, but also were actively involved in political movements and organizations, and accustomed to defending their interests and those of their families and communities. Once political independence had been secured, women in the emergent African nations seized the opportunity to further their education and secure jobs in the formal sector, albeit in gender-segregated ways. A small but significant minority occupied key political offices in newly independent countries, notably Ghana, Sierra Leone, and Nigeria. Some entered academia and brought their perspective to feminist debates, mounting a double-sided protest against the western domination of knowledge production within women's studies on the one hand and the male domination of African scholarship on the other.

Challenge by African Women

By the time of the UN Decade of Women, sub-Saharan African women were beginning to challenge both western feminist scholarship and the dominant development discourse of international forums. The formation of the Association of Africa Women for Research and Development (AAWORD) in 1977 marked the beginning of self-defining scholarship by African women. The first AAWORD workshops and publications were critical of the dominant development discourse—at that time focused on industrialization—and of theories and methods imported from the West. It was almost two decades, however, before the regional Council for the Development of Social Science Research in Africa acknowledged the importance of bringing gender analysis to bear on scholarly pursuits and held a cross-disciplinary workshop on the subject in Dakar 1991 (Imam et al, 1997).

Women's Research Centers and Institutes

By this time, African women had formed their own study groups and centers in several countries, beginning with the Women's Research and Documentation Project at the University of Dar es Salaam, Tanzania, in 1978 and the Women's Research and Documentation Centre (WORDOC) at the University of Ibadan, Nigeria, in 1986. Between the end of the 1970s and the early 1990s women's studies courses were established on campuses all over the continent, beginning with Ahmadu Bello University in Nigeria in 1979.

In addition to these more formal structures, a number of NGOs and research networks engaged in gender research in specific fields such as health and reproductive rights, secular and Islamic law, and violence against women. All these initiatives worked to generate locally grounded and locally relevant knowledge about African women's live and realities. The Zimbabwe Women's Resource Centre and Network and the Tanzania Gender Networking Programme, both established at the end of the 1980s, marked a more strategic attempt to generate knowledge that would challenge gender oppression and contribute to the establishment of more just and equitable societies. In 1996, the establishment of the African Gender Institute at the University of Cape Town built on these earlier initiatives, retaining a commitment to linking theory and practice in order to generate gender studies grounded in African contexts and conditions. The African Gender Institute draws on state of the art information technology and international resources to strengthen the region's intellectual and technical capacity for realizing the goals of gender equality and social justice.

African women have organized a diverse range of other interest groups outside traditional academic and research institutions, many of which have made significant contributions to knowledge about women and gender in particular national contexts.

The Harare-based Zimbabwe Women's Resource Centre and Network (ZWRCN) is a fine example. ZWRCN has been in existence since 1990. This nongovernmental organization has established a library and resource centre and involved itself in a range of activities that involve research, lobbying, and advocacy. The main objective of ZWRCN is to enhance the position of women through the collection and dissemination of material on gender and development issues. Since its inception, ZWRCN has established contacts with women's organizations, NGOs, research institutes, donor agencies, individuals and government departments.

The Tanzanian Women's Research and Documentation Project (WRDP) at the University of Dar Es Salaam began as an informal study group in 1978 and formally constituted itself in 1980. The Tanzanian Association of Media Women (TAMWA) was also formed in Dar Es Salaam in the 1980s. For over a decade TAMWA has been actively contributing to raising gender awareness in government and civil society, and publishing a women's journal, *Sauti ya Siti*, in English and Kiswahili. As of this writing, the most recent initiative in this country was the Tanzania Gender Networking Programme (TGNP), bringing together an array of academics, activists, and practitioners concerned with advancing gender equality in Tanzania.

In Botswana, Emang Basadi (Women Stand Up) was established in 1986 with the goal of liberating women through activism and research. In Ghana, local women established the Development and Women's Studies (DAWS) project to advance gender and women's studies in the universities, and to foster linkages between researchers, activists, and practitioners. It also set about developing a postgraduate curriculum for teaching women's studies under the rubric of the Centre for African Studies at the University of Ghana.

In Nigeria the growth of interest in women's studies was facilitated by Women in Nigeria (WIN), a national NGO formed at Ahmadu Bello University in 1982. WIN established chapters all over Nigeria and carried out gender activist projects, many of which included research and public education. Subsequently, a national network of scholars and researchers based in Nigeria's forty universities was formed at a workshop, "Setting an Agenda for Gender and Women's Studies," held in Kaduna in January 1996. The Network for Women's Studies in Nigeria, supported by the British Council, carried out a program of national and local training workshops to build the intellectual and institutional capacity for gender and women's studies relevant to the Nigerian context.

Regional Networks

In addition to these national initiatives, women in Sub-Saharan Africa have also established a range of networks, many of which are contributing to knowledge about women and gender issues, often in specific areas. All of these regional groups have Web sites that can be accessed through the African Gender Institute's website.

The African Centre for Women (ACW), based in Addis Ababa, is a division within the Economic Commission for Africa. ACW is the regional Women in Development structure in the United Nations system in Africa. The Centre services national, regional, and sub-regional structures involved in the advancement of women, and produces regular publications.

ABANTU for Development (ABANTU) is a nongovernmental regional network organization founded in 1991 by women wishing to mobilize development resources for the benefit of African people. Abantu means "people" in many languages, and symbolizes the organization's people-centered philosophy. The main focus of Abantu's work is on training, providing information and advice on mobilizing resources towards sustainable development in Africa. In addition, the ABANTU network has carried out research in six of the countries in which it operates, mainly to gather information on the capacities of NGOs for intervening in policy making in the interests of advancing gender equality.

African Gender Institute (AGI) is a regional resource involved in various aspects of building intellectual capacity for African women. A major program of the AGI is the associates program that enables African women to complete writing projects in a supportive intellectual environment. Supported initially by the Carnegie Foundation and subsequently by the Rockefeller Foundation, the AGI has hosted 30 women from all over Africa. There they spend time utilizing the resources of the institute and the University of Cape Town, and interacting with the faculty to develop their writing skills and complete publications.

FEMNET stands for the African Women's Development and Communication Network. The network, based in Kenya, is concerned with the sharing of information and ideas between African NGOs so as to enable a better and more effective focus on women's development.

With a regional secretariat in Nairobi, Kenya Forum for African Women Educationalists (FAWE) has national chapters in a growing number of African countries. FAWE's work has included an array of interventions in the sphere of girls' academic achievement and education, and awarding the Agathe Prize, which is dedicated to the memory of the late Rwandan prime minister Agathe Uwilingiyimana, founding member of FAWE. FAWE has run capacity building workshops for its various branches, has carried out lobbying of national governments, and has produced a booklet on gender analysis for educators. It publishes a regular newsletter that carries details of FAWE projects and initiatives.

Women in Law and Development in Africa (WiLDAF) is a pan-African women's rights network dedicated to promoting and strengthening strategies which link law and development to increase women's participation and influence at the community, national, and international levels. WiLDAF brings together organizations and individuals who share this objective and who are operating at local, national, and regional levels to make it a reality. WiLDAF has carried out a range of research activities in the area of women and the law in Africa.

Women in Development Southern Africa Awareness (WIDSAA) Programme provides information access, working closely with the Southern African Development Community (SADC) and national partners in the 14 member countries. Regional in focus and action-oriented, the WIDSAA program aims to be a catalyst and service to the region's governments, NGOs, agencies, and media—and the public—in formulation of policy affecting women.

Some of the best examples of contemporary African women's studies include recent books on gender, nationalism and national politics; on culture and religion; on women's organizations and grassroots movements; on sexuality and economic activity; on agricultural development; and on the impact of international development industry. The main issues facing women's studies in Africa have been discussed in two reviews (Mama, 1996; Snyder, 2000). These two reviews point to a proliferation of gender research across the region, but point out that the bulk of this relies on external funds and the internationally available literature is still dominated by expatriate researchers rather than by local scholars. Thus the literature does not fully reflect a reality in which African women have organized in numerous ways and on multiple fronts under challenging circumstances.

Nevertheless, the relevance of gender research to policy analysis and development planning remains incontrovertible, and in some ways this fact has secured the expansion of African gender studies in spite of the wider setbacks and failures being endured by African tertiary institutions and the constraints on independent research activity. The form and direction of gender and women's studies in the African region are often directed toward servicing international development agencies and government interests, rather than addressing the concerns and issues being identified by African women's organizations and movements. These are not always incompatible, however, and scholarly work must respond to the financial exigencies if it is to flourish in the twenty-first century.

See Also

COLONIALISM AND POSTCOLONIALISM; DEVELOPMENT: SUB-SAHARAN AND SOUTHERN AFRICA; EDUCATION: SUB-SAHARAN AFRICA; FEMINISM: SUB-SAHARAN AFRICA; NONGOVERNMENTAL ORGANIZATIONS; WOMEN'S STUDIES: SOUTHERN AFRICA

References and Further Reading

Boserup, E. 1970. *Women's role in economic development*. London: George Allen and Unwin.

Imam, I., A. Mama, and F. Sow, eds. 1997. *Engendering African social science*. Dakar: CODESRIA.

Mama, A. 1996. *Women's studies and studies of women in Africa in the 1990s*. Dakar: CODESRIA.

Mba, N. 1982. *Nigerian women mobilised: Women's political activity in southern Nigeria 1900–1965*. Institute of International Studies, Berkeley: University of California Press.

Paulme, D., ed. 1963. *Women of tropical Africa*, Berkeley: University of California Press.

Rogers, B. 1980. *The domestication of women: Discrimination in developing societies*. London: Tavistock.

Snyder, M. 2000. Women and African development. *Choice* 37(6): 1035–1051.

Walker, C. 1982. *Women and resistance in South Africa*. London: Onyx.

Urdang, Stephanie. 1989. *"And still they dance": Women and resistance in Mozambique*. London: Earthscan.

Amina Mama

WOMEN'S STUDIES: United States

Women's studies in the United States is both a success story and an emblem of the elusiveness of success in a rapidly changing world where entrenched power, with its guardian institutional structures, stubbornly and by habit resists change. As the following analysis will demonstrate, on the one hand, women's studies has had three decades of remarkable achievements. It has established just under 700 women's studies academic undergraduate programs, spawned more than 100 graduate programs, founded dozens of feminist journals, transformed the contours of many disciplines, reformed the way classes are taught, and transformed the lives of million of students. On the other hand, on most of the 3,500 college campuses in the United States, women's studies continues to be underfunded, typically without designated faculty positions, and often marginalized, and the intellectual implications of its scholarship are not fully recognized. Its two most distinctive accomplishments are the intellectual power of its inquiry and the success with which women's studies has become institutionalized. Its most telling challenge will be whether that foothold will enable it to alter the structures, policies, and practices of the academy that pose barriers to more wide-sweeping intellectual and societal transformation.

Historical Origins

Women's studies in the United States has its deepest roots in the women's movement of the 1960s and 1970s, a movement itself deeply shaped by the civil rights movement for equality for African-Americans, the antiwar movement against the Vietnam War, community-based urban and rural organizing on behalf of the dispossessed, and the small but influential group of professional women in local, state, and federal government positions. The 1960s in particular, a period of questioning and political turmoil, unleashed a grassroots conviction that individuals in a democracy could create change, that mass organizing could accelerate that change, and that significant interconnections existed between these parallel movements for racial and gender equality, peace, and economic justice.

Many of the most visible early leaders of the women's movement themselves came of age politically through the other social movements of the decade. It seemed only natural to extend the quest for equality and justice to women's lives. College campuses that had nurtured so many of the thinkers and been the arena of political expression for other social movements of the decade were a logical arena for the women's movement as well. It was, in fact, a commonplace

for the early founders of women's studies programs to define women's studies as "the academic arm of the women's movement." Women's studies was particularly influenced by the efforts to establish black studies courses and programs. For almost the first two decades of black studies, however, gender was not addressed, and black women were largely invisible as a focus of study, just as they were less visible in the first decade of women's studies. Although black studies preceded women's studies, the fact that there were so many more women faculty members and students than there were African-Americans as a group contributed to the far more rapid and expansive growth of women's studies.

In the United States higher education was effectively segregated until the mid-1960s, by law in the South and by practice almost everywhere else. African-Americans overwhelmingly were educated at historically black colleges and universities. Less than 3 percent of all racial minorities in the United States were educated at predominantly white institutions before 1960. It was not until civil rights legislation, activism, and a shift in U.S. immigration policies in 1965 that the complexion of undergraduate students began to change across the nation. Some 27 percent of undergraduates are students of color, as are 12 percent of the faculty. Because women's studies had its origins in such a racially imbalanced setting in the 1960s and early 1970s, the earlier programs were dominated by white women, white students, and largely white concerns. Decentering those origins in a society that continues to favor whiteness has been one of the most difficult tasks for women's studies in the United States. But women's studies continues to tackle that challenge and has proved over the decades to be an important site of activism for racial equality and other liberation movements within the academy. Debate about exclusion and power inequities has characterized women's studies since its inception. If it sometimes fractured alliances, such critiques have also been a source of the continuing vibrancy and political edge of women's studies. As women's studies and ethnic studies began to find more common ground over the years, together they have proved a powerful source for keeping social change at the heart of the educational enterprise.

During the late 1960s, the first wave of women's studies courses began to appear. Some were spurred by the intellectual and political commitment of the faculty; some were spurred by the insistence of students; almost none were instigated by administrative leadership from the top. By the 1970s, women began to attend college in expansive new numbers and would by 1984 constitute the majority of undergraduate students. Title IX, a major piece of federal legislation about women and girls, passed in 1972, required colleges and universities that received federal funds to provide data each year to the government demonstrating that there was no sex discrimination in programming at their institution. The establishment of women's centers, women's student groups, women's commissions, and women's research centers created a critical mass on many campuses that nurtured the growth of women's studies. Private foundations and a few governmental agencies also began to contribute funds to support the development of new scholarship and faculty development initiatives in women's studies and to help establish women's studies programs. Professional associations like the Modern Language Association, the American Historical Association, and the American Sociological Association became vehicles for promoting and legitimating women's studies scholarship. Members of women's studies faculties also turned repeatedly to one another for professional support as they invented this new interdisciplinary field. They shared syllabi, ran small conferences, established local and state women's studies organizations, and eventually, in 1976, established the National Women's Studies Association.

If the 1970s were a period of establishing an ever-expanding number of courses and was defined principally by the discovery that sisterhood is powerful, the 1980s were a period of institutionalizing the courses into more permanent programs and were defined by the discovery that not all sisters are alike. If the celebration of women as a group characterized the 1970s, the 1980s were marked by sometimes painful and fractious explorations of differences within women as a group. Although articulating those differences across race and religion, sexuality and class, age and ability was not easy, the critical questioning that is at the heart of women's studies inquiry allowed the scholarship to become more sophisticated, more honest, and more inclusive.

If the 1980s were dominated by delineating differences between women, the 1990s explored the points of connection, spawning such terms as *intersectionality, borderlands, multiplicity,* and *hybridity.* The 1990s also witnessed the consolidation of women's studies programs, the development of postgraduate degrees, and an even deeper engagement with theories connected to but not necessarily rooted in women's studies: postmodern theory, cultural studies, queer theory, and critical race theory. The 1990s were also a decade that more definitively challenged women's studies in the United States to see itself in a global context as practitioners became increasingly influenced by international women's conferences and postcolonial studies. Now in the twenty-first century, women's studies in the United States is proving itself resilient, adaptive, and intellectually flexible. But it faces challenges about the relationship between theory and practice, the implications of its evolving location in the academy, and how women's studies, nested in an ever more corpora-

tized university, can assume leadership in the dramatic liberatory movements in the academy in the opening decades of the twenty-first century.

A Statistical Profile

Although hundreds of women's studies courses were offered at colleges and universities during the late 1960s, the first women's studies program to receive formal approval was at San Diego State University in California in the spring of 1970. After that, there was a deluge. By 1973 there were 78 undergraduate women's studies programs nationwide; three years later, in 1976, the year the National Women's Studies Association (NWSA) was founded, the number had catapulted to 276. By 1988 that number had almost doubled to 519. The last official count of programs by NWSA in 1990 listed 621 programs, a 20 percent increase. In 1999 NWSA estimated that there were 680 women's studies programs. More than 425 programs have formalized their course offerings as minors, certificates, or concentrations, while just under 200 programs offer majors in women's studies.

As stunning as the rapid growth of formal programs is, such data do not begin to capture the pervasiveness of the new field, even on new campuses without formal programs. A survey by Elaine El-Khawas (1984) for the American Council on Education's *Campus Trends Report* said women's studies courses were offered at two-thirds of universities (68.1 percent), one-half of four-year colleges (48.9 percent), and one-quarter of community colleges (26.5 percent). Given the steady growth in programs, one could safely surmise that percentages have climbed even higher since then. More students, however, choose to take women's studies courses than to major in the field. A college with only 10 women's studies majors, for example, might teach anywhere from 500 to 2,600 students each year in various women's studies courses.

Predictably, the newly educated undergraduates in women's studies and the burgeoning production of scholarship about women and gender stimulated new programs at the graduate level as well. NWSA's *Guide to Graduate Work in Women's Studies* (1991) reported that in 1986, the first year graduate programs in women's studies were tracked, there were 23 graduate programs. By 1991 that number had tripled in just five years to 69. The second edition of NWSA's *Guide to Graduate Work* (1994) lists 111 graduate programs—a 60 percent increase in three years, or approximately 14 new programs per year since 1986. As in the growth of the undergraduate programs, most graduate programs are offered as minors or concentrations taken within doctoral study in a traditional discipline. In 1990 only a handful of institutions offered an M.A. in women's studies. By 2000 self-standing master's-level work in women's studies had expanded steadily. Not surprisingly, nearly a dozen new doctoral programs in women's studies are offered as well. Marilyn Boxer reports that *Dissertation Abstracts International* lists 10,786 women's studies titles between 1978 and 1995, with the numbers accelerating as the years go by (1998).

Women's studies programs grew so rapidly in the United States in part because they were inexpensive to initiate and because the academy permits a good deal of faculty autonomy over course development. The most common structure for a women's studies program is to release a full-time tenured faculty member from several courses to administer the women's studies program. Most programs have no faculty assigned specifically to them, but instead borrow faculty from various departments and assemble as best they can a set of offerings that have intellectual integrity. A student will usually take several interdisciplinary courses in women's studies along with some discipline-based courses cross-listed in women's studies and another department. In larger programs there are faculty appointments, sometimes as many as a dozen, a growing number of joint appointments, and an impressive array of affiliated faculty. In the past several years an increasing number of programs became departments, which usually affords additional access to institutional resources like travel budgets, faculty lines, authority over promotion and tenure, and physical space. Even when they are departments, women's studies programs continue to draw from affiliated faculty in other departments and therefore continue to have permeable borders, which in turn fosters an interdisciplinary base of inquiry. Even as they are institutionalized, women's studies programs still function as a matrix in an otherwise hierarchal structure.

Mapping the Intellectual Debates in Women's Studies

The early years of women's studies focused largely on two main intellectual enterprises: (1) analyzing the various systems that oppressed women over centuries and (2) retrieving the lost history and culture of women's lives. The resulting scholarship taught a great deal about women's victimization and women's agency. It also forced feminist scholars to examine the ways in which women themselves were sometimes agents of oppressing other people, including other women, which resulted in a far more complicated feminist theory and politics. The scholarship of difference spawned a rigorous delineation of new areas of study about particular groups of women: lesbians, Jewish women, African-American women, Latinas, Asian-Pacific American women, American Indian women, working-class women, older women, immigrant women, disabled women—the list

continues to expand with the investigation of women outside the boundaries of the United States, especially in third world countries.

But the delineation of different identity groups also revealed that these groups were not monolithic. Those investigations, in turn, generated comparative studies between groups, linking once more what had heretofore been studied separately. It became difficult not to acknowledge the gendered nature of race, the raced nature of gender, or the inflection of sexuality in religion. A more inclusive and integrated theory came to characterize the best of feminist scholarship.

Women's studies professors in the 1980s initiated what in the United States is called the curriculum transformation movement. In addition to offering to separate women's studies courses, feminists in the academy began a strategy of integrating the new scholarship about women and gender into traditional disciplinary courses and into what are called general education courses. Although there was heated debate for several years in the 1980s about whether this integration would weaken women's studies, funnel off its funds, and ultimately dilute a feminist analysis, the majority came to see curriculum transformation as an important strategy for institutional change. The movement also helped women's studies move toward its goal of not simply producing new knowledge about women and gender but transforming all knowledge.

One of the benchmarks of success of women's studies has been its influence on traditional disciplines. As Dale Spender and others have attested, feminist scholarship has had a leavening force, modifying, expanding, and redefining the knowledge base and methodologies in the disciplines. A testimony to the success is the larger arena in which feminist research and teaching now occur outside of women's studies programs per se. This success, however, presents some second-generation questions for the field. How can women's studies programs keep their vital link with the disciplines, some of which may no longer need the institutional shelter of a woman's studies program? What kind of translation capacities do we need to develop in the face of scholarship that is, in some instances, written in a less accessible kind of disciplinary-specific dialect? And how might women's studies more effectively promote the interdisciplinary focus so critical to its formulation by connecting with the interdisciplinary frameworks that often are masked behind a traditional discipline while also connecting with other self-standing interdisciplinary programs?

Some people worry from within that women's studies in the United States may have grown complacent with success, abandoned its activist roots, succumbed to the preference for theory in academia, wed itself to outmoded and discredited identity constructions, and rigidified into an oppositional stance. These are troubling questions that should not be ignored. If women's studies is true to its core principles, then questions will be debated and examined with open-eyed candor and through passionate, articulate exchanges. Most women's studies practitioners, however, continue to see women's studies scholarship and programs as a seedbed of intellectual challenges, an ethical compass for social responsibility, and a source of institutional and personal renewal. Many have proposed an agenda for the decades ahead: globalizing women's studies, integrating feminism and science studies, tackling the implications of technology on society, generating new public-policy formulations, renewing a commitment to interweaving theory and practice in the service of social change movements and movements for justice, and continuing to invest in curriculum and faculty development with a special focus on interdisciplinary frameworks.

Assessing the Impact of Women's Studies

A national report, *A New Vitality in General Education* (1988), singled out the special intellectual rigor of women's studies: "Women's studies' questioning of accepted explanations of topics and problems has motivated an emphasis on accurate development, analysis, synthesis, and theory building." In a survey by the Association of American Colleges and Universities that compared 11 different majors, women's studies was rated the highest in 10 out of 14 categories that ranged from connecting different kinds of knowledge and exploring values and ethics to investigating important societal questions and designing assignments about personally significant questions. The fact that women's studies challenges students to rethink all they have learned prompted one student at Old Dominion University to quip, "I felt as if I had a completely new brain."

An assessment of the impact of women's studies courses on students' learning in the United States is found in the present author's *The Courage to Question: Women's Studies and Student Learning* (Musil, 1992), which drew from data collected over a three-year period at seven different institutions, each of which had women's studies majors. Although the report was meant to spur more attention to the educational outcomes of women's studies, little has been published since that date. Such studies should be on the agenda for women's studies programs in the future. Students reveal in the research thus far that women's studies engages them intellectually and makes education a way of life—not merely a collection of course credits. It reestablishes the centrality of teaching and student-focused learning. Students talk of finding their own

voices, engaging in robust debates, and developing critical perspectives. They also say that women's studies has helped them understand different viewpoints and diverse people. Finally it challenges them to actively shape their society. Capturing the complexity of students' learning, one student at Wellesley College described women's studies as generating "learning that does more than fill your brain. It fills your body, it fills your heart, and it makes you grow."

In differentiating between women's studies and non–women's studies courses, one student at Hunter College explained that women's studies courses, "open with questions... that's really the biggest difference... you question all the time, all the time." Students moved from being objects of study to being subjects with a voice of their own, thus reinforcing a developmental link between voice, empowerment, self-esteem, and critical thinking. Distinguishing itself from many traditional disciplines, women's studies is unabashedly value-centered, poses tough-minded ethical questions, and confronts students with, as the University of Colorado's women's studies program put it, "knowledge inconvenient for students to know." *The Courage to Question* provided evidence that women's studies students debate issues far more frequently both in and out of the classroom than do students in non–women's studies classes. The differentials ranged from 21 percent to as high as 25 percent. Students in that study repeatedly affirmed that women's studies professors presented, prodded, and welcomed divergent points of view. After taking women's studies courses, students expressed a desire to improve things not only for themselves but for other people, and they translated that new commitment to citizens' action after graduation.

While critics portray women's studies as academically "soft," students in *The Courage to Question* argued that women's studies is *more* difficult because its subject matter challenges not simply what you think but also how you feel about what you think and what you do because of what you know. How a course is taught is discussed almost as much as feminist scholarship. Women's studies classrooms are typically more participatory, experiential, and structured to encourage students' voices. They also seek to foster dialogue, create an arena in which to express disagreements, and challenge students to engage with difference. There is more attention in most cases to group work, spatial arrangements in the classroom, varieties in course assignments, and invitations to tie theory to personal experience.

Women's studies is, then, an entire new body of knowledge, a critical framework for evaluating older bodies of knowledge, and a vehicle for engaging in dialogue and debate about competing truths. It offers its own self-standing interdisciplinary programs of study while also connecting, as few other disciplines do, with almost every other academic area of study. Serving as a web linking many areas of study within the academy, women's studies also derives some of its most incisive intellectual insights because it lives on the margin. It offers new ways to connect intellectually and personally across difference and therefore offers higher education new models for preparing students to be boundary crossers, critical questioners, and engaged citizens seeking a more equitable society.

See Also

CULTURAL STUDIES; EDUCATION: CURRICULUM IN SCHOOLS; GENDER STUDIES; GIRL STUDIES; POSTMODERNISM: FEMINIST CRITIQUES; QUEER THEORY

References and Further Reading

Boxer, Marilyn Jacoby. 1998. *When women ask the questions: Creating women's studies in America.* Baltimore: Johns Hopkins University Press.

Hedges, Elaine, and Dorothy O. Helly, eds. 1997. Looking back, moving forward: 25 years of women's studies history. *Women's Studies Quarterly Anniversary Issue* 25(1–2: Spring/Summer).

Learning. Washington, D.C.: Association of American Colleges and Universities.

Musil, Caryn McTighe. 1992. *The courage to question: Women's studies and student learning.* Washington, D.C.: Association of American Colleges.

Pearson, Carol S., Donna L. Shavlik, and Judith G. Touchton, eds. 1989. *Educating the majority: Women challenge tradition in higher education.* New York: Macmillan.

Spender, Dale, ed. 1981. *Men's studies modified: The impact of feminism on the academic disciplines.* New York: Pergamon.

Stimpson, Catharine R., with Nina Kressner Cobb. 1986. *Women's studies in the United States.* New York: Ford Foundation.

Task Group on General Education. 1988. *A new vitality in general education.* Washington, D.C.: Association of American Colleges and Universities.

Caryn McTighe Musil

WOMEN'S STUDIES: Western Europe

History and Development

Women's studies as an academic discipline and a social movement has been developing in western Europe since the 1960s and 1970s, both in educational settings and in the grassroots activities of women. The extent and direction of this development have depended in part on the political, social, and cultural influences and movements of particular countries and in part on their educational and other institutional structures.

Economic factors also have influenced the development of women's studies, with a north-south divide as well as a west-east one, with Greece, Portugal, Ireland, and Spain less wealthy than their northern neighbors (Zmroczek and Duchen, 1991). In Spain, the alliance of feminist movements in resistance to the Franco regime led to developments in the growth of women's studies outside the academy, and in Denmark, women's studies is one of the main sources for feminist political action (Delhelz et al., 1998). In France, women's studies developed through a strong and radicalized feminist movement in the 1970s, coupled with an institutional distrust (see Duchen, 1987; Ezekiel, 1992); and in the Netherlands, women's studies in the academy developed from the emergence of women's liberation movements in the late 1960s (Brouns, 1992). Similar patterns developed in many European countries, including Germany, where "women's studies was born of needs and responded to energies freed by the new wave of the feminist movement" (Gerhard, 1992: 98). In the United Kingdom, early women's studies courses were established through women's socialist commitments and through adult education and community-based study arising from the growth of the women's movement (Jackson, 2000). In Ireland, the development of women's studies can be positioned against the structural and legal discriminations faced by women. Social changes for women have informed both grassroots activities and the beginnings of the development of academic women's studies:

> Women's studies programs have emerged within a context of other changes for women in Irish society, such as the introduction of equal pay, equal employment opportunity legislation, improved access to contraception, the establishment of two government commissions on the status of women, and the initiation of social welfare schemes for women. (Byrne, 1992: 16)

These social and political developments were coupled with a substantial growth in voluntary groups run by and for women, such as rape crisis centers and divorce action groups. This led to a corresponding growth in local daytime educational groups for women and the development of women's studies. Women's studies has, then, developed from the growth and development of women's movements throughout western Europe (and elsewhere), predominantly active from the late 1960s.

Academic Women's Studies

As in most countries throughout the world, women's participation in higher education in western Europe has a comparatively short history, with the doors of the academy locked against them until the later nineteenth or early twentieth century. Although there is no unified system of higher education, in recent years women have constituted almost half of the undergraduate population in most western European countries. Within the universities, the history of women's studies as an academic discipline is relatively new in western Europe, with grassroots women's studies starting to develop from the 1970s onward. What has been apparent in many institutions across western Europe is both the difficulties in getting women's studies courses agreed to by universities and feminists' commitment to keep trying. Early courses in women's studies often relied on the commitment and goodwill of feminist academics to supplement the program, often in addition to already heavy workloads. At the turn of the twenty-first century, it was still rare for women's studies departments to employ dedicated women's studies staff, and many feminist academics worked both within and without women's studies (Braidotti, 1996).

The inherent problems that arose in the institutionalized setting-up of women's studies courses meant that although throughout the 1980s some form of women's studies was evident in many higher educational institutions, this was variable throughout western Europe. In Britain, for instance, it was not possible in the 1970s or 1980s to earn an undergraduate degree in women's studies. Although the first postgraduate degree was launched at the University of Kent in 1980, it was not until a decade later that the first British single subject undergraduate degree in women's studies was launched, at the then Polytechnic (now University) of East London. It is still not possible to take an undergraduate degree in women's studies in many countries in western Europe, with most institutions beginning with postgraduate rather than undergraduate programs. It is these postgraduate programs that remain most firmly institutionalized.

A report from the International Office of Women's Studies in the University of Utrecht, Netherlands, has explored the institutionalization of gender studies and women's studies in Europe (Delhez et al., 1998). The report highlights issues of definition in cross-European comparison. The interdisciplinary field of women's studies, for example, also appears (in differing forms) as gender studies and feminist studies, and, according to the report, there are "striking differences in organisation, funding and shape in this academic field" (13).

It is clear, however, that women's studies in western Europe has been institutionalized in the academy, with women's studies departments, research centers, or Ph.D. programs in almost every country. How this institutionalization happens, though, varies widely between countries. In Norway, for example, the strong research centers that developed in women's studies led to difficulties in the integration of teaching women's studies in the academy. In Austria, the integration of women's studies or feminist teaching into other academic disciplines has led to the invisibility of women's studies, whereas in the United Kingdom the separate departments of women's studies have enabled some institutions to close these departments completely. In France, the academy has remained resistant to the inclusion of women's studies or gender studies as an academic discipline, with career success of feminist academics firmly linked to their "nonfeminist" research. The University of Utrecht report cites Dutch women's studies as "exemplary of a successful type of integration, which combines the rigour and accountability of autonomous structures with their own resources and staff and specific programmes, while remaining firmly embedded in a faculty structure" (Delhez et al., 1998: 21). Throughout western Europe, where women's studies courses are offered (and they are offered in almost all countries) they are most commonly integrated into existing disciplines, with very few countries offering women's studies education at both the undergraduate and the postgraduate levels, and even fewer countries offering degrees or diplomas in women's studies.

Institutional support for women's studies has varied widely. In the Netherlands, for example, the Ministry of Education established programs of women's studies and provided the funds for the appointment of women's studies coordinators and professors, so that women's studies programs exist in all of the Dutch universities, with about 20 professorships and personal chairs (Bird, 1996). In France, however, women's studies is barely recognized by the Ministry of Education, with only 5 women's studies lectureships out of a total of 50,000 lecturing positions, although France does have vibrant and active feminist research. There are, indeed, many active centers throughout western Europe, including WERCC (Women's Education, Research and Resource Centre), University College Dublin; NIKK (Nordic Institute for Women's Studies and Gender Research), Oslo; the Department of Feminist Studies, Odense, Denmark; Centre for Women's Studies, Antwerp; Department of Women's Studies at Utrecht University; and the Centre for the Study of Women and Gender, Warwick, England.

Organizations and Associations

As well as institutional centers, some countries in western Europe have established their own networks and associations. The Women Studies Network (U.K.) Association, for example, is a national network, with international feminist and professional links. It has regional subgroups and encourages networking among women. It is mainly an academic organization, however, and is involved in lobbying national education bodies about women's studies and feminist issues. The network has a newsletter that stimulates debates on new issues in women's studies and includes book, conference, and Web site reviews and an up-to-date events listing. In addition, one of the main focuses of the network is its annual conference and the ensuing publication of conference papers. Although the network is an organization of professional academic women, and its main concern is with higher education issues, the conferences engage in a range of themes and issues developed from feminist perspectives and politics, making clear the links between academic women's studies and feminist grassroots political activism (Jackson, 2000). A good example of countries working together is the aforementioned Nordic Institute for Women's Studies and Gender Research, NIKK, which is financed by the Nordic Council of Ministers. NIKK aims to advance, initiate, and coordinate women's studies and gender research in Denmark, Finland, Iceland, Norway, and Sweden, and through the production of a newsletter, conferences, and events has established a firm network of feminist researchers and women's studies practitioners.

There are other organizations and associations operating in western Europe, however, which have a wider brief. AOIFE (Association of Institutions for Feminist Education and Research in Europe) is a European association for women's studies. Pronounced "eefa," it is named after the Gaelic Eve (Eefa). The association is based on institutional membership and in western Europe has about 80 member institutions across 15 countries. AOIFE operates on several levels to support women's studies in Europe: to collectively address issues; to act on those issues; to network and work cooperatively; and to encourage and support funding applications to the European Union (EU) and other organizations. AOIFE initiates a range of activities and projects for its affiliated membership.

One such project is ATHENA, created by AOIFA in 1996 and selected as a Socrates Thematic Network Project in 1998. ATHENA's central coordination is located at Utrecht University in the Netherlands, although 80 women's and gender studies programs across Europe participate in the project. ATHENA has undertaken a comparative study of degrees, qualifications, and professional outlets of women's-gender-feminist studies in western Europe. The project was concerned with investigating how far feminist work and theorizing are recognized as a core content of academic degrees in Europe and the extent to which degrees in women's studies open employment opportunities. With a concern that most women's studies curricula are dominated by North American perspectives, one of ATHENA's main activities is a survey of European curriculum development in women's studies.

WISE (Women's International Studies Europe) is a feminist studies association that was formally constituted in 1990. The aims of WISE are the promotion of women's studies research, teaching, and publications and the defense of women's studies as an academic discipline in Europe. WISE offers a guide to fund-raising to enable and support research. The "divisions" of WISE, set up to encourage networking and the dissemination of ideas and research, give an indication of some of the issues being discussed in European women's studies. They include contemporary feminism and its strategies; lesbian studies; research on violence; women, work, and state policies; race and racism; women, science, and technology; and women as professional teachers in higher education. WISE publishes a regular newsletter for its members and also supports the *European Journal of Women's Studies*. In addition, it has a Web-based discussion list, WISE-L, open to all women doing women's studies in Europe or on European topics, which is an exchange for information and for networking between practitioners of women's studies.

The *European Journal of Women's Studies* (*EJWS*) is supported by WISE. It is a major international journal that has as its focus theoretical and empirical relationships between women in a European context. Although the journal does engage with women in eastern Europe, and indeed its first issue (Spring 1994) indicated a need for both an eastern and a western European context, the majority of its articles are written by western European women's studies practitioners. The special issues of the journal indicate something of these interests and concerns and have included "The Family" (1994); "Gender and Technology" (1995); "The Body" (1996); "Women, War, and Conflict" (1997); "The Idea of Europe" (1998); "Simone de Beauvoir" (1999); "Women in Transit: Between Tradition and Transformation" (2000); and "Lesbian Studies, Lesbian Lives, Lesbian Voices" (2001).

In 1995, SIGMA, European interuniversity network for evaluation, cooperation, and the development of new perspectives in higher education, completed a report evaluating the state of women's studies programs in European universities (Braidotti et al., 1995). It included national reports from a range of countries in western Europe, including Austria, Belgium, Denmark, Finland, France, Germany, Greece, Ireland, Italy, the Netherlands, Norway, Portugal, Spain, Sweden, and the United Kingdom. The report indicated that women's studies had developed throughout almost all academic disciplines, while challenging the male domination of these disciplines. In particular, the report found that the development of women's studies had provided methodological and theoretical tools for the study of power relations that influence and determine women's access to social, political, economic, intellectual, and cultural life.

Although the report noted the uneven development of women's studies in Europe, it was well enough developed to give a Europe-wide brief to evaluate and promote European women's studies. The report also noted the need for increased funding and institutional interest, called for stronger European coordination and sharing of information about European women's studies research and teaching. The report concluded:

> In the light of the role it has played and can continue to play in issues related to European integration, it is recommended that Women's Studies be identified at the European, national and institutional levels as an important vehicle for (a) the promotion of European policies in the area of equal opportunities in higher education; (b) the promotion of gender equality in European social policy and in areas of training related to this; and (c) the promotion of a European cultural and multi-cultural dimension in teaching and research. (Braidotti et al., 1995)

NOISE (Network of Interdisciplinary Women's Studies in Europe) is a program for women's studies student exchanges in Europe and is managed by the Centre for Women's Studies, Utrecht. It is part of the European Union's Erasmus scheme to facilitate cooperation in higher education between its member states. There are a range of anticipating universities in western Europe, including Antwerp, Bologne, Dublin, Madrid, Paris, and York.

Following the conception of an idea by GRIF (Groupe de Recherches et d'Informations Feministes), the Commission of the European Communities initiated a new European women's studies database—GRACE. It has been supported since its inception in 1991 by the Equal Opportunities Unit of the European Commission. GRACE has become an important database for work on women's stud-

ies in western Europe, containing references for more than 2,000 researchers from all over the European Union, as well as data about 250 women's studies courses. It aims to advance and spread feminist studies and research toward engagement with social, economic, and political change in Europe. One of the ways it does this is through the promotion of research and teaching about women's inequality in European countries, coupled with a concern for an improvement of the state of knowledge about the situation of women in Europe.

Women's Studies in Western Europe in the Twenty-First Century

Women's studies in western Europe has a long, interesting, and powerful history. What, though, is its present and its future? Feminist research is active in most of the countries in western Europe, and all countries in western Europe have some form of women's studies in the academy, although the form and extent are highly variable. The Women's Studies EuroMap <http://hgins.uia.ac.be/women/>, which offers information about European women's studies and research programs, shows a very healthy list of activities, organizations, and centers in western Europe, both for academic women's studies and for feminist activism (including feminist research activities). Nevertheless, many involved in women's studies programs are concerned about the lack of institutional support and lack of funding, and some programs face closure. Women's studies continues to be tied in part to the economic, social, cultural, and political climate of its country of origin and to the institutional and educational structures of those countries. It has been suggested that for the survival and consolidation of women's studies in the twenty-first century, it needs increasingly to explore its profile in different directions (Delhez et al., 1998). Although its current position in the academy might be tenuous or insecure, at least in some countries, there are several ways in which women's studies has transcended the borders and boundaries around it and has found ways to continue to develop in a wider western European (as well as international) context.

See Also

EDUCATION: HIGHER EDUCATION; FEMINISM: SECOND-WAVE BRITISH; FEMINISM: SECOND-WAVE EUROPEAN; HOUSEHOLDS AND FAMILIES: WESTERN EUROPE; POLITICS AND THE STATE: WESTERN EUROPE; WOMEN'S STUDIES: OVERVIEW; WOMEN'S STUDIES: RESEARCH CENTERS AND INSTITUTES

References and Further Reading

Bird, Elizabeth. 1996. Women's studies in european higher education. *European Journal of Women's Studies* 3(3): 151–165.

Braidotti, Rosi. 1996. Women's studies curricula in European universities. *European Journal of Women's Studies* 3(4): 173–176.
———, Ellen de Dreu, and Christine Rammrath. 1995. *Final report of the evaluation of women's studies in Europe for the SIGMA network and Directorate General DGXXII of the Commission of the European Union.*

Brouns, Margo. 1992. The Dutch development: Women's studies in the Netherlands. *Women's Studies Quarterly: Women's Studies in Europe* 20(3–4): 44–57.

Byrne, Anne. 1992. Academic women's studies in the Republic of Ireland. *Women's Studies Quarterly: Women's Studies in Europe* 20(3–6): 15–27.

Delhez, Evelien, Rosi Braidotti, and Christine Rammrath. 1998. *Institutionalisation of gender studies/women's studies in Europe.* Berne: Swiss Science Council.

Duchen, Claire, ed. 1987. *French connection: Voices from the women's movement in France.* London: Routledge.

Ezekiel, Judith. 1992. Radical in theory: Organised women's studies in France, the women's movement, and the state. *Women's Studies Quarterly: Women's Studies in Europe* 20(3–4): 75–84.

Gerhard, Ute. 1992. German women's studies and the women's movement: A portrait of themes. *Women's Studies Quarterly: Women's Studies in Europe* 20(3–4): 98–111.

Jackson, Sue. 2000. Networking women: A history of ideas, issues and developments in women's studies in Britain. *Women's Studies International Forum* 23(1): 1–11.

Zmroczek, Christine, and Claire Duchen. 1991. What *are* those women up to? Women's studies and feminist research in the European Community. In Jane Aaron and Sylvia Walby, eds., *Out of the margins: Women's studies in the nineties,* 11–29. London: Falmer.

Sue Jackson

WOMEN-CHURCH

Women-church is one expression of feminist spirituality, a global, ecumenical movement of feminist base communities that gather in sacrament and solidarity to live their religious faith in egalitarian, democratic styles. Women-church is not a new denomination, sect, or organization. Rather, it is a way in which women from biblical traditions live out feminist spirituality while transforming patriarchal religions. It has many different expressions around the world, summarized here.

The term *women-church* originated in U.S. Roman Catholic circles among feminists scandalized by hierarchical oppression, especially the exclusion of women from priestly ordination. The feminist biblical scholar Elisabeth Schüssler Fiorenza coined the term *ekklesia gynaikon* in 1983; Diann L. Neu translated it into English as *women-church*. The original term was *woman church,* a usage that was replaced in the United States by the plural and hyphenated form by 1987 when the "Women-Church: Claiming Our Power" conference was held in Cincinnati, Ohio. The linguistic change reflects a rejection of the essentialist notion that any one "woman" could be construed as representative of all women. It signals a feminist, not feminine, approach to religion.

Scope

Comprehensive data do not exist on its size or scope, but publications and reports make clear that women-church is increasingly ecumenical and international. Active women-church groups are found in Canada and the United States; various European countries, especially Germany, Switzerland, and the Netherlands; Australia, New Zealand, and the Philippines; and Chile, Argentina, and Brazil. Most groups have small meetings in homes and focus primarily on liturgy and ritual, social change, and community building.

In some countries—Switzerland, for example—there are coalitions of groups that sponsor national gatherings, educational programs, and publications. The Women-Church Convergence is a coalition of groups in the United States that meets twice a year for education, strategizing, and conferences. In other settings—for example, Argentina—the term *women-church (mujer iglesia)* is rejected because of its ecclesial connotation, but groups function in a similar manner and consider themselves part of the movement.

Women-church is mistakenly understood as a church for women only. In fact, women-church means an inclusive community in which feminist women, men, and children join together in what Dr. Schüssler Fiorenza calls "emancipatory communities," which strive to live as a "discipleship of equals." In women-church, in contrast to patriarchal churches, women as well as men are part of democratic processes of decision making and leadership. The theologian Rosemary Radford Ruether offers a vision of women-church as a "feminist exodus community" from patriarchy, taking the Eucharist and feminist forms of ministry into a promised land of equality.

The theology of women-church is drawn from feminist revisions of Jewish and Christian sources, as well as from Goddess, Wicca, and other religious traditions. Membership is equally eclectic. Some members belong simultaneously to women-church and a traditional denomination, while others have left institutional churches and simply enjoy women-church groups.

Worship in women-church groups takes on a variety of forms: naming celebrations for children; life-cycle rituals for women, including first menstruation and menopause; political actions such as demonstrations and protests; celebrations of the seasons such as harvest and the solstice; and feminist reconstructions of the traditional liturgical forms such as the seder and Easter vigil, among others.

A Movement Both Political and Spiritual

Women-church is a political as much as a spiritual movement. It undertakes the transformation of patriarchal religious institutions as part of a larger political project. Women-church regards patriarchy as made up of interlocking forms of oppression in which children; women; the earth; animals; persons from racial-ethnic minority groups; lesbian, gay, bisexual, and transgendered people; and those who are poor are subordinated and abused. Patriarchal religions therefore contribute the ideology for many forms of discrimination—notably, notions about hierarchy and inferiority that are used to ground social structures. Structural changes will not be accomplished without changes in the fundamental images, symbols, and beliefs that undergird patriarchy. Thus, women-church groups provide spiritual "safe places" and function as base communities that engage in systemic social change.

Women-church is distinct from "women and church" or "women in church" efforts insofar as it signals an agenda set by those who have been marginalized, not by those who have discriminated. "Women-church" means a desire to "be church" on women's terms rather than simply changing hierarchical churches on patriarchal terms, placing the priority on women's human right to spiritual integrity. There is a great deal of cooperation between women-church and women in institutional churches, these differences notwithstanding. Backlash against the women-church movement by hierarchial church officials is predictable given that many groups celebrate the Eucharist without an ordained priest or minister presiding.

The women-church movement in its first decade and a half has comprised predominantly women who are faced with the strongest opposition in their churches. For example, in many groups, women from the Roman Catholic tradition predominate, claiming that for them it is women-church or no church. For women who can be ordained or participate in decision making as lay members of their denominations, being part of the women-church movement is a way to avoid being co-opted by their institutions as they pursue their feminist faith.

Next steps for the movement include intensified global networking so that groups can share resources and learn from one another. Religious education of children having their formative religious experience in women-church needs to be developed. The role and participation of feminist men in the women-church movement is another concern. All of these projects signal the continued growth of the movement.

See Also

CHRISTIANITY: FEMINIST CHRISTOLOGY; CHRISTIANITY: STATUS OF WOMEN IN THE CHURCH; SPIRITUALITY: OVERVIEW

References and Further Reading

Neu, Diann L., and Mary E. Hunt. 1993. *Women-church sourcebook.* Silver Spring, Md.: WATERworks.

Ruether, Rosemary Radford. 1986. *Women-church: Theology and practice.* San Francisco: Harper and Row.

Schüssler Fiorenza, Elisabeth. 1992. *But she said: Feminist practices of biblical interpretation.* Boston: Beacon.

———. 1993. *Discipleship of equals: A critical feminist ekklesialogy of liberation.* New York: Crossroad.

Troch, Lieve. 1989. The feminist movement in and on the edge of the churches in the Netherlands. *Journal of Feminist Studies in Religion* 5(2): 113–128.

Mary Elizabeth Hunt

WOMEN: Terms for Women

The connotations and denotations of words designating women show that in the process of acquiring language, girls also acquire derogatory images of and metaphors for themselves. The language they learn disparages the women they strive to become.

Words used to name or describe a concept reveal much about a society's attitudes, prejudices, and fears regarding that concept. A rich stock of terminology designating various kinds of snow, for example, is relevant, and perhaps even necessary, to the management of everyday life in Nordic cultures. A choice between negative and positive terms for a person (as, for example, the choice between *terrorist* and *freedom fighter*) reveals the presence or absence of prejudicial feelings toward that person. And taboos disclose underlying fears cloaked in the disguise of euphemisms (*passed away*) and dysphemisms (*croaked*). Thus, an analysis of the vocabulary of a language can reveal much about the people who created the language.

If, as is generally assumed, men are the primary creators of the language in societies where they are dominant, then terms used by that society to name and define women provide evidence of male obsessions, prejudices, and fears about females. Obsession is evident in the wealth of vocabulary for women in many languages. Although Chinese, for example, provides just a single set of kinship terms for males, it has two sets for females: one identifies married and the other, unmarried women. Hong-Fincher (1995) has shown that the extra set—those designating spinsters—has usually acquired negative connotations in Chinese. That trend of language—a surplus of terminology for women and a tendency for those terms to acquire negative connotations—is found in other languages as well. Rolv Blakar (1975) found the same plurality of synonyms in Norwegian for *kvinne* ("woman") and a similar striking abundance of negativity associated with them, versus the neutrality adhering to the smaller set of terms denoting *mann* ("man").

In English one finds a much richer taxonomy of endearments (*honey, tootsie, cutie pie*) and descriptive terms (*tomato, broad*) for women than for men. In addition, in a study of the historical evolution of such terminology Muriel Schulz (1975) demonstrated that words that began as neutral, or even positive, designators for females usually have gradually acquired negative implications, at first only slightly disparaging, but after a period of time strongly abusive and including a sexual slur in their allusions (*tart, nymph*). It is as though the concept *female* contaminates any word designating females. The phenomenon—common in other languages as well—is stunningly illustrated in Chinese: 90 percent of the words that are written using a female radical in the Chinese script either develop negative connotations or connote highly negative stereotypes of women (Ng and Burridge, 1993).

Masako Hiraga (1991) also finds a sexual derogation in terms designating women in Japanese. The same word—*yogoreta*—means simply "dirty" when used to describe a man; for a woman, it signifies "sexually loose." And in Spanish, Iris Gonzalez (1985) points out that *un rea* is a criminal; *una rea* is an impoverished prostitute; *honesto* is used for a man who is "sincere, honest"; *honesta* is used for "a woman who does not have illicit sexual relations"; and *un patrono* is "an employer, a protector"; *una matrona* is a euphemistic cover term for "a madam."

In England, titles have undergone a similar semantic change. Where parallel titles for men and women exist, the latter have been degraded in a way not paralleled by those for men. *Lord, baronet,* and *governor* are still used for people entitled by tradition to a degree of special respect. *Lady* is no longer always an honorific (in fact, it was for a period derogatory); today it can name any woman. *Dame* has a lower status in common usage than *lady* or *woman*; and *gov-*

erness is used only for nursemaids and baby-sitters, much diminished in stature from when Queen Elizabeth I was acknowledged to be "the supreme majesty and governess of all persons." *Sir* and *master* seem to have remained as titles of courtesy without taint; however, both *madam* and *mistress* have pejorated, becoming euphemisms for respectively "a mistress of a brothel" and "a woman with whom a man habitually fornicates."

The latter titles illustrate the most frequent course followed in English by pejorated terms designating women. They cease to designate respectable women, then acquire sexual connotations, and finally serve as cover terms for prostitutes and mistresses. "Pejoration," a semantic process whereby a neutral word acquires negative connotations over a period of time, occurs when a word names a concept about which society is uncomfortable.

Words identifying women have repeatedly suffered the indignity of degeneration, many of them becoming sexually abusive. One generally looks in vain for the operation of a similar pejoration of terms referring to men. Languages do have many derogatory labels for men (such as *scoundrel, rascal, bounder,* in English, for example), but these are words that began as negative epithets. The dismaying downward spiral of terms for women finds no counterpart in words denoting males. As they acquire language, boys are presented with male models setting out which behaviors are approved and which are stigmatized; girls throughout the world, on the other hand, learn that the female role itself is stigmatized sufficiently so that any term used to describe it is subject to semantic pejoration.

See Also

LANGUAGE; LINGUISTICS; MISOGYNY; NAMING; SEXISM

Reference and Further Reading

Abd-el-Jawad. 1989. Language and women's place with special reference to Arabic. *Language Sciences* 11(3): 305–324.

Blakar, Rolv. 1975. How sex roles are represented, reflected, and conserved in Norwegian. *Acta Sociologica* 18(2–3): 162–173.

Gonzalez, Iris. 1985. Some aspects of linguistic sexism in Spanish. In Marlis Hellinger, ed., *Sprachwandel und feministische Sprachpolitik: Internationale Perspektiven*, 48–63. Opladen: Westdeutscher Verlag.

Hiraga, Masako K. 1991. Metaphors Japanese women live by. *Working Papers on Language, Gender, and Sexism* 1(1): 38–57.

Hong-Fincher, B. 1995. Indications of the changing status of women in modern standard Chinese terms of address. In D. Laycock and W. Winter, eds., *A word of language: Papers presented to Professor S. A. Wurm on his 65th birthday,* 269–270. Canberra: ANV.

Ng, Bee-Chin, and Kate Burridge. 1993. The female radical: Portrayal of women in the Chinese script. *Australian Review of Applied Linguistics* (supplement 10): 54–85.

Schulz, Muriel. 1975. The semantic derogation of woman. In Barrie Thorne and Nancy Henley, eds., *Language and sex: Difference and dominance,* 64–75. Rowley, Mass.: Newbury House.

Muriel Schulz

WORK: Equal Opportunities

See EQUAL OPPORTUNITIES.

WORK: Equal Pay and Conditions

Over the last three decades of the twentieth century, throughout the world, there has been a dramatic increase in women's participation in the formal economy (United Nations Development Program, 1998). But, despite this change, labor forces everywhere remain segregated by sex, with women concentrated in the least attractive work. Although there are overlaps and variations, every country has women's work and men's work, women's pay and men's pay, women's conditions and men's conditions.

In the Republic of Korea, for example, women are paid 47 percent of the male wage; in Japan, 51 percent; in Canada, 70 percent. The size of the gap varies from country to country and over time, but the gap remains. Similarly, among countries of the European Union (EU), there are variations in the proportion of women employed in education and general public service activities. However, in most of the EU countries, more than 50 percent of those employed in textiles and the distributive trades are women, and so are nearly 50 percent of those in banking and insurance (Statistical Office of the European Communities, 1992: 84–85). In fact, there has been little change in the proportion of women employed in top jobs in major industrial nations since the 1980s (OECD, 1998).

Differences between Women and Men at Work

Women's relations in their labor force jobs are also different from those of men. Women are less likely than men to have control over their work, to direct the work of others, or to have opportunities for promotion. Women are also much more likely than men to have part-time or temporary employment. But in every country women have developed strategies to change the kinds of jobs they hold, the kinds of pay they receive, and the kinds of conditions and relations they face.

Using Laws to Improve Work Conditions

Many women have looked to the law as a way of improving their work. Labor law has seldom been on the side of women. Indeed, it has often served to reinforce women's segregation into the least attractive jobs and to justify their low pay or lack of promotion when they do gain access to traditional male work. Yet because labor legislation has a significant impact on the conditions and relations of work, women have often looked to the law to provide both protection and improvements in their paid jobs. But women have not relied on the law alone. They have joined or organized unions to demand decent work and working conditions. In general, unionized women fare much better than women without union protection. However, unions too have not always been on the side of women. Women have had to struggle both within and outside unions to assert their claims (Peters and Wolper, 1995; Rowbotham and Mitter, 1994). While women have worked individually and collectively in a wide variety of ways to change their paid jobs, legislation and collective agreements have produced the most visible results. For this reason, they constitute the main subjects here.

Law reflects particular national power relations and conditions. In most countries, however, women are significantly underrepresented in governments, in courtrooms, and in other places where many of the decisions about the law are made. This politics is involved not only in the development of legislation but also in its interpretation and implementation. Because law both reflects and becomes part of a political process, it often has implications far beyond, or contrary to, the designers' intent. And it usually has a differential impact related to sex, class, race, location, and age. Moreover, the impact of labor legislation is not necessarily limited to particular workplace practices. It can have a much more pervasive impact on ideas about what is legitimate in relations at work. In assessing any legislation, then, it is important to understand the historical context in which it was developed. But it is also important to understand the short- and long-term consequences for both practices and ideas and for different kinds of women.

Obviously, legislation will vary from country to country, and any kind of systematic survey is well beyond the scope of this article. But there are significant commonalities among labor laws related to women—commonalities that reflect women's subordination and segregation throughout the world (Kerr, 1993). This article focuses on the patterns in legislation that, despite local variations in content and impact, are found wherever women work for pay.

For women working for change, there is always a tension between stressing their similarities with men and stressing their differences from men. An emphasis on difference can lay the basis for discriminatory practices. On the other hand, an emphasis on similarities can mean ignoring differences that must be acknowledged in order to ensure equity (Bacchi, 1990). This tension is evident in what are here classified as four major kinds of labor legislation that affect women's paid work.

Household Law

One of the oldest forms of labor legislation that has a direct impact on women could be called household law, because it is based on assumptions about women's household relations and domestic labor. Country after country has had legislation that required women to leave the labor force when they married or became pregnant, assuming that these women had a man to support them and work responsibilities at home. Lower minimum wages for women have been justified on the grounds that either women support only themselves or they have a husband who pays most bills. Employment was seen primarily as a brief interlude before marriage.

In Australia, for example, the Harvester Arbitration decision early in the twentieth century provided for a "family wage," defined as the minimum necessary for a man to support his wife and family. Such legislation legitimated both lower wages for women and women's economic dependency. Although the unions then officially supported equal pay for women and men, they strongly opposed women's lower wages only when women were competing directly with men.

Not all women opposed this kind of legislation. Women living with an employed man who supported them economically, women who had no good employment opportunities, and women who had heavy domestic responsibilities benefited from such laws, at least in the short term. But the many women who had no such support were sentenced to wages sometimes as low as half those of men. In the long term, all women suffered from the unequal pay and employment opportunities. Indeed, as more women enter the labor market and fight for change, household labor laws have become increasingly difficult to maintain, at least in their earlier form.

Protective Legislation

Protective legislation constitutes a second category of labor law that is aimed particularly at women. Such legislation is most commonly based on assumptions about women's specific health and safety needs and about women's capacity to

protect themselves (Messing, 1998). In many cases, these restrictions were based on concern about the consequences for the fetus or the potential fetus, although they also reflected a recognition of women's greater vulnerability to harassment and attack. Some women's groups have cooperated with unions in demanding legislation that "protected" women from working in certain industries or underground, from working certain hours and shifts, or from working in jobs with requirements that were considered beyond women's strength or ability. Over the years, the International Labor Organization has adopted a series of conventions calling for restrictions on women's work, and so have many countries.

In the late nineteenth century, for example, ironmongers in the United States successfully argued that women must be excluded from foundries because such work could threaten their future as wives and mothers. The United States has now abandoned most similar legislation, but a century after the American ironmongers' efforts, Japanese unions were calling for mandatory menstrual leave and stronger prohibitions against women working at night. The current Convention 1 of the League of Arab States prohibits the employment of women in mines and hazardous jobs or in night work.

Much of this work was indeed dangerous for women, and many women have benefited from the protection. Much of it was also harmful to the fetus. But the restrictions on women too often have allowed employers to avoid introducing the kinds of changes that would make jobs safer for all workers or that would allow all workers to participate in domestic work. Yet anything that can harm a fetus can also harm an adult of either sex, although the consequences may be less immediate and visible (Stellman, 1977). Moreover, protective legislation aimed at women frequently serves to protect men's jobs from women by excluding women. This exclusion is particularly problematic for women without formal credentials or alternative economic support, because they are often denied access to the highest paid of the blue-collar jobs. In the long term, protective legislation has reinforced occupational segregation and saved some high-paying jobs for men.

There is no way around protective legislation for maternity leave, however. Only women have babies. Women need special laws to guarantee that their jobs will be there if they leave to have children and that leaving to have children will not jeopardize their pay, benefits, seniority, or chances for promotion. Most western countries provide some form of maternity legislation. Many also provide child care leave for women, although such protection has not necessarily ensured that women will not suffer for their interrupted work. Led by Swedish legislation introduced in 1974, an increasing number of countries have paternity leave, allowing men to participate in child care without fear of losing their paid jobs. Only a minority of men have taken such leave, but the more men participate, the less likely maternity will be grounds for discrimination against women.

Antidiscrimination Law

While both household law and protective legislation are based on women's assumed differences from men, antidiscrimination legislation is based on women's assumed similarities with men. While the former prevents women from doing certain kinds of work, the latter is designed to ensure that the same criteria apply to women and men. Antidiscrimination legislation makes it illegal to discriminate on the basis of sex in such areas as pay, working conditions, hiring, promotion, benefits, and training. Many countries in both the developed "North" and the developing "South" have antidiscrimination legislation, although there are significant differences in the areas covered, the exclusions allowed, the means of enforcement, and the penalties for contravening the law.

The Directives for the European Union, for instance, set out the principle of equal pay and of equal treatment for women and men in terms of access to jobs, promotion, vocational training, working conditions, and occupational social security systems (European Commission, 1999). The directives also require that member states take all necessary steps to ensure that these principles are put into practice. Although member states are free to develop their own legislation and strategies, the European Court of Justice can determine whether individual members have fulfilled their obligations. In 1982, the court ruled that a worker in the United Kingdom was denied these rights because "equal pay for work of equal value" applied only in workplaces where a job evaluation scheme had been developed with the consent of the employer. As a result, the United Kingdom introduced new legislation that allowed equal pay claims even where no job evaluation or classification study was in place.

Equal treatment practices can lead to significant gains for women. Australia provides a case in point. When equal pay was formally introduced in 1969 and the family wage policy abandoned, the national awards system meant that women's wages grew considerably. The gap between male and female wages that remains can be attributed primarily to occupational segregation. And here is where much of the problem with antidiscrimination legislation can be found.

Because many women do jobs that are different in kind and location from those of men, because women have different family responsibilities from men, and because many women have less power than many men, equal treatment legislation may do little to improve women's conditions of work. In the case of pay, for instance, "equal pay for equal work" legislation makes it illegal to discriminate against women by paying them less money to do the same jobs as those done by men. But such legislation allows employers to pay higher wages to many males, given that women and men for the most part hold different jobs. Moreover, employers can avoid such legislation by simply requiring different duties from their male and female employees. In many western countries, groups of women addressed these problems by demanding equal pay for work of equal value or comparable worth rather than for equal work. In other words, the legislation should recognize that women and men do different jobs, but these different jobs may be equally valuable to the organization.

In the U.S. state of Oregon, for example, the comparable worth initiatives set out to compare female and male jobs in terms of the skill, effort, responsibility, and conditions involved in the work. The aim was to ensure that female-dominated jobs that were evaluated as comparable to male-dominated jobs in terms of overall worth to the organization should be paid the higher male wage (Acker, 1989). However, the women working with the legislation found that the schemes used to record and value women's work favored men's jobs both because they were developed on the basis of men's work and because they were designed to reflect existing unequal wage rates. Learning from this experience, women's groups in the Canadian province of Ontario insisted that their legislation require job evaluation that is free of gender bias. With this legislation as a background, various unions were about to argue that existing job evaluation schemes were biased against women and must be replaced by methods that recognize and value the too often invisible skills, effort, responsibilities, and working conditions that are specific to women's work. In this case, antidiscrimination legislation means recognizing differences, not just treating women in the same way as men.

Similarly, workers' compensation regulations that allow claims mainly for accidents that cause visible physical injury primarily benefit those in male-dominated jobs such as construction, mining, and forestry. They often leave out the many women who develop eye and nerve problems from long hours of doing detailed work making computer chips and jewelry, who develop varicose veins from standing at the cash register and the assembly line, or who develop repetitive strain injury from typing on keyboards or from folding linen. Instead, women's work-related illnesses are often dismissed as products of their biology rather than as products of their labor. For example, when women break down in tears at their computer, the problem is often attributed to menstruation or menopause, not to the stress of the work. Likewise, women's breast cancer is assumed to be genetic, not the results of work conditions (Zahm et al., 1993).

Problems arise not only from those jobs covered by universal legislation but also from those jobs not covered by universal legislation. In Italy, for example, the law limiting layoffs does not apply to small firms, and unions do not exist in small firms. Given that women make up the majority of those working in small firms, it is women who are the least protected by what appears as a universal law free of discrimination. In Germany, part-time workers are eligible for fewer benefits than full-time employees, and women account for the majority of part-time workers. In Canada, much of the labor standards legislation specifically excludes domestic workers. Most of such workers are women.

Even in those areas where the equal application of the law would benefit women, antidiscrimination legislation may be ineffective or unequally applied. In African countries, for example, laws require equal pay and equal working conditions for all women. However, an employed women's survivors have no right to benefits after her death, and she cannot receive family allowances, even though she makes the same contributions to these schemes as her male counterparts (Diagne, 1993: 48). Similarly, even though it is against Mexican federal labor laws, it is common for employers to have women examined before they are hired to determine whether they are pregnant (Tirado, 1994: 105).

In addition, antidiscrimination laws are useful to women only if they are consistently enforced. Most countries rely on complaints to reveal and resolve problems of discrimination. But the complaint-based procedure often means that only the most secure unionized workers can take the risk of charging an employer with discrimination or can afford the time and expense of proceedings. As a result, many employers can simply ignore the law.

Affirmative Action Legislation

One response to these problems is what has been called proactive or affirmative action legislation; that is, laws that require employers to initiate programs that assist women. Such legislation is based on the assumption that employers will resist equality measures primarily because they benefit from women's subordination. Here, the focus shifts from an emphasis on equal opportunity and equal treatment to a stress on treating women differently so that they can achieve equality in results. Proactive legislation recognizes that women are not equally able to become equal or to ensure that equity legislation is put in practice (Abella, 1984). For

instance, Labor Law 91, introduced in Egypt in 1954, made special provisions for married women and mothers that helped them retain their labor force jobs. In the United States, some states have introduced legislation requiring particular kinds of employers to provide information on recruitment, hiring, and promotion procedures, indicating what steps they are taking to ensure equal results for women and men. In Canada, some provinces have introduced pay equity legislation that requires employers to develop and post pay equity plans based on the principle of equal value. In the German Democratic Republic, the state provided good maternity leave, benefits, and subsidies for child care and children's clothes as a means of keeping young mothers in the labor force (Rai, Pilkington, and Phizacklea, 1992).

Although legislation, especially in its proactive form, has helped many women improve their conditions and relations of work, the law is not sufficient in itself. Indeed, unions have often been much more effective than legislation both in establishing and in enforcing women's rights. Throughout the world, women in unionized jobs have better pay than women doing the same work without the benefit of a collective agreement, whatever the existing equal pay legislation. Unions frequently mean women have the right to say no to dangerous work conditions, to sexual advances, and to unreasonable work requests. Unionized women are often the only ones eligible for paid maternity leave or pensions and the only ones with workplace child care. Unions can also help women come together to discuss the issues that are specific to women's work. They provide women with experience in organizing that is extremely useful outside the workplace as well. Moreover, unions have been central in bringing about changes in social programs or legislation that are directly beneficial to women and that allow them to participate more equally in the labor force. Unions in Sweden, for example, were important in developing a law that pledges "that all children whose parents worked or studied would be assigned an opening in the public child care system from the age of 18 months until they began regular school" (Swedish Institute, 1993: 14). The combination of unions and the women's movement can be particularly effective in these terms. In Korea, a sit-in by female employees in a textile company triggered a national demonstration that contributed to the end of a dictatorship (Women Working Worldwide, 1991: 24).

However, unions have not always served women well. Some unions have fought to prevent women from being hired or have refused to protect women employed part-time. Others have refused to have women's committees or to make women's issues a concern of their organization. Many are dominated by men who simply do not understand the issues women are raising and thus fail to fight hard for women's demands. Some unions have become so closely connected to the employer that they cannot defend women's rights. Women have responded by fighting within unions for their concerns, by organizing their own unions, and by seeking other means of defending their collective interests. In Hong Kong, for instance, many women in the Philips electrical plant felt that unions focused too much on political differences, and they organized a Women Workers' Club to defend their interests.

In addition, many women have no union protection. The high turnover in areas where women work, the large proportion of part-time employees, managerial strategies designed to prevent unionization, and state regulations about organizing, combined with practices and policies that make it difficult for women to do both their domestic work and their union work, have all contributed to women's lower rate of unionization. In whole sectors of economies, women face employers alone. For example, none of the women electronics workers employed in the U.S. "Silicon Valley" are unionized, and thus they have no organized means of defending their interests.

Employers' strategies in the new global economy constitute a further threat both to unions organizing for women and to legislative protection for women. While many companies have long demanded not only union- and regulation-free workplaces but also a downgrading or worsening of women's condition before investing in Free Trade Zones, this situation increasingly prevails in other areas and other countries as well. In an attempt to attract investment, many states are giving in to these demands.

Furthermore, the restructuring of economies both within and among countries is making it difficult to organize unions or even retain members under old rules. More and more firms are contracting out to small firms whose size both makes them difficult to unionize and often puts them outside legislative restrictions applied only to larger employers. Sectoral bargaining becomes difficult, and such bargaining accounts for women's greatest gains. Women in the former Soviet Union are particularly at risk as old protections disappear. At the same time, restructuring includes a dramatic increase in the number of part-time and temporary jobs. Existing legislation frequently makes it difficult to unionize these workers, and such workers are often excluded from legal restrictions as well. In any case, it is much harder to enforce legislation or to organize when there are an enormous number of small firms and organizations appearing and disappearing. Similarly, what is in some countries called homework and in others outwork is growing rapidly, and it is very difficult to protect those who work for pay in their own homes. The overwhelming majority of part-time and temporary workers, homeworkers, and those employed in small firms in most countries are women.

In sum, most improvements in women's work have resulted from women's successful struggles for legislative change and collective agreements that serve their interests. However, many of the gains made through these means are now under threat owing to global restructuring practices.

See Also

ANTIDISCRIMINATION; DIVISION OF LABOR; ECONOMY: OVERVIEW; EQUALITY; FAMILY WAGE; INDUSTRIALIZATION; UNDEREMPLOYMENT; UNION MOVEMENTS

References and Further Reading

Abella, Rosalie. 1984. *Equality in employment: A Royal Commission report.* Ottawa: Minister of Supply and Services Canada.

Acker, Joan. 1989. *Doing comparable worth: Gender, class and pay equity.* Philadelphia: Temple University Press.

Bacchi, Carol. 1990. *Same difference.* Sydney: Allen and Unwin.

Diagne, Seny. 1993. Defending women's rights—The facts and challenges in francophone Africa. In Joanna Kerr, ed., *Ours by right: Women's rights as human rights:* London: Zed.

European Commission, 1999. Forum Special, *Five years of social policy.* Brussels: European Communities.

Kerr, Joanna, ed. 1993. *Ours by right: Women's rights as human rights.* London: Zed.

Messing, Karen. 1998. *One-eyed science: Occupational health and women workers.* Philadelphia: Temple University Press.

OECD. 1998. *The future of female-dominated occupations.* Paris: OECD.

Peters, Julie, and Andrea Wolper, eds. 1995. *Women's rights, human rights.* New York: Routledge.

Rai, Shirin, Hilary Pilkington, and Annie Phizacklea, eds., 1992. *Women in the face of change: The Soviet Union, eastern Europe and China.* London: Routledge.

Rowbotham, Sheila, and Swasti Mitter, eds. 1994. *Dignity and daily bread.* London: Routledge.

Statistical Office of the European Communities. 1992. *Women in the European Community.* Luxembourg: Office of the Official Publications of the European Communities.

Stellman, Jeanne. 1977. *Women's work, women's health.* New York: Pantheon.

Swedish Institute. 1993. *Equal worth: the status of men and women in Sweden.* Stockholm: Swedish Institute.

Tirado, Silvia. 1994. Weaving dreams, constructing realities: The Nineteenth of September National Union of Garment Workers in Mexico. In Sheila Rowbotham and Swasti Mitter, eds., *Dignity and daily bread.* London: Routledge.

United Nations Development Program. 1998. *Human development report.* New York: Oxford University Press.

Women Working Worldwide, eds. 1991. *Common interests: Women organizing in global electronics.* London: Women Working Worldwide.

Zahm, S. H., et al. 1993. Inclusion of women and minorities in occupational cancer epidemiological research. *Proceedings of the International Conference on Women's Health: Occupation and Cancer.* Panel 4.

Pat Armstrong

WORK: Feminist Theories

Western feminist theories about work have focused on the way paid and unpaid work has been divided between women and men, why these patterns persist, and their implications for women. In the late nineteenth century theorists argued for women's access to paid work outside the home and anticipated that gender equality would follow from women's involvement in "public production." Contemporary feminists have looked more skeptically at paid work as a strategy for emancipation and identified how inequalities between women and men are perpetuated in the labor market. Feminist theorists have also challenged definitions of "work" that exclude unpaid domestic work and voluntary work. The tendency in the last 20 years has been for abstract theorizing to be replaced by careful analysis of particular contexts in which work is gendered. Differences between women as well as differences between women and men have also received more attention. This article traces some of the shifts and changes in feminist theorizing about work and addresses some of the issues that have persisted over the last 100 years.

Private Property, Privatized Labor, and Work outside the Home

In the 1970s many feminist theorists turned their attention to *The Origin of Family, Private Property, and the State,* an analysis of the origins of gender inequality written nearly a century before by Friedrich Engels, close friend and political associate of Karl Marx (Engels, 1884, 1972). Engels argued that the first division of labor was the division of labor between women and men. Male domination, however, emerged only when men as individuals and family members began to assume private control of productive resources like land and animals. As property became privatized, women were confined to work in privatized households, their sexuality controlled by men who wanted to ensure that only their biological offspring would inherit their property. "Father right" (descent through the male line) replaced "mother right" (female descent) and "conjugal fidelity" was demanded of women to ensure that they produced children of "undisputed paternity." Engels referred to this shift from "mother right" to "father right" as "the world-historical defeat of the female sex."

Engels tended to overemphasize the extent to which women's work in preindustrial societies involved attention to food preparation and child care and paid little attention to the ways in which human communities depended on women's gathering, horticultural labor, and care for domesticated animals (Moore, 1988: 43–72). He assumed that women were dependent on men's labor and considered that men's control of herds and land was an outcome of their involvement in hunting, herding, and cultivation. Since the development of private property was the source of women's oppression, women's liberation, according to Engels, required the overthrow of capitalist relations of production. This overthrow would precipitate women's incorporation into "public industry"—work that was oriented toward the production of goods and services for large numbers of people rather than individual households.

The U.S. feminist writer and public speaker Charlotte Perkins Gilman shared Engels's enthusiasm for the absorption of women into work outside the home, but she paid more attention to the specifics of how this might be achieved. (One of her suggestions was the construction of "kitchenless" apartments with communal eating facilities.) Gilman argued that human development depended on the intensification of the division of labor. If human progress depended on specialization, the expectation that all women would do unpaid domestic work was inconsistent with the direction of human social evolution. Child care, cooking, and cleaning should be performed professionally by those who had these skills. Other women, less suited to domestic work and child care, would then be able to pursue a variety of different occupations (1898/1966).

The Sexual Division of Labor

Gilman assumed that, freed from the requirements of domestic work, women would join men as workers in a complex and increasingly specialized market for labor. However, few women with children have experienced the freedom from domestic responsibilities that she envisaged. Women have also continued to be concentrated in a narrow range of occupations, predominantly occupations in which other women are employed.

While some women did move into male-dominated jobs, gender divisions in employment remained remarkably stable during the twentieth century. Many people see women's location in clerical work, sales, teaching, nursing, clothing, and textile manufacture and in domestic and social services as the outcome of women's interests, inclinations, inherent abilities, and personal choices. Feminist theorists, however, have argued that the concentration of women in certain jobs is the outcome of "gender segregation at work"—systematic social processes that have the effect of limiting women's access to certain forms of paid work (Bradley, 1989; Dex, 1985; Walby, 1986) and hence their access to rates of pay associated with jobs in which men predominated.

Western feminist scholars have attempted to analyze the processes in schools, workplaces, and trade unions that make it difficult for women to enter traditionally male spheres of employment. While the term *segregation* is often used to refer to situations where individuals experience direct exclusion because of their personal attributes like skin color, ethnicity, or gender, feminist theorists have used *segregation* to refer to a range of overt and covert practices that have the effect of excluding women from certain occupations or discouraging their advancement in those jobs.

Gender segregation at work has "horizontal" and "vertical" components (Hakim, 1979). Women on average do different jobs from those done by men (horizontal segregation), but they are also more likely to be located in the lower levels of occupational hierarchies (vertical segregation). Women are likely to be concentrated in teaching but less likely to be school principals; they may be most of those who are clerical workers but less likely than men to be office managers. Women are also overrepresented among those in part-time and casual work with few prospects of upward mobility in the organizations that employ them (Beechey and Perkins, 1987).

Dual Labor Market Theory

In the 1970s some feminist theorists attempted to assess the ways in which the dynamics of capitalism contributed to gender differentiation in employment. They argued that capitalist economies needed sets of workers who could be drawn into paid work when needed and discharged in times of recession. Employers had to retain skilled workers, especially if these were in short supply, but other sets of workers could be hired or discharged depending on expansion and contraction in the economy. These lower-paid workers might be immigrants, ethnic minorities, or women—the ideal workers to occupy positions in what some analysts

began to refer to as the dual labor market (Barron and Norris, 1976).

Dual labor markets are characterized by two sectors. The "primary" sector includes jobs with higher pay, training, promotion opportunities, fringe benefits, and continuity of employment. In the "secondary" sector wages are lower, there is little opportunity for upward mobility in the organization, there are no fringe benefits, and job security is meager. The social characteristics of young people, immigrants, women, and ethnic minorities are often used to explain why they are overrepresented among those in low-paid and insecure jobs. Those using dual labor market theory argue that their location in these jobs needs to be explained—in terms not just of the attributes of these workers but also of the dynamics of a capitalist labor market.

Dual labor markets are distinguished by a pronounced division into higher- and lower-paid sectors and little opportunity for movement between sectors (Barron and Norris, 1976: 49). Barron and Norris argued that the properties of jobs tended to become associated with the types of people who filled those positions, so if women were in low-paid casual work with little opportunity for promotion, women in general might be defined as those with no interest in career advancement. They advocated unraveling the different strands of "individual" and "structural" factors that contributed to gender segregation at work.

Women and the Industrial Reserve Army

While some feminist scholars used dual labor market theory to explain certain aspects of women's experiences in paid work, others drew on Marx's analysis of the "industrial reserve army." Marx argued that the production of a reserve army of labor was a consequence of the dynamics of capitalist accumulation. Without such a reserve of unemployed potential workers, wages would rise and the opportunities to produce surplus value would be reduced. Some feminists in the 1970s suggested that married women in particular were overrepresented in this industrial reserve army—drawn on as paid workers in expanding phases of capitalist economies and discarded at times of economic retraction. According to Veronica Beechey, "married women function as a disposable and flexible labor force.... The specificity of the position of women arises from their domestic role in the family and the prevalent assumption that this is their primary role" (1978: 190).

Other feminists drew attention to the way women's access to paid work depended most significantly on expansion and contraction in the industries and occupations in which they were concentrated (Milkman, 1976), rather than their use as a reserve for male-dominated occupations. Irene Bruegel, in her defense of the "reserve army of labor" thesis, argued that women's overrepresentation in part-time and casual work meant that they were often vulnerable to periods of unemployment or were more likely to have to move between firms as small businesses expanded, contracted, or ceased to operate (1986: 50). Women may act as a labor reserve for jobs in which women generally are concentrated, and their use in this way may undermine job security and wages.

Men, Women, and the Preservation of Gendered Work

By the late 1970s explanations that focused on the dynamics of capitalism as the basis of gender segregation at work were under attack. A key contribution to this critique was a paper by Heidi Hartmann (1979) that explored the way some male guilds and unions in the United States had excluded women from entering paid work in the skilled trades. According to Hartmann, while aspects of men's control over women had been disrupted by the development of capitalist relations of production, the labor market had become a new site for male dominance. Men, acting in concert with other men, could control women's labor by excluding them from paid work in particular occupations. Hartmann concluded that "job segregation by sex... is the primary mechanism in capitalist society that maintains the superiority of men over women" (108). Women's exclusion from certain occupations limited their access to paid work and intensified the possibility that they would be dependent on a male breadwinner.

Cynthia Cockburn's analysis (1983) of the British print industry also highlighted the way men had organized with other men to advance their interests as male workers at the expense of women. These forms of exclusion were often at odds with the interests of capitalist employers who might otherwise have employed female printers at lower rates of pay. The dynamics of capitalism could not adequately explain these forms of job segregation.

Ann Game and Rosemary Pringle (1983: 15) also looked critically at attempts to understand women's position in paid work exclusively through an analysis of the dynamics of capitalism. Reversing the standard Marxian approach to gender inequalities, they argued that an understanding of capitalism demanded attention to the gendered features of work. They highlighted the need for analyses of gender segregation that attended not just to women but also to men and masculinity. In their discussion of gendered work in the white goods industry, banking, retailing, computing, nursing, and unpaid housework, Game and Pringle avoided the often static models developed by other theorists and empha-

sized the gendering of work, the existence of contradictions, changes in the labor process, and the agency of different sets of workers.

In the mid-1980s Sylvia Walby argued that strategies used by men to limit women's access to paid work were an example of "patriarchy at work" (1986: 55). Instead of seeing women's position in paid work as an outcome of women's domestic responsibilities, Walby suggested that gender divisions in workplaces and state policy contributed to women's availability for unpaid domestic work. Walby also looked critically at the assumption that capitalist entrepreneurs always benefited from job segregation, arguing instead that "the relations between patriarchy and capital should be seen as historically and spatially variable and riddled with conflict" (89).

Domestic Labor

Just as Marxist and socialist feminist theory dominated attempts to analyze women's position in paid work in the 1970s, so attempts to analyze unpaid work were cast in terms of the relationship between domestic labor and capitalist relations of production. According to Benston (1978), household work was productive work, even though it was unpaid and performed outside capitalist relations of production. The women who did most of this unpaid domestic work were engaged in "pre-capitalist" production of "use values" since their labor was not directly exchanged for money and occurred outside the relations of trade and commodity production. Inequality between women and men in capitalist economies was an outcome of women's involvement in work that had no monetary value in contexts in which money determined value.

Christine Delphy (1984) argued that the relations between men who controlled material resources in households and women who were dependent on them for economic support constituted a distinct mode of production—the "family mode of production." Delphy focused on the material relations between women and men operating small family farms in France. Because their wives supplied much of the labor and men controlled the resources used in that labor, Delphy concluded that the relationship was a "class" relationship, analogous to the relationship between those who sold their labor power and entrepreneurs who controlled the means of production. According to Delphy, the difference between the family mode of production and the wage mode lay not so much in the work that was done but in the relations of production. In the wage relation the amount to be paid and the services to be provided were fixed, while in the family relation both were fluid. On the other hand, it was more difficult for women to change husbands than for wage workers to change employers. For these reasons, according to Delphy, the mode of family production constituted "patriarchal exploitation."

Sylvia Walby (1986: 51–55) drew on Delphy's ideas in her discussion of the "patriarchal mode of production," which consists of a producing class of unpaid "housewives" or "domestic laborers" and a "non-producing" class of husbands. According to Walby, women in this mode of production produced "labor power"—the capacity to work, which was sold to employers in the wage exchanges that characterized the capitalist mode of production.

In the late 1970s, Bettina Cass suggested that a "sex–class" system operated in households in which women were dependent on male partners or husbands for the material resources they needed in order to do their domestic work. Because so many adult women were involved in the "sex–class" system of domestic production, all women occupied a disadvantaged position in the labor market. Women were paid less because they were expected to return to unpaid work at home if they were made redundant.

Voluntary Work

By the early 1980s what was referred to as the "domestic labor debate" (Kaluzynska, 1980) was seen as an intellectual and political dead end. Some feminist analysts were, however, still interested in looking at unpaid work as "work." This included studying voluntary work (unpaid work done for a voluntary agency providing social services) as "work." Cora Baldock's research on "volunteer work" explored the dependence of voluntary agencies on unpaid female volunteers who combined this work with unpaid domestic work. Just as some feminists had explored the ways in which housework sustained the process of capital accumulation, so Baldock argued that "the voluntary sector appears to further the process of accumulation" (1983: 283). Money saved by the state through the use of voluntary agencies and volunteers could be diverted to other purposes that might benefit the expansion of capitalist enterprise.

What Women Are Worth:
The Market Value of Unpaid Work

In the late 1980s Marilyn Waring published *Counting for Nothing: What Men Value and What Women Are Worth*, a sustained case for calculating the economic value of unpaid productive and reproductive work. She argued that this work should be recognized in the national accounts of all members of the United Nations. Chris Beasley (1994) indicated that this strategy of calculating the value of unpaid work left the framework of institutional economics intact. It also

obscured what was specific about this type of work. Beasley advocated the development of a feminist political economy that "begins with women, sex relations and women's private labor" (74). She argued that exploring sexual forms of power might involve taking sexual-emotional relations in households as the starting point for studies of paid work. Her work resonated with the analysis American sociologist Arlie Hochschild (1983) had offered of "emotion work." It was also consistent with arguments that economic models of "work" could not adequately explain the place of sexuality in workplaces in which sexual services were not overtly for sale.

The Sexualization of Paid Work

Attention to the relationship between sexuality and market relations has received increasing attention from feminist theorists. Catharine MacKinnon (1979) analyzed the pressures on women to respond to sexual overtures by men in the workplace, particularly in contexts in which men had the power to hire, fire, or promote women. Jeff Hearn and others (1989) looked in some detail at the place of sexuality in organizations, and Rosemary Pringle (1988) examined the sexualization of secretarial work. More recently, Lisa Adkins (1995) explored the significance of sexual relations in the hospitality industry. Linda McDowell (1995) highlighted the way even jobs in banking were characterized by "sexualized performances" through which individuals constructed gendered selves that were used to sell their professional services.

Gendered Bodies, Gendered Organizations

Joan Acker (1990: 139) focused on the "embodied nature of work" in complex organizations. She argued that hierarchical bureaucratic organizations were significant sites of male dominance, sites that organization theorists peopled with "abstract," "bodiless" workers. The failure to address how bodies mattered in organizations concealed the ways in which male and female bodies were differentiated in supposedly gender-neutral bureaucracies. While ostensibly gender-neutral, the abstract worker, according to Acker, was actually a man. Women's bodies were marked as pleasurably or problematically different. Their difference from the supposedly "neutral" body of the abstract male worker could lead to their sexualization or their exclusion from certain jobs.

Power in the workplace has been associated with male embodiment, even when job descriptions are gender-neutral. While few men were managers. Acker asserted that many men gained financially from the "organizational gender hierarchy" (153) because their advancement in organizations might depend on barriers to the promotion of potentially competitive women.

The detailed operation of particular gender hierarchies was the focus of Cynthia Cockburn's investigation (1991) of the responses by men to equal employment opportunity initiatives in four British organizations: a large private sector retailing firm, a government department, a local body, and a national trade union. Cockburn's research illustrated the ways in which equality initiatives in workplaces involved struggles that took different forms in different organizations. These struggles occurred regardless of agreement in principle to equality between different sets of workers. They might also involve struggles between different sets of men, including men defined by Cockburn as "pro-equality" and those hostile to change. Struggles over equal employment opportunities were, however, not just struggles over gender divisions in workplaces but also struggles over "race" and ethnicity, and this demanded attention to theorizing about the relationship between ethnicity and gender.

Work, Gender, Class, and Ethnicity

In the 1980s, against the background of critical responses to western feminist theory from African-American women, indigenous women in former colonies, immigrant women in Britain, and those who identified as "women of color" or "working class," the intersection of gender, class, and ethnicity began to receive more attention by feminist scholars (Collins, 1990; hooks, 1984; Phizacklea, 1988; Ramazanoglu, 1989). Generalizations about "women" were challenged by studies that indicated the diversity in women's experience depending on their age, ethnicity, sexual orientation, and status as descendants of white settlers, indigenous people, or immigrants (Larner, 1993).

Those women most likely to be located in the secondary labor market are African-American and Chicano women in the United States, Asian and African Caribbean women in Britain, Aboriginal women in Australia, and Maori, Samoan, and Fijian women in New Zealand. Phizacklea (1988) analyzed how, in the British context, racism and sexism contributed to the overrepresentation of black women in subordinate positions within the labor market. Patricia Hill Collins (1990) examined the position of African-American women in gender- and racially segmented labor markets. African-American women's experiences in paid work were measured against the experiences of middle-class, white American and European families in which there were often sharp distinctions between the "public" sphere of paid work and the "private" sphere of unpaid work. Collins argued that the experiences of most African-American women did not fit this model. For them survival often depended on fluid boundaries between "public" and "private" spheres and paid and unpaid work.

Differences between women were dramatically illustrated in Jackie Cock's analysis (1980) of the relationship between South African domestic servants and the white women who employed them, but women's purchase of other women's domestic services does not occur exclusively in South Africa (Collins, 1990: 55–58; hooks, 1984: 49; Huggins, 1987–1988; Ramazanoglu, 1989: 106–110), nor is control by women over the work of other women confined to situations in which women are domestic servants. Women supervisors and managers exert control over other women, exercising this control as they simultaneously experience sexualization in the workplace or exclusion from informal networks of association open to men. Collins (61) highlighted the contradictory positioning of some professional African-American women whose work identity might be at odds with their political identity, their position in their families and communities, and the gendered expectations associated with managerial work.

Challenges to Grand Theory

Over the last 20 years feminist theorists have become increasingly wary about highly generalized statements about "women," "capitalism," and "patriarchy." The focus has shifted to more nuanced, contextually specific analyses of differences between women and men with respect to access to paid work, experiences on the job, and rewards for different types of work. Those interested in analyzing gender and work often focus on particular occupational fields like secretarial work and nursing (Marks, 1994; Pringle, 1988; Witz, 1988), particular industries like the printing, clothing, and hospitality industries (Adkins, 1995; Cockburn, 1983; Phizacklea, 1990), and particular companies or firms (Kondo, 1990; McDowell, 1995). The focus is on gendering as a complex process and on the interactions and tensions between economic relations, gender relations, sexuality, and ethnicity.

Contemporary feminist theorists are now more interested in examining gendered processes and less convinced that they can discover underlying patriarchal structures that can explain inequalities between women and men. They are less likely to assume that women are heterosexual, mothers, and located in nuclear family households. At the same time they remain convinced that work, whether paid or unpaid, is usually gendered—significantly shaped by the gender identities of those doing that work and the social practices that have developed over time in particular industries and workplaces.

See Also

CAREGIVERS; DIVISION OF LABOR; DOMESTIC LABOR; ECONOMY: HISTORY OF WOMEN'S PARTICIPATION; ECONOMY:

INFORMAL; PART-TIME AND CASUAL WORK; PATRIARCHY:
DEVELOPMENT; VOLUNTEERISM; WORK: OCCUPATIONAL
SEGREGATION; WORK: PATTERNS

References and Further Reading

Acker, Joan. 1990. Hierarchies, jobs, bodies: A theory of gendered organizations. *Gender and Society* 4(2: June): 130–158.

Adkins, Lisa. 1995. *Gendered work: Sexuality, family and the labor market*. Buckingham, England: Open University Press.

Baldock, Cora. 1983. Volunteer work as work: Some theoretical considerations. In Cora Baldock and Bettina Cass, eds., *Women, social welfare and the state in Australia*, 278–297. Sydney: Allen and Unwin.

Barron, R. D., and G. M. Norris. 1976. Sexual divisions and the dual labor market. In Diana Leonard Barker and Sheila Allen, eds., *Dependence and exploitation in work and marriage*, 47–69. London: Longman.

Beasley, Chris. 1994. *Sexual economyths: Conceiving a feminist economics*. New South Wales, Australia: Allen and Unwin.

Beechey, Veronica. 1978. Women and production: A critical analysis of some sociological theories of women's work. In Annette Kuhn and AnnMarie Wolpe, eds., *Feminism and materialism: Women and modes of production*, 155–197. London: Routledge and Kegan Paul.

———, and Tessa Perkins. 1987. *A matter of hours: Women, part-time work and the labor market*. Cambridge: Polity.

Benston, Margaret. 1978. The political economy of women's liberation. In Alison Jaggar and Paula Struhl, eds., *Feminist frameworks*, 188–196. New York: McGraw-Hill.

Bradley, Harriet. 1989. *Men's work, women's work: A sociological history of the sexual division of labor in employment*. Cambridge: Polity.

Bruegel, Irene. 1986. The reserve army of labor 1974–1979. In Mandy Snell and Mary McIntosh, eds., *Waged work: A reader*, 40–53. London: Virago.

Cock, Jackie. 1980. *Maids and madams: A study in the politics of exploitation*. Johannesburg: Ravan.

Cockburn, Cynthia. 1983. *Brothers: Male dominance and technological change*. London: Pluto.

———. 1991. *In the way of women: Men's resistance to sex equality in organizations*. London: Macmillan.

———. 1985. *Machinery of dominance: Women, men and technical know-how*. London: Pluto.

Collins, Patricia Hill. 1990. *Black feminist thought: Knowledge consciousness and the politics of empowerment*. New York: Routledge.

Delphy, Christine. 1984. *Close to home: A materialist analysis of women's oppression*. London: Hutchinson.

Dex, Shirley. 1985. *The sexual division of labor: Conceptual revolutions in the social sciences*. Brighton, England: Wheatsheaf.

Engels, Friedrich. 1884/1972. *The origin of the family, private property, and the state*. New York: Pathfinder.

Game, Ann, and Rosemary Pringle. 1983. *Gender at work*. Sydney: Allen and Unwin.

Gilman, Charlotte Perkins. 1898/1966. *Women and economics: A study of the economic relations between women and men as a factor in social evolution*. New York: Harper and Row.

Hakim, Catherine. 1979. *Occupational segregation: A comparative study of the degree and pattern of the differentiation of men and women's work in Britain, the U.S. and other countries*. London: Department of Employment.

Hartmann, Heidi. 1979. Capitalism, patriarchy and job segregation by sex. In Zillah Eisenstein, ed., *Capitalist patriarchy and the case for socialist feminism*, 206–247. New York: Monthly Review.

Hearn, Jeff, Deborah L. Sheppard, Peta Tancred-Sherrif, and Gibson Burrell, eds. *The sexuality of organization*. London: Sage.

Hochschild, Arlie. 1983. *The managed heart: Commercialization of human feeling*. Berkeley: University of California Press.

hooks, bell. 1984. *Feminist theory: From margin to center*. Boston: South End.

Huggins, Jackie. 1987–1988. Aboriginal women domestic servants in the interwar years. *Hecate* 13(2): 5–23.

Kaluzynska, Eva. 1980. Wiping the floor with theory—A survey of writings on housework. *Feminist Review* 6: 27–54.

Kondo, Dorinne. 1990. *Crafting selves: Power, gender, and discourses of identity in a Japanese workplace*. Chicago: University of Chicago Press.

Larner, Wendy. 1993. Changing contexts: Globalization, migration, and feminism in New Zealand. In Sneja Gunew and Anna Yeatman, eds., *Feminism and the politics of difference*, 85–102. New South Wales, Australia: Allen and Unwin.

MacKinnon, Catharine. 1979. *Sexual harassment of working women*. New Haven, Conn.: Yale University Press.

McDowell, Linda. 1995. Body work: Heterosexual gender performances in city workplaces. In David Bell and Gill Valentine, eds., *Mapping desire: Geographies of sexualities*, 75–95. London: Routledge.

Marks, Shula. 1994. *Divided sisterhood: Race, class and gender in the South African nursing profession*. Johannesburg: Witwatersrand University Press.

Milkman, Ruth. 1976. Women's work and economic crisis. *Review of Radical Political Economy* 8(1): 73–97.

Moore, Henrietta. 1988. *Feminism and anthropology*. Oxford: Blackwell and Polity.

Oakley, Ann. 1974. *Housewife*. London: Allen Lane and Penguin.

Phizacklea, Annie. 1988. Gender, racism and occupational segregation. In Sylvia Walby, ed., *Gender segregation at work*, 43–54. Milton Keynes: Open University Press.

———. 1990. *Unpacking the fashion industry: Gender, racism and class in production.* London: Routledge.

Pringle, Rosemary. 1988. *Secretaries talk: Sexuality, power and work.* Sydney: Allen and Unwin.

Ramazanoglu, Caroline. 1989. *Feminism and the contradictions of oppression.* London: Routledge.

Walby, Sylvia. 1986. *Patriarchy at work: Patriarchal and capitalist relations in employment.* Cambridge: Polity.

Waring, Marilyn. 1988. *Counting for nothing: What men value and what women are worth.* Wellington: Allen and Unwin and Port Nicolson.

Witz, Ann. 1988. Patriarchal relations and patterns of sex segregation in the medical division of labor. In Sylvia Walby, ed., *Gender segregation at work,* 74–90. Milton Keynes: Open University Press.

Rosemary Du Plessis

WORK: Informal

See ECONOMY: INFORMAL.

WORK: Occupational Experiences

Women's occupational experiences in both developed and developing nations occur in a context in which they undertake paid labor in conjunction with, rather than as an alternative to, unpaid labor. Paid work frequently must accommodate familial and household responsibilities, and these responsibilities can place significant restrictions on women's occupational experiences and opportunities over the life cycle.

The gendered division of labor that gives women primary responsibility for work within the household also structures their experiences of paid work in important ways. Despite substantial increases in the workforce participation of women in developed countries in recent decades, the labor force remains heavily sex-segregated. In both developed and developing countries, women are disproportionately located in particular occupations and particular industries. Female-dominated sectors (sales, clerical work, teaching, nursing, subsistence farming) tend to be less well paid and less highly valued than male-dominated ones (skilled trades, engineering, medicine, cash-crop farming). Women are frequently more tenuously attached to the formal economy and are often employed as outworkers, as casual workers, and in the so-called informal labor market. The contexts within which women work, whether in the home or in the informal sector, in tradi-tional (female-dominated) areas or in nontraditional (male-dominated) areas, play an important part in structuring their occupational experiences.

The Context for Women's Work

In developed and developing societies alike, most women who undertake paid employment do so in addition to their domestic and household responsibilities, not as an alternative to them. Arlie Hochschild's *The Second Shift* (1989) is one of the better-known texts describing the "double shift" worked by women in western industrialized societies. Similar findings across countries and over time suggest that while the proportion of women in the labor market has increased, even among those in full-time paid employment, women continue to bear the brunt of responsibility for domestic labor. The preponderance of women among part-time workers and women's movements in and out of the paid labor force are important corollaries of such trends.

The ideology supporting the domestic division of labor appears remarkably resistant to change, both across cultures and over time. Under state socialist systems in eastern Europe, attempts were made to socialize private-sphere responsibilities in order to help women to reconcile their "dual" responsibilities. Although this effort at state intervention met at best with limited success, since 1989 there has been evidence of a reversal of such trends. The demands of economic transformation have led to retrenchments that appear to have been concentrated in the female labor force. In *Cinderella Goes to Market* (1993), Barbara Einhorn argues that women in east central Europe are being actively pushed back toward their "primary field of responsibility"—the family.

Women in poor, developing countries are especially disadvantaged by the domestic division of labor. Occupational choice, for example, is more restricted by the requirements of the wife, housekeeper, and mother role, partly because of the more onerous nature of the work involved (for example, carrying water and fuel, or grinding grain), and partly because women do not have the resources to pay for substitute services (housekeeping, child care, fast food, and the like), as do many women in the developed world. Women in poor countries have fewer employment opportunities than do men, and where they do find employment, they earn less and work longer hours (Dasgupta, 1993).

Working without Pay

Domestic labor. Much of women's work involves the production of goods and services consumed within the household. This includes domestic labor (meal preparation, cleaning, shopping, water carrying, fuel collection), caring labor (feeding, supervising, teaching, washing young children or disabled family members), and the production or collection of food and goods consumed by the household (hunting, gathering, care of livestock, subsistence farming, spinning, weaving, making of clothes, and so on).

When Ann Oakley (1974) published her influential work on the sociology of housework in the early 1970s, perhaps the major point that she sought to establish was that housework was work and that women experienced it as such. The social and physical isolation, the routine and monotonous nature of the work, the fragmentation and time constraints, and the low status of such work were compared, often unfavorably, with aspects of the work environment of factory workers. Moreover, the housewife was financially dependent, subjugated within the domestic sphere. Oakley's solution, consistent with that era of feminism, involved the rejection of the "housewife and mother" role and the pursuit of activities and occupations that were more highly valued in society. A more radical departure in recent years has been the attempt to assert and identify the value and skills associated with women's domestic and caring labor, together with a recognition of the economic, social, and psychological consequences of the invisibility of much of women's labor (Waring, 1988).

Women as caregivers. Women undertake the vast majority of caring work (paid and unpaid) in contemporary society, whether for children, for the disabled, or for the frail aged. Community care has long been favored in industrialized nations as the preferred option for the care of the disabled and frail, as the process of deinstitutionalization is largely regarded as a self-evident good by policy makers and social reformers alike. The critique of community care that emerged in the British social policy literature in the 1970s, however, drew attention to the assumptions implicit in such policies concerning the role of women as unpaid and underpaid caregivers and led to the often-quoted statement that community care was really family care, and family care was really care by women. Community care was thus revealed as exploitative of female labor (Land, 1978). In subsequent years, study after study has drawn attention to the realities of caring for seriously disabled children and adults—the all-too-frequent devolution of responsibility on one or two family members, the isolation, the physical and emotional labor involved, the inadequacy of the support provided by formal services, and the consequent stress and burden involved for caregivers (Braithwaite, 1990; Ungerson, 1987). For many years, the weight of feminist opinion was firmly set against community-based care, at least insofar as it presumed substantial unpaid female labor, and often included a criticism of its reliance on poorly paid female labor. In a more recent

development, an interesting autocritique of feminist work on caring has emerged, exemplified by the work of the disabled feminist Jenny Morris (1993), who has argued that because most of those cared for are also women, feminist scholarship should not ignore their rights and interests.

Women's traditional responsibility for unpaid caring work is, not surprisingly, reflected in the division of labor in the paid labor force. Women predominate in caring work, and that work is generally poorly paid and often perceived as requiring little skill or training. Personal care attendants in nursing homes dealing with frail or seriously disabled human beings are not, for example, classified as skilled workers, nor are those engaged in providing personal care services to aged people living in the community. These issues are a useful reminder that the nature of "skilled" work, or rather what is defined as skilled work, is a historically determined category rather than an objective determination. Even where the occupations involved are classified as professional or paraprofessional, the occupations in which women predominate (nursing and teaching) remain at the lower end of the status hierarchy.

Women's work for men's jobs. It is not only in terms of their domestic and caring labor that women's work is invisible. There is also the unpaid work contributed by women to family farms and family businesses and the labor that women contribute to their husbands' jobs.

On family farms, wives frequently combine the roles of farm laborer, secretary, and accountant, as well as providing domestic labor. In hard times, they may also undertake paid "off-farm" work, in order to keep the family farm afloat financially. In rural communities, which frequently have fewer social and support services than their urban counterparts, these same women often undertake a significant volunteer workload. While wealth may protect a proportion of these women, the more typical experience of farm women is of fragmented labor, limited financial independence, and long hours of work.

In both developed and developing nations, farming and rural landownership have typically been extremely patriarchal. Even today, in developed nations the inheritance of family farms is largely the province of sons rather than daughters. Rural communities are among the most conservative with regard to women's occupational roles, and given smaller and more constrained local labor markets, women are often more limited in the job opportunities open to them. As marriage takes women into farming communities, they are frequently more heavily constrained in obtaining off-farm work than are their urban counterparts by a combination of their own skills, the size and nature of the local labor market, the state of the regional economy, the demands of their spouse's occupation, familial obligations, and more limited replacement labor facilities (for example, child care centers).

In developing countries, the pattern of women's engagement in agricultural work is complex, but some generalizations are possible. It is most commonly women who are involved in production for domestic consumption—that is, subsistence-type agriculture. Where cash crops are produced, these tend to be a male preserve: they are grown and marketed by men, giving men control over the household income and allowing a construction of men as breadwinners even where both spouses are engaged in crop production. Even in a matrilineal society such as Ghana, recent work demonstrates that where farms are bought and worked by women, cocoa-producing (cash-crop) land is inherited by the sons, with the daughters receiving the subsistence plots.

Farming thus provides an effective illustration of the persistence of the sexual division of labor and its effects on women's occupational experiences and broader life chances. While involving virtually the same labor, women's activities remain segregated either through the nature of the crop (subsistence versus cash) or in the perception of their contribution (helper rather than farmer) or in their status as laborer rather than farm owner. While there are obvious consequences for individual income, the failure to recognize the value of women's labor can also have prejudicial consequences for society at large.

Other small businesses and family businesses can absorb women's labor in similar ways. Men who own small businesses, whether they be plumbers, electricians, butchers, or doctors, frequently rely on their wives to mind the shop, act as receptionists and telephonists, send out quotes, manage the books, deal with difficult clients or employees, and so on (Finch, 1983). In addition, the wives of politicians, clergymen, and diplomats are expected to undertake certain activities and responsibilities in support of their husbands' chosen occupation, almost regardless of whether these are consistent with their own interests and capacities.

As Finch (1983) points out, however, it is not only by these direct contributions that women support their husband's work. Their assumption of primary responsibility for domestic labor frees men to undertake paid work, and women's emotional and caring labor underpins the social and psychological well-being of the family unit.

Women as traders. Women are disproportionately active in the informal labor market, including such tasks as doing housework and minding children, whether for cash or on an exchange basis, as well as a range of trading or bartering activities, to supplement their formal income. In modern welfare states, these behaviors have been documented with

regard to the wives of unemployed men, who cannot undertake formal employment without their husbands' losing eligibility for the unemployment benefit.

Brydon and Chant document a striking pattern in *Women in the Third World* (1989), whereby women figure in small-scale manufacturing of goods and work as itinerant tradespersons, seamstresses, laundrywomen, domestic servants, stallholders, and ambulatory traders. These are all activities closely associated with women's traditional work and have the advantage that they can be carried on in association with women's domestic responsibilities. So, for example, stallholders in marketplace trading have the advantages of flexible hours, baby-sitting by other market women, and so on.

Even within these informal labor markets, however, there is often a sexual division of labor. For example, among the Yoruba of Nigeria, women tend to sell subsistence foods in the open marketplace and from small stalls, whereas men are involved in selling more substantial consumer goods from larger stalls and stores. In countries such as Mexico and Ecuador there is evidence that women traders are prevented by a combination of domestic duties and male authority from venturing out of their houses, leaving a greater share of commercial profit making available to the male traders. In these countries, then, the disadvantages that women face in the formal labor market are actually replicated in the more heavily female-dominated informal sector (Brydon and Chant, 1989: chapter 7).

The Formal Labor Market

Contemporary feminist research has demonstrated that despite the continuing existence of men's jobs and women's jobs, the sexual division of labor in the paid workplace is not fixed. Game and Pringle (1983), for example, illustrate the changing sex-typing ascribed to particular jobs under the impact of technological change in a range of established (for example, manufacturing) and "new" (for example, computing) industries. What remains constant, however, is the tendency for certain occupations to be readily identifiable as either male- or female-dominated.

At the same time, gender regimes differ significantly in different workplaces, and it is important to recognize that the mechanisms by which the sexual division of labor is maintained vary quite significantly in different contexts. Cynthia Cockburn's work (1983) documents the collusion of trade unions and management to mutual (predominantly male) benefit; Ruth Cavendish's study of factory workers (1982) exemplifies the strategies by which a malleable and cheap (predominantly female) workforce is effectively exploited and controlled. In some of the other examples that follow, the processes of exclusion are centered more directly on the collective consequences of particular decisions by individual bosses that involve overt and covert discrimination. Not only is there a sexual division of labor, but these and similar studies point to a gender-based structuring of production that serves both to reinforce and to justify women's exclusion from particular labor market areas.

Women as factory workers. Some of the most consistent examples of the gendered division of labor in the workplace come from research on women as factory workers. Cavendish (1982) presents a classic account of these distinctions in her detailed study of assembly line work in a car components factory. The assembly line work was semi-skilled, highly repetitive, labor-intensive, and undertaken entirely by women. Men, in contrast, occupied a range of grades, with variations in skill and pay levels and with opportunities for promotion. The women had lower pay, with no opportunity for moving "off the line." Cockburn (1983) provides a compelling analysis of the ways in which the interests of male workers and management converge to ensure that female labor is restricted to less well paid and less skilled segments of the labor force. Drawing her examples from the printing industry, Cockburn describes the processes by which historically defined "male" jobs are maintained as bastions of male privilege despite the onslaught of mechanization and technological change. Where their engagement in the printing workforce was permitted, women were effectively excluded from skilled positions.

Women as secretaries. The gendered nature of work is further revealed in Rosemary Pringle's analysis (1988) of the stereotypically female role of secretary. Pringle points to the unequivocally feminine and maternal characteristics associated with secretarial work, and uses her research to assert the ubiquitous nature of sexuality in the workplace. While secretaries are clearly structurally disadvantaged in relation to their bosses in terms of pay, conditions, status, and authority, Pringle explores a variety of ways in which secretaries accommodate or resist such power. She returns at numerous points to the varied circumstances in which women as secretaries find themselves, their different reactions to those circumstances, and the various strategies that they employ in dealing with them. The variability of women's working experiences even within a seemingly coherent category such as "secretary" is a recurrent theme.

Women and professions. The status of women within the professions is generally taken as a benchmark of women's progress toward equality in the labor market. Although patterns vary across countries and across professional groups, some general trends can be identified. The proportion of women in the traditionally male-dominated professions (which are generally held to include medicine, the law, science, academia, and engineering) is increasing. However, a status and income differential remains, with women concentrated in less well paid, less prestigious, and less influential areas within particular professions. In medicine, for example, women are more likely to be general practitioners and less likely to be found in prestigious specialties such as surgery or ophthalmology. Women continue to predominate in lower-status professions such as teaching, nursing, and social work. Even in female-dominated professions, however, the senior positions are disproportionately held by males. There is a well-documented process of attrition as women move through the career path in both male- and female-dominated professions. In Australia the proportion of women entering medical schools is approximately 50 percent, yet the proportion graduating is lower, and that practicing less than 20 percent. While some of the explanation lies in the increasing participation of successive cohorts of women in professional careers, the comfortable expectation that women would progressively gain equality through that "natural" process has been increasingly eroded, as women fail to secure an equal share of senior positions. A variety of practices of marginalization and exclusion underlie such patterns.

In the legal profession, where the increase in the proportion of women graduating has been substantial, women are more likely to be salaried than partners, to work for the state rather than in private enterprise, and to work in lower-status areas such as family law rather than in commercial law, and they are less likely to be barristers and judges than are their male counterparts. Where women enter the judiciary, they do so at the lower levels, as local magistrates rather than as supreme or high court judges.

The law as a profession remains both male-oriented and male-dominated. Many male lawyers defend the status quo, basing the failure of women to reach senior and high-status positions on the "aggressive" and "masculine" nature of the law, the difficulties that women encounter in dealing with that environment, and the unwillingness of clients to accept female lawyers as adequately representing their interests. Domestic and family responsibilities are generally held to be antithetical to successful legal work, where a strong ethic of 60-to-70-hour working weeks prevails among those destined to "get ahead." Women who choose to have children are expected to leave the profession, unless employed in the public sector. Those women who do leave provide further reinforcement for the dominant professional norms that militate against the promotion of women to senior and central positions on the grounds that family and marital responsibilities will lead sooner or later to their resignation.

The legal profession encapsulates the difficulties that women face in succeeding in a male-dominated profession. Spencer and Podmore (1987: 129) sum up the classic double bind that women face by reference to the basic mismatch between a personal identity that is feminine and a workplace culture that is masculine: "Women lawyers are essentially marginal members of their profession and can find themselves in a 'no-win' situation. If they attempt to conform to the dominant male norms of the profession, they will be regarded as 'unnatural women'; while if they distance themselves from professional norms they will not be regarded by men as competent professional colleagues." A confounding factor discussed by these and other authors is the persistent evaluation by some men of women as sexual objects, rather than as professional colleagues.

In academia, too, women remain concentrated at the lower levels and are less likely to hold tenure. Even in areas such as the social sciences and humanities, where they constitute a majority of undergraduate students, women constitute only a small minority of senior academic staff. In science, women are more likely to be found in particular areas, such as the biological sciences, than in the physical sciences, such as chemistry and physics. In a well-known work, Ruth Bleier (1984) has argued that science itself is structured in ways that are antithetical to women.

Academia holds itself to be an institution in which promotion is based on merit. But recent work suggests that the very nature of merit in academia may be imbued with male cultural norms. Counting published works is one obvious example of the difficulties that women encounter if they have taken time out from their career for family obligations. But the more subtle and probably more effective components are the ways in which merit is perceived and constructed: communication strategies (the "authoritative male voice," for example), behavior in meetings, and the recognition of traditional (and hence male) areas of scholarship (political theory) as of more weighty intellectual significance than emerging areas of interest to feminists (family policy).

Several explanations are offered for these patterns. Some are based on the conflict between women's familial and career obligations, particularly over a professional career where there may be significant penalties for temporary withdrawal from the workforce associated with child rearing. Other related arguments cite the nature of the professional culture, the expectation that successful members of the professional group will have the kind of domestic support system usually provided by wives. While some arguments

continue to be made concerning women's intellectual capacity and interest in (particularly male-dominated) professional careers, these hold decreasing legitimacy. Nonetheless, the need for stereotypical "male" qualities such as rationality and aggression continues to be cited as a rationale for women's underrepresentation in fields such as the physical sciences, on the one hand, and the legal profession, on the other. Other explanations lie in overt or covert discrimination, including the failure to perceive and reward competence among women, and access to mentoring relationships and professional networking, which facilitate career development in highly competitive fields.

Women and management. The proportion of managers who are female has increased in many parts of the world. While this is particularly so in North America, even there female managers are underrepresented in the top levels of governments and corporations. So, for example, in Britain, women constitute some 30 percent of those entering in the administrative categories, but only 10 percent of the senior categories, and only 21 among 700 men in the top civil service grades (Walters, 1987). Historically, there is clear evidence of overt discriminatory practices against women in government in a number of countries. Until the 1940s, women in Britain (and Australia) were required to resign when they married, and equal pay was not granted until the 1950s (the 1960s in Australia). And the pattern of inequality described above exists in a context where the British Sex Discrimination Act has been in place for 20 years.

Government bureaucracies are characteristically staffed at their higher levels by a group of people who have one employer, are engaged in a style of work very similar to that of their colleagues, are members of a relatively small group, and interact with one another frequently over a lifelong career. Career civil or public servants do not generally have as large a range of alternative opportunities open to them as managers. Sometimes referred to as occupational encapsulation, this results in a certain homogeneity and a shared sense of an occupational community with a particular uniform culture. It is also predominantly male, and those women who enter are consequently judged in terms of this predominantly male culture. Here, as elsewhere, there is evidence that women experience a conflict between career and familial requirements; as is the case for senior professional areas, there is little acceptance of part-time work at very senior levels of government, and withdrawal from the labor market associated with child rearing disadvantages women. While governments generally have been among the vanguard of equal opportunity employers, it may well be that part of the reason for differential success lies in the definition of merit as applied by predominantly male superiors in a strongly male-dominated culture.

The patterns are similar, albeit more disheartening, in private managerial patterns. Karen Legge (in Spencer and Podmore, 1987) provides an account of a number of aspects of women's performance in bureaucracy with her description of women in personnel management. She found that while personnel was regarded as a low-status area of managerial responsibility, women were indeed represented in senior areas of the corporate ladder. The pattern as described echoes the general claim that women are systematically underrepresented in the powerful, well-paid, and high-status area of professional and managerial work.

The problems that confront women in the third world are somewhat different—in countries such as Iran, China, and India the issues are more likely to be concerned with the absence of equal access to education and employment rather than with equal representation in upper levels of bureaucracy and management. One must be wary of such blanket statements, however; in India, for example, the effects of gender are mediated through a rigid caste system. Women of higher social status will therefore have access to education and professional advancement not available to those belonging to lower social groups (whether male or female). However, in relation to males of their own social grouping, gender remains a disadvantage for women.

Conclusion

While women's progress toward equality may be mapped in terms of their progress in the professions and in management, the majority of women are not employed in such areas. Most women are employed in the sales and service sectors, often in areas characterized by part-time work, casual work, poor conditions, limited job security, and few prospects for promotion. The negative aspects of such work are often outweighed by the fact that such jobs allow women to undertake familial and domestic responsibilities. Globally, an increasing number of women are engaged in outwork or homework, in which they have the advantages of combining domestic and paid labor responsibilities but also the disadvantages of isolation, often coupled with low wages, insecurity, and fluctuating income and hours of work. Women's occupational experiences, while showing significant variations, all too frequently both reflect and serve to reinforce the continuing sexual division of labor.

A major aspect of women's occupational experiences remains the invisibility of their labor and the undervaluing of its worth. Women's work has often not been regarded as work by mainstream economic, social, and philosophical traditions. Redefining what constitutes productive labor in contemporary society has been a major contribution of feminism.

See Also

DISCRIMINATION; DIVISION OF LABOR; DOMESTIC LABOR; ECONOMY: HISTORY OF WOMEN'S PARTICIPATION; ECONOMY: INFORMAL; FEMOCRAT; MANAGEMENT; NURSING; PROSTITUTION; SEXUAL HARASSMENT; WORK: OCCUPATIONAL SEGREGATION; WORK: PATTERNS

References and Further Reading

Bleier, Ruth. 1984. *Science and gender: A critique of biology and its theories on women.* New York: Pergamon.

Braithwaite, Valerie A. 1990. *Bound to care.* Sydney: Allen and Unwin.

Brydon, Lynne, and Sylvia Chant. 1989. *Women in the third world: Gender issues in rural and urban areas.* Aldershot, England: Edward Elgar.

Cavendish, Ruth. 1982. *Women on the line.* London: Routledge and Kegan Paul.

Cockburn, Cynthia. 1983. *Brothers: Male dominance and technological change.* London: Pluto.

Dasgaupta, Partha. 1993. *An inquiry into well-being and destitution.* Oxford: Oxford University Press.

Einhorn, Barbara. 1993. *Cinderella goes to market.* London: Verso.

Finch, Janet. 1983. *Married to the job.* London: Allen and Unwin.

Game, Ann, and Rosemary Pringle. 1983. *Gender at work.* Sydney: Allen and Unwin.

Hochschild, Arlie. 1989. *The second shift.* New York: Avon.

Land, Hilary. 1978. Who cares for the family? *Journal of Social Policy* 7(3): 257–284.

Morris, Jenny. 1993. *Independent lives: Community care and disabled people.* London: Macmillan.

Oakley, Ann. 1974. *The sociology of housework.* New York: Pantheon.

Pringle, Rosemary. 1988. *Secretaries talk: Sexuality, power and work.* Sydney: Allen and Unwin.

Spencer, Anne, and David Podmore, eds., 1987. *In a man's world: Essays on women in male-dominated professions.* London: Tavistock. (See articles by Legge and Spencer and Podmore.)

Ungerson, Clare. 1987. *Policy is personal: Sex, gender and informal care.* London: Tavistock.

Walters, Patricia A. 1987. Servants of the crown. In Anne Spencer and David Podmore, eds., *In a man's world: Essays on women in male-dominated professions.* London: Tavistock.

Waring, Marilyn. 1988. *Counting for nothing: What men value and what women are worth.* Sydney: Allen and Unwin.

Diane Gibson

WORK: Occupational Health and Safety

See OCCUPATIONAL HEALTH AND SAFETY.

WORK: Occupational Segregation

Occupational segregation by sex is the relationship between the sex of workers and their employment in gendered occupations and refers to the separation of men and women at work. It denotes the degree to which there is "women's work" or "men's work" and the ways in which women and men are unevenly distributed in the workforce. It is also related to the concentration of women and men in different sectors of employment. Debates about segregation are fundamental not only to liberal perspectives on gender equality and discrimination but also to feminist theories of patriarchy.

Types of Segregation

Segregation is of two types, vertical and horizontal. Horizontal segregation is the division across occupations or sectors, such as women's overrepresentation in nursing, the garment trade, or services, while men are overrepresented in engineering or construction. The great majority of workers are in sex-typed occupations. In the United States in 1981 two-thirds of women and 7 in 10 men were in occupations where their sex formed 70 percent or more of the workforce. This pattern was still true in Britain in 1991 (Hakim, 1992, 1993).

Vertical segregation is the unequal distribution of men and women within occupational hierarchies, such as women's greater share of classroom teaching and men's greater share of senior posts, including headships. In many sectors, women dominate clerical work, with men having the greater share in administration and management. In manufacturing, women tend to be in unskilled grades, while skilled work is typically synonymous with men. Vertical segregation can also mean women's concentration in lower-status occupations, a classic example being nurses compared with doctors.

Occupational segregation is, therefore, a key component of sex inequality, linked to questions of sex discrimination. It restricts women's (and men's) right to choose their work, whether the constraints lie in sex stereotyping of jobs, formal barriers to entry, custom and practice, or subtle exclusionary processes. But most of all, occupational and job segregation are the chief barriers to equal pay. The gender gap in earnings is mainly due to men's domination of better-remunerated, higher-status work. The causes of this domination are complex, but often at stake in its persistence are strong vested interests. In avoiding equal pay in Britain, employers, supported by male workers, often segregated women from men, thus making their jobs noncomparable. This is why laws that support equal pay for work of equal value are so crucial.

Occupational segregation is, then, of great importance for policy makers, especially since it appears to have become more marked, not less so, with economic development. It is also of particular concern that most cross-national studies, including those undertaken by the Organization for Economic Cooperation and Development (OECD), indicate the highest levels of segregation in countries with a strong state interventionist approach to sex equality—Norway, Australia, and the United States, for example. But this paradox results essentially from difficulties in measuring segregation. The methodological issues (and disputes) are sometimes highly technical, but they matter because of their implications for conclusions about the role of equality policies, of economic growth, or of changes in the workforce in reducing segregation.

Measuring Segregation

The most widely used measure, the dissimilarity index, is very sensitive to the size of the occupational classification. It is largely for this reason that segregation levels appear so high in industrialized, as compared with developing, economies. Southern European countries, such as Greece, Italy, and Portugal, along with Japan and India, have a large agricultural sector and high proportions of the workforce in nonwage employment, and they lack the detailed occupational distinctions associated with manufacturing and services (Ferreira, 1994). The smaller the number of occupational groups, the lower the index of segregation. The use of broad categories can help deal with national variations in occupational classifications or their changes over time, but as a result, comparative research based on this index is often misleading and can exaggerate the amount of integration. Another popular measure, the sex ratio index (or a variant of it) compares the proportion of women or men in an occupation with their share of the workforce as a whole. It thus measures over- or underrepresentation (Hakim, 1992). Typically it is not affected by the size of occupations and so does not alter simply because of changes in the occupational structure, like the growth of the service sector. But it is not independent of changes in the proportion of women in the labor force. Such difficulties have led to a number of additional measures, including those that reflect the growth of integrated occupations (Hakim, 1993). These measures show that segregation has declined among women working full-time but the opposite is true of part-timers. The female workforce is becoming more polarized in economies like Britain, where the expansion of women's employment has been largely part-time.

There are differences of interpretation here too, and it is important to treat national and international findings with much caution, as only indicative of trends, not as absolute statements. In particular, vertical segregation may be underestimated since there are many relatively integrated occupations, such as university teaching, where women remain concentrated in the lower echelons. National studies also underestimate segregation in the workplace since this never mirrors aggregate patterns, and the job structure of firms is usually much more segregated than occupations.

Case studies of organizations, sectors, or particular occupations best capture the social reality of segregation and identify the causes of change or lack of it (Cockburn, 1991; Humphrey, 1987). There is great value in historical studies, since gender segregation is often reconstituted, and in considering other forms of segregation and social division.

Historical Study of Segregation

Segregation has connotations of rigid racial boundaries from South Africa during apartheid or the southern states of the United States, and studies of segregation by sex initially adapted research instruments used in the United States to study ethnic dimensions of residential or labor market segmentation. Although there is rarely absolute exclusivity, it is only in the past hundred years or so that legal restrictions on women's entry into many occupations have been lifted. In England women were barred from many professional bodies until 1919, and men have been allowed to practice modern midwifery only since 1975. Legal barriers can be reimposed, as in Iran, where the Islamic revolution of 1979 banned women from the legal profession and some other areas of work. Formal exclusion also applies to the Roman Catholic and Orthodox priesthood; the Anglican church in England approved the ordination of women only in 1993, after a long and bitter struggle.

The historical variability of segregation is well illustrated by the case of coal mining, since it was nineteenth-century protective legislation in Europe and North America that excluded women and children from certain areas of work or restricted their hours of employment. Then, as now, the issue of segregation was highly charged, with opinion strongly divided, among women as among men. Male trade unionists often fought alongside middle-class reformers to return women to their "proper" domestic sphere, and it is this fact that leads feminists to argue that patriarchy actively reproduced the sexual division of labor. However, some working-class women also supported restrictions, while some men, including male miners, pressed the case for women's right to work.

Job Segregation

Debates about the role of patriarchy in job segregation have often centered on the question of skill. Many feminists have argued that the association of skilled work with men and unskilled work with women rarely corresponds to real differences of expertise and that women's skills are socially devalued in most cultures. It is men's greater bargaining power, exercised through trade unions, that has enabled them to claim the title of skill only for themselves and to define women as merely semi- or unskilled. Skill is socially constructed, not immutable, and a product of a political struggle within and beyond the workplace that both maintains and presupposes the subordination of women and the domination of men (Phillips and Taylor, 1980). These processes are particularly evident when the jobs of male craftsmen (such as clothing cutters or compositors) are being challenged by technological or other changes to the labor process—changes that in destroying old skills (deskilling) may enable employers to draw on cheaper, often female labor. During the two world wars, for example, women were recruited into skilled work, but only "for the duration" and provided they were paid at men's rates, to prevent employers from using women's labor to undercut the economic and political power of engineers and riveters.

Such arguments persuasively account for the differentials of skill status and the processes of exclusion from formally skilled (often apprenticed) labor. But they are relatively weak at explaining why many men are also excluded from skilled manual trades, unless patriarchy is more widely conceived as a process wherein men subordinate other men as well as women. Nevertheless, some men may have more in common with unskilled women, and there are circumstances under which male-dominated trade unions have pursued genuinely inclusive, collectivist, even equality strategies (Milkman, 1983).

Many theories of occupational segregation emphasize economic factors. In sectors of the economy where labor costs are at a premium or market conditions dictate fluctuations in employment, employers tend to prefer cheaper and more disposable workers, who can be easily laid off or rehired as needed. This explains the ghettoization of women in labor-intensive work throughout manufacturing and services. Also, the feminization of occupations often follows their decline in status and prospects (such as reduced opportunities for self-employment in pharmacy). However, these theories do not explain why, for example, women can be hired more cheaply than men in the first place, except with reference to claims that women have lower human capital. Women may have lesser experience or qualifications, because of their primary family commitments and low investment in employment and training. Such arguments are often used to explain women's concentration in junior grades and their lower chances of promotion to administrative, managerial, or higher professional levels. But as women become increasingly well qualified and acquire better credentials, they do not always reap their due rewards. Instead they frequently encounter an invisible "glass ceiling." The gender hierarchy in organizations and professions is reinforced through several processes: male networks, the privileging of men's careers, corporate cultures, and sexuality itself (Cockburn, 1991). Among the prejudices is that women are suitable only for "women's work."

What counts as gender-appropriate varies across time and space. "Women's work" in manufacturing is often deemed light and intricate, but these terms merely correspond to the detailed hand processes of assembly and other labor-intensive work. In agriculture, women's work is typically heavy and arduous. Occupations once male-dominated can become feminized and vice versa, although the general principle of gender segregation appears extremely resilient (Reskin and Roos, 1990). Women are almost everywhere also associated with domestic work, in caring for others and servicing their needs. Typical feminized occupations are those in social and personal services. Women's reproductive role may naturalize this, but a most telling characteristic of women's work is that it is a "labor of love," unpaid domestic labor in the household, and low-paid employment. There are powerful associations between domestic tasks and low social status. However, although women are therefore candidates compared with men, other socially inferiorized groups may carry out domestic or dirty work—untouchables in India, Gypsies, and others who are marginal or powerless in most parts of the world. Those who work as domestic servants are typically working-class and very often of ethnic minorities. Occupational segregation by sex is a potent indicator of gender inequalities, but it also highlights the complex, interrelated role of class and racial divisions.

See Also

ANTIDISCRIMINATION; DISCRIMINATION; ECONOMY: HISTORY OF WOMEN'S PARTICIPATION; ECONOMIC STATUS: COMPARATIVE ANALYSIS; WORK: FEMINIST THEORIES

References and Further Reading

Cockburn, Cynthia. 1991. *In the way of women: Men's resistance to sex equality in organizations.* London: Macmillan.

Ferreira, Virginia. 1994. Women's employment in the European semiperipheral countries: Analysis of the Portuguese case. *Women's Studies International Forum* 17(2–3): 141–155.

Game, Anne, and Rosemary Pringle. 1983. *Gender at work.* Sydney: Allen and Unwin.

Hakim, Catherine. 1992. Explaining trends in occupational segregation: The measurement, causes and consequences of the sexual division of labor. *European Sociological Review* 8(2): 127–152.

———. 1993. Segregated and integrated occupations: A new approach to analyzing social change. *European Sociological Review* 9(3): 289–314.

Humphrey, John. 1987. *Gender and work in the third world: Sexual divisions in Brazilian industry.* London: Tavistock.

Milkman, Ruth. 1983. Female factory labor and industrial structure: Control and conflict over "women's place" in auto and electrical manufacturing. *Politics and Society* 12(2): 159–203.

Phillips, Anne, and Barbara Taylor. 1980. Sex and skill: Notes towards a feminist economics. *Feminist Review* 6: 79–88.

Reskin, Barbara, and Patricia Roos. 1990. *Job queues, gender queues: Explaining women's inroads into male occupations.* Philadelphia: Temple University Press.

Jackie West

WORK: Patterns

The patterns of women's working lives are very diverse and shaped by a multitude of factors: their age, life expectancy, and place in the life cycle; their culture and class; geographical mobility; and their educational qualifications, to name a few. The diversity is also a product of their differing responses to the opportunities that present themselves and the constraints they face. Perhaps one need think only of the life and work experiences of one's mother and grandmother to appreciate the changes that have occurred across time and space, class and culture, and to recognize, across that diversity, some similarities in the constraints women must deal with in their working lives.

The first thing to appreciate about the patterns of women's working lives is that they frequently encompass both paid and unpaid work: work that generates an income and equally maintains and sustains a household but that is rarely directly remunerated in either cash or kind. Because this work is unpaid, the mainstream (masculine) economy has typically regarded it as nonwork and women who do unpaid work as unemployed or not productively employed. The distinction makes most sense for the citizens of societies more or less shaped by the development of a capitalist economic system, in which the notion of "productive employment" usually connotes work undertaken outside the home for wages. (It would be nonsensical to differentiate between paid and unpaid work, or even "real" work and "nonwork," in a hunter-gatherer society, for example.) As a result of the linking of "work" with "pay," the productivity of women's unpaid labor and of themselves as unpaid workers is routinely left uncounted by measures of a nation's economic well-being and systems of national accounts (Beneria, 1982; Waring, 1988). Nor is it just as housewives and mothers that women's work is uncounted; so, too, is much of the unpaid work done by women in the "public" sphere, as unpaid family workers in agricultural production or in small businesses, as volunteers in community organizations, and as wives whose labor is directly incorporated into their husband's careers (Finch, 1983).

Expanding Definitions of Work

Beginning with Gavron (1966) and Oakley (1974), feminists have consistently challenged the implications of this distinction between paid and unpaid work and have argued, for example, that housework *is* work. It is not necessarily the same as what passes for "real" work—the productive, income-generating work men are usually assumed to be doing—and it is organized differently from much paid labor, but it is work nevertheless.

Worldwide, women are largely responsible for the bulk of domestic labor, although it varies in the extent to which it is time-consuming and arduous. An example that is both is the fetching of water and fuel; in 1980, upward of 1.2 billion people were dependent on women and girls collecting water from village standpipes or wells—a journey undertaken several times each day and, in some places, from up to six miles away (Lewenhak, 1992: 52). No matter what the particular conditions under which housework is done, however, it is never trivial. Even in industrialized countries, where technological innovations have over time eased the arduousness of domestic tasks, there may be no discernible decrease in the amount of time devoted to them. Lewenhak, for example, reports on surveys showing that in the United States "women had less free time in 1965–1966 than they had in 1930 despite the massive introduction of electrically powered domestic apparatus" (64).

To deprive housework of the status of "real" work because it is usually unpaid not only makes it invisible, thus lowering the status and worth accorded women, but also—as Marxist feminists contributing to the debate over domestic labor in the 1970s pointed out with respect to capitalist economies—denies the reliance of paid on

unpaid work (Baxter, 1990; Kaluzynska, 1980). Equally significant for the purposes of this article, the dichotomy disguises a constraint women must negotiate in order to take up various kinds of paid or income-generating work.

The periods in a family's life cycle when the pressures of reconciling paid work with domestic work become most intense for women are during their childbearing and early child rearing years. Pregnancy itself is work, but work that is considered to have no value because it is "natural" (Lewenhak, 1992: 36). More readily accepted as work are the tasks of child care, which both increase the amount of domestic labor to be accomplished and, during early infant care, do so under conditions that make labor, domestic or paid, more difficult. Along with domestic responsibilities, women are primarily, and in some cultures solely, responsible for infant care. Baxter reports on Australian studies which found that the number of hours spent on housework increases dramatically with the addition of young children to the family but that "men's participation in domestic...labor was not affected by the presence of young children" (1990: 137). (Indeed it appears that the variable that most closely accounts for the amount of time Australian men spend on domestic labor is the amount of time *they themselves* spend in paid employment.)

While the expectation that women are primarily responsible for infant care seems fairly pervasive, the extent to which the state and other institutions provide support can vary widely, as can the availability and use of other family members to share the care of infants and small children. The relatively widespread provision of some form of maternity leave, and the corresponding lack of paternity leave (or parental leave), indicates the degree to which women and not men are responsible for children. With the notable exception of the Nordic countries (Lewenhak, 1992: 47–48), government policies are instrumental in discouraging men from taking up child care as much as or more than they encourage women to take up paid work (Baldock, 1988: 45). In a similar example, Katz and Monk (1993: 12) report a range from 37 percent of preschool children in Sweden attending child care centers to less than 1 percent in Nicaragua. Where formal child care is limited, women may be able to cooperate with and utilize others to share the care of children (older siblings, other female relatives, and perhaps partners). Among West Indian extended households (houseyards), for example, girls may have their first child at 14 or 15 but will find that child care is undertaken by older kin and other adult females, leaving them to return to school or paid work (Pulsipher in Katz and Monk, 1993: 113). No matter what arrangements women make to deal with their caretaking responsibilities, the organization of the care rests with them. For the hunter-gatherer woman, for example, that may mean carrying her baby with her as she goes about her daily tasks. For the rural village woman, it may mean involving older siblings in child care or allocating to them some of her domestic tasks. For the working woman in most nations, it means carrying with her into her paid work, at least in her mind if not in the practical organization of her day, the demands and responsibilities of child care.

Constraints on Women's Paid Work

The extent of the constraints placed on women's paid work by their domestic and family responsibilities varies historically and culturally. For some women, a primary responsibility for domestic work and early child care, as well as their greater confinement to the home and its immediate environs, may prevent them from engaging in wage labor at all. In developing countries, for example, women's responsibility for the household may contribute to their exclusion from income-generating activities as men take up opportunities for cash-cropping or migrate to cities for waged labor, leaving the women responsible for subsistence production for domestic consumption (Rogers, 1980). An increased "feminization" of the agricultural workforce results, which is often ignored by official agencies and agricultural development workers because much of the agricultural work women undertake is as unpaid family workers whose work is done in or near the home is small in scale, seasonal, and primarily for home consumption.

Similarly, it has been the case in some industrialized nations that marriage, with its attendant possibility of children, formally signaled the end to a right to permanent paid employment for women. In Britain, for example, "marriage bars" requiring women in certain occupations to resign on marriage were gradually removed between 1946 and 1963 (Walby, 1986). Even in the absence of formal barriers, for many women convention still presumes that mothers, especially mothers of young children, should not "work." This convention is not evenly applied, however, as is demonstrated by the differences in maternity leave benefits available to women workers or variations in government policies on single supporting parents' benefits and family allowances: in 1984, for example, the government of Singapore used family allowances to pursue a eugenicist policy of discouraging more than two children per couple for the majority of the population while encouraging highly educated women to leave the paid workforce and have more children (Lewenhak, 1992: 41).

If childbearing does not cause a woman's formal departure from the workforce and the beginning of a life as a full-time mother and housewife, it will usually mean a short period of leave from paid employment. In industrialized countries the number of women who quit paid work permanently once they start a family became a minority over the latter part of the twentieth century. Among Swiss women, for example, this pattern fell from 37 percent of women who married between 1940 and 1950 to 18 percent of those who married between 1960 and 1970 (Streckeisen, 1991: 77). In Australia until 1947 more than 90 percent of married women stayed home; by 1986 the proportion of married women in the labor force had risen to 47 percent (Baldock, 1988: 27). A career interrupted or slowed down by a period or periods of maternity leave, a discontinuous employment history, and multiple jobs are common effects of women bearing children and being accorded primary responsibility for child rearing. Streckeisen's previously cited study of Swiss women's work patterns (1991) showed that the number of women who worked continuously throughout their adult lives had remained constant over past decades at about 20 percent. The majority of adult Swiss women experienced "interruptions" of six months or more in their paid working lives, with the majority of mothers in the study going back to work before their children started school. For more than half of the sample of 989 of these women with interrupted patterns of employment, the effect of interruptions due to the arrival of a child was often a change of profession on return to work. The longer a woman stayed out of paid work, the more likely it was that her return to work would be in a different occupation (1991: 77).

Just as childbearing affects women's paid work patterns, their paid work affects their patterns of childbearing and child care. A Canadian study (Ram and Rahim, 1993) that used a life-table analysis to relate women's paid employment history to their patterns of childbearing found that women with a longer paid work experience, a less interrupted early career, and a greater "work commitment" tended to space their births at longer intervals than those with less and more discontinuous work experience and greater "attachment to home." Working women were also likely to have fewer children.

In addition to a discontinuous paid employment pattern, many women find that domestic and family obligations constrain their choices of paid work: restricting the hours they can work and meet both obligations, or the places they may work, or the kind of work they can undertake and still successfully meet those obligations. Thus, women with family responsibilities may find shift work—particularly the night shift, when partners are available to supervise children—a feasible option. Equally, women in industrialized nations routinely make up the larger proportion of part-time workers, apparently so as to better manage both kinds of work. The consequences of making such "choices," particularly contingent work (temporary, casual, part-time, seasonal), are that for women paid work is frequently associated with poorer industrial conditions, lower wages, limited opportunities for promotion, and poorer working conditions. Part-time and casual work, for example, rarely carry the same rights to leave, retirement, and other benefits as full-time work.

Home-based paid work may provide another approach to the juggling of unpaid domestic and family responsibilities and paid work. Maria Mies's study (1982) of lace workers shows how homework provides an accommodation of income-generating work with both the cultural mores for upper-caste Indian women and their domestic tasks (a typical lacemaker worked 13.5 hours a day—7.5 on lacemaking and 6 on domestic chores). Home-based work carries quite different consequences for women and men. Walker (1989), for example, reports on a study of home-based computer workers that found that the men "had chosen to work at home because there were *less* distractions and stress," and eliminating commuting time had given them more leisure time to spend with their children. All the men had wives at home to ensure that their working time was uninterrupted by children and chores. For women, "working at home was associated with a *lack* of choice and the need to combine wage labor and domestic responsibilities, particularly child care. The result was *increased* levels of stress" (63). The regulation of such work at home (for example, monitoring home-based secretarial work through log-ins and keystrokes at the terminal) may also lead to working conditions akin to the sweated labor of older forms of outwork in, say, the garment industry (Allen and Wolkowitz, 1987).

Not only the hours and the location of paid work but also the kind of work readily available to women may be dictated by domestic contingencies: in southeast Asia adult women take up economic niches like local agricultural work, weekly market work, smallholder food stalls, making and peddling traditional medicine, or providing services like midwifery because they are compatible with their family obligations and domestic location (Manderson, 1983: 6). In a similar way, cottage industry and local cooperatives may provide more flexible forms of work organization, enabling women to integrate rather than separate their many roles in time and place. Where women's access to mainstream financial resources and wage income is limited, these forms of local industry may provide a practical economic alternative (Lewenhak, 1992: 106–108).

Globally, women work significantly longer hours than men do and have reduced opportunities for leisure. For many women, paid work exacerbates an already heavier load: they effectively do a "double shift" or suffer from a "double burden" wherein women undertaking paid work are still responsible for the larger share of housework, fitting these chores around their paid work hours. Australian data, for example, show that even among couples where both are in full-time paid employment, women spend about twice as much time as men on child care and housework. Moreover, there is little evidence that the time Australian men spend in domestic labor significantly increases as women take up paid employment; rather, there is a decrease in the time the women spend on domestic chores (Baxter et al., 1990: 23–25). Among women, those in full-time paid employment spend the least time on housework, while those who work part-time spend almost as much time as those who have no paid work at all. Women who work part-time, fitting their paid work into their established family obligations, experience the longest working week and the greatest double burden (Baxter et al., 1990: 28). This double burden can become a triple burden if women continue to undertake voluntary labor for their communities as well. The marginal status attributed to women's paid work, and the ideological linkages between caring labor done in the family and at home and caring labor done in the community, mean that women are frequently called on to do additional unpaid voluntary work for the public sector such as running children's play groups and school snack shops, hospital visiting, and other forms of welfare work. Ironically, because only paid work is regarded as real work, women are understood to have the "leisure" and the "flexibility" to fulfill these community needs.

It is crucial to recognize that patterns of women's work that result from these various negotiated solutions to the balancing of domestic roles with paid employment or income-generating activity are not simply driven by women's socially prescribed responsibility for domestic labor. The other side of this coin is that the organization of paid labor presumes that the normative "worker" is a man who has a woman to relieve him of responsibility for his own daily maintenance and the care of any children they may have. For this reason, single women and women without children or no longer responsible for children—women who are nominally likely to be able to participate in paid labor on the same terms as men—will exhibit work patterns different from those discussed above, although they will continue to find that the sexual division of labor and government policies premised on the assumption that women's primary role is that of housewife and mother still limit their opportunities (Pratt and Hanson, in Katz and Monk, 1993). Similarly, when aid programs and development policies in the third world take up and duplicate this assumption of women's proper domestic role in development planning, they erode women's traditional economic base (Rogers, 1980).

Generally, the manner in which paid work is organized—for example, around large discrete periods of concentrated single-minded labor—does not readily or easily accommodate disparate, repetitive, and cyclical tasks that daily or weekly constitute the bulk of domestic labor. Still less does the organization of paid labor accommodate the unpredictable, fragmented, and intense activities involved in infant and early child care. Without considerable adjustment to the way paid work is organized, and considerable change in men's freedom from domestic work and child care, the pressure of reconciling the public responsibilities of paid work and the private responsibilities of domestic life will fall more heavily on women. The accommodations will be made in the patterns of their working lives and how those working lives are experienced.

See Also

CAREGIVERS; CHILD CARE; DOMESTIC LABOR; ECONOMY: HISTORY OF WOMEN'S PARTICIPATION; ECONOMY: INFORMAL; HOUSEHOLD WORKERS; VOLUNTEERISM; WORK: EQUAL PAY AND CONDITIONS; WORK: OCCUPATIONAL SEGREGATION

References and Further Reading

Allen, Sheila, and Carol Wolkowitz. 1987. *Homeworking: Myths and realities*. London: Macmillan.

Baldock, Cora V. 1988. Public policies and the paid work of women. In Cora V. Baldock and Bettina Cass, eds., *Women, social welfare and the state*. Sydney: Allen and Unwin.

Baxter, Janeen. 1990. Domestic labor: Issues and studies. *Labor and Industry* 3(1): 112–145.

———, Diane Gibson, and Mark Lynch-Blosse. 1990. *Double take: The links between paid and unpaid work*. Canberra: Australian Government Publishing Service.

Beneria, Lourdes, ed. 1982. *Women and development: The sexual division of labor in rural societies*. New York: Praeger.

Finch, Janet. 1983. *Married to the job: Wives' incorporation in men's work*. Sydney: Allen and Unwin.

Gavron, Hannah. 1966. *The captive wife*. London: Routledge.

Kaluzynska, Eva. 1980. Wiping the floor with theory: A survey of writings on housework. *Feminist Review* 6: 27–54.

Katz, Cindi, and Janice Monk, eds. 1993. *Full circles: Geographies of women over the life course*. London: Routledge.

Lewenhak, Sheila. 1992. *The revaluation of women's work*. London: Earthscan.

Manderson, Lenore, ed. 1983. *Women's work and women's roles: Economics and everyday life in Indonesia, Malaysia, and Singapore*. Monograph no. 32, Development Studies Centre. Canberra: Australian National University.

Mies, Maria. 1982. *The lace-makers of Narsapur*. London: Zed.

Oakley, Ann. 1974. *The sociology of housework*. New York: Pantheon.

Ram, Bali, and Abdur Rahim. 1993. Enduring effects of women's early employment experiences on child-spacing: The Canadian experience. *Population Studies* 47: 307–317.

Rogers, Barbara. 1980. *The domestication of women: Discrimination in developing societies*. London: Tavistock.

Seager, Joni, and Ann Olson. 1986. *Women in the world: An international atlas*. London: Pan.

Streckeisen, Ursula. 1991. More and more women work: Inquiries into the work patterns of adult Swiss women. *Women's Studies International Forum* 14(1–2): 77–84.

Walby, Sylvia. 1986. *Patriarchy at work: Patriarchal and capitalist relations in employment*. Cambridge: Polity.

Walker, Jill. 1989. The production of exchange values and employment in the home. *Australian Feminist Studies* 9: 51–84.

Waring, Marilyn. 1988. *Counting for nothing: What men value and what women are worth*. Wellington, New Zealand: Allen and Unwin.

Beverly Thiele

WORK: Temporary

See PART-TIME AND CASUAL WORK.

WORKING-CLASS WOMEN

See CLASS.

WORLD WIDE WEB

See CYBERSPACE AND VIRTUAL REALITY; DIGITAL DIVIDE; INFORMATION TECHNOLOGY; *and* NETWORKS: ELECTRONIC.

XENOPHOBIA

See RACISM AND XENOPHOBIA.

Y

YOUTH CULTURE

Scholarship on youth culture was set in motion by G. Stanley Hall's "discovery" of adolescence in 1904, which brought together a range of analyses about young people and their relationships to education, family life, peers relations, sexuality, biology, and employment. Hall's dominant definition of *adolescence* is still relevant—it is a biological state when young people's bodies undergo the often perilous transition to adulthood and is a vulnerable time, a period of "storm and stress," when puberty's rioting hormones render young people both physically and emotionally unstable. This model has exerted tremendous influence in shaping contemporary understanding of youth culture internationally. When a cultural trend becomes popular among young people, arguments about its danger to an already unstable segment of the population often result in restrictions of one form or another, which are passed off as protection. Moreover, feminist scholars have pointed out that when "storm and stress" is applied to young women, the resulting restrictions are often much harsher than they are for young men, because women are understood as "naturally" more susceptible, more in need of protection. So we can see that this model provides a rationale for limiting girls' access to certain cultural forms of consumption and production.

When we discuss *youth culture,* we are referring primarily to how groups of young people use resources in their environment to help them to make sense of their lives, to experiment with and forge identities, and to express meanings about themselves and their relationship to their contexts. Although a cultural resource can be anything from a paper clip to a love song, because of the dominance of mass media forms such as popular music, fashion, television, and video games in our lives today, many scholars have argued that youth cultures are mediated primarily by popular cultural forms. Young people therefore make use of cultural resources and organize themselves in real, material ways, and popular media, government officials and policy makers, and academics (in other words, the adult world) interpret and explain young people in symbolic, discursive ways (often resulting in material consequences, of course).

Approaches Taken by Scholars

Two related approaches have shaped the development of scholarship on youth culture. First, youth itself is a social construction, an "invented" category that serves a heavily symbolic purpose; and, second, debates about and constructions of youth take place in historically specific contexts, using terms and arguments that resonate with particular social conditions. Because feminist scholarship has been integral in developing richer, more sophisticated, and more self-reflective understandings of youth culture, it has helped these tenets evolve to better reflect the experiences of young women.

Youth appears to be a function of economic, social, and political trends that have been gaining force internationally since the advent of industrialism. Even today, however, the time we think of as "youth" can vary tremendously as we cross social classes. Regardless of location, poor and working-class young people tend to experience the shortest period of youth, as many are forced to enter full-time employment and take up adult responsibilities much earlier than young people from other backgrounds. Among the reasons for a shift toward what we would call a more "discursive" understanding of youth is that most societies do not apply a consistent, empirically driven definition of youth. Moreover, even on reaching the age of majority, one is still usually considered a youth, because most societies define youth culturally—that is, symbolically.

We see socially constructed ideas about youth functioning internationally—for example, in the United States there are genX and Y, in Taiwan there are "new new human beings," in mainland China "the lucky generation." Each of these labels is infused with connotations of youth that resonate with meanings relevant to their respective contexts. And when we examine what is at stake in these cultural characteristics, we see that the idea of youth operates in ways that reveal how social anxieties about the future are constructed, amplified, and worked out. This internationally recurring theme—popular culture + youth = danger!—is articulated in different contexts in different ways, but feminists document the gendered development of moral panic. Thus, discussions about youth culture often are attached to fervent debates about policies designed to stitch youth more firmly into the social fabric, by restricting young people's access to forms of popular culture. Feminists have remarked that this point is particularly salient for young women, because for them, being stitched back into the social fabric often involves a very big needle and a tiny swath of cloth, resulting in significant regulation of young women's voices and bodies. The dominant stereotype that youth is rebellious, resistant, and threatening to the social order is inflected differently, depending on issues at stake in particular contexts. What this means is that in order to understand youth culture, we must make every attempt to consider what a particular cultural activity means to the young people experiencing it and how these meanings relate to the broader social arrangements that shape it. What navel piercing means to young people in Bulgaria is not necessarily what it would mean in Sweden, Nigeria, or the United States, and how different societies and contexts interpret young people's body decoration is shaped by issues at stake about youth in respective places.

Studying youth culture in its social context is anything but straightforward. Feminist scholars of youth culture have pointed out that traditional mainstream ("malestream") scholarship has a distinctly male understanding of youth, making generalizations about all youth from the study of primarily male youth. It fails to consider the role gender plays in shaping the social context itself. Many of the canonical texts were derived from ethnographic studies in which male academics observed and in some cases participated in the lives of groups of young men. Young women were largely absent from these narratives—either because much of the action took place on the streets or in places where young women were typ-

ically not welcome or because male researchers could not gain young women's trust, a crucial factor in motivating research subjects to share details about their private thoughts and experiences. When young women were described, the description is so "thin" that the young women appear to be nothing more than stereotypes. Besides the obvious implication that any generalization about youth culture deduced from such methods must be presented as a provisional one, feminist researchers have found that much scholarship on youth tends to render young women (and their use of cultural resources) invisible, expendable, or insignificant.

Culture Associated with Young Women

Feminist scholars also have argued that when a cultural form or product is enjoyed by, produced by, or associated primarily with young women (for example, "teen heartthrobs"), it is infantalized, denigrated, and not taken seriously. Yet, at the same time, when young women gain cultural visibility for using cultural resources in a manner not in keeping with prescribed norms of traditional femininity, they are either vilified in ways that tell us something of a society's views of all women or symbolically rehabilitated and reabsorbed back into the mainstream. We see in this description a recurrent critique feminists have made about cultural products associated with girls and young women. What is perceived (by popular media as well as social critics) as "girl culture" tends to be denigrated and dismissed, thought of as "soft" and "fluffy" or threatening in a way that reflects broader anxieties about women. In this case, the threat of unfettered, "abnormal" female sexuality can swell into an organized effort to contain and rehabilitate it. From another perspective, in the United States, with the astounding popularity of the movie *Titanic,* there was a spate of strident narratives in the popular media about the "tweening of American culture." In this case, commentators expressed fear that by pandering to the lucrative market of girls who were not quite teens but "tweens," popular cultural forms were dumbing themselves down even further. The way that young girls threaten the status quo, then, is by lowering its intellectual standards.

Feminists who study youth and culture do so from a variety of geographic locations and disciplinary moorings, and they share certain perspectives and commitments with these areas of emphasis. How can we best understand the cultural forms that young women engage and are engaged in, the cultural practices that young women participate in, and the cultural products that young women both consume and produce? Feminists also ask: How can we intervene in cultural forms, practices, and products that seem to restrict the lives and mobility of young women? Or how can we reconfigure young women's relationships to cultural products so that their experience is empowering rather than disempowering (keeping in mind that what we deem "harmful" or restrictive may not be experienced as such by young women). For example, there is a rich feminist literature that has addressed how cultural norms of femininity, often expressed symbolically through a woman's clothes, hairstyle, and use of cosmetics, allow for the perpetration of systems of gendered oppression. Yet feminists tend to be aware that a young woman who appears to embrace cultural norms of femininity can be doing so in order to serve her interests in manifold ways. She is not docile or passive but is making decisions about how to express herself given the tools she has at hand and her evaluation of her situation. Likewise, young women who become invested in cultural forms and products that appear to be misogynistic are not to be dismissed out of hand or simply thought of as self-hating. When we are able to understand the complexities of the context in which these investments are taken up, we might be surprised at what we find.

Feminist work on young women and culture, then, has focused on how young women make use of cultural resources, on how a culture's resources circumscribe young women's abilities to express their experiences in satisfying ways, on the stultifying effects of a profit-driven culture industry, and on the implications of popular cultural forms shot through with misogyny. Whereas literature on youth culture by male academics tends to emphasize how (male) young people *resist* forms of oppression by using cultural artifacts in creative, dynamic ways, feminists have been concerned with how cultural products and practices work to initiate young women into a system that restricts their mobility, their possibilities, and their ability to express themselves in satisfying ways. To be sure, feminist scholarship addresses how young women resist forms of oppression and celebrates young women's creativity and dynamism in their use of cultural resources. Yet most feminists argue that these forms of creativity are circumscribed by the limited tools made available and by how patriarchal social arrangements represent young women and their use of cultural resources in ways that perpetrate myths about young women, in effect stripping a situation of the conditions responsible for producing it. In the end, feminist research in this area works to demythologize young women by calling attention to the contexts in which young women make use of cultural resources. Feminists hold that we make

meanings with the tools made available to us because this is all we have—at least in the beginning. Culturally mediated signs of struggle can be reason enough for feminists to be cautiously optimistic about youth culture and the next generation of feminists.

See Also

ADOLESCENCE; DISCIPLINE IN SCHOOLS; GIRL STUDIES; GIRLS' SUBCULTURES; GRRLS; POPULAR CULTURE; SEXUALITY: ADOLESCENT SEXUALITY

References and Further Reading

Allison, Anne. 1996. *Permitted and prohibited desires: Mothers, comics, and censorship in Japan.* Boulder, Col.: Westview.

Bennett, Andy. 2000. *Popular music and youth culture: Music, identity, and place.* New York: St. Martin's.

Bhavnani, K., K. Kent, and F. Twine, eds. 1998. Feminisms and youth cultures. *Signs: Journal of Women in Culture and Society* 23: 575–881.

Cohen, Stanley. 1972. *Folk devils and moral panics.* London: Granada.

Fornas, J., and G. Bolin, eds. 1995. *Youth culture in late modernity.* London: Sage.

Gillis, J. R. 1974. *Youth and history.* New York: Academic.

Giroux, Henry A. 2000. *Stealing innocence: Youth, corporate power, and cultural politics.* New York: St. Martin's.

Griffin, Christine. 1993. *Representations of youth: The study of youth and adolescence in Britain and America.* Cambridge: Polity.

Grossberg, Lawrence. 1992. Rock and youth. In *We gotta get out of this place,* 171–200. New York: Routledge.

Hebdige, D. 1978. *Subculture: The meaning of style.* London: Methuen.

Johnson, Norine G., and Michael C. Roberts, eds. 1999. *Beyond appearance: A new look at adolescent girls.* Washington, D.C.: American Psychological Association Press.

Kan, Katharine. 1998. Not just a guy thing. *Voice of Youth Advocates* 20: 380–381.

Kinsella, Sharon. 1998. Japanese subculture in the 1990s: Otaku and the amateur *manga* movement. *Journal of Japanese Studies* 24: 289–316.

McRobbie, Angela. 1991. *Feminism and youth culture: From Jackie to Just Seventeen.* Boston: Unwin Hyman.

McRobbie, Angela, and Mica Nava, eds. 1984. *Gender and generation.* London: Macmillan.

Mizra, H. S. 1992. *Young, female, and black.* London: Routledge.

Nava, Mica. 1992. *Changing cultures: Feminism, youth, and consumerism.* London: Sage.

Pointon, Susan. 1997. Transcultural orgasm as apocalypse: Urotsukidoji: The legend of the overfiend. *Wide Angle* 19: 41–63.

Skelton, Tracey, and Gill Valentine, eds. 1997. *Cool places: Geographies of youth cultures.* New York: Routledge.

Skov, Lisa, and Brian Moeran, eds. *Women, media, and consumption in Japan.* London: Curzon.

Springhall, J. 1977. *Youth, empire, and society.* London: Croom Helm.

United Nations Centre for Development and Humanitarianism. 1993. *The global situation of youth in the 1990s: Trends and prospects.* New York: United Nations.

Watabe, Chiharu. 1999. Going gaijin. *Creative Review* 19(May): 77–78.

Maria Mastronardi

Z

ZEN

Women have been engaged in Zen Buddhist practices for more than a millennium. The existing record reveals that women have been active in Zen as leaders, teachers, patrons, and respected monastic and lay practitioners.

In Chinese Zen (Ch'an), the first recognized female teacher was Mo-Shan Liao-jan (tenth century), from the dominant school of Zen, the southern school. During the southern Sung (late eleventh century to thirteenth century), women participated in the pinnacle of Zen as teachers and practitioners—both monastic and lay.

In Japanese Zen, female disciples received direct tutelage from the founder of Sōtō Zen, Dōgen (1200–1253). Ever since then, women have participated in Sōtō Zen monastic and lay practice while contributing to the development of its teachings, practices, and institutional structures. Dōgen's first female monastic disciple, Ryōnen-ni (ordained in 1231), was attributed with being the primary influence in Dōgen's most explicit teaching on the equality of male and female practitioners in the *Bendōwa*. Another nun, Shōgaku Zenni (ordained in 1225), donated the funds to construct the Dharma Hall at Dōgen's first monastery, Kōshō-ji. Among other nuns, Egi-ni received Dōgen's tutelage for 19 years, including assisting him while he was ill before his death.

During the twentieth century several advances were made by Sōtō Zen nuns. They began the century with little recognition from the male-dominated sect authorities, and they ended the century with equal regulations. Kojima Kendō (1898–1995) led the nuns in the effort to compel the sect administration to revise sect regulations, eradicating regulations that had given male monastics preferential treatment. The first steps the nuns took were to gain equality in education and monastic training. On 10 August 1902, regulations for official degree-granting Sōtō Sect Nuns' Monastery Schools were established. By 1907 nuns had established monastery schools in Toyama, Aichi, Nagano, and Niigata prefectures. The largest is in Aichi, and it was established in 1903 by four nuns, Mizuno Jōrin (1848–1927), Hori Mitsujō (1868–1927), Andō Dōkai (1874–1915), and Yamaguchi Kokan (1875–1933). Aoyama Shundō (b. 1933) has been the abbess of Aichi Women's Monastery since 1976.

Female nuns of the Rinzai Zen sect in Japan participated in the Nuns' Five Mountain temple system known as Ni-gozan. The Five Mountain system is associated with the movement that gave rise to what is commonly referred to as Zen culture: painting, calligraphy, tea ceremony, flower arranging, and gardens.

In Korean Zen (Son), the nun Manseong (1897–1975) founded a Son monastery for women named T'aesong, located outside Pusan. A small order of T'aego Son nuns was founded in 1972. A large order of Chaogye Son nuns was founded in 1985.

In Vietnamese Zen (Thiem), Chan Khong (b. 1938) is a nun in the order Tiep Hien, founded by Thich Nhat Hanh. The experience of Zen Buddhist women during the Vietnam War is included in Khong's book, *Learning True Love* (1993).

In the United States and Europe women started lay and monastic Zen Buddhist practice in the late nineteenth century. A number of female teachers are engaged in acculturating Zen to occidental cultural contexts. The first woman recognized for her contribution to the introduction of Zen to the West is known as Mrs. Russell. In 1905, the Zen master Soyen Shaku (teacher of D. T. Suzuki) wrote a poem to Mrs. Russell that ends: "Someday my [fifth patriarch of Zen] teaching will surely go to the West,/Led by you." During the 1930s and 1940s, Ruth Fuller Sasaki was a principal supporter of the Buddhist Society of America in New York. Jiyu

Kennett Roshi founded Shasta Abbey in 1970. Elsie Mitchell established the Cambridge Buddhist Association in 1957; it was headed by Maurine Myoon Stuart Roshi from 1979 to 1990. Barbara Rhodes helped found the Providence Zen Center, becoming master dharma teacher in 1978. Since 1983, Charlotte Joko Beck has run the Zen Center of San Diego. Patricia Dai-en Bennage Roshi founded the Mount Equity Zendo in 1991.

See Also

BUDDHISM; NUNS

References and Further Reading

Aoyama, Shundō. 1990. *Zen seeds: Reflections of a female priest.* Trans. Patricia Daien Bennage. Tokyo: Kosei.

Arai, Paula K. R. 1999. *Women living Zen: Japanese Sōtō Buddhist nuns.* New York: Oxford University Press.

Beck, Charlotte Joko. 1993. *Nothing special: Living Zen.* Ed. Steve Smith. San Francisco: HarperSanFrancisco.

Khong, Chang. 1993. *Learning true love: How I learned and practiced social change in Vietnam.* Berkeley, Calif.: Parallax.

Levering, Miriam. 1998. Dogen's *Raihaitokuzui* and women teaching in Sung Ch'an. *Journal of the International Association of Buddhist Studies* 21(1): 77–110.

———. 1999. The nun Miao-tao and her teacher Ta-hui Tsung-kao. In Peter Gregory and Daniel Getz, eds., *Buddhism in Sung China.* Honolulu: Kuroda Institute Series, University of Hawaii Press.

Paula Arai

ZINES

A zine (pronounced *zeen*) is an independently produced, noncommercial magazine, traditionally with a small circulation and a narrow scope of interest. Zines are most often characterized by a casual, intimate writing style and typically address topics not covered by the mainstream media. The 1990s saw a boom in the creation of zines by and for women. These zines are frank, personal documents of subjects of specific concern to women—from angry, uncensored accounts of sexual abuse to tips on combating street harassment to critical dissections of representations of women in traditional "women's magazines." Zines are most commonly distributed through one-on-one contact between creator and reader, by hand distribution, mail order, or trades with other zine makers. In this way, zines are also an effective, grassroots means of building an alternative international feminist community.

Factsheet Five, a triannual directory that, in the 1990s, cataloged thousands of zine reviews, but is now defunct, defined a zine as "a small handmade amateur publication, done purely out of passion, rarely making a profit or breaking even." Beyond this very loose definition, however, the defining characteristic of a zine is that anything goes. Zines range in format from folded documents of a few pages to perfect-bound magazines of more than one hundred pages. Their design and production run the stylistic gamut from simple, photocopied cut-and-paste techniques to slick, professional-looking layouts created using desktop publishing software and printed on an offset press.

Roots of Zines

Zines have their roots in the "little magazines" of the 1920s, the science fiction newsletters of the midcentury (from which sprang the term *fanzine*), and the underground press of the 1960s counterculture. Contemporary zines developed out of the North American punk rock subculture of the late 1970s and 1980s. One hallmark of the punk scene was its support of a "do-it-yourself" (DIY) attitude toward cultural production. Rejecting conventional notions of expertise and skill, this DIY ethic encouraged people with little or no experience to start bands, make art, and write zines. Most early punk zines were primarily focused on underground music and served as a means of disseminating information about the music scene to a loose international community of like-minded musicians, fans, and other zine makers.

With the growing availability of reproduction technologies and the boom in personal computer use, both the number and the production quality of zines have increased appreciably. No longer strictly concerned with the minutiae of the underground music scene, zine writers now write about everything from politics to pop culture trivia. With the phenomenal growth of zine culture in the 1980s and 1990s, zines produced by and for women came to play an increasingly visible and vocal role in the world of zines.

"Girl Zines"

"Girl zines," as they are commonly known in zine-speak, are not just by or for girls but are created by a wide variety of women, young and old. The use of the word *girl* (rather than *woman*) reflects the impact of "riot grrl" on girl zine making. Riot grrl, a grassroots political movement of young punk women, used the DIY principles of the punk scene to encourage other young women to speak out and fight back against sexism and violence by creating their own bands and zines.

Riot grrl zines address such traditionally feminist concerns as rape, sexual abuse, and violence against women, but in the idiosyncratic, personal voice of the writer rather than in the removed, objective tone of the journalist or academic. Other girl zines are strictly personal, focusing on explorations of growth, self-esteem, and relationships. Still others may be less explicitly feminist yet still political, more concerned with questions of race and class. Some might be just for fun. Not all girl zines are riot Grrl zines, but all provide a critical forum for self-expression for women who feel marginalized by the punk community, the feminist community, or mainstream culture more generally. Unlike straight journalism, zine writing prefers the individual story.

Zine making offers a means of combating the gender roles and assumptions about lifestyle propagated by the dominant culture. Zine writers replace these often ill-fitting stereotypes with their own stories, defining their own identities and worldview. With evocative, often confrontational titles such as *Bitch, FaT GiRL, Harlot, hip Mama,* and *Lezzie Smut,* girl zines concisely assert a fiercely individual vision of female identity.

Mainstream Media Attention

In the past decade zines have attracted a significant amount of attention from the mainstream media . Some zines have become quite professional and are practically indistinguishable from commercially produced magazines. With international distribution of more than 10,000 copies, glossy four-color printing, and pages of advertisements, the New York City–based *Bust* is perhaps the most visible zine of this genre. Some more politicized zine editors are critical of such crossover attempts, feeling that zine editors have a responsibility to remain outside mainstream channels of distribution and commerce. Such bids for large-scale publication are seen as "selling out" and antithetical to the independent, DIY spirit of zine culture. Others feel that despite the external trappings of commercial success, *Bust* and other "successful" zines retain an independent, uncensored voice. In addition, those zines that secure popular distribution—in chain bookstores and on newsstands—can serve as a much needed introduction to zines for girls and women living outside of urban areas, who may not have immediate access to the independent book and record stores that support an urban zine culture.

Zines and Internet Technology

The explosive growth of Internet technology has opened a multitude of further possibilities for zine production. Although Internet access is still available only to those with the education and relative wealth to take advantage of it, the World Wide Web has already seen the creation of a network of girl zine Web sites. Sites such as *gURL, Maxi,* and *exoticize this!* provide original writing and art, as well as links to other Web zines and on-line feminist resources. Other sites are Web adjuncts of already existing print zines (*Bust, hipmama*), while still others consolidate and organize information about feminist sites on the Web and provide a convenient, reliable jumping-off point for further exploration (*Estronet*). Web zines require as much labor and financing as print zines and probably will not supplant the printed product anytime soon, but the democratic, non-hierarchical nature of the Web bodes particularly well for the creation of a strong international community of zine makers.

As Karen Green and Tristan Taormino (1997) note in the introduction to their anthology of girl zine writings, zines are "sites for communication, education, community, revolution, celebration, and self-expression." Because they are distributed by hand—sold at rock shows, given away to friends, or mailed to foreign readers intrigued by a listing in another zine, they are one of the only unmediated means of communication left in a mediascape increasingly dominated by corporate interests. By encouraging women to tell their own stories and become actively involved in creating their own zine, rather than being passive consumers of commercial media, zines are part of an ongoing, dynamic process of empowerment and subversion.

See Also

AUTOBIOGRAPHY; CARTOONS AND COMICS; CYBERSPACE AND VIRTUAL REALITY; GRRLS; MAGAZINES; MEDIA: ALTERNATIVE; MEDIA: GRASSROOTS; PUBLISHING: FEMINIST PUBLISHING IN THE WESTERN WORLD; YOUTH CULTURE

References and Further Reading

Duncombe, Stephen. 1997. *Notes from underground: Zines and the politics of alternative culture.* New York: Verso.

Green, Karen, and Tristan Taormino, eds. 1997. *A girl's guide to taking over the world: Writings from the girl zine revolution.* New York: St. Martin'.

Vale, V. 1996, 1997. *Zines!* Vols. 1 and 2. San Francisco: V/Search.

Zines

Bitch, 3128 16th Street, P.O. Box 201, San Francisco, Calif. 94103

Bust, PO Box 319, New York, N.Y. 10023

FaT GiRL, Fat Girl Collective, 2215-R Market Street, San Francisco, Calif. 94114

hip Mama, Ariel Gore, PO Box 9097, Oakland, Calif. 94613

Lezzie Smut c/o Hey Grrrlz Productions/Robin Hand, PO Box 364, 1027 Davie Street, Vancouver, British Columbia V6E 4L2, Canada

Web Zines

Bust <www.bust.com>
Estronet <www.estronet.com>
exoticize this! <members.aol.com/Critchicks>
gURL <www.gURL.com>
hip Mama <www.hipmama.com>
Maxi <www.maximag.com>
Rockrgrl <www.rockrgrl.com>

Martha Bayne

ZIONISM

There is no single definition for the term *Zionism.* As with many other contested terms, the meanings and practices associated with Zionism depend on the particular standpoint of the person or group defining it. While there are different strands of Zionism—such as socialist and nonsocialist, religious and secular—for most Jews, Zionism is a movement for Jewish national self-determination that eventually led to the establishment of Israel as a Jewish state (Hertzberg, 1962). Palestinians and many others, by contrast, view Zionism as a racist ideology that underlies the settler–colonial movement responsible for the occupation of Palestine and the dispossession of its indigenous Palestinian population (Abdo, 1992; Zunes, 1994). The Zionist movement emerged in the late nineteenth century in Europe in response to the rise of European nationalism and anti-Semitism. With the Holocaust, which increased the flow of Jewish immigrants to Palestine, the Zionist movement gained significant international recognition and support. For the most part, however, the history of Zionism and the contested debates about its nature and politics did not address its gendered dimensions.

Through consistent references to the survival of Israel and of the Jewish people as a whole, Zionism has, arguably, constructed particular notions of femininity, masculinity, and gender relations. The assertion of an aggressive and highly militarized masculinity, for example, was justified by the need to end a history of weakness, suffering, and persecution. Images of Israeli-Jewish men that are exceedingly masculine—pragmatic, protective, aggressive, and emotionally tough—have been contrasted with fairly traditional notions of femininity, on the one hand, and with images of the helpless and powerless Jew in the diaspora most commonly associated with the collective traumatic memories of the Holocaust, on the other. In addition to the negative juxtaposition of the Israeli-born Jew with women and with Jews in the diaspora, the Zionist conception of masculinity has been contrasted with images of the so-called enemy. In sum, Jews who were not born in Israel or do not live there, women, and Arabs (especially Palestinians)—all characterized as nonmasculine—became the background against which the "new" Jewish men were encouraged to assert their masculine identity (Sharoni, 1995).

Zionism's conception of femininity, by contrast, was far less elaborate and did not represent a drastic departure from traditional women's roles. In principle, the Zionist project, like other nationalist projects, provided women with a compelling vision of collective identity, with a community in which they could be members, and with incentives to become political actors. In reality, however, women did not have much say in determining the terms of their social and political inclusion; their participation in the Zionist project depended, to a great extent, on their willingness to comply with the gendered division of labor and power within the movement. While men were expected to be the liberators and protectors of the Jewish people, women, who were cast as symbols of the nation and the land, were viewed as vulnerable and in need of protection and were assigned primary responsibility for the reproduction of the nation and for the transmission of its culture (Katz, 1995; Sharoni, 1995).

Zionist women who settled in Palestine around the turn of the century were inspired by the nationalist-socialist ideology prevalent in the Zionist movement at the time. They called into question the limited roles assigned to women in the emerging society. These women had come to Palestine to participate more fully in social life than they had been permitted to do in the middle-class circles of their Jewish communities in eastern Europe; they expected that gender equality would be an accompanying feature of their move to the new homeland. Reality, however, did not meet their expectations; women were relegated to secondary roles in the new society. Since domestic work was still considered by many—both men and women—as women's responsibility, women were automatically assigned to the kitchen and the laundry. At the same time, farmers in the agricultural villages refused to employ women, considering them inefficient as workers and immoral because they lived on their own among men (Bernstein, 1992).

With the escalation of tensions between Zionists and Palestinians opposed to their settlement in Palestine in the mid-1930s, the problem of gender equality was further marginalized and relegated to a secondary status. Many women acceded to this. Some contended, however, that equality of rights depended on equality of duties and, therefore, sought to participate in various paramilitary organizations that operated underground. Still, women's participation in these organizations was limited to auxiliary roles on the home front; women were not allowed to take part in civil defense or in military operations. This gendered division of labor and power was further institutionalized with the establishment of the state of Israel.

See Also

JUDAISM; KIBBUTZ

References and Further Reading

Abdo, Nahla. 1992. Racism, Zionism and the Palestinian working class, 1920–1947. *Studies in Political Economy* 37(2): 59–93.

Bernstein, Deborah, ed. 1992. *Pioneers and homemakers: Jewish women in pre-state Israel.* Albany, N.Y.: State University of New York Press.

Hertzberg, Arthur, ed. 1962. *The Zionist idea: A historical analysis and reader.* New York: Doubleday.

Katz, Sheila Hannah. 1995. Adam and Adama, Ird and Ard: Engendering political conflict and identity in Jewish and Palestinian nationalisms. In Deniz Kandiyoti, ed., *Gendering the Middle East: Emerging perspectives.* London: Tauris.

Said, Edward. 1979. Zionism from the standpoint of its victims. In *The question of Palestine.* New York: Vintage.

Sharoni, Simona. 1994. Feminist reflections on the interplay of racism and sexism in Israel. In Ethel Tobach and Betty Rosoff, eds., *Challenging racism and sexism: Alternatives to genetic explanations.* New York: Feminist Press.

———. 1995. *Gender and the Israeli–Palestinian conflict: The politics of women's resistance.* Syracuse N.Y.: Syracuse University Press.

Shohat, Ella. 1988. Sepharadim in Israel: Zionism from the standpoint of its Jewish victims. *Social Text* 19–20: 1–35.

Stasiulis, Daiva, and Nira Yuval-Davis, eds. 1995. *Unsettling settler societies: Articulations of gender, race, ethnicity and class.* London: Sage.

Zunes, Stephen. 1994. Zionism, anti-Semitism, and imperialism. *Peace Review* 6(1): 41–49.

Simona Sharoni

Index

Note: Page numbers in **boldface** indicate article titles.
Volume key: 1, pages 1–499; 2, pages 500–1096; 3, pages 1097–1714; 4, pages 1715–2167

Commission on the Status of Women (U.S.). *See* President's Commission on the Status of Women (1961)

Committee for Abortion Rights and against Sterilization Abuse (CARASA), 1756

Committee of Soviet Union (CSW), 740

Committee of Women for Progress (Jamaica), 727

Committee on Asian Women (CAW), 1709

Committee on Equality for Women (Canada), 822

Committee on South Asian Women (U.S.), 714

Committee on the Causes and Cures for War (U.S.), 1522, 1524

Committee on the Elimination of Discrimination against Women (CEDAW). *See* United Nations Convention on the Elimination of Discrimination against Women

Committee on the Status of Women in India, 2103–2104

Committee on Women, Population and the Environment (U.S.), 930

commodity culture, 139, **194–195**, 197

Common Catalog, The (directory), 2103

Commoner, Barry, 1638

common law, 1190, 1200

    on adoption, 14

    as discriminatory against women, 657, 677, 678, 687, 759, 1194, 1195, 1380

    onjustifiable self-defense, 1195

    patriarchal family themes in, 657, 802

common law marriage, 189, 1020–1021

Commonwealth of Independent States

    abortion law, 3

    child care provisions, 159

    comparative economic status, 438

    economic development, 341–344

    education, 482

    environmental problems, 575–578

    feminism, 739–745

    health care, 961–963, 966

    households and families, 1028–1031

    literature, 1275–1277, 1287–1289

    political representation, 1584–1588

    suspension of legal support for women workers, 1201

    violence against women, 2000–2002

    women's studies and research centers, 1236, 2062, 2072, 2104

    See also Armenia; Azerbaijan; Belarus; Georgia; Kazakhstan; Kyrgyzstan; Moldova; Russia; Soviet Union (former); Tajikistan; Turkmenistan; Ukraine; Uzbekistan

communalism

    China and, 336, 337

    collectivism organizations, 997

    community and, 209, 210–211

    ecofeminist, 1186

    feminist epistemology and, 1185

    as feminist response to patriarchy, 1495

    first-wave feminist advocates of, 760, 764, 766

    kibbutz, 1179–1181

    liberalism vs., 1227–1228

    Native North American, 686

    networking and, 1445–1447

    utopian socialism and, 801

    women as symbol of, 1432–1433

    See also cooperation

Communication for Change (N.Y.C.), 1985

communications: audience analysis, **196–200**

    black female oppositional gaze and, 276, 876

    of European images of women, 1116

    feminist film theory on, 861–862

    gendered film spectatorship and, 857–858, 858–859, 861–862

    gender preferences in media type and, 1116

    hard and soft news and, 1163–1164

    improved images of women and, 1100

    lesbian perceptions, 1208

    for mass media political coverage, 1340–1341

    media studies and, 1327

    politics of representation and, 875–876, 1100–1101

    "reading against the grain," 1338

soap operas and, 1920–1921

    stereotypes, awareness of, 1338

    television representations and, 1920

    women as consumers of culture and, 274–276

communications: content and discourse analysis, **201–202**

    content analysis, 201, 1099–1101, 1243

    discourse analysis, 201–202, 1243–1244

    gendered differences, 96, 1188–1189, 1242, 1243

    gendered play studies, 907

    media content, 1326–1327

    media representations of women and, 1099–1101, 1107

    oral tradition and, 1480–1481

    postmodernism and, 1650–1652

    See also conversation; *écriture féminine*

communications: overview, **195–196**

    advertising industry, 22–24

    assertiveness training, 95–96

    computer-mediated, 1761

    cyberspace, 283–286, 1448–1449

    digital divide and, 382

    dress as nonverbal form of, 422–423

    gatekeeping, 898–899

    global feminism and, 924, 933

    global health movement and, 927

    globalization of, 931, 933

    information technology, 1141–1144

    silence as alternative to, 1850–1851

    studies, 194, 898

    zine culture and, 276, 277, 278, 920, 922, **2164–2166**

    See also Internet; media, *specific entries*; networks, electronic; video

communications: speech, **202–205**

    analysis of nonwestern women's patterns, 1242

    conversation, 233–238, 1188–1190

    oral tradition, 1479–1481

    silence and, 1849–1852

    See also language; linguistics

Communication, Technology, and Society: Conceptions of Casuality and the Politics of Technological Intervention (Slack), 1143

communism, **205–208**

    anarchism and, 46

    central and eastern European economic development and, 327, 328, 329

    child care system, 158, 159

    Chinese economic development and, 335, 336–338, 339–340

    Chinese feminism and, 737–738

    Chinese media and, 1332–1333

    conservative gender politics as backlash against, 224–225

    Cuban women under, 1581–1582

    eastern European, 205–206, 207, 1593–1594

    eastern European education under, 494

    eastern European feminism under, 750, 751

    family policy, 903, 1024, 1033–1034, 1613

    fascism and Nazism as enemy of, 638, 696

    folk music and, 1394

    genocide and, 913

    green movement and, 942

    health care system, 966

    households and families under, 1023–1024, 1029–1030

    legal systems, 1200–1201

    Maoist, 738, 1865

    Maoist education model, 492–493

    Nicaraguan women under, 1581–1582

    preschool provisions, 515

    socialist parties and, 1865

    Soviet economic development and, 341–343

    as Soviet literature influence, 1275–1276

    theory vs. reality of women's emancipation under, 157, 205–207, 341–342, 552, 575–576, 739–740, 743, 1232, 1585–1587, 1592, 1593–1594, 2085

    women's peace activists and, 1522, 1523

    women's studies legacies, 2077–2078

    See also feminism: Marxist; Marxism; "Red scares"; socialism; Soviet Union

Communist Manifesto (Marx), 1308, 1864, 1865

Communist Party of China. *See* Chinese Communist Party

Communist Party of the Soviet Union (CPSU), 740, 1275, 2055

Communist Party of the United States, 1394, 2058

communitarians. *See* communalism; utopianism

community, **208–209**

    and bookstores, women's, 117–118

    built environment and, 126

    convents as, 1450

    creation of, 208, 210–211

    different definitions of, 208, 209, 210

    and domestic violence, coordinated response, 416

    history of concept of, 209

    long-term care services, 1293–1294

    settlement house movement and, 765

    women-only, 746

    See also community politics; socialism; utopianism

Community Action Program (European Union), 72

community gardens, 34

Community of Feminist Lesbians in Israel, 776

community politics, **209–211**

    anarchist feminists and, 49

    definitions of, 209

    identity politics and, 1097–1098

    immigrant women's services, 1125

    Internet politics and states, 1154–1155

    Latin American feminists and, 732

    multiculturalism and, 1389

    neighborhood organization, 88–89

    nongovernmental organizations and, 1451

    services offered by, 87

    women's roles in, 210–211, 940, 1583

    See also political participation

Comnena, Anna, 1250

Comninou, Maria, 62

Como Agua para Chocolate (film), 1112

Comolli, Jean-Louis, 861

Compagnia Drammatica dell Città di Roma, 1934

companionate union (term), 1020–1021

comparable worth, 612, 2134

    See also work: equal pay and conditions

Compensation for National Debt movement (Korea; 1907), 781

competitiveness, androcentrism supporting, 59

complementary medicine

    health care and, 954

    holistic health and, 1006

    in western Europe, 980

composers. *See* music: composers

composition theory, 97

compound families, 692

Compton's Cafetereia Riot (San Francisco), 1968

compulsive eating, 432

compulsory altruism, 45

Compulsory Education Act (1921; Thailand), 1279

compulsory heterosexuality. *See* feminism: lesbian

"Compulsory Heterosexuality and Lesbian Existence" (Rich), 785, 996, 1215, 1270

computer games, 215

computer-mediated communication (CMQ), 1761–1762

computer science, **211–213**

    ability and, 1–2

    components of, 211

    programming history, 99, 211

    role of women in, 211–212, 213, 214, 1331, 1807

    See also computing: overview; information revolution; information technology

computing: overview, **213–216**

    automation and, 99, 100

    cyberspace and, 284–286

    cyberterrorism and, 1927

    digital divide and, 381–382

    distance education application, 487

    effects on women's traditional jobs, 1917

    global restructuring and, 453

    historical background, 99, 211, 213–215

    masculinity associated with, 215

    occupational ergonomic risks, 1478

Devi, Siddeshwari, 1412
devil. *See* demonization
Devillers, Marina, 88
Devimahatmyam (Hindu text), 999
DeVore, Irven, 66–67
devotional literature, 1290
Dewey, John, 484, 1526
Dewey, Melvil, 489
de Wolfe, Elsie, 1147
Dhanammal, Vina, 1412
Dharmastrasas (Hindu text), 143
diabetes, 957, 984
Diablo Canyon nuclear power plant, 2051
Diaghilev, Serge, 290, 292
Diagnostic and Statistical Manual of Mental Disorders
    (DSM-III, DSM-IV), 64, 312, 1701–1702
Dialectic of Sex, The (Firestone), 821, 822, 1808
Diallo, Assitan, 745
Dialogues in Paradise (Can Xue), 1260
Dialogues of the Dead (Montagu), 114
Diamond, Elin, 1532
Diamond, Irene, 430
Diana, princess of Wales, 107, 128, 991
Diana of Dobson's (Hamilton), 1936
Diana Press, 1712
Dianic Wicca, 2037
diaphragm (contraceptive), 229, 231, 1549, 1633, 1752,
    1753
diaries and journals, **375–378**
    editorial intervention in, 375–376
    Japanese, 1265
    Latin American, 1257
    themes in, 376–378, 1268
    travel, 377
diarrhea, 966
Diary of Izumi Shikibu, The, 1265
Diary of Murasaki Shikibu, The, 1265
diaspora space, 1088, 1089
Dibo, Amal, 1519
Dick (film), 1327
Dickinson, Emily, 375–376, 854, 1217, 1263, 1268,
    1269, 1556–1557
Dick-Read, Grantly, 1475
dictionaries, feminist, 1188
didanosine (Videx), 36
Diderot, Denis, 46
"Did Women Have a Renaissance?" (Kelly-Gadol),
    1249
Dien, Cut Nyak, 839
diet. *See* cooking; food and culture; nutrition I
    and II
dietary chaos syndrome, 432
Diet for a New America (Robbins), 1981
Diet for a Small Planet (Lappé), 1981
diethylstilbestrol (DES), 137, 556, 616, 650, 1343, 1536,
    1537, 1627, 1753, 1952
dieting. *See* eating disorders; food and culture
Dietrich, Marlene, 861, 1122
difference I and II, **378–380, 380–381**
    ethnicity and, 634–635
    female writing tradition and, 1246–1247
    feminists theoretical questions on, 1097, 1098,
        1247, 1823–1824
    formal equality theory and, 1195, 1565
    French linguistic debate on, 378–379
    gendered play and, 907
    global feminism concerns, 924–925
    health education considerations, 988
    identity politics and, 1097–1098
    images of women and, 1100
    indirect discrimination and recognition of, 397
    linguistic theories, 1188–1190, 1242–1244, 1851
    nature-nurture debate and, 1441
    occupational health and safety issues, 1477
    organizational structure and, 1482
    pedagogies of, 1525, 1526–1529
    political representation and, 1565
    politics of, 1571
    as popular postmodern term, 1651
    postmodern critique and, 1651–1652, 1824
    sisterhood and, 1855

stereotyping and, 876
    among women, 1851–1852
    woman-centeredness, 2045
    See also other; sexual difference
difference feminism, 380–381, 612–613, 614
    concepts of, 380–381
    critique of, 379, 380
    deconstruction of, 807, 808, 828
    feminist legal critiques and, 1176, 1196
    legal theory and, 1195
    lesbian studies and, 1215–1216
    origins of, 381
    pedagogical theory, 1525
    on roots of oppression of women, 380–381
    See also feminism: cultural
differentialist racism, 1724
differently abled. *See* disability
DiFranco, Ani, 919, 1417
Digambara (Jain sect), 145
digital divide, **381–383**
digitalis, 1785
Dike, Fatima, 1937
Dilemma of a Ghost, The (Aidoo), 1285
Diller, Phyllis, 1087
"Dill Pickle, The" (Mansfield), 1848–1849
Dima (Senegalese women's association), 40
Dimitrova, Blaga, 1263
"Dimples" (cartoon strip), 141
Dines, Gail, 1639
Dinesen, Isak, 1848
Ding Ling, 1260
Dingman, Beth, 1712
Dinka (people), 1857
Dinner Party (artwork by Judy Chicago), 868, 878,
    1640–1641, 1930
Dinnerstein, Dorothy, 1684, 1791, 1792
Dinnerstein, Myra, 281
Dion, Celine, 919
Dionysian mysteries, 1424
Dionysos (deity), 428
dioxin, 1627
diphtheria, 966
direct democracy, 303
direct discrimination
    definition of, 69, 396
    in financial market, 864–865
    forms of, 396
    legal, 1190
Directors Guild of America, 855
Directory of National Women's Organizations, 1736
disability
    ability vs., 1
    abortion and, 4
    assisted technology for, 386
    black women's simultaneous oppression, 1852–1853
    definition of, 2
    descriptors for, 385–386
    independent living and, 384
    as infanticide motive, 1135
    information technology's aids, 1143
    long-term care services, 1293–1294
    and Nazis, 390, 913
    negative eugenics and, 637
    as socially constructed, 383, 390
    special needs education and, 530–532
disability: elite body, **384–385**
disability: health and sexuality, **385–389**
disability: quality-of-life debate, **389–391**
    euthanasia and, 642–643
    genetic screening issues, 383, 389–390, 910–911
disability and feminism, **383–384**, 385
    prenatal testing debate, 389–390
    simultanous oppression situation, 1852–1853
Disability Awareness in Action, 383
Disabled People's International, 383
"disappeared" persons (Latin America), 225, 245, 732,
    1509, 1582, 1926
disarmament, **391–394**, 1989
    nuclear weapons protests, 1459, 1514–1515, 2030
    U.S. and Canadian peace activists for, 1522
    women as innovative thinkers on, 392–393

See also pacifism and peace activism; peace
    movements, *specific entries*
disasters. *See* environmental disasters
discipline in schools, **394–396**
Discordes, 1951
discourse analysis. *See* communications: content and
    discourse analysis
Discourse and Society (journal), 202
discrimination, **396–397**
    affirmative action and, 27–29
    as African-American feminist issue, 708–711
    ageism as, 29, 1463, 2059
    antiracist and civil rights movements, 74–76
    caste and, 142–144
    definition of, 69, 396
    direct and indirect, 69–70, 396–397, 864–865,
        1190–1191, 1194–1195
    disabilities and, 386, 387
    ethnicity and, 633
    feminist legal critiques, 1194–1196, 1197
    in financial markets, 864–865
    genetic screening and, 910
    heterophobia and homophobia as, 992–993
    in housing, 1076
    hypertension linked with, 1093–1094
    against indigenous women, 1133
    in Internet use, 1140–1141
    legal, 1190–1191, 1194–1195
    nature-nurture debate and, 1440–1441
    Nazi policies, 696–697
    neoclassical economic theories of, 444–445
    by New Left males, 771
    occupational safety and, 1477
    occupational segregation as, 2149–2151
    in political asylum grants, 1191, 1558
    in reproductive technology availability, 1749
    sexual harassment as, 1824–1825
    sports and, 1888–1890
    systemic, 397
    taboos as, 1910
    in unemployment benefits access, 1972
    union movements and, 1975–1976
    See also antidiscrimination; anti-Semitism; apartheid,
        segregation, and ghettoization; equality; equity;
        heterosexism; racism and xenophobia; sexism;
        work: equal pay and conditions
disease, **398–399**
    in central and eastern Europe, 966
    culture-specific, 398
    definition of, 398
    genetic, 910–911, 1720–1721
    genocide and, 912
    health education on, 986
    historical women's ailments, 1342–1343
    holistic health view of, 1005, 1006, 1007
    internal medicine and, 1345–1349
    pharmaceuticals and, 1536
    race and, 1720–1721
    sexually transmitted. *See* sexually transmitted
        diseases
    in southeast Asia, 970
    in sub-Saharan Africa, 975
    vulnerability to, 952
    as women's health challenge, 985
    See also health: overview; health care, *specific
        entries*; health challenges; specific diseases and
        disorders
Disney Company, 24
Disney Productions, 1119
disordered eating. *See* eating disorders
Disorders of Sexual Desire (Kaplan), 1832
displaced persons. *See* refugees
Dispossessed, The (Le Guin), 1808
Distance Education (journal), 486
distance learning. *See* education: distance education
diuretics, 127
Divan (E'tesami), 1273
Divar (Farrokhzad), 1273
diversity
    as affirmative action goal, 28
    See also multiculturalism

postcolonial theory and criticism as reaction to,
1646
postmodern challenge to, 1649
race and cosmetic use and, 242
racial taxonomy and, 1720
settler societies promulgating, 1812
Europe. *See* eastern Europe; European Union; western
Europe; *specific countries*
European American Studies Association, 627
European Commission, 1115
European Community (EC). *See* European Union
European Convention on the Protection of Human
Rights, 227
European Economic Community (EEC). *See*
European Union
European Journal of Women's Studies, 2127
European Monetary Union (EMU), 369
European Network for Policewomen, 1193
European Network of Women in the Audio Visual
Arts, 1334
European Network of Women's Studies (ENWS), 541,
2094, 2103
European Parliament (EP), 605, 1561
equal opportunity politics, 181, 817
women members, 1622
European Union (EU)
antidiscrimination measures, 72–73
child care, publicly funded, 158–159
competition from third world cheap female labor,
437
economic development, 371, 372
environmental action plan, 604, 605
equal access to education resolutions, 540, 1623
equal pay and working conditions provisions,
72–73, 369, 1623, 2134
Erasmus scheme, 2128
maternity leave provisions, 440, 813
and new borders, 119
part-time emploment rates by sex, 465
part-time worker directive, 438–439
violence against women and children directives, 9
women's higher education provisions, 541
women's networks, 817, 1861
women's studies support, 2076, 2103
European University (St. Petersburg, Russia), 744
European Women in Mathematics, 1317
European Women's Studies Guide, 1737
European Women's Thesaurus, 1235
Europride Festivals, 1210
Eurynome (deity), 247
euthanasia, **642–644**
Nazi program, 390
and quality of life, 389
evangelicalism, 170
nineteenth-century feminism and, 800–801
See also fundementalism, religious
Evans, Mari, 1271
Evans, Mary Ann. *See* Eliot, George
Evatt, Elizabeth, 71
Eve and the New Jerusalem (Taylor), 760
Eve (biblical figure), 85, 168–169, 170
curse of, 283, 430
demonization of, 310
misogynistic view of, 1376
nature and, 1437
racial designation for, 1720
as sinful, 1842
Evelina (Burney), 1457
Evelyn-White, Hugh G., 429
Even (musical performer), 919
Eve's Garden (woman's sex store), 1313
evil. *See* demonization; sin
evolution, **644–647**
anatomical sex differences and, 51, 82–83, 83–84,
1548–1549
ancestral mother groups, 631
biological anthropology and, 65, 66–67, 68
biological determinism and, 108, 109, 644–646
concepts of nature and, 1437–1438
eugenics and, 635–636, 639, 1440
Gaia hypothesis and, 897

genetics and, 908
nature-nurture debate and, 1440
"ontology recapitulates phylogeny," 1720–1721
racial taxonomy and, 1720
social Darwinism as misapplication of, 639
women-centered models, 646
Ewart, Florence, 1396
Ewe (people), 1857
Ewen, Stuart, 1338
Ewha Hakdang (Korea) mission school, 492
Ewha Women's University, 2065, 2091
examinations and assessment, **647–648**
ability vs. test bias, 2
psychometrics, 1698–1699
excision (female genital mutilation), 700
Exclusion Act (1882; U.S.), 713
Exclusion Act (1924: U.S.). *See* Immigration
Restriction Act
executive positions. *See* management
exercise and fitness, **648–649**
benefits of exercise, 648–649
definitions of, 648
excessive exercise issue, 649
good health role, 920–921
as leisure activity, 1203
physical education, 510–512
See also sport; sport and discrimination
existential feminism. *See* feminism: existential
exogamy, 1301, 1303, 1614, 1839
experimental critical writing. *See* autobiographical
criticism
experimental method, 1442–1443
experiments on women, 631, **650–651**
disparities in, 1344
gynecological surgery, 1901–1902
oral contraceptive testing, 1957
reproductive technology clinical tests as, 849
See also contraceptives: development
Exponent II (Mormon feminist journal), 1382
Export, Valie, 1530, 1542
Export Processing Zones (EPZs), 401, 451, 452, 459
austerity measures' effects on women, 1149
in east Asia, 1590
in Mexico, 332
in southeast Asia, 338
union movements and, 1977
extended family, 658, 669, 692–694
African-American, 658, 688
in Caribbean region, 1021
in central and South America, 1025
child care and, 157, 692, 1386
in Commonwealth of Independent States, 1030
in east Asia, 1032, 1033
elderly care and, 694
family planning and, 1632
gender constructions, 901
household role, 1017
in Micronesia and Polynesia, 1037–1038
in Middle East and north Africa, 1040–1041, 1042
Native North American, 685–686, 1045
in south Asia, 1050–1051
in southern AFrica, 1055
Exter, Alexandra, 877
extramarital sex. *See* adultery
Eyrick, Elizabeth, 756
Ezrat Nashrim (Jewish feminist organization), 776

F
Fabella, Virginia, 1662
Faber, Friar Felix, 1948
Fabio, Sarah Webster, 1271
Fabiola, 950
fabric. *See* textiles
Face (Dimitrova), 1263
Facett, Millicent Garrett, 797
factory system. *See* industrialization
factory workers, women as, 2146
Factsheet Five (directory), 2164
Faderman, Lillian, 1215, 1217
Faery Tradition, 2037
Fairbairns, Zoë, 654, 1808

Fairbanks, Douglas, Sr., 855
FAIR (Fairness and Accuracy in Reporting), 1164–1165
fairness. *See* equity
fairy tale, **653–654**
archetype, 85, 311
demonization in, 310, 311
eastern Europe, 1262
literary reworking of, 1292
myth vs., 1426
oral tradition and, 1480
romance portrayal, 1767
as sacred texts source, 1774
short stories based on, 1849
women as perpetuators of, 165
faith, **654–656**
Jewish women's concerns, 777–778
Faith, Karlene, 486
Faith Keepers, 686
Falk, R., 933
Falkenmark, Malin, 564
Fall, Aminata, 1286
Fallon, Mary, 854
false memory syndrome, 6
FALTA (Feminist Alternative; Moscow), 742
Faludi, Susan, 1165, 1327, 1337, 1629
Falwell, Jerry, 892
family, definition of, 1016, 1057, 1067–1068
Family, The (Ememcheta), 1286
family: extended. *See* extended family
family: households and women's roles. *See* households
and women's roles. *See* households
and families: overview
family: power relations and power structures,
669–674
abuse and, 5–10
battery (domestic violence) and, 101–103, 413, 415,
702
in Caribbean region, 1021–1022
in central and South America, 1026
consumption and, 671–672
dimensions, conditions, and sources of, 672–673
in east Asia, 1032
Engels's theory on, 791
English common law and, 802
ethnic studies on, 631
family law and, 656–661
femicide and, 703
gender constructions and, 902
grandmothers and, 940–941, 1021, 1318
headship and kinship factors, 671, 687
household resources issues, 1074
incest and, 1130
in indigenous cultures, 670, 671
Islamic brother's control over sister, 1854–1855
Islamic women's manipulation of, 794
liberal feminist argument on, 786–787, 788
liberal vs. patriarchal approach to, 1226, 1227
marital, 675, 802
in matriarchy, 1317–1320
in matrilineal systems, 1021–1024
in Middle East and north Africa, 1042
Napoleonic Code and, 788, 802
in nuclear traditional structure, 669–670
in Pakistan, 359
patriarchal, 1226, 1227, 1494–1495
Protestantism and, 687–688
in Russia, 1029
as site of woman's oppression, 670, 791
socialization for inequality and, 1870–1873
stress from, 1895
television viewing patterns and, 1921–1922
violence against women linked to, 2021
west African women's religious activities and, 690
women's sexuality/fertility and, 673
See also battery; domestic violence; family:
property relations; family: religious and legal
systems; gender construction in the family;
households and families: overview
family: property relations, **674–676**
ancient indigenous cultures: women's roles, 54
ancient nation-states: women's roles, 56
customary law and, 1533–1534